MARLBOROUGH

HIS LIFE AND TIMES

SARAH CHURCHILL, FIRST DUCHESS OF MARLBOROUGH

Watercolor miniature by Bernard Lens the Younger, 1720 (detail),
courtesy Victoria and Albert Museum, London/Art Resource, NY.

MARLBOROUGH

HIS LIFE AND TIMES

BY

WINSTON S. CHURCHILL

BOOK TWO

CONSISTING OF VOLUMES III AND IV
OF THE ORIGINAL WORK

The University of Chicago Press

The University of Chicago Press, Chicago, 60637
Copyright © 1936, 1938, 1947, 2002 by Winston S. Churchill
All rights reserved.
Volume III first published in October 1936 by George G. Harrap & Co., Ltd.
Volume IV first published September 1938
This edition in two books first published in 1947 by
George G. Harrap & Co., Ltd.
University of Chicago Press edition 2002
Printed in the United States of America
11 10 09 08 07 06   2 3 4 5

ISBN: 0-226-10636-5 (cloth)
ISBN: 0-226-10635-7 (paper)

The Press acknowledges the very generous contribution of
The John M. Olin Foundation
toward the publication of this edition

Library of Congress Cataloging-in-Publication Data

Churchill, Winston, Sir, 1874–1965.
    Marlborough : his life and times / by Winston S. Churchill.
        p.   cm.
    Originally published : London : Harrap, 1933–1934.
    Includes bibliographical references and indexes.
    ISBN 0-226-10634-9 (v. 1 : alk. paper) — ISBN 0-226-10633-0
    (v. 1 : pbk. : alk. paper) — ISBN 0-226-10636-5 (v. 2 : alk. paper) —
    ISBN 0-226-10635-7 (v. 2 : pbk. : alk. paper)
        1. Marlborough, John Churchill, Duke of, 1650–1722. 2. Great Britain—
    Politics and government—1660–1714. 3. Great Britain—History,
    Military—18th century. 4. Great Britain—History—1660–1714—
    Biography. 5. Great Britain—Court and courtiers—Biography.
    6. Statesmen—Great Britain—Biography. 7. Generals—Great Britain—
    Biography. I. Title.

DA462 .M3 C45   2002
941.06'9'092—dc21
[B]

2002072179

ABBREVIATIONS

B.M. = British Museum Library.

H.M.C. = *Report of the Royal Historical Manuscripts Commission.*

P.R.O. = Public Record Office.

S.P. = State Papers at the Public Record Office, London.

Documents never before made public are distinguished by an asterisk (★) and left for the most part in their original form.

All italics are the Author's, unless the contrary is stated.

In the diagrams, except where otherwise stated, fortresses held by the Allies are shown as black stars and those occupied by the French as white stars.

METHOD OF DATING

Until 1752 dates in England and on the Continent differed owing to our delay in adopting the Reformed Calendar of Gregory XIII. The dates which prevailed in England were known as Old Style, those abroad as New Style. In the seventeenth century the difference was ten days, in the eighteenth century eleven days. For example, January 1, 1601 (O.S.), was January 11, 1601 (N.S.), and January 1, 1701 (O.S.), was January 12, 1701 (N.S.).

The method used has been to give all dates of events that occurred in England in the Old Style, and of events that occurred abroad in New Style. Letters and papers are dated in the New Style unless they were actually written in England. In sea battles and a few other convenient cases the dates are given in both styles.

It was also customary at this time—at any rate, in English official documents —to date the year as beginning on Lady Day, March 25. What we should call January 1, 1700, was then called January 1, 1699, and so on for all days up to March 25, when 1700 began. This has been a fertile source of confusion. In this book all dates between January 1 and March 25 have been made to conform to the modern practice.

CONTENTS

VOLUME THREE

CONTENTS

GENERAL MAP OF EUROPE

KEY

Grand Alliance and Allies

Territory of the Two Crowns and Allies

Neutrals

Boundary of Empire

English Miles
0 50 100 200 300 400 500

ILLUSTRATIONS

ILLUSTRATIONS

VOLUME THREE

Volume Three

PREFACE

I HAD purposed to finish the story of Marlborough and his Times in this volume; but as the massive range of the material came fully into view it was clear that this could not be done without altering the balance and proportion of the work and failing to give a level, comprehensive account. I have therefore ended this volume after the campaign of 1708.

At this point Louis XIV saw himself to be definitely defeated, and his whole desire was for peace, almost at any price. On the other hand, the Allies, although war-wearied and discordant, had extended the original objects of the war, raised their terms, and hardened their hearts. At the same time Marlborough's power, triumphant in the field, and now accepted as paramount throughout the Grand Alliance, was completely undermined at home. He and his faithful colleague Godolphin had lost all effective hold upon Queen Anne, had no control of the Whigs, and were pursued by the malignity of the Tories. The Whig Junto had at last forced themselves upon the Queen, and established for the first time a powerful party Administration supported by majorities in both Houses of Parliament. Upon this rigid, tightly built, but none the less brittle platform Marlborough and Godolphin were still able to act, and Marlborough was to be furnished with greater means to conduct the war than he had ever before possessed. But the hollowness of his foundations was apparent to Europe, and especially to the enemy. It was known at Versailles that the Queen was estranged from Sarah, that she wished to extend her favour to the Tories, or Peace Party, as they had now unitedly become, and that she was in intimate contact by the backstairs through her bed-chamber woman Abigail Masham with Harley, the leader of the Opposition. The knowledge of these deadly facts, coupled with the harsh demands of the Allies, encouraged France to struggle forward, until the fall of Marlborough broke the strength and blunted the action of the Grand Alliance, and brought it to a situation incomparably worse than that of 1708.

The constitutional and European issues debated in this present volume are peculiarly apposite to the times in which we live. At home they involve and portray, first, the Union of Great Britain; secondly, the establishment of party government as the expression of a Parliamentary Constitution; and, thirdly, the shaping of the Cabinet system, in the forms in which these arrangements were destined to survive for over two hundred years. By the Great Rebellion against Charles I, and by the Revolution of 1688, the House of Commons had gained the means of controlling policy through the power of the purse. But in the reign of Anne the Sovereign still preserved, not only in theory but in practice, the right to choose Ministers. Naturally the Crown, lifted above party, sought to maintain its own power by forming Court Governments, or, as we should now call them, national Governments, from both the organized political factions and from outside them. The stresses of a prolonged world war and the vast pre-eminence of Marlborough favoured such an inclination. He understood with his deep sagacity that only a peace party can make or wage a war with united national strength. His fears that a Tory Party in opposition would weaken, if not destroy, the war effort of England, and the Queen's fears that, without the Tories in the Government, she would fall wholly into the hands of the Whigs, with all that that implied in Church and State, constituted a bond of harmony between servant and Sovereign which carried on our weak country and the loose confederacy of which it was the prop through the darkest, and at times apparently the hopeless, years of the struggle.

But after the glories of Blenheim had roused the martial enthusiasm of the English nation the Whigs, with their ardour for Continental war and leadership, obtained in very large measure, and in the end entirely, control not only of the Lords but of the Commons. It was not surprising that they insisted upon predominance in the Government. The dismissal of the high Tories, the intermediate system of the moderates of both parties which Harley rendered possible, and the steady incursion of the Whig leaders into the Cabinet Council comprised an evolution which in the compass of this volume led from a royal or national to a party administration in the height of a prolonged but successful war. Marlborough and Godolphin were forced step by step to yield to remorseless Parliamentary pressures, and make themselves the reluctant instruments of bringing them to bear upon the Queen. In so doing they, and still more Sarah—that keen Whig partisan—lost with the stubborn Queen the influence which alone had enabled them to cope with so many difficulties, and found themselves ultimately shorn of every source of organized domestic strength. All that remained was Marlborough's universally acknowledged indispensability, whether for the victorious waging of war or the successful negotiation of peace.

The reader will be able to judge for himself whether they could have taken any other course. Upon the whole I incline to the view that greater risks should have been run in 1707 to preserve the coalition character of the Government, to placate the Queen, and to work with Harley. On the other hand, the House of Commons was master of the money, and no Minister, however magnificent and successful, could long withstand its hostility. Secondly, the Cabinet system in its rapid adolescence presented insoluble problems to its members. Great nobles and famous statesmen sat round the Council Board united by no party bond, and owing allegiance to rival factions engaged in bitter Parliamentary conflict. Once the Queen's loyalties began to be in doubt, divergent personal and party interests manifested themselves in treacherous disclosures and intrigues. When Marlborough's sword brought home the triumphs of Ramillies and Oudenarde, when all men saw the princes and states of Europe arrayed against France under his supreme direction, these disruptive tendencies were held in suspense, and all bathed their hands in streams of martial glory and growing British power. But a barren or adverse campaign relaxed all ties, and Marlborough's defeat in the field, or even failure in a major siege, would have destroyed them. When in Marlborough's conduct of war we see now violent and sudden action with armies marching night and day, and all hazards dared for a decision, now long delays and seeming irresolution, the dominating fact to be remembered is that he could not afford to be beaten. So he never was beaten. He could not bear the impact of defeats such as his warrior comrade Eugene repeatedly survived. Neither in his headquarters at the front nor behind him at home did he have that sense of plenary authority which gave to Frederick the Great and to Napoleon their marvellous freedom of action. It is the exhibition of infinite patience and calculation, combined upon occasion with reckless audacity, both equally attended with invariable success, which makes his military career unique. When British generals of modern times feel themselves hampered by the tardy or partial action of allies, or embarrassed by the political situation at home, let them draw from the example of Marlborough new resources of endurance, without losing his faculty of "venturing all."

In these pages I also show the seamy side. A shorter account would, if justice were done, be compelled to dwell almost entirely upon the broad achievements. I have faithfully endeavoured to examine every criticism or charge which the voluminous literature upon this period contains, even where they are plainly tinctured with prejudice or malice, even where they rest on no more than slanderous or ignorant gossip. In the main Marlborough's defence rests upon his letters to Sarah and Godolphin. It is strange that this man who consciously wrote no word of personal explanation for posterity should in his secret, intimate correspondence, which he expected to be destroyed, or at least took no trouble to preserve, have furnished us with his case in terms far more convincing than anything written for the public eye. The reader's attention is especially drawn to these letters, not only those that have never been published, and which are now printed in their quaint, archaic style, but to the immense series drawn from Coxe's *Life* and Murray's *Dispatches*. I have sedulously endeavoured to reduce them, in the interests of the narrative, but in so many cases they *are* the narrative, and tell the tale far better than any other pen. They plead for Marlborough's virtue, patriotism, and integrity as compulsively as his deeds vindicate his fame. Although no scholar, and for all his comical spelling, he wrote a rugged, forceful English worthy of the Shakespeare on which his education was mainly founded. He held the whole panorama of Europe in his steady gaze, and presented it in the plainest terms of practical good sense.

How vain and puerile seem the calumnies with which the Deputy Goslinga has fed Continental historians, and with which Thackeray's *Esmond* has familiarized the English-speaking world, beside Marlborough's plain day-to-day accounts of his hopes and fears in the long-drawn struggle for Lille! How base appear the slanders with which Tory faction assailed him in those vanished days! Everything Marlborough writes to his wife and cherished friends rings true, and proves him the "good Englishman" he aspired to be.

I have not sought to palliate his vice or foible in money matters. In his acquisitive and constructive nature the gathering of an immense fortune and artistic treasures wherewith to found and endow his family was but a lower manifestation of the same qualities which cemented the Grand Alliance and led England to Imperial greatness. His avarice never prejudiced his public duty. For the sake of petty economies, mostly affecting himself, he let himself become a joke among the officers and soldiers who trusted and loved him; while at the same time he made generous benefactions of which the world knew nothing to his children, friends, and subordinates, and to strangers in distress; or spent large sums upon buildings which would long outlast him. An instinctive hatred of waste in all its forms, private and public, and particularly where his own comfort was concerned, was his dominant motive. Narrowly he scrutinized the expenses of the army; but the soldiers praised the precision with which their food and rations reached them through all the long campaigns. With zest he collected the percentages for which he held the Royal Warrant on the bread contracts and on the pay of the foreign troops; but never was Secret Service money more lavishly or more shrewdly expended. Given only a small addition to the great authority he wielded, he would have brought the war to a victorious end with half its havoc and slaughter; would have made a wise and stable peace in harmony with the highest interests of England and of Europe; and at the same time blandly pocketed the largest possible commissions on these august transactions. We see him in the midst of his hardest struggles cheered by the prospect of a small perquisite of plate, and yet unhesitatingly brushing aside the revenues of a viceroyalty when his acceptance of that princely office would have impaired the cohesion of the Allies. Half the money which he gave in private kindness, if spent upon his table in camp, would have doubled his popularity. It would not have affected his worth.

Most of the English characters of the earlier campaigns present themselves again in this volume. Marlborough is everywhere attended at the front by his devoted friends Cadogan and Cardonnel, the former combining the functions of Chief of the Staff and Quartermaster-General, the latter presiding over and conducting a correspondence which extended from the Duke's Headquarters to every capital in Europe. We find again Marlborough's brothers— George managing the Admiralty, and Charles at the head of the Infantry; and his great fighting officers Orkney, Lumley, Argyll, and his younger men, Brigadiers Meredith and Palmes. The war in Spain introduces remarkable personalities. Peterborough, Galway, Stanhope, each in his own way shows the plethora of quality and ability at the disposal of the Crown in these famous years. Godolphin still guards Marlborough's home base; Heinsius and Hop and Buys preserve his profound relations with the Dutch republic. Wratislaw is his contact with the Empire. There are some grand German princes and warriors in the heroic Hesse-Darmstadt, the Prince of Hesse, and the Prussian cavalrymen Rantzau and Natzmer. Always through the drama runs the brotherhood in arms of Marlborough and Eugene.

In one other main aspect the story of this volume has a peculiar interest for us to-day. We see a world war of a League of Nations against a mighty, central military monarchy, hungering for domination not only over the lands but over the politics and religion of its neighbours. We see in their extremes the feebleness and selfish shortcomings of a numerous coalition, and how its weaker members cast their burdens upon the strong, and sought to exploit the unstinted efforts of England and Holland for their own advantage. We see all these evils redeemed by the statecraft and personality of Marlborough, and by his military genius and that of his twin captain, Eugene. Thus the causes in which were wrapped the liberties of Europe were carried to safety for several generations.

In a final volume I design to describe the fall of Marlborough after his main work was done. Here again the tale is rich in suggestion and instruction for the present day; for it illustrates what seems to have become the tradition of Britain—indomitable in distress and danger, exorbitant at the moment of success, fatuous and an easy prey after her superb effort had run its course. Here we shall see harsh and excessive demands producing innumerable unforeseen reactions upon the defeated nations. Here in foretaste we may read the bitter story of how in the eighteenth century England won the war and lost the peace.

I have followed in these pages the method of the earlier volumes. The reader should consult the preface to Volume II for some comments upon the authorities to whom I have recurred. The bibliography has been extended to cover the new years through which the story now runs. It will be seen that I have drawn deeply upon the records of foreign archives and the writings of Continental historians. There is no doubt that they give a more vivid and vital picture of Marlborough's life and times than anything which had appeared in the English language until the illuminating and impartial work of Professor Trevelyan.

I have tried as far as possible to tell the story through the lips of its actors or from the pens of contemporary writers, feeling sure that a phrase struck out at the time is worth many coined afterwards. Great pains have again been taken with the diagrams and maps in order that the non-military reader may without effort understand 'what happened and why.' I am again indebted to Brigadier R. P. Pakenham-Walsh in this respect, and for his assistance in the whole technical field. Commander J. H. Owen, R.N., has helped me in naval matters. I again renew my thanks to all those who have so kindly allowed me to reproduce pictures and portraits in their possession, and also to those who have placed original documents at my disposal. I make my acknowledgments in every case. I also record my thanks to the present Duke of Marlborough for continuing to me all that freedom of the Blenheim archives without which my task could neither have been begun nor pursued.

WINSTON SPENCER CHURCHILL

CHARTWELL
  WESTERHAM
    August 13, 1936

Chapter One

THE WHIG APPROACH

1705

THE General Election which began in May 1705 produced changes in English politics which at first seemed only slight and beneficial, but which set in train events of decisive importance to Marlborough and his fortunes. The Captain-General was capable of enduring endless vexations and outfacing extreme hazards. But he had one sensitive spot. In the armour of leather and steel by which in public affairs he was encased there was a chink into which a bodkin could be plunged. He sought not only glory but appreciation. When according to his judgment he had done well he yearned for the praise of his fellow-countrymen, and especially of those Tory squires—'the gentlemen of England,' as they styled themselves—to whom he naturally belonged, but with whom he was ever at variance. They were the audience whose applauses he sought to compel; and when instead of admiration he received their sneers and belittlings his indignation was profound. "Blenheim indeed!" quoth they. "What was that? A stroke of luck, and the rest the professional knowledge of Eugene." Rooke was the man and the sea war the theme. The campaign of 1705, was it not a failure? All this Continental exertion and expense were follies which should be stopped. How much longer must the blood and treasure of England be consumed in European struggles while rich booty glittered neglected across the oceans and the Church was in danger at home? Thus the Tories. On the other hand stood the Whigs, logical, precise, resolute, the wholehearted exponents of the great war on land and of England rising to the directing summit of the world.

Sarah, as we can judge from John's replies, must have confronted him with this contrast in many a letter. She saw, with a woman's unsentimental discernment, that his illusions about the Tories were vain. They would ever be his foes, and would in the end work his ruin. Her hatred of them ran bitter and strong. With deft hand she picked and shot at him the Tory taunts that would sting him most; and others no doubt wrote in the same strain. Usually the Duke was proof against all minor assaults; but when the Moselle campaign was ruined by the desertion of the German princes and his fine conceptions in Brabant were one after another frustrated by the obstinacy and jealousy of the Dutch commanders, many shafts got home, and he palpably winced under the pangs.

The Parliamentary manœuvre of the Tories in trying to 'tack' the Occasional Conformity Bill to the main supply of the year was undoubtedly a breach of the solemn unwritten convention by which Whigs and Tories were alike bound—that, however party strife might rage, the national war effort must not be weakened. Reluctantly but remorselessly during 1705 Marlborough took the resolve to break with the Tories. His resentment burned through his letters to Godolphin from the front:

April 14

> As to what you say of the tackers, I think the answer and method that should be taken is what is practised in all armies—that is, if the enemy give no quarter, they should have none given to them.[1]

And on June 24:

> I beg you will give my humble duty to the Queen, and assure her that nothing but my gratitude to her could oblige me to serve her after the disappointments I have met with in Germany, for nothing has been performed that was promised; and to add to this they write to me from England that the tackers and all their friends are glad of the disappointments I meet with, saying that if I had success this year like the last the Constitution of England would be ruined. As I have no other ambition but that of serving well her Majesty, *and being thought what I am, a good Englishman, this vile, enormous faction of theirs vexes me* so much that I hope the Queen will after this campaign give me leave to retire and end my days in praying for her prosperity and making my own peace with God. . . . I beg you will not oppose this, thinking it may proceed at this time from the spleen; I do assure you it does not, but is from the *base ingratitude of my countrymen.* . . .[2]

Even before the scandal of the 'tack,' not only Marlborough and Godolphin but Harley too seem to have made up their minds to lean upon the Whigs, as Sarah ceaselessly urged. The first sign of this was Marlborough's willingness in the spring of 1705 to demand the Privy Seal from the Duke of Buckingham, whose intrigues with the Tory leaders had become obvious. This might

---

[1] Coxe, *Memoirs of John, Duke of Marlborough* (second edition, 1820), ii, 70.
[2] *Ibid.,* 127.

have seemed a delicate matter; for Buckingham had romantic, if faded, claims upon the Queen's favour. He had been her first and sole flirtation. He was her personal appointment. Anne, however, seems to have made little difficulty about this. He was succeeded by the Duke of Newcastle, possibly the richest man in England and, though not a Junto stalwart, the fountain of Whig hospitality. On the night of March 28, 1705, when Buckingham retired, Portland (King William's favourite and friend Bentinck, now become one of the most important sources of information on London affairs to the Dutch Government) wrote exultingly to Heinsius, "The liaison is thoroughly effective between the Whigs and 22 and 23 [Marlborough and Godolphin]."[1] A more significant step was the supersession of Admiral Rooke in the command of the Fleet. This ran directly counter to the resolution which the Tories had carried in the Commons, coupling his victory of Malaga with that of Blenheim, and may well have been the royal and ministerial rejoinder to it. Indeed, Harley's agent Defoe described Rooke in one of his pamphlets in these blistering terms:

> A man that never once fought since he was admiral: that always embraced the party that opposed the Government, and has constantly favoured, preferred, and kept company with the high furious Jacobite party, and has filled the Fleet with them.[2]

At the beginning of April the Lord-Lieutenancies, so important in elections, were shuffled in favour of the Whigs. On April 7, two days after the dissolution, political society was astonished to see the Queen sit down to luncheon with Orford (Admiral Russell) and other Lords of the Junto.[3] These steps showed, and were meant to show, the electorate which way the royal favour inclined.

Yet it is remarkable with what restraint Marlborough and Godolphin tried to measure the blow which must now be struck. There was no sense in weakening the Tories only to fall into the hands of the Whigs. Enough force must be used to beat them, but not so much as to produce a Whig triumph; for then the balance would be deranged, and the two super-Ministers and the Queen would but have exchanged the wrong-headed grumblings and intrigues of the Tories for the exacting appetites and formulas of the Whigs. Marlborough wrote to Sarah from The Hague (April 19/30):

[1] Von Noorden, *Europäische Geschichte im achtzehnten Jahrhundert* (1870), ii, 248.
[2] Portland Papers, *H.M.C.*, viii, 136.
[3] Dispatches of Spanheim (Prussian Resident in London), April 9, 1705; von Noorden, ii, 248.

[Neither] You nor anybody living can wish more for the having a good Parliament than I do, but we may differ in our notions. I will own to you very freely mine; which is, that I think at this time it is for the Queen's service, and the good of England, that the choice might be such as that neither party might have a great majority, so that her Majesty might be able to influence what might be good for the common interest.[1]

Such sentiments were, of course, agreeable to the Queen. Thus the Cockpit circle, still intact, embarked upon the election with a desire to chastise the Tories, but not too much, and to procure a Parliament in which, the Whigs and Tories being equally matched, the "Queen's servants," as the placemen were called, and the moderates would hold the balance.

Such nicely calculated plans rarely stand the rough tests of action. The rank and file cannot fight hard to win only half a victory; and once the party forces were launched to the attack they strove with might and main. Everywhere the Tories proclaimed the Church in danger. Sir John Pakington rode to the hustings of Worcester under a banner which portrayed a toppling steeple. The high-flying Tories were furious at what they called the Queen's desertion of the Church, which they epitomized thus:

> When Anna was the Church's daughter,
> She did whate'er that mother taught her;
> But now she's mother to the Church
> She leaves her daughter in the lurch.[2]

A pamphlet called *The Memorial of the Church of England*, by Dr Drake, attributed this desertion of the Church to Marlborough and Godolphin. Everywhere the Tories railed against the expense of the Continental war and denounced the meanness of Britain's allies and the mistakes of her leaders on the Continent and at the Admiralty. The oppressive land-tax upon the country gentlemen and the growing National Debt were contrasted with the fat profits of the upstart financiers and money interest of the City of London. Lust for war by those whom the war paid, and greed for self-advancement by those whose hypocritical conformity exposed the Church to mortal peril, were the Tory accusations.

To modern eyes this would seem a good platform. It marshalled all the prejudices of the Old England against the fighting effort of the New. But the vision of the English people was not clouded.

[1] Coxe, ii, 232.
[2] Quoted by Agnes Strickland, *Lives of the Queens of England*, viii, 241.

Out of the brawl and clatter of the polls one dominating fact emerged—the battle of Blenheim. From the depth of the national heart surged up a glow of pride and of desire for British greatness. Mighty France, four times as populous, the Grand Monarch, tyrant of Europe in all his splendour, cut to the ground by island blades and English genius; his proudest regiments led off captive in thousands by the redcoats, his generals and nobles brought home in droves and tethered about the countryside; conquest, glory, the world to win and the man to win it—these scenes and thoughts stirred the English imagination.

Thus, although the Tories, both Tackers and Sneakers, as they called one another, fought with deep-rooted local strength, it was apparent by the beginning of July that the voting would carry their defeat beyond the calculations of the Ministry. Godolphin succeeded in breaking Sir Edward Seymour's ascendancy in Cornwall. Cadogan was easily elected through Marlborough's influence for Woodstock. The Tackers, indeed, though they suffered heavily, and all their names were on a special black list, returned seventy-five or eighty strong out of a hundred and thirty-four. But a good many moderate Tories fell, and the Whig Party gained at the expense of both. They had been but one-fifth of the old House of Commons. They were now nearly equal to the Tories. Hitherto, with their ascendancy in the House of Lords, they had been able to maintain themselves vigorously in the State. Now, with the Commons so much more evenly divided, their predominance became apparent. If they joined with the extreme Tories in a general opposition the new House of Commons would be unmanageable. If they supported the Government what price would they ask in return? This now became the crux.

The Queen scented the danger at once. To Godolphin, on the other hand, it seemed obvious that the Ministry would have to depend on Whig support. Marlborough, impressed by the toughness of the Tackers, was of the same opinion.

Marlborough to Godolphin

Lens les Béguines
July 6, 1705

★Upon my examining the list you sent me of the New Parl: I find so great a number of Tackers and their adherents that I should have been very uneasy in my own mind, if I had not on this occasion begged of the Queen as I have in my letter, that She shou'd be pleas'd for Her own Sake, and the good of Her Kingdom to advise early with You, what incoragement might be proper to give the Whigs, that they might look upon it as their own Concern, to beat down and oppose all such proposals as may prove uneasy to Her Maty's government. . . . When I have said this, You know my opinion, and I am sure it is yours also, that all the Care imaginable must be taken that the Queen be not in the hands of any Party, for Party is always unreasonable and unjust.[1]

He wrote in this sense more at length to the Queen ten days later, adding at the end:

By the vexation and trouble I undergo I find a daily decay, which may deprive me of the honour of seeing your Majesty any more, which thought makes me take the liberty to beg of your Majesty that for your own sake and the happiness of your kingdoms you will never suffer any body to do Lord Treasurer an ill office. For besides his integrity for your service, his temper and abilities are such that he is the only man in England capable of giving such advice as may keep you out of the hands of both parties, which may at last make you happy, if quietness can be had in a country where there is so much faction.[2]

The Lords of the Junto surveyed the scene on the morrow of the elections with cool and determined eyes. They might well have been tempted to claim their rights with the same pedantic rigour with which they held their doctrines. Their turn, they felt, was coming. Why should not the war party wage the war? They had the strength, they had the talents, they had the experience, they had the Cause—why should they be proscribed? Why, indeed, should they not have the Government? Their wishes were no more than the workings of the Constitution would nowadays automatically concede. But at the beginning of the eighteenth century the Crown was still the prime factor in actual politics. The Queen might not be able to choose the policy of the State, but she could still choose the agents to conduct it. To entrust her beloved Church to the freethinking Whigs and their Dissenter supporters, to surround her person with men who in their hearts, as she believed, were the inveterate enemies of monarchy, to part with faithful Tory Ministers and household friends under Parliamentary pressure, was all against the grain to her.

The conflicts and disputations between Lords and Commons which had lasted since 1698 were now ended by Whig control and influence in both Houses. But in its place there opened a wearing struggle in which the Whigs, using all the resources and pressures of Parliamentary government, sought to force themselves upon the

[1] Blenheim MSS. [2] Coxe, ii, 131.

Queen. The Tory Party was splintered into four sections: the Jacobites, who claimed to be the only true exponents of the Tory creed; the anti-Jacobite Tories, generically dubbed the Sneakers, or more courteously "the Whimsicals"; the Tackers, whose embittered opposition was led by Rochester and Nottingham and found a new and eloquent mouthpiece in the converted Whig, Haversham; and the placemen, the "Queen's Servants" and independent moderate forces who followed Harley and St John, deferred to the Court, and sustained the Government. Although the whole party had an underlying sense of unity, and felt alike on many questions of peace and war, they were for the time paralysed by their feuds. Indeed, in the Commons they could not find a single man of sufficient distinction and aptitude to be their leader. Their opposition was effectively vocal only in the Lords. Yet, resting as they claimed upon the Land and the Church, commanding as they did the support of the squires and parsons, they constituted the strongest political force in the realm. If at any moment Tory divisions were healed, their inherent power would assert itself.

The five Whig nobles, on the other hand, had the advantages of unity and leadership. They controlled a disciplined party, inspired by broad and logical principles, which in its most active branches, interests, and classes accepted their guidance with almost military obedience. Long and frequent were the conclaves of the Junto in their great country houses. They knew well the prejudices of the Queen against them. They acted at first with the utmost moderation and with admirable adroitness. They decided to put forward Sunderland, their youngest member—the only one who had not held high office under King William—as their candidate for official favour. Sarah, as usual, was ardent in their cause. Her influence both with the Queen and with her husband was regarded as irresistible. How could that influence be more easily and more naturally exerted than in pressing the claims of her own son-in-law? Sunderland would be the thin end of their wedge. Behind it were the sledgehammers of action in both Houses of Parliament.

The impact of all this fell, as the months passed, upon Godolphin. He had to procure a Parliamentary majority to carry on the war. From this there was no escape. It must be there, on the benches and in the lobbies of both Houses, from day to day. Without it there would be no Supply, the armies would wither, the Grand Alliance would crumble, and the war would be lost. Since he had broken with the Tory Party and the Queen was increasingly reluctant to admit the Whigs in numbers, his task soon became arduous and ungrateful to the last degree. His days were spent in begging the Whig Junto to forbear and the Queen to concede. Marlborough understood perfectly that his colleague's vexations and anxieties at Whitehall were scarcely less wearing than his own distresses and dangers in the field. His letters breathed a lively sympathy, and again and again he assured the Lord Treasurer that he would stand or fall with him.

The idea of sending Sunderland to Vienna upon the mission of mediation between the Emperor and the Hungarian insurgents seemed to Godolphin the least difficult expedient. It was the wedge at taper-point. The Queen, relieved at not having this obnoxious politician obtruded upon her Council, accepted his emloyment abroad as a compromise. After all, Sunderland was Mr and Mrs Freeman's son-in-law, and surely for the sake of old friendship they would keep him in his place and out of her sight. Thus in June 1705 one of the Lords of the Junto, formally representing the power and interest of the Whigs, became an envoy of Queen Anne. This was a considerable event. A minor appointment of a young Whig Member named Walpole to the Admiralty Board attracted little notice. But further encroachments upon the Queen's peace of mind were in store. Sir Nathan Wright, the Lord Keeper, a Tory, was well known to be incompetent. His knowledge of Chancery business was woefully defective, and his praiseworthy efforts to acquaint himself late in life with the great profession of which he was the head, by studying a manual of practice compiled for his own use, evoked no confidence among his friends, and mockery from his foes. On the other side stood Cowper, the Whig, with far higher abilities and credentials. As the time for the meeting of Parliament approached the Whigs demanded with bluntness that Cowper should be appointed Lord Keeper. Under this pressure and that of the Parliamentary situation Godolphin recommended the change to the Queen. Anne was greatly distressed. The office of Lord Keeper was intimately concerned with Church patronage. To admit Whig influence in this sacred preserve was more than she could bear. Her letter of July 11 to Godolphin is well known.

> . . . I cannot help saying I wish very much that there may be a moderate Tory found for this employment. For I must own to you I dread falling into the hands of either party, and the Whigs have had so many favours shown to them of late that I fear a very few more will put me insensibly into their power, which is what I'm sure you would

not have happen no more than I. I know my dear unkind friend [Sarah] has so good an opinion of all that party that to be sure she will use all her endeavour to get you to prevail with me to put one of them into this great post, and I cannot help being apprehensive that not only she but others may be desirous to have one of the heads of them [the Junto] in possession of the Seal. But I hope in God you will never think that reasonable, for that would be an unexpressible uneasiness and mortification to me. There is nobody I can rely upon but yourself to bring me out of all my difficulties, and I do put an entire confidence in you, not doubting but you will do all you can to keep me out of the power of *the merciless men of both parties,* and to that end make choice of one for Lord Keeper that will be the likeliest to prevent that danger.[1]

Against this resistance Sarah strained her influence in vain. Stiff letters passed. The Queen refused. In a personal letter (now lost) she appealed to Marlborough. Marlborough's reply of September 29, from which we may infer its character, deeply disappointed her.

Sept. 29/Oct. 10, 1705

Your Majesty has too much goodness for your servant in but thinking of an excuse for your not writing. . . .

Not knowing when I may have the honour of seeing your Majesty, I cannot end this letter without lamenting your condition; for I am afraid I see too plainly that you will be obliged by the heat and malice of some that would not stay in your service, to do more than otherwise would be necessary. What I say is from my heart and soul for your service; and if I had the honour of being with you, I should beg on my knees that you would lose no time in knowing of my Lord Treasurer what is fit to be done, that you might be in a condition of carrying on the war and of opposing the extravagances of these mad people. If your Majesty should have difficulty of doing this, I see no remedy under heaven, but that of sending for Lord Rochester and Lord Nottingham, and let them take your business into their hands, the consequences of which are very much to be feared; for I think they have neither courage nor temper enough to serve your Majesty and the nation in this difficult time, nor have they any support in England but what they have from being thought violently at the head of a party, which will have the consequence of the other party opposing them with all their strength.

As I am sure your Majesty has no thoughts but what are for the good of England, so I have no doubt but God will bless and direct you to do what may be best for yourself and for Europe.[2]

[1] Godolphin Papers; Add. MSS. 28070, f. 12.   [2] Coxe, ii, 235.

On this the Queen yielded, and the Great Seal was transferred to Cowper on October 11.

It was inevitable that this long, unceasing, day-to-day friction should destroy the relations between Anne and Sarah. The Queen's friend became no more than the advance agent of the Whig Party, so ardent for tangible proofs of royal favour. She not only over-rated her influence on public matters with the Queen, but she mistook its character. She sought to win byargument, voluble and vociferous, written and interminable, what had hitherto been the freehold property of love. She undertook to plead every Whig demand with her mistress. For Sunderland, her son-in-law, that might be understood. There the Queen could suppose a personal desire which in old friendship she still wished to meet. But the acceptance of a Whig Lord Keeper, guardian of the Queen's con-science, adviser upon the Church patronage, seemed to Queen Anne not a matter for the judgment of her favourite and con-fidante. As for all the propaganda of Whiggery of which Sarah made herself the advocate, this only encountered an obstinacy, and in the end wore out a patience, which in conjunction were unique.

The result of the elections and its effect upon the Government manifested themselves as soon as Parliament met on October 25, and the House of Commons proceeded to choose a Speaker. The Tories put forward the pious 'tacker' Bromley, Member for Oxford University, long identified with the Occasional Conformity Bill. The Whigs found a respectable figure in a certain John Smith. The attendance was enormous for those days of difficult travel. Out of 513 Members 454 were in their places. It soon became evident that the Ministry would support Smith. Sir Edward Seymour, now desperately ill, could think of no better argument against him than that, being a Privy Councillor, he was ineligible for the Speaker-ship. On this Harley was able to make a rejoinder which must have been effective. Seymour himself, he recalled, had been Speaker and Privy Councillor at the same time in the reign of Charles II. Smith was elected by 249 votes to 205 for Bromley. The majority of 44 did not represent the full combined strength of the Whigs and the Government. A number of Tory placemen were either genuinely unable to believe that the Court wished a Whig Speaker to be chosen, or else resented their instructions. They voted in the wrong lobby. They made haste, with many apologies for tardiness, to set their sails to the new breeze.

The Queen's Speech dwelt upon the now familiar theme of Marlborough and Godolphin—"war abroad and peace at home."

If the French king continues master of the Spanish monarchy, the balance of power in Europe is utterly destroyed, and he will be able in a short time to ingross the trade and the wealth of the world. *No good Englishman* [Marlborough's phrase] could at any time be content to sit still, and acquiesce in such a prospect; and at this time we have good grounds to hope, that by the blessing of God upon our arms, and those of our allies, a good foundation is laid for restoring the monarchy of Spain to the house of Austria; the consequences of which will be not only safe and advantageous, but glorious for England.[1]

Such declarations went far beyond the original objects of the Grand Alliance, and proclaimed England's direct interest in the most extreme form of victory. They confirmed the arguments and assurances which Marlborough had used to the Dutch a few weeks earlier in urging them to reject the peace overtures of France. War on the greatest scale with implacable spirit for the highest demands was the message. The second main appeal was for the union with Scotland. For these high purposes the Queen called for another union—a union of men's spirits in England and the laying aside of party strife.

In every point except the last both Houses of Parliament cordially sustained the Sovereign. The addresses of the Lords and the Commons repeated the sentiments of the Queen's Speech about the war in even stronger language. They overflowed with praise for the Queen's person, her zeal for the Church, and her devotion to the harmony of her subjects. "We want words," said the Commons, "to express the deep sense we have of the many blessings we enjoy under Your Majesty's happy government."[2] Although both addresses were tinctured with Whig censures against those whose wicked rumours that the Church was in danger had disturbed men's minds, and thus acquired a partisan character, they were carried by large majorities. The Commons then proceeded to vote unprecedented supplies of money for the war, and to make large additions to the armed forces by land and sea.

The reactions of Whig pressure upon Godolphin affected Harley, and not only reveal the key to his future conduct, but form the true defence of his career. Harley knew the Tory Party alike in its

[1] *Parliamentary History of England* (Hansard), edited by William Cobbett and J. Wright, vi (1810), 451.
[2] *Ibid.*, 455.

temporary weakness and in its latent strength. He saw that it was his foundation in public life. He knew that his relations with the Queen were at this stage on an entirely different plane from those of the Cockpit circle. Godolphin and the Captain-General could perhaps, but only perhaps, afford to be careless of party attachments. That was their own affair. But Harley would never in any circumstances cut himself finally adrift from his Tory moorings. He might co-operate as an honoured colleague and as a real contributory force with a national Government such as the Queen and her two chief Ministers desired. He might even quarrel fiercely for the time being with the unreasonable elements of Toryism; but ever before his eyes there glinted the prospect of a Tory reunion at the head of which he would be no longer an agent, however indispensable, but the real, natural leader.

Therefore we find Harley from the very outset deprecating the Whig infusion. Large concessions must no doubt be made. As a House of Commons man and a master of that assembly, he recognized their practical necessity. He was prepared to give way step by step and month by month; but he meant it to be known both by the Queen and by the Tory opposition that he was a resisting force to Whig ambition. To the Queen the language he used was highly agreeable; indeed, it was her own. "Persons and parties must go to the Queen, not the Queen to them." The Queen had chosen the Tory Party as her basis. There must be no party domination, certainly no Whig domination: "If the gentlemen of England [*i.e.*, the Tory country gentlemen] are made sensible that the Queen is at the head and not a party [*i.e.*, the Whig Party] everything will be easy, and the Queen will be courted, and not a party."[1] In other words, Harley was prepared to serve in a national coalition provided it remained national; but he would not serve in a Whig Government veneered with Tory elements. Gradually, but at the same time decisively, Harley made this fact apparent to Godolphin and Marlborough. The differences which opened between the Lord Treasurer and the Secretary of State, though at present vague and veiled, were deep. Godolphin could never go back to the Tories: Harley had never left them. Godolphin was prepared to lean upon the Whigs and rule with their aid; Harley would never accept such a system. Godolphin sought always an effective, clear-cut majority upon which Marlborough could wage war triumphantly. Harley felt much more coolly about it all. The war would not go on for

---

[1] Harley to Godolphin, September 4, 1705; Bath Papers, *H.M.C.*, i, 75.

ever; it might even end disastrously. What would happen then? It was not his war. But it would be his Tory Party.

Nevertheless, at this stage the Whig assertion had not been pushed to such a pitch that he was seriously disturbed. On the contrary, he showed himself well disposed towards an accommodation with them. He soothed and reassured the Queen, who already found him expressing her instinctive thoughts, about the appointment of a Whig Lord Keeper. He was entirely favourable to the Sunderland mission. He it was who had tripped up Seymour in the Commons at the election of the Whig Speaker. In all this he served the Government, and at the same time made the Queen feel a certain measure of comradeship in the sacrifices which both must make for longer ends.

Their resentments now betrayed the Tory leaders into further acts of extreme unwisdom. Once again they tried by an insincere manœuvre to entangle the Whigs, and once again they were themselves upset. Their spokesman, Haversham, put forward in the Lords a proposal that, in order to ensure the Protestant succession, the Electress Sophia should be invited to take up her residence in England.[1] No one knew better than Rochester and Nottingham that this suggestion was insupportable to the Queen. Yet it seemed a plan for which no Whig could refuse to vote without repudiating the whole doctrines of his party. If the Whigs endorsed it, they made a new breach with the Queen. If they refused it, they falsified their principles, and staggered their party. Such was the plan upon which the Tories were led into the enemy's lines masquerading in their uniforms.

This insidious form of attack naturally drew Godolphin, Harley, and the Whig lords into common consultation, and all were found equally desirous of pleasing the Queen. The political sagacity of the Junto and the discipline of their party enabled them easily to defeat the fantastic assault, and to turn it to their own advantage. They supported the Government in meeting Haversham's motion with a plain negative. The Queen herself was encouraged to be present 'incognito,' as it was called, in the House of Lords during the debate. She heard the Tory orator putting forward the project most deeply repugnant to her. Buckingham, furious at his recent dismissal, wasted little sentiment. The Queen heard him at a few yards' distance discuss the possibility of her soon being physically incapable of reigning. She heard the Whig debaters, whom she had

[1] *Journals of the House of Lords*, xviii, II, 19.

so long regarded as her enemies, displaying all their brilliant gifts of argument and rhetoric upon her side. Never had the Whigs more nearly won the heart of Queen Anne than on this occasion. The motion was rejected by an overwhelming majority. The Queen returned to St James's with the feeling that her lifelong friends had outraged her, and her lifelong foes had come to her rescue. How profoundly shaken she was alike in her faiths and her prejudices can be judged by the letter which she wrote to Sarah.

> I believe dear Mrs Freeman and I shall not disagree as we have formerly done; for I am sensible of the services those people have done me that you have a good opinion of, and will countenance them, and am thoroughly convinced of the malice and insolence of them that you have always been speaking against.[1]

This royal mood might render possible the formation of a real national Government in which Harley and St John and many respectable Tories could work heartily with the Lords of the Junto, the whole under the auspices of Marlborough and Godolphin. Such a system would command ample Parliamentary strength for the vehement prosecution of the war. It was plain, however, that the Whig leaders could not rest upon the mere rejection of the disingenuous Tory proposal to bring the Electress Sophia into England. Had they done so they would have been disavowed by their party. They therefore in close accord with the Government brought forward their counter-plan for assuring the Hanoverian succession should the Queen die without a natural heir. This was the Regency Bill, by which upon the demise of the Crown a Council of Regency would automatically come into existence for the express purpose of placing the Hanoverian heir upon the throne. The Queen, in her relief from what she regarded as an odious proposal of the Tories, relegated into the background of unrealizable sentiment any compunction which she nursed about the "pretended Prince of Wales." ("Maybe 'tis our brother."[2]) She cordially welcomed the Regency Bill. It was carried without serious difficulty. The Whig leaders reassured their party, and the Tories lay like beetles on their backs.

At this time we must imagine the Tories, morose and chagrined by what they considered the unworthy defection not only of their own men, but of their own Queen, making every conceivable blunder, while the Whigs caracoled before the throne displaying their matchless skill in political equitation, and eager to persuade

---

[1] *Account of the Conduct of the Duchess of Marlborough* (1742), p. 171.
[2] Vol. I, p. 239

íts occupant to make them her champions. One final exhibition remained. The Tories came forward with their cry, "The Church in danger." Rochester, Nottingham, and the newly dismissed Buckingham set forth their threefold case. The Act of Security— which in that dark hour before the victory of Blenheim brought new life Godolphin had advised the Queen to sign—authorized the Presbyterian Government in Scotland to arm a fierce, fanatical anti-episcopalian peasantry. The Occasional Conformity Bill had been for three sessions handspiked. The invitation to the Electress Sophia had been rejected. Thus (moaned the Tories) Presbyterians and Dissenters had gained the upper hand both in England and in Scotland.

Anne again attended as an auditor, and sat impassive through eight hours of speeches, often directed at her. But neither the issue nor the ill impression produced by the Tories upon the Queen was for a moment in doubt. Somers derided the Tory ex-Ministers. "Those lords who see the Church in danger take this view because they are excluded from office. They cannot, it seems, take their eyes off the danger, nor can the danger itself be removed until they are embraced in the Government, and an Act is passed to make their tenure of office eternal. But they are mortal: religion is immortal. The only final solution is to discover some means to make them immortal."[1]

Upon this question of the danger to the Church and to the episcopacy the Bishops had a rightful say. King William's bishops, still a majority, plumped for the Whigs and the Administration. By sixty-one votes to thirty the Lords declared that

> the Church, which was rescued from the extremest danger by King William III, of glorious memory, is now, by God's blessing, under the happy reign of her Majesty, in a most safe and flourishing condition; and whoever goes about to suggest and insinuate that the Church is in danger under her Majesty's administration is an enemy to the Queen, the Church, and the Kingdom.[2]

The Commons at the request of the Lords made a similar declaration; and, the Queen assenting in cordial terms, it became a penal offence to speak of danger to the Church of England. Notwithstanding this threat, the country clergy and the fox-hunters continued to ingeminate their griefs with general impunity; and the pamphleteers were artful, virulent, hard to catch, and harder to convict.

[1] Lords Debates, II, 161. [2] *Journals of the House of Lords*, xviii, II, 43.

Chapter Two

PRINCE OF MINDELHEIM

1705 —OCTOBER–DECEMBER

THE fruitless outcome of the campaign of 1705 in the Low Countries, the bitter controversies which it had aroused in all the camps, Courts, and Diets of Europe, and the revival of the French power on almost every front, might well have smitten Marlborough's reputation on the Continent and in consequence impaired his strength. On the contrary, he emerged more obviously than ever before as the brain and impulse of the Grand Alliance. The victories which had been denied him in the field were to be gained during the winter by his personal influence in diplomacy. If the confederacy was to bear the strain of another year's war its members must be regathered by a master-hand. There was but one, as all men could see. The island Power, which, though seemingly more detached from the struggle than its Continental allies, was making remarkable exertions, possessed in Marlborough an agent upon whom all eyes were turned, and to whose tent appeals from every quarter were addressed.

Once again the fortunes of the Alliance had ebbed.[1] Though the fame of Blenhem still resounded, its advantages had largely disappeared. The plight of the Empire, if not immediately desperate, seemed forlorn in the last degree. The Hungarian revolt had become monstrous. It dominated the life and swallowed the public revenues of four out of five of the hereditary provinces of the Austrian crown. It was the first call upon the Emperor's men and money. The rebel leader, Rakoczy, bulked larger in the Emperor's mind than Louis XIV. The Imperial armies on the Upper Rhine and in Italy were starved for the sake of the deadly intestine conflict. The failure of Marlborough's design upon the Moselle and the lack of any victories in Brabant had wasted the superiority of the main allied army during the whole year. This had enabled the French to maintain an unrelenting pressure with numerous forces upon Savoy. Nearly a hundred and fifty thousand troops were acting continuously

[1] See the general map of Europe facing p. 1040.

39

in the Italian theatre. Victor Amadeus, the reigning Duke of Savoy, was hopelessly outnumbered. His fortresses, stubbornly defended, had fallen one by one. The genius of Prince Eugene and the terror of his name could not make good the wants of his army in numbers, munitions, equipment, and money. His hazardous battle against Vendôme at Cassano[1] had yielded nothing more than a momentary diversion. His ragged, unpaid, disintegrated force, of which the eight thousand Prussians whom Marlborough had procured from the Court of Berlin in the previous year, now greatly reduced, were the core, could do no more than cling to the foothills of the Alps by Lake Garda. Victor Amadeus himself was at variance with Starhemberg, the Imperial general at his side. The French under Vendôme and La Feuillade were steadily overcoming every form of resistance. The total collapse of the Allies in the Italian theatre seemed to await only the return of spring. The French conquest of all Italy was imminent, after which the whole army of the two Marshals would be speedily transported to the northern fronts.

Godolphin was anxious that Marlborough should return to England, if possible in time for the meeting of the new Parliament, and assuredly the Duke himself was longing to be home. The state into which the Grand Alliance had fallen quenched these desires. All through September a series of letters from the Emperor, from Wratislaw, and from Eugene unfolded their new distresses and implored him to come himself to Vienna, and settle there, in the distracted capital of the Hapsburgs, whatever measures were possible to meet the dreaded opening of another campaign. Sunderland, now at Vienna, wrote urgently endorsing these requests. "If he does come," he wrote to Godolphin, "there is nothing in the power of this Court that he will not persuade them to."[2] Marlborough seems from the first to have been sure he ought to go. He laid his plans with his customary care. In forwarding the Emperor's appeal to Godolphin and the Cabinet he represented himself as disinclined to undertake so arduous a journey. Certainly it would not be worth while making it if he were not armed with authority first from England and then from Holland to bring effective financial and military aid to the Emperor. Unless this were forthcoming, and both the Sea Powers felt such a mission to be his unavoidable duty, he would not go. If he went so far as Vienna, he would return by the Courts of Berlin and Hanover to The Hague and reach

[1] August 16, 1705. [2] Coxe, ii, 225.

London early in the new year, having done what he could, and at any rate with full knowledge upon which to advise the Cabinet. Thus he made himself begged from all quarters before he committed himself to the course he desired.

At this time his thoughts were centred upon the Italian theatre. "It seems to me," he wrote to Wratislaw (October 5), "that it is high time to think seriously about this war in Italy, which employs so great a number of enemy troops, who would fall upon our backs everywhere if we were driven out of it."[1] His prime object was to secure money from England and Holland, and men from Prussia and the German princes, to sustain the army of Prince Eugene. It may well be that he had already in his mind a design for a decisive campaign in Italy, in which after a march longer and more adventurous than the march to the Danube he would himself join his glorious and now beloved comrade upon the plains of Lombardy for a battle that should outshine Blenheim. At any rate, he began by every means and from every quarter setting the flow of troops and supplies towards the south.

He planned his tour of Germany so as to meet every one who mattered on the way. He must visit the Elector Palatine and the authorities of the Electorate of Trèves. At Frankfort he must find d'Almelo and Davenant, the Dutch and English financial agents, and Geldermalsen, the Dutch Deputy, whose removal at least from the front he had been promised before the new campaign, but who still held his office unwitting; and here too he hoped to conciliate the Margrave, if Prince Louis's toe and temper would permit the rendezvous. To all these he wrote cordial letters specifying the business that must be transacted. Rantzau, the Prussian general, asked that his son might accompany the Duke upon his journey, and Marlborough invited the young man to join him at Ratisbon, "whence we will drop down the Danube together, and I will make it my task that his voyage shall be as agreeable to him as possible." To Stepney, the English Ambassador, he wrote:

> I must entreat the liberty when I come to Vienna to set up my field bed in your house, and if you find that preparations are making to lodge me elsewhere, I pray you will let the Prince of Salm . . . know that I expect this retirement as a particular mark of the Emperor's favour, and cannot on any terms admit of being elsewhere.[2]

Meanwhile he remained at his headquarters with the army until the

---

[1] Sir G. Murray, *Marlborough's Letters and Dispatches* (1845), ii, 293.
[2] *Dispatches*, ii, 296.

last possible moment, "spinning out the time" by the siege of Sandvliet "so that Prince Louis may not be interrupted in his operations on the Rhine," and paying only flying visits to The Hague.

Bavaria had revolted against its conquerors of the year before. The Bavarian army had continued a local resistance after the battle of Blenheim. It had surprised and routed with heavy loss the small Imperialist force left to besiege, or rather to blockade, Ingolstadt. The treaty signed with the Electress was repugnant to the Bavarian generals, who, now that the main allied armies had left Bavaria, desired to continue fighting. It was, however, enforced throughout the country by the Munich Government, and the bulk of the Bavarian army was disarmed and disbanded, and all the fortresses, with one single exception, were garrisoned by Imperial troops. The reader will remember M. de la Colonie, the "Old Campaigner," whose account of the Schellenberg is so valuable. It was due to La Colonie that Ingolstadt alone continued its resistance. This brave officer and his regiment of French grenadiers in the Bavarian service found themselves forgotten in the treaty, which covered only Bavarian subjects. They were without a military status of any kind, and opinion was divided upon whether they would be shot as deserters from the Empire, or hanged for the marauding for which they were notorious, or allowed to make their way back to France as unarmed individuals, with the certainty of being massacred by the infuriated Swabian peasantry. It would have gone hard with these men if they had not held together under their resolute leader.

In their desperation they animated the resistance to the terms of the treaty of all the Bavarian troops in Ingolstadt. Thus strengthened, they held the fortress, and declared themselves resolved to perish in their bastions unless they were granted honourable safe-conduct to France. The Allies in due course protested against the breach of the treaty. The Electress from Munich declared the recalcitrant garrison mutineers; but the deadlock continued. Superior forces at length arrived before Ingolstadt, and it seemed that a bloody event was inevitable. However, Prince Eugene, returning from the siege of Landau, took the matter into his own hands. He patiently inquired into the dispute. He treated La Colonie with soldierly respect, and entertained him at his table. He decided that the soldiers were entitled to their arrears of pay, and that the French grenadiers, together with the remaining French residents, should be escorted back to Strasburg as an armed force evacuating a foreign territory with the honours of war. Accordingly, La Colonie, after several private adventures, duels, legal processes, and a marriage, found himself by the end of 1705 commanding the remnants of his regiment under the Elector in the Low Countries.

The rancours in Bavaria had not ended with the dispersal of its military forces. The Bavarian nobility and people had not shared in their Elector's guilt, but they had paid the penalty. The devastation of the countryside before Blenheim had roused a fierce, abiding hatred of the Allies. The efforts of Vienna to recruit Bavarians for the Imperial service met with sullen and often savage resistance from all classes. Disorder and bloodshed spread throughout the ravaged principality. The dragon's teeth had been sown, and murder and revolt sprouted everywhere.

No enemy prince had suffered more at Marlborough's hands than Max Emmanuel, Elector of Bavaria. His country had been laid waste; his armies had been destroyed in the Blenheim campaign; his remaining cavalry and personal adherents had been routed at Elixem. He was a fugitive ruler serving far from home and family in the Low Countries as a French Marshal. A crowning disaster impended upon him. But at least he must have his sport. The wild boar which infested the Forest of Soignies afforded him the prospect of a hunting season, and he wrote to Marlborough early in September asking various passport courtesies and, above all, facilities to pursue the chase undisturbed in regions which the Allies now controlled. The Duke answered on September 25 in his most ceremonious style:

> Indeed I should be enchanted were it in my power to give the orders which His Highness desires to favour his hunting. When, however, he has thought the matter over carefully, he will see that it is not in my power to exempt so great a stretch of country from the movements of patrols; but as for the passports, they are at his service, and shall be couched in whatever terms he judges most convenient, there being nothing that I would not do to prove to his Electoral Highness the most submissive respect with which I have the honour to be Monseigneur's devoted, humble, and obedient servant.[1]

The Elector persisted, and on October 4 Marlborough expressed his "despair" not to be able to give orders forbidding his patrols to enter the Forest of Soignies.

"I flatter myself," he said,

[1] *Dispatches*, ii, 278.

that your Electoral Highness is convinced that if it depended upon me I should hasten with eagerness to accord everything he should ask, if only in order to mark the deference which I shall always have for his orders, begging him to do me the justice of believing that no one could be with more veneration and respect than I am Monseigneur's devoted servant.[1]

Making all allowance for the manners of the period between opposing commanders, there was more in these exchanges than their trivial topic would warrant. We have seen the distrust with which Max Emmanuel in his capacity as Vicar-General of the Netherlands was viewed at Versailles. The possibility of his making a separate peace for Belgium at the expense of France was never excluded from the French precautions. Sometimes it is convenient for public men to keep up a correspondence on slight matters with their opponents in order to preserve a certain personal intimacy and an easy approach should it become desirable. The extravagant flattery and humility with which Marlborough caressed the Elector were not only characteristic of the age and of Marlborough, but a measure of the situation, with, as we shall see, a bearing on the future.

Ailesbury has given us a picture of Marlborough at this very time more intimate than any other which his campaign records provide. The old Jacobite Earl had made repeated requests to be allowed to go back to his native land. He felt he had claims of friendship upon Marlborough dating from the Fenwick trial.[2] The Duke pitied his plight, liked his company, used him with tender courtesy, but was inflexible upon reasons of State. At the end of 1703 they had dined together on two nights at the Albemarles'. "The last night," says Ailesbury,

> the Duke drinking to the Lord and Lady of the house to all that could give us most satisfaction, Mr Meredith [one of Marlborough's rising brigadiers], who was diverting the company and ever towards me and my wife most obliging, cried out, "My Lord, I love deeds and not words. We are here all friends and in good humour, and pray let the whole company go to England in the same ship." My poor wife, that knew better, let fall some tears, on which my Lord Marlborough said somewhat [something] obligingly, but what was taken for Court holy-water, the expression in French when Ministers say what they do not think to perform.

Ailesbury, still eating his heart out in exile, had refused to call

---

[1] *Dispatches*, ii, 291.   [2] Vol. I, p. 405.

upon the Duke either on his return from Blenheim ("Hockster" he calls it) or in the spring of 1705. But now in October Count Oxenstiern urged him to come to Headquarters, "for that I had sufficiently mortified my Lord Marlborough for going from his promise (the year before) given to my wife." The Duke was quartered in a convent outside the gates of Tirlemont.

He supped not, so was generally alone. My host invited several of our nation to sup with me; the next morning he carried me to my Lord's, who was in business, and the Generals in chief and of the Auxiliary troops also were attending; but he sent for us two into his chamber, and, it being post-day that morning, he desired Count Oxenstiern to amuse me as well as possible until dinner time, and at his little table, a great word with him, he seldom having a great one save Sundays. He embraced me much, and made me many protestations. At dinner, sitting by me, he would continually take me by the hand, but politickly (of which he was a great master) putting his hand under the napkin. That night my Lord Orkney gave me a vast supper, and of consequence much company of all those he knew that had a regard for me; he had the hautboys of the regiment of foot-guards, and the Marquis, now Duke, of Lavalière that was at Aix, [taken] prisoner with Maréchal Tallard, had obtained by great favour liberty on his parole and permission to live in France, and out of gratitude he sent my Lord Marlborough, as Colonel of the Guards, a great number of books with the best airs, and all sorts of instruments, and of all countries, fit for hautboys, and the symphony was admirable;[1] and who should come in but my Lord Marlborough, with this expression (for he was not invited, as not supping), "My Lord Orkney, do not take it ill, if I say I come here for the sake of this Lord"—pointing to me. He was perfectly merry, and for him ate much and drank heartily, and we all found the effects of the excellent wine, and I never saw more mirth. The next day he asked me where I dined. I told him [at the same place] where he was [himself] [expected] to dine—at Count Oxenstiern's. "I shall not be so happy," he said, "for I am condemned to dine with base company, and shall have as base dinner." The three States Deputies of the Army had invited him, and that year they were three sad fellows and great pedants, and continually thwarting him.

The next day we were all invited to my Lord Albemarle's at Landen. That morning Maréchal Overkirk posted his troops and auxiliaries, the left line of the army in review, and my Lord Marlborough promised to come, but, we going to see him in the morning, he entertained us and the company so long that I put him in mind

[1] See *Dispatches*, ii, 194, 308.

of going. He whispered me in the ear that it was very indifferent to him. At last he went in his chaise for one person and one horse, and in getting up he set foot on ground again, and told me he had forgot to show me the plan of his house and gardens at Woodstock, and so went up again, and in pointing out the apartments for him and his lady, etc., laid his finger on one, and told me, "that is for you when you come and see me there"; and yet it was he that, out of policy and by a timorous temper, kept me on this side, together with my Lord Godolphin, and yet both in their hearts wished me most well.

I asked him who was his Architect (although I knew the man that was), he answered "Sir Jo. Van Brugg." On which I smiled and said, "I suppose my Lord you made choice of him because he is a professed Whig." I found he did not relish this, but he was too great a Courtier for to seem angry. It was at my tongue's end for to add that he ought as well to have made Sir Christopher Wren, the Architect, Poet Laureate. In fine, I understand but little or nothing of this matter but enough to affirm (by the plan I saw) that the house is like one mass of stone, without taste or relish.[1]

Sandvliet surrendered on October 29, and the armies dispersed into winter quarters thereafter. Marlborough had started on his journey on October 26. He passed through Dusseldorf on the 28th, and the next day he met the Elector Palatine. In order not to draw him from his road this prince entertained him in rustic state by the wayside. After a banquet in a tent they came to business. The States-General had tardily reached the conclusion that Count d'Aubach should be tried by a court martial for his shameful abandonment of Trèves in the spring. Marlborough had to procure the assent of the Elector, whose general Count d'Aubach was, to this process.

More serious was the question of troops. The Duke asked that three thousand Palatines should go to Italy. The Elector would only agree that the number of his subjects in the pay of the Sea Powers should be raised from seven to ten thousand; and there for the moment the matter rested. On the 31st Marlborough, having been escorted by the notables of Trèves through the electorate, entered Frankfort under triple salutes of cannon. Here the Margrave awaited him. They had not met since the Margrave had wrecked Marlborough's campaign on the Moselle, and Marlborough had rated him before Europe. Many shrewd, anxious eyes watched the demeanour of these two captains between whom there were so many griefs, just and unjust. But all was honeysweet. The out-

[1] *Memoirs of Thomas, Earl of Ailesbury*, ii, 585–587.

side world received the impression of a complete reconciliation, and Marlborough, after long closetings with D'Almelo, Davenant, and the Frankfort bankers, resumed his journey to Vienna, where he hoped to secure the Margrave's removal from the Rhine command.

At Ratisbon, which he reached on November 6, the Imperial yachts were moored. One might have thought that floating down the Danube in these sumptuous barges would have been a welcome interlude after the fatigues of the campaign, of the journey, and of such tangled affairs. But, on the contrary, Marlborough in two of his letters describes the voyage as "tedious." He landed at Vienna on the 12th. Sunderland was on the quay with Stepney and an array of Austrian magnates. A palace had been prepared for his reception, but he stuck to his plan of "setting up his field bed" at the British Embassy. He intended to transfer Stepney to another post, and it was therefore necessary to uphold this able agent in the most public manner, and make both him and the Austrians feel that his services were not undervalued by his countrymen. The young Emperor, who was still under Marlborough's spell, received him with all the honours which the tottering yet august Court could bestow. But the next day our hero was laid up with an attack of the gout, and most of the conferences took place in his bedroom.

Everything was settled as well as the bleak facts admitted. The first need was money; the credit of the Empire was sunk so low that immediate local bankruptcy threatened the Austrian Government. Marlborough had to engage his private fortune with the bankers of Vienna to procure a hundred thousand crowns to pay the wages. He promised in the name of the Sea Powers a loan of £250,000 for Prince Eugene's army; but care was taken that none of this money passed through the hands of the Imperial Court. It was eventually sent through Frankfort to a financial house in Venice and thence paid direct to the order of Prince Eugene. The Emperor explained the impossibility of removing the Margrave on account of his influence in Swabia and Franconia. Marlborough exposed to the Emperor and his Ministers the grievances of the Prussian King and the imperative need of satisfying them. The harassed Court placed their affairs in this quarter in his hands. The most delicate topic was Hungary. There had been for some weeks an armistice which Rakoczy had accepted but encroached upon, and which the Imperial generals observed only for the purpose of revictualling their isolated fortresses in rebel territory. The counsels

47

which Marlborough had given his son-in-law at the camp on the Dyle had borne fruit: Sunderland had acquitted himself with tact and good sense. He had formed an independent opinion that the rebels were asking for more than any sovereign could give. The Whig doctrinaire and republican, whose advent had been dreaded by the Austrian Court, was now cherished. All their reproaches were directed upon Stepney; but even these were abated. The English envoys undertook to tell the Sea Powers that the faults at this time lay with Rakoczy and that mediation was impossible.

Here we must digress upon the princely rank and principality which the late Emperor Leopold had offered Marlborough during the march to Blenheim. The Duke certainly desired this honour, extraordinary for a private person. He had procured the Queen's permission and overridden Sarah's objections with his usual skilful management. After the victory on the Danube he had made Wratislaw press the old Emperor to fulfil his promise, and in lengthy correspondence had made it clear that he would not take the dignity without the actual grant of lands and a seat and vote in the Diet of the Empire. When difficulties of public business arose between him and Wratislaw at the end of 1704 and thereafter, the artful Austrian more than once brought into his letters references to the principality and the trouble he was taking to meet Marlborough's wishes, as if he thought he had him on a hook. Marlborough was determined not to accept anything that was not a reality. He would not take the empty title. The promise must be redeemed in fact as well as in form. If not he would have none of it, and as soon as he perceived Wratislaw's thought he immediately brushed the whole project aside and quite curtly told the great diplomatist not to cumber their correspondence with such minor matters. Thereafter there had been a long silence upon the topic. In none of Wratislaw's lengthy letters appealing to Marlborough to come to Vienna is there the slightest suggestion that the visit would afford an occasion for imparting substance to the princely title by which Marlborough was already recognized in Europe. No one can read the correspondence without seeing how entirely Marlborough excluded his personal vanities from the great affairs he handled.

Now at Vienna the new Emperor Joseph was able to redeem his father's promise. Mindelheim, a small but *bona fide* principality, was produced. This estate had been bought by an Elector of Bavaria in the sixteenth century, and had been held more or less continuously by his successors since then. It was confiscated in 1704 from Max Emmanuel after his treachery, and effectively occupied after Blenheim. But, like other war-conquests, its fate depended on the ultimate peace treaty. The grant was made with all possible ceremony, and the princes of the Empire were summoned by Imperial rescript to meet together and accept the Englishman as a brother-prince. Even now the difficulties were not at an end. Mindelheim produced an annual income of fifteen hundred pounds; but by ancient law its yield was charged in war-time with an Imperial tax about four times as great. Moreover, the expense of being made a prince of the Empire amounted to from twelve to fifteen thousand pounds, payable by the recipient of the honour. On this basis it was a negative gift. Marlborough, though attracted by the dignity, had equally clear views, as we have seen, upon the value of money. Archdeacon Coxe devotes an entire chapter to the laborious negotiations which followed and the stately ceremonial in which they culminated. In the upshot Marlborough was prepared to pay £4500 for his installation, but no more, and the Imperial Ministers had to arrange that the war surcharges did not apply to him, so that the net income of about fifteen hundred pounds a year was free. This might in itself be taken as a profitable though precarious return upon the Duke's capital investment.

These details being eventually settled after many months' decorous haggling, the Diet of the Holy Roman Empire assembled at Innsbrück in April 1706, and a high festival was held after the custom of ancient times with as much magnificence as Marlborough's £4500 would warrant. The King of Prussia by all his representatives, through the mouth of the valiant Prince of Anhalt-Dessau of Blenheim fame, moved that the title should descend successively to all the heirs of Marlborough's body. The princes of the Empire would not swallow this. The fact that he was without a male heir had been essential to their agreement. Marlborough the Victor they would have, if necessary, in their sacred circle; but they were disinclined to see his remote descendants taking their seats and casting their votes in the Imperial Diet.

Marlborough does not seem to have cared about this. He thought the rank was worth paying £4500 for, and probably that was about its real value to him in his relations with princely commanders. Apart from this there was the income, if realizable. It did not prove so for long. The Treaty of Utrecht restored Mindelheim to the Elector of Bavaria, provided no compensation to the

Captain-General, now fallen from favour and command, and had no thought of repaying the £4500 which he had invested in his installation. Charles after he became Emperor seems to have had some pricks of conscience, and went out of his way in 1712 to write apologetic letters about it, which Marlborough in due course accepted with proper gratitude. The title of Prince of the Holy Roman Empire has, however, descended to this day.

On November 23 Marlborough and Sunderland set out for Berlin, and such were the pains taken to smooth and speed their journey that they covered the five hundred and thirty miles in eight days in their coaches, in spite of the bad roads and winter weather. The Prussian capital was at this moment the danger-point of the Alliance. The irritation of the King expressed a grave political crisis. There never was a milestone at which Prussia had more obviously a choice. The northern war lapped her frontiers, and created problems and also opportunities which the rest of the Allies did not share. The Swedish dare-devil, Charles XII, was victorious on every side. The home lands of Brandenburg might suffer his invasion. On the other hand flickered a sinister temptation. What could resist the union of Prussian and Swedish ambitions, and of Prussian and Swedish troops? Such a revolution on the part of Prussia would overturn the historic system of Europe. It would force immediately all the Germanic princes to withdraw for their own protection not only the troops they owed to the service of the Empire, but their mercenaries serving under the Sea Powers. The grievous losses suffered by the eight thousand Prussians with Prince Eugene at the battle of Cassano had roused a natural emotion in Berlin. Their withdrawal alone meant the downfall of the Italian front against France. That these ideas were not outlawed from Prussian thoughts is evident. Against them stood the solemn veto of past ages. Deep in the heart of the Prussian state and race lay the antagonism to France. Such a desertion of the Teutonic principle spelt the triumph of the Gaul.

Surely, however, short of an act of irrevocable betrayal, there were infinite means of extorting favours from the wealth of England and the ancient majesty of the Empire. The raw Prussian monarchy with many troops and little money had men to sell. There was no lack in Prussia then, as in every century, of brave, docile, faithful soldiers. These, then, must be marketed on terms which would most conduce to the strength of the Prussian state. The mere withdrawal of the Prussian troops from Italy and from the Rhine would almost certainly be fatal to the Allies. But this was not so easy as it looked. It was shrewdly realized throughout the Alliance that the Prussians could not be withdrawn by a simple decision from Berlin. Without the money of the Sea Powers they could not even be fed except by rapine in the countries through which they must make their homeward march. And who would keep all these soldiers when they came home? What would they do if they were not kept? All the materials, therefore, existed for an interminable series of hagglings, bargainings, and blackmailings. In the shadows of the background lay a greater danger still.

Louis XIV, alive to all these aspects, offered recognition of the Prussian kingship and important territories, including Guelderland, merely for non-reinforcement of the Prussian troops in the allied ranks. The Czar and Augustus II of Saxony and Poland were suitors of Frederick I in other interests.

The recital of these facts shows the delicate, unpromising, and critical quest on which Marlborough must now engage himself. Nevertheless, such was the wonder and curiosity with which he was regarded by this ambitious King and his military Court that his arrival steadied the balance, and the weight of England in his hands turned the scale. The King was frankly delighted to see him again. His diplomatic ill-humour disappeared. In a week of conferences and festivities Marlborough convinced the Berlin Government that the main foe of Prussia was France, and her sure stand-by England. To achieve this he took great responsibility. He promised that if Prussian territory should be in danger anywhere England would protect it. At the general peace Queen Anne would treat the interests of Prussia as her own. He bore authority from Vienna to guarantee the assent of the Emperor to the conditions of the renewed treaty which he proposed. In December Prussia agreed that her contingents, raised to their full strength, should serve with the Allies in Italy and upon the Rhine during the whole of 1706. When he left for Hanover bearing with him a jewelled sword, the gift of the King, he had once again staved off for the time being the collapse of the Alliance and the loss of the war.

The Court at Hanover had been thrown into the liveliest perturbation by the news which reached them from London. The debate in the Lords on Haversham's motion produced the worst impression. That the Whigs, the sworn friends of the house of Hanover, should have joined with the Ministers of Queen Anne in rejecting so fair-seeming a Tory proposal was to these eager foreign students of our affairs incomprehensible. As is usual in small countries deeply concerned in the internal politics of a powerful ally or neighbour, the royal family and the leading politicians cultivated different sympathies, so that some of them would be good friends with whatever faction in the larger state was uppermost at any given moment. The aged Electress thus held that the Tories would prove the truest friends of the house of Hanover. Her son, the Elector, put his trust in the Whigs. The Electress now vaunted her superior judgment: the Elector deplored the inconstancy of his Whigs, and both were disgusted to the point of threatening to recall their troops by the behaviour of Queen Anne's Ministers. Both fell upon Marlborough with demands for explanations and assurances. Happily, that diligent servant had not been left unprovided with instructions from home. A letter from the Queen left no doubt upon the main point.

The Queen to Marlborough

Nov. 13 [1705]

The Prince is [so] very desirous of having his niece, the Princess of Denmark, married to the King of Prussia that I cannot help giving you this trouble to desire you to try if there be any hopes of bringing it to pass, for I doubt unless you can do anything towards it, it will never be compassed. . . .

The disagreeable proposal of bringing some of the house of Hanover into England (which I have been afraid of so long) is now very near being brought into both Houses of Parliament, which gives me a great deal of uneasiness, for I am of a temper always to fear the worst. There have been assurances given that Mr Shutes[1] should have instructions to discourage the propositions, but as yet he has said nothing of them, which makes me fear there may be some alterations in their resolution at the Court of Hanover. I shall depend upon your friendship and kindness to set them right in notions of things here, and if they will be quiet I may be so too, or else I must expect to meet with a great many mortifications.[2]

With these commands arrived also the Ministerial and Whig justifications of the course they had been forced to adopt. More important still, Marlborough was furnished with the drafts of the Bills providing for a regency upon the demise of the Crown and for the British naturalization of the Electress and of all her Protestant

---

[1] Schütz, the Hanoverian Agent in London.

[2] "This letter shews the great aversion the Queen had to the King [*sic*] of Hanover."
—Sarah's endorsement. (*H.M.C.*, 8th Report, Marlborough Papers, p. 103.)

descendants. Armed with these, Marlborough soon convinced the Elector of the fidelity of the Whigs, and the Electress Sophia of the good intentions of the Government. Some little umbrage was at first taken that a reigning German sovereign and heir-designate to the English throne should require to be naturalized like an ordinary person. But it was easy for Marlborough to show how necessary this was to meet the peculiar laws of the islanders and to place the British friends of the house of Hanover in a strong position to deal with common enemies. His personal glamour and the impression of weight, magnitude, and command which he always inspired abroad did the rest. Hanover became happy. All difficulties about the troops disappeared. Compliments and flatteries were the order of the day. Marlborough was presented with a coach and six horses, although he deemed his Blenheim coach still good enough, and Sunderland with "a set of horses." Sarah, no doubt apprised in good time, had sent the Electress a portrait of the Queen, which the old lady acknowledged in terms which left no doubt of her satisfaction:

> I think that after all the kindness you have had the goodness to show me you will be pleased with my acquainting you with the joy we felt in having had my Lord Duke here in person, and in finding that his manners are as obliging and polished as his actions are glorious and admirable. I have testified to him the esteem I feel for the present you have made me of the Queen's portrait, which I prize much more than it is possible to prize that of the whole universe, which I send you in tapestry.

"The day after I came," wrote Marlborough,

> I had a very long conversation with this Elector, who did not want many arguments to convince him that his and the Queen's interest were the same. He has commanded me to assure her Majesty that he will never have any thoughts but what may be agreeable to hers.[1]

A certain amount of irritation remained, however, beneath the surface. We find on January 1 Sir Rowland Gwynne, the English Resident in Hanover, writing an indiscreet letter to an English peer, full of bitter complaints against the Whigs, which, when it became public, both Houses declared to be a libel, ordering the printer to be mulcted. For the next six months Halifax, Somers, and other leading Whigs were occupied in making their peace with the Hanoverian Court, and trying to explain to them the intricacies

---

[1] Coxe, ii, 260–261.

of party manœuvres at Westminster. Marlborough during his three-day stay at Hanover was forced to deal with an extremely tangled dispute about the winter quarterings of the allied troops in the various electorates along the Rhine, and he settled the matter satisfactorily by eleven letters to the Electors, Bishops, Princes, Landgraves, Deputies, and other notables concerned.[1] Then he set out for Holland.

He reached The Hague on December 15 after a journey by coach and barge in mid-winter of nearly two thousand miles. Delayed by contrary winds and the consequent lack of battleship convoy, he did not arrive in London till December 31/January 11. He was weary and worn, but he had restored for the moment the cohesion of the Grand Alliance, and made the preliminary dispositions for the coming campaign.

[1] *Dispatches*, ii, 337–344.

Chapter Three

THE WAR IN SPAIN

1705–1706

GIBRALTAR had fallen into English hands in August 1704. It had successfully withstood Louis XIV's formidable efforts at recapture. The allied invasion from Portugal had languished. The youthful Archduke, brother of the Emperor Joseph, whom the Allies under British instigation had proclaimed King Charles III of Spain, had perforce lingered in Lisbon endeavouring to animate King Pedro II, and comforted by the indefatigable ambassador, Methuen. We have not broken the chain of events in the main theatre to describe the course of the Spanish diversion; but the curtain must now rise upon a scene where striking episodes and personages play their part.[1]

In Spain from the summer of 1705 to the autumn of 1706 the cause of the Two Crowns fell to so low an ebb that the War of the Spanish Succession seemed to be settling itself in the country primarily concerned. The failure of the large Franco-Spanish army under Marshal Tessé to recover Gibraltar at the end of 1704 had been followed by a complete lull in the Spanish war. It was throughout a war of petty armies, occasionally fighting small, fierce battles and making long marches about an enormous country in the main stony and desolate. The fortresses, ill-protected by defences or garrisons, easily changed hands. The sympathies of the countryside, however, played a serious part in the fortunes of the wandering armies, and a surge of national feeling was almost immediately decisive. So far the Allies, advancing eastward with the Portuguese, had made little or no progress. The Marquis de Ruvigny, who commanded there, was one of King William's generals, a French Huguenot refugee raised to the English peerage. The Earl of Galway, to use the title by which he was henceforward known, was an heroic figure in the resistance to the tyranny and persecution of Louis XIV. He had been Deputy-General of the Huguenots. Connected by marriage to the Russells, he had acquired English

[1] See general map of Spain facing p. 1041.

nationality as early as 1688. He had commanded for King William in Ireland. He had fought in his Continental campaigns. Saint-Simon has recorded the moving story of his adventure at the battle of Landen.[1] His French captors, knowing that his life was forfeit, in the heat of battle refused with soldierly magnanimity to hold him prisoner. They found him a horse and set him free. He was a gallant and faithful man, and a skilful, experienced professional soldier. A contemporary record describes him as "one of the finest gentlemen in the army, with a head fitted for the Cabinet as well as the camp; is very modest, vigilant, and sincere; a man of honour and honesty, without pride or affectation; wears his own hair, is plain in his dress and manners."[2] His right hand had recently been shattered by a cannon-ball at the siege of Badajos, and he had henceforth to be lifted on to his horse like a child.

Marlborough had known him long and held him in the highest esteem. He had himself chosen him for the command of the Portugal expedition. Without approving some of his operations, he upheld him through the worst misfortunes. He defended his military character in strong and even passionate terms when Galway was censured by Parliament in 1711.

But now a far more brilliantly coloured personality was to enter upon the Spanish scene. Early in 1705 the English Government decided, under Marlborough's impulse, to use their sea-power in the Mediterranean. A wide latitude was necessarily accorded to the commanders of the fleet and army. Their prime purpose was to assist the Duke of Savoy upon the Riviera coast. Their second was to act in Spain, as they might decide upon the spot. The preference of the Cabinet was for the succour of the Duke of Savoy. Already Marlborough hankered for an attack upon Toulon. As early as April 1705 he described Toulon to Briançon, the Savoy envoy in London, as a main English objective.[3] The slow, precarious communications forbade them to prejudge the issue from Whitehall. In order to avoid repeating the naval and military discordances which had wrecked the Cadiz enterprise in 1702, it was resolved that the general should not only command the troops, but should have equal power with the admiral in the strategic movements of the fleet. Sir Cloudesley Shovell was appointed to the naval command, and Charles Mordaunt, Earl of Peterborough, became Commander-in-Chief in Spain with additional commission as Admiral,

---

[1] *Mémoires* (1873), i, 95.   [2] John Macky, quoted in *D.N.B.* (1909), xiii, 21.
[3] Briançon's dispatch; Pelet, v, 629.

jointly with Shovell. Peterborough's appointment was delayed till Parliament had separated, as it was known to be unacceptable to both political parties.

We cannot attempt here to appraise the character and quality of one who is called by his admirers "the great Earl of Peterborough," but merely to present the reflections cast upon his memorable deeds and misdeeds by Marlborough's judgment and actions. Hoffmann reported to his Government upon him, "He is of such a temperament that he cannot brook an equal. He is a thoroughly restless and quarrelsome character, incapable of dealing with anybody, . . . and on top of that he has had no war experience on land or sea."[1] This seems to have been well informed. John and Sarah had known Peterborough all his life, and had tasted his malice and mischief as far back as the trial of Sir John Fenwick in 1696.[2] In the closing years of King William, and since the opening of the new reign, friendly and even cordial relations seemed to have subsisted between the Marlborough and Peterborough families. We have seen how Peterborough's intrepid son, the hero of the forlorn hope at the Schellenberg, had wooed but not won Marlborough's youngest daughter, Mary.[3] Peterborough certainly regarded the Marlboroughs, especially Sarah, as friends who rated him at his own valuation. He corresponded with the Duchess in terms of gay affability, and with the Duke with almost obsequious respect. Sarah, whose sure scent for genius had led her in her youth to marry the penniless John Churchill, and was to lead her in old age to bestow ten thousand pounds upon the great Pitt, then equally undistinguished, was evidently conscious of the Peterborough spell. Certainly she sang his praises to Marlborough during 1705, and Marlborough bears responsibility both for the appointment and for its exceptional conditions.

It is strange that he should have chosen a commander for Spain whose character, qualifications, and methods were so utterly different from his own. Peterborough had, as Hoffmann reported, no training as either soldier or sailor. He lacked patience, reserve, and persistency. He was quarrelsome and boastful. His caprice, or inspiration, was incalculable. His recklessness, his violence and profusion, were well known. How far, then, did Marlborough act upon his own

---

[1] Hoffmann's dispatch, April 7; Kunzel (German life of Hesse-Darmstadt), p. 555, quoted in Klopp, *Der Fall des Hauses Stuart*, xi, 489. Hoffmann was one of the two Imperial envoys in London.

[2] Vol. I, p. 405. [3] Vol. II, p. 657.

judgment and how far did he trust himself to Sarah's instinct? At any rate, at the end of May 1705 an armada of sixty-six British and Dutch battleships, with many smaller vessels and 6500 soldiers, sailed from Portsmouth to Lisbon under the command of Peterborough and Shovell.

In issuing their orders to an expedition which once launched passed almost completely out of control the English Cabinet, guided by Marlborough, had pondered deeply upon their past experience. Although there was much friction, upon which historians have dilated, the arrangement at first worked well, and the results were splendid. All the leaders of the Allies for the war in Spain met at Lisbon in the last week of June 1705. Charles III, with his handful of personal officers, awaited them. Das Minas, the Portuguese general, and Galway rode in from the front a little beyond the Portuguese boundary. The valiant Prince George of Hesse-Darmstadt, an Imperial Field-Marshal at thirty-six, came in an English frigate fresh from his six months' defence of Gibraltar. To these were now joined Peterborough, with Stanhope at his side, and Shovell, with Leake his second-in-command. This symposium of forceful, competing personalities was gathered to debate problems offering many alternatives. Their subsequent quarrels have led historians to dwell upon their differences. But the outstanding fact at the beginning is their agreement and its successful execution. Peterborough, fresh from Whitehall, leaned to the succour of Savoy. The Archduke, the Allies' King of Spain, naturally regarded this as desertion of his cause. He had been sent by the Allies to fight for the Spanish crown in Spain. What was this talk of Italy?

Darmstadt, as we may call him, seems first to have recommended a march on Madrid through Valencia; but he was also agreeable to an attack on Barcelona. He had defended Barcelona against the French in 1697. He had been Viceroy of Catalonia. The Catalans regarded him with gratitude and admiration. He had played a decisive part in the capture of Gibraltar, and was the soul of its defence. Whether under his influence or not, the Lisbon Council chose Barcelona as their goal. Their discussions and the necessary preparations were protracted, but at length the great fleet resumed its progress. Galway authorized the exchange of the seasoned regiments at Gibraltar for the raw English and Irish recruits, and contributed two regiments of Dragoons. All were confirmed in their resolve by a dispatch from London giving the Queen's permission for a landing in Catalonia.[1] Marlborough had learned from the English envoy with the Duke of Savoy, Richard Hill, that an attempt upon Toulon was not to be contemplated. He therefore relaxed his dominating control, and was content to see a Spanish venture in 1705.

On the voyage along the eastern coast of Spain the fleet touched at Denia, in Valencia. They were received with enthusiasm by the people. The magistrates of Philip V made immediate submission. All reports declared the acceptance by Valencia of the Hapsburg claim. Peterborough was excited. He saw the merit of Darmstadt's first suggestion. "Land here," he urged, "and march directly upon Madrid." The distance was but a hundred and fifty miles through easy, unravaged country. In a fortnight, he suggested, King Charles III would be enthroned in the Spanish capital. This was widely different from his previous counsel; but no one can say it was wrong. However, Darmstadt had now been rallied by Charles III to the capture of Barcelona. He believed and protested that all Catalonia would rise to welcome him. Ultimately what he said proved true. The youthful sovereign, with the proved officer whose name seemed to be magic upon these doubtful coasts, prevailed. Peterborough, the Commander-in-Chief, submitted, and the fleet sailed northward to Barcelona. By this time there was sharp disagreement in this hydra-headed enterprise. Probably if Marlborough had been in Peterborough's shoes in the Lisbon discussions he would have refrained from advocacy of any course. He would have been content if all were agreed that the fleet, having on board the strongest possible force, should pass the Pillars of Hercules and enter the Mediterranean. He would have left the partisans of various plans to exhaust each other and so gradually transform a nominal command-in-chief into effective control. But Peterborough struck with all his force in one direction, and now, valid reasons having arisen, with equal vehemence in another. Thus he lost much power.

In the third week of August the armada anchored before Barcelona. This was the most populous and wealthy city of Spain. It was a fortress of no mean repute, tested within a decade by siege. Its fortifications could not compare with the wonderful creations of Vauban in the Low Countries. But they comprised a complete perimeter of bastioned ramparts and ditches, and the most vulnerable quarter was guarded by the strong stone star-fort of the Montjuich upon its dominating height three-quarters of a mile south of

[1] Klopp, xi, 497.

the city. The Spanish Governor, Don Velasco, was a resolute, vindictive champion of the Bourbons. He had about three thousand trustworthy soldiers under his command. On August 22 Charles III landed north of Barcelona, and was greeted and acclaimed by the Catalans, who flocked to his banner. The sympathies of Catalonia were manifestly favourable. Crowds of countryfolk and local nobility assembled to welcome him. Of armed forces only fifteen hundred Miquelets, as the Catalan rebels were called, presented themselves.

Velasco saw in the local hostility a military advantage for the defence of Barcelona. The Allies could not afford to destroy their popularity with the Catalans by starving the citizens or bombarding their dwellings, still less by delivering them to storm and sack. With all these facts present in their minds also, the councils of war upon Sir Cloudesley Shovell's flagship became distracted. Charles, animated by Darmstadt, demanded a siege. Shovell supported him. No one has ever been able to plumb Peterborough's mind. Whether he was actuated by caprice and day-to-day events, or whether he prepared a profound design with all Marlborough's dissimulation, may well be indefinitely disputed. Certainly he could exert his influence most strongly by urging his Lisbon proposal to proceed at once to Italy. The armed support which Darmstadt had predicted—nay, promised—in Catalonia was lacking. The Council had rejected his own bold plan of a march from Valencia on Madrid. What hopes were there of capturing a fortified city which could not even be bombarded for fear of alienating local sympathy? Peterborough played this card for all it was worth. Thus, with a shrewdness unusual in him, he forced all his colleagues to try to conciliate him. From weakness or from craft he yielded to their wishes, but he stipulated—and all agreed—that eighteen days was to be the limit of the siege.

Accordingly the guns were landed and siege approaches made from the north side of the town, supported by sixteen thousand soldiers and sailors, mainly British. The ground was marshy and difficult, and Governor Velasco protected his ramparts at the threatened point by a preliminary lunette. No practicable breach appeared, and Peterborough continued to baffle the council of war by the alternatives of a march to Valencia and thence to Madrid, or preferably an immediate departure for Italy. After a fortnight when everything was thus in the most perfect confusion he suddenly emerged with an audacious surprise. He informed Darmstadt that he was about to assault the Montjuich. The Prince, who, according to some, had already pressed this course, was delighted. Neither of them told Charles III or the admirals of their plan till the troops were already marching.

On the evening of September 13, 1705, a thousand men, of whom eight hundred were English, set off under Peterborough and Darmstadt ostensibly for Tarragona, the first stage in a march southward to Valencia. A reserve of twelve hundred men under Stanhope followed later. The fleet cannon had already been re-embarked, and Governor Velasco was preparing his celebrations. Peterborough and Darmstadt marched all night by the circuitous route shown on the map at p. 62, and at daybreak appeared from the contrary quarter upon the most accessible side of the Montjuich. There followed a comedy of chance which was also an epic. The assailants stormed the outer works. They placed their ladders in the stone ditch, but these proved too short by seven or eight feet, and they found themselves stopped. The scanty garrison sent frantic messages for help to the city. Governor Velasco dispatched at once a hundred dragoons, each with an infantryman riding pillion. The garrison, seeing this help approaching, raised a cheer which Lord Charlemont, who commanded the British brigade, mistook as the signal for surrender. Thereupon the English leaped into the covered way, assuming themselves the victors. In this exposed situation they received a series of deadly volleys from the cannon and musketry of the fort. Many fell and two hundred surrendered. Darmstadt, hastening to intercept Velasco's reinforcement, was wounded. A bullet severed the major artery in his thigh, and in a brief space he bled to death. Aghast at this catastrophe, Charlemont's remaining men retreated. They had already abandoned the action when Peterborough, arriving, behaved in a most becoming manner. Seizing a half-pike and declaring he would conquer or die, he rallied his surviving soldiers and led them back to the outworks. This would have availed him nothing but for a curious turn of luck.

The two hundred prisoners were being hustled down the hill towards Barcelona, three-quarters of a mile away, when they met virtually the whole garrison of the city advancing to the rescue of the Montjuich. Interrogated, they admitted that both Peterborough and Darmstadt were assaulting the fort. The officer in command of the relief was staggered by the presence of these great personalities. He concluded that the bulk of the allied army must be with them; he therefore returned to Barcelona, and sealed its fate. By extraordinary exertions ships' cannon, relanded, were dragged into the captured outworks, and from this deadly position launched a bombardment which after three days compelled the commandant of the fort to surrender. The fall of the Montjuich broke the spirit of Velasco. He agreed to capitulate unless relieved within four days. Hostages were accordingly exchanged, Stanhope representing the

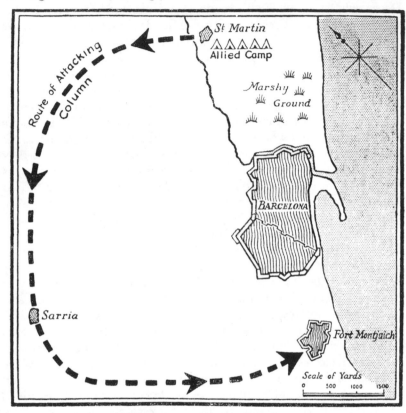

THE CAPTURE OF BARCELONA

Allies. The terms could not however be executed. The excitement of the Barcelona populace rose to an uncontrollable pitch. The Miquelets from the surrounding hills penetrated the city. The massacre of Bourbon adherents without respect to age, sex, or quality was imminent. The Governor invoked the aid of his hostage, Stanhope. Peterborough with strong forces entered the city while it was in wild confusion, and had the crowning and romantic satisfaction of personally saving a beautiful and terrified duchess from the fury of the mob. Even the King, who suffered so much from his arrogance, wrote to Queen Anne that Peterborough had saved the city from "a veritable blood bath."[1]

However it happened, Barcelona was captured. Whosoever's conception it was, whether it arose from accident, caprice, or profound design, the glory belongs to Peterborough, who lost no time in claiming it. Forthwith he sent Stanhope to England with dispatches couched in a grandiloquent vein, with letters to the Ministers, and to all his friends and his family, clamouring for praise, reinforcements, and appointment as commander-in-chief of all the forces in Spain, with sole control of the fleet.

Conflicting accounts reached Marlborough from Barcelona. On September 29 he wrote to Hedges, the Secretary of State for the Southern Department:

> When the Duke of Savoy receives these dispatches, and sees how earnest the Queen is in giving him all the assistance that is possible, it will encourage H.R.H. to continue firm in the interest of the Allies, which, I believe, he must needs be sensible is his own too, though he may suffer for the present. And if the good news we have from Catalonia be confirmed, no doubt but it will have a great influence upon our affairs in Italy, and likewise in Portugal. By letters I received yesterday I am advised that the whole country had owned King Charles, and that even at Barcelona the inhabitants had taken arms to oblige the garrison to surrender, so that it was not doubted but H.M. was in possession of the city likewise.[2]

And three weeks later:

> A great deal will depend on what we do in Catalonia, from whence the news you send me is the freshest we have that we can depend upon. The last letters from Paris of the 16th pretend that Barcelona held out still, but we have no reason to doubt our affairs going well on that side, since they tell us nothing to the contrary. We were still in hopes, till the receipt of your letters, that the news of the Prince of Darmstadt's death might not be true.[3]

The news of the capture of Barcelona had been hailed in London with unbridled enthusiasm. The highest opinion was held of King Charles's conduct. Godolphin was impressed by his detailed report to the Government. The English bias, especially Tory bias, was so strong for Spanish operations and for using the naval power that the capture of a fortress in Spain was judged at double the far stiffer similar prize in Flanders. Stanhope's mission met with the

---

[1] G. de Lamberty, *Mémoires pour servir à l'histoire du xviii siècle*, iii, 543.
[2] *Dispatches*, ii, 284.   [3] *Ibid.*, 312.

warmest response. Parliament presented addresses acclaiming the prowess and conduct of Peterborough. Five thousand British infantry and two hundred and fifty thousand pounds, together with a strong squadron under Byng, were eagerly devoted to the Peninsular campaign of 1706.

Success, however, had not assuaged the quarrels of the allied commanders. Everybody hated Peterborough, and Peterborough struck at all. His differences with "the Germans," or "the Vienna crew," as he described Charles III and his Imperialist advisers, soon made even formal relations difficult. "If another general," wrote Prince Lichtenstein, one of Charles's Austrian counsellors and his old tutor (November 5, 1705), "had been in command, it would have been easy to take Majorca or Minorca, and to conquer the whole of Aragon and Valencia." He added, "All the officers under Lord Peterborough seek to leave for home. But I see no hope they will send us out a better general from England."[1] On the other hand, Peterborough himself was vociferous. "God protect this land," he wrote to Stanhope (November 18), "from even the best of the German Ministers."[2] Peterborough's vanity, his violence, his giddy shifts of view and of mood, made him quarrel with the young King, with the allied generals and the English admirals. Shovell had sailed for home with most of the heavy ships. But Leake, who remained upon the coast, regarded this human firework with equal dislike and distrust. In December Charles appealed to London to send Galway from Portugal to take the command.

The effects of the fall of Barcelona and the ardour of the whole province enabled the small allied forces to become speedily masters of every stronghold in Catalonia and on the Aragon frontier. At the same time the Spanish officers whom Darmstadt with sure knowledge had selected to uphold King Charles's causes in Valencia met with unbroken success. Peterborough after several minor successes entered Valencia at the end of January 1706, and Charles was then in effective possession of all eastern Spain with the overwhelming support of its inhabitants. These conquests—easy come and easy go though they were to prove—threw a glowing light upon the Spanish scene at the end of the year, when all else was black or grey.

Yet beneath the surface of success were causes of deep anxiety. Charles III, writing to Marlborough from Barcelona (October 22, 1705), described his condition in gloomy terms:

[1] *Feldzüge*, Series 2, viii, 552   [2] Klopp, xi, 507.

64

*. . . We are in want of everything necessary for the war, having neither the money nor the ammunition required to defend Catalonia, which is all for us, except Rosas, . . . but the country very devoted. . . . We are in great danger, whatever Lord Peterborough's efforts may be, without prompt and extraordinary succours. . . .[1]

And Peterborough, amid his gay diversions in Valencia, was himself under no illusions.

Peterborough to Marlborough

VALENCIA
3 *February*, 1706

*MY LORD,

How long we can resist such odds I know not. It is very uncomfortable to receive no letter this four months. My Lord, it is a hard shift I am put to to sustain a war against French Generals and French troops with a Spanish horse—the best that be seen anywhere—without troops, without baggage, without money, in a country without an Officer speaking the language but myself. . . . The greatest honours imaginable have been paid in Valencia to the Queen, and we have been received with unexpressible marks of joy. I think we have deserved to some degree the kindness they have expressed. Under all fatigues I endure and dangers I undergo my comfort is that I have done my duty and that I am confident I shall continue to do so. I wish My Lord a happy campaign. I believe Your Grace has had a good winter one, and I hope whenever we are overpowered the enemy shall pay a reasonable reckoning. It is a great pity, My Lord, that we should have made such false steps as those I have given much account of, and that we must languish so long without relief or support.[2]

The active prosecution of the war in the Peninsula had really sprung from English Parliamentary circles. The Cabinet and Marlborough became conscious of a strong impulse of support for this theatre. They yielded somewhat easily to a genial breeze. Many writers have censured the dispersion of forces as improvident and unorthodox. There is no doubt that Marlborough was influenced by politics rather than by strategy in the tolerance, and more than tolerance, which he showed to the Spanish venture. Still, he could have cited facts and figures in deprecation if not in defence. The English expenditure in the Low Countries in 1706 was £1,366,000 and in Spain no less than £1,093,071.[3] The number of English troops, apart from those in English pay, sent to Spain was above

[1] Blenheim MSS.   [2] *Ibid.*
[3] *Letters and Accounts of James Brydges. Cf.* G. M. Trevelyan, *Ramillies and the Union with Scotland*, p. 159 *n.*

ten thousand. On the other hand, the French had at least fifteen thousand regular troops in the Peninsula during 1706, and eighteen thousand in 1707. Whether, if there had been no war in Spain, Marlborough could have gained these troops for Flanders is more than doubtful. Probably if they had not fought there they would never have been granted him. Fighting there, they actually contained through the ups and downs of three critical years superior numbers of the enemy. We feel sure that he regarded all troops sent to Spain as a concession to London opinion. He would have rejoiced to have them in his own hand. Nevertheless, they were by no means wasted in the general application of available forces. A substantial military compensation, apart from political convenience, could be adduced in the grim account. When we deplore the absence of ten thousand redcoats from the campaigns of Ramillies and Oudenarde, and all the extra weight that this would have given to Marlborough's control over the main confederate army, we are by no means entitled to assume that this alternative was ever open to him.

The attitude of the Emperor Joseph was different. He had a natural sympathy for his brother in his trials. But the sending of the young Archduke to the Peninsula was a London and not a Vienna plan. It was not until after the capture of Barcelona that a surge of enthusiasm for the effort in Spain rose in the Emperor's heart. Certainly thenceforward he was deeply moved. In a dispatch to Gallas[1] in London (December 23, 1705) he offered to provide troops for Spain, and urged that transport, and of course money, should be furnished by England. He would even, so Gallas was instructed to state, pawn his own jewellery rather than allow Charles's life and honour to be cast away.[2]

But—and on this point all opinions converged—Peterborough must be removed, and if possible Galway appointed in his stead.

[1] Hoffmann's colleague in London.
[2] From Gallas's family archives in Prague; Klopp, xi, 509.

Chapter Four

THE TOTTERING ALLIANCE
1705–1706

EVER since the disaster of Blenheim Louis XIV had been anxiously seeking by this road and that for a peace based on compromise. He no longer sought victory; but until the beginning of 1709 he hoped to escape a treaty of absolute defeat. In its military and financial weakness the Empire claimed the most from the war; in its strength and ardour England sought the least. The Dutch occupied the decisive position; they maintained the largest army in the field; they made a substantial money contribution; they played their part at sea. Nevertheless, their aims were practical and compact. They wanted their barrier of Belgian fortresses, with as many French fortresses to broaden it as possible. They hoped for a barrier on their southern and south-eastern frontiers stronger than that which they had so incontinently lost in 1701. The article of the original treaty of the Grand Alliance, while deliberately vague upon the question of the sovereignty of Belgium, was explicit about its strategic destiny. The Spanish Netherlands must be recovered "to the end that they may serve as a dyke, rampart and barrier to separate and keep France at a distance from the United Netherlands."[1] After Blenheim at various times, through successive agents, Louis XIV intimated secretly to the Dutch that he was willing to partition Belgium and divide its fortresses with them.

At the end of 1705 the French negotiations, hitherto intangible, took a more definite form. The Marquis d'Alègre, a French Lieutenant-General, had been captured by the Scots Greys in Marlborough's cavalry charge after the forcing of the Lines of Brabant in July 1705.[2] To this high personage the Duke granted a parole of two months to settle his affairs in France, and charged him to convey to Louis XIV a message of ceremony. Arrived at Versailles, d'Alègre was taken into Torcy's confidence and became a secret

---

[1] Treaty of the Grand Alliance, Clause V; Lamberty, i, 620–628.
[2] Vol. II, p. 959.

67

emissary of peace. The instructions which were given him deserve particular attention.[1] On his return to Holland at the expiry of his parole he was to seek out Marlborough, express the pleasure with which the King had received his compliments, and, if permitted, open decisively the question of peace. D'Alègre was to dwell upon the vexations Marlborough was bound to suffer at the hands of the Dutch, upon the hazards of war, and the many shifts and insecurities of private fortune. How success, however brilliant, brought envy in its train; how often ingratitude alone repaid the efforts of great servants; how peace would consolidate the glories which Marlborough had gained; and how earnestly the King desired that just and lasting peace. If these overtures were well received by Marlborough, d'Alègre was to broach a very delicate topic. So ardent was his Majesty for peace that he would bestow a kingly reward on anyone who could bring it about. "It might perhaps have been wished," d'Alègre was instructed to say,

> that the Duke of Marlborough had not already received all the honours which have been bestowed upon him, in order that there might be room for his Majesty to offer him, after the peace, rewards worthy of a man of his standing. Since he possesses them all, the King has no resource but munificence: but whatever benefits he had received from his own sovereign, two millions of French livres [about £300,000] would raise him above the dangers to which eminence is always exposed in England, if not sustained by great wealth.[2]

It was further suggested that the payments should be spread over the first four years after the Peace. If all this went down well with Marlborough, and d'Alègre sustained no rebuff, he was then to outline the actual terms on which the King would treat.

These were curious, and widely different from all later versions. Philip V was to keep Spain and the Indies, also the Milanese. Charles III was to become, as an Archduke, Elector of Bavaria, thus strengthening the house of Hapsburg exactly where it had been most imperilled. Max Emmanuel was to be indemnified for the loss of his native land, Bavaria, and for abandoning his Vicar-Generalship of the Spanish Netherlands, by becoming king of the "Two Sicilies." France was to hold all the bridgeheads of the Upper Rhine. Holland was to have her Barrier fortresses, to be held by Swiss garrisons, and the full possession of Guelders and Limburg.

---

[1] "Instructions pour d'Alègre," October 6, 1705; *Instructions des Ambassadeurs de France*, "Hollende," ii, 131 *et seq.* (ed. André and Bourgeois).

[2] *Ibid.*, p. 147.

The Duke of Lorraine, whose balancing attitude during the campaign of 1705 had been noticeable, was to be consoled for French acquisitions on the Rhine by the Vicar-Generalship of such parts of the Spanish Netherlands as remained after the Dutch claims had been met. This French proposal contemplated for the first time since the outbreak of the war the division of the Spanish inheritance. Nevertheless, it was a French peace. The Great King paid his debt to Max Emmanuel, but held him in his power. He maintained his grandson in Spain. He kept his grip on Northern Italy.

All this was set forth in Torcy's instructions to d'Alègre of October 5, 1705, but we have no record of what passed at d'Alègre's interview with Marlborough. It is, however, certain from the sequel that the Duke allowed the captive peace agent to unfold the whole story. Imperturbably he listened to the proposal of a vast bribe to himself, and thereafter to the French terms for a general peace. He must have been all smiles to d'Alègre, who departed without an inkling of where Marlborough stood. Clearly Marlborough was not at all attracted by the French peace proposal. He did not think that the French power was as yet sufficiently broken to give England the security which she needed and deserved. He doubted the French sincerity in view of their great remaining military strength and the disappointing close of his late campaign. He suspected a manœuvre to spread disunion between the Allies. He was resolved to continue the war and bring France low. When d'Alègre unfolded four days later his peace terms to Heinsius, Marlborough set himself to discredit and frustrate them. He was neither offended nor seduced by the personal bribe. He put it by in his mind as something which might be of interest some day, but which could not in the slightest degree affect his judgment or his action.

The political scene in London seemed vastly better than any the Captain-General and the Lord Treasurer had known before; and probably the first three months of 1706, which he spent in England, were not merely comfortable, but even gave the illusion of security. He was cordially thanked by both Houses of Parliament. Extraordinary supplies were forthcoming for the prosecution of the war. The loan of £250,000 which he floated in the City for the Empire, or rather for Prince Eugene and his army, to whom it was conveyed direct, was fully subscribed between a Thursday and the following Tuesday. The war effort of the island in men and munitions each month assumed a larger scale. He was thus able to turn his mind very definitely to the new audacious military adventure on which he had set his heart for 1706. Meanwhile he cultivated the Whigs.

Many accounts have come to us of a dinner-party which seemed to seal an all-powerful confederacy in British politics. It is remarkable in this period that, while opposing commanders in the field lavished courtesies upon each other across the lines of actual war, the politicians at home adopted a stiffer attitude in their own circles. Nevertheless, in January 1706 we see united round Harley's table Marlborough and Godolphin; Harley and St John; Halifax, Sunderland, Boyle, and Cowper. Somers was absent only by inadvertence. An incident of this festivity recorded by Cowper is well known. On the departure of Lord Godolphin,

> Harley took a glass, and drank to love and friendship, and everlasting union, and wished he had more Tokay to drink it in; we had drank two bottles good, but thick. I replied, his white Lisbon was best to drink it in, being very *clear*. I suppose he apprehended it (as I observed most of the company did) to relate to that humour of his, which was never to deal clearly or openly; but always with reserve, if not dissimulation, or rather simulation; and to love tricks even where not necessary, but from an inward satisfaction he took in applauding his own cunning. If ever man was born under the necessity of being a knave, he was.[1]

Historians generally have taken this statement as illustrating the distrust which undoubtedly still prevailed. But that chaff of this kind could be indulged in without offence is surely a measure of prevailing sincerity and good will. Undoubtedly the Whigs expected to be partners in the Government. Marlborough and Godolphin earnestly desired their aid. Even Harley was caught by the enthusiasm of the hour. Only one obstacle remained—Queen Anne.

The end of this session saw the furthest unbending of Queen Anne to the Whigs. The Tory Party had driven her far from her innate convictions. Godolphin, whose whole aim was the prosecution of the war and the sustaining of Marlborough and his armies, might be truly thankful. Harley, while thoroughly helpful, had made a special virtue of going so far. The curious, intricate machine of English politics worked more smoothly for practical ends than it had ever done. Out of the innumerable stresses and intrigues there arose a spell of commanding harmony. Never had domestic affairs conformed more perfectly to Marlborough's ideals than at

---

[1] *The Private Diary of William, First Earl Cowper* (Roxburgh Club, 1833), p. 33.

this beginning of 1706. It was too good to be true, and it was too good to last. Well might Seymour warn a group of Whigs who were exulting in his presence upon the triumph of their party, "Don't be too sure. Whatever the Queen may look like to you, she never hated you more."[1] But while it lasted the sun shone brightly upon the English scene, and the island Power could plunge again with united authority into the murk and storm of Europe.

On the Continent in the ranks of the Grand Alliance all was again turning to chaos. The agreements Marlborough had made with the allied princes and sovereigns threatened to crumble as soon as his personal influence was withdrawn from the various Courts. All the Electors saw the chance of making money and local advantage out of the weakness of the great confederacy and out of the astonishing readiness of England to make exertions far beyond her apparent stake. No doubt each had ground for complaint. Every signatory had entered the war upon the promise that the Empire would maintain a hundred and twenty thousand men against France. Actually about forty thousand men, ill-clothed, worse equipped, unpaid, the bulk under the now rapidly failing Margrave of Baden, were all that was forthcoming. The Empire, deemed so mighty, had in fact fallen down. The thoughts of Vienna were riveted upon the civil war in Hungary and Transylvania. Compared to these terrible and near obsessions, dominion over Italy, Spain, and the New World became now a faint and far-off thing.

The Prussian extortions and threats had not hitherto implied any serious resolve to change sides. But in the early months of 1706 the behaviour of Frederick I began to excite Marlborough's anxiety. There are indications in his letters that he feared his positive desertion of the common cause. He suspected him of being actually in negotiation with Louis XIV. Marlborough's letters cite no proofs. We have adduced many evidences of the excellence of his secret service, but it may well be that in this he was guided mainly by his instinct. Certainly the English Cabinet do not seem to have been themselves at all alarmed. Modern research has, however, shown how truly Marlborough divined or measured facts, for, as we now know, the Prussian King was advancing far on the path of treachery. Indeed, it is doubtful whether anything but an overwhelming military event could at this juncture have kept him from a separate peace with France.

[1] Hoffmann's dispatch, December 22, 1705; Klopp, xii, 18.

Next in importance were the Danes. Thirty thousand Danish troops served as mercenaries in the allied armies. They earned an invaluable revenue for the Danish State. These good soldiers who never failed on any battlefield had also to be marketed by their rulers. Denmark had been led to seize the town of Eutin, and this raised dangerous questions not only with the Swedes, but with the Empire. Meanwhile, the payments of the Sea Powers for the Danish troops being in arrear, those warriors became tardy in moving up to their necessary strategic positions.

These political situations were aggravated by the actual state of the fronts. Spain was an adventure, costly, precarious, and on the whole ill-judged. But Italy was capital. There French armies, almost equal to those in Flanders and upon the Rhine, advanced against the exhausted Imperialists and the desperate remnants of Savoy. The year opened with the capture of Nice on January 4 after a siege of some weeks by a detachment of seven thousand men under the Duke of Berwick. By the express orders of Louis XIV the fortifications were destroyed. So thoroughly was this executed, says Berwick, "that no trace remained where the fortress of Nice had once stood."[1] Thus Victor Amadeus found himself cut from any effective contact with the Allies by sea. While their armies used ruthless force, the French lavished their seductions upon the harassed Duke of Savoy. His wife and his daughters were princesses of France.[2] The Grand Monarch could forgive his own family without loss of dignity. Let the Duke once more turn his coat, however tattered, and the parable of the Prodigal Son would be re-enacted. Victor Amadeus was made of stubborn if untrustworthy stuff. It was plain, however, in February and March of 1706 that the complete extinction of all resistance to France in Italy was imminent.

Against all these dangers and incoherences there remained to the Allies the greatness of their cause, which still held good in spite of every disappointment and disloyalty throughout the whole vague, vast block of the Germanic peoples. There were the sturdy, stubborn Dutch, and the rich, busy, and strangely resolute English; there was Prince Eugene, the hero of a Europe which had been for nearly twenty years at war; and lastly there was John, Duke of

---

[1] *Memoirs*, i, 194.
[2] His wife was Anna of Orleans, daughter of Charles II's sister. His daughters were Marie Adelaide, who married the Duke of Burgundy, and Marie Louise, who married Philip V.

Marlborough, deemed by all in those days to be the Champion. By a ceaseless correspondence, obstructed sometimes for several weeks by adverse winds in the Narrow Seas, Marlborough worked untiringly to prevent the transient harmony which his personal journey had achieved from falling into ruin. The seventy pages of his letters to high personages which Murray's *Dispatches* contains for these ten or twelve weeks must be read by those who wish to understand his difficulties and exertions. Now the new, fierce campaign was about to begin. The eight French armies were already almost gathered upon their respective fronts. Every promise of the German states had been at the best half kept; all the contingents were weaker and later than arranged. Every single ally had his special complaint. The Empire, the most helpless, the most failing, was the most arrogant and querulous of all. The Margrave maundered over a mouldering army on the Rhine. The King of Prussia held all his troops back from the fighting fronts to which it had been agreed they should march. The Danes, even after their Eutin incursion had been adjusted, were set upon their arrears of pay. England was the milch-cow of all, and Parliament was already voluble upon that pregnant point. But England, detached yet dominant in the distracted Continent, was still resolved upon war and victory. She was to have both.

D'Alègre had lingered in Holland, hopeful of his peace mission and reluctant to face the rigours of captivity and the English climate. When all was ready for the new campaign his presence at The Hague was no longer desirable. "Since we have no more business to do together," wrote Heinsius (February 19), "it would be better that he should leave."[1] On his arrival in England at the end of March he found himself reduced effectively to the position of a prisoner of war by the following characteristic letter from Marlborough, which marked the extinction of his mission:

WINDSOR PARK
March 29, 1706

Colonel Macartney, having gone yesterday evening to Windsor and having apprised the Queen of your safe arrival, has this morning informed me that her Majesty wishes you to start to-morrow for Nottingham. I am truly sorry to be out of town and thus deprived of the pleasure of saluting you. I will however send this evening

---

[1] G. G. Vreede, *Correspondance diplomatique et militaire de Marlborough, de Heinsius, etc.* (1850), p. 3.

M. Cardonnel [le Sieur Cardonnel] to receive your instructions, begging you to be persuaded of the very sincere feelings with which I have the honour to be, etc.[1]

The whisperings of peace which d'Alègre had begun continued while the armies were being painfully gathered from intriguing Courts and war-worn peoples. Two separate lines of discussion persisted. Apart from the more general objects of the war, England had a special reason for courting the Dutch. Queen Anne's Ministers and Parliaments of every hue, especially before the Union with Scotland was achieved, centrèd their desires upon securing a Dutch guarantee of the Protestant Succession. This could not in English opinion be secured, nor their effort repaid, until France was thoroughly beaten. They were therefore wont to encourage the Dutch to gain their Barrier by a vigorous combined prosecution of the war; while Louis XIV tempted them at least with a large portion of it as the reward of a speedy, and if necessary a separate, peace. These two opposite winds blew for several years alternately upon Holland according to the varying fortunes of the armies. Marlborough knew well that the Dutch claims would be exorbitant; that, whatever the London Cabinet might feel, they would deeply offend the Empire; and that the heavy hand of "Their High Mightinesses" would infuriate all parts of the Netherlands that might fall under their rule. He foresaw also the complications which must arise with Prussia and other signatory states of the Grand Alliance concerned with the Lower Rhine. We find him, therefore, dilatory and obstructive in all that concerned the Barrier Treaty, and in fact he staved it off till after Malplaquet.

The idea of the reciprocal guarantee of the war-aims of the two Sea Powers, as a preliminary to a draft of general peace terms, grew steadily in England. The Whigs, naturally attaching the highest importance to anything assuring the Protestant Succession, were prepared to go almost all lengths to meet the Dutch over their Barrier. As it was already necessary to carry them along, Halifax was at Marlborough's wish associated with him in all the preliminary negotiations. When at length, at the beginning of April, it became imperative that Marlborough should return to The Hague and to the army, Halifax went with him. We do not need at this stage to enter upon the details of the Anglo-Dutch discussions, which did not reach a settlement till the end of 1709. It is sufficient here to indicate the very different angles from which Marlborough and Hali-

[1] *Dispatches*, ii, 464.

fax approached their common task. Halifax in one of his regular letters to his party leader, Somers, neither being at the time a Minister, wrote, "I think it is our interest that their Barrier should be as good as we can obtain for them, and if they insist on too much, it will be a greater tie on them not to make peace until it is procured for them."[1] He thought from his talks with Marlborough that the Duke agreed with this. It is probable, however, that, whatever civilities Marlborough may have practised towards the eminent Whig, his opinion was not different from what he expressed three years later in his well-known letter to Godolphin: "Be assured that whenever England shall comply with the States as to the Barrier . . . they will think it more their interest to be well with France than with England."[2] Two more contrary opinions could hardly be expressed, and it must be noted that Marlborough's view of the Dutch reaction was not borne out in different circumstances by the ultimate result.

Their differences did not emerge in public. The two envoys were not long together at The Hague. Marlborough had very soon to take the field. Except for a month's stay in Hanover in the Whig interest and for occasional visits to Marlborough's headquarters, Halifax remained throughout the year at The Hague in parley with the Dutch. His negotiations were soon to be affected by events.

The Bourbon power in Spain had sunk to its lowest ebb at the end of 1705, but a stern rally marked the opening months of 1706. Louis XIV refused to accept the sudden change of fortune in the Peninsula. He was deeply conscious of the danger to his interests in the western Mediterranean which arose from the capture by the Sea Powers of the fortified naval base of Barcelona. Just as at the end of 1704 he had sent a great army to recover Gibraltar, so now he exerted himself to recover the Catalonian capital. Tessé, with all the French troops confronting Galway, about twelve thousand men, was moved into Aragon. Arrived there, he was ordered, in spite of his misgivings, to drop his communications and march on Barcelona. Here he met the new reinforcements from France, and found himself at the head of twenty-one thousand men, two-thirds of whom were French regulars. This concentrated army outnumbered all the allied formations dispersed throughout the conquered provinces. It lay however in the midst of a bitterly hostile population.

[1] Quoted in R. Geikie and I. A. Montgomery, *The Dutch Barrier*, 1705–19, p. 46 n.
[2] August 1709; Coxe, iv, 409.

It could be fed and supplied only from the sea. A comprehensive plan was framed. The Toulon fleet carrying the munitions and cannon for the siege reached the coast in the first days of April, and in perfect timing with the junction of all the forces, Philip V arrived in the camp from Madrid.

This sudden apparition completely turned the tables upon the Allies. Peterborough's troops were widely scattered, the bulk being in the province of Valencia, in whose pleasant cities their commander had disported himself with the gallantry and profusion of a knight-errant. Charles, menaced and invested both by land and sea, threw himself into Barcelona with four thousand men, of whom one-third were English. The second siege of Barcelona began. Marshal Tessé not unnaturally regarded Montjuich as the key of the city. He hoped in his turn to carry it by assault. The defence of the famous fort was confided to seven hundred English redcoats under Lord Donegal. It was necessary to use against them the heavy batteries and the greater part of the French army. At nightfall of the 21st the breach was stormed by overwhelming numbers, and Donegal, refusing all quarter, and striking down his foes on every side, perished gloriously, sword in hand, with the greater part of his men. The attack on the city now began in earnest. Aided by the fidelity of five thousand citizen levies, the young King Charles—he was but twenty-one—conducted the defence with conspicuous personal valour. Donegal's stubborn resistance in the Montjuich had given time for the population to strengthen the ramparts. A bitter conflict ensued. This was the great episode in the career of the future Emperor. Although he could easily have quitted the city by sea in the early days, he proclaimed his resolve to conquer or die among his ardent Catalans. His death in action, and still more his capture alive, would have violently transformed the whole policy of the Grand Alliance.

Almost everything about Peterborough is disputed. A sombre writer of Victorian times, Colonel Parnell,[1] has, with remarkable erudition, laboured to strip him of all his laurels and to represent him only as a nuisance and impostor. These aspersions are still deemed extravagant and unjust But certainly Peterborough's conduct at this crisis shows him at his worst. On March 30, when the French design upon Barcelona was fully apparent, he wrote a letter to Duke Victor Amadeus of Savoy which reveals the black treachery of his mood.

[1] *The War of the Succession in Spain* (1702–11).

May God preserve his Majesty, . . . but it is my duty to your Royal Highness that in case of his death *I shall give Spain to he who has the right to it.* . . . The most fatal event for the public will be a captive King of Spain. The game will be difficult and delicate, and I can only say that I will do my best; . . . for your interests, Monseigneur, will always be [illegible: paramount?] and your Royal Highness cannot wish for a more devoted or faithful servant.[1]

To this limit did he push his personal feuds and public presumption.

Alike in thought and action he proved himself utterly indifferent to the fate of the sovereign in whose interest he had been sent to Spain. He seemed prepared to face the loss of Barcelona. Admiral Leake, reinforced by Byng's squadrons and transports carrying five thousand men, was now sailing up the coast from Gibraltar to the relief of the city. Peterborough, asserting his commission as a joint-admiral of superior rank, sent him reiterated orders to land his troops in Valencia before engaging the Toulon fleet. "Any forces sent to Barcelona are sent so far out of the way." He wished himself to march from Valencia to Madrid and seize the capital, as an offset to the fall of Barcelona.

Leake treated Peterborough's thrice-reiterated orders with perfect disdain. He pressed his voyage to Barcelona with the utmost speed. King Charles from the beleaguered city sent him imperative appeals to hasten "without stopping or disembarking the forces elsewhere, as some other Persons may pretend to direct you; for there can be no one so necessary in this town, which is on the very point of being lost for want of relief."[2] Peterborough, finding his orders disobeyed, and beginning to be at length conscious of the storm that would break upon him if Barcelona fell, gathered a small force, hastened along the coast, and joined Cifuentes, the Miquelet leader, in the blockade of Tessé's army. When the fleet, delayed by adverse winds, drew near, he boarded the flagship, hoisted his admiral's flag at the mainmast, and sought to present himself as the saviour of the city and the organizer of its relief. No one could have behaved worse. The whole credit belongs to Admiral Leake.

The Toulon fleet did not accept Leake's proffered battle. On the approach of his superior forces their admiral, the Count of Toulouse, sailed without loitering for Toulon. Tessé, whose land communications were cut and himself blockaded by the Catalan bands, had no

---

[1] Add. MSS. 28057, ff. 93-94.   [2] Parnell, p. 166.

choice but immediate retreat. Leaving his whole siege-train, all his cannon, stores, supplies, and the bulk of his wounded, he withdrew, harassed by the guerrillas, northward into France. Such was the first refreshing news which greeted the allied captains at the opening of the main campaign of 1706.

Chapter Five

FORTUNE'S GIFT

1706—MAY

MARLBOROUGH had reached The Hague full of a great military design. Our chief source for this is in the letters which he wrote after it had been decisively prevented. But there is ample evidence how far he had carried his plan for marching all round France into Italy. For months past he had been setting everything in motion to that end. There were the eight thousand Prussians who were anyhow to stay in Italy. There were the seven thousand Palatines and three thousand Saxe-Gothas. There was the English Government subsidy of three hundred thousand crowns, there was the £250,000 loan, both of which were payable only to Prince Eugene's account in Venice. Well-equipped in the Italian theatre would stand Eugene, and thither Marlborough would march with the renowned redcoats and such other contingents as he could scrape. We can see to what point his actual staff work had proceeded by the issue of the six hand-mills to every British battalion for grinding corn, utensils which had never been needed in the Low Countries.[1] He had procured the assent of the Cabinet, and was now strong enough to have his plan embodied in a solemn commission from the Queen authorizing him to act, if he thought fit, independently of the Dutch.[2]

[1] Captain Robert Parker, *Memoirs* (1746), pp. 108, 109.
[2] The document is as follows. The original, with signature and seal, is in the Queen's hand.

April 14/25, 1706

Additional Instructions for our Right Trusty and Right intirely beloved cousin and councillour John Duke of Marlborough our embassador extraordinary to the States Generall of the United Provinces and captain General of our Forces &c.; Given at our court at Kensington the fourteenth day of April 1706, in the fifth year of our Reigne.

Whereas we have by our instructions to you bearing date the tenth day of April in the fifth year of our reign given you our directions to press the States Generall of the United Provinces with the utmost earnestness to joyne their proportion of forces with ours for the compleating forty squadrons and forty battalions to march forthwith into Italy, for the effectuall carrying on of the warr there, and the relief of H.R.H. the Duke of Savoy; which service we take to be of the last importance to the common cause.

Armed with this vigorous document, he now opened the matter boldly at The Hague. The States-General showed much more imagination and confidence than they had done in 1704. Their terms were simple. If he went he must take no Dutch troops: that would cost them their lives at the hands of the Dutch populace. But for the rest they would run all risks to help him. He had already directed eighteen thousand men upon the Italian theatre. If with twenty thousand English, who were to make another long pilgrimage, and certain auxiliaries of quality he could reach Lombardy, he and Eugene might do a deed the fruits whereof would be inestimable and the fame immortal.

To take the pressure off the Dutch, while he was fighting in Italy, Marlborough had resolved upon an important diversion. A French refugee, the Comte de Guiscard, a man whose dark and explosive nature was armed with much address, had for many months past pressed upon the London Cabinet a plan for the landing of a strong force upon the coasts of France far behind the fortress barrier of the Low Countries. St John was much impressed with Guiscard. He wrote of him to Marlborough in the highest terms: "His conduct has been full of zeal, very discreet and very moderate." Guiscard proposed that a number of battalions should be raised from the Huguenot refugees, and that these, reinforced by several brigades of British infantry and regiments of dragoons,

---

And altho' we wil not permit our selves to doubt of the concurrence of that Government in so reasonable and so necessary a proposition, yet the consideration that we are not only obliged in justice to do this, but also we are mov'd by the thoughts of the fatal consequences which would befall the whole confederacy in case the French prevail there, and that the warr on our part be not effectually carryed on. That we might not, therefore, be wanting to do our utmost for this necessary and important service; we do hereby require you, upon the refusal or delay of the States General, or their ministers to joyne with us in ordering a proportion of their troops for that service; that you do, in such time and manner as you shal think most proper, cause to march into Italy of the troops in our pay as near the said number of forty squadrons and forty battalions as you can possibly provide. And that you take the proper methods for concealing the said designe and also that you give al the necessary directions for the time and manner of the said march of our troops and for making provision for them in their march, and after they arrive in Italy, as you shal judge most convenient.

And we are so fully perswaded of the necessity of this enterprize and withall knowing your zeale for the common cause, and how absolutely necessary your presence will be to command our troops in this expedition; we do therefore hereby permit, and require you to take the command of our said troops upon you in person as soon as they have entered into Italy. And we leave it to your care and prudence to order and direct all other things relating to the said expedition as you shall judge most conducing to the promoting the intended service.

should be landed by surprise somewhere between Blaye and the mouth of the Charente. Xantes was to be occupied and fortified, and the French Huguenot officers were from thence to rouse the Cevennes and reanimate the Camisards, carrying rebellion supported by invasion into these smouldering regions. Marlborough thought well of the venture and of the part it would play in his general strategy. Five Huguenot regiments were raised at the end of 1705, and nearly a dozen British battalions were gathered at Portsmouth and in the Isle of Wight. "I hope to be able," he wrote to Heinsius from London (February 12/23, 1706),

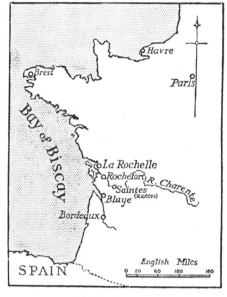

THE DESCENT

before I seal this letter to send you a project of the Comte de Guiscard, which has been communicated to M. de Buys; we keep it here as a great secret and do not doubt that you will do the same; but if we can make it practicable to make such an attempt, I should think this year is more proper than any. For by what we see of the French disposition for this year's service, there will be very few troops left in the body of the kingdom—I beg you will give me your opinion of this project so that I may know how to govern myself.[1]

Heinsius, who had already had relations with Guiscard, favoured this use of amphibious power. It was of course entirely in harmony with Tory Party war-conceptions, and was bound to command a strong backing in Parliament once it became known. Marlborough always referred to it as the 'descent' (alas! he wrote it 'decent'), and we shall see it play an appreciable part in the operations of the next three years. Guiscard too was to make his own contribution to history when in 1710 he attempted to assassinate Harley, the Prime Minister, in the Council Chamber. The troops, together with their shipping and stores, were prepared and provided during the

[1] Vreede, p. 4.

81

winter of 1705–6, and their use lay in Marlborough's hand when he reached The Hague.

The Italian scheme was destroyed by the earliest events of the campaign of 1706. The French forestalled the Allies in the field both on the Rhine and in Italy. In March Vendôme, unseasonably mobilized, inflicted at Calcinato a savage minor defeat upon Reventlau, who commanded the Imperial forces in Eugene's absence at Vienna. Eugene arrived, not indeed to stem the rout, but to reorganize and reanimate the beaten army when they reached the Trentino. Here was a loss in capture, and still more in desertion, of ten thousand men. In Germany Villars fell upon the Margrave, who with feeble forces was blockading Fort Louis, and on May 3 chased him over the Rhine. The blockade of Fort Louis was abandoned, and the blockaders were thankful, or even proud, to have made their escape. Hagenau and Duremberg were captured with their garrisons, and almost all those conquests which the triumphant Allies had made on the left bank after Blenheim were lost. Not only the line of the Moder, but also that of the Lauter, was devoured, and Landau, into which a garrison of four thousand men was thrown by the Margrave, alone remained. The siege and recapture of this key fortress seemed set for the next scene.

Marlborough's correspondence at this time with the King of Prussia and with Wartenberg, the Prussian Prime Minister, deserves study. The English Ambassador at Berlin, Lord Raby, was a gentleman of spirit, ardent for military repute, and inclined to carry diplomacy into dangerous channels. Marlborough's comment upon him as "impertinent and insignificant" is severe. However this may be, his intrigues, amorous and political, caused ill-feeling at the Prussian Court. He was accused roundly of being the lover of Countess Wartenberg, the Prime Minister's wife. This was a complication the advantages and disadvantages of which might well become the subject of dispute. In April the King demanded Raby's recall. However, in those days letters passed slowly.

A personal relationship had been established between Marlborough and Frederick I. The King, markedly emphasizing Marlborough's new dignity as a prince of the Empire, addressed him as "my cousin," and his letters breathed a spirit of comradeship and admiration. But he still delayed the moving of his troops. Those which should have been at Mainz were only at Wesel. Those which should have hastened to help the Margrave on the Upper

Rhine were proceeding sluggishly towards Maestricht. The King complained that he had not been told of Marlborough's plans. Nor had he, for the project of the Duke's marching into Italy could not risk disclosure beyond the most limited circle. In fact, though Marlborough did not yet know it, a courier with an exposing dispatch from Victor Amadeus had already been captured by the enemy. The Prussian King wrote to Marlborough on April 20 a most severe and challenging letter couched in terms, probably sincere, of high personal regard. Considering the great number of troops Prussia was furnishing to the Allies, her King felt he should be party to all secrets. To this Marlborough replied personally with all ceremony. To Wartenberg, the Prime Minister, he was more blunt: if the King went on writing to him in this style, he would not find it necessary to give him any more information about military movements. But the moment that the Margrave was defeated upon the Upper Rhine and the Italian scheme was no longer possible Marlborough became expansive about his ruined plans. In a dozen letters he informed the Emperor, the King of Prussia, and all the German Electors what he had purposed and what he could no longer do. This was a cheap currency, but it was as much as he had to give. They were all now fully informed of the discarded plan.[1]

All this time the French armies were steadily concentrating, and further rude shocks impended on all European fronts. In these circumstances the States-General made Marlborough another simple offer. They would approve the sending of an extra ten thousand men to the aid of Prince Eugene, provided that he would himself command the Dutch armies on the Flanders front. Moreover, he should not be hampered in any way by Deputies or generals. If he, their Deputy Captain-General, would stay to guard the Dutch homeland, he should be master in the field, and he might send this further substantial aid to his comrade Eugene. Marlborough closed with this. Assuredly the Dutch kept their word. Slangenberg smouldered in sullen obscurity. Three new field Deputies, Sicco van Goslinga, Ferdinand van Collen, and Baron de Renswoude, were appointed with instructions to obey the Duke and with no prohibitions against fighting a battle, which however seemed most unlikely. Collen seems to have been a nonentity, and Renswoude was a friend of Marlborough's.[2] We shall have much to say about Goslinga as the story unfolds. He was no doubt picked for his

[1] See *Dispatches*, ii, 496–497 (to Wratislaw).   [2] *Ibid.*, 468.

office because of his personal courage and fiery, aggressive nature. Here was a man eager for battle. He would be no clog. But another series of difficulties arose. New trials, different in character, were henceforth to fall upon Marlborough's patience. Goslinga was a military-minded civilian, fascinated (without any professional knowledge) by the art of war, who would have liked to command the army himself. He combined the valour of ignorance with a mind fertile in plans of action. His military judgment was almost childishly defective; his energy was overflowing. Day after day, as his memoirs recount, he waited upon the Duke in his tent, offering freely his best advice. When this was not taken his mood became not only critical but aspersive; and from an early stage in their relations his writings accuse Marlborough of "prolonging the war for his own advantage," instead of ending it speedily and easily by adopting one or other of the numerous Goslinga plans. On the battlefields the pugnacious Deputy bustled into the hottest fighting, galloping to every quarter, helping to rally and lead disordered battalions, making happy suggestions to the generals in the heat of action, and sometimes even giving orders upon his vaguely defined but impressive authority. All this, however, will become apparent.

It was with melancholy thoughts that Marlborough began his most brilliant campaign. "I cross the sea," he wrote to Wratislaw, "with sufficiently sad reflections."[1] "The little concern of the King of Denmark and almost all the other princes give me so dismal thoughts that I almost despair of success."[2] These expressions can be multiplied. But this was his dangerous mood. Just as he had written before starting upon the Blenheim march that he saw no prospect of doing any good that year, so now he was in the deepest gloom. It was not the abysmal despair into which he was plunged in the two or three days before Oudenarde, but it was black as night. Yet he had his consolations, and his poise remained perfect. There is a letter of his which we like as much as any he wrote to his wife.

John to Sarah

May 4[/15], 1706

★I am very uneasy when Your letters do not come regularly, for without flatterie my greatest support are the thoughts I have of your kindness; hether too I really have not had tim to write to my Children, but when I do, be assur'd that I shal let them know my heart and soul,

[1] March 29; *Dispatches*, ii, 462.
[2] Marlborough to Godolphin, April 23/May 4; Coxe, ii, 330.

as to their living dutyfully, and kindly with You, and let mee beg for my sake of my dear Soull, that she will passe by litle faults and consider thay are very Young, and that thay cant do other then love you withal their hearts, for when thay consider how good a Mother You have been to them, thay must bee barbariens if thay did not make a kind return; You will see by my letters to Lord Treasurer that *in all likely-whode I shal make the whole Campagne in this country, and consequently not such a one as will please mee, but as I infinitely vallu Your estime, for without that You cant love mee, let mee say for my self, that there is some merit, in doing rather what is good for the publick, then in prefering ons private satisfaction and Intirest, for by my being here in a condition of doing nothing that shal make a noise, has made me able to send ten thousand men to Italie, and to leave Nyntien thousand men on the Rhin til the Mareshal de Marsin shal bring back his detachement to this country*; the ffrench are very positive that thay must succeed at Barcelone but,I trust in God our ffleet will relieve it, and then we may end this Campagne so as that the ffrench may have nothing to brag off, for I fflatter my self that the ten thousand men we are sending to Pr. Eugene will put him in a condition of acting offensively; for Garmany I expect nothing but ill news, and for this country I do not doubt but You will be so kind as to believe if I have an opertunity I will do my best; the decent [descent] is what I have also a great opinion off.

pray lett mr Travers know that I shall be glad to hear sometims from him how the Building goes on at Woodstock; for the Gardening and Plantations I am at ease, being very sure that mr Wise will bee dilligent.[1]

This is the most splendid period in Marlborough's career. Every personal need urged that he should win a battle for himself. At home the wolves, though temporarily baffled, were always growling. Already Sarah was losing her influence with the Queen: already her contacts were becoming a hindrance, not a help. His dream of another epic march across Europe and an Italian "Höchstädt" won side by side with the man he loved had faded. But there still remained the duty of a soldier and the dominating responsibility of the working Head of the Alliance. Not without pangs, but certainly without the slightest hesitation, Marlborough divested himself of troops which would have secured him a large superiority in the Low Countries and the chance of some deed "that shall make a noise." What an example to admirals and generals of the Great War through which we have passed, to fight for the common cause and not to be 'local commanders,' grasping at all the ships or troops they could reach or extort, so as to make themselves secure

[1] The part in italics is quoted in Coxe, ii, 335–336; the rest is from the Blenheim MSS.

in their own sphere, even if all else went to rack and disaster! We know of no similar instance in military history where a general-in-chief, thus pressed, has deliberately confined himself to a secondary rôle while furnishing colleagues, who were also rivals, with the means of action. There is nothing in the career of Napoleon which stands upon the level of the comradeship of Marlborough and Eugene. Napoleon's relations to Davout during and after Jena are the exact contrary. Only with Lee and Jackson have we a similar self-effacement among warriors of genius; and even then more with Lee than Jackson. So Marlborough wrote, and so he decided. He strove to reconcile himself to "a whole campaign" with indecisive forces in the fortress zone of Brabant at a time when personal success seemed most necessary to his public existence.

A small incident at this moment throws a pleasant light upon John and Sarah. An unfortunate divine, one Stephens, who had already published in the interests of his party a memorial on *The Church in Danger*, illustrated his theme by disparaging comments upon Marlborough's military performances, and found himself in consequence of the Lords' Resolution condemned not only to a fine but to the pillory. Horror-struck at his approaching ordeal, he implored Sarah's mercy and protection. These were not denied. Availing herself of her partially restored friendship with the Queen, she begged that he should be let off the physical punishment, which he piteously protested would break the hearts of his wife and children. The reluctance with which Anne agreed to suspend this is a measure of her mood at this time. She wrote:

> I have upon my dear Mrs Freeman's pressing letter about Mr Stephens ordered Mr Secretary Harley to put a stop to his standing in the pillory till farther orders, which is in effect the same thing as if he were pardoned. Nothing but your desire could have inclined me to it, for in my poor opinion it is not right. . . .[1]

Marlborough shared Sarah's compassion.

May 9/20

> I agree entirely with you that Stephens ought not to be forgiven before sentence, but after he is in the Queen's power, if her Majesty has no objection to it, I should be glad he were forgiven; but I submit it to her Majesty's pleasure, and the opinion of my friends. I do not know who is the author of the review [a favourable pamphlet by another hand]; but I do not love to see my name in print, for I am

[1] *The Private Correspondence of Sarah, Duchess of Marlborough*, i, 22.

persuaded that an honest man must be justified by his own actions, and not by the pen of a writer, though he should be a zealous friend.[1]

And a little later:

I am very glad you have prevailed with the Queen for pardoning Stephens. I should have been very uneasy if the law had not found him guilty, but much more uneasy if he had suffered the punishment on my account.

The Captain-General quitted the endless discussions at The Hague and set out in his coach for Headquarters on May 9. Here he found little to comfort him.

Marlborough to Godolphin

May 4/15

When I left The Hague on Sunday last I was assured that I should find the army in a condition to march. But as yet neither the artillery horses nor the bread-wagons are come, so that we shall be obliged to stay for the English, which will join us on Wednesday, and then we shall advance towards Louvain. *God knows I go with a heavy heart; for I have no prospect of doing anything considerable, unless the French would do what I am very confident they will not;* unless the Marshal de Marsin should return, as it is reported, with thirty battalions and forty squadrons; for that would give to them such a superiority as might tempt them to march out of their lines, *which if they do, I will most certainly attack them,* not doubting, with the blessing of God, to beat them, though the foreign troops I have seen are not so good as they were last year; but I hope the English are better.[2]

Louis XIV had brooded deeply upon the danger and ignominy which his finest army had sustained under Villeroy in the late campaign. To stand upon the defensive in the Low Countries seemed to promise only the renewal of those affronts. The genius of the French soldier could not, the King felt, flourish without not merely offering, but seeking battle. Long fortified lines were plainly no barrier to the kind of manœuvres of which Marlborough was capable. Moreover, the old lines were gone. Forty miles of them had been diligently levelled by him before the armies went into winter quarters. What, then, was to prevent the "mortified adventurer," backed by his bloodthirsty English Parliament, from again packing ten days' food upon his wagons, marching into the midst of the fortress zone, and confronting the French commanders with the kind of hideous situation from which, as they now knew, only

[1] *The Private Correspondence of Sarah, Duchess of Marlborough,* i, 22.   [2] Coxe, ii, 335.

the Dutch Deputies had saved them last August? To avoid this, Villeroy must be free to show the same eagerness for a decisive trial of strength as his opponent. The initiative must be seized and held from the beginning of the campaign. The will-power of the aggressive antagonist must be bent by a sincere readiness to fight, and if possible broken by a great battle. Chamillart encouraged these (in themselves) sound military conceptions of the Great King by counsels which had less sound foundations. Marlborough was an adventurer; his knowledge of war was mediocre; Blenheim was a fluke. The surrender of twenty-seven battalions of the French flower in Höchstädt was not a fact from which to draw general conclusions. It was easily explained by the blunders of Tallard and the misconduct of Clérambault. But for these this monstrous imposition of a unique defeat and of irresistible hostile fighting power would never have depressed the morale of the royal armies. France must now re-establish true values, and for this there was no way except battle. And why shrink from it? The successes of Calcinato in Italy and of Hagenau on the Rhine justified a confident temper. Their news about Marlborough was, moreover, encouraging. "On trouve en Hollande," wrote Torcy to Tallard on May 11, "M. de Marlborough moins vif sur la guerre qu'il était les années précédentes."[1] Thus King Louis and his overburdened Minister of War and Finance stirred one another.

They then proceeded to stir Villeroy. They wrote him successive letters in the spirit that he should not hesitate to fight, that he should not shirk a pitched battle. Let all be arranged to give a good superiority, and then make some offensive movement to which Marlborough must submit or take the consequences. "The brusque and proud spirit of Villeroy," says Saint-Simon,

> was wounded by these reiterated admonitions. He had the feeling that the King doubted his courage since he judged it necessary to spur him so hard. He resolved to put all at stake to satisfy him, and to prove that he did not deserve such harsh suspicions.[2]

The mental processes of a general should lead him first to put himself faithfully in the position of his enemy, and to credit that enemy with the readiness to do what he himself would most dread. In the next stage idiosyncrasies of the hostile commander, the temper and quality of his troops, and the political background come into play. But these are secondary. The safe course is to assume that

---

[1] French Foreign Office Archives, vol. 221, f. 101.   [2] Saint-Simon, iv, 422.

the enemy will do his worst—*i.e.*, what is most unwelcome. With that provided against, lesser evils can be resisted. Marlborough, surveying the campaign of 1706 as if he were King Louis's adviser, was convinced that the true French effort should be made in Italy and in Spain. If more force was available it should be used against the Margrave on the Upper Rhine. A period of sieges in the fortress zone of the Low Countries might lead to a few French strongholds being lost, but would gain much precious time for action elsewhere. Accordingly, in various letters Marlborough had formally advised the Dutch Government that no French offensive in the Low Countries need be expected.[1] Also to Heinsius:

> In my opinion there is nothing more certain than that the French have taken their measures to be this campaign on the defensive in Flanders and Germany, in order to be the better able to act offensively in Italy and Spain.[2]

And again:

> 26 *March*, 1706
>
> I am very much of your opinion that the placing of the King of Frances Housold [*sic*] so that they may be sent either to Germany or Flanders is a plain instance that they intend to take their motions from what we shall do, which confirms me in my opinion of their being resolved to act in both places defensively.[3]

He was wrong only because the French were wrong. He judged their hand as he would have played it himself. Hence the despondency with which he resigned himself to a difficult, wearisome, and limited manœuvring among the fortresses. His costly Intelligence service could give him no clue to the personal reactions which his operations of 1705 had produced upon Louis XIV, nor to the pressures which the King was putting upon his Marshal. Up till May 18 we see Marlborough sombrely resigned to the path of duty, having cleansed his heart of personal ambition, and acting solely in the common cause.

King Louis's dispositions for the northern front comprised an army of forty thousand under Villars to operate against the Margrave on the Upper Rhine, and an army under Villeroy of sixty thousand to confront Marlborough in Brabant. Marshal Marsin, with 25 battalions and 30 squadrons, lay so as to operate in either theatre, and likewise the famous Maison du Roi (the "Housold")

---

[1] Letter to Geldermalsen, *Dispatches*, ii, 516.
[2] February 22, 1706; Vreede, p. 8.   [3] *Ibid.*, p. 16.

was so posted as to be capable of intervening either way, but with a strong bias towards Brabant. The King's plan was that both these important forces should join Villeroy, and thereafter seek Marlborough, and put him to the test.

The reader will remember the minor fortress of Léau, which

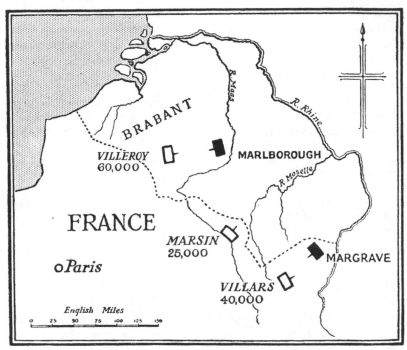

THE NORTHERN FRONT (MAY 1706)

surrendered to the Allies after the Lines of Brabant were forced in July 1705.[1] Louis XIV held, and was advised, that the siege of this place would either inflict painful humiliation upon Marlborough or force him to a battle at odds and disadvantage.[2] Villeroy's instructions were therefore definite. Moreover, that Marshal had newly lighted upon one of Marlborough's many intrigues. A prominent citizen of Namur was believed to be in treacherous correspondence with the Captain-General for the purpose of delivering that important fortified city into the hands of the Allies. This was no more than the truth. Villeroy's counterstroke to such designs was well expressed in an aggressive siege of Léau, and he became most anxious

[1] Vol. II, pp. 958, 983, 989. See map on opposite page.   [2] Pelet, vi, 40.

to forestall his opponent. He knew that none of the Prussians had passed the Rhine. He learned that the Danes would be absent from any immediate concentration Marlborough might make. It there-

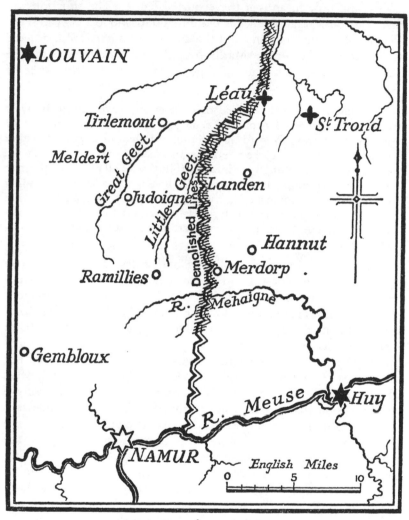

VILLEROY'S OPENING

fore seemed necessary to reckon only with the Dutch and the English, and over these the Marshal conceived he had an ample superiority.

On May 18 the Intelligence service reported heavy French

assemblings on the left bank of the Dyle between Wavre and Louvain. On the 19th decisive news arrived. The French army had
crossed the Dyle and advanced to within four miles of Tirlemont.
This could only mean that they courted battle. The situation was
instantaneously transformed. Doubt and despondency vanished;
all became simple and dire. All the allied contingents were ordered
forthwith to concentrate. Marlborough's first thought was for the
Danes. He sent an urgent message to their general, the Duke of
Würtemberg:

> Having this moment learned that the enemy have passed the Dyle
> and almost reached Tirlemont, I send you this express to request your
> Highness to bring forward by a double march your cavalry, together
> or in separate units as they lie upon the road, so as to join us at the
> earliest moment, letting your infantry follow with all the speed possible
> without exhaustion. In case your Highness is not with the leading
> corps, the officer commanding that corps is hereby instructed to march
> without waiting further orders, and to forward this letter forthwith
> to your Highness and all commanders in rear so that they also can
> conform.[1]

The whole region was familiar to both sides. It had long been
regarded as a possible ground of great battles. It was one of the
most thoroughly comprehended terrains in Europe. We remember
how Marlborough had wished to force the Lines hard by this point
in the autumn of 1703, and how the Dutch generals had warned him
against the dangers of the Ramillies position, which lay three miles
behind them and in which there was "a narrow aperture of but
1200 paces."[2] We must remember also that the French engineers
who traced the Lines of Brabant had discarded the Ramillies position
for the reason that it was concave and thus had lengthy sideways
communications. For this reason they had decided to construct the
Lines somewhat in advance of it. Marlborough, of course, knew the
ground perfectly. His autumn headquarters, while he was levelling
the Lines, had been for more than a month at Meldert, five miles
from Tirlemont. He was accustomed to keep himself fit and hard
by riding every day. We have seen how a week before Blenheim he
and Eugene reconnoitred all the neighbourhood south of the
Danube where a battle might be fought.[3] We cannot doubt that he
had examined this part of Flanders and measured its possibilities in
his mind as in a newly read and deeply pondered book.

Indeed, his topographical memories went back to the wars of

[1] *Dispatches.* ii, 517.   [2] Vol. II, pp. 676–678.   [3] Vol. II, p. 834.

King William. The whole area had been thoroughly mapped by English and French engineers. Maps of those days reached a high level of information and accuracy, and we must imagine besides that Marlborough could visualize the whole of these areas and their military potentialities in exceptional clarity and detail. Moreover, though in no way he expected the French advance, he would mark the Ramillies position as one which the French might be inclined to occupy if he could not get there first, and where a battle might very well be fought. This knowledge, his eye and memory for country, together with his belief in his own troops and in his own capacity, explain the amazing wave of confidence which swept over him as soon as he divined the purpose of the French advance, and the spontaneity of his subsequent action on the battlefield. During the 19th, 20th, and 21st of May he wrote seven letters to the various high personages upon whom his system depended, proclaiming his belief that a battle was imminent, and that a great victory would be won.

To Harley:

The enemy having drained all their garrisons, and depending on their superiority, passed the Dyle yesterday and came and posted themselves at Tirlemont, with the Geet before them, whereupon I have sent orders to the Danish troops, who are coming from their garrisons, to hasten their march. I hope they may be with us on Saturday, and then I design to advance towards the enemy, to oblige them to retire, or with the blessing of God to bring them to a battle.

To his friend Hop, the Dutch Treasurer:

We design to advance in order to gain the head of the Geet, to come to the enemy if they keep their ground. For my part, I think nothing could be more happy for the Allies than a battle, since I have good reason to hope, with the blessing of God, we may have a complete victory.[1]

To the King of Prussia's general, Bülow:

We are making a halt for the Danes, who should arrive to-morrow, and then we shall be ready to advance in such a fashion that if the enemy hold firm you should soon learn the news of a battle in which I trust that God will bless the just cause of the Allies.[2]

He repeated these words to Wratislaw, adding, "Cela nous mettrait en état de rétablir nos affaires partout."

[1] *Dispatches*, ii, 518.   [2] *Ibid.*, 520.

And, finally, to Lord Raby, at Berlin, a sentence obviously meant to be repeated: "If it should please God to give us a victory over the enemy, the Allies will be little obliged to the King for the success; and if, on the other hand, we should have any disadvantage, I know not how he will be able to excuse himself."[1]

These were awkward hostages to give to the future, but we now see him, with all doubts and fears swept away, in the full, joyful plenitude of his powers. At the same time, while rapidly concentrating his army, devouring all the scraps which his far-reaching Secret service could procure, and proclaiming before the battle his impending triumph, he seemed wrapped in a perfect serenity. All the ordinary business of Cardonnel's office proceeded, and on the 20th Marlborough wrote the agreeable letter to Sarah about not punishing the delinquent Stephens for his libel.[2] He wrote latest of all to Wartenberg begging that the King of Prussia would make some provision for the widow of a gallant Prussian officer who had died after long service and many wounds. Purged from all dross and self-seeking, his genius flying free, he was in these days and those that followed sublime. In all his circle of high personages there was but one from whom the coming shock was hidden. Sarah had no inkling.

And now Fortune, whom Marlborough had so ruefully but sternly dismissed, returned importunate, bearing her most dazzling gift.

[1] *Dispatches*, ii, 521.   [2] *Sarah Correspondence*, i, 23.

Chapter Six

THE BATTLE OF RAMILLIES

1706—MAY 23

THE Confederate army was concentrated around Cors-waren by the evening of the 22nd. The English had joined the Dutch the day before, and the Danes were only a league behind. Marlborough mustered 74 battalions and 123 squadrons, with exceptionally strong artillery and pontoon trains (100 guns, 20 "hawbitzers," 42 pontoons). The suddenness with which the campaign had opened found the Dutch with four hundred officers absent; but otherwise the army was in excellent condition, and comprised about sixty-two thousand men. Marlborough's intention was to march through the gap of firm ground between the headstreams of the Geet and those of the Mehaigne in order to occupy the plateau of Mont Saint-André, which formed a part of the Ramillies position. He purposed thereafter to seek Villeroy in the neighbourhood of Judoigne and bring him to battle or drive him across the Dyle.

An hour after midnight he sent Cadogan and the quartermasters, with an escort of six hundred horse, to scout ahead of the army and if unopposed to mark out the new camp. The prescribed march was about twelve miles. The whole army, in four columns, started at three A.M. in dense fog and darkness. The organization by which these large masses found their way across country deserves respect; but of course their progress was very slow. Three hours after daylight, at about eight o'clock, Cadogan, far ahead of them, reached the high ground beyond the hamlet of Merdorp, and here in thick mist his escort struck into advance parties of French hussars. There were shots and scamperings. Cadogan halted. The mist lifting a little, he was able to see moving objects on the farther side of the valley; this was the Mont Saint-André plateau, upon which it seemed the enemy also had designs. He sent word at once to Marlborough. The Duke had already started, and, passing through his marching troops, joined his trusted and treasured lieutenant at ten o'clock. Almost at the same moment the mist curtains rose, and the whole western horizon was seen to be alive with men whose armour and weapons flashed back the bright sunshine from ten thousand sparkling points.

Marlborough could not know at this moment whether the enemy would fight or retreat. He resolved forthwith to attack them in either event. If he was in presence only of a rearguard, he

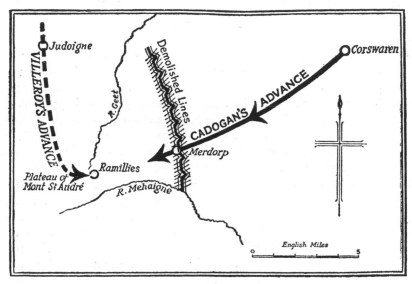

CONTACT

would fall upon them with all his cavalry; if, on the other hand, they were prepared to defend the Ramillies position, a general battle would at once be fought. Orders were sent back to all the columns, and especially to the cavalry, to press their march; for the enemy awaited them. At about eleven the allied army were traversing the Lines which Marlborough had demolished in the autumn, and here they subdivided into eight columns preparatory to forming the line of battle. The Danish horse was already close to the Dutch cavalry on the left wing.[1]

<hr />

[1] Goslinga records his own opinion that if at this time in the morning Villeroy had himself attacked with his whole army he would have taken the Allies at a great disadvantage, because their infantry were lagging far behind and only part of their cavalry had come up. We quote this nonsense merely to measure its author as a military critic. Obviously, if the French army had advanced Marlborough would have fallen back with his cavalry, and formed his line of battle somewhere about the old levelled Lines of Brabant. By this time the Danes would have come up, and an encounter-battle on equal terms, save that the French would be further exhausted by their additional march, would have followed. Since we see so many writers gravely parading Goslinga's

We must now recur to M. de la Colonie, the "Old Campaigner," who at the head of his Franco-Bavarian brigade had marched with the French army from Judoigne in the morning:

> So vast was the plain at Ramillies that we were able to march our army on as broad a front as we desired, and the result was a magnificent spectacle. The army began its march at six o'clock in the morning, formed into two large columns, the front of each consisting of a battalion; the artillery formed a third, which marched between the two infantry columns. The cavalry squadrons in battle formation occupied an equal extent of ground, and, there being nothing to impede the view, the whole force was seen in such a fine array that it would be impossible to view a grander sight. The army had but just entered on the campaign; weather and fatigue had hardly yet had time to dim its brilliancy, and it was inspired with a courage born of confidence. The late Marquis de Goudrin, with whom I had the honour to ride during the march, remarked to me that France had surpassed herself in the quality of these troops; he believed that the enemy had no chance whatever of breaking them in the coming conflict; if defeated now, we could never again hope to withstand them.[1]

About eleven o'clock the Duke began his personal reconnaissance. There rode with him only Overkirk, Dopff, Cadogan, a couple of ex-Spanish officers (Belgians) who knew every inch of the ground well, and the new Deputy, Sicco van Goslinga, whom it was so important to captivate. We are indebted to Sicco for a naïve account. As they stood on the slopes opposite Ramillies the ex-Spanish officers said boldly and positively to the Duke "that the enemy's left could not be attacked with any prospect of success: for the hedges, ditches and marshes were a complete barrier *to both sides*: that therefore the whole of our cavalry should be massed on our left, even if they had to be three or four lines deep: and that all thereabouts was fair open plain." The Duke listened impassively; but, adds Goslinga, "he left the order of battle as it was with an equality of cavalry on each wing."[2]

The new field Deputy saw the mistake at once, and, writing years afterwards, pointed it out to his children. In spite of the advice which he had received that the cavalry could only act upon his

---

military opinions it is necessary to expose them, though otherwise they are of no significance.

Goslinga's diary (*Mémoires relatifs à la guerre de succession de 1706–9 et 1711 de Sicco van Goslinga* (Leeuwarden, 1857), p. 19) is almost the whole substance of Klopp's account of he battle of Ramillies.

[1] *The Chronicles of un Old Campaigner*, p. 305.   [2] Goslinga, p. 19.

left, Marlborough supinely let them remain equally divided according to the conventional order of battle. Luckily, notes Goslinga, "the enemy made the same mistake as the Duke did, and did not remedy it as he did during the combat." These inane comments should strip Goslinga of any military credential except that of being a stout-hearted Dutchman. We can see Marlborough, bland, inscrutable, on his horse at the head of this small group, making the great mistake of dividing his cavalry more or less equally upon each wing, so that Villeroy fell into the same error and kept no fewer than fifty squadrons massed upon this impracticable flank. No doubt Marlborough did not at this moment forget that the French occupied the well-known crescent position of which he commanded the chord. However, he said nothing. He deceived Goslinga. The poor man missed the whole point. He deceived Villeroy, which was, of course, more important.

Meanwhile the eight columns had arrived on the rolling upland of Jandrinol and were deploying into line of battle, eating their dinners as they arrived at their preparatory stations. A little after one all along the line the French artillery began to fire. The Allies replied a few minutes later with far heavier metal. Whereas at Blenheim the French had used a 50 per cent. superior artillery, the case was almost reversed at Ramillies, for Marlborough had not only more guns, but nearly thirty 24-pounders. Although artillery in those days was not a decisive weapon, the fact should be noted. The roar of the cannonade resounded, and the smoke clouds drifted across the broad undulations of a battlefield unchanged and unobstructed to this day.

Contact between armies began about half-past two. The Allies advanced in magnificent array on a four-mile front; but at both ends of the main line, and nearly half an hour ahead of it, two separate attacks of pregnant consequence projected like horns. Towards the extreme French right, now lodged in the villages of Franquenay and Taviers, a column of Dutch infantry rapidly advanced. Next to them, but nearly a mile behind, all the cavalry of the left wing, Dutch and Danish, approached the gap between Taviers and Ramillies, where eighty-two French squadrons, including the long-renowned Maison du Roi, stood to receive them. The main allied infantry attack, comprising forty thousand men ranged in two heavy lines, advanced slowly towards the enemy's centre between Ramillies and Autréglise. The massive onset of the whole army, drawing momentarily nearer with intent to kill and destroy, made its impression upon Marshal Villeroy and his troops, as it had upon Tallard and Marsin at Blenheim. The French command observed the scene from the high ground to the north of Offus, and one fact riveted their thought. This was the northern horn of Marlborough's line of battle led by Orkney. Against their left, towards the village of Autréglise, considerably ahead of the Allies' general line, there steadily developed a Red Thing. The two scarlet columns on this flank had now formed into lines, and were rapidly descending the slopes about Foulz. Already their skirmishers were paddling and plodding in the marshy bottom, using bridging equipment, finding tracks, and wending their way across. Intermingled with this infantry were considerable bodies of red-coated cavalry, also plashing forward mounted or leading their horses towards Autréglise.

When in contact with immeasurable events it is always dangerous to have fixed opinions. Villeroy's opinions had been fixed for him by the Great King. "It would be very important," Louis XIV had written a fortnight earlier, "to have particular attention to that part of the line which will endure the first shock of the English troops."[1] With this the Marshal was in full agreement. He had therefore no doubt what to do. He saw with satisfaction that this dreaded attack, which also threatened his line of retreat upon Louvain, was about to fall upon that part of the French army which was most strongly protected by the accidents of the ground. A fine opportunity offered itself. Forthwith the sector between Autréglise and Ramillies was heavily reinforced by troops brought up from the rear or transferred from the French right and right centre. The choice battalions of the French Guards and the Swiss were urgently brought into the line to meet, under the most favourable conditions, the impending collision with the redoubtable islanders. The whole of the cavalry of the French left wing, about fifty squadrons, was held in close readiness for the decisive moment. That moment would come when this red attack was half across the sloppy meadows of the valley, and enough British had breasted the upward slope to make the prize worth taking. That moment could not be long delayed. Evidently the marsh was not so grievous an obstacle as the French engineers had deemed it. Not only had considerable bodies of British infantry made their way across it and formed on the farther side, but several squadrons of the same kind of horsemen could be observed in order at the foot of the slope. A definite line of battle, much inferior to the troops who awaited them, was

[1] Louis XIV to Villeroy, May 6, 1706; Pelet, vi, 19.

already moving upward towards Offus and Autréglise. The Marshal judged his presence necessary at this dominating point. By his side rode the Elector, Max Emmanuel, who, summoned at the last

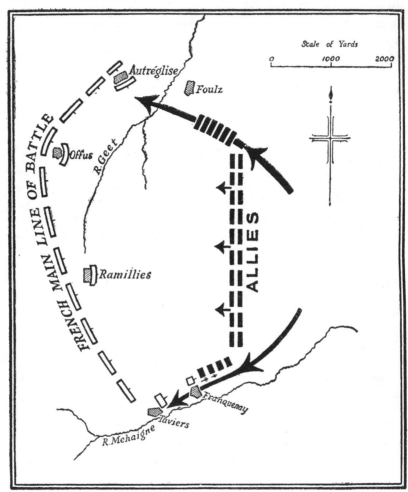

THE HORNS

moment from his pious exercises of Pentecost, had just arrived at a gallop from Brussels. For all that they counted in the main decision, we may here leave the French High Command. This we must regard as Act I of the battle of Ramillies.

But three or four miles away, at the other end of the line, there had been an overture. It was essential to the French occupation of the Ramillies position that the village of Taviers, to which Franquenay formed an outwork, on the extreme right, should be strongly held. A mile and a half of perfect cavalry country separated Taviers from Ramillies. Here must be the scene of the great cavalry encounter. The cannon of those days could not effectively sweep so

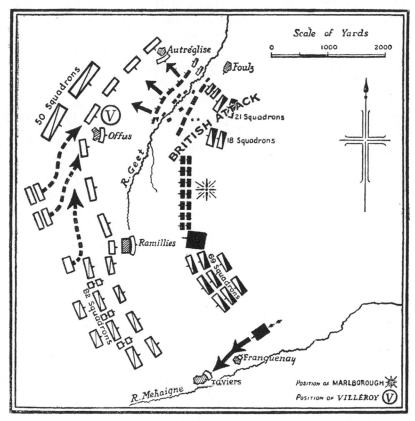

THE BRITISH ATTACK

wide a space with cross-fire, but the position of both these strong villages would make the intervening ground most adverse to his assailants. Thus Villeroy had occupied Franquenay and Taviers with five battalions, but not apparently with artillery. Against Taviers a little after 2.30 P.M. there marched four battalions of the Dutch guard, under General Wertmuller. Behind them to their right, opposite the cavalry gap, the solid masses of Dutch and Danish cavalry could be plainly seen.

Almost everything about the battle of Ramillies is clear, but none of the accounts explain how these four battalions managed so swiftly to storm the villages of Franquenay and Taviers, and expel the larger number of French troops from their houses and enclosures. An ancient map[1] throws light on this. This map was drawn for General Overkirk, probably under his personal directions, a year after the victory. It throws a sharp gleam of light upon this operation. The two cannon[2] were apparently brought forward in the very van of the Dutch attack. So unusual was the employment of artillery in those days in the front line, and so remarkable was the effect of these pieces, that a special reference in the explanatory table is devoted to them—a departure from the whole proportion of the map. Evidently these two cannon were attached to the Dutch Guards by orders of the supreme command, probably by Overkirk himself. Brought into action at close range, they smashed the houses and garden walls, and opened the way for the violent assault of these fine Dutch troops. By a quarter past three, just about the time when the English attack on the other end of the line was preoccupying the French headquarters, the Allies gained both these extremely important villages, which should have guarded the French right flank, and, together with the Ramillies batteries, have swept and protected to a very large extent the gap of open plain in which the mass of the French cavalry were ranged.

The serious nature of this loss was instantly realized by the French command in this quarter. Two battalions of Swiss and fourteen squadrons of dragoons were ordered to retake Taviers. La Colonie's Bavarian brigade, which had reached the battlefield south of Ramillies at about half-past two, was ordered to support them. The dragoons withdrew from the array of French cavalry in the plain, dismounted, and parked their horses about midway between Taviers and a wooded eminence called the Tomb of Ottomond. From this point they advanced on foot upon Taviers. The counter-attack upon Taviers, because of the urgent need to recover the place, was delivered before La Colonie's brigade could reach the scene. It was repulsed by the Dutch, now firmly ensconced. But worse was to follow; for while the Swiss and the dismounted dragoons were falling back, a whirlwind of hostile cavalry broke upon them, and destroyed or routed them utterly. These were the Danes, who, supporting the success of the Dutch battalions, slipped

[1] Facing p. 118. This map should also be consulted for the general aspect of the battle. [2] Marked 'M' in the map.

in between Tabiers and the French right, and, already reaching forward round the French right, exacted this cruel forfeit. The dismounted dragoons never saw their led horses again. Thus, before the main cavalry shock occurred the French cavalry in the plain had been reduced from eighty-two to sixty-eight squadrons, while losing all security for their right.

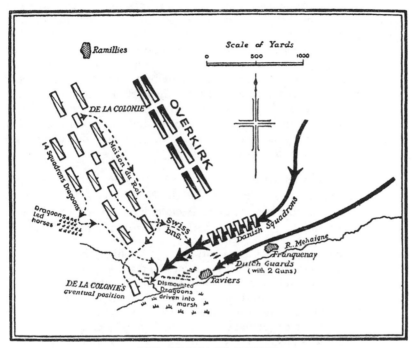

THE COMBAT BY TAVIERS

At this point we must return to the Old Campaigner. The orders he had received "to reinforce the village of Taviers" drew his Bavarian brigade across the front of the Maison du Roi under long-range cannon fire to which he replied, ordering

flourishes upon our hautboys, to entertain us the while; but the booming of the guns that went on all round so startled our musicians that they disappeared like a flash before anyone noticed it, and transported the melodious sounds of their instruments to some quarter where the harmonies were not quite so discordant. However, we set out, and passed along the right of our line to reach the marsh without knowing if any other troops had preceded us, or if others were to follow us.

La Colonie records two impressions—first, "that the enemy

were moving troops from their right to their left: but it was impossible to define their intentions." His second impression is not less significant:

> I noticed, when passing the Maison du Roi, that there were large
> intervals between the squadrons, and that their formation was disproportionately extended. This made me think that the principal
> attack was not to be made here; that there was some other and more
> dangerous point that had had to be provided for; and that reliance
> had been placed upon the Maison du Roi, all picked men, at this point.
> When these gentlemen saw us pass the head of their squadrons, they
> evidently thought that we were coming to support their right on the
> marsh, and by the graceful applause with which they greeted my
> grenadiers, this seemed to give them some pleasure; they recalled the
> action of Schellenberg, and made known to us how much they counted
> on our valour in the coming engagement; but they soon found that
> they could hardly reckon upon us, as we continued our march and
> crossed the swamp [towards Taviers].

Arrived near this point, the Old Campaigner became sharply conscious that a mishap had occurred. Not only had the troops originally sent to occupy Taviers been driven out of the village, but the Swiss and dragoons who had been thrown in to recapture it.

> came tumbling down upon my battalions in full flight, just at the time
> when I was re-forming my men after their crossing; they brought
> such alarm and confusion in their train that my own fellows turned
> about and fled along with them. It appeared that they had attacked the
> village without waiting for us, and had been repulsed with much
> loss by the fourteen [actually four] battalions the enemy had there,
> which were well posted, and outnumbered them by two to one. The
> Swiss perished almost to a man, and it is not surprising that a small
> body of troops attacking others more than double their strength in an
> advantageous position should have been vigorously repulsed and driven
> back in disorder. M. d'Aubigni was killed, and his lieutenant-colonel
> and many others wounded. The runaways threw themselves amongst
> my men, and carried them off with them, and I was never more surprised in my life to find myself left standing alone with a few officers
> and the colours. I was immediately filled with rage and grief; I cried
> out in German and French like one possessed; I shouted every epithet
> I could think of to my grenadiers; I seized the colonel's colour, planted
> it by me, and by the loudness of my cries I at last attracted the attention
> of some few of them. The officers who had stood by me rushed after
> the fugitives, also shouting and pointing out the colonel's colour,
> which I still kept in my hands, and at last they checked the stampede.

I gradually rallied my French grenadiers and several companies of the Cologne regiment, making in all four small battalions, very much shaken with the manœuvres they had just gone through.[1]

With this small force behind the marshes the colonel maintained himself throughout the afternoon, and from this point had a fine view of the tremendous cavalry battle which was now about to begin.

The second act of the drama opened. Overkirk, with the Dutch cavalry and twenty-one Danish squadrons well forward on his left, advanced against the Maison du Roi and the mass of the French forces between Taviers and Ramillies. At the same time the infantry of Marlborough's centre began to come into close contact with the Ramillies defences. The main fronts of both armies were now in action. Marlborough with his staff and retinue must at this time have been on the high ground before Offus and Ramillies. Indeed, he was practically opposite to Villeroy and the Elector, though somewhat farther south. But whereas Villeroy's gaze, fascinated by the advance of the English, was turned to the northern flank, Marlborough was watching the cavalry struggle beginning in the contrary quarter. It is probable that he had no certain knowledge of what had happened in Taviers; but he could see plainly the surge and shock of Overkirk's resolute advance, and that this was not impeded by any cross-fire. He saw the forty-eight Dutch squadrons crash into the Maison du Roi. Measuring and timing the forces now launched, he was entitled to the same assurance of success as he had felt before the final attack at Blenheim.

Forthwith he began the simple yet superb manœuvre to which the preliminaries had led—namely, the transference of all his cavalry to the left wing. He sent peremptory orders to Orkney to break off the attack on Offus and Autréglise and retire, and to withdraw the British to the high ground behind Foulz. Casting aside his veil of secrecy and deception, he exclaimed, "I have five horses to two." Actually he now had the power to bring first four to three, and finally five to three;[2] but it was enough. Leaving Cadogan to enforce Orkney's withdrawal and to rearrange the right, he ordered eighteen squadrons from the cavalry of that wing to trot across the rear of his infantry attack on Ramillies to the support of Overkirk's cavalry

---

[1] *The Chronicles of an Old Campaigner*, p. 309.

[2] 69
$69 + 18 \quad\ = \quad 87$
$69 + 18 + 21 = 108$ $\Big\}$ to 68.

attack. He galloped on ahead of them with his personal staff. He arrived at a crisis. The Dutch, knee to knee in a solid mass, had charged the Maison du Roi. These splendid warriors, the pride of the French nobility, advanced in countercharge to meet their foes.

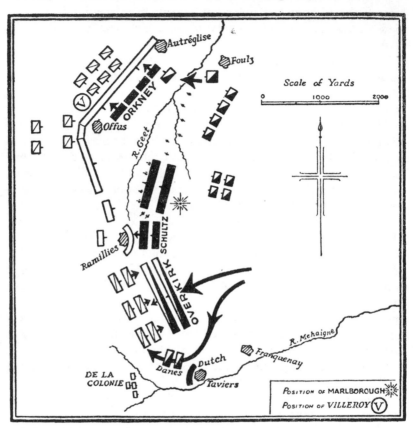

THE GENERAL ENGAGEMENT

Where their squadrons engaged front to front they conquered, but the Dutch, penetrating the intervals between the French squadrons, assailed them in flank and even in rear. In this mêlée the French cannon could not meddle; and the horsemen were free to fight it out alone. Nevertheless, such was the vigour of the French cavalry that they drove in the Dutch right, and were about to fall upon the left flank of the allied infantry now engaging upon the outskirts of Ramillies.

It was at this moment that Marlborough arrived with his handful of English officers and orderlies. The long column of eighteen squadrons was still traversing the front, and had not yet assembled. The Duke sent instant orders to bring from his right the whole remaining cavalry except the English, twenty-one squadrons more,

and, riding himself with his personal attendants into the whirlpool, he rallied the nearest Dutch squadrons. Transported by the energy of his war vision and passion, he led them himself again to the charge. This lapse from the duty of a commander-in-chief nearly cost him his life, and might well have cost the Allies the war.

The mile and a half space between Ramillies and Taviers had now become the scene of the largest cavalry battle of which there is any trustworthy account. In all nearly twenty-five thousand horsemen were brought into collision hand to hand, charging and countercharging with varying fortune for two hours. If we can imagine seven or eight modern cavalry divisions

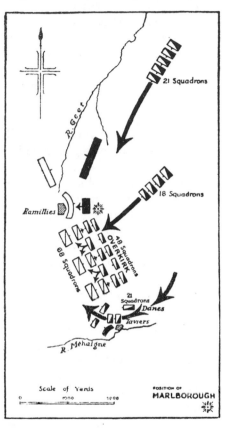

THE CAVALRY BATTLE

fighting in close order on such narrow ground, we shall realize that it was densely thronged with solid masses of flesh and blood in every stage of symmetry or dissolution. Wave after wave of charging horsemen, each trooper seeking with his sharp sword to slay his foe, were hurled in mob violence one upon another. Here numbers told. Where nearly all did their duty bravely the last reserves prevailed. The finest troops of France and the pride of French society, all the military splendour of the Court and age of Louis XIV, met the onslaught of the stern, tough Dutch in a white heat of disciplined passion. But

107

then came Marlborough, with his inspiration and new lines of formed squadrons crashing in; and on the Taviers flank the twenty-one Danish squadrons, lapping round till Taviers village was at their backs, outflanked and rode down all in their path. The fourteen squadrons of French dragoons who had been dismounted to help retake Taviers and had been repulsed therefrom sought in vain to regain their led horses near the Tomb of Ottomond. These had stampeded in the tumult and galloped riderless about the countryside, some even finding their old winter quarters twenty miles away. Their masters, running away on foot, fell victims to the swords of the Danes.

Still more waves of allied cavalry rolled upon the Maison du Roi as Marlborough's orders to bring all the cavalry, except the English, from the right wing were obeyed. Twenty-one fresh squadrons fell upon the harassed, over-pressed chivalry of France. The odds against them were now five to three. In vain were their glorious golden banners, the royal emblems, the lilies of France, borne forward in sublime devotion. Nothing could withstand the hammer-blows of repeated and seemingly inexhaustible reinforcements. The whole of the French cavalry of the right wing was shattered by superior numbers of very good troops who attacked them in front, in flank, and at the end almost in rear, and thus set about them from all sides.

It is difficult in this grand confusion to settle what actually happened to Marlborough himself. That he regarded the struggle at this point as decisive for the whole battle, that he led two charges by the Dutch in succession, that he remained trying to dominate events within a few hundred yards of the left of his infantry attack upon Ramillies, and was in the cavalry mêlée for about twenty minutes, is indisputable. Upon details, as would be natural, all accounts conflict. But certain definite impressions emerge. Marlborough charged for the second time against the victorious left flank of the Maison du Roi at between a quarter and half-past three. The Dutch squadrons which he led or which he succoured were broken. There was a pell-mell to the rear. Amid these blue- and grey-coated troops[1] the scarlet uniforms of the Commander-in-Chief and his personal retinue were conspicuous. The French troops recognized him; they fired their long pistols at him, and individuals breaking from the ranks rode at him and overthrew him. Or, again (a better account), he turned his horse with the crowd of fugitives and tried to jump a sunken pathway or ditch. His horse

[1] *Uniformenkunde*, xvi, 1; quoted in *The Cavalry Journal*, July 1931.

pecked, and he fell to the ground. He was ridden over by the throng. Napoleon's historian, perhaps under direction, makes this point:

> Here we see how important it is to a general to be loved by the soldiers he leads. At the very sight of the danger which threatened their commander his squadrons thought above all of making themselves his rampart. They returned upon their own impulse to the charge. They hurled back the French who had penetrated their ranks, and the rescue of Marlborough was identified with a military success.[1]

More grim versions are found in the letters of British officers, actors in and eye-witnesses of the drama. Colonel Cranstoun, usually an acid critic, wrote a week after the battle:

> Major-General Murray, who was posted on the left of the second line, was so happy visibly to save the Duke of Marlborough, who fulfilled that day all the parts of a great captain, except in that he exposed his person as the meanest soldier. The attack being to be made by the Dutch on our left against the enemy's right where all the King's household and their best troops were, the Duke put himself at the head of the Dutch horse; and the guards du corps, mousquetaires, and gens d'armes happening to encounter them, ten of the Dutch squadrons were repulsed, renversed and put in great disorder. The Duke, seeing this, and seeing that things went pretty well elsewhere, stuck by the weak part to make it up by his presence, and led still up new squadrons there to the charge, till at last the victory was obtained. It was here where those squadrons being renversed and in absolute déroute and the French mixed with them in the pursuit, the Duke, flying with the crowd, in leaping a ditch fell off his horse and some rode over him. Major-General Murray, who had his eye there and was so near he could distinguish the Duke in the flight, seeing him fall, marched up in all haste with two Swiss battalions to save him and stop the enemy who were hewing all down in their way. The Duke when he got to his feet again saw Major-General Murray coming up and ran directly to get in to his battalions. In the meantime Mr Molesworth quitted his horse and got the Duke mounted again, and the French were so hot in the pursuit that some of them before they could stop their horses ran in upon the Swiss bayonets and were killed, but the body of them, seeing the two battalions, shore off to the right and retired.[2]

It is clear that Marlborough had to run in the scrimmage some considerable distance on his feet towards the friendly Swiss battalions. His devoted aides-de-camp were about him, thinking only of saving him. Captain Molesworth got off and gave him his horse

---

[1] Duclos, *Histoire de Jean, duc de Marlborough* (1808), ii, 160.
[2] Portland Papers, *H.M.C.*, iv, 309.

—"we got the Duke mounted again." He reached Major-General Murray's battalions a few minutes later. Behind their bayonets he was able to resume the control of the battle—at least in the centre. He must have remained at this point for more than an hour. It was under the close and continuous fire of the French batteries in

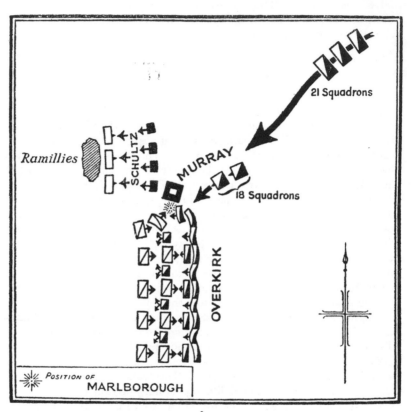

MARLBOROUGH'S INTERVENTION

Ramillies; but it was well placed for watching both the end of the cavalry conflict and the infantry onslaught now about to break on that village. Marlborough's staff, scattered in the fray, gradually rejoined him here. Presently his equerry, Colonel Bingfield,[1] arrived with his second charger.[2] The Duke changed horses. Bingfield was holding the off-side stirrup, and as Marlborough threw his leg over the saddle a cannon-ball cut off the faithful colonel's head. Orkney, who was on the other flank and no eye-

---

[1] Or Bringfield.   [2] Parker says he rode Molesworth's horse for an hour.

witness, but had the view of the senior officers, writing the next day, said:

> Milord Marlborough was rid over, but got other squadrons which he led up. Major Bingfield holding his stirrup to give him another horse was shot with a cannon ball which went through Marlborough's legs; in truth there was no scarcity of 'em.[1]

This incident became popular not only in England but in Europe: it was even commemorated on at least one pack of playing-cards.[2]

We must now return to the British on the right. Orkney's attack upon Autréglise had made unexpected progress at the moment when Marlborough had ordered its recall. Ten or twelve British battalions, including the 1st Guards, had crossed the morass, and their first line had already broken into the houses and enclosures of the village. Lumley, with several English squadrons, made a show of covering their right. The French advanced large bodies of troops from their main line to resist the assault, but always retired as it advanced, with the purpose of drawing it into the open country where their overwhelming numbers of cavalry would be decisive. Fighting became severe. "Indeed," wrote Orkney the next day, "I think I never had more shot about my ears—both musketry and cannon."[3]

It was at this moment, when the British were advancing in the highest confidence, that an aide-de-camp from the Duke brought an order to retire. Marlborough, in order to impart the more reality to this attack, had not informed his valiant lieutenant that it was a feint. Orkney thought that the order had been sent him in the belief that it was impossible to traverse the marsh, whereas he had in fact traversed it and was in full action. He therefore persisted. Messenger after messenger reached him in quick succession, but his blood was up and his vigorous infantry seemed to be driving all before them. Autréglise was in his grip. "But as I was going to take possession, I had ten aides-de-camp to me to come off." Last of all came Cadogan himself. The two generals argued in the storm of shot. Orkney urged that the High Command did not know how good were the prospects. Cadogan explained that the Duke had gone to the left with all the cavalry of the right wing, and that there was no horse to sustain the British foot. It

---

[1] "Letters of the First Lord Orkney," *English Historical Review*, April 1904, p. 315.
[2] An example of this quaint pack is kept at Windsor Castle in the alcove where Queen Anne received the news of Blenheim.
[3] "Letters of the First Lord Orkney," *loc. cit.*

was, he said, impossible to attack everywhere at once. It took all this to recall the vehement assault once it had been launched. When Orkney at length obeyed, he had to make a similar exertion to force his troops to retire. Many of them, in spite of the victory, nursed the grievance for years. They would not believe that the

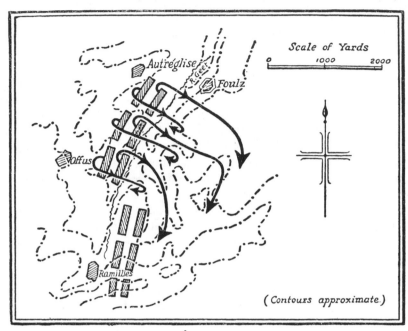

ORKNEY'S WITHDRAWAL

orders had come from the Duke; Cadogan, they grumbled, had relied too much on maps and theory, and acted on his own responsibility and thus baulked them of their prey. However, the whole line was made to retire. Slowly and indignantly they withdrew, the Guards covering the harassed retreat. Once again they floundered through the marsh—re-formed and ascended the slopes of Foulz.

Then followed under Cadogan's eye a manœuvre which we cannot doubt was part of Marlborough's original design. When the two red lines reached the summit of the hill from which they had started, the original first line faced about and stood displayed upon the crest, while the second, which had not been engaged, descending into the dip in the rear, wheeled into column, and began marching towards the centre of the battle to form an additional reserve for the main attack on the Ramillies-Offus front.

Some writers have assigned to this transference of part of the British infantry from the right wing to the centre an importance which it does not deserve. It was a highly ingenious feature which would have played its part if the resistance of the enemy had been more obdurate. But events outstripped it. The decision of the cavalry struggle had already gained the day. The British infantry commanders, angry, eager to act, and excited, were for the most part only spectators, and not until the French in their front recoiled did their battalions join independently in the fighting.

The battle moved at such a pace that all the troops of both sides on the northern flank were left behind its headlong course. Marshal Villeroy and the Elector were still ardently awaiting the climax of the British assault upon the French left when grave news reached them from their right. The cavalry of the right wing had been broken; the Maison du Roi was defeated. Moreover, the flank was turned. Forthwith they spurred their horses from Offus along the main line of the army to the rear of Ramillies. They encountered a tide of fugitives, and were soon involved in the rout. Half an hour earlier they had been expecting the battle to begin. They now saw that it was lost beyond repair. They set themselves to form a new front bent back from Ramillies at right angles to their original line. At the same time they ordered a general retreat upon Judoigne. Ramillies was the pivot upon which all this turned. Here Count Maffei, a Bavarian general and the writer of valuable memoirs, commanded a strong brigade.[1]

Marlborough's central conception of the battle had been the storm of Ramillies by the mass of his infantry; and his feint with Orkney on the right, the capture of Taviers, and his onslaught with the whole of his cavalry on the left were but to be the preliminary and ancillary phases of this crowning result. In fact they had already decided it. The main infantry struggle had been growing in severity during the cavalry battle in the plain. Long lines of foot, backed by the whole reserves of the army, including now the British second line from the right, all aided by the fire of twenty heavy cannon and the bulk of the allied artillery, impended upon the enemy's centre.

With the destruction of the French right wing and the flower

---

[1] Two Maffeis figure in this volume—(1) Marquis Alessandro Maffei, the Bavarian general, who eventually became a Field-Marshal, and (2) Count Annibale Maffei, the Savoyard diplomat, Minister in London, Plenipotentiary at Utrecht, and later (1713) Viceroy of Sicily.

of their cavalry the third phase of Ramillies began. A series of decisions was taken by Marlborough and Overkirk, evidently working in full comprehension and harmony. About five o'clock the immediate pursuit of the French horse was stopped, and the whole of the victorious cavalry was ordered to wheel to the right and form a line facing north, in order to attack and roll up the French army from their exposed flank. Just as at Blenheim Marlborough delayed his final attack until Eugene could re-form and strike at the same time, so now the infantry advance on Ramillies was suspended or slowed down until the cavalry got into their new position.

We have no record of these orders. We only see them in execution. The allied infantry, who had begun their advance at about three o'clock, had little more than a mile to cover. Their leading brigades were on the outskirts of Ramillies by half-past three. Since then they had been in heavy action, attacking and counter-attacked. On the other hand, the allied cavalry, victorious at about five, did not resume their advance until they were completely formed upon the new front. This marked pause in the battle, in order to deliver a final blow in thorough combination, when Marlborough must already have felt assured of victory, gives us a measure of the way in which his mind worked on the battlefield. Neither the dazzle of success nor the ordeal of personal combat, neither the fall from his horse nor the breathlessness of his run, affected in the slightest degree his sense of proportion, or his perfect comprehension of the whole problem—at least from the moment when he was once again in his saddle. He had wrongly descended from his high station upon an immediate local need. He emerged from this violent personal experience, and instantly, as after the charge at Elixem, resumed his normal poise.

It was now six o'clock. Marlborough and Overkirk had re-formed the whole of the allied cavalry almost at right angles to their original attack. They stretched in overwhelming strength from behind Ramillies to the Tomb of Ottomond. Both generals must have been brilliantly served by their staffs and subordinate commanders; for the feat of wheeling the whole front of more than a hundred squadrons, disordered by fierce action and triumphant pursuit, although it flowed naturally from the course of the battle and the Danish turning movement, is remarkable in cavalry history. This grand array now began a second resolute and orderly advance. Villeroy and the Elector by their personal exertions had managed to form a new cavalry front facing south against them, composed partly of rallied squadrons from the plain, but mainly of the fifty fresh squadrons hitherto idle upon the French left. This new front rested upon the remnants of Maffei's unlucky brigade, which now clung to the rear of Ramillies, also facing south, and manning a sunken road. Thus the French army was re-formed in a right angle,

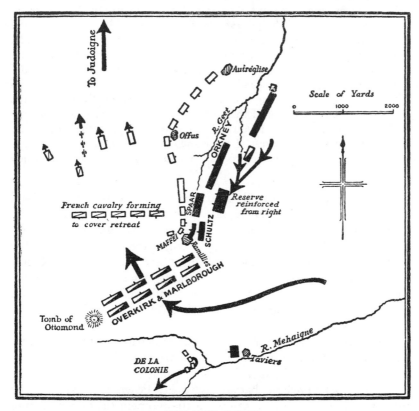

THE NEW FRONT

one side of which comprised the whole of their cavalry remaining on the field; and the other (from Ramillies to Autréglise) of their infantry. Behind this evidently shaken screen the Marshal hoped to withdraw his artillery and transport wagons and make a respectable retreat through Judoigne across the Dyle.

This picture was no sooner created than it was dissolved. The advance of the allied cavalry was not resisted. The fifty squadrons from the French left, appalled by the disaster to their comrades in the plain and to the whole army, would not face the coming charge.

They turned their horses' heads and melted from the field. Count Maffei at the angle or hinge of the position suffered the same shock as the Old Campaigner had sustained at the Schellenberg.

> I then saw coming towards us a line of hostile cavalry who, having broken our right, were advancing to surround the village; but as this cavalry was coming from the side from which I naturally had expected our own to arrive, I thought at first that they must be our people, and I had not even the slightest suspicion to the contrary when I saw that they stopped two or three hundred paces from us without doing anything, although they could have attacked us from the rear. I did not notice the green cockade which they wore in their hats, which was indeed so small that it could hardly have been discerned at the distance. Thus convinced that they were our friends, I made up my mind to collect all the infantry I could to [complete the front] . . . I went towards the nearest of these squadrons to instruct their officer, but instead of being listened to was immediately surrounded and called upon to ask for quarter.[1]

This he was compelled to do at the point of sword and pistol, and thereafter became prisoner of war. The hinge was broken.

And now the whole of the allied infantry, including several English battalions from Orkney's command, crashed into the French line between Ramillies and Offus, and to the north of Offus. Lumley, with the British cavalry, hitherto inactive on the extreme right, at length got across the Geet, followed by Orkney, and, piercing the crumbling front, cut directly on to the line of the French retreat.

We have the definite record from numerous witnesses of that almost unknown feature in European warfare of that epoch, charges at the gallop. The King's Dragoon Guards and the Royal Scots Greys compelled whole battalions to lay down their arms. The infantry Régiment du Roi, caught at the moment they were picking up the knapsacks they had discarded for the battle, were cut to pieces or captured almost to a man.

Now the whole French army broke and collapsed together. Their left drew off northward across country in fair order. Orkney relates how Lumley asked him to hurry on with his infantry, as the cavalry could not deal alone with that part of the French infantry which was unbroken. "If," says Orkney, "I could only have got up in time we should have taken eight or nine battalions." The main part of the French centre fled along the road to Judoigne, but this road

[1] *Mémoires du Marquis Maffei* (1740), ii, 129.

was blocked by the transport of the army. The remaining troops, impeded by the obstacle, dispersed and scattered over the countryside, for the main part throwing away their arms to hasten their flight, which achieved itself by its rapidity. Another long stream fled panic-stricken westward towards Wavre. The Old Campaigner

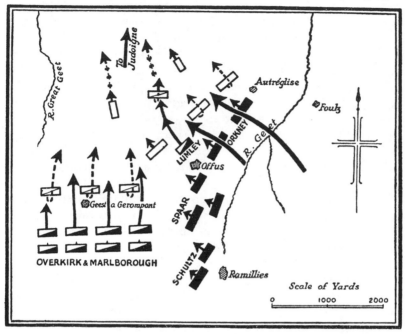

THE PURSUIT

behind Taviers found himself completely cut off by the floods of allied cavalry which covered the plain as far as the Tomb of Otto-mond, and were everywhere charging and pursuing the flying French. He was by no means at a loss. As the shadows fell upon the battlefield he marched off with his four battalions and many fugitives who accompanied him, or whom he had rescued from the swamp, in the opposite direction towards Namur, which he reached the next morning.

Thus, in the space of four hours, between three and seven o'clock, the entire magnificent French army was shattered and scattered into utter rout and ruin. All their baggage, their cannon, trophies innumerable, five thousand unwounded prisoners, fell to the victors. The pursuit for a considerable time was merciless, and thousands of flying men were denied all quarter and cut down. So rapid had been the transformation, and the day was already so far advanced, that darkness fell without the full realization of their victory coming home to the allied commanders. Nearly all the accounts of Ramillies written immediately after the battle give the impression that their writers only very imperfectly understood the completeness of their triumph. Under the burden of their long march to the battlefield, worn by the excitement of the day, baffled by the rapidity with which the French recoiled and ran before them, scattered and unlinked by the sudden collapse of the hostile front, they fell forward as through a suddenly opened door in very great disorganization. The orders and the urge of every one were to press forward into the night; and when each brigade or regiment halted they had only vague ideas of their own whereabouts, and still less of that of their friends and foes. "We might have been a defeated army," says Orkney, "for the confusion we were in." They had, in fact, fought a great battle and marched twenty-five miles across country in as many hours.

The pursuit roared away to the north. At midnight Marlborough and his headquarters staff, with a heavy column of cavalry, was near Meldert, more than twelve miles beyond the field of battle. He still wished to press on, but his guide was lost, and he was forced to a brief halt. He had been nineteen hours in the saddle. He was bruised and shaken by his fall, and worn by his physical exertions. He knew he had gained one of the greatest battles of history. His cloak was spread upon the ground, and he was about to throw himself upon it for a few hours' sleep, when one more thought—eminently characteristic at this moment—occurred to him. Goslinga, the field Deputy, who might be either so great a help or hindrance in future operations, was at hand. Marlborough saw the opportunity of paying him the finest compliment that could be conceived. He invited him to share the cloak of the Commander-in-Chief on the night of victory. However, as the reader will learn, this pearl was cast in vain.

Chapter Seven

THE CONQUEST OF BELGIUM

1706—JUNE

UNRELENTING pursuit magnified the victory of Ramillies. No battle in the eighteenth century produced comparable direct results. The fortress-barrier was for a while shorn away like grass before the scythe. As Blenheim saved Vienna, so Ramillies conquered the Netherlands. Cities and towns, the masterpieces of Vauban, any one of which would have been the prize of a campaign of King William, capitulated on all sides. The rout and temporary destruction of the French field army led to a collapse so far-reaching and so unexpected that it dwarfed even the shock of battle. To measure rightly this prodigy we must recall the mile-by-mile methods of those days, the limited means of offence and movement, and the habits of thought engrained in military minds by a generation of this kind of war.

Before midnight of May 24 Orkney's British and the leading brigades of Dutch infantry under General Churchill had orders to force the Dyle. The pontoon train and all available cannon were pressed forward along the crowded roads. The British cavalry were soon upon the head-streams of the river. As he knew he had captured all the French artillery on the field, Marlborough was sure he could not be withstood. In fact there was no resistance. By noon on the 25th his advance-guards appeared before the gates of Louvain. This stronghold, which he had longed to possess in the autumn of 1703 and in the summer of 1705, surrendered to the trumpet. At midnight after the battle Marshal Villeroy and the Elector had held haggard, dishevelled council by torchlight in the market-place. Fugitives of high distinction, veteran leaders of so many years of strife, gathered as they rode in, stained and seared. Survivors of the Maison du Roi clustered about them. There was no difference of opinion among the generals. All were agreed that neither the Dyle nor even the Senne could be held. The French army could only be rallied behind the Scheldt if there. In that direction all formed bodies of troops remaining were ordered to retreat with the utmost speed. Of the brilliant army of sixty-three thousand men which had set out so confidently in the morning to seek a decision of arms, barely fifteen thousand were under control. Twelve thousand had fallen killed or wounded in the clash. Nearly six thousand were prisoners of the Allies.[1] The rest had dispersed to every quarter of the compass, seeking the gates of some friendly

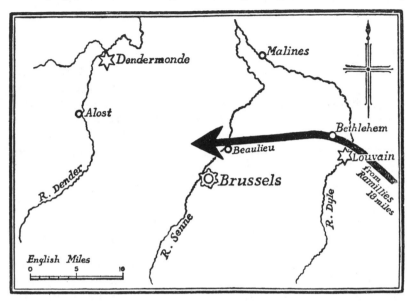

THE DIRECT PURSUIT AFTER RAMILLIES

town. For more than a month no semblance of a French army could keep the field.

Marlborough could not know all this. Indeed, his standard of values, inculcated by so many years of war in this obstinate theatre, expanded itself only day by day. At first no one realized how overwhelming had been the victory, still less its reverberations. But the Duke thrust forward with every scrap of moral and physical energy he could extort from himself or from his soldiers. In this temper, but always with considerable precaution and always against the stubborn drag of supplies, he traversed Louvain on the 25th, and encamped on the heights of Bethlehem with above fifty thousand men. On the 26th his headquarters stood upon the Senne at the

[1] John Millner (*Journal of Marches* . . . (1733)) says: killed, 6759; wounded, 5328; prisoners, 5729. Abel Boyer (*Annals of the Reign of Queen Anne* (1703-13)) says: killed, 5000; wounded, ——; prisoners, 4600.

castle of Beaulieu, midway between Malines and Brussels. Both these places were summoned to surrender. On the 28th the army halted for two days, having since the 23rd advanced fifty miles. Detachments were sent forward to secure the crossings of the Dender and the Scheldt.

Intent upon these new gains, and especially of the capital, Marlborough had already forgotten Ramillies. The French cannon lay where they had been abandoned among the dead; and while the allied army rolled forward on its irresistible career the French command in Namur had the enterprise to send out teams of horses and drag them inside their ramparts. The heave of Marlborough's advance and the exclusive intensity of his forward impulse cannot be better judged than from this curious lapse. This was no time to count or even collect spoils and trophies. The dominating military objectives lay ahead: to drive deep into the fortress zone and to keep the French from the sea flank; to isolate and perhaps soon besiege Antwerp; to strike at Ghent and Oudenarde on the Scheldt, were prizes which threw past triumph into twilight.

And now a political revolution in Belgium supervened. Spectators of the French disaster, confronted by the massive invasion of the allied army, dazzled by the sword of the Captain-General, not only the magistrates of Brussels and the Estates of Brabant, but the whole Spanish authority in the Netherlands deserted the cause of the Two Crowns and declared their allegiance to Charles III. The prolonged French occupation, with its insolences and exactions, not less than the fear of hostile armies, sustained the decision of the rulers with the ardent support of the entire population. In a trice the conquest of Belgium by the Allies became the act of its deliverance from the thraldom of Louis XIV.

Marlborough was not furnished with formal powers to deal with so surprising a transformation. There was no time to communicate with London or even The Hague. He therefore took everything upon himself. Keeping in close accord with Goslinga and the other Deputies, he received on the 27th at Beaulieu a joint delegation from the Brussels magistracy and the Estates. He accepted their change of allegiance. He guaranteed all religious and civil rights. He renewed the famous charter of "La Joyeuse Entrée"; and in an order to the allied army he threatened "death without mercy" to any officer or soldier found guilty of plundering or molesting the inhabitants. These measures were far-reaching, and not only the citizens but the whole countryside came over to the Allies. The

Spanish garrisons in several fortresses turned the French out of the citadels, and held them for Charles III. Food and forage poured in from the farms in response to British and Dutch cash. French stragglers were caught and brought in by the peasantry. French detachments hurried to disentangle themselves from the hostile population, and overtake the general retreat. Meanwhile the Allies were able to draw troops from their garrisons. The Prussians, Lunebergers, and Hanoverians began to move forward from the Rhine, and Villeroy was justified in reporting that Marlborough was soon to be at the head of ninety thousand men. Early on the 28th Charles Churchill took possession of Brussels, and that evening Marlborough made his public entry into the city. The magistrates received him with the pomp of ancient ceremonial, and the populace welcomed him with hectic enthusiasm and every sign of gratitude. Flanked by his own garrisons in Brussels and Malines, he could now march forward to the Scheldt.

Villeroy and the Elector had hoped to halt near Ghent, behind the Lys and the Scheldt, whence they could cover Bruges and Ostend and thereby flank any allied movement on Antwerp. Up to this point, and especially while the French were under immediate shock of the battle, the pursuit had been direct. Now Marlborough moved across Villeroy's communications with France.[1] His impending passage of the Scheldt at Gavre threatened these to such an extent that Villeroy withdrew to Courtrai.

Marlborough's letter to Sarah after the battle is a moving document. In its tenderness, its modesty, its reverence and composure, and in its thought for others, it reveals his natural glory. Amid the press of events and in extreme fatigue his chief thought was for Bingfield's widow and mother.

Monday, May 24, 11 o'clock

I did not tell my dearest soul in my last the design I had of engaging the enemy if possible to a battle, fearing the concern she has for me might make her uneasy; but I can now give her the satisfaction of letting her know that on Sunday last we fought, and that God Almighty has been pleased to give us a victory. I must leave the particulars to this bearer, Colonel Richards, for having been on horseback all Sunday, and after the battle marching all night, my head aches to that degree that it is very uneasy to me to write. Poor Bringfield, holding my stirrup for me, and helping me on horseback, was killed. I am told that he leaves his wife and mother in a poor condition. I can't write to any of my children, so that you will let them know that I am well,

---

[1] Marlborough to Heinsius, May 30-31; Vreede, pp. 29-30.

and that I desire they will thank God for His preserving me. And pray give my duty to the Queen, and let her know the truth of my heart, that the greatest pleasure I have in this success is that it may be a great service to her affairs; for I am sincerely sensible of all her goodness for me and mine. Pray believe me when I assure you that I love you more than I can express.[1]

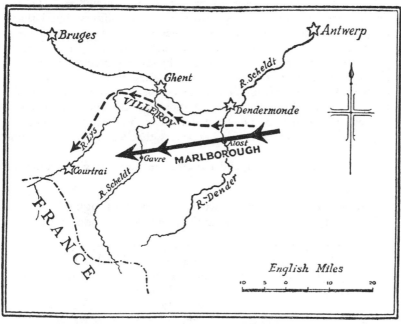

MARLBOROUGH THREATENS VILLEROY'S COMMUNICATIONS
(MAY 30)

To Godolphin he presented some details:

Monday, May 24

I believe my last might give you expectation of an action. We have been in perpetual motion ever since; and on Sunday last we came in presence with the enemy, who came with the same intentions I had, of fighting. We began to make our lines of battle about eleven o'clock, but we had not all our troops till two in the afternoon, at which time I gave orders for attacking them. The first half-hour was very doubtful, but I thank God after that we had success in our attacks, which were on a village in the centre; and on the left we pursued them three leagues, and the night obliged us to give it over. Having been all Sunday, as well as last night on horseback, my head aches to that degree that I must refer you to the bearer. I shall only add that we beat them

[1] Coxe, ii, 354.

into so great a consternation that they abandoned all their cannon; their baggage they had sent away in the morning, being resolved to fight. They had 128 squadrons, and 74 battalions; we had 123 squadrons and 73 battalions; so that you see the armies were near of a strength; but the general officers which were taken tell us that they thought themselves sure of victory by having all the King of France's household, and with them the best troops of France. You will easily believe this victory has lost us a good many men and officers; but I thank God we have but three English regiments that have much suffered; the Dutch horse and foot have suffered more than we. I am going to get a little rest, for if our bread comes by six this evening, I will then march to Louvain this night, in hopes to find them in such disorder as that we may be encouraged to attack them behind their lines, for they can have no cannon but what they can take out of Louvain. I beg you will assure the Queen that I act with all my heart, and you know how necessary it is for her affairs that we should have good success.

Poor Bringfield is killed, and I am told he leaves his wife and mother in bad condition.[1]

There was a courier twice a week, and Marlborough's letters tell the tale incomparably. On the 27th he wrote to Godolphin:

Since my last we have not only passed the Dyle, but are masters of Louvain, Malines, and Brussels; you will see by what I send to Mr Secretary Harley what has passed between me and the states of Brabant, which I found assembled at Brussels. As there could not be time for orders from England, I hope her Majesty will approve of what I have done. . . . *The consequence of this battle is likely to be of greater advantage than that of Blenheim; for we have now the whole summer before us, and with the blessing of God, I will make the best use of it.* For as we had no council of war before this battle, so I hope to have none this whole campaign; and I think we may make such a campaign as may give the Queen the glory of making an honourable and safe peace; for the blessing of God is certainly with us. . . .[2]

And to Sarah:

I have been in so continued a hurry ever since the battle of Ramillies, by which my blood is so heated that when I go to bed I sleep so unquietly that I cannot get rid of my headache, so that I have not as yet all the pleasure I shall enjoy, of the blessing God has been pleased to give us by this great victory. My Lord Treasurer will let you see what I send by this express to Mr Secretary Harley, by which you will see that we have done in four days what we should have thought ourselves

---

[1] Coxe, ii, 355. [2] Ibid., 365.

happy if we could have been sure of it in four years. I bless God that He has been pleased to make me the instrument of doing so much service to the Queen, England, and all Europe, for it is most certain that we have destroyed the greatest part of the best troops of France. My dearest soul, I have now that great pleasure of thinking that I may have the happiness of ending my days in quiet with you.

I have appointed next Sunday for the army to return thanks to God for the protection He has been pleased to give us. For on this occasion it has been very visible, for the French had not only greater numbers than we, but also all their best troops. I hope the Queen will appoint a speedy thanksgiving day at St Paul's, for the goodness of God is so very great that if He had suffered us to have been beaten, the liberties of all the allies had been lost. . . . My dearest life, I am ever yours.

Brussels has submitted to King Charles the Third, and I am promised that in eight days the states of Brabant will also proclaim him.[1]

On the 31st he wrote to Godolphin:

MERLEBECK, NEAR GHENT

We did this day design the passing the Scheldt at Gavre, by which we should have cut the French army from their old lines; but they rather chose to abandon Ghent, which they did this morning at break of day, so that I have camped the left of the army at Gavre and the right at this place. I shall send to-morrow a detachment to Bruges, they having also abandoned that town. As soon as we can have the cannon, and what is necessary, we shall attack Antwerp; after which I should be glad the next place might be Ostend; for unless they draw the greatest part of their army from Germany, they will not be able to hinder us from doing what we please on this side their lines. I tell you my thoughts, but if you think there is anything better for the Queen's interest, I shall endeavour to do it, having that more at heart than my own life.[2]

To Sarah:

MERLEBECK, NEAR GHENT
June 1

We are now masters of Ghent, and to-morrow I shall send some troops to Bruges. *So many towns have submitted since the battle, that it really looks more like a dream than truth.* My thoughts are now turning to the getting everything ready for the siege of Antwerp, which place alone, in former years, would have been thought good success for a whole campaign; but we have the blessing of God with us, and I hope we shall do more in this campaign than was done in the last ten years' war in this country. . . .[3]

---

[1] Coxe, ii, 366.   [2] *Ibid.*, 368.   [3] *Loc. cit.*

On June 3:

Every day gives us fresh marks of the great victory; for since my last, which was but two days ago, we have taken possession of Bruges and Damme, as also Oudenarde, which was besieged the last war by the King, with sixty thousand men, and he was at last forced to raise the siege. In short there is so great a panic in the French army as is not to be expressed. Every place we take declares for King Charles. . . .

You are very kind in desiring I would not expose myself. Be assured I love you so well, and am so desirous of ending my days quietly with you, that I shall not venture myself but when it is absolutely necessary; and I am sure you are so kind to me, and wish so well to the common cause, that you had rather see me dead, than not to do my duty. I am so persuaded that this campaign will bring us a good peace that I beg of you to do all you can that the house at Woodstock may be carried up as much as possible, that I may have a prospect of living in it.[1]

To Godolphin:

MERLEBECK
June 3

. . . I have sent Brigadier Cadogan with six squadrons of horse, to offer terms to the town and citadel of Antwerp. If I can have that place without a siege, it will gain us a month. I am doing all I can to gain the governor of Dendermonde, which place would be of great consequence. They have let out the waters, so that we cannot attack it. As soon as we have Antwerp, and can get our artillery to Ostend, we shall attack the place, at which time it would be necessary that the Dunkirk squadron should help us. *You see that I make use of the consternation.*

Marsin will join them to-morrow with 18 battalions and 14 squadrons, and I am assured that orders are gone to Marshal de Villars to send 30 battalions more, and 40 squadrons; so that Prince Louis [the Margrave] may act if he pleases. I have ordered the Hanover troops to join me, and we hope to have the Prussians, which will enable me to make the detachment for the descent. If Prince Louis makes use of this occasion to press the French in Alsace, as I will, with the blessing of God, in this country, the King of France will be obliged to draw some troops from Italy, *by which Turin may be saved.* We have nothing now that stops us but the want of cannon; for the French cannot have their troops from Germany in less than three weeks. We march to-morrow to Deynse, and the French are retired behind Menin, by which you see we are at liberty to attack Ostend and Nieuport, if we had our artillery.[2]

[1] Coxe, ii, 369.　　　　　[2] *Ibid.*, 371.

And to Heinsius, June 1: "Dendermonde is under water, but I am endeavouring to make the Governor propositions that may tempt him to declare for King Charles; *for if we had that place, Ostend, and Audener [Oudenarde], all this country would be covered by those three places.*"[1]

The Duke could now write letters to the chiefs and princes of the Alliance, which followed hard upon the announcements he had made to them of the impending battle. His first, on the 24th, to the King of Prussia, contained both sting and appeal. "I profoundly regret that Your Majesty's troops have not had a share in this glorious action; however, I will not despair yet of seeing them join the army. I am sure that not one of Your Majesty's generals would take more care of them."[2] The Prussian Colonel Grumbkow was the bearer of this. Marlborough waited till next day, when he had passed the Dyle, to address the States-General: "It is with double joy," he wrote, "that I give myself the honour of writing to their high and mighty Lordships this letter from Louvain. . . ." And then, looking back on his frustrated efforts in 1703 and 1705, he added, "où il y a longtemps que je souhaitais être pour le bien de la cause commune."[3]

Twelve of these letters reporting the victory are printed in the *Dispatches*. They were as important a part of his warfare as the military movements. They are in the main variants of one another. Cardonnel was a master of correspondence; but to the Emperor and ruling sovereigns the Duke wrote in his own hand, and the labour of scribing must alone have been severe. These personal letters from this extraordinary English general announcing his victories fortified the whole Alliance. To Eugene he sent a detailed account of the battle and its preliminary movements. He had marched on the Saturday "to seize the gap between the Mehaigne and the Great Geet." His information was that the enemy did not mean to fight before Monday, "ne croyant pas que nous oserions aller à eux." The armies were in presence before noon: both sides waited to range their lines of battle and to plant the batteries, which began to fire a little after midday, and at two o'clock

> we attacked the village of Ramillies, which sustained the right of their infantry and where they had their strongest battery *avec beaucoup de monde*. The fight warmed up and lasted for some time with very great fury, and at last the enemy were compelled to bend. We there took their cannon and made many prisoners and having continued the action with the same vigour, infantry as well as cavalry, up to four or five o'clock, when the enemy began to retreat, we pursued them continually

[1] Vreede, pp. 30–31.   [2] *Dispatches*, ii, 521.   [3] *Ibid.*, 523.

till long into the night. . . . We halted for only two hours in the night and were on the march before daybreak to gain the Dyle, of which we had determined to force a passage to-day at dawn. But the enemy have spared us the trouble, having retired last night towards Brussels, so that we have already occupied Louvain and our whole army has passed the river without any opposition. . . . Your Highness can judge from this the losses of the enemy and the consternation in which they lie. We propose to march to-morrow upon Brussels to exploit their disorder and try to close with them or compel their further retreat. Nothing could justify making such demands upon the troops after so violent an engagement except the need of pushing them to extremes before Marshal Marsin can join them, as he might do in four or five days.[1]

The account which he gave to the Margrave mentioned that "the Maison du Roi has been almost all cut to pieces," and he added, "I am sure Your Highness will soon feel the advantages of our success by the detachments which will have to be drawn from the Rhine, and that will give you a chance of acting on your side."

The return messengers from England brought a flood of congratulations. "I want words," said the Queen,

to express my true sense of the great service you have done to your country, and I hope it will be a means to confirm all good and honest men in their principles, and frighten others from being troublesome. . . . I must repeat my earnest request that you should be careful ot yourself.[2]

She wrote again (May 21/June 2) a letter which gains from being printed in its original form:

★The great Glorious Success wch God Almighty has bin pleased to Bless you wth, & his preservation of your person, one can never thank him enough for, & next to him all things are oweing to you; it is impossible for me ever to Say or doe much as I ought in return of your great & faithful Services to me, but I will endeavour by all ye actions of my life to Shew you how truly Sensible I am of them. The account you Send by mr Pitt of ye great progress you have made since ye Batle is astonishing, the Blessing of God is Sertinly with you, may he Still continue to protect you, & make you the happy instrument of giveing a lasting peace to Europe; I never durst venture to Send ye enclosed by ye post for feare of any accident but Stanhope[3] going to

---

[1] *Dispatches*, ii, 525. In French.   [2] *Conduct*, p. 207.
[3] Mary Stanhope, one of the Queen's maids of honour, a daughter of Alexander Stanhope, Envoy at The Hague, sister of the famous Stanhope (at this time in Spain).

see her father I would not miss yt opertunety it being what may be usefull on some occasions, I intended to have made use of this opertunety to writt my mind more freely then I can by ye post, but I have bin in Such a Continual hurry these three or four days & am Soe still yt I can only now desire you to forgive all ye faults in my letter of fryday last wch was writt when I was soe Sleepy I could hardly keep my eyes open, & to be assured yt I Shall ever be wth all truthy our humble Servant.[1]

St John and Harley vied with each other in their enthusiasm. Godolphin showed signs of the pressures to which he was constantly subjected. He wrote on May 17/28:

> God be thanked for the good news you sent us by Richards, who arrived here yesterday evening, and more particularly for the great escape you have had in your own person. I am very sensible you could not avoid exposing yourself upon this occasion; but where so much consequence turns upon one single life, you must allow your friends the liberty to think and say it ought not to be done without an absolute necessity. . . . You may depend that her Majesty will not fail to take care of poor Mr Bringfield's widow.[2]

And again, on May 24/June 5:

> The Queen is come to town to give God thanks next Thursday for your victory. I assure you I shall do it from every vein within me, having scarce anything else to support either my heart or my head. The animosity and inveteracy one has to struggle with is unimaginable, not to mention the difficulty of obtaining things to be done that are reasonable, or of satisfying people with reason when they are done.[3]

It was not until he woke on the morning of May 26 that Louis XIV learned that his finest army had suffered disaster in Flanders. No formal dispatch conveyed the details, but the courier from Louvain brought a short letter from Marshal Villeroy to Dangeau, the Court Chamberlain, telling him how bravely his son had fought, and that he would surely recover from the scalp wound he had received from a sabre. Thereafter there was a silence of six days. "I was at Versailles," says Saint-Simon. "Never has one seen such anxiety and consternation. . . . In ignorance of what had happened and of the consequences of such an unfortunate battle, and amid every one's fears for their kith and kin, the days seemed years."[4] The King was reduced to asking his courtiers what they had heard. At

[1] Blenheim MSS. [2] Coxe, ii, 357. [3] Ibid., 361. [4] Saint-Simon, iv, 427.

E   129

length, finding suspense intolerable, he astonished Versailles by sending Chamillart in person to Villeroy's headquarters, thus leaving the Ministries of War and Finance headless. Chamillart reached Lille on the 31st, and found Villeroy, reinforced by Marsin, around Courtrai. He had retired successively from the Dyle, the Senne, the Dender, and the Scheldt; he had abandoned the whole of Spanish Flanders. He was content if he could hold the French fortress line along the Lys. Chamillart spent three days in long separate discussions with the Marshal and the Elector, and heard versions of the battle and the retreat from all quarters. He found Villeroy dominated by the sense of Marlborough's power; but equally convinced of his own blamelessness, and, indeed, that he had saved the remnants of the army by his prolonged, rapid retreat.

French writers have blamed the Marshal for giving up so much territory, so many fine positions and important places. They overlook the alternative. This was to fight another battle. All Marlborough's marches had shown that this was what he sought. Fortresses were not his primary aim. His quarry was the French army; and the French army could not face him. Its condition was such that if caught in grapple it would be utterly destroyed. Therefore Marshal Villeroy comforted himself in defeat with the fact that in giving ground he had taken no half-measures.

To the King he wrote with dignified assurance. Three main criticisms were focused upon him by his generals: first, that he had accepted battle without knowing the strength of the enemy, and without waiting for the troops of Marshal Marsin; secondly, that he had not reinforced his right and held the village of Taviers in superior strength; and, thirdly, that he had so marshalled his army that the battle had been lost without its main strength being engaged. To all these points the Marshal addressed himself pertinaciously, observing, however, that as a man of the world he knew well "that good reasons are no explanation for catastrophe." He finished his lengthy justification, "I have said more than enough. I end by taking the liberty of telling Your Majesty that the only happy day which I foresee in my life will be that of my death."[1]

To this Chamillart, having returned to Versailles, replied in due course (June 16) with severely reasoned rebuttal. It was resolved to remove the Marshal from his command. The feelings of his army and even such public opinion as the French Court could nourish made this step imperative. But Villeroy was a personage of high

[1] Pelet, vi, 41.

consequence. He was a veteran general; he was a great gentleman. He was also the personal friend both of the King and of Mme de Maintenon. Napoleon's maxim "Dur aux grands" had not been born. The King's egotism, which now wore the guise of magnanimity, led him to treat Villeroy, who enjoyed the privilege of being in his inmost circle, with an extreme consideration. Elaborate procedures were accordingly used towards the defeated Marshal. He was offered alternative appointments, and for several weeks discreetly urged to resign. But when he continued as obstinate in holding his command as he had been in retreating from the enemy, patience was at length discarded. He was dismissed. Yet, even when forced to abrupt action, Louis practised the utmost politeness. "At our age," he said to Villeroy when he received him, "we must no longer expect good fortune."

The next measure was to re-create the field army. The resources of France seemed inexhaustible. Marlborough has given his own account of this process.

> The method the King of France has taken to make good his word to the Elector of Bavaria, of putting him at the head of an army of 80,000 men, are the 18 battalions and 14 squadrons which came with the Marshal de Marsin; the detachment that is now marching from Alsace, of 30 battalions and 40 squadrons; and 14 battalions, which the Comte de Gassy commanded in the lines, which were not at the battle. These, joined with the troops that were at the battle, would make above 100,000 men. . . .[1]

Thus, after making provision for garrisons, there was speedily built up the largest French army with which Marlborough had been confronted. In that hour only one man was deemed capable of leading it. The Duke of Vendôme was recalled from Italy.

The strategic pursuit had lasted nearly a fortnight, had cleared all Brabant and much of Flanders, and had rendered the French army for the time being wholly ineffective. The easy gains of panic now ceased. The French were withdrawing into the main fortress zone and towards France. Further advance by Marlborough, especially if any siege was involved, depended upon the waterways. The rivers were still blocked by the French possession of Antwerp and Dendermond. Their fortresses at Ostend and Nieuport controlled the entrance to the canals leading to the Lys and the Scheldt. Marlborough was compelled to suspend his advance in order to clear

---

[1] Marlborough to Godolphin, June 28; Coxe, iii, 2.

the communications. He could take whichever fortress he wished and no one could gainsay him, but every siege took time and strength, and it was soon plain that half a dozen captures would be the limit of the campaign in Flanders and Northern France. On June 5 the allied army crossed the Scheldt and the Lys and camped at Arsele, where it could cover any siege necessary to open the communications.

The joyous news here reached Marlborough that Antwerp had capitulated. Summoned by Cadogan, the Spanish grandee in command declared for Charles III. The burghers endorsed his action; the Spanish and Walloon regiments came over to the Allies, and the French troops marched out upon terms. The gaining of this great prize, with all its strategic and commercial attributes, without the firing of a shot was deemed a wonder. "The hand of God," wrote Marlborough to the States-General, "appears visibly in all this, spreading such fear among the enemy as to compel them to surrender so many strong places and whole districts without the least resistance."[1] Leaving the army to wait for its artillery around Arsele, the Duke paid a flying visit to The Hague in order, as he wrote to Heinsius, "to settle with you what is proper for the descent, as also to let you know my thoughts for the plan of this campaign, which, with the blessing of God, I think may be such a one as may make France glad of a reasonable peace this winter."[2] He also wished to make arrangements for the administration of the conquered cities and territories, and above all to press that the Dutch garrisons should join the army forthwith and to the last man possible. This would enable him to pursue his advantage in Flanders, and at the same time to provide the necessary troops for the descent upon the French coast so dear to the hearts of the English Cabinet, and now regarded by Marlborough as a timely operation. All was agreed with the utmost cordiality.

On the way back to the army Marlborough passed through Antwerp. On the night of the 11th the keys of the city were presented to him by the authorities with the remark that "they had never been delivered up to any person since the great Duke of Parma, and that after a siege of twelve months." He was greeted with enthusiasm by great crowds and escorted through the streets by all the notables in torchlight procession to the bishop's palace, where he was "splendidly entertained." On the 13th he rejoined the army, whose siege artillery was now drawing near.

[1] *Dispatches*, ii, 558.　　　　　　　　　　[2] Vreede, p. 30.

Marlborough to Godolphin

ARSELE
June 7, 1706

. . . I am extremely obliged to you for your kind concern for my safety. I am now at an age not to take pleasure in exposing myself but when I think it absolutely necessary. You can never say enough to the Queen for her goodness to me in the letter you sent me. Though I take myself to be a good Englishman, and wish well to the common cause, yet my great joy in this success is that it hath pleased God to make me the instrument of doing that which must be of great consequence to her service. . . . I take this time of going to The Hague, we being at full stand for want of cannon; for the French being retreated into their own country behind their strong towns, have put the greatest part of their foot into Ostend, Nieuport, Ypres, Menin, Tournay, and Lille. The Marshal de Villeroy is camped with the rest of the French at Saint-Amand, and the Elector of Bavaria is at Lille. The capitulations for the surrender of the town and citadel of Antwerp were signed yesterday; so that we are now in possession of all Brabant. Our next thoughts will be for the attacking Nieuport and Ostend, which I see you have a great mind we should; so that I beg there may be no time lost in sending such ships as are ready to cruise before those two places, which will be of great use to us. By the letters from Paris, we see they would have us believe that they are taking the necessary measures to have a superiority in this country, which I think they will never be able to do, unless they put themselves on the defensive in Italy, as well as in Germany. For the good of the common cause, I wish they may endeavour it, *for the men they have here will very unwillingly be brought to fight again this campaign.*[1]

Marlborough to Godolphin

June 14, 1706

If we take Ostend in any seasonable time, it will be much the best place for the transports to come to, and I will take care to have the troops there [*i.e.*, for the descent]. The efforts the French are making to have a strong army I am afraid will make it impossible for us to take Dunkirk this year; but whenever we can have it, I agree with you that the best thing we can do is to spoil the harbour.[2]

Marlborough to Godolphin

ARSELE
June 17, 1706

The troops designed for the siege of Ostend marched that way two days ago, and I shall march with what remains of the army to cover the siege to-morrow; I have with me 50 battalions of foot and 99 squadrons

[1] Coxe, ii, 380.   [2] *Ibid.*, 376.

of horse. I hope to have the Prussians and Hanoverians with me before the enemy can have their detachment from Germany.[1]

Overkirk, deflected from Nieuport by the opening of the sluices at the mouth of the Yser, conducted the siege of Ostend. Admiral Fairborne blockaded the harbour with a squadron of battleships from the main fleet and small craft from the coast flotillas, including the bomb-ketches *Blast* and *Salamander*. The citizens of Ostend adhered to the French garrison, and for three days both the fortifications and town were subjected to a severe bombardment from land and sea until, according to contemporary accounts, "the place was near reduced to a heap of rubbish"—not for the last time in its history. On the second day, July 4, a Dutch battalion, preceded by a storming party of fifty British grenadiers, formed a lodgment upon the counterscarp, and after a vigorous sally by the besieged Ostend surrendered. The French garrison, undertaking not to serve for six months, marched out "without marks of honour," and the Spaniards mostly joined the Allies. Two Bourbon men-of-war of seventy and fifty guns and a quantity of smaller shipping, together with many colours, ninety cannon, and much ammunition, were captured with the fortress, the casualties of the Allies being five hundred men. Ostend deprived the enemy of a hitherto useful port for their galleys and privateers; it gave Marlborough a base nearer to the army than the Dutch rivers, and it placed in his hands the chief port of entry for English cloth into the reopened markets of Belgium.

Blackadder, of the Cameronians—now a major—had fought with the British right against Autréglise. After Blenheim he had drawn the moral that the victory was due to the goodness of the cause, and the slaughter among the English to their blasphemous language. Now at Ramillies, while the victory which God had granted had been no less remarkable, the English troops had got off very lightly. Another explanation was readily supplied by the valiant major's piety.

I observe also that the English had but small part in this victory. They are the boldest sinners in our army, therefore God will choose other instruments. Also the English have got a great vogue and reputation for courage, and are perhaps puffed up upon it; and so God humbles their pride, as it were, by throwing them by. I was easy, and helped to discharge my duty well. We were very much fatigued with the pursuit, and lay all night in the open fields without cover.

[1] Coxe, ii, 381.

134

Give me grace, O Lord, never to forget this great and glorious day at Ramillies.

The effects of this battle are most surprising; towns that we thought would have endured a long siege are giving up and yielding without a stroke. Even the thoughtless creatures in the army observe the hand of Providence in their rapid success. Bruges, Antwerp, and, in short, all Brabant and Flanders almost yielded! What the French got in a night by stealth at the King of Spain's death they have lost again in a day. That old tyrant who wasted God's church is about to be wasted himself.[1]

Meanwhile French soldierly admiration of Marlborough rivalled their fears. Upon a nation so responsive to chivalry, valour, and prestige the genius of the English leader exercised an abnormal fascination. His courtesy to the captured nobles, his humanity to the wounded, the care he took about the well-being of the humbler prisoners, find testimony in all contemporary records. It was noted that he allowed no distinction between the treatment of the French and allied wounded. The Duke always showed the utmost attention to his prisoners. "Marlborough treated his prisoners of mark," writes Saint-Simon, "with an infinite politeness and set many of them at once at liberty for three months upon their parole."[2] He was most careful to shield the aristocracy of France from any reflection upon their courage. French historians of successive generations cherish and repeat his words of praise. They are probably not authentic, but this was the strain in which he spoke: of Villeroy's army, "With thirty thousand men as brave as that I could go to the end of the world"; of the Maison du Roi, "These were more than men, and I knew them so well that I was forced to set six men against each one of them."[3] Thus we see to what perfection he carried the art of conquest, and while inflicting the most terrible injuries made the vanquished grateful for his praise. Thus he anticipated the modern Japanese field orders which enjoin that the valour of the defeated enemy must always be praised. Thus he created the hold upon the French mind which lasted for generations after English contemporary politicans and writers had done their worst.

Marlborough cannot be robbed of the laurels of Ramillies. The Schellenberg, his detractors said, had been won by the Margrave. Blenheim was the conception and achievement of Prince Eugene. But neither of these explanations covered the amazing event of

[1] A. Crichton, The Life and Diary of Lieutenant-Colonel J. Blackader (1824), p. 280.
[2] Mémoires, iv, 427.   [3] Duclos, ii, 170.

May 23. Here the world saw Marlborough alone, without a council of war, achieving a military masterpiece seldom equalled and never surpassed. This was his victory and his alone. Ramillies belongs to that rare class of battles fought between equal forces of the highest quality wherein decisive success at comparatively small loss is gained through the manœuvres of a commander-in-chief. It will rank for ever with Rossbach and Austerlitz as an example of what a general can do with men.

Chapter Eight

THE REVERSE OF THE MEDAL

1706—JULY–OCTOBER

THE consequences of Ramillies rolled forward in every
quarter. Louis XIV, responding to the event, stripped
all other fronts to make head against Marlborough.
The distresses and perils of Flanders dominated the
enemy mind. The King of France was not incapable of taking the
sweeping decisions required at intervals from the head of a mighty
state assailed upon every side by a coalition. All his orders were
obeyed. Indeed, if the French military power had not been so highly
organized in the person of its ruler, France might have escaped the
disaster which was to befall her in Italy. Marlborough, after all,
was still only half-way through the fortress zone. More than
twenty fortresses of the first order barred all the roads, rivers, and
canals by which he could enter France. Every one of these would,
if resolutely defended, count in the recognized schedule of weeks
and days, of life, money, and gunpowder, before capture. The
temporary dispersion of the French field army enabled them to
receive ample garrisons. There is such a thing in war—it must be
stated with all reserve—as over-precision of thought and action.
Probably the King's best plan was to take his punishment among
the fortresses with phlegm, and to finish the war in Italy by defeating the Imperial army under Prince Eugene and destroying the Duke
of Savoy. A less highly sensitive organism or an even more comprehensive mind might have taken this chance.

But Louis XIV felt in his own bosom the shock of Ramillies,
the overthrow of his household troops, the slaughter or capture of
his intimate courtiers, the stigma of rout upon the armies of France.
Thus he devoted every effort to rebuilding his Flanders army. He
drained the Rhine and the Moselle of French troops. He resigned
his successes at Hagenau and on the Lauter, and all prospects of
recapturing Landau. Here the Margrave, defeated, broken, and
now dying in his half-finished palace and gardens at Rastadt, might
remain unmolested at the head of the hungry, ragged, dispirited

137

remnants of the Germanic armies. All the weight was taken off them. But in Italy, where final French victory was already in sight and where the allied cause seemed hopeless, an even greater submission to the battle was enforced. The whole flow of French reinforcements was stopped. Considerable forces were actually withdrawn, and Vendôme, who thought he had all the fruits of success in his hands, was ordered to the north. Thus did the victory of Ramillies prepare the rescue of Turin.

The effects upon the Allies were not less pronounced. Prussian loyalties returned to the allied cause, and the Prussian troops hitherto dawdling at Wesel had already marched to join Marlborough's army. All the German princes were heartened to make at least a renewed gesture of putting their shoulders to the wheel. But there were other less favourable reactions. The Court at Vienna was confirmed in their mood that all the Empire had to do was to lean heavily upon these marvellous Sea Powers, to be prompt in asserting its judicial rights to any conquests they might make, and as a prime endeavour stamp out the Hungarian revolt. In Holland the evil went much farther. The victory, the revolution in the Spanish Netherlands and their reversion to the Allies, created a new European situation which hinged directly upon Marlborough. The reconquered lands and cities were by every principle of the Grand Alliance a province of the monarchy of Charles III. That prince, now planning a march upon Madrid, had left behind him in Vienna, on the chance, however remote, that the French would be driven out of the Low Countries, a series of blank commissions for their government. These were in the hands of his brother, the Emperor, who since correspondence with Spain was slow and irregular had plenary powers to act in the general Hapsburg interest. Besides this, Count Goes, the Imperial Ambassador at The Hague, had lawful authority to take possession in the name of Charles III of any territory or fortresses that might be recovered. The major part had now suddenly fallen into the hands of Marlborough's army; and the Emperor and all his agents made haste to claim them.

On the other hand, the Dutch regarded Belgium as their longed-for Barrier, their indispensable dyke against France and Louis XIV. Here was their means of self-preservation, their prime objective of the war, as they saw it, in their grip. Moreover, Ramillies was to them above all a Dutch victory. Their native troops had borne the brunt. They had lost more blood than all the allied contingents together. It was the Dutch guards who had stormed Taviers against surprising odds. Dutch troopers had ridden down the Maison du Roi. The English had been but lightly engaged. The Prussians had stood aloof. The gallant Danes were the mercenaries jointly of the two Sea Powers. The Dutch acknowledged cordially that the battle had been won by the genius of an English Commander-in-Chief. But was he not also Deputy Captain-General of the Republic? Was he not their salaried officer? Had they not had the foresight to choose him and sustain him when the Queen of England would have set some ninny in his place? As the broadening tale of glory and of conquest flowed in to The Hague and Amsterdam, accompanied by lengthening lists of the Dutch killed and wounded, the States-General and every warlike element in Holland felt that the prize was theirs. There was, in fact, a renewal of the Limburg quarrel of 1703[1] between the Dutch and the Empire on a scale magnified many-fold alike by the wonderful gains of the battle and the bitter weariness of the unending war.

From the first moment when the Dutch realized what had happened they were very rough with Count Goes. He produced his patent of administration, dated the previous October in case the Netherlands should be regained. He formally notified the States-General and demanded a conference. His demand was refused. Three interests, he was told, must be satisfied: first, the practical interest of making the Estates of Brabant support the maximum number of troops; secondly, the Dutch financial interest of collecting the Belgian revenue and distributing it later by agreement; and, only thirdly, the Spanish interest, as the interest of King Charles III was described. This, it was intimated, would consist of formal homage to his sovereignty pending a general treaty of peace. Thus the Dutch claimed the substance, and in so far as they conceded the form conceded it only for their own convenience. Indeed, they needed to invoke the symbols of the Hapsburg claimant to the Spanish throne; for it was to this alone that the Estates of Brabant had so suddenly sworn allegiance, and they knew well that no rule would be more disliked in Belgium than the rule of Holland. By the third week in June Hop, the Dutch Treasurer, was already there arranging the taxation. When Count Goes spoke of going to Brussels to protect the rights of Charles III he was warned in terms almost of menace not to inflame the Government of the Republic against his person.

In his distress Goes turned to Marlborough during the Duke's

_____
[1] Vol. II, pp. 685–686.

brief visit to The Hague. He reported the conversation to Vienna in his dispatch dated June 8.[1] The Duke said that he had found the secret Deputies of Holland so prejudiced against the Hapsburg claims that he had not felt able to assert them. Pending a general peace settlement, an interim military contribution must be agreed between the Estates of Brabant and Flanders and the Dutch authorities without reference to King Charles III. The Imperial Ambassador declared he would use his powers to the utmost against this. Marlborough, calmer than ever on the foam of success, counselled patience. "Wait," he said; "I will concern myself with the interests of the King." "But what am I to report?" asked Goes. "Write merely to the Emperor and the King of Spain," replied Marlborough, "that the Netherlands are for his Catholic Majesty; that the Queen claims nothing in them, nor any part of the Spanish monarchy; that besides there are some claims she will not suffer the Republic to raise. And," he continued, "this delay I am now demanding of you is only for the satisfaction of these people and for the great good of his Catholic Majesty himself, as I certainly imagine you could not in a dignified manner bring the Estates of Brabant and Flanders to do the things that will be asked of them, although those things are just, reasonable, and fair."

The Ambassador became more composed. He asked Marlborough whether he still agreed with the view that France must be reduced to the frontiers of the Pyrenees treaty. Marlborough answered, "You must discuss this question with the Pensionary. After the campaign is over I will myself make efforts to secure unity upon it. I have hopes of success, particularly [he threw in this point of reproach] *if peace should be made in Hungary. If this occurs I hope to engage the Republic in the reconquest of the whole Spanish Monarchy.*"[2]

This conversation reveals the simple, sober ruthlessness of Marlborough's political aims. The allied armies had now advanced to the point where many important conquests seemed open. The Dutch always suspected that the British would try to keep Ostend and Nieuport for themselves, with all that followed them in trade and strategy. Marlborough, on the other hand, sought to overthrow the French domination of Europe by the sundering from France of the whole Spanish monarchy, of which the Hapsburgs were to be the

---

[1] Marlborough did not reach The Hague till the 9th; so the Ambassador must have completed his dispatch on the 10th or 11th. See R. Geikie, *The Dutch Barrier,* 1705-19, p. 12.

[2] Goes' dispatch, June 8. The original French is in Klopp, xii, 87 *n.* Goes added, "These are his own words."

custodians. He set an incidental value upon Dunkirk, that nest of privateers whose depredations were a curse to the revenue and a perpetual nuisance to Godolphin in Parliament; and he deemed it a substantial British interest that fortified harbours like Dunkirk, Rochefort, and Toulon should be permanently demilitarized. But, apart from this, England must covet nothing on the continent of Europe. Her reward would be in the success of the causes for which she fought, which would open the future to her in a manner not to be measured by territorial gains. "I see by yours," he wrote to Godolphin (June 21), "that you do not expect any great advantages for England, when the treaty of peace is once begun. I ask your pardon on being of another opinion, for I think you may expect everything that is for the safety and good of England. I do not mean by that any places in this country, for I am persuaded that it is much more for her Majesty's service and England not to be master of any towns in this country, since it would create a jealousy both at home and abroad. I know this should not be the language of a general, but I do it as a faithful subject."[1] It was also the language of a statesman.

It was natural, and soon became obvious, that the completeness of their local victory would make the Dutch more ready for peace and better able to obtain it. They were the vital factor in the English policy to break irretrievably the power of France, which Marlborough animated and executed, and at the same time they were the power most susceptible to proposals to start separate peace negotiations. While French armies contended on the frontiers, French diplomacy was at work in all the capitals. We have seen how narrowly they had failed at Berlin. But it was at The Hague that Louis XIV and his advisers always felt their best chance lay. The Dutch fought against misfortune with unconquerable stubbornness and vigour. But in success they fought only for their definite, limited purpose. All this extension of the war to Bavaria, Spain, and Italy, and across the oceans, they regarded as markedly subordinate to their clear-cut, practical aim—the Dyke, the Barrier, behind which lay their safety, freedom, Protestantism, and trade.

Far gone were the days of 1702, when their army crouched under the ramparts of Nimwegen, and when this new English commander, whom, to bind the English to their cause and keep out more overweening servants, they had made their Deputy Captain-General, had invited them to take the offensive, sword in hand. The Meuse

[1] Coxe, ii, 377.

was clear to the gates of Namur. The whole course of the Rhine, and all its strongholds, were in allied hands. Brussels had fallen. Antwerp, the greatest prize of all, for which the utmost sacrifices might well have been made, had surrendered without a siege. Bruges, Ghent, Oudenarde, Ostend, even Tournai and Mons, were already theirs or were within their grasp, and Nieuport, Ypres, Menin, Ath, might well be gained. Behind these bristled the fortresses of the French frontier—Dunkirk, Aire, Saint-Venant, Lille, Valenciennes, Douai, Bouchain, Maubeuge, and Philippe-ville. But were these trophies essential to the preservation of the Republic? They wanted to humble the power of France. Surely it was humbled already. Were not the great King's envoys busy through half a dozen channels with proposals for a separate peace, based primarily and without question upon a good Barrier for Holland? And what of England? Her schemes ranged far. While with one hand she animated and led the armies of Europe to the invasion of France, with the other she calmly took possession of trade, of the oceans, and of the fabulous regions that lay beyond. How far should Dutchmen be drawn by this island incantation? If Marlborough wielded a glorious sword, did he not also wave a magician's wand? They might be grateful; they must not be bewitched.

The majestic events of history and the homely incidents of daily life alike show how vainly man strives to control his fate. Even his greatest neglects or failures may bring him good. Even his greatest achievements may work him ill. If Marlborough had merely won the battle of Ramillies, taken Louvain, and perhaps entered Brussels, the campaign of 1706 might have carried the allied cause to victory in 1707. But he now began to experience a whole series of new resistances and withholdings from the Dutch, as well as their grabbings and graspings, all of which were destined to bring the fortunes of the Allies once again to the lowest ebb.

Marlborough to Godolphin

July 14, 1706

Now that the siege of Ostend is over, I was in hopes we might have lost no time in attacking Menin; but M. Geldermalsen sends me word that they have not the necessary preparations ready. But as soon as they come to Ghent he will let me know it. I am afraid we shall find at last that some of our friends are of opinion that we have *already done too much*;[1] for notwithstanding what I said when I was at

[1] Marlborough's italics.

Ostend, that two regiments would be enough to leave in that place, they have left six. But I have written to The Hague, and if they do not give orders that some of them be sent to the army they do not intend to have much more done this year. This will appear strange to you, but we have so many of these refined politics that it is high time we had a good peace. At the same time that I say this to you, the greatest part of the people are very honest, and wish well to the common cause; but those that are of the contrary faction are more active and diligent. Everything goes so well in Spain that if we have success with the descent France must submit to a reasonable peace.[1]

"It is amazing," wrote Godolphin at this time,

that after so much done for their advantage, and even for their safety, the States can have been capable of such a behaviour. Those of the French faction must have seen their advantage upon this occasion, to fill them with jealousy of your having, and consequently of England's having, too much power; and if this be at the bottom we shall soon see that argument made use of on other occasions, as well as this. But your prudence and good temper will get the better, I hope, of all this folly and perverseness.[2]

Marlborough to Godolphin

HELCHIN
July 15, 1706

I find we must not expect all our cannon till the end of this month; but on the 22d. I think to invest Menin, and employ the first six or seven days in covering some of the quarters; for we cannot spare above thirty-two battalions for the siege. There will remain with me seventy-two, which I hope will be a sufficient strength to oppose whatever they can bring, though the Elector of Bavaria says he is promised 110 battalions. They have certainly more horse than we; but if they had greater numbers I neither think it their interest not their inclinations to venture a battle; for *our men are in heart, and theirs are cowed.*[3]

Marlborough to Godolphin

HELCHIN
July 19, 1706

I think I have convinced the States-General that their resolution of the 19th of last month, in which they reserved to themselves the signing all the powers, and consequently governing this country in their names, was excluding her Majesty and England from being able to perform to these people, what I promised in her Majesty's name, which, if they had persisted, must have produced a very ill effect; *for the great towns depend [count] much more upon the Queen's protection than upon that of the States.*[4]

[1] Coxe, iii, 57, 58. [2] July 15; *ibid.*, 394. [3] *Ibid.*, 2, 3. [4] Coxe, ii, 400.

These hindrances continued throughout the campaign. "It is publicly said at The Hague," wrote Marlborough to Godolphin (August 30),

> that France is reduced to what it ought to be, and that if the war should be carried farther, it would serve only to make England greater than it ought to be. In short, I am afraid our best Allies are very fond of a peace, and that they would engage England to quarrel with the emperor, to have a pretext to come at a peace.[1]

And again (September 20):

> The success with which it has pleased God to bless the arms of the Allies this campaign has made them [the Dutch] very jealous of the great power, as they term it, that England has in the greatest part of the courts in Christendom. It is certain that the Dutch carry everything with so high a hand that they are not beloved anywhere.[2]

In those days, when to our minds news travelled slowly, grave decisions of State were often taken with promptitude, few having to be consulted. In the middle of June the Emperor filled in and signed one of the blank commissions which his brother-sovereign had confided to him. He appointed the Duke of Marlborough Viceroy of the Netherlands. In the instructions to Goes the Court of Vienna gave their reasons. Marlborough would be acceptable to the Belgians. His appointment would bind the English more closely to the interests of the Empire. His prestige both in England and Holland would alone preserve the Netherlands intact for Charles III. He controlled "the heart of the war," and would, they thought, also control the peace negotiations. On its merits this was a fine stroke of policy. It offered far the most agreeable arrangement to the Belgians, and safeguarded in the highest degree possible Hapsburg interests. Who else but Marlborough had a chance of persuading the Dutch? The courier bearing this important news reached Marlborough's headquarters on June 28. The proposal confronted him with one of the testing decisions of his life. It was no doubt the best military and political arrangement conceivable. Combining the command of the army with a virtual sovereignty in the theatre of war, his control would for the first time be perfect. It would, if adopted, adjourn the rending question within the Alliance till peace was gained. It invested him with almost royal status, and offered him a revenue of sixty thousand pounds a year.

From every point of view, personal and public, British and

---

[1] Coxe, iii, 56, 57.   [2] Ibid., 60.

European, it met all needs. There is no doubt that Marlborough greatly desired to accept it. Goslinga insinuates that he had himself applied for the post to Charles III. He suggests that Count Le-cheraine, who was in almost continuous movement between Düsseldorf, Barcelona, and Vienna, had borne the request from the victorious Duke to the struggling King of Spain. There is not the slightest evidence that Marlborough made any such request to Charles III. There is no question but that the offer originated spontaneously in Vienna, and a mere comparison of dates and distances shows that it was utterly impossible for Charles III at Barcelona to have corresponded with his brother in the time. But even if it were true that Marlborough had asked the King for the appointment it would only make his conduct on receiving the offer from the Emperor more to be respected. Nothing in his whole career shows in more striking fashion how far he could rise on great occasions above all those private advantages which in the ordinary swing of life he counted so carefully. Here was the greatest prize ever within his reach. Moreover, it was the best arrangement. Let us see how it weighed with him in comparison with what was now already a hackneyed phrase, but none the less to him a grand reality—the common cause.

Marlborough to Godolphin

June 28, 1706

I received last night an express from Vienna, with the enclosed letter, in Latin, from the Emperor. I shall keep it here a secret, till I know from you what her Majesty's pleasure is, as also I shall take measures with my friends in Holland to know how they will like it; *for I must take care that they take no jealousy, whatever the Queen's resolution may be.* I beg no notice may be taken till the Emperor's Minister shall apply to her Majesty. I beg you to assure the Queen that I have in this matter, nor never shall have in any other, any desire of my own, but with all the submission in the world be pleased with what she shall think is for her interest.[1]

It happened that the Dutch Treasurer was in his camp at Rousse-laer almost immediately after the Emperor's letter had been received. The Duke laid it before him. Hop said at once that it would raise ill-humour in Holland. The States-General would say that the Emperor wished to make use of Marlborough and the Queen of England to keep the wealth of Belgium out of the hands of the Dutch. This only confirmed Marlborough's own opinion. He saw

[1] Coxe, ii, 388.

that his acceptance of this great and lucrative office might deeply injure the Allies. If that were so he would have none of it.

Marlborough to Godolphin

ROUSSELAER
July 1, 1706

M. Hop is come this day from Brussels, and I have communicated to him the Emperor's letter, and the powers from the King of Spain. He made me great compliments, but I find by him that he thinks this may give uneasiness in Holland, by thinking that the Court of Vienna has a mind to put the power of this country into the Queen's hands, in order that they may have nothing to do with it. If I should find the same thing by the Pensioner, and that nothing can cure this jealousy but my desiring to be excused from accepting this commission, I hope the Queen will allow of it; for the advantage and honour I might have by this commission is very insignificant in comparison of the fatal consequences that might be, if it should cause a jealousy between the two nations.[1]

Every one consulted in England was delighted. Not only Godolphin but the Whig leaders, Somers and Sunderland, whom he apprised, accepted the proposal cordially. England would have Belgium in her hands. What could be better, whether for the war or for the peace? The Queen, still under the impression of Ramillies, was entirely content that Mr Freeman should have this great honour which he had won with his sword. She was glad when her Ministers moved her to authorize him to decide the matter as he thought fit.

Meanwhile Count Goes brought the dispatches he had received from the Emperor to the notice of the Dutch authorities. Certainly Goes, smarting under his rough usage from the Dutch, took the worst way. Instead of submitting the documents to the Pensionary in due routine, he handed them, as we may suppose with some air of triumph, to the President of the States-General for the week. The letters of the Emperor were read out to the Assembly. There was general astonishment. The Pensionary, assailed by a storm of questions, was completely unprepared. The Dutch view was overwhelmingly expressed that the Emperor had no right to dispose of the government of Belgium without previous consultation with the Republic, whose Barrier it must be. Pensionary Heinsius quitted the stormy meeting, indignant at having been thus inconsiderately exposed. He fell upon Count Goes, and reproached him vehemently with not having warned him beforehand. "He was more beside

---

[1] Coxe, ii, 392.

himself," reported Goes, "than I have ever seen him, though I have had frequent opportunities of observing him."[1] The Ambassador then quoted the terms of Marlborough's letter; but this merely asked him "to inform Messieurs les États," and certainly had never prescribed the omission of Heinsius, or any departure from the usual custom. Heinsius addressed himself by letter to Marlborough. He complained of the proposal; he complained of the procedure. Marlborough replied in terms of the utmost good will. He would on no account allow any question of his personal interest to impair the unity of the Alliance. Never was disinterested renunciation more forthcoming or more complete. But his own letters had better be read.

Marlborough to Heinsius

ROUSSELAER
July 3, 1706

. . . I shall take no step in this matter, but what shall be by the advice of the States; for I prefer infinitely their friendship before any particular interest to myself; for I thank God and the Queen I have no need nor desire of being richer, but have a very great ambition of doing everything that can be for the public good; and as for the frontier, which is absolutely necessary for your security, you know my opinion of it. In short, I beg you to assure yourself, and everybody else, that I shall with pleasure behave myself in this matter, and all things else, that you may think for the good of the republic, as you would have me; for next to serving the Queen and my country I have nothing more at heart than to have your good opinions. And let me on this occasion assure the States that I serve them with the same affection and zeal that I do my own country, so that they need be under no difficulty; for if they think it for their service I shall with pleasure excuse myself from accepting this commission.[2]

Marlborough to Godolphin

HARLEBECK
July 6, 1706

The enclosed letter [from the Pensioner] of the same date confirms me that if I should accept the honour the Emperor and the King of Spain do me, it would create a great jealousy, which might prejudice the common cause, so that I hope her Majesty will approve of what I have done. And I beg you to be so just and kind to me as to assure the Queen that, though the appointments of this Government are three-score thousand pounds a year, I shall with pleasure excuse myself, since I am convinced it is for her service, unless the States should make

---

[1] Klopp, xii, 93.   [2] Coxe, ii, 392.

it their request, which they are very far from doing; for they have told me that they think it not reasonable that the King of Spain should have possession of the Low Countries till they had assurances of what barrier they should have for their security. I hope this compliance of mine will give me so much credit as to be able to hinder them from hurting themselves; for it is certain, if they follow their own inclinations, they will make such demands upon this country as will very much dissatisfy the house of Austria, and be thought unreasonable by all the Allies, of which the French would be sure to make their advantage.[1]

Marlborough hoped that his renunciation of great advantages would give him all the more influence in inducing the Dutch to abate their own ambitions. In a formal letter to Heinsius, after repeating his refusal of the Emperor's offer, he opened this argument.

Marlborough to Heinsius

CAMP OF HARLEBECK
July 10, 1706

. . . On this occasion I take the liberty of reminding their High Mightinesses that when the army came to Louvain, and in the farther progress which we have made with the advice of the army Deputies, we jointly gave assurances, in writing, to all the towns and people of the country, in the name of the Queen, of their High Mightinesses, and of his Catholic Majesty, that those should regain the same rights, privileges, and advantages which they enjoyed in the time of King Charles the Second; and to these assurances, with the help of God, I am persuaded we must partly attribute the facility with which we entered into possession of so many strong places, where every one testified universal joy. . . .

However, according to what I have learned, or have been able to comprehend hitherto, it has always appeared that the States had nothing else in view but a good barrier, and a reasonable security for their country. I beg, then, you will, with all submission to their High Mightinesses, entreat them to reflect maturely on such a step, which is perhaps not the true means of attaining those objects. . . .[2]

Marlborough to Godolphin

HELCHIN
July 12, 1706

By my last letter, which I sent by way of Ostend, you will see the measures that the Dutch are desirous to take concerning the management of this country, *which would certainly set this whole country against them*; so that I hope you will find some way of not letting them play

---

[1] Coxe, ii, 393.   [2] *Ibid.*, 395.

the fool. You know that I am always very ready to speak freely to them, when I think it for their service. But in this matter I am not at liberty, fearing they might mistake me, and think it might proceed from self-interest. I am sure, in this matter, I have with pleasure sacrificed my own interest, in order to make them reasonable, which I hope will be approved by my friends; for should I have acted otherwise, the party that is for peace would have made a very ill use of it. For the favourers of the French faction endeavour all they can to persuade the people in Holland that the King of Spain will be governed by the Queen, and that this success will all turn to the advantage of England, so that they must not rely upon any body, but secure their frontier now that they have it in their power. This is so plausible in Holland that I am afraid the honest people, though they see the dangerous consequence this must have, yet dare not speak against it; *and I can assure you these great towns had rather be under any nation than the Dutch.*[1]

Marlborough to Godolphin

HARLEBECK
July 14, 1706

You will see by three or four letters that I have lately writ to you the care I have taken not to give any occasion of jealousy in Holland, and that I was in hopes that my declining the honour the King of Spain had done me would give me so much power with the States as that I might be able to hinder them from doing themselves and the common cause hurt. But such is their temper that when they have misfortunes they are desirous of peace upon any terms, and when we are blessed by God with success they are for turning it to their own advantage, without any consideration how it may be liked by their friends and allies . . .[2] I dread the consequences of this matter, for I cannot write so freely to the States as I should otherwise, if I were not personally concerned. You may be sure the French have too many partisans in Holland, not to be informed of this proceeding, so that they will be sure to make their advantage of it.[3]

Thus we see this man, described by so many historians as the most self-seeking and avaricious of his generation, rejecting without apparent mental hesitation a personal advantage of the greatest magnitude. It came to him as the fruit of his victory. He longed to have it. The Emperor wished it. The English Government warmly approved. The plan was good in itself. There was no obstacle but the Dutch. But if the Dutch disagreed, if the structure of the Alliance were thereby endangered, Marlborough was ready at once to discard the whole scheme.

---

[1] Cona, ii, 397.   [2] Some words omitted in the original.   [3] Coxe, ii, 398.

He was also ready to make another personal sacrifice. His intense military exertions after Ramillies were accompanied by a remarkable diplomatic intrigue equally designed to exploit the victory. We have seen the elaborate procedure which Marlborough had observed towards Max Emmanuel about his boar-hunting proclivities in the autumn of 1705. While he could not meet his wishes, he sought by every means to establish a personal and friendly contact with the Prince who seemed marked on every occasion to be the nearest victim of his sword. On the morrow of Ramillies came a new occasion. A Dutch courier had been captured by the Elector's cavalry with letters from the field Deputies to Marlborough. The Elector was at pains to forward the letters unopened to Marlborough with studied compliments. Marlborough replied from Nivelle on June 4, 1706:

> I render a thousand most humble thanks to your Electoral Highness for the kindness of sending my letters captured near Antwerp. I wish with all my heart that some occasion may offer to prove my most respectful gratitude. I beg your Highness to be assured that I should seize it with extreme pleasure. . . .[1]

Hot-foot amid the marches of the army, and the surprising fall of fortresses, Marlborough appointed an agent, one Sersanders, a distinguished Belgian functionary, to visit the Elector. There was a secret interview at Mons on August 3. Sersanders urged Max Emmanuel to desert the cause of France. He cited the example of the Duke of Savoy. In Marlborough's name he offered the fugitive Elector the full restoration of his hereditary Bavarian lands. He held out the hopes that these might be stretched across the Brenner Pass to include the Milanese. Lastly, to clinch the matter and to prove Marlborough's sincerity, Sersanders was authorized to throw in the principality of Mindelheim which Marlborough had gained at Blenheim and by laborious negotiations with the Emperor. It was the trophy which had most tempted his vanity. But now in a larger grouping of ideas it might play a different part. Sersanders in Marlborough's name offered the Elector "all his Bavarian estates without any exception, not even that of the principality of Mindelheim."[2]

It will now be seen how important it had been for Marlborough to learn d'Alègre's terms of the previous year. Those that he now

[1] *Dispatches*, ii, 562.
[2] French Foreign Office Archives, "Bavière," tome 56, f. 161.

outlined were their complete reverse. Max Emmanuel, instead of being forced to exchange Bavaria for an Italian kingdom, was to be restored to Munich, Ulm, the Danube, Donauwörth, Ingolstadt, and his own people. More than that, he might aspire to the Milanese, which he had tried vainly to invade before Blenheim. All the original ambitions which had induced this prince so traitorously to abandon the Empire were to be achieved at the price of a counter-desertion. If ever there was a bribe it was here. But one item remained: the four key-fortresses which Marlborough could not see his way to conquer within the limits of the campaign—namely, Namur, Mons, Charleroi, and Luxembourg—at this moment garrisoned by the Elector's troops, were to be surrendered to the armies of the Sea Powers.

Max Emmanuel, at first staggered, was captivated by this plan. We have seen the long suspicion with which he had been regarded by the French Court. To no one did the Great King in chivalrous honour owe a greater service than to this luckless, hunted exile, who had sullied and ruined himself for his faith in the arms of France. Of no one was the King less sure. He saw the temptation and he knew the man. What followed casts a cold light upon the temper of Versailles. It happened that the French also had a secret agent in the Elector's camp. Rouillé, a former ambassador of France and President of the Parliament of Paris, was at Mons when Sersanders arrived. The Elector did not conceal from him the proposals he had received. Rouillé reported the whole matter to Versailles. The campaign was in full swing. The tide of Marlborough's conquests was at its height. Here were the four vital fortresses, by which alone the soil of France could be defended, about to be betrayed. The counsellors who gathered around Louis XIV and Madame de Maintenon, and the princes of the blood so far as they were informed, were neither shocked nor indignant. They faced the reality. They at once sought to broaden the negotiations. Vendôme, as well as Rouillé, was in the camp. Together they framed the counter-proposals of a general peace and sent them through Sersanders to Marlborough.[1]

These proposals mark a shrinkage of French claims induced by the military situation. Not only the Spanish monarchy, but Spain itself, was to be partitioned between Philip V and Charles III. The choice of which part each should have was offered to the Allies, provided that, whatever happened, Philip V had the province of

---

[1] French Foreign Office Archives, "Bavière," tome 56, f. 213.

Guipúzcoa and Charles III the sovereignty of the Spanish Netherlands. As for Max Emmanuel, not only would he be restored to
Bavaria with some additions at German expense, but he for his life
and his son after him should be entrusted with the government of
the Netherlands, as a vassal or servantof Charles III, with whom
he was at the moment at war, and of whose house he had long been
a deadly foe.

It is not difficult to see how this fantastic plan struck Marlborough.
The partition of Spain would have been violently rejected in England.
The proposal about the Viceroyalty of Belgium was inherently
absurd, and finally closed any prospect which might still remain to
Marlborough. Above all, he was not to have the four fortresses.
This supreme immediate military objective was at all costs denied
him. He therefore ruptured the negotiations. He left the French
counter-proposals unanswered. He bent again to his sieges. The
French, taking no avoidable risks, replaced all Max Emmanuel's
Spanish garrisons with their own troops, and the campaign was
ended only by the winter.

During the autumn both the Anglo-Dutch bargainings about
the Barrier and the Succession Treaty and the French overtures for
peace continued fitfully. Early in October the Dutch "preliminaries" after long debatings with Halifax were drawn up and dispatched to England. They included the whole of the Spanish
Empire for the Hapsburgs except for an extensive Dutch barrier.
Godolphin approved the Dutch "preliminaries" as they stood;
and Marlborough was able on November 19 to inform the Elector
of Bavaria, with whom he still remained in contact, that Queen
Anne was willing to enter into peace negotiations with Louis XIV.
It would be a mistake to suppose, however, that the Barrier-Succession Treaty was so far settled between the Sea Powers as to make it
possible for them to address the French unitedly upon a general
peace at this time. The inter-allied negotiations never, in fact, got
far enough for any formal discussion with the other side. The draft
terms which the Allies were arranging with each yther were incomparably more severe than anything France was at that time prepared
to concede. Marlborough, no longer attracted by the four fortresses
and by the hopes of detaching Max Emmanuel from France, was
now implacably adverse. "You must give me leave," he wrote to
Slingelandt, Overkirk's future successor in command of the Dutch
(October 10, 1706), "to tell you that I am one of those who believe

that France is not yet reduced to her just bounds, and that nothing can be more hurtful to us on this occasion than seeming over-forward to clap up a hasty peace."[1] The English refusal of the Dutch demand for Ostend as a "barrier-fortress" caused another deadlock. The Sea Powers found themselves unable to agree with one another upon the foundations, and never even reached a point at which they could try to come to an agreement with the enemy. As soon as the French Government realized that there was no chance of dividing the Maritime Powers they in their turn abandoned all hope of fruitful negotiation in 1706.

Fate with sardonic smile ordained that the most brilliant victory gained by Marlborough for the Dutch Republic should raise new hindrances to his action in their name; and that his most generous of personal sacrifices should leave behind it in Dutch hearts only embarrassing suspicions. From the day on which the Emperor offered him the Viceroyalty of the Netherlands a sense of divergent interest arose inevitably and irresistibly between the Dutch leaders and their Deputy Captain-General. Henceforward, whatever Marlborough might declare, they could not help believing, first, that he owed them a grudge for having been the obstacle, and, secondly, that he still hoped to obtain the prize. Henceforth they must regard him as an interested supporter of Hapsburg and Imperial claims rather than of their own. It is no reproach to Marlborough that persisting elements of truth underlay the Dutch misgivings. His conduct had been spontaneous, high-minded, and scrupulously correct. He bore no grudges; he pursued no conscious designs. But of course he was gratified by the offers of the Emperor and of Charles III, and hoped, indeed, that a day might come when without prejudice to the common cause he might accept and enjoy them. How far in the deep springs of human action this fact influenced his policy and counsel no one can measure; but certainly in every negotiation about the Barrier, in every overture for peace with France—nay, almost in every march of the Confederate army—Dutch opinion sought to trace a prevailing and personal motive; and from this cause his influence throughout Holland suffered a partial but none the less profound and incurable decline.

Ramillies, with its prelude and its sequel, was the most glorious episode in Marlborough's life. Whether as the victorious commander, the sagacious Minister, or the disinterested servant of the allied cause, his personal conduct was noble. Before the battle he

---

[1] *Dispatches,* iii, 165–166.

had sacrificed as he believed his prospects of a fine campaign in the Low Countries for the sake of the armies in other theatres, and especially for Prince Eugene. He had gained a great battle by consummate art. He had used the military pursuit and the political consequences to such deadly profit as to drive the French out of the Netherlands. After the victory he had handsomely renounced his own interests in order to preserve the harmony of the Alliance. To procure from Max Emmanuel the four French key-fortresses he had not hesitated to throw his own principality of Mindelheim into the scale. How vain are those writers in so many lands who suppose that the great minds of the world in their supreme activities are twisted or swayed by sordid or even personal aims. These, indeed, may clog their footsteps along the miry road of life; but soaring on the wings of victory all fall away. It is Marlborough's true glory that the higher his fortune, the higher rose his virtue. We must at a later stage present the reader with some contrasts, and show how Marlborough's conduct contracted with his power. But in 1706 he shines as genius and hero, wise, valiant, and stainless, striving only for the best for England and the best for all.

Chapter Nine

MADRID AND TURIN

1706—MAY–SEPTEMBER

THE relief of Barcelona, the quitting of Spanish soil by Philip V, the effective possession by the Allies of Aragon, Catalonia, and Valencia, and the fact that there was no longer any force to oppose an invasion from Portugal —all in combination offered to Charles III his fairest opportunity in Spain. The need for an immediate march on Madrid from all sides—Galway from Portugal, Peterborough from Valencia, and above all the King himself from Catalonia—blazed before every eye.[1] In congratulating Peterborough upon his relief of the city Marlborough pointed out in his most persuasive manner the next step.

Marlborough to Peterborough

I have no doubt that your Lordship has already escorted the King to Madrid, and take this opportunity to felicitate you on this glorious exploit, which is everywhere attributed to your valour and conduct. All the Allies exult in the advantages which are likely to result from this splendid success, and I particularly rejoice in the new lustre which it will shed on your glory. After such astonishing actions there is nothing which we may not expect from you; so that I flatter myself you will not consider our hopes as ill-founded if we reckon upon the speedy reduction of Spain to the obedience of its legitimate sovereign, since it seems as if Providence had chosen you to be the happy instrument. I heartily wish you all success till you have completed the great work.[2]

These brilliant prospects were swiftly wrecked by personal jealousies. To escape from Peterborough's malicious control King Charles III, with the troops from Barcelona, first delayed on petty pretexts, and eventually made a long, needless circuit through Aragon. Peterborough, obsessed by his feud with "the Vienna crew," left all his forces dispersed throughout Valencia, and when eventually imperative orders forced him to march to a junction

[1] See map at p. 157; also general map of Spain facing p. 1040.   [2] Coxe, ii, 374.

with King Charles, he set out with only a few hundred dragoons. Galway, with the main army, nearly nineteen thousand strong—chiefly Portuguese—had, as soon as Tessé withdrew, advanced into Spain from the west. The Portuguese commander, Das Minas, preferred sieges and pillage to marches or battle. Precious time was lost in the capture of Alcantara and Ciudad Rodrigo; but Marshal Berwick, sent in haste to the scene from the Cevennes, and out-numbered two to one, could at first do no more than observe, and fall back before, the invaders. The sloth of Das Minas so angered Galway and his English officers that extreme measures were used with King Peter. Methuen, the ambassador, told him plainly that, unless the Portuguese forces marched forthwith upon Madrid, all the British and allied troops would be withdrawn from Portugal, carried round by sea, and thrust in from the opposite side of the Peninsula.

It may be that this was the best plan. The main advance would have been through friendly regions, leaving Castilian pride un-affronted by the sight of hereditary Portuguese foes. However, King Peter, who was failing fast, submitted to the threat. Impera-tive orders were sent to Das Minas, and Galway plodded stead-fastly forward upon his long, remarkable march. Berwick, with less than eight thousand men, retreated before him to Madrid. Here he was joined by Philip V and reinforcements from Valencia which raised his army to fourteen thousand men. By the end of June he was equal in numbers and superior in quality to Galway, whose strength had wasted during his advance. Berwick, with his cool, adept professionalism, rejected the temptation of fighting a battle for the capital. He had also to consider Charles III approaching from Aragon, and Peterborough, who, for all he knew, might bring nearly six thousand English from Valencia. He therefore aban-doned Madrid, and, accompanied by Philip, retired to Burgos. On June 27 Galway entered Madrid, and proclaimed Charles III King of all Spain and the Indies. But the capital was deserted, and its Hapsburg monarch still tarried at Barcelona.

At Burgos Berwick was joined by almost all the Castilian nobility. At the same time the population of the two Castiles, of Leon and Estremadura, rose against the insult of a Portuguese invasion. In every town and village of western and central Spain levies and guerrilla bands sprang to arms. All Galway's communications with Portugal were obliterated by a veritable tide of popular uprising. By the middle of July General Légal from France joined Berwick with eleven thousand men. Although the gathering of the fruits might be delayed, the Marshal was henceforward master of the situation. Once again the fortunes of this sporadic war had been reversed. Galway could do no more than wait for a while in or near Madrid imploring King Charles and Peterborough to join him. The three leaders eventually met on August 6 at Guadalajara, thirty-

THE CAPTURE OF MADRID

five miles north-east of Madrid. But where were their armies? The King had barely five thousand men, instead of eight thousand expected. Peterborough arrived with a paltry four hundred horse, and Galway's own army after garrisoning Madrid was reduced to little more than ten thousand. The rejoicings of a friendly population, the assemblage of so many notable personages, could not veil the fact that the great opportunity was already lost. If further proof were needed it was to be speedily supplied. On the very day of the allied junction at Guadalajara a detachment from Berwick's army re-entered Madrid.

157

The allied commanders for a while nursed the belief that united they were stronger than Berwick. Gradually it became apparent that he had twenty-five thousand men, while they had but fifteen thousand. Unless the Allies were anxious for battle at these odds, there was no choice but retreat, and in the only direction open. To Valencia therefore the leaders made their way; and Charles and his Court wintered there. It seems strange that Berwick did not force a battle or at least pursue with vigour. Doubtless he had soldierly reasons. Perhaps the shadow of Ramillies falling upon this minor theatre forbade the hazard of the only success gained by France in 1706.

Peterborough did not share the asperities of the retreat. He saw with selfish intuition that the sunshine days in Spain were gone. Characteristically he had thrown the blame on Charles for the delayed junction of the allied forces. To Sarah he had given the following version:

> Your Grace . . . will wonder when I tell you that we cannot prevail with the King of Spain to go thither [to Madrid]: and his wise Ministers have thought fit to defer it from the time it was possible at least two months, if some accident do not prevent it for ever. . . .
> . . . Your Grace has not been without some great mortifications of this kind, when want of power has prevented the amazing success which always attended the Duke of Marlborough when at liberty; but mine of this kind are eternal. and no history ever produced such an everlasting struggle of Ministers against the interest of their master.[1]

Upon his arrival at Guadalajara he proposed to the council of war that he should go on a mission to the Duke of Savoy. Some echo of authority for this was derived from his original instructions. Time and events had made these instructions so obsolete that Godolphin describes his use of them as a "pretension." Indeed, the Treasurer, who was shrewdly informed, had other suspicions. "I don't find," he wrote to Marlborough (September 30/October 11),

> he [Colonel Hamilton: a messenger] can give any other account of my Lord's journey to the Duke of Savoy than to get some dismounted German troopers, and to carry them back to Spain and mount them. This seems so slight an occasion for a general that I cannot help thinking it might be worth your pains to engage Count Maffei *to let you know what he says to the Duke of Savoy; for my opinion is, it fully deserves your curiosity.*[2]

[1] *Sarah Correspondence*, i, 35–36.   [2] Coxe, iii, 40.

If the careful Lord Treasurer had also known the moneys which Peterborough was to borrow for the public from the Jews of Genoa and their rate of interest, he would have felt that his own attention should also be engaged.

Peterborough's proposal to quit the Headquarters was received with such ill-concealed feelings of joy from all his colleagues that the matter was decided in a single day. "The whole council," wrote Godolphin, "agreed to it, by which we may conclude they were as well content to be rid of him as he was to go."[1] We need not follow the romantic and dangerous adventures of Peterborough's journey. How he was robbed by brigands of his enormous baggage, with its abundance of delicate provisions; how he gave the law to the towns through which he passed; how he beguiled the path of duty with the exploits of gallantry; how he sailed on a frigate commanded by his second son, who fought a stiff action with a French squadron; and how he eventually reached Genoa and the Duke of Savoy, are not necessary to our tale.

We may now observe the repercussion of these events as after long delays it reached Whitehall and the allied Headquarters in Flanders. Marlborough learned through many channels of the evil turn in Spain. All the quarrelling chiefs laid their cases before him. At first he seemed to accept Peterborough's versions, and certainly Peterborough sought by every means to hold his approval.

Peterborough to Marlborough

BARCELONA
May 13, 1706

★You cannot imagine, my Lord, how much the dependence on your protection has given me heart in the great difficulties, and I flatter myself so far as to think that I assure myself the continuance of your friendship, which I value at a high rate, and shall endeavour to preserve by all means in my power.[2]

May 26, 1706

★Our successes must plead for the extraordinary expenses the Queen is put to, which are such as I hope will soon make us amends, unless some fatality attends the Portuguese army [*i.e.*, Galway's invasion], which in all human probability should determine the fate of Spain in a short time. The last news we had gave account they were at Almenara, within a few miles of Madrid. . . . Notwithstanding the extraordinary delays which upon all occasions we may hear, I embark aboard the Fleet to-morrow with 3000 foot . . . and I think the King

[1] Coxe, iii, 40. [2] Blenheim MSS. Extract.

will follow, though our great Prince of Lichtenstein is somewhat surprised that he is not furnished with 100,000 pistoles for the King's equipage, and I think he is equally angry with England as Catalonia with Mr Stanhope and me. . . . About £50,000 came in the ships from Italy . . . but being brought to Barcelona it has only been applied to orders of the King and the uses of the siege.[1]

27 June 1706*

★. . . As to what relates to Spain, I am a stranger and a heretic, yet I have the power of a dictator, of a tyrant; when the King is absent, in truth I do all; but the King himself is made use of to obstruct me upon almost all occasions, and it may easily be conceived how I am with his Ministers, whose avarice I cannot satisfy and whose blunders I am obliged to obstruct, being condemned to contradict them in almost everything or suffer all to come to ruin.[2]

Marlborough was already well informed of the state of Peterborough's relations with the King. Upon a suggestion, which came to nothing, that troops should be sent from Spain to the relief of Turin, he wrote to Godolphin (June 18, 1706):

The Duke of Savoy has desired that Lord Peterborough may go with the succours. That part is left to the King of Spain, who, I suppose, will not be sorry to part with him, and his Lordship will be naturally willing enough to go, if he does not suspect that it will make the King of Spain easy.[3]

Godolphin, while increasingly distressed by all he heard from Spain, was for a while uncertain as to where the blame lay. Lord Peterborough's letter, he wrote (July 18),

is full of extraordinary flights and artificial turns. But one may see by it that there is room for everything that has been thought or said of his conduct there; and, at the same time, by that and other letters of more credit, nothing ever was so weak, so shameful, and so unaccountable, in every point, as the conduct of the . . . King of Spain's German followers.[4]

And the next day: ". . . Vanity and passion are capable of carrying people who have no principle to do strange things." The Cabinet were by now unanimous that Galway should assume the supreme command. "I think this is right for the service," wrote Godolphin, "but how it may make him [Peterborough] fly out, I cannot answer." Marlborough on August 5 concurred. "The Cabinet Council are certainly in the right in advising the Queen to give the command to Lord Galway."

[1] Blenheim MSS. Extract.   [2] *Ibid.*   [3] Coxe, iii, 35.   [4] *Ibid.*, 36.

"I agree with you," he wrote to Godolphin (August 16),

> that the Germans that are with King Charles are good for nothing;
> but I believe the anger and aversion he has for Lord Peterborough is
> the greatest cause of taking the resolution of going to Saragossa,
> which I am afraid will prove fatal; for Mr Crowe told me that he once
> said to him that he would never have anything to do with Lord
> Peterborough, that he would not accept of health from him; I suppose
> this expression is better in Spanish than English.[1]

Towards the end of August Godolphin's judgment had turned
finally against Peterborough. He wrote to Marlborough (August
13/24):

> Lord Peterborough has written a volume to Mr Secretary Hedges.
> It is a sort of remonstrance against the King of Spain and his Ministers,
> in the first place; and, secondly, a complaint against all the orders
> and directions sent from hence, and as if he had not authority enough
> given him, either at sea or land. In a word, he is both useless and
> grievous there, and is preparing to be as troublesome here whenever
> he is called home.[2]

Of Peterborough's letter he wrote (August 15/26):

> . . . It is a sort of two-edged sword; first, a remonstrance against
> King Charles, in terms as unmannerly as unjust; and, secondly, it is
> prepared to fall on anybody here that shall be in his displeasure.[3]

By mid-September Peterborough had entirely lost Marlborough's
confidence.

> I hope he [the King of Spain] will also advise with Lord Galway;
> but I must confess, if my opinion were to be taken, Lord Peterborough
> should not be consulted. *I do not think much ceremony ought to be used
> in removing him from a place where he has hazarded the loss of the whole
> country.*[4]

Peterborough, however, continued to write to Sarah in his
sprightly style, to which she was by no means insensible.

> *September* 4, 1706
> . . . The most disagreeable country in the world is Spain; the most
> pleasing, England; our German Ministry and Spanish statesmen
> much alike; their officers the greatest robbers, and their soldiers the
> greatest cowards; the only tolerable thing, your sex, and that attended
> with the greatest dangers. Judge then, madam, of my joy and dis-
> appointment when I soon expected the honour of seeing your Grace,
> after a war ended in a year, and a treaty finished in two months.

[1] *Cove*, iii, 30. [2] *Loc. cit.* [3] *Ibid.*, 39. [4] *Loc. cit.*

These pleasing thoughts I had, but I submit to the faults and misfortunes of others, not my own. Hitherto I have been only acquainted with success, but attended with inconceivable fatigues. Perhaps I may now have a reprieve or at least the satisfaction of submitting to whatever the Queen shall desire or command.[1]

Marlborough's comment upon Sarah's correspondence with Peterborough was withering.

John to Sarah

What you say concerning Lord Peterborough and his fair lady is certainly very just, for there is nothing that may not be expected from them. I have observed, since I have been in the world, that the next misfortune to that of having friendship with such people is that of having any dispute with them, and that care should be taken to have as little to do with them as possible.[2]

As the summer advanced the London Cabinet became deeply concerned to reinforce the armies in Spain. Charles III, Galway, and all their agents vied with one another in appeals for troops. Where could they be found? At the beginning of August all the preparations for the "descent" were complete.[3] Lord Rivers had Guiscard, at the head of 8200 men, convoyed and carried by Sir Cloudesley Shovell with a strong squadron, sailing on August 10 for the Charente. All were forced back by a gale on the 14th into Torbay. There had been lively discussion in secret circles whether the Spanish theatre was not a more promising and, indeed, more necessary alternative. When the whole expedition was thrown back upon the English coast the debate renewed itself with vigour. Guiscard was searchingly re-examined upon the prospects of a local rising. Naturally he could not give precise guarantees of the effect which such a landing would produce. Only the attempt could prove the facts. The Cabinet, therefore, after weeks of disputing, resolved to divert the ships and troops to the Peninsula. On October 1/12 they sailed for Lisbon, upon what ultimately proved a melancholy errand. Marlborough, though he submitted with good grace, was deeply disappointed. Guiscard, his dream of playing a great part in the war destroyed, seems to have been thrown completely off his balance, and drummed his heels in the antechambers of Whitehall, corroded with bitterness. To the public in England and Holland the great event in Spain had been the

---

[1] Coxe, iii, 42.   [2] *Ibid.*, 43.   [3] See p. 81.

entry of King Charles into Madrid; and it was not until late in the
year that this favourable impression faded. Meanwhile a new triumph
in another quarter had cheered the whole Alliance.

The Relief of Turin

Louis XIV and his circle at Versailles had harboured solid hopes
of the Italian campaign. The Duke of Vendôme there commanded
150 battalions and 180 squadrons. If Saint-Simon's account of the
filthy habits and arrogant manners of Vendôme is well founded,
the Marshal must have also possessed extraordinary personal force
and military qualities to have been so long employed as the first
soldier of France. The blood of Henry IV, which flowed through
a bastard channel in his veins, gave him a sure position at the
Court; but no one reading the successes and shortcomings of his
many campaigns can doubt that he was a man recognizably built
upon a larger scale than the common run. His victory at Calcinato
had driven the Imperialists round the corner of Lake Garda, across
the Mincio, and into the foothills at the mouth of the Brenner Pass.
The King had prescribed an early offensive, well knowing how
tardy were the Imperialist preparations, and the approach of the
German reinforcements which Marlborough had laboured so long
to set in motion. Once this success and the delay resulting from it
had been gained, the King's directions were precise. The French
troops in Italy should form two equal armies, one under Marshal
La Feuillade to besiege Turin, and the other under Vendôme, who
was also commander-in-chief, to cover the siege and the French
conquests by holding the Adige both in Lombardy and Piedmont.
Here was the most forward line that could be chosen. Behind it
the Mincio, the Po, and a succession of streams from the Alps lay
between Turin and all relief. The best of all protective positions is
one where the covering army is close enough to the besieging
troops for easy transference of forces from one front to the other.
The distance of over two hundred miles from the Adige to Turin
threw the two French armies out of joint. On the other hand,
Eugene would have to make his long journey across an almost
indefinite series of obstacles.

That prince had reached and rallied the Imperialist army on the
morrow of Calcinato: "I succeeded so well," he wrote, "that the
same day the greater part was reassembled in a few hours."[1] He

[1] Letter to Count Daun, April 22: *Feldzüge*, Series I, viii, Suppt., 86.

163

had confronted Vendôme at Limone in such a posture that, although the Marshal was twice as strong, he did not attack. Eugene withdrew at his own discretion and sheltered in the mountains until he could restore his army. While he awaited his reinforcements Vendôme and his generals fortified the eighty-mile course of the Adige from Verona to the Adriatic. The defences which the French built were remarkable in strength and extent; but reinforcements of very good troops were approaching Prince Eugene. His field

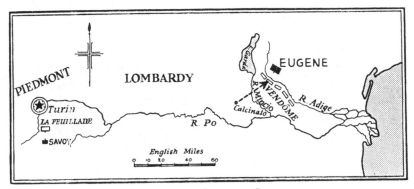

ITALY (MAY 1706)

strength on May 12 amounted to twenty-nine thousand men, including five thousand Prussians, and there were marching down to him over twenty-one thousand drafts and accretizns, including seven thousand five hundred Palatines and Saxe-Gothas, the whole constituting a compact army of fifty thousand men, of which nine thousand were cavalry.[1]

[1] The following is the order of battle in Eastern Italy (May 12, 1706) (*Feldzüge*, Series I, viii, 130):

	In Eugene's Army	Expected Reinforcements
12 Imperial infantry regiments . . .	12,100	4,850
Hayducken	1,000	
Wolfenbüttel	800	
Hildesheim	500	300
Prussians : 11 battalions .	5,000	
Palatines : 2 regiments . . .	1,400	1,000
10 new battalions . . .		5,000
Saxe-Gothas		1,500
7 Imperial Piedmontese regiments . .	5,250	2,180
Infantry totals	26,050	14,830

In this somewhat tense situation Vendôme received the King's orders to take the command against Marlborough. He was asked by Chamillart his opinion upon Marshal Marsin as his successor. "Marsin," he wrote,

> is a brave man, just and honourable, but he always adopts the opinion of whoever speaks to him last, which is a great defect in a commander-in-chief, whose business it is to lead others. A will of iron is needed to confront the difficulties here, and if the King orders me to leave Italy, Marshal Berwick is the only man who can fill my place. But I must also say to you that my recall before the capture of Turin, and at a time when we are assured that Prince Eugene intends to take active measures, involves the hazarding of everything. Once Turin is captured all the difficulties of the war here would be levelled out, and there is reason to think that the town will fall before Marlborough has taken any of the towns which the King holds in Flanders.[1]

He added the next day a strong recommendation that Marsin, if he were sent, should be sustained by a prince of the blood. "In Italy a name is required even more than in any other land, for the Italian princes are far from having the same respect for a marshal of France as for a prince. . . . The loss of Italy would involve the loss of everything, and therefore it is impossible to be too careful."[2] This advice, implying as it did that Vendôme himself possessed both the iron will and the princely quality which were indispensable, was well received by Louis XIV. He appointed his nephew Philip, Duke of Orleans, to the Italian command, with Marsin as his coadjutor. Vendôme was in full accord with their general instructions to prevent Prince Eugene from crossing the Adige while the siege of Turin proceeded. Highly pleased, he wrote:

	In Eugene's Army	Expected Reinforcements
Cavalry now serviceable	2,800	
Imperial reinforcements		4,300
Palatine recruits		300
Palatine reinforcements		1,200
Saxe-Gothas		600
Cavalry totals	2,800	6,400
Grand totals	28,850	21,230

Final total: 50,080, including 9200 cavalry.

[1] Letter of June 16, 1706; Pelet, vi, 639–640.   [2] *Ibid.,* 642.

All other lines of defence [than the Adige] are very dangerous. We should rather sacrifice the army than give up this river and admit the enemy to the Brescianese. We are now, God be thanked, in strong positions everywhere here, and well entrenched, so that it will be easy for us to hold our ground, and if, as is rumoured, the enemy intends to make an attempt, he will suffer for it.[1]

It was agreed that he should not quit the Italian command until the Duke of Orleans and Marshal Marsin arrived, and he could explain the position to them.

The siege of Turin began before May 15[2] as prescribed from Versailles. Duke Victor Amadeus, with the remnants of his faithful Savoyard army, sustained by a loyal population, was aided by a modest Imperial force under General Daun. The French round the greater part of Turin built lines of circum- and contravallation from within which they prosecuted the siege by sap and battery. Victor Amadeus did not remain inside this unfinished circle. With about six thousand cavalry he quitted his capital, moved freely about his domains, and hampered the siege from the open country. Marshal La Feuillade's reputation, never high in the French service, had suffered during the campaigns of 1704 and 1705. His marriage in 1702 with a "cruelly ugly" daughter of Chamillart, the apparently indispensable Minister, had alone secured him in his command. He was a light and vain man, whose considerable energies were not guided by sagacity or proportion. Saint-Simon's scathing comments are perhaps excessive. "... A heart corrupted through and through, a soul of mud, a jaunty and avowed unbeliever."[3] The capture of Turin in the shortest possible time was evidently the supreme French objective. With the fall of the capital, and the addition of La Feuillade's besiegers to Vendôme's covering army, the conquest of Savoy and Northern Italy would be complete. Naples and the south of Italy should fall automatically to the victors. But, instead of bringing the siege forward by the daily personal presence of the commander, La Feuillade left this dominant operation to subordinate generals, and set off in pursuit of Victor Amadeus and his vexatious cavalry. He hunted him near and far among the foothills of the Alps, and through a countryside where every peasant was against France.

History must admire the military conduct of the Duke of Savoy. He proved himself an adversary at once fugitive and dangerous. Day after day a swarm of French horsemen followed the Pied-

[1] Pelet, vi, 642. [2] Actually May 14. [3] Saint-Simon, iii, 196-197.

montese flying column; but the Duke was always a day ahead. After three weeks of marches and ambuscades he was still at large as a dangerous fighting factor. He was even suspected of a design upon Nice. From his changing bivouacs La Feuillade presumed to control the siege operations, and studied the reports of his engineers. The defenders and citizens of Turin were stubborn. They knew they guarded the title-deeds of Savoy and its existence as a state. Most severe bombardments not only of the works but of the city were resolutely endured. The siege went forward at a snail's pace.

As soon as the situation was realized in Paris Chamillart, as Minister and as father-in-law, wrote his warning. How imprudent to neglect the siege! Old Vauban had delivered an adverse opinion. At the Court voices already called La Feuillade a self-seeker, hoping to boast the capture of a reigning prince, while following a will-o'-the-wisp. "Your honour is at stake," wrote Chamillart.[1] But La Feuillade, although disconcerted by what he saw on his fleeting visit to the trenches on July 7, obstinately continued his chase, and finally brought his quarry to bay as far afield as the mouth of the Luserna valley. Here the Duke was found so strongly posted that he could not be assailed.

As the weeks had passed the French victory at Calcinato was eclipsed and effaced by the relief of Barcelona and the thunderbolt of Ramillies. The Venetian republic, vexed by the exactions of Vendôme's troops, leaned in its neutrality towards the Empire and Prince Eugene. Through the bank in Venice Marlborough, side-tracking Vienna, paid upon his own note of hand direct to Eugene 200,000 ducats, part produce of the loan he had raised and subscribed to in London. English cash flowed steadily by this channel. The army of the Empire and Sea Powers was fed, paid, and equipped by the end of June. Strict behaviour and ready money gained the inhabitants of the Venetian mainland territories to the allied cause. Eugene felt himself able to infringe Venetian neutrality with impunity. This fact doubled the front which Vendôme must watch from Lake Garda to the Adriatic. He might be struck at any point. He feared particularly an attack between the lake and Verona. But Eugene had already decided to pierce the line nearly sixty miles to the southward. On June 27 he wrote to Victor Amadeus, "I have brought boats to a number of places to alarm the enemy everywhere, but I think of attempting the real passage below Badia."[2]

[1] Pelet, vi, 194.   [2] *Feldzüge*, Series I, viii, Suppt., 174.

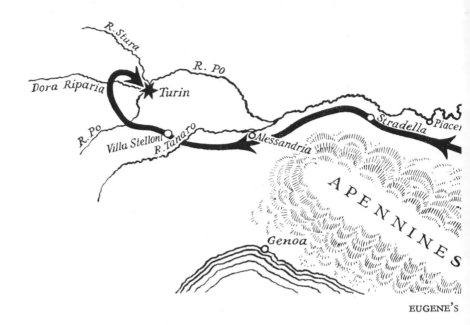

EUGENE'S

We now see another of the examples, numberless in the text-books, of the difficulties of defending lengthy river lines at right-angles to the advance of a determined enemy. Eugene in the last days of June, without waiting for his final reinforcements, the Hessians, and leaving garrisons in Verona and opposite the various bridge-heads on the Upper Adige, marched southward through Venetian territory with between twenty-five and thirty thousand men. Vendôme's forces were probably somewhat superior. But what are thirty thousand men spread along a hundred miles of river and fortifications, when an almost equal force may thrust at one of the many passages, all of which must be guarded? Vendôme had been much pressed by his anxious subordinate, General Saint-Frémont, to abandon that river altogether and take up the less ambitious line of the Mincio, about twenty miles farther west. He inveighed against such suggestions. He had stigmatized the line of the Mincio as the worst that could be adopted.

But while he was watching vigilantly his defences between Verona and the lake, Eugene, on July 4, 5, and 6, passed about

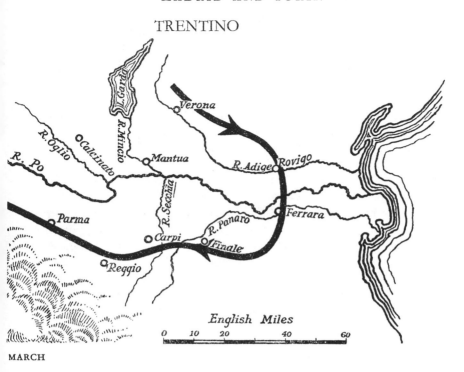

TRENTINO

MARCH

twelve thousand men in various detachments across the Adige near Rovigo and moved to attack the French posts, which retired to Badia. Vendôme obstinately believed this was a feint. "You can be sure," he reported on July 10 to Versailles, "that Prince Eugene will not be able to disturb the siege of Turin. We have too many positions in which to stop him, for his even dreaming of bringing relief."[1] That very day Eugene had driven in General Saint-Frémont's posts over a wide front and was himself approaching the banks of the Po.[2] He had thus turned the whole line of the French defences. Eugene was astonished at his own easy advance. "I cannot imagine at all," he wrote to the Emperor, "why the army has abandoned all its works at such speed."[3] Vendôme now made haste to accommodate himself to circumstances, and explained airily to Paris that his general retreat had placed him in a much better position. This was the moment of Marshal Marsin's arrival. Vendôme handed over his command, and, perhaps with less reluctance

[1] Pelet, vi, 200.
[2] See map above.
[3] *Feldzüge*, Series I, viii, Suppt., 184.

than he would have felt a fortnight sooner, entered his coach and set off through Milan to face Marlborough in Flanders.

A few days earlier the Duke of Orleans had arrived before Turin. He found the siege-works progressing slowly in the face of stubborn resistance and heavy cannonading. Marshal La Feuillade was still absent pursuing the Duke of Savoy, and the attack had palpably languished. Orleans had left Versailles under the impression of Vauban's pessimistic predictions. The aged engineer had from the winter onward declared vehemently that the way to attack Turin was by first securing the fortified eminence of the Capuchins' monastery. This gained, the town would become untenable, and as a second major operation the reduction of the citadel could begin. But he had recognized that for this task eighty-five battalions were required instead of sixty-five, which was all the King could spare La Feuillade. In that case, said Vauban, it would be better to leave Turin for another year. The young French Prince, who had, as his mother wrote to the Electress Sophia, "appeared three fingers taller" on being given his first important command, found that out of La Feuillade's sixty-five battalions as many as thirteen battalions and several cannon were diverting themselves before the walls of Cherasco, forty miles to the south of Turin, whither the Marshal had followed the elusive Duke. He wrote long and by no means sanguine letters to the King.[1]

Marshal Marsin had no sooner assumed command and ranged the French covering army along the Mincio and the Oglio than these lines were in their turn compromised by the steady advance of Prince Eugene. On July 17 he crossed the Po and marched through Ferrara to Finale, which he occupied on the 24th. The Duke of Orleans, having visited the siege, joined Marsin on the 19th. There being no doubt that Eugene was marching to the relief of Turin, the French command resolved to concentrate the covering army and keep pace with him along the northern bank of the Po. Orleans wished to bar his path at the defile of Stradella, but Marsin, who seemed strangely despondent, dissuaded him. At the worst, by the method adopted they would join La Feuillade's army and meet Eugene with superior forces on the lines of circumvallation at Turin. However, the Prince of Hesse, with the Hessian contingents tardy but four thousand strong, had now joined the six thousand men Eugene had left at Verona. The arrival of this new corps, which had immediately become active, forced Marsin to leave a

[1] Pelet, vi, 231 et seq.

large detachment of at least the same number under General Medavi to face them south of Lake Garda. Eugene's long westward march was therefore virtually unresisted. By August 5, having crossed the Secchia unopposed, he entered Carpi. On the 14th he was at Reggio and on the 19th at Piacenza. To avoid the fierce heats he marched by moonlight, but the difficulties of finding food and water were serious and the sufferings of the Imperialists severe. He found the pass of Stradella undefended, and, turning south to avoid Alessandria, which held a French garrison, he crossed the Tanaro on the 29th and entered Piedmont. On September 1 he joined Victor Amadeus at Villa Stelloni, about twenty miles due south of Turin. The six thousand Savoyard cavalry raised Eugene's strength to thirty thousand men, besides several thousands of armed peasants and local militia from the countryside. The moment had come for what might well have seemed a desperate feat of arms.

The French combined army amounted to nearly sixty thousand men. Their obvious course, and one which Vendôme might well have taken, was to suspend the siege, form the order of battle, and march with every available man to attack the daring enemy wherever they could be found in the open country. The Duke of Orleans urged this upon Marsin; but the Marshal, plunged in ever-deepening gloom, would not agree. The unfortunate Prince, nominally at the head of the army, had all the right ideas, but, bred in the strict family discipline of Versailles, he had not the personal authority to enforce them upon marshals experienced in so many campaigns. La Feuillade consumed much strength in two furious and unsuccessful assaults upon the fortress, and for the rest the French army awaited passively whatever stroke Eugene and the warlike Duke might launch upon them.

This was not long delayed. Never in his fifty years of war was Prince Eugene more cool and confident. The French were already in his judgment "half beaten" by strategic manœuvres, and the rest would be settled on the field of battle. On the 4th and 5th he crossed the Po and the Dora Riparia, seized Pianezza, and began to form the allied army between that place and the Stura river, on the north-west side of the city. His headquarters that night were three miles from Turin.

The siege-works and their exterior protecting lines had never, as we have seen, been completed, and the allies were now drawing up opposite the gap by which Victor Amadeus had always maintained a precarious communication with the city. Frantic efforts were made by the French during the 6th to fortify the threatened sector. Again Orleans pleaded that the siege should be suspended and all forces concentrated to meet the impending attack. He was over-

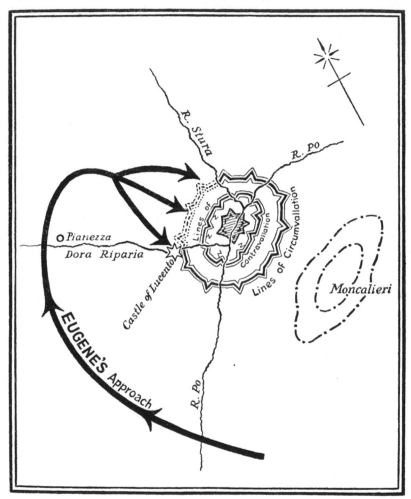

THE BATTLE OF TURIN

ruled at the council of war, and, since he insisted, Marsin reminded him that he had no authority over La Feuillade's besieging troops. Thus the French actually faced the Allies with about fifty squadrons and only seventeen battalions in such entrenchments as could be raised in twenty-four hours. They had the benefit neither of lines of circumvallation nor of their large superiority.

At daybreak on the 7th Eugene ordered the general attack. As he mounted his horse he was asked to fix his headquarters for the night. "In Turin," he replied gaily, and rode forward into the battle. Palatines and Prussians led the assault upon the enemy's right, and the whole front was soon engaged. Eugene, Victor Amadeus, and the Prince of Saxe-Gotha fought throughout in the van. Eugene's horse was shot under him. Twice the assailants were

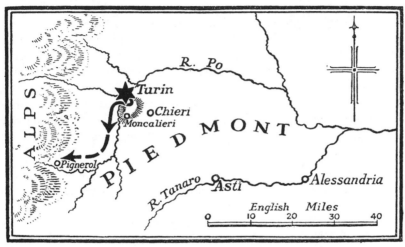

THE FRENCH RETREAT FROM ITALY

repulsed; but at the third attack the sturdy Brandenburgers stormed and pierced the French right wing. The centre gave way in consequence; and only the left wing, which had strong assistance from the batteries in La Feuillade's siege-works, made an orderly retreat into these defences. Marshal Marsin, exposing himself devotedly, fell mortally wounded into the hands of the Allies. The Duke of Orleans, having recorded his protest in writing the night before, set an example to all soldiers. He was twice wounded before he quitted the field. By one o'clock the French were completely broken. Count Daun, the governor of Turin, sallying out upon them with a large part of the garrison, completed their ruin. They lost three thousand killed and wounded, and six thousand were taken prisoner. The Allies lost more than five thousand men. The road into the city was now open.

As soon as the Duke of Orleans learned that Marsin had fallen he ordered the raising of the siege, and took it for granted that the retreat would be eastward through Chieri and Asti towards

Alessandria. His coach was proceeding in that direction when he was informed that the enemy already held the heights of Moncalieri. These were no more than the armed peasants and militia who had appeared in this quarter. They were sufficient, however, to drive the French out of Italy; for, instead of marching back into Lombardy, with its many fortresses and numerous detachments of French troops, including the strong force under General Medavi, they now turned west and marched on Pignerol and towards France. La Feuillade's army came off in good order with some of their field guns, and the bulk of the cavalry joined them by various routes. They abandoned the whole of the siege artillery and munitions in the lines. They abandoned more: they abandoned the war in Italy.

It was not till some time afterwards that the secret of Marshal Marsin's morbid depression was explained. On the day before the battle he had given his confessor the following painful letter for Chamillart:

. . . Your generous sentiments compel me to make you an avowal of my weakness, which makes me feel that all is mortal, and I must soon submit to this general law.

As this letter is not to be given you till after my death, should it come this year, I beg you to preserve the secret of the weakness which haunts me. Ever since I received the orders of the King to go to Italy I have not been able to clear from my mind the conviction that I shall be killed in this campaign; and Death, in the workings of God's pity, thrusts itself upon me at every moment and possesses me day and night; since I have been in this country nothing can relieve my presentiment except my hope in God. . . .

P.S. At this moment the enemy are crossing the Po.[1]

As if to mock the ignominious retreat of the French army, Fortune favoured General Medavi by Lake Garda. The Prince of Hesse with his powerful corps had captured Goito, and was moving upon Castiglione when Medavi attacked him with slightly superior numbers. A fierce action was fought near this town on September 9. Hesse was driven from the field, nearly half his force being killed or captured. The successful general was preparing to exploit his victory when the news of the disaster at Turin and the retreat of the army reached him. He at once marched southwards and distributed his twenty battalions among the fortresses of Mantua, Pavia, Ales-

---

[1] The original of this letter is still preserved in the Archives du Dépôt de la Guerre, vol. 1966, No. 460. See also Pelet, vi, 277.

sandria, and Milan, thus imparting to all these strongholds a serious defensive power. If the main French army had retreated eastward, instead of yielding to a homing instinct, they would have remained masters of the Milanese, and the relief of Turin with all its glory might have remained but a local episode. In the event, however, it decided the fate of Italy. The impulsive plans which were formed at Versailles for a renewed invasion, chilled by the approach of winter, never bore fruit. The fortresses of Piedmont were blockaded or reduced one by one, and presently there began that series of negotiations both military and political which before the opening of 1707 had brought the war in Italy to a close.

Chapter Ten

THE YEAR OF VICTORY

1706—JUNE–OCTOBER

STRONG reinforcements had joined Marlborough at the end of June. The Prussians, the Hanoverians, and the Palatines, in all nearly twenty thousand admirable troops, crossed the Scheldt and were posted from Alost to Brussels. Here they isolated Dendermonde and the towns of Brabant, and were within easy reach of the main army in case of need. After Ostend had capitulated Marlborough advanced to Courtrai, with his headquarters at Helchin, and thence menaced the three fortresses of Ypres, Menin, and Tournai. This movement puzzled Villeroy, who saw the need both of strengthening their garrisons and forming a field army to preoccupy the besiegers. He felt, however, unable to withdraw any of the twenty-five battalions and nine squadrons with which the aged Vauban was covering the coast fortresses, since Marlborough could so easily march west against Nieuport and Dunkirk.[1] The dispersion of the French armies in Flanders was now grievous. One hundred and ten battalions of field troops were scattered in eleven fortresses from Nieuport to Namur; yet none was safe. The detachments arriving from the Rhine were distributed here and there as rumour mentioned the next point of attack.

This was in fact, as we have seen already, decided. Menin, on the soil of France, "reckoned the key to the French conquests in the Netherlands,"[2] enlisted the desires and would presumably engage the energies of the Dutch, and was acceptable to Marlborough. It was a first-class fortress, one of Vauban's later conceptions, built since the Peace of Nimwegen. This model of the defensive art was garrisoned by six thousand men under a group of distinguished generals and engineers, among whom the resolute Caraman will be remembered. The French controlled the sluices, and further protected it by inundations which robbed the Scheldt and the Lys so seriously that the allied siege train had to come by

[1] See Pelet, vi, 69 *et seq.* [2] Lediard, ii, 99.

road. From this cause, although Menin was invested on July 23, the trenches could not be opened and the batteries established till August 4. After a fortnight's sapping and bombarding, the moment for the attack of the counterscarp was reached. Marlborough came himself from the covering army to superintend this serious attempt. The contingents which had suffered least in the battle, or had not been engaged in the campaign, were chosen for the ordeal. The

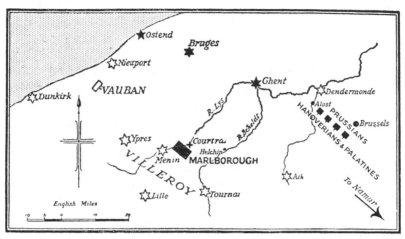

FLANDERS (JULY 1706)

Duke, having spent the previous day in preparation, entered the trenches on the evening of the 18th, and at seven o'clock the explosion of two mines heralded the storm. Eight thousand British and Prussian infantry under Lord Orkney and General Scholtz marched to the assault of the work called the "Half-moon of Ypres." After two hours' stubborn fighting they mastered the covered way and established themselves along the ramparts. The assailants lost fourteen hundred men (the French assert four thousand). Among these the British bore the brunt. Ingoldsby's regiment alone had fifteen officers killed or wounded. The Royal Irish suffered heavily. "Here," says Captain Parker, "we paid for our looking on at Ramillies, having had two captains and five subalterns killed and eight officers wounded, among whom I was one."[1] In the judgment of the armies it was the sharpest siege-fighting since Kaiserswerth in 1702; but it was decisive.

The next day the signals for parley were made, and on the morning of August 22 the end came. "Yesterday morning," wrote

[1] *Memoirs*, p. 115.

Marlborough, "the enemy at Menin planted a white flag on their breach, and as I was there I immediately ordered an exchange of hostages."[1] The highest honours and accommodations of war were conceded to the garrison, who marched off to Douai five or six days before, in Marlborough's judgment, the place need have fallen. They had lost 1500 men and the Allies 2500, almost as many as at Ramillies. Thus for the first time had British soldiers trod "the bloody road to Menin."

Vendôme had arrived at Valenciennes from Italy and superseded Villeroy on the day the trenches were opened before Menin. He found himself in command of an army which, though almost as numerous as the enemy and every day increasing, was dispersed among the fortresses and utterly discouraged. "No one," he wrote to Chamillart (August 5),

> would answer for the fidelity of the Spanish troops, but that vexes me much less than the sadness and prostration which surrounds me here. I will do my best to reanimate our people, but it will be no easy task, if indeed I can manage it, *for every one is ready to doff his hat when one mentions the name of Marlborough.* If the soldiers and troopers were in the same mood, there would be nothing for it but to throw up the campaign. But I hope for something better. I do not despair of rallying the officers by appeal and example, . . . but let me tell you candidly that the job is much harder than I expected. Whatever happens I can promise you I will not lose heart.[2]

Marlborough as soon as he knew Vendôme was coming to Flanders had asked Eugene for his opinion of him. The reply was:

> He is beloved by the common soldiers, and once he has taken a decision he adheres to it, so that nothing whatever can shake him. He is great at entrenching. If his plans are at all upset, he finds it difficult to adjust himself even in an action, and leaves the remedy to chance. In sieges he is full of enterprise. He is ever ready to challenge an army, but unless he has a large superiority he will not attack if he finds that it intends to stand its ground.[3]

Marlborough's own first impressions can be judged from his letters:

August 9

M. de Vendôme has given orders to all the troops to be in readiness to march at twenty-four hours' warning, so that in three or four days he may draw them together. By his language we ought to expect another battle, but I cannot think the King of France will venture it;

---

[1] Coxe, iii, 7.   [2] Pelet, vi, 94.   [3] *Dispatches*, iii, 29.

if he should, I hope and pray that the blessing of God may continue with us.[1]

August 23

The Duke of Vendôme continues to talk more than I believe he intends to perform; however, he strengthens himself every day with all the troops he can possibly get.[2]

Vendôme set himself at once to restore the morale and to gather a field army from the fortresses and reinforcements. He proposed to mix the Spanish among the French troops and to stand behind the Lower Deule and the Lys. He was in no condition to interfere with the siege of Menin. But in a cavalry skirmish on August 19 he cut up a party of Marlborough's foragers and captured Quartermaster-General Cadogan, who was riding too far afield. This news reached Marlborough before the attack on the Menin counterscarp. His distress was acute.

"An officer is just come to me," he wrote to Sarah,

to give me an account of the forage we have made this day, and he tells me that poor Cadogan is taken prisoner or killed, which gives me a great deal of uneasiness, for he loved me, and I could rely on him. I am now sending a trumpet to the Governor of Tournai to know if he be alive; for the horse that beat him came from that garrison. I have ordered the trumpet to return this night, for I shall not be quiet till I know his fate.[3]

Marlborough's fears were groundless. Vendôme, knowing how high Cadogan stood in Marlborough's affection, released him at once on parole as an act of personal courtesy to his adversary, and Marlborough made haste to exchange the Baron Pallavicini, a Lieutenant-General taken at Ramillies,[4] in order to regain Cadogan's services.

Later in the year he wrote about Cadogan to Godolphin:

CAMERON
Oct. 24, 1706

I find by your last letter that applications are made by Mr Mordaunt and others for my brother's place in the Tower.[5] I beg you will not be engaged, and that the Queen will gratify me on this occasion. I would not have this place disposed of as yet; but when I shall think it a proper time, I would then beg the Queen would be pleased to let

---

[1] Coxe, iii, 5–6.   [2] *Ibid.*, 7–8.   [3] *Ibid.*, 6.

[4] A Savoyard who had entered French service when Victor Amadeus joined the Allies.

[5] General Charles Churchill had accepted the governorship of Guernsey.

Brigadier Cadogan have it, since it will be provision for him in time of peace. As I would put my life in his hands, so I will be answerable for his faithfulness and duty to the Queen. I have for the Queen's service obliged him this war to expose his life very often, so that in justice I owe him this good office.[1]

By the 19th Vendôme had mustered 63 battalions and 163 squadrons from Armentières to Lille in the angle of the Lys and

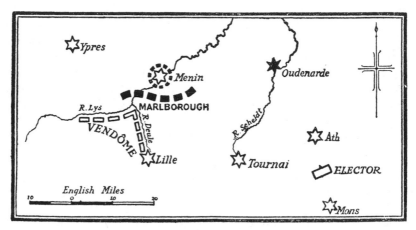

THE SIEGE OF MENIN

the Deule.[2] The Elector thought this line dangerously extended, and there was considerable argument, in which Versailles supported him. Nevertheless, a formed French army now being in the field, Marlborough was limited to undertaking only one siege at a time. The most promising towns were Ypres, Dendermonde, and Ath. The capture of Ypres would open the coast for clearance, but it was now late in the year to exploit success in that quarter. More-over, if Marlborough moved towards the sea he would have to leave heavy detachments to protect Brussels and Brabant. The capture of Ath, on the other hand, would cover Brabant; it would keep the allied army closely in touch and broaden the front for further operations. To bring forward the artillery for the siege of Ath it was necessary to free the navigation of the Dender by the capture of Dendermonde. This siege, though impeded by excep-tional physical difficulties, was the least exposed to French inter-ference. Accordingly on August 26 Churchill was sent against Dendermonde with strong forces.

[1] Coxe, iii, 6–7.   [2] See also general map of Western Flanders, facing p. 488

Marlborough to Godolphin

HELCHIN
August 26, 1706

. . . I saw the garrison of Menin march out yesterday; they were near 4500 men. The fear they had of being made prisoners of war made them give up the place five or six days sooner than, in decency, they ought to have done.

My brother will be to-morrow before Dendermonde, and I hope the cannon may fire by Monday; and if we have no rain, five or six days may make us masters of that place, which has always been thought unattackable; and in truth we should not have thought of it, but the extraordinary drought makes us venture. If we succeed at Dendermonde, and can in time have more ammunition from Holland, we shall then make the siege of Ath, which will be a security to our winter quarters, notwithstanding the Duke of Vendôme's army. If we could have been sure of having the necessaries for the siege of Ypres, I believe we should have undertaken it; for that place is very difficult to be relieved when the posts [by which it can be invested] are once taken; but we can't expect the stores that are sent for in less than three weeks. . . . I give you the trouble of all this that you may see that I should have preferred Ypres before Ath, but the Dutch like Dendermonde and Ath much the best; so that I hope they will not let us want ammunition for them.[1]

And on August 30: "The engineer sends me word that he finds much more water at Dendermonde than he expected. I go there in three or four days, and then I shall be able to send you the certainty of what we may expect."[2]

Marlborough to Godolphin

September 9, 1706

In yours of the 23rd you were afraid that if there were any good news from this country, it would find the way over, whereas you had three packets due. When they come to you, you will find everything you could expect from hence. That of Dendermonde, making them prisoners of war, was more than was reasonable, but I saw them in a consternation. That place could never have been taken but by the hand of God, which gave us seven weeks without any rain. The rain began the next day after we had possession, and continued till this evening.

. . . The express that carried the good news to the States of our being masters of Dendermonde was dispatched in such haste that I could not write to you. I believe the King of France will be a good deal surprised when he shall hear that the garrison has been obliged

<hr>

[1] Coxe, iii, 9.   [2] *Ibid.*, 10.

to surrender themselves prisoners of war; for upon his being told that preparations were making for the siege of Dendermonde he said, "They must have an army of ducks to take it." The truth is God has blessed us with a very extraordinary season. . . . What makes it the more remarkable is that this place was never before taken, though once besieged by the French, and the King himself with the army. I hope in seven or eight days we shall have in this town all the cannon and ammunition that is necessary for the siege of Ath.[1]

From the battlefield of Turin Prince Eugene wrote to Marlborough. His letter, sent on the night of his victory, took a fortnight to reach Marlborough's headquarters at Helchin.

Your Highness will not, I am sure, be displeased to hear by the Baron de Hondorff of the signal advantage which the arms of his Imperial Majesty and his allies have gained over the enemy. You have had so great a share in it, by the succours you have procured, that you must permit me to thank you again. Marshal Marsin is taken prisoner, and mortally wounded. The troops have greatly signalized themselves. In a few days I will send you a correct account; and in the meantime refer you to that which you will hear from the bearer of this letter, who is well informed, has seen everything, and is competent to give an accurate relation. Your Highness will excuse the shortness of this letter, as I have not a moment of time.[2]

Marlborough's delight at his comrade's success, and, indeed, at the fruition of his own plans and labours, roused him to unusual expressions. "It is impossible," he wrote to Sarah on September 26,

for me to express the joy it has given me; *for I do not only esteem, but I really love that Prince.* This glorious action must bring France so low that if our friends can be persuaded to carry on the war one year longer with vigour, we could not fail, with the blessing of God, to have such a peace as would give us quiet in our days; but the Dutch are at this time unaccountable.[3]

To Heinsius (September 27) he magnified his friend's victory: "I am assured that the French take more to heart their misfortune in Italy than they did that of Ramillies."[4]

John to Sarah

GRAMETZ
October 7

I am to return you my thanks for five of yours, all from Woodstock. I could wish with all my heart everything were more to your mind;

---

[1] Coxe, iii, 10.   [2] *Ibid.*, 20.   [3] *Ibid.*, 21.   [4] Vreede, p. 131.

for I find when you wrote most of them you had very much the spleen, and in one I had my share, for I see I lie under the same misfortune I have ever done, of not behaving myself as I ought to the Queen.

I hope Mr Hacksmore will be able to mend those faults you find in the house, but the great fault I find is that if the war should happily have ended this next year, I might the next after have lived in it; for I am resolved to be neither Minister nor courtier, not doubting the Queen will allow of it. But these are idle dreams, for whilst the war lasts I must serve, and will do it with all my heart; and if at last I am rewarded with your love and esteem, I shall end my days happily, and without it nothing can make me easy.

I am taking measures to leave the army about three weeks hence, so that I shall have the happiness of being above one month sooner with you than I have been for these last three years.[1]

In these great days the English Press began to present itself for the first time as a definite, permanent factor in affairs. There were already, besides the official *London Gazette*, of which Steele became editor in 1707, the *Daily Courant* and the *Postman*, both dull and semi-official. There were Defoe's *Review* and Tutchin's *Observator*, both Whig and entertaining. *The Flying Post* was another Whig paper. *The Post Boy* was Jacobite, and *Mercurius Politicus* high Tory. Many of the sharpest and some of the greatest pens in English literature sustained these fierce and sprightly rags of Grub Street. They passed from hand to hand in the coffee-houses, and post-boys carried them to lonely halls and vicarages throughout the country. It is difficult for dwellers in the twentieth to realize the power of print in the eighteenth century. Then every word was devoured and digested, and grave persons of narrow, bitter convictions fortified themselves thereby in their prejudices and their passions. Several scores of editors, news-letter writers, and pamphleteers vied with each other in distinction, virulence, and poverty. Great nobles, astute Ministers, clubs, groups, and factions sustained a literary clatter which excited England and even echoed upon the Continent with Marlborough's cannonades.

The maxim "There is safety in numbers" was never more true than about a free Press. If enough is printed nothing in particular counts. The larger the organ, the less an executive Government has to fear from its personal director. But in those days glittering or terrible words were written anonymously; facts or scandals, revealed by personages who had access to secret or private knowledge or gossip, were flung out by writers of genius upon a fierce and earnest

---

[1] Coxe, iii, 102–103.

public. The authors and often the printers lay hidden in obscurity. The powerful politicians of the day exploited them or hunted them down according to circumstances, but usually left them almost starving. Naturally high Tory and Whig scribes were stirred and prone to loose their arrows upon Marlborough and his wife, and also upon Godolphin. These were the largest targets. Marlborough was protected from time to time by his victories, but Godolphin, without victories and without party, was enjoyably vulnerable.

We have seen Marlborough behaving with temper and even with magnanimity about the unlucky divine Stephens, who was caught for the pillory. But during 1705 and 1706 he shows himself acutely sensitive to malicious, or, as he judged it, untruthful, criticism, especially when directed against his military conduct. He was less resentful of taunts upon his rebuffs, or disappointments in the field, than of disparagements of his successes. For these he claimed justice. When he found justice denied he was keenly distressed, and at rare moments his calm was broken by a surge of wrath. In August 1705 when he had read Dr James Drake's *Memorial of the Church of England*, wherein he had been accused of betraying the Church, he wrote to Godolphin:

> I think it is the most impudent and scurrilous thing I ever read. If the author can be found I do not doubt he will be punished; for if such liberties may be taken of writing scandalous lies without being punished, no Government can stand long.[1]

The author of the *Memorial* was then unknown, but Godolphin set to work to find him. It was also unknown at the time that Dr Drake was the author of *Mercurius Politicus*, the high Tory anti-Government paper which from 1705 onward maintained a continuous stream of abuse against Marlborough and Godolphin in a vein that would hardly be tolerated in the freest of countries to-day. The Duke was disturbed to find the news-sheets and the coffee-houses buzzing like the Parliamentary lobbies with the rival merits of Whig and Tory generals. He did not relish officers in his Army grouping themselves upon these lines, and writing anonymous letters home according to their personal or political affections. He would have liked to put a stop to the whole process in the Army, and range them with himself upon a purely professional basis. When this proved impossible, he was forced to some extent to favour those who were loyal to him. He was plainly conscious

[1] Coxe, ii, 278.

throughout all his later campaigns that savage, implacable forces were ceaselessly striving to tear him down while he lived under the hazards of war, and that success alone could hold the wolves at bay. One single disaster would destroy him, yet all the time he had to cope with the unknowable and often, as he would put it in his habit of under-statement, "to venture."

In the weeks before Ramillies when he had deliberately condemned himself to a bleak campaign in the fortress zone he showed his anxiety that his operations should be properly represented in the Press. On May 6 he wrote to Harley:

> As all truths may not be proper to be in the *Gazette*, I desire the favour of you that during this campaign when I send you in your letter, as I do now, a paper of news, you will let it be inserted in the *Postman*, and what is to be in the *Gazette* Mr Cardonnel will send it to the office as formerly. I shall depend on your friendship and judgment to leave out what you may think improper.[1]

This was not unreasonable. There were to be the dispatches in the official *Gazette*, but in addition there should be a bulletin or news-letter which would describe events from the standpoint of the Commander-in-Chief and his Headquarters, and in case of disputes would give his own version to his countrymen. Few generals, even in our own generation, have been so modest in their claims. Ramillies for a spell silenced the critics. They were dazzled by the lightning flash and scorched by the conflagration which followed. It was nearly a month before the voice of disparagement could be raised, and even a few weeks more before it could be heard. Then a letter from the Army found its way to London and became the talk of the town. It was from Cranstoun, of the Cameronians. This brave and accomplished officer, after paying the highest tributes to Marlborough's conduct as "a great Captain" and censuring him gently for "exposing himself like the meanest soldier," proceeded to explain how much better the battle could have been won. Cranstoun voiced the complaint of the British infantry under Orkney who had been forced by the order to retire from Autréglise and Offus, and thereafter, as they believed, from cutting the retreat of the French army. All these veteran soldiers saw this point so clearly that they saw nothing else in the whole battle. Cranstoun imagined that Cadogan had given the order out of jealousy or ignorance, and had not had Marlborough's sanction first. At any rate, this was the line he took.

[1] Bath Papers, *H.M.C.*, i, 81.

Harley, all his spies and vigilance at Marlborough's disposal in this hour of triumph, intercepted one of the copies of the letter (which was unsigned) and informed Marlborough. The Duke was somewhat upset, and further vexed by the renewal of the *Observator's* attacks.

"I am obliged," he wrote to Harley on July 12,

> to you for your friendly care, and I will have Major Cranstoun observed, and should be glad to have a copy of the letter concerning Ramillies, and if possible be certain of the author. I am told the *Observator* is angry with me.[1]

There may have been other critical letters from the British troops under Orkney's command who brooded morosely upon having been denied what they deemed their prey, and their chance of distinction, for we have another letter of Marlborough's on July 8 addressed "for yourself."

> I thank you for what you mention of the letters and the care you have taken to find out the authors. I should be glad to know them. . . . If you send me the copies of the letters from the army I should be glad to see them.[2]

Several references to this matter occur in the official correspondence. On August 5 Marlborough returns to Cranstoun: "If you could let me have a sight of the original letter of Ramillies, I could then be sure of knowing the author, having in my custody an original letter of the major's." And on August 26: "You have forgot to send me copies of Cranstoun's letters."

All this has a modern flavour. Finally in September Harley obtained Cranstoun's original letter, and Marlborough was able to identify with certainty the author. He addressed himself immediately to Cranstoun's criticism. He defended Cadogan and took the responsibility to himself. "The part in which he mentions Cadogan he is very much in the wrong, for if those troops had not been brought back they must certainly have been cut to pieces." No one aware of the masses of French cavalry drawn to the left of the hostile line by Orkney's attack, and hungrily awaiting the moment to destroy their unsupported assailants, can doubt the finality of this answer. Viewed in retrospect and with full knowledge, the secret of Ramillies is obvious; but the British infantry continued to feel they had been sacrificed, in the sense of being pulled out of the battle, so that its glory had shone on foreign blades. They had been cheated of the

---

[1] Bath Papers, *H.M.C.*, i, 82.   [2] *Loc. cit.*

brunt; and this in the name of their own Captain-General. But then, thought they, it was Cadogan with his Staff mind and his maps who had misinterpreted him.

It may be noted that Marlborough, having found out the critic and replied to the criticism, never visited his displeasure upon Major Cranstoun. That officer was unconscious of the State correspondence which had passed concerning him. Indeed, what he wrote was in other respects so complimentary to Marlborough that the Duke could not really have been offended. In the following year he promoted Cranstoun Lieutenant-Colonel, and in that rank at the head of his Cameronians he was to fall heroically at Malplaquet.

There is, however, one rougher tale to tell of these times. In October 1706 Marlborough wrote in wrath to Harley:

> I have by this post sent an *Observator* to Mr St Johns [*sic*]. I should be extremely obliged to you if you would speak to Lord Keeper, and see if there is any method to protect me against this rogue, who is set on by Lord Haversham. If I can't have justice done me, I must find some that will break his and the printer's bones, which I hope will be approved by all honest Englishmen, since I serve my Queen and country with all my heart.[1]

This "rogue" was Tutchin, an enthusiastic Whig, described by contemporaries as "the scourge of the Highfliers," whose work took the form of dialogues between a "countryman" and the "Observator." For each of these articles of deadly malice and admirable prose Tutchin drew from his paper no more than half a guinea. The Ministry was at first reluctant to arrest Tutchin. They had already tried to punish him for seditious libel in November 1704; but the judges had ordered his acquittal on technical grounds. According to one story,[2] Tutchin in 1707 was "waylaid and beaten to death." Marlborough was not guilty of any violent act. But the law pursued the pamphleteers with heavy hand.

> Earless on high, stood unabashed Defoe,
> And Tutchin flagrant from the scourge below.[3]

In fact Tutchin, after being flogged, died in the Queen's Bench Prison at the Mint in September 1707. In justice to the *Observator* it must be mentioned that its files contain many fine tributes to Marlborough. It recognized throughout his reluctance to enter the

---

[1] Bath Papers, *H.M.C.*, i, 82.
[2] Contrast Bourne, *English Newspapers*, i, 60; and *D.N.B.*, *sub* Tutchin.
[3] Pope, *The Dunciad*.

literary lists or to encourage others to write on his behalf. It emphasized his reliance on deeds instead of words: "I don't think," it remarked on one occasion in 1706, "the Duke of Marlborough will thank any one for being his Praise Trumpeter, that's a post for a pedant and a sycophant." And again: "My Lord Duke is one of the best authors this country has possessed. He's the author of conquests and victories."

"I should be glad to know the authors of letters against me," Marlborough himself told Harley in 1706, "though as long as God blesses us with success, their writing can have little weight."

And to Sarah in 1705:

> I see that there is another scandalous pamphlet. The best way of putting an end to that villainy is not to appear concerned. The best of men and women have in all ages been ill-used. If we could be so happy as to behave ourselves so as to have no reason to reproach ourselves, we may then despise what rage and faction do. . . .[1]

Godolphin seems to have hopefully tried to endorse this opinion: "If Marlborough can conquer animosities as well as armies, his presence will be very useful in this island of Britain." Judged by the standards of those days, they were both astonishingly patient, tolerant, and merciful men. In our own enlightened and scientific epoch it will probably be felt in many great countries that if they had been more ruthless they would have been more successful.

The wonderful successes in Flanders, Italy, and Spain found no counterpart in the Empire. Under all the varied but persistent pressures of England and Holland the new Emperor had striven to the utmost limit for peace in Hungary. Although the Imperial generals had made good headway against the rebels in 1705, full rein was given to the mediations of the Sea Powers. The line which they had drawn between the contending forces was scrupulously observed by Vienna, while behind it Rakoczy made himself master of all Hungary and Transylvania. The truce for negotiations began on May 12, 1706. At the end of the month the rebel terms were presented. Austria must abandon all sovereign rights beyond the Carpathians. The Army, finance, justice, administration, were to be the sole concern of the Hungarian assembly. Sullen, grudged recognition of the kingship of the Emperor was conceded as a matter of form. When these terms became known in Vienna the

---

[1] September 7; Coxe, ii, 278–279.

population surrounded the palace in fury against the Hungarians. "All the world," wrote the Dutch Ambassador at the Imperial Court (June 5), "is shouting 'Crucify them—crucify them!'"[1] All classes were clamouring to break the sworn truce. The Emperor at his parley made very generous offers. These were at once rejected by the insurgents.

The effects of Ramillies extended swiftly to this sphere. There is a quaint letter from Rakoczy to Marlborough which shows the close relationship prevailing between the rebels and the would-be conciliators:

Prince Rakoczy to Marlborough

NEYHEYSEL
July 22, 1706

★The glorious exploits which your Highness continues to perform during this war and the love which you have for liberty makes me hope that the Hungarian nation is not indifferent to you. For in truth, my Lord, the kingdom is being overwhelmed by your frequent victories. Cannot your generous heart find some means of compensating us for the sufferings which your victorious arms bring upon us. We are affected even here through the insupportable arrogance which your rapid conquests breed in the hearts of the Imperial Ministers. They become more intractable every day, in spite of the efforts of the mediators [Stepney and the Dutch envoy, Bruyninx] and of my own attempts to smooth the path of peace negotiations. I am quite persuaded, my Lord, that this conduct is by no means in accordance with the pious sentiments of Her Britannic Majesty, nor with the equitable intentions of your Highness. Thus I flatter myself the letter which I give myself the honour to write will influence your natural clemency to take us effectively under your protection.[2]

The Sea Powers, impatient at the distraction of this internal struggle, still pressed for conferences. They were able to induce the Emperor to observe the truce till July 24, and urged him to continue it longer. They were still pressing conciliation upon him when Joseph I bluntly declared through all his envoys and agents that the Imperial House would rather give up Spain and Italy than Hungary and Transylvania. This was final. Apart from Eugene's exploits in Italy, the remaining effort of the Empire was now devoted to the civil war.

It was upon this adverse tide that the Margrave, Prince Louis of Baden, ended his career. The Imperial Government, ignoring his

[1] Von Noorden, ii, 505.   [2] Blenheim MSS.

needs, sought to pay their way with the insistent Allies by hounding him to action. They pretended he had forty thousand men. He declared he had not the half, and invited them to come and count them. The offer was accepted, and the Imperial Commissioner, Count Schlick, visited the army. With his position at stake he closed his eyes to the facts, and his report was hostile. He declared the Margrave was strong enough to recover the line of the Moder, and undertake an operation in Alsace.

At this moment the Margrave's toe, which had now infected his whole leg, burst into deadly inflammation. He asked for sick leave to seek curative waters. The Emperor, in whose eyes he was now a recalcitrant and almost a mutineer, ordered his second-in-command to carry out the offensive. This was, of course, an impossible task. Thungen could only moulder till the winter came. Meanwhile the French raiding parties rode deep into Germany, harrying the circles of Swabia and Franconia.

The Margrave was now a dying man. His last letter to Marlborough contains tragic passages.

> . . . I have been for several weeks so ill that I can neither concern myself with the command nor with other affairs. I do not know whether I shall ever get well—yes or no; having had no sleep for nearly three weeks. His Imperial Majesty, my master, seems unconvinced of the truth of the lists [numbers and strengths] which I have sent him about the army under my command. I have been made to feel in terms which are plain enough that his Majesty has received contrary accounts from his Quartermaster-General, who has assured him that this army comprises 40,000 combatants equipped with everything. As for the figures I have given, I am sure that I have not made a mistake. But for the rest of the troops, which are added in with all the equipment they are supposed to have, and for the nineteen hundred thousand odd florins, of which Count Schlick has boasted to the Elector of Mainz, at Cologne and everywhere else that he brought into these regions—of all that we know nothing in this army, having no money at all.
>
> . . . I have been forced by his Majesty's orders to hand over to Field-Marshal Thungen charge of affairs, not doubting that the 40,000 men which the Imperial Court knows with scientific certainty are massed upon the Upper Rhine will succeed in all that is desired of them. . . . The result will clear up the whole affair; and I am only too grieved to be entirely incapable of working either with my body or my head. . . .[1]

[1] September 7, 1706; Blenheim MSS.

On January 4, four months later, he expired in his unfinished palace at Rastadt, from grief and blood-poisoning. Thus ended the career of the famous general of the Turkish wars, a brave warrior who had long held aloft the German standard on the Rhine, but who had neither been endowed with the troops or skill to beat the French himself, nor with the magnanimity to share as a loyal subordinate the fortunes of Marlborough.

When we recount the famous victories of 1706 and set forth the long tale of captured cities and conquered or reconquered lands which built up the allied triumph, it seems amazing that all this good fortune should not have prompted the comparatively small effort of good comradeship needed to bring the war to a successful conclusion. The victories of Ramillies and Turin; the relief of Barcelona; the capture of Antwerp and a dozen famous fortresses in the Low Countries; the French expelled from Italy; Charles III entering Madrid; the complete suppression of France upon the seas and oceans —all these prepared a broad, an easy road along which the signatory states of the Grand Alliance, who had striven so hard against misfortune, could walk to peace and plenty. But by the mysterious law which perhaps in larger interests limits human achievement, and bars or saves the world from clear-cut solutions, this second revival of the allied cause led only to a second decline. Twice now the genius of Marlborough and Eugene had lifted the weary, struggling signatory states to the level where their will could be enforced, and most of their needs secured. But again, in despite of their champions, they were to cast themselves down into peril and distress. The Empire represented nothing but moral and military decay and legal or territorial appetite. The German principalities and the strong kingdom of Prussia cast off their responsibilities and sponged for subsidies upon their Anglo-Dutch deliverers in proportion as they were relieved of their dangers. The Dutch themselves, with their Dyke at their fingertips, were "unaccountable." In Spain the incursions of the Allies, especially the Portuguese, had roused a national spirit similar to that which a hundred years later wore down Napoleon. The Hapsburg king imposed by foreign troops had become to Spanish eyes usurper and invader; while the Bourbon claimant, though more alien, seemed to embody the continuity and grandeur of the Spanish past.

In England, now the hub of this Juggernaut wheel, not only party strife, but the prejudices and failings of a handful of men and women, including and circling round the Queen, were to crack and splinter the inefficient but still august league of nations which hitherto had successfully defended the liberties of Europe against the intolerance of totalitarian monarchy. Thus success bred failure, and prosperity prepared collapse, by which again new, larger, and more painful efforts were extorted.

Chapter Eleven

SUNDERLAND'S APPOINTMENT

1706—AUTUMN

WHILE in the field Marlborough and Eugene carried all before them a series of English party and personal rivalries prepared the general reversal of fortune. Sunderland had been chosen by the Whig Junto as the thin end of the wedge by which they would force their way into the controlling circle of the Queen's Government. According to modern ideas, their majority in both Houses of Parliament gave them the right, and even at this time it gave them the power, to acquire pre-eminence in public affairs. Sunderland, admonished and guided by Marlborough, had acquitted himself with high discretion in his mission to Vienna. He had shared or adopted Marlborough's view that the Hungarian insurgents, and not the Imperial Court, were to blame for prolonging an intestine war, in view of the offers made to them by the Emperor. Whiggism comprised at this time the quintessence of aristocracy, plutocracy, and oligarchy at home, coupled with the ruthless application of Radical, Nationalist, and Republican principles abroad. Instead of fulminating these doctrines, Sunderland had judged the situation of the Empire in a matter-of-fact mood. He went to Vienna a political theorist and partisan. He had acquitted himself like a statesman facing the actual facts.

His colleagues and the tensely organized party they ruled were not at all displeased with his behaviour, and may even have recommended it. Their foresight and understanding taught them that at this phase in their party advance office was more important than principle. They must get their hands on some at least of the levers of the machine. They must work their way by all measures into the councils, and if possible the confidence, of the Queen. They now decided that their move must be to make Sunderland Secretary of State. To this end they combined his recent serviceable conduct, his relationship to the Marlboroughs, and their own party power in both Houses. They concentrated their assaults upon Godolphin. Politically they had him in their grip. The Lord Treasurer, hunted by the Tories upon the Scottish Act of Security and the Union, had for some time past been dependent upon Whig protection. By this means alone he had acquired the power to use martial law against Scotland at this critical juncture in the life of the two countries. Without this overriding force added to all other argument the Union could never have been achieved. But the union of the two kingdoms was a deadly blow at the hopes of a Jacobite restoration. Godolphin was led by his vision of British unity to renounce alike by his action and by his new connexions those Stuart memories which he had long illegally cherished, and which were a strange but real bond of sympathy between him and the Queen. By these sacrifices, assuredly made for no personal motive, from no weakness of character, and in what all must now regard as the long interest of the British Isles, Godolphin obtained the votes and the force to lay strong hands on Scotland and clinch the Union.

This now approached its closing stage. The Scottish Parliament had made a number of minor amendments to the original English proposals. The Union party in Scotland urged that another session of the Scottish Parliament would add to their difficulties. Therefore they requested that the English Parliament should accept the Act exactly as they had passed it. Marlborough, who was one of the Commissioners, regarded the Union as vital to the strength of the nation. From the camp at Helchin he had written in the summer (August 9):

> What you say of both parties is so true that I do, with all my soul, pity you. Care must be taken against the malice of the angry party; and notwithstanding their malicious affectation of crying the Church may be ruined by the union, the union must be supported; and I hope the reasonable men of the other party will not oppose the enlarging of the bottom, so that it may be able to support itself. . . .
>
> I had last night the honour of yours of the 13th, and am very glad to find that the commission has so unanimously agreed. I do with all my heart wish the Parliament of both nations may do the same, so that her Majesty may have the glory of finishing this great work, for which she will not only deserve to be blessed in this, but also in future ages.[1]

It was in fact the supreme object in domestic politics to which he and Godolphin bent all their power. When in 1707 the Act was finally passed Guenin, the French agent, wrote from London (January 18):

[1] Coxe, iii, 145.

This Union gives much satisfaction to the Treasurer and the Duke of Marlborough. The latter has really done more than anyone to put it through, although he has not seemed to have played much part in it.[1]

But the Lord Treasurer, who had long lost all hold upon the Tories and had only a temporary working agreement with the Whigs, now found himself in daily contact with a highly discontented Queen. Anne's thoughts strayed often to the "young man in France." "Maybe 'tis our brother." She knew—every one knew—he was her brother. She would not give up the throne to him, even had she the power to do so. She would fight to the last against it. But was she bound to ensure the succession to the house of Hanover she detested so cordially? And to the very prince who had insulted her maiden charms? This Act of Union which her trusted friends the General and the Treasurer pressed upon her forced her to rob James of almost his only remaining hope—the crown of Scotland. Perhaps it must be so. What could she do, one woman among these domineering statesmen with their passions, their intense personalities, their fierce rivalries, their massive arguments? She thought it was necessary to bring about the Union. It was right and wise; it was her duty; but she was not in the mood at any moment to rejoice in that duty. Her heart did not warm to those, even her most trusted friends and proved, sagacious guides, who held her so firmly to her task. Mr Freeman was at the wars—he was always at the wars. She was deeply conscious of the glory and power with which his sword had invested her reign. But Mr Montgomery—she did not often call him that now—was pressing her too hard. He had not the same claim to her favour. Anyone can be a Minister. All her ablest subjects were seeking, contriving, and conspiring to be Ministers. He asked too much. After all, he hung only by a thread which she could cut; but perhaps she hung by that same thread herself. Thus the Queen.

We can see how extremely hazardous was the Lord Treasurer's position. A false step in his personal relations with the Queen on his part, an emotional crisis on hers, and he would see himself delivered to the competitive fury of both bitter factions. In the autumn of 1706 Godolphin seemed to foreign eyes to have gained a position of immense security, unrivalled by any statesman in Europe. But in fact, at the very moment when, in spite of endless war, the finances flourished under his skilful, honest administration, when his great colleague had conquered the Netherlands, when

<hr />

[1] French Foreign Office Archives, tome 221, f. 48 v.

Eugene, upon whom he had lavished money and men, was chasing the French from Italy, when the Scottish Parliament bowed to the inevitable union, Godolphin felt himself in awful jeopardy, and almost without a friend. Almost—but there was one friend, an old friend, the greatest man alive, whom he knew he could count upon till death. He was sure that Marlborough would never desert him; and thus he persevered, and with his perseverance grew the unity of Britain and her power among the nations.

It was in the situation which we have thus briefly outlined that Godolphin was now subjected to the extreme pressure of the Whigs. Sunderland must be Secretary of State. They asked nothing more; they would take nothing else; and now was the moment. Let him pay the price, let him extort the price from the Queen, and all would be well. The skilful Whig politicians would shield him from any reproaches about his past. They even sent a Member to the Tower for insinuating that he had corresponded with Saint-Germains. Great Whig orators and famous ex-Ministers would produce substantial majorities for his defence, for his policy, for the support of Marlborough's armies, and for the insatiable prosecution of the war. On their broad shoulders, in their competent hands, he and all the causes he believed in could rest; and the General overseas would ride on to the decisive defeat of France and the lasting greatness of England. Otherwise they would paralyse the Government and break Godolphin in pieces. This they imparted to him with many bows and scrapes during the summer of 1706.

Accordingly Godolphin, under remorseless pressure, and having, as he said, "no other bottom [than the Whigs] to stand on," addressed himself to Queen Anne. He directed upon her the forces to which he was himself subjected. He added all that long friendship, faithful service, and his personal ascendancy could command. It is astonishing that most of our native historians have depicted Queen Anne as an obstinate simpleton, a stupid, weak creature, in the hands of her bedchamber women; and that it should have been left to foreign writers to expose her immense powers of will-power, resistance, and manœuvre. She fought a harder fight than Godolphin. On her throne she was as tough as Marlborough in the field. She would not have Sunderland—she could not bear him. He was, she felt, a brazen freethinker, and at heart a Republican. The Queen, the embodiment of Church and Monarchy, recognized in him, as she conceived the case, her true foe. Was he not the vanguard of those "tyrant lords" who, as she saw truly, meant to force themselves and their nominees into her Government in order to rule the land and, if they could, Europe. But the Whigs continued to make it clear to Godolphin that he must either compel the Queen to make Sunderland Secretary of State or face the immediate inveterate hostility of both Houses of Parliament. Accordingly all means were employed to persuade the Queen. Godolphin enlisted the vigorous advocacy of Sarah. He himself tried his utmost, exposing his difficulties and threatening resignation. The Queen used every art; she appealed to his friendship, to his loyalty and chivalry. But what could he do? He could not resign and abandon Marlborough. He could not carry on the government unless he forced Sunderland upon the Queen. That she was wrong on the merits of the situation and making needless trouble may be admitted without detracting from the personal quality which she displayed.

Sarah also was, of course, made use of by the Whigs to press Sunderland upon the Queen. Both as a Whig and as a mother-in-law she was by no means reluctant to do this. She immediately encountered an impenetrable resistance. The Queen affected to regard her advocacy as the natural expression of family interests. Evidently there must have been awkward conversations. Sarah was at pains to assert that her zeal for Sunderland had nothing to do with his being her daughter's husband. In fact, however, Anne would have been more tolerant of this motive than of Sarah's Whig partisanship. We notice immediately signs that the Queen took offence at her Mistress of the Robes meddling in high politics. She used much less patient processes with her old intimate confidante than with her Lord Treasurer. She reasoned with Godolphin; she repulsed Sarah. The following notable correspondence ensued:

Sarah to the Queen

August 1706

I conclude your Majesty will believe my arguments upon this subject proceed chiefly from the partiality which I may have for my Lord Sunderland, tho' I solemnly protest that I never had any for any person, to the prejudice of what I believed your interest. And I had rather he had any other place, or none at all, if the party that most assist you would be satisfied without it; for, besides the very great trouble of that office, executed as it should be, he is not of a humour to get anything by such an employment; and I wish from my soul that any other man had been proposed to you, that you could not have suspected I had any concern for. But 'tis certain that your Government can't be carried on with a part of the Tories, and the Whigs disobliged, who, when that happens, will join with any people to torment you and those that are your true servants. I am sure it is my interest, as well as inclination, to have you succeed by any sort of men in what is just, and that will prevent what has been done from being thrown away. Your security and the nation's is my chief wish, and I beg of God Almighty, as sincerely as I shall do for His pardon at my last hour, that Mr and Mrs Morley may see their errors as to this *notion* before it is too late; but considering how little impression anything makes that comes from your faithful Freeman, I have troubled you too much, and I beg your pardon for it.[1]

We have italicized the word "notion," because the Queen read it as "nation," and so took it as a general charge of high disrespect. She left the letter unanswered for some time. Sarah had never experienced such treatment before. She made inquiries and learned hat her letter had offended the Queen. She was quite at a loss to know why. Indeed, she was indignant.

Sarah to the Queen

August 30 [1706]

Your Majesty's great indifference and contempt in taking no notice of my last letter did not so much surprise me as to hear my Lord Treasurer say you had complained much of it, which makes me presume to give you this trouble to repeat what I can be very positive was the whole aim of the letter, and I believe very near the words. It was, in the first place, to show the reason why I had not waited on your Majesty, believing you were uneasy, and fearing you might think I had some private concern for my lord Sunderland. I therefore thought it necessary to assure your Majesty that I had none so great as for your service, and to see my Lord Treasurer so mortified at the necessity of quitting it, or being the ruin of that and himself together. Then I took the liberty to show, as well as I could, that it was really no hardship nor unkindness to Sir Charles Hedges; and I think I might have added, though I believe I did not, that your Majesty, to carry on your government, must have men that neither herd with your enemies nor that are in themselves insignificant. At last I concluded, if I am not more mistaken than ever I was in my life, with these following words, that I did pray to God Almighty, with as much earnestness as I should at my last day for the saving of my soul, that Mrs and Mr Morley might see their errors. This is the whole sense of the letter; and, having had the honour to know your Majesty when you had other thoughts of me than you are pleased to have now, and when you did think fit to take advice and information, I could not reasonably imagine that you should be offended at my earnest en-

[1] Coxe, iii, 111.

deavours to serve you, and pray that you nor the prince might not be deceived. But, finding that no proofs nor demonstrations of my faithfulness to your interest can make anything agreeable to your Majesty that comes from me, I will not enlarge on this subject. I will only beg one piece of justice, and that I fancy you would not refuse to anybody, if you believed it one, that you will show my Lord Treasurer the letter of which your Majesty has complained; and I wish from the bottom of my heart that he, or anybody that is faithful to you and the prince, could see every word that ever I writ to your Majesty in my life.[1]

On this the Queen opened the matter to Godolphin, and pointed to the phrase "errors as to this *nation.*" Godolphin told Sarah, and Sarah made it clear that she had written "*notion.*" This disposed of the grievance, but the Queen's answer contained a phrase of challenge certainly not warranted by anything Sarah had written.

The Queen to Sarah

Friday morning
[*September* 4, 1706]

Since my dear Mrs Freeman could imagine my not taking notice of her letter that was writ before she went to St Albans, proceeded from indifference or contempt, what will she think of my not answering her other in another week's time? But I do assure you it was neither of the reasons you mention that hindered me from writing, *nor no other*[2] but the concern I have been in since the change of the Secretary was proposed to me. *I have obeyed your commands* in showing your letter to my Lord Treasurer, and find my complaint was not without some ground, and a mistake anybody might make upon the first reading; for you had made an *a* instead of an *o*, which quite altered the word. I am very sensible all you say proceeds from the concern you have for my service, and it is impossible to be more mortified than I am to see my Lord Treasurer in such uneasiness; and his leaving my service is a thought I cannot bear, and I hope in God he will put all such out of his own mind. Now that you are come hither again, I hope you will not go to Woodstock without giving me one look, for whatever hard thoughts you may have of me, I am sure I do not deserve them, and I will not be uneasy if you come to me; for though you are never so unkind, I will ever preserve a most sincere and tender passion for my dear Mrs Freeman.[3]

Sarah's reply (September 5), although well suited to an argument with a Cabinet colleague, reads in the circumstances as the height of tactlessness. Instead of fastening on the gracious ending of the

[1] Coxe, iii, 112–113. [2] The Queen's italics. [3] Coxe, iii, 114–115.

Queen's letter, and going to see her in a mood of clouds dispersed, she plunged into a conscientious recapitulation of her arguments.

> By the letter I had from your Majesty this morning, and the great weight you put upon the difference betwixt the word notion and nation in my letter, I am only made sensible (as by many other things) that you were in a great disposition to complain of me, since to this moment I cannot for my life see any essential difference betwixt these two words, as to the sense of my letter. . . .
>
> . . . If you can find fault with this, I am so unhappy as that you must always find fault with me, for I am uncapable of thinking otherwise as long as I am alive, or of acting now but upon the same principle that I served you before you came to the crown for so many years, when your unlimited favour and kindness to me could never tempt me to make use of it in one single instance that was not for your interest and service. . . .

She proceeded with several pages of admonition to the Queen, and disparagement of Sir Charles Hedges, the threatened Secretary of State, and ended, "I beg your Majesty's pardon for not waiting upon you, and I persuade myself that, long as my letter is, it will be less troublesome to your Majesty."[1]

These letters show how far the mischief had gone between Sarah and the Queen. The Duchess made a profound mistake in supposing that she could convince her mistress by argument or compel her by remonstrance, when she could no longer persuade her by love.

Marlborough was from the first averse to the appointment of Sunderland. He did not like him much as a son-in-law. He did not agree with him as politician. He learned with misgivings of the efforts of the Whigs. He did not share Sarah's party feeling. He thought her imprudent to put herself forward in the matter. He would certainly have disapproved of her procedure. Still, at the request of Godolphin he joined in the concerted appeal to the Queen. He wrote his mind bluntly to Sarah.

John to Sarah

HELCHIN
August 9, 1706

You know that I have often disputes with you concerning the Queen; and, by what I have always observed, when she thinks herself in the right, she needs no advice to help her to be very firm and positive. But I doubt but a very little time will set this of Lord Sunderland very right, for . . . she has a good opinion of him. I have writ

[1] *Conduct*, pp. 165–170.

as my friends would have me, for I had much rather be governed than govern. But otherwise I have really so much esteem and kindness to him, and have so much knowledge of the place you would have for him that I have my apprehensions he will be very uneasy in it; and that, when it is too late, you will be of my opinion, that it would have been much happier if he had been employed in any other place of profit and honour. I have formerly said so much to you on this subject, and to so little purpose, that I ought not now to have troubled you with all this, knowing very well that you rely on other people's judgment in this matter. I do not doubt but they wish him very well; but in this they have other considerations than his good, and I have none but that of a kind friend that would neither have him nor my daughter uneasy. Writing this by candle light, I am so blind that I cannot read it, so that if there be anything in it that should not be seen, burn it, and think kindly of one who loves you with all his heart.[1]

As the dispute deepened he became more concerned. Amid the ceaseless exertion of commanding an army, the marches, the sieges, the trenches, the sluices, gunpowder, Vendôme, and the Dutch, he became acutely conscious of the dangerous disputes now rising to intensity at home. In the fullness of his military success he felt the foundations of his power being sapped and undermined. He resented being forced to turn his eyes from the enemy in a great campaign to the petty, but at the same time poisonous, intrigues at home. At times he gave way to despondency.

John to Sarah

HELCHIN
September

What you write me concerning the Queen and the Lord Treasurer gives me a great deal of trouble; for should the consequence be what you say, that there is no relying upon the Tories, and that the Whigs will be out of humour, it must end in confusion, which will have the consequence of the Dutch making peace with France. I am afraid this is what will gratify many of the Tory Party; but I can see no advantage that can come to the Whigs by the ruin of the Lord Treasurer; so that I hope they are too wise a people to expose themselves and the liberties of Europe, because some things are not done with a good grace. I would not have you mistake me; for as far as it is in my power, for the sake of my country and the Queen, for whom, had I a thousand lives, I would venture them all, I would have everything that is reasonable done to satisfy the Whigs, of which I think the Lord Treasurer is the best judge.

[1] Coxe, iii, 89–90.

If it were not for my duty to the Queen, and friendship to Lord Treasurer, I should beg that somebody else might execute my office. Not that I take anything ill, but that the weight is too great for me, and I find a decay in my memory. Whatever may be told you of my looks, the greatest part of my hair is grey, but I think I am not quite so lean as I was.[1]

At some moment in this quarrel we have a letter from Godolphin to the Queen, which is poignant when the circumstances are remembered. The Treasurer was, with Marlborough, the head of a Government which was dazzling Europe by its triumphs in the field and achieving the Union of Great Britain. The Queen was being carried forward by her Ministers to a world eminence to which none of her predecessors had attained. Yet in this autumn of the year of victory Godolphin was forced to write:

Godolphin to the Queen

Saturday morning, at nine
[August 31, 1706][2]

I come this moment from opening and reading the letter which your Majesty gave yourself the trouble to write to me last night. It gives me all the grief and despair imaginable to find that your Majesty shows inclination to have me continue in your service, and yet will make it impossible for me to do so. I shall not therefore trouble your Majesty with fruitless repetitions of reasons and arguments. I cannot struggle against the difficulties of your Majesty's business and yourself at the same time; but I can keep my word to your Majesty.

I have no house in the world to go to, but my house at Newmarket, which I must own is not at this time like to be a place of much retirement; but I have no other. I have worn out my health, and almost my life, in the service of the Crown. I have served your Majesty faithfully to the best of my understanding, without any advantage to myself, except the honour of doing so, or without expecting any other favour than to end the small remainder of my days in liberty and quiet.[3]

There is no doubt that Godolphin was at the end of his resources. He longed to quit. Marlborough alone sustained him.

Marlborough to Godolphin

VILAINE
September 9

In yours of the 20th you say it would be an ease to you to retire from business, the weight of which you cannot bear, if you are not

[1] Coxe, iii, 96.
[2] The Queen's letter dated August 30 is in Add. MSS. 41340/1.
[3] Coxe, iii, 92-93.

allowed some assistance. I hope the Queen will do everything for your ease but that of parting with you, in which, should you have a serious thought, you could not justify yourself to God or man; for without flattery, as England is divided, there is nobody that can execute your place but yourself.[1]

And from Grametz on September 16:

> . . . I am positively of the opinion that should you quit the service of the Queen, you would not only disturb the affairs of England, but also the liberties of Europe; so that I conjure you not to have a thought of quitting till we have obtained a good peace; and then I hope the Queen's interest may be so well settled that she may allow of our living quietly. But as the affairs of Europe and those of the Queen in particular are at this time, I think both you and I are in conscience and honour bound to undergo all the dangers and troubles that is possible to bring this war to a happy end, which I think must be after the next campaign, if we can agree to carry it on with vigour.[2]

Finally: "Allow me to give you this assurance, that as I know you to be a sincere, honest man, may God bless me as I shall be careful *that whatever man is your enemy shall never be my friend.*"[3]

With the personal stresses at this height the Queen suffered as much as anyone. Towards the end of September she proposed a compromise to Godolphin. It was a hard thing, she said, to remove Sir Charles Hedges, and

> I can never look upon it other ways. As to my other difficulties concerning Lord Sunderland, I do fear for the reasons I have told you we shall never agree long together; and the making him Secretary, I can't help thinking, is throwing myself into the hands of a party. They desire this thing to be done, because else they say they can't answer that all their friends will go along with them this winter. If this be complied with, you will then, in a little time, find they must be gratified in something else, or they will not go on heartily in my business. You say yourself they will need my authority to assist them, which I take to be the bringing more of their friends into employment, and shall I not then be in their hands? If this is not being in the hands of a party, what is? I am as sensible as anybody can be of the services Lord Sunderland and all his friends have done me, and am very willing to show I am so, by doing anything they desire that is reasonable. Let me therefore beg of you once more to consider of the expedient I proposed, of bringing Lord Sunderland into the Cabinet council, with a pension, till some vacancy happens.

When I mentioned this before, I remember your objection against

[1] Coxe, iii, 97.   [2] *Ibid.*, 97-98.   [3] *Ibid.*, 103.

it was that so young a man taken into the Cabinet council, without having any post, might look more like an imposition upon me than a desire of my own. Maybe some people may find this fault; but I confess I can but think if he was made Secretary, others would say *that* were also an imposition upon me. One of these things would make me very easy, the other quite contrary; and why, for God's sake, may *I* not be gratified as well as other people? . . . If they are not satisfied with so reasonable a thing as this, it is very plain, in my poor opinion, nothing will satisfy them but having one entirely in their power.

This is a thing I have so much at my heart and upon which the quiet of my life depends that I must beg you, for Christ Jesus' sake, to endeavour to bring it about. I know very well that you do not serve for advantage or ambition, but with entire duty and affection, which makes me that I cannot bear the thoughts of parting with you; and I hope, after what the Duke of Marlborough has said to you, you will not think of it again, for to use his words, "you cannot answer it neither to God nor man, but are obliged both in conscience and honour not to do it." Let his words plead for her who will be lost and undone if you pursue this cruel intention.[1]

No one would have been more happy than Godolphin had it been in his power to accept this offer which had cost the Queen much to make. But the Whigs were inexorable. They had made what they considered a just and moderate claim. All had subscribed, and none would recede from it. They could hardly sympathize with the Queen's repugnance to them. The Treasurer's troubles were his own affair. As for Marlborough, surely his beloved wife spoke for him, and she was as keen as any. Thus they held to their demand.

Godolphin's misery presents itself vividly after two centuries. He could not bear to coerce the Queen. Wrong though she was, every loyalty in his nature revolted against the task. Well might he long for Newmarket, compared to such an odious duty. But Marlborough, British interests, and the allied cause would not let him go. This chivalrous, disinterested man, inspired by deep reverence for the Crown and by devotion to the Queen, wearied by so many years of service in four reigns, had now to compel the Queen to accept an intruder whom he himself distrusted, at the demand of a party with whom he had no tie save procuring the money votes for the war. Those who envy the glitter of great office are usually unseared by such ordeals. Godolphin remained to force Sunderland upon the Queen at the cost of his life's friendship with her.

[1] Coxe, iii, 104-106.

Finding nothing but despairing resistance from her Treasurer, Anne, obstinate to the end, knowing what he thought of the Whigs, regarding him but as their mechanical tool, finally appealed to Marlborough.

The Queen to Marlborough

September 10, 1706

. . . I have been considering the business we have so often spoke about ever since I saw you, and cannot but continue of the same mind that it is a great hardship to persuade anybody to part with a place they are in possession of, in hopes of another that is not yet vacant. Besides I must own freely to you I am of the opinion that making a party man Secretary of State, when there are so many of their friends in employment of all kinds already, is throwing myself into the hands of a party, which is a thing I have been desirous to avoid. Maybe some may think I would be willing to be in the hands of the Tories; but whatever people may say of me, I do assure you I am not inclined, nor never will be, to employ any of those violent persons that have behaved themselves so ill towards me. All I desire is my liberty in encouraging and employing all those that concur faithfully in my service whether they are called Whigs or Tories, not to be tied to one, nor the other; for if I should be so unfortunate as to fall into the hands of either, I shall not imagine myself, though I have the name of queen, to be in reality but their slave, which as it will be my personal ruin, so it will be the destroying all government; for instead of putting an end to faction, it will lay a lasting foundation for it.

You press the bringing Lord Sunderland into business, that there may be one of that party in a place of trust, to help carry on the business this winter; and you think if this is not complied with, they will not be hearty in pursuing my service in the Parliament. But is it not very hard that men of sense and honour will not promote the good of their country, because everything in the world is not done that they desire! when they may be assured Lord Sunderland shall come into employment as soon as it is possible. *Why, for God's sake, must I, who have no interest, no end, no thought, but for the good of my country, be made so miserable as to be brought into the power of one set of men? and why may not I be trusted, since I mean nothing but what is equally for the good of all my subjects?*

There is another apprehension I have of Lord Sunderland being Secretary, which I think is a natural one, which proceeds from what I have heard of his temper. I am afraid he and I should not agree long together, finding by experience my humour and those that are of a warmer will often have misunderstandings between one another. I could say a great deal more on this subject, but fear I have been too tedious already. Therefore I shall conclude, begging you to consider how to bring me out of my difficulties, and never leave my service, for Jesus Christ's sake; for besides the reason I give you in another letter, this is a blow I cannot bear.[1]

No one reading this able, powerful State paper can doubt the reality of the part played by Queen Anne. Marlborough allowed nearly a month to pass before he rejected this appeal of his sovereign and benefactress.

Marlborough to the Queen

October 7, 1706

As I am persuaded that the safety of your government and the quiet of your life depend very much upon the resolution you shall take at this time, I think myself bound in gratitude, duty, and conscience to let you know my mind freely; and that you may not suspect me of being partial, I take leave to assure you, in the presence of God, that I am not for your putting yourself into the hands of either party. But the behaviour of Lord Rochester, and all the hotheads of that party, is so extravagant that there is no doubt to be made of their exposing you and the liberties of England to the rage of France rather than not be revenged, as they call it. This being the case, there is a necessity, as well as justice in your following your inclinations in supporting Lord Treasurer, or all must go to confusion. As the humour is at present, he can't be supported but by the Whigs, for the others seek his destruction, which in effect is yours. Now pray consider, if he can, by placing some few about you, gain such a confidence as shall make your business and himself safe, will not this be the sure way of making him so strong that he may hinder your being forced into a party? I beg you will believe I have no other motive to say what I do, but my zeal for your person and friendship for a man whom I know to be honest and zealously faithful to you.[2]

Still the Queen resisted both Marlborough's advice and Godolphin's despair. Still the Whigs demanded their rights.

Marlborough to Godolphin

GRAMETZ
October 12

This has given me some trouble, but nothing of what I now feel by a letter I have received this morning from the Duchess, concerning the temper and resolutions of the Whigs, by which I see all things like to go to confusion. Yours of the same date mentions nothing of it, which makes me fear you have taken your resolution, which if it be to retire I must lay the consequence before you, which is that certainly the Dutch will make their peace, which will be of fatal consequence,

[1] Coxe, iii, 90–92. [2] *Ibid.*, 100–101.

especially considering the advantages we now have; for in all probability one year's war more would give ease to all Christendom for many years.[1]

And again, on the 14th:

You will have seen by my last how uneasy I was at some news I have heard from England. I shall continue so till I have your thoughts on that matter; for my trouble proceeds from my friendship to you, and my duty to the Queen. *For the consequences of what may happen to the rest of Europe, mankind must and will struggle for their own safety*; and for myself, I shall be happier in a retired life, when I have the Queen's and your leave for it.[2]

To Sarah he showed a sombre resolution.

CAMBRON
October 18

. . . I hope you will order it so that after I have been some days at London we may go to the lodge and be quiet, for I am quite weary of the world; and since I am afraid there is a necessity of my serving in this country as long as this war lasts, let me have a little more quiet in England than I have been used to have, and then I shall be the better able to go through what I must endure in this country; for upon the success we have had this year, our friends grow less governable than when they were afraid of the French. . . .

As I have no farther prospect of doing any more service to the public this campaign but that of putting Courtray in a condition, every day is very tedious; and for the two or three days I shall be at Brussels I shall be torn to pieces, there being twenty pretenders to every place that must be given; for I have not been able to prevail with the Deputies to declare them before my arrival, which would have given me ease.

I have already more than once writ my mind very freely, so that my conscience is at ease, though my mind is very far from it; for I did flatter myself that my zeal and sincerity for the Queen were so well known to her that my representations would have had more weight than I find they have. *But nothing can ever hinder me from being ready to lay down my life when she can think it for her service; for I serve [her] with an entire affection, as well as the utmost duty; for you and I, and all ours, would be the most ungrateful people that ever lived if we did not venture all for her good. By this, do not mistake me; for I am very sensible that if my Lord Treasurer be obliged to retire, I cannot serve in the Ministry.* But when these projectors have put all in confusion, I shall then readily not only venture my life, but all that I have, to show my gratitude. When the express comes by which I shall see all that has passed, I shall once

[1] Coxe, iii, 98.   [2] *Ibid.*, 14–15.

more write, as becomes me, and will yet hope it may have its effect; if not, God's will be done.[1]

And a few days later in response to her Whig girdings:

I have had the good luck to deserve better from all Englishmen than to be suspected of not being in the true interest of my country, which I am in, and ever will be, without being of a faction; and this principle shall govern me for the little remainder of my life. I must not think of being popular, but I shall have the satisfaction of going to my grave with the opinion of having acted as became an honest man; and if I have your esteem and love I shall think myself entirely happy.

. . . Since the resolution is taken to vex and ruin the Lord Treasurer because the Queen has not complied with what was desired for Lord Sunderland, I shall from henceforth despise all mankind, and think there is no such thing as virtue; for I know with what zeal the Lord Treasurer has pressed the Queen in that matter. I do pity him, and shall love him as long as I live, and never will be a friend to any that can be his enemy.

I have writ my mind very freely to the Queen on this occasion, so that, whatever misfortune may happen, I shall have a quiet mind, having done what I thought my duty. And as for the resolution of making me uneasy, I believe they will not have much pleasure in that, for as I have not set my heart on having justice done me, I shall not be disappointed, nor will I be ill-used by any man.[2]

Sarah forwarded the first of these letters to the Queen

Sarah to the Queen

Sunday morning, October 20, 1706

I must in the first place beg leave to remind you of the name of Mrs Morley, and of your faithful Freeman, because without that help I shall not be well able to bring out what I have to say. . . . I will tell you the greatest truths in the world, which seldom succeed with anybody so well as flattery. Ever since I received the enclosed letter from Mr Freeman I have been in dispute with myself whether I should send it to Mrs Morley or not, because his opinion is no news to you, and after the great discouragements I have met with only for being faithful to you, I concluded it was no manner of purpose to trouble you any more. But, reading the letter over and over, and finding he is convinced he must quit Mrs Morley's service if she will not be made sensible of the condition she is in, I have at last resolved to send it you; and you will see by it how full of gratitude Mr Freeman is by his expressions, which were never meant for Mrs Morley to see. He is

[1] Coxe, iii, 116–117.   [2] *Ibid.*, 101–102.

resolved to venture his life and fortune, whenever it can be of any use to you, and upon recalling everything to my memory that may fill my heart with all that passion and tenderness I had once for Mrs Morley I do solemnly protest I think I can no ways return what I owe her so well as by being plain and honest.

The sting was in the tail: "*As one mark of it, I desire you would reflect whether you have never heard that the greatest misfortunes that have ever happened to any of your family had not been occasioned by having ill-advice and an obstinacy in their tempers.*"[1] Anyone can see the harm that this would do. It probably destroyed the whole effect of Marlborough's moving words. What pleasure could the Queen derive from such a friend? What patience could survive such endless intimate assaults, what love such endless candour?

Marlborough put the practical point with deep respect but uncommon bluntness.

Marlborough to the Queen

CAMBRON
October 24

. . . The Lord Treasurer assures me that any other measures but those he has proposed must ruin your business, and oblige him to quit his staff, which would be a great trouble to him, and I am afraid will have the fatal consequence of putting you into the hands of a party, which God only knows how you would then be able to get out of it. It is true that your reign has been so manifestly blessed by God that one might reasonably think you might govern without making use of the heads of either party, but as it might be easy to yourself. This might be practicable if both parties sought your favour, as in reason and duty they ought. But, madam, the truth is that the heads of one party have declared against you and your government, as far as it is possible, without going into open rebellion. *Now, should Your Majesty disoblige the others, how is it possible to obtain near five millions for carrying on the war with vigour, without which all is undone.*

. . . As I would in return for your many favours die to make you and your Government easy, makes me take the liberty, with all submission on my knees, to beg for your own sake, the good of your country, and all the liberties of Europe, that you would not lose one day in giving the Lord Treasurer that necessary assistance he thinks proper, for carrying on of your business in Parliament, by which you will not only enable him to make your business go well, but also that of governing the only party that can be made use of. I am very confident the Lord Treasurer thinks he shall be able to govern them to your

[1] Strickland, *Lives of the Queens of England*, viii, 163.

ͻatisfaction, or he would not say so much as he does; and as for myself, I beg your Majesty's justice in believing that I shall take all the care I can to make them sensible of the obligations they have to you, so that you may never have reason to repent the measures, I hope in God, you will now take.[1]

Thus deprived of her last hope, the Queen gave way. Many strongholds fell as the result of Ramillies; many dangers to the Grand Alliance passed away. The power of England mounted in the world. The union with Scotland was sealed. But more difficult to pluck than any of the other fruits of victory was the appointment of Sunderland. There is no doubt that an immense volume of English opinion supported the Queen in her resolves to have a national rather than a party Administration. The bitterness and ambitions of both factions were dreaded by all outside their ranks. The extreme politics of either would throw the whole country into turmoil. But this was not the case that had yet arisen. It was an extremely modest request for a party which dominated both branches of the Legislature and represented half of the nation that one of their members should have high executive office. The issue was in fact painfully simple: Anne was a Stuart, and England was ungovernable except by Parliament.

For four months the Queen had withstood all her advisers as well as the broad facts of politics. It was now the end of October. The meeting of Parliament approached, when even Stuarts must face realities. Yet it was not till December 3 that Sunderland received Hedges' seals as Secretary of State. He shared that office with Harley, who had hitherto been a deeply attentive spectator. The Whigs had gained their point; they were jubilant, discreet, and helpful. They had, to use terms which in those days were familiar to the educated world, captured the counterscarp and entered the covered way. They paused, as the Queen had so clearly foreseen, only to regather their forces for a more decisive assault. The casualties were grievous. The loyalties of the Cockpit circle were destroyed. The friendship between Anne and Sarah was finally ruptured. Godolphin's favour had withered. Only Marlborough, resplendent in the field, vital to every party and to every combination, still preserved a solid claim in the Queen's regard; and even here there was a change. The Whig Junto observed these losses, and bore them stoically. They fell upon others. But this was not the end.

[1] Coxe, iii, 117-119.

Where should the Queen turn? She was amazed that her old friends should use her thus. Surely they might be contented with their great commands and offices, and with the favour and affection she had shown them. Why must they force this obnoxious Whig into her circle? Was there no one who would stand by her? Such a one undoubtedly there was. We have seen how Harley had felt uncomfortable since the results of the 1705 election had produced a Whig Parliament. It must be emphasized that his attitude in these early stages of the quarrel was reasonable, consistent, and sincere. His admiration for Marlborough, though often fulsomely expressed, was genuine. On the main issues he agreed with the Marlborough-Godolphin policy. With his unrivalled Parliamentary knowledge, he understood every move in the Whig game. He did not mean to become their prisoner. Not for him the plight of Godolphin, who now had no party whom he could join or to whom he could make his way back. Never would he put himself at the mercy of the Whigs. Never would he break the ties which joined him to the Tories. Neither would he separate himself from that considerable body of Tory moderates who had followed him so faithfully, and had proved of invaluable support to the Government. The intrusion of Sunderland might be accepted; but if it was, as seemed to him certain, only the first step to general Whig supremacy, he would oppose the process at every stage.

Anne therefore found in her Secretary of State a very able Minister, admittedly master of House of Commons politics, who spontaneously sympathized with her feelings and took her view. When she talked with Godolphin everything ran against the grain. When she talked with Harley she felt he understood her distress, and she was fortified in her convictions by the vast knowledge and good sense of this admirable servant. Godolphin vexed her. Harley soothed her. To consult with the Treasurer became a duty. To consult with the Secretary of State became a relief.

Harley was not at this stage disloyal to Godolphin, nor did he encourage the Queen to resist his advice. But swiftly and surely there grew up between him and the Queen an easy, confidential relation. It was impossible that this should be lost upon Godolphin. Harassed with the uphill work he had to do, and with the latent insecurities of his own position, he was not unnaturally suspicious of his powerful colleague, renowned for craft. He could not fail to understand that but for Marlborough—there was his rock—he would have been supplanted. To resign is one thing, to be forced out another. The relations of the two Ministers became less cordial. They were soon to become bleak. It was but a step from a perfectly just appreciation of the facts for Godolphin to believe that Harley was adding to his difficulties with the Queen, and seeking to oust him from her favour by intrigue. Nor was this further conclusion long to be untrue. Less than a year had to pass before Harley became Godolphin's rival and foe.

Nevertheless Harley in the autumn of 1706 had no reason to reproach himself. He believed his views were right. He was sure the war could not be carried on except with the support of the moderate Tories. Let the Government once fall into the hands of the Whigs and there would be an end to national unity upon the war. The Tories, banned from office, would be openly and whole-heartedly a peace party. Harley was the first English statesman to systematize his contacts with public opinion. He had, as we have seen, a regular staff, including men as brilliant as Defoe, who moved continually about the country, and reported to him what they heard and saw. He learned—and he did not hide his knowledge from the Queen—that there was much war-weariness beneath the surface. Nothing, of course, could stand against glorious episodes like Ramillies and Turin. At any moment in the campaigning season these tremendous generals might produce some prodigy, and all men would follow their triumphal car. Therefore it was necessary to proceed with all propriety and prudence. But if, which God forfend, misfortune overtook the arms of the Allies, or a cannon-ball cut off the Captain-General's head instead of that of his equerry, the peace party, which was the Tory Party, would become very powerful. It must not lack a responsible leader. Surely all this ran along the high road of public duty. If the Queen began to like him better than she did the Treasurer, was it for him, in these days when favour was so much, to complain of it?

Parliament did not meet till December. By that time the Parliament of Scotland had carried the decisive article of the Treaty of Union adopting the Hanoverian succession. Thus fortified, the English Cabinet could plan the session around the final Act which ratified and solemnized the creation of the United Kingdom of Great Britain. The Whigs, squared by Sunderland's appointment, made haste to prove what their friendship was worth. The Queen's Speech was for war to such a finish that "it shall no longer be at the pleasure of one prince to disturb the repose, and endanger the liberties, of this part of the world." Both Houses acclaimed these sentiments. In unanimous addresses they declared their gratitude to the Queen for her conduct of national affairs, their joy at the glories of the campaign, and their admiration for the achievements of the Duke of Marlborough. To back words with deeds, the Commons proceeded forthwith to vote the unprecedented Army and Navy supply of six million pounds for the hearty prosecution of the war. When Queen Anne went down to the House of Lords to give her assent to these startling Money Bills the Speaker said, on submitting them to her, "As in the glorious victory of Ramillies it was so surprising that the battle was fought before it could be thought that the armies were in the field, so it was no less surprising that the Commons had granted supplies to her Majesty before her enemies could well know that her Parliament was sitting."[1]

The opposition of the irreconcilable Tories did not venture to show its head until the stage of details was reached. It asserted its vitality upon a supplementary estimate for the overspending of nearly a million pounds in the previous year, largely upon the payment of the German contingents with which Prince Eugene had conquered Italy. The Whig leaders allowed this debate to develop before they declared their position, in order no doubt to keep Godolphin alive to his dependence upon them. On this occasion Harley intervened dramatically. Although so ill that he had been bled the day before, he came down to the House to defend the treaties which had led to the excess expenditure. In his final words he craved leave to withdraw from the debate because of his weakness. He did not know, he said, whether he would recover from his illness. If not, he asked for an inscription on his tomb that he was one of those who had advised the Queen to spend these sums of money in the public service. The Whigs rolled up upon this wave of emotion, and it was voted by 253 to 105 that the money had been expended for the security and honour of the nation.

Nevertheless, Marlborough came home from the most fortunate of all the campaigns of the Grand Alliance and from his year of noblest service to an altered scene. Europe saw him at the summit of glory. Abroad all the doubters were convinced; in London all the detractors were for the moment silenced. Both Houses of Parliament received him with addresses of unbounded admiration. The pension refused in 1702, settled only for his life in 1704, was now, with his titles and estates, made perpetual upon his heirs, male or

[1] Lediard, ii, 150.

female, for ever, "in order," as the statute set forth, "that the memory of these deeds should never lack one of his name to bear it." The City welcomed him with spacious hospitality. The common people gazed upon him as a prodigy and cheered him as their protector. The captured standards of Ramillies could not be hung in Westminster Hall: it was already decked with the standards of Blenheim. To the Guildhall therefore the splendid cavalcade made its way, and here were displayed the trophies of the second greatest defeat which the arms of France in the reign of Louis XIV sustained. Amid thunderous salutes of cannon all the notables of British life knelt in thanksgiving in St Paul's Cathedral on New Year's Eve in celebration of "the wonderful year" that had ended.

But underneath all was insecure. The Queen's heart was estranged. The Tories saw themselves definitely consolidating as an Opposition. Harley and St John began to look about them.

Chapter Twelve

MARLBOROUGH AND CHARLES XII

1707—SPRING

DISASTER is the name affixed by history to the Allies' campaign of 1707. On the Rhine, on the Riviera, and in Spain the French won or even triumphed. In Flanders, the main theatre, where the best and far the largest armies faced each other, where Marlborough commanded, no victory was gained. At the same time the slow, subtle processes by which Marlborough's foundations in England were sapped made steady progress, and grew from an intrigue into a crisis. At the end of 1706 the Grand Alliance was once again found incapable of enduring success. Each partner was balancing the hopes of extortionate gains against the risks of a separate peace. Ramillies and its companion Turin had removed from short-sighted Governments the fear of general defeat at the hands of France. The war was hard and long. Why pursue the theme of victory farther? The cruel need which had called into being the disjointed federation of so many states, kingdoms, republics, empires, principalities, had been banished by the swords of Marlborough and Eugene. The temptation to rush for the spoil, to grab and depart, was strong. The Dutch could have their dyke; Austria saw herself mistress of Italy; Prussia was sure of important satisfactions in status and in territory; Germany, incoherent and ineffectual, at this time felt scarcely less fear of Charles XII than of Louis XIV. Thus every common impulse was relaxed, every contribution was neglected, and every preparation for 1707 delayed.

But the power of France was still unbroken. Louis XIV was forming his armies for the new campaign. Twenty-one thousand militia were drafted into the front line. Vendôme and the Elector in Flanders, Villars on the Upper Rhine, Noailles in Roussillon, Tessé in Dauphiné, and Berwick and the Duke of Orleans in Spain confronted the Allies. The Great King sought peace, but still only a French peace: and at any moment a turn of fortune would revive his full claims. Between equals and similars there always is much to be said for peace even through a drawn war; but to a wide, numerous, disconnected coalition, faced by a homogeneous military nation and a grand autocracy, a drawn war embodied in a treaty spelt permanent defeat. One man, still carrying with him the British island in its most remarkable efflorescence of genius and energy, stood against this kind of accommodation. Marlborough, harassed and hampered upon every side, remained unexhausted and all-compelling.

After the day at Blenheim had shifted the axis of the war he had planned the decisive invasion of France by the Moselle. In the sun-shine of unhoped-for prosperity the German states had failed him. The surest, easiest road into France would never be trodden by the Allies. The chance had fled. But now 1706 had restored the Blen-heim situation, and once again he formed a plan which if it were executed—as with ordinary loyalties it could be—would bend or break France to the will of England. This plan lay in that high region of strategy where all the forces are measured and all the impulsions understood. Since it had proved impossible to lead Germany into France directly by the Moselle, a wider operation was required. His conception was now a double invasion from north and south. This used the resources, the war-will of England, and above all her supreme naval power, at the highest pitch. With his present ascendancy in Holland, with his redcoats and the British-paid contingents and subsidies, Marlborough and the Dutch would hold and press hard upon the principal army of France in the fortress zone of the Netherlands. Simultaneously Eugene, with the forces of the Empire sustained by the allied mercenaries and the whole strength of the English and Dutch fleets in the Mediterranean, and based upon sea-borne supplies and munitions, would invade France from the south. For this purpose they must first of all seize a safe fortified harbour through which the amphibious power of England could exert itself to the full, and also animate the Imperial armies. The mighty French monarchy would be taken between hammer and anvil. This he deemed would be irresistible and final.

According to the recognized and enduring conventions of war, an attack on a central body by opposite forces can normally be met by the simple expedient of masking both assailants, and organizing a mobile central force which can be thrown against either in over-whelming strength as opportunity suggests. But this school-book diagram, like all other strategic manœuvres, is governed by the facts of time, distance, and numbers. When the two fronts threatened are so far apart that it takes many weeks to transfer troops from the one to the other, and when the weight of the two attacks or invasions is almost insupportable in either quarter, the manœuvre which looks so obvious and has so often succeeded in a restricted theatre ceases to work. The separate inroads forge ahead, and no decisively superior concentration can be made against either. This was the basis of Marlborough's strategy for the year 1707. But all hung on the sea base. And there was only one. Toulon must be taken: it must become the root of an immense rodent growth in the bowels of France, leading to a fatal collapse either on the northern or the southern front, or perhaps on both. Here was the way to achieve the full purpose of the Allies and finish the war.

This scheme, for which Marlborough toiled and ran great and drawn-out hazards, reveals to us his true views about the Spanish theatre. We have seen him repeatedly and genuinely supporting the war in Spain, always ready to send trusted generals and good, sorely needed troops from England or from Flanders to the Peninsula: always ready to accept this large, costly, and disconnected diversion. Although, as has been shown, there were substantial offsets, such a policy cannot easily be reconciled with the canons of true strategy. Political and commercial factors had launched the Allies into a great war in Spain. Not only the Tory Party, but on the whole the bulk of English opinion, preferred an alliance with Portugal and an expedition to Spain to the grim ding-dong in Flanders. To Parliament Spain seemed the easy and clever road. It was in fact an additional detour on a journey already only too long. Why, then, did our great commander acquiesce so tamely in this questionable exertion? Did he agree or did he submit? There is no doubt that he submitted. He paid off at great cost Tory and English prejudices, and did the best he could with what was left. Otherwise even that might have been lost.

But now we shall see how truly he measured the war in Spain. The capture of Toulon and a real thrust up towards Lyons into the vitals of Southern France would, in his judgment, instantly clear Spain. The French, no matter how few there were to drive them, would flow out of the Peninsula as naturally as water flows out of a cistern when its bottom tap is opened. Therefore in the winter of 1706–7 Marlborough's central aim became the siege and capture of Toulon.

* * * * *

The victory at Turin had roused Victor Amadeus to a high degree of war vigour and of territorial desire. He hoped to have the concessions he had been promised in Lombardy endorsed by treaty with the French, and to spread his sovereignty in Provence by conquest. He was therefore eager to invade Southern France. All his ideas and efforts were in harmony with Marlborough's plans. The Empire, on the other hand, had contrary ambitions. After the rough treatment they had received from the Dutch in Belgium, and with the proofs of extreme Dutch claims about the Barrier before their eyes, they were resolved to take physical possession not only of Lombardy, but also of the Kingdom of Naples. They were not interested in aiding the general victory by carrying the war into Southern France. They developed an obstinate resistance even to the transfer to Savoy of those parts of Lombardy which had been specifically promised to Victor Amadeus in the original treaty by which he had joined the Grand Alliance. Naples, as a conquest or at least as a counter for the peace treaty, now became their supreme desire. The whole urge of the Imperialist policy was therefore divergent from the purpose of common victory which Marlborough steadfastly pursued.

As early as December 6, 1706, Marlborough wrote a guarded but none the less pointed letter to Wratislaw in which he complained of the ill-treatment by the Empire of the Duke of Savoy, and hinted that he might not be able to prevent the twenty-eight thousand Prussians, Palatines, and Hessians in the pay of the Sea Powers, without whom the victorious campaign of Turin could never have been undertaken, being withdrawn at the instance of the Dutch from the Italian theatre, unless the Imperialist efforts were loyally devoted to the common cause, and justice done to Savoy.[1] The Imperial Court were alive to the consequences of this threat, which was, in fact, the only lever which Marlborough could use upon them. Nevertheless, they were recalcitrant in the last degree. They retarded every concession to Savoy; they raised every possible objection to the invasion of Provence and the siege of Toulon; and they remained bent above all things on the seizure of Naples. Upon this last forward project they paraded an additional grievance. Peterborough, during his self-imposed mission to the Duke of Savoy in the autumn of 1706, had without the slightest authority held out expectations of a landing force of five thousand British troops for the capture of Naples. Marlborough rejected this

[1] *Dispatches*, iii, 245.

demand on the very same day (December 11) that it was presented to him in London, and wrote to Eugene accordingly.[1] He insisted upon the siege of Toulon, and refused to countenance the excursion to Naples. An acrimonious correspondence ensued in which, in language which became increasingly blunt, he reminded Wratislaw of the immense aid which the Sea Powers were rendering to the Empire, of its helplessness if that aid were withdrawn, and of the grievous disappointment of the Allies at the failure of the Emperor's war-effort.

It was impossible for the Imperialists to march on Naples unless the English Fleet by its command of the sea prevented French sea-borne reinforcements forestalling the long, slow overland expedition. This potent factor, added to the menace of the withdrawal of the troops of the Sea Powers, forced the Emperor to transfer some of the fortresses of Lombardy to the Duke of Savoy, and to agree to the Toulon plan. But nothing could persuade him to abandon the design upon Naples. Early in February Marlborough made a detailed written agreement with Victor Amadeus for the attack upon Toulon. England would furnish forty ships of the line to sustain the advance along the Riviera of the Savoyard and Imperialist troops. The fleet would supply money, powder, and food upon a very large scale. It would land cannon and sailors in strong force for the siege and the preliminary operations. Article XV was laconic and precise: "The proposed expedition to Naples is excluded, being judged at the present time impracticable, and harmful to the interests of the campaign in France."[2]

This document was presented to Vienna as decisive upon the controversy. Confronted with a virtual ultimatum, the Imperial Court behaved in the worst manner. They agreed sullenly to allow their troops to share in the Toulon expedition, and to the vital point that Prince Eugene should command it. They persisted in their plans against Naples. They were taking a far more disloyal and selfish step. They entered ardently into a military convention with France which resulted in the Treaty of Milan. This amounted to a separate local peace. The Emperor agreed with Louis XIV to close down the Italian front altogether. The twenty thousand French troops who were blockaded in the various fortresses of Northern Italy and must in a few months have become prisoners of war

---

[1] *Dispatches*, iii, 250.

[2] *Feldzüge*, Series I, ix, 335 *et seq.* Printed from the copy communicated by Victor Amadeus to Prince Eugene, January-February 1707.

were accorded free passage to rejoin the main hostile armies. Portions of them reinforced Vendôme in Flanders; the rest strengthened Marshal Tessé, who was guarding the passes of the French southern front.

The history of all coalitions is a tale of the reciprocal complaints of allies; but the conduct of the Imperial Court at this juncture stands forth remarkably as an example of wanton, reckless self-seeking. If the Dutch were too narrowly set upon their Barrier, if English ambitions sought a disproportionate humiliation of France, at least the Sea Powers backed their aims with enormous and generous exertions for the common cause. But the Empire, saved from disaster in Bavaria in 1704, restored to success in Italy in 1706 by the resources of England and Holland, dependent upon them not only for the inestimable prizes to which it aspired, but also for its very existence, stands guilty of folly and ingratitude of the basest kind.

Through all this Marlborough, working from a distance, using his control in London and his influence at The Hague, strove tirelessly for the larger strategy of the war. His faith was in Eugene. In 1706 he had provided him with the core and substance of the army which had conquered at Turin. In 1707 he placed at his disposal overwhelming naval power, and encouraged him by every practical means to strike another equally glorious and possibly final blow for the allied cause at Toulon. "I not only esteem, but really love that Prince." To arm him for another splendid achievement he would be himself content to face Vendôme with a smaller army and to conduct a campaign in Flanders under most unpromising conditions. Never mind! He would manage it somehow, and far to the south his great comrade would gather the fruits which would make amends for all. We shall presently recount how these hopes were blighted.

During the successes of 1706 the Northern War encroached ever nearer to the main quarrel. Charles XII was now at his zenith. His triumphs over the Russians were followed at the beginning of 1706 by his crushing defeat of King Augustus of Poland, also Elector of Saxony, at the battle of Fraustadt (February 13). At the head of his veteran and victorious Swedish army Charles marched into Saxony, and, establishing himself at Altranstädt, a few miles from Leipzig, proceeded to exact his terms. These were at once humiliating and sinister. Augustus must renounce his title to the crown of

Poland. He must recognize Charles's nominee, Stanislaus, as Polish king. He must write personally to felicitate him. He must abandon the Russian alliance. In order to make his breach with Russia mortal, he must perform a deed of infamy which the Czar could never forgive, which, indeed, destroyed all basis of faith and honour between the Saxon and the Russian Courts. He must surrender Patkul.

The reader will remember how Patkul, a Livonian patriot and Swedish subject, in revenge for his own and his country's ill-usage had made himself the mainspring of the coalition against Charles XII. The influence which this impressive personage, waging what was almost a private war, had been able to exert upon so many states and princes was a remarkable feature in these times. Patkul was now General and Plenipotentiary of the Czar. He was his envoy to the Court of King Augustus. He had come there in the sanctity of laws and customs sacred even to barbarian rulers. Although his diplomacy had latterly been tortuous, he had entered Saxony as a friend and ally. King Augustus must now deliver him foully and treacherously to the vengeance of Charles XII. That there might be no hitch in the execution of these grisly terms, a final condition prescribed that the Swedish army should have free quarters in Saxony during the winter of 1706–7, levying their contributions on the countryside by force in so far as their needs were not supplied by the Saxon Government. It was not till September 1706 that Augustus could subjugate himself to these conditions. By the Treaty of Altranstädt he bowed to his fate and his shame. At midnight on April 7, 1707, the Swedish general Meyerfeld halted before the gates of Königstein with a band of soldiers. Patkul, who had been for some months detained in the fortress and had neglected a proffered opportunity to escape, was handed over to Charles's representative, and forthwith chained hand and foot as a Swedish deserter and high traitor. From the King of Sweden's point of view this was no doubt a true bill. After some months of rigorous confinement and a vain hunger-strike Patkul was brought before a Swedish court martial, and thereafter the General and Ambassador of Peter the Great was broken upon the wheel and expired in excruciating torment.

Charles XII was now twenty-five. Encamped in the heart of Germany at the head of forty thousand devoted, ruthless, athletic, disciplined Swedish co-adventurers whom no troops had yet been able to withstand, he became the object of the most earnest anxiety, and solicitation from all parts of Central Europe. He recognized no law but his grand caprice; and Christendom, divided against itself, competed for his sword. It was no easy matter to obtain access to him. He lived the life of a general on active service. He saw no ambassadors, and referred all diplomatic notes to Stockholm, where nothing could be settled without his approval. Louis XIV had already sent M. Besenval to wait at his tent-pegs. The Swedish King found it difficult to decide between his various revenges and opportunities. His hatred for the Czar was equalled by his hatred for King Augustus. His dislike of France and the religious persecutions of Louis XIV was matched by his many points of quarrel with the Empire. He conceived himself the champion of Protestantism, particularly of the Lutheran Churches. Personal brawls and fisticuffs had flared up between his agents and the Imperial representatives. An Imperial ambassador had received a box on the ear. There were tangled disputes with the Emperor about Muscovite troops who had taken refuge in the Reich, about supplies, and of course religion. To which quarter would Charles XII turn his fierce and as yet invincible bayonets? Throughout all Germany in the winter of 1706 this was the main preoccupation. To the Sea Powers it was a monstrous irrelevance. But there he poised, with the choice of plunging into the Russian wilderness or marching into the very heart of world affairs.

We shall not weary the reader with the intricate details of the disputes and negotiations which centred round the youthful conqueror's tent. The main outlines will suffice. Marlborough was alarmed at Charles XII's attitude as early as September 1706. "I am very much afraid," he wrote to Heinsius, "that this march of the Sweeds [*sic*] into Saxe will create a great degree of trouble. . . . Whenever the States or England write to the King of Sweden, there must be care taken that there be no threats in the letter, for the King of Sweden is of a very particular humor."[1]

In February he wrote again to the Pensionary:

If you thought it might be of any advantage to the Public, I should not scruple the trouble of a journey as far as Saxony, to wait on the King, and endeavour, if need be, to set him right, or at least to penetrate his design, that we may take the justest measures we can not to be surprised. I have mentioned this to nobody here, neither will, till I have your opinion. . . .[2]

[1] Vreede, pp. 117-118.   [2] February 17, 1708; *ibid.*, p. 220.

There was a general feeling in the shuddering Courts of Germany and in the dour Cabinets of the Sea Powers that Marlborough, with his military glamour and almost equally renowned diplomatic arts, was the man who of all others could penetrate the King's designs, could tip the balance, if it were possible, and cushion this formidable, romantic, ruffianly genius and his grim phalanx into the Russian wastes. Accordingly on April 20 the Captain-General set off in his coach from The Hague through Hanover to the tent of Charles XII. Many picturesque accounts have been given of their meeting, which fascinated contemporary Europe as a "topic of wonder" to all men. They met as commanding generals each fresh from glowing victories. Whatever effects could be produced depended upon personal contact. Biographers of Marlborough usually claim that his mission at once transformed the purposes of Charles XII. This seems unreasonable. It established a relationship upon which Marlborough negotiated all the summer with results which eventually reached their conclusion in 1709 upon the battlefield of Pultawa.

The interest for our purpose which attaches to the details of the meeting is Marlborough's personal demeanour and management When he arrived at Altranstädt from his tiringjourney through. Hanover he went to see Count Piper, who was a kind of Prime Minister to Charles XII. The Count, for reasons which are not worth examining, sent out word to say that he was engaged, and kept Marlborough in his coach waiting half an hour behind his appointment. Then the Swede, having asserted his dignity, came down the steps of his house to the gate to receive Queen Anne's envoy. Marlborough got out of the coach at the same moment and, putting on his hat, walked past Count Piper without recognizing him or saluting him, and turned aside on to the grass "as if to make water."[1] After a delay more protracted than would have seemed necessary he came back into the path, and with courtly gestures and ceremonious phrasing began his embassy. Count Piper meanwhile had stood embarrassed in the roadway.

A good general would probably have the knack of retorting affronts so as to retain for himself the advantages of a discussion. There was a day when Murat and Joseph Bonaparte forced themselves upon Napoleon in his bedroom. The Emperor was standing by a large hip-bath filled to the brim with hot water, and as his defence against this intrusion of public business into private affairs

---

[1] Lediard, ii, 167. He was at Altranstädt at the time, and is a credible witness.

had only his towel. The others were dressed in full uniform of blue and gold for a great parade. As they approached him Napoleon threw himself back into the hip-bath and splashed them from head to foot, while, being in a state of nature himself, he underwent no corresponding disadvantage. He then proceeded to deal with the matter in hand.

Charles XII and Marlborough were interested in each other— the first a knight-errant pursuing glory through all hazards, at all costs, and irrespective of reward; the other the statesman and commander, trying to shield large public purposes from capricious disturbance. Charles stands for all time as an example of the firmness of the human soul under every freak of fortune. John was a monument of practical sagacity. The young King, since he leaped from his throne at the throat of Europe at seventeen, had only experienced measureless triumph. The elderly General, reared as a courtier, with all the ups and downs of a lengthening life behind him—a little heavy with the weight of all that weighed upon him, and webbed by the combinations of which he was the motive power —had a different status and outlook. But War and Victory were a theme, a basis, and a bond. At their meeting Marlborough presented a letter from Queen Anne: "Had her sex not prevented it, she would have crossed the sea to visit a prince admired by the whole universe. I am in this particular more happy than the Queen, and I wish I could serve in some campaign under so great a commander that I might learn what I yet want to know in the art of war."[1] Charles XII appeared to accept the compliment, and it was frequently repeated by his devoted army. He was not to be easily flattered, and it is said that he deemed it overdone. He thought, we learn from Voltaire, that Marlborough in his scarlet uniform and Garter star and riband looked less like a soldier than he himself in his austere dress and with his studied abhorrence of all show.

Marlborough, for his part, took trouble during his stay to find out personally and through his officers about the Swedish army. What was it worth? How could it be dealt with, if need be? He found the Rev. John Robinson, the English envoy to Sweden, an invaluable companion. Robinson, who had thirty years' experience of the Swedish Court, has left various letters upon the visit. He says that Marlborough remarked about the Swedish army, "It has no artillery-train, no hospitals, no magazines. It is an army which lives on what it finds, *et qui dans une guerre de chicane périrait bientôt.*"

[1] Lediard, ii, 166.

Even the captious Klopp is provoked to comment, "These seem to be the words of a soothsayer."[1] In fact Marlborough was measuring the ugly, but none the less possible, prospect of having to deal professionally with an abominable disturbance of the War of the Spanish Succession.

Often in the casual remarks of great men one learns their true mind in an intimate way. In this expression "*a war of chicane*" there lies a fund of reflection. A war of chicane is a war of artifice and bickering, of pettifogging even, a war where a fortnight's delay before some awkward lines or fortress would run an enemy short of bread or cash, a war where time would count more than action, a baffling war; a war of deadlocks, a war where the enemy must face continually an ebbing tide. This was not Marlborough's kind of war. He was entirely modern. The offensive, the aggressive, the grand, sharp decision in the open field, and the rest would follow, as Napoleon would say, *par surcroît*. But if nothing could be done with the King of Sweden, *a war of chicane* was the war which Marlborough and his friend Eugene, with many a comprehending nod, might find themselves not incapable of waging against him.

The meeting was, however, both memorable and important. The two men had a long talk about what they understood best. Marlborough spoke French, which the King understood but did not speak, and Robinson translated the Royal replies. Charles XII, with the reports of Blenheim and Ramillies in his mind, asked whether, and if so why, Marlborough thought it necessary to charge at the head of his troops. Marlborough replied in effect, "Only because otherwise they would not think so much of me." The King agreed with this. They were together for about four hours, until, in fact, his Majesty's "kettledrums called him to prayers."

Marlborough to Godolphin

KING OF SUEDENS QUARTERS

April 16 [1707]

★I gote to this place last night so early as to have one hours Conversation with Comte Pyper, and this morning a litle after ten I waitted on his Maty. He keep me with him til his hour of dyning which was at twelf, and as I am told set longer at diner by half an hour, then he used to do. He also took me again into his Chamber wher wee Continued for above an hour, and then his kettledroms called him to prayers. Mr Robinson was with mee all the time, so that I must refere

[1] Klopp, xii, 387.

You to the account he gives the Secretary,[1] for I am come soe lait into my Quarters, that I have not time to send for a Copie of his letter, nor to say more to You, than that I am in hopes my Journey may do good.[2]

The King expected Marlborough to make him proposals upon the international situation, but all accounts show that Marlborough kept entirely upon personal and professional ground. He did not even, though he had been pressed to do so, presume to intercede on behalf of Patkul. Voltaire in his romantic but none the less profound *Histoire de Charles XII* wrote:

> Marlborough, who was never in a haste to make his proposals, and who, by a long course of experience, had learned the art of diving into the real characters of men, and discovering the connexion between their most secret thoughts and their actions, gestures, and discourse, studied the King with close attention. When he spoke to him of war in general, he thought he perceived in his Majesty a natural aversion to France, and noticed that he talked with pleasure of the conquests of the Allies. He mentioned the Czar to him, and observed that his eyes always kindled at the name, notwithstanding the calm tone of the conversation. He remarked, besides, a map of Russia lying on a table. He wanted no more to convince him that the real design and sole ambition of the King of Sweden was to dethrone the Czar, as he had done the King of Poland. He divined that if Charles remained in Saxony it was only to impose some hard conditions on the Emperor of Germany. He knew the Emperor would make no resistance, and so the whole affair would be wound up without difficulty. He left Charles, therefore, to follow his own bent; and, satisfied with having read his mind, made him no proposals.[3]

Voltaire asserts that this version was given him by Sarah after Marlborough's death.

It is alleged that more precise methods were adopted with Count Piper; that he was bribed with large or at least substantial sums of money to push his master to the east instead of to the west. Historical argument has developed about this, and no one would wish to do injustice to the memory of the gallant, faithful servitor of Charles XII, who became one of the many victims of the defeat at Pultawa in 1709. But we know that Marlborough made arrange-

---

[1] In *Dispatches*, iii, 347–348.

[2] Blenheim MSS. This letter seems to dispose of Voltaire's story, against which Lediard argues at length, that Marlborough did not visit Count Piper immediately on arriving, but first addressed himself to Count Piper's subordinate, Baron Gortz. See Lediard, ii, 165 *et seq.*

[3] Voltaire, *Histoire de Charles XII*, in *Œuvres Complètes* (1878), xvi, Part 2, 225.

ments to procure considerable sums of money for this avowed purpose before starting on his mission; and there is a matter-of-fact business letter from him on July 9, 1708, to Mr Secretary Boyle which contains the following blunt paragraph: "As to what you mentioned in your former relating to Count Piper and the two other Swedish Ministers, it is very true what Mr Robinson writes that they were promised the yearly allowance of £2500; but whatever may be thought fit hereafter, I do not see any necessity for the present payment of it."[1] Most people nowadays will consider this decisive upon the point.[2]

The practice of Ministers receiving gifts from foreign Powers in the course of negotiations was not unusual, and often known and tolerated by their masters. Torcy accustomed himself to mention his receipts to Louis XIV. The entry of Portugal into the war had been preceded by a veritable auction. Stanhope in this same year 1707 accompanied the commercial treaty which he obtained from Charles III by substantial payments to Count and Countess Oropeza.[3] At the moment in Leipzig Besenval, the French envoy, had received precise instructions from Versailles. "If the King of Sweden helps to bring about the general peace of Europe, the King of [France] will reward the labours of Count Piper, and his Majesty has already taken the resolution of giving him 300,000 livres as a reward for his exertions."[4] Against this were the English counter-offers.

It must not, however, be inferred that any of these payments induced their recipients to fail in their duty. Other and far more drastic processes awaited such defaults. In almost every case the Ministers did their work in accordance with their country's interests or with the wishes of the sovereigns they served; but they were very glad to be able to pick up large sums of money from one side or other, or preferably from both, in the course of their public duties, according to the lax conventions of that age. These gains were regarded as no less respectable than the large profits which nowadays so often come to the organizers of a sound and

[1] *Dispatches*, iv, 100.

[2] But see also a letter from Robinson to Harley: "LEIPZIG
"*April* 19/30

"By his Grace's orders I have acquainted Count Piper, M. Hermeline and Cederheilm that her Majesty will give yearly pensions: to the first £1500 and to each of the other £500; but the second for the first time £1000, and that the first payment should be made without delay." (Quoted in "Marlborough and Charles XII," *Transactions of the Royal Historical Society*, vol. xii (New Series).)

[3] See B. Williams, *Stanhope*, pp. 60–61.

[4] *Instructions des Ambassadeurs de France*, "Suède," p. 229.

successful flotation in the markets. The facts should nevertheless be recorded.

The day after the talk of the two warriors Charles XII set off according to his custom (and Napoleon's) at full gallop for Leipzig, where he had arranged to meet Augustus, dethroned King of Poland and vanquished, but still ruling, Elector of Saxony. More than that, Stanislaus, Charles XII's nominee and actual holder of the Polish crown, was in attendance. Queen Anne had not recognized this usurping pawn of the Swedish victories. Charles therefore asked Marlborough, whom he kept at his side, whether he could meet him. The Duke made no difficulty, and when Stanislaus arrived through the double doors he bowed and addressed him as "Your Majesty," which committed England to nothing, but was received with evident gratification by both the conqueror, Charles, and his puppet, Stanislaus. Apart from compliments he was careful to hold no intercourse with the unrecognized sovereign. The King of Prussia did not wish to be left out of these conversations, and Marlborough on the next day therefore repaired to Charlottenburg, where he met King Frederick. He thus, according to the biographers of his day, "met four kings in four days." His comment to Sarah is the instructive "If I was obliged to make a choice, it should be [the] youngest [Charles XII]."[1]

He returned by hard stages from Leipzig to Brussels to meet the news of the worst disaster which had yet befallen the Allies.

[1] Coxe, iii. 182.

Chapter Thirteen

ALMANZA AND STOLLHOFEN

1707—APRIL AND MAY

THE departure of Peterborough for Italy in August 1706 had deprived the allied chiefs in Spain of the only objective upon which they were agreed. They resumed their quarrels with added zest, and a new figure, Lord Rivers, arrived presently from England with novel complications. Peterborough, for his part, returned to Spain for Christmas. His credit with the London Cabinet was extinct. To the convinced disapprobation of Godolphin and Marlborough was now added the active hostility of Sunderland. The new Secretary of State had no sooner received the seals than he set himself to examine Peterborough's conduct. In accordance with the Whig Party view, he stood by Galway, "one of King William's men." His prim, pedantic nature was affronted by Peterborough's extravagances. His taste for controversy was excited by Peterborough's boastful, acrimonious, and endless dispatches. He determined to break him. Meanwhile the mercurial Earl reached the allied headquarters at Valencia in the middle of January 1707 to find discord at its height. The hatreds against him had in his absence been supplanted by a different, a more recent and more lively crop. Indeed, he even seemed about to capture the favour of Charles III. But the hounds were on his trail. Along the slow sea communications with England Sunderland's directions made their way. Galway was appointed to the supreme command in Spain. Peterborough, thus superseded, continued to disport himself gaily in council, and no one was quite sure of his actual position.

Strong reinforcements had arrived. We have seen how the whole of the British and Huguenot troops, above eight thousand strong, so long held in readiness for a "descent" on the French coasts, had been deflected in August 1706 to the Peninsula. They had lingered at Lisbon till the end of the year. They arrived in Valencia in February 1707. In all, the Allies disposed of nearly thirty thousand men. The three proverbial alternatives presented themselves to the council of war held on January 15 at Valencia. Galway and Stanhope, in accordance with Marlborough's general directions, proposed to combine all forces and march on Madrid, challenging a decisive battle on the way. Charles III and the "Vienna crew" urged that the troops should be dispersed in garrisons for the defence of the loyal provinces of Valencia and Catalonia. He was backed by Noyelles, whom we last saw leading Marlborough's advance guards to the forcing of the lines of Brabant in 1705.[1] Noyelles had served in Spain during 1706, and he was rapidly replacing Lichtenstein in the King's confidence and favour.

Peterborough ridiculed both plans, and proposed to lead a large detachment to join the Duke of Savoy. All were therefore opposed to Peterborough, and as disaster attended their action he was subsequently able to claim that all were wrong. Indeed, it is hard to understand how experienced generals could have drifted into the feeble-fatal compromise which they adopted after all reasonable argument had burned itself out. In the upshot King Charles, with Stanhope and the Austro-Spanish troops, marched northward to garrison Catalonia and Aragon, while Galway, with the flower of the allied infantry and Das Minas and his surviving Portuguese, set forth, cruelly weakened in numbers but in considerable optimism, for Madrid. Peterborough did not accompany them. Sunderland's later dispatches had arrived. He was stripped of all his commissions ashore and afloat, and peremptorily recalled to explain his measures, his excursions, and the bills he had drawn upon the British account.

Marshal Berwick, soon to be reinforced by eight thousand men released from Italy by the Treaty of Milan, lay in the field before Madrid. He had prepared magazines in Murcia to enable him to manœuvre there. Galway marched upon these magazines as a preliminary to his advance upon Madrid. The population of Murcia were hostile, and sickness made inroads upon the new recruits from England. Galway, who found it difficult to obtain intelligence of the real strength of the enemy, hardened his heart and resolved to force a battle upon Berwick. He had fifteen thousand men, of whom five thousand were British, while Berwick commanded twenty-five thousand, half of whom were French, and was now daily expecting the arrival of the Duke of Orleans with the eight thousand reinforcement. It is not surprising in these circumstances that Berwick was equally desirous of battle. While Galway was besieging the small town of Villena, he heard that the main

French army was but four hours distant. He heard also that Orleans had not yet joined it. This was true so far as concerned that tardy Prince. But the bulk of his forces had already reached Berwick, and their royal commander was moving with leisurely gait some days behind them. Forthwith Galway and Das Minas set out against Berwick. At daybreak on April 25 the Allies advanced into the plains before the walled town of Almanza. Here Berwick awaited them in order of battle, with certainly thirty thousand men against fifteen thousand. However, the wine was drawn and must be drunk.

Berwick drew up seventy-six squadrons and seventy-two battalions in two lines in front of Almanza. He placed the Spanish cavalry on his right, the infantry in the centre, and the French on his left. Galway's army was so weak in cavalry that it was necessary to intersperse the English on his left with infantry detachments. His main body of infantry faced Berwick's centre. Their right was protected by the Portuguese horse, who under Das Minas demanded this post of honour. The battle was begun about three o'clock by the horse and foot of the English left. They broke the first line of the Spanish cavalry. Inspired by this, the infantry of the Allies— English, Dutch, and Huguenots—attacked the greatly superior forces opposite to them with admirable spirit and actually drove this large mass of French and Spanish foot almost to the walls of Almanza. Meanwhile, however, the cavalry of the French left observed that the Portuguese in their post of honour on the right had not conformed to the general advance, and that the right flank of the allied infantry was therefore uncovered. They therefore rode forward upon both. The Portuguese cavalry galloped from the field before any collision was possible. Das Minas and a handful of his officers threw themselves into a square of Portuguese infantry which made a stand; and when this broke they rode round to fight it out with Galway on the left, or quitted the field. The whole French cavalry then fell upon the naked flank of the allied centre, breaking up and cutting down whole battalions and throwing at least a third of it into disorder.

The battle now became most fierce and bloody. The one-armed Galway, blinded by the blood from a sabre-cut above his eyes, could no longer command. Berwick, relieved by the partial confusion among the allied infantry, transferred his best French battalions to sustain the yielding Spanish horse. The English cavalry in their turn were driven back, and now not only the right but the left of the British, Dutch, and Huguenot infantry was exposed to the full fury of cavalry and infantry attack. Practically all the Portuguese troops had now fled, and little more than eight thousand infantry remained to face the exultant onset of at least three times their number. Galway, whose wound was now bandaged so that he could again see, led forward his reserve of English infantry to

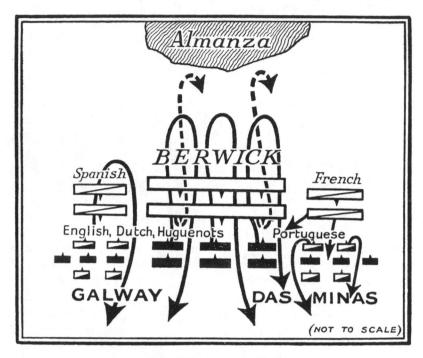

THE BATTLE OF ALMANZA

protect and cover the retreat of the centre. An orderly withdrawal from the field began; and, surprising as it may seem, this was effected. Galway, with 3500 English and Dutch, made good his retreat in unbroken order. The remnants of the centre under Count Dohna, one of Marlborough's veterans, and Major-General Shrimpton likewise retired in a disciplined array, but in a different direction. They found a respite in darkness and among the mountains. The separated fragments of the allied army lay for the night nearly twenty miles apart. With the dawn Galway saw himself bound to continue his retreat upon Valencia. Shrimpton, with about two thousand British, resisted all attacks for two days, but, being then surrounded on all sides without food or hope of succour, he surrendered at discretion upon the third.

History has noted the oddity that in this battle the English commanded by the Frenchman, Galway (Ruvigny), were beaten by the French commanded by the Englishman, Berwick. The proportion of casualties was unusual. The Allies left on the field four thousand killed and wounded and three thousand prisoners, or half their total force. Berwick's own casualties were also severe. He admitted only two thousand, but most authorities compute them at at least five thousand.[1] There were five thousand allied stragglers, most of whom rejoined the army. Galway retreated rapidly to Alcira, where he reorganized his troops and arranged for the defence of the frontier fortresses of Valencia. Here he was joined by two thousand six hundred reinforcements newly landed by Admiral Byng.

Considering the memorable character and consequences of this savage battle, the accounts are both scanty and obscure. It is therefore right to print a few new letters upon it from the Blenheim archives.

Galway to Stanhope

ALCIRA
April 28

*I have given you an account of our march to Yecla and Montelegre and our mining the enemy's magazines there. Upon our return we endeavoured to take the Castle of Villena, but failed there on account of heavy cannon and our men being stopped by the rocks. The enemies having assembled all their forces marched back to Montelegre and from thence to Almanza. You know your resolution was taken this winter at Valencia to march to the enemy and give a battle if they set for us before our forces should diminish; which was always yours and my opinion. We accordingly, all the Generals being of the same sentiment, thought this the best opportunity, our forces being fresh and very good. We marched on the 25th into the plain of Almanza. The enemy waited for us near the town where we gave them battle and were defeated; both our wings being broke and routed. Our foot was hounded by the enemy's horse, so that none could get off. Don Juan de Alayda and fifty horse got to the mountains and Comte Dohna and Mr Shrimpton, and with them considerable body of English, Dutch and Portuguese foot. He would then have marched away at break of day Tuesday morning, but Comte Dohna judged he should not, because he had sent a parley to the Duke of Berwick, so Don J. de A. left them, and met no enemy on the way. Last night a Captain of Miquelets came to me as from thence for succours and bread. He says that he left Tuesday at six in the afternoon, that they had been

_____
[1] Parnell says six thousand.

attacked and taken the enemy's cannon with which he had left them firing at the enemy. This man came by way of Xativa to get some men to conduct them home, being laden with bread; it being impossible for us to send any convoys by the open road or help them with any horse to favour their retreat.

All the Generals that are here assembled yesterday to consult what was now to be done. All agreed we were not in a position to think of defending this kingdom, and resolved to retire to Tortosa with what horse is left us, embarking baggage and sick and wounded on board the fleet at Denia or at Valencia, according to which I have wrote to Sir George Byng to take the troops on board again and not to land for money, biscuits or other provisions, but to sail to Tortosa and land all there; after which I am of the opinion he should sail with the fleet to Barcelona. These are too bad news for me to write to the King, which I broke to you, and acquaint him with it that he may send us his orders, if he has any to give us, and that he may take his measures to assemble all those troops in Catalonia and Aragon to defend the Ebro, which I do not know of what use it will be in the situation we are now in, or if there are more to take on this action.

Galway to Byng

28th April, 1707

I suppose you have already heard the bad news of the battle having been lost. . . . I did not write to you [sooner], not being in a condition, and having a desire to inform you more exactly of the particulars thereof. *We have lost our Artillery*[1] and as to our foot, none is returned in a body unless a few officers and some scattered soldiers. As to ye horse I believe there may be about 3000 or more saved. You are sensible that with that we shall not be in a position to form an army able to protect the kingdom of Valencia. We just now resolved to pass off what we have here and at Valencia with all ye diligence we can to Tortosa to see if we can with the troops his Majesty has in Aragon and Catalonia make up an army. . . .

Charles III to Marlborough

BARCELONA
May 3, 1707

★My Lord Gallway and the Marquis Das Minas had received news that the enemy were camped four hours from them with a great number of cavalry. The forces of the enemy consisted of 9000 horse and 12–14,000 infantry, taking up the position at a place called Almanza as their centre. After this news the two Generals without any other

---

[1] All extant British accounts declare that the cannon were saved. Evidently this is not true.

This extract is quoted from *The Byng Papers* (Navy Records Society), i, 171.

counsel marched on the 25th at dawn their whole army these four
good leagues without a halt and without giving any rest to the troops
except to put themselves in line of battle, and with their tired soldiers
ordered an attack on the enemy who remained in their position at
two o'clock in the afternoon. Our cavalry and particularly the Portuguese gave way without waiting for any charge, abandoning all alone
on the plain our infantry without any Commander, My Lord Gallway
then having been wounded by a sabre over his eye and the Marquis
Das Minas and the greater part of the Generals having retired with the
Cavalry in such disorder and precipitation without looking behind
them and without pulling rein until they reached Xativa, eight good
leagues from the field of battle. The Infantry have been completely
defeated and the Comte Dohna and a Portuguese General after having
rallied the debris of fourteen battalions, about 2000 men, and after
having defended themselves on a height against the enemy for two
days without bread or help, which the Generals, all lost and confused,
had not sent them any; and at last as far as one knows they have
capitulated on terms. The Cavalry has lost hardly anything, as it
escaped at the beginning. Of the Infantry one does not know exactly
yet how many have been saved.

Methuen to Sunderland

LISBON
19 *May*

*One of the worst circumstances of this fatal accident is in my
opinion its happening so early in the year, by which the enemy will
have too much time before them to make the most of this victory. I
heartily wish that My Lord Galway may with the battered remnants
of his army and what the King of Spain has with him make head against
them from the other side of the river Ebro, and preserve Catalonia
during the whole campaign. I have already written to his Lordship
and Mr Stanhope that the only remedy that can be applied must
come from Italy if that be possible, for I am afraid that anything which
may be sent from England or Holland will come too late.

Considering how destructive was the defeat of Almanza, the rally
and front presented by Galway were praiseworthy in a high degree.
Crippled, wounded, beaten, discredited, distrusted in the vilest
manner, a foreigner hated in England, an intruder in the Spanish
brawl, he never for a moment ceased to wage war upon the enemy.
He gathered together the fragments of his shattered army; he yielded
no post without stubborn fighting, and in October, after five months
of apparently hopeless struggle, he was still at the head of a coherent
force of upwards of fifteen thousand men. He was of course greatly

aided by the withdrawal in September of French troops in Spain for the rescue of Toulon. There is nothing known about Galway that is not to his honour.

"This ill success in Spain," wrote Marlborough stubbornly (May 23), "has flung everything backwards, so that the best resolution we can take is to let the French see we are resolved to keep on the war, so that we can have a good peace."[1]

Galway's personal position engaged his attention. "God knows," he wrote to Sarah (June 6), "what is to be done for the recovery of the great disorders that are now in Spain. For by what Lord Rivers says it is too plain King Charles apprehends that Lord Galway betrays him, which can never enter into my head; however if they believe it, it will poison all the undertakings on that side." To Godolphin (June 13): "I find Lord Galway in very bad circumstances. For my own part I think him incapable of being guilty; but if there be no confidence, the consequences must be fatal." (June 23) "It is impracticable for Lord Galway to continue in that service." And, finally, to Lord Sunderland on June 27: "Nobody can have a better opinion than I have of Lord Galway, but when I consider the Court and King of Spain, I think it would be the most barbarous thing in the world to impose upon Galway to stay; for I am very confident he would rather beg his bread—I am sure I would."

His own opinion about the tactics of Almanza was equally decided (Meldert, June 16): "I had this morning yours of the 30th of the last month, with the order of battle, by which it appears that the enemies were very much stronger than Lord Galway, which makes it very strange that by choice they should go to attack them in a plain."[2]

On May 21 the Duke had assumed command of the army which had assembled under Overkirk near Brussels, and advanced at once to the south of Hal. He drew out ninety-seven battalions and 164 squadrons with 112 guns, in all about ninety thousand men. Vendôme had assembled around Mons 124 battalions and 195 squadrons —say, about a hundred and ten thousand men, not including the detached cavalry (sixteen squadrons) of La Motte.[3] Vendôme was operating from a frontier well guarded by many fortresses of the first class; and his instructions were not to hazard a battle without urgent need. Marlborough, on the other hand, had to cover several

[1] Coxe, iii, 207 *et seq.*   [2] *Ibid.*, 239.   [3] Pelet, vii, 299.

important but poorly fortified towns, especially Brussels. He had thought earlier of making a dash for Mons or Tournai before Vendôme was ready. His journey to see the King of Sweden had prevented this, and the moment had now passed. He was too far outnumbered to undertake a siege, and must content himself with covering Brabant, hoping for a chance of battle on favourable terms. All his letters show him anxious for battle, though not at

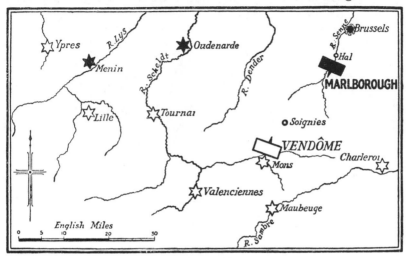

MAY 1707

undue risk. The Dutch had instructed their field Deputies that they were not to allow a battle. He was careful "not to let the army know that the Dutch are not willing to venture, since that must have an ill effect."[1] He tried to obtain some latitude by assuring Heinsius that he would not fight except at a marked advantage. The Dutch Government only enjoined more strict caution upon their Deputies. Marlborough was thus thrown back into the conditions he had found intolerable in previous campaigns. He had to create a situation where the superior enemy were at great disadvantage, and where at the same time the Dutch had no option but to fight. This double problem was incapable of solution. Thus unhappily circumstanced, he took the field.

At midnight on May 25, after he had ordered the army to march the next day to Soignies, his spies reported that the French were also to move forward at daybreak. These movements brought the two great armies into critical relation. On the 27th Marlborough,

[1] Coxe, iii, 210.

taking with him the field Deputies, made a reconnaissance in force towards the enemy but failed to find them. They had in fact moved eastward to Gosselies, where they formed a strong camp. This was not known till late in the day. The French movement deliberately uncovered the fortress of Mons, as if to challenge its siege. Had the Allies attempted this, Brussels, Louvain, and, indeed, all Brabant

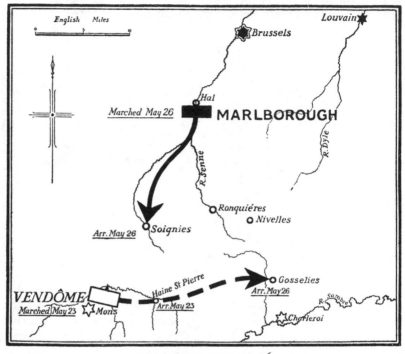

MOVEMENTS, MAY 23–26

would have been exposed. The choice remained of moving eastward across the Senne to converge upon the enemy with the chance of battle, or of retracing the marches along the Brussels road and standing between him and Brabant. A council of war debated the question. Marlborough proposed to remain where he was, and send a detachment to demolish the abandoned French lines before Mons. Evidently he wished to lead Vendôme to believe that he was about to commit the error which the Marshal's movement had invited. Upon this pretence he would await Vendôme's next move. The general opinion was against this apparent adoption of an unsound policy.

According to Goslinga, Marlborough then proposed to retire on Brussels. At this the Deputies, supported by many of the generals, Dutch and English, raised an outcry. A sudden retreat at the very opening of the campaign would be injurious to the prestige and morale of the army; it would give the French, already comforted by Almanza, exactly the tonic they required. The council wished to cross the Senne and march on Nivelles. Marlborough consented to this, and orders were issued accordingly. Goslinga slept in his boots, expecting to move at two A.M. But at three o'clock he could hear no movement in the headquarters, and at four he learned that Marlborough had changed the plan and persuaded Overkirk, and that the army would fall back on Brussels. The reason given was that Cadogan had personally reconnoitred the passage of the Senne at Ronquières, and found it both occupied and difficult. The other passage was even less satisfactory. There was therefore no alternative but the "humiliating" withdrawal, which was, in fact, in full progress. Obviously Marlborough was doing what he chose, and finding facts and excuses to baffle the contrary argument. Filled with wrath at what he calls *cette foutue démarche*, the fiery, opinionated Dutchman mounted his horse and accosted the Captain-General during the march: "I used full freedom in thrusting before the Duke face to face [*entre quatre yeux*] how much this ignominious retreat at the opening of the campaign would stain his fine reputation, raise that of the Duke of Vendôme, and reanimate the castdown courage of the French soldiers. He said little in response [*pas grand chose*]; but persisted in his course." Such is Goslinga's tale.

On the other hand we have Marlborough's letter written to Godolphin on May 30, while the facts were well known to the principal officers of the army:

> This caution of mine is absolutely necessary; for instead of coming to this camp I would have marched yesterday to Nivelles, but the Deputies would not consent to it, telling me very plainly that they feared the consequence of that march might be a battle. So that unless I can convince the Pensioner that I am not for hazarding, but when we have an advantage, they will give such orders to their Deputies that I shall not have it in my power of doing good, if an advantage should offer itself. . . .[1]

There is thus a conflict between Goslinga's retrospective memoirs and Marlborough's report written at the time to Godolphin; but

---

[1] Coxe, iii, 209.

the explanation of Marlborough's decision seems plain. Had he possessed the powers which are the right of every commander of an army, he would have marched to meet Vendôme through Nivelles after encouraging him to commit himself more deeply by a feint by Mons; and perhaps the chance of battle would have come. But it was not primarily against Vendôme that he was in this instance manœuvring. He hoped that this super-prudent retreat, and the heart-burnings it caused to the Dutch field Deputies and generals, would convince Heinsius of his extreme cautiousness, and procure him the freedom without which it was not possible to handle an army with success. If he gained that freedom from his friends, and if the enemy, inflamed by his apparent weakness, would "grow insolent," then something might be made of the campaign. Meanwhile he had no intention of forcing the Senne and bringing about a situation where he could offer battle, when he knew that at the culminating moment the Deputies would produce their written instructions to veto such hazards. As the somewhat crestfallen confederates passed by Brussels and their columns bent eastward towards the Dyle and their former fighting-grounds, the news of a second major disaster reached Marlborough. The Lines of Stollhofen had been captured by Marshal Villars.

Prince Louis of Baden was dead, and the Margrave of Bayreuth, appointed by Vienna because, though a bad general, he was a good Catholic, led the armies of Germany in his stead. Prince Louis had left behind as his monument that renowned system of defences upon the Upper Rhine known as the Lines of Stollhofen. It had become a joke in the armies that the late Prince's whole conception of the world war was the defence of the Lines of Stollhofen. He had originally expected to command on the Rhine the hundred and twenty thousand Imperial troops which had been promised by the old Emperor in the treaty of the Grand Alliance. These had not appeared; but as the successive campaigns passed with their twists of fortune Prince Louis when in doubt had always persevered in the fortification of his lines. In fact, it was said that in exact proportion as the military strength of Germany diminished so his fortifications grew. They had never been more impressive than in the spring of 1707. From the impassable mountains of the Black Forest to Fort Louis stretched the double and triple lines of bastions, redans, redoubts, trenches, strong points, inundations, marshes, which had hitherto in the War of Succession effectively prevented all invasion of Germany along the Rhine valley. Now, after the Margrave had been driven out of Alsace, the defences had been perfected along the whole course of the river to the fortresses of Landau

THE LINES OF STOLLHOFEN

and Philippsburg. Counting round the angle of Fort Louis, these fifty or sixty miles of elaborate earthworks and water-shields constituted the finest manifestation of passive defence which war in those times had seen. Within them stood the ragged remnants of the Emperor's Rhine army, recently stripped and stinted for the sake of the expedition to Naples. Behind them lay Germany, defenceless, disunited, but, thanks to the Sea Powers, to Blenheim

241

and Ramillies, hitherto unravaged. But behind them also had risen at Rastadt the magnificent palace and gardens of the late Margrave, on which he had lavished hundreds of thousands of pounds, and by which he proclaimed his confidence that his lines were inexpugnable. The mercy of God, manifested through his toe, had laid him in his tomb before the striking of the fatal hour.

Marlborough's accurate Secret Service, and his own military instinct, had led him to fear some sudden stroke by Villars on the Rhine. Already from St James's on March 18 he had sent a plain warning. "I am glad," he wrote to M. de Janus,[1] "that you are beginning to settle down in your quarters. It is reported, however, from France that M. de Villars seems to have some project in view which he would explode [*ferait éclater*] at the first chance; but I do not doubt that all necessary precautions will be taken on your side to frustrate it [*le faire avorter*]."[2] No notice had been taken by the Margrave of Bayreuth's headquarters, although nearly two months had passed.

On the night of May 22 Marshal Villars gave a grand ball at Strasburg. This festivity and its date had become widely known. The news had crossed the gulf between the armies, and upon the staff of the new Commander-in-Chief, the Prince of Bayreuth, entire confidence prevailed. But while Villars arranged his general officers in the minuet, their troops, mobilized with the utmost stealth, were marching fast, and when they received their orders from him in the ballroom they rode off to play their parts in a great surprise. The famous lines which for five years had protected the German Fatherland were overrun at numerous points without loss of life, almost without the firing of a shot. The most impregnable section, between the river and the mountains, was the first to fall. The French clambered in succession over tiers of permanent defences. The Reich troops fled in disorder towards Durlach, and Villars fixed his headquarters in the palace and castle of Rastadt on the evening of the 23rd. By then the entire system of defence which had hitherto served Central Germany in the place of an army was in French hands. The roadway into Germany was now barred neither by ramparts nor soldiers. The dyke had broken, and the bitter waters flowed onward in a deluge. This was no more than the Germanic states deserved for their meanness to the Empire, and the Empire for its incompetence. Fortune committed an injustice

---

[1] Chief Staff Officer of the Rhine Army.
[2] *Dispatches*, iii, 336.

when the main penalty was paid by the Circles of Swabia and Franconia, which had done the most to defend their country.

Such was the opening of the campaign of 1707. In a trice the entire face of the war had changed. In Italy an improvident separate peace; in Spain a shattering defeat; in Germany unstemmed invasion; in Flanders deadlock and veto. There remained Marlborough's hope: Eugene and Toulon.

Chapter Fourteen

TOULON

1707—SUMMER

THE attack upon Toulon in 1707 was one of the greatest naval enterprises ever undertaken by England. Marlborough's power and the whole authority of the Government sustained the Fleet. They found in Sir Cloudesley Shovell an admiral who brought to the enterprise a strong surge of his own. Marlborough understood from his youthful service afloat the difficulties and uncertainties of sea war. There was no need to tell him, as Shovell was at pains to explain to Victor Amadeus, that the Navy sometimes took three weeks or a month to arrive at a place which they might with a fair wind reach in twenty-four hours. Marlborough realized what Napoleon would never believe until Trafalgar—that a land commander cannot drive a fleet. Admiral Shovell was, however, from the outset as keen and convinced as Marlborough about taking Toulon. He saw the profit to the naval war of securing this excellent Mediterranean base. He saw from his quarterdeck across the short, wind-whipped seas of the Gulf of Lions exactly what Marlborough saw in his headquarters at Meldert —the destruction of the French fleet and its base, and the command of the Mediterranean for England during the war and perhaps longer. Both Shovell and Admiral Norris, his representative in the Duke of Savoy's army, also comprehended the strategic consequences upon the whole struggle of the organized invasion of Southern France from a conquered Toulon and an English-dominated Mediterranean.

Peterborough had written in 1705 a description of Shovell which certainly seems borne out by his conduct before Toulon.

> ★Sir Cloudesley Shovell is a man possessed of many good qualities.
> . . . He is brave if I may say to a fault, and in matters he does not
> understand thinks that whatever is directed first must be begun, and
> when begun must be carried on what accidents soever occur, or what-
> soever improbabilities come in the way. He sticks close to what he

calls orders, and will conceive no latitude in such instructions that I think were calculated for the greatest.[1]

Marlborough ceaselessly urged the attack upon Toulon. The disasters at Almanza and Stollhofen only increased its importance in his eyes. "Our greatest hope is on the Italian front, although the expedition to Naples in which they [the Imperialists] are persisting with so much obstinacy may cause much difficulty."[2] To Admiral

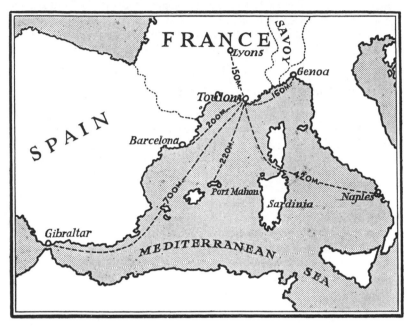

STRATEGIC SITUATION OF TOULON

Norris, on June 5, "You will have heard of our misfortune upon the Rhine. Our chief hopes are from the projects on your side, wherein I am confident nothing will be wanting on the part of our fleet."[3] To Wratislaw, "England and Holland base all their hopes on the Italian plan and are convinced that the whole future of the campaign and even of the war depends upon it." To Sinzendorf, the Imperial Ambassador at The Hague, on June 6, "The maritime powers have set their hearts upon the entry into France, and it is there that they expect the greatest fortune that can come to the

[1] Peterborough to Godolphin, September 9, 1705; Add MSS. 39757.
[2] Marlborough to Noyelles, June 3; *Dispatches*, iii, 388.
[3] *Ibid.*, 389.

high allies to restore our affairs."[1] Chetwynd, the English Minister to the Court of Savoy, kept Marlborough constantly informed.

Chetwynd to Marlborough

24 *May*, 1707

★Lord Peterborough is still here as inquisitive as anybody else, but Your Grace may depend upon it he will know nothing from myself nor anyone else, none knowing of the matter. . . . I hope your letters to the Court of Vienna after the news of our misfortunes will oblige the Emperor to countermand the troops who are on their march for Naples. This will make the enemy believe our real designs are to send the troops to Spain, and would be the only way to recover our late misfortune.[2]

To Chetwynd Marlborough wrote on June 8:

I find the only difficulty you are like to labour under is the want of ball and powder, concerning which you will certainly have orders immediately from England, whither I had written that though the provision were never so great, it can be no prejudice, since what is not used will remain in store. In the mean time the service must not be delayed for want; the fleet will certainly furnish a good quantity of powder besides ball for their own guns, and in my opinion it would not be amiss that care were taken to secure a quantity of ball of the same calibre, and some powder at Genoa and Leghorn, as you propose; . . . if you stay for orders or a supply from England, if it be not already sent, the time for operations will be lost; and I must tell you the greatest hope we have for the campaign . . . is from your side.[3]

Although the nominal command rested with the Duke of Savoy, everything turned upon Eugene. Eugene, as we shall have further occasion to remark, was a land animal, a denizen of Central Europe. He did not understand the sea; what he knew of it he disliked and distrusted. He had no comprehension of amphibious strategy. But the attitude of the Vienna Government with which he was himself bound up also reacted upon him. He knew they had been forced into the plan by Marlborough. The Empire had no army of its own worthy of the name in Italy. It was as feeble and ragged on the Po as on the Rhine. But twenty-eight thousand Germanic troops, to be revived by the Sea Powers with nearly fifteen thousand recruits, were a force upon which they might ride, if not to victory in the South of France, at least to annexation in the South of Italy. The threat of withdrawing these twenty-eight thousand northern soldiers

---

[1] *Dispatches*, iii, 392.   [2] Blenheim MSS.   [3] *Dispatches*, iii, 399.

had compelled them to consent to the Toulon enterprise. They resented both the menace and the task; and Eugene to some extent shared their mood. Thus we see before Toulon a Prince Eugene different from any of the gleaming pictures with which he illuminated the warfare of his age. We shall show how in 1708 Marlborough, worn down, leaned upon Eugene and was in a dark hour sustained by him; but now in 1707 it must stand on record that the ever-glorious prince and warrior who with his own dauntless heart constituted the fighting power of the Holy Roman Empire allowed himself to fall below the level of the event.

We therefore have the spectacle of Marlborough inspiring Shovell, and Shovell trying to animate Eugene: of a half-hearted military command and an overflowing fleet stimulus. Shovell was obliged by the agreement to furnish large specified quantities of powder and shot. But he never considered these limits. He would land more than a hundred guns for the siege. Most of his marines had been dropped in Spain to plug the gap of Almanza; but he proffered his seamen. Forty rounds a gun was considered the lowest reserve tolerable in an English fleet; Shovell cut it down to thirty-five without express authority. Acting on Marlborough's suggestion, he sent to Leghorn and Genoa to purchase ammunition. He pledged his own personal credit pending sanction from the Treasury. Throughout the operation the Navy never failed to give more material aid than was contracted beforehand or asked under necessity. The spirit of the Admiral and his stubborn, audacious counsels thrust themselves upon the Duke of Savoy and still more upon Prince Eugene. At every moment he was at hand to aid, to encourage, to reassure. In our history the Navy has sometimes stood by to watch the Army do the work. Here was a case where a navy tried by its exertion and sacrifice to drive forward an army. It did not succeed.

Marlborough's wish and endeavour were to begin the advance against Toulon in early May. But many insuperable obstacles intervened. The snow melted late upon the passes; both the Imperialists and the Duke of Savoy were behindhand with their preparations; and even the allied fleet, delayed in Spain, did not "come on to the coast" till the middle of June. In spite of this and of the lengthy and embittered discussions between the Allies, no hint of the Toulon plan had reached Versailles till June 10, when it was reported that Eugene would shortly march on Nice. It was the end of the month before it was recognized that Toulon was the allied aim, and that Provence and not Dauphiné was threatened. Marlborough's Secret Service gives the date as precisely as the French records. "The French," he wrote to Chetwynd on July 1, "seem to have penetrated our grand design, so that the longer it is delayed the greater the difficulty you must expect."[1] Toulon was at this moment an easy prey. Its defences were neglected; its garrison less than eight thousand men. Forthwith Marshal Tessé, leaving the forces on the coast to delay the advance, began to concentrate all his available troops upon Toulon, and set to work to fortify an extended position north-east of the city.

Eugene, having feinted at Susa, began his march on June 30 with about thirty-five thousand men. Of these scarcely a sixth were provided by the Empire. Over eight thousand Imperialists under General Daun, the defender of Turin, were slowly wending their way down the leg of Italy towards Naples amid the protests of the Papal States. The first charge on whatever recruits, supplies, and transport the Empire could procure had been for Naples. All the engagements which the Imperial Ministers had signed with the Sea Powers, particularly England, about the supplies of food, powder, shot, mules and horses, had hopelessly collapsed. Every attempt to borrow money on the Imperial credit had failed. Eugene's letters to the Emperor are a painful exposure of military and financial prostration.[2] On his side, however, stood the redoubtable German mercenaries of the Sea Powers. There were the ardent Savoyards who followed their Duke; and there was the fleet and Sir Cloudesley Shovell, upon whom all burdens could be thrown, and by whom nearly all were accepted.

Up till the last moment Eugene and the Government he served hugged the hope that they would persuade the Sea Powers to abandon the attempt and to send five thousand of their paid troops to Spain. Eugene mooted this to Shovell. The Admiral, supported by the representatives of England and Holland, flatly refused to consider such a desertion, and as they were the masters of the men, ships, and money it could not be pursued. The disputations with Vienna about Toulon were continued by the London Cabinet. The Imperial Ministers made unceasing complaint. "We risk our army," wrote Wratislaw to Marlborough on July 13, "in the sole view of pleasing England." "Had they ever," scornfully exclaimed Godol-

---

[1] *Dispatches*, iv, 450.
[2] Eugene to the Emperor, Sospello, July 8; *Feldzüge*, vii, Suppt., 72.

phin, "had Italy or an army, but for the extraordinary efforts and expenses of England?"[1]

One feature long unknown to Marlborough and the Allies must be noticed here. Lamberty tells a story of secret Swedish intervention at Turin at the instance of the French envoy to Charles XII.[2] The Swedish King is said to have brought decisive pressure to bear upon Victor Amadeus to frustrate the attack upon Toulon. The King of Sweden had, it seems, been under a ten-years secret alliance with France. This engagement was limited to mutual aid only in the event of mortal danger. Charles XII recognized such danger in the fall of Toulon. His treaty with France did not expire till the end of 1708. It is alleged that he told the Duke of Savoy's agent that if Toulon fell he would invade the Empire. If the Allies invaded Dauphiné or Provence he and his Swedes would winter in Saxony and Bohemia. At the same time Marshal Villars, who was already across the Rhine ravaging Swabia and Franconia, made vehement appeal to the Swedish King to join hands with him, and consummate the destruction of the Hapsburg power; and anyone can see how fatal such

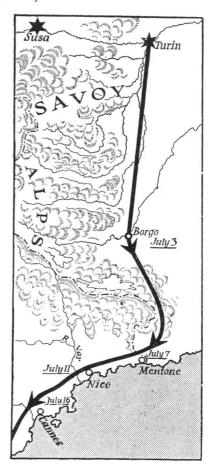

EUGENE'S MARCH TO TOULON (I)

a combination would have been. Victor Amadeus, it is suggested, deliberately spoiled the Toulon expedition. His apologists present him as being willing to bear silently and secretly all the odium of military treachery committed out of loyalty to the common cause.

It was under these depressing auspices that Eugene came down

---

[1] Coxe, iii, 112.　　　　　　　　　　[2] Lamberty, iv, 569.

through the Alps, reached the sea, and marched along the Riviera through Nice and Cannes. The picture presented to modern eyes of shores lined with endless pleasure cities, villas, and gardens, and striped with mighty causeways at every level, affords no suggestion of the stern country that confronted Prince Eugene. Only one ill-kept road wound its way across the innumerable spurs and water-courses with which the mountains meet the sparkling sea. Primitive hamlets of goatherds or fisher-folk offered neither food nor shelter to an army. Small, impoverished coastal towns, few and far between, scowled from amid their fortifications upon open roadsteads, with here and there perhaps a jetty or a quay; and the Mediterranean, for all its smiles, afflicted a sailing fleet with constant uncertainty and frequent peril.

Wishing to be informed by an eye whose measure he knew well, Marlborough now sent Brigadier Palmes, the young cavalry officer who had distinguished himself at Blenheim, "to the Duke of Savoy and Prince Eugene with orders to stay there till they can judge how the campaign will end on that side, and then to have their thoughts on a project for the next campaign. . . . I expect him back about the middle of September."[1] The importance of this liaison appoint-ment is shown by the fact that the Queen's sanction was officially obtained. Thus Palmes was more than Marlborough's personal representative.

On July 11 Eugene came in contact with the French delaying force in redoubts behind the Var. The English fleet with its Dutch squadron had kept pace with the army. Shovell now stood in, and four ships of the line, one of seventy guns, sailed into the mouth of the river and bombarded in flank the seaward works. These, speedily abandoned, were occupied by landing parties of seamen, while at the same time the advanced troops of Eugene's army forced the passage inland.

Chetwynd to Marlborough

July 15, 1707

★Yesterday His R.H. and Prince Eugene were on board the flag-ship where it was resolved to march straight to Toulon in order to besiege that place, upon the assurances Sir Cloudsley gave his R.H. and the Prince of leaving the Fleet in Toulon all the winter if we could take it, and upon those I gave them of her Majesty's vigorous assistance to support His R.H. in all his just designs. [This] was abso-lutely necessary to calm the fears they had of leaving Antibes, Villa

[1] Marlborough to Godolphin, August 1; Coxe, iii, 296.

Franca and Monaco behind them and to determine them to begin with Toulon. In this I hope we have acted according to the Queen's intentions. . . . All our advices say that the enemy are sending troops from all sides to oppose us, and I find our two great men are afraid they shall have enough to do . . . to keep their ground should we take Toulon, since we shall run the risk of losing all communications except by sea. His R.H. and Prince Eugene desire Your Grace will send them a courier with accounts of what troops the enemy may detach from the Rhine, which is what they are most afraid of.[1]

Eugene to Marlborough

ST LAURENS
July 14, 1707

★ We are about to march now straight for Toulon with the intention of besieging it unless we meet such obstacles as will make the enterprise completely impracticable, leaving in our rear all the other strong places. You will be able to judge by our having set aside all difficulties, the eagerness of my zeal for the august desires of the Queen and for the good of the common cause, and will believe that the army is united upon the same goal. Since you have much at heart the success of this important expedition on which depend such essential consequences, I am persuaded that you will also wish to contribute to it by all means in your power, employing all your efforts to force vigorous action on the offensive of your front to cause considerable diversions, and prevent the enemy augmenting their forces against us by detachments from all parts—especially the Rhine. That is what I beg you most earnestly, and I refer to what I have written more in detail to Comte Maffei. I renew my most sincere protestations of friendship to you. . . .[2]

This letter is signed "Your affectionate Cousin."

After the Var only seventy miles now stood between the Allies and Toulon. For an army whose artillery and supplies were largely carried by sea a week's marching should have sufficed. Actually a fortnight was consumed. ★ "It was the opinion of almost every officer," wrote Chetwynd to Marlborough a month later, "that if before coming to Toulon, we had not been so dilatory and cautious, we might have done a great deal."[3] It was not until July 26 that the allied army and fleet arrived before Tessé's new lines at Toulon. The Marshal had managed to gather about twenty thousand men for their defence, the last of whom only reached their position some days after the Allies.

Now came the crux. The Admiral proposed the immediate storm

[1] Blenheim MSS.   [2] *Ibid.*   [3] August 14, 1707; *ibid.*

of the newly constructed and still only partially garrisoned defences. Victor Amadeus appeared favourable, but, though nominally in chief command, he threw the burden upon Prince Eugene. A year before he and Eugene with barely twenty thousand men had not hesitated to attack the French lines before Turin, although there were on the spot or in the neighbourhood more than fifty thousand enemy troops. At Toulon these proportions were almost reversed.

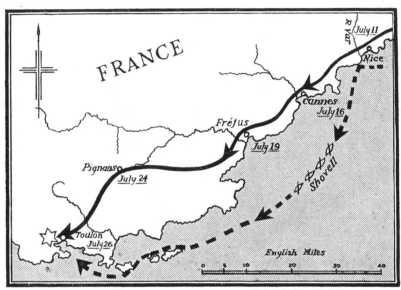

EUGENE'S MARCH TO TOULON (II)

There were the same Prussians, Hanoverians, and Saxe-Gothas— all at their full strength. There was now besides the mighty fleet: fifty battleships with a score of ancillary vessels. Moreover, every day's delay meant the arrival of French reinforcements and the strengthening of their fortifications. Should the signal be given?

Eugene refused. All the dislike he had for the enterprise, all his misgivings, broke forth. The place was no longer lightly defended. The enemy were there in strength. Surprise had miscarried. Prudence commanded immediate retreat before the army was cut off from Italy by a French descent through a choice of passes upon its communications. A council was held at headquarters. Shovell reacted vigorously. He renewed the assurances he had already given at Nice. Why fear for the line of supply? He would feed the army from the sea. Why fear for the line of retreat? The cavalry could ride away, and he would embark all the infantry in his ships and land them on the Italy side of any intercepting position which the French might occupy. Grave, tense debate! Finally a compromise; no grand onslaught, but an attack upon the lines by bombardment and local assaults. Trenches were accordingly opened, and a dead-lift effort began.

Chetwynd to Marlborough

July 29, 1707

*I have had the honour to see His Highness [the Duke of Savoy], who has returned from the post that was to be attacked this morning, far from being satisfied with his day's work and of the dispositions made there. From the conversations he has had with Prince Eugene I find he [Eugene] has little hopes of our succeeding here. I cannot tell what to make of all this and much less what the Prince could mean. I know he never had a liking for this project, but I thought when he was here he would have acted with his usual vigour. How this will end God knows, but I have yet reason to fear it will not be to our satisfaction.[1]

The section of the defences resting upon the height of St Catherine was stormed on July 30, not without severe casualties, and a first parallel of the attacking works was completed by August 7.

Eugene's outlook and feelings are exposed in his letter to Wratislaw of August 4:

... What you write to the Duke of Marlborough is just. With regard to myself, I will go wherever they wish me, if I have an army; *and I declare that I will no longer be subaltern*, except to my masters, unless conjunctures should oblige me to pass the winter in this country, of which I am very doubtful.

The Duke [of Savoy], with his usual policy, seeing the great difficulties, not to say impossibilities, of this operation, throws it entirely on me, *in order not to disgust England and Holland, who press him extremely*, without listening to any reason. He does it with the more cunning, because he praises me on my capacity, and says I can do what I will. He answers them on everything that they must address themselves to me, that he is much inclined to this operation, that he knows the consequence of it, but that he can do nothing, which I do not deem proper.

They are all enraged with me, and think that I wish not to risk the troops. I answer clearly that I am accustomed to act according to the rules and reasons of war, every one knowing that I readily hazard when I have the least appearance of succeeding; and that I shall not,

[1] Blenheim MSS.

from complaisance for England, *and for a little envoy* [*un petit d'Envoyé*] who is here [Chetwynd], advise a thing if I see it impossible; but that if, in spite of all, the Allies and the Duke will have it so, the troops of the Emperor will not abandon them, and that I will omit nothing to succeed.

This is the state in which we are. By the journal and my relation you will see the detail. It is the most difficult operation I have seen in my life. We are working at the batteries; we will see the effect of them before we decide on a bombardment or a siege—at least, this is my sentiment.

I do not doubt that strong detachments will arrive on all sides, the enemy having repassed the Rhine in Germany, being retired into quarters of refreshment in Spain, and the armies of Flanders inactive.[1]

Properly speaking, it was no siege, but only an attack by the fleet and one field army upon the fortified position of another. Eugene, whose sentiments are only too apparent, bent to his task against his mood and judgment in fulfilment of his promise to Marlborough "that he would do his best." Besides this, however, he formed a certain contact, comprehensible to fighting chiefs, with Shovell and the English admirals. No soldier of high quality can be unmoved by the ardour and comradeship of the naval service in a joint operation. Eugene was evidently affected by Shovell's grit, resource, and zeal. "In spite of the representations I have made to the Admiral," he wrote to the Emperor (August 5), "he absolutely insists upon carrying on with the enterprise of Toulon. . . . If they wish to proceed to its serious undertaking in spite of all the difficulties they see with their own eyes, the troops of Your Imperial Majesty will certainly not separate from them."[2] And later, "Although the Admirals do not understand the land service, they refuse to listen to facts, and adhere obstinately to their opinion that for good or ill everything must be staked on the siege of Toulon. Yet the pure impossibility of this is clearly before their eyes."[3]

For a while the fierce and costly fighting for the outworks of Toulon flowed forth and back as the days drew into weeks, and all the bombardments of Shovell's landed cannon of the fleet could not master the adverse tide. The strategic excellence of the Toulon design made itself only the more intelligible. Louis XIV and those who sat around him could not see the deep divisions and underlying despondency in the allied camp before Toulon. What they

[1] Coxe, iii, 349.   [2] *Feldzüge*, Series I, ix, Suppt., 179.
[3] Eugene to the Emperor, August 14; *ibid.*, 182.

weighed with increasing clarity were the consequences of its fall. They saw, in fact, what Marlborough had seen. They put the same value upon it as he did. Both the high centres from which the war was directed now measured with the same rod. The Versailles Council, through the difficulties of communication, were from three

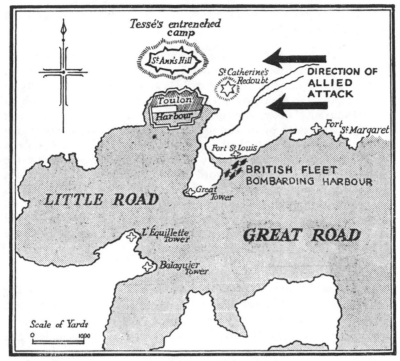

THE SIEGE OF TOULON

weeks to a month behindhand in their power of intervention. But as soon as they knew that a violent struggle was proceeding on the heights to the east of Toulon, and that the fate of the harbour hung in the balance, they laid their hands on every other theatre and clawed troops away even from the most urgent need. Exactly what Marlborough had foreseen and predicted happened. First of all they denuded Spain. Marshal Berwick in full exploitation of Almanza was ordered on August 18 to gather his troops and quit the Peninsula, recross the Pyrenees, and march to the succour of Toulon. The foolish descent, prayed for by the Empire, of five thousand men at Barcelona would not have shifted a French battalion out of Spain. The attack upon Toulon denuded Spain of French troops. The

255

remnants of the allied forces were suddenly conscious that everywhere pressure upon them was relieved.

On August 15 a French counter-stroke expelled the Allies from the heights of St Catherine, which they had gained on July 30. The gallant Prince of Saxe-Gotha, who had led the right wing at Turin a year before, was killed. By the 20th it was resolved to retreat. There were the recriminations usual in failure. Eugene reveals his own vexation in his letter to the Emperor of August 20:

> Something fresh keeps cropping up with the English, whose nature is that once they have got anything into their heads they stick to it. At the moment they would like to believe that we are not really in earnest about the operation before Toulon, but, to tell the truth to Your Imperial Majesty with all submission and respect, this is sheer nonsense, suggested by the English envoy to the Duke, a young man without experience in military affairs.[1] Others, who have only a partial understanding of war but are more sensible, say exactly the opposite and of their own accord comprehend matters in the right way; indeed, it might well be possible to throw blame on the English themselves because they were not prepared to seize the enemy's booms at the very first, although I represented the urgent need to do so, and offered to deal with this end myself, and to embark troops to force the other end with the assistance of the fleet.[2]

But all was over.

The fleet embarked the sick, wounded, and artillery in its transports. Before he sailed away Shovell determined to attack the French fleet in the dockyard basins from the sea. Battleships had already prepared the way for bombardment: they had cannonaded the batteries that prevented the approach of their vulnerable bomb vessels, and had landed men to spike the deserted guns. On August 21, the first day calm enough for bombarding, Rear-Admiral Sir Thomas Dilkes anchored the flotilla of bomb-ketches near the shore. That afternoon and throughout the night under his direction they hove shells and explosive carcasses over the neck of land into the dockyard, setting ships and storehouses alight. What was thought in those days to be immense damage was done, and Toulon was shrouded in the smoke of many fires. That same night the army retreated along the coast in five columns. They were neither pursued nor intercepted. They crossed the Var on the 31st, reached Pignerol about the middle of September, and with the object of

---

[1] Chetwynd.
[2] *Feldzüge*, Series I, ix, 185–186.

securing a more favourable line of advance in another year wound up the campaign with the siege and capture of Susa.

Thus ended the memorable effort against Toulon. The design and will-power were Marlborough's and the impulse English: but nothing could prevail against the selfish divergencies of the Empire or the signs of oppression which seemed to rest throughout upon Prince Eugene. There may have been a deeper cause, but these were enough. Marlborough and the London Cabinet threw the blame upon the Empire, and never harboured or tolerated suspicions against Victor Amadeus. "You will therefore understand," wrote Marlborough to Wratislaw (October 2, 1707),

> that this prince should be humoured [*ménagé*] without being allowed to dictate to us, and I don't mind telling you that I have a high opinion of his sincerity and good faith.

The voice of suspicion suggested that Marlborough's favourable view of Victor Amadeus was not entirely impartial. According to a Dutch report printed in Lamberty:

> The Duke of Marlborough was not in favour of weakening His Royal Highness of Savoy, and it was because he was convinced of that Prince's wise conduct that the latter sent him a rich present. This consisted of a set of hangings of seven or eight pieces, made of gilded leather. It was very much worn, but its value was greatly increased by the paintings by the hand of Titian in the middle of each piece. These were of nude figures in diverse lewd and lascivious postures, but the parts that might offend one's delicacy were covered over. Its high value was due to the fact that it was an original which had never been copied. The King of France had in vain offered 100,000 crowns for it, to hang in his abode of pleasure called Trianon. The Duke of Marlborough had the pieces hung in the house of the English envoy Stepney [at The Hague].[1] On the latter's death in London about this time the Duke brought them away with him, when he crossed the Channel.[2]

It is far more likely that Marlborough accepted the gift than that his judgment or actions were influenced thereby. Indeed, as we shall see, he rigorously subordinated the interests of Victor Amadeus and the Savoy front to the main campaign of 1708 in Flanders.

> Likewise [his letter to Wratislaw continues] I cannot quite agree with you about Toulon. You may take it from me that no Englishmen

[1] Stepney, after leaving Vienna, succeeded A. Stanhope at The Hague. He died in London on September 15, 1707.
[2] Lamberty, iv, 598.

will be found ever to disavow this enterprise: on the contrary, I am sure that if we had had more troops, *or had arrived five days earlier,* it was a certainty [*immanquable*].[1]

No one, on the other hand, must ignore the estimate of the difficulties presented on the spot by so sincere and noble a warrior as Eugene. He may well have been right that the task was impossible. It does not look in retrospect so hard as many of the feats of arms which he performed both before it and after. But it had failed, and with it failed the best hope of redeeming for the Allies the year 1707. Nevertheless good strategy even in failure often produces compensations. The secondary evils of the defeat at Almanza were avoided, and the Allies regained a fleeting control of the Peninsula. The results afloat were decisive and enduring. The French had scuttled their fleet in shallow water to save their hulls from the Allies' fire. When the time came to raise these ships again, all but a few were found to be past repair. Others were burned or fatally injured by the English and Dutch bombardment. The dockyard, its cordage-stores and factories, were largely destroyed. Never again in the War of the Spanish Succession did France attempt to dispute the English command of the Mediterranean, which has been maintained with occasional interludes up till the present day. "The war of squadrons is finished," wrote the French naval historian. "Toulon is safe; but our Fleet is defunct."[2]

[1] *Dispatches*, iii, 607.
[2] La Roncière, *Histoire de la marine française* (1932), vi, 395.

Chapter Fifteen

MARLBOROUGH IN TRAMMELS

1707—SUMMER

I T is hard across the gulf of time to represent the magnitude of the effort which the siege of Toulon cost Marlborough. Upon this enterprise he staked all his power to plan the next move which the Ramillies campaign had won him. It was his design. His wishes had been obeyed by the Cabinet in London, by the States-General at The Hague, by the princes of Germany so far as they were concerned or were capable of action. Even Vienna had conformed sullenly, disloyally, but still decidedly. So far as lay in his power, then so far-reaching, he had set all things moving in one direction. Was he right or wrong? Would the fall of Toulon have been the death-blow of France? Marlborough's own authority and conviction must carry the chief weight; but Louis XIV and his military circle thought the same as their opponent; and Charles XII from his entirely different standpoint arrived secretly and spontaneously at a similar conclusion. Thus the three supreme exponents of the military art were in accord upon the merits of the plan. But the cost was measureless. A year's campaign must be used; a year of political attrition at home; a year of waning comradeship throughout the Alliance. High stakes for Toulon!

Nothing remained for Marlborough at Meldert but to await the result, and meanwhile to hold the main French army close gripped upon the Flanders front. His smaller numbers prevented him from making a siege; the Dutch veto forbade him to force a battle. There was only the faint hope that Vendôme, like Villeroy, would himself seek a decision. But Vendôme, although from his fortified camp at Gembloux he pressed various projects upon Versailles, was himself restrained from running any serious risks by Louis XIV, who was listening at this time to the cautions of the Elector Max Emmanuel. He continued to make proposals for action, and accepted his master's refusals without undue chagrin. Thus both the main armies lay motionless within a couple of marches of one another during the height of the campaigning season for more than ten weeks. When we reflect upon the poverty and rudimentary organization of the warring nations, and try to measure the daily cost of keeping these enormous forces watching each other month by month in intense readiness for battle, we may realize the waste and strain involved.[1]

The Captain-General's letter-bag reveals the whole European scene. In the forefront stood the catastrophe upon the Rhine. The incompetent Margrave of Bayreuth had made no attempt to defend the line of the Enz. Exposing the crossing at Pforzheim, he had retired towards Muhlacker pursued by Villars with forty thousand men. Leaving detachments to demolish the famous Lines of Stollhofen, the Marshal pressed forward impetuously, unhampered by considerations of reserves, bases, siege-train, or supply columns. His aim was to burst into Germany before a militia could be collected, to grind down the defenceless Estates of the Reich, and roam through the land with colours flying, spreading terror before him. On June 8 his headquarters were at Stuttgart. From here he made it plain that the French Treasury would be replenished from the purses of German princes, nobles, burghers, and peasants. Messengers were sent in all directions to demand contributions in kind and payments in money. Threatened by fire and sword, the princes and cities of Swabia produced millions to ransom what they had neglected to defend. Advancing from Stuttgart, Villars drove the Margrave back upon Nördlingen. French raiders traversed the battlefield of Blenheim. French detachments and exactions spread throughout Franconia. There was even a possibility of the general revolt of the Bavarian countryside against the Allies.[1] Marlborough did what he could to stem the tide. He begged a regiment of cavalry, one of dragoons, and three battalions of infantry from the Elector Palatine. He requested Vienna to return Danes from Bavaria, and eventually diverted Saxons who were approaching his own army.[2] To the Margrave of Bayreuth he wrote on June 7:

> I dare flatter myself that if all the troops Your Highness has in hand were concentrated the army of the Empire would be at least equal and perhaps superior to the enemy's forces, of which it is certain that at least half are but militia. . . . I invite Your Highness to consider whether some helpful diversion cannot be made with the numerous garrisons of Philippsburg and Landau. . . . Moreover, there would be no purpose in having such strong garrisons at such a juncture, if no use is made of them. Your Highness may well believe that if the

---

[1] See also von Noorden, ii, 556.   [2] *Dispatches*, iii, 395.

advantage had been on our side, and we had made an irruption into their country, the French would not leave six thousand men at Strasburg with their arms folded [*les bras croisés*], as ours are at Philippsburg.[1]

To Harley: "If all their troops were together with a good head, they might themselves remedy this disaster."[2] To Wratislaw he prescribed a more personal remedy. "We were right to press you

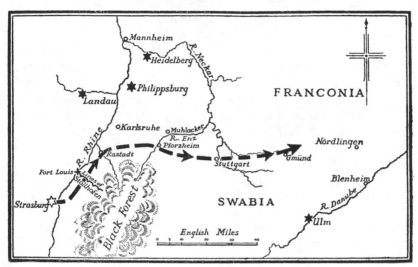

VILLARS'S INVASION OF GERMANY

for so long a time to send a general there, I do not propose to say which; but in the name of God do not lose a moment in getting rid of the Margrave and sending thither a general on the active list [*un général en poste*]."[3] And to Count Sinzendorff:

> We might make you many reproaches about the disaster on the Rhine. If the least attention had been paid to the pressing requests which have been so often repeated to you to send there a general of authority, capable of commanding the troops, our affairs would not be in this vexatious condition. On the contrary, if M. de Starhemberg had been sent there in good time, the enemy would never have ventured on any undertaking, and we should perhaps have had the advantage on our side.[4]

To Harley (June 9): "If they had a good general in Germany, I am persuaded they can bring together troops enough of their own to oblige the French to retire over the Rhine."[5] And to M. de

[1] *Dispatches*, iii, 396.　　[2] June 6; *ibid.*, 394.　　[3] June 6; *ibid.*, 389.
[4] *Ibid.*, 392.　　[5] *Ibid.*, 400.

Janus: "I am sure that all Villars has beyond his sixteen thousand men are militia and local levies on which he would never dare depend."

These extracts are typical of the authority and vigour of the correspondence which made Marlborough's headquarters the centre of the whole Alliance. For the ten weeks of his stay at Meldert from June 1 to August 10 the more important letters printed in the *Dispatches* fill a hundred and twenty-five pages, and this takes no account of his private correspondence with Sarah and Godolphin.

The Hungarian revolt at this time had entered upon a new phase. The French Government sought to commit Rakoczy to an irreconcilable breach. Louis XIV offered him an official alliance, but only on condition that the Diet of Hungary formally deposed the Emperor Joseph I from the kingship. Rakoczy yielded to this pressure. Perhaps he had little choice. But the consequences were fatal to the rebellion. The Hungarian movement was split from top to bottom. The majority of the nation wished to secure their rights by coming to terms with their legitimate ruler. His attempted deposition meant a fight to the death. The Catholic elements on the whole favoured the French view, but the Lutherans were vehemently opposed to it. Rakoczy was himself compelled to coerce Hungarian opinion by violence. A Diet was summoned to meet at Onod. The leader of the Lutherans, one of the enormous family of Okolicsany, was seized and executed, and two of his friends were murdered by Rakoczy's orders at the instigation of French officers. This event produced a profound impression throughout Hungary. The "bloody Diet of Onod," as it was called, marked the collapse of Hungarian unity. The revolt was wracked with other difficulties. The peasants of Moravia and Austria had now taken refuge in strongholds; the fields and farms were ruined. Raids were no longer profitable, and the patriot soldiers could only live by preying on their own countrymen. The demand that the Emperor should abdicate the Hungarian Throne redoubled the fury of Vienna. Marlborough, well informed as ever, held back the Sea Powers from further efforts at conciliation. Rakoczy's position became increasingly precarious, and his insurgent troops began to flinch. During 1707 the resistance of Hungary absorbed the main Imperial effort, but under that effort it steadily weakened, although its final defeat at the battle of Trentschin was not reached until the spring of the following year.

The need for a victory in Flanders became only the more apparent.

Marlborough continued to coax and persuade the Pensionary Heinsius to grant him the necessary freedom to fight, without which he could only manœuvre up to a fiasco. Geldermalsen had by this time returned to the army, apparently with Marlborough's consent. His colleague Goslinga continued to cavil and malign. His charges are not obscure. Upon the retreat at the end of May from Soignies by Brussels to the camp at Meldert Goslinga says:

> I made up my mind from that moment that the Duke had no intention of achieving anything in the whole campaign, and that, seeing himself deprived of the hope of ever obtaining (except in the last extremity) the agreement of the States-General to his governorship of Belgium, his obsession [*sa marotte*], he would drag out the war in order to checkmate us while he from time to time gave orders, and filled his purse.[1]

On the other hand, he writes on almost the same page of his memoirs:

> We received in this camp positive orders from our masters to risk nothing. The reasons for these fine orders were the uncertain outcome of the Toulon expedition and the superior strength of the enemy. Geldermalsen and I, who suspected already from the Duke's entire conduct that he had no desire to accomplish much in this campaign, managed to get them kept secret until we had new ones, meanwhile explaining [to The Hague] our reasons. We foresaw that the Duke would be delighted to be able to exculpate himself for his own inaction by such orders, and would throw the blame of an abortive campaign upon the States and their deputies. Our representations were vain, and we were ordered anew to *avoid all occasions where there would be any risk of coming to an action, until the outcome of the Toulon enterprise was known or until the Duke of Vendôme had made a substantial detachment.*[2]

Thus we see Goslinga blaming Marlborough for sluggishness and lack of zeal against the enemy, while at the same time he had in his pocket the explicit orders of his "masters" to avoid every occasion where there would be a "risk of coming to an action" till news was received of the upshot of Toulon, which might not be for two or three months. It may be thought hard upon a general to be blamed for not fighting, and foully aspersed in his motives, by the very man whose highest function was to prevent him. Goslinga was no judge of the military possibilities. Neither was he Marlborough's channel to the Dutch authorities. The Duke suffered Goslinga with an eighteenth-century patience. He dealt with

---

[1] Goslinga, p. 34.   [2] *Ibid.*, p. 35.

Heinsius. On the very day, June 2, when Goslinga depicts himself as deploring the veto on battles because it would give Marlborough an excuse to wriggle out of fighting and meanwhile to continue to draw his salaries, we find a hitherto unpublished letter:

Marlborough to Heinsius

MELDERT
June 2d, 1707

★By the march of the Enemy to Perwis this morning, it lookes as if thay despair'd of gaining Bruxelles, and it is said the Siege of Huy is resolv'd; I hope You will be of opinion that this Victorious Army aught never to suffer such an affront, for shou'd we let them make that siege in quiet, the next step wou'd bee the taking of Liege, and after that be in a Condition of doing what thay please. I am sure the Army is in good heart, and where ever the grownd will permit us to engage, with the blessing of God we shou'd beat them, the Consequences of which must be a good peace, which is much wish'd for. . . .[1]

John to Sarah

MELDERT
June 13, 1707

★But for the public good it were to be wished it [the battle] might be had, for our affairs go very ill in Germany as well as Spain, and for my part, notwithstanding the noise the French have made, I think they would less care to venture a battle than our friends; for if they had a real mind to it it must have been decided before this time. In the army I must do them right that there is all the desire imaginable to venture their lives for the publick good, but all other sorts of people on this side of the water are so very wise that I am afraid at last they will bring us to an ill peace. For myself I am old and shall not live to see the misfortunes which must happen to Christendom if the French be suffered to get the better of this warr.[2]

These proofs both from published and unpublished documents can be multiplied to an extent which would be wearisome. Day after day during this injurious, costly paralysis Marlborough's intimate letters to Sarah and Godolphin show him using the whole influence he had with The Hague and also with the Deputies and generals in the camp to procure freedom of action and manœuvre. In particular he pressed upon the Deputies a march to the west of Vendôme's position—a minor manœuvre which would, he declared, immediately oblige the French to retreat. Always he begged for the right to fight a battle if he thought fit. He stooped to every kind

[1] Blenheim MSS. [2] *Ibid.*

of promise not to fight a general engagement unless he had undoubted advantage. But the only response was from The Hague
reiterated negation to their Deputies, and from Goslinga the insertion of renewed calumnies in his diary. The Dutch Government,
with the power placed in their hands by Ramillies, did not intend
to jeopardize their gains. "Our friends will not venture," wrote
Marlborough compendiously, "unless we have an advantage,
which our enemies will be careful not to give."[1] They were chilled
by Almanza and Stollhofen. They used the protracted operations
against Toulon as a valid excuse for delay. When this was exhausted
they found others, and never during the whole of 1707 did they
allow the Duke more than a shadow of the freedom he had used so
remarkably in the previous year.

It was said of Marlborough that he could refuse a favour with
more grace than others could grant one. The business of exchanging prisoners of mark afforded many opportunities for the courteous
usages of the day. He had, it will be remembered, after Ramillies
given large numbers of French officer prisoners immediate leave of
absence upon parole to arrange their affairs. These were bound
by a code of honour, accepted throughout Europe, to return when
called upon. However, there were many excuses on the grounds
of ill-health, private affairs, or old friendship with the Duke. His
letter to the Marquis du Plessis-Châtillon-Nonant is a model.

> I have received your letter of the 8th and am indeed grieved to learn
> that your health is so bad, all the more because it no longer depends
> upon me to allow the extension of leave which you desire. All your
> friends will bear witness to the promptitude with which I always
> busy myself in meeting their wishes, but the orders which the Queen
> has given me to direct those whose leave is expired to surrender to
> their parole have quite tied my hands; thus I must await a more
> favourable occasion of marking the veritable esteem with which I
> subscribe myself.[2]

And to the Comtesse de Lionne, who had written on behalf of
her husband:

> I should indeed have one of the hardest and most insensible hearts
> in the world were I not extremely touched by the letter you have been
> so good as to write me about the leave of M. le Comte de Lionne;
> and what greatly increases the pain that I feel is that the remedy which

---

[1] To Harley; Bath Papers, *H.M.C.*, i, 173.
[2] June 20; *Dispatches*, iii, 428.

you propose for your troubles no longer depends upon me; for . . . the Queen has given me orders which entirely tie my hands, and do not permit me to give you the proof which I should wish of my sympathy in your distress; and although I have always obeyed the Queen's orders with pleasure, it is with much regret that I execute those which concern the Comte de Lionne.[1]

The explanation of these stern orders from Queen Anne is found in Marlborough's letter to Harley of June 23.

> Enclosed you have the copy of a letter from the French commissary wherein he proposes a general exchange of all the French prisoners we have in England, Holland, Germany, and Italy, against a like number they have lately taken in Spain. . . . As the French seem very pressing, I guess they do it in hopes of having their people to serve in their armies during this campaign, which is what we can hardly expect on our side; and therefore I am of opinion we ought to spin out two or three months, which we may easily do before we come to any conclusion of this matter. As I find the French begin in their usual manner to be a little haughty upon their success in Spain and the number of prisoners they have taken, I have written to M. Chamillart to desire he would send over all the French general officers and others that ought to have been in England before now.[2]

We do not propose to complicate this chapter of misfortune in the field and all the great strategic designs that went awry or were spoiled with any account of the royal and party intrigues at home. Our concern is with Marlborough, in his camp at Meldert, waiting and longing for the good news from Toulon which his comrade Prince Eugene might presently send him, and for the consequent change in the military conditions which would render so many European, domestic, and Cabinet perils obsolete. It is enough here that the Whigs in their anger and alarm had recourse to their usual and hitherto unfailing method of putting the screw on Godolphin, and that Godolphin poured out his troubles into Marlborough's bosom. Certainly the ten weeks of inaction at Meldert "eating and drinking," as Goslinga insolently observes about this remarkably frugal and abstemious man, "making his fortune from his pay and allowances," could not have been among the most agreeable in Marlborough's laborious life. The story of Job might well be rewritten in the terms which the historical facts of this period provide. But always there was the hope of Toulon. "I have been uneasy in my head," he wrote to Godolphin (August 4), "ever since

[1] June 26; *Dispatches*, iii, 443.   [2] *Ibid.*, 438.

I left off the Spa water; *but if the siege of Toulon goes prosperously, I shall be cured of all diseases except old age.*"[1]

The repercussion of the attack at Toulon had been protracted. Marlborough used language which spread over the high circles of the Confederate army an expectation that presently Vendôme would be ordered to send troops to Toulon. Even Goslinga records this impression. It was justified. By August 1 Louis XIV had sent peremptory orders to Vendôme to dispatch thirteen battalions and six squadrons to the southern front. As soon as this news reached Meldert Marlborough declared that the hour for action had struck. Vendôme was weakened. His superiority was gone. Marlborough demanded the right to attack him in his fortified camp at Gembloux. He appealed to The Hague. The Hague referred the matter to its Deputies and generals. Goslinga may speak for himself. "The Duke of Vendôme having at last received the order to send a large detachment to France, Milord appeared anxious to use the chance to attack the camp of the enemy, whose strength was still about equal to ours."[2] This should surely have been Goslinga's moment to spur the hitherto recreant Captain-General out of his lucrative inertia. But alas, all he remarks is, "This seemed risky" (*C'est ce qui paroissoit téméraire*). Therefore he, Geldermalsen, and the Dutch generals with whom they consorted unleashed their veto. "Nothing remained," says Goslinga, "but a secret sudden march which might compel him [Vendôme] to quit his unattackable camp. This is what the Duke resolved. I may say without vanity that I encouraged him in it as much as possible, and that when he made up his mind it was to me and Geldermalsen that he first told the secret."[3]

Here was, in fact, the march which Marlborough had for six weeks past been suggesting to The Hague, to the Deputies and the generals. He was almost certain, through his Secret Service and from his calculations, that Vendôme would resist nothing but a frontal attack, and that a movement upon his communications would send him scurrying back towards his main fortress line. He did not hope for a decisive battle. That could only be obtained by paying the high price of a direct assault. Still, there was the chance of mauling his rearguard or his flank-guard, and once these clashes began no one could fix their limits. The Deputies deemed an attempt of this kind not barred by their instructions. After all, they could

[1] Coxe, iii, 382. [2] Goslinga, p. 35. [3] *Ibid.*, p. 36.

always recur to them if undue risk threatened by ordering the Dutch troops to halt or retire at any moment, which would effectually arrest the Confederate army. It seemed a good opportunity for a spirited gesture with restricted commitments. Thus on the late afternoon of August 10 the splendid army of the Sea Powers, the best and largest that Marlborough had yet commanded, sending its baggage by daylight towards Louvain as a feint, broke camp at dusk.

There ensued the second brief series of rapid movements by the great armies which marked the campaign of 1707. Marlborough, marching south-west through Wavre, reached Genappe in the afternoon of August 10.[1] Here he threatened to attack the left flank of Vendôme's position, or alternatively to cut him off from Mons and his fortified lines and feeding-base. Vendôme, realizing at midnight (10th/11th) what his adversary was doing, abandoned his strong camp and retreated instantly by Gosselies towards Seneffe. The two armies therefore marched all day, converging in the same direction. But Vendôme by his promptitude in retiring kept ahead of Marlborough. The former distance of ten miles between the armies was perhaps halved, but in spite of their greater exertions no contact could be made by the Allies. The weather had suddenly become frightful; torrents of rain descended, making the few roads by which these large masses were moving most painful. Marlborough, who had intended to march early, postponed his further advance till noon to give his tired troops a rest. He reached Arquennes at six P.M. on August 12. Vendôme, who had halted when his pursuer halted, moved on again as soon as the chase was resumed, and thus kept a lead. Still the armies converged, and when the Allies reached Arquennes the French were but three miles away.

Both generals were under veto of the Dutch and French Governments respectively against wilfully fighting a battle. Marlborough's only chance was to stamp on the French rearguard. Such an event might have involved a general action. On the other hand, Vendôme, who might, if well posted and entrenched, have been ready to withstand an onslaught, was bound by his orders from Versailles to avoid this contingency if possible. Marlborough tried during the night of the 12th/13th to compromise Vendôme's rearguard. This operation miscarried, not only because of the general intentions of the French but also by an accidental delay in the pursuit.

Marlborough sent written orders to Count Tilly to march with

[1] See map on opposite page.

forty squadrons and five thousand grenadiers and attack the French rearguard. Count Lottum, with thirty squadrons and twenty battalions, was to support him. Tilly reached the point upon which he had been directed and opened his orders.

It rained heavily, was pitch dark, and no house near, so that it was an hour before a light could be got for him to read and know

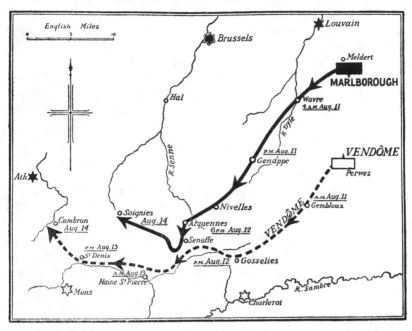

AUGUST 11–14, 1707

his orders, and no guides being there who knew the country and many defiles before him. It was another hour before guides were found, and, it still continuing dark and raining the whole night, he was shy to venture to march the detachment so near the enemy in the dark, so that in reasoning upon this the night was spent.[1]

Two allied squadrons who pushed on through the darkness reported at daylight the French army already in retreat under a strong rearguard of twenty-five squadrons and two thousand grenadiers. Tilly's men doubled for six miles; but the rearguard, using sunken roads to delay the pursuit, and withdrawing as fast as possible, got themselves out without serious ill-treatment. Thus

---

[1] Cranstoun; Portland Papers, *H.M.C.*, iv, 443.

the attempt to pin the French tail failed, and with it the last chance, if ever there had been a chance, of bringing about a battle under the limited conditions prescribed. The next two marches could not alter the relations of the armies. Vendôme moved through Haine-Saint-Pierre and on to Saint-Denis, where he was close to his fortified lines about Mons and where further chase was useless. In terrible weather Marlborough moved on August 14 to Soignies; and Vendôme, resting his right wing on Mons, continued a little farther to the westward towards Ath. Both armies, exhausted and dripping, then settled down in almost the same positions they had occupied in May. Vendôme now drew reinforcements from Charleroi and Namur. Marlborough remained about Soignies, being only able in the continuous heavy rain to feed himself by the stone-paved turnpike from Brussels.

The best-known accounts of this swift, abortive manœuvre of the main armies come down to us from Goslinga and Colonel Cranstoun. Both criticize Marlborough. Goslinga complains that he did not move early enough on the morning of the 12th, and that he did not move at all on the 13th. Both he and Cranstoun say that Count Tilly was too old a man to have been entrusted with an operation that required the greatest vigour and daring. Cranstoun blames Marlborough for not having seen Count Tilly beforehand and explained to him orally what he was to do. This is one of those exceptional cases where the commander-in-chief is censured for having given written instead of verbal orders. Goslinga, of course, construes the series of events, the delayed march on the 12th, the choice of Count Tilly, and the halt on the 13th, as evidence that Marlborough did not mean to bring Vendôme to battle; and he further assumes, though without any warrant, that he could have done so by different decisions. Marlborough's good faith is vindicated by his critic Cranstoun:

> I believe most certain that no general in the world ever desired more sincerely and anxiously to fight, and to push the war in earnest than my Lord Duke does, yet by not taking all the right measures at that critical time . . . the enemy escaped out of our hands.[1]

And he agrees with Goslinga about Count Tilly: "An old man, and though a notable officer, yet by his age become perhaps too cautious and slow for such an enterprise."

It may well be that these strictures are valid. They do not in

---

[1] Portland Papers, *H.M.C.*, iv, 443.

any way affect the main issue. Vendôme was under orders to avoid a battle, and had a good start; Marlborough was not allowed to fight one unless he could bring it about inevitably. Considering that Vendôme marched light and free from all impedimenta, without pitching tents in spite of the cruel weather, and so fast that he lost four thousand straggler-prisoners, and that Marlborough carried with him all his cannon, and was clogged by the roads besides the veto, it is scarcely remarkable that there was no decision. Moreover, Vendôme could at any moment turn south towards his fortresses and bridgeheads on the Sambre at Charleroi and Maubeuge. Marlborough must therefore have been certain throughout that only by some gross error on the part of his enemy, or some piece of good luck, could he bring him to action. Vendôme committed no error, and the odd mischance fell against Marlborough. To catch Vendôme was a forlorn hope which failed.

Peterborough had accepted his dismissal from his military and naval appointments and his recall with outward nonchalance and inward wrath. He made his homeward journey in the spring of 1707 through the capitals of the Alliance. The Secretary of State lost no time in advising the various Courts that he had no commission or authority. Nevertheless Peterborough's fame, his rank, his energy of mind, his audacious personality, soon won him in most cases not merely ceremony but attention. His method was simple. He took the opposite line to the British Government on all points in dispute. He encouraged the Duke of Savoy to set his pretensions at the highest. Wratislaw he captivated by dwelling on the advantages of the Imperial expedition to Naples, which it was one of Marlborough's chief objects to prevent. Charles XII refused to receive him. Peterborough galloped after him on a groom's horse, and overtook and accosted him on the way to Altranstädt. The grim Swede listened in spite of himself.[1] While Marlborough's every effort was directed to turning Charles's thrust to the eastward, Peterborough of course exhorted him to remain and mediate between France and the Grand Alliance. Fortunately the King regarded him with undue contempt. In Hanover he naturally advised the Electress to press her claims to visit England. These marplot peregrinations finally brought the errant Earl to the camp at Soignies. Wratislaw had written Marlborough a highly favourable account of Peterborough's mood and quality. The Duke, who thought

[1] Besenval (an intercepted letter); Coxe, iii, 185.

he had better find out what might be his intentions on reaching England, and unruffled by his vexatious conduct, sent him a ceremonious invitation. "I am willing to flatter myself," he wrote, "that your curiosity of seeing this army, as well as your friendship to me, will give me the pleasure of seeing you very quickly."[1]

The Almanza defeat had been a godsend to Peterborough. He was on record as having condemned beforehand the advance which had led to the disaster. Had he not denounced Galway as incompetent? And was this not now terribly proven? Had he not spent and mortgaged his private fortune in the public cause? Had he not been dismissed, as he declared, in the full flow of his genius and success? Peterborough arrived at Marlborough's headquarters with a somewhat formidable self-justification supported by "several letters and resolution of councils of war."[2] He was well aware that his case would appeal to the Tory Party. Galway was obnoxious to them as a French refugee, as one of King William's importations, as a Whig *protégé*, and as a defeated general. Peterborough embodied a first-class Parliamentary quarrel, rich with facts, armed with prejudice, and touching the most irritable spots of English politics.

The English Cabinet were increasingly incensed by Peterborough's conduct. Both Secretaries of State were hot against him. Harley, in fact, wished to make him show that he had obeyed his orders, and in default to try him for misdemeanour before a common jury. "It would be better," he remarked, "to find him work to defend himself than to leave him at leisure to do mischief."[3] The natural logic, pedantry, and partisanship of the Whig lords sustained this temper. Marlborough saw farther ahead. He warned Godolphin against the crude processes suggested by the Secretary of State. But all were agreed that Peterborough should sooner or later be invited to explain why in 1706 he had not marched to Madrid with the forces under his command; secondly, why he had not fulfilled his instructions by advancing to the King of Spain the moneys entrusted to him for that purpose; and, thirdly, why he had quitted Spain for Italy without orders, and there borrowed large sums of money for the Government on improvident terms.

The Commander-in-Chief received his guest with his customary courtesy, and listened for hours at a time to all he had to say. During ten long days the Duke surpassed himself in patience, urbanity, and reserve. His current comments are illuminating.

---

[1] *Dispatches*, iii, 365.   [2] Coxe, iii, 323.   [3] *Ibid.*, 350.

To Godolphin (August 15): "My lord Peterborough has been here ever since Friday, and I believe he thinks of staying some days longer." To Sarah:

> Since my last we have had one continued rain so that neither the enemy nor we can stir out of our camps. I have at this time my winter clothes, and a fire in my chamber, but, what is worse, the ill weather hinders me from going abroad, so that Lord Peterborough has the opportunity of very long conversations; what is said one day the next destroys, so that I have desired him to put his thoughts in writing.[1]

And to Godolphin (August 18):

> Lord Peterborough has said all that is possible to me, but says nothing of leaving the army. By what he tells me, he thinks he has demonstration to convince you that he has been injured in everything that has been reported to his disadvantage.[2]

And again to Sarah (August 25): "If Lord Peterborough should, when he comes to England, at any time write to you, pray be careful what answer you make, for sooner or later it will be in print."[3]

Notwithstanding these drab reflections, Marlborough was evidently impressed with Peterborough's case. He gave him a letter of recommendation to the English Government which, though studiously non-committal, ended with the decisive sentence, "As far as I am capable of judging, I verily think he has acted with great zeal."

Towards the end of August Chetwynd's reports from Toulon were gloomy. "There is not that friendship and reliance between the Duke of Savoy and Prince Eugene as should be wished, for making so great a design succeed."[4] Rumours of a failure in the south floated across from the French lines in Flanders. The facts gradually spread. At last the truth was known.

Marlborough bore this crowning disappointment with his usual calm. He set himself at once to minimize the evil effects, and to encourage every one. "We have no direct letters," he wrote to Count Maffei, the Savoyard Minister in London (September 5),

> since those of August 13. But all the letters from France make it only too clear that His Royal Highness abandoned the siege of Toulon on the 22nd. We know nothing since of the movements of our army,

---

[1] Coxe, iii, 320.   [2] Ibid., 321.   [3] Ibid., 325.   [4] Quoted in Taylor, ii, 49.

which gives me some reason to hope that His Royal Highness may have had some other less difficult plan in view; at least you may comfort yourself that all accounts are agreed that His Royal Highness has acted in this enterprise with all the zeal and ardour that could be wished, after which the decision upon events must be left to God.[1]

And to General Rehbinder (commanding the Palatine troops in Spain) (September 7):

We have learned from France that the Duke of Savoy has quitted the siege of Toulon and retreated, which as you may well believe has caused much chagrin after the hopes we had founded on the capture of this place.[2]

And to Sunderland (September 19):

I agree entirely with you that the success the French have had is very discouraging, and if care be not taken in the manner you mention the consequences may be dangerous with Holland; for I have received very desponding letters from these parts. Either we were in the wrong in the beginning of the war, or we have reason to continue it with vigour, or content ourselves with losing our liberties; for the French are very insolent in success, notwithstanding their very great desire for peace.

If the Allies continue firm this winter, I am of opinion the enemy will at the entrance of the next campaign venture a battle in this country, since they see that success in any other part of the world cannot give them peace. You may be sure that I long extremely for quietness; but at the same time I am very sensible that during this war I must continue in the galley. . . .[3]

During the whole summer Marlborough conducted the allied correspondence with Charles XII. He wrote repeatedly to Count Piper in order to maintain the ties established by his visit. He urged the Emperor through every channel to make the concessions which the imperious Swede demanded. During the whole summer these critical negotiations hung in the balance. They may be studied in Marlborough's dispatches and in Continental histories. Marlborough tried to keep the King of Sweden in good humour, and eventually persuaded the Emperor to sacrifice his offended pride to grave need. There were moments when he feared that nothing but force would bring Charles XII to reason. He began sombrely to consider ways and means. He let Count Piper feel that the Sea Powers had other resources besides argument and presents, and that if all else failed they would aid the Emperor to defend his territory

---

[1] *Dispatches*, iii, 548. [2] *Ibid.*, 549. [3] Coxe, iii, 367.

and rights. He managed to convey this impression to the King without enraging him. It was not till September that the "hero of the North" declared himself appeased. It is significant that he waited till he had news that the siege of Toulon was definitely abandoned. The treaty was ratified on the 12th; and on the 25th his terrifying army turned its bayonets to the east and crossed the Oder into Silesia. The Imperial Court freely attributed to Marlborough the main credit for this result. It was one of his most notable successes in diplomacy.

General Schulenburg gives us a convincing instance of Marlborough's judgment and of his comprehension, which held all Europe in its gaze. He recounts a conversation which he had with him in 1708 in the presence of Eugene upon Charles XII's affairs. "Milord duke believes that one cannot do better than let him act exactly as he wishes in the direction of Moscow, where he could never reach his end [*venir au bout*] but will ruin himself to such an extent that he will not be able to do any more mischief, and that we shall find ourselves altogether rid of him."[1] It is curious that Prince Eugene, with all his knowledge of Europe, took the opposite view. He thought that "the attack upon the Czar might go too far and might well produce regrettable consequences; and that the King of Sweden at the head of forty thousand men would be able to over-turn the Empire as often as he chose."[2]

But Marlborough was right. His measurements of men and affairs were so sure that he seems almost gifted with prophetic power. By the end of 1709 Charles XII was irretrievably ruined by the battle of Pultawa. Every word of Marlborough's had come true.

This was for the future; and it was with sorrow that the Captain-General surveyed the results of 1707. The recovery of France seemed complete in every theatre. Grievous defeats had overtaken the allied arms at Almanza and Stollhofen; cruel disappointment at Toulon. His own campaign had been fettered and ineffectual. The Empire pursued its woebegone, particularist ambitions. Southern Germany had allowed itself to be ravaged without any rally of the Teutonic princes. The Dutch, angry and disappointed, hugged their Barrier, and their grasping administration had already cost the Allies every scrap of Belgian sympathy. There had been no lack of political malice in England even after the glories of 1706.

---

[1] *Leben und Denkwürdigkeiten Johann Mathias Reichsgrafen von der Schulenburg* (1834), i, 340.　　[2] *Loc. cit.*

What would be the temper now when there was nothing to show but vast expense and general miscarriage? In this adversity the Confederate armies sought their winter quarters; and Marlborough returned home to face a Cabinet crisis, the Parliamentary storm, and, worst of all, a bedchamber intrigue.

Chapter Sixteen

ABIGAIL

1707—SUMMER

SUNDERLAND'S appointment rankled in the heart of the Queen. Ignoring the straits to which her two chief Ministers were put, closing her eyes to the Parliamentary situation and the needs of Supply and War, Anne set herself to vindicate her royal authority. Her heart was estranged from Mr Montgomery and from Mrs Freeman. She listened to what they said to her on public business, and complied with all the requirements of State. But she made them feel that the tie which bound her to them was one of duress or convenience and no longer of affection. Nor did the void in the Queen's bosom remain unfilled. Who would deliver her from the Whigs? This became her obsession. The many glories of her reign, the wonderful position she now held in Europe, which was then the world, the united island, the loyal people, the lustre of immortal victories, all faded in the sullen glow of her resentment. Her search for a deliverer was not long or fruitless. Always at hand was her trusted, well-liked Secretary of State, Mr Harley. What a comfort it was to talk to him! He understood her difficult position; he sympathized with her in the oppression to which she was subjected. He never asked her to do disagreeable things. On the contrary, he made her feel how unnecessary was Godolphin's subservience to the Whigs, how wrongful and injurious were their insatiable demands. In this business of modern politics, in the House of Commons, in the party intrigues, the money votes, and all that, he was unrivalled. What he did not know about the management of the Commons was not worth knowing. He was there in the assembly which he had led or presided over so long, and could sway. Unlike Godolphin, he had a following, and it was composed of exactly those very elements, the moderate Tories, which Anne conceived to be the true nucleus of any national Government.

Mr Freeman was always at the wars. This was necessary, because he was a wonder-worker at the head of armies. There was none like him in the whole world. It was a pity he could not be at home. If only he would protect her from the Whigs! She would not then have to listen to their hateful voices conveyed shamefacedly through the mouth of their puppet Godolphin. He would keep Sarah from making scenes, writing endless political letters, and giving her unwelcome lectures on matters far beyond the province of a woman subject. There was nothing the Queen would not do for him if in return he could only render her this reasonable and rightful service. With him at her side, all would be well; but he was abroad.

The time came when Anne addressed herself to Harley in terms which were disloyal to her principal Ministers. One day a gardener handed him a secret letter from the Queen. She appealed to him to give her his help.[1] No greater temptation could have been cast before an eighteenth-century statesman. Moreover, it harmonized with Harley's deep political calculations and his innate love of mystery and subterranean intrigue. Forthwith he began to organize a group out of which, with the Queen's exclusive favour, an alternative Government might be formed. He held nightly meetings with his Tory friends, with the law officer Simon Harcourt, and with the Secretary-at-War, St John, to devise a plan of action. It was obvious that this must comprise as its first decisive step the supplanting of Godolphin. But what of Marlborough? Harley was not at all sure which way Marlborough would go. He knew that, on the whole, Marlborough agreed with him, that he wished to preserve contact with the Tories, that scarcely less than the Queen he dreaded falling into the hands of the Whigs. Had not Marlborough visited the Duke of Shrewsbury, now returned from his long self-imposed exile, and spoken to him of the tyranny of the Whig lords? This suggestive fact had been disclosed to the Harley group, who were in touch with Shrewsbury. Shrewsbury was a fresh factor in the combination. A strong rally of the sensible Tories, with new, vigorous support from the Queen, might give Marlborough all that he wanted as the basis for his campaigns.

Up to a point Harley could persuade himself that he was acting in Marlborough's practical interest. Was Marlborough the man to allow this interest to be prejudiced for the sake of saving an old friend like Godolphin, who had definitely exhausted his political

---

[1] We incline to the view of Herr Salomon that this incident occurred in the autumn of 1707 or early in 1708, and not in 1710, as dated by Swift. We will not burden the reader by repeating the complicated but convincing argument. (F. Salomon, *Geschichte des letzten Ministeriums Königin Annas von England, 1710–14* (1894), p. 15.)

usefulness? Like other people then and in later generations who have studied this enigmatic being, Harley could not measure Marlborough. He therefore deemed it probable that the Captain-General would desert Godolphin—for whom every kind of ceremonious and lucrative compensation would no doubt be provided—and accommodate himself to the new arrangement.

But still it might not be so. Marlborough might stand by Godolphin through thick and thin. The Secretary of State did not shrink from this awe-inspiring contingency. It would no doubt be bad for the war and the allied cause to oust Marlborough from the command of the armies; but when Harley was dealing with exciting personal and party forces, external events seemed to take on a new and temporarily reduced proportion. There was the Elector of Hanover, now at last persuaded to accept the command of the Imperial forces on the Rhine. Even the Whigs would be reassured in their party future by the appointment to the supreme command of the lawful Protestant successor to the crown of England. Apart from questions of victory, the lives of soldiers, the honour of the nation, the glint of the flag, all this looked promising and perhaps practicable, if need be.

But here arose the case of St John. Without St John's brilliant oratory, his splendid mental equipment, his fire, his ruthlessness, everything would go awry. What would St John do? He was Marlborough's Secretary-at-War, in the closest touch with the armies, sharing the burden of their labours, fascinated by their prowess. Still revelling in wine and women, he was none the less in office eager, vigilant, and tireless. He was a whole-hearted admirer of Marlborough. He was one of his young men. A comradeship subsisted between them, for Marlborough had come to like and trust St John. They corresponded freely and intimately. The Duke interested himself in St John's private affairs. He had been made acquainted with the young Minister's perpetual financial embarrassments. He had concerned himself in having his emoluments raised. More than that, this miser and skinflint, as he is represented, had on one occasion, it is asserted,[1] paid St John's debts from his own carefully accumulated fortune. Again the question presented itself to Harley: Would St John go the whole length?

Harley on this occasion did not deal in half-confidences. He let his associate see quite clearly that the ruin of Marlborough might,

---

[1] Von Noorden, *Historische Vorträge* (1884), p. 70.

if the worst came to the worst, have to be faced as part of the plan. On what process St John made up his mind we cannot tell. To cast aside a benefactor and hero, and perchance wreck the policy of the state and the Alliance, and lose the war for the sake of a leap at real political power, must have been to him a tremendous personal issue. In the upshot, however, St John decided, should the need arise, to go with Harley in compassing the overthrow of Marlborough. For the sake of office, for a share in the management of the war, for contact with the Duke, he had very readily four years before let the Occasional Conformity Bill, and all that it meant to those he had incited, go to the devil. Now the same operation must be performed upon a larger scale. It was Marlborough now who must be sacrificed, and possibly the allied cause as well. These were important decisions for the bankrupt gambler and genius to take. They were not, however, decisions to which his audacity was unequal, or his nature a bar.

The next stage carries us into the ecclesiastical sphere. A series of important vacancies occurred. The sees of Chester and Exeter fell vacant, and also the Regius Professorship of Divinity at Oxford. All these were key-posts in religion and party politics. Any dilution of King William's bishops would affect the small but solid Whig majority in the House of Lords. Oxford was at that time virtually a High Church seminary, from which the country clergy were mainly recruited. Every force at the disposal of the Whigs was set in motion. Sarah had already exhausted her influence, and her long letter of the preceding year and the Queen's reply explain the opposing points of view very clearly.[1] In January 1706/7 Somers had persuaded the Archbishop of Canterbury, Tenison, to wait upon the Queen and ascertain her feelings about one of the bishoprics. The Archbishop's reception was chilling. "My discourse," he reported, "was short, it being said to me on my entrance that the thing was already determined, though the person was not declared."[2] Godolphin's pleadings were equally vain and unwelcome. Upon the Oxford appointment Marlborough had been induced to exert his whole influence in favour of Dr Potter, the Whig nominee. Although under this heavy intervention the Queen gave way, the concession only strengthened her will upon the bishoprics. She was, in fact,

[1] See Coxe, iii, 272.
[2] Professor Sykes, "Queen Anne and the Episcopate," *English Historical Review*, July 1935, p. 441.

resolved to regain in the episcopal what she had lost in the Ministerial sphere. If Godolphin in the hands of the Junto made her
swallow Whig Ministers, she would make the Junto swallow Tory
bishops. Who could defeat her here? Was she not the acknowledged Head of the Church? Was not this a matter of conscience?
It was no mere party prejudice. Her duty to God was involved.
Founded upon the Eternal Rock and her own desires, no one could
presume to shake her. She nominated Dr Blackhall, a prominent
Tory partisan, to Exeter, and Dawes, another Tory, to Chester.
Both did homage in August.

Not only were party politics involved in a sharp, practical form,
but behind lay a more disquieting question. If these appointments
represented the Queen's spontaneous personal convictions, it was
bad enough. If some one was secretly influencing her, it was far
worse. If that some one was a Secretary of State acting behind the
backs of his colleagues, and behind party agreements on which
the Supplies had been voted and all Parliamentary difficulties
removed—that surely was worst of all. The very doctrine fundamental to the British Constitution, that the Monarch can do no
wrong, directed this blast of Whig suspicion and reprobation upon
Harley and his agents. What agents? And here the keenest minds
in England anticipated the French maxim, "Cherchez la femme."

It may be remembered that as far back as 1689 Sarah had discovered with some surprise that she had a poor relation named
Hill, a Levantine merchant ruined by speculation, who had four
children, among them a daughter, Abigail.[1] When the parents died
Sarah became the benefactress of the orphans, and provided for all
of them in various ways. Abigail, the eldest, lived at St Albans
with the Churchills and their children, and Sarah treated her as a
sister. Thus the years passed. When Anne came to the throne
Sarah introduced Abigail into the royal household, and during the
course of 1702 she became one of the Queen's dressers. She figured
in the list of bedchamber women of 1704 [2] In this post of humble
intimacy Abigail faithfully and tenderly waited upon the Queen in
her daily life and frequent illnesses. To beguile the long hours, she
played with skill the harpsichord, greatly to the Queen's enjoyment.
But at first and for some time their relations were those of mistress
and servant, or of patient and nurse. There is a curious letter of
Anne's in 1703 in which she chides Sarah, with a touch of

---

[1] Vol. I, pp. 433-435.　　　　[2] E. Chamberlayne, *Anglia Notitia* (1704).

jealousy, for her friendship for "Mrs [Mistress] Hill," as Abigail was called.

> Dear Mrs Freeman hates writing so much I fear, though she would stay away two or three days, she would hardly let me hear from her, and therefore for my own sake I must write to get a line or two. I fancy now you are in town you will be tempted to see the opera, which I should not wonder at, for I should be so too, if I were able to stir, but when that will be God knows, for my feavor is not quite gone, and I am still so lame I cannot go without limping. I hope Mrs Freeman has no thoughts of going to the Opera with Mrs Hill, and will have a care of engaging herself too much in her company, for, if you give way to that, it is a thing that will insensibly grow upon you. Therefore give me leave once more to beg for your own sake, as well as poor Mrs Morley's, that you would have as little to do with that enchantress as 'tis possible, and pray pardon me for saying this.[1]

Gradually, however, an attachment grew in the Queen's heart towards one who rendered her so many small offices.

We have noticed the change in Sarah's relations with Anne which followed the Queen's accession. They were no longer united by common dislike of King William, and they had widely different feelings about politics and religion. We have traced the growing tension and estrangement which Sarah's advocacy of Whig interests produced between her and her royal mistress. At the same time Sarah's habits also changed. She had now become a great lady—after the Queen the greatest in the land. She dwelt at the centre of politics, and with her strong, clear-cut views, powerful, practical mind, and caustic tongue was bound to play a prominent part in all the business transacted by Ministers with the sovereign. In her husband's absence at the wars she was his link with the Queen. Her relations with Godolphin were those of an indispensable Cabinet colleague. Courted by all, besought on every side for favours, united to the Queen by what the world believed to be a tie of life-long and undying affection, Sarah seemed endowed with power to make or mar. To do her justice, she set singularly little store by the dispensation of patronage and favours. Her interests were in the great spheres of war and affairs; her pride was to manage the Queen for the glory of the realm.

But Sarah had also her own four daughters to guide. She had her pleasant home at St Albans; she had her loving life with John in his fleeting visits, and her daily correspondence with him when

---

[1] Blenheim MSS.; quoted in Stuart Reid, *John and Sarah*, p. 146.

he was at the wars. Can we wonder that now she found her constant attendance upon Anne, their endless privacies, the dull, exacting routine of the palace, a companionship almost stifling? Insensibly she began to bring Abigail forward to bear some of the burden of entertaining the Queen. Abigail showed herself apt in this, and Anne made less difficulty about being separated from her beloved Mrs Freeman as the early years of the reign slipped by. There was no doubt, up to 1705 at least, that Anne would much rather have had Sarah with her than anyone else in the world except her husband. Nor can we doubt that had the Duchess of Marlborough continued the same assiduous and unceasing attentions which had been for nearly twenty years Sarah Churchill's task in life she would have kept her strange dominance over the royal heart. However, as the splendid reign unfolded and Marlborough's triumphs raised him to the pinnacle of Europe, Sarah saw less and less of Anne, and Anne increasingly leaned on Abigail.

It was also unfortunate that when the two women were together conversation should turn so often on the tiresome politics about which they disagreed, or upon proper and necessary requests by Sarah for decisions and promotions. Unsuspected at first on both sides, affection cooled. By the summer of 1705 Anne had become at least as dependent upon Abigail as upon Sarah. Till about this time Abigail never seems to have "talked of business" to the Queen; but she gradually became conscious of the reality of her influence. She was the witness on many occasions of hot disputes about politics between Sarah and the Queen. She saw Anne's distresses; she comforted her after stormy scenes. Presently she began not unnaturally to make comments upon public affairs which pleased the Queen. She always said what her mistress liked to hear. This process became pronounced as the divergence between Harley and Godolphin developed, and here we must note, though Sarah appears to have been long unconscious of it, that Abigail stood in about the same family relation to Harley as she did to Sarah. She was bound by a cousinly tie to both. She would naturally see the Secretary of State in his audiences and on many occasions. She cultivated this intimacy, as well as that with the Queen.

It is not till June 2, 1707, that the name of Abigail figures in Marlborough's correspondence. Evidently Sarah had become aware of a marked change in the demeanour of her poor relation. She felt herself in contact with a new power, hesitating, tentative, furtive, undefined, but in all senses real. She wrote in alarm to the

Duke. Marlborough, into whose category of values Abigail had not yet swum, replied, "I should think you might speak to her with some caution which might do good; *for she is certainly grateful and will mind what you say.*" This optimism did not last long.

Sarah was deeply disturbed. Instead of increasing her attendances upon the Queen, using all her arts upon her, and acting as if she were entirely at her ease, she indulged in the haughtiness of offended friendship. She stayed away from Court, and taxed the Queen roundly in letters with departing from their old affection and talking politics with her chambermaid. Sarah's eyes ought surely to have been opened by Anne's letter of July 18.

Anne to Sarah

Friday, five o'clock, July 18 [1707]

I give my dear Mrs Freeman many thanks for her letter, which I received this morning, *as I must always do for everything that comes from her*, not doubting but what you say is sincerely meant in kindness to me. But I have so often been unfortunate in what I have said to you that I think the less I say to your last letter the better; therefore I shall only, in the first place, beg your pardon once more for what I said the other day, which I find you take ill; and say something in answer to your explanation of the suspicions you seemed to have concerning *your cousin Hill*, who is very far from being an occasion of feeding Mrs Morley in her passion, as you are pleased to call it; *she never meddling with anything.*

I believe others that have been in her station in former times have been tattling and very impertinent, but she is not at all of that temper; and as for the company she keeps, it is with her as with most other people. *I fancy that their lot in the world makes them move with some out of civility rather than choice*; and I really believe, for one that is so much in the way of company, she has less acquaintance than anyone upon earth. *I hope, since in some part of your letter you seem to give credit to a thing because I said it was so*, you will be as just in what I have said now about Hill for I would not have anyone hardly thought of by my dear Mrs Freeman for your poor unfortunate but ever faithful Morley's notions or actions.[1]

This evidently was not one of Anne's genuine, forceful, effusions. It is, indeed, a masterpiece of sarcasm and polished hostility. It may well be that two or three people sat together upon this and chuckled in exclusive comradeship over its many stabs and gibes. We have little doubt that Harley pointed the pen with which the Queen wrote. Such a letter nowadays would chill relations between

[1] Coxe, iii, 259–260.

equals. Between Sovereign and subject it wore a graver aspect. The relations could not be ended. The sword of Marlborough upheld Britain and the Grand Alliance. His authority and connexions at home were on a vast scale, not easily to be measured. Sarah was his wife. Her office of Mistress of the Robes was as important as that of the Lord Keeper. She and the Queen were bound together and had to bicker it out. All political forces converged upon the point. Besides, in the Queen's heart there still perhaps sometimes lurked a fading wish to kiss, and let old days come back.

At the end of July 1707 Sarah learned that Abigail had been married some months previously to a Mr Masham, one of the Prince's gentlemen. Abigail, taxed with the concealment of this important fact from the author of her fortunes, admitted it with her mutinous deference. It was not until Sarah learned that the Queen had been present at the ceremony and had made a substantial donation that she realized how closely organized was this inner world from which she was excluded. We have to measure not only the wrath of an arrogant woman, but a political situation which held all Europe in its grip.

Here again Sarah lost her poise. Says Coxe very truly:

> In this case the Duchess, instead of attempting to conciliate her royal mistress and regain her favour by renewing her former attentions, assailed her with bitter reproaches, which were the more revolting because partly just. On the first intelligence of the marriage she burst into the royal presence and expostulated with the Queen for concealing the secret which nearly regarded her as a relation. The mortifying replies of the Queen, who warmly vindicated the silence of her favourite by imputing it to fear of offending, rather inflamed than soothed her resentment, and from this period their correspondence exhibits a tone of dissembling humility on one hand, and, on the other, of acrimonious reproach.[1]

By this time the real facts had dawned on Marlborough. In the midst of this year of misfortune in the field he felt himself struck a deadly blow. He always measured the Queen's temper far better than his wife. He knew the Stuart qualities, that the breach was irreparable and the danger capital, not only to himself but to the whole cause of the Allies. From this moment a sombre fatalism began to steal over him. Henceforth he considered himself less the responsible master of events, but rather a servant who must do his duty as well as he can, and as long as he is bidden or allowed to do

[1] Coxe iii, 260.

it. Some commentators suggest he should have submitted to the Queen, made terms with the moderate Tories, and thrown all his weight against the Whigs. This involved a wrong and disastrous strategy for the war, and the sacrifice of Godolphin. The opposite course of joining with the Whigs and coercing the Queen to expel Abigail was clearly repugnant to him. He would never take any measure against the Queen except that of leaving her service. Nothing would induce him to be the political tool of either party. He would do his job as General until he was turned out of it. Beyond that at his age he would not go. All this must be remembered when we come to judge his conduct during the Peace negotiations. Abigail was probably the smallest person who ever consciously attempted to decide, and in fact decided, the history of Europe. The first extant account of her is contained in a letter of a lady of fashion dated May 12, 1707:

> This makes me think of a match yours mentioned, our relation the Dresser with Colonel Masham, whom the Queen hath lately advanced. If the same is young have heard her greatly commended for a sober woman. I believe she is the same Aunt Brom[field] used to talk of, lived with Sir George Rivers' lady when first we went to Greville Street. The great Lady Duchess in that deserves great commendations, that hath taken such care of her relations, who when low are generally overlooked. Is her brother Colonel Hill married, as was reported, to one of the Queen's maids? [1]

Abigail can speak for herself in her own way.

Abigail Masham to Harley

LONDON
September 29th, 1707

All that has happened new since you left us relates to myself which is: the 22nd day I waited; and in the evening about eight o'clock a great lady came and made a visit till almost ten. I was in the drawing room by good luck, and as she passed by me I had a very low curtsey, which I returned in the same manner, but not one word passed between us, and as for her looks, indeed, they are not to be described by any mortal but her own self. Nothing but my innocence could have sup-

[1] Lady Pye to Abigail Harley, at Eywood, Derby, May 12, 1707; Portland Papers, *H.M.C.*, p. 406. These names are superficially misleading. Abigail Masham, the dresser, conducted her famous political intrigue with Robert Harley, the Secretary of State. Abigail Harley is a different person altogether and has nothing to do with either of them. The name of Lady Pye, the writer of the letter, is sometimes used by Abigail Masham in her letters to Robert Harley as a blind for the Duchess of Marlborough.

ported me under such behaviour as this. When she had ended her conversation with the Queen, I was gone to my lodging to avoid seeing her again that night, but she was so full, she could not help sending a page of the back stairs to speak with me. When I came to her she told me she had nothing to say to me and was easiest to me, and then she would trouble me no more. I desired I might wait upon her where and when she pleased; then, says she, I will send for you to-morrow. I waited all day, expecting to be sent for, but no message came; at last, between eleven and twelve o'clock the next morning, this letter was sent by her footman, which I have taken the liberty to enclose with a copy of my answer[1] before she went her journey to Woodstock, if you care to give yourself the trouble of reading them; and I beg you will let me have her letter back again when we meet.[2]

Dartmouth describes Abigail as "exceedingly mean and vulgar in her manners, of a very unequal temper, childishly exceptious and passionate."[3]

Swift, on the other hand, wrote:

A person of plain, sound understanding, of great truth and sincerity, without the least mixture of falsehood or disguise; of an honest boldness and courage, superior to her sex, firm and disinterested in her friendship, and full of love, duty, and veneration for the Queen, her mistress.[4]

These are opposite opinions, equally biased. The reader will be able to judge from the sequel.

The climax in Sarah's relations with Abigail at the end of 1707 can best be described in Sarah's own words.

After some time it was thought proper that she should write to me, and desire I would see her; to which I consented, and appointed her a time. When she came I began to tell her that it was very plain the Queen was much changed towards me, and that I could not attribute this to anything but her secret management; that I knew she had been very frequently with her Majesty in private, and that the very attempt to conceal this, by artifice, from such a friend as I had been to her was alone a very ill sign, and enough to prove a very bad purpose at bottom. To this she very gravely answered that *she was sure the Queen, who had loved me extremely, would always be very kind to me.* It was some minutes before I could recover from the surprise with which so extraordinary an answer struck me. To see a woman, whom I had raised out of the dust, put on such a superior air, and to hear her

---

[1] Not found. [2] Portland Papers, *H.M.C.*, p. 454.
[3] Burnet, vi, 37. [4] *Works*, vi, 33.

assure me, by way of consolation, that the Queen would be always very kind to me! At length I went on to reproach her with her ingratitude and her secret management with the Queen to undermine those who had so long and with so much honour served her Majesty.[1]

No one reflecting on the relationship which had subsisted for so long between Sarah and Abigail can wonder at Sarah's inability to address herself adroitly to the new situation. It was more than could be expected from human nature, least of all from Sarah's nature. Jealousy gnawed her vitals, affront inflamed her proper pride, ingratitude aroused her moral indignation. Hatred and contempt of Abigail inspired her every thought, word, and gesture. Every expression she gave to these uncontrollable feelings drove deeper the wedge between her and the Queen.

Marlborough's letters to Sarah and Godolphin, written from the camp during the summer and autumn, give a revealing picture, alike of his own mood and of the impending Court and party crisis. He wrote under strain and disappointment to his wife and to his closest friend, unconcerned with the eyes of the future.[2]

John to Sarah

MELDERT
June 6, 1707

. . . It is true what you say of Woodstock, that it is very much at my heart, especially when we are in prosperity, for then my whole thoughts are of retiring with you to that place. But if everything does not go to our own desire, we must not set our hearts too much upon that place, for I see very plainly that whilst I live, if there be troubles, I must have my share of them. This day makes your humble servant fifty-seven. On all accounts I could wish myself younger; but for none so much as that I might have it more in my power to make myself more agreeable to you, whom I love with all my soul.[3]

And (June 13):

I do from my heart assure you that I should be much better pleased to live with you in a cottage than in all the palaces this [world] has without you.[4]

June 26, 1707

The weather is so very hot, and the dust so very great, that I have this hour to myself, the officers not caring to be abroad till the hour of

---

1 *Conduct*, pp. 245–246.
2 The letters are severely abridged to avoid repetition and irrelevancy.
3 Coxe, iii, 231.   4 *Ibid.*, 212–213.

orders obliges them to it. It is most certain that when I was in Spain, in the month of August, I was not more sensible of the heat than I am at this minute.[1] If you have the same weather, it must make all sorts of fruit very good; and as this is the third year of the trees at Woodstock, if possible, I should wish that you might, or somebody you can rely on, taste the fruit of every tree, so that what is not good might be changed. On this matter you must advise with Mr Wise, as also what plan may be proper for the ice-house; for that should be built this summer, so that it might have time to dry. The hot weather makes me think of these things, for the most agreeable of all presents is that of ice.[2]

June 27, 1707

I am glad to hear that the Duke of Shrewsbury is easier than the last year. I do not think he can ever be of much use, but it is much better to have mankind pleased than angry; for a great many that can do no good have it always in their power to do hurt.[3]

Marlborough to Godolphin

MELDERT
June 27, 1707

That which gives me the greatest trouble is what you say concerning the Queen; for if Mrs Morley's prejudice to some people is so unalterable, and that she will be disposing of the preferments now vacant to such as will tear to pieces her friends and servants, that must create distraction. But you know my opinion was, and is yet, *that you ought to take with you Mr Secretary Harley,*[4] and to let the Queen see, with all the freedom and plainness imaginable, her true interest; and when she is sensible of that, there will be no more difficulty; if there should, you will have performed your duty, and God's will be done. For my own part, I see in almost every country they act so extremely against their own interest that I fear we have deserved to be punished.[5]

John to Sarah

MELDERT
July 4, 1707

If I were ever capable of giving advice, it would be rashness to do it at this distance; but I believe nothing can cure this matter, if I guess right, but Lord Treasurer's giving himself the trouble of writing very plainly what he thinks is wrong, and send it to the Queen, without offering to quit, or expecting any answer; but, as in duty bound, to leave it to her consideration. I should hope this would do it; but if

---

[1] This remark may refer to his youthful service at Tangier; and it is possible, though we have no record of it, that he travelled in Spain at that time.
[2] Coxe, iii, 262–263.
[3] *Ibid.,* 264.
[4] Marlborough's italics.
[5] Coxe, iii, 265–266.

it should not, the last and only thing must be, that the Solicitor-General speak very freely to Mr Harley. . . .[1]

Apparently this process of communication with a delinquent colleague through a Law Officer was reserved for the most serious differences and for decisive steps. We shall see it in use later on— a kind of writ, a legal process entirely different from the usual elaborate courtesies, however formal.

Marlborough to Godolphin

MELDERT
July 11, 1707

Since you think it will be of no use to take Mr Harley with you to the Queen, you must find some way of speaking plainly to him; for if he continues in doing ill offices upon all occasions to Lord Somers, Lord Sunderland, and Lord Wharton, it will at last have so much effect upon the Queen, whose inclinations are already that way, it must occasion that no measures will be followed. If Mrs Morley writes to me, I shall be sure to send you a copy of my answer.

You have so much business that I am afraid you have forgot to settle with Mr Bridges the allowance out of the poundage, which I desired for Mr St John. I beg the favour of your doing it.[2]

John to Sarah

MELDERT
July 11, 1707

. . . Your expression of the ice-house, that it can't be of use this three years, is a very melancholy prospect to me, who am turned on the ill-side of fifty-seven.

I am very sorry that you think you have reason to believe that Mr Harley takes all occasions of doing hurt to England. If Lord Treasurer can't find a remedy, and that before the next winter, I should think his wisest and honestest way would be to tell the Queen very plainly which way he thinks her business may be carried on; and if that be not agreeable, that she would lose no time in knowing of Mr Harley. I am very confident the latter would not dare undertake the business, and then everything might go quietly.[3]

John to Sarah

MELDERT
July 21, 1707

My head is full of things that are displeasing, that I am at this time a very improper judge of what would be best for the work at Woodstock; for really I begin to despair of having any quietness there or

[1] Coxe, iii, 266–267.   [2] *Ibid.*, 272.   [3] *Ibid.*, 273–274.

anywhere else. What you say of Mr Prior has given me uneasiness; but when you shall know the reason why any consideration was had for him, you will rather pity than reproach me; but as I am taking my measures so as to be out of the power of being censured and troubled, I am resolved to be ill-used for a little time longer. I see by yours of the 30th that I am to be mortified by the prosecution of my brother George. I have deserved better from the Whigs; but since they are grown so indifferent as not to care what mortifications the Court may receive this winter, I shall not expect favour. My greatest concern is for the Queen, and for the Lord Treasurer. England will take care of itself, and not be ruined, because a few men are not pleased. They will see their error when it is too late.[1]

This letter is of interest because of its reference to the poet Prior. Prior had a small post at the Board of Trade, and wrote odes glorifying Marlborough's victories. For some time he had been suspected by Godolphin of intriguing with Harley and writing anonymously in the opposite strain. In April 1707 he was dismissed from his appointment. Prior was a friend of Cardonnel. Marlborough did not believe him guilty of a double part. "When I first heard of yours and my master Blathwayt's remove," wrote Cardonnel to Prior (July 14, 1707), "I took the liberty to tell His Grace in the most friendly manner I could what I thought of your circumstances, and he was pleased to answer me, under the injunction of the greatest secrecy, that he had and would take care of you."[2] Marlborough's behaviour in this incident is interesting. He did not attempt to reverse Godolphin's decision. He did not argue the point with Sarah. On being convinced by Cardonnel that the dismissed poet was destitute he gave him a pension from funds under his control of four hundred pounds a year, which lasted until 1710. It then appeared that Sarah and Godolphin had been right in their suspicions. The hostile Tories on coming into power immediately restored Prior to his place at the Board of Trade, and he subsequently distinguished himself by the malevolence of his attacks upon Marlborough in *The Examiner*. We shall meet him again at a later stage in this account. But here we see a Marlborough deceived and generous.

Admiral Churchill's affairs, which reached their climax in the following year, already began to cause anxiety. "When my brother," Marlborough wrote to Godolphin (July 18), "spoke to you about his renewing, I could wish you had encouraged him in his resolution

---

[1] Coxe, iii, 279-280.   [2] Bath Papers, *H.M.C.*, iii, 436.

of being quit, for it would be very disagreeable to me to have him receive a mortification. . . ."[1]

And to Sarah (July 22):

I have sent to Lord Treasurer a copy of my letter to the Queen, tho' I own to you I am desponding as to the good it may do; however, I have done my duty, and God's will be done. By my letter you will see that I have endeavoured to do the Whigs the best office I can; but I shall think it a very ill return if they fall upon my brother George. I do with all my heart wish he would be so wise as to quit his place; but I hope nobody that I have a concern for will appear against him. After the usage I had from Lord Halifax I am concerned but for very few; therefore, if there should be occasion, pray say, as from yourself, two words to Lord Sunderland; for it would be very uneasy to me to have reason to take anything ill of him, and it is impossible for me to be unconcerned in this matter. I expect no more than what I would do if he had a brother attacked. This, and many other things, shows there is no happiness but in retirement.[2]

Evidently Sarah was still championing the Whigs to her husband, urging him to make their interests his own, and to help her press the Queen on their behalf. Under this persistent solicitation Marlborough now showed an utter weariness and despondency. Neither the threats against his brother nor Sarah's pleadings and remonstrance would stir him. He would do no more.

SOIGNIES
August 22, 1707

I do assure you I did not mean the Whigs when I spoke of ingratitude, but I meant it in general to England; and if you will do me justice, you must believe that I have done all the good offices that are possible at this distance. I do not say this to make my court to the Whigs, but that I am persuaded it was good for my country, and for the service of the Queen; for I do really believe that the Tories will do all they can to mortify the Queen and England; for I am now both at an age and humour that I would not be bound to make my court to either party, for all that this world could give me. Besides, I am so disheartened that when I shall have done my duty, I shall submit to Providence. . . .[3]

And again (August 29):

If you have good reason for what you write of the kindness and esteem the Queen has for Mrs Masham and Mr Harley, my opinion should be that the Lord Treasurer and I should tell her Majesty what

[1] Coxe, iii, 280.   [2] *Ibid.*, 280–281.   [3] *Ibid.*, 324–325.

is good for herself; and if that will not prevail, to be quiet, and let Mr Harley and Mrs Masham do what they please; for I own I am quite tired, and if the Queen can be safe, I shall be glad, . . . for as I have served her with all my heart, and all the sincerity imaginable, I think I deserve the indulgence of being quiet in my old age.[1]

At this stage Harley was aware that his attitude and activities were exciting the suspicions not only of the Whigs but of his colleagues. A single specimen of his letters will suffice.

Harley to Marlborough

September 16/27, 1707

I have desired my Lord Treasurer to ask leave for me to go into the country, which I hope to do this night se'nnight. I entreat your Grace will permit me now, upon my taking leave, to assure you I never have writ anything to you but what I really thought and intended. For near two years I have seen the storm coming upon me, and now I find I am to be sacrificed to sly insinuations and groundless jealousies. I have the satisfaction, not only of my own mind, but my enemies and friends witness for me, that I have served your Grace and my Lord Treasurer with the nicest honour and by the strictest rules of friendship; and [that] I have sacrificed everything to this, the world knows; and that what credit I have with the clergy or laity has been all employed to no other end but the service of both your Lordships.

I have not interposed in, or contradicted directly or indirectly, by myself or any other, the putting in or putting out any person, or meddled with any measures which are taken; for I have avoided knowing them. And yet I am now first charged in general, and when I desired that particulars might be told me, nothing is specified but the two nominated bishops. I must therefore say the same to your Grace I did when it was mentioned to me yesterday, that I never knew those two persons, I never spoke of them, nor ever thought of them, or directly or indirectly ever recommended them to the Queen, or to or by any other person. And, my Lord, I must do myself this justice, that I am above telling a solemn lie; that I scorn the baseness of it; and that if I had known or recommended those persons, I would not have been so mean as to deny it, but would have owned it, and given my reasons for it. And now, my Lord, since I am going into the country, and perhaps Sunday next may put an end to any farther opportunity of my troubling your Grace with letters, I beg leave to assure your Grace that I shall always preserve an entire duty and service for your Grace. And I will add but this, that if there be any uneasiness in the Queen to comply with any proposals, I heartily wish that the true reason of it may be found out; for as I have no hand in it, nor any

[1] Coxe, iii, 328–329.

friend or acquaintance of mine that I know of, so I believe that half the pains which are taken to accuse and asperse the innocent would discover the true cause, and provide the remedy.[1]

"I dread the thoughts," Harley wrote to Godolphin (September 10/17), "of running from the extreme of one faction to another, which is the natural consequence of party tyranny, and renders the Gov[ernment] like a door which turns both ways to let in each party as it grows triumphant, and in truth this is the real parent and nurse of our factions here."[2] It was hardly possible to express more tersely implacable opposition to the whole system of party government as it was to flourish in England for the next two hundred years. But Harley's attempt to overturn the Government cannot be translated entirely into terms of subsequent or modern politics. In 1708 the party system, though inconceivably violent and bitter, was in the infancy of its power. The use of an organized party to impose a phalanx of Ministers upon a reluctant sovereign had not become respectable. The Whigs could not fight the coming election upon the principle that a victorious faction is entitled to dictate to the Crown its choice of advisers. Such a suggestion would have at once discredited them in the eyes of many worthy persons. If it came to a clash between the Whig Parliamentary doctrines and the Queen it was certain that large numbers of Whigs would stand by her. Public coercion of the Crown on personal issues was impossible.

Harley, armed with the Queen's favour, planned to regain his control of a great part of the Tories and at the same time to woo the moderate Whigs and isolate their extremists. The language which he held was that he represented the Queen, was fully in sympathy with her, and that she was even willing to take certain moderate Whigs into her Cabinet. Were the Junto, then, prepared to defy her wishes, to stand together against her, and to go to the polls as the declared enemies of the Prerogative? His early moves, as reported to Shrewsbury by Vernon, the former Secretary of State, indicate that Harley was beginning to take up this national position by grouping friends of the Prerogative against the Junto.[3] Thus at the same time he undermined Godolphin and sought to drive the Whigs to argumentative extremities which would divide and ruin them. Moreover, once Harley became the probable head

[1] Coxe, iii, 395–397.   [2] Bath Papers, *H.M.C.*, p. 181.
[3] James Vernon, *Letters illustrative of the Reign of William III* . . . (1696–1708) (edited by G. P. R. James, 1841), iii, 345.

of a Government he could rely upon a flow of recruits from Whig ranks. Whig discipline, though remarkable for the age of Anne, could not compare with twentieth-century caucus control. "I never in my life," Swift wrote to the Archbishop of Dublin,

> saw or heard such division or complication of parties as there have been for some time. You sometimes see the extremes of Whigs and Tories driving on the same thing. I have heard the chief Whigs blamed by their own party for want of moderation. . . .[1]

The swift and decisive failure which overtook Harley's schemes, and the rejection by following generations of his views, must not blind us to their deadly sagacity and force at this time. Nor can we say that upon the merits Harley was wrong. The issue, apart from personal rivalries, was to him one of national *versus* party government at the height of a great war. His methods are not to be reconciled with any standard of honour or good faith. But at this juncture he came within an ace of frustrating the development of the party system, and ruling by a composite majority on the principles which St John in his old age afterwards embodied in the idea of a Patriot King.

Neither must we underestimate the quality and resources of Godolphin. His Pole Star was Marlborough and Marlborough's war. He saw his supreme duty in forming a Parliamentary foundation upon which Marlborough could bestride Europe, and in furnishing him with supplies of money, men, and ships. To this purpose he used all the ruse and artifice with which forty years of Parliamentary and Court intrigue, in times most of them rougher than the age of Anne, had made him familiar. While Harley calculated upon the collapse of the party system, Godolphin relied upon its feuds. The Lord Treasurer's strength consisted, according to Briançon, in his supreme gift for applying the maxim 'Divide and govern.' His skill lay in the management of business in such a way that, immediately any party assault on the Ministry threatened to become dangerous, some question would be raised to set the Tories and Whigs by the ears. Therefore he worked for national government through the equipoise and cancellation of the parties, whereas Harley sought it by the fusion of their central elements.

[1] February 12, 1708; *The Works of Jonathan Swift* (edited by Sir Walter Scott, 1883), xv, 283.

Chapter Seventeen

THE FALL OF HARLEY

1707–1708—WINTER

AS the meeting of Parliament approached it became known that a serious attack impended upon the administration of the Navy. Naval circles debated in those days, as in our own, whether our sea effort should be directed to keeping open the lines of communication or expended on main military purposes in support of the armies. During the first six years of the war Marlborough's strategy, always aiming at decisive results, had been ready to suffer heavy losses on the trade routes for the sake of gaining command of the Mediterranean and all that followed therefrom. Part of the price paid for the immense naval effort against Toulon had been the marked weakening of trade protection, with consequent heavy forfeits on the oceans and elsewhere. Never in our history has the Fleet been used so much for the military purpose, or so little for the comfort, convenience, and profit of trade. The losses of the merchants had been severe. No fewer than eleven hundred merchant ships belonging to London River alone had been lost during the war. In this very year of 1707 French cruisers had raided three great trading fleets, and taken a heavy toll off Brighton, off the coast of Lapland, and between Scilly and Ushant, capturing or destroying six battleships of the escorting squadrons. The Whigs, apart from their political manœuvres, were naturally sensitive to the bitter complaints of the merchants and the City financiers. We may measure the classic vigour of the war administration by the fact that it was capable in the pursuit of victory of imposing such hardships upon these powerful and vital interests. But now victory was lacking; there was naval miscarriage and defeat. The brunt of all this fell upon George Churchill, virtually, in modern terms, First Sea Lord, who under the Queen's husband, Prince George of Denmark, managed the Admiralty in harmony with his brother's strategic aims.

To these serious, debatable public issues private friction was added. Halifax, better known to history as William III's famous Finance Minister, Montagu, one of the lords of the Junto, a brilliant, powerful man, for years excluded from office, was at this time in a fury with Marlborough. Having been associated with him in the Barrier-Succession negotiations of the previous year, he ardently desired to be nominated a plenipotentiary in the peace discussions which always lay just beneath the threshold of the war, and might at any moment become all-important. He had paid his court to Marlborough. He had even stood, hat in hand, to Sarah as she entered her carriage. His wish had not been gratified. His anger is recorded in vehement letters now extant. He made little secret that he would retaliate for this rebuff, and his means were ready to hand. He would when Parliament met attack George Churchill and the administration of the Admiralty.

Admiral Churchill, Marlborough's faithful naval wing, was personally vulnerable. He was a vehement Tory, probably in his heart a Jacobite. Rumour said graft was rife in the Admiralty; and, indeed, there was evidence of convoys denied to the merchants or delayed on insufficient grounds, and of officers who must be bribed to do their duty. Marlborough's brother was, then, to be accused by Halifax and the Whigs at once of maladministration which had proved disastrous and of feathering his own nest. Upon the first count he has a good answer to later times. He steadfastly pursued the major objects of the war. Upon the second count no very satisfactory rebuttal is forthcoming. In the event nothing was brought home against him. But whether this was due to his innate purity, or to the fact that the Whigs for larger reasons, which will appear, eventually abandoned the hunt, is a dubious matter.

Marlborough was distressed and worried by the attack upon his brother, of which he had learned early. As his letters from the camp show, he was well aware of Halifax's intentions and their cause. He tried to placate that offended magnate by a ceremonious and conciliatory letter. Halifax had no mind to be paid off in such light coin. He left the Duke's letter unanswered—a marked affront —and continued his hostile preparations. There was, however, one helpful reaction. Any attack on the Admiralty was an attack upon the Queen's beloved husband, the Lord High Admiral. Prince George had been friendly to Marlborough even before the days when they both rode off at Salisbury from James II to William III. He was under the Duke's spell. All his influence with the Queen was steadily exerted for Marlborough. He was in these years, for all his simplicity, ailing health, heavy meals, and heavier potations, one of the linchpins in that marvellous coach of State that drove so triumphantly along the roads of Europe. Anne would tolerate no reflection upon her husband. To attack Admiral Churchill was to attack George of Denmark. The Queen would have liked to see him commanding the armies of the Grand Alliance, and winning the great battles of the age. This through Dutch obstinacy and other difficulties had failed. Mr Freeman had had to do it all in his own name. But the Admiralty and the sea war and all that the Royal Navy meant to Britain were in the Queen's eyes embodied in her husband. That sphere should certainly be his. Moreover, Prince George readily made common cause with Admiral Churchill. He let himself be managed by him, felt that thereby he was helping the Duke, was loyal to the now broken Cockpit circle, and pursuing the surest road to victory in the war. It is by no means certain that this limited man had not laid hold upon the root of the matter. Thus the Queen's husband stood by George Churchill, and the Queen resented the attack upon the Admiralty as a personal insult to herself. She expected such treatment from the Whigs. She was perturbed but not unduly dismayed to find not only high but moderate Tories joining in it.

A catastrophe at sea had closed the year of disaster. Sir Cloudesley Shovell, returning late in the year from Toulon with the battle fleet, approached the mouth of the Channel in the third week of October 1707. We are prone in these days of steam, perfect charts of rocks, shoals, and currents, well-lighted coasts, and wireless telegraphy to ignore the awful dangers of the sea in the early eighteenth century. We may remember Rooke's repugnance to a late return of the heavy ships.[1] But in this period the fleet was used as roughly as the armies, and all risks were run for main objects. These mighty oak vessels, carrying sometimes ninety guns and more than seven hundred men, were in the narrow waters at the mercy of gale, mist, and current. So unsure were the methods of fixing a position within twenty or thirty miles that the Admiralty was wont to send out frigates to cruise about to pick up the homeward-bound battleships and cross-check their position by their recent contacts with the land. This precaution was not neglected in October 1707. Unhappily, the helping frigate was too late to find the fleet. The weather was thick and violent; and there was a current, not then known to navigators, which carried Admiral

[1] Vol. II, p. 573.

Shovell forty miles out of his reckoning. The evening of October 22 found the battle fleet with a deadly wind amid the sharp rocks of the Scillies. Two great ships and a capital frigate were dashed to pieces, fifteen hundred sailors perished, and, worst of all, our finest admiral, cast upon the beach exhausted and unconscious, was let die for the sake of his emerald ring by an island woman, who a generation later at the point of death confessed her crime.

Such were the elements of the storm, about to break upon the Admiralty, which the foundations of Marlborough's political structure must now withstand.

The first Parliament of Great Britain met on November 6/17, 1707. The forty-five new members from Scotland were solidly favourable to the Government, and the re-election of Mr Speaker Smith was uncontested. The Commons replied dutifully and without demur to the gracious Speech. When the management of the Navy was arraigned they listened contentedly to the cogent defence presented by a young Minister—Robert Walpole by name—who had lately been appointed to the Admiralty Board. Not so the Lords: on the contrary, while the Commons were voting even larger Supplies than in the previous year and increasing the army from fifty to sixty thousand men, the Upper House opened a series of debates on the most thorny questions of the day. They declined to acknowledge the Queen's Speech until the state of the nation had been reviewed. They actually delayed their reply for six weeks. Never had such action been taken by the Peers. It seemed, as the Queen said, to deny her "even ordinary politeness." The Whig lords led the way in the attack on the Admiralty, and no sooner was this launched than the Tories came in behind it. The Government was called to account by both the great parties. Marlborough, reaching England on November 16/27, found Godolphin in dire straits.

When we review the situation which the two friends had to face after the year of disaster one must admit that it required strong nerves. The Queen, estranged from Godolphin, severed from Sarah, bridling at the Whigs, loyal only to the Admiralty; the high Tories in Church and Parliament intent to smash the Government and the war; the Whigs resolved to use the public difficulties to assist their constitutional claims and oust and humble their party foes; the maturing of Harley's profound schemes, St John at his side, Abigail in his hands! But Marlborough's weight and fame were immense. In spite of his own barren campaign and the many misfortunes that had befallen the Allies, he seemed to bulk even larger in men's minds than after Blenheim and after Ramillies. The very fact that things were going wrong restored him an authority denied on the morrow of his victories. When he landed at Dover all eyes were turned upon him. We have glimpses of him at this time from contemporary pens. His levees were thronged as if they were those of a sovereign. He seems to have fallen into the habit, used by the greatest personages of those days, of receiving in his bedroom as he did in his tent. Like the kings of France, though he did not carry it to the same extremes, he made his toilet in public. "Every morning when he is in London he has in his antechamber gentlemen of the first quality including ambassadors and Ministers of foreign princes; he dresses, even shaves and puts on his shirt, in public; yet he behaves in a manner calculated to offend no one, at least by words, and affects a gentle and gracious air with all."[1]

Marlborough's conception of the campaign of 1708 was, in fact, a renewal of the double invasion of France which had failed in 1707. If he could have ordered it, Prince Eugene, with the Duke of Savoy, would have broken into Dauphiné at the head of the forces, brought up again to full strength, which had attempted Toulon in the previous year. He was extremely set upon this, and the reports which Brigadier Palmes brought back showed Victor Amadeus well disposed to the scheme. Marlborough was resolved to stand on the defensive in Spain and make the main effort in the Low Countries. Eugene, for his part, was more inclined to come round to the northern theatre and fight upon the Rhine or the Moselle in conjunction with Marlborough. However, English politics and Parliamentary strategic fancies complicated the problem. Many Whigs, as well as the Tory Party, were unduly fond of the Spanish scene. They had worked themselves up year by year to the exorbitant principle "No peace without Spain," thus vastly extending the aims of the war. They supposed that the conquest of Spain could best be achieved on the spot. They wearied of the severe fighting in Flanders, and imagined the Iberian peninsula the shorter and easier road. They wished to avenge the defeat at Almanza locally.

These views were constantly pressed by Charles III and all directly interested in the Spanish enterprise. Stanhope had returned home after the disaster as the mouthpiece of the young King. No

---

[1] Report of the Genoese envoy; *Relazioni di Ambasciatori Sabaudi, Genovesi e Veneti,* 1693–1713 (edited by C. Morandi, 1935), p. 179.

more competent representative could have been chosen. Stanhope ranks high among the heroic and brilliant figures of the age of Anne. He was an accomplished soldier. He had gained the entire confidence of Marlborough when serving under him in the campaign of 1705. He was one of the Duke's most trusted informants upon Spanish affairs. Although his military record is chequered by one grievous defeat, his reputation even for skill survived, while his personal prowess was to be adorned by the astounding feat which the Romans exalted as *spolia opima*. During the battle of Almenara in 1710 he actually, as Commander-in-Chief, cut down with his own sword the opposing commander. When it is remembered that to these unfading laurels he subsequently added the successive discharge of the duties of Foreign Secretary and eventually Prime Minister, his title to rare distinction cannot be disputed.

Stanhope, with his already acknowledged force and ability, now urged upon Marlborough and the Cabinet a halt in Flanders and a decisive campaign in the Peninsula. This was pressed through every channel. "I hope," wrote Charles III later (January 1708) to Wratislaw, "that you will at last recognize that it is a chimerical conception that one ought to act upon the defensive here. They must either put me in the position to advance and act on the offensive, or they must clearly determine to sacrifice my person and the whole affair here."[1] And again, later, to Marlborough (January 18, 1708): "Stanhope's secret project consists in that you should come yourself to Spain with 25 or 20,000 men with which, you entering by one side, and Prince Eugene and I from the other, you will end with one glorious stroke this long and so bloody war."[2]

These appeals are typical.

Such strategy found no foothold with Marlborough. He was inflexibly resolved not to shift the axis of the war to Spain. He was willing to recruit the English forces already there sufficiently to enable them to mark time without collapse. He was willing that the Empire should send new contingents; but the bulk of the drafts and all the reinforcements under British control must be reserved for the main army in Flanders. One grievous concession he would make if absolutely forced: he would consent to Prince Eugene's going to Spain. He had foreseen and admitted the attraction of the step and even the need for it in a letter to Godolphin in September.

[1] 1708, correspondence between Charles III and Wratislaw; Klopp, xiii, 107.
[2] Vienna Archives, quoted in Arneth, *Prinz Eugen von Savoyen*, ii, 460.

As to your desire of Prince Eugene's going to Spain, I think he can serve nowhere else; for I dare say [*i.e.*, I am sure] he will not serve under the Elector of Hanover, nor can he serve with the Duke of Savoy. I shall incline to think, as Sir Edward Seymour said in the House of Commons, that he never knew admiral or general that had ships or troops enough.

I am of opinion that the war will be decided in this country by a battle early in the next campaign, for they [the enemy] see that no success in any other part of the world can get them peace; so that I am persuaded they will have a very great struggle here at the opening of the field.[1]

He had written to Wratislaw (November 21), "One sees that the last resource of the King is in the presence of Prince Eugene at the head of the army next year."[2] The English Cabinet was ardent for such a decision. Nothing could be more popular in London. Marlborough therefore lent himself to suggestions of this character which were freely made during the late autumn to the Emperor and to his glorious general. Nevertheless we do not believe that Marlborough ever thought there was much likelihood of Eugene's consenting to go. Obviously, if the whole burden of the Spanish theatre was to be thrown upon him, Eugene would stipulate for a strong, effective army. Indeed, he had already written that he would not serve without "a real army, not on paper, capable of acting offensively."

Marlborough was sure that with his authority in London and his influence at The Hague he could prevent any large diversion of forces. Thus there would be no army to satisfy Eugene. Meanwhile, if necessary, great play could be made in England with the Prince's name, and the Cabinet could safely go all the way with Parliament in asking for Eugene's services, which would almost certainly not be granted. This seems to be the key to Marlborough's inner policy and to the voluminous correspondence which arose between the Allies. On November 29 the Queen wrote to the Emperor asking that Eugene should be sent to Spain. On December 9, however, we know that Marlborough said in great confidence to Primoli, a secretary of Count Gallas, the Imperial Ambassador, that he "did not intend to send troops into Catalonia for the new campaign."[3] This is the decisive fact.

[1] Coxe, iii, 353–354.   [2] *Dispatches*, ii, 627.
[3] Primoli's letter; Klopp, xiii, 10.

The second debate in the Lords on Peterborough's conduct drew from Marlborough his most memorable Parliamentary performance. It is the more remarkable because, although he had made up his mind what ought to be done and what he meant to do, his handling of the debate was at once spontaneous, dissimulating, and entirely successful. As on the battlefield, he changed his course very quickly indeed and spread a web of manœuvre before his opponents. He made candour serve the purpose of falsehood, and in the guise of reluctantly blurting out the whole truth threw his assailants into complete and baffling error. Under the impulse of an emotion which could not have been wholly assumed, he made a revelation of war policy which effectively misled not only the Opposition but the whole House, and which also played its part in misleading the foreign enemy, who were of course soon apprised of the public debate. He acted thus in the interests of right strategy and of the common cause as he conceived them. He was accustomed by the conditions under which he fought to be continually deceiving friends for their good and foes for their bane; but the speed and ease with which this particular manœuvre was conceived and accomplished in the unfamiliar atmosphere of Parliamentary debate opens to us some of the secret depths of his artful yet benevolent mind. But to the scene!

Rochester opened the debate. The Queen was present incognito in her box "till five of the clock in the afternoon." The high Tory leader embraced the interests of Peterborough the Whig, who had thrown himself upon the good offices of his party opponents. He dilated upon Peterborough's courage and skill. He recounted his services. Was it not usual and fitting that an officer of such rank and achievement, recalled from the front, should either be thanked by Parliament or called to account for his conduct? Halifax, speaking for the Whigs, took a line which would enable his party to throw its weight for or against the Government as they might later decide. He supported the demand for a full inquiry. Several Tory peers, headed by Haversham, followed with open attacks upon Galway as an incompetent foreigner responsible for a British defeat. Then Rochester rose again. He broadened the issue. In the temper of the House he felt able to impugn the whole principle of a major offensive in Flanders: "We seem," he said, "to neglect the principal business and mind only the accessories. I remember the saying of a great general, the old Duke of Schomberg, 'that the attacking France in the Netherlands is like taking a bull by the horns.'" He proposed that we should stand on the defensive in Flanders, and send from that army "fifteen or twenty thousand men into Catalonia." Nottingham, the other Tory ex-Minister, followed in the same strain: "Spain, the principal object of the war, is almost abandoned."

Marlborough had certainly not expected this development, nor the evident swing of opinion with which it was received. He rose at once. Every eye was upon him, and his anger was apparent to all. He spoke of "undigested counsel." He declared that the need was to augment rather than lessen the armies in Flanders. He gave two reasons, blunt and solid. The first "which induces me to object to this proposal is that in Spain most of the enemy's strong places may be kept with one battalion in each, whereas the great towns of Brabant which we have conquered require twenty times that number of men for their preservation." This implied that relaxing pressure in the main theatre would liberate incomparably more French troops for the struggle in Spain than any allied reinforcements which could be spared. His second reason was: "If our army in the Netherlands be weakened and the French by their great superiority should gain any considerable advantage, which is not improbable, the discontented party in Holland, who are not a few, and who bear with impatience the necessary charges of the war, will not fail to cry aloud for peace." These massive truths delivered tersely did not stem the tide. Spain was uppermost in all minds, and Marlborough had not even mentioned Spain.

For the third time Rochester rose. He declared himself astonished that "the noble peer, who had ever been conspicuous for calmness and moderation, should now lose his natural temper." The House was set upon the succour for Spain. "Would not his Grace oblige their lordships by apprising them how they might attain troops to send thither for that purpose?" "The obligation," he added, "is the greater as Lord Peterborough has reported the opinion of Prince Eugene that the Germans would rather be decimated than be sent into Spain."

Thereupon Marlborough resolved to make public the idea of sending Prince Eugene. He excused himself for his warmth. Such a vital issue could scarcely be discussed without profound concern. He would take the House into his confidence:

"Although it is improper to disclose secret projects in so numerous an assembly, because the enemy will not fail to be informed of them; yet I am authorized by the Queen to gratify your lordships by the assurance that measures have been already concerted with the Emperor for forming an army of forty thousand men, under the command of the Duke of Savoy, and for sending succours to King Charles. *It is also to be hoped that Prince Eugene may be induced to take the command in Spain*, in which case the Germans will gladly follow him. The only difficulty which may be objected to this scheme is the usual tardiness of the Court of Vienna; and it must be admitted that if the seven thousand recruits, which the Emperor promised for Piedmont, had arrived in time, the enterprise against Toulon would probably have been attended with success. But I dare engage my word that for the future his Imperial Majesty will punctually perform his promises."[1]

The peers were staggered by his declaration. They felt they had been made party to the secrets of the Cabinet and of the Captain-General. They rejoiced to find how much they had misjudged the policy. The opposition collapsed. Rochester even said, "Had we known sooner how well all things had been managed, this debate might have been spared." Somers clinched the matter for the Whigs by moving "That no peace could be reasonable or safe either for her Majesty or her allies if Spain and the West Indies were suffered to continue in the power of the house of Bourbon," and a resolution was passed unanimously thanking the Queen for pressing the Emperor to send a considerable force to Spain under the command of Prince Eugene. The action of the House moved so rapidly that the Whigs had to be very agile in adding a rider-resolution in favour of also "reinforcing the Duke of Savoy and strengthening the army on the Rhine," and further setting up a committee to cast this resolution into the form of an address, upon which Marlborough, Godolphin, and Peterborough were named to serve, but no Tory except Rochester. Thus was affirmed the Whig thesis, "No peace without Spain," but at the same time there was safeguarded the main effort in the main theatre. The long-delayed acknowledgment of the Queen's Speech embodied these conclusions.

When the Ministers met to consult on the morrow of this memorable debate they set themselves to implement Marlborough's declaration, with which they themselves were in hearty accord. The idea of Eugene conquering Spain for the Allies captivated London opinion. Accordingly solemn appeals were renewed to the Emperor to send him there. Marlborough joined in these. He wrote letters to Wratislaw. He held conversations with the Imperial Ambassador which presented the view of the British Parliament.

---

[1] Coxe, iv, 12–13. The report is, of course, only a summary.

But all the time he had continued obstinately and calmly to strengthen the main theatre, to prepare for the double invasion of France, and to withhold all reinforcements from Spain except a meagre draft of eighteen hundred men. He submitted as little to the strategic conceptions of the Lords and Commons in 1707 as he did during the march to Blenheim.

On December 22/January 3 the hopes of the Cabinet were dashed by a dispatch from the English ambassador at Vienna, in reply to their earlier requests, stating that the Emperor could not consent to send Eugene to Spain. The Ministers, with the assurances given to Parliament only three days before vivid in their minds, and the general applause which had greeted them ringing in their ears, were consternated. Indeed, they were furious. Hoffmann, the Imperial Ambassador, was summoned before them. His excuse was blunt: there were not enough troops in Spain to make a worthy command for Prince Eugene. "I must admit," he reported to his Government, "I have never seen the English Ministers in such a state of excitement as over this refusal."[1] Marlborough appeared to share the general feeling, and he lent his weight to their appeals both orally to Hoffmann and, three days later, in a strong letter to Wratislaw. Inwardly, we may suppose, he was able to bear the disappointment with his customary composure.

Eventually, in February, for it is convenient here to anticipate, the Emperor made a counter-proposal. He had recourse to one of those expedients which even now have not gone entirely out of fashion. He suggested a conference at The Hague, where the war leaders of England, Holland, and the Empire should settle among themselves the final plan of campaign. This was found acceptable by all. In the first place it seemed to put everything off for a time. The Ministers could feel that the question of sending Prince Eugene to Spain was still open, and as it gradually appeared that the conference could not assemble until April, Marlborough saw that there was very little prospect of his going. In fact, the procedure adopted after all the political storms left everything in Marlborough's hands under the exact conditions which he desired. Little wonder, then, that on the very day (February 17/28) when Hoffmann received his instructions from Vienna Marlborough saw him, and personally urged him to frame his proposals for a conference in a formal memorial to be presented to the Queen.[2] From that moment he never said another word about sending Prince Eugene to Spain.

---

[1] Hoffmann's dispatch; Klopp, xiii, 15.　　　　[2] *Ibid.*, 19.

There can be no doubt that he got what he had wanted all along
But he had certainly been guilty of dissimulation.

The first month of Parliament had been dominated by the Whig
attempt to link Supply with the attack on Admiral Churchill. This
did not prove so formidable as Marlborough and Godolphin had
feared. The Tories gave it only partial and lukewarm support. The
more the Whig agitation prospered the cooler the Tories became.
Their sympathies were more easily aroused by the distress of the
Queen's husband than by that of the City merchants who had lost
their trading ships. In the end Parliament was made content by
the passing of an Act "for the better securing the Trade by Cruisers
and Convoys," which regulated the service of trade defence on the
lines which had been proposed by Admiral Churchill, among others,
fifteen years before. Prince George's Council had in fact followed
these principles so far as the means allowed after providing for the
offensive function of the main fleet abroad. After the passing of this
Act in March 1708 the losses of merchant shipping diminished
sensibly; but this may well have been because the state of the war,
especially after the destruction of the French fleet at Toulon, no
longer required so great a force in the Mediterranean, and thus
more cruisers could be found for the North Sea and the mouth of
the Channel. The strategy of the first part of the war appears in
the final sentence of the answer the Lord High Admiral made to the
Committee of the House of Lords in January 1708.

"His Royal Highness does hope their Lordships will believe that the
Queen's fleet has not been useless and unemployed during this war,
which cannot be carried on agreeable to the declared sense of their
Lordships, but by supporting a superiority at sea upon the coasts of
Portugal, Spain, and Italy, in all which places the Queen's fleet hath
done great services the last four years, and attempted some things
which might have secured Britain for one age from all the naval power
of France."[1]

Both Houses seemed glad when in the fifth week of the session
the Spanish question, with all the exciting scandals about Peterborough and the Almanza disaster, came upon the scene and
diverted attention from what threatened to become a very dangerous Whig electioneering cry. It seems probable that both Godolphin
and Harley, for opposite purposes, were favourable to this development. At any rate, it was from the Ministerial bench that on

[1] *Journals of the House of Lords*, xviii, 410.

December 9/20 the matter was originally opened in the House of Commons. The first phase of the conflict of the session was ended on December 19/30 by Marlborough's triumphant speech. The Address had been voted in the Lords; the Supplies had been given by the Commons: the Ministry still held together; and it seemed that the crisis was past. Exhausted, as one may readily believe, by all they had gone through, Marlborough and Godolphin retired to Woodstock and Newmarket for Christmas, and both remained in the depths of the country for a full fortnight.

At the moment when Harley's underground movement was in its most delicate and critical condition a sudden startling incident plunged him in grave personal weakness and embarrassment. A certain William Greg, one of the various confidential agents whom he was wont so wisely to send about the country to report on the public temper, had been placed by him in the sub-department which dealt with the correspondence of the French prisoners of war. The letters of all these French nobles and generals from Marshal Tallard downward were forwarded to France after being censored. When the mail was being made up for the Continent the Secretary of State's letters and dispatches dealing with the most secret matters were sent to this same room, and often left lying on the table till they were put in their proper bags for The Hague, Berlin, Vienna, Lisbon, Barcelona, or Turin. Daniel Defoe, the most famous of all Harley's political scouts, shocked at this lax procedure, had already warned his chief of its dangers; but the Secretary of State had taken no action.

This was a period in the war when French espionage attained its highest efficiency and success. Already in May 1707 Chamillart had corrupted and gained the secretaries employed by the Savoyard Ministers both at The Hague and St James's. The plan against Toulon had in fact been betrayed, though somewhat tardily, from Briançon's office in London. Now, in the winter of 1707/8, the tentacles of the French secret service penetrated the office of the Secretary of State and lapped themselves around William Greg. The wretched man, poorly paid, financially hunted, sought to procure from the French Government immunity from capture for an English merchant-ship whose owners had promised him two hundred guineas. He therefore slipped a sealed envelope into the bag of the French prisoners' correspondence. This contained nothing less than a copy of the letter which Queen Anne had written with her own hand to the Emperor asking for the services of Prince Eugene in Spain. Suspicion had already been aroused by previous leakages; the bag was opened in Holland, the treachery exposed, and Greg, arrested (December 31/January 11), made a full confession of his villainy. At the same time two smugglers whom Harley had employed to procure intelligence between Calais and Boulogne turned out to be double spies. Upon arrest they of course protested that they had only been telling some tales to learn better. In truth they had trafficked with both sides for personal gain. On January 8 Briançon's secretary, who had sold the Toulon plan in the previous year, was detected, exposed, and after an exciting chase through London laid by the heels. Both the English scandals touched the Secretary of State at a time when the very air seemed poisonous.

It would be an error to ascribe the fall of Harley to his clerk's treason. It must however have played an important part in this evenly balanced struggle for power. At any rate, when in the middle of January Godolphin and Marlborough came back to town they felt strong enough to consider definitely his expulsion from the Government. Godolphin, with Marlborough's assent, discussed with the Whig leaders the promotion of the moderate-Whig Chancellor of the Exchequer, Boyle, to the Secretaryship of State in Harley's place. The Whigs cared little for Boyle's advancement, but much for Harley's fall. They saw that their pressure had worn out Godolphin's favour only to exalt a far more hostile and obnoxious personage, with all his train and designs. Thus in the middle of January the whole blast of these internal passions was concentrated upon Harley, already somewhat smitten in public opinion and under grievous personal imputation. Such was the power of the Queen's support and his own following that he maintained an equal and now open war within the Cabinet and in Parliament for nearly a month.

Harley, at bay, marshalled his forces. He assembled the elements of his alternative Government. He drew the Duke of Buckingham into his combination. He persuaded the Queen directly, and through Abigail, to encourage the Tories with the near prospect of a moderate Tory Administration. The public need created Parliamentary opportunities. Twenty thousand men were wanted for the army, fifteen thousand of whom must be found with the utmost speed. The most strained interpretations of voluntary recruitment had now failed. A Conscription Bill was brought before Parliament in the early days of the new year. The plan for the campaign of 1708 depended upon it.[1] This measure stirred parties and individual members alike to their roots. All those deep-seated sentiments of personal freedom innate in English hearts were roused. The press-gang for the Navy was an old custom. Stimulating the constables by bonuses to entice, cajole, or peaceably persuade the unemployed, or to coerce vagabonds, to take the Queen's shilling had run its course. Now, either the war effort must languish or young men at work in the fields, or even possessed of some property or the heirs to property, must by compulsion don the scarlet coat. In extreme perturbation the House of Commons sat in committee upon the demand.

Harley's attempt to overturn the Government developed very rapidly. It is to be distinguished both in nature and form from the previous Whig and Tory party manœuvres. These had aimed far lower—points of prejudice for the election, a working agreement with the Ministry, perhaps Cabinet rank for one or two of the leaders. Harley's was a deliberate attempt to upset the whole Government, to detach men from both parties, and to form an entirely new Ministry of the middle. Shocking!

The first unexpected difficulties arose in the Committee of Friday, January 16, upon the conscription proposals. On the Tuesday following these were defeated by 185 votes to 177. This was the first defeat in the House of Commons which any Ministry of Queen Anne had sustained. While both Houses were wrestling with conscription and vehemently probing the causes of the Spanish disaster, St John, no doubt at Harley's instigation, committed an indiscretion calculated to bring any Ministry down with a clatter. Harley had on January 12 asked him for the figures for the troops in British pay in the Peninsula and at Almanza on the date of the battle. St John had at first replied that none were available. Now suddenly on January 29 in the course of a tense debate the Secretary-at-War blurted out to the House of Commons that out of 29,595 men voted by Parliament for service in Spain only 8660 had fought in the decisive action. This produced a tremendous sensation. Other Ministers disputed their colleague's statement, and an interchange of searching addresses to the Queen and Ministerial replies as from the Queen's hand followed. During the same week the Government majority, even upon a financial measure, fell to twenty-nine, and then to fifteen. On the Saturday a majority of fifty-one was

[1] Briançon to the Duke of Savoy, January 23/February 3; Turin State Archives, Lettere di Ministri, Gran Bretagna, Mazzo 16.

recorded "against the Court." Finally a hostile resolution about the numbers at Almanza was carried "without a division." The House of Commons was completely out of control. In the Lords the Whigs were still pressing the Admiralty. Following this week of Opposition triumph, the Queen "told Mr St John that she was resolved to part with the Lord Treasurer. She sent him with a letter to the Duke of Marlborough which she read to him to that purpose; and she gave him leave to tell it about the town, which he did without any reserve."[1]

Harley was now sure he had won. He spoke openly of his new Administration and of the favour of the Crown. Nothing remained but the supreme trial of strength. All that royal intrigue and Parliamentary manœuvre could do was achieved. Against it stood Marlborough, virtually alone. No one outside the circle of Harley's most daring adherents had faced what the nation, Europe, and the Queen would do if he were overthrown. It was generally believed, or at least hoped, that he would consent to the sacrifice of Godolphin, and serve the Queen at home and abroad in the new combination. All this was now to be put to the test.

On January 29, the very night of St John's disclosure, Godolphin instructed the Attorney-General to tell Harley officially that he no longer possessed the confidence of the Lord Treasurer.[2] Harley met this formal and final challenge with imperturbable effrontery. He professed himself at a loss to understand what complaint could lie against him. He volubly defended his loyalty and good faith as a colleague. He declared himself the victim of a conspiracy. He demanded an interview with Marlborough. He appealed to him as his patron and protector. But Marlborough had slowly been brought to regard him as an inveterate liar and a mortal foe. He showed that he did not believe a single word that Harley uttered, and he cited with particularity a number of odious but now established details. Even after this Harley wrote Godolphin one of those dishonest letters of injured innocence which have but to be read in the light of the established facts to prove him a base and hardy hypocrite. Godolphin's answer stands upon its own simplicity:

> I have received your letter, and am very sorry for what has happened, to lose the good opinion I had so much inclination to have of you; but I cannot help seeing, nor believing my senses. I am very far from having deserved it of you. God forgive you.[3]

[1] Swift to the Archbishop of Dublin, London, February 12, 1708; *Works*, xv, 282.
[2] Bath Papers, *H.M.C.*, i, 189. [3] Coxe, iv, 22–23.

Marlborough meanwhile had been at grips with the Queen. Those who depict Anne as a weak woman should reflect upon the marvellous tenacity of her will-power, right or wrong. Upon her lone head and worn, ailing frame descended the whole weight of the quarrels of her realm. The mightiest men of that brilliant age contended for her verdict. The passions of great parties, inflamed by faction and impelled by real needs, collided in her bosom. The storms which now exhaust themselves over enormous electorates beat upon her. Alone she had to face in personal confrontation the reason, knowledge, and appeal of her most famous servants and counsellors. We can see from her vigorous letters the skill with which she selected her lines of resistance. When these became untenable she fell back on woman's tears. But she would not yield. At all costs she would stand by Harley. When Marlborough declared that he would not sit again in Council with such a man she made no response. When he made plain his determination to resign she answered that "he might as well draw his dagger and stab her then and there as do such a thing."[1] But she would not dismiss Harley. She wept convulsively, she seemed about to suffocate; but never would she agree. Such were the scenes inseparable from the discharge of public business in these antique conditions. Marlborough, with his tenderness and chivalry to women, his romantic, almost mystic reverence for the Queen, must indeed have felt that life was not worth living.

Marlborough to the Queen

MADAM,

Since all the faithful services I have endeavoured to do you, and the unwearied pains I have taken for these ten days to satisfy and convince your Majesty's own mind, have not been able to give you any such impressions of the false and treacherous proceedings of Mr Secretary Harley to Lord Treasurer and myself, but that your Majesty is pleased to countenance and to support him, to the ruin of your own business at home, I am very much afraid it will be attended with the sorrow and amazement of all Europe, as soon as the noise of it gets abroad. And I find myself obliged to have so much regard to my own honour and reputation as not to be every day made a sacrifice to falsehood and treachery, but most humbly to acquaint your Majesty that no consideration can make me serve any longer with that man. And I beseech your Majesty to look upon me, from this moment, as forced out of your service as long as you think fit to continue him in it.

[1] L'Hermitage, Dutch Agent in London; Add. MSS. 17677.

No heart is fuller of duty to your Majesty than mine; nobody has more sincere wishes for your prosperity, nor shall more constantly pray for your Majesty's long life, and for your happiness both here and hereafter.[1]

But Queen Anne was determined to see the quarrel through. On February 9 in a brief, tense audience she received the resignations of her illustrious servants. She made some final entreaty to Marlborough, but showed herself glad to let Godolphin go. The two Ministers who had raised her strength so high at home and carried her fame so far abroad quitted her presence, entered their coaches, and drove away from St James's. The scene which followed at the Cabinet Council is well known. The Queen seated herself in her State chair at the head of the table. Harley rose with a confident air to open the first business of the day, which happened to relate to his department. "The members at first," says Coxe, whose account is based on Swift and Burnet, "appeared as if absorbed in reflection: half-smothered murmurs were then heard, and the Secretary paused. A momentary silence ensuing, the members turned to each other, with looks of surprise and uneasiness, till the Duke of Somerset arose, and, with warmth, exclaimed, 'I do not see how we can deliberate, when the Commander-in-Chief and the Lord Treasurer are absent.'"[2] Swift gives a rougher and probably truer version. "If your Majesty suffers that fellow," pointing to Harley, "to treat of affairs of the war without the advice of the General, I cannot serve you."[3] It was plain that every one agreed with him except Harley and the Queen. Harley faltered. The Duke repeated his remark, and neither the Queen nor her favourite said another word. The Council broke up in confusion. The Queen was assisted from her chair half stifled with anger and distress amid the bows of her agitated advisers. But even now—this is the measure of her grit—she did not abandon Harley. She showed in that hour in magnificent fashion the quality which had sent her grandfather to the scaffold and her father to Saint-Germains. She would not have shrunk from either fate. Absolute deadlock gripped the Government of Great Britain at a time when London was the dominating centre of world affairs.

The news spread far and wide that Marlborough and Godolphin

---

[1] Coxe, iv, 24. Coxe gives no date, but it was probably written on February 8, ten days after the open challenge to Harley (see p. 311). Klopp thinks that this was never intended for the Queen's eye, but was Marlborough's draft for his remarks at the audience the following day.

[2] *Ibid.*, 24–25.   [3] *The Works of Jonathan Swift*, xv, 297.

had been dismissed by the Queen. The effect was devastating. The calculations of adroit intrigue, the hot blood of partisanship, suddenly seemed of no account. The larger values asserted themselves in a sobered London. Both Houses of Parliament—the Commons by a definite resolution—decided to conduct no business till they were better informed of these transactions. The City, with its vast new financial power, was in consternation. George of Denmark, appalled by what he heard and saw of the public mood, and strengthened by what he felt himself, implored his wife to bow to the storm. Even then it was Harley, not the Queen, who gave way. During the afternoon and evening he succumbed to the fury of pressures which bore in upon him from every side. He furled his standard for a better day. He advised the Queen to accept his resignation. She wept; and he departed.

Anne was now absolutely alone; apart from Abigail, with the pillows, with the harpsichord and the Tory gossip, she could find no one to whom she could turn. Then, and then only, did she yield. On the 10th she summoned Marlborough to her presence, and after bitter lamentations and reproaches informed him that he had his way. The dismissal of Harley was announced on February 11. The Whig Boyle, from the Exchequer, became Secretary of State; and John Smith, the Whig Speaker of the House of Commons, took his place at the Treasury. St John, Mansell (the Comptroller of the Household), and Harcourt went out with Harley. The office of Secretary-at-War had grown enormously in importance during St John's tenure. Previously it had scarcely counted as Ministerial. In theory the Secretary-at-War was little more than a private secretary of the Commander-in-Chief. But St John had assumed charge of all military questions in the House of Commons, and with his extraordinary gifts and under war conditions had held the centre of the stage. Another Parliamentarian of the first order must be found. Marlborough chose the young Robert Walpole, who had distinguished himself by his vigorous defence of the Admiralty. In St John and Walpole he seems to have picked or found the two young men of destiny in that day for the office, the efficient conduct of which was an essential part of his power to wage war.

The Whigs now fell upon the fallen Harley. Had this master of political intrigue been content to undermine his colleagues by backstairs influence; or was he a Jacobite betraying war secrets to the enemy? Who could be sure that his machinations stopped short at the English Channel? The torments to which he was subjected were merciless. Greg was condemned to death on January 19/30. The execution was postponed from week to week while a Lords Committee examined him, and it was freely asserted that Greg was offered his life if he would incriminate the ex-Secretary of State. Harley was, of course, innocent of anything except culpable negligence in public business. But the ordeal through which he passed was terrible. He endured it with characteristic phlegm. He asserted his innocence, he offered no explanation and declared that his life and honour were in God's keeping. William Greg, however, withstood all pressures and temptations; and history has pondered over the mysteries of his nature, which could sell his country for a paltry sum, and yet face a grisly death rather than bear false testimony against his master. When at length in April he was brought to Tyburn to be hanged, drawn, and quartered, he handed the sheriff a paper proclaiming his sole guilt and Harley's innocence.

There had been also a final scene in the House of Commons. When on February 18/29 the Government admitted that St John's figures about Almanza were true, so staggering was the fact that the crowded House sat for nearly half an hour dumbfounded, not one man caring to attempt to express its feelings. This oppressive silence brings home to us the magnificent earnestness of that long-vanished Parliament, and we feel the beating of those resolute English hearts which, in spite of so many failings and follies, built up the greatness of our island. At last the spell was broken by some member moving formally to thank the Queen for her reply.

The injuries given and received in this struggle were of the kind that men do not forget. They seared and destroyed all fellow-feeling and comradeship between the antagonists. In this bitter month will be found the explanation of the ruthless ill-usage which Marlborough was to receive four years later at the hands of Harley and St John.

Thus ended one of the decisive constitutional conflicts of our history. The authority of the Crown was once more definitely restricted. The public interest, the power of Parliament, the force of party organization, all combined might not have prevailed against the will and courage of this wrong-headed Stuart sovereign. For her part, in pursuance of her conviction, she would have squandered Marlborough, the Grand Alliance, and all that was bound up in their cause. But she was beaten by Marlborough's prestige without the slightest distortion of the Constitution, without a vote, without even an address. She submitted only with undying resentment. She never forgot and she never forgave. Henceforth she set herself to plan revenge. If we have called her a great queen, it is not because of her benevolence or her understanding, though both were considerable; certainly not because of her right judgment —but because of her toughness and will-power, and the part they played both for good and for ill in this expansive and glorious period.

Chapter Eighteen

THE JACOBITE RAID

1708—SPRING

SCOTLAND chewed the thongs of union morosely throughout the misadventures of 1707. Harley's political travellers had warned him of widespread disaffection. Hooke, who toured Scotland for him in the early summer, reported that nine-tenths of the people were against the Union. Highland clansmen, Lowland Jacobites, Whig noblemen, Covenanters, Catholics and Presbyterians, were all ripe for rebellion, though with different objects. Now, if ever, was the hour for the rightful heir to Scotland's ancient crown to set foot upon Scottish soil. Versailles, long sceptical, as we have seen, of Jacobite hopes, was convinced by far-reaching inquiry that a serious revolt would follow the landing of the "rightful sovereign of the three kingdoms" with arms, money, and supplies, and the French nucleus of an army. James Edward, *Prætensus*, now twenty, was ardent for the attempt, and around him clustered the faithful exiles of Saint-Germains. During January Dunkirk hummed with preparation. Five French battleships, a score of frigates to serve as transports conveying twelve battalions, thirteen thousand stand of arms, the gold plate, the liveries and insignia of a royal Court, were assembled. The blessing of the Pope and the proved skill of Admiral Forbin were cast into the scales for no less an object than the conversion of England and Scotland[1] and the dethronement of the usurper Anne.[2] Berwick would himself have liked to command the troops, and his services were implored by the Scottish Jacobites. But Louis XIV drew the line at risking the victor of Almanza upon so hazardous a stroke. A squadron of French frigates, six thousand soldiers—these might be staked upon an outside chance, but Berwick—no.

The stir at Dunkirk and elsewhere was reported to Marlborough by his Secret Service in France and Holland, and it may be also through some of those strange personal channels the traces of which

[1] The Pretender's mother's letter.   [2] James's proclamation.

317

are deeply marked in history. At any rate, by the middle of February we see this alleged friend of the Jacobite cause, this persistent correspondent with the exiled Court, suddenly active in many directions. On the 17th he ordered Cadogan in Flanders to watch "the preparations making at Dunkirk," and

> by all possible means to inform yourself of the enemy's designs, giving notice of what you can learn, by every opportunity, and if you find it requisite, by frequent expresses, both by Ostend and the Brill. . . . In case there be any good grounds to believe the enemy have formed a design of landing in these parts or in North Britain, that there be a proportionable number of her Majesty's foot forces, not only kept in readiness to embark immediately, but . . . if the enemy should embark with the intention of landing in Great Britain, before you have any other orders from hence, that then you put her Majesty's troops on ship-board with all possible speed, either at Ostend or in Zealand, and come yourself with them, to the first convenient port you can make.[1]

He wrote also to Lumley about the selection of the battalions, to Overkirk about replacing them in the various garrisons, and to the States to supply warships, transports, and facilities, enjoining upon all the utmost secrecy. He began to prepare and mobilize the home forces. Household troops, Foot Guards, nine battalions of infantry, and some dragoons were all that remained in England. The drafts for the English regiments in Spain depleted by Almanza were formed into provisional battalions. A regiment of horse and two of dragoons in the north of Ireland were also prepared for service. By the end of February Marlborough had from all sources a substantial force in hand. Still greater exertions were enjoined upon his high Tory, even Jacobite, brother, George Churchill, at the Admiralty. Without upsetting their arrangements for reinforcing the Mediterranean, the Admiralty fitted out at this rigorous season of the year fifteen British battleships, which sailed from Deal under Sir George Byng, and, together with three Dutch ships, blockaded Dunkirk before the end of February. Within a fortnight this force was nearly doubled. "Since we have got a greater strength of shipping than in all likelihood they can put to sea," wrote Marlborough, "I think we have nothing to apprehend, whatever their design may be."[2] Actually the British strength in the end was five times as great as the French.

Parliament was informed on March 4/15 alike of the impending

[1] Coxe, iv, 35, 36.   [2] February 20/March 2; *Dispatches*, iii, 686.

invasion and of the measures taken to cope with it. It was added that the States-General desired to assist the Queen with their whole disposable force by land and sea. The double effect was remarkable. All parties rallied round the Throne. Drastic legislation against Jacobites, avowed or suspected, was voted. The Habeas Corpus Act was suspended. The Pretender and his adherents were proclaimed traitors and rebels. Lavish funds were provided for the defence of the realm. Yet at the same time the Commons proclaimed "that no attempts of this kind shall deter us from supporting Your Majesty in the vigorous prosecution of the present war against France until the monarchy of Spain be restored to the house of Austria, and Your Majesty have the glory to complete the recovery of the liberties of Europe."[1]

Meanwhile at Dunkirk the event occurred. Gales drove off the blockading squadrons, and Forbin put to sea with his warships, his transports, six thousand men, and the Pretender, convalescing from measles but indomitable. Twelve hours behind them Admiral Byng, leaving a division of English and Dutch ships under Admiral Baker to guard the Flanders convoys, sailed in chase. Simultaneously all the troops waiting in England, Ireland, and at Ostend set forth for Scotland by land and sea. Private Deane has left us a laconic record:

> The English Fleet was commanded to sea to wait their [the enemy's] motion, and wth all possillety to prevent y[e] designe. And a Command likewise from his Grace y[e] Duke of Marlborough for y[e] 10 Eldest Regiments of foot, whereof 7 were quartered in y[e] Citty of Ghent; namely y[e] first Batallion of Guards, y[e] Earle of Orkneys[2] battalion, y[e] Duke of Arguiles,[3] Maj[r] Gen[ll] Webbs,[4] my L[d] Norths,[5] Left[t] Gen[ll] Ingoldsbyes[6] and Co[ll] Tattons.[7]
>
> March y[e] 8th y[e] aforesaid Regiments marcht to Bruges Port; and there imbarqued in vessels, and were towed by horses that day to Bruges 8 leagues from Ghent, commanded by Maj[r] Gen[ll] Cudagon, and Brigadeir Sabin: where we continued untill such times as Shipping was fitted, and a Convoy ready; on y[e] 15th y[e] Reig[mts] before mentioned . . . marcht from Bruges to Ostend, a very strong Sea Port, being 4 leagues from Bruges, and there was shipt on board y[e] Men

---

[1] *Parliamentary History*, vi, 727.
[2] Later the First Foot, the Royal Scots.
[3] Later the Third Foot, the Buffs (Royal East Kent).
[4] Later the Eighth Foot, the King's Regiment (Liverpool).
[5] Later the Tenth Foot, the Lincolnshire Regiment.
[6] Later (since disbanded) the Eighteenth Foot, the Royal Irish Regiment.
[7] Later the Twenty-fourth Foot, the South Wales Borderers.

of War and Transports; for that purpose we lay till ye 17 att wch time ye winde presenting, it blowing a fresh gale, about 10 a clock in ye morning we sett sail under [protection of] 10 Ships of War English and Dutch: under ye Command of Admirall Baker Rear Adm^ll of ye White Squadron . . .

March ye 21st about 1 a clock in ye afternoon we came to anchor att Tinmouth, where we lay for further orders, laboring under many ilconveniences, haveing only ye bare Deck to lye upon, wch hardship caused abundance of our men to bid adieu to ye world.[1]

By the time these much-tried soldiers reached Tynemouth the danger was over. Forgin entered the Firth of Forth and anchored near the Isle of May on the 12th/23rd. Signals made to the shore met with but vague responses. Byng was already at the mouth of the Forth. A lucky turn of wind prevented the whole expedition from being trapped. The Pretender still hoped to land at Inverness; but all the rest now thought only of home. The sufferings of the soldiers, crowded upon the open decks in storm and icy rain, were extreme. Our own losses, as Private Deane reveals, were heavy. The French lost several thousand men from sickness and exposure. All the French vessels escaped except one, the *Salisbury*, taken from England in 1703 and "the best ship" in Forbin's fleet. This was boarded by the *Leopard*, and yielded a crowd of luckless Jacobites. Among these was the aged Lord Griffin, whom we may remember with John Churchill in James II's shipwreck of 1681 saving himself "by catching hold of a hen-coop."[2] The unfortunate nobleman was again in dire peril. In fact, he had but one hope—his comrade of those early days. This, however, did not fail him.

The news of the arrival of the invaders in the Firth of Forth, the rumour of their landing, and of an alleged Scottish uprising caused a panic in London. The funds fell fifteen points. The Goldsmiths' Company, which was in some respects the Tory rival of the Bank of England, started a formidable run upon that institution. The Queen, Marlborough, the Dukes of Somerset and Newcastle, Dutch merchants, Huguenot refugees, and Jewish financiers, together with all the Whig wealth, hastened to the rescue. Godolphin transferred all the Treasury gold to the Bank. The shareholders of the Bank prepared to meet a 20 per cent. call. The run was stopped. The good news arrived. The funds soared, and general rejoicings were the order of the day. No severities darkened

[1] J. M. Deane, *A Journal of the Campaign in Flanders*, 1708 (1846), p. 4.
[2] Vol. I, p. 158.

the success. Lord Griffin, indeed, was condemned to death, but Marlborough successfully, though under much criticism, prevented his execution. This caused some disappointment. "The boys of the town," wrote Swift sardonically, "are mighty happy; for we are to have a beheading next week, unless the Queen will interpose her mercy." Eventually the old Lord, respited from month to month, died in the Tower in 1710, of old age, and perhaps of a not unnatural depression.

Thus ended somewhat ignominiously the first of the Jacobite descents. It led, however, to consequences of far-reaching importance in the party sphere. Parliament was approaching the end of a triennial term. What more deadly prelude could there be to a General Election than the seeming or imputed identification of the Tories with the frustrated invasion of the island by foreign troops? All Whig suspicions of Marlborough and Godolphin were swept away by their proven vigilance and zeal. The Queen, having felt the throne shake beneath her, her every instinct of self-preservation stirred, was glad to give expression to her feelings in language which went far beyond her normal mood. Ministers found her willing to declare her obligation "to place her chief dependence on those who had given such repeated proofs of the greatest warmth and concern, for the support of the Revolution, the security of her own person, and of the Protestant Succession."[1] In closing the session she allowed herself to say, "All which is dear to you is perfectly safe under my government, and must be irrecoverably lost, if ever the designs of a popish Pretender, bred up in the principles of the most arbitrary government, should take place."[2]

It was indeed the hour of the Whigs. Even before the election they renewed their efforts to press themselves upon the Queen. Once again they selected one of their number behind whom all their efforts should be concentrated. Somers, William III's Lord Chancellor, was, for his gifts, his dignities, and his record in history, the accepted head of the Junto. During Anne's reign he had been removed with other Whig Lords from the Privy Council. His associates now resolved that he should become its President. The demand by the victorious party for the inclusion of so eminent a statesman in the councils of the sovereign was amply justified. Indeed, the Whigs might boast their moderation in asking only for this. Not only did the five Lords sustain the request, but it was endorsed by the moderate Whig members of the Cabinet, the Dukes

[1] *Parliamentary History*, vi, 729.   [2] *Ibid.*, 731.

of Devonshire and Newcastle. The Queen met their first overtures with the answer that she could not displace Lord Pembroke, with whom she was entirely pleased. The Whig Dukes then reduced their claim to the simple inclusion of Somers in the Cabinet. Anne, taken by surprise at the audience, could think of no grounds for refusal other than that the Cabinet was full enough already. Pressed from all sides, the Queen carried her complaints to Marlborough.

The Queen to Marlborough

KENSINGTON
April 22/May 3, 1708

The occasion of my writing to you, at this time, is to give you an account of a visit I had yesterday from Lord Privy Seal and Lord Steward, in which they proposed my taking Lord Somers into the Cabinet Council, without giving him any employment, since I could not be prevailed upon to make him President, laying a great stress on its being necessary for my service. Their arguments did not at all convince me of the reasonableness nor the propriety of the thing. But all the answer I made was that the proposition was a very new thing, and that I thought there were enough of the Cabinet Council already; that I depended upon their assistance in carrying on my business; and had no thoughts of employing any but those that served me well in the Parliament, and had no leaning to any others, and would countenance all that served me faithfully. This is the sense of what I said to them; and this morning I gave this account to Lord Treasurer, who had heard nothing of this matter before, but joined in the two Dukes' proposal, using a great many arguments to persuade me to comply with it; and, I must own to you, did not convince me any more than what I had heard before on the same subject, though I have a much greater respect for him than for either of the others, *looking upon it to be utter destruction to me to bring Lord Somers into my service.* And I hope you will not join in soliciting me in this thing, though Lord Treasurer tells me you will; for it is what I can never consent to.

You are very happy to be out of the disagreeable and vexatious things that I am more or less continually made uneasy with, which makes me not wonder at your not coming back as you promised. I pray God bless and direct you in everything, and never let it be in anybody's power to do me ill offices with you, but be assured that I am, and will be ever, your faithful servant.[1]

Marlborough, now at the front anxiously watching the French army gathering around Mons, urged her to comply. His letter shows that he was as good a judge of electioneering as of military

[1] Coxe, iv, 72–73.

matters. Evidently the Queen, presumably on Harley's forecast, hoped that the Tories would hold their own at the polls, and Marlborough was at pains to undeceive her.

Marlborough to the Queen

GHENT
May 9, 1708

. . . I do not doubt but care is taken to incline your Majesty to believe that the Tories will have, this next Parliament, a majority in the House of Commons. But I beg your Majesty to consider, before it is too late, how that is possible, after the attempt that has been made by France for the Pretender; and that the greatest part of that party is suspected, either to have known, or at least to have wished success to the attempt. Besides, their continual endeavours to incline the people to a peace which, in the circumstances we are in, can only tend to the lessening your Majesty, and consequently the advancement of the Pretender's interest.

This being the truth, how is it possible, madam, that the honest people of England, who wish well to you, and the carrying on of the war, can be prevailed upon to choose such men as they believe would ruin all that is dear to them? If what I have the honour to write to your Majesty be the truth, for God's sake consider what may be the consequences of refusing the request of the Dukes of Newcastle and Devonshire; since it will be a demonstration not only to them, but to everybody, that Lord Treasurer and I have no credit with your Majesty, but that you are guided by the insinuation of Mr Harley.

We are assured that the Duke of Burgundy is coming to the head of this army with the King of France's leave and orders to venture a battle. I shall be so far from avoiding it that I shall seek it, thinking it absolutely necessary for your service; so that God only knows whether this may not be the last I may have the honour to write you which makes me beg with the same earnestness as if I were sure it were to be my last that your Majesty will let no influence or persuasion hinder you, not only in this, but in all your worldly affairs, to follow the advice and good counsel of Lord Treasurer who will never have any thought but what is for your honour and true interest.[1]

Marlborough attached grave importance to the reception of his advice. "If she be obstinate," he wrote to Godolphin, "I think it is a plain declaration to all the world that you and I have no credit, and that all is governed underhand by Mr Harley and Mrs Masham."[2]

The Queen ignored Marlborough's advice about Somers, but in a letter of European importance assured him that she would in no way lend herself to peace negotiations.

[1] Coxe, iv, 74–76.   [2] May 8; *ibid.*, 75.

The Queen to Marlborough

. . . I have been so tired to-day with importunities that come from the Whigs that I have not spirits left to open my afflicted heart so freely and so fully as I intended. . . .

I can now only tell you that as to what you mention, and what the Lord Treasurer told me some time ago, of your being pressed in two conferences for the making steps towards a peace, I am entirely of your opinion, thinking it neither for my honour nor interest; and do assure you that whatever insinuations my enemies may make to the contrary, I shall never at any time give my consent to a peace, but upon safe and honourable terms. Excuse my answering nothing more of your letter at this time, and be so just to me as not to let any misrepresentations that may be made of me have any weight with you, for that would be a greater trouble to me than can be expressed. I cannot end without begging you to be very careful of yourself, there being nobody, I am sure, that prays more heartily for your preservation than her that will live and die most sincerely your humble servant.

The Prince desires his service to you.[1]

The election was fought out in May. A month before both Harley and the Queen nursed secret hopes of a Tory victory. Now the Tories were taken at a hopeless disadvantage. The shadow of the frustrated invasion overlay the land. The Whigs exploited the occasion to the full. In manifestos and speeches they endeavoured to confound the Tories with the Jacobites, and their political antagonists with the French. Brutally accused by their opponents of bringing the curse of civil war and foreign invasion upon the land, distrusted by important moderate elements, abandoned at this critical moment, though only for the moment, by the Queen, in whom their hopes were set, it was marvellous the Tories were not annihilated in the constituencies. They were stubborn folk, and in those days Englishmen did not run in droves, like their modern descendants. Harley, in spite of the invasion scare, in spite of Greg's treason, and all the odium thrust upon him both by the Whigs and the Court, was returned for his Welsh seat (New Radnor). St John, having quarrelled with his father, patron of the family borough of Wootton Bassett, sought a refuge in over-represented Tory Cornwall. He failed to find it. No doubt his cynical discarding of the Occasional Conformity Bill for the sake of office three years before had left an impression upon the Tory Party managers, both national and local, which not all his brilliancy and eloquence could efface.

[1] Coxe, iv, 83–89.

He passed for the moment into complete eclipse. Burying himself in the depths of the country, he affected to find in horse and hound, in books and agriculture, a solace for his exile from affairs. As the election results flowed in it became certain that the Whigs would be masters of the new House of Commons. In fact, they secured a majority of over a hundred, and thus the Lords of the Junto became possessed of lawful and predominant power in both Houses, exercisable as soon as Parliament should meet.

Parliament only sat in the winter. It was now no more than June. The Whigs felt that the Queen should recognize the results of the polls by embracing them forthwith in a definitely party administration. The event, however, struck Anne differently. She was surprised and chagrined by the Tory defeat. All her prejudices against the Whigs were redoubled by their triumphs. She understood, and Harley must have explained to her, how narrow and accidental had been the margins by which their previous plans had been cast down. When Secretary of State, Harley had looked forward upon a very solid basis to forming a Government with or even without Marlborough in January or February 1708, and, aided by the favour of the Crown, to winning the General Election. Marlborough's prestige and his fidelity to Godolphin had ruptured Harley's scheme of government. The Jacobite raid had spoiled his chances in the constituencies. The Queen resented these unforeseeable happenings. In the face of what Sunderland called "the best Whig Parliament that has been since the revolution,"[1] Anne was more cordially Tory than ever before. Already she had forgotten the Jacobite scare. She would not hear of new Whigs in the Cabinet. The supplies had been voted for the year; Marlborough was in the field at the head of the armies, and until the money ran short the Whigs could drum their heels in the coffee-houses, or the antechambers—if they could get so far.

Anne's distress and discontent vented itself upon Sunderland. The Whig Secretary of State had used his office, his influence, and, as far as he dared, the Queen's name to rig the election of the Scottish peers in his party interests. In a letter to the Duke of Roxburgh he had written: "I would not have you be bully'd by the Court-Party, for the Queen herself cannot support that faction long."[2] This undoubted disloyalty to the principles upon which the

---

[1] Sunderland to Newcastle; B.M., Lansdowne MSS., 1236, f. 242.
[2] Ralph, *The Other Side of the Question* (1742), p. 380. Author anonymous: "A Woman of Quality." Ralph is the name of the journalist who probably compiled it.

compromise of the Queen's Government was framed, and which Marlborough and Godolphin represented, was exposed to her up the backstairs by Harley. All her dislike of Sunderland, all her resentments at his having been forced upon her, now found vehement expression. Her name had been used for a party purpose, contrary, not only to her feelings, but to the whole character of the Government, which Marlborough's authority had wrung from her as a final settlement. She became so enraged that only her respect for Marlborough and for Marlborough's power prevented her from taking the seals of office out of hand from his son-in-law. She protested to him indignantly in two letters of June 18/29 and June 22/July 3.

The Queen to Marlborough

June 18/29, 1708

. . . There is no wonder opposition should increase when one of my own servants is at the head of it, as you will see by the enclosed, which I could not forbear sending you to give you a view of the ill-treatment I receive from the person that is mentioned in it: there are larger accounts come to-day from other hands, all to the same purpose; it is such a behaviour, I believe, as never was known, and what I really cannot bear, nor what no other I dare say would one minute; but I am willing out of sincere kindness and consideration I have for you to defer taking away the seals till I receive again more confirmation of what the enclosed contains; not that I have doubt of the truth of it; all Lord S.'s own actions having shown so much of the same spirit. . . . It is impossible to bear such usage; and I am sure you are too reasonable, if you consider this matter impartially, to blame me when I send for the seals, and be assured I shall ever be the same sincere and faithful friend to you as ever.[1]

The Queen to Marlborough

June 22/July 13, 1708

*I believe you expect to hear from me this post, and therefore I writt to lett you know I have had better succession [sic] in ye Election in Scotland than could be expected after such Opposition. . . . Ld Sunderland has assured me he had neither directly nor indirectly made use of my name, but at ye same time owned he had writt his own thoughts about ye Election to some Lds of ye Squadron, as they call them, . . . tho he did not mention my name I think in effect what he has done is ye same thing, . . . soe I cannot but still resent this usage very much. . . .[2]

[1] Marlborough Papers, *H.M.C.*, p. 42.   [2] Blenheim MSS.

Apparently the Queen was disconcerted by his silence, for she wrote again on July 3/14, when, unknown to her, her armies were gathering the spoils of victory, a more equable and mollifying letter.

The Queen to Marlborough

WINDSOR
July 3/14, 1708

I am very sorry you continue still in the desire you mentioned to the Lord Treasurer of retiring after the campagne, . . . but though you are never so desirous to be at quiet, I conclude, till you see in what condition you can leave things abroad and how you find things at home, you can take no resolution, and therefore I will not now trouble you with everything I could say to persuade you out of this melancholy thought; but leave it to you to consider how mortifying a thing it must be for me if ever you put it in practice. . . . What you desire concerning Lord Treasurer was not at all necessary, for I have so true a sense of his friendship to me, and so real a value and esteem for him, that if ever anybody should endeavour to do him any ill office, it would have no effect upon me. . . . Great care must be taken that no cause be given to our friends abroad to think that there is any fear of business going ill in England, and you may be sure I will advise in everything with those you desire; the parties are such bugbeares that I dare not venture to write my mind freely of either of them without a cypher for fear of any accident. I pray God keep me out of the hands of both of them.[1]

Marlborough received the earlier menacing or disquieting messages in the crisis of marches and manœuvres which preceded battle. So obvious an affront as the public dismissal of his own son-in-law at such a moment seemed likely to undermine his authority before all men. Harassed by the Queen's attitude, he was also incensed by Sunderland's behaviour. All that we know of Sunderland during the summer of 1708 shows that his only loyalty was to the Junto. For the Queen, for the compromise Cabinet of which he was a member, for Marlborough, his father-in-law, to whom he owed so much, for Sarah, who had wrecked herself to help him—nay, for the cause of the Alliance, he cared in comparison nothing: the party pledge was his only tie. Thus we see him using throughout the year language about Godolphin and even Marlborough which in cold hostility equalled the worst that from the opposite angle Harley could whisper through Abigail to the Queen.

[1] Marlborough Papers, *H.M.C.*, p. 42.

Marlborough, at grips with a superior French army, worn and wearied, ill and fevered, was, as we shall see, roused after a brief collapse to the mood of Napoleon before Wagram; "La bataille répondra." He cast political intrigues from him with inexpressible loathing. He left the Queen's letters unanswered, and mounted his horse.

Chapter Nineteen

EUGENE COMES NORTH

1708—SPRING

PRINCE EUGENE, according to Schulenberg, said of the campaign of 1708, "He who has not seen this has seen nothing." This remark is typical of the accounts of eyewitnesses of all ranks on either side. The captious Goslinga ends his tale with the words, "Thus ended this dangerous and remarkable campaign, one of the most glorious which was ever made." And our Private Deane, of the First Guards, calls it "very long, tiresome, troublesome, mischievous and strange, yet very successful." Indeed, it is not easy to find operations more novel and suggestive to the student of military affairs. We have the two greatest commanders of the age at the head of troops from many confederate states, surmounting the vices of coalitions, beginning under a serious misfortune, courting undue risks to gain victory in the field, and undertaking the greatest siege till then recorded, with their communications cut. We see besiegers besieged while still besieging; preserving existence from day to day only by the narrowest margins and chances; isolated and invested in the midst of enemy territory, yet never relinquishing their prey; fighting on in defiance of custom and season till the end of December; finally overcoming every obstruction and succeeding in every detail against the forces of a homogeneous French army, which never outnumbered them by less than six to five.

It is worth while, in order the better to recognize the sequence of events, to set forth the major episodes beforehand: namely, the loss of Ghent and Bruges; the battle of Oudenarde; the investment of Lille; the convoy of the siege-train from Brussels; the French attempt to raise the siege; the severance of the communications with Brussels; the opening of new communications with the sea; the critical action of Wynendael; the bombardment and assaults of the city of Lille; the inundations and aquatic warfare for supplies; the total isolation of the allied armies; the timely surrender of the city of Lille; the opening of a third line of communications from the sea; the French diversion against Brussels; the forcing of the Scheldt and the relief of Brussels by Marlborough and Eugene; the fall of the citadel of Lille; the final recapture of Ghent and Bruges by the Allies.

Encouraged by his success in 1707, Louis XIV resolved, as Marlborough had predicted,[1] to gain the mastery in Flanders. By a hard effort he brought to the field the most numerous army which the world had seen for centuries. Nearly a hundred and ten thousand men, forming 131 battalions and 216 squadrons, assembled during May around Mons. His intention was to give the effective command against Marlborough to Marshal Vendôme. His eldest grandson, Fénelon's pupil, the blameless Duke of Burgundy, having, however, expressed a desire to serve, was placed nominally at the head of the army, and the Elector of Bavaria was constrained to transfer himself to the Upper Rhine. Vendôme favoured the change, thinking that the inexperienced prince of the blood would hamper him less than the able, war-toughened Elector.

Max Emmanuel, on the other hand, was loath to leave Flanders. What Marlborough had foretold in 1706 had come to pass. The cities of Belgium were seething with discontent under the rule and exactions of the Dutch. The Elector felt himself possessed of real influence with the Belgian people. Moreover, he feared lest his removal should be the prelude to peace negotiations with Holland at his expense. The French Court, however, consoled him with the prospect of so strong an army upon the Upper Rhine that by a brilliant campaign he might even regain his own Bavaria. "On account of the disgust that subsisted"[2] between the Elector and Villars, the latter was made to exchange commands with Berwick, who had already been appointed to the southern front (Dauphiné). Berwick, when he arrived on the Rhine, like Vendôme in Flanders, was held responsible commander, with the extra duty of keeping a royal or exalted figurehead out of mischief and in good humour, and of securing to such personages the glory to which their birth entitled them. Neither of them was, however, willing to be a puppet or even a passenger. When we dwell upon Marlborough's troubles with the Dutch field Deputies and recalcitrant allies, it must not be forgotten that similar vexations often afflicted the marshals of France. Not only had they to endure a divided authority, but also a persistent interference by almost daily couriers from the Great King himself, to whom all decisive issues were referred.

[1] See p. 274.   [2] Berwick, *Memoirs*, ii, 3.

Indeed, once Eugene had joined Marlborough their perfect comradeship and pre-eminence established a higher unity of command
than had ever been seen in the war. "The Princes," as they came
to be called in the confederacy, settled everything between themselves. Neither ever allowed a whisper of disagreement to circulate.
They were apparently immune from any kind of jealousy of each
other, were proof against every form of mischief-making or intrigue,
and in the field at any rate were in practice absolute. The councils
of war were frequent, and many opinions were heard. But once
"the Princes" had finally spoken all bowed to their judgment.
Without this new fact at the allied headquarters the extraordinary
operations which these chapters describe, so intricate, so prolonged, and contrary on many occasions to the accepted principles
of war, could never have been achieved.

Marlborough, Eugene, and Heinsius met at The Hague on
April 12 to concert the general strategy of the year. It immediately
became obvious that Eugene would not go to Spain. The Emperor
would not agree; Eugene did not want to go; Marlborough did not
mean him to go. Thus the pet project of the British Parliament and
Cabinet which had been referred to this conference was promptly
dismissed. The theatre was judged minor, and the policy should be
defensive. Who, then, should command? This also had been largely
settled by Marlborough. A fortnight earlier Stanhope had been
appointed Commander-in-Chief of the British forces there. He had
travelled to The Hague in Marlborough's company. He attended
all the meetings. But it was not Marlborough's policy to send any
important British detachment to Spain. Only about two thousand
British troops were actually capable of taking the field. Marlborough therefore had procured from the Cabinet authority to pay
the expense of a considerable reinforcement of Imperial troops. He
also proposed that the Palatine contingent in Italy, seven thousand
strong, under General Rehbinder, hired jointly by England and
Holland, should be sent to the Peninsula. This was the most he
could do; it was also the least. The great preponderance of Germanic
troops made it necessary that an Imperial commander should also
be appointed. Starhemberg, reputed "the best General of the age
for the defensive,"[1] was at that time commanding against the
Hungarian rebels. It was decided to transfer him to Spain. This
implied that Stanhope's military rôle would be minor or nil.

[1] N. Tindal, *Continuation of Rapin's History of England*, iv, 97.

However, as he was entrusted with the payment of £10,000 a month from the British Government to Charles III, he was assured of some attention; and his instructions from the Cabinet charged him to "enlarge the bounds" of the operations in Spain by land and sea. To console the British Parliament upon the withholding of Eugene from Spain special emphasis was laid upon the naval aspect of the campaign—namely, the need of capturing a safe sea-base.

It was already plain that no forces could be provided for an important offensive in Dauphiné under Victor Amadeus. Marlborough, serenely unmoved by the Titian hangings, acquiesced at once in this restriction of the southern front. Every one at The Hague welcomed the idea that Eugene should fight in the north. But a further complication remained.

The Elector of Hanover had with great difficulty been at last induced to accept the Rhine command as Imperial Generalissimo. He had viewed the arrival of Prince Eugene in the north with disfavour. He saw himself eclipsed in reputation, and feared—with justice, as it proved—that his troops would be diverted or that his rôle would become subsidiary. Not only because of the difficulty of finding an Imperial commander-in-chief, but as a substantial ally, and heir to the British throne, Elector George Lewis of Hanover was a figure of the highest importance throughout the confederacy, and especially to Marlborough. Nevertheless, when Marlborough and Eugene came together their war-thought prevailed over all other considerations. Eugene at first proposed to Marlborough that the main allied effort should be made along the Moselle and also across the Rhine. Thirty thousand men should be withdrawn from Flanders to Coblenz, making a Moselle army of seventy thousand, which Eugene would command. In conjunction with the Elector of Hanover's Rhine army of forty thousand men, Marlborough's abortive plan of 1705 would be tried again under more hopeful conditions. But the States-General would not agree, in the face of the heavy French concentration proceeding daily on their front, and magnified by rumour, to strip themselves of so large a part of their defence. Marlborough was unwilling to weaken the Flanders army. He could use the frustrated invasion of Scotland against moving his forces away from the sea. He warned Eugene from his own bitter experience that the assembly of the German contingents upon the Moselle would be fatally delayed; and the French would seize the initiative in Flanders long before the Moselle army could be assembled.

Accordingly he proposed to Eugene that, although the three armies should be formed, and every pretence made of an invasion of France by the Moselle, yet at the proper moment secretly and suddenly Eugene should carry whatever troops had gathered on the Moselle to join the main army in Flanders; and that in the few days before the French could bring similar reinforcements from the Rhine he and Eugene should fall upon them with the superior strength of a hundred and twenty thousand men, and force a decisive battle. This idea of a super-Blenheim commended itself to Prince Eugene. The two agreed to confine their secret to the narrowest circle. By these plans the French were remarkably deceived. With the impressions of Toulon strong in their minds, they still feared a major offensive in Dauphiné. Everything that leaked out from Briançon's office in London about such schemes misled them. Completely mystified in this theatre by the allied strategy, they provided a substantial army to guard their southern front and sent Marshal Villars to command it.

As a part of his main scheme Marlborough was still attracted by the idea of a "descent." He believed that practically all the French regular troops were engaged on the various fronts, and that nothing but encampments of militia guarded the long coasts of France. Even if a serious landing was not made he hoped that the appearance of a substantial force in transports, escorted by a fleet, now here, now there, would draw far more than its own numbers from the main armies. We have seen the fate which awaited the troops of the first "descent." Now, at the beginning of 1708, a second force under General Erle of eleven English battalions was assembled in the Isle of Wight with the necessary shipping and escort, to be used on the Belgian coast or against the French Channel ports in conjunction with Marlborough's operations as he should direct. This, as we shall see, played a decisive part.

Thus it was settled that Starhemberg and Stanhope should stand on the defensive in Spain; that Victor Amadeus should play a minor rôle in Dauphiné; that Eugene should concentrate upon the Moselle, as if to work with the Elector of Hanover on the Rhine, but that suddenly thereafter he should join Marlborough for a surprise battle in Flanders; and, lastly, that an amphibious descent should be prepared as a contributory diversion.

The first step in pursuance of this general plan was to reconcile the Elector of Hanover to the preparatory formation of the three armies in the north. For this purpose Eugene insisted that Marlborough should accompany him to Hanover. Disregarding the entreaties of Godolphin and Sarah that he should return home, if only for a fortnight, to save the political situation, of which more later, Marlborough set out for Hanover in the third week of April. His report to Godolphin (The Hague, May 3) speaks for itself.[1]

> I am now thoroughly convinced, if I had avoided being at Hanover at the same time with Prince Eugene, not only the project made at The Hague had miscarried, but also these people would have laid the fault at my door.
>
> After a very great deal of uneasiness the Elector has consented to the project for three armies; but we have been obliged to leave on the Rhine two Imperial regiments more than we designed, so that Prince Eugene will have 2000 horse less on the Moselle; and *as for the joining the two armies* [*Marlborough and Eugene*], *we thought it best not to acquaint the Elector with it, so that I expect when that is put in execution, he will be very angry*; but since the good of the campaign depends upon it, I know no remedy but patience.

In fact, though Marlborough's letter does not mention it, he had been forced also himself to transfer five thousand troops to the Rhine army, thus providing the Elector with forty-seven thousand men, who were destined to stand virtually idle during the whole of the campaign. Moreover, the Elector never forgave him for the concealment, and afterwards, as George I, he was not without opportunities of marking his displeasure.

Lastly, it was understood between the princes that Marlborough might have to fight a battle before the junction of the armies could be made. "We are assured," he wrote to the Queen (May 9),

> that the Duke of Burgundy is coming to the head of this army with the King of France's leave and orders to venture a battle. I shall be so far from avoiding it that I shall seek it, thinking it absolutely necessary for your service, *so that God only knows whether this may not be the last I may have the honour to write you . . .*[2]

This histrionic note mingles more than once in Marlborough's later letters to Queen Anne. It marks the decline in their relationship. He never wrote like this in any campaign before 1707. Its lack of reserve is excusable only by the crises of the Queen's personal attitude and the political factions at work around her. But the same conditions that prompted the Captain-General to strike the note led the Queen to disregard it.

[1] Coxe, iv, 62.   [2] *Ibid.*, 76. For full text see p. 323.

The months of May and June were one of Marlborough's periods of silent stress. In England the impact of the Whigs upon the Queen had produced a dangerous deadlock. All Holland, especially the burghers of Amsterdam, lent themselves to the demand for peace negotiations, even negotiations to be opened by the Allies. All Belgium was utterly wearied of the Dutch, and its great fortress towns were alive with conspiracy. Eugene's army, as Marlborough had foreseen, had scarcely begun to assemble. The French were ready to take the field with about a hundred and ten thousand men collected around Mons, and Marlborough faced them with 112 battalions and 197 squadrons, or almost ninety thousand, in his camps to the south of Brussels. Indeed, Louis XIV announced to his Court on May 24 that his reports from the armies led him to believe that a general engagement would be fought before the end of the month.

A wealth of alternatives presented themselves to the French High Command. Vendôme persuaded Louis XIV to approve the siege of Huy as a provocation to battle. It was a small undertaking, and if Marlborough sought to interrupt it the whole army could meet him in country favourable to the more powerful French cavalry and offering no helpful enclosures to the much-respected Confederate foot. Burgundy wished to march directly towards Brussels to threaten the Dutch Barrier and test the alleged disaffection of the Belgians. Marlborough himself apprehended a third plan towards the coast, beginning with a siege of Ath and aiming at Ghent, Bruges, and Antwerp. Later on we shall see that his instinct proved sound. For the moment Vendôme agreed with Burgundy's view, and on May 26 the French army marched suddenly by night to Soignies. Marlborough advanced to Hal to confront them, and a battle seemed imminent. On June 1, however, the French moved eastward towards Nivelles, threatening Louvain; whereupon Marlborough repeated his retreat of the previous year by a very long march (thirty-six miles in thirty hours and drenching rain). He passed around Brussels, and reached Terbanck, behind the Dyle, on June 3. The French, again confronted, halted between Genappe and Braine l'Alleud. In these positions both armies lay for the rest of June, the French in doubt what to choose, and Marlborough waiting on their choice and for Eugene. The Deputy Goslinga deemed Marlborough's retirement pusillanimous, and recorded his usual calumnies upon it. But the Duke pursued his strategy with phlegm. At Terbanck he was safe. There he covered Brussels and

Louvain, and thence he could move by his many prepared routes to parry attacks so divergent as upon Huy on the Meuse or Ath on the Dender. Meanwhile he contained a superior hostile army; but time was precious.

One discerning eye had early pierced his secret. Berwick had ridiculed the airy plans of an invasion of Germany with which the

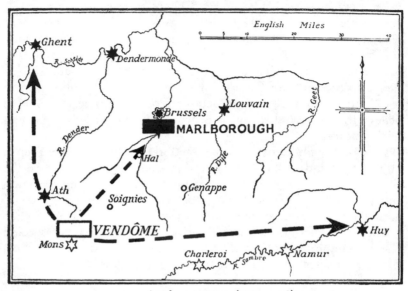

VENDÔME'S CHOICES (MAY 1708)

French Court had soothed Max Emmanuel. He persuaded the Elector by soldierly argument that

> they [the Allies] would . . . be well pleased to see us amuse ourselves with operations which would be to no other advantage but merely that of saving the reputation of the general; while Prince Eugene, *in imitation of the Duke of Marlborough's conduct in* 1704, would make a sudden incursion into Flanders with a suitable force to crush the King's army and invade France upon that side.

Berwick therefore thought it his duty "principally to watch the movements of the enemy," in order to send the Duke of Burgundy "troops in proportion as detachments should be made by them."[1]

Marlborough was soon conscious, from the way Berwick disposed his troops, of his nephew's suspicious vigilance. Gradually prospects of making a superior concentration against Vendôme

[1] *Memoirs*, ii, 7.

faded. "The disappointment of the Palatine troops,"[1] he wrote to Godolphin (June 11),

> and Eugene not being able to put in execution, by at least a fortnight, what was agreed between him and me, gives great disadvantage. However, I have taken my measures that nothing may be wanting at

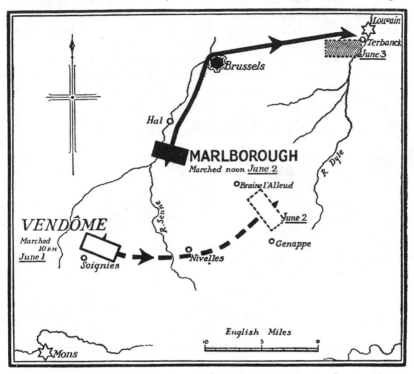

MOVEMENTS IN THE FIRST WEEK OF JUNE 1708

> his arrival, being persuaded that our greatest hopes must be in what we shall be able to do in the first four or five days; for their [Berwick's] foot will be able to join them as soon, if not sooner than ours. But if Prince Eugene uses that diligence he has promised, he may, with his horse, join me some days before they can, by stealing a march, which time we must make use of. . . . I have been busy every day in reviewing the troops. The great part are in extreme good order.[2]

And to Sarah:

> Whenever I have any reason, and my mind a little at ease, I make sure of that time to write to my dear soul. The post does not go till

[1] A separate contingent additional to those ordered to Spain.
[2] Coxe, iv, 112–114.

to-morrow, but as I am that morning to see the left wing of horse, I make use of this time to tell you that I am in my health, I thank God, as well as one of my age, and that has not his mind very much at ease, can be; for what I concerted with Prince Eugene will not be executed by fifteen days so soon as was resolved, which will be an advantage to the Duke of Vendôme, by giving him time; but the slowness of the Germans is such that we must always be disappointed. . . . As for us in this country, we have a very good army, but the French think themselves more numerous; however, I hope, with the blessing of God, that this campaign will not pass without some good success on our side. You may easily believe me when I tell you that I do from my heart wish that the favourable account I now give you of the posture of our armies may meet with no disappointment. . . .[1]

To Eugene he wrote on the same day:

June 11, 1708

You will have learned on your arrival that the Elector of Bavaria [advised by Berwick] has sent a strong detachment towards the Moselle, which will doubtless march forward, in proportion as your troops advance, so you will easily judge that for a beginning we can rely only on the cavalry, *with which I request you to hasten in all diligence*; for we can only reckon on a surprise which will depend on the little time you may take for your march between the Moselle and the Meuse. *If the Palatines are not now arrived, you will please not to wait for them*; and as soon as I know the day you will be at Maestricht, I will send some one to meet you, and acquaint you with my projects.

If you can gain only forty-eight hours, I will make my dispositions for the moment of your arrival, and with the blessing of heaven we may profit so well by these two days as to feel the good effects of it the rest of the campaign. *You will order the infantry to hasten as much as possible to Maestricht, where they will receive directions for their further march.*

The two armies have remained in their present camps, and there is no appearance of a change, till I have the news which I expect from your Highness. I have employed this time in making an exact review of the troops, which are in so good a condition that it would gratify your Highness to see them.[2]

This letter is interesting because it shows the relations between Marlborough and Eugene at this time. We see Marlborough giving the definite orders of a superior commander. Moreover, Eugene fully accepts the position. "Your Highness," he wrote, "may be convinced I will omit nothing to press on my march from Rheinfels. I will give you due notice by courier, being myself extremely impatient to assure you in person of my respect . . ."[3]

---

[1] Coxe, iv, 112.   [2] *Ibid.*, 116–117.   [3] *Ibid.*, 118.

Marlborough used the protracted delays in reviewing the army. Napoleon was accustomed in his greatest days to take every opportunity of inspecting his troops division by division. He used to assemble ten thousand men at a time, and spend the whole day with them, studying their condition, hearing complaints from all ranks, and becoming personally known to the men. Marlborough may well have been his exemplar in this, for during this month he saw the whole allied army in detachments of eight to ten thousand a day, and was increasingly satisfied with its quality and spirit. But the delays of the Germans began to have serious results. To Godolphin he wrote on June 28:

> Prince Eugene thinks the Elector will not approve of his march, which is the reason of his not acquainting him sooner with my letter, *so that he might not have it in his power to hinder the march, which he thinks otherwise he would do.* That which gives me the greatest uneasiness is that I find Prince Eugene thinks that their horse cannot join me in less than ten days, and that their foot must have fourteen or fifteen days. If they cannot make greater expedition, I fear the horse of the Duke of Berwick will get before them. . . . Since the disappointments Prince Eugene has met with have lost us above a month, and that the enemy know too much of our design, the best thing we can hope for is that we may be able to oblige them to come to some action.[1]

On June 29 the Prince started on his 150-mile march from Coblenz with forty-three squadrons and eighteen battalions—only fifteen instead of the originally hoped-for forty thousand—but still a formidable reinforcement. But Berwick was also hastening to Flanders with fifty-five squadrons and thirty-four battalions (twenty-seven thousand men), and Eugene could not hope to be more than two or three days ahead of him even with his cavalry. The impending climax was apprehended in the secret circle at home. Sarah evidently bent beneath her anxieties, but who should reproach a soldier's wife in such an hour?

"You are so kind," wrote Marlborough (June 25), "as to be in pain as to what may happen when Prince Eugene comes. Put your trust in God, as I do, and be assured that I think I can't be unhappy as long as you are kind."[2]

At this time, as was usual in a crisis, his mind played placidly with homely topics. Sarah had long desired a great house in London, and John made no difficulty about the heavy expense. His economies were usually upon small matters mostly affecting himself, and arose

---

[1] Coxe, iv, 120–121.   [2] *Ibid.*, 90.

from his dislike of frittering money. A hundred thousand pounds for some important object dear to his wife did not afflict him. But his opinions about Marlborough House, and especially about house-building, deserve the attention of all who lack that experience.

John to Sarah

July 1st, 1708

★I have receiv'd yours from St Albans, and am glad to find the Windows you are making please you. But as for myself, I am so desirous of living at Woodstock that I should not much Care to do anything but what is necessary anywhere else. In my Opinion what you write of Vanbrugh ought to please any reasonable Man. And besides the reasons you give against a Pension, 'tis more for his Interest to stay till something happens that may be lasting. You ask my Opinion, which is best for building your House at London, three lifes, or 50 years. I should think the Term of Years much the best. But I would have you follow your own Inclination in it. You know I never lik'd to build it at all. And I am Confident you will find 'twill cost you much more Mony than the thing is worth. You may build a better Apartment than you have now, but you will never have as many Conveniences as in your Lodgings. *And you may depend on it, 'twill cost you double the Mony they have estimated.* 'Tis not a proper Place for a great House: And I am sure, when you have built a little one, you won't like it. So that if you have not set your Heart upon it I should advise you to think well of it. *For 'tis more advisable to buy a House than to build one.*[1]

The moment (July 2) had now come to inform the States-General that the whole Moselle army was marching to Flanders.

Having reflected on the situation of our affairs in this country, and considered those on the Moselle, and observing the little probability of supplying the army of Prince Eugene with all the requisites, so as to act offensively and with vigour; and being confirmed in my opinion by a resolution of your high Mightinesses, communicated to me by the Deputies, I have imparted to Prince Eugene and to Count Rechteren my opinion that it will be more advantageous to the interests of the common cause for the army on the Moselle to join us in Brabant without delay, and entreated them, should they be of my opinion, to communicate the same to the Elector of Hanover, and to begin their march as soon as possible. These measures being taken in conformity with the approbation of the field Deputies, I doubt not but they will give notice to your high Mightinesses. Nevertheless, I would not fail

[1] Blenheim MSS. The remainder of this letter, beginning, "Though we are in the Month of July, I am now by a fire," is printed in Coxe, iv, 90–91.

to inform you that I have just received from Prince Eugene intelligence that his army commenced their march last Friday, the cavalry advancing by long forced marches, while the infantry rapidly followed; and that it was his intention to arrive in our camp on the 5th or 6th, to concert with me the operations, according to our arrangement; that as soon as the cavalry shall approach we shall move directly upon the enemy, and bring on a battle, trusting in God to bless our designs, and hoping that I shall soon have an opportunity of sending you good news.[1]

The ink was scarcely dry upon this letter when news arrived that the French army was about to move.

[1] Coxe, iv, 123–124.

Chapter Twenty

THE SURPRISE OF GHENT AND BRUGES

1708—JULY 4–10

THE hatred which the Dutch occupation had aroused in the Belgian people in the two years since Ramillies had made the former French yoke seem light by contrast. Count Bergheyck, a Flemish noble of high repute, headed and organized a widespread pro-French conspiracy. His partisans prepared themselves to deliver the great fortress towns of Belgium to the French at the first favourable opportunity. In May Marlborough had detected and nipped in the bud the plot to surrender Antwerp. He had grave reasons to be anxious about the feelings in Brussels itself. He was under no illusions about Ghent and Bruges. Indeed, he had stationed Major-General Murray in that region with a whole brigade for the express purpose of giving timely aid to any threatened garrison.

During June Count Bergheyck unfolded a design for delivering Ghent and Bruges to France. The plan was considered immediately both by the French headquarters and at Versailles. Burgundy himself resolved upon the sudden flank march across the Dender towards Ghent. Vendôme thought it too hazardous, and advised a longer detour to the south. But the young prince took the plunge. On July 4 his strong advance forces under Grimaldi, ostensibly foraging to the westward, crossed the Dender at Ninove, and moved fast on Ghent. Simultaneously a flying column under the Comte de la Motte moved from the French lines at Comines to summon Bruges. The French Grand Army broke camp at seven P.M. They marched all night and all through the day of the 5th. At three A.M. La Motte entered Bruges without opposition. At dawn the French army was crossing the Senne at Tubize. At eight in the evening, having thrown out strong detachments under Albergotti to cover their right flank, they were crossing the Dender at Ninove. Here they learned that the town of Ghent had surrendered, and that the governor had agreed to yield the citadel by July 8, if not sooner relieved. This continuous march of more than thirty miles, part in

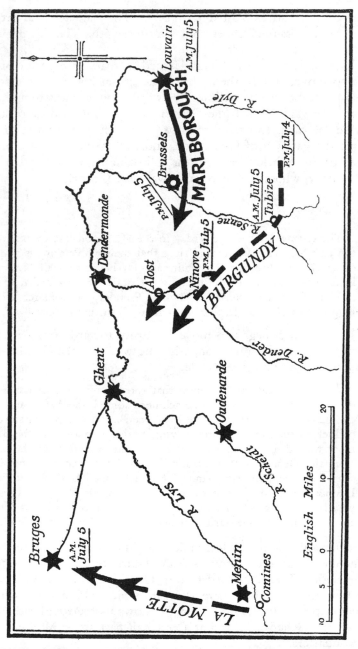

BURGUNDY'S MARCH

heavy rain, had exhausted the army. The baggage and artillery could not cross the Dender till dawn on the 6th. They lay protected only by their rearguards.

Late on July 2 Marlborough learned that the enemy were preparing to move, and on the night of the 4th at about ten o'clock he heard that they were marching westward, having sent strong detachments forward towards the Dender. He gave immediate orders to strike the camp and stand to arms. His first concern was to reinforce the garrison of Oudenarde, and thus make sure of a bridgehead on the Scheldt. He sent the following significant instructions to Murray, whose mobile brigade was near Ghent:

> CAMP AT TERBANCK
> *July 5, 1708*
> *Two in the morning*
>
> The enemy detached yesterday in the afternoon five thousand men towards Ninove. We are told since that their whole army is marched, of which we only expect the confirmation to begin ours, all things being in readiness for it. In the meantime I desire that immediately upon receipt of this you cause Sir Thomas Prendergast to march with his regiment to Oudenarde, there to remain till further orders.[1]

Marlborough began to move his army towards Brussels at the same hour. In the afternoon, when he was near the city, he wrote to the Secretary of State, Boyle:

> Having had advice last night that the enemy were decamped and that they had made a strong detachment some hours before under the command of M. Grimaldi, we have been upon our march since two o'clock in the morning, and, having notice at noon that the detachment was advanced as far as Alost, and had broken down the bridges over the Dender, I immediately detached two thousand horse and dragoons under the command of Major-General Bothmar, to pass at Dendermonde to observe them and protect the Pays de Waes. By what we can learn hitherto their army is advanced as far as Ninove, and we shall continue our march according to their further motions.[2]

After a march of eighteen miles the Allies came into camp about Anderlecht, on the south-western outskirts of Brussels, during the afternoon. Their advanced troops, the right wing, lay as far west as Lombeek. We have here a picture which, although drawn by a spiteful pen, is too rare to omit. It shows us the rough side of the tapestry. Goslinga arrived at about half-past six at Marlborough's headquarters.

[1] *Dispatches*, iv, 95.   [2] *Ibid*, 96.

We found him ready to mount his horse. He had received an hour earlier a report from the right that they were in touch with the enemy and there was a chance of striking at their rear-guard. . . . It was upon this message from the generals of the right that the Duke had got up from his bed, pale and worn out and disconsolate, to go and reconnoitre

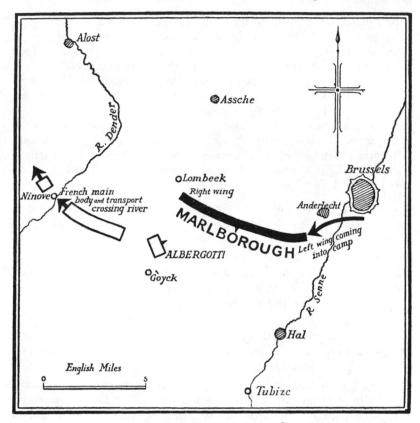

EVENING OF JULY 5, 1708

for himself the situation of the enemy. We had scarcely ridden a couple of miles when he said that there was no use in going further, that it was too late to begin an operation, and thereupon he turned his horse and rode back to his quarters.[1]

Goslinga followed him thither, and urged an attack next morning upon the French rearguard, which must be exhausted by an extra-ordinary march. The Duke replied that the ground was not favour-able. However, upon further reports that the whole French army

[1] Goslinga, p. 45.

was before him in position and might even itself attack at daybreak, he reinforced his right or advanced wing with thirty battalions and thirty squadrons of his weary troops, only just camped after their heavy march. "I was wakened at one in the morning," continues Goslinga,

> by Milord's adjutant, who told me that the Duke was getting up to go to the right wing. I dressed forthwith and presented myself before two o'clock at his quarters. I found him at prayers. These finished, he got into his carriage. M. Dopf and I followed him. It was at the first gleam of dawn that we arrived at the mill of Tombergh [Lombeek]. We there found Bulow with other generals of the right. All were under the strong conviction . . . that we should find the enemy army in battle array ready to fall upon us. Several even in the dawn and darkness, when no objects could yet be distinguished, imagined that they counted squadrons and battalions. But at length broad daylight dissipated these phantoms, and we found not one living soul before us.[1]

A detachment sent in pursuit captured a French baggage column and two or three hundred prisoners, but thereafter came in contact with the infantry of the enemy's rearguard posted in hedges and enclosures, and returned with their booty to camp about noon. It was evident that the French, by a sudden and extremely daring forced march, had carried their whole army beyond the Dender, and that they stood between the Allies and Ghent. They were thus in a position to adopt the third alternative plan, which Marlborough had always apprehended, and to attack the allied fortresses and bridgeheads on the Scheldt and the Lys, including particularly Oudenarde and Menin.[2]

To give an idea of the trials of the Commander-in-Chief we must dwell a little longer on Goslinga's account. The Deputy pursued the Duke back to his headquarters. In ignorance of the measures which had been taken for its defence, he opined that Oudenarde was probably already lost. He clamoured for an immediate march south-westward in order to protect Menin and the conquered territories of Flanders. All his account is designed to portray Marlborough as a vacillating sluggard whom the Deputy was endeavouring to arouse to a sense of his duty. The correspondence which has been set out shows that Marlborough was only waiting

---

[1] Goslinga, p. 48.
[2] See map at p. 343; also where necessary the general map of the Western Netherlands facing p. 488.

for the arrival of Eugene's cavalry to strike his blow. In the meantime he must cover Brussels. He had been without sleep the whole
night, moving the army, marching himself, and striving to measure
the unknown. He was, by Goslinga's account, physically very hard
pressed. Nevertheless, he endured with patience the prolonged
irresponsible solicitations of the Deputy, and, remarking that "your
masters would not be particularly edified if we thus abandoned our
own Flanders," ordered the army to march to Assche. Here,
guarding Brussels and the crossings of the Dender, he could await
developments and Eugene. Goslinga did all he could to create
prejudice and marshal opinion against this prudent strategy, but of
its massive good sense there can be no doubt.

We have seen that on the evening of the 5th the generals of Marlborough's right wing conceived themselves in presence of the
main French army and even liable to attack. It was not, however,
till daylight on the 6th that all the French vehicles and cannon passed
the Dender safely, followed during the morning by Albergotti and
the rearguard. There is little doubt that if Albergotti had been
strongly attacked about four in the afternoon of the 5th Burgundy
might have paid for his audacity with the loss of the whole of his
artillery and baggage, as well as of his flank and rearguards. This is
made a reproach against Marlborough. The question remains
whether such an attack was physically possible. Marlborough could
not move from Terbanck on the night of the 4th till he knew for
certain which way the French main army was marching. Grimaldi's
advance to Ninove might be a feint to cover a stroke in the opposite
direction at Louvain, and bring about a disastrous separation of the
converging allied armies. When Marlborough moved he moved
as fast as the French; but the French had started ten miles nearer to
the Dender and seven hours before him. He did not come in touch
with their rearguard till half-past five in the afternoon. His own
troops had been under arms for eighteen hours and had made a
full march. His left wing had not yet arrived. Darkness must have
fallen before he could attack in force. When about seven o'clock he
said it was too late and turned his horse, he was unquestionably
right. If, of course, he had known with certainty the day before
what the French intended, if even he could have known what they
were doing when they started on the evening of the 4th, a better
chance would have offered itself. But Burgundy was protected by
the secrecy of his plans and by the very rashness of his march.

Civilian spectators like Goslinga often perceive opportunities which are not in fact open to responsible generals moving large armies in the fog of war, and bound to provide against many dangers which as soon as they are warded off are not remembered or even noticed. Fine stories can always be told of what might have happened *if* the facts, times, and information had been different. Nor would a Deputy, driving about in his comfortable berlin, appreciate the strain upon the marching troops, or the imperative nature of

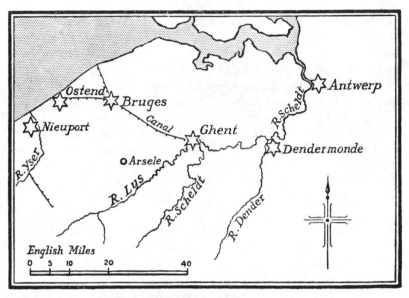

FRENCH CONTROL OF THE WATERWAYS

their need for food and rest. It is not that these factors would be unknown to him, but rather their emphasis and values. We can, however, see from his account Marlborough's intense fatigue at this time, his despondency and grave anxiety, his unrelenting care and discharge of duty. He was ailing and about to become ill. The prolonged and varied stresses to which he was subjected—the Queen estranged, his political system tottering, the hounds upon his track at home, a superior enemy upon his front, Eugene's unavoidable delays, Goslinga's endless officious carping and chatter—had found the limits of his hitherto unconquered spirit.

The worst was to come. On the march to Assche the news he must inwardly have dreaded of the loss of Ghent and Bruges arrived. To Marlborough this seemed for the moment disastrous to the whole campaign. Ghent was, in Berwick's words, "the key to all the rivers and all the waterways of Flanders." It seemed to govern the movement of siege artillery. Bruges was only less important. By its loss the direct line of communication with England by Ostend was destroyed. The fruits of Ramillies could be torn away piecemeal. The climax of the new campaign seemed ruined. What wonder if the Captain-General yielded to an hour of gloom? He was only a man.

Brigadier Grumbkow, the Prussian commissary at the British headquarters, wrote to Frederick I:

> The blow which the enemy dealt us did not merely destroy all our plans, but was sufficient to do irreparable harm to the reputation and previous good fortune of My lord Duke, and he felt this misfortune so keenly that I believed *he would succumb to this grief early the day before yesterday, as he was so seized by it that he was afraid of being suffocated.*[1]

It was in this mood that Eugene found him. They met at Assche. The Prince, escorted by a hundred Hungarian hussars, had driven on in his post-chaise four days ahead of his cavalry, and here he was fresh and gay with Cadogan at his side. Now for the first time the Army of the North saw the hero of the Empire in their midst. "Eugene had," we are told, "at first to live down the disappointing impression given by his stunted frame, his slouch, and the pock-marked cheeks which sagged in his pale face. Although thirteen years younger than Marlborough, he was called the 'old Italian Prince.' At headquarters and in the heat of the fighting, in deliberations and bold, calculated deeds, in his domination of councils of war and his irresistible power of command, he revealed his worth as a man and a soldier."[2]

Marlborough was overjoyed to see his heroic comrade. He was also very glad to have Cadogan back from Ostend. He had noticeably missed his Quartermaster-General and Intelligence chief during these exhausting days. He "tenderly embraced"[3] Eugene, saying, "I am not without hopes of congratulating your highness on a great victory; for my troops will be animated by your presence." But this was for the public. The two shut themselves up together for some hours with their maps. No one knows what passed. Eugene was certainly surprised at Marlborough's depression. ". . . I did not remain in Brussels, but passed straight through the town to the army

---

[1] Grumbkow to Frederick I (undated, but presumably July 9, 1708); K. W. von Schöning, *Des General-Feldmarschalls Dubislav Gneomar von Natzmer Leben und Kriegsthaten* (1838), p. 286.

[2] Von Noorden, iii, 44.   [3] Grumbkow to Frederick I; *loc. cit.*

in order to discuss with the Duke of Marlborough what is to be done. I have found him also in full march and pretty consternated [*ziemlich consterniert*]."[1]

Eugene's Austrian biographer says that

the Prince was astounded to see such despondency in a general like Marlborough over a misfortune not relatively very important. They were closeted together for several hours, and Eugene succeeded in convincing the Duke that his affairs were not in anything like so bad a state as he saw them.[2]

Grumbkow's account tallies with this:

While Mylord Duke was writing to the Queen, the Prince drew me aside and asked me what exactly all this meant. The Duke was incomprehensibly exhausted, and talked as though everything was lost, which the Prince did not consider appropriate, for unless he [Marlborough][3] lost his life we should with God's help obtain satisfaction.

This morning Mylord Duke had a severe fever and was so ill that he had to be bled. He is very exhausted, and I believe it would do him a great deal of good if your Majesty could write him something consoling and assure him of your continued well-wishing in spite of the losses he has suffered, leaving out of consideration that there will be opportunities for the Duke to display his gratitude.[4]

Natzmer, the Prussian cavalry general, says:

All Flanders was being lost, and there was deep depression in the army.

Mylord Duke was inconsolable over these sad happenings and discussed with me in touching confidence this sudden turn in events which would have become even worse for us, had the enemy exploited their advantage with persisting boldness. But our affairs improved through God's support and Prince Eugene's aid, whose timely arrival raised the spirits of the army again and consoled us.[5]

Eugene's encouragement to Marlborough at this moment is a bright feature in their comradeship. He brought a draught of new life to a hard-pressed man. But Marlborough had summoned Eugene from the Moselle for the express purpose of fighting a battle, and no other thought but procuring it was ever in his mind. It was obvious that a movement across the French communications was the

---

[1] Eugene to the Emperor, Brussels, July 9, 1708; *Feldzüge*, Series II, vol. i, Suppt., p. 148.　　　　　　　　　　　　　　　　　　　　　　[2] Arneth, ii, 19.

[3] We think this is what Eugene suggested. The alternative would be contrary to his character.

[4] Grumbkow to Frederick I; *loc. cit.*　　　　　　　　[5] Natzmer, p. 286.

effective answer to their daring march, and the best way of bringing on the long-sought decision. When "the Princes" emerged, their plans were made. Their original design of joining forces and attacking in superior strength had failed. It was resolved to rest the army at Assche for two or three days until Eugene's cavalry could reach Brussels and his infantry come into the theatre. Then they would strike south and west across the Scheldt to prevent or interrupt any siege of Oudenarde or Menin, to attack the French communications along the Belgian coast with France, and if possible to force a battle and to fight it *with Marlborough's army alone*. These clear-cut decisions were endorsed by the council of war.

There followed a three days' lull. Marlborough succeeded in throwing Chanclos, the governor of Ath, with all the troops he could collect (about seven hundred men), into Oudenarde, thus fully manning its defences. He was forced to send four infantry battalions into Brussels on account of the panic and excitement there. His pioneers were busy on the roads to the southward, and the army was preparing itself for march and battle. Eugene returned to Brussels for a private reason. There dwelt in that city an aged lady, his mother, the Comtesse de Soissons. He had survived twenty years of glory and danger since they last met. Now after a day of reunion they must part again, and on the eve of battle. By the 9th his cavalry would be near enough to the capital to make it safe, and Marlborough's army thus acquired full freedom of movement.

On the evening of the 7th Marlborough collapsed. He was forced to abandon business. His doctor advised his removal to Brussels. He refused to quit the camp, but the orders of the 8th were issued from Overkirk's tent. "His Grace," wrote Hare, "has been confined to his bed to-day by a hot fever fit, but something he took in the afternoon carried it off with a gentle sweat and he was much mended."[1] Cadogan, with a strong detachment, started south at dusk with pioneers to make sure of the ways. At two A.M. on Monday, the 9th, the army marched in four columns, two of infantry in the centre, with cavalry on either flank. Thirty squadrons under Albemarle covered their rear and interposed as long as possible between the enemy and Brussels. Marlborough's condition improved greatly in the night, and he was able in the morning to ride his horse in the sight of all men. "In all appearances," says Hare, "he was very well." The army reached Herfelingen, where Eugene overtook them, before eleven o'clock, having marched

[1] Hare Papers, *H.M.C.*, p. 218.

fifteen miles, and the Duke ordered a halt and camp to be pitched. From this place Marlborough wrote a letter to Godolphin which deserves careful attention.

July 9

. . . The treachery of Ghent, continual marching, and some letters[1] I have received from England have so vexed me that I was yesterday in so great a fever that the doctor would have persuaded me to have gone to Brussels; but I thank God I am now better. . . . The States have used this country so ill that I no ways doubt but all the towns in this country will play us the same trick as Ghent has done, whenever they have it in their power. I have been desired by the Deputies to write that her Majesty would be pleased to let *the troops, now in the Isle of Wight,* be sent for their relief to Ostend; so that it is likely you will be desired the same thing by M. Vriberg;[2] *but I hope the Queen will continue in the resolution of employing those troops as she first designed; for I think that will be much more for hers and the nation's honour;* but Vriberg must not know my opinion. . . .

Having made a halt of five hours, I am continuing my march, as I intend to do all the night, in hopes of getting to the camp of Lessines before the enemy, who made yesterday a detachment of sixteen thousand men for the investing of Oudenarde. If I get to the camp of Lessines before them, I hope to be able to hinder the siege, being resolved to venture everything, rather than lose that place.

Lessines the 10*th*

Mr Cardonnel telling me that by a mistake the letters were not gone, I have opened mine to let you know that the head of the army is got hither. I have received advice this morning from the Governor of Oudenarde that he was invested on both sides of his town yesterday morning. I should think myself happy, since I am got into this camp, if they continue their resolution of carrying on that siege.[3]

The pith of this lies in the reference to the eleven battalions of British troops, over six thousand men, who were held in the Isle of Wight under General Erle ready with shipping for the "descent" upon the French coast. Marlborough's request that the Deputies' advice should be ignored, and that the force should be held suspended, reveals his far-reaching thought. He looked across the impending great battle, with all its chances, to the exploitation of victory. Later on we shall see the form which he wished that exploitation to take.

Meanwhile the French had not been able to make any use of their

[1] From the Queen and Sarah. [2] Dutch envoy in London.
[3] Coxe, iv, 133–134.

leisure since the 6th. They had received the surrender of the citadel of Ghent, they had rested their army, they still lay in the angle of the Scheldt, and obviously believed themselves to have the advantage. After sharp discussions it was decided to besiege Oudenarde rather than Menin, to attack it only from the western bank of the Scheldt, and to cover the siege from a strong position at Lessines. The investment of Oudenarde began early on July 9. About three o'clock it

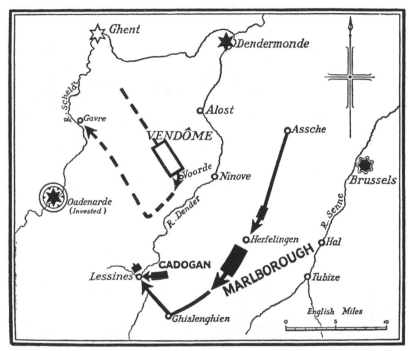

THE MAIN ARMIES (JULY 10, 1708)

was learned that the Allies had camped at Herfelingen. This seemed to the French command to portend a movement on Namur or Charleroi. For precaution they decided to move at once upon Lessines. By midnight their vanguard had reached Voorde, ten miles short of it. But at four o'clock on the afternoon of the 9th Cadogan, with eight battalions and eight squadrons, had set off quietly from the camp at Herfelingen, and by midnight eight hundred of his men had actually crossed the Dender and occupied Lessines. By four in the morning the rest of Cadogan's forces had come up. They spent the night building bridges for the army and establishing themselves in the naturally strong Lessines camp. Marlborough moved throughout the night with the whole army, and after a short halt at Ghislenghien his head reached the Dender at Lessines at eleven A.M. on the 10th, having marched in extremely good order over thirty miles in thirty-three hours. All day long his columns were crossing the bridges and closing up. In the early morning from Cadogan's outposts he saw with pleasure the steel flashes of the

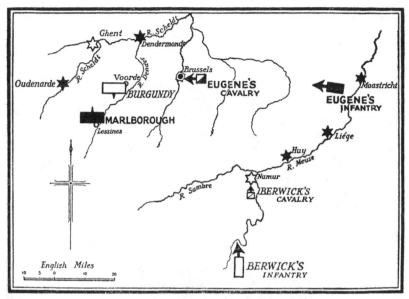

GENERAL SITUATION (JULY 10, 1708)

French troops still on the heights before Voorde. The corner was turned and the Dender passed.

Finding themselves forestalled at Lessines, the French held a council of war. They could, of course, have marched to the attack, in which case the battle would have been fought a day earlier and upon the Dender instead of the Scheldt, with the difference that Cadogan already occupied a strong position, and the allied main army was deployed or close at hand. But neither Burgundy nor Vendôme, although numerically stronger, was thinking of an offensive battle. They were constrained to raise the siege of Oudenarde. The investing cavalry was ordered to return, and their great army of over a hundred thousand men turned right-handed, withdrew northward by an easy march, and lay for the night near the crossings of the Scheldt which they were preparing at Gavre. Their general intention was to hold the line of the Scheldt, and establish a thoroughly secure communication with Lille, and eventually with Berwick's army. Their sense of security was enhanced by the fact that Marlborough had left some of his tents standing at Ghisleng-hien. They had no idea that his main body was already at Lessines. None of the experienced French commanders expected a serious event. They might wrangle about future action, but all thought themselves in control of the situation.

Certainly many choices lay open to them. The normal position of the great armies was reversed. The French looked towards France, the Allies towards Holland. Each might threaten the com-munications of the other. Each could count upon powerful rein-forcements. Eugene's cavalry had reached the outskirts of Brussels. Berwick's advance guard was already at Namur. Whichever side could combine its whole force first would enjoy for some days a decisive superiority. Burgundy's stroke on Ghent and Bruges had been crowned by substantial and sensational success. The price of the long French marches to the north and west was, however, that Marlborough and Eugene could now certainly join forces a week before Burgundy could be strengthened by Berwick. In fact, the armies of Marlborough and Eugene were already in strategic relation, while the recent French movements had left Berwick on the balance six marches farther from the decisive scene. The realiza-tion of this potent fact explains the hesitancy of the French behaviour. They wanted to guard their stolen prizes in the north; but vital safety enjoined them to come nearer to Lille and to Berwick's approaching army. This they thought easy to achieve from their central position in the angle of the rivers. They held the chord, while the Allies to forestall them must move around an arc three times as long. It was therefore with complacency that they lay on the night of the 10th within a few miles of the Scheldt, over which their bridges were a-building. Even if Marlborough's advance troops were holding Lessines, they had plenty of time to blockade the bridgehead of Oudenarde from the west and thus put themselves behind a secure river line and within two marches of Lille.

But they had no idea of the astonishing speed with which Marl-borough's army was moving.

Chapter Twenty-one

THE BATTLE OF OUDENARDE

1708—JULY 11

AS the campaign of 1708 opened new conceptions of the art of war, so its decisive battle was quite different in character from any previously fought. Apart from the primitive types of firearms and the slow movements of the artillery, Oudenarde was a twentieth-century battle. The chance encounter by forces of unknown strength, the gradual piecemeal broadening of the fighting front, the increasing stake engaged willy-nilly by both sides, the looseness and flexibility of all the formations, the improvised and wide-ranging manœuvres, and, above all, the encircling movement of the Allies, foreshadowing Tannenberg, present us with a specimen of modern war which has no fellow in the rest of the eighteenth century. This was no set piece of parade and order. The troops fought as they came up on the unknown ground where they collided. There was no fixed plan nor formal array. Opportunism and a hardy pugnacity led the victors. The French High Command never understood what was happening till they realized they had sustained a most grievous defeat. And thereafter, also in accordance with modern practice, they lied zealously to prove that nothing had happened. Yet the day at Oudenarde reversed the fortune of war, upset the odds, and dominated the whole campaign.

When the Allies sank into their bivouacs about Lessines, as they arrived during July 10, the soldiers scented battle in the air. Men deserted their duties as escorts of the baggage wagons in order stealthily to take their places in the fighting ranks. "It was expected," wrote Private Deane, whose regiment of Foot Guards so often guarded Marlborough's headquarters, "yᵉ Duke's quarters would have been att Gillingen [Ghislinghien], but his grace being carefull lay in yᵉ feild wᵗʰ yᵉ Army that night."[1] Regarding the long marches, he says, "And all for to force them to a battle, although on great unequallety, they being 21 Battalions of Foot and 24 Squadrons of Horse more than we att this juncture."

[1] Deane, *Journal*, p. 11.

At one A.M. on the 11th Cadogan set off along the Oudenarde road with sixteen battalions, eight squadrons, strong detachments of pioneers, thirty-two guns, and the whole of the pontoon train. Although Marlborough's rear had hardly crossed the Dender before dark on the 10th, he marched after Cadogan with the whole army at seven. Goslinga, judging backwards, snarls at Marlborough for not starting even earlier. Those who ride in carriages have their own point of view. Eugene's diary, on the contrary, says, "The army could not follow until the roads had been repaired."[1] This seems conclusive; but we must remember also what the troops had done and what they had to do. The rank and file must stand to arms for a considerable time before the columns can move. "We marcht at dawn," said Private Deane, and that no doubt was how it seemed to him. In fact, not a moment was lost in this surprising march.

SITUATION, DAYBREAK JULY 10

This was the greatest day in Cadogan's splendid military career. It was nine o'clock when he reached the high ground overlooking the Scheldt below Oudenarde. His scouts could see that the great masses of the French army six miles away were still east of the Scheldt. He instantly sent this all-important news back to Marlborough, and proceeded with his engineers to pick the sites of the bridges. At 10.30, while his infantry columns were closing up, his pontoons arrived, and the throwing of five bridges began.[2] There were also two stone bridges inside the fortress of Oudenarde. These were supplemented by two temporary bridges in order that if necessary the whole of the Dutch, who formed the rear and left wing of the army, could cross thereby. In all, nine bridges for eighty thousand men.

---

[1] Werwicq, July 18; *Feldzüge*, Series II, i, Suppt., 154.
[2] Eugene's "Diarium," dated Werwicq, July 18; *loc. cit.*

Meanwhile the French, in complete ignorance of these activities, had begun to cross the Scheldt in a leisurely fashion. Lieutenant-General Biron, a nobleman of the highest repute, had been ordered to command the advance- or flank-guard of twenty squadrons and seven Swiss battalions. He was delayed for some time because the French bridges were still unfinished; but during the morning he made his way into the plains beyond, occupied the village of Heurne with his infantry, four battalions of which, apparently in error, moved on a mile farther to the village of Eyne. He remained himself with his cavalry astride of the Ghent road, and his foraging parties scattered themselves about the peaceful fields.[1]

As soon as Cadogan's news reached Marlborough at about ten he advanced, with Prince Eugene, at the head of the cavalry of the right wing as fast as possible to the river. Indeed, the two generals, with twenty squadrons of the Prussian horse, made a large part of the way at the gallop. Natzmer, their general, says:

> On the march we received the cheerful news that Cadogan had thrown bridges over the Scheldt at Eename, near Oudenarde, without any resistance, and also that the enemy, coming up from Alost, were planning to cross the river at Gavre.
> This news filled us with joy and in our eagerness we sought out my Lord Duke to allow us to advance at a faster pace.[2]

Marlborough disposed the whole cavalry of the left wing as a flank guard to the northward in case the French should advance against him instead of crossing. He ordered the whole army to press on with the utmost diligence. The troops were told that they could surely pass the river before the French. This aroused an intense excitement among all ranks. Forgetting the fatigues of their tremendous marches, the infantry columns strode out manfully. Many intelligent men and veteran soldiers in every rank understood what was at stake. They were also deeply angered by what they considered the treacherous filching from them of Ghent and Bruges. Their exertions were wonderful. "It was no longer a march," says Goslinga, "but a run." A fierce enthusiasm, noted by all observers, and most unusual in those times, inspired the private soldiers. The strictest orders had been given against the baggage of high personages being intermingled with the troops. Such breaches as occurred were punished out of hand. The soldiers hurled the wagons from the track, scattering or pillaging the contents, and overtook their marching

[1] See general map of the battle of Oudenarde, facing p. 380.   [2] Natzmer, p. 288.

comrades with hoarse cries of satisfaction. Never was a battle more consciously fought by the rank and file. Trust in Marlborough, admiration for Eugene, and hatred for the enemy filled their sturdy hearts. "Towards 12 o'clock [actually 12.30] the head of our cavalry of the right wing reached the bridges and crossed by the pontoons at a brisk trot; but the infantry took longer to move and it was several hours later that they began to cross."[1]

Cadogan's bridges had been completed shortly before noon, and all his troops assembled near them. Leaving four battalions to guard the passage, he crossed the river with the other twelve, and, with his eight squadrons under Rantzau, the general in command of the Hanoverian cavalry, guarding his left, moved cautiously towards the village of Eyne. Rantzau's patrols almost immediately brushed into Biron's foragers. Shots were fired, and some foragers were captured. Others carried the alarm to the rear. Biron thereupon advanced sharply with twelve squadrons, and Rantzau fell back behind the left of Cadogan's infantry, now in line and approaching the Diepenbeck rivulet and the village of Eyne. Biron, advancing under the belief that he had only a raiding party in front of him, suddenly saw a little after one o'clock a considerable force of hostile infantry already deployed for action. Conspicuous among these was a brigade of redcoats. The presence of allied infantry in such a place at this time was most surprising to the French generals. They were nearly seventeen miles beyond Lessines, where the allied vanguard had been reported the previous evening. But much more broke upon him. Advancing to the windmill of Eyne, he saw the bridges and the battalions guarding them. He saw an endless column of cavalry streaming down the hillside above Eename, crossing the bridges at a trot, and swiftly forming on the near bank. Above all, on the opposite uplands he saw the dust-clouds of an approaching army. Evidently something very serious and totally unexpected by the French command was in progress. He sent a succession of messengers spurring back to the French headquarters as these successive apparitions confronted him.

His aide-de-camp found Vendôme and the royal princes already over the river, dismounted and lunching by the road-side. Vendôme at first refused to believe the news. He thought it incredible that strong enemy forces, especially of foot, could have crossed or even reached the Scheldt at this hour, still less that the allied generals would attempt to carry any large proportion of their troops across

[1] Eugene's "Diarium"; Natzmer, p. 288.

the Scheldt within such close striking distance of the whole French army. A study of the distances on the map will show that there were solid reasons for this opinion. After all, it was but two days since Marlborough had been located at Assche, nearly fifty miles away. But successive messengers amplified Biron's facts, and it is with facts that soldiers have to deal. The Marshal, whose temper had been rising under the pressure of unwelcome news, at length

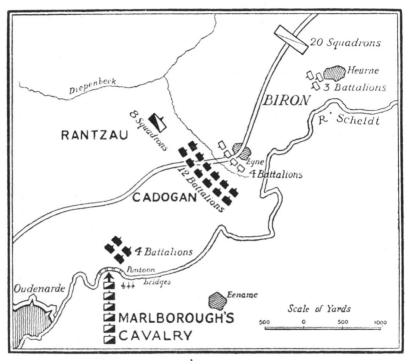

BIRON'S DISCOVERY

got up furiously from the improvised table and mounted his horse. "If they are there," he exclaimed, "the devil must have carried them. Such marching is impossible!" But when he looked across the rolling plain to the southward he too saw the dust-clouds from Marlborough's marching columns. These showed the heads of the allied main body only a mile or two from the bridges. So far, however, it seemed that only their vanguard had crossed. He sent Biron's aide-de-camp back with an order to attack at once, adding that he would come himself and support him with ample forces. Telling the princes to follow gently with the main body now across the river and close at hand, he rode in no great haste to the head of the leading columns, composed of the cavalry of the right wing, and turned them in Biron's direction.

There was much dispute among the French after the battle about the hour when Vendôme first realized that the Allies were crossing the river in force. Vendôme declares, and his secretary, Alberoni, in the letter which Saint-Simon analyses so scathingly,[1] pretends absurdly, that it was as early as ten o'clock; that Vendôme wished immediately to attack; but that Burgundy would not move till four in the afternoon; and then only when Vendôme deemed it too late. Saint-Simon, on the contrary, declares with a wealth of argument that it was two in the afternoon before Vendôme understood what was happening. There can be no doubt that Alberoni's letter is a tissue of lies. It must have been at least half-past one before Biron's third aide-de-camp aroused Vendôme to his danger. By that time Marlborough and Eugene had crossed in person with the Prussian horse, and the Duke himself was posting a six-gun battery on Cadogan's left behind the village of Schaerken.[2]

When Biron received Vendôme's order he was hardly in a position to execute it. The hostile front had broadened; it now extended almost to Schaerken village, behind which the battery of cannon was now visible. It was protected by the marshy rivulet of the Diepenbeck. The enclosures and hedgerows behind Eyne and about Schaerken were lined with enemy infantry. Their strength across the river was increasing every moment, and large bodies of cavalry were now formed on the slopes above Bevere. Biron did not know the ground, and was evidently outnumbered. While in these circumstances he was reflecting how to obey the orders he had received, Puységur, a Lieutenant-General of high reputation, afterwards well known as a writer on military subjects, arrived to lay out the camp. Puységur warned him that the ground in his front was impassable. Marshal Matignon, another of the principal staff officers of the army, who had ridden up and heard this discussion, thereupon forbade Biron to charge, and assumed responsibility for so doing.

After another quarter of an hour Vendôme was seen approaching

---

[1] Saint-Simon, vi, 70–86.

[2] This was almost the only allied artillery which fought in the battle. The bridges must have been so continuously blocked with troops, or the pressure upon the commanders so great, that not even the rest of Cadogan's thirty-two guns found their place at the crossing, and the remainder of the artillery was outstripped by the infantry and the event.

along the Ghent road at the head of considerable forces of horse and foot. He asked why Biron had not attacked as ordered. Puységur intervened. He declared that a morass lay between them and the enemy, and as he was supposed to have unique personal knowledge of the ground his judgment prevailed. Vendôme, still more angry, submitted. He withdrew his reinforcement west of the Ghent road, leaving Biron's seven battalions in Eyne and Heurne unsupported.

While this was passing Burgundy, "following gently" at the head of the main body of the army, began to descend the slopes towards the Norken stream; and, seeing that no action was in progress, and that Vendôme's squadrons were halted or moving westward, he and his advisers decided not to cross the Norken, but to draw up the army in order of battle along the high ground behind it with the centre about Huysse. This was accordingly done. In the circumstances, with no special instructions and having regard to the ponderous masses moving steadily behind him, this seems to have been a prudent measure. It must have been half-past three before the movement was completed. Vendôme, who was certainly no more than a mile away, does not seem to have made any attempt to prevent this deflection of the army. It was, however, essentially a refusal of battle, and inconsistent with any idea of driving the allied vanguard into the Scheldt. Moreover, it left Biron's seven battalions, particularly the four in Eyne, most perilously detached and exposed to Cadogan's assault.

It was a quarter to three. Although the Allies were morally they were not yet physically committed to the hazardous operation of crossing the deep, broad river, and forming on the other bank in the face of a superior enemy. There was still time to withdraw Cadogan. But the moment of final choice had come. Argyll and the leading corps, including all the British infantry, had reached the bridges. The hesitating movements of the French, their unaccountable delays, their deployment behind the Norken, confirmed Marlborough's resolve. With Eugene at his side in resolute accord, he allowed his dusty, ardent redcoats to trample across the pontoons. At this moment, when the main action was about to begin, these infantry had marched over fifty miles in sixty hours. For the Allies the die was cast; but even now the French could refuse battle. If they were content to let Marlborough dominate the region between the Scheldt and the Lys, and themselves to stand where they were to cover Ghent, no general attack could be made upon them that day. But their great opponents were playing confidently and high.

No record exists of any order sent to Cadogan; but it is certain that he acted in the very closest concert with his chief. The Swiss battalions in Eyne had been for some time at his mercy. All his preparations were complete. He had filled in the Diepenbeck at numerous points with fascines. He now called up his fourth

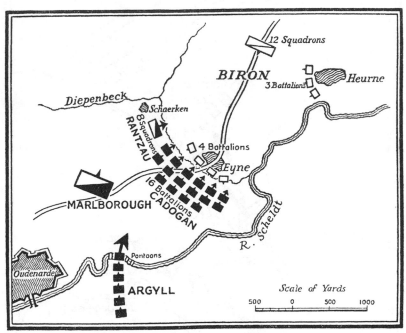

CADOGAN'S ATTACK, 3 P.M.

brigade, no longer needed at the bridgehead, and at three P.M., with his whole force of sixteen battalions and Rantzau's cavalry guarding his left, advanced to storm the village of Eyne.

Sabine's British brigade was in the centre opposite the village. In perfect order, with shouldered arms, they moved slowly forward without firing a shot; nor did they bring their bayonets to the charge until they were within twenty yards of the Swiss who lined the enclosures. There was a roar of musketry, and the battle of Oudenarde began. The Swiss brigade, feeling themselves forgotten or abandoned by the French army, now nearly three miles away, left alone far from any help, made practically no resistance. Three battalions out of four surrendered at once. The fourth sought to retreat along the road to Heurne. But Rantzau's squadrons, circling around the western outskirts of the village, rode in upon them, broke them up, and cut them down. At this grisly spectacle the

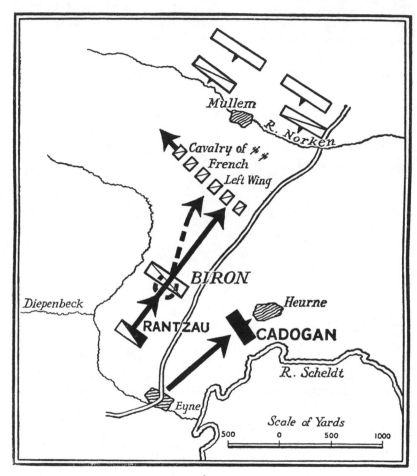

RANTZAU'S CHARGE

three battalions in Heurne, who had advanced some distance to support their comrades, fled in disorder beyond the Norken.

Rantzau now saw before him in the open plain Biron's twelve French squadrons. With him was the young Electoral Prince, the future King George II, and a group of daring notables. Rantzau charged the twelve French squadrons. These good troops, oppressed by the destruction of the Swiss, feeling no firm grip behind them to counter the aggressive will-power of the enemy, were broken and scattered by the Hanoverian charge. They all fled towards the main French army. The cavalry of its left wing, or rearguard, was slowly defiling across the front to take their positions in the battle array drawing up beyond the Norken. Into their left flank suddenly drove a disorderly crowd of fugitives, and behind them Rantzau and his eight squadrons still in hand and in good order. In hot blood no doubt, but as a definite military decision, Rantzau charged into the whole cavalry of the French left wing. There was a wild confusion. Prince George's horse was shot. The squadron commander with whom he rode, Colonel Loseke, gave him his own, and was himself killed as he helped the Prince to remount. Many French squadrons, unable under the impact to wheel left into line, were thrown into disorder. Numbers speedily prevailed. A French battery between Mullem and the Ghent road came into action. A dozen squadrons advanced at the gallop. Nevertheless Rantzau got out of the mêlée with surprisingly small loss, carrying with him a mortally wounded colonel, numerous officer prisoners, ten standards, kettle-drums, and horses.

This audacious and affronting exploit, much of which was plainly visible to the proud army of France, brought on the general battle. It was an insult not to be borne. Those who had previously favoured caution now clamoured for revenge. The mood was valiant, but the hour was late, the ground unstudied, the plan unformed, and the leadership divided.

All the while the allied deployment across the river was proceeding. Natzmer with his twenty squadrons had already passed the bridges. They met "heaps" (*haufen*) of prisoners coming back from Cadogan's attack. "Cadogan himself," says Natzmer,

> came to me in great joy at our arrival and at my coming up in his support. I traversed the village of Eyne, where the fighting had just ended, and formed beyond it. Soon afterwards Prince Eugene came and accosted me, "Je vous trouve bien avancé" [You are pretty far ahead]. He then sprang forward to examine himself the enemy's position. In a little while he returned in great spirits, and exclaimed, "Il faut que nous en ayons poil ou aile" [We have got to get 'em plucked or winged].[1]

At four o'clock the French, more from impulse than design, began to advance from behind the Norken to the attack. Burgundy sent sixteen squadrons under Grimaldi to reconnoitre the approaches

---

[1] Natzmer, p. 289.

to Cadogan's left. This movement, if the prelude to a general attack, was most dangerous to the Allies. Fortunately the ground west of Groenewald and Schaerken was difficult and broken. Farms and enclosures, small woods, avenues of poplars, and above all three rivulets, of which the chief was the Diepenbeck, with their surrounding thickets and boggy patches, arrested Grimaldi. Marlborough, riding through Heurne with the Prussian horse, drew them out in the open plain beyond in order to afford some protection to Cadogan's right. Two of Cadogan's four Prussian battalions, drawn from the bridges, were already lining the hedges about Groenewald along the rivulet towards Schaerken. Sabine's British brigade was marching to extend his left. Grimaldi reported that the ground was unfit for cavalry, and was held in strength, and that infantry alone would serve. He withdrew towards the mill of Royegem. From the ladder-ways of this large structure, which itself stands on a small eminence, a fair view of the country towards Oudenarde is offered. Here Burgundy and his younger brother, Berri, and the Pretender, the Chevalier de St George, gathered with their staffs and suites.

Practically the whole of the French infantry of the right wing had now crossed successively the Norken and the road from Royegem to Oycke, and were now entering the entangled country on a broad front. This formidable movement was necessarily slow, but at present there were no troops to resist it. Unless it could be stopped it would be fatal. Burgundy ordered six battalions to drive the Prussians from Groenewald. A fierce fire-fight at close quarters along the hedgerows began. The Prussians made good their defence against heavy odds. The six French battalions recoiled in some disorder. The loud, increasing fusillade drew Vendôme to the spot. He would better have discharged his duties as a commander had he joined the princes on the steps of Royegem mill. Instead he plunged into the local conflict. He rallied the six battalions; he brought up another six, drawn from the French centre, along the road from Mullem, and ordered a renewed attack.

All Cadogan's sixteen battalions were now in line about Groenewald and behind the rivulet towards Schaerken. Cadogan found time before the second attack to occupy the avenues leading to Herlegem, even to seize that hamlet. When Vendôme's troops came forward again they found themselves unexpectedly galled and delayed by the flanking fire from this advanced position. After a fierce encounter they were again repulsed. Marshal Vendôme was

now in a fighting frenzy. The violence of his nature, which so often
cowed or quelled his equals and superiors, determined him to have
Groenewald whatever the cost. He drew lavishly for that purpose
upon the French centre. Brigade after brigade was hurried forward,
arriving breathless. Many battalions were even sent into the fire-

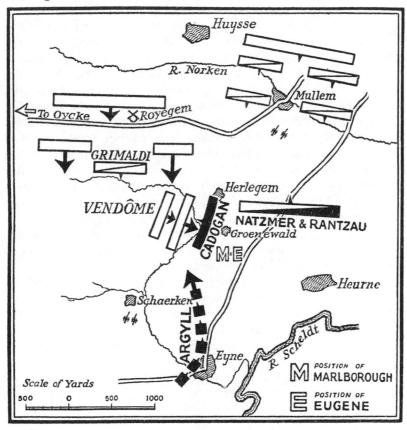

OUDENARDE, 5 P.M.

and bayonet-fight as they arrived in column. A very heavy mass
of troops was crowded upon Cadogan's front. He was outnumbered
and hard pressed. His men fought with devoted courage, helped
by the congestion of the enemy and the broken ground, to every
feature of which they clung tenaciously.

At five o'clock Vendôme sent orders to Burgundy to bring the
whole of the left wing into action by attacking to the east of Groenewald and across the Ghent road. Here, where Marlborough had

posted them, stood Natzmer's twenty squadrons of Prussian horse and Rantzau's eight squadrons, reorganizing after their charge. That was all. Not a single infantry battalion was available. The ground thereabouts was favourable for cavalry, but cavalry alone could not have withstood very long the thirty thousand men—horse, foot, and artillery—constituting the French left wing.

Vendôme's order reached Burgundy at the mill a few minutes after five. The Prince was assured by his staff and Puységur that the ground was obstructed by a morass. He therefore did not endorse or pass on Vendôme's order. He sent Captain Jenet, an aide-de-camp who had brought it, back to Vendôme to explain the reason. Jenet was killed before delivering his message by the heavy fire under which the Marshal stood. In consequence Vendôme did not know that the French left would not co-operate in the renewed attack he was about to make upon Cadogan. Had he known that his order was countermanded and the reason he could in a few minutes have reassured Burgundy about the ground, for, as Vendôme stridently repeated ever afterwards, he had himself ridden over it with considerable forces only two hours before.

We must regard the paralysis of the French left wing at this moment as most fortunate for the Allies. No one can pretend to measure what would have happened had Cadogan been driven, as he surely would have been, back upon Eyne by the concerted onslaught of overwhelming numbers. But ill-luck does not exculpate Vendôme. He should not have indulged himself by entering the local fight around Groenewald unless he could keep a sense of proportion and a comprehensive grip of his great army. Half an hour later it was apparent that the left wing was still motionless; but by that time he was fighting with a pike, like a private soldier rather than a marshal of France charged with the supreme control of ninety thousand men.

Another mortal danger confronted the heroic Cadogan. Overweighted in front, his right flank in the condition we have described, he was now momentarily being overlapped and turned on his left by the advance of the French right wing. This alone rendered his situation desperate. But help was at hand. The Duke of Argyll, with twenty battalions of British infantry, advancing in perfect order, now came into line on his left, and met foursquare the masses of French infantry, who assaulted along the whole front from Herlegem to Schaerken.

The first main shock of the battle now began. Along the rivulet

368

upon a mile of front Cadogan and Argyll, with twenty British and sixteen German battalions and the single battery which Marlborough had posted, fought nearly fifty battalions of the French right and centre. The intensity of the musketry fire was said to have surpassed all previous experience. The troops repeatedly fought hand to hand. Each side advanced and recoiled several times in the struggle, and every battalion had its own tale to tell.

Marlborough and Eugene remained together between Groenewald and the Ghent road. They were in equal anxiety both for their right and their left. But the immediate peril was on the left. All the bridges were now disgorging infantry in great numbers. Lottum's corps of twenty battalions was already close at hand, fully formed in line, and as the weight and breadth of the French right wing began to lap round Argyll's left, this powerful reinforcement advanced in its turn to meet the extending attack. Cadogan's action had long been flaring. Argyll was in deadly grip. The inn at Schaerken was captured by the French about 5.30, and the enemy were everywhere across the Diepenbeck. Here they were within a mile of the pontoons. Lottum became heavily engaged at 5.45, and by six o'clock his counter-attack drove the French back over the Diepenbeck and recovered Schaerken. To and fro swayed the struggle. Always the French brought up superior numbers and reached round the allied left. Always Marlborough's infantry poured across the bridges and advanced to make new head against them.

Hitherto Eugene had sat by Marlborough's side discharging, as was said, the functions of a counsellor, staff officer, and aide-de-camp. The critical situation in the centre and on the left required Marlborough's immediate personal control. Lottum's fight was hanging in the balance. But there was another reason which made Marlborough's presence at the other end of the battlefield indispensable. Overkirk, with the flower of the Dutch army, all their national troops, horse and foot, was now crossing by the Oudenarde bridges. This force of nearly twenty-five thousand men seemed likely to come into action exactly where and when they were most needed. They could deliver the decisive stroke of the battle. The fighting front was now developing fast in both directions. Marlborough wished to be on the spot to concert Overkirk's entry into the field. On the other hand, his main preoccupation was still the attack which he must expect at any moment from the French left wing, whose great intact masses of cavalry and infantry could plainly be

seen a mile away beyond the Norken. There was a crisis at each end
of the line. The "two bodies with one soul" must now separate.
At six o'clock, therefore, Marlborough placed Eugene in command of the whole right of the battlefront, including Cadogan
and Argyll, Natzmer's twenty squadrons of Prussian and German
horse, and Rantzau's Hanoverians. Eugene henceforward conducted
the main action and commanded all the British troops. Marlborough
galloped to the centre of Lottum's front, and concerned himself with
this, and with bringing Overkirk and the allied left wing into action.

Overkirk, with the whole of the Dutch horse and foot, was
engaged in crossing by the two stone bridges through the town
of Oudenarde, and it was evident that if he could debouch in time
he would reverse the position in this quarter of the field, and turn
the French right decisively. But Marlborough still feared that
Eugene would not be able to support an attack by the French left.
Lottum's successful entry into the action and his advance had given
a precious breathing-space. A new corps of eighteen Hanoverian
and Hessian battalions was already in line behind Lottum.

We now witness one of those intricate manœuvres in the height
of action of which Marlborough's battles afford several notable
examples. There is no evidence that Eugene asked for further help.
There is undoubted proof that he needed it. Vendôme's third attack
was actually at its height. At 6.15 he drove Cadogan from both
Herlegem and Groenewald. Eugene was at full strain. His comrade felt his burden as if it were his own. At this very moment,
therefore, Marlborough brought up the eighteen Hanoverian and
Hessian battalions as if to reinforce Lottum's attack, and then
ordered Lottum to withdraw through the intervals of these fresh
battalions, and march to the right to strengthen Prince Eugene.
We remember how in the crisis of Blenheim Eugene instantly parted
with his one remaining cuirassier brigade at Marlborough's call.
Now Marlborough repaid this glorious debt. There was, indeed,
also a high economy of force in the manœuvre. Lottum's troops,
which had been fighting heavily, would now march to the right,
and be out of the fire for a space before they came again into action.
The Hanoverians and Hessians, who had marched so far and fast
but not yet fought, would come for the first time into action. The
presence of both these forces simultaneously in Marlborough's
array gave the enemy the impression of double weight on this sector.
Discipline and drill enabled this complicated evolution to be
executed with precision under Marlborough's eye. It took Lottum

over twenty minutes after coming out of the line to reach Eugene on the right flank a mile away. The arrival of his twenty battalions stemmed the adverse tide. At this moment, therefore, Marlborough had placed Eugene in command of fifty-six engaged battalions,

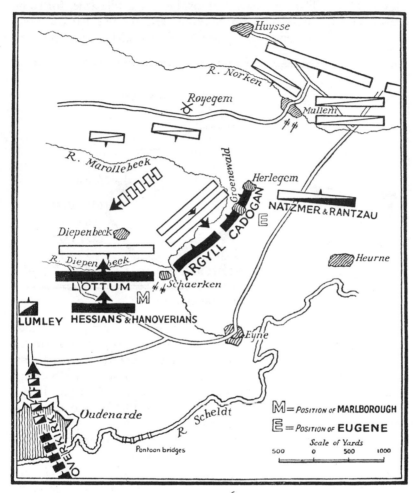

OUDENARDE, 6 P.M.

while keeping only eighteen under his own hand for the hard fight on his immediate front. Of this, while waiting for Overkirk, he now assumed personal direction.

At six o'clock Overkirk's intervention in force had seemed imminent. There were still two and a half hours of daylight, and

Marlborough might feel, as he did before the final charge at Blenheim, that very great results lay surely within his grasp. On the Danube he had broken the hostile centre. On the Scheldt he could roll the French up from their right flank. But now a misfortune fell upon him. The supplementary bridges in Oudenarde, for some reason not explained to us, broke down, and the two narrow stone bridges could not secure the passage of Overkirk's great force at

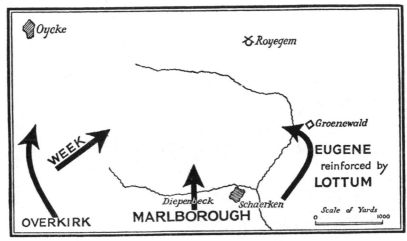

THE ENCIRCLEMENT

the rate expected. Overkirk, with most of his cavalry, was already by 6.15 upon the slopes of Mooregem. There was grievous congestion in the fortress, and the delivery of the infantry into the plain behind Mooregem was delayed for at least an hour. Marlborough found himself hard pressed and overlapped in his turn. It was necessary to attack with the first troops available, and Overkirk received orders to do so at 6.45 P.M.

A high control of the battle is evident at this moment. For the first time the whole allied fighting front advanced together. Overkirk sent his two leading infantry brigades under General Week through a gap in the woodlands to strengthen Marlborough's left. Marlborough with his eighteen battalions drove the French across the brook as far as Diepenbeck village. On Eugene's front Lottum arrived with his twenty battalions in the nick of time, and the French were driven from Groenewald and Herlegem. The musketry fire of all the infantry engaged at close quarters in the enclosed, broken country was now perhaps the most intense that had yet been heard anywhere. But a third of the French army had not yet been engaged. Their reserves were enormous. Large masses could be seen moving to reinforce their right, while the greater part of their left wing and all its cavalry still overhung Eugene. The Captain-General could no longer expect the supreme results he had hoped for from Overkirk's intervention on his left. But neither need he any longer fear defeat in that quarter, for the Dutch infantry were now flowing fast out of Oudenarde, and their leading columns, undeployed, were already beyond Mooregem. His dominant thought was for Eugene. The whole of the British cavalry, seventeen squadrons under Lumley, were now at Bevere. Once Overkirk was in action they were no longer indispensable to the safety of the army. Marlborough therefore at seven o'clock sent his second great reinforcement to Eugene. The brilliant regiments which had charged so finely at Elixem trotted swiftly across the field, and drew out behind the Ghent road to strengthen Eugene's right flank against the expected onslaught of the French left wing.

Thus we see Marlborough, himself in the height of action only a few hundred yards behind the swaying, quivering infantry fighting line, having also a momentous hope in his heart, depriving himself first of Lottum and then of Lumley for the sake of the general battle. It is these qualities of perfect comprehensive judgment, serene in disappointment or stress, unbiased by the local event in which he was himself involved, this fixing with untiring eye and absolute selflessness the problem as a whole, that deserve the study and respect of soldiers of every age.

Just as Lottum had arrived in time to throw back the French assault and recover the villages of Groenewald and Herlegem, so did Lumley and the English horse reach their new station on Eugene's right when they were needed. The strain upon Eugene was, as Marlborough had truly felt, almost overwhelming. So bitter was the struggle, and yet so good the hopes that a further advance could be made, that Eugene a little before seven at Count Lottum's appeal launched the whole of his available cavalry upon a desperate charge. "It was only an hour before dark," records Eugene in his diary,

> when the Prussians and Hanoverian cavalry managed to reach the small plain in a little valley, to the left of which they formed into ten or twelve squadrons [actually twenty] on the flank, after the infantry ranks had been opened and room had been made by two battalions.[1]

[1] "Diarium"; *Feldzüge*, Series II, i, Suppt., 154.

General Natzmer, with the Prussian gendarmes, had time to draw up in strict array before leading the charge against very superior numbers. He broke the French squadrons. Behind them lay intact battalions of French infantry. The Germans rode straight

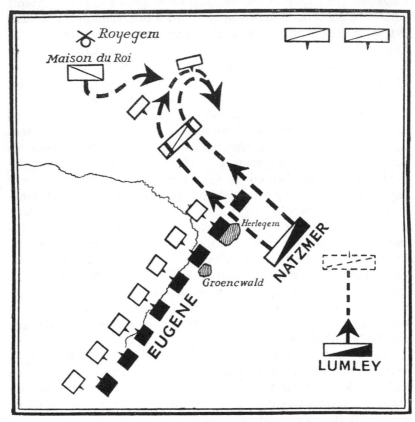

NATZMER'S CHARGE

at these and were received with a deadly fire. Swerving to the right, they encountered more infantry lining the hedgerows. The Prussian gendarmes broke two battalions, capturing their colours; but the command was now dispersed. The Maison du Roi, "rich in scarlet with silver facings,"[1] arriving in force, fell upon these remnants. Natzmer, left quite alone in the midst of the enemy, received four sabre-cuts, and escaped only by leaping a broad ditch, "full of water in which a half-dead horse was lying."[2] Survivors of

[1] Natzmer, p. 292. [2] *Loc. cit.*

374

his twenty squadrons found refuge behind the ranks of Cadogan's and Lottum's battalions. Three-quarters of the gendarmes perished. The twenty squadrons existed no more as a fighting force; but precious time had been gained. The initiative had been held. The charge of the gendarmes, as we can see from Marlborough's dispatches and from many Continental records, was long deemed memorable throughout the armies. This death ride of a cavalry division has been rightly compared to the charge of Bredow's brigade at Mars-la-Tour in 1870.[1] The cavalry of the French left wing, deranged by the incursion, now saw before them in the distance the seventeen English squadrons in perfect order in their path. Ill-led by their chiefs on this day, they forbore to attack them. Lumley's regiments, now the only shield on Eugene's right, remained by the prince's order motionless till darkness fell.

Marlborough, with his small numbers all now heavily engaged and without any reserves, could do no more in the centre than hold the line of the Diepenbeck against a renewed attack. But Overkirk's great operation upon the left was now in full swing. Week's brigades were in hot action against the French right flank. The old Veldt-Marshal was already in possession of the high ground called Boser Couter, and a whole division of his infantry, sixteen battalions, occupied the hill of Oycke. From this point the entire field was visible. He saw himself in a position almost to surround the French army. He wheeled to the right and, having received an express order from Marlborough, advanced from Oycke towards Royegem. This deadly attack was delivered by four brigades of Dutch infantry, sustained by twelve squadrons of Danish cavalry. At the head of the Dutch, commanding for the first time the troops of the Republic, rode the young Prince of Orange. He was but nineteen years of age. This was his first battle. Down the slopes before Royegem he marched irresistibly. The French infantry in his path were swept away. The Maison du Roi failed to stop him. At the same time upon the other flank Cadogan attacked successfully from Groenewald. The entire French right and a great part of their centre were now almost surrounded. The straight line had become a vast horseshoe of flame within which, in a state of ever-increasing confusion, were more than fifty thousand Frenchmen. It was now half-past eight. But for the failure of the bridges in Oudenarde this situation might have been reached an hour earlier.

For more than two hours the enemy princes had clustered around

[1] F. Taylor, *The Wars of Marlborough*, ii, 138.

or upon the mill of Royegem. With them was the numerous train of military courtiers and nobility who enjoyed the coveted privilege of personal attendance. The slopes about the mill were crowded with several hundreds of orderlies, grooms, and valets, holding the led horses of the royal circle and of the headquarters staff. The Duke

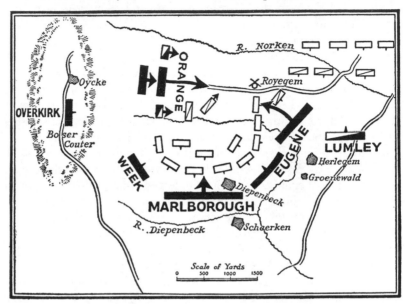

8.30 P.M.: THE NET CLOSES

of Burgundy and his younger brother, with the pathetic figure of the English Pretender neglected in the background, gazed with anxious, fascinated eyes upon the battle which was raging along a wide crescent a mile away to the south-east. They could see from Herlegem, on their left, almost to the castle of Bevere, on their right, the infantry of the two armies in the meadows between the thickets and woodland, locked together in fierce fight, swaying forward and back, charging and counter-charging amid a ceaseless roar of musketry and drifting wreaths of smoke. They had witnessed the confusion and surging masses of horsemen which had marked the charge of Natzmer's cavalry division. Reassuring reports had arrived. The assailants had been driven back and cut to pieces. But the left was none the less receding. The line of smoke and flame was now drawn nearer than the villages so lately captured. Masses of enemy infantry could be seen advancing across the open spaces behind Groenewald, while out on the slopes beyond the Ghent

376

road long lines of scarlet horsemen sat motionless upon their horses as if at a reveiw.

Sombre reflections held the mind of Fénelon's pupil, and gnawing anxiety. Here was the army of France, at whose head he had been marching a few hours before, short of ammunition and in increasing disorder, locked in deadly grapple with an enemy whose strength seemed inexhaustible, whose numbers were growing every moment, and whose confident aggression proclaimed the presence and the genius of Marlborough and Eugene. This was the battle which he, heir to the crown of France, had been sent forth to win. War, yesterday the jaunty boon-companion, now glared upon him with lineaments of fury, hate, and doom. Where was Vendôme? Where was that brutal, bestial, but none the less tremendous warrior who had been placed at his side to win him military glory, whose advice he could lean upon, whose decisions in the end he had been directed to obey? The Marshal was in the cauldron fighting hand to hand, organizing and reorganizing attacks, sending messages which were incomprehensible and orders which were obsolete by the time they arrived. The one thing the Great King had always forbidden, and which Burgundy had above all others resolved to avoid—namely, an infantry battle in enclosed and broken country—was now burning away the grand army of France. Such is the chastisement of those who presume to gain by easy favour and pretence the glories which the gods reserve for their chosen heroes.

But what is this stir close at hand? Why has every one about him turned so suddenly their backs upon the battle? What is this at which they are all staring in the opposite quarter? Who are these troops in ordered lines and masses who are crowning the skyline by Oycke village, and now already rolling forward down the grassy slopes less than a mile from the mill? Horse and foot in great numbers far behind the French flank—nay, upon its rear, driving all before them, their volleys flashing red in the fading light! Messengers gallop up with terrible news, followed by fugitives and riderless horses. The Maison du Roi in the fields by Chobon hamlet can be seen wheeling to the rightabout to meet this new appalling peril. A wave of panic swept the courtly group; the royal princes scrambled to their saddles. The troops of the French right, says Saint-Simon, "gave ground so fast that the valets of the suites of all who accompanied the princes fell back upon them with an alarm, a rapidity, and a confusion which swept them along with extreme speed and much indecency and risk towards the main battle on the left."[1] But here too they met masses of French infantry retreating and dispersing in disorder before Cadogan's final effort. Unhappy princelings, far astray from the mirrored halls and obsequious glitter of Versailles! We are assured by those who attended them that they behaved with courage and composure, that they encouraged the troops, praised the officers, asked the generals they met what ought to be done, and told Vendôme when they found him what they thought themselves. This may well be so. But over their actions, as over the carnage of the field, night and the increasing dissolution of the army now cast an impenetrable cloak.

It is this phase of the battle of Oudenarde which suggests so strongly the German victory at Tannenberg. But with weapons that shot no more than a hundred yards there was no means of covering the many gaps between the encircling brigades. The fish were in the net, but the meshes were large enough to let the greater part of the catch escape. Nevertheless, the circle was in fact completed. The Prince of Orange and Cadogan from the opposite ends of the line of battle actually fired into each other near the mill of Royegem. Total darkness descended upon the wild confusion of the field. Marlborough at nine o'clock ordered all allied troops to cease fire, halt where they stood, and lie on their arms till daybreak.

It must have been nearly ten o'clock when the defeated leaders met in the village of Huysse on the high ground behind the Norken, and on horseback a tragic council of war was held. Two-thirds of the army were in a welter, surrounded by the enemy, and to a large extent beyond control. No one knew how to lay hands upon the remaining third which had not yet been engaged, including all the cavalry of the left wing. Vendôme, habitually careless of his appearance, now dishevelled with the sweat and dust of physical combat, arrived furious with the enemy, with Burgundy, and above all, for good reasons, with himself. What should be done? Burgundy sought to speak, but the Marshal, drunk with authority and anger, told him to hold his tongue. "Your Royal Highness must remember that you only came to this army upon condition that you obeyed me."[2] We have to transport ourselves into that vanished age to realize what Saint-Simon calls the "enormity" of these words, spoken as they were before a score of officers of all ranks. They seem, moreover, important in judging Vendôme's reponsibility for the misconduct of the battle. If this was the relation established

[1] Saint-Simon, vi, 56. [2] *Ibid.*, 57.

between him and Burgundy by the King, nothing can relieve Vendôme's military reputation. He had without purpose or reason delayed crossing the Scheldt. He had been completely surprised by Marlborough's march. He had flung the army piecemeal into a disastrous action; he had abandoned the functions of commander; he had quitted the centre, from which alone they could be exercised. He had crashed about in the front line like an enraged animal, squandering the strength and cohesion of the troops, and upon his head rested, and rests, the burden and shame of an easily avoidable disaster.

The Marshal was for fighting it out. A little more than half of the army, he said, had been engaged. Let them spend the night in reorganizing the front. Let them bring up the intact reserves from the unused left wing. Let them fall to at dawn and see what was left at the end of the day. But this personal ardour did not correspond with the facts. No one dared outface him, but the silence struck its chill. Officer after officer, Puységur, Matignon, Cheladet, arrived in succession. All declared that the army was in total disorder, and that to await the onslaught of the Allies at daybreak was to court certain destruction. The only course was an immediate retreat upon Ghent. The consensus was overwhelming. It was also right. If the French had engaged little more than half their army, the Allies had fought during the greater part of the day with scarcely a third of their strength. Another third had hardly been in action for two hours; and, according to Prince Eugene,[1] "there were still troops crossing the Scheldt late on into the night."

When Vendôme saw himself alone in opinion, and was also probably himself shaken in his own mind, he relieved his passions in the most cowardly manner. "Very well, gentlemen," he said; "I see you all think it best to retire. And you, Monseigneur," fixing the Duke of Burgundy, "have long had that wish." With this crowning insult he gave the order to retreat to Ghent, and disappeared into the night. Once this signal was given the French army fled from the field of Oudenarde. The brave troops still in close contact with the enemy were left to their fate. The masses imperfectly surrounded could take their chance. All the rest set off along the highroad at their best pace. There had been some discussion whether the princes should be taken in their carriages under escort to Bruges, but Vendôme had dismissed this as shameful, and the royalties jogged along on horseback with the rest. No one knew

[1] "Diarium"; *Feldzüge*, Series, II, i, Suppt., 155.

the whereabouts of General Rosen and the cavalry of the left wing. However, they were in fact marching off with the rest in the darkness. The Maison du Roi had cut their way through the encircling Dutch, many squadrons of dragoons being sacrificed to secure their retreat. Ghent became the only thought for the great majority; but large numbers broke out through the thin cordon of the Allies in all directions. Some fled to Courtrai. Nearly ten thousand men struck across the Scheldt towards the French frontier.

Meanwhile the Allies could do no more in the pitch dark but stand their ground and arrest all who collided with their front. Many regiments and battalions surrendered. Stragglers in great numbers were collected. By a stratagem of Eugene's, Huguenot officers in the allied service were sent into the darkness calling out the names of famous regiments, "A moi, Picardie," "A moi, Roussillon," etc., and taking prisoner those who rallied to these calls. It had now begun to rain, and the victors sank worn out upon the ground and slept on their arms. Marlborough and Eugene remained on horseback throughout the night. Reinforcements were brought up, and at least twenty thousand weary troops, who had not yet been engaged, were guided to their places for a general attack at dawn. But dawn disclosed the battlefield occupied only by the prisoners, the wounded, and the slain.

THE BATTLE OF OUDENARDE

Chapter Twenty-two

THE MORROW OF SUCCESS

1708—JULY

BATTLES are the principal milestones in secular history. Modern opinion resents this uninspiring truth, and historians often treat the decisions of the field as incidents in the dramas of politics and diplomacy. But great battles, won or lost, change the entire course of events, create new standards of values, new moods, new atmospheres, in armies and in nations, to which all must conform. The effects of Oudenarde, both moral and material, transformed as by magic the campaign of 1708. The hasty retreat of the French did not stop at Ghent. They did not feel safe until they had crossed the canal from Bruges beyond the town. Some one—the honour is disputed—had organized an effective rearguard, and the forty squadrons which Marlborough sent in pursuit met with a stiff resistance. Dismay and disorder none the less gripped the French troops, and their leaders resigned themselves to waiting upon the Allies. Marlborough and Eugene were united: Burgundy and Berwick were widely separated, the former behind his canal, the latter now the sole defence of France. The French army never recovered during the whole of 1708 from the shock, and the remarkable operations of the Allies are only to be explained by this fact.

When Marlborough rode into the fortress of Oudenarde about nine A.M. on the 12th the fine old square—which stands little touched to this day—was already filled with French prisoners, and they continued, as Hare says, "to come in by droves for many hours."[1] He sent Lord Stair, with whom he had contracted a friendship, to London with the news. He wrote forthwith to Godolphin.

July 12

I have been so very uneasy, and in so great a hurry for some days, that I should not be able to write, were I not supported by the good success we had yesterday. The particulars you will have from Lord

[1] July 12, 1708; Hare Papers, *H.M.C.*, p. 218.

Stair, who will give you this. . . . I must ever acknowledge the goodness of God, in the success He was pleased to give us; for I believe Lord Stair will tell you they were in as strong a post as is possible to be found; but you know when I left England I was positively resolved to endeavour by all means a battle, thinking nothing else would make the Queen's business go on well. This reason only made me venture the battle yesterday, *otherwise I did give them too much advantage*; but the good of the Queen and my country shall always be preferred by me before any personal concern; for I am very sensible if I had miscarried, I should have been blamed. I hope I have given such a blow to their foot that they will not be able to fight any more this year. My head aches so terribly that I must say no more.[1]

And to Sarah:

CAMP AT OUDENARDE
July 12, 1708

I have neither spirits nor time to answer your last three letters; this being to bring the good news of a battle we had yesterday, in which it pleased God to give us at last the advantage. Our foot on both sides having been all engaged has occasioned much blood; but I thank God the English have suffered less than any of the other troops; none of our English horse having been engaged. I do, and you must, give thanks to God for His goodness in protecting and making me the instrument of so much happiness to the Queen and nation, *if* [and this is a phrase to which we must recur later] *she will please to make use of it.*

He summoned a council of war for four o'clock, and meanwhile, after snatching a few hours' sleep, discussed and decided the next moves with Prince Eugene. The council met in Governor Chanclos' house. Marlborough and Eugene in preconcerted agreement proposed to march westward at once across the Lys, and threaten the French frontier and its fortresses. The strategic situation was peculiar. While Vendôme continued at Ghent he paralysed the whole water communications of the Lys and Scheldt by which the siege-train could reach the allied army. The French frontier was protected by a strong line of fortifications which ran from the fortress of Lille through Warneton and Ypres, and was thence prolonged to the sea by the water defences controlled from Dunkirk. To pierce and level these lines before they could be occupied by Berwick's army was to lay bare the path into France. Such a menace, it was hoped, would force Vendôme to evacuate Ghent and Bruges and bring his army to the defence of France. Such was the advice of "the Princes."

[1] Coxe, iv, 153–154.

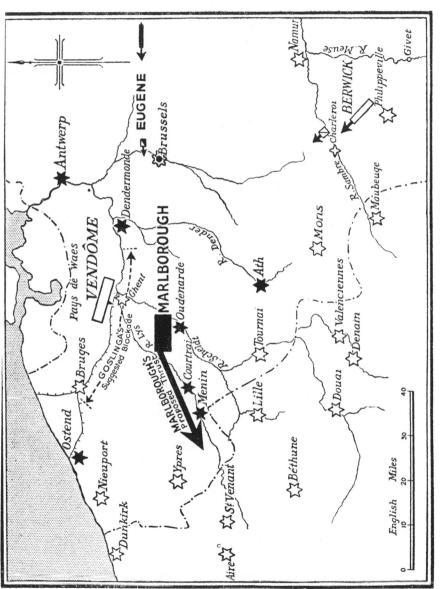

ALTERNATIVE COURSES AFTER OUDENARDE

Overkirk, Dopff,[1] Cadogan, and most of the Dutch Deputies concurred. But Goslinga had a different plan. After making what he calls "a pretty compliment" about opposing such illustrious commanders, he urged that Burgundy and the French army at Ghent and Bruges, with their backs to the sea, should be blockaded, walled in, and starved out. There is no need to ridicule this plan as some writers have done. He had previously half gained his colleague Geldermalsen to his ideas. It was a large and plausible proposition of war. All the generals, following the lead of "the Princes," were against it. It was pointed out, first, that the line of investment was nearly fifty miles long and could thus be pierced at any time by a desperate sortie; secondly, that the area in which Burgundy would be confined was very extensive and comprised a considerable Dutch population, which would certainly starve first; thirdly, that the French communications along the sea-coast by Nieuport and Dunkirk would be hard to close; finally, that Berwick's army, gathering all the troops from the fortresses, would fall at a concerted moment upon the allied rear. These reasons were deemed solid, and Goslinga's project was, not without regrets and respect, dismissed by every one present. Even Geldermalsen, with whom Marlborough had become reconciled, fell away from him. Nothing could be more reasonable and straightforward than this discussion and decision. To measure Goslinga we must read his comments on it in his own words, and note the discreditable motives which it was his habit of mind to impute to every one who differed from him or stood between him and the military career which he fondly pictured for himself.

> The two Deputies who followed me supported the Princes (God knows why. I fear however that their jealousy of *some glory I had gained in the battle* [this will be perceived later] can only have had too much influence). Geldermalsen inclined to my opinion, it is true, but feebly like a courtier, as he had been by profession. . . . Besides that, he is by nature weak and too much of a politician. Cadogan and Dopff also followed the Princes, the first because he had the same interest as others in prolonging the war. The other is naturally feeble, irresolute, and a courtier, not daring to take responsibility and feeling his way.[2]

Of Eugene he says besides, that "he always adopted the views of Marlborough out of the deference which the Court of Vienna had for England."[3] Yet the essence of his account of the battle is

---

[1] One of the Dutch generals. See Vol. II, p. 728.
[2] Goslinga, p. 64.   [3] *Ibid.*, p. 70.

the complete ascendancy of Eugene and Marlborough's passive submission to his leadership!

Thus there is not one of these colleagues, commanders, and generals for whom some insult is not reserved. Marlborough was bent on prolonging the war for his own corrupt gains. Cadogan shared his profits. Eugene was politically under Marlborough's influence, and as a military man had an interest in delaying peace. Overkirk was "quasi-moribund" and subservient to the favour of the Princes. Dopff was a dolt.

The fact that Marlborough had placed Eugene in command of so large a part of his army in the height of Oudenarde was eagerly seized upon by his detractors in England as a proof that it was Eugene who had won the battle. "The 'moderate' party attributes the glory of Oudenarde to Eugene."[1] Marlborough's friends naturally resented this. Every effort was made by letters and insinuations to breed jealousy between the two commanders. Not the slightest impression was produced upon either. "I dare say," wrote Marlborough (July 30) to an English correspondent, "Prince Eugene and I shall never differ about our share of laurels. While the public has any real benefit of my services, I shall not be much concerned at any endeavours that may be used to lessen them."[2]

We may contrast this Olympian calm with Goslinga's insolent tale of the battle.

A large part [of the army] had passed the river towards 4 o'clock; but since Milord [Marlborough] had not yet chosen his field of battle, and appeared visibly embarrassed upon the issue, and gave no positive order for the arrangement of the troops, Count Rechteren and I, seeing how things stood, set ourselves to consider what should be done about it. We were however soon in mutual agreement. We resolved to address ourselves to Prince Eugene, to beg him to be so good as to take upon himself in this dangerous juncture the command of the army. He answered that, like us, he was convinced that without delaying a moment it was necessary to take a decision [*il falloit prendre son parti*]; but, finding himself without troops and a volunteer in the army, it would not become him to interfere in the command. We pressed him afresh, and set before him our danger and that of the whole common cause, the safety of which depended on this fine and formidable army; at last we conjured him by all that he held dear, his country, his master, his glory, and that so effectively that he said to

[1] Archives of the French Foreign Office, July 24, 1708; *Correspondance Politique, Angleterre*, tome 225.   [2] Coxe, iv, 164.

us in a gay and confident tone, "All right, gentlemen, I give in to you and will do what you ask of me." He crammed his hat upon his head at the same time and set spurs to his horse, and advanced to the head of the line. He first gave orders to fill in and cross a little stream which ran across the fields and to deploy in an open plain to the right. This was done there and then; the movement compelled the enemy, who had already shown signs of occupying it [the plain], to abandon it in haste.[1]

If this were true it would indeed be a striking episode. The scene is supposed to have occurred beyond the bridges where Marlborough, surrounded by his staff—several scores of persons—was regulating the deployment of the troops as they came over. We are invited to believe that Goslinga and his fellow-Deputy in these circumstances conferred the command of the army upon Prince Eugene, and persuaded him in this dramatic fashion to accept it, while Marlborough was left sitting on his horse supine and dumbfounded amid his abashed staff officers of several different states.

The field Deputies had, of course, no authority to supersede the Captain-General of England and Deputy Captain-General of the Republic. They had, in fact, in this campaign been instructed to obey his orders whatever they were. Still less had they the power to confer the command upon Prince Eugene. Least of all is it credible that Prince Eugene at Marlborough's side, consulted by him and acting with him, and, as we have seen, under his orders, would have paid attention to such effrontery. Could such a transaction, formal or informal, have taken place without causing an open scandal to the numerous persons who must have witnessed it? Would none of the British and foreign officers present at the bridges have commented upon it? There is no scrap of confirmatory testimony. On the contrary, Goslinga himself, with the other five Deputies, signed a report the next day in which the only mention of Eugene is that he "was present at this action." Eugene himself in his "Diarium" says nothing which could even remotely suggest such an occurrence. Biron, fresh from a captivity in the allied headquarters and full of gossip, told Saint-Simon that "Prince Eugene took command wherever he went by courtesy of Marlborough, *who preserved the entire authority*."[2] Grumbkow, an impartial witness, wrote to the King of Prussia:

Mylord Duke shone in the battle, giving his orders with the greatest sangfroid, and exposing his person to danger like the commonest

[1] Goslinga, p. 56   [2] Saint-Simon, vi, 63.

soldier. Prince Eugene showed much spirit under the heaviest fire, and was with the Prussians, whom he had specially sought out.[1]

Goslinga continues:

We had *towards five o'clock* all our first line engaged in battle. I found myself at this time with Geld [Geldermalsen] on the right, *in the presence of the two Princes*, at the head of our cavalry. . . . We did not know at this stage if our left, or how much of it, had crossed, nor what disposition of it had been made. It was to be informed upon this point, but still more to give an order to our generals to hurry, above all to take if it were possible the enemy upon their right flank, that Prince Eugene begged Geld and me to go there as fast as possible to carry these orders and have them executed by our authority as Deputies. I asked that the Prince would give us one of his adjutants, but he said that our order would have more weight than the word from a simple adjutant. We set off accordingly, wishing the *two Princes* a glorious day.[2]

This statement confirms the fact that Marlborough and Eugene were still together at five P.M. They were, as we have described, upon the extreme right flank in front of Heurne, and the command had not yet been divided. It was a cardinal moment in the battle. The movement of Overkirk with the left wing through Oudenarde was, of course, an integral part of Marlborough's dispositions for crossing the river. Bridges had been built many hours beforehand for that express purpose, and the orders to hasten the movement, which could have no other effect but turning the enemy's right flank, had been reiterated throughout the march. It may well be that Eugene, pestered by the continued suggestions of the two Deputies, disembarrassed himself and Marlborough of their presence by sending them on a superfluous errand. This would certainly be a natural explanation.

Goslinga's account of his further personal exploits at Oudenarde has received merciless ridicule at the hands of Taylor. The Deputy assures us that he and his colleague at length found Marshal Overkirk, accompanied by the other generals of the cavalry, and gave them the "*orders of the two chiefs*." "The brave but altogether exhausted old fellow could hardly answer me, and stammered out that he *would neglect nothing*."[3] He was at that moment engaged in his extremely toilsome and difficult enveloping movement which decided the battle, and his answer to the excited Deputy seems to have been all that civility required at the moment. Goslinga,

[1] Natzmer, p. 293.   [2] Goslinga, pp. 55-56.   [3] *Ibid.*, p. 67.

shocked to see Overkirk's cavalry making what he thought was a meaningless movement in the direction of Courtrai, galloped off to animate the infantry. Here he tells us that, when he gave orders to one of the lieutenant-generals to attack, this officer "turned a deaf ear to him." Thereupon Goslinga dismounted from his horse and put himself at the head of Sturler's two battalions of Swiss, "after a little compliment which I made them of wishing to fight with such brave men."[1] He led them to the assault, followed by five other battalions, and eventually captured a pair of kettle-drums and performed other feats of arms in such a fashion and to such effect that only his innate modesty prevents him from claiming to have won the battle of Oudenarde himself. He preferred that this conclusion should be drawn naturally from his narrative by his children, for whose delectation it was written. It is not strange, indeed, that Goslinga did not choose to publish his memoirs in the lifetime of any who could contradict him. The wonder is that serious historians like Klopp should have cumbered their pages with these malicious inventions, and forced us to deal with them.

Lieutenant-General Biron was among the prisoners. He was personally well known to both Marlborough and Eugene, and had many friends in the allied army. The Duke released him almost at once on special parole, prescribing only that he should go direct to Paris without passing through the French army. The object was no doubt to make sure that Louis XIV had an early and independent account of the magnitude of the defeat. Meanwhile Biron lived at the headquarters, and was treated with intimacy and consideration. Some of his statements recorded by Saint-Simon are illuminating. "He told me that the day after the fight, being at dinner at Marlborough's quarters with many officers, the Duke asked him all of a sudden for news about the "Prince of Wales," adding excuses for referring to him by [no more than] that title."[2] Biron was astonished at this, and smilingly replied that there need be "no difficulty on that point because in the French army the prince carried no other name than that of the Chevalier de St George." He then praised the character and behaviour of the young prince. Marlborough listened with deep attention, and said before every one that it was a deep satisfaction to him to learn so much good about him, because he could not help being "keenly interested in this young man." The Frenchman noticed the gleam in Marlborough's

[1] Goslinga, p. 69.   [2] Saint-Simon, vi, 64.

eye, and that the stern faces of the English officers around the table lit with pleasure. No incident reveals more clearly the latent streak of sentimental Jacobitism which Marlborough and the English Army cherished and, oddly enough, felt able to indulge more particularly in their hours of triumph over the French supporters of the Jacobite cause. Even on the morrow of a battle in which the exiled claimant and heir to the throne had committed the great error of drawing his sword for France against England, these resolute and faithful officers of Queen Anne were thrilled by news of the Pretender. It is a strange commentary on these times that had Anne herself been able to overhear Biron's account her heart would have made the same unbidden response. "Maybe 'tis our brother."

Biron summed up his impressions of the allied camp as follows:

> He was struck by an almost royal magnificence at Prince Eugene's quarters and a shameful parsimony at those of the Duke of Marlborough, who ate the more often at the tables of others; a perfect agreement between the two Captains for the conduct of affairs, of which the details fell much more on Eugene; the profound respect of all the generals for these two chiefs, but a tacit preference on the whole for Prince Eugene, without the Duke of Marlborough being at all jealous.[1]

Marlborough could no doubt have enormously increased his popularity with the high officers if, in accordance with the custom of those days, he had dispensed a lavish hospitality, and lived in the field, as he could well afford, with the style and magnificence of a prince. His frugal, thrifty habits and the great fortune he was known to be saving were a handicap which his genius accepted and carried at a disproportionate cost. Regimental officers and private soldiers of the army, however, saw none of this seamy side. They would not, in any case, have been invited to the entertainments and banquets of the Commander-in-Chief. They continued to admire the manner in which the affairs of the army were conducted, the regularity of their promotions, pay, clothing, and food amid all the difficulties of war, and the assurance, now in their minds a certainty, that they would be led only to victory. As one of his privates wrote, "The Duke of Marlborough's attention and care was over us all."[2] Without palliating the fault of stinginess when displayed in the circles of rank and fashion, it is only just to remember the other side. The generals shrugged their shoulders at the foible of their illustrious chief; the rank and file, and the mass of the officers who,

---

[1] Saint-Simon, vi, 64.
[2] *The Life and Adventures of Matthew Bishop*, p. 194.

often with families at home, lived on nothing but their pay, may well have thought his conduct a good example to the 'fighting sparks' and wealthy nobles whose baggage-wagons flicked the dust over the marching columns.

Most of the great masters of war have preferred to live with simplicity in the field. Cæsar, Frederick, Napoleon—all avoided the banquetings and junketings which marked the aristocratic organization of eighteenth-century wars. Modern opinion and practice has inculcated austere personal habits in commanders whose duty it may be at any time to send men by the thousand to their death. Luxurious ostentation of any kind would have been fatal to any general in the American Civil War. The utmost plainness of living, brief meals, and formal demeanour were the rules of the British, French, and German headquarters in the Great War. No one grudged a colonel or a brigadier when out of the front line the best feast he and his officers could procure; but upon the High Command and their staffs an almost monastic simplicity was enforced. Thus the vices of one age become the virtues of another. Marlborough's habit of dining frequently with different commanders in his army of course saved him money. It may have had other conveniences. He got to know the officers of the army as a whole. They no doubt felt cheered and honoured by a visit from the Commander-in-Chief. He was personally most abstemious, and did not like sitting long at table. As a guest he could leave whenever he chose to resume his work. In fact, there are many excuses to be made for his behaviour.

Every effort to minimize the defeat was made by Burgundy and Vendôme to the King and by the Paris *Gazette* to the world. There had been, it was alleged, a partial and indecisive combat, and the losses had been moderate but equal. These absurdities find repetition even in the instructed pages of Pelet. It was some weeks before Louis XIV himself realized the gravity of the event. His army had left six thousand killed and wounded on the field. Nine thousand prisoners, including eight hundred officers, were taken. At least another fifteen thousand men were scattered about the countryside and separated from the main army. Many of these, however, eventually returned to their duty, or were put to some other service. "It is most certain," wrote Marlborough a fortnight later,

that the success we had at Oudenarde has lessened their army at least 20,000 men, but that which I think our greatest advantage consists in the fear that is among their troops, so that I shall seek all occasions of attacking them. But their army is far from being inconsiderable, for when the Duke of Burgundy's army shall join that of the Duke of Berwick, they will be at least one hundred thousand men. If it had pleased God that we had had one hour's daylight more at Oudenarde, we had in all likelihood made an end of this war.[1]

The casualties of the Allies were almost exactly three thousand, and this loss was more than repaired by recruitment from deserters and captured mercenaries. All our friends, the diarists, Colonel Kane, Major Blackadder, Captain Parker, Sergeant Millner, Privates Deane and Matthew Bishop, fought in the battle. Blackadder noted (June 30, O.S.), "This is another great Ebenezer of my life, to be added to Hochstet, Ramillies etc. We fought the French, and by the great mercy of God, beat them. I was liberally supplied with courage, resolution and a calm mind. *All is the gift of God.* . . . My frame was more serene and spiritual than ordinary. My thoughts were much upon the 103d Psalm, which I sung (in my heart) frequently upon the march."[2]

[1] Marlborough to Godolphin, July 26; Coxe, iv, 167–169.
[2] *Life and Diary of Lieutenant Colonel J. Blackader* (1824). pp. 318–319.

Chapter Twenty-three

THE THWARTED INVASION

1708—JULY–AUGUST

MARSHAL BERWICK had reached the Meuse at Givet on the day of the battle. His army of 34 battalions and 56 squadrons was still toiling by forced marches; but on the 12th its head lay on the Sambre. Here he learned from the governor of Mons that "there had been an engagement on the 11th near Oudenarde . . ., that the enemy had had the advantage, and that our army was retreating towards Ghent in great disorder." In spite of the need of resting his troops and allowing his rear to close up, the bad news determined him to hasten forward to Mons, which he reached on the 14th with twenty squadrons. He found great numbers of stragglers and small bodies who had escaped south and homeward from the battlefield, streaming in upon the fortress. He collected and organized these into a force of nine thousand men, with which he reinforced the garrisons of Tournai, Lille, and Ypres. None of these troops were found capable of further service in the field, and in the French accounts of the campaign they are frequently referred to as "*débris* of the Grand Army." Here we have another measure of the gravity of Oudenarde.

Berwick's sure instinct made him fearful for Lille. Ordering his army to concentrate upon Douai, he went himself to Lille on the 14th to prepare for the coming shock. "I took care to supply the fortresses with all sorts of stores, and as my infantry came up I distributed it among them, in order that, which way soever the enemy should take, they might meet with opposition."[1]

Marlborough's army lay during the 12th on the battlefield recovering from its immense exertions; but at midnight on the 13th, in accordance with the decision of the council of war, the Duke dispatched Count Lottum with thirty battalions and forty squadrons to seize and level the French lines about Warneton and Comines. He followed himself with the main army the next day. Eugene went

[1] *Memoirs*, ii, 12.

to Brussels, where his infantry was now expected. Berwick, who had scented this danger also, made every effort to occupy the almost undefended lines. But Count Lottum, marching fast, reached the fortifications in time, before dawn on the 15th. "We slung our Firelocks," says Private Matthew Bishop,

> and every man had a Shovel in his hand; and when we came to the place appointed, we ran up upon their works. It was like running up the side of a house. When we got to the top we began to throw it down as fast as possible in order to make way for the Army.[1]

Five hundred prisoners were taken. The pathway into France was now laid bare and open. During the afternoon Marlborough arrived at Werwicq, which became for some time his headquarters.

From here he wrote a series of letters to English agents abroad in order to repair the injury which the fall of Ghent had done. His postscript to Stanhope led to a memorable result.

CAMP AT WERWICQ
July 15 [1708]

... You have here the Copy of a Letter from the Admiralty to the Earl of Sunderland, about the wintering of a Squadron in the Mediterranean. I send it only for your own information, that you may, by your insinuations, prevent the Courts putting too great a stress upon it, in case it should be found impracticable, for 'tis certain our Sea Officers are the best judges what may be done with safety in this case.

I am so intirely convinced that nothing can be done effectually without the fleet, that I conjure you if possible to take Port Mahone, and to let me have your reasons for any other Port, so that I may continue to presse them in England.[2]

John to Sarah

WERWICQ
July 16

... I was in good hopes that the diligence I have made in getting into the French country (for I am now behind their lines) would have obliged them to abandon Ghent; but as yet it has not had that effect, but on the contrary M. de Vendôme declares he will sacrifice a strong garrison rather than abandon that town, which, if he keeps his word, he will give me a great deal of trouble; for till we are masters of Ghent we can have no cannon. ... The Duke of Berwick came to Lille the day before yesterday, but his troops will not be here these three or four days; those of Prince Eugene came last night to Brussels, so that

[1] *The Life and Adventures of Matthew Bishop*, p. 162.   [2] *Dispatches*, iv, 108.

both our armies will be abundantly recruited. However, I believe the French will be careful not to venture any more this year; *but the greatest mischief they can do is the venturing all for the preserving of Ghent. . . .*[1]

It is curious to notice how Vendôme and Marlborough from their opposite standpoints were in complete accord upon strategic values. Marlborough hoped, however, that he would succeed in forcing Louis XIV to overrule Vendôme's correct decision.

Marlborough to Godolphin

July 16

My blood is so extremely heated that I must refer you to what Mr Cardonnel will write to the Secretary's office of what has passed since my Lord Stair left the army. If we had been six hours later, I am afraid we should not have been able to force these lines; for M. de Motte was got with his little army to Ypres, and the Duke of Berwick was at the same time at Lille. We are now masters of marching where we please, but can make no siege till we are masters of Ghent, from whence only we can have our cannon. The camp the French are now in, behind the canal of Bruges, makes them entirely masters of Ghent and Bruges; but at the same time they leave all France open to us, which is what I flatter myself the King of France and his council will never suffer; so that I hope by Thursday M. de Vendôme will receive orders from Court not to continue in the camp where he is, from whence we are not able to force him but by famine.

I am taking measures for attacking Ghent as soon as he marches; and if the Duke of Vendôme's resolution of staying where he is be approved at Court, I shall then endeavour to cut off all provisions, as much as possible, from going to him; for if he stays, and we can ruin that army, France is undone; but if they can subsist longer than we can, they will be able by that to hinder us from doing anything considerable from want of our cannon. Upon the whole the hazard to them is so very great that I cannot think the King of France will venture it. Four or five days will let us see their intentions. In the meantime I shall take what rest I can, in order to be the better able to serve, for this minute my head is so very hot that I am obliged to leave off writing. . . .[2]

Marlborough to Godolphin

July 19

. . . That which hinders us from acting with vigour is that as long as the French are masters of Ghent we cannot make use either of the Scheldt or the Lys. But we are using our utmost endeavours to get some cannon by land, which meets with infinite difficulties; but

[1] Coxe, iv, 156–157. [2] *Ibid.*, 158–159.

we must overcome them, or we shall have very little fruit of our victory. The Duke of Vendôme is not contented with having the canal before him, but he is also retrenching, as if he intended to stay there the rest of this campaign. But when the King of France shall see that we have a probability of getting a battering train, I believe he will not let his own country be abandoned for the maintaining their treacherous conquest of Ghent.[1]

Marlborough to Godolphin

July 23

. . . We continue still under the great difficulty of getting cannon. . . . We have ordered twenty battering pieces to be brought from Maestricht, and we have taken measures for sixty more to be brought from Holland. The calculation of the number of draught horses, to draw this artillery, amounts to sixteen thousand horses, by which you will see the difficulties we meet with; but we hope to overcome them. In the meantime we send daily parties into France, which occasions great terror. . . .

I am very glad you have sent Lieutenant-General Erle to hasten the troops on board, for though the number is not great, they will much alarm the coast. I hope you will not determine to send these troops for Portugal, till we first see *whether they may not be of much use more on the coast of France. You know formerly you sent me a project for Abbeville: I have looked for it, but cannot find it. I should be glad if you would send it me, for I think something of that kind might be practicable, and in that case those troops, as well as the fleet, will be necessary.*

The Duke of Vendôme's army is so frightened, I am very confident if we could get them out of their retrenchments, and from behind the canal of Ghent and Bruges, we should beat them with half their numbers, especially their foot. This is one of the reasons for their staying where they are. . . .[2]

Vendôme believed that by holding his key position he could prevent any important siege. He certainly showed remarkable constancy in his opinion, and it was his will-power that kept the French army at Ghent in spite of every strategic pressure or moral provocation that the Allies could apply. Marlborough, however, with his knowledge of the resources of Holland, conceived it possible to undertake a first-class siege, although deprived of the Belgian waterways. Immense masses of munitions and stores and more than a hundred heavy cannon were moved towards Brussels from Antwerp and Maestricht through such canals and rivers as the Dutch controlled. From Brussels all must be drawn forward by road. Two

[1] Coxe, iv, 159–160. [2] *Ibid.*, 165–166.

great convoys would be required merely to begin the operation. Marlborough's army had been separated from its heavy baggage since the first movements in July, and to transport this to them and replenish the field parks was urgent. The second and far larger convoy would carry the siege-train and the heavy projectiles. The process of collecting the necessary sixteen thousand horses from Holland and from the armies, and of extorting them from the

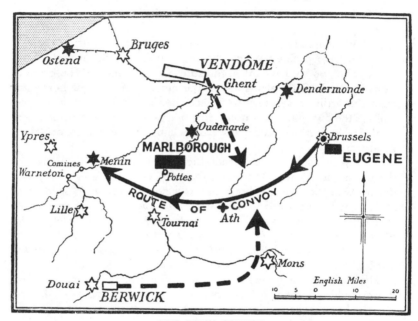

THE FIRST CONVOY

countryside and from French territory, must take several weeks, and was at once begun.

A glance at the map will show that both these convoys had very nearly seventy-five miles to traverse through a region in which they could be attacked from opposite sides by both French armies separately or in combination; Vendôme could descend from Ghent, and Berwick could strike north from Mons. The securing of each of the convoys was therefore a major operation of war requiring the use as escort of all the troops at the disposal of the allied command. The passage of the first was accomplished during July 22–25. Eugene covered the wagon-train to the Scheldt with his army; and Marlborough advanced to receive it from him at the bridgehead he had prepared near Pottes. Berwick, who wished to attack Eugene on the way, was by the King's order held at Douai to safeguard France, and Vendôme, in spite of Berwick's timely and repeated warnings, remained obdurately behind the Bruges canal.

Critics have asked why Marlborough did not march directly upon Lille, into which place Berwick was daily sending troops and supplies. The first and sufficient answer is clearly that he did not wish to involve himself in a premature attack upon any one particular fortress, until he knew the siege-train could come through from Brussels. He could not have encircled Lille for at least a week, and once the factor of uncertainty had gone the whole French effort and succour would pour in through its open gorge. By moving to Werwicq and levelling the Comines line he threatened equally Ypres, Lille, and Tournai. This uncertainty continued to the end. Even as late as August 11 Berwick was writing to Burgundy, "I have no doubt that in less than two days Lille, Tournay, or Ypres will be invested." It was only on the 12th, the day before the investment, that he could state, "The enemy are determined to lay siege to Lille."[1]

This advantage had to be balanced against the undoubted strengthening of the defences and garrison of Lille which was in progress. Suppose Marlborough had tried to carry the town of Lille by assault without artillery, suppose even that he had succeeded, everything in the theatre of war would have become quite clear, and all the French commanders could have acted upon certainties. There is no reason to believe that he could have stormed the fortifications on July 17 or 18 with his field troops. But if he had achieved this questionable venture, he would have been obviously tethered to the citadel of Lille without any of the means of carrying the operation through. Goslinga, furious at the rejection of his blockade plan, pours out his calumnies. This needless levelling of the lines of Comines was, he asserts, in part the revenge of prolonging the war which Marlborough was taking upon the States-General for having baulked him of his desire to be Governor of Belgium in 1706, and the rest was sordid love of his pay and allowances. During the next ten days, he declares, no doubt with much truth, the resisting powers of the fortress of Lille were enormously strengthened. Marlborough and Eugene decided to face this disadvantage, and on the merits, apart from the high authority of these masters of war, their case is good. But Marlborough had yet another reason for not entangling himself prematurely in the siege of Lille.

[1] Berwick to Burgundy, August 11 and 12; *Memoirs*, ii, 390, 391.

In the days following Oudenarde he imparted to Eugene his greatest strategic design. The whole combined army should invade France, ignoring the frontier fortresses and abandoning all land communication with Holland. A new sea-base of operations should be seized and formed in French territory. Abbeville was in every way suitable. General Erle, with his six thousand men, would descend upon it from the Isle of Wight. The English and Dutch sea-power would be used to escort and ferry round from Holland in the calm summer weather the whole mass of stores, cannon, and equipment required for the armies, and thereafter would maintain a constant flow of supplies. From Abbeville Marlborough and his illustrious comrade would march on Paris through unravaged country at the head of a hundred thousand men, and bring the war to a swift and

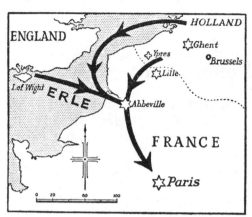

THE THWARTED INVASION

decisive close. This movement the Duke believed would irresistibly draw in its train all the French armies and fortress garrisons. It would free Holland from the menace of Burgundy's army. It would avoid the cost, labour, and peril of reducing the great fortresses on the French frontier. It would clear or render impotent Dunkirk, Calais, and all fortresses, naval bases, and garrisons on the sea-coast. Such was the secret project of the general who was represented by his detractors as prolonging the war for his own ends.

Marlborough had convinced the London Cabinet. He had, of course, expected a stubborn resistance from the Dutch. He hoped that with Eugene's aid he might overcome this. But, as we have already observed, Eugene was a land animal. He was staggered at the proposal. The dangers of leaping forward to a new base to be formed from the sea, with the terrible fortresses and strong hostile armies barring all return, seemed to this prince of tireless audacity to involve an unnatural hazard.

Without Eugene there was no hope for the plan. "By what I hear from Buys," wrote Marlborough to Godolphin (July 26), it is plain that they [the Dutch] think enough is done for peace, and I am afraid they will not willingly give their consent for the marching of their army into France, which certainly, if it succeeded, would put a happy end to the war. . . . I have acquainted Prince Eugene with the earnest desire we have for our marching into France. He thinks it unpracticable till we have Lille for a *place d'armes* and magazine, and then he thinks we may make a very great inroad, but not be able to winter, though we might be helped by the fleet, unless we are masters of some fortified town. . . .[1]

And again (Marlborough to Godolphin, August 3):

I have spoke of it to nobody but the Prince; for by several observations I have of late made of the Deputies of our army I am afraid the States would not be for this expedition, nor anything else, where there is a venture. . . . After we have succeeded at Lille, and that [if] we shall think it feasible to support the project of Abbeville, I should agree with you that Lieutenant-General Erle should have the chief command [there] this winter. . . .[2]

And, finally, to Halifax, "Were our army all English, it would be feasible, but we have a great many among us who are more afraid of wanting provisions than of the enemy."[3] Yet at this time the gossip of the French Court credited Eugene with the desire of raiding Paris.

★People exaggerate with lively pleasure the offer which Prince Eugene has made to the Duke of Marlborough, of whom he has asked for 8000 horse to go to Versailles, when he promised to bring back the King's five best pictures, and give Marlborough three of them.[4]

While all this was being debated Marlborough from his headquarters at Werwicq sought by every means to torment Vendôme out of Ghent. He sent cavalry detachments northward to cut off all supplies which Berwick might try to send to the main French army. He ordered the governor of Ostend to impede the communications between Bruges and Nieuport by opening such sluices as were under his control. Strict injunctions deterred the Belgian population from offering their produce to the enemy's camp. By these means he subjected Vendôme to scarcity. It was beyond his power to invoke famine. The French communications along the coast were never effectually severed. But Marlborough's greatest hope lay in raiding the French province which now lay open and

---

[1] Coxe, iv, 168.   [2] *Ibid.*, 173–174.   [3] *Dispatches*, iv, 127.
[4] Archives of the French Foreign Office, August 28, 1708; *Correspondance Politique, Angleterre*, tome 225, f. 115.

exposed. He repeated in Artois, and to some extent in Picardy, the same severities, though greatly modified, which he had inflicted upon Bavaria in the month before Blenheim. Using fifty squadrons, sustained by infantry and guns, he entered many French towns whose names have hallowed memories for our generation. On July 23 he occupied Armentières; on the 26th La Bassée, and his cavalry burned the suburbs of Arras; on the 27th Lens. From these positions during a whole week the allied horse ravaged Artois. Crossing the Scarpe, they harried the countryside, molesting Doullens, Guise, Saint-Quentin, and Péronne. In the last week of July he had at least twenty-five thousand men in Artois gathering food, booty, and hostages. Louis XIV, unable to protect his subjects, authorized the unhappy province to compound for a contribution of fifteen hundred thousand livres. Picardy was also summoned. Following the precedent set by Villars in the previous year in Germany, they were invited to fix their indemnity, having regard to the arrears due from 1702. Burning and pillage enforced these extortions, and many violent deeds were done. Berwick, with such forces as he could spare from the fortress line, resisted with energy; there was sharp cavalry fighting, but the French were everywhere outnumbered.

All that happened shows how easily the first stages of Marlborough's strategic adventure could have been achieved. He might have moved at this time the whole allied army into France behind the fortress lines, fed himself comfortably upon the country, and received his munitions and reinforcements through Abbeville. Such an invasion would have dominated the war. The lesser processes to which he was confined, although yielding immediate necessary supplies, did not procure the strategic result. Wrath and panic rose in Paris. Here was war, so long fought in foreign lands, now raging upon French soil. The Great King, who had for more than a generation laid his rod upon his neighbours, must now endure the same measure for his own people. But Vendôme stubbornly insisted that so long as he held the waterways at Ghent and strangled the Scheldt-Lys no great siege could be undertaken by the Allies, nor any lasting invasion. He induced Louis XIV to bear the woes of his subjects with fortitude. He clung to his invaluable position. He could even retaliate to some extent by harrying the Dutch province of the Pays de Waes, which was in his grip. If the siege of Lille was to be attempted Marlborough's incursion could only be temporary. He would need all his troops to bring the convoys through.

By the early days of August therefore this bitter phase of the war subsided. Marlborough's garrisons still held La Bassée, Armentières, and Lens, but his whole strength was required to receive the great convoy from Eugene.

We must regard the refusal of the Allies to accept Marlborough's scheme for the invasion of France at this juncture as one of the cardinal points of the war. Although Louis had borne the injuries and humiliations which Marlborough had thus far inflicted upon him, the strain was near breaking-point. He forbade Berwick to quit Douai and attack the convoy. He warned Burgundy on July 30, "If the enemy resolve to cross the Somme or the Authie you should not hesitate for one moment to march towards them, taking none the less all proper measures in concert with Marshal Berwick."[1] And Chamillart's order of August 1 to that Marshal contains this significant passage: "You must be very attentive to any movement which the enemy may make with a considerable corps towards the Somme or the Authie. That would be a sure way of completing the ruin of Picardy and of spreading terror throughout Normandy and to the very gates of Paris."[2]

Thus it is certain that the spell would have worked had Marlborough been allowed to use it. If his strategy had prevailed, not only would Ghent have been freed, but all the French armies and garrisons would have been recalled to defend the capital and to confront the invasion. Great battles would have been fought in the heart of France, and victory would have provided in 1708 that triumphant peace which after so much further bloodshed the Grand Alliance was still to seek in vain.

The question arises, ought not Marlborough to have been able to enforce his conception upon Eugene and the Dutch? He had the English Cabinet behind him. The Whigs were ardent to carry the war into France. Godolphin, faithful and trusting, was still at the helm. If Eugene had been gained the Dutch could hardly have demurred. But Marlborough's admiration for Eugene, his respect for his vast experience and mastery of the art of war, made it impossible for him to force Eugene beyond his will. In the previous year he had tried to press him unduly about Toulon. It had not succeeded. Indeed, when Eugene differed from him he may well have questioned his own instinct. His infinite labours, the stresses to which he was being subjected at home, and the physical weakness and weariness which lay heavy upon him in this campaign

[1] Pelet, viii, 57.   [2] Chamillart to Berwick; Berwick, *Memoirs*, ii, 406.

constrained him to acquiesce, and the supreme opportunity was gone, as fate decreed, for ever. "... As I think," he wrote sadly on another miscarriage at this date (August 2), "most things are governed by Destiny, having done all that is possible, one should submit with patience."[1]

It was with a heavy heart that Marlborough now bent his thought and energies to the siege of Lille. In doing so he did not finally relinquish his design. He hoped that a ten days' bombardment would suffice for the city, and another fortnight for the citadel. If so, Eugene's condition would be established. There would still be time in the middle of September to march into France. If not, the plan must stand over to the next year. He was therefore most careful to keep General Erle's force free for the Abbeville descent, and not to disturb that place prematurely. "It will be impossible for us," he wrote to the Secretary of State (August 3),

> to take our just measures for seconding Lieutenant-General Erle's design upon Abbeville till we are masters of Lille, and therefore the fleet with the troops should go directly to the coast of Normandy, and land and make what impression they can there till this siege be over, and then I shall give you timely notice when it may be proper to come this way, for we are of opinion that no attempt should be made on Abbeville, nor the least jealousy given that way, till towards the end of September.[2]

The coasts of Normandy and Brittany might be alarmed, but Abbeville was sacrosanct.

Marlborough to Godolphin

WERWICQ
August 2

... We have got a great part of our cannon to Brussels, so that now our greatest application is to have it here. ... We have an account that our parties have occasioned very great terror in Picardy, and that they exclaim very much against M. de Vendôme staying where he is; but by the measures he takes, there can be no doubt of his intention of staying there all this campaign. If we can succeed in our undertakings *we must not think of winter quarters, till we have obliged him to quit that country.* It must be by force, for it is not in our power to hinder them from having subsistence, even for the whole winter, if they should be permitted to stay. ...[3]

---

[1] To Godolphin; Coxe, iv, 172.
[2] Marlborough to Boyle; *Dispatches*, iv, 147.
[3] Coxe, iv, 172.

The great convoy had now assembled at Brussels. The sixteen thousand horses had been procured.[1] Every district of Belgium and France in Marlborough's control had been compelled under threats of fire and sword to deliver every suitable horse or vehicle. In vain had Berwick ordered all horses to be brought into the French fortresses. The threat of military execution was decisive upon the country folk, who were under the impression of the ravages in Artois and Picardy only a week before. They had to choose between yielding their horses and having their homes burned. Louis XIV could not ask this sacrifice of subjects he could no longer protect. Strict and stern measures were also used with the farmers and peasants around Oudenarde and Ath. The armies were combed of every horse not needed for fighting. "All the generals, we ourselves," says Goslinga, "the battalions and even the vivandiers were obliged to furnish horses and chariots; the number used was incredible."[2] Finally the tale was complete.

The operation was studied with the utmost care. Eugene rode through from Brussels to Werwicq, and spent several days with Marlborough. Cadogan, in almost daily correspondence with the Duke, had been for some weeks at Brussels preparing all. At length the moment came. To an official letter of August 2 to Cadogan, prescribing various precautions and directing him to come with the convoy himself, and slip away with it "on the sly" (à la sourdine), Marlborough added this unusual and imperative postscript, written in his own hand:

> For God's sake be sure you do not risk the cannon, for I would rather come with the whole army than receive an affront. You must have people towards Ghent to be sure that, when you begin your march, they have no considerable body of their troops between the Scheldt and the Dender.[3]

On August 4 Eugene left Marlborough's headquarters at Werwicq for Ath, where the bulk of his own army was concentrated. Marlborough sent him in addition twenty-five squadrons and twenty-five battalions. Together with the escort of the convoy numbering thirty-five squadrons under the Prince of Hesse-Cassel, who guarded the opposite flank to Eugene, and a powerful rearguard, Eugene disposed of more than fifty thousand men. Thus covered, the convoy started on the 6th. Eighty heavy cannon, each drawn by twenty horses, twenty mortars drawn by sixteen horses, and

---

[1] For more details upon this operation Taylor's admirable and accurate account should be read (*The Wars of Marlborough*, ii, 165 *et seq.*).

[2] Goslinga, p. 72.   [3] *Dispatches*, iv, 144.

three thousand four-horse munition wagons, formed two columns, each fifteen miles long, marching by separate roads. They took the direction not of Lille but of Mons, thus keeping as far as possible from the main French army, and incidentally deceiving Berwick, who, thinking Mons was after all the objective, reinforced that garrison by seven battalions from his field forces. By nightfall on the 7th the convoy reached Soignies unmolested. Here they found

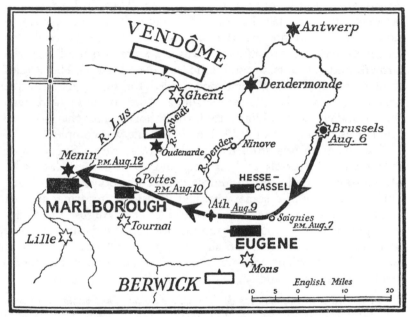

THE GREAT CONVOY

Eugene with a fighting force of forty thousand men. Marlborough's anxiety may be judged from the fact that, besides the troops with which he had already supplied Eugene, he had sent on the 5th twelve squadrons to Oudenarde to scout towards Ghent, and on rumours of a French detachment at Ninove reinforced them on the 7th by another thirty squadrons. At the same time he strengthened the garrisons of Antwerp and Brussels from various reserves in Holland, and ordered the keenest alert in both cities. He himself, with the rest of his own army, was ready to march at an hour's notice.

On the 8th before dawn the convoy turned at right angles on to the road to Ath, and marched throughout the day under shield of Eugene's army and Hesse-Cassel's cavalry. They had slipped away from Brussels "on the sly," and Vendôme could scarcely reach them during their first two marches. But the 8th, 9th, and 10th were the critical days. Upon this stage of the journey Vendôme and Berwick could combine by the shortest route. Marlborough's forty-two squadrons near Oudenarde were, however, a screen against Vendôme, and would have given timely warning to Eugene had he moved to strike the convoys between Ath and the Pottes bridgehead. The Dender was crossed at Ath on the 9th, and the march towards the Scheldt began the next morning. Had Vendôme moved south in force he could have been encountered on this day by the whole of the allied armies. The Oudenarde squadrons would have fallen back before him, and Marlborough from Werwicq could have reached the battlefield as soon as he. But Vendôme had no thought of moving. He remained deaf to the appeals of Berwick. He suppressed Burgundy. He declared himself incredulous that any great siege could be undertaken while he held the Ghent waterways. He affected to disbelieve all reports about the great convoy. At the root of this attitude lay the fact that he did not mean to fight a battle. In this resolve he was right. He measured truly the havoc Oudenarde had wrought in the Grand Army. Thus the convoy crossed the Scheldt at Pottes in tranquillity during the 10th. Here they were in the midst of Marlborough's army. Thirty battalions and thirty-four squadrons under the Prince of Orange masked the fortress of Lille, while thirty squadrons at Petegem guarded the northern flank. The Duke himself marched with his remaining troops to Helchin on the 12th, and that night the siege-train safely entered the allied fortress of Menin.

This operation was watched with intense curiosity by the soldiers of all countries. Feuquières, whose pretentious and faulty judgments upon military matters have received too much respect from later writers, opined, in this case truly, that posterity would have difficulty in believing that such a feat had ever been performed. Certainly no general of those days, studying the positions of the armies upon the map, would have pronounced it possible. French military historians have criticized with extreme severity the negligence of Vendôme. Berwick roundly condemns him. Nevertheless, the terror of Oudenarde and the combined skill and prowess of Marlborough and Eugene were facts which maps and documents cannot convey. On the 13th—Blenheim Day—Eugene, crossing the stream of the Marque, joined both hands with the Prince of Orange, and the investment of Lille was complete.

Marlborough wrote that night to Count Maffei: "The Prince of Savoy has invested the town of Lille on all sides, and the cannon has arrived at Menin within reach of the siege, which will be pressed with all possible vigour, and this may at last convince the enemy that they have lost the battle of Oudenarde."[1]

[1] *Dispatches*, iv, 165.

Chapter Twenty-four

THE HOME FRONT

1708—JULY—OCTOBER

WE have followed during a quarter of a century Marlborough's relations with his royal mistress. They were never as intimate as those which she had cherished with Sarah, but they stood throughout at a higher level and on a broader foundation. Sarah had been the playmate of her childhood, the loved companion of her youth and prime, her partisan and comforter in every struggle as princess, a high participant in the glories of her reign. But Marlborough was to the Queen an august friend, a guide who had never led her wrong, a rock where she could always find safety, a sword never raised in vain. Although the fact was concealed for some time from the world, the Queen had now broken with Sarah. Not only had she cast her from her heart, but in its recesses she had installed another. From 1707 onward the Queen began to hate Sarah as much as she had loved her, and to hate her the more because of the language of outworn affection and the candour of vanished friendship which still prevailed between Sovereign and subject.

Marlborough remained: her general, her counsellor, at the head of Europe, by all consent the most remarkable man alive, her lifelong friend, her own triumphant choice! To Marlborough the Queen now addressed herself. She had shown herself prepared in January 1708 to let him go rather than part with Harley, and lose contact with the Tories. She had come in contact for a moment with the appalling weight of national and international force which forbade such a decision. She had submitted: she had been compelled to submit. But she bore no resentment against him. Godolphin, the Junto, Sarah, she regarded as her opponents, even as her foes; but Marlborough was still her hope, almost her last hope. He was, she still believed, the prop of her throne, the only man who could win the war and keep the crown on her head.

Naturally from time to time in former years letters had passed between the Queen and the Captain-General. No great number had been needed when they were agreed upon so much. But in 1708 there grew a correspondence which is little less than an epitome of British history at that time. During this hazardous, grinding campaign, both before and after Oudenarde, the Queen wrote at least a dozen lengthy letters in her own hand to Marlborough, and Marlborough at intervals perhaps half as many in reply. No one can read Anne's letters, most of which—whatever advice she got or wherever she got it from—obviously sprang from her own heart and fell pithily and passionately from her pen, without realizing across the wastes of time what a woman she was, what a prince she was, and—what a Stuart!

Marlborough's letters are also revealing. His reverence and affection for the Queen were his dominant sentiment. "I can't entirely agree with your opinion of the Queen," he wrote to Sarah. "I must own I have a tenderness for her; I would willingly believe that all that is amiss proceeds from the ambition and ill judgment of Mrs Masham, and the knavery and artfulness of Mr Harley."[1] But against this ran the conduct of the war, the cause of the Allies, the necessities of politics, the brutal force of faction, his loyalty to Godolphin and his own personal interests. He loathed being made to put pressure on the Queen by the impulsion of the Whigs. But he was bound in honour to Godolphin, and Sarah was in their hands. Moreover, the Whigs had both Houses of Parliament at their command, and without Parliament the armies of the Alliance, with victory almost in their grasp, would fall prostrate. Also, on the merits the Queen was utterly wrong. Her personal interventions hampered the prosecution of the war, and delayed and eventually frustrated a victorious peace. Thus we see Marlborough in his letters sometimes descending perforce below the natural and manly simplicity of his earlier correspondence. He sets himself to manage the Queen, to play upon her sentiments. References to his own ill-health, to the services he had rendered her, to the risks he was running, to the drum-beats of approaching battles, none of which he would have mentioned in the days of Blenheim and Ramillies or in the earlier campaigns, creep into his letters. And always throughout them jars the threat of resignation. If he had neglected these measures, he feared that perhaps the war would be lost, and all his toils consumed for nothing.

In these years there arose in his heart an intense desire to be quit of politics. Why could he not be free from the factions, and serve

[1] Coxe, iv, 213.

at the head of the armies as a soldier? To cease to be a Minister and to remain a General was his heartfelt wish. How easy to bear were the trials and toils and hazards of war compared to this—to him hateful—pressure, the coaxing, cajoling, and coercing of the Queen for the sake of a set of men for whom he cared nothing, but that they alone could support the war! Moreover, as will be seen, he drew a very clear line between pressing the Queen on direct public issues and taking advantage of her weakness or her prejudices. He would argue with her, he would appeal to her, he would warn her; but he would not help the Whigs in their schemes to blackmail her.

At the same time Marlborough had no illusions about Anne. His eye, which measured things so exactly and pierced into the thoughts and motives of men and women, had told him the truth about the Queen. Abigail had got her. The political consequences were plain. "I do not take Mr Bromley for a great negotiator, but a less able man than himself will reconcile Lord Rochester and Mr Harley at this time. I believe you may depend upon it that they will all be of one mind, and that they think themselves assured of the hearts of the Prince and of the Queen, which is a very dismal prospect."[1]

In the middle of July Lord Stair arrived in London with the news of Oudenarde. Many circumstances contributed to make this triumphant victory agreeable to the British nation. It was the largest battle yet fought in the war. It had been fought against odds and under conditions which, according to professional opinion, were deemed unprecedented. The defeat and rout of the main army of France, reputed a hundred and twenty thousand strong, seemed to assure the future of the campaign. The hopes of a speedy and victorious peace rose high in both Whig and Tory bosoms. The accounts of the bravery of the Electoral Prince, heir presumptive to the throne, stirred all Protestant and constitutional circles, and many unfair comparisons were made between his behaviour and that of the 'pretended' Prince of Wales.

> Not so did behave
> Young Hanover brave
> In the Bloody Field, I assure ye:
> When his War-Horse was shot
> He valu'd it not,
> But fought it on foot like a Fury.[2]

[1] August 23; Coxe, iv, 201–202.
[2] "Jack Frenchman's Lamentations"; Jonathan Swift, *Poems*, iii. 6.

The Queen to Marlborough

I want words to express ye Joy I have yt you are well after your Glorious Success, for wch next to God Almighty my thanks are due to you & indeed I can never say enough for all the great & faithfull Services you have ever don me, but be soe just as to beleeve I am as truly Sensible of them as a gratfull hart can be, & Shall be ready to Shew it upon all occasions; I hope you can not doubt of my esteeme & freindship for you, nor think yt becaus I differ wth you in Some things, it is for want of ether; no I do assure you, if you weare heare I am Sure you would not think me Soe much in ye wrong in Some things as I feare you do now, I am afraid my letter Should Com to late to London, & therfore dare Say no more, but yt I pray God Almighty to Continue his protection over you & Send you safe home againe, & be assured I shall ever be Sincerly your humble Servant.[1]

There was a shout of triumph from all classes which for a moment, but only for a moment, drowned the clatter of faction. Marlborough's answer shows how little his judgment was affected by success. Except perhaps where Sarah was concerned, he was a man without illusions. He saw all the facts in a cool, clear, steady light. After expressing his thanks to the Queen he wrote (July 12/23):

As I have formerly told your Majesty that I am desirous to serve you in the army, but not as a Minister, I am every day more and more confirmed in that opinion. And I think myself obliged, upon all accounts, on this occasion, to speak my mind freely to you. The circumstances in this last battle, I think, show the hand of God; for we were obliged not only to march five leagues that morning, but to pass a river before the enemy, and to engage them before the whole army was passed, which was a visible mark of the favour of heaven, to you and your arms. Your Majesty shall be convinced from this time that I have no ambition, or anything to ask for myself or family; but I will end the few years which I have to live in endeavouring to serve you, and to give God Almighty thanks for His infinite goodness to me.

But as I have taken this resolution to myself, give me leave to say that I think you are obliged, in conscience and as a good Christian, to forgive, and to have no more resentments to any particular person or party, but to make use of such as will carry on this just war with vigour, which is the only way to preserve our religion and liberties, and the crown on your head. . . .[2]

---

[1] Blenheim MSS. Printed in the *Conduct*, pp. 215–216, in modernized form.
[2] Coxe, iv, 182–183; *Conduct*, p. 258.

Almost while he was writing these solemn words the Queen was freeing herself from the exhilaration of Oudenarde. We have seen the letter which Marlborough had pencilled in the exhaustion after the battle to Sarah, which she had shown to the Queen. The final sentence ran: "I do, and you must, give thanks to God for His goodness in protecting and making me the instrument of so much happiness to the Queen and nation, *if she will please to make use of it.*" The chance phrase at the end nettled her; she did not let it pass.

The Queen to Marlborough

WINDSOR
July 13/24

. . . I was showed a letter the other day by a friend of yours that you writ soon after the battle, and I must beg you will explain to me one expression in it. You say, after being thankful for being the instrument of so much good to the nation and me, *if I would please to make use of it.*[1] I am sure I will never make an ill use of so great a blessing, but, according to the best of my understanding, make the best use of it I can, and should be glad to know what is the use you would have me make of it, and then I will tell you my thoughts very freely and sincerely.[2]

A week later her Majesty replied to Marlborough's restrained acknowledgment of her gracious congratulations. Her bitterness against the Whigs and fears of their encroachments were unallayed, and this time it must be admitted she had good cause. The Junto, who saw that in the winter Parliament they would be able to carry any fair-seeming project through both Houses, were determined to assert their rights. Incensed by the Queen's scornful hostility, they devised a new plan to make her yield. The reader will remember how in 1705 the Tories had, with grotesque folly, sought to vex the Queen by proposing to invite the Elector of Hanover or the Electress Sophia, or both, to England; and how serviceable the Whigs had made themselves in burking this manœuvre by their Regency Bill.[3] Now it was the Whigs who had recourse to this envenomed weapon with which to prod and prick their estranged Sovereign. Both their position and their case seemed overwhelming. They had the majorities; the Tories were compromised upon the point; and what could be more natural than that the young Electoral Prince, fresh from his gallant charge at Oudenarde, should pay a visit to London and receive the hearty acclamations of his future subjects?

[1] The Queen's italics.   [2] Coxe, iv, 184.   P. 35.

The proposal struck the Queen far more deeply than the Whigs or almost any of her contemporaries were aware. We must remember her letter to her dying father, James II, before she assumed the crown, and the reply of Mary of Modena.[1] Anne had compromised with her conscience on the grounds that her duty to the Church of England compelled her to ascend the throne, lest chaos engulfed both Church and State.

Thus she had reigned, praying always for a son who would assure her of the blessing of heaven and prolong her line. But this hope was now extinct. Her husband was seriously ill with an affection of the chest which grew as the summer passed; and she herself knew she could hardly expect another pregnancy. Henceforward increasingly, the Act of Settlement notwithstanding, the Queen found comfort in the dream that her brother would succeed her. Bound as she was hand and foot by the laws, the Parliament, and the nation, she might not attempt to aid such restoration. Sarah, with her Whig prejudices and rough common sense, did not attach sufficient importance to this mood. But Godolphin and Marlborough knew and understood. They were vigilant and picked their steps with care. Indeed, this sentiment—it was no more than a sentiment—was a secret bond which still united them to the Queen. They knew that Anne would never tolerate the presence of any representative of the house of Hanover in the island while she drew breath. The Whigs, without realizing how sensitive was the spot upon which they directed their thrust, had nevertheless a pretty plain notion that this was a deadly and at the same time a practical method of pressure or revenge.

Accordingly it had been put about, and whispered to the Queen by Abigail, that Marlborough liked the idea of bringing the young Electoral Prince back to England after the campaign.[2] When this rumour gained some currency the Whig Lords exposed what they designed when Parliament met. They made through Sunderland, and perhaps through Sarah, every promise of active support for Marlborough, for Godolphin, and for the war, if only Marlborough

[1] Vol. II, p. 506.

[2] "All the letters from Hanover say positively the Elector Prince is to make the campaign under the Duke of Marlborough, though our prints do not mention it, and I think it may be observed that our news writers are more cautious what they say in relation to that family than on any other subject. I am further told that the Duke will next winter bring him or his grandmother over hither, in such a manner that they shall have the obligation neither to Whigs or Tories, but entirely to himself and Lord Treasurer; whether they will think fit to communicate it to the Queen I cannot tell."— E. Lewis to Harley, May 22, 1708; Portland Papers, *H.M.C.*, iv, 490.

would join with them in this push. Lord Haversham in the Tory interest waited upon the Queen and exposed the intrigue. Anne now wrote again to Marlborough a letter which certainly did not shirk the issue.

The Queen to Marlborough

WINDSOR
July 22/August 2, 1708

For tho' you say you will serve me as general, but not as a Minister, I shall always look upon you as both, and never separate those two characters, but ask your advice in both capacities on all occasions. You seem to waive giving any answer to these two letters I have mentioned, and, after answering my sincere congratulations on your last glorious success, you tell me you think I am obliged in good conscience as a good Christian to forgive and forget all resentments I may have to any particular person or party. I thank God I do forgive all my enemies with all my heart, but it is wholly impossible in human nature to forget people's behaviour in things so fresh in one's memory so far as to have a good opinion of them, especially when one sees for all their professions they are still pursuing the same measures, and you may depend upon it they will always do so, *for there is no washing a Blackamoor white.* I am truly sensible and thankful for God Almighty's Great Goodness showered on your head and mine, and hope He will give me grace never to make an ill use of his Signal Blessings, but I can never be convinced that Christianity requires me, nor that it can be for my service to put myself entirely into the hands of any one party.[1]

She then described how Lord Haversham had warned her of the Whig plan.

What I have to say upon this subject, at this time, is to beg you would find whether there is any design where you are, that the young man should make a visit in the winter; and contrive some way to put such thought out of his head, that the difficulty may not be brought upon me of refusing him leave to come, if he should ask it, or forbidding him to come, if he should attempt it; for one of these two things I must do, if either he or his father should have any desires to have him see this country, it being a thing I cannot bear, to have any successor here, though but for a week.[2]

We have no record of any reply of Marlborough's to the Queen upon this issue. But it is certain that he refused to give the Whigs the slightest countenance upon it. He had never favoured the visit of the Electoral Prince; indeed, he had expressed surprise that his

---

[1] Marlborough Papers, *H.M.C.*, p. 42.   [2] Coxe, iv, 194–195.

father, the Elector, should wish him to serve with the main army in Flanders instead of on the Rhine. He explained himself clearly to Sarah.

John to Sarah

[Some time in July]

. . . In the first place, you may depend upon my joining with the Whigs, in opposition to the Tories, in all things; but as to the invitation, or what else may be personal to the Queen, in regard to myself, as well as concern for her, I must never do any thing that looks like flying in her face. But as to everything else, I shall always be ready to join with the Whigs, in opposition to the Tories, for whom I shall have no reserve. . . . I must be master of my own actions, which may concern the Queen personally . . . You judge very right of the Queen, that nothing will go so near her heart as that of the invitation. I think the project very dangerous; I wish the Whigs would think well of it, but I am at too great a distance to be advising. . . .[1]

Marlborough wrote (August 2) in the form of a grave protest and warning a general reply to the Queen's letters both before and after the battle.

He complained of his treatment at her hands. "The uneasiness of my mind, upon receiving your Majesty's letters of the 18th and 22nd of June, had such an effect upon my body as to make me very ill, till it pleased God to bless me with such good success, as in great measure recovered me."[2]

He reproached her about Sunderland.

Though he may have done what your Majesty does not like, I did flatter myself nobody could have prevailed with you, to carry your resentment so far against him in my absence as is mentioned in your letters, and to give me so great a mortification in the face of all Europe, at a time when I was so zealously endeavouring to serve you at the hazard both of my reputation and of my blood.

. . . For God's sake, madam, consider that, whatever may be said to amuse or delude you, it is utterly impossible for you ever to have more than a part of the Tories; and though you could have them all, their number is not capable of doing you good. These things are so plain that I can't doubt but your Majesty will be convinced nothing can be so fatal to your service as any way to discourage the Whigs at this time, when after the blessing of this victory you may be sure that if you show a confidence in their zeal for your interests, they will all concur very cheerfully to make you great and happy, as I wish. God Almighty bless and preserve you.

[1] Coxe, iv, 196–197.   [2] *Ibid.*, 186.

He then explained and justified in a very plain manner the phrase that had ruffled the Queen.

Your Majesty might see by the shortness of the letter that was shown you that I was in great haste when I writ it, and my fulness of heart for your service made me use that expression. What I then meant, as I must always think, is that you can make no good use of this victory, nor of any other blessing, but by following the advice of my Lord Treasurer, who has been so long faithful to you; for any other advisers do but lead you into a labyrinth, to play their own game at your expense. Nothing but your commands should have obliged me to say so much, having taken my resolution to suffer with you, but not to advise, being sensible that if there was not something very extra-ordinary, your Majesty would follow the advice of those that have served you so long, faithfully, and with success.[1]

To Sarah he wrote (August 6):

. . . The account you give me of the commerce and kindness of the Queen to Mrs Masham is that which will at last bring all things to ruin; for by all you write I see the Queen is determined to support, and, I believe, at last own her. I am of the opinion I ever was of, that the Queen will not be made sensible, or frightened out of this passion; but I can't but think some ways might be found to make Mrs Masham very much afraid. The discovery you have made of the Queen's having the opinion that she has friends which will support her can be no other than the Tories; and it is true they would ruin Lord Treasurer and me, and will be able to bring it about, if it can be thought ruin to be put in the condition of quietness, which of all things I wish for. . . . The temper of England is such that nobody in any great station can be liked; for if they are lucky, they do not make use enough of their advantage; if unfortunate, they run the risk of being called fools and traitors. . . .[2]

Nothing moved the Queen. She defended herself obdurately from the suggestion that she had other advisers than her Ministers. She was conscious that she could hardly expect Marlborough to believe her. But she made no concession.

The Queen to Marlborough

[Undated]

I received yours of the 2/13th of this month on Saturday last, which was in answer to three of mine. I am very sorry to find you persist in your resolution of not advising me concerning my home affairs; but I would beg your pardon for disobeying your commands in that

[1] Coxe, iv, 187–188.   [2] Ibid., 191–193.

particular, it being impossible for me, who have on all occasions spoke and writ my mind very freely, as I think every friend ought to do to one another, to forbear doing the same still, and asking your opinion in everything; there being nobody but you and Lord Treasurer that I do advise with, nor can rely on, which I will yet hope you will believe, since I tell you so, you having more than once or twice assured me you would credit what I said. Though I must confess, by what I am told every day of my being influenced by Mr Harley, through a relation of his, and your saying you are sensible that if there were not something very extraordinary, I should follow the advice of Lord Treasurer and you, I fear you have not a thorough good opinion of me, and if that be so, it is in vain for me to say anything. However, I can't help asking why my not complying with some things that are desired, and which you know I have ever been against, should be imputed to something extraordinary? Is not one body of one opinion, and *one of another*?[1] and why then should it be wonderful that you and I should differ in some things, as well as other people, especially since my thoughts are the same of the Whigs that ever they were from the time that ever I have been capable of having notions of things and people; and I must own I can see no reason to alter mine.[2]

This response to his remonstrance made the worst impression upon Marlborough. It "has thoroughly convinced me," he wrote to Sarah (August 9), using with asperity one of the Queen's phrases,

that there is no washing a blackamoor white, and that we must expect this winter all the disagreeableness imaginable; for the Tories have got the heart and entire possession of the Queen, which they will be able to maintain as long as Mrs Masham has credit.

But he added loyally:

I do earnestly beg, when Mr Montgomery has read Mrs Morley's letter and this of mine to you, that they may both be torn to pieces, so that they may never hurt Mrs Morley, whom I can't but love, and endeavour to serve, as long as I have life; for I know this is not her fault, otherwise than by being too fond of Mrs Masham, who imposes upon her.[3]

John to Sarah

August [9]/20

. . . I am doing my best to serve England and the Queen, and, with all my heart and soul, I pray for God's protection and blessing; but I am so tired of what I hear, and what I think must happen in England, that I am every day confirmed that I should be wanting to myself, and ungrateful to God Almighty, if I did not take the first

[1] The Queen's italics.   [2] Coxe, iv. 189–190.   [3] *Ibid.*, 193–194.

occasion that can be practicable to retire from business. And as I have for several years served my Queen and country with all my heart, so I should be glad to have some time to recollect and be grateful for the many mercies I have received from the hand of God. I would not live like a monk, but I can't with patience think of continuing much longer in business, having it not in my power to persuade that to be done, which I think is right. I foresee the difficulty of retiring during the war, which is my greatest trouble at this time; but even that difficulty must be overcome, if I must be in some manner answerable for the notions of the Queen, who is in no ways governed by anything I can say or do. God knows who it is that influences; but as I love her and my country, I dread the consequences. . . .[1]

Queen Anne had received the news of Oudenarde in the little house she had occupied at Windsor to nurse her poor prince. Her instinctive comment reveals her mood to the depths: "Oh, Lord, when will all this dreadful bloodshed cease?"[2] But now it was the day of thanksgiving for the victory. The Queen left her ailing husband's couch, and journeyed to St James's to be robed for her progress to St Paul's. It was Sarah's duty to lay out the jewels she was to wear. We may be sure that the Duchess, full of politics, full of the victory, discharged her duty punctiliously. She, the wife of the victor-general, her idolized "Lord Marl," would drive by the Queen's side through the cheering crowds to St Paul's Cathedral, and receive on her husband's behalf a British triumph. Suddenly she perceived that the Queen was not wearing the jewels her Mistress of the Robes had selected, or, according to some authorities, any jewels at all. Instantly Sarah saw the hand of the hated Abigail. It was not only feminine anger which stirred her. Sarah was also a politician. She knew well that these jewels, or no jewels, would be the talk of every Court in Europe. All the ambassadors who now crowded in the greatest state upon the once-neglected Court of St James's would write that night the story of Marlborough's failing favour. For weeks thereafter statesmen, diplomats, commanders, princes, would shake their heads or grin upon it.

As they rode along through the joyful streets she reproached the Queen for wounding her upon Lord Marlborough's festival. No one knows what the two women said to one another in the coach. They had more than thirty years of intimacy, most of it joyous intimacy, behind them. But Anne was Queen, and extremely capable of making her will felt. Probably very few interchanges

[1] Coxe, iv, 200. [2] N. Tindal, *Continuation of Rapin's History*, iv, 104.

passed between them. But at the top of the steps of St Paul's, at the entry where all the functionaries were arrayed, the Queen began to speak with warmth, and Sarah said, "Be quiet—not here," or words to that effect. The courtiers and dignitaries gaped and stared, and Queen Anne and the Duchess of Marlborough proceeded to offer their thanks to Almighty God for having blessed the arms of Britain with the timely and glorious victory of Oudenarde.

It may well be that not one word was spoken by either the Queen or Sarah on the return journey from this somewhat grim celebration. An adherent of Harley's wrote to him:

> The solemnity of the day has been performed with a great deal of decency, but I cannot say with any visible marks of real joy and satisfaction. There were very few people in the windows and balconies, and it was to be read in everybody's countenance that they looked upon the giving of thanks for a victory at Oudenarde to be a mocking of God. However, the men in office acted their parts, and put on their wedding garments.[1]

This is a jaundiced account. But we must remember that it was the seventh year of the war, and that in twenty years there had only been three years of peace.

Sarah, upon the return to St James's, was conscious that something had happened. Evidently she thought the best course was to pass it off by going on with the interrupted argument. A day or two later she wrote:

> I cannot help sending your Majesty this letter,[2] to show how exactly Lord Marlborough agrees with me in my opinion, that he has now no interest with you: though when I said so in church on Thursday, you were pleased to say it was untrue. And yet I think he will be surprised to hear that when I had taken so much pains to put your jewels in a way that I thought you would like, Mrs Masham could make you refuse to wear them in so unkind a manner, because that was a power she had not thought fit to exercise before. I will make no reflections upon it; only that I must needs observe that your Majesty chose a very wrong day to mortify me, when you were just going to return thanks for a victory obtained by Lord Marlborough.[3]

Anne's reply was freezing:

Sunday [August 22/September 2, 1708]

After the commands you gave me in the church, on the thanksgiving, of not answering you, I should not have troubled you with

---

[1] E. Lewis to Robert Harley, August 19, 1708; Portland Papers, *H.M.C.*, iv, 501.
[2] Printed at p. 416.   [3] *Conduct*, pp. 260–261.

these lines, but to return the Duke of Marlborough's letter safe into your hands, and for the same reason do not say anything to that, nor to yours which enclosed it.[1]

Sarah was not disposed to relinquish her right, so long enjoyed, of free discussion with the Queen. Her answer yielded nothing, and does her no discredit. It was also utterly futile for any purpose she sought to serve.

Sarah to the Queen

[Undated]

I should not trouble your Majesty with any answer to your last short letter, but to explain what you seem to mistake in what I said at church. I desired you not to answer me there for fear of being overheard: and this you interpret as if I had desired you not to answer me at all; which was far from my intention. . . . I should be much better pleased to say and do everything you like. But I should think myself wanting in my duty to you if I saw you so much in the wrong as, without prejudice or passion, I really think you are in several particulars I have mentioned, and did not tell you of it. And the rather because nobody else cares to speak out upon so ungrateful a subject. The word *command*, which you use at the beginning of your letter, is very unfitly supposed to come from me. For though I have always writ to you as a friend, and lived with you as such for so many years with all the truth and honesty and zeal for your service that was possible, yet I shall never forget that I am your subject, nor cease to be a faithful one.[2]

Her sincerity and a certain broad justice in her complaint drew from Anne a further reply:

Tuesday evening

. . . I shall only just touch upon two things, the first as to what you say that it shows plainly by what the Duke of Marlborough says in the end of your letter he thinks he has not much credit with me; to this I answer I am of opinion, and so I believe all impartial people must be, that I have all my life given demonstration to the world he has a great deal of credit with me. The other is to beg you would not mention that person any more who you are pleased to call the object of my favour, for whatever character the malicious world may give her, I do assure you it will never have any weight with me, knowing she does not deserve it, nor I can never change the good impressions you once gave me of her, unless she should give me a cause, which I am very sure she never will. I have nothing further to trouble my dear Mrs Freeman with at this time, but that whatever

---

[1] *Conduct*, p. 262. [2] *Ibid.*, pp. 262–263.

opinion she may have of me, I will never deserve any that is ill, but will always be her faithful Morley.[1]

Some may think that even at this hour Sarah could have saved some way of living with the Queen in decorum and even amity. She would have had to drop politics, smile upon Abigail, and discharge her Court duties with kindly, cool detachment. She could never have done it. The best and the worst of her was her candour and blunt common sense. Anne, apart from her sovereign authority, had immense powers of reserve and dissimulation. Sarah resembled in some respects the kind of woman we are familiar with in the public and social agitations of our own day. But no personal accommodation could alter the antagonism. Behind the Queen lurked Harley, the Tories, and Peace. Behind Sarah stood Marlborough, the Whigs, the Grand Alliance, and the War; and against them all, still magnificent and seemingly inexhaustible—France.

John to Sarah

August [12]/23

You say Mrs Morley has taken no notice of your letter. I think that is a true sign she is angry. There being three or four posts come from England since she has received Mr Freeman's last letter, I take it for granted the same method will be taken of giving no answer. I am in no ways dissatisfied at that manner of proceeding, for till the Queen changes her humour and resolutions, the less the conversations are the better. . . . I should never trouble the Queen with any of my letters, but that I can't refuse Lord Treasurer and you, when you desire anything of me.

Marlborough had at this time in fact become almost indifferent to the political scene. In the next chapter we shall see what he was facing in the field.

I am sure that the interest of Mrs Masham is so settled with the Queen that we only trouble ourselves to no purpose; and by endeavouring to hurt, we do good offices to her; so that in my opinion we ought to be careful of our own actions, and not lay everything to heart, but submit to whatever may happen.[2]

This continued to be his sage opinion. "I am glad," he reiterated to Sarah (September 17), "that you have taken the resolution of being quiet; for you are certainly in the right, that whatever is said or writ by you, the Lord Treasurer, and me, serves only for information to do hurt."[3] And (October 1), "For the resolution you have

[1] Marlborough Papers, *H.M.C.*, p. 52.   [2] Coxe, iv, 201–202.   [3] *Ibid.*, 212.

taken of neither speaking nor writing is so certainly right that I dare assure you that you will find a good effect of it in one month."[1]

Neither the Queen, nor Harley in the background, was prepared at this moment of all others to face the consequences of Marlborough's or even Godolphin's resignation. The country was still ringing with the Whig triumph at the polls. The new Parliament, in which the Whigs must be supreme, was to meet in a few months. What madness to provoke a constitutional crisis! Marlborough, however treated by the Tories, would defend the Queen's throne against the Whigs and all comers. But Harley could feel no such assurance that the same defence would be forthcoming for his interests or even his head. Patience! Accordingly Anne appealed vehemently to Marlborough not to resign.

The Queen to Marlborough

[Undated, but endorsed by the Duchess August 27]

I am sorry to find you in such a splenetic way as to talk of retiring it being a thing I can never consent to, and what your country, nor your truly faithful friends can never think right, whatever melancholy thoughts they may have all this time. Besides, in my poor opinion, when after all the glorious successes God Almighty has blessed you with He is pleased to make you the happy instrument of giving a lasting peace to Europe, you are bound in conscience, both to God and man, to lend your helping hand; and how can you do that if you retire from business? You may be as grateful to God Almighty in a public station as in a private one; but I do not wonder at your desiring quiet, after all the fatigues and vexations you go through daily; for it is certainly the most valuable blessing in this world, and what every one would choose, I believe, that has ever had anything to do in business, if there were nothing to be considered but one's self.

Lord Treasurer talks of retiring too, and told me, not many days ago, he would do all he could to serve me, by advising with people, and settling a scheme for the carrying on my business in the Parliament, before he went to Newmarket; but that he would not come back from thence. I told him that must not be, that he could not answer it either to God or himself; and I hope you will both consider better of it, and not do an action that will bring me and your country into confusion. Is there no consideration to be had for either? You may flatter yourselves that people will approve of your quitting; but if you should persist in these cruel and unjust resolutions, believe me, where one will say you are in the right, hundreds will blame you.

She proceeded to restate her own position. The Whigs, she

[1] Coxe, iv, 213.

421

declared, were "disputing her authority, certainly designing," when the new Parliament meet, "to tear that little prerogative the Crown has to pieces," and "have none in any employment that does not entirely depend upon them." "Now, how is it possible," demanded the Queen, closing her eyes to Parliamentary majorities, "when one knows and sees all these things, as plainly as the sun at noonday, ever to take these people into my bosom?"

> For God's sake [her letter ran], do but make it your own case, and consider then what you would do, and why a handful of men must awe their fellow-subjects. There is nobody more desirous than I to encourage those Whig friends that behave themselves well; but I do not care to have anything to do with those that have shown themselves to be of so tyrannizing a temper; and not to run on farther on those subjects, to be short, I think things are come to, whether I shall submit to the five tyrannizing lords or they to me. This is my poor opinion on the disputes at present, which could not be, if people would weigh and state the case just as it is, without partiality on one side or the other, which I beg, for the friendship you have ever professed for me, you would do; and let me know your thoughts of what may be the best expedient, to keep me from being thrown into the hands of the five lords.[1]

But what possibility was there of denying office to a great party, newly placed by the constituencies in control of both Houses of Parliament? To do so was to strain the Constitution, even as then interpreted. Nor would another Dissolution have been effective. It would have been a violent abuse of the Prerogative; and there was no reason to suppose a different answer would be given by the electors.

Marlborough's reply could not therefore offer the slightest prospect of any agreement with the Queen. On the contrary, he seems to have been at pain to set the differences forth in terms as blunt and hard as any which an English sovereign ever received from a loyal servant.

Marlborough to the Queen

[Undated 1708]

As to the reflections your Majesty is pleased to make upon my real inclinations to retire, tho' it be very natural and very desirable, after one has lived a great many years in a hurry, to enjoy some quiet in one's old age; yet I will own freely to your Majesty, my inclinations to retire proceed chiefly from finding myself incapable of being of any

[1] Coxe, iv, 202–205.

further use to your Majesty. The long and faithful services I have endeavoured to perform to your Majesty, and the goodness you had expressed to me upon several occasions, had created a general opinion, both abroad and at home, that your Majesty placed entire trust and confidence in me; and upon that foot I was the more capable of doing many great and effectual services, both here abroad and in England. But your Majesty will give me leave to say, with all imaginable duty, that is now reduced singly to serving you at the head of the army this campaign; for your Majesty, having shown so publicly last winter and this spring that you have no more trust and confidence in me, nor any reliance upon my opinion, but much more upon the opinion of those who have neither honesty nor capacity to serve you, and who visibly ruined your service last winter in several undeniable instances, it is no longer possible for me to be of any further use to you; and to continue in your council to advise, without credit enough to prevail with you to follow good advice, would only expose myself and my reputation in the world, by making myself answerable for other people's follies, or worse.

And by what your Majesty is pleased to say in your letter of the Lord Treasurer, tho' I have nothing so far as that from himself, I believe his opinion, and his reasons for that opinion, must be the same with mine. Your Majesty is pleased to think we shall be blamed for quitting; but, not to reflect upon that coldness, and that behaviour in yourself which forces us to quit, by withdrawing your trust and confidence from us, to give it to insinuating, busy flatterers, who can't serve you one month this winter *without danger of being torn in pieces in the streets.* I don't doubt but these things are very sensible to the Lord Treasurer, as I am sure they are to me. However, I shall not trouble your Majesty any farther with the consequences that must follow, since I find plainly by your Majesty's letter that all I have said and written hitherto is to no purpose, nor, indeed, ever can be, while your Majesty's heart is possessed by all the false and malicious insinuations which are possible to be suggested by our enemies; and therefore I shall conclude this head with wishing your Majesty may find abler servants than we have been; more faithful and affectionate, I will beg leave to say, you never can.[1]

Such was the melancholy and dissolving background at home upon which Marlborough had to conduct the greatest siege of the eighteenth century while surrounded by superior French armies. It is only by surveying the double set of pressures and cares weighing upon him that his fortitude of spirit and tenacity of purpose can be judged.

[1] Coxe, iv, 205–208.

Chapter Twenty-five

THE SIEGE OF LILLE

1708 — AUGUST–SEPTEMBER

AFTER Paris Lille, the capital of French Flanders, was the greatest city of France. It was almost the earliest, and certainly the most splendid fruit of Louis XIV's lifelong aggressions. For forty years it had been the monument of his military fame. It was also the staple of all the trade between the Netherlands and France. Its wealthy merchants financed and profited by the privateering from Dunkirk. Its name, Lisle, sprang from its secure position amid the pools and swamps of the Deule. Since the most ancient times it had been a stronghold and refuge. All the art of Vauban, unhurried by time, unstinted in expense, had been devoted to the fortifications. Broad double moats filled with water, massive masonry of covered ways and galleries, surmounted by enormous earthworks armed with heavy cannon, and an intricate system of outer defences made the town itself as strong as a citadel. But, besides the fortifications of the town, a large and wholly independent pentagon-shaped fortress afforded the garrison the means of standing what was virtually a second siege. These defences would have been formidable in the last degree if manned only by six or seven thousand troops. But Berwick, with the King's cordial agreement, concentrated a miniature army of fifteen thousand men within them, including twenty-one battalions; and Marshal Boufflers, Marlborough's old adversary of Maestricht days, had claimed the honour of commanding the resistance. It was evident that Lille would be the greatest siege operation since the invention of gunpowder. All Europe watched with wonder what seemed to those times a prodigy of human effort. That it should be undertaken by armies inferior in numbers to the French forces actually in the field, whose water communications were cut by fortresses in their rear, whose road communications seemed to lie at the mercy of Vendôme and Berwick, constituted an act of temerity only possible when allied to the authority and fame of Marlborough and Eugene. Vendôme, among his many miscalculations of 1708, declared that "so wise a commander as Prince Eugene would not venture upon such an enterprise," and the French Court boasted that "without striking a blow they would oblige the Allies to abandon the siege."

All these facts are cited by historians to extol the indomitable firmness of the Allies in choosing such a trial of strength. They were, indeed, the very reasons which had made Marlborough earnest to find some other course. Compared with the perils of the siege of Lille and the limited objects obtainable by its capture, the hazards of a new sea-base and of a march to Paris seemed attractive. Thus in our own time we have seen the minds of men and all resources absorbed by the great offensives on the Western Front which were driven forward on both sides regardless of bloodshed or any other exhaustion of war-power, while the dangerous prudence of conventional opinion prevented unexpected and so-called eccentric alternatives. Nevertheless, Marlborough, anticipating Lord Kitchener's dictum, "One cannot wage war as one ought, but only as one can," addressed himself with zeal and confidence to the inevitable step. He was glad to welcome in his camp as spectators and volunteers King Augustus of Saxony and the Landgrave of Hesse-Cassel. Marlborough entertained—we trust not too parsimoniously—King Augustus at his quarters, and no doubt his silver plate and the massive wine-coolers were displayed at several unavoidable feasts. The Landgrave of Hesse-Cassel lived with his son, who was one of Marlborough's most active generals.

Marlborough to Godolphin

HELCHIN
August 13

You will know by this post that our cannon is arrived safely at Menin, and that I have reinforced Prince Eugene's army with thirty-one battalions and thirty-four squadrons. That, with the detachments we have made for Flanders and Brussels, makes this army to consist only of 140 squadrons and sixty-nine battalions, with which I am to observe the motions of the Duke of Burgundy's army. That of Prince Eugene is for the siege, and observation of the Duke of Berwick. Prince Eugene's army consists of ninety squadrons and fifty-three battalions, by which you will see that when we join, which I believe we shall do, the whole will be 230 squadrons and 122 battalions. This day Lille is invested; I pray God to bless the undertaking. What I most fear is the want of powder and ball for so great an undertaking, for our engineers fear we must take the town before we can attack the citadel.[1]

[1] Coxe, iv, 222.

John to Sarah

. . . The siege of Lille, which was begun on Monday last, is of that consequence to France that I nowise doubt of their drawing all the troops that is in their power together, to give us what disturbance they can. I pray God to bless this undertaking, and all others that may tend to the bringing of us to a safe and lasting peace, and then I will not put the visit of Lord Haversham to Abigail much to heart. . . .

But I think we are now acting for the liberties of all Europe, so that, . . . tho' I love the Queen with all my heart, I can't think of the business of England till this great affair is decided, which I think must be by another battle; for I am resolved to risk rather than suffer Brussels to be taken, tho' the number of this army is very much diminished by the siege. But I rely on the justness of our cause, and that God will not forsake us, and that He will continue to keep our troops in good heart, as they are at present. I beg you to be so kind and just as to be assured that my kindness for you is such that my greatest ambition is bounded in that of ending my days quietly with you.[1]

The Great King was vehemently stirred by the siege of Lille. Like Vendôme, he had not believed it would be begun. He was resolved that it should be prevented. He ordered that Marshal, and, of course, Burgundy, not to hesitate to fight a decisive battle to relieve the city. Weariness of war lay heavy upon this old monarch. For more than forty years he had been the scourge of Europe. But war had lost its glamour with its laurels. One final, supreme battle to rescue Lille or lose the war; and then peace—peace now become dear and precious even on the worst terms. Such was his mood. But the French army and its generals, with the doubtful exception of Vendôme, whose conduct we shall examine later, did not find it so easy to court such dire decisions. They still felt the mauling of Oudenarde. Marlborough judged the facts with perfect accuracy. The siege was a grave hazard and might fail, thus spoiling the campaign, but that the enemy would fight a decisive battle for its relief was too good to be true. Only one movement would force a decisive battle—the march on Paris. That the army he commanded would win any pitched battle he was sure; but he did not think it probable that any decisive result would be reached in the field in 1708.

[1] Coxe, iv, 198-199.

John to Sarah

*I have had none of Yours since my last, so that I have no answere to any of Yours which will make my letter the shorter. Our canon being arriv'd in safety we are devid'd in two Armes, that of Pr. Eugene is to invest Lisle this day, I am to observe as well as I can the motions of the Duke of Vandoms Army. If his designe shou'd be on Bruxelles, he has it in his power of being there 2 days before me, but we having ten Redgts in it, if he has not intelligence in the place, I hope to come time enough for the relief of it; but the truth is that 116 [the Dutch] has been so very insolent, that we have generally the people against us, which att this time creates great difficultys. I cou'd strugle with all this knowing as I think the worst of itt, but that which gives me the greatest concern is, the prospect we have in 108 [England] for by the enclos'd letter I sent you by the last post, it appeares plainly to me that 239 [the Queen] is determined to do everything that will hurt themselves, which will have the consequences of hurting everybody, and everything; I have this evening Yours of the 27th and thank you for the Verses which I think very good; I shou'd have been glad to have known the auther.

He added a comic touch. "I have read in a news paper that the Queen had given mr. Harley myself and severall others our Plate, I suppose it is not treu since you do not mention itt."[1] Actually Harley had been called upon by the Attorney-General to restore the plate furnished him for his official use during his tenure as Secretary of State. He had made difficulty about this, alleging his poverty; and the Queen was disposed to make him a gift of it. But the question arose, Should this principle be applied to other office-holders? Marlborough, at grips with the Queen, and in all the stresses of the campaign, was at once attentive to this. Anything in the nature of a perquisite stirred him, and gave him real pleasure even in his most magnificent exertions, and under his most wearing ordeals.

Marlborough to Godolphin

By the threatening of M. de Vendôme I did not think we should have continued thus long in this camp; but as yet he is not marched from behind the canal. But the Duke of Berwick is drawing to his army, with all the troops he can, from their several towns. M. de Vendôme declares in his army that he has *carte blanche*, and that he will

---

[1] Blenheim MSS.

attempt the relief of Lille; that when the Duke of Berwick joins him, they shall then have 135 battalions and 260 squadrons, which he flatters himself will be much stronger than we can be. If we have a second action, and God blesses our just cause, this, in all likelihood, will be the last campaign; for I think they would not venture a battle, but that they are resolved to submit to any condition, if the success be on our side. . . . If God continues on our side, we have nothing to fear, our troops being good, though not so numerous as theirs. I dare say, before half the troops have fought, the success will declare, I hope in God on our side, and then I may have, what I earnestly wish for, quiet; and you may be much more at ease than when you writ yours of the 31st of the last month, which I received yesterday.[1]

The story of the siege is set out fully with many striking anecdotes by Lediard, to whom full reference should be made. The attack was delivered from the north. Prince Eugene commanded the fifty battalions, of whom ten were always in the trenches, which were assigned to the task. Of these thirty were provided from Marlborough's army. Lines of circumvallation were drawn, and the work of mounting the batteries began. The youthful Prince of Orange, who commanded the sector of assault, fixed his headquarters in close shot of the Lille artillery. His house was pierced by several cannon-balls, and when on the morning of the 18th he was being dressed for his duties a round shot, passing over his shoulder, smashed his valet's head and "besmeared his clothes and face with blood and brains." He was thereupon persuaded to find a safer abode. As it was known that not only the ramparts but the town was to be bombarded, a large number of ladies sought permission to leave the dangerous area. Prince Eugene chivalrously accorded them facilities; but his engineer officers, disguised as common soldiers among the troops who received them, were able to study the approach to the St Mark and St Magdalen gates, which were the selected points of attack. Two immense hornworks protected these entrances, and were the main defences of the northern side.

The magistrates of Lille, by Boufflers' leave, sent a deputation "with compliments and refreshments" to Prince Eugene, appealing to him to spare the burghers as much as possible. But he answered

that a besieged town ought to be kept very close; so that he could not yet admit of their civilities; but when he should be master of the place, the burghers might be assured of his protection, provided he should

[1] Coxe, iv, 223.

be satisfied that they had endeavoured to deserve it, by their impartial carriage during the siege.[1]

So strong was the garrison that fierce fighting developed upon the approaches. The chapel of St Magdalen and the neighbouring mill were scenes of carnage. However, on the 21st the lines of contravallation and circumvallation were perfected. Thus Eugene and his besiegers dwelt in a double ring of earthworks several hundred yards apart and nine miles in length, facing outward and inward around the city, and Marlborough with the field army protected them from interference. Trenches were opened on the 22nd, and five days later the heavy batteries began to play with eighty-eight pieces. The object of this process in a siege was to shatter the masonry and crumble the earthworks, so that as they fell in ruins they filled up the moats, and made a breach in which hand-to-hand fighting proceeded till the moment of assault was ripe. The large cannon-balls of those days and primitive shells from the mortars, after a certain number of days of firing, which could usually be accurately estimated, were capable of producing such a result. But all depended upon the powder and ball. By the early days of September deserters reported that the breach was very wide, that the ditch was almost full with the ruins of the wall, and that Marshal Boufflers had ordered a good part of his best cannon to be withdrawn from the ramparts into the citadel. The assault of the counterscarp was accordingly fixed for the 7th. But now the French grand army, united with that of Marshal Berwick, arrived upon the scene.

John to Sarah

CAMP AT AMOUGIES
August 27, 1708

★I begin to write to my dear soull early this morning beleiving I may be oblig'd to march, so that I shou'd not have time in this afternoon; for if the intelligence I receiv'd an hour ago that the Duke of Vandomes Army as well as that of the Duke of Berwick were on their march to join be true, I must march. Our canon began this morning to fyre at Lisle, so that in ten days we hope to have the town, and after that we must attack the citadel, which we think will give us full as much trouble. My hopes are that God will bless us, in this undertaking which will very much forward my being at quiet with You, especially if we have another success against the Duke of Burgundy who has the King of ffrance's possitive orders to ventur every thing rather then suffer Lisle to be taken.

[1] Lediard, ii, 308.

We have for these last ten days had extreame hott weather, which I hope may give You good peaches att Woodstock, wher I shou'd be better pleas'd to eat even the worst that were ever tasted, then the good ons we have here, for every day of my life I grow more impatient for quiet; having write thus farr I have notice that Monsr de Vandome has begone his march, in order to camp this night at Gavre, which is not above one league and a half from Gand, so that I shall not march til to morrow, when I shall be more certainly inform'd of his intentions. I intend to stop the post til then, so that if there be any thing new, I may writt itt.

By the slow motions of Monsr de Vandome it lookes as if he resolv'd not to march to join the Duke of Berwick, but to make that Duke march his Army to Gramont where thay will then join.[1]

This is exactly what they did.

Marlborough to Godolphin

. . . When we are once masters of the town, we shall have no occasion for so great a circumvallation, by which the army will be much stronger; so that if the enemy will venture, it must be before we take the town. Our troops are in good heart, and their foot in a bad condition. They are, in horse, stronger than we, but upon the whole I cannot think they will venture a battle, though it is said they have positive orders to succour the place. . . .

As I am now posted, it is impossible for him to get between me and the siege; and I have taken such measures with Prince Eugene, for the strengthening each other, that I no ways doubt of preventing anything they may flatter themselves with. . . .

As to point of time, it is equal to us whether the Duke of Vendôme marches by Mons, or obliges the Duke of Berwick to make the tour of Brabant. One day will inform us of his resolutions. . . .[2]

In a letter to reassure Sarah he forecasted with perfect comprehension the future action of the enemy. His power of putting himself in the enemy's shoes, and measuring truly what they ought to do, and what he himself would most dislike, was one of his greatest gifts. He was only wrong in his anticipations when the enemy made a mistake. But this also had compensations of its own.

PÉRONNE[3]
September 3, 1708

*I have receiv'd the pleasur of Your three letters of the 6. 7. and 13th with copies of those You write, and receiv'd from mrs Morley . . . I shall not answer mrs Morleys til I see the success of this siege,

---

[1] Blenheim MSS.   [2] Coxe, iv, 226–228.   [3] A village near Lille.

which goes much slower than were to be wish'd, when I came into this Campe last Saturday I imeditely went to Pr. Eugene, where I found the Siege at least six days backwarder then I was made to believe by my letters, so that mr. Crags[1] wagers in all likelywhode will be lost; Pr. Eugene dined with me yesterday, and we have mark'd a Camp, where we are resolved to receive the ffrench if thay will make their threats good; *the post we have chose I think to be so very much for our advantage, that I am confident You may be at ease, that the ffrench with the blessing of God will be beatten, which makes me think thay must be mad if thay ventur itt; I believe their greatest application will be the endeavouring to starve us*; thay having already in the King of ffrances name forbid on pain of death for any of his subjects to bring us any provisions, *this is the greatest hurt I think thay can do us, but I hope we shall be able to strugle with itt*; yours of the 17th I had last night, by which I find Your kindness makes You in pain for fear of a battaile. I hope this letter will make You easy, for I really think if thay do ventur a Battaile on the disadvantages thay must have, it is the will of God thay shou'd be beatten, for tho thay have more Redgments then wee, I think we have as many men. What ever happens, do me the justice to beleive, I am and ever will be tenderly. . . .[2]

After protracted discussions and long letters to and from the King, Burgundy and Berwick marched towards each other at the utmost speed on August 27. They joined, as Marlborough had forecast, at Grammont on the 29th, and reached the Scheldt at Tournai together on September 1. Berwick, who refused to serve under Vendôme, resigned his command, and became Burgundy's rival adviser. It was learned that Marlborough had left Helchin on the 31st and that he was moving on an inner circle between them and Lille, which, they heard, had been since the 27th under the heaviest bombardment by Eugene. They spent September 2 in crossing the Scheldt, camped at Orchies on the 3rd, and reached Mons-en-Pévêle during the 4th. Here they were joined by their heavy cannon from Douai. Burgundy and Vendôme climbed the heights behind the camp, and thence saw the allied army spread in a wide arc before them. Their best chance was to draw out their line astride of the Lille-Douai road, and begin the battle that very evening. Although all their troops had not come up, they had on the spot or close at hand nearly double Marlborough's strength. Berwick's account agrees with Vendôme's view that the hour was

---

[1] There were two Craggs, father and son. The former was secretary to the Ordnance Board at this time; the latter was Stanhope's able secretary and the newly appointed English Resident at Barcelona. The son is probably the one mentioned here.

[2] Blenheim MSS.

too late. It was, however, earlier than that on which Marlborough had stormed the Schellenberg. Thus night fell in silence. But all seemed set for battle on the 5th. The fate of Lille and of the campaign was at stake. The orders of the King to fight a decisive engagement were imperative and reiterated.

Marlborough's concentration was effected with precision. Before dawn on the 5th Eugene, with seventy-two squadrons and twenty-

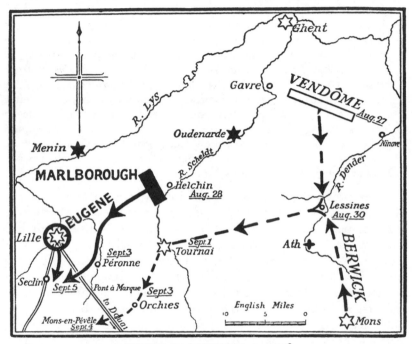

AUGUST 27–SEPTEMBER 5, 1708

six battalions, arrived from the siege and took his station on Marlborough's right. General Fagel, with seven battalions, by "incredible" marches from Dutch Brabant reached the battle front as the sun rose. The Captain-General drew out 209 squadrons and 109 battalions, between seventy and eighty thousand men, to face the combined French army of a hundred and ten thousand.

As this was the only occasion when Marlborough seemed prepared to fight a defensive battle on a large scale, his dispositions are of interest. The position he had selected permitted the French to attack only on a narrow front. He narrowed the gap further by strong infantry bodies on either flank supported by cavalry. In the gap he placed his cavalry in two lines, covered by guns and backed by infantry. To prevent the enemy's capturing Ennetières village on his front and so breaking the cohesion of his cavalry attack, and also to disrupt the French cavalry attack, he occupied it with a brigade of infantry. He clearly intended to disorganize

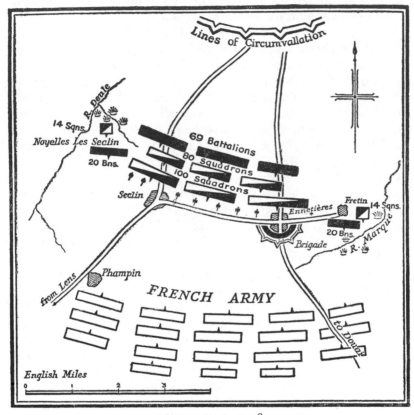

SEPTEMBER 5, 1708

the more numerous French cavalry by artillery fire, and then to charge them down-hill with cavalry supported by infantry, trusting to the training and morale of his cavalry as proved at Blenheim, Elixem, and Ramillies. The position he had selected was four miles outside the lines of circumvallation. He made no attempt to impede the approach and deployment of the enemy. In order to leave himself full freedom to counter-attack early in the action, he did not at first entrench. When Eugene proposed this Marlborough

433

answered that "since he had commanded he had never accustomed his army to entrench in the presence of the enemy." Eventually he allowed digging to begin at Ennetières; but he kept the whole of the rest of the field open to a gigantic manœuvre-battle once the enemy had committed themselves to the attack. Thus we may measure his confidence in his troops and in himself, and his readiness to risk all upon the stroke of the day.

A different mood held the French High Command. At daylight their chiefs began a prolonged reconnaissance. Vendôme wished to attack at once. Berwick pointed out the particular marshes and wood which would interfere with the advance. Burgundy decided that the approaches must be improved before the attack could be made. This work was accordingly begun, and it soon became apparent that there would be no general battle on the 5th. Boufflers, as prearranged, took advantage of Eugene's absence from the siege to make a vigorous sortie upon his denuded lines. We are told by several authorities[1] that as early as ten A.M. orders were issued to Eugene's troops to return to the siege. But this is absurd. Even the infantry did not move off the field till darkness fell; and the cavalry not till the next day.[2] Marlborough, although now only half the strength of the enemy, but with confidence confirmed by their indecision, was still reluctant to entrench. Bidding high for battle, he was prepared to run what seemed desperate risks to tempt the enemy. But the opinion of Eugene, and, indeed, of all the allied generals, was so strong that during the evening of the 5th he began to break the ground, and by the 8th important works stretched from Noyelles to Fretin. As he was now confined to defensive action, he reorganized his array, the infantry being in two lines behind the trenches and the cavalry massed in rear of the wings. The difference between these dispositions and those of the 5th reveals very clearly the kind of battle he had hoped to fight.

Marlborough to Godolphin

FRETIN
September 7

Since my last, I have had yours of the 20th, and am very sorry to see, by the journal and letters from the fleet, that we are not to expect much from the expedition; for it is certain, if the sight of tents and militia can hinder them from landing, they will, in some degree, find them all along the coast.

M. de Vendôme having drawn all the troops possible from the

---

[1] Lediard, ii, 318. [2] Marlborough to Godolphin; Coxe, iv, 233.

garrisons, and having a great train of artillery joined him from Douay, made his own army and ours believe we should have had a battle on the 5th, which was the King of France's birthday, so that Prince Eugene joined me that morning with seventy-two squadrons and twenty-six battalions; but they not moving from their camp, which is in sight of ours, we sent back the foot the same night to the siege, resolving to entrench the front of our camp, which we began to do yesterday. The entrenchment is so far advanced that I have this morning sent him back all his horse, as also a detachment of 2000 foot, to assist him in the attacking of the counterscarp this night, and for the carrying on the siege with more vigour than hitherto; for it is certain our engineers find much more work than they expected. By the success of this night we shall be able to guess when we may have the town, for should we be obliged to fire much more powder and ball, we should be very much put to to find enough for the citadel, this being the twelfth day our batteries have fired. . . .[1]

The three French marshals spent the 5th and 6th in personal reconnaissance. All day they examined the hostile front with a curiosity which frequently drew the fire of its field batteries. All night they argued in Burgundy's tent. Vendôme still had no doubts; he urged an immediate onslaught, first upon the allied left and then extending to their centre, which lay across a wide plain. Berwick took the opposite view. The allied flanks were secure. It could only be a frontal attack in a country "where ten thousand could stop thirty thousand." Burgundy, torn between these conflicting views of eminent commanders, resorted to his customary habit of consulting his grandfather. So on the night of September 6 they all wrote letters to the King. Vendôme wrote:

> I cannot resist saying that the most part of the general officers of this army care nothing about losing Lille, nor for the glory of the Duke of Burgundy and your Majesty's arms. What I see makes my heart bleed. However, these are the same men who are leading the mind of the Duke astray and in whom he has all confidence. From the brigadiers down to the soldiers the spirit is unsurpassable, but it is far otherwise among the generals.[2]

In a second letter, to Chamillart, he begged to be relieved at the earliest moment of all responsibility. Berwick wrote:

> Even if our troops were as vigorous as I have seen them in the other war, it would not be possible to attack an enemy at least as strong as we, well-posted, entrenched, whose flanks are covered and

---

[1] Coxe, iv, 233–234.   [2] Pelet, viii, 89.

who cannot be dislodged; but with an infantry *already rebuffed* and with battalions under strength we should risk not only a repulse, but even total overthrow thereafter. It is sad to see Lille taken, but it would be even more sad to lose the only army which now remains to us or which can stop the enemy after the fall of Lille.[1]

Burgundy balanced between these opinions, but in the main agreed with Berwick.

Faced with this grim decision, Louis XIV showed no weakness; he resolved to play the stake. He expressed his surprise that his positive orders had been questioned, and renewed his commands to Burgundy to attack even at the risk of "suffering the misfortunes inseparable from failure, less dishonouring however, both for his person and for the army than to become spectators of the capture of Lille." He sent Chamillart to the camp to enforce his will.

In the midst of this tension the Allies found themselves strong enough to prosecute the siege. The assaults upon the counterscarp were delivered on the prescribed day, although upon the opposite side of the city at this very moment the largest battle of the war seemed imminent. On the south of Lille Marlborough faced Vendôme at heavy odds. On the north side the great assault was launched. Fourteen thousand men reinforced the troops in the trenches, and at half-past seven in the evening attacked the whole front from one hornwork to the other. Four great mines exploded under the feet of the assailants, "which destroyed abundance of men."[2] All through the night the struggle raged with varying fortune in the intricacies of the fortress system. The counterscarp was stormed; but, owing to the engineers who were to direct the second phase being all killed, and the workmen in their charge "departing under the Favour of the Night,"[2] the enemy were able to retire to their capital works, from whence they maintained a terrible fire for some hours. It was impossible to advance beyond "the Angles of the Glacis of the two Hornworks and of the Tenaille."[2] Des Roques, the chief engineer upon this sector, recorded, "This unhappy Accident retards the Taking of the Town, which may yet hold out eight or ten Days."[2] The slaughter among the allied troops in this assault by all accounts was nearly equal to their loss in the battle of Oudenarde. The French claimed that five thousand men had fallen. Certainly between two and three thousand, of whom the most part perished, covered the few acres of the saps and breaches with their gay uniforms and mangled bodies.

[1] Pelet, viii, 91.   [2] Lediard, ii, 323.

Marlborough to Godolphin

Since my last, M. de Vendôme is come so near to us that we did begin to believe that his intention was to attack us, but yesterday and the day before he did nothing but fire a great quantity of cannon, and this day we have been very quiet, he having drawn his cannon from the batteries on our left, as we think, with a design to see what he can do on our right. We are encamped so near that there is no possibility of being at ease till Lille is taken. I have been so disturbed these two last nights and days that I am as hot as if I were in a fever, so that you will excuse my saying no more by this post.[1]

Had the French grand army forced a general battle on the morning of the 5th, as Marlborough hoped, every scrap of force at the disposal of the Allies would have been cast simultaneously into the fateful scales. The interest of these operations to posterity, and to military annals, consists in the odds against which Marlborough and Eugene preserved their ascendancy, and the absolute conviction with which they acted upon narrow and impalpable margins. Marlborough courted the decisive battle. He was ready to face with less than sixty thousand men the possible onslaught of a hundred and ten thousand. Yet at the same time five miles away Eugene involved himself in the tremendous and necessarily bloody assault of the breaches. The two captains were disappointed in both respects; the assault did not capture the capital works, and the French army did not face a battle. Even more difficult trials lay ahead.

As long as Burgundy and Vendôme were threatening a general battle to the south of Lille, the road from Brussels was fairly free from molestation. Although Marlborough had had to recall General Fagel from the duty of protecting the communications in order to strengthen the line of battle, several important replenishments of ammunition came safely through just in time to enable the bombardments to be continuously maintained. "Last night," writes the Chief Engineer, Des Roques, on September 10,

we lodged ourselves in the covered way; and this night we shall work on a battery of thirty pieces of cannon, in order to widen the breach. The battery of eighteen guns having fired this day, with success, we may this evening make an attack upon one of the hornworks.[2]

While the siege was thus at its crisis and great numbers of troops involved in deadly grapple in the *débris* of the ramparts, the quagmire

---

[1] Coxe, iv, 235. [2] Lediard, ii, 323.

of the ditch, and the labyrinth of the counterscarp galleries, Vendôme threatened again to force a battle. Very heavy cannonades and the deployment of the whole French army once more aroused the Allies' hopes. Eugene rejoined Marlborough on the south front with his cavalry and spare troops. But this time battle was no longer offered in the open field, and it was hardly to be conceived that the enemy would pay the price of demanding it against entrenchments. The only effect of the French demonstrations and bombardments of the 11th was to divert Eugene from the siege for a few hours, and to supply the Allies with a large quantity of cannonballs, which were diligently collected and fired into Lille. On this day also an important munitions convoy which had left Brussels on the 8th was escorted into camp by Albemarle.

At a council of war on the 14th the proposal was made to open passages through the newly constructed works, march out, and actually attack the French army. Berwick in his memoirs says that Vendôme would in this case have suffered a total defeat. He states that Marlborough and Eugene favoured an offensive, but that the Dutch Deputies forbade them. Goslinga, who in later years discussed the war with Berwick, declares on the other hand that he and his colleagues urged the daring course, and that it was "the Princes" who were adverse. War in retrospect, like life, seems rich in opportunities; but at the time one opportunity shuts out another, and the choices are neither so numerous nor so obvious as appears.

All French Society—indeed, France itself—waited in protracted suspense. A freezing hush fell upon the Court. The card-tables, the supper parties, were deserted. The churches were thronged with rank and fashion praying for the life of husband, lover, son. It was known that Chamillart had been sent to the army for the express purpose of compelling its leaders to fight. This had seemed a very plain and obligatory course amid the galleries of Versailles and in the presence of Louis XIV. He arrived clear and decided. On the spot, in contact with the realities and the atmosphere of doubt which infected the French command, the War Minister soon lost heart. He watched the desultory cannonades. He heard the talk. He saw the ground and the defences along which flaunted the standards of the Allies, and behind which the shapes of Marlborough and Eugene seemed crouched to spring. On the night of the 14th Vendôme was left alone in his opinion; Burgundy, Berwick, Chamillart, and almost all the generals were for retreat. At this point it cost

Vendôme little to persist in valorous opinions. No one would take him at his word. Were there not other methods of succouring Lille? They knew the besiegers were short of powder. Although two convoys had lately arrived, a third was urgently expected. Any prolonged interruption of the supplies must be fatal. All the communications were exposed. If the main French army were used, it should be possible to cut Marlborough and Eugene both from Brussels and the sea. There is little doubt that the painful and humiliating decision was right. Comforting themselves with these hopes, the French army fell back by Orchies to Tournai. Burgundy's headquarters were at Saulchoi on September 17, and Marlborough observed him from behind the Marque.

John to Sarah

September 17

Whenever I have a minute to myself, I make use of it to write to my dear soul; for M. de Vendôme, having gathered much more strength together than we could imagine, and being camped *so near that in one hour's time we might be engaged*, obliges us to be so very diligent that we have very little rest, by reason of the troops we are obliged to have at the siege, which makes him have near twice as much foot as I have in this army; but I am so well entrenched that I no ways fear their forcing us. But the siege goes on so very slowly that I am in perpetual fears that it may continue so long, and consequently consume so much stores, that we may at last not have wherewithal to finish, which would be very cruel. These are my fears, but I desire you will let nobody know them. I long extremely to have this campaign well ended; for of all the campaigns I have made this has been the most painful; but I am in the galley, and must row on as long as this war lasts. . . .[1]

Marlborough to Godolphin

September 20

. . . It is impossible for me to express the uneasiness I suffer for the ill conduct of our engineers at the siege, where I think everything goes very wrong. It would be a cruel thing, if after we have obliged the enemy to quit all thoughts of relieving the place by force, which they have done, by repassing the Scheldt, we should fail of taking it by the ignorance of our engineers and the want of stores; for we have already fired very near as much as was demanded for the taking of the town and citadel; and as yet we are not entire masters of the counterscarp; so that to you I may own my despair of ending this campaign, so as in reason we might have expected. I beg you to assure

[1] Coxe, iv, 235–236.

the Queen that my greatest concern is on her account; for as to myself, I am so tired of the world that were she not concerned my affliction would not be great.

When the fate of Lille is once known, we shall endeavour all we can to bring the French to a general engagement; *but as that is what we shall desire, I take it for granted it is what they will avoid.* . . .[1]

This just reflection was fully confirmed by events.

[1] Coxe, iv, 238-239.

Chapter Twenty-six

WYNENDAEL

A GREAT battle being denied him, Marlborough, as he had foreseen, must face a far more harassing attack. The siege batteries were firing at full blast. The defence of Lille had been already maintained for nearly three weeks beyond the scheduled time. The bombardment was living from hand to mouth. To suspend it even for a few days was to take the pressure off Marshal Boufflers, who, for his part, watched with anxiety the daily diminution of his own limited magazines. Unless he could continue his counter-battery, the front would clearly break. The King had prescribed a proportion of powder to be reserved for the defence of the citadel. The losses of the garrison had been severe. If Eugene's bombardment and the progress of his saps continued, Boufflers must within a definite time retire to the citadel. But if the cannonade ceased he could stand where he was indefinitely. All therefore turned upon the convoys. Now upon the communications with Brussels came the main French army. In the last fortnight of September Vendôme and Burgundy occupied the whole line of the Scheldt from the Lille approaches to Ghent. They held and fortified every crossing. They made a curve around Oudenarde, at which point their defences became more like a fortress than field entrenchments. By this means they cut absolutely all communication between the Allies and Brussels, and beyond Brussels with Holland. Marlborough and Eugene were thus isolated. They were separated both by road and river from their base, from the homeland, and from all supplies, while they had the greatest siege of modern history on their hands, and when any slackening in their attack meant almost certain failure. From this time forward the siege of Lille became a desperate operation.

Only one resource lay open. Marlborough's eyes turned to the sea-coast. The fortress and harbour of Ostend were in his hands. The road, often a causeway amid the canals, streams, and inundations of the coastal region, ran through Thourout, Roulers, and Menin

441

to the siege, a distance of less than fifty miles. But on either side of this life-line lay the hostile fortresses of Ypres, Nieuport, and Bruges.[1] From Nieuport the French controlled the sluices of the Yser, and could flood a large and indefinite area. The road from the coast was now alone left to the besiegers of Lille, and the French gathered heavy forces on both sides of Ostend, but especially from the north, to attack the convoys. Possessing the command of

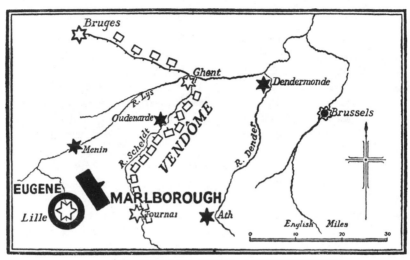

VENDÔME CUTS THE ALLIED COMMUNICATIONS

the sea, Marlborough had directed large supplies of munitions upon Ostend. On September 21 General Erle with his six thousand British infantry was brought under a strong escort of the fleet from the Channel into Ostend. Marlborough sent a trusted officer to him with full instructions,[2] and set him to work to prepare a heavy convoy.

Meanwhile the siege and bombardments proceeded with all possible vigour in the teeth of an obstinate defence. Eugene prepared for another major assault on the St Andrew and St Magdalen sectors. This was delivered on the evening of the 21st by about fifteen thousand men. At first good progress was made, and it seemed that the grand breach would be carried. But a violent sortie from the city robbed the assailants of most of their gains. In this savage night they lost at least a thousand men. Among the wounded was Eugene. With Hesse-Cassel at his side, he conducted the attack

[1] See general map of the Western Netherlands, facing p. 488.
[2] *Dispatches*, iv, 231.

at close quarters. Seeing the grenadiers repulsed, he advanced into the deadly fire to rally and animate his troops. He was soon struck by a musket-ball which grazed his forehead above his left eye. The force of the blow was broken by his cocked hat, which was "beat off" his head.[1] Hesse-Cassel gave him his own hat, already pierced by a bullet. Eugene, according to his usual habit when receiving a wound, made light of his injury and insisted upon remaining in action. But as it was apparent that he was half stunned and dazed his officers prevailed upon him to withdraw. He was led or carried to his headquarters while the struggle at the breaches was at its height. Although his injury was bloodless, he was suffering from severe concussion of the brain. It was clear to all about him that he would be incapacitated for some time. This serious news was carried to Marlborough during the night. Early the next morning the Duke arrived at Eugene's headquarters. He found his comrade, among an expostulating staff, preparing to go up to the trenches. He was only prevailed upon to return to his couch by Marlborough's undertaking to conduct the siege himself, as well as to cover it, till he was restored.

From September 21 till the end of the month the double burden was borne by Marlborough. This was a period of incredible strain. The besiegers were in extremities. The batteries were approaching the end of their ammunition. The engineers were scandalously at fault in their estimates. Around Lille all was in arrears and in confusion. A critical and hazardous operation was required to bring the convoy through from Ostend in the face of superior forces and ever-spreading inundations. Riding to and fro between the covering army and the siege, Marlborough effectively "sustained the weight of the command."[2] He looked narrowly into the siege-stores and munitions, and was shocked at his discoveries. On the 23rd he renewed the assault on the fortifications. He directed it himself from the trenches, and after hard fighting a substantial improvement was achieved. In these days he reorganized the siege operations like a careful housekeeper. The bombardment and trench-grapple were ceaselessly maintained. Meanwhile Eugene began to throw off his concussion.

The remorseless attack and heavy firing reduced Marshal Boufflers's magazines to very near the last reserve for the defence of the citadel. A French captain from Burgundy's army, creeping through the lines,

[1] Lediard, ii, 331.   [2] Ibid., 332.

stripped himself stark naked, and, having hidden his clothes, swam over seven canals and ditches and got in that manner into the town. He returned the same way, and, finding his clothes again, brought the Duke of Burgundy a letter from the Marshal, which was so contrived that he carried it in his mouth secure from being damped by moisture.[1]

The letter showed that without more powder the defence of the city must be abandoned. This emergency provoked a dramatic enterprise. The Chevalier de Luxembourg, a Major-General, with about two thousand dragoons, who "besides their arms carried each a fusee and a bag of sixty pounds' weight of powder," set out during the night of the 28th along the Douai road. In order the better to conceal their identity in the darkness they wore green boughs in their helmets, as was often done by the Allies on battle occasions. They arrived at the lines of circumvallation at a point near Pont-à-Tressin held by the Palatine troops. Their officers pretended to be Germans carrying prisoners to the camp. In this war of many nations and all languages spoken indifferently on either side they were suffered by carelessness—other accounts say by corruption—to pass the barrier. Several hundred were already safely over when a subaltern officer, "having some distrust, advanced to examine them." There was a challenge, an altercation, shouts, shots, and pandemonium. The whole two thousand galloped along the road

COMMUNICATIONS, OSTEND–LILLE

[1] Lediard, ii, 329.

towards the city. About half got through, the rest turned back in disorder. The road from Douai to Lille was paved with cobbles. Horses slipped: sparks struck out from their hoofs, or fire from the muskets, ignited powder-bags. A succession of loud explosions alarmed the camps and covered the road with scorched fragments of men and horses. About thirty prisoners were taken, but Luxembourg brought into Lille nearly sixty thousand pounds of powder for the fortress batteries. Marlborough's and other allied accounts minimized this grave annoyance, but it was regarded throughout Europe as a brilliant feat of arms.

During this last week of September the fate of Lille hung in the balance. At several agonized councils the raising of the siege was debated by the allied commanders. Goslinga, as usual, declares that he and his colleagues were for fighting it out, and that Marlborough was in despair. All accounts agree that Eugene, rising from his sickbed, declared "that he would be responsible for the success *provided he was supported with ammunition.*" But this begged the question. It is certain that Marlborough, who was engaged in the important operation of bringing in the convoy, allowed it to be known that, unless the convoy came through, the siege must be abandoned. Here we must let him speak for himself.

Marlborough to Godolphin

CAMP AT LANNOY
September 24, 1708

Since my last Prince Eugene has received a wound in his head, which I thank God is no ways dangerous; and I hope to-morrow or next day he may be abroad. Ever since Friday, that he was wounded, I have been obliged to be every day at the siege, which, with the vexation of its going so ill, I am almost dead. We made a third attack last night, and are not yet masters of the whole counterscarp; but that which is yet worse, those who have the charge of the stores have declared to the Deputies that the opiniatrety of the siege is such that they have not stores sufficient for the taking of the town. Upon which the Prince has desired to speak with me to-morrow morning. My next will acquaint you of what is resolved, but I fear you must expect nothing good.

I have this afternoon a letter from Lieutenant-General Erle from Ostend. He is ill of the gout. The enemy has cut in three several places the canal of Nieuport, by which they have put that country under water, to hinder our communication with Ostend. However, I shall find ways of letting him know what I desire. I am so vexed at the misbehaviour of our engineers that I have no patience, and beg your excuse that I say no more till the next post.[1]

Marlborough to Godolphin

September 27

You will have seen by my last letter the unhappy circumstances we are in, by the very ill conduct of our engineers and others. Upon the wounding of Prince Eugene I thought it absolutely necessary to inform myself of everything of the siege; for before I did not meddle in anything but the covering of it. Upon examination I find they did not deal well with the Prince for when I told him there did not remain powder and ball for above four days, he was very much surprised. I own to you that I fear we have something more in our misfortunes than ignorance. Our circumstances being thus, and the impossibility of getting a convoy from Brussels, obliged me to take measures for getting some ammunition from Ostend, which we could never have attempted *but for the good luck of the English battalions being there.*

Having time, I begin to write in the morning, but as the letters are not to go till the evening, I hope to send you some certainty of the convoy; I having sent yesterday Major-General Cadogan with twenty-six squadrons and twelve battalions to meet them, so that they might come with the greater safety, with which we must do our best; for should this not come safe, I am afraid we must not flatter ourselves of hoping to get any other, though you may be sure we shall leave nothing unattempted. It is impossible to express the trouble this matter has given me; for I am sensible that not only her Majesty but all the common cause must suffer if we miscarry in this undertaking, which we have but too much reason to apprehend. . . .[2]

General Erle, whom Marlborough had reinforced at Ostend till he had perhaps seven thousand British infantry and a large number of vehicles and horses, in spite of his gout behaved with zeal and skill. He succeeded in draining a large part of the inundation between Nieuport and Ostend. He occupied Leffinghe, and there built a bridge over the canal. Communication was thus for the moment restored with the main army. Marlborough had sent twelve battalions and as many squadrons towards Leffinghe to receive the convoy. But now Vendôme ordered La Motte to advance southward from Bruges with no fewer than twenty-two thousand men, a small army, and seize the prize. Marlborough had early information of this movement, though he underrated its strength. On the 25th he sent twelve more battalions and some horse to reinforce the convoy guard. The command of these troops was confided

[1] Coxe, iv, 243.   *Ibid.,* 253–254.

to General Webb. We are familiar with this picturesque personage through Thackeray's malicious pages. Webb was a high Tory, at heart a Jacobite, a man as vain as he was brave, but also a competent and experienced veteran of the long wars. He was now to

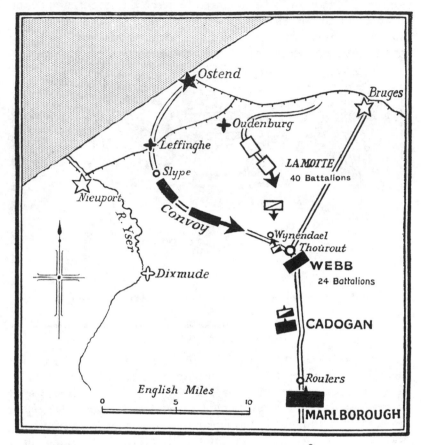

SITUATION, MORNING, SEPTEMBER 28

fight a most brilliant and glorious action, no small part of whose lustre falls upon the British infantry.

Early on the morning of the 28th the precious convoy was trailing along the road from Leffinghe to Thourout when the news came that La Motte, rebuffed by the allied defences at Oudenburg, was advancing at right angles upon it. All French historians have condemned his dispositions. His pathway to strike the convoy led him between two thick woods a thousand yards apart. It is contended

447

that his great numerical superiority—far beyond what Marlborough had expected—should have been used to outflank one or the other of these woods. But La Motte felt that the thickets on the one hand and the Château de Wynendael on the other debarred him from this. Accordingly he advanced between the woods, and about two P.M. found himself confronted by General Webb with twenty-four battalions drawn up in the gap, and, as he was soon to learn,

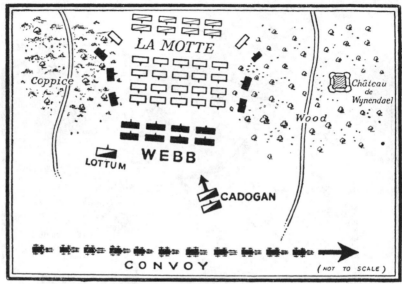

THE ACTION OF WYNENDAEL

in the woods on either side. He deployed his whole force, line behind line, and after three hours' cannonade advanced to the assault, being in superior strength of at least two to one. His troops found themselves fired upon not only by the British infantry on their front, but by strong forces hidden on both their flanks. The slaughter was heavy, and for those days unusually swift. His leading lines, largely composed of so-called Spanish infantry—that is to say, Belgian battalions adhering to the French—melted under the fusillade, and the rest refused to renew the battle. Here was a striking instance of the superior fire-discipline which was so marked a feature of Marlborough's infantry training. Three or four thousand men lay killed or wounded in the narrow space, and none would face the allied line, which stood unbroken and invincible. In the intense fire which preceded this decision Webb himself lost nearly a thousand men. But the repulse of the French was utter. Marlborough, who had come with strong forces of the main army to Roulers, had the day before sent Cadogan with twenty-six squadrons and infantry support to strengthen Webb. Cadogan arrived with a handful of squadrons as the victory declared itself. He offered Webb to charge the defeated French corps. Webb thought the odds were too great, and did not ask this effort of his comrade. Meanwhile the convoy had slipped safely past the point of intersection and was coming within the ambit of Marlborough's main army. The victory of Wynendael had sealed the fate of Lille.

It had another sequel. The Prince of Hesse-Cassel on the 29th sent the States-General a report explaining the unpleasant incident of Luxembourg's dragoons carrying the powder into Lille. In a paragraph at the end he added:

> Your High Mightinesses will, no doubt, have had direct advice of the advantage which the troops, lately arrived from England, sustained by those Mons. Cadogan carried with him from the army, have obtained near the canal that goes from Ostend to Newport over the Duke of Berwick's troops which attacked them. The great convoy is arrived at Menin. I congratulate your High Mightinesses on both these accounts. . . .[1]

Hesse-Cassel lay, of course, on the far side of Lille, and had no personal knowledge of what had happened nearly forty miles away at Wynendael. But, as it chanced, his was the first report that arrived. It was instantly published in Holland and, as soon as it reached England, in the *Gazette*. Thus the whole credit of the action was officially ascribed to Cadogan, and the name of Webb, the Tory General, was not even mentioned. When the truth was known later on the Tory Party raised a furious outcry. Here was a proven case of Marlborough stealing away the credit from an heroic Tory commander and bestowing it upon his own personal favourite and follower Cadogan. From this in the winter arose a bitter debate in the House of Commons, when all the spite of the Tory Opposition was discharged upon Marlborough's head. In fact no one can be more easily proved guiltless. His official dispatch to the Secretary of State, written as early as Hesse-Cassel's casual paragraph, made no reference to Cadogan and did full justice to Webb. Cadogan himself evidently told the tale in a fair and soldierly manner. Marlborough on his report wrote immediately to Webb as follows:

---

[1] Lediard, ii, 336.

Mr Cadogan is just now arrived, and has acquainted me with the success of the action you had yesterday in the afternoon against the body of troops commanded by M. de la Motte at Wynendael, which must be attributed chiefly to your good conduct and resolution. You may assure yourself I shall do you justice at home, and be glad on all occasions to own the service you have done in securing this convoy, upon which the success of our siege so much depends.[1]

His private letters to Godolphin, as we shall see, were earnestly concerned about Webb's immediate promotion. Webb himself was eventually satisfied that the Duke had done him no injustice. But the malice of the Tory Party spread the impression of an act of personal meanness jealously perpetrated against a subordinate who was also a political opponent. The Duke, struggling with the siege, only gradually became aware of what had occurred. Meanwhile his own letters clear him from this as from so many other reproaches.

Marlborough to Godolphin

In my last I had not time to give you any account of our last action but that of referring you to what was writ to the Secretary's office; I have since had a particular account. Our loss in killed and wounded is very near 1000; by what the enemy left dead on the place they must have lost at least three times as many as we. They had above double our number, all our horse, except 300, and 2000 foot, being sent on before, for the security of the convoy, so that there were not above 8000 men; and it is said by the officers who were left wounded on the field of battle that they had forty battalions and forty-six squadrons, as also cannon.

Webb and Cadogan have on this occasion, as they always will do, behaved themselves extremely well. The success of this vigorous action is, in a great measure, owing to them. If they had not succeeded, and our convoy had been lost, the consequence must have been the raising of the siege the next day. All her Majesty's subjects have had the good fortune this campaign in all actions to distinguish themselves; so that I should not do them justice if I did not beg the Queen that when this campaign shall be ended, she will be pleased to make a promotion among the generals of this army only, which will be a mark of her favour and their merit; for hitherto, though almost all the action has been in this army, yet every general has advanced equally with them, though two parts of three of them have not so much as

[1] *Dispatches*, iv, 242.

served this war. If the Queen and Prince approve of what I desire, in favour of this army, I should be glad it might not be known to anybody, till I have an opportunity of giving the names for their approbation. Count Corneille, M. Overkirk's son, has on this occasion behaved himself extremely well.[1]

Great if haggard rejoicings saluted the arrival of the new convoy in the camps before Lille. Above two hundred and fifty thousand pounds of powder, with cannon-balls and shells sufficient in those days for a fortnight's bombardment, had reached the besiegers. Besides this Eugene, now fully recovered, began to appear among the troops, and in the early days of October resumed the conduct of the siege, which was prosecuted night and day. However, a new and even more dangerous attack impended upon the communications. Vendôme, stung by the disgrace of Wynendael, came down on October 3 through Bruges to Oudenburg with thirty thousand men. He reinforced Nieuport and threatened Ostend and Leffinghe. He broke the dykes, opened the sluices in all directions, and "drowned the country." The French were still capable of moving freely all along the coast across the allied communications, which now seemed finally cut. This mortal challenge was instantly accepted. On the morning of the 7th Marlborough divided his army. He left twenty battalions and as many squadrons to aid Eugene in case of need, and with sixty battalions and 130 squadrons, or about forty-five thousand men, marched at daybreak directly upon Vendôme. At Roulers he learned that Vendôme was still at Oudenburg, and there seemed to be good prospects of pinning him against his own inundations. The expectation of battle ran high. King Augustus hastened from the siege to see the day. In an intercepted letter Vendôme had assured Louis XIV that "he engaged his honour the Allies should have no further communication with Ostend." Indeed, the Marshal was disposed to stay and fight. This hardihood was not shared by his generals. Finding remonstrance useless, they adopted, according to Berwick, a more compulsive argument. They opened the sluices higher up the coast, and before it was too late flooded him out of his camp. Marlborough, arriving on the field of Wynendael with his vanguard, heard that the French had retreated to Bruges, laying the countryside under water to the utmost extent. He accordingly halted his army at Roulers.

Ostend was now completely isolated by the floods. Another heavy convoy of munitions, brandy, salt, and other necessaries had

[1] Coxe, iv, 255.

been transported thither by sea from Holland and England. Eight or ten miles of flood-water, rising with the full-moon tides, stretched between these supplies and the ravening batteries and straitened army before Lille. Hitherto the want of food had not been felt. The forays into France had provided for men and horses. The convoys

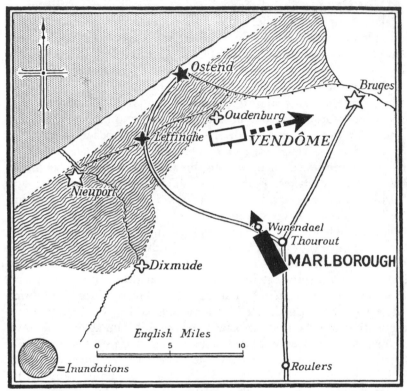

OCTOBER 7, 1708

had been reserved almost entirely for powder and ball. In the third week of October, however, Marlborough was forced to reduce the bread ration by one-third, four days serving for six. He ordered the other two days to be paid in money. "Particular care," he wrote to Cadogan, "must be taken that the officers pay the two days in money, that the soldiers have less reason to complain."[1] He had in the middle of October to push his foraging parties ever more deeply into France around Armentières and La Bassée. Both besiegers and besieged were in dire straits. All hung on the passage

[1] *Dispatches*, iv, 268.

of supplies. Marlborough now took possession of the region round
Dixmude with strong forces. Erle on one side of the floods collected
a flotilla; Cadogan on the other procured high-wheeled vehicles.
By these means the powder and shot was ferried across the inundations, drawn through the shallow waters by Cadogan's high wheels,
and finally transferred to Marlborough's supply wagons. Every day
and night small quantities came through. The Duke's letters record
each arrival, and give instructions for drying any bags of powder
which were wetted. Thus the cannon and the siege were fed
literally by handfuls.

Forthwith there developed an aquatic warfare. The French sent
light-draught galleys from Dunkirk to attack the munition boats on
their daily journeys. The English brought a number of armed
small craft to combat these by day and night. The struggle continued in an archipelago of villages and unsubmerged hillocks. The
key to all was Leffinghe, now a strong place, but almost flooded at
high tide. The French had begun to attack this post on the 13th.
With their galleys they mounted a battery on an island knoll, and
maintained a severe bombardment to which there could be no reply.
By night they attacked in galleys and flat-bottomed boats. The
garrison, twelve hundred strong, defended themselves vigorously
for eight days, and on the 24th they were relieved by fresh troops.
The French pressure increased continually, and the waters spread.
". . . The enemy," wrote Marlborough to Sunderland on October 13,
"having cut the dykes in other places, the spring-tides threw in so
much water, that their galleys and armed boats rowed over the very
places where we had posted our men, whereby they have destroyed
a great tract of land for many years and prevented our drawing anything more from thence; however we have got over nearly seventeen
hundred barrels of powder. . . ."[1] Thus by many desperate shifts
and contrivances the bombardment of Lille was maintained. The
siege batteries were now entrenched amid the ruins of the fortifications. "They have mounted nearly fifty pieces of cannon, besides
a battery of mortars," wrote Marlborough, "upon the counterscarp,
and hope to begin to fire from them to-morrow."[2] This intense
fire at close quarters marked a well-known phase. The breaches
gaped. Boufflers had already withdrawn most of his cannon into
the citadel. The hour of summons and of general storm drew near.

Marshal Overkirk did not live to see success. He died in his
headquarters at the siege on the night of October 18. Marlborough's

---

[1] *Dispatches*, iv, 269.   [2] *Loc. cit.*

faithful comrade, the indomitable Dutch veteran, had known since Oudenarde that his end was approaching. He sunned himself in the glory of that victory, to which he had himself given the crowning stroke. We are indebted to Goslinga for a striking picture of the old marshal during his last few weeks.

I saw on one of those days a magnificent spectacle, which struck me by its singularity. The generals and colonels had been ordered to have all the flags, standards, and kettle-drums brought to the heads of the army, the Duke, the Prince, and the Field-Marshal. . . . Ours were the greatest number. They were arranged as trophies around the walls of a long, spacious hall. The worthy M. Overkirk, virtually moribund, was seated in his best clothes in a great armchair at the end of the hall, surrounded by all these glorious trophies. I found him in this state one morning when I went there with Prince Eugene. The Prince was as much impressed as I was, and said to me that he was reminded of one of the old Roman generals displaying the spoils of a victory. In fact, nothing could be finer nor more striking.[1]

Marlborough's letters carry on the story of the campaign.

Marlborough to Godolphin

THOUROUT
October 8

The uneasy march of this day cannot hinder me from repeating again the obligation the Queen and all the Allies have to Major-General Webb, who will give you this letter; and I beg you will present him to the Queen; and were it not for measures I am obliged, for the Queen's service, to keep with the States-General [about the relative promotion of British and Dutch officers], I should desire her Majesty would declare him a Lieutenant-General, which he does extremely deserve. But as it must be done with management with them, I humbly desire the Queen will assure him that when she makes a promotion this winter, he shall be one; and I will be answerable that not only now, but at all times, he shall deserve it from her.[2]

Marlborough to Godolphin

ROUSSELAER [ROULERS]
October 9

You will know by this post that we are in great want of another convoy, so that I marched on Sunday morning, with 110 squadrons and sixty battalions, and camped that night at Rousselaer; and yesterday I was in hopes to have been in sight of the Duke of Vendôme, who was encamped at Oudenburg, to hinder our having anything

---

[1] Goslinga, p. 72. [2] Coxe, iv, 260.

from Ostend. But as soon as he was informed of my being at Rousselaer, he decamped, and marched to Bruges. During the time he has
been at Oudenburg, he has cut all the dikes; so that the whole country
is under water, which makes it impracticable for our carts to pass;
but I have sent to Ostend, to see if they can put the powder into bags
which may be brought by horses; for we hope to find a passage by
which they may come. God knows how this siege may end; I have
but little faith, and am quite uneasy, but resolved to persist, as long
as there is the least hope.

Major-General Webb goes for England; I write to her Majesty
by him. I hope she will be pleased to tell him that she is very well
satisfied with his services, and that when she makes a promotion this
winter, he may be sure of being a Lieutenant-General, which really
this last action makes his due. . . .[1]

Marlborough to Godolphin

October 19

Poor M. Overkirk died yesterday, by which her Majesty will save
the pension. . . . It would be an act of goodness and generosity if
the Queen would be pleased to give some part of it to Count Corneille
[Overkirk's son], who is as virtuous and as brave a man as lives. His
father has been able, I fear, to leave him nothing. . . .

We hope in four or five days to give a general storm, if they will
venture [to stand] it, which I fear they will [*i.e.*, instead of surrendering
the town]. I wish I may be mistaken, since it will cost a great many
lives. God continues to bless us with good weather.[2]

On the 22nd, all the troops being at their stations for the final
assault, which if successful would deprive the garrison of quarter
and expose the city to sack, Marshal Boufflers beat a parley and
offered to surrender the town. The hostages and courtesies were
immediately exchanged. Eugene imposed upon Boufflers the task,
difficult and exacting to an accomplished soldier and a man of honour,
of fixing himself the terms of capitulation. "Whatever you think
right I will agree to." Boufflers asked for a three days' truce to
withdraw to the citadel, leave to send his movable sick and wounded
into Douai, and that the attack upon the citadel should not be
directed from the town side. Eugene, sending presents of wine and
fresh provisions for the Marshal's table, subscribed to these conditions without demur. Little was lost by these gestures of chivalry.
Every inducement was offered to Boufflers to state his terms for the
surrender of the citadel, and when the old Marshal deprecated the
raising of such unseasonable questions, Eugene began the opening

[1] Coxe, iv, 258–259.   [2] *Ibid.*, 261.

of his trenches and moving his cannon even before the three days had expired. There was an unpleasant difference of opinion as to whether or not the truce precluded this. Of the garrison of fifteen thousand who had defended the fortress three thousand burghers laid down their arms upon parole, four thousand sick and wounded were carried to Douai, and between four and five thousand men retired to the citadel. The rest had perished. Besides the casualties of Wynendael and upon the communications, the Allies admitted 3632 men killed and 8322 wounded, of whom in those days about half died. The French asserted that they had inflicted more than double this loss. The price of Lille, although less than King William had paid for Namur twenty years before, was regarded as terrible throughout Europe.

Chapter Twenty-seven

THE WINTER STRUGGLE

1708—WINTER

WHILE their success was reverberating throughout Europe Marlborough and Eugene were for a space completely cut off from the outside world. The city had no sooner been surrendered than the communications with Ostend were finally closed. The garrison of Leffinghe, who had distinguished themselves by their stout resistance, were relieved on the 24th by an English, Dutch, and Spanish force. The newcomers proceeded forthwith to celebrate the joyous news in such a fashion that both officers and men were surprised drunk and incapable by a French attack during the night of the 24th, many being put to the sword. The gateways to the sea were shut but luckily too late. The situation of the allied armies was nevertheless still precarious. In every direction lay the French fortified positions and lines. Not only the sea-coast but the entire line of the Scheldt was sealed against them by superior forces. In their midst bristled the citadel of Lille with its ample garrison, its powerful artillery, and sacredly hoarded separate reserves of ammunition. On the other hand, the greatly contracted lines of circumvallation liberated more than half the besieging army for service in the field and both siege-works and bombardment were upon a far smaller scale.

The Treasurer gave full expression to his anxieties.

Godolphin to Marlborough

19th/30th Octr. 1708

★. . . By your Lres to Mr Erle, I see you always set much weight upon keeping of Leffinghe. You did not know it was lost, when Sr R: Temple left you, yet he tells me you expected it, wch makes me hope you have had in your thoughts how it was to bee supplied.

However I cant help being uneasy to think, we are not to have any Communication with you, but what is so very precarious as by the holland post; how will you have your money from Antwerp or Brussels? how will you be sure of provisions & subsistence for your Army?

457

Can you be secure the french will not destroy all Artois, & even Picardie too, rather than they shall furnish subsistance to your Army? I could ask a great many more of these wch perhaps you will call idle questions, but I must own, I should be glad to be sure they were so, and I think your business were more than half done, if you were once master of a port that could give your army a free communication wth us in England from whence you might have your money, your provisions & any other wants supplied not only with ease but wth a great deal of satisfaction. . . .[1]

The fall of Lille wrung further efforts from Louis XIV. He drew reinforcements both from the Rhine and Dauphiné to the Flanders theatre. Grave differences of opinion, aggravated by personal bitterness, distracted the French headquarters in the field. Berwick, without a command, had established his ascendancy over Burgundy. His keen eye and military sagacity detected every fault in Vendôme's successive projects. That Marshal was throughout very loud for battle. Whether, if he had exercised the sole command, he would in fact have fought is doubtful. But as he knew the bulk of the generals would not agree with him, that Berwick and Burgundy would overrule him, and together had greater influence at Court, he ran little risk in assuming an heroic rôle and forcing every one else to hold the only brave man back. Certain it is that Marlborough wished for nothing better on three or four separate occasions than that Vendôme should have his way. It is difficult, therefore, to believe that Vendôme's attitude, if sincere, was right.

At any rate, the French command had him well restrained. On November 3 there was a council of war at headquarters. Vendôme, as usual, clamoured for battle. His plan to attack Marlborough was vetoed. He then proposed to hold all the canals and rivers from Nieuport and Bruges through Ghent round to Tournai, in order to reduce the Allies to the alternative of being "starved to death or suing for peace." He might have added "or fighting." But the ill reception of his first proposal warned him of the unwisdom of dwelling on this theme. Chamillart favoured the scheme, but Berwick mercilessly pointed out that the Allies had enough ammunition to reduce the citadel, and that, as for food, they could live far better on the plenty of Artois and Picardy than the French in war-worn Flanders. Berwick advised that serious garrisons should be left in Ghent and Bruges while the whole of the French army concentrated to cover the rich French provinces. The council decided

[1] Blenheim MSS.

to hold their ground and wait events. The relations of Vendôme and Berwick were now so intolerable that Berwick quietly allowed himself to be withdrawn from the main army to his original command on the Rhine. Thus a fortnight passed during which Eugene battered and bored into the citadel of Lille.

In the third week of November the Elector of Bavaria returned from the Rhine, where the armies had gone into winter quarters, and joined the princely circle at the French headquarters at Saulchoi. He had no command, but he had a plan. A renewed attack should be made upon Brussels, and he would lead it himself. The inhabitants, he declared, were his devoted subjects, and would rally to his call. The garrison was thought to be meagre, and the defences were certainly weak and defective. With a small force drawn from various neighbouring fortresses he would capture the city. The idea caught fire; it prevented other plans. The Elector, at the head of fourteen battalions and eighteen squadrons with a minor siege-train, camped at Hal on November 21, and presented himself before Brussels the next day. Marlborough's unfailing Secret Service, although he lay surrounded by the French forces, gave him warning of this enterprise almost as soon as it had been conceived. He had already some weeks before reinforced the garrison of Brussels. It now consisted of ten battalions, comprising about six thousand men. He enjoined a spirited resistance upon the governor, Colonel Pascal, an officer of exceptional quality.

At the same time he began one of those elaborate strategic farces which on several notable occasions served him so well. We have an account of this, which has not hitherto seen the daylight, from that aide-de-camp of his, Colonel Molesworth, who had saved his life at Ramillies.

> *This design of the enemy's I am credibly informed my lord Duke had private intelligence of at least six days before we de-camped from Rousselaer [Roulers], and from the moment he knew it formed the design of passing the Scheldt to prevent it, and began to take all necessary measures for that purpose. But no common methods could have been of any effect in so uncommon an undertaking, and had my Ld Duke immediately made a movement with his army towards the Schelde, the enemy had taken the alarm and been prepared for the defence on't, in which case we had found the passage impossible or must have sacrificed half our army to have effected it. Therefore the point to be labourd for was to deceive the enemy and lead em, if possible, into an opinion that we had no such design at that time; and

to bring this about orders were given for two or three days before we march't, for the carrying of all forage from the camp to Courtray and Menin. The two artillerys english and dutch marcht to Menin as to their winter quarters. The Quartermasters were sent to Courtray and ordered to take up convenient lodgings for my Ld Duke, his family and equipage, and to take out billets for all the Generalls and officers of distinction; and it was given out that the army was to move to the neighbourhood of Courtray and from thence to be distributed into cantoonments where they might refresh till the Cittadell of Lille were over, and then that the passage of the canal [the Bruges canal] would certainly be attempted. This farce was so well managed that our whole army was imposed upon by it, and I'me confident all our Generalls except those few whom it was necessary to admit into the bottom of the design, really thought it was intended (as was given out) to cantoone and refresh the army for a while.[1]

The sanguine hopes which the Elector, Max Emmanuel, had nourished about Brussels proved ill-founded. He summoned Colonel Pascal in imperious terms to surrender. "His Electoral Highness knows that the commandant is not in a condition to defend himself with the few troops he has; wherefore if he obliges his Electoral Highness to begin the attack, he should not know capitulation for himself or his garrison. Let not the commandant flatter himself that he can retire with his garrison to Antwerp if he delays to surrender; for he is to know that he will soon find troops posted to hinder his retreat." But the governor replied with some spirit, "The commandant of Brussels is very unfortunate in not having the honour of knowing Your Electoral Highness. He dares assure you that he will do all that a man of honour ought to do, that he is satisfied with his garrison, and that he has the honour, with profound respect, to be, Monseigneur, Your Electoral Highness's most humble servant."[2]

Colonel Pascal proceeded to animate his troops. He ordered a pound of flesh, two quarts of beer, and four glasses of brandy to be distributed every day gratis to each soldier. Thus fortified, the garrison resisted with vigour; and the inhabitants remained mute and motionless. The Elector, instead of making a happy pounce, found himself committed to a grievous assault, if not, indeed, to a regular siege. He clamoured for reinforcements, and, the business having been started, these perforce had to be supplied. Bloody fighting ensued, and for a week the attempt to break into Brussels —siege it could not be called—became the feature of the campaign.

[1] Blenheim MSS.   [2] Lediard, ii, 92.

Although the French command were reassured by the news they had of Marlborough's preparations to move into winter quarters, Burgundy harboured misgivings about his own power to defend the line of the Scheldt if heavy forces were brought against him.

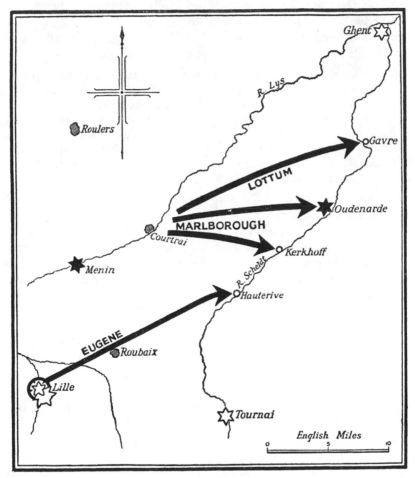

MARLBOROUGH FORCES THE SCHELDT

Vendôme, on the other hand, appeared to be serenely confident, and had the misfortune to assure the King, in a letter dated the 26th, that the French positions were impregnable. The piercing of long lines by selected attacks was familiar to Marlborough and Eugene. Nevertheless, the decision to force the fortifications of the Scheldt defended by the French main army was deemed most serious in the

461

small circle of veteran officers who were privy to it. It was a major operation which might entail heavy slaughter even if all went well. During the 26th Marlborough marched upon the river at three widely separated crossings, Gavre, Oudenarde, and Kerkhoff, while Eugene, leaving only the barest screen before the citadel, moved on Hauterive. The fortified line was seventy miles long, and the four attacks covered twenty miles of front. The principle of Marlborough's plan is explained by Captain Molesworth.

> *It was so ordered beforehand that when any one of these [four] bodies had made their passage and lodged themselves on the other side, whichever of the others met with more than ordinary difficulties and opposition should repair to the bridges of that body that had passed, and likewise make their passage there. Each body after passing was to direct its march to the right or left towards the hauteurs near Oudenarde, which was appointed to be the rendezvous of the several bodies when passed.[1]

When on the night of the 26th all the columns found themselves in movement towards the Scheldt a ripple of excitement spread through the hard-bitten Confederate army. We may find some comic relief and also some gleams of contemporary colour in the memoirs of Deputy Goslinga. Indeed, a patient study of his contacts with Marlborough throws a rare light upon these vanished scenes. Goslinga repaired to the Duke's tent at four in the morning when the throwing of the bridges was already in progress: "I found him in bed weary and ill, as he himself said, but sad and cast down to a far greater extent. He had just taken medicine." A little later Cadogan arrived, soon followed by Chanclos, the governor of Oudenarde, who was to accompany Count Lottum, the commander of the north column of attack. Chanclos, perfectly acquainted with the ground, would show him where the bridges could be thrown at Gavre. As usual, Goslinga, who thought that "the fate of the army and of the common cause" was at stake, had his plan to save the situation. If Count Lottum got across at Gavre he must not stop there—he must immediately turn southward and cut off the French troops masking Oudenarde. He pressed this development strongly upon the company. The Duke, whose medicine was no doubt working, "listened to him but did not make up his mind." In order to encourage him Goslinga volunteered to march himself with Lottum's corps. Cadogan and Chanclos kept up the conversation, while Marlborough maintained an attentive civility. Finally

---

[1] Blenheim MSS.

he indicated that the Deputy's idea must not be neglected; indeed, he would direct six battalions upon Oudenarde in order to profit by Goslinga's far-flung turning movement. This brought the Duke's trials to an end, and Goslinga departed, satisfied and thrilled. He was in no mood, so he tells us, to allow the other Dutch Deputies to share the martial honours which he foresaw. "Indeed, in their presence I gave my people orders to put my baggage and my berlin near the baggage column which should follow the princes' head-quarters"; and it was only when Lottum was already some distance on his road that he found himself honoured and refreshed by the arrival of the Deputy.

Amid the mists of morning Lottum's troops made the passage near Gavre with little or no opposition. But there Lottum halted. Goslinga at once exhorted him to march upon the rear of Oudenarde. The general drew him into a neighbouring house. Here, to his intense disgust, Goslinga discovered the two other Dutch Deputies whom he thought he had shaken off. A long debate ensued. Lottum said he had his orders from the Duke. He was to cross at Gavre and wait at Gavre. Goslinga declared he had it from the Duke's own mouth that he should hurry on to Oudenarde. Lottum refused to budge. He said politely that the Deputy was right, but he could not depart from his instructions. Goslinga, exasperated, appealed to the other Deputies to give a formal command:

> But my two colleagues, God only knows the reason, although I suspect it only too well and attribute it to a damnable jealousy, said that they would not act: that Count Lottum was the general; that it was for him to know what orders he had received from the Duke, and that they would not countermand them.[1]

Nothing would shake these obstinate men. Orkney—our dashing Orkney—joined with Count Lottum in pressing Goslinga's plan, but alas, the other two Deputies would not consent to give the necessary order, and without that they could not depart from their instructions. Then at last did Goslinga begin to realize that he had been fooled. We can see the scene in this cottage room: three or four of the most experienced soldiers in the army, trusted lieutenants in Marlborough's near circle, and this officious civilian lecturing them on their duty while his two colleagues, sent for that express purpose, paralysed his authority and left him a laughing-stock, or would have done so had his mischief-making powers not

---

[1] Goslinga, p. 88.

inspired a more elaborate procedure. Here, then, thought Goslinga, was another of Marlborough's tricks to prolong the war and line his pockets by depriving a Dutch Deputy "of an occasion so finely to serve Holland." It was not till the afternoon, while they were still at loggerheads, that Marlborough's aide-de-camp came with news that the Scheldt had been forced at all points with very little resistance and that Lottum was to march on Oudenarde.

We have dwelt upon this trifling incident because it illustrates the conditions under which Marlborough and his officers had to toil. The essence of his plan was to make sure at all costs of any bridge-head taken. Lottum led the flank column, and there were important French forces about Ghent. It may well be that with greater latitude Lottum could have done more that morning; but if every column commander had been accorded a similar discretion the clockwork precision of the operation might have been destroyed.

By the afternoon of the 27th the whole French army was chased from the fortifications of the Scheldt. Some fell back on Ghent and the rest on Tournai. The position of the Elector of Bavaria at Brussels became at once forlorn. Saving himself at the loss of all his artillery, and leaving eight hundred wounded behind him, he escaped to Mons. Meanwhile the strong post of Saint-Ghislain, which he had denuded of its garrison for the siege of Brussels, was captured by a raid of the governor of Ath, and many troops and much time and trouble were required to recover it for France. The moment the passage of the river was known to be secured Eugene hastened back to reinforce his scattered cordon around the citadel of Lille. The whole of this swift and fine operation marks the ascendancy which the Allies under Marlborough and Eugene had gained over the still numerically superior French armies. The fate of the citadel was now only a question of days. By this operation Marlborough had not only relieved Brussels, but had reopened the eastern line of supply to the besiegers of Lille and to the country in which his troops must winter. The morale of the French army had suffered a further shock. On December 9 the citadel of Lille capitulated. Boufflers marched out with honours of war, never more justly earned, and with the remnants of his garrison retired into France.

When the news of the loss of the Scheldt, of the failure before Brussels, and of the surrender of the citadel of Lille reached Louis XIV, he was so mortified that he incontinently ordered his armies to abandon the field and disperse into winter quarters. To protract the campaign further into the depth of winter no doubt meant a severe disorganization of all the recruiting and recuperative processes upon which the efficiency of his armies must depend in the new year which scowled upon France. It was believed at Versailles that Ghent and Bruges could stand prolonged sieges, and that the Allies would find it impossible to continue fighting incessantly. They too would have to break up, and by the late spring of 1709 the grim board might be set afresh. But this decision took little account of the forfeits which must be paid when one side ceases fighting and the other continues. Vendôme protested violently. The King remained obdurate. Berwick makes the pithy comment, "It is astounding that the King should have agreed to all the Duke of Vendôme's extraordinary proposals during the campaign, and should then have persisted in rejecting the only reasonable one he had made."[1]

One final, vital stroke was required to complete this glorious, remorseless campaign. The French must be driven from Ghent and Bruges. With a piercing eye Goslinga discerned the obvious. "While we were in this camp [on the Dender] to cover the convoys I said to the Duke one day that I feared very much that, if the enemy remained in possession of Ghent," the opening of the next campaign would be impeded. "The Duke listened to what I said with attention; he said that he would ponder over it maturely and asked me to come back the next day to thrash it out anew."[2] When on the morrow at eight o'clock the Deputy repaired to the Duke's quarters, he was received by Cadogan, who seemed very ready to be convinced in favour of the project. Thus fortified, Goslinga pressed the plan upon the Commander-in-Chief as soon as he emerged from his bedroom. If Marlborough was a good general, he was also a consummate actor. Like Cadogan, but more slowly, he yielded his mind gradually to Goslinga's audacious plan; and finally he adopted it. Goslinga, thrilled, full of having given this important turn to strategy, hurried off to write enthusiastically to The Hague in its support, leaving Marlborough and his Quartermaster-General to exchange smiles and confidences which can readily be imagined. The historian Klopp, who adopts every word of Goslinga, as if it were the Bible, writes, "Field-Deputy Goslinga suggested to Marlborough the idea of rounding off the work of this campaign by the recapture of Ghent and Bruges."[3] However, the reader will remember that on August 2 Marlborough had written to Godolphin:

[1] *Memoirs*, ii, 53.   [2] Goslinga, p. 95.   [3] Klopp, xiii, 158.

"If we can succeed in our undertakings we must not think of winter quarters till we have obliged him [Vendôme] to quit that country [Ghent and Bruges]."[1] And on August 20, "When I wrote you that I must drive the French from Ghent and Bruges I had no other thought than that it was absolutely necessary for the common cause."[2] Molesworth, the Duke's aide-de-camp, writing to his brother (December 3), says:

> I do not think it improbable that we may cantoon our horse, and that our infantry finish this prodigious campaign with the reduction of Ghent and Bruges. . . . Upon the whole I must tell you I can hardly flatter myself with the hope of keeping this Christmas with my friends in England, but I wish them a happy one with all my heart. We must yet give the finishing stroke to the campaign. Then, if you do not caress us excessively when we come amongst you, and say we have done like honest fellows, you do us wrong. . . .[3]

Having long held these intentions, it was no doubt most agreeable to Marlborough to see the officious Deputy going forward with the plan as if it were his own, and to make him its spontaneous advocate with the Dutch. No doubt it was a help for him to be able to say to the members of the Dutch Government or the States-General, "Goslinga's plan is sound. We should be culpable if we neglected it." How right was Goslinga when he described Marlborough as a man of "extreme dissimulation"! How glad must Marlborough have been to find this insufferable pest volunteering to pull the cart forward in the right direction! The incident illustrates Marlborough's method of using the foibles, the vanities, the virtues, and the vices of those with whom he had to work to further his own designs. He made even enemies work for him and for the victory of the Allies without their knowing it. Let us, then, proceed to Goslinga's master-stroke, the regaining of Ghent and Bruges.

Within an hour of Boufflers's surrender at Lille Marlborough began his concentration against Ghent. The French garrison consisted of thirty-four battalions and nineteen squadrons well supplied. The population of eighty thousand dreaded the siege, declared they would observe neutrality, and begged Marlborough not to bombard the city. The Duke could give them no comfort. On the 11th he approached; but in view of the strength of the place and its garrison he decided that Eugene must aid and cover him. Accordingly on December 16–17 Eugene marched north to the neighbourhood

---

[1] Coxe, iv, 172. [2] *Ibid.*, 224. [3] Blenheim MSS.

of Grammont, and sent his infantry forward to the siege. On the 18th Ghent was invested. The weather was obliging. Hitherto the frost had been intense, but now a sudden thaw without any rain freed the waterways for the barges carrying the siege cannon. On the 24th the trenches were opened; on the 27th Fort Rouge, on the north, was captured, and by this time the batteries were planted. There was no reason why Ghent should not have stood a prolonged siege, but the disheartenment of the French armies produced a surprising collapse. To the indignation of the King, Count de la Motte on the 29th opened negotiations. In his justification before a French court-martial he pleaded that his supreme duty was to preserve his army. Marlborough's judgment was thus expressed: "I believe Monsieur de Lamotte will not be able to give good reason for what he has done."[1] Following La Motte's example and orders, Grimaldi evacuated Bruges, Plassendael, and Leffinghe. All the French troops withdrew along the coast upon Dunkirk. The very next day the weather broke completely; it poured, and Marlborough dispersed the allied armies to their winter quarters.

John to Sarah

Dec: 17th, 1708

★ . . . If You have had the same weather we have had, it has been so very cold that it must have done You hurt, for it has frozen so excessive hard that the rivers have been al shut up, so that we cou'd have nothing come to us, which if it had continu'd must have oblig'd us to have gone to our Garrisons; but I thank God we have now a gentle thaw, by which I hope the rivers will in a few days bring us our canon and amunition. The ffrench knowing the consequence of this town have now in itt 30 Battalions and 19 Squadrons, so that I have desir'd the assistance of the ffoot of Pr. Eugenes army, which will be with me to morrow, and then I shall invest the place on all sides. The ffrench hope by their numerous garrison to make such a defence, and by the advantage they have of the season that we shall be forced to raise the siege, but my hopes are that God will enable us to deceive them, for to be in some quiet this Winter, and to enable the making a good Campagne the next Yeare, wee must be masters of this town. I have had this evening a Deputation from the Clergy Nobillity and Citizens of the town in the Name of al the people, desiring thay might not be bombard'd; with all my heart I wish it cou'd be taken without doing hurt, but in kindness to our own soldiers we must use all means for the reducing in the shortest time.[2]

[1] Marlborough to Godolphin, Brussels, January 7.
[2] Blenheim MSS.

467

John to Sarah

Dec: 31st, 1708

I write yesterday by the Expresse I sent by the Way of Ostend to lett You know that the Comte de la Motte had capitulated to march out of Gand next wensday if not succord sooner. The Marishal Boufflair is at Tournay, but we do not hear he has troupes enough to do that service; I have this morning write to the Governor and Town of Bridges [Bruges] to offer them the same Capitulations I have given to this place, but I fear thay will only return a Civill answere, and oblige me to march with part of the Army thether which if possible [I] wou'd avoyd, especially now that it lookse like weat weather, the rain having begaone yesterday, and God having hethertoo bless'd us with extreme good weather, we may now reasonably exspect a great deal of rain. My next letter will lett You know what I shall be oblig'd to do, for if I do not go to Bridges, I shall then go for two or three days to The Hague with Pr. Eugene, and then return to this country, where I must continue til the end of febuarie; the months of March and April, will be under the care of the Pr. of Savoye [Eugene]. By this You will see that I shall enjoye but a very little time with my dear Soull this Winter in England. If we must have Warr next summer, I do hope that the taking of these two towns will oblige the Enemy to wish for a Peace. I have this minute receiv'd Yours of the 14th but have not time to say more by this post, then that mr Bromleys and other Gentlemen's good nature join'd with the trouble I have here makes me quit weary of serving.[1]

Marlborough to Godolphin

GHENT

January 3, 1708[9]

I was yesterday from ten in the morning till six at night seeing the garrison of Ghent and all that belong'd to them march by me. It is astonishing to see so great numbers of good men to look on, suffer a place of this consequence to be taken at this season with so little a loss. As soon as they knew I had possession of the gates of this town, they took the resolution of abandoning Bridges. *This campaign is now ended to my own heart's desire*, and as the hand of the Almighty is visible in this whole matter, I hope her Majesty will think it due to Him to return public thanks, and at the same time to implore His blessing on the next campaign. I can't express enough to you the importance of these towns, for without them we could neither be quiet in our winter quarters nor have opened with advantage the next campaign. I shall to-morrow give the necessary orders for the separating the army, so that in two days they will be all on their march for their winter quarters. I must go with Prince Eugene for some

[1] *Sarah Correspondence*, i, 164.

few days to The Hague, after which I shall take a little care of my health. . . .[1]

A result of the first importance was also achieved in the south. The land campaign in the Peninsula, as, indeed, in Dauphiné, was comparatively uneventful. The new Imperialist commander, Star-hemberg, landed with four thousand reinforcements at Barcelona in April, and on the arrival of Stanhope and the English contingent took the field in the following month. The operations centred around the fortress of Tortosa, on the Ebro, now become one of the last Ally strongholds in Eastern Spain. Starhemberg was unable to prevent its fall on July 10. When his main body of some six thousand troops eventually arrived from Italy he attempted, in conjunction with Stanhope, its recapture. This effort miscarried dismally, and with it closed the military operations of the campaign. The armies settled down in winter quarters in almost the same posi-tions as they had occupied at the opening of the year. The French had, however, lost nearly five thousand men in the fighting at Tortosa, and had been seriously weakened by the withdrawal of troops for Flanders after the battle of Oudenarde.

It was, however, at sea that the decisive event took place. The possession of Gibraltar enabled the Allies to prevent the junction of the Brest and Toulon fleets; but up till now heavy ships had been forced to sail to Lisbon every winter to refit. We recall Marl-borough's exhortation to Stanhope, "I conjure you . . . to take Port Mahon."[2] Earlier (June 1708) he had written:

> You know I am sufficiently convinced of the necessity of a squadron wintering in the Mediterranean, but it is certain all our seamen are against it, alleging the men of war cannot be secure and have all the necessities to keep them at sea in the port of Spezzia, so that you must continue to press this matter as of the greatest consequence, advising the King to do the same.[3]

The whole plan depended upon naval co-operation. Sir John Leake had succeeded the ill-fated Shovell in January 1708. During the summer he had been active. He had fed the army in the Penin-sula, transported the Imperialist reinforcements, had fetched Charles III's Wolfenbuttel bride, captured the island of Sardinia with its valuable corn supplies (August 1708), and now was free to attack Minorca. For this, however, troops were necessary.

[1] Coxe, iv, 298. [2] *Dispatches*, iv, f. 3.
[3] Chevening MSS. (Stanhope family papers); B. Williams, *Stanhope*, p. 72.

Stanhope provided seventeen hundred men, who were embarked at Barcelona. A rendezvous with Leake was arranged off Minorca, and the squadrons met on September 14. To Leake might have fallen the honour of the event. However, with the gale weather approaching he refused to hazard the fleet. Leaving Admiral Whittaker with seventeen ships to aid the land operations, he sailed for England. Stanhope was undaunted. His arrival off the island led to the surrender of the whole place except Port Mahon. This

longed-for harbour was defended by the strong Fort Philip, garrisoned by a thousand men. Stanhope landed his troops and guns, and prepared for a regular siege. But on September 30, after a week of reconnoitring, the garrison surrendered to an offer of good terms. With the fall of this main defence the harbour was soon occupied, and thus, at a cost of less than fifty killed and wounded, the English fleet secured their coveted base in the Mediterranean. To Stanhope belongs the credit, and it certainly seems that the admirals were not so forward in the capture of this great naval prize as might have been expected. "I may in confidence," wrote Stanhope somewhat bitterly to Sunderland, "tell your lordship that I have in all this affair met with ten times more difficulty in dealing with the sea [officers] than with the enemy."

Henceforward the English fleet had a secure, unapproachable island base in the Mediterranean, and their command of the inland sea became perennial. The importance attached to the possession of Minorca by the soldiers, sailors, and statesmen of all parties in England became a continuing tradition which fifty years later, when the island was lost, explained the pitiless execution of Admiral Byng. To Marlborough in 1708 the capture of Port Mahon was the achievement of a major strategic aim decisive upon the future course of the war.

Thus ended, according to his "heart's desire," Marlborough's grand campaign of 1708. Throughout the supreme command had rested unquestioned in his hands. He often deferred to Eugene's advice, and the two commanders always presented themselves in full agreement. Marlborough's decisions, supported by Eugene, were accepted invariably by the councils of war. The noble Prince not only served and aided, but inspired Marlborough in anxious days. But the responsibility and authority rested with the Duke and five-sixths of the troops in the field were under his own command. Success was joyously shared between the two, but failure would have fallen upon Marlborough alone. Constantly ailing in health, reduced once to despair, gnawed by his political anxieties at home, harassed by every kind of pressure and appeal from Godolphin, Sarah, and the Whig leaders, conscious of his waning favour with the Queen, pursued by the inveterate malice of the Tory Party, he nevertheless continuously took great risks, and wished to take more.

The answer to the innumerable criticisms passed upon his operations must be their complete success. While always audacious, in every case he made the most careful plans based upon wonderfully accurate information. He had studied attentively the character of his chief opponent, Vendôme. He realized quickly the divergence of view among the French commanders, and played upon it. From the battle of Oudenarde onward he was sure that the morale of the French army was broken. Weighing all these factors and making his plans, he did not allow himself to be distracted by the closing of his communications or converging superior forces. He was unaffected by the terrible appearance of the war-map. Although baulked in his design of marching into France, he contrived to produce outstanding success by a second alternative. He persevered, undaunted by hazards, unsatisfied by victory, until every antagonist and almost every adherent was worn down by physical and mental strain, and he was left unchallenged master of the whole theatre of war. "I think," he wrote to Sarah on December 10, "we may say without vanity that France will with terror remember this campaign for a long time."

Chapter Twenty-eight

CULMINATION

1708—WINTER

ENGLAND had now been raised by Marlborough's victories to the summit of the world. Many living men could remember the island as a paid dependant of France. The Constitution and the religion of the nation had repeatedly lain under mortal challenge. Only twenty years before, with Ireland in rebellion and Scotland separate and estranged, the English people, led by the aristocracy, had been reduced to the desperate remedy of bringing in a foreign ruler and foreign troops to protect them against betrayal by their own sovereign and invasion by Louis XIV. Even after the wars of William III, as it seemed but yesterday, the nation, disarmed by an insensate economy, had quaked to see the Grand Monarch occupying without the firing of a shot all the fortresses of the Spanish Netherlands, and adding, apparently without opposition, the mighty empire of Spain and the Indies to the already paramount and overweening power of France. Protestantism and Parliamentary institutions crouched behind the dykes of Holland or stood ill-guarded and downcast beyond the Strait of Dover. The discordant petty states of Germany could make no headway against the gleaming arms and all-embracing diplomacy of France. Not only European hegemony, but even the dominion of the whole world seemed about to fall to a glorified, triumphant, Catholic ruler, as intolerant as he was cultured, as cruel and ambitious as he was strong, and sole autocrat of twenty million Frenchmen.

One man and three battles had transformed all. The Grand Monarch was beaten to his knees. His armies would no longer face in the open field the men who had conquered at Blenheim, Ramillies, and Oudenarde, or the Commander who led them. The whole of the Netherlands, all their fortresses, had been regained and now stood as the barrier of salvation for world causes dear to Dutch and English hearts. The three parts of the British Isles were united under one Queen and one Parliament. The French fleets had

472

been driven from the seas. The Mediterranean had become an English lake. The treasures of the ocean, the wonders of the New World, seemed to be the appointed inheritance of the islanders.

An intense desire to take part in these splendid events inspired the nobility, the country gentlemen, and even the city merchants. There was a galaxy of talent at the disposal of the Crown. Not merely profit, though profit there was in plenty, but even more fame and the chance to attempt great deeds, allured with their magnetic spell ability and rank. Eloquence in Parliament, valour in the field or afloat, wealth, broad acres, ancient lineage, bore the eager competitors to the arena. Political intrigue, party faction, royal favour, prescribed the conditions of their strife for power. The Continent laboured to understand the English political system. The eyes of Europe were fixed upon the Court of Queen Anne. Every word, every whisper, every gesture, every combination or counter-combination of the leading figures of British public life, were eagerly reported. Above all, the minutest indications of the Queen's mood and leanings were reported far and wide. The persons she saw, the bishops she made, the honours she bestowed, the jewels she chose to wear, the bedchamber women who presented them to her—all these were scrutinized by rulers of a score of states with as much attention as was paid to the march of a substantial corps from one theatre to another.

We have seen by what narrow margins, against what adverse chances, the Grand Alliance had three times been rescued by Marlborough's war and policy from ignominious collapse. The external difficulties were now virtually at an end. With Eugene at his side, his military command was undisputed. The princes and sovereigns of the Grand Alliance had in general yielded themselves to his leadership. From The Hague, from Hanover, from Berlin, from Vienna, from Turin, from Barcelona, all roads led to his tent. The Russian excursion of Charles XII had removed that formidable irrelevancy from the scene. To dictate terms of peace to France, either upon her frontiers or in Paris itself, seemed a prospect near and sure. But now a new and fatal burden was bound upon those shoulders which had borne so much. The Queen's heart, it was said, was changing. The Captain-General and his wife were losing—nay, had lost—the favour they had used to such effect. The Tories, the peace party, the Jacobite party, were gaining in royal favour. Henceforth the Court of Louis XIV pondered the question, If reasonable peace is denied, can France hold out till Marlborough falls? Thus every scrap of gossip about Queen Anne, about her relations with Sarah and Abigail, about Mr Harley and the back stairs, about Whig obtrusiveness and Godolphin's helplessness, exercised its influence both upon the conduct of the war and every peace negotiation. Queen Anne was the axis upon which the fate of Europe turned: and Queen Anne had now become her own worst enemy.

As the meeting of Parliament approached the Whigs professed themselves highly discontented with the exertions which Godolphin, Marlborough, and even Sarah—who had broken herself in their interests—had made to bring them into office. Sunderland was deputed to inform the Duchess that unless Lord Somers received promotion, and unless Law Officers more agreeable to their party were appointed, they would withdraw their support. Sarah passed this on to Marlborough, besieging Lille, and did her best herself. When it was seen that she no longer had any influence with the Queen some of the Whig lords even stooped to make their court, with poor success, to Abigail. They realized that Marlborough alone still possessed exploitable credit with the Queen. They therefore sought to spur him to their service by renewing the attack upon his brother, which had been called off at the beginning of the year. Whether or not Admiral Churchill was vulnerable in his financial record, or in his naval administration, he was certainly obnoxious to them as a politician. The Admiral had during the year stimulated the Toryism of his chief, Prince George of Denmark, and given full vent to his own. He had embarrassed Godolphin and Marlborough by circulating the report that the Duke had given a regiment to a certain Colonel Jones at the instigation of Harley. He had cited the Secretary-at-War, Walpole, as his authority for this. Much mischief was made thereby. He meddled besides in the intrigues about Oxford patronage. Sarah became deeply incensed against him. In vehement letters she importuned her husband to free himself of a brother who had become an encumbrance. For a long time Marlborough resisted. He was attached to his brother George, through whom he controlled naval strategy. He yielded only to the arguments of Godolphin.

Godolphin to Marlborough

June 11/22, 1708

The case with the Prince is little better. He is sometimes uneasy at the apprehensions of what he shall meet with, but unadvisable in what is proper to prevent it; whether from his own temper, or made so by your brother, I cannot judge. But your brother is not, at least seems not to be, without his own uneasiness too, in which I always confirm him when we talk together, and he appears to be upon those occasions very much of my mind; however, he has great animosities and partialities, and either cannot, or will not prevail with the Prince to do any good.[1]

John to Sarah

August 2, 1708

I am sorry that my brother George is gone to Oxford, fearing he may do what I shall not like. I can't hinder being concerned for him, though I find he is not at all sensible of the trouble he is like to have this winter, so that I shall certainly have mortifications upon his account.[2]

Godolphin to Marlborough

WINDSOR
July 6/17, 1708

You may do me the right to observe that I never trouble you with stories from hence, being sensible I ought not to make you uneasy, upon whom all our hopes and safeties depend. But since you required an account of the noise about your brother George and Mr Walpole, I cannot but think he was very much to blame in that whole affair from the beginning to the end; but nobody is able to give so exact an account of the particulars as Mr Craggs, who was himself a witness to the most material part of it. I must needs add, upon this occasion, that your brother does certainly contribute very much to keep up both in the Prince and in the Queen the natural, but very inconvenient averseness they have to the Whigs in general, and to Sir George Byng in particular, though Mr Montgomery took all imaginable pains to reconcile them, and to give promises and assurances to each other; and nothing is more certain than that the general dislike of your brother in that station is stronger than ever, and much harder to be supported; but nothing less than your express command should have made me say so much to you upon so disagreeable a subject.[3]

It was not till October that Marlborough was finally convinced that his brother must go. Then he wrote him a truly devastating letter.

Marlborough to Admiral Churchill

October 19, 1708

Finding you still continue in the Prince's council, and the Parliament now so near, I cannot be so wanting either to you or to myself as not to tell you plainly, with all the kindness of a brother and the sincerity of a friend, that if you do not take an unalterable resolution of laying down that employment before the Parliament sits, you will certainly do the greatest disservice imaginable to the Queen and

---

[1] Coxe, iv, 89.   [2] *Ibid.*, 185.   [3] *Sarah Correspondence*, ii, 288.

Prince, the greatest prejudice to me, and bring yourself into such inconveniences as may last as long as you live, and from which it is wholly impossible to protect you. Whereas, on the other side, if the considerations of making the Queen's affairs more easy next session, of avoiding a great deal of trouble and disagreeableness to the Prince, and of real danger to yourself, as well as prejudice to me, prevail with you to comply with my earnest desire in this thing, I think I could be answerable to you that you could not fail of finding your advantage in it, doubly to what you do now, both in profit and quiet. These motives being all of them as strong as it is possible for me to suggest, I hope you will give me the satisfaction of letting me know very soon, that my mind may be at ease in this matter, and that you have virtually laid down before my coming over.[1]

Both Marlborough and Godolphin hoped that the sacrifice of the Admiral would placate the Whigs and spare the Queen the distress of a Parliamentary attack upon George of Denmark. All through this summer the Prince had lain grievously ill in the little house the Queen had occupied at Windsor. Here she and Abigail nursed him with every care. The poor Prince "had his astma, a spitting of blood, a lethargie, a hidropsie and something of a palsie."[2] The summer of 1708 was hot, and the Prince suffered much in the small house from the weather, from his maladies, and no doubt from the remedies of those days. The house was backed upon the park, and, according to Sarah, gave easy access to Harley, who was frequently admitted by Abigail to the Queen.

Who can wonder at Anne's hatred of the Whigs, whose cruelty and greed of employment sought to hound her stricken husband out of place and reputation? Her sorrow as a wife, her wrath as Queen, were flames that fed each other. Heedless of this, and, indeed, of every decency, but strong in their sense of constitutional injustice, the Whig lords expanded their claims. Nothing would now content them but the removal of the Prince, the transference of Lord Pembroke to the Admiralty, the distribution of Pembroke's existing offices to Somers and Wharton. Sunderland collected the Junto leaders at Althorp in October to concert their demands. In the Lords Haversham excelled himself: "Your disasters at sea have been so many a man scarce knows where to begin. Your ships have been taken by your enemies, as the Dutch have your herrings by shoals, upon your own coasts; nay, these are pregnant misfortunes, and big with innumerable mischiefs." The Whigs believed this was

---

[1] Coxe, iv, 316–317. [2] Marlborough Papers, *H.M.C.*, p. 469.

their only way. They struck at Marlborough through his brother and at the Queen through her husband. Their calculations were proved correct, their methods efficacious. To spare her husband's last days from pitiless public attack, Anne flung the hungry Whigs their offices. What she would not give to Marlborough's wise and loyal counsel, to Godolphin's entreaties, and to the obvious facts of the Parliamentary situation, she yielded to this peculiarly mean form of personal pressure. "The Queen," wrote Godolphin to Marlborough on the day Anne surrendered (October 22/November 2),

> has at last been brought to allow me to make such condescensions, which, if done in time, would have been sufficient to have eased most of our difficulties; and would yet do it, in great measure, if the Whigs will be but tolerably reasonable; and I am really of opinion that if you were in England at this moment but forty-eight hours, all might yet go well—I mean as to the public.[1]

The Junto were indignant to find that after the promise had been extorted its fulfilment was delayed. On October 28 they learned the cause. Death had discharged the Lord High Admiral from his office. ". . . Nature," wrote Godolphin,

> was quite worn out in him, and no art could support him long. The Queen's affliction and the difficulty of speaking with that freedom and plainness to her which her service requires, while she has so tender a concern upon her is a new additional inconvenience, which our circumstances did not need, and will make it more necessary than ever that you should not delay your return to England; for I really foresee that unless that can be compassed very, very soon, it will be next to impossible to prevent ruin. . . .[2]

The crisis had, however, passed. The Whigs obtained their posts. Lord Pembroke became Lord High Admiral. Wharton, from whom Anne had once so summarily demanded his staff on account of his evil character, went to Ireland as her Lord-Lieutenant; and Somers became Lord President. Thus in the teeth of the Queen, somewhat to the concern of the country, but in accord with the will of the House of Commons, a characteristically Whig party Administration was installed in power. The events of the next four years were to make this expedient the rule for the future. A memorable, milestone in British constitutional history had been passed.

Admiral Churchill's appointment lapsed with the death of the Prince. "He continues in town," wrote one of Harley's correspondents

---

[1] Coxe, iv, 318. [2] Ibid., 318–319.

"till the funeral is over, and then retires to Windsor with the intention not to appear this winter in Parliament."[1] Indeed, he never appeared in Parliament again. He retired to a villa which he had built himself at Windsor, and amused himself for the remaining eighteen months of his life with a remarkable aviary, which he bequeathed to the Duke of Ormonde and the Earl of Torrington. He does not seem to have amassed a large fortune; but he was able to leave twelve thousand pounds to his natural son, and the like sum to his nephew Brigadier Godfrey.[2] He had been the mainspring of the Admiralty for seven war-time years, when the British fleets were stronger than all other navies combined, and when they were used more whole-heartedly in support of the main strategy than at any other period in our naval history.

Neither Sarah nor, indeed, the doctors had realized how rapid Prince George of Denmark's end would be, but when she heard that his condition had become critical she wrote:

WINDSOR LODGE
Oct. 26

Though the last time I had the honour to wait upon your Majesty your usage of me was such as was scarce possible for me to imagine, or for anybody to believe, yet I cannot hear of so great a misfortune and affliction to you as the condition in which the Prince is without coming to pay my duty, in inquiring after your health; and to see if in any particular whatsoever, my service can either be agreeable or useful to you, for which satisfaction I would do more than I will trouble your Majesty to read at this time.[3]

This letter grates upon the ear, and it is not surprising that when the next day Sarah, who had driven all night from Windsor, presented herself at Kensington, she was, as she records, received "very coolly, and like a stranger," by the afflicted Queen. She returned, however, the next day and was present at the moment of the Prince's death. Archdeacon Coxe, writing for the England of 1820, says:

She again waited on the Queen the ensuing morning. With affectionate zeal she removed her royal mistress from this sad spectacle to her closet, and desiring the other attendants to withdraw, she knelt down, and endeavoured to soothe the agonies of her grief, continuing in that posture till the first emotions had subsided.[4]

---

[1] Lewis to Harley, November 2; Portland Papers, *H.M.C.*, iv, 510.
[2] Luttrell, vi, 58. [3] Coxe, iv, 321. [4] *Ibid.*, 322.

Such rigmarole probably does justice to what occurred. Sarah was in a false position. She would have been universally condemned if she had abandoned her mistress and former beloved friend in her grief; yet her presence could only be an intrusion. One person alone in the whole world could be of any comfort to Anne. It was to Abigail she turned. She suffered herself to be led and advised by Sarah, whose duty it was; but she only wanted Abigail. Sarah directed affairs with her customary precision. The Queen must leave Kensington for St James's in order that the funeral arrangements should be made. Anne, reluctant to quit her husband's body, resisted feebly for a while and then submitted. The Duchess, putting aside the Queen's requests for Abigail by saying, "Your Majesty may send for her at St James's, when and how you please," conducted her in her own coach to that palace.

No fault can be found with Sarah's behaviour on this difficult occasion. It was correct, capable, and considerate; but on neither side was there a spark of loving companionship. All that was dead. Even its afterglow ended with the breath of the poor Prince. He had always been a good friend to Sarah and a staunch admirer of the Duke. Now he too was gone. Sarah in her memoirs wrote of her relations with the Queen in the succeeding weeks:

> She would make me sit down as formerly and make some little show of kindness at night when I took my leave; but she would never speak to me of anything, and I found I could gain no ground, which was not to be wondered at, for I never came to her without finding Mrs Masham had just gone from her, and I went to her seldomer.[1]

Sarah's behaviour would lie under no reproach but for her subsequent writings upon these events. She thought fit to record that the Queen, in spite of her grief, "ate a very good dinner" on the day of her husband's death. When Anne took the habit of sitting alone for long hours in her husband's little workroom at St James's Palace, she made a reflection which does only herself discredit. "But the true reason of her Majesty choosing this closet to sit in was that the backstairs belonging to it came from Mrs Masham's lodgings, who by that means could secretly bring to her whom she pleased."[2] These aspersions, uninspiring as thoughts, unpleasant as statements, recoil upon their author when contrasted with one of Anne's scribbled notes to Sarah:

I scratched twice at dear Mrs Freeman's door, as soon as Lord

---

[1] *Sarah Correspondence*, i, 415–416.   [2] *Conduct*, p. 265.

Treasurer went from me, in hopes to have spoke one more word to him before he was gone; but, nobody hearing me, I wrote this, not caring to send what I had to say by word of mouth; which was, to desire him that when he sends his orders to Kensington he would give directions there may be a great many Yeomen of the Guards to carry the Prince's dear body, that it may not be let fall, the great stairs being very steep and slippery.[1]

When Archdeacon Coxe says of this that it "marks the Queen's minute attention to all the details of the interment" he also seems to fall below the level of feelings which simple folk understand.

Low, low lay the Tories in the trough of misfortune after Harley's fall. Harley's ordeal, until Greg's dying breath had exonerated him, had been shattering. That at least was over; but he had quitted office and the Court to find his party split into at least three sections, each abusing the other, and all laying the blame of their plight upon him. The Jacobite attempted invasion ruined Tory prospects at the polls. Mauled and diminished, they awaited the meeting of a Parliament where, for the first time during the reign, the Whigs would be masters. St John, seatless, buried himself in the country. Harley was returned; but to a scene how changed! For nearly a decade he had practically led the House of Commons, either from the Speaker's Chair or as Secretary of State. All that time he had been its principal figure. Now, stripped of his official trappings, without a majority to support or even a party to cheer him, and lacking the power of dramatic and eloquent speech by which an individual position can be maintained, his prospects seemed at first forlorn.

But Harley's political knowledge taught him that a healing process would soon begin in the Tory Opposition. Common misfortunes would beget a common partisanship. He felt sure the party would come back to him. He knew its great strength if united. Meanwhile, as was notorious—and notorious to his advantage—he was, through Abigail, in the closest contact with the Queen. Abigail signalled her loyalties and information in her own cryptic way.

Abigail Masham to Harley

April 18th, 1708

I was at Court this day, and if I have any skill in physiognomy, my old mistress is not pleased with me. I told you 'twas my thought on Thursday night. If I guess right am to seek why 'tis so. My Lady

[1] Coxe, iv, 324.

Giggster [?] was there very gay and seemed extremely at ease. Ailligo's mother [?] was also there. I was asked by a very sensible man and one that knows Courts whether any or all of us four were not with my old mistress when she last was in town. The reason for the question I had not, and the answer I made you may guess. I shan't go till Thursday; therefore you may be sure I shall wait on you first.[1]

July 21st, 1708

I repent heartily my telling my aunt [the Queen] the reason why I desired to go to Walton [London], but did not question having leave, as I told you in my last. I thank you for your kind advice, and I hope God Almighty will give me more grace than to be taken in any of their snares. I am very ready to believe they will try all ways to ruin me, but they shall never do it by any indirect action of my own. If theirs will take effect against me, God's will be done: I must submit to what He permits. Oh, my poor aunt Stephens is to be pitied very much, for they press her harder than ever. Since what happened lately she is altered more than is to be imagined; no ready money [courage] at all to supply her with common necessaries. Really I see it so bad and they come so fast upon her I have no hopes of her deliverance, for she will put it quite out of her friends' power to save her. I have heard of the court they make to Mrs Packer [Hanover family] from several people and *told her all*; while she is leaving it, she is very melancholy, but says little to the matter.

My Lady Pye [Duchess of Marlborough] is here still. I have not seen my aunt since my duty called me, which was Saturday and Sunday in the morning; to-morrow I go again to do my duty. I don't think it any unkindness in my aunt, but because my Lady Pye is here. My friend that is gone the journey you need not fear will be led into any inconvenience by the person you mentioned to my brother, for my friend is as cautious as anybody can be; he knows them very well.

I shall be glad to have a line from you Saturday. God bless you and give you health. The papers are safe which you left with me, but if you want them let me know when you write.[2]

Apart from his hopes in Court intrigues and party strife, Harley might at any time receive a valuable windfall from abroad. Oudenarde, indeed, had been a heavy blow, setting the town agog again with Marlborough's fame. But as the autumn advanced it seemed almost impossible, if one took a map and studied the positions of the armies and Marlborough's communications, to believe that he could capture Lille. Expert military opinion was predominantly adverse throughout Europe. Marlborough as he now stood with the Queen was in no condition to sustain so grievous a reverse as the

[1] Portland Papers, *H.M.C.*, iv, 486–496.   [2] *Ibid.*, 495–496.

abandonment of the siege. There were always, besides, the personal dangers of the trenches and the field.

Harley, out of office, still preserved his group of correspondents. One such, Erasmus Lewis, a Cambridge man with diplomatic experience, Harley's private secretary in 1704, made a series of reports to his chief which reveal only too clearly their common point of view. "The business of our little world," he wrote to Harley (September 28), "stands still in expectation of the great event in Flanders, and till that be decided all things are in suspense. . . ."[1]

> I conceive [October 17] . . . our affairs to be in such a miserable posture that it cannot but affect anyone who has a subsistence . . . in his country. I see, however, that this ill blast blows this good, that I dare go, without fear of being insulted, into public places, which I could not have done some months since; . . . and you would be surprised to hear men say publicly we have spent so many millions to find out this great secret, that our General does not understand the *métier de la guerre*, that he has indeed twice or thrice thrown a lucky main, but never knew how to play his game, and that he is but a little genius, of a size adapted to getting money by all sordid and dishonourable ways, which I think never was the vice of a warlike, nor, indeed, of a great spirit of any sort.[2]

And (October 8), the fruits of eavesdropping:

> Lord Sunderland, Lord Coningsby and Sir James Forbes dined yesterday at Pontacks with their City Friends, where they took Lille and raised six millions in a trice without the assistance of any but their own party, as the two gentlemen last named declared last night in all the public places, adding that Lord Treasurer had promised to drop the Duke of Queensberry, and to surrender himself up entirely to the sage advices of the Junto.[3]

Refreshed by these streams of malicious gossip, flowing in perfect detachment from national interest, Harley and the leaders of the Tory Opposition watched the heartshaking drama of the famous siege run its course, and awaited with equal eagerness bad news from the front and the meeting of Parliament. As this approached, St John from his country retreat gave signs of life and recovery.

St John to Harley

October 11, 1708

I have thought a good while that you could expect from one quarter nothing but that you have met with, and this prepossession used to

---

[1] Portland Papers, *H.M.C.*, iv, 505.   [2] *Ibid.*, 507.   [3] *Ibid.*, 508.

make me very uneasy when we were building up the power of a faction which it was plain we should find it necessary in a short time to pull down, and when we entered into some engagements which would prove clogs and fetters upon us whenever we came in our own defence to play a contrary game, This has been and this is our case, and what can redeem us from more than Egyptian bondage? There is one person [no doubt Marlborough] who with a fiat resolutely pronounced might do it; but when I recollect all I heard and saw last winter I despair of any salvation from thence. There is no hope I am fully convinced but in the Church of England party, not in that neither on the foot it now stands, and without more confidence than is yet re-established between them and us. *Why do you not gain Bromley entirely?* The task is not difficult, and by governing him without seeming to do so, you will influence them. Your Friends, I mean such of them as are in Parliament, will I dare say take their parts and do everything which they possibly can without direct contradiction to themselves. *You broke the party, unite it again*; their sufferings have made them wise, and whatever piques or jealousies they may entertain at present, as they feel the success of better conduct these will wear off, and you will have it in your power by reasonable measures to lead them to reasonable ends.

If they are not at first strong enough to conquer they will be too strong to be broken. *This hollow square*[1] will defend you who seem to be singled out for destruction, and will be in condition whenever the propitious day comes to lodge power where it naturally should be, with property.[2]

Harley needed no prompting where Bromley was concerned. For some weeks he had held his written pledge. "I can now assure you," Bromley had written (September 18), "of my own very sincere disposition to enter into measures with you and the gentleman you mention, for serving our common interest, and that I verily believe you will find the like in others."[3]

St John to Harley

November 6, 1708

I am as much convinced as it is possible to be that going out of employment at the time and in the manner we did was equally honest and prudent. No man's opinion can add any weight to confirm me in this thought.

I must say further that the merit of this action depends, according to my apprehension, on the use which you and your friends make of that

---

[1] Evidently the late Secretary-at-War had in his mind Caraman's brilliant retreat from the field of Elixem in 1705.

[2] Bath Papers, *H.M.C.*, i, 191.   [3] Portland Papers, *H.M.C.*, iv, 504.

state of freedom which they placed themselves in by laying down their employments.

No one living is able to do so much as you yourself towards removing our present evils, and towards averting those which a very short-sighted man may perceive to impend over us. But you are the mark at which every dart of faction is levelled, and it is impossible either that you should be safe from daily insults or that the least progress should be made towards those views which you propose, unless a number of gentlemen be satisfied of their danger, unless they be convinced that to preserve themselves they must follow you, unless you inspire your party with industry and courage, which at present seem only to be possessed by the factions, and with as much of that virtuous love of the country as this vile generation is capable of receiving and which at present seems to have the least share in the guidance of any side. The fiery trial of affliction has made the gentlemen of the Church of England more prepared to form such a party than from their former conduct it might have been expected. . . .[1]

Thus, while the Queen and Abigail had been holding the fort against the Whigs and obdurately resisting the advice of her two great counsellors, Harley quietly and deftly rallied the Tories. The spectacle which greeted the new Parliament of a purely party Whig Administration monopolizing all the important offices, though certainly not the favour of the Crown, was all that was necessary to unite the "gentlemen of England" into a solid opposition. To whom could they look but Harley, who had suffered for resisting Whig pretensions, and whose relations with the Queen gave him the key to the spacious patronage of any new Administration?

The intense constitutional struggle recorded in the letters between the Queen and Marlborough had proceeded unknown to Parliament or the nation. It was fought out sternly in secret. To the outer world the Constitution seemed to work with perfect smoothness. The Queen was seen to extend her gracious favour increasingly to those statesmen who had the greatest influence with the new Parliament. The new Parliament extolled its happy relations with the Crown; and the Commons voted ever larger supplies for the prosecution of the war, even before the campaign of 1708 reached its long-drawn, glorious conclusion. Such was the world parade. But underneath how strangely different! The victorious General broken and begging to retire; the faithful Treasurer a black-mailed agent of the Junto; the world-revered Sovereign working by the backstairs with the publicly discredited leader of the Opposi-

[1] Bath Papers, *H.M.C.*, i, 193.

tion against the Parliament which sustained her throne and the great Ministers who had made it safe and almost all-powerful!

We have now reached the culmination of the eighteenth-century world war, and also of this story. The foundations of Marlborough's authority in England had been destroyed, and the national and European cause which he served was triumphant. His power had gone, but his work was done. We have witnessed a spectacle, so moving for the times in which we live, of a league of twenty-six signatory states successfully resisting and finally overcoming a mighty coherent military despotism. It was a war of the circumference against the centre. When we reflect upon the selfish aims, the jealousies and shortcomings of the Allies, upon their many natural divergent interests, upon the difficulties of procuring common and timely agreement upon any single necessary measure, upon the weariness moral and physical which drags down all prolonged human effort; when we remember that movement was limited to the speed of a marching soldier or a canal barge, and communication or correspondence to that of a coach, or at the best of a horseman, we cannot regard it as strange that Louis XIV should so long have sustained his motto, "Nec pluribus impar." Lying in his central station with complete control of the greatest nation of the world in one of its most remarkable ebullitions, with the power to plan far in advance, to strike now in this quarter, now in that, and above all with the certainty of implicit obedience, it is little wonder how well and how long he fought. The marvel is that any force could have been found in that unequipped civilization of Europe to withstand, still less to subdue him. In Marlborough the ramshackle coalition had found, if not its soul, its means of effective expression, its organic unity, and its supreme sword. Thus the circle of quaking states and peoples, who had almost resigned themselves to an inevitable over-lordship, became a ring of fire and steel, which in its contraction wore down and strangled their terrible foe.

This result had in fact been achieved. Behind the lines of the French armies, beneath the glitter of Versailles, all was exhausted, all lay in ruin. The Grand Monarch still stood magnificent at bay; but his heart was broken. When he looked out upon his wasted realm, upon the depleted manhood of France, upon his pillaged treasury and half-tilled fields, upon his cowed armies and sunken fleet, despair and remorse swelled upon him in a dark flood, and peace at any price became his dearest, all-compelling wish.

Marlborough, Heinsius, Eugene, the Triumvirate of executive action, could not as yet see the dust and ashes which lay behind the fortresses, the rivers, and the mountain-chains of the French front. They saw that front was still unbroken; they were sure it was crumbling. One more campaign, one effort stronger than any yet made, and the prize of their long toils would be won. This was their conviction at the fall of Ghent and Bruges. They could not foresee the crowning calamity of the great frost which was to fall on France in the winter of 1708. Neither, on the other hand, were they or any of their generation conscious of the new strength which the French people could supply if a war of monarchical aggrandizement should be transformed into a war of national survival. They all three underrated both the present prostration and the latent final resources of France. None of these facts presented themselves to the breathless actors in this struggle in the clear light, shape, and proportion in which we now see them. They could not tell how soon or with what exertions they were going to win. But that they were winning, and had only to hold together and drive on, was their absolute conviction.

But when they looked behind them to their own countries they saw themselves at the last gasp. The Empire, including Austria and all Germany, could not put forty thousand men in the field, apart from the troops paid for by the Sea Powers. The Dutch were worn to the bone by the endless struggles of the Republic. Their Barrier was in their hands to take and hold. They longed for peace. All future war-effort depended upon Marlborough and England, and from this moment Marlborough and England were no longer one.

The Captain-General and the Lord Treasurer, Marlborough and Godolphin, had spent upon the seven campaigns all their political capital. The Queen was estranged. Instead of being their strength, she was henceforth their bane. Sarah and Godolphin were her aversion, Marlborough a splendid but oppressive fact. The Tories banished from power, united by misfortune, nursed revenge. The Whigs had arrived. They had forced their way into what the Queen regarded as her own apartments. They had gained control of all the great offices and assets of State, including the services of Marlborough. They had the majorities of the Lords and Commons at their backs. They cared nothing for Sarah and Godolphin; for these were blunted tools which could be thrown aside. They knew they owed nothing to Marlborough. He constantly vowed that he would align himself with no party. In so far as he had used his influence in their behalf upon the Queen it had been in vain. He had not only had no part in their success, but had even been grievously offended by the actual methods by which they had succeeded in gaining their ends. They recognized him as their greatest possession. They were sure he was in their hands, or at least that without them his power was at an end. He knew this too. He was inflexibly resolved not to play the game of any party. From the bottom of his heart, and with forty years' experience in court, camp, and council, he despised both Whigs and Tories with a cordiality which history has readily understood. Henceforward he regarded himself not as a leader, but as a functionary. He would serve the Government as a soldier or as a diplomatist. He would not be answerable for their relations with the Queen or with Parliament. He would lead such armies as they provided, and negotiate such treaties as they prescribed. In this humbler guise he might still procure the means to fight the find campaign and march to Paris.

GENERAL MAP OF THE WESTERN NETHERLANDS

English Miles

488

VOLUME FOUR

Volume Four

PREFACE

THIS volume upon the fall of Marlborough completes the story of his life which I began nearly ten years ago. It exposes and explains the lamentable desertion by England of her leadership of the Grand Alliance, or League of Nations, which had triumphantly broken the military power of Louis XIV. It shows how when victory has been won across measureless hazards it can be cast away by the pride of a victorious War Party and the intrigues of a pacifist reaction.

In the spring of 1709 we see England, or Great Britain, as she had recently become, at the summit of power and achievement. Queen Anne, seated securely upon her throne, was the centre of the affairs of the then known world. The smallest incident at her Court was studied with profound respect or attention by all civilized countries. Louis XIV, old, broken, bereaved, brooded disconsolately amid the stricken splendours of Versailles. The tyrant of Europe, who had let loose a quarter of a century of war upon his neighbours, had become a suppliant. The Whig Party in England, possessed of majorities in the Lords and Commons, had forced themselves into power. They no longer sought the liberation of Europe, but the destruction of France. They lost the victorious peace which might have closed the struggle. In France they roused the patriotism with which Frenchmen have always defended their soil, and in England they fell a prey to the designs of their party foes. The terrible battle of Malplaquet, the bloodiest and best contested for a hundred years, marked the climax of their efforts. Thereafter all became shameful and confused. Queen Anne abandoned the purposes of her reign. Abigail led Harley up the backstairs. The Queen devoted her great power to driving out the Whigs. England was dominated by party politics and the jealous emulation of great nobles. Marlborough and Godolphin were undermined. The Whigs were ejected and chased from office, and a Ministry was installed resolved upon peace at any cost. But by these very facts the French were incited to continue their resistance, and after three more years of conflict they found themselves, though exhausted, still erect.

This process depended upon the political drama in London, which in its various acts and scenes illustrates vividly the life of a Parliamentary nation, and reveals at many points the foundations of our Constitution. Marlborough was hunted down. His wife was driven from the Court. He himself, though he served the Tories faithfully in the field, was subjected to the cruellest humiliations and vile, undeserved reproach. The British army was forced to abandon its comrades in the field, and a peace was made contrary to every canon of international good faith. All Europe, friend and foe, was staggered by the perfidy of the Tory Ministers; but while the Queen lived they ruled with unchallengeable authority. Marlborough chose exile rather than the ill-usage he must receive in his native land. The name of England became a byword on the Continent, and at the moment of Queen Anne's death the Protestant Succession itself was in danger, and our island on the verge of a second Civil War. This supreme disaster was averted, but when Marlborough returned to his native land and to a great position, time and age, which cast their veils over the fierce impulses and scenes of action, had led him to the dusk of his life.

I have tried to show Marlborough in his wonderful strength, without concealing his faults. I am not aware of any charge brought against him that has not been fully exposed and discussed. My impression of his size and power has grown with study. His genius in war, his statecraft, his virtues as a man, may be judged by these pages; nor is it necessary to dwell further upon them here. Happy the State or sovereign who finds such a servant in years of danger!

I have followed the method used in earlier volumes of always endeavouring to make Marlborough speak whenever possible. I have drawn upon the admirable foreign histories of this period— Klopp, Salomon, Von Noorden—and have been guided by them to the vivid reports of Hoffmann, Gallas, and other ambassadors and envoys to the English Court. From these sources a more intimate picture can be obtained of the political life of our country than in any of our domestic records.

The Blenheim archives have been found more fertile than in the preceding volume; in particular the reports of the British spy in Paris seem of high interest.

I must express my acknowledgments to the authorities of the Rijksarchief at The Hague for the courtesy with which they have laid their archives open to me; and also to the Huntington Library in California, to the Hon. Edward Cadogan, Lieutenant-Colonel Gordon Halswell, and others who have contributed original material.

I have been greatly assisted in the necessary researches by Mr F. W. Deakin, of Wadham College, Oxford, and again by Brigadier R. P. Pakenham-Walsh and Commander J. H. Owen, R.N., in technical matters. I accord my thanks to all those who so kindly allowed me to reproduce pictures and portraits in their possession, and to the present Duke of Marlborough for continuing to give me the freedom of the Blenheim archives.

WINSTON SPENCER CHURCHILL

CHARTWELL
WESTERHAM
August 13, 1938

Chapter One

OO

THE whole of Europe was now weary of the almost unceasing wars which had ravaged its peoples for twenty years. Peace was desired by all the warring states. It was in all men's minds. The Allies wished to reap the fruits of victory. Louis XIV, resigned to the decision of arms, sought only a favourable or even a tolerable escape. The enormous quarrel had been fought out, and the exorbitant power of France was broken. Not one of the original objects of the war was not already gained. Many further advantages were open. Why then was this peace not achieved in the winter of 1708 or the spring of 1709? Upon Marlborough has been cast the responsibility for this lamentable breakdown in human affairs. How far is this censure just? The issue is decisive for his fame. Before it can be judged his authority and the foundations on which it stood in Holland and in Britain must be measured.

From the day in 1706 on which the Emperor had first offered him the Viceroyalty of the Netherlands a sense of divergent interest had arisen between the Dutch leaders and their Deputy Captain-General. Although Marlborough had at a very early stage refused the offer, the Dutch could not help suspecting first that he owed them a grudge for having been the obstacle, and secondly that he still hoped to obtain the prize. It was known in Holland that both the Hapsburg brothers were intent upon this plan. After Oudenarde Marlborough had been sent a patent for life of the Governorship of the Netherlands. In August 1708 King Charles had written, "I do not doubt but that you will never allow the Netherlands, under the pretext of that pretended Barrier, to suffer any diminution either in their area or as regards my royal authority in them, which authority I wish to place in your hands."[1]

In reporting the arrival of the patent to Godolphin Marlborough

[1] Charles to Marlborough, August 8, 1708; Brussels Archives, quoted in L. P. Gachard, *Histoire de la Belgique*, p. 337.

494

had written, "This must be known to nobody but the Queen; for should it be known before the peace, it would create inconveniences in Holland." But, he had added, if when the time came Anne "should not think it for her honour and interest that I accept of this great offer, I will decline it with all the submission imaginable."[1]

Nothing, indeed, could be more correct than his conduct. But the Dutch increasingly regarded him as the interested supporter of Hapsburg and Imperial claims rather than of their own. Rumours of the arrival of the patent were rife in The Hague in December. There is a report in the Heinsius Archives of an interview in December 1708 between Marlborough and the Dutch Intendant at Brussels, a certain Pesters, with whom he was particularly friendly and from whom he gained much information. Marlborough spoke with vehemence.

> "In God's name, what have I to expect from King Charles? He has more than once bestowed on me the government of the Low Countries. I have the patent" (pointing to his strong-box). "No, I have left it in England. But when I learned that it was displeasing to your Republic I renounced the idea, and I renounce it for ever. No, in truth, Pesters" (he always calls me "Pesters" when he wishes to speak with sincerity), "if they offered me in Holland the office of Stadt-holder, I swear by God and by my own damnation I would not accept it. I am greatly misjudged. I know of what I am suspected; but my sole thought, after I shall have done my utmost to secure a good and durable peace, is to retire into private life. Nevertheless, if a Governor were required for the Low Countries I do not know why I should be less agreeable to the Republic than another, but I assure you that I have no thoughts of it."[2]

During the summer of 1708 a correspondence sprang up between Heinsius and Torcy, the French Foreign Minister, the tendency of which was a separate understanding between Holland and France which might well bring about a general peace conference. This was irregular, but not necessarily disloyal. The preliminaries of the Treaty of Ryswick, in spite of the passionate resentment of England, had been arranged for the whole coalition by Holland, and the Dutch Republic conceived itself upon this precedent practically entitled by custom to test for itself, without consulting its allies, the readiness of the enemy to make peace. Louis XIV also was obstinately convinced that the path to peace lay through an initial

[1] W. C. Coxe, *Memoirs of John, Duke of Marlborough* (second edition, 1820), iv, 246.
[2] H. Pesters to Heinsius, December 17, 1708; Heinsius Archives. See also R. Geikie and I. Montgomery, *The Dutch Barrier* (1705–19), pp. 93, 373.

and separate understanding with The Hague. A means of communication had long existed in the person of Herman von Petkum. Petkum, "Petithomme," as Marlborough once, perhaps accidentally, spelt his name, was officially the agent at The Hague of the Duke of Holstein-Gottorp, but he was in fact the Pensionary's servant, reserved for just this kind of work. Although he was paid not only by Heinsius and Vienna, but by Torcy,[1] his faithful and skilful labours for peace none the less deserve respect. At the end of May 1708, even before the battle of Oudenarde, Torcy had invited Petkum secretly to Paris, and in August, with the knowledge and approval of Heinsius,[2] he had conversations with Torcy at Fontainebleau. Torcy complained of the obduracy of the Allies. Petkum said this was due to the shifting propositions of France through different channels, and insisted that France must as preliminaries agree to yield Spain and the Indies, and all allied conquests in Brabant, Flanders, and Alsace; must recognize Queen Anne and undertake not to interfere with her or with the order of succession established by Parliament; must restore English trade in France to its former footing, and accord to Holland the tariff of 1664 and a satisfactory Barrier.

Torcy said that France would hazard everything sooner than submit to these excessive demands. On the other hand, he contemplated the partition of the Spanish Empire, was prepared to yield the bulk of it, and also declared that "the maritime Powers should receive security for their trade, and the Low Countries their tariff and their Barrier."[3]

Having remained at Fontainebleau for five or six days, Petkum returned to Holland and reported everything to the Pensionary. But Heinsius told Marlborough nothing.[4]

It was not proper nor did it prove possible to keep all this from the vigilant Captain-General. During August the news of Petkum's Paris visit·leaked out in high circles at The Hague, and it cannot be doubted that it soon reached Marlborough. In fact, at the beginning of 1709 his Secret Service obtained the whole file of the current Torcy-Petkum correspondence. It was in cipher; but one of his

[1] Eugene's report to Vienna, Vienna Archives; W. Reese, *Das Ringen um Frieden und Sicherheit* (1708–9) (1933), p. 16. See also O. Klopp, *Der Fall des Hauses Stuart*, xiii, 217. See also *Recueil des instructions données aux Ambassadeurs de France*, tome xxiii. Petkum received from France 3000 livres a year after 1703; on October 6, 1709, 4000 livres, on March 6, 1720, 3000 livres (French Foreign Office Archives, "Correspondance de Hollande," tome 200, ii, 117).

[2] Klopp, xiii, 219.   [3] Round Papers, *H.M.C.*, p. 329.

[4] Marlborough to Heinsius, November 6/17, 1708 (Heinsius Archives); Marlborough to Wratislaw, September 25, 1708 (Vienna Archives); Reese, pp. 27–28.

agents, Blencowe,[1] a gentleman from Northampton, succeeded in penetrating the code, and translations of eleven letters are now in the Public Record Office.[2] In the autumn of 1708, however, Marlborough was dependent mainly on oral accounts. He was conscious that his relations with Heinsius were far from sure. He was not willing that Heinsius should pursue separate negotiations behind his back or that of the British Government, and in his turn he sought contact with France.

Throughout the long campaigns Marlborough had maintained correspondence, written in English and under his secret sign "00," with his illustrious nephew Berwick. In the main this had been concerned with the courtesies of war, and cherished kinship amid national quarrels. It also served to keep alive that link with the exiled family at Saint-Germains which had persisted for so many years. But Marlborough's civilities, although they always excited tremors of hope, had long ceased seriously to deceive the Shadow Court. It was not till 1708 that the correspondence touched any serious matter. Communication was easy, for Berwick at Château l'Abbaye was but a day's ride from Marlborough's headquarters at Helchin, and there was much traffic between the hostile commanders upon the exchange of prisoners, safeguards, and complaints of various kinds. To and fro went the messengers with their trumpets and flags of truce, bearing letters of routine, and other letters also, in their sabretaches. Marlborough took every possible precaution. He enjoined secrecy. He requested Berwick to return each of his letters with the answer. He seems to have trusted him absolutely, and as it proved rightly. Nevertheless, he ran a very high degree of risk in confiding himself to those upon whom he was inflicting such grievous injuries when, without consulting the Queen or the Cabinet, Sarah or Godolphin, Heinsius or Eugene, he at last, in mid-August 1708, definitely set on foot a peace negotiation.

Marlborough to Berwick

August 24

00. I had not had time when I returned your trumpet to answer your last letter. You have no doubt heard of the commotion caused by the respite accorded to mylord Griffin, and that the malcontents

[1] William Blencowe was a Fellow of All Souls and barrister-at-law. He received two hundred pounds a year from the Secret Service fund for his decoding work. Hearne, the Oxford antiquary, calls him "a proud fanatical Whig." He lost his employment on the arrival of the Tories in office, and shot himself in August 1712. See *Remarks and Collections of Thomas Hearne* (edited by C. E. Doble, 1889), iii, 439.

[2] B.M., Add. MSS. 32306, 34518.

say that they will raise the matter when Parliament meets. However, you may be sure that at the first opportunity I shall render a similar service to my lord Middleton's sons.[1] I would also assure you that no one in the world wishes for peace with more sincerity than I. But it must be stable and lasting, and in conformity with the interests of my country. Circumstanced as I am, I am inclined to think that the best way to set on foot a treaty of peace would be for the proposal to be first made in Holland, whence it will be communicated to me, and then I shall be in a better position to help, of which you may assure the King of France. And if there is anything which he wishes me to know upon this, I beg him that it may not be by other hands than yours, for then you may rest assured that I will tell you my opinion frankly. 00.[2]

It will be seen that Marlborough's intervention took the form, not of superseding any negotiations already in progress between France and Holland, but rather of broadening their basis, and bringing himself and Britain into them. Berwick replied cordially to this letter, and sent it to the King. Louis and his advisers Chamillart and Torcy were all set on dealing with the Dutch alone. They did not welcome the intervention at this stage of Marlborough, and still less of Britain. They also inclined to regard Marlborough's letter as only another of his innumerable traps and stratagems. Chamillart thought that it confessed a precarious military position. The answer which Berwick was at length directed to send reflected these views. "It is not now for his Majesty to make such overtures, but for the Dutch."[3] He invited Marlborough to continue to use him as a channel, and thanked him for his efforts to save the lives of Lord Griffin and Middleton's sons. Marlborough could only reply, "The King is alone the judge of what is best for his honour and his interest. . . . If ever the King wishes to let me know his intentions about peace, I desire that it should be by your agency, for I shall have no reserve with you, being sure of the care you will have for my safety and my honour."[4] And a day or two later: "I beg you to believe that I have no other reason for asking you for the return of my letters than the fear of accidents, for I will always trust you willingly with my life and my honour. So pray return me in your first letter that which I wrote you on the 14th."[5]

[1] Lord Griffin and Middleton's sons were among those captured in the Jacobite descent of 1708. Marlborough had exerted himself to save the aged Lord Griffin from the scaffold. See Vol. III, p. 321.

[2] French Foreign Office Archives, "Angleterre," tome 226, f. 121; A. Legrelle, *La Diplomatie française et la succession d'Espagne*, v, 381.

[3] *Loc. cit.*   [4] Dépôt de la Guerre, tome 2083, p. 68.   [5] *Loc. cit.*

During the next two months Petkum continued his activities: "I have promised Heinsius," he wrote to Torcy (September 11), "to treat with him alone and let him communicate to Marlborough no more than he thinks fit." But Marlborough had already heard many things. Petkum wrote (September 25), "Marlborough suspects some secret negotiation, and will do what he can to thwart it."[1] By the end of October the Duke feared that the Dutch were about to quit the Alliance.[2] No answer had been returned to his urgent request for an augmentation of their army for the campaign of 1709, and he saw that the fall of Lille would encourage the Dutch to a quick separate negotiation. Boufflers[3] beat the chamade on October 25, and on the 29th Marlborough received an unsatisfactory reply from Heinsius about the augmentation. Confronted with a grave menace to the Alliance and to British interests, he made a renewed and far more direct effort to gain control of the peace negotiations, and to bring London and Vienna into them.

On October 30, the night that the capitulation terms of Lille were finally agreed, and the day after receiving Heinsius' refusal to increase the Dutch army, he wrote again to Berwick. This time he proposed that France, counting on his aid, should ask for an armistice and openly seek a peace.

Marlborough to Berwick

October 30

. . . You know that I have formerly assured you of my desire to contribute to peace whenever a favourable occasion should present itself. In my view it is at this moment in our power to take such a step as will produce peace before the next campaign. . . .

My opinion is therefore that if the Duke of Burgundy had the King's permission to make proposals by means of letters to the deputies, to Prince Eugene, and to me, requesting us to communicate them to our masters, which we should be bound to do, that would have such an effect in Holland that peace would certainly ensue.

There follows this remarkable passage:

You may be assured that I shall be wholeheartedly for peace, *not doubting that I shall find the goodwill [amitié] which was promised me two years ago by the Marquis d'Alègre [i.e., the douceur of two million livres].* If the King and the Duke of Burgundy do not feel that this time is suitable for peace proposals, I beg you to have the friendship and

[1] Round Papers, *H.M.C.*, p. 330.
[2] Marlborough to Heinsius, October 6, 1708; Hague Archives; Reese, p. 28 *n.*
[3] The governor of Lille.

justice to believe that I have no other object than to end speedily a wearisome war.

As I trust you without reserve I conjure you never to part with this letter except to return it to me.[1]

It is indeed amazing that any man should have the hardihood to write such a letter to those who regarded him as their most terrible foe—indeed, their only foe. Marlborough is justified before history in pursuing these unauthorized negotiations. In his supreme position, both military and political, he was entitled, on his own judgment and at his own peril, to act for the best for his country, for the Alliance, and for Europe, all bleeding and ravaged by interminable war. It is often inevitable that the first overtures of peace should be made by secret and informal means. Marlborough, for his part, combined all the qualities both of the military and the civil power; he was the soul of the war, and if he thought it was time to make peace he was right before God and man to do so. But to introduce into this grave and delicate transaction a question of private gain, a personal reward of an enormous sum of money, however related to the standards of those times, was, apart from moral considerations, imprudent in the last degree. Yet this conduct has a palliative feature curiously characteristic of several of Marlborough's most questionable acts. It served interests national, European, and personal at once and equally. It was the one thing capable of convincing the French King and Cabinet of his sincerity. It affected Berwick in this sense immediately. "Although naturally," he wrote to Torcy on November 2, "I am not taken in by all he says, nevertheless I am inclined to believe in his good faith on this occasion, *all the more because he speaks in it of a certain matter by which you know he sets great store.*"[2]

It certainly shook the advisers of Louis XIV. "If he is sincere," wrote Chamillart to Torcy (November 2), "use should be made of his goodwill, which would not be bought too dearly at Monsieur d'Alègre's figure."[3] The dreaded conqueror placing himself in their hands in this way, and revealing his personal weakness so nakedly, went far to sweep away their inveterate suspicions. They addressed themselves with renewed concern to his proposal. In the course of their anxious confabulations a memorandum was written, assembling all the arguments for and against the project, which throws a revealing light upon the inmost thoughts of the hard-pressed yet mighty monarchy.

[1] Legrelle, v, 385.   [2] *Ibid.*, 387.   [3] *Ibid.*, 386.

The Duke of Marlborough must amidst all his prosperity fear the envy and antagonism of his own class, the general hatred of his countrymen, whose favour is more inconstant than that of any other people, the fickleness of his mistress and the credit of new favourites, perhaps the death of the Princess [Queen Anne] herself, the resentment of the Duke of Hanover[1] and the residence of his son in England, and lastly the breaking up of the Alliance. . . . If the war could last for ever, a man like Marlborough, who rules absolutely the councils of the principal European Powers and who conducts their armies, might have to make up his mind whether the fear of the future should induce him to abandon so fine a personal position. But in one way or another the war is drawing towards its end. . . .

He might well be satisfied with his glory if he could win peace for his country. . . . He will be no less satisfied upon the point of possessions, which the war has procured him in plenty. It is not just that peace should deprive him of all the advantages which the command of the armies brings him. We might well, therefore, give him to understand, and that without undue circumlocution—scarcely necessary, indeed, with him—that if he worked sincerely for peace he would be rewarded on its conclusion with a sum of two or even up to three million livres, payable at the earliest date, which would be a matter of arrangement.

The influence which Cardonnel has upon his mind is such that it is absolutely necessary to persuade the secretary in order to succeed with the master. The sum of three hundred thousand livres would be usefully employed to this end, and the King agrees to the Duke of Berwick proposing this by the person whom he chooses to speak to the Duke of Marlborough.[2]

In the end, however, King Louis and his councillors could not bring themselves to take the momentous step which Marlborough required. They still saw plainly the shattering effects upon French prestige and French means of resistance which were involved in suing for an armistice or initiating a peace proposal to Holland on the morrow of the fall of the city of Lille. It spelt defeat, acknowledged for all time in letters of fire. Well might they believe that Marlborough was sincere; for what better conclusion could the war hold for him? His sword would have struck the final blow. They would have surrendered beneath its impact, and he would quit the field of war loaded alike with glory and booty. More grievous distresses were needed to bring them to their knees. So,

---

[1] The Duke, or Elector, of Hanover was offended at not having been fully consulted in the Oudenarde operations.

[2] Legrelle, v, 674 *et seq.*

hearkening principally to Chamillart and his false ideas about the immediate military situation, clinging to the hope that the French armies could winter on the Scheldt and that Lille could be regained in the spring, the King directed Berwick to say in reply:

November 5, 1708

You know that the Kings of France and Spain desire peace. . . . You are aware that so far [the Allies] have made no response indicating a genuine desire for a settlement. Their situation, although most brilliant in appearance, cannot prevent those who have experience of war from perceiving that it is strained in all sorts of ways, and may at any moment be so transformed that even if you took the citadel of Lille you might be thrown into extremities which would destroy your armies and put it out of your power to supply with munitions and food the strong places you occupy beyond [*depuis*] the Scheldt, to recruit and re-establish your forces, and to put your armies in a state to resume the war in the next campaign.

I cannot but think that these reflections, joined to the desire which you have always shown me to contribute to a peace, have led you to write me the letter which I have received from you, which I will send you back if it has no happy results, and which I would return with great pleasure if it proved to have hastened the moment for me to thank you for the part you have allowed me to play in this important negotiation. . . .

If you think it would help the negotiation that the proposals for an armistice should come rather from the Duke of Burgundy than from the Allies, but without any mention of peace proposals, it is for you to bring us to that step in the best way. But in my opinion the conditions under which a suspension of arms could be arranged with your armies still in the midst of territories in his Majesty's rule, and Prince Eugene besieging the citadel of Lille, will be more difficult to settle than those of a general peace, *and it is in this last case that you would receive all the marks of friendship of which the Marquis d' Alègre has given you assurances on behalf of the King.*[1]

Berwick was sorry to have to send such an answer. He had arrived by very different paths at the same estimate of the war facts as Marlborough. "Nothing," wrote Berwick,

could have been better for all than this idea of the Duke of Marlborough's. It opened to us an honourable doorway to finish a burdensome war. . . . Monsieur de Chamillart from political excess made himself believe that this proposal of Marlborough's was extorted only by the plight in which the allied armies stood. I confess that this

---

[1] Legrelle, v, 390–391.

reasoning was beyond me; and from the manner in which Marlborough
had written to me I was sure that fear had no part in his action, but only
his wish to end a war of which all Europe began to weary. There was
no sign of bad faith in all that he said to me, and he only addressed
himself to me so as to make the negotiation pass through my hands,
believing that this would be helpful to me. Monsieur de Chamillart
prescribed the answer for me to make, and I thought it so extraordinary
that I *sent it in French* in order that the Duke of Marlborough might see
that it did not come from me. He was, in fact, so affronted by it that
nothing fruitful for peace could be gathered from this overture. I
even believe that this was the main cause of the aversion which the
Duke of Marlborough always showed afterwards to a friendly settlement.[1]

That Berwick was right upon the personal and military issues
cannot be disputed. Marlborough felt himself violently rebuffed.
He does not seem to have minded at all asking the King of France
to give him a fortune if he brought all things to a happy conclusion.
He had no consciousness of how disdainfully posterity would view
this incident. But he was deeply angered that the other side should
dispute his opinion upon the military situation. He was sure he
could beat their armies wherever they chose to stand. His peace
proposals had been sincere. He had made the French what he deemed
a fair offer. They had rejected it. Let them, then, since they were so
proud, learn the consequences. In a few weeks he had broken their
lines along the Scheldt, recaptured Ghent and Bruges, and driven
Burgundy and Vendôme helter-skelter into France. "I am much
mortified," he wrote to Berwick,

> to see that you believe I had any other motive for my letter except
> a wish for peace and the promise which I had given to let you know
> when I thought the proper time had come to take the steps necessary
> to secure it. . . . If the King and the Duke of Burgundy feel that secret
> conferences would be a surer and quicker path, they can propose this
> to the Pensionary and to some of the States at The Hague, so that
> when the campaign is finished and I arrive there, I can be informed
> of what has passed.[2]

He would, he added, continue to do his best to reach a just and
lasting peace before the next campaign, "and meanwhile the two
armies will be free to make the best use of the advantages which they
each suppose they possess. Please send me back my letters with your
next." Marlborough's request for the return of his letters was

---

[1] *Memoirs*, ii, 51-53. [2] Legrelle, v, 392.

evidently complied with by Berwick. The French archives contain only unsigned, undated translations from Marlborough's English in Middleton's[1] hand, with comments by Berwick.[2] This fact has a bearing on a future transaction.

So failed Marlborough's personal effort for peace. That it was wisely and justly founded at the time few can doubt. It is tarnished for us by the alloy of a sordid pecuniary interest. But this, indeed, in that age added to its chances of success. Some writers have actually maintained that Marlborough only inserted this suggestion in order to convince the French Court of his sincerity; and they point to his refusals, to the astonishment of Torcy, of all bribes when these were eventually offered. But the suspicion remains. It reflects more upon Marlborough as a man than upon Marlborough as a worker. He was a greater worker than man. No personal interest or failing turned him from his work. He toiled and schemed with all his power for a reconciled and tolerant Europe, a chastened France, and a glorious England to inherit the New World. As a part in these purposes he delighted in military success. All these conditions being satisfied, and without prejudice to their achievement, he would take pains and stoop for a commission. Supreme sanity, profound comprehension, valiant, faithful action, and if all went well large and punctual money payments!

[1] Secretary of State to the Pretender.   [2] Legrelle, v, 664–665.

Chapter Two

THE WHIGS AND PEACE

1708–1709—WINTER AND SPRING

THE Lords of the Junto had held together through many baffling years. They now formed the core of a party Cabinet which controlled ample majorities in both Houses. We must not underrate their contribution to the course of public affairs. For years in their splendid country houses, in their clubs, in their party groupings and assemblies, they had examined and discussed every aspect of British politics and of the European war. They conceived themselves the heirs to the majestic estate which Marlborough's sword and their policy had raised for Britain. They proposed to manage it in their own way, and in accordance with the matured and defined principles of their party, and, above all, in accordance with its interest. On no point did the Whigs ever consciously diverge from that.

The arid, pedantic Sunderland was no longer their chief representative in the Cabinet. Somers had become Lord President of the Council. His outstanding ability, his experience, his learning, his eloquence and aptitude in speech and writing, once joined to a great office, ensured him leadership in the political world. Godolphin, divorced from the Tories, evidently weakened with the Queen, was, in spite of his Treasurership, eclipsed at the council board. His political authority, apart from his long fame, amounted to no more than his unbreakable association with Marlborough.

On the other hand, the fact that the Whigs were now effectively in power, and for the first time satisfied with their treatment by the Crown, removed for the moment all Parliamentary difficulties. For the first time in Anne's reign the organized dominant forces in the Cabinet and in Parliament had a clear-cut, coherent policy upon the war, upon peace negotiations, and in domestic affairs. The Whig leaders regarded Marlborough as their most valuable instrument. They were at last also contented with Godolphin. Few scruples had governed the pressures they had exerted upon the Crown or upon the Captain-General and Treasurer in order to gain office; but it must be admitted that, once installed, they showed themselves resolute, efficient, and helpful in all the processes of government. They managed the Parliamentary machine with deft and sure touch. Queen Anne had hoped that in practice the Whig Party would be split between the Junto and its moderate elements; but the Junto showed themselves too clever for this. They withdrew their own nominee for the Speakership in favour of the candidate of the moderates, and carried him with a solid party vote. The Royal Speech in November breathed inflexible resolution to continue the war with the utmost vigour. The addresses in reply from both Houses praised the Queen's conduct of affairs in glowing terms. The successes of the campaign were extolled, and the thanks of Parliament were once again voted unanimously to the Duke of Marlborough for his latest successes and for the energy which he was displaying in the national service. Since he was still abroad, a delegation was sent to present these tributes to him. Without waiting for any similar decision by the Dutch, an augmentation of ten thousand men was voted for the army in Flanders.

Finance was the field in which the Whig mastery was greatest. The whole force of the City, of the Bank of England, of the moneyed classes, obeyed the Ministerial requirements with the enthusiasm of confidence and interest. The largest estimates yet presented were cheerfully accepted by the House of Commons. All Europe marvelled that in the seventh year of so great and costly a war, when every other state was almost beggared, if not bankrupt, the wealth of England proved inexhaustible. Indeed, it seemed that the Government held a magic purse. The yield of high taxation was reinforced by internal borrowing upon the largest scale yet known. The Bank, in exchange for a twenty-one years' extension of their charter, bound themselves to provide four hundred thousand in cash and issue two and a quarter millions of bank-bills. The lists were opened on February 11. Within four hours of nine o'clock the whole amount was subscribed, and eager would-be lenders were turned away in crowds.[1] Hoffmann dilated to the Emperor upon

1 *Boyle to Marlborough*
February 9, 1709
★. . . At a general court held this morning they [the Bank] agreed to open their banks for an additional subscription of two million two hundred thousand pounds. We shall make the way easy for them to supply the Government with any amount my Lord Treasurer proposes.
P.S. *February* 11.—The subscription of the bank was filled to-day, not lasting for four hours. [Blenheim MSS.]

these prodigies, as they then seemed to the world. "Outside England," he wrote,

> it would appear incredible for this nation, after it has provided four hundred million Reichsthaler during nearly twenty years of war, to be able to produce a further ten millions in a few hours at the low rate of interest of 6 per cent. It must be observed that this has not been done in cash, which is now difficult to obtain, but in paper, particularly banknotes. Indeed, not a penny of these ten millions was paid in cash, but all in banknotes. These banknotes circulate so readily here that they are better than hard coin. So the whole of this wealth appears to be based almost entirely upon the credit of the paper money and the punctual payment of the interest.[1]

In the ordinary tactics of party also the Whigs easily out-manœuvred the Tory Opposition. They freed Marlborough and Godolphin from the minor annoyances which they had so long endured while unprovided with a disciplined majority. If there were losses and arrears in the yield of the Land Tax they would allow no censure to fall upon the Treasurer. Godolphin's name was deleted from the hostile motion by 231 votes to 97. If there were reproaches that the measures to defend Scotland at the time of the invasion had been inadequate, these were converted into votes of confidence and thanks to the Queen's Government for the great and effectual precautions they had taken and for their success. If "warm speeches were made against him, and he was roasted, as they call it,"[2] the Whigs hastened to his aid. There was another little matter in which the Whigs made themselves obliging to the two non-party or super-Ministers. An act of general pardon was passed for all correspondence with the Court of Saint-Germain, and, indeed, for all past treasonable actions of any kind except treason upon the high seas. This last provision was designed to exclude the Jacobites who had actually sailed in the invading fleet the year before. Thus the slate was cleaned, and a very large number of Tories and Jacobites both in England and Scotland, who lay under anxieties for what they had done or planned to do if the

---

Sunderland to Marlborough

February 11, 1709

★This day was appointed for taking the subscriptions of the Bank, and the whole sum was subscribed by twelve o'clock; the like I believe was never known in any country. I hope it will have its weight in France. [*Ibid.*]

[1] Hoffmann's dispatch, March 5, 1709; Klopp, xiii, 206–207.

[2] Peter Wentworth to Lord Raby, March 1, 1709; J. J. Cartwright, *The Wentworth Papers* (1705–39) (1883), p. 77.

Pretender landed, were generously released by those who might have been expected to be their chief prosecutors. Gratitude from this quarter was neither expected nor received.[1]

Marlborough had always pursued his devious way serene and imperturbable. He did not concern himself with the Amnesty Bill. But Godolphin, whom Wharton had recently confronted with one of those customary sentimental letters to Mary of Modena which the Treasurer persisted in writing, was certainly well pleased to have an Act of Parliament between him and future reprisals by his enemies. It is perhaps of significance that the Queen gave consent to the Bill on the very day of its passage. To have the Whigs showing themselves so accommodating to her Tory and Jacobite friends and to Mr Harley, lately harried again over the Greg affair, was at any rate some compensation for their presence at her Council.

But the incident most illustrative of these times concerned the Queen herself. A number of young Whig Members moved an address to the Queen urging her to marry again. This striking proposal was not only supported by the House of Commons, but endorsed by the Lords. At this time Queen Anne was in the depths of mourning for her husband. She had already been eighteen times disappointed of an heir by death or miscarriage; she was within a few days of her forty-fifth birthday. It had, in fact, been decided to omit from the accession service the prayer that the Queen might be "an happy mother of children, who, being educated in Thy true faith and fear, may happily succeed her in the Government of these kingdoms." What wonder then that many regarded such a suggestion to the Queen as ill-timed and indecorous? Indeed, Mordaunt, Peterborough's younger brother, who sat in the Commons, raised a general laugh when he suggested impudently that the address should be presented only by Members who had not yet reached their thirtieth year. The explanation was, however, simple to those who were behind the scenes. The bitterness which the Whig triumph aroused in the Tory Opposition had led them once again to bait the Queen with the prospect of bringing over the Electress of Hanover or her son to visit or, perhaps, to reside in England. The Whig counter-move was to urge the Queen to marry again, for she could hardly be urged to do this one day and to bring over the existing heir the next. It seems certain that the Queen fully understood the tactics of both the attackers and the defenders. She replied by message sedately the next day: "The subject of the address is of such

[1] Cartwright, p. 83.

a nature that I am persuaded you do not expect a particular answer."[1] But if the Queen, weighed down by her grief and increasing infirmities, was thus quaintly protected by the Whigs from a Hanoverian intrusion, and might even recognize their Parliamentary dexterity, she nevertheless sought their expulsion from office as her chief desire.

At this time one would suppose Marlborough and Godolphin had all they could ask in Britain for themselves or for their policy. Yet their intimate letters reveal their profound misgivings and discouragement. Godolphin harps again on vexations to which "the life of a slave in the galley is paradise in comparison."[2] Marlborough replies that nothing but his loyalty to his colleagues and his duty to the Queen would make him endure the burden and hazards of his command. There is so much bewailing in the Marlborough-Godolphin correspondence, written for no eye but their own, that many writers have questioned the sincerity of these tough, untiring personalities who, in the upshot, held on with extreme tenacity and to the last minute to every scrap of power. It was surely, then, no mere desire to keep up appearances before each other, but rather to fortify their own minds for action by asseverating their own disinterestedness, that made it worth while to set all this on paper? It is certain that neither was deceived by the favourable surface which British politics had assumed. Both knew too much of what was hidden from Parliament and even from the foreign envoys in London. They knew Queen Anne with the knowledge of a lifetime. They knew the Tory Party to its roots. They had enjoyed the best opportunities of measuring ex-Secretary of State Harley. Thus their eyes were necessarily fixed upon Abigail and the visitors she brought to the Queen by the backstairs.

Party government in time of war might show management and efficiency, but it lacked the deep-seated, massive strength of a national combination. This was revealed only too clearly upon the question of conscription. The fighting had lasted so long in 1708 that the regimental officers concerned in recruiting not only for reinforcements, but even for drafts, were very late in coming over. Parliament had voted an extra ten thousand men for the coming campaign, but had not yet faced the difficulties of recruiting them. Several proposals had been put forward in Ministerial circles. One

---

[1] *Parliamentary History of England* (Hansard), edited by William Cobbett and J. Wright, vi (1810), 778.
[2] Coxe, iv, 356.

was the Swedish plan that owners of houses and land should be organized in groups, each group being responsible for the maintenance of a recruit. Walpole, the Secretary-at-War, proposed recruiting the English Army after the French pattern, based on the obligations of each individual parish. But the Cabinet did not feel strong enough to adopt either scheme in the face of high Tory and Whig opposition. Even the tightening up of the existing recruiting laws upon the unemployed and idle was not carried through.[1] In fact, apart from hired foreign contingents, the proportion of British soldiers in the allied ranks was smaller in 1709 than ever before.

Neither could the Whigs bring to the peace negotiations the real force of a national decision. A Whig Government might in 1707 and earlier years have been most helpful to vigorous war. In 1709 their peculiar qualities, prejudices, and formulas were a new obstacle to the peace now within reach. England had little to ask for herself. The recognition of the Protestant Succession, the expulsion of the Pretender from France, and the demolition of the harbour and fortifications of Dunkirk seemed modest requirements for the State and nation which had formed, sustained, revived, and during so many years led to victory the entire coalition. But upon the general objective of the war the London Cabinet was implacable. The whole of the original Spanish Empire—Spain, Italy, and the Indies— must be wrested from Philip V, the Duke of Anjou, and given to Charles III. As early as 1703 Rochester and the high Tories, intent upon colonial acquisition, had raised the cry "No peace without Spain." The Whigs, while holding a different view about strategy, were for their part more than willing to associate themselves with this sweeping demand. What had become for years a Parliamentary watchword was now to be made good. This was not only an extension of the original purposes of the war; it was a perversion of them. The first aim had been to divide the Spanish inheritance; now it was to pass it in a block to the Austrian candidate, himself the direct heir to the Imperial throne of the Hapsburgs. From the rigid integrity of this policy there was not to be even the slightest concession. Nothing was to be offered to the Duke of Anjou. Nothing was to be offered to Louis XIV. In order to carry into history their English Parliamentary slogan, the British Government, with Parliament behind them, were ready to shoulder all the

[1] Report of L'Hermitage, January 1 and February 1, 1709; C. von Noorden, *Europäische Geschichte im achtzehnten Jahrhundert*, iii, 385.

demands of the Empire upon the Rhine, including Strasburg, all the demands of the Duke of Savoy, and almost all the demands of the Dutch for their Barrier.

There is no doubt that responsibility for the loss of the peace in 1709 lies largely upon England, and that the cause arose unconsciously out of her Parliamentary stresses. In Parliament the Spanish theatre always commanded vivid and abnormal interest. Money for Spain; troops for Spain; ships for Spain; a base for the fleet in Spanish waters; war in the Peninsula; no peace without its entire surrender—these were phrases and ideas popular not merely for a session but year after year, and enlisting a very general measure of active support. Marlborough throughout regarded the whole of this Spanish diversion as a costly concession to wrong-headed but influential opinion. By one device or another he had contrived to reduce it to the least improvident dimensions. He scraped away troops and supplies on various pretexts. He sought his results in Flanders or at Toulon. Nevertheless, as in the famous debate of December 1707,[1] he found it necessary to his system to humour Parliament in these ideas which were so strangely cherished by them. No doubt he found it convenient to gather support for the general war by adopting and endorsing the watchword "No peace without Spain."

Indeed, at this juncture in 1709 we find Marlborough mouthing this maxim, to which he had become accustomed, as fervently as its ill-instructed devotees. He was committed to it by the shifts to which he had been put to gain supplies from precarious majorities in former years. It had become a sort of drill, a parade movement, greatly admired by the public, of doubtful value on the battlefield, but helpful in recruiting. So now, at the culmination of the war, Marlborough marched along with the Cabinet and Parliament upon this Spanish demand; and the whole influence of England, then paramount, was used to compel the Dutch and incite the Empire and German states to conform. The Whigs in the brief morning of their power invested this demand with their own sharp precision. Upon it was placed an interpretation which certainly had not been adopted by any English party at an earlier stage. 'Spain' was made to include not only the Indies, but Italy. The interests of the City and of the Whig merchants in the Levant trade now found full expression in the Cabinet. "Let me tell you," said Sunderland in April to Vryberg, the Dutch envoy, "that any Minister who gave

---

[1] Vol. III, pp. 303–305.

up the Sicilies would answer for it with his head."[1] There could be no compromise with the Whigs about Sicily and Naples.

It has been remarked as curious that each side in the great war, while remaining in deadly conflict, had in fact largely adopted the original standpoint of the other. The English, who under King William had seen their safety in the partition of the Spanish Empire, now conceived themselves only served by its transference intact to the Hapsburg candidate. The Spanish nation, which at the outset cared little who was their king so long as their inheritance was undivided, were now marshalled around their Bourbon sovereign, and were almost indifferent to what happened outside the Peninsula. The insistence by England upon her Parliamentary formula destroyed the victorious peace now actually in her grasp. The incidents of the negotiations which will presently be recounted followed inevitably from this main resolve. But although England with her wealth and Marlborough's prowess could, as the event showed, over-persuade the Allies to her point of view, her resulting position was unsound and even absurd. Neither the Dutch nor the German states had the slightest intention of making exertions to conquer Spain after they had made a satisfactory peace with France. Austria, at once famishing and greedy, was impotent for such a purpose. Upon England alone and the troops she paid must have fallen the burden of conquering not only Spain but, as it had now become, the Spanish nation. It is certain that this was a task of which she would soon have been found incapable.

The Dutch demands were more practical, but no less serious. They had fought hard and long for their Dyke against France. It was now certain they would gain it. Exactly which fortresses, how many of them, where the flanks of the line should lie, were to be matters of sharp discussion with the French, with the English, with the Prussians, and still more with the Empire. But in all that concerned military security friend and foe were agreed that the Dutch rampart should be established. During the course of the war the Dutch trading interests had come to regard the conquest of the Barrier of fortress towns as carrying with it control over the commerce of the whole countryside between the fortresses. The Empire, the Allies, King Charles III, several of the most important German states, and also England had rights or interests which this Dutch demand affronted. In those days the wishes of the local population, with their charters and long-established customs, also counted. The

<hr />

[1] Vryberg to Heinsius, April 26, 1709; Heinsius Archives.

Belgian people, Flemings and Walloons alike, were no friends of France. They were prepared in the circumstances to be ruled by Charles III of Spain, by the Elector of Bavaria, or, if that could be brought about, by the Duke of Marlborough. The one solution which was abhorrent to them was the intimate exploitation of their Dutch neighbours. We have seen how, as Marlborough predicted in 1706, eighteen months of Dutch rule over the Belgian cities had produced a universal disaffection, culminating in the treachery of Ghent and Bruges. A hundred and thirty years later the severance of Belgium from Holland arose from the very same antagonisms which surged within the victorious Grand Alliance and beat upon the head of Marlborough. It was not only fortresses the Dutch wanted but the trade of Belgium. The London Cabinet was, however, in no position to read the States-General a lecture. In the summer of 1707 Stanhope had induced King Charles III to give special trading rights in the Indies—ten ships a year—to England. This was a minor, though none the less vexatious, breach of the pledge binding on all signatories of the Grand Alliance not to seek special favours at the expense of their confederates. The Dutch might claim that this liberated them from their own undertakings.

The Tories were prepared to make a stand for British trading interests in the Low Countries. But the Whig Junto dwelt upon the Dutch guarantee of the Protestant Succession which assured their ascendancy in Great Britain. Marlborough, whose outlook was European and covered at the least the whole compass of the Grand Alliance, saw from the beginning that if the Dutch had their way in the Spanish Netherlands, not only about the Dyke but about trade and government, the Empire would be fatally estranged. Charles III would be virtually stripped of his dominions in the north, Prussia would be indignant, the cohesion of the Alliance would be ruptured, and the English Tories would make the satisfaction of Dutch pretensions at the expense of British trade a mortal grievance against the Minister responsible. The argument which Marlborough used so often, that, once satisfied about their Barrier, the Dutch would desert the war, was disproved by the event. After the Barrier Treaty, which gave them their fill, had been signed by the Whig Ministers, the Dutch, so far from abandoning the war, fought all the harder for this dear prize. Indeed, it was only England who quitted the field.

Why did Marlborough not see that it would always be possible for England in conceding the Dutch demand about the Barrier to stipulate, as was in fact done, for a still more vigorous prosecution of the war by the Republic? His contention, though valid in the controversy of 1709, was stultified by the final outcome. He had, however, broad as well as particular reasons for opposing the Barrier Treaty. It seemed to him the highest unwisdom to give one of the members of the Alliance all that they desired, thus offending and unsettling the others, before the military power of the common enemy was decisively broken and it was certain the war could be ended. Moreover, his personal influence upon events must be seriously prejudiced. He saw, with his customary clarity, that if his were the hand that signed this invidious pact the wrath of all the disappointed members would be vented upon himself. His own countrymen were turning against him. The Dutch found themselves able, and preferred, to deal over his head with the Whigs. Must he then break with the Empire, with the two Hapsburg sovereigns who wished to make him almost a king, and with Eugene, his faithful comrade? Must he, by accepting the Dutch view of the Prussian claim to Guelderland, alienate that jealous Prussian Court, with whom his influence stood so high, for whose splendid troops he was in constant entreaty? Thus smitten, how could he conduct the war, if after all it had to be resumed? Whatever else a Barrier Treaty agreeable to the Dutch might mean, it was certain that Marlborough could not make it without destroying the whole system upon which he had hitherto led the Alliance through so many perils and shortcomings to what in the spring of 1709 seemed to be almost unbridled victory. For all these reasons, public and also more personal, which nevertheless on the whole corresponded to the essential needs of Europe, Marlborough, as we have seen, had hitherto delayed the Barrier Treaty and was bent on persevering in that course.

The divergence between Marlborough and Heinsius was thus inevitably serious. The Pensionary had been vexed by Marlborough's obstruction of the Barrier negotiations in 1706. He had for months been conducting secret parleys with France on the basis that Marlborough was not to be told about them. Already in December 1708 Heinsius had gone so far as to instruct Vryberg to discuss the Barrier Treaty directly with Somers[1] and to appeal to the new Whig Ministers apart from Marlborough. In December Vryberg reported that he had done so, and had found the Whig leader very desirous of a settlement with Holland on the basis of a reciprocal

---

[1] Heinsius to Vryberg, December 14; Hague Archives.

guarantee about the Barrier and the Succession. Godolphin wrote to Marlborough that he agreed with Somers. The formal proposals for a Barrier Treaty which he was expected to negotiate reached Marlborough on his way from Ghent to The Hague, and on arrival he was officially told about the French peace offers through Petkum.

At this time he believed that any peace offer from France would only be an attempt to amuse and cheat the Allies. Accordingly when the Pensionary harped upon the Barrier Marlborough diverted the discussions to the Dutch quota of troops for the new campaign. As the mails from England were weatherbound, he was able to profess himself without sufficient instructions. Heinsius had, however, already threatened Godolphin that he would send Buys, the Amsterdam leader and a friend of Harley, to London to conduct the Barrier negotiations there if Marlborough proved obdurate. He appealed to the Whig Junto over Marlborough's head, and with success. The Cabinet, and especially Godolphin, who feared Buys' Tory contacts, was anxious to prevent a Dutch mission arriving in London. Sunderland did not hesitate to criticize Marlborough to Vryberg, the Dutch Ambassador. When he was told that Marlborough pretended to have no powers Sunderland said, "I cannot imagine what reasons my Lord Duke can have for doing so."[1] Vryberg lost no time in telling Heinsius that Marlborough was disavowed by the Secretary of State, "who does not hesitate even to gainsay his father-in-law's opinions when he thinks they are not right."[2] Thus at the outset of these all-important negotiations Marlborough found himself to a large extent isolated. He was divided both from the Dutch and from his own Government upon large issues of principle and procedure.

His main wish was to convince the Dutch that he cared more for their confidence in the conduct of the war than for the Viceroyalty of the Netherlands. For this he took during the spring and summer a series of steps which were painful to him. The question of the Viceroyalty did not slumber. In February Charles pressed him further.

Charles III to Marlborough

February 2, 1709

★On the return of Mr Craggs I have received yours of October 29 in answer to that which I had entrusted to him upon his departure for England. He has given me an ample account of all you had commissioned him to say, and in particular of your zeal in working for

---

[1] Heinsius Archives, quoted in Geikie, p. 104.   [2] *Loc. cit.*

all that can help my interests. . . . I am sure you will continue to respond in the same manner as you have always done. Indeed, you could not better employ your zeal than for a Prince whose interests are always and will ever be so tightly bound up with those of your Mistress, the Queen. . . . As to what I have written you formerly concerning my Low Countries, you will find me always ready to keep my word. I should indeed feel a keen regret [*déplaisir*] if by any accident or consideration you should be turned from accepting this mark [*marque*: this word is added in Charles's own handwriting] of my gratitude and of the esteem which I have formed of your merit. I approve, however, the prudent dissimulation which you have used up till now in the direction of the Dutch; although it would be equally useful to the Common Cause, and necessary for the repose and comfort of my Low Countries, if the States-General would allow them at least to take the oath of fidelity. I need not desire you to uphold my interests in the present session of Parliament, because your own zeal will lead you to do that yourself, and particularly in all that can re-establish our affairs, and put us in condition to wage an offensive war in Spain. . . .[1]

Marlborough conveyed through Stanhope, with whom he had relations of close confidence and friendship, an account of the difficulties which prevented him from accepting the Viceroyalty.

King Charles replied (June 16):

I had thought to give you some evidence of my goodwill in this matter in the message which I sent you formerly by the resident Craggs, but what General Stanhope has just told me on your behalf has caused me trouble and disquiet. I hope none the less that the consideration which you wish to have for the Dutch in this juncture will soon cease to carry weight with you, and that in other circumstances you will have the pleasure of enjoying this small mark of my gratitude—to put it better, that I shall myself profit by your good government and the good order which you would bring into the Low Countries.[2]

Up to this moment Marlborough had still nourished hopes of ultimately receiving the appointment. But in the middle of 1709 he took a decisive step to exclude himself. At all costs to himself he must regain the confidence of the Dutch. A letter from Charles III to Wratislaw on June 30, 1709, shows how far he went. Not only did he three times specifically refuse this magnificent office, but he urged that it should be conferred upon Eugene. He thought that only by the substitution of another name for his could the misunderstandings between him and the Dutch be finally removed.

[1] Blenheim MSS. [2] *Ibid.*, and Geikie, p. 373.

Reluctantly he had reached the conclusion that only this sacrifice would preserve that Anglo-Dutch unity, the keystone of the whole Alliance, which was now in jeopardy.

Charles III to Wratislaw

June 30, 1709

[As to] what concerns the person of the Duke of Marlborough, to whom I alone upon the advice of Moles[1] have given the patent of the Governor in the Netherlands, which he has three times resigned and bidden me rather to name another 'actualen' [in order] to placate the jealousy of the Dutch. He has also written about this matter to the Emperor to ask if he does not think that it would be better to send Prince Eugene himself there, for he is very popular with the Dutch, and it is at the moment very necessary to bring order into the whole Barrier affair, and thereby to animate the Dutch further.[2]

It would no doubt have been agreeable to Marlborough, since he was resolved not to accept the Viceroyalty himself, to have it conferred upon his friend and comrade Prince Eugene. With Eugene in control of the Spanish Netherlands, he could be sure that the treatment of the Belgian inhabitants and the general course of the government would be no hindrance to the military operations. But to propose Eugene for the appointment was by no means to secure it for him. The question became a burning one as soon as Eugene reached Vienna. The Prince himself was anxious to accept. He had been baulked by internal jealousies in 1706–7 of his desire to remain Viceroy of the Milanese. Here now was the opportunity of gaining a finer kingdom, where he would be more closely knit with Marlborough for any further campaigns in the Low Countries. His enemies, however, were as persistent as ever against him. They were now reinforced by the apprehensions of his friends, who saw themselves likely to be deprived in the future of his leadership and protection in Vienna. Thus Marlborough's proposal was never made public by the Emperor or by Charles III, and it was only after a lapse of a hundred and fifty years that the fact became known.

[1] The Duke of Moles was Charles's principal councillor and Austrian representative at Barcelona.
[2] Ritter von Arneth, *Prinz Eugen von Savoyen* (1864), ii, 467.

Chapter Three

THE GREAT FROST

1709—JANUARY–APRIL

THE campaign of 1708 had ended according to Marlborough's "heart's desire," and although it had been
protracted beyond all custom into the depth of winter
and over the end of the year, his warlike energy was
entirely unabated. "This has been," he wrote to Godolphin
(January 31, 1709), "a very laborious campaign, but I am sensible
the next will be more troublesome; for most certainly the enemy
will venture, and do their utmost to get the better of us; but I trust
in the Almighty that he will protect and give success to our just
cause."[1] Neither his own fatigues and worries nor his deep desire
for peace had slackened his preparations for 1709. While peace
negotiations regular or secret, now by this channel, now by that,
made The Hague a whispering-gallery, Marlborough had already
for two months past been concerting with Godolphin, the British
Cabinet, and throughout the Grand Alliance the marshalling for
1709 of the largest armies yet seen in Europe. In order that the
whole movement of the Alliance towards its goal should be unfalter-
ing, it was planned that he and Eugene should take it in turns to
remain in Holland driving forward the gathering of men, munitions,
food, and forage, and making sure that no signatory state fell out
of the line. Eugene's presence in Vienna being judged at first
indispensable, Marlborough stood on guard in Holland during
January and February. As soon as the fall of Ghent liberated the
confederate armies for what remained of the winter he repaired to
his headquarters at Brussels, and thence, with occasional visits to
The Hague, began to pull all the levers of the vast, complicated,
creaking machine of which he was still master.[2]

---

[1] Misdated January 10 by Coxe (iv, 356).

[2]   *Marlborough to Godolphin*   BRUSSELS
                                                       January 7, 1709
★I have receiv'd the favour of Yours of the 17th by which I see the Augementation
is Votted. I cou'd wish it had been for 20000 Men, for the measures the ffrench take of
bringing their Troupes from all parts, even from Spain, makes it very necessary that we

518

He seems to have quartered himself when at The Hague upon the Prussian commissary, General Grumbkow, who wrote some droll accounts to his master:

My lord Duke has obliged me to take a furnished house opposite the Orange palace and is living there himself. This costs me twenty louis d'or a month, and as I have very good Tokay, *qu'il aime à la fureur,*

shou'd do our utmost, for I think it is evedent their intentions are to act if possible this Winter, or so early in the Spring, as that the fatt of the Warr may be desided in this Country before our Armys can think of taking the field wither in Italie or on the Rhin. Pr. Eugene assures me that the ffrench troupes on the Rhin receiv'd such pressing orders for their march, that they left their Cloathing behind them. We see by the orders given by the Marishall de Boufflaires, that the ffrench King design'd the relieving of Gand, reconing that that town might defend itt self six weekes. I believe Monsr. de la Mott will not be able to give good reason for what he has done. I shall be sure to follow Her Majestys Commands in pressing the Dutch to their augementations but I fear one thirde is the most we can expect, but I shall presse them to a *Moittié* [*i.e.*, to pay half the cost of the extra mercenaries]. I shall also follow your directions as to the intercorse of letters, but as to the hindering all intercorse by letters from ffrance, is what Amsterdame I am afraid will never consent to, & [peace] being extreamly desir'd by all those people; I shall by my next send You an account of the forage and Copie of the treaty I have sign'd in Conjunction with the Deputys, for the fforage and bread for the Imperiall troupes, in this thay bare one half of the Expence. From the Hague I shall send over Major G. Palms. I hope You will send him back in ten days, so that he may do what may be thought proper at Vienna and be early enough at Turin for the pressing of the Duke of Savoye to take the field early, for if wee will have a good peace it must be by taking the field early, and acting with Vigor; I am uneasy at the little hopes You give mee for the Recrutes, for if there be not some way taken for the getting them, we shall be at a lose, for our officers can not have time for the doing of itt. The Dutch garrison is at Ostend so that the English Redgts stay only for a Convoye. I beg orders may be given to the Comander of the Convoye, that he give notice of his arrivall to Lt. Generall Lumley at Gand, so that those which are to be sent for Recrutes maybe immediately sent to Ostend, for thay will lose to much time in going by Holland. We have now the hardest frost and coldest weather I ever felt, which will make our gitting to the Hague very troublesome, we shall not begine our Journey till after to morrow. [Blenheim MSS.]

Marlborough to Heinsius

BRUSSELS
January 28, 1709

★I gote safe to this place on Friday last, and we have had ever since a thaw so that I hope in a few days the rivers will be open so that we may be able to send the stores to the severale garrisons, and I beg you will take care that there be no time lost in sending from Holland the Magazines promised to Prince Eugene, on which our safety depends. . . . [Heinsius Archives.]

Marlborough to Heinsius

January 31, 1709

★By the extraordinary measures the enemy take in marching troupes from Spain, Dauphiné, and the Rhin notwithstanding our augmentation, they will have superiority, the consequences of which may be fatal, for should we receive an affront in this country, no success in any other parts could make amends, so that I think in prudence we should omit nothing that might strengthen us in this country, for the French do neglect all their other armies in order to make this strong, knowing very well that success in this country must decide the whole. [*Ibid.*]

I gave his Highness a supper yesterday, which was attended by Prince Eugene, my lord Albemarle, Cadogan, and Lieutenant-General Ros. They were all in the best spirits in the world. I recommended the matter of exchanging the prisoners to my lord Duke in the most pressing manner yesterday; he was almost angry and said to me, "I will stake my fortune on what you want; you will have your people before the end of this month." "Good," I said; "I will wager you ten pistoles." "Done," replied the Duke, and soon afterwards, with a violent gesture, "Mordieu, if these people make me lose this money I will make them suffer so much that they will have cause to regret their surliness." Prince Eugene laughed loudly over the effect which a bet of ten pistoles had upon the spirits of my lord Duke, and I cannot help assuring your Majesty that if I had foreseen that my lord Duke would take this matter so much to heart I should have offered him fifty pistoles and gladly lost them so that your Majesty should be more certain of getting back two battalions and two squadrons. The bet has at any rate resulted in the Duke's sending precise and threatening commands to the French commissary over the matter.[1]

Marlborough lavished his flatteries and persuasions upon the King of Prussia, using exactly the kind of arguments which were most likely to appeal to a military monarchy.

Brussels
January 31

"Imagine for a moment," said my lord Duke in the further course of the conversation, "that we make a celebrated campaign and conclude peace, would not the King of Prussia be held in greater esteem if he had had twenty thousand men in the field than if he had had fourteen thousand? And in what ultimately does the greatness of a king and his might consist except a large army and good troops—*le reste n'est que chimère!*"[2]

Brussels
February 17

Yesterday, while at table with My lord Albemarle, My lord Duke received letters from Berlin and told me with great joy that he was informed that your Majesty had allowed the Crown Prince to serve in the campaign; in his view, he added, your Majesty could do nothing more glorious for yourself or more advantageous to your interests than to send the Crown Prince to the school where great men are formed and princes are only esteemed so far as their valour and good conduct make them worthy of it. All good Englishmen, he added, would be enchanted, and he for his part would give a good example and exert himself to let your Majesty see by his devotion and atten-

[1] *Des General Feldmarschalls Dubislav G. von Natzmer Leben und Kriegsthaten* (1838), p. 303.   [2] *Ibid.*, p. 309.

tion to the Crown Prince the extent of his sentiments in this direction for the sacred person of your Majesty yourself. If your Majesty would permit it he would himself undertake the duties of a father from time to time, giving his Royal Highness the best advice of which he is capable in order to effect the purpose which your Majesty has laid down —that is, to make the Crown Prince ever more and more fitted for the time when he has to rule, and enable him to follow the noble examples of his father and his great and illustrious ancestors. When we had risen from table he added that he hoped his Royal Highness would arrive in good time, as in order to obtain a true picture of the war it was necessary to see how the armies were formed and how they made their first movements, for these usually determined the issue of the campaign.[1]

These attentions produced remarkable results. Frederick I was more amenable to Marlborough's solicitations than to any other. But here is another odd illustration of Marlborough's attitude towards money. Because of the need for reinforcements, he gave up the $2\frac{1}{2}$ per cent. commission on the pay of the contingent to which he was entitled by the Queen's warrant and which formed the fund under his unchecked control by which his Intelligence and Secret Service were maintained. How this was applied is not recorded, but it turned the scale at Berlin, and King Frederick by an addition of 6210 men raised the Prussian troops to the magnificent figure of twenty-two thousand for the coming campaign.

It was not until the Prussian negotiations were completed, and he had also made his arrangements for the Würtembergers and the Palatines, that he once again addressed himself to the Dutch. He was now in a position to display to them the powerful succours which he had obtained, and the States-General were threatened with the reproach of being the sole defaulter. Thus spurred, they in the end produced an increase of six thousand hired troops, and this, added to the ten thousand expansion sanctioned by the British Parliament, would raise the confederate army to an unprecedented strength during the currency of the peace negotiations. We must admire the dual process to which the Allies were now committed of earnestly seeking peace while at the same time preparing for war on an ever greater scale. Nearly always Governments which seek peace flag in their war efforts, and Governments which make the most vigorous war preparations take little interest in peace. The two opposite moods consort with difficulty in the human mind

[1] *Des General Feldmarschalls Dubislav G. von Natzmer Leben und Kriegsthaten*, pp. 310-311.

yet it is only by the double and, as it might seem, contradictory exertion that a good result can usually be procured.

On February 7 Marlborough gained possession of a letter written by a Minister at the Court of Madrid to the Duke of Orleans stating that "The most Christian King is resolved to turn the brunt of the war against Flanders in order to make a new siege of Lille from the beginning of April, with 150,000 veteran troops." "This," he said to Henry Boyle, the Secretary of State, "agrees with the advices we have from all other parts of the great efforts the French design to make the next campaign in this country."[1] And to Godolphin: "I am far from thinking the King of France so low as he is thought in England."[2]

The grim winter held Spain with the rest of Europe in its grip.[3] In Barcelona, overcrowded and short of provisions, Charles and Starhemberg, the commander of his army in Catalonia, wearily composed long memorials of complaint to the English Government and plans for an offensive against Madrid in the next campaign. But while these strategic disputations followed their usual course Charles's last fortress in Valencia was the scene of an heroic feat of arms. Major-General John Richards, with a mixed force of English, Huguenots, Spaniards, and Miquelets, about two thousand strong, still held out in the castle of Alicante. At the end of November a Bourbon army under d'Asfeld of twelve thousand men advanced down the coast to lay siege to the town, having captured Denia on the way. The town itself was quickly taken. Richards withdrew into the castle, which stood upon a rock, two hundred feet above the town. For three months the French, in spite of the fire of the defence, drove a long gallery under the western wall. This threatened annihilation. In the middle of January five men-of-war of Byng's fleet arrived in Alicante Bay on their way from Lisbon to Barcelona, but, failing to establish communication with Richards, sailed on to Port Mahon. On February 20 the governor was summoned to surrender. Two of his officers were invited to inspect the completed mine. They went into the gallery under the castle, where 117,600 lb.[4] of gunpowder was packed. They reported to Richards that all was ready to be sprung. After two more appeals to capitulate Richards prepared himself. On the morning of March 3, sur-

[1] Sir G. Murray, *Letters and Dispatches of John, Duke of Marlborough* (1845), iv, 429.
[2] February 13; Coxe, iv, 373.   [3] See the map of Spain facing p. 1041.
[4] Trevelyan says 17,600. This is a misprint. See A. Parnell, *The War of the Succession in Spain*, p. 262. Twelve hundred barrels of gunpowder, each containing a quintal (98 lb.), were used.

rounded by his senior officers and a small guard, he took his stand upon the parade ground immediately above the mine. Just before six o'clock puffs of smoke were seen climbing the face of the castle rock, and the corporal of the guard on the west side shouted that the train was lit. The inhabitants of the adjacent houses poured forth in panic. On the stroke of the hour a shattering explosion convulsed the castle. The parade ground gaped asunder, and the governor, three senior officers, five captains, three lieutenants, and forty-two soldiers vanished in the abyss. Undaunted by their fate and inspired by their example, the survivors held out for another six weeks. In April Stanhope and Byng sailed into the bay, signed a capitulation, and took on board the remaining six hundred men of the garrison.

The last town in Valencia had been lost to Charles.

Elsewhere the military misfortunes of France were numerous and heavy. The disastrous campaign in Flanders has been recounted. The Hungarian revolt, mortally smitten by Rakoczy's defeat at Trentschin, was dying down. Turkish intervention against Austria was no longer likely. The Empire, freed from these distractions, must be regarded as a less feeble enemy in the future. The capture of Port Mahon confirmed upon a permanent basis the absolute English command of the Mediterranean. Nevertheless, Louis XIV prepared indomitably to meet in 1709 the onslaughts of the Allies, and from every quarter troops were gathered to face Marlborough and Eugene. Further intercepted letters in January confirmed the reports that the French Grand Army would reach a total of a hundred and fifty thousand men by the early summer, that Villars would command it, and that the objective would be Lille. At the same time by Marlborough's exertions there were gathering over a hundred and fifty thousand men around the Allies' standards in the Low Countries. The campaign was therefore planned by both sides upon an unexampled scale.

But now there fell upon France a new and frightful misfortune. Since the beginning of December there had been a hard and almost unbroken frost. On January 6, after a brief thaw, it set in again with a bitterness so intense that two days later the rivers of France, even the Rhône, one of the most rapid rivers in Europe, were almost completely covered with ice. All the canals of Venice were frozen, and the mouth of the Tagus at Lisbon. Masses of ice appeared in the Channel and the North Sea. Communications between England and Holland were suspended; Harwich and the Dutch ports were ice-bound. Olives and vines split asunder. Cattle and sheep perished in great numbers. The game died in the forests, the rabbits in their burrows. From January 25 to February 6 there was an interval of snow followed by a few days' thaw, and then another month, until March 6, of extraordinary cold. Thereafter gradually the weather became less severe. Thus this almost glacial period had lasted into the fourth month. On February 4 it was known at Versailles that the seed corn was dead in the ground. The English fleet, now active in the Mediterranean and in the Baltic throughout the winter, intercepted supplies of grain from Africa, the Levant, and Scandinavia.[1] After more than sixty years of his reign, more than thirty years of which had been consumed in European war, the Great King saw his people face to face with actual famine.

Their sufferings were extreme. In Paris the death-rate doubled. Even before Christmas the market-women had marched to Versailles to proclaim their misery. In the countryside the peasantry subsisted on herbs or roots or flocked in despair into the famishing towns. Brigandage was widespread. Bands of starving men, women, and children roamed about in desperation. Châteaux and convents were attacked; the market-place of Amiens was pillaged; credit failed. From every province and from every class rose the cry for bread and peace. Meanwhile the northern horizon darkened continually with the menace of impending invasion.

The peace discussions wended onward. A secret meeting between Dutch and French agents had been arranged in February under the authority of Heinsius and Torcy. In March the burrowings of Petkum were replaced by public negotiations which originated in another quarter. Philip V had, apparently on his own impulse, in the early days of the New Year sent an agent from Spain with full powers to make peace offers on his behalf. The Dutch had replied through van der Dussen, the Pensionary of Gouda, that a minimum offer of Spain, the Indies, Milan, and Belgium, and a favourable treaty of commerce were the essential basis of conversations. Louis XIV saw in this reply the possibility of compensating and consoling his grandson with Naples and Sicily, and grasped the opportunity. In January he had been vigorously

[1] *Cabinet Council Minutes*

February 21, 1709
★To the Council of Trade to inquire into the scarcity of corn, and if not scarce not fit to be exported; what methods can be found to prevent its being carried to France under the cover of passes to Spain? [Blenheim MSS.]

preparing for a new campaign pending negotiations. But during February, appalled by the full realization of the calamity which had befallen France, he resolved upon peace at all costs. In March[1] he sent Rouillé, one of his ambassadors, the President of the Parlement of Paris, to meet the two Dutch plenipotentiaries, Buys and van der Dussen, at Moerdyk, an obscure village within the Dutch frontier.

It was several weeks before the Allies understood this change of mind and the extent of the disaster which had enforced it. Marlborough sailed on a flying visit to England on February 25/March 8. He was still under the impression that another campaign must certainly be fought, and that it would open early in Flanders with unexampled fury. ★ "I think the only good step that we can make towards a peace is to get early into the field. I have given my orders for all officers to be at their commands by the end of this month, and I beg the Queen would show a dislike of any that should stay after that time."[2]

Before he reached London on March 3/14 the Whig leaders Somers and Halifax had carried an address in the Lords defining the minimum terms of an English peace. ". . . That the French King may be obliged to own your Majesty's title and the Protestant Succession as it is established by the laws of Great Britain; and that the Allies be engaged to become guarantees of the same. And that your Majesty would take effectual methods that the Pretender shall be removed out of the French Dominions. . . ." To this Boyle, in the Commons on the 13th, added the demolition of Dunkirk. The purpose of this address was to proclaim the main outlines of the Government policy, and to rouse and reveal its support in Parliament and the country. It was in essence a vote of confidence in Whig foreign policy, emphasizing the popular side and putting foremost the guarantee of the Protestant Succession. There was no mention of Spain. Somers and Halifax knew that the public were indifferent to this Parliamentary counter. It was better to dwell on the guarantee of the Protestant Succession, which every one understood, and in which the Whigs and the majority of the nation were one. The loud demand by the Commons for the razing of Dunkirk was a warning signal to the Dutch negotiators. "The Pensionary," wrote Petkum, "is scarcely pleased by the latest address of the English Parliament, or the Queen's reply. He let me know in

---

[1] Legrelle, v, 446-448.
[2] Marlborough to Godolphin, The Hague, March 11; Blenheim MSS.

confidence that he suspects that the Duke of Marlborough is the author of both."[1]

Marlborough on his arrival in England was conscious of a somewhat restrained welcome, especially from his colleagues. He was expected in many circles to be the bearer of definite peace proposals. He had none. He had not sought to have any. His position was sensibly undermined. William III's old friend Portland, who was an extremely well-informed Dutch agent in England, and Vryberg had been equally successful in convincing the Whigs of the Duke's obstruction and the Dutch of his loss of influence. When the news of Rouillé's apparition and the details of the first Moerdyk conversations reached London, the startled Whig leaders looked askance at Marlborough. How could this detrimental situation have arisen without his knowledge? Marlborough no doubt had realized that some one was coming from Versailles. He had not expected that a peace mission would be made public before Heinsius had even mentioned it to him. He was thus proved to the Cabinet not to be in the confidence of the Dutch. He had a just grievance against Heinsius, and their relations were never quite the same as before. The Cabinet showed itself much disturbed by the Dutch proceedings. ★ "It has," wrote Marlborough to Heinsius (March 8/19), "given here a very great allarum. . . . I do believe by this proceeding of Rouillé, that the chief design of the French is to occasion a jealousy amongst the Allies."[2] Cadogan, who was in charge at headquarters during Marlborough's absence, was ordered at once to The Hague to assure the Pensionary that the British Government were willing to take up the Barrier negotiations.

Rouillé's coming caused equal alarm in Vienna. It was, of course, believed that Marlborough was behind it. His disclaimers to Wratislaw,[3] although true, did not convince. "It seems almost incredible," replied Wratislaw, "that you should not have been informed."[4] Marlborough's position was further prejudiced. Hitherto his influence with the Dutch had helped him with the British and the Empire, and his influence with these had helped him with the Dutch; now the British and Dutch began to talk together directly, and the Empire still held Marlborough responsible. Portland wrote from London to Heinsius, "There are jealousies here as elsewhere, and he knows that many are watching him."[5] In the Cabinet

---

[1] Petkum to Torcy, March 21; French F.O. Archives, "Hollande," vol. 217, f. 240.
[2] Heinsius Archives. [3] Marlborough to Wratislaw, March 11/12; *Dispatches*, iv, 471.
[4] Blenheim MSS.; quoted by Geikie, p. 111. [5] Heinsius Archives; Geikie, p. 108.

Somers and his tightly knit group were vexed at the friction between the Pensionary and themselves. They were inclined to lay this upon Marlborough. Nevertheless, they disliked the Rouillé discussions as much as he did. Portland informed the Pensionary on March 25, "The jealousies on account of these pourparlers in Holland increase in England and will soon be growing to unkind distrust."[1]

Meanwhile Marlborough's Secret Service had intercepted Rouillé's correspondence describing the conversations at Moerdyk. The Dutch seemed prepared to go very far to meet France upon the crucial issue of Naples and Sicily. The French proposal was not only that Naples and Sicily should be guaranteed to Philip V, but that the guarantee should be enforced if necessary by a Franco-Dutch (and possibly English) expedition. It is noteworthy that this is the first appearance in the negotiations of the idea of enforcing peace terms upon recalcitrants by war, and that it came from France. Clearly the French envoy was suggesting to the Dutch hostilities in the last resort against the Empire. It also appeared from Marlborough's intercepts and decipherings that the Dutch were not prepared to go so far as that.

The new instructions, based upon the Parliamentary address of March 6, with which Marlborough reached The Hague on April 9/20, emphasized among other matters "that no negotiations for peace should be concluded with France until preliminaries were adjusted between England and the States." This sealed the fate of the Rouillé mission. Eugene had arrived from Vienna the day before. "My lord and I are agreed," wrote Eugene, "that we should press for the dismissal of Rouillé out of the country."[2] Marlborough,[3]

---

[1] Reese, p. 132.   [2] *Feldzüge*, Series II, ii, Appendix, 62.

[3] *Marlborough to Godolphin*

HAGUE
April 12, 1709

★I cant send You so much news as I thought I shou'd have been able to have done by this post, since the Messinger dispatch'd by Monsr. de Roullee to ffrance will not return til towardes the end of the next weake.

Monsr. de Buys and Vanderdussen both assure me that thay have been Carefull in not making any demand, but that thay had explain'd the treatys and obligations thay lay under to their Allyes, and the ferm resolutions the States had taken of not treating without the aprobation and Concurance of their allyes, and particularly the Queen of England; I have endeavour'd to Convince the Pensioner and others of the dainger thay may run by the Jealoussy the Allyes may take to this Secrit negocation. Thay seem to be of opinion that if thay have not much more Satisfaction by the return of this Courier then thay have hethertoo had, that that must put an end to this matter; what I fear is that if ffrance gives a satisfactory answer as to their Barier, we shall find great difficulty in putting a stop to this unseasonable Negocation, but Pr. Eugene and some

supported by Eugene, interpreted his instructions as authorizing him not to open the Barrier negotiations until the Franco-Dutch talks were cleared out of the way. If the Dutch wanted to discuss the Barrier let them first get rid of Rouillé. Heinsius realized that the only point on which the Duke was in agreement with the English Government was deep distrust of the Dutch relations with Rouillé. If these were severed, Marlborough, save for his personal contacts with Eugene, would again be isolated. Heinsius saw himself at his weakest in preserving the Rouillé mission. He saw Marlborough at his weakest if the Barrier Treaty came to the fore. He therefore resigned himself to the dismissal of Rouillé. The last formal interview took place between the Dutch and the French envoys at Bodegraven, another obscure village by the banks of a small, remote canal where the French envoy had been deposited by Heinsius. Rouillé was informed that there could be no guarantee of the use of allied force to procure the cession of Naples and Sicily to France. The very idea was impossible, and ought never to have been suggested. The French envoy then asked for an armistice. Such a request exposed the weakened will-power of France, but the Dutch delegates had no authority to grant it. This was the end of Rouillé's

---

others whome I trust are of opinion, that we shou'd bee quiet til we see what answer ffrance makes. In the mean time I have acquaint'd the Pensioner with my Instructions, and he is of opinion that I shou'd att the first Conferences avoid speaking [of] any thing but what may Concern their Barier, and the Protestant succession, by which we shall gain time and know the answer ffrance will make by this last Courier. This whole Negociation was yesterday under greatt Secrisy Communicat'd by the Pensioner to the States of Holand, so that I fear this man cant now be sent back but by their Consent. [Blenheim MSS.]

Marlborough to Godolphin

HAGUE
April 16, 1709

★. . . You will have seen by my letters that the second Conference produced nothing more then the adding of ffurnes [Furnes] to the first proposall, which inclines these people to beleive that ffrance is not in that bad Condition wee think them in. But I indeavour to perswaid them that the true reason of the Enemies offering no more proceedes from the hopes thay have given them from some of this Country that the Conditions thay offer will be accept'd by this Republick, and that I no ways doubt that as soon as the ffrench shall be Convinced of the Contrary, that thay will Consent to what ever we shall insist upon, even before the opening of the Campagne; the Pensioner and such others as are the most reasonable assure me that the States will make no farther step but in conjunction with their allyes and in particular with England, but att the same time the Pensioner tells mee in Confidence and which he desires his name may not be made use of, and that the thing it self shou'd be known to very few, as You will see the necessity for the good of the Service it shou'd be a Secritt, for if the ffrench shou'd come to know itt, we must despaire of a good peace; that which he has told mee is that their Circomstances are such that thay shall be necessitated to take

mission. He brushed from his shoes the dust of the Dutch pothouses to which he had been relegated, and set off for the challenged splendours of Versailles.

Heinsius was now resolved that Marlborough should face the definite Dutch demands which he had so long staved off, but upon which he had been instructed by his own Government to negotiate. On April 19, when Eugene was away at Amsterdam, a deputation of the States waited on Marlborough and with all ceremony unfolded their claim. They opened their mouths very wide. "You will see," reported Marlborough afterwards, "it encloses what might be thought a great kingdom." In the course of the discussion it was plainly hinted that if Marlborough objected too much or dallied too long the rumour would be circulated that personal aims—for instance, the Viceroyalty—were his motives. The Duke listened urbanely. When at length he spoke he criticized only the two points which his instructions from the Whigs authorized him to resist. He protested against the inclusion of the coast towns, particularly Ostend, in a military Barrier against France. He drew attention to the weight of the contribution demanded from the Belgians to maintain the Dutch garrisons. He could not resist at the end asking what

---

such a peace as thay can gett, for thay are not able to go on with the Warr. The Pensioner of Amsterdame has been with me this morning, and after many expressions of esteem and freindshipe to the Queen and English Nation has declar'd to mee in the name of the Burgemasters very near the same thing, as was told me by the Pensioner, who in the discourse I had with him told mee that if the Allyes and England shou'd insist upon having every thing in the Prelimenaries, the Consequences of that must be, the breaking off the Confirences which thay cou'd never bring their towns to Consent to, so that thay shou'd be oblig'd to lett the Queen see the necessity thay lay under of a Peace; after the return of the Courier from ffrance I shall be better able to make a Judgement of what maybe proper steps for the Allyes and particularly England to make in this Conjunctur; I hope Her Maty will approve of my not having writt any thing Contain'd in this letter by this post to Mr Secritary, as the letter shou'd be Communicat'd but to very few.

I hope by the next post to be able to give You some account as to the Barier. You know my opinion that thay must be humour'd and pleas'd as far as it is possible, but by what I can larn their expectations and desires growes every day so that thay will not only meet with difficultys from the house of Austria, but give also Jealoussies to the King of Prussia and the rest of their Neighbours, I must not flatter my self to have the same Creditt with them in this affaire, as I may have in that of the Peace, *notwithstanding the resolution You know I have taken of not accepting the offer of the King of Spain. This resolution of mine is not yett proper to be known to the house of Austria, fearing thay might name some other Governour,* which wou'd make the ajusting of the Barier much more difficult; I beg I might have the Queens Commands, and the opinion of such as You Communicat this too. As to my own behaviour, I cou'd wish I might hear from You by munday or tuesday next for I beleive I shall not be acquainted with what Comes from ffrance til about that time. [Blenheim MSS.]

was to be left to King Charles III of his possessions in the north. Having thus met the attack on ground which even the Whigs must occupy, he dismissed the subject with the soothing remark, "The matter is not yet ripe for discussion." Thus he had broken the Rouillé mission by invoking the priority of the Barrier, and now put the Barrier once again for the moment upon the shelf.[1]

During March and April the allied Governments became convinced that Louis XIV was finally defeated. The reports which poured in upon them seemed to show that France was incapable of fighting another campaign. To the lamentable tales of the frost havoc, of the widespread famine, of the desperate condition of the French troops, without bread and forage, had been added the bankruptcy of the great French banker Bernard of Lyons, whose efforts to found a French State Bank with an official paper currency had been remarkable. Whereas the Allies had previously overrated the remaining resources of their antagonist, they now set them as far beneath the truth. Marlborough was not immune from this process. Apart from his manœuvring against Heinsius, he was now sure that the French would grant the whole allied demands. All the more had it been right to drive away Rouillé! Why prolong these partial local chatterings when Louis XIV was forced to beg before all the world for armistice and peace? To drive away Rouillé was not to drive away peace. A far fuller offer was impending.

But how long would it be before France made a new proposal of peace, not secretly to Holland, but publicly to the Grand Alliance? Evidently the Duke thought it was a matter of days. But days were now very important. Heinsius was demanding the Barrier. The Whig Cabinet was set upon the Barrier and Guarantee Treaty as a preliminary to peace. But if the French opened a general peace negotiation all preliminaries between the Anglo-Dutch allies would be superseded. The discussion would be with the three great allied Powers. Marlborough's instructions were to negotiate the Barrier, and he knew that within a few days of Rouillé's departure Heinsius would force him to a decision. That decision must cause

[1]   *Heinsius to Portland*
                                                        April 26, 1709
We have pressed my lord Duke in the conference upon the Barrier. He has asked to be given a list of the towns claimed, with the reasons why I have not found it convenient to do this. . . . I had thought that we should have been able to finish this business in a conference, because it was thought he was sufficiently empowered, but he has handled the affair differently from what I expected. [Heinsius Archives; *Correspondence of William and Portland*, ii, 456.]

great dissensions among the Allies. "I tremble," he wrote to Godolphin on April 19, "when I think that a very little impatience may
ruin a sure game."[1]

Heinsius at length felt himself certain of his preliminary Barrier
treaty. Marlborough was convinced that much larger events were
at hand. The question was whether Heinsius would corner him upon
the Barrier before France publicly appealed for a general peace. In
order to gain time he returned to London.[2] No one could stop
him. While Heinsius and the Deputies were arranging their plans,
their Captain-General was at sea on one of the "yachts," sailing for
home. How could he have negotiated the Barrier Treaty? He did
not agree with it. He thought the Dutch demands monstrous in
themselves, ruinous to the Alliance. Besides—here he turned the
argument which had damaged him against those who used it—the
Dutch would never believe he was impartial after the offers of the
Viceroyalty had been made to him. The Whigs must appoint a
colleague to deal with the Barrier question, some one who felt as
they did and commanded their entire confidence; some one who
was not hampered as he was by all that had happened in the past
and by all that might happen in the future. So Marlborough sailed
from the Brill to Margate, leaving Heinsius to extract what consolations he could from the frosty, sepulchral glitter of Eugene.

[1] Coxe, iv, 388.   [2] *Dispatches*, iv, 496.

Chapter Four

THE FATAL ARTICLE

1709—APRIL AND MAY

WHEN Louis XIV read in Rouillé's report the "hard replies" which were the sole fruit of peace efforts he had never dreamed he would be forced to make, he broke into tears before his Ministers, and with a gesture of despair said he would give up all—yes, even Lille and the Sicilies. To this point, then, had he been reduced by Marlborough's seven campaigns and the terrible frost. After the Council had been dismissed, Torcy loyally offered himself to carry the humiliating acceptance to Holland.[1] Upon the mood of the moment this offer was accepted.

The sending of the French Foreign Minister into Holland to sue for peace was a signal acknowledgment of defeat by France. Marshal Villars, when he heard of it, was convinced that peace was already agreed; for otherwise how could so devastating an admission have been made? It was a proof of sincerity and of stress which none could mistake. Henceforth no longer would there be merely attempts to make sectional treaties with the Dutch, but a grand negotiation for a general peace on the part of a Power which could, it was apparent, no longer continue the war. "Had not Torcy come himself," wrote Petkum, "the Allies would never have asked for such preliminaries."[2] On May 4 Eugene reported to the Emperor that an unknown man with the passport of an ordinary courier had passed through Brussels, where the Prince lay, and that rumour said he was Torcy.[3] Most writers suppose that Heinsius had no previous notice. It is certain, however, that when on that May night the Pensionary heard Torcy's knock at the door he was already expecting him.[4] Thirty years before Heinsius, acting in Paris too zealously in the interests of the Dutch Republic, had been menaced by Louvois with the Bastille. The Great King had in his

---

[1] *Mémoires du Marquis de Torcy* (1850), edited by Michaud and Poujoulat, p. 588.
[2] Round Papers, *H.M.C.*, p. 355.   [3] *Feldzüge*, Series II, ii, 84.
[4] May 6. Torcy was accompanied by the Rotterdam banker, Senserf. Reese, p. 203.

long reign patronized as well as maltreated the Dutch. This small Republic of the Dykes now found mighty France suppliant upon its threshold.

Heinsius received Torcy with courtesy, but informed him that he could only confer with him by the authority of the States-General; and thereafter the States-General declared "that the States did bind themselves to nothing until they knew the sentiments of the Queen of Great Britain by the return of the Duke of Marl-borough." The second stage of the parleys thus began, but on a footing entirely different. An excessive admission of weakness had been made, disastrous to France, but destined in the long swing of events to be fatal to the Allies.

Torcy's plan was first to gain the Dutch by extreme concessions upon their Barrier, then to induce them to bring pressure upon Marlborough, and at the same time to win Marlborough's goodwill by a colossal bribe. He believed that "at the present conjuncture Marlborough holds the key and that there are means of making him choose peace."[1] Marlborough had just left the second time for England, and the French Minister anxiously awaited his return. In the meanwhile he received the detailed assent of the King to his proposed procedure. He was to tell Marlborough how astonished the King was that he should be making efforts to break off the negotiations after his previous overtures for peace. The King would be glad to see Marlborough receive the reward which had been promised him. A precise tariff was set up. If Philip V received Naples and Sicily, or even in extreme necessity Naples alone, two million French livres; if the fortifications and harbour of Dunkirk were spared, or Strasburg was left to France, two millions: a total, if all these objectives were obtained, of four millions. Such was the view which the French took of their conqueror. They can hardly be blamed for doing so after his letter to Berwick. However, as we shall see, Marlborough was not to be bought for money. He would accept it as a reward, but not as an inducement. There is no doubt a real distinction between the two cases; but it is not one of which the French could be aware, nor upon which posterity will bestow any large measure of respect.

But Marlborough was in England. His second visit to London taught him further how his power had declined. The Whigs had full control of the Cabinet and both Houses, while the Queen was cool with him and hot against Sarah. The Whigs, and Godolphin

[1] *Mémoires*, p. 592.

with them, were convinced that France was at her last gasp, and would submit to whatever terms were imposed. Marlborough, upon whom the reports of the ruin wrought in France by the frost had made their impression, did not contest the general view. He understood only too well that henceforward in all negotiations he was no longer to be executor of his own policy, but only spokes-man of the Cabinet. His keen instinct and knowledge of men must have apprised him of the little goodwill which his new colleagues bore him; but whether he had any inkling of the ingratitude of his son-in-law may be doubted. He did not make a quarrel with the Whigs because he had been overruled or because he found himself in a strait-jacket. He set himself, as usual, to bring about the best results possible with the means at his disposal. But he was deter-mined not to become responsible for the kind of Barrier Treaty which the Dutch demanded. Already on April 24 he had written to Godolphin asking for a colleague plenipotentiary representing the view of the Whigs and accountable to them.[1]

This request was not entirely welcome. Somers, Sunderland, and others would have been content to have Marlborough obey their will, and yet bear full responsibility. They would thus have been all-powerful and quite safe. But when Marlborough made a move, whether in war or politics, he had usually reasons behind it which could not be disregarded. During all these months he had been busily preparing for a new campaign. The greater part of his time was spent in extorting or enticing contingents from the Allies, in organizing the depots, in assembling the armies, and above all in gathering food and forage. In spite of the rigorous weather, it was expected that the great armies would on both sides have to take the field before the end of May. A request, therefore, by the Captain-

---

[1]   *Marlborough to Godolphin*

HAGUE
24 *April* 1709

★. . . I have taken my measures with Prince Eugene that he returns to Brussels next Saturday, we having agreed upon the assembling of the army, which will be ten days later than usual by the backwardness of the season. So that if the wind is favour-able I shall take the opportunity of returning to England for five or six days to give an account of the Barrier as well as my observations of the humours of these people as to the peace. In the meantime you may depend upon it that if the King of France does not recall Monsieur Rouillé, he may continue in this country all this campaign; so that there will be a necessity of having here, at the same time I shall be obliged to leave for the army, one of the lords which her Majesty shall design to be in the treaty of peace. I think it may be for the service that he shall be ready to come hither at the same time as I shall return, for at my return I shall not be able to stay here above two or three days. [Blenheim MSS.]

General for relief in one branch of the peace negotiations could not be resisted.

The Whigs deferred to the logic of facts. Their first choice fell upon Halifax, who was still fuming out of office, and for whom they wished to provide. Halifax had been much concerned in the earlier peace overtures, and had made public his resentment at not having been associated with Marlborough in 1706. He refused his friends' offer with a taunt directed at Marlborough. "If the Duke had anticipated that the treaty to be concluded with the Republic would be to the satisfaction of the English people, he would not share it with anyone else; but the fact that he is asking for a colleague shows that he wishes to push off some of the odium upon this colleague."[1] Several writers have associated themselves with this sneer. It is hard to see how it can be justified. Marlborough would no doubt have gladly accepted the whole control and borne the whole responsibility. If he was to be merely the instrument of the Whigs, surely they should have one of their own band to share the consequences of their decisions. Moreover, his personal influence over the many states of the Grand Alliance was indispensable to the power of resuming the war effectively if the negotiations failed. Nothing could be more fatal to that influence than that he should have to drive through this hard bargain of the Dutch upon the Barrier Treaty, of which he strongly disapproved, and which was bound to be intensely unpopular with every other member of the Alliance.

The Cabinet next considered Sunderland, and all were speedily agreed that he would never do. So the choice fell upon the young Lord Townshend. He was an amiable and well-informed politician, a recent convert to the Whig Party, and a friend and protégé of Somers. He was a student of foreign affairs, and had much personal charm. "Everybody who knew Townshend loved him."[2] This last must always be considered a dubious qualification. But Townshend was prepared to serve as Marlborough's colleague, and the Junto were able to conceal themselves united in the background. Hoffmann said of him, "He is pliant and manageable."[3] Marlborough announced Townshend's appointment at once,[4] treated

---

[1] Hoffmann's dispatch of May 7; Geikie, p. 122.

[2] F. Taylor, *The Wars of Marlborough*, ii, 320. John Macky, *Characters of the Court of Great Britain* (Roxburgh Club, 1895), p. 89.

[3] Hoffmann's dispatch, May 7; Klopp, xiii, 227.

[4]   *Marlborough to Heinsius*   LONDON
                                                 April the 29, 1709
★I have had the favour of yours of the 3d, and that of the eighth this morning by

him with the greatest ceremony, and made him bear the responsibility for those parts of the Cabinet policy to which he himself had from the beginning been inveterately opposed.

The second matter to be settled was the official British attitude towards the Barrier. Marlborough had brought over with him for the Cabinet the latest Dutch project. Parliament had been prorogued before his arrival. Even the Whig Ministers felt bound to support his main objections to it, and their counter-project was framed on this basis. Ostend, which governed the sea trade of Belgium, and Dendermonde, which controlled the sluices affecting Brabant, were definitely refused. The Dutch right to place an army in the Spanish Netherlands was limited to the unique occasion in which France was the attacking Power and war had been declared. The revenues for the upkeep of the Dutch garrisons must be related only to those fortified towns which had not belonged to the Spanish monarchy before the death in November 1700 of Charles II of Spain. The clause forbidding Charles III before the general peace to take possession of Belgium was deleted. Upper Guelderland was reserved for the decision of the Queen. On the other hand, the Dutch guarantee for the Protestant Succession, the sending of the Pretender out of the French dominions, and the demolition of Dunkirk were demanded in explicit terms.

Meanwhile in Holland the negotiations had made great progress. According to his discretion, inch by inch Torcy yielded to the Dutch demands about their Barrier. Heinsius was able to announce to Eugene that the Dutch were content with the terms so far as they concerned themselves alone; they had only to consider their allies. On this they had newly given explicit assurances. Torcy was forced to recognize that there was no chance of a separate settlement with the Republic. "I believe I could deal with you more easily," remarked Heinsius to him (May 15), "perhaps even more independently of the Dutch nation, if Marlborough and Eugene were

---

which I see that you have Monsr. de Torcy att the Hague; I stay only for a fair wind, and shall bring Lord Townshend with mee who will be impower'd both for the Peace and Barier. I wish for my own sake that you cou'd be here, tho but for one day or two, to see the Zeal every body has for the carrying on of the Warr til we have a safe and lasting Peace. You wou'd then think mee a very moderat man; for the Prelimenarys I acquaint'd you with in the Queen's name, are by many not thought sufficient, for thay wou'd have had Newfoundland, and Hudson Bay, as well as our Treaty of Comerce, and some other pretentions to have been in the Preliminarys; I hope to be with you as soon as this letter, so shall say no more till I have the happiness of being with you. [Heinsius Archives.]

with me." The mood of the Pensionary had changed considerably since the early months of the year. As the desperate plight of France became every day more understood, both he and his countrymen stiffened towards the French and warmed towards the Allies.

Buys now raised the question of what guarantee the French could offer that the Spaniards would accept the terms. Torcy answered that Philip would be given three months to submit on pain of the complete withdrawal of French support. Heinsius also continued to demand, though without great enthusiasm, the entire Spanish monarchy for Charles III. Even this was no longer to be resisted by the French. But now every one hastened to put in his claim. From the Emperor, from the Diet at Ratisbon, from Victor Amadeus of Savoy, and from Portugal there arrived new demands upon the humbled monarchy. All had suffered from Louis XIV in his days of power. All hastened to reclaim with interest in this moment of his apparent prostration what they had lost. "Every sovereign prince," wrote Torcy to the King, "assumes that he has a right to formulate his claims against France, and would even think himself dishonoured if he had extorted nothing to the injury of the French crown."[1]

When we look back on the long years of terror and spoliation to which these princes had been subjected from the might of the Great King, it would be surprising if they had acted otherwise. Moreover, the allied armies were now gathering in the field. Contingents, in former years so tardy, were this time hurried to the front by rulers who saw the prey in their grasp, and were anxious to be in at the death and establish their rights to a handsome share. Marlborough's exertions for five months to have large forces at his disposal during the negotiations had succeeded beyond his hopes. "All the facts," wrote Eugene (May 17) to the Emperor, "go to show that France is quite unable to prolong the war, and we can, therefore, if we wish obtain everything we ask for. We have only to hold together and preserve a good understanding among ourselves."[2] Even those Dutchmen who at the beginning of the year were willing to make a separate peace were now convinced that France was at their feet. Van der Dussen, the leader of the Dutch peace party, himself wrote, "The policy of this province [Holland], the largest of all, depends upon more than five hundred persons, most of whom regard France as brought to bay [aux abois], and who are so embittered by the memories of the past that they are resolved without compunction to make an end once and for all

---

[1] *Mémoires*, p. 605.   [2] *Feldzüge*, Series II, ii, Appendix, 101 ff.

of their puissant foe."[1] In this mood van der Dussen had advised Torcy not to hesitate or wait for the arrival of Marlborough, which would only create fresh complications. Let him now, while time remained, concede all that was demanded. But Torcy still had hopes of Marlborough, and one remarkable reason for those hopes.

On the 18th the two Englishmen arrived.

Marlborough to Godolphin

HAGUE
May 19th, 1709

★ I had so bad a passage that I was not able to gett to this place til yesterday morning; my Lord Townshend was drove into Zealand so that he did not get hether til the afternoon. I must refer You to Mr Secretary Boyle, by which You will see that the intier Monarque [entire Monarchy], Dunkerk, the Qeens tytel, the Succession and the sending the Pretender out of ffrance will be allowed of in the Prelimenarys, and I am not out of hopes the getting of Newfoundland also in, which is in effect all that England askes; for the pretentions of Hudsons Bay must be ajuste'd by Commissions; the Cessation of Armes will be the difficult point, of which You shall have an account in our next; I can't end this letter without assuring You that the Pensioner's behaviour in this whole affaire has been very honest and friendly to England; the Pensioner tels me that Monsr. de Torcy is under some difficultys as to the maner of removing the pretender. Upon the whole matter, I think Monsr de Torcy has offer'd so much that there can be no doubt, but it will end in a good Peace; my head eakes extreamly, that I can write no more.[2]

The situation had simplified itself and vastly improved. The French were ready to submit; the Dutch had no thought of a separate treaty; Heinsius was content to shelve the idea of preliminaries with England. Marlborough saw all going as he had wished, and evidently thought the peace as good as made. Torcy, who was staying with Petkum, asked at once through his host to see him. Marlborough met the French envoy that very night. Torcy has given his own account of the discussion. Marlborough was all smiles and blandishments. He protested profound respect for Louis XIV, and presently mentioned Berwick. Torcy replied that he was familiar with the correspondence and that the attitude of the King had not changed. He would have enlarged upon the details, but Marlborough at once dismissed the subject.[3] So far from suggesting any mitigation, he asked, in accordance with his

---

[1] Torcy, *Mémoires*, p. 605.   [2] Blenheim MSS.   [3] *Mémoires*, p. 606.

instructions, for the restoration of Newfoundland. This was a fresh demand, and Torcy was shocked by it. To ease the situation they talked about Saint-Germain. Torcy had spoken of the Pretender as "the King of England." Marlborough referred to him always as "the Prince of Wales." He expressed an earnest desire to do some service to the Prince as the son of a king for whom he would gladly have sacrificed his blood and life. Speaking of Townshend, he said, "He is here to keep watch over me [*en surveillant*] in person. He is a very good fellow, whom I chose myself, but he is a Whig party man. Before him I must speak as an obstinate Englishman. But I wish with all my heart it were in my power to serve the Prince of Wales, and that your good offices may give me an opportunity." Marlborough went on to emphasize his desire for peace, and how he longed to end his days quietly. Torcy, who knew how fast the armies were gathering, was not comforted. He saw that there could be no hope of saving any part of the Spanish monarchy through Marlborough. He had that morning received permission from the King to drop Naples and Sicily if need be. He now announced this to Marlborough. The Duke, gratified, assured him that this was the only way to make peace. The interview ended. Torcy went to the Pensionary and informed him of the fresh sacrifice he had been prepared to make for the sake of peace.

The culminating phase in the negotiations was now reached. Together Marlborough and Townshend drafted their report for the Cabinet. Torcy had admitted willingness to concede not only Spain but Italy. He had, however, in telling Heinsius used a phrase which had attracted immediate attention.

> . . . *As far as in him lay*, by which expression it seems as if he thought the King would not be able to do it of himself in the manner we expect, or that he has some further reserve. To this the Pensioner tells us he gave him a very good reply by letting him know that he did not doubt that he had already seriously weighed the matter so essential and of such great concern that it would be expected they [the French] should propose the proper expedients.[1]

Here was the first glimpse of the rock on which all was in the end to split. It was not immediately approached.

On May 20 the three leaders of the Alliance met Torcy and Rouillé in formal conference. The Dutch and English demands were discussed first. These were easily conceded by the French plenipotentiaries. But then Prince Eugene began to say that France

---

[1] May 8/9, P.R.O.; quoted by Reese, p. 222.

had given way to England and Heinsius in order to gain them to her interest. He took his stand for Germany on the terms of the Treaty of Westphalia, which had ended the Thirty Years War in 1648. He must now on behalf of the Emperor ask for Strasburg and Alsace. At this Torcy appeared to lose patience. "We were practically at one with Torcy," wrote Eugene to the Emperor, "but when mention was made of the lands of the Holy Roman Empire he began to stutter, and answered he must leave, and demanded to depart and asked for his passports, so that without any further resolution the conference broke up."[1] Neither Eugene nor Marlborough thought that Torcy was in earnest. The Frenchman saw himself faced by united enemies. Later on in private van der Dussen warned him that the war spirit was rising in Holland, and there was no more hope from the pacifists. Torcy returned to the conference when it met again next day. He had powers to abandon Strasburg, but not Alsace. He fought for both, and no agreement was reached. There was a similar dispute over the claims of Savoy. In the end Torcy offered to dismantle Strasburg; but Eugene still continued to demand Alsace, and the Dutch and English supported the claims of Savoy. The deadlock continued.

Alone with Marlborough, Torcy made a final effort to seduce him. We have only the French Minister's account. Marlborough, who had himself proposed the interview, urged submission. He used all his most obsequious arts. If the peace was made he would earnestly desire the favour and protection of the King. He spoke again with sympathy about the Pretender. He referred to his desire for peace, to his uprightness, to his conscience, to his honour, and frequently to God. Torcy, thinking his moment had come, renewed his offer of a vast bribe. He received at once the same rebuff. "When," says Torcy, "I spoke about his private interests, he reddened and appeared to wish to turn the conversation."[2] "It was in vain," says the latest of German writers on these negotiations, "that Torcy offered the Englishman uncommonly high sums of money for the slightest concessions. He got no further than hints."[3] It was hopeless. We are left wondering why Marlborough should have wanted to repeat this unpleasant scene. Did he wish to expose Torcy to a second rejection of his offer? Did he wish to convince Louis XIV how vain it was? Did he, perhaps, take a personal relish in being offered these immense sums of money and seeing himself reject them? No one can tell, but the fact remains that this

[1] *Feldzüge*, Series II, ii, 108.   [2] *Mémoires*, p. 606.   [3] Reese, p. 208.

hardy, avaricious man, who could at this juncture without the slightest injury to the interests of England have helped the French towards the peace he himself desired, and gained an immense sum thereby, proved incorruptible. There is nothing to boast of in this.

On the night of May 21, after the negotiators had separated, a letter from the King to Torcy was intercepted with news from the Spanish peninsula. Galway, advancing from Portugal, had fought an unfortunate action on the Caya. The Portuguese cavalry had fled precipitately, and it was only with loss and difficulty that the English infantry had made good their retreat across the frontier. It was deemed striking that the victorious army was for the first time composed entirely of Spanish national troops without any French contingent. This was no great encouragement to the French envoys, for the victory of a Spanish army could not relieve the desperate position of France. The importance of the news was its effect upon the Allies. For the last two days their discussions had been going on in the rather unreal atmosphere of Germanic territorial claims. Now with Spain there came to the forefront the question of security and guarantees.[1]

When the conference met on May 22 the two questions, Alsace and the claims of Savoy, were still in dispute. Torcy and Rouillé therefore—perhaps a little stiffened by the Spanish news—begged to take their leave. Heinsius replied that they had all gone too far to part without a treaty. On this appeal the French envoys remained, but only provided they could send a courier to Versailles for instructions on these two points, and could present to the conference a memorandum on those which had already been settled. As soon as this memorandum had been presented on the 23rd the new divergence came to the fore. The Allies complained of the inadequate security which was offered for the surrender of Spain. They asked that they should not have to carry on the war in Spain while France was enjoying peace. They demanded guarantees. It had been realized at Versailles for some weeks that security for the fulfilment of the peace treaty would be required.[2]

---

[1] *Marlborough to Godolphin*

★My lord Townshend's letter and mine having in it all that has passed since our last, joined with the spleen I have for the ill news we have received from Petkum of Lord Galway's being beaten, will shorten my letter. I think the worst effect of this unseasonable defeat will be the disheartening of these people [the Dutch], who will not conclude this negotiation, which, if the French perceive, they will not be brought to give much more than they have already consented to. [Blenheim MSS., modernized.]

[2] Vetes to Rakoczy, end of April; Reese, p. 223.

King Philip was established in Spain. His kingship was championed by the Spanish people. His armies were victorious. He had declared to his grandfather, "I will only give up my crown with my life." He had created his one-year-old son Prince of Asturias, and the Cortes had acclaimed the infant as heir to the monarchy. Here were grave realities. Louis XIV was not necessarily able to answer for the King of Spain. He may have been aware of the strong feeling of the Dauphin against any desertion of his son, who had fought successfully at odds amid perils. All the more did the old King hope that some compensation would be secured for Philip V which, added to his own pressures, might procure compliance with the unrestrained demands of the Allies under the leadership, as must be owned, of the English Government. "There are occasions," he wrote (April 29) to his Ambassador at Madrid, "when courage must yield to prudence; and since the people, at the moment so zealous, may well not always think the same, nor may my grandson, it would be better to reconcile oneself to reigning somewhere rather than lose at a stroke all one's dominions."[1] Such expressions show a sincere will to peace.

But now Torcy violently opposed the idea of any guarantee. The Pensionary on behalf of his colleagues asked as proof of good faith for three French and three Spanish fortresses actually still occupied by French troops over and above all that had been conceded. Eugene, the land animal, wanted permission to march the allied armies into Spain through France. During the conference Marlborough sat silent. But on the night of the 23rd he expressed his doubts upon the possibility of forcing Louis XIV to act against his grandson.[2] "Marlborough even suggested schemes to turn the article so as not to commit his Majesty to war against Spain."[3]

"The French Ministers absolutely refused," wrote Townshend,

an amendment which might, they sayd, possibly engage their master to a condition so unnatural as to make a war with his grandson; but it was sayd there are no reason[s] to aprehend so harsh a consequence from the amendment, but [it] might have the good effect of making the Spaniards readily declare for King Charles when they saw the French King was under an obligation to joyn with the allies to force them to their new alleys [sic].[4]

For two days the discussion turned around this crux, and as it became the ultimate cause of the disastrous breakdown it is neces-

---

[1] Quoted in Klopp, xiii, 227.　　　　　　　[2] Reese, p. 235.
[3] Torcy, quoted in Reese, p. 235.　　　　　[4] Reese, p. 235.

sary to realize its importance. Many writers think it monstrous that, when these immense issues were so nearly settled, all should have been wrecked on such a point. It is certain that the Allies would have been wrong and unwise to break upon it, and without doubt they did not mean to do so. None the less it was a matter of far more importance than many of the terms over which both sides haggled so long. To England, with her strident demand for the surrender of the whole Spanish Empire, it was specially important. She would be left alone in all probability to conquer Spain. Marlborough had for some time been aware of the danger. A month before he had written to the Duke of Moles on the urgent need of gaining Spanish support.

> . . . It seems to me that one ought from this moment to take all possible measures to tame and win over the spirit of the Spanish nation, especially the notables who by a perversion are the most estranged from their duty, . . . so that when we come to make peace, and when France is forced to give orders for the recall of the Duke of Anjou, we shall not meet any setback in this quarter.[1]

The allied chiefs were, however, at this time convinced that King Philip would obey the orders of his grandfather if these were given to him *in earnest*. Torcy was evidently of the same opinion. All that was necessary, therefore, was for the King to give gages that he would issue these orders in good faith. It never occurred to anyone on either side at this moment that Louis XIV was really to be compelled to use armed force to expel his grandson from Spain. The allied leaders were surprised and shocked at a later stage that this colour could be put on their requests. The alternative for them was a new war, perhaps a very grievous war, a war of conquest and subjugation in Spain. It might impose enormous expense in blood and treasure on the Allies, already exhausted, while defeated France, whose ruler could by a word have prevented it, would rebuild her prosperity in peace.

Marlborough had his plans ready for a Spanish war. It would have been on the largest scale. The great armies would be transported to the Peninsula. One army under Marlborough would advance from Portugal, and the other under Eugene from Catalonia. They would meet in Madrid. Marlborough himself considered that a single campaign would suffice. It may well be that he greatly underrated the resisting power of a nation, and thought of it in

Dispatches, iv, 478.

terms merely of professional armies. He might have fallen into the same trap as was a hundred years later to ruin Napoleon. There was always the possibility which Bolingbroke, basing himself on Stanhope's opinion, was many years later to describe: "That armies of twenty or thirty thousand men might walk about that country till Doomsday . . . without effect; that wherever they came the people would submit to Charles III out of terror, and as soon as they were gone proclaim Philip V again out of affection. That to conquer Spain required a great army, *and to keep it a greater*."[1] But at least the Allies saw the conquest of Spain as an operation of the first magnitude, and if they could avoid this by merely extorting from Louis the effective exercise of his royal and family authority no one can fail to see why they pressed the point and pressed it hard. It would have been far better to concede the Sicilies as consolation for the Duke of Anjou. Here is the obstinacy for which the Allies are blameable. It is not, however, certain that even so Philip would have accepted the concession.

As no agreement could be reached on the outstanding points and no solution was forthcoming of the guarantee problem, Torcy invited the Allies in their turn to put their whole proposals in the form of a memorandum. Heinsius undertook to draw it up. The days following were occupied with the final drafting of the preliminaries. The Dutch statesmen worked throughout the nights of May 24 and 25 to frame the project. During that time the memorable Articles IV and XXXVII were drawn up.

> IV. . . . But if it should happen that the said Duke of Anjou does not consent and agree to the execution of the present convention, before the expiration of the term aforesaid, *the Most Christian King, and the Princes and States concerned in the present treaty, shall in concert take convenient measures to secure the full execution thereof.*
>
> XXXVII. . . . *In case* the King of France executes all that is above mentioned,[2] *and that the whole monarchy of Spain is delivered up and yielded to King Charles III as is stipulated by these articles, within the limited time,* 'tis agreed that the cessation of arms between the parties in war shall continue till the conclusion and ratification of the treaties which are to be made.[3]

No documents have come down to us showing how this wording was reached. It must be remembered that the Dutch did not feel

---

[1] *Defence of the Treaty of Utrecht,* edited by G. M. Trevelyan (1932), p. 108.

[2] Including the cession of the cautionary towns.

[3] Torcy, *Mémoires,* p. 619; G. de Lamberty, *Mémoires pour servir à l'histoire du XVIII siècle,* v, 288.

themselves so much concerned as the British or Imperial Governments either in the recovery of Spain or in the means of enforcing it.
They themselves did not mean to conquer Spain for anyone. Thus
perhaps these two Articles did not receive the profound study at
Dutch hands which would have been accorded to purely Dutch
interests. Heinsius certainly rested upon his original assumption
that, as Louis XIV would bring decisive influence to bear upon
Philip V, they would never have to be put into force. The clauses
were merely to be a threat of action, and the Allies were prepared
to accept alternative guarantees from Torcy. In this sort of atmosphere Marlborough and Townshend sponsored the whole plan of
the Forty-four Articles without demur. The Austrians raised only
minor objections. It was proposed to arrange an armistice of two
months from June 1 in which the final peace would be signed.

On the morning of May 27 Heinsius laid what were called the
"preliminaries" before the Frenchmen. Invited to comment upon
it, they made various reserves, but it is remarkable that they made
no specific objection to Articles IV and XXXVII, which, read
together, obliged France, under penalty of losing the cautionary
towns, to procure the submission of Philip V. The document must,
of course, be sent to Versailles for the King's final decision. Would
the French envoys sign it first themselves? Torcy refused point-
blank. Rouillé was inclined to sign. "You knew," he remarked to
Torcy, "the state of affairs when you came to Holland. Your journey
was proof of its gravity. If you leave without concluding peace,
however onerous it may be, make no mistake about the disappointment of the whole of France."[1]

Marlborough to Godolphin

May 25, 1709

★ffor Yourself

Since this business of Portugale [*i.e.*, Galway's defeat], the ffrench
have thretned us with desiring their passports, but I think thay are
now resolved to Comply with what is reasonable, so that I hope by
Munday we shall be able to send You the Project. Monsr de Torcy
not having sufficient power to Conclude til he first speak with his
Master, I thought it the safest way to send the Project before we
signe to Her Maty, tho every thing of Moment desir'd by England
is agreed too; You will see that there is so litle left to the Negotiation
that it maybe worth Your Consideration whether You will [need to]
ogment the number of Ambassadors, especially if You meet with

[1] Torcy, *Mémoires*, p. 629.

difficulty in the personne to be sent; besides I believe the humour of 4 [Halifax] is such that *in order to have business and merit, he may Creat difficultys*, and 14 [Townshend] heithertoo, is just the Contrary; so that if You can do itt without offence, You might save Your mony and wee not be troubled.

Since the writting of this wee think it the best way to signe, and give france a perumtary day, which I think is necessary for the preventing 110 [Dutch?] to make alterations. Monsr Torcy returns tomorrow and will have time til the 4th of the next month for the signing and sending back of the Conditions we insist upon.[1]

And on the 29th:

*Mr Walpole brings the Preliminarys signed by the Emperor the Queen and the States, and the ffrench are allow'd time till the fourth of the next month, Monsr Torcy not having powers sufficient to agree to all we insist upon, the particulars of which I must refer You to Mr Secretarys letter; the dutch were so desirous to insert their Barier into these Preliminaries, that I thought last saturday all had been undone, Pr. Eugene and Sinzendorff resolving not to Complye; You will see by the Project that we have a mind to finish all in two months, and to do it without a Mediator and as litle Cerimony as possible. If the ffrench Comply as I think thay must, I have hopes of seeing You before the end of the Summer. You will see that we have alter'd the Article Concerning the Pretender, I think it much better then what was at first insist'd upon. As soon as we have setled the Barier, we shall in the next place aplye our selves for the Treaty that all may be Garant to this Peace. Pr. Eugene goes for Bruxelles tomorrow, in order to have the Army in readyness on the fourth, so that we might lose no time if the ffrench shou'd not comply. I am to stay here til the fourth, but keep only two or three servants, for we shall open the Campagne with two Armys.[2]

The French were requested to give an answer by June 4. Thus the "memorandum" acquired the character of an ultimatum. This had not been the original intention. Into this position the Allies had been manœuvred by Torcy's skill. The document he had obtained presented the issues to his master in such a way as to enable him to refuse, should he choose to do so, on the broadest grounds.

[1] Blenheim MSS.   [2] *Ibid.*

Chapter Five

THE LOST PEACE

1709—MAY AND JUNE

YOUR Majesty," wrote Torcy on May 28 in sending the preliminaries to Versailles, "is thus entirely free to reject absolutely these conditions, as I trust the state of your affairs will permit; or to accept them if unhappily you conceive it your duty to end the war at any price."[1] If the King decided to break, his Minister advised that the odium should be thrown upon Alsace and the claims of Savoy, rather than upon the methods of ensuring the surrender of Spain. It is thus clear that Torcy had in no way taught the allied negotiators to recognize that Article XXXVII possessed a fatal character. On the contrary, it is evident that he took it for granted that Philip V would obey his grandfather without the slightest hesitation. Indeed, he had even remarked in the conference that the King of Spain would very likely be at Versailles before him.[2] With heavy heart the unhappy Frenchman followed the woeful ultimatum he had sent forward to his master. On the journey he passed through Villars's headquarters at Douai. He showed the terms to Villars. The Marshal, mortified, indignant, indomitable, conjured him to tell the King that he could count upon the army.

London and The Hague, as well they might, made haste to ratify the preliminaries. Vryberg reported that he had never seen Godolphin so cheerful. There was not even a Cabinet meeting. Every one was confident that peace was made. Marlborough began to arrange for the transport home of the British troops after the paying off of the foreign contingents in Flanders. "Everything goes so well here," he wrote to Sarah, "that there is no doubt of its ending in a good peace. . . . You must have in readiness the sideboard of plate, and you must let the Lord Treasurer know that since the Queen came to the crown I have not had either a canopy or chair of state, which now of necessity I must have, so the wardrobe should

---

[1] *Mémoires*, p. 619.
[2] Resolution of the States-General of July 27, 1710; Lamberty, vi, 70.

have immediate orders." And he adds—a characteristic touch—
"I beg you will take care to have it made so as that it may serve
for part of a bed, when I have done with it here, which I hope will
be by the end of the summer."[1] Nevertheless, he found the suspense
irksome, and from time to time he had misgivings about this
Article XXXVII which neither Torcy nor any of Torcy's allied
opponents thought would be a serious difficulty. It is recorded that
he said privately in these trying days, "I fear Article XXXVII may
spoil everything."[2] Certainly, to be prepared for either event, he
put the armies at twenty hours' notice to march.

Torcy reached Versailles on the evening of June 1, and made his
report to the King in the apartments of Madame de Maintenon.
All next morning the Council sat. The highest dignitaries of France
swelled the throng of courtiers in the anterooms, and although
they were nourished only upon rumour, the sharpest division prevailed. Peace was the cry of the realm. But did they know what
peace meant? Meanwhile behind the closed doors Louis, his son,
and his councillors faced the awful alternatives. No authoritative
account transpired. Torcy's memoirs, Dangeau's diaries, Saint-
Simon's ample pages, give no clues. It was only in 1855, says
Klopp, that the publication of the memoirs of Rakoczy's agent, the
Hungarian Vetes, who might well have been in a position to know,
threw a light upon this grim debate. Vetes' report is dated *lundi au
soir*, the Council having been held on the Sunday. He attributes
the decision entirely to the action of the Dauphin. This Prince,
usually so tranquil, appeared to be transported with wrath at the
idea of his son, the crowned King of Spain, at that time idol of the
Spanish people, being abandoned, even dragged from his throne,
by Louis XIV. He bitterly reproached the Council with the shameful deed they were about to commit, and apostrophized his father
the King himself in terms so little marked by respect that the
listeners were petrified. Furiously he reminded the Ministers who
had spoken for peace that one day he would be their master, and
that if the King by their advice abandoned his son they should
render a long account to him. He rose from the table and left the
room. The doors closed behind him, and there was a lengthy interval; but presently Torcy emerged, and, pursuing the indignant
Dauphin, told him and the whole Court that the resolve had been
taken to stand by the King of Spain. Rouillé was sent post-haste to
tell the Allies that their ultimatum was rejected.

[1] Coxe, iv, 393.　　　　　　　　　　[2] Lamberty, v, 288.

Klopp, for all his research, is wrong in stating that Vetes alone left a record of the dispute in the Council. Frequent mention has been made of Marlborough's Secret Service. One cannot tell where this begins and ends. The Blenheim Papers contain above four hundred reports from Paris dealing with the events of 1708 to 1710. Twice or three times a week a letter was written from the French capital. These reports, never yet published, are remarkable both for their accuracy and their prescience. They are all in French and, of course, unsigned. The writer must have been a man of position and intelligence, and his contacts were wide and various. Evidently he was accustomed to meet high personages at luncheon or dinner. One of his agents is mentioned who "lunches regularly with the clerks of the Foreign and War Ministries" fresh from the Council of the King. It is also probable from certain domestic details in the reports that some valet or female servant in close attendance upon Louis XIV or Madame de Maintenon gave to the British spy all he observed. They are remarkable because they show how soon and how truly Marlborough was advised. They give pictures of the private life and routine of Louis XIV sometimes more intimate than anything that Saint-Simon and Dangeau have recorded, and these pictures were swiftly, punctually, and regularly transmitted to his principal foe.[1]

Marlborough's spy at this juncture was as well informed as Vetes; and Marlborough within a few days had knowledge of the Dauphin's intervention which Klopp supposed to have been buried for a hundred and fifty years.

Advices from Paris

June 3, 1709

*Monsieur de Torcy arrived Saturday evening at Versailles, and found the King at Madame de Maintenon's. The King at supper said

---

[1] The series at Blenheim is found not in the Marlborough, but in the Sunderland Papers. It has therefore been ignored by those who have previously examined the archives in order to write about the Great Duke. All these reports are addressed to the Secretary of State, Sunderland, through a clerk in his office named Pringle. It is certain that they were sent direct from Paris to Marlborough's headquarters, because we find him frequently reflecting their contents in his home letters; and, besides, to send them roundabout by Whitehall would have involved at least a fortnight's and often, with adverse winds, a month's delay, thus rendering military Intelligence useless. On the other hand, from some of Godolphin's letters it seems that he was receiving them too.

The spy reports cease abruptly on the dismissal of Sunderland by the Queen. One may suppose that on his son-in-law's coming into the Cabinet Marlborough after receiving his agent's reports sent them on to him, but that before and after the Sunderland tenure he kept them to himself and probably destroyed them. This view would appear to be confirmed by the fact that the Record Office contains no documents of this character.

nothing, and seemed sad and gloomy. Yesterday from eleven o'clock till half-past one the Council dealt with the peace proposals of the Allies, which were found very hard. *The Dauphin opposed them with heat,* and so did the Duke of Burgundy, and a general assured me on good grounds that the Council did not think fit to accept them, and letters from Versailles state that the negotiations are broken off. However, the Council meets again to-day or to-morrow on the same subject. I am told that Monsieur de Beauvillier[1] will ask for peace on behalf of all his followers.

The King after dinner yesterday went for a walk, and told Monsieur de Torcy to be at Madame de Maintenon's about six o'clock. It is certain that one sees reigning at the Court a great agitation mixed with consternation. Many people are of opinion that the peace will be made whether the King accepts the hard conditions imposed upon him or whether he refuses them. They flatter themselves that the States-General, who wish for peace, and to whom the King has in a sort of way entrusted his interests, will put a brake upon the boldness of Prince Eugene and Milord Marlborough, and oblige them to soften upon several articles for the sake of peace. But the fate of peace or war will have been decided yesterday evening at Madame de Maintenon's. . . .[2]

"Is there, then, no counter-proposal?" asked Marlborough, when he learned the staggering news. He was deeply shocked. For some days he nursed a project for some compromise upon Article XXXVII.[3] In much despondency he set out for the front. He wrote to Godolphin (June 7):

The Marishall de Villars has given his advice to the King for the venturing a Battel. There is no doubt a Battel in the plains of Lens wou'd put an end to this Warr, but if that shou'd happen, and God Almighty as hethertoo bless with Success the Armes of the Allyes, *I think the Queen shou'd then have the honour of insisting upon putting the ffrench Government upon their being againe govern'd by the three Estates which I think is more likely to give quiet to Christendome, then the taring provences from them for the inriching of others.*[4]

This is one of the most revealing insights which we have into Marlborough's statecraft. The idea of substituting for the despotic rule of France a Parliamentary régime had long commended itself to him. It is a strange speculation how the course of history would have been changed if he had been able to enforce his policy upon

[1] This French Duke was the son-in-law of Colbert and tutor to the three sons of Monseigneur the Dauphin. He was personal enemy of Madame de Maintenon at Court.
[2] Blenheim MSS.   [3] Reese, p. 266.   [4] *Sarah Correspondence,* ii, 324.

France. The French Revolution might have accomplished itself gradually and beneficently in the course of the eighteenth century, and the whole world have moved on to broader foundations without paying the awful price in war and horror. There might have been no Napoleon! To pursue such thoughts beyond their earliest suggestions is vain; but Marlborough's words show how far in this respect he stood ahead of his times—and our own.

Petkum made a last futile effort with Heinsius for the exclusion of Article XXXVII. The Pensionary said it was too late. Marlborough and Eugene wished, however, to charge Rouillé, who had lingered in Holland, with the offer. On June 9 they made an attempt to interview him on his way through Brussels. "M. Rouillé," wrote Marlborough to Townshend, "came to Brussels on Tuesday evening. Both the Prince and myself designed to have seen him, and ordered that no post horses should be given to anybody without our direction, but through a mistake we were disappointed." He added in his own hand a postscript: "The Prince of Savoy is of opinion that we should have explained the XXXVIIth article, and have made it easy, thinking the French were sufficiently in our power when they had put us in possession of the towns. . . ."[1] But all was over.

The question which is capital for Marlborough is whether he strove for peace or war. The immense tangle of the negotiations and the multitudes of letters written by the principal actors baffle history by their bulk and by their contradictions. A full account from day to day of all that passed would carry little meaning. Sometimes we see Marlborough rupturing what looks like a pacific move. Often he is arguing a minor point. Sometimes he presents himself in sharp opposition to Dutch, Prussian, or Imperial desires. Sometimes he is their champion. At each of the numberless phases of the negotiations the attitudes of the various principals shift. At one moment it is the Dutch who are sincere, at another the French; and always when there is agreement between any two, friend or foe, it is because the interests of others have been put in the shade.

But there can be no doubt where Marlborough stood. To Heinsius, to Godolphin, to Torcy, he wrote a series of urgent and at times impassioned appeals, the only aim of which was peace with France, leaving Spain, if necessary, to be dealt with separately and later. These appeals and warnings began from the moment when the XXXVIIth article, or, in other words, the question of guarantees,

---

[1] June 13; *Dispatches*, iv, 505.

became crucial. He was the first to state in open conference, in the presence of the enemy representatives, that Article XXXVII ought not to be pressed. Torcy bears witness to this. When, to Marlborough's consternation, the negotiations were ruptured and the French envoys took their departure he tried to intercept them, and his first thought, in harmony with Eugene, was to condemn the obstinacy on this point which had led to disaster. His letters to Heinsius, and above all their secret postscripts "For Yourself Only," most of which have hitherto reposed in the Dutch archives, are the pith of the whole debate and the revelation of his inward mind.

At the moment of the rupture, later as the year advanced, and up to the eve of the great battle, his exhortation to Heinsius not to let Article XXXVII become a fatal obstacle was vehement. After the demand of the Allies had shifted from cautionary towns in France, which Louis XIV could undoubtedly deliver, to a demand for cautionary towns in Spain, which he certainly could not, Marlborough solemnly warned Heinsius that the consequence of obstinacy was the continuance of the war.

"I find the Prince is of opinion," he wrote to Heinsius (June 11), "that it will be impossible for the French to comply with the Article for the giving up of the Monarque of Spain by the last of July."[1] And on June 19:

★ *For Yourself Only.*

What you say as to the ffrench if thay are sincere, thay might propose some expedient for the evacuating of the Spanish Monarque is very trew; on the other side may thay not apprehend, if we shou'd not approve of their expedient, that thay expose the honour of their King and Nation.

The opinion of the Pr. of Savoye and your humble servant is, that if the ffrench had delivered the possession of the towns thay promis'd; and demolish'd Dunkerke and the places nam'd on the Rhin, thay must after that have comply'd with whatever we shou'd have thought reasonable, but as their is an end of the Negotiation, we must now do our best, to make it their intirest to renew the Negotiation.[2]

In reply to Sarah, who had reported that the talk in England was that he had obstructed peace, he wrote (July 1):

As to the good-natured turn of some of my countrymen, it is what must ever be expected as long as parties are in being; which I believe must be as long as England has a being. Notwithstanding their

---

[1] Heinsius Archives.   [2] *Ibid.*

remarks, I am very well assured that 39 [himself] would have been very glad if 43 [Louis XIV] had consented.[1]

Again to Heinsius (July 4):

For Yourself Only.

The positive orders that my Ld Townshend has for the insisting on the three towns in Spain makes it impossible for me to express myself otherways than I do in my letter; *but I call God to witness that I think it not in the power of the King of France, so that if you persist in having three towns in Spain, it is in my opinion declaring the continuation of the war.* I am told that some letters from the army pretend to know my opinion. I do assure you on my word that I never speak to anybody on this subject but the Pr. of Savoye and sometimes to M. de Sinzendorf.[2]

And (July 10):

If I were in the place of the King of France I should venture the loss of my country much sooner than be obliged to join my troops for the forcing of my grandson.[3]

The Pensionary revealed his own and reflected the prevailing Dutch view when he wrote to Marlborough (August 17), "There is vehement opposition here to continuing the war in Spain, after peace has been made with France."[4] Marlborough's rejoinder cuts to the root:

* *For your self only.*

August 22, 1709

You say that you find many that have great difficulty in continuing the Warr with Spain; thay are of the same opinion and have the same difficulty in England; but for God ake will not this difficulty be the same two yeares hence, and Spain the more time thay have given them be the better able to defend themselves, for I think it is plain that the ffrench Ministers have it not in their powers to recal the Duke of Anjoue; and I think it is as plain that if Holand England, and the Emperor will take Vigorous resolutions the Warr in Spain maybe end'd in six months.[5]

He revealed his convictions on this point at any rate to Townshend with perfect candour.

TOURNAY
August 31, 1709

* . . . As I never shall have any other thought of acting in this or any publick business, but agreeable to the orders I shall receive from

---

[1] *Sarah Correspondence*, i, 182.
[2] Heinsius Archives; partly quoted in Geikie, p. 137.
[3] Geikie, p. 131.   [4] Heinsius Archives.
[5] *Ibid.*; mentioned in Noorden, iii, 589.

England, I beg as a friend you will assure everybody where you think it may do good, that my judgment is entirely guided by the orders you received from England; *but to you as a friend I will own very freely, by all the observation I can make, I do not think it in the power of the French King and his ministers to recall the Duke of Anjou. On the other hand I do think it very practicable to force him out of Spain in less than six months if just and vigorous measures are taken by England and Holland.* This opinion of mine I desire should be known to nobody but yourself; and be assured that I will be directed and guided in this whole matter by yourself and the Pensioner.[1]

And again, as the crisis of the campaign approached:

TOURNAY
September 2, 1709

★As to the three towns in Spain it is impossible for me to express myself more positively than I have done in few words to the Pensioner, by assuring him that I can never be of any other opinion than what is agreeable to the orders you have from the Queen; but to you as a friend I must repeat that my private opinion is that the King of France has it not in his power to deliver three towns of consequence in the Kingdom of Spain, so that insisting on these towns, in my opinion, is declaring that the war shall continue, but this opinion of mine is only to yourself, *for you and I must obey the orders we receive*; the Comte de Sinzindorff will give you the names of the towns the Prince of Savoy and I think should be insisted upon. . . .[2]

Although at the beginning of the conferences Marlborough recognized his own weakness unduly, although he affected an extreme deference to the London Cabinet and the Whig power, although his letters dutifully breathe the form and spirit of his instructions, although no doubt he made wrong estimates of the forces at work, and used many arguments which were not his own, nevertheless it can be proved that at every stage he threw the whole of his weight upon the high personages with whom he was in the most intimate relation in favour of a settlement.

The far shrewder criticism has been launched that he failed to assert his authority and his genius. This view was actually recorded at the time by his critic, Colonel Cranstoun (July 28):

It is certain the Imperial Ministers and Prince Eugene were not for breaking upon that point [Article XXXVII], and however the Duke of Marlborough went into the opinion of the Pensionary and those who were for standing to all we demanded, yet it is not believed to

[1] B.M., Add. MSS. 41178.   [2] *Loc. cit.*

have been his real judgment, but, on the contrary, that he was for passing from that article, but in prudence would not take it upon him knowing what advantage his enemies at home would have made of it if any cross accident had fallen out thereafter.[1]

We are told by later writers that he had become so used to conciliating divergent interests, to finding a middle course, to avoiding awkward points, to submitting to the mistakes of others and devising new expedients to achieve his own plans, that now, at this culminating moment in his career, he gave in fact no clear, real guidance, and resigned himself with sombre complacency to the drift and sequence of events. Marlborough, say these critics, had become an institution rather than a man, a function rather than an actor. To keep the Grand Alliance united, and himself at the head of it, till final victory was secured had so long been his duty that he thought it his sole duty. In a certain degree he had become the creature of his task. He had gained so often by being patient that he had lost the quality of revolt. He had conducted so many ill-assorted, antagonistic forces through endless toils and hazards to safety and success that the Common Cause had become more to him than the rightful cause. If his countrymen and colleagues, if the States-General, if the Empire, chose to frustrate the French desire for peace, and conjured him to lead the strongest armies yet known to the invasion of France and the march to Paris, he would willingly, too willingly, be their servant and commander.

The great decline in Marlborough's personal power must not be ignored by those who censure him. He had since 1700 woven together a Grand Alliance and carried it forward by management, tact, and great victorious battles to mastery. At every stage he had had to hold in check divergent and competing aims. The fear of being defeated and destroyed had joined the Allies together. Now his own victories had destroyed that fear. Thus at the moment when his work should have given him the greatest authority, and when that authority might have been most beneficently exercised, he found himself alone, with no party and no country at his back. In England he was the servant of a Queen with whom his favour was gone, and the agent of a Government to whom he was in one aspect the survivor of a period during which they had been excluded from office. In Holland Heinsius and the leaders of the Dutch Republic were convinced that he was no longer their advocate. The Empire and the Hapsburg brothers still hoped to bind him to their

1 Portland Papers, *H.M.C.*, iv, 497.

cause and to sever him from the Dutch by proffering him almost a kingdom. But otherwise they thought, with General Schulenburg, "My lord Duc est l'homme le plus fin et le plus rusé du monde."

The circumstances of May and June 1709 were very different from those of October 1708. If Louis XIV had at that time accepted Marlborough's offer in the spirit in which it was made, when the armistice and peace conference would have broken out, as it were, from the surrender of Lille, Marlborough would probably then have been able to gather the conduct of the affair into his own hands. The Whigs had not yet forced their way completely into the Cabinet. The Dutch were comforted by the surrender of Lille, but were still oppressed by the French positions on the Scheldt and their grip on Ghent and Bruges. The great frost had not begun. No one can say with certainty that Marlborough would have had the power to carry a good peace, and end the waste and carnage from which Europe had suffered so long. The negotiations might, however, have lain in his skilful, tolerant, comprehending, if interested, hands. Whatever the military conditions may be, peace can never be established between great civilized countries upon the brutal execution of the rights of one side over the other. Marlborough's desire was peace; his interest was peace; perhaps he had then the power to procure peace.

This later phase shows Marlborough's efforts to guide events without any real control of the new forces at work. He was admittedly the indispensable agent. But for that very reason he could not use the last weapon at the disposal of a public servant who is resolved to carry his point of view. He could not compel by threatening resignation. This, if accomplished, would only wreck any chances of peace. His fall would be sufficient to encourage France to a point where all hopes of an agreement would have vanished. He must continue Generalissimo and plenipotentiary of the Allies, while at the same time consciously and unconsciously he was divested of the necessary power. Whereas up to this point Marlborough has been leading forward the whole Alliance for the most part along paths which he had chosen, we now see a cluster of magnificos bearing him shoulder-high on their own courses, but in great difficulty in deciding, and still more in agreeing, what those courses shall be. We see also efforts and manœuvres by Marlborough to free himself from these ceremonious maulings and to regain independent authority.

In the process everything was lost. Marlborough did not regain his control, and the Allies did not secure their terms. Europe was long denied the peace so sorely needed. Confusion and disaster were destined to cloud the end of this triumphant war. Peace was achieved only after further years of waste and torment, and then at the price to Britain of an act of desertion and dishonour. And Marlborough, who had performed a prodigy of loyalty, skill, valour, and effort, was condemned to be the scapegoat of universal disappointment. He had won the war. Some one, somehow, had lost the peace —his peace—and lost it for ever. Between them all they had let the splendid opportunity slip through their fingers. There were too many powers and potentates engaged, and no commanding leadership was tolerated. No one can be convicted of malice. All wanted peace. At the end two great Captains were still striving for it. They all failed. They all suffered for their failure.

The disappointment of the Allies found vent in a vain and furious clamour that they had once again been tricked and fooled by Louis XIV. The drums beat in the allied camps, and the greatest armies those war-worn times had seen rolled forward to the carnage of Malplaquet.

Chapter Six

DARKER WAR

1709—JUNE

WHEN Torcy had declared at the peace congress that Louis XIV could not wage war upon his grandson to dethrone him Marlborough had replied at once that he agreed with that. But now the die was cast to fight it out, and for the first time in his reign of more than sixty years the Great King appealed directly to French public opinion. In a circular letter addressed to the governors of his provinces, but intended for the widest audience possible in those days, he fastened the blame of the broken negotiations upon this cruel and unnatural demand. It had not been made, but there was enough appearance of it in the excessive claims of the Allies and in the protracted discussions upon them. Many famous verbal manœuvres have been less justly founded.

From this time the character of the war was profoundly affected. Justice quite suddenly gathered up her trappings and quitted one camp for the other. What had begun as disjointed, tardy resistance of peoples, Parliaments, and Protestantism to intolerant and aggressive military power had transformed itself for some time gradually, and now flagrantly, into invasion and subjugation by a victorious coalition. From this moment France, and to a lesser degree Spain, presented national fronts against foreign inroad and overlordship. Many generations had gone since Joan of Arc had struck this gong, and three were to pass before its harsh, reverberating clang was heard again. In those days, when all the large populations were controlled and their life expressed only by a few thousand notables and educated persons, there was, of course, no conscious movement of the masses. Nevertheless the governing classes throughout France, and also in Spain, derived a strange invigoration from the national spirit. The French people reverenced and almost loved their monarch; and a strong unity reaching far beneath the official hierarchies now made itself felt. A new flood of strength, welling from depths which the early eighteenth century had not plumbed, revived and replenished an enfeebled nobility, exhausted professional armies, and a ruined treasury. The Spanish were already fighting a national war on behalf of Philip V. Now the French nation moved against foreign oppressions with some rude foretaste, even at that time formidable, of the passions of 1792.

The King's circular letter invoked a haggard but none the less genuine surge of indignation through all the circles upon which the French Government was accustomed to rely. "I cannot express to you the wrath of this nation," wrote Vetes, "against the Allies at the news of their stiff demands, and the general joy at the King's resolve to sustain his grandson, the King of Spain."[1] In Court circles there was a wave of emotion. Marshal Boufflers sent his plate to the Mint. The royal Princes and the aristocracy followed his example. Louis XIV melted down his gold dinner service and made efforts to pawn or sell the Crown Jewels. His example was followed by the Duke of Grammont and all the Ministers. No one in Paris dared to dine off silver. In the provinces the Church, the bankers, and the merchants responded to this mood. ★ "It is an emetic," wrote Marlborough's Paris spy,

> which is being given to France, and I believe it is the last resource. It was said yesterday at the Duke of Albe's that Spain would send 40 or 50 millions to the King, silver plate taken from all the churches. . . . It is not believed that the true Spaniards are deserting Philip. The Duke of Linares, with whom I found myself, told me in Spanish that never had Spain been more firm and less intimidated. . . . If the King has consented to abandon Philip and to withdraw his troops from Spain, they are quite sure here that we are maintaining an understanding to sustain Philip secretly; and to dislodge this the King would have to join his troops to those of the Allies, which it is not likely he will ever do.[2]

In France, even a foe turned ally. Famine, which had brought the realm so low, now led the strongest peasantry to the Army. "They follow the bread wagons," remarked the King unworthily. They followed also the promptings of the French heart, of which he had so long been unconscious.

At the Court much of the exaltation was on the surface and short-lived. The King and his morganatic wife set no great store by it. "When it became known that the King refused the shameful terms of peace," wrote Madame de Maintenon to the Duke of Noailles

---

[1] J. Fiedler, *Fontes Rerum Austriacum*, i, 133; quoted in Klopp, xiii, 245.
[2] Advices from Paris, June 10, 1709; Blenheim MSS.

(June 9), "every one cheered and called for war; but this impulse did not last, and people soon fell back into that prostration which you saw and despised." There was also a fierce temper around, of which the shrewd woman was sharply aware. "How many times," she wrote,

> have you heard it said, "Why are we left our plate? It would be a pleasure if the King took all." Now, however, that the most zealous have set an example there is consternation; there are murmurs. They say that it is for the King to begin to economize. All his spendings are criticized. . . . Let him give up his horses, his dogs, his servants. . . . In a word, they wish to strip him the first. Where are these murmurs? At his door! From whom? From those who owe him everything. As for me, they want to stone me because it is thought that I don't say anything to him; as if he didn't give his own orders.[1]

In July there were serious riots at Dijon and Rouen. At Rouen the mob cried, "Vive Marlborough."[2] In the capital bitter tongues repeated a new Lord's Prayer. "Our Father which art at Versailles, unhallowed is thy name. Thy kingdom is no longer great. Thy will is no more done on land or sea. Give us this day our daily bread, which we are short of on all occasions. Forgive our enemies who have beaten us, but not your generals who have allowed them to do so. Do not fall into all the temptations of the Maintenon, but deliver us from Chamillart."[3] This appeal was answered. Chamillart's obstinacy, it was declared, had lost the chance of peace. His improvidence had neglected the preparations to resume the war. In June he was replaced by Voisin. For the eighth campaign the French armies assembled. Money drawn from every recess trickled into the military chest. Rations, though not enough, were gathered into the magazines, and in the old hero Boufflers, and even more in the ardent, indomitable Villars, the army of France found leaders worthy of the greatest nation in its greatest need.

The unfolded map of history now shows us that Louis XIV was right in rejecting the peace terms and renewing the war. He wavered long; but the outcome vindicated his final plunge, and in the after-light his grandeur amid appalling stresses shines forth. Here is another triumph for perseverance against the enemy. His decision was condemned at the time by some of the clearest minds in France. Fénelon has left his reasoned censures upon record. More-

---

[1] *Lettres de Madame de Maintenon* (1758), v, 120.
[2] Advices from Paris, June 8; Blenheim MSS.
[3] M. T. Sautai, *La Bataille de Malplaquet* (1904), p. 2.

over, the final result of the war was not determined by the fortitude of the sovereign, nor by the magnificent efforts of the French armies. It was settled by the obscure intrigues upon the backstairs and around the couch of Queen Anne and by the consequent reversal of British policy which produced and followed the fall of Marlborough. None of this was guessed or even dreamed of by Louis XIV at the time. It was unknown and unknowable. Who could foresee that in little more than a year the dominating Whigs would be hurled from power or that England, so long the implacable soul of the confederacy, would become the active agent of its destruction? All the more must the moral be drawn—"Fight on."

Claude-Louis Hector de Villars, Marshal of France, has already played some part in this account. When Marlborough in 1705 had wished to enter France by the Moselle, Villars had confronted him; and the fact that, owing to the tardy arrival of the German contingents, the Duke had been forced to abandon the project constituted a French success. Villars's three campaigns on the Rhine had prospered and at moments shone. His surprise of the Lines of Stollhofen in 1707 and his subsequent inroad into Germany had gained him glory and booty. He had regained in full the confidence of the King. The discrediting of Vendôme had thrown the brunt of the defence of France on Villars. Placed at the head of the main army to face the gravest attack, his buoyant assurance had sustained the spirits of Versailles, and was no doubt a factor in the decision to persevere in the war.

Villars was a being into every atom of whose texture vanity and valour entered in equal proportions. Both were serviceable to his country in those dark days. He boasted, he postured, he gesticulated, but at the same time he organized, inspired, and acted. His self-admiration was matched by his patriotism. He was a great-hearted braggart. When disasters befell the armies on other fronts he was heard to exclaim, "I can't be everywhere." His indomitable ardour in facing adversity and the foe was of the highest service to his country. To few of her great soldiers does France owe more. But the conditions at the front in March were shocking. "I was unable before starting to formulate a plan of campaign because I did not know whether I should find an army there. . . . In fact I found the troops in a deplorable condition, without clothes, without arms, and without bread."[1] The soldiers starved in their camps. The officers were demoralized. Even more than when Vendôme

---

[1] *Vie de Villars* (1784), ii, 30.

had taken the command after Ramillies, every one was "ready to doff his hat when one mentions the name of Marlborough." By every device of discipline and every trick of propaganda he had set himself in the face of these aching deficiencies to revive the spirit of the army.

But at this stage the facts left Villars no choice of action. He could aim at nothing more than keeping the army together behind entrenchments. He affected throughout the campaign the desire to fight a great offensive battle. But his means were never equal to this, and the King's permission was only given intermittently. He spread the tale that before leaving Paris he had required as a condition of accepting the command that nine million livres in cash should be placed in the army chests. The famished soldiers looked upon him as a man fighting for their daily bread and trusted him as their sole champion. Here at least was stubborn material. The men driven into the ranks by famine were the best the French peasantry could breed. They had a feeling that they were fighting not only for their King but for their country. Since it was so hard to keep body and soul together, why not die fighting? Thus there were desperate troops and an indomitable chief. As he moved about among them in his ceaseless inspection of garrisons and camps he often heard the words, "The Marshal is right. There are times when one has to suffer."[1] "Villars," says Saint-Simon, writing in the safety of Versailles, "set to work to boast like a madman and to advocate insane proposals in his usual style. He breathed nothing but battles. He gave out that nothing but a battle could save the state, and that he would fight one in the plains of Lens at the outset of the campaign."[2] But this is a shabby account of exertions which saved France.

Marlborough's spy took a far truer view. ★ "The King has written," he reported (June 10),

that peace is at an end. Mons. de Villars was delighted [*ravi*] at this letter. He read it to the whole army, and asked the soldiers and officers if they did not wish to avenge the honour of the King which his enemies were insulting. So saying, he called for cheers from them all, and when they threw their hats in the air he threw his up too. It is felt here that this General, although light and vain in his talk, inspires audacity in the soldiers and leads them well *and as the French like to be led*, and that he is a lucky risker. Thus all hope he will do well. Besides he foresees and provides for everything. He is the first Munitioner

[1] *Vie de Villars*, ii, 34.   [2] Saint-Simon, *Mémoires*, xiii, 95.

and Treasurer of his army. He has obtained the King's leave not to pass things through the channel of the Minister of War, who is an imbecile. He has himself formed a body of six munitioners for the army. On the other side Mons. Desmarets sends him money direct, which he spends at his discretion. It is said that Mons. Desmarets has sufficient funds not only for the food and munitions of the army, but for its pay, up to the month of September. His assistant [*second commis*] said this in my hearing. . . .[1]

Of Chamillart's successor, Voisin, the spy wrote (June 14), "He is a creature of the Lady's, and described as a turned-coat."[2]

The allied army was already assembled about Ghent, and Marlborough and Eugene set out thither along the causeway road on June 12 under an escort of two hundred horse. As reports had been received that French raiding parties were in the woods near Alost with intent to seize the High Commanders, considerable detachments of allied troops were drawn out in this direction. The army at Ghent was the most powerful yet known, and more numerous than Europe had seen for many centuries. The order of battle comprised 194 battalions and 320 squadrons. Of these 152 battalions and 245 squadrons[3] were already marshalled, amounting to between 110,000 and 120,000 men for active operations, apart from a much larger number in garrisons and on the communications.

The cruel winter was followed by a cold, wet spring. The fields were sodden. Even by June the grass could scarcely support the cavalry horses. The magazines which Marlborough had sought to establish at Ghent and Lille were only half filled. "The account we have concerning forage is so terrible," he wrote to Godolphin (June 9), "that I fear *that* much more than the Marshal de Villars's gasconading."[4] Even if there had been no peace conference the campaign could not have begun sooner. Moreover, it was plain from the state of the French countryside that famine-stricken regions alone awaited the invader. Not only did the campaign open late, but it was already obvious that it would have to end early. There was no chance of repeating in 1709 the winter struggle of 1708. A mighty, well-equipped army, the best-fed community in Europe, stood at the orders of the renowned Chiefs. But the time at their disposal was short, and the fortress barrier of France after all these years of siege and battle, though worn thin, was still unbroken. If

---

[1] Blenheim MSS.
[2] "C'est une créature de la Dame, et on l'appelle un justaucorps retourné."
[3] *Sarah Correspondence*, ii, 328. [4] *Loc. cit.*

forecasts were to be made upon the military facts only, the prospect to those who had lost so good an opportunity of peace was certainly bleak. But we find at this time an overwhelming conviction among all the allied leaders, soldiers and statesmen, that the economic and internal misery of France would compel a peace. Merely leaning the weight of the great army upon the enemy would, it was believed, confront them with stresses they could in no wise sustain. The blockade was rigorously enforced.[1]

Marlborough to Heinsius

GHENT
June 13, 1709

*. . . You will know by your deputys that Pr. E. and I have had a conference with the Generals, who are all of opinion that till we have three or four days of sunshine we must not march fearing to ruin the ffoot, for there being no straw in the country, if they are obliged to lye on the wet ground the greatest part of them will fall sick.[2]

And to Godolphin:

We make use of this delay in sending up the Lys all that may be necessary for a siege; for when we shall get to the plains of Lens, we must have a battle or a siege, the greatest difficulty of the latter will be the want of forage.[3]

---

[1]

Godolphin to Marlborough

June 14, 1709

*My Lre of yesterday, which you will receive at the same time with this, was so long that I shall now give you the trouble only of telling you what Care has been taken here to stopp the Corn from France.

Sr John Norris is sent to the Sound, as the most proper Station to intercept it from the Baltick. Sr John Leake is going to Sea to Supply his place before Dunkirk & my Lord Dursleys squadron of 9 ships cruises in the Soundings to protect our own trade, & to lie in their way, in Case they Come north about; orders are also sent to Sr. G. Bing in the Mediterranean for Some ships to cruise betwixt the ports of Barbarie & the South of France.

This seems to bee as much as is possible for us to doe here in this matter. I hope [the Dutch] will send ships also to ye Northward, and some to watch the other channell of Dunkirk, ours not being able to doe both.

June 17

*All possible care is taken on our part in the Channel, in the Sound, in the Mediterranean, to intercept the corn from coming to France as the most pressing means, in case they can avoid fighting, to bring them to reason.

June 20

*Our endeavours to keep the corn from France have improved so very successfully, Sir John Norris having stopped all the neuter ships laden with corn in the Sound, and Sir John Leake having taken three French privateers . . . which went on purpose to have had corn from Dantzick. [Blenheim MSS.]

[2] Heinsius Archives.
[3] *Sarah Correspondence*, ii, 330–331.

Marlborough to Heisnius

★I was yesterday to see the Prussien troupes, which are in very good order. I hope we shall find the whole army in the same condition, wee being assur'd that the Marishall de Villars has orders to ventur a Battel. *The same man that gave me the first notice of the resolution taken last yeare for the attacking of Bruxelles, has been with me this morning,* and assures me that I may depend upon itt, that the Marishals orders are to take the first opertunity of attacking us, thay declaring that thay have nothing else to save them from the barbarity of the allyes. The same man tels me that the Marishals confidence is in his horse, great part of their foot being in ill condition, he also tels me that thay expect a body of troupes from the Rhin, which makes mee incline to think thay will not attempt any thing till thay have those troupes, and that we are devid'd in order to make a siege. Upon the whole in my opinion if we must have Warr, the most desirable thing for us wou'd be that the ffrench wou'd ventur a battelle, for we shall meet with very great difficultys as to forage and the subsistance of the army. . . .[1]

And again (June 19):

★I had the honour of writting to you yesterday, since which Monsr. de Goslinga is come which I am very glad off, for I am afraid we shall meet with some difficulty in forming the order of Battel to every bodys content, which may prove a very great *Contretems*. It is occasion'd by the resolution of the States concerning their own troupes; I do assure you that I shall in conjunction with your deputys do all that is in my power to make itt easy, for union is absolutely necessary if we will have the blessing of God with us.

A glance at the map reveals the strategic situation. The French front line stretched from Dunkirk to the Meuse. It had been bent back by the capture of Lille. Marlborough, with the Lys and the Scheldt up to Tournai in his control, could advance through his captured strongholds of Courtrai and Menin in several directions. The gap between Ypres and Tournai was blocked by the French army. If that army would give battle, as Villars loudly boasted, in the plains of Lens, all would be brought to a speedy issue. But nobody believed that Villars would be so foolish. All available information about his army showed it weaker in numbers than the Allies and subsisting only with extreme privation. It was already known that, far from seeking battle in the open field, he had constructed

---

[1] Heinsius Archives.

strong defensive lines running from the minor fortress of Saint-Venant through La Bassée to the great stronghold of Douai. Here, almost in the trenches in which two centuries later the descendants of the French and British troops together faced the remorseless bombardment of the descendants of the Prussian and German contingents, Villars had drawn his line. At first it was a single trench, with a parapet fifteen feet thick and a ditch deep and broad.

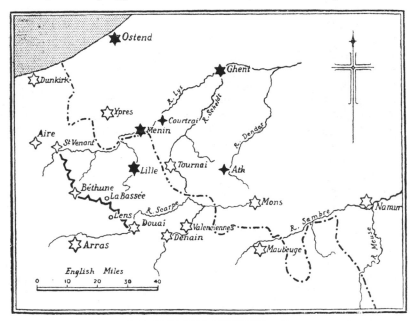

THE SITUATION EARLY IN 1709

But a second line fifty paces in front of this was in process of construction, and every use was made of all the water which the control of the headstreams of the rivers could give after a season of exceptional rains.

When Marlborough and Eugene reached Ghent several councils of war were held. The headquarters of the confederates had now become an assembly of the leading warriors of Europe after nearly thirty years of war. So many states had sent their contingents to Marlborough's army that his own British redcoats actually in the field army were barely a seventh of the international force which now awaited his orders. The commanders of all these forces, and representatives from all the countries from which they came, made a gathering of notables and potentates at once imposing and top-heavy. Nevertheless, so nicely were the distinctions drawn and so unquestionable was the authority which flowed from Marlborough, acting with Eugene, that it was not only possible to discuss the war measures in a considerable body without leakage, but for sudden and surprise action to be taken. The councils of war surveyed the situation, and many alternatives were examined or aired, but afterwards orders were issued by Marlborough which embodied what he with Eugene decided. Only in this way can the repeated deceptions of the enemy be explained.[1]

Apparently both Marlborough and Eugene at first spoke freely of their disapproval of the way in which the negotiations had been conducted; and to such an extent that offence and some alarm were caused at The Hague. Goslinga's secret letters to the States-General are revealing:

GHENT
June 16, 1709

★I will not repeat what Mons. Geldermalsen has written to you about the views of the two Princes on the recent negotiations. They make no bones about saying [*ne font pas la petite bouche*], particularly the Prince of Savoy, that we have displayed too much stubbornness. . . . The reasons that they give are known to you, . . . but it is discussed pretty openly here, [and] I entirely agree with you that this could not

<hr/>

[1] *Marlborough to Heinsius*

ABBY DE LOOS
June 23, 1709

★I have had the favour of yours of the 19th and by the account you give me of Monsr. de Torcy's letter to Pettecum, it is very plain thay do not think of proposing any expedient, this campagne. We ought on our side to think of every thing that may make it more difficult for them to continue the Warr, as that of hindering any corn going by sea to them, and if it were possible that the States wou'd consent to a prohibition of comerce which wou'd very much hearten the Allys, and discorage the Enemys, but this matter you can Judge so much better than my self, that I beg your pardon for mentioning itt. . . . [Heinsius Archives.]

June 23

★I have had the favour of yours of the 19th and I am very sure that you will know from Monsr. de Goslinga that I have acted very sincerely in the endeavoring to content every body as to the forming of two Armys, so as that the troops of the States might have the left Wing, the right being to consist of the English, Prussiens, and the Hanovers, and by the assurances Monsr. de Goslinga gives me, I do noways doubt when the service shall requier our being in one army, we shall make itt very easy; the ffrench army will be all form'd to morrow behind their line near La Basse, and it is possatively said that the Elector of Bavaria is comand the whole; by the ffrench not offering any expedient I think it is very plain that thay think them selves in a Condition of making this campagne; lett me once more assure you that nothing shall be wanting on my side for the having a good Corispondance with your Generals, which I think can't fail since I am sure of the assistance of Monsr. Goslinga; I need not repeat to you how usful it wou'd be to have Gelder-Malsen this Campagne; but I am afraid he has no mind to it. [Heinsius Archives.]

produce any good effects. Our enemies will be encouraged by it, and ourselves discouraged. But, since this is the case, judge for yourselves whether it is impracticable to reopen the matter.

And the next day, evidently after some remonstrance on his part:

★The Prince told me that in public he speaks in agreement with the resolution of the State, and does not express to anyone that he holds himself a different opinion. . . . Milor appears to me to have the excellent intention of cultivating the friendship of our generals: at least, he has made great protestations to me on the subject.

And from Lille on June 23:

★Regarding the behaviour of the Princes, there is no reason to complain. In public they reveal the same views as we do. I see with regret that at The Hague people are too anxious upon this subject. . . .

He adds:

The Prussians refuse absolutely to serve in the army of Prince Eugene.[1]

It is to be hoped that in the face of this and similar evidence the many historians and writers who have condemned Marlborough and his comrade for prolonging war for their own ambition or profit will no longer be credited.

Public opinion in England expected that a great battle and a victorious advance to Paris would follow the impudent rejection of the Allies' peace terms. This was not unreasonable, considering the mood of Ministers. Godolphin was worried. ★ "Though," he wrote to Marlborough (June 1/12),

there did not want a great many people here to find fault with the peace while it was thought sure, yet upon yesterday's news of it broken off to show the general opinion which the bulk had of it the stocks fell 14 per cent. in one day. 'Tis true they had risen 20 per cent. upon the news of peace. I own, however, that it vexes one to have them fall so much since I can see no ground to think the condition of France so better, . . . and in my opinion the insincerity in their dealing with Spain does not deserve the least endurance from our state.

I am nettled besides with the advantage they have already got by keeping us long in uncertainty whether we were to have peace or war. It has plainly stopped the dispatch of our ships and troops at least a month, and if cross-winds should come it may render them useless during the whole season. Supposing this should prove to be our case,

[1] Hague Archives.

which is not improbable, I should be glad to learn from you . . . what views you may have for this year of entering into France with any part of our army towards the sea coast, and how far we might be of any use to you from hence in furnishing and supplying provisions. I remember there were thoughts of this kind last year after the taking of Lille. . . .[1]

Tory criticism was loud and captious.

Peter Wentworth to Lord Raby

LONDON
10 *June*, 1709

At our coffee-houses we are very angry that the news talks of our beseigeing Douai; for their opinion is that we ought not to amuse ourselves in taking towns, but march directly to Paris. When they are told that an army can't march without having before provided magasins . . . they give no answere to this but—How did Prince Eugene march his army over the mountains without such a train or mony, and his march to the releif of Turin was in like manner; 'tis but to employ him and the business is done. . . . If they are told 'tis too late to provide such provision then they fall upon the credulity of those that gave so much into the faith of the French King's sincerity to peace. . . .[2]

At the front the matter was less easy, although the strategic issues were simple. Could the confederate army pierce the lines of La Bassée? Could it defeat the French, no longer in the open field, but behind entrenchments amounting almost to fortresses? If so the march would lie forward into the heart of France. But if these lines and the troops which held them were judged too strong for frontal assault, then they must be turned on one flank or the other. The approaches to both these flanks were protected by fortresses— on the north Ypres, on the south Tournai. The reduction of either of these places would probably occupy a large part of the all-too-brief campaigning season which was open. It was therefore first of all necessary to decide whether a frontal attack should be made or not. Great reconnaissance was made of the whole of Villars's front during the latter part of June. Cadogan and Dopff not only pressed at this point and at that with powerful escorts, but also it is said that the former, descending from his high position as Marl-borough's Chief of Staff and Quartermaster-General, traversed at the peril of his life, disguised as a labourer, a large section of Villars's front. The spy in Paris reported:

[1] Blenheim MSS.   [2] *The Wentworth Papers*, p. 90.

June 24

★There is complete confidence in M. de Villars. It may be said that the fate of the kingdom is in his hands, and that he is playing a fine rôle, if he can keep it up, as he promises in all his letters. Two days ago 500,000 francs was sent to him for the troops. He takes great care of his men, going in detail into everything to do with the pro-vision of the Army.

June 28

★I have seen the letters of the 29th from Flanders, which show that M. de Villars is encamped in a very favourable position, that the morale of the army is good, that Villars has withdrawn all the garrisons from Mons, Tournai, and Ypres, and has sent them to join the main army. This shows an attack is feared.

It is said that the allied plan is to pierce through on the sea flank and penetrate into Normandy, so as to support a landing from the fleet, which has spies in Cherbourg.

It is also reported that M. de Villars suspects some of his staff officers of giving the enemy information of his plans, and had thought fit to warn them that if he discovered any traitor in touch with the enemy, even if he were a prince, he would have his head off on the spot and send it to the King.[1]

On June 24, in the light of all information procurable, the ques-tion of frontal attack was put to the council. There was no doubt about the conclusion. Villars supposes that Marlborough and Eugene were overruled by the Dutch Deputies. But there is no truth in this. Marlborough's letters show that he accepted Cadogan's view that a frontal attack would not be justifiable. It was unanimously resolved that the French lines were too strong to be attacked. The only question in dispute was whether Ypres, on the one flank, or Tournai, on the other, should be besieged. Considering how France had begged for peace and the terms which could have been obtained, it was a poor and damaging outcome that the main effort of the Allies could compass no more than a siege. Indeed, Villars by his lines, by his forays, by his gasconades, had already gained an unfought victory when he compelled his indignant enemies to content them-selves with such local and stony fare.

Which, then, should it be? The allied commanders debated in deep conclave. Marlborough still hoped to pursue his design of the previous autumn. He wished to advance along the coast by Boulogne upon Abbeville and then up the Somme to Amiens and towards Paris. As a preliminary to this it would be necessary to besiege Ypres.

[1] Advices from Paris; Blenheim MSS.

We know now from Villars's memoirs that this was the movement which he dreaded most. It would be difficult for him to feed his own army in opposing it; and he saw as clearly as Marlborough that here alone could the Allies make use of their command of the sea in supplying their forces or in establishing a new base. There seems little doubt that Marlborough's view was right. But Eugene opposed it. He advocated the attack on Tournai, and he found great support. On political grounds the whole inclination of the German states and the Dutch was to draw the British away from the sea and carry the war as far inland as possible. Goslinga, who was present at the council, says:

> The Duke voted for the siege of Ypres, the Prince for that of Tournai. Our people [*nous autres*], as well as Count Tilly, ranged ourselves with the Prince. The principal reasons which led us to this choice were, first, the extreme weakness of the garrison [of Tournai]; second, the importance of the place; third, the convenience and security of the convoys; and, fourth, the lay of the land [around Tournai], which made the raising of the siege by a battle almost impossible; and finally the protection of Brabant, which we should cover, while making the siege.

All these reasons were no doubt just; but in war, as in peace, there is rarely any lack of good arguments for doing all sorts of things. "The Duke," continues Goslinga,

> did not set forth his reasons, except [the Goslinga touch] for mentioning the considerable revenues of the Châtelainie of Ypres. I believe, however, that his principal motive was to get nearer the sea, and once Ypres was taken to begin another siege on the coast, preferably that of Dunkerk, in order to put it into the hands of England; he took care, however, not to let this come out; on the contrary, he submitted without hesitation to the views of the Prince [Eugene].[1]

Thus we see Marlborough deferring as easily to the opinions of Eugene and the Deputies in the field as he had to those of the Whigs in council. In the one case, as in the other, he was evidently conscious of diminished authority. Besides this, it had become a habit with him to try to get everybody together and yield to majority opinion in the hope that at some moment or other a situation would be created out of which his ingenuity might draw some great event. He was ageing and worn with incessant exertions, and perhaps unduly conscious of the decline of his power in England. He could

[1] Goslinga, *Mémoires* (1857), p. 104.

not well, when the British contingent was so modest, force the commanders of the confederate army into courses which were unwelcome to them. It was rash even to persuade them against their will. He believed at this time that the state of France was so desperate and the war so nearly over that unity among the Allies was more important than true strategy. He underrated the remaining strength of France. He perhaps still more underrated his own strength, ebbing though it now was. He thought the Grand Alliance would gain an inevitable victory if only it kept together; and this was no doubt true if it had kept together long enough. Lastly, he was in favour of a siege of Tournai if the other alternative was excluded. The rapidity and precision of the operation which follows makes it certain that there was no friction in the allied High Command.

Chapter Seven

TOURNAI

1709—SUMMER

THE decision to besiege Tournai was taken on June 24. The operation was executed with masterly precision, and, according to Pelet,[1] "with such extreme secrecy that no one was able to divine the true objective." Marlborough, in pursuance of his Ypres plan or alternatively as a feint, had brought all the siege-train down to Menin. Its position there was known to Villars, and seemed to him proof that it was his left that was about to be attacked. Dompré, one of the Ally commanders, who was marching with twelve battalions and as many squadrons from Alost, was ordered the same afternoon to rejoin the army at Tournai. Another reconnaissance in force of Villars's lines before La Bassée was made as a blind on the 25th, and on the 26th a full council of war assembled ostensibly to take proper measures to assault them. At tattoo the allied camps were struck, the baggage loaded, and the whole army stood to arms ready to march. Once it was dark the heavy baggage started back to Lille, and the mass of Marlborough's and Eugene's forces moved in the opposite direction south-west towards La Bassée. By these manœuvres Marshal Villars was convinced either that he would have to face a frontal attack upon his lines at daybreak, or more probably that a feint at La Bassée was to cover the turning of his left. Accordingly, "fearing much more for his left than for his right, and above all for the neighbourhood of Saint-Venant, which was the most important and the most exposed, he sought the means of protecting it without moving his army from the La Bassée position."[2] He reduced the garrison of Tournai, reinforced those of Saint-Venant and Aire, and proceeded himself to Béthune with five hundred men, who lighted fires along three leagues of the front as if he had moved his main army towards his left. Finally he sent a detachment towards La Gorgue with orders to spread the tale that they were the vanguard of the French army.

[1] J. J. G. Pelet and F. E. de Vault, *Mémoires militaires relatifs à la succession d'Espagne*, ix, 37.　　　　　　　　　　　　　　　　　　　　[2] *Loc. cit.*

"This ruse," writes Pelet, "had all the success which was hoped for. Eugene stopped short. . . . The Duke of Marlborough's march towards Douai produced no effect." It is surprising that so able an historian, writing long after and with much knowledge, should remain under the deceptions of the French headquarters at the moment. In fact, at eleven P.M. on June 26, after marching southward towards La Bassée for about two hours, Eugene turned northwest and later east towards Tournai. At the same time the long strings of barges carrying the siege-train and its ammunition began

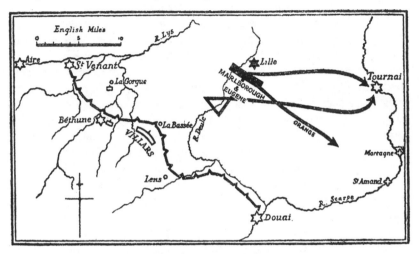

THE FEINT BEFORE TOURNAI

to float down the Lys back to Ghent, in order to be towed up the Scheldt. Marlborough's right and centre, moving at first south through Seclin, turned simultaneously in the same direction, while his left, which had not yet quitted camp, marched due east directly upon Tournai. Agreeably with these changes, the Prince of Orange with 30 squadrons and 10 battalions moved against Mortagne and Saint-Amand, on the Scarpe before it joins the Scheldt above Tournai.

The confederate troops, whose wagons carried six days' rations, did not know where they were going, and at first expected to be called upon for a general assault on the lines in the morning. But the turns in the darkness completely mystified them as well as the enemy, and when day broke they were astonished to see the towers of Tournai Cathedral rising at no great distance before them. Dompré, from the north, arrived simultaneously on the eastern side

of the Scheldt, where he was soon joined by Lumley with 30
squadrons, including the British cavalry, and 10 battalions. Marlborough's army deployed during the day, facing south with its right
on the Lille-Douai road. Mortagne and Saint-Amand were captured
without opposition by Orange; and Eugene, coming in later, filled
the gap between Marlborough's left and the Scheldt. By nightfall
on the 27th Tournai was invested in force on all sides. The surprise
was complete, and the fortress was caught with barely five thousand
men, or half the proper number to man its defences. It was well
supplied with munitions and had some bread, but the hostile apparition was so sudden that Surville, the commander who had distinguished himself at Lille, had no time even to drive in the cattle
from the surrounding fields. The attempts by Villars on the 29th
to throw in seven or eight hundred horse from Mons and Condé,
and on the 30th by Luxembourg, who had orders to repeat his
brilliant exploit at Lille with a thousand dragoons each carrying a
foot soldier behind his saddle, were effectually frustrated.

John to Sarah

June 27

If it had been reasonable, this letter would have brought you the
news of a battle; but Prince Eugene, myself, and all the generals, did
not think it advisable to run so great a hazard, considering their camp,
as well as their having strengthened it so, by their entrenchments;
so that we have resolved on the siege of Tournai, and accordingly
marched last night, and have invested it, when they expected our going
to another place, so that they have not half the troops in the town
they should have to defend themselves well, which makes us hope it
will not cost us dear. I am so sleepy that I can say no more, but
am entirely yours.[1]

Marlborough to Godolphin

VILLEMEAUX
June 27, 1709

The bringing our battering cannon to Menin has had the success
we wished, for the French took it for granted that we intended the
siege of Ypres, and accordingly put sixteen battalions in that place,
and drew ten battalions from Tournai, so that we marched last night,
and this day, by twelve of the clock, the town was invested. And as
they have not above half the troops in the town they ought to have
for a vigorous defence, we intend to attack the town and citadel at
the same time.

. . . We cannot have our cannon brought to us by the Scheldt in

[1] Coxe, v, 6.

less than ten days, but when we have them once on our batteries, I believe it will go very quick. . . .[1]

Although the pretence of French historians that the Allies had been forced to alter their plans by Villars's nocturnal measures cannot be maintained, the Marshal had nevertheless no serious ground for self-reproval or disappointment. It was beyond human wit to guess which way the cat would jump. It had jumped in the least dangerous direction. The siege of Tournai, begun as late as midsummer, meant, even with the favour of surprise, the indecisive consumption of the greater part of the campaigning season. Villars was relieved that the danger of operations against his left in conjunction with the naval power of the Allies might now be definitely set aside. He therefore expressed himself well content with what had happened. "It was a great relief," he says in his memoirs. He set himself at the time to interpret the events of the preceding days in the manner most satisfactory to his reputation. Marlborough and Eugene had sought, he suggested, to lure him from his lines into a battle in the open field. He had baulked them. Fearing their movement by his left, he had purposely left Tournai weakly garrisoned as a bait. "The fortress should hold out," he declared publicly, "at least four or five months." His private estimate carried its defence to the beginning of October. These views commended themselves to Louis XIV. "I count for much," he wrote on July 2, "that by your wise dispositions and the precautions which you have taken all the vast projects [of the enemy] are reduced to the single enterprise [of the siege of Tournai], and you could not at the beginning of this campaign render me more important service."[2]

Marlborough's letters to Godolphin speak repeatedly of the hardships of the troops and of the misery of the countryside. (June 24) "All the wheat is killed everywhere that we have seen or heard of."[3] (July 4) "It grieves my heart to see the sad condition all the poor country people are in for want of bread; they have not the same countenances they had in other years."[4] To Sarah (July 11): "It is not to be imagined the ill weather we have, insomuch that the poor soldiers in the trenches are up to their knees in dirt, which gives me the spleen to a degree that makes me very uneasy, and consequently makes me languish for retirement."[5] (July 18) "If we have not peace, I shall be sooner with you this year than any of this war, for in all likelihood we shall not find forage to enable us to make a long cam-

[1] *Sarah Correspondence*, ii, 338–339.   [2] Louis XIV to Villars; Pelet, ix, 47.
[3] *Sarah Correspondence*, ii, 336.   [4] *Ibid.*, 344.   [5] *Sarah Correspondence*, i, 187.

paign, and that is what I fear the French know as well as we."[1]
And (July 30): "The misery of all the poor people we see is such
that one must be a brute not to pity them."[2]

The strains were increasingly hard in all directions. Godolphin
wrote to Marlborough (July 4):

> *I am glad to find you continue to have so hopeful an opinion of the
> siege of Tournai; the people are a good deal prejudiced against it here,
> but if it succeeds . . . we shall be as sanguine as ever, which is too
> necessary; for unless our credit be not only supported but also aug-
> mented by successes abroad, our provision in Parliament for the
> expenses of the present year will fall short before the end of it by at
> least twelve hundred thousand pounds.[3]

Meanwhile the vessels carrying the battering-cannon had passed
Ghent and were being towed up the Scheldt. The French had
blocked the fairway by sinking barges filled with stone, and it was
necessary to cut a new channel. The first thirty barges passed the
obstruction on the 8th, and by the 10th the whole of the siege artillery had arrived. The work of constructing the batteries and mounting the cannon absorbed the energies of the besiegers. Marlborough,
with sixty battalions, undertook the siege. Eugene commanded the
covering army. Thus the rôles at Lille were reversed. Three separate
attacks were launched against the town: Lottum the Prussian against
the citadel from the Valenciennes road; Schulenburg the Saxon
against the Sainte-Fontaine gate from the left bank of the Scheldt;
Fagel the Dutchman against the Manville gate. Keen rivalry existed
between these commanders, and wagers were laid as to which would
win the prize. The difficulties of the siege were vastly increased not
only by the unseasonable rains, but by the enemy's control of the
sluices of the Upper Scheldt, which enabled them to flood the siege
works suddenly in various places. The Town Ditch opposite
Fagel, which was in fact a branch of the Scheldt, was filled with
a deep stream running so fast that it washed away the debris as fast
as the bombardment cast it down. To this was now added an
intensity of mining and countermining novel and horrible in that
age. "This is a siege," wrote Schulenburg, "quite different from
any hitherto made; the most embarrassing thing is that few officers
even among the engineers have any exact knowledge of this kind
of underground works, and even less of the way of attacking them."[4]

---

[1] *Sarah Correspondence*, i, 189.   [2] *Ibid.*, 193.   [3] Blenheim MSS.
[4] *Leben und Denkwürdigkeiten Johann Mathias Reichsgrafen von der Schulenburg* (1834),
Part II, 397.

T   577

"The great quantity of waters," Marlborough wrote to Godolphin (July 25), "which this garrison are masters of gives us great trouble now that we should pass the Fosse, so that our being masters of the town is retarded for some days."[1]

On the 19th Marlborough had determined not to press Fagel's attack, but to concentrate upon the other two. The garrison, although active and frequently successful with their mines, were clearly saving themselves for the defence of the citadel, and on the 28th, when preparations for a general storm were far advanced, Surville hung out a white flag and beat the chamade on the fronts of all three attacks. The terms of capitulation resembled those of Lille. Eight hundred French wounded and invalids were allowed to proceed to Douai. The town was yielded, and Surville after dining ceremonially with Prince Eugene withdrew into the citadel with about four thousand men. Taking the town cost the Allies over 3200 men—800 in Lottum's, 1800 in Schulenburg's, and 600 in Fagel's attack.

Colonel Cranstoun was, as usual, critical of Marlborough. "All those amongst us here," he wrote to a friend (August 5),

> who are reckoned High Whigs or in with the Junto, as you call them, seem pleased at continuing war, and reason on all occasions to persuade the world that all the offers and advances made by France were a trick to impose upon us, though, indeed, I could never hear a good argument given to prove this, and I doubt that if we do no more than take Tournai this campaign there will be many in St Stephen's Chapel next winter of opinion we were in the wrong to push things so far and refuse offers that appeared both so reasonable and sincere. It has cost us twenty-two days open trenches to take the city of Tournai and about 3000 men killed or wounded, officers and all, though I believe there are not above 1500 men can be said truly to be killed or so wounded as to be *hors de combat.*"

The hardest part was yet to come. The citadel, a five-bastion fortress of earthworks and masonry, was reputed "one of the best fortify'd Places by Art that is in the World."[3] The garrison was sufficient for the defence of their reduced lines. Powerful as were the visible defences, the underground works were soon found by the assailants to be even more formidable. A bitter subterranean warfare began. "We have to fight with moles," the British complained. Mining parties met each other below the surface and fought

---

[1] *Sarah Correspondence*, ii, 351.   [2] Portland Papers, *H.M.C.*, iv, 497.
[3] R. Kane, *Campaigns of King William and the Duke of Marlborough* (1735), p. 79.

with picks and shovels, and, as the process developed, with sword
and musket. The men in the batteries and trenches heard the ceaseless tapping of the miners beneath their feet. Explosions where
soldiers were buried thirty or forty at a time, and one in which no
fewer than four hundred men perished, made the siege terrible in
the memories of veteran troops. All our diarist friends confirm this.
"The siege," wrote Blackadder (August 18),

> goes on slowly, and in the dark underground. . . . There is a great
> mortality among the boors through the country, occasioned, no doubt,
> by the famine, and scarcity, and unwholesome food they are forced to
> eat. And as pestilence often treads upon the heels of famine, so we
> are getting melancholy and alarming accounts of the plague being in
> several places in Germany, and some say in France.

The pious major had other griefs.

> *July* 8. Involved all night in a multitude of promiscuous company.
> But they put the conversation on such a footing, either by swearing, pro-
> fane talking, bantering, or some impiety or other, that I can take little
> part in it. To reprove would be needless, and to join them is sinful.[1]

Private (afterwards Corporal) Matthew Bishop, whose moving
life-story is too little known,[2] writes:

> I remember after our Army had completed twelve Saps, we mounted
> the Trenches, and sat upon the Foot Banks, when of a sudden the
> Enemy sprung a Mine, which made the Earth tremble under us; but
> it ceased in a Moment. We were surprised it had not taken us up into
> the Clouds; for, comparatively speaking, it ascended like unto a Cloud.

[1] A. Crichton, *The Life and Diary of Lieutenant-Colonel Blackader* (1824), p. 343.

[2] A young man with some property and an insatiable desire for warlike adventure,
he had served afloat till the end of 1704. When his ship was paid off he addressed his
captain, with whom he had much credit, as follows: " 'Sir, I have a favour to beg. . . .
You know, sir, my behaviour hitherto. . . . I am of a roving nature; and ever since
I heard of the Action that was performed on the Danube by the Duke of Marlborough,
I promised to myself, in God's name, that if nothing prevented I would go and assist
the Duke, for so noble a General cannot have too many good men; and as my inclinations are already with him, I hope your Honour will not deny me; There have been
many instances that our enemies' defeat has been owing to the success of one blow,
and it may be my fortune to strike that lucky blow; and if you please to release me I am
determined to stand to all events, for I find there will be nothing more done at sea,
and I will go where I can be employed, for I have . . . no ambition but to carry arms,
so that I may call myself a Man of War and Arms Bearer.' " The captain consenting,
Matthew obtained his discharge from the Navy, took to himself a wife, upon whom he
settled all his property, and set forth in Flanders as a private in Webb's regiment.
Thenceforward he served in all the bloodiest fighting, and his account of his ordeal
at Malplaquet is of high value. His admiration for the Duke grew with his campaigns.
I must refer the reader to his own book (*The Life and Adventures of Matthew Bishop*,
p. 80) for the tragedy which caused his neglected wife's melancholy death.

This private soldier's diary finds exact confirmation in Schulenburg's report to King Augustus: "They exploded several mines, which caused but little damage. In one case there was not enough powder in the mine; for those who were up above [merely] jumped a foot into the air. If it had been effective it would have killed more than eighty men."[1] "We were prodigious hard at Work," Bishop continues, "in sapping the Enemy, who sapped under us, and sprung several Mines, which stifled great Numbers of our Men. Then those that were above would work with all their Might, in order to give them below Air. By that Means we did save some alive." One day he saw when out of the trenches "a prodigious Blaze, and it ascended up into the Air like unto a Cloud. We could distinguish they had sprung one of their grand mines. . . . But at our return I found there was almost a whole Regiment of the Scotch Hollanders[2] blown up. There was likewise a kind of report spread through all our Army, that it was their intention to blow us all up; but to prevent them we were continually in Motion."[3]

Surville was prepared to make a resolute defence of the citadel, and his underground works gave him great advantages. He had, however, been guilty of the fatal neglect of not laying in sufficient provisions. His resistance was limited to little more than a month by his food. He therefore proposed to Marlborough that the citadel, unless relieved before September 5, should then be surrendered and that in the meanwhile the siege operations should be suspended. He asked leave to send an officer through the lines to obtain the King's approval. Marlborough was agreeable to this, "since it will save the lives of a great many men, and we cannot hope to take it much sooner."[4]

---

[1] Schulenburg, Part II, 396. [2] Scots troops in the Dutch service.

[3] In lighter vein Bishop tells the story of "another Man that was remarkable for a great Eater, his Name was John Jones, who belonged to Captain Cutler's Company: He said he was prodigious hungry. With that the Men asked him how many Cannon Balls he had eaten for his Breakfast. Then I said to him, Thou deservest Preferment, if thou canst digest Cannon Balls. Then Sergeant Smith came up to me, and told me, He had eaten four or six twenty-four Pounders, and as many as six twelve Pounders in a Morning for his Breakfast. Now this Sergeant was not addicted to tell fabulous Stories, though it seemed incredible to any one's Thinking. But he explained it in this Manner, that the Man often frequented the Fields in Search of those Cannon Balls; that he had used to dig them out of the Banks, and had brought a great Number in a Morning to the Artillery, in order to dispose of them for Money; and the Money he bought his Provision with. Had there been no Cannon Balls flying he certainly could not have subsisted; for he both eat and drank more than ten moderate Men; So that his daily Study was to provide for his Belly."

[4] Letter to Sarah, August 5; Coxe, iv, 14.

Villars, when he heard of the shortage of food, vented his wrath upon Surville in cruel terms. He alleged that the proposal for a local armistice had come from the Allies. He advised the King to reject it. Louis XIV accepted his view. It seemed to him unwise not to compel the Allies to spend their munitions upon the siege. Surville was therefore sternly forbidden to go forward with his proposal, unless the allied commanders would consent to a general armistice throughout the whole of the Flanders theatre. This, of course, was in turn rejected.

Marlborough to Godolphin

TOURNAI
Augt. 15*th*, 1709

★By the enemys dayly springing of new Mynes our Ingeniers advance so very slowly that the Pr. of Savoye and myself thought it for the Service to Come hether in order to push on the attacks, but as this is the first Siege where we have met with Myns, we find our soldiers apprehend them more then they aught, so that we must have patience for some little time, that thay may be used to them.

We have no further Confirmation as yett of the battel between the Swedes and Moscovit, but shou'd it be trew of the first being so intierly beaten as is report'd, what a mallincolly reflection is it, that after a Constant Success for ten Years, he shou'd in two hours mismanagement and ill success ruin himself and Country. . . .[1]

Marlborough's reaction to the defeat of Charles XII at Pultawa gives us a glimpse of his own inward feelings. "Constant success for ten years; two hours' mismanagement!" How easily in the dangerous game of war might these words find a new application! There is no doubt he liked the tremendous Swede, and, in spite of the advantage which his removal from European affairs spelt to the Allies, Marlborough was sorry for him, and fortified in his own prudence.

John to Sarah

Aug. 26

This afternoon I have received a letter from Prince Menzikoff, favourite and general of the Czar, of the entire victory over the Swedes. If this unfortunate king had been so well advised as to have made peace the beginning of this summer, he might, in a great measure, have influenced the peace between France and the Allies, and have made his kingdom happy; whereas now he is entirely in the power of his neighbours.[2]

[1] Blenheim MSS. The remainder of this letter, which deals with politics, will be found in the next chapter.

[2] Coxe, iv, 97.

The siege went forward in a severe and bloody style. Nothing like the mining and counter-mining had ever been known. On August 5 a hundred and fifty besiegers who had gained a footing upon the defences were blown into the air. Through the nights of the 16th and 17th there was fierce fighting in the mining galleries, ending in the expulsion of the French. On the 20th the blowing up of a wall smothered thirty or forty Ally officers and men. On the 23rd the besiegers discovered a large mine when it was about to destroy a whole Hanoverian battalion. But while they were rejoicing in this good fortune another mine below it was sprung, causing very heavy losses. On the 26th a townsman of Tournai offered to reveal one of the principal mines of the citadel on condition that he should be made head gaoler of all the prisons in Tournai. His offer was accepted, and the mine gallery was occupied by three hundred men. The French, however, again sprung a mine below this gallery, and the whole three hundred were destroyed, and a hundred more besides.

"The manner of Fighting in this Siege," says the author of *The Tatler*,

> discovered a Gallantry in our Men, unknown to former Ages; Their Meeting with adverse Parties under Ground, where every Step was taken with Apprehensions of being blown up with Mines below them, or crushed by the Fall of the Earth above them, and all this acted in Darkness, has something in it more terrible than was ever met with in any other Part of a Soldier's Duty: However this was performed with great Chearfulness.[1]

In the face of grievous losses and ordeals the Allies persevered remorselessly in their attacks. On August 31 Surville, almost destitute of food and exposed to imminent storm, when no quarter would be shown, hung out the white flag of capitulation. Marlborough demanded that the garrison should be prisoners of war, and on Surville refusing another two days' bombardment ensued. On September 3 it was agreed that the garrison should march out with the honours of war and be permitted to return to France on condition of not serving again until duly exchanged. On September 5 the Allies were masters of Tournai.

The advices from Paris were never more full of information, true and false, than during this period. The extracts which follow show the variety of contacts which the spy must have made at Versailles.

[1] Lediard, *Life of John, Duke of Marlborough* (1736), ii, 482.

July 10, 1709

★In spite of the war people here still believe in peace and talk a lot about it. I don't know how this campaign will end, but at Court M. de Villars is highly praised for having up till now prevented the enemy from giving battle and invading the realm.

July 12, 1709

★I tell you for certain that there is a plan to throw reinforcements into Tournai by means of inundations and flat-bottomed boats, and for this purpose they sent off three days ago a certain Galliot with the title of "Amiral des Galions du Canal de Versailles," who has a pension of 2000 écus from the King. He is a navigation expert, and has left with all his workmen to join the Flanders army and carry out the above plan. *This information is certain.*

People in Paris are frightened of a revolution on account of the tax on bread.

July 15, 1709

★The terrain from Tournai to Douai is being prepared so that the inundation, caused by means of the Tournai sluices, will fill up and form a canal as far as Douai. On this they will be able to launch flat-bottomed boats each capable of holding a hundred men.

People here are quite pleased that M. de Villars has converted the enemy plan for a campaign of invasion into a campaign of bluff.

July 26, 1709

★The King has sent M. de Villars permission to attack the enemy in accordance with his plan for relieving Tournai, and Princess d'Epinoy, who has just arrived from Versailles, tells us the same. According to report, they are going to open the sluices in two or three places to create a big inundation. By this means they hope to break the bridge of communication and at the same time attack in three places—such is Court rumour. *Others say it is a rumour that the Court circulates by design, and that no attempt will be made to relieve Tournai.*

Two days ago a crowd of fifty poor people gathered round a dead horse at the end of the Pont Neuf, fighting over it and each one taking away a piece.

There are 15–20,000 workmen out of employment. They beg in their leather aprons. All these people added to the mob cause fears of a rising at any moment. The first thing they would do will be to pillage the Mint, the Louvre, and the customs.

July 29, 1709

★Really it is impossible to understand the idea of forbidding our generals to undertake anything—for the rumour which was spread that M. de Villars had permission to carry out the plan (a draft of which has been sent to the Court) was only to occupy people's minds with the expectation of some event. To-day the story goes round that M. de Villars, tired of making war in this fashion, has written to the King asking to be relieved of his post, as he is forbidden to do anything.

August 2, 1709

★It is said that M. de Villars, furious at having his hands tied and not being able to undertake anything, screams like an eagle because he is held back. Nothing is clear. The Court is in complete confusion, caused by the two factions which reign there. This makes everything go wrong, and from bad to worse.

The same confusion reigns in Spain.

August 5, 1709

★In regard to Madame de Maintenon, it is certain that she still rules the King's mind. This is how she sets about seeing that her wishes prevail and are carried out.

She never omits discussing with the King the matters which are to come up at the *conseil secret* held in her apartment every day. The King asks her advice, which she always seasons with something flattering to him; and sometimes she scares him, according to the circumstances—but this happens seldom. Then she sends for her creature (it used to be M. de Chamillart, and now M. Voisin) and orders him to hold such a view on such a matter, so that the King shall not suspect that she governs.

The number of those present is not fixed: sometimes it is only the King, she, and M. Voisin, and sometimes another Secretary of State, according to the business transacted; sometimes M. de Beauvillier and M. de Bourgogne, and, rarely, Monseigneur.

This *conseil secret* is held in her apartment from seven till nine o'clock. The King is there an hour beforehand and works with her, and then summons those who are to attend. While the *conseil* is sitting she busies herself with some piece of needlework and never fails to express her views in the discussions—that is to say, to support those views with which she has inspired the King and her favourite Minister.

At nine o'clock the *conseil* leaves. She has supper with the King, who waits on her in almost bourgeois fashion. Then she goes to bed while the King chats to her, et souvent fait apporter par une de ses femmes une chaise percée, et pousse une selle auprès de son lit.

He then takes leave of her, embracing her. Then word is sent to Madame de Bourgogne, who is in a neighbouring apartment with her attendants, and the princesses, who are to dine with the King. All this is certain.

With regard to the *conseil du matin*, which is held in the King's apartment from after Mass till one o'clock, when the King dines:

This *conseil* is more numerous, but the spirit of the lady reigns here too—for the King is always influenced by her. Monseigneur is often at this *conseil*, and the Chancellor, the Ministers, and Secretaries of State. It is here that one sees the two factions. That is to say, the princes and their puppets against M. de Bourgogne, Madame de Maintenon, and hers. The latter are entirely in favour of peace so as to bring back King Philip, and the others are opposed to this and would rather everything went to blazes.

August 10, 1709

★I don't forecast favourably for us in a battle if one takes place. For all the letters from the Army show that our troops are very much discouraged, and the officers write home that there is no longer profit or honour in making war. It is true that the officers are very badly paid, the soldiers rather better. It is certain that this week 500,000 francs of the old coinage have been sent to our Army. As fast as they are brought to the Mint they are dispatched thither. Up till now only piastres and plate have been melted down, and the new coinage is not popular in Flanders. That is why they will have to have the old. It is also certain that 6000 sacks of flour have come in from Brittany for the Army.

The King has thus no further resources than his ordinary revenues, which have contracted by half through the universal.distress, the corn monopoly, the poll tax, the taxes called *aises*, and finally a new tax which is to be levied of 10 per cent. on all capital and incomes of individuals and nobles of the kingdom without exception. Added to this is the profit on the coinage. It is true that the King can carry on for a short time with these exactions and by not paying his debts, but in the end everything will collapse. There is no lack of money— there is plenty of it—but it is hidden away for lack of confidence. It seems that violence and brigandage abound.

Meanwhile, in spite of all this distress, the King is amusing himself by making a waterfall which will cost 200,000 francs.

I am told further that he is nearly always humming a tune, either to give a false impression of firmness or, more likely, from dotage and the weakness of a failing mind which needs constant distraction.

August 12, 1709

★It is learned that Prince Eugene is marching towards Marchiennes and apparently intends to cross the Scarpe to catch M. de Villars. This has forced the Marshal to strike camp and get on the move in order to frustrate the plan of Prince Eugene. On the way he has picked up the Marquis de Coaquin, who was at the head of eighteen battalions. He has also with him the Duke of Guiche, with the French and Swiss and Walloon guards, and is marching in the direction of Douai.

It seems he is to join M. d'Artagnan and Count of Luxembourg. He has some artillery with him, and letters from the army lead us to expect an action near Marchiennes. We shall see how M. de Villars comes out of it. Many people have a poor opinion of him. It is believed that our troops are discouraged, discontented, and badly paid.

They say that the allied generals don't want to pass the time in sieges and are determined to break through and fight. One of M. Voisin's clerks assured me yesterday that affairs in Spain are in a fine muddle, and that there is a faction of grandees against Madame des Ursins, who is planning to decamp and has already sent out of Spain more than two millions' worth of belongings. He also told us that the Archduke is ill, and that it is on the cards that King Philip and his wife might go back to France, but that the Prince of Asturias would remain as King and would be educated as a Spaniard by the Regency, without any interference by the French Ministers, who would have no finger in the pie, and that the Allies would be on the same footing in commercial matters as in the reign of the late King, and that the little Prince of Asturias, not having known his father or grandfather, would one day be entirely Spanish and perhaps our worst enemy.

In fact, the policy adopted by France in Spain is sufficient to weaken and ruin us for ever, and is putting new strength into a nation which one day will cause her a lot of trouble. Such is the 'system' of the Duke of Burgundy and his followers.

August 23, 1709

★There is still talk of peace being negotiated in secret. It is passionately desired here, and the *conseil* and the Ministers are at the end of their tether, and in the present state of public affairs I know of no further resources.

August 26, 1709

★There is still the fear of sedition in Paris, and the King has appointed M. de Boufflers to command the troops in the city. There are guards at all the gates, night and day. Last night the musketeers remained booted and spurred in their quarters ready to ride at the first order. One has the impression of being in a town in the war area, or of awaiting a surprise attack. Everywhere there are alarming posters, and the price of bread is going up, instead of down. There is complete bewilderment. The parish clergy exhort the people to pray hard for the prospering of the royal armies. There is a babel of voices in the churches crying aloud, "The Devil away with him!" . . . Marshal de Tallard's valet arrived here a few days ago from London on his master's business. He said that every one in England is crying for peace too, as eagerly as we are, and that makes us hope to obtain it at least some time this winter. But, whatever happens, if England and Holland make it appear that they still have the means to carry on the war, you will see our Court change its tune. It is only held back by the impression it has been given that England, and particularly Holland, have as much need of peace as we have.

August 30, 1709

Calm is being restored in Paris. Two days ago the guards and soldiers were disbanded, and M. de Boufflers has returned to Marly.

Thus did this deadly personage feed Marlborough with knowledge.

Chapter Eight

THE INVESTMENT OF MONS

1709—AUGUST AND SEPTEMBER

THE fall of Tournai was followed by an explosion of war-fury strangely out of keeping with the policy and temper in which the campaign had hitherto been conducted. Up to this moment the French had been virtually forbidden by Louis XIV to fight a battle. Villars was told that their interest enjoined a strategy of delay. On the other side, Marlborough, Eugene, and the Dutch Deputies, convinced that France must collapse under the weight of the war through economic and financial pressure, had also been wedded to caution. Repeatedly they had examined Villars's lines, and always it had been decided that to incur the risks and costs of forcing them was not warranted in the favourable position of the allied cause. Thus the campaign seemed relegated to the sphere of manœuvre, with no more serious objective than making a further inroad upon the French fortress line.

Now suddenly, upon the capitulation of Tournai, an access of mental rage seems to have taken possession of both sides simultaneously. They discarded their cold calculations. They flung caution to the winds. The King gave Villars full freedom. The Marshal used it to court an encounter battle. Marlborough and Eugene two days later assaulted him frontally in a position already strong by nature, and now fortified by serious entrenchments and defences. The contagion of this mood swept through both armies like a fever. A terrible ardour inspired all ranks. They thirsted to be at each other's throats, and slay their foes. The soldiers of every nation, national and mercenary alike, fell upon each other with a ferocity hitherto unknown to the age, and in the largest and bloodiest battle of the eighteenth century quarter was scarcely asked or given.

But the source of this new temper is to be found in the allied Governments even more than in their troops or their generals. A hitherto unpublished letter of Marlborough's shows that his own instinct was against a supreme trial of strength, but that both the

Empire and the Dutch were pressing him to it. In this letter is revealed for the first time the origin of Malplaquet.

Marlborough to Heinsius

August 18, 1709

*Monsr. de Heems, who staid two days with the Pr. of Savoye, has given us an account of his commissions for Vienne, and the great desire the *Comte de Sinzindorff* and others att the *Hague that* we shou'd undertake *some*[1] thing of consequence; I am sure you do the Pr. and myself the justice to beleive that we shall neglect no opertunity of undertaking what we can judge practicable, and as a friend I own to you that I think our affaires are in so good a postur, and that of the Enemy in so very ill condition, that I shou'd think wee aught not to ventur, but where in reason wee shou'd hope for success; but if you Judge otherways, and that the temper of your people are such, that thay will not be satisfied unless there be action, we must then take our measures agreable to that; for what ever is in my power You may command, for I have a Confidence in your Judgement, besides you know the temper of England is always for action; but I can't think it for the service to attempt, without hopes of success.[2]

As the fall of Tournai citadel approached the next step was considered by the Allies. It was realized that the situation would not be greatly changed by its capture. On the one hand, the course of the Scheldt would be open up to Saint-Amand; on the other, Villars's army was better organized, his supply was less stringent, and his defences more complete. The season was far advanced, and no important invasion of France could be made that year. There remained, as it seemed, only the possibility of prolonging the pressure upon the French to renew the negotiations, or, if that failed, to secure a good start for the army in 1710. An advance in the centre between the Lys and the Scarpe would be confronted by the French prepared positions. Eyes therefore turned again to the flanks. In the west Ypres, Aire, and Saint-Venant offered themselves as costly prizes. Ypres was strong and well prepared, and Marlborough and Eugene judged the country round it bad for manœuvre late in the season. Our own experience at Passchendaele in 1917 in no way contradicts their impressions. On the other flank lay the fortresses of the Sensée—Condé, Valenciennes, the entrenched camp at Denain, or perhaps Bouchain.

A wider turning movement would be facilitated by the capture of Mons. But this fortress of the first order controlled no river

---

[1] Marlborough's underlining.   [2] Heinsius Archives.

communication. High ground stood between it and the valley of the Sambre. There is no account of the discussions which took place, though Goslinga, as usual, condemns what was actually done. Politics may well have been the deciding factor. During the peace negotiations nothing should be done to sow dissension among the

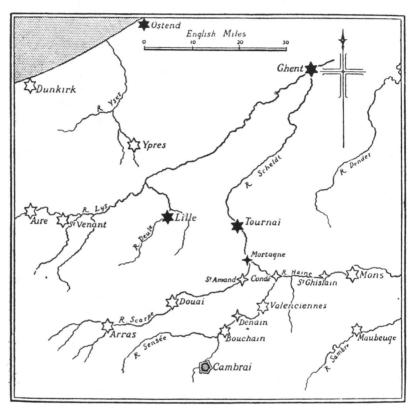

FORTRESSES AFTER THE FALL OF TOURNAI

Allies. Mons may have been chosen because it completed the occupation of the Barrier required by the Dutch. There was always the chance that Villars would fight a battle for the sake of Mons; but neither Marlborough nor Eugene counted upon his doing so. Actually the Marshal does not appear to have considered the likelihood of an attack on Mons. He was with reason more concerned about Valenciennes and Bouchain, and also about his lines stretching west to Aire. If Villars foresaw the allied plan, and occupied the line of the Haine and the strong position behind the Trouille stream, the siege of Mons might be prevented. Thus quick movement and surprise were necessary to Marlborough.

The first step was to seize the fort of Saint-Ghislain, on the Haine. Orkney, with the Dutch general Pallandt, twenty squadrons, and the grenadiers of the army, was entrusted with this task. There is conflicting testimony whether he started before or immediately after Surville offered to surrender.[1] The French accounts record his arrival in front of Saint-Ghislain at one A.M. on September 3. He was followed on that day by Hesse-Cassel with sixty squadrons and four thousand foot. They were to help Orkney take Saint-Ghislain, and if successful to cross the Haine and invest Mons from the south-west. If Saint-Ghislain could not be taken, both forces were to pass round the north of Mons and capture the line of the Trouille to the eastward. After dark on the same day Cadogan with forty squadrons followed Hesse-Cassel. At midnight, leaving 26 battalions and 20 squadrons to clear up at Tournai, the main army marched to Brissœil. The operation was hazardous, and Goslinga was full of misgivings. ★ "This is only to tell you," he wrote to Heinsius on the 4th, "that the army marched this night [i.e. the 3rd]. They aspire to invest Mons, but, according to my humble view, it is impossible to succeed. We are going to follow to-morrow and join the army on the march. If all goes as wished, Mons will be invested to-morrow; but, as I had the honour to tell you, I doubt myself whether even our leaders are convinced that the thing is possible. . . ."[2]

Saint-Ghislain had been reinforced from Condé, and resisted Orkney. He therefore turned northward. On September 5 the main army marched to Sirault, where Orkney rejoined them. On the 6th, at two A.M., Hesse-Cassel crossed the Haine at Obourg, driving a small French force before him. At seven A.M. he formed his line south of Mons, and at noon crossed the French lines on the Trouille. Three French regiments of dragoons withdrew back into Mons. Luxembourg, with thirty squadrons, arriving too late for an action, retired to join Villars at Quiévrain. By nightfall Hesse-Cassel held the heights south of Mons on the line Frameries-Jemappes. That

---

[1] Millner says Orkney started on August 31. Coxe and Taylor, possibly following, agree. Villars says it was on September 2, and Pelet adopts his view. It is certainly unlikely that Marlborough disclosed his intention before Surville asked for terms, which he did not do till the 2nd. A hitherto unpublished letter of Goslinga's (Tournai, September 1) seems decisive. ★"Pallandt has an enterprise against Saint-Ghislain which should be executed to-night." (Goslinga to Heinsius; Heinsius Archives.)

[2] Goslinga to Heinsius; Heinsius Archives.

same night (the 6th) Marlborough reached Obourg, and marched south at dawn to support Hesse-Cassel. By these swift operations, which won Hesse-Cassel much praise, Mons was effectually cut off and invested.

The Paris spy sent the following decisive intelligence:

September 6, 1709

★M. de Boufflers has left for Flanders. It was thought at first that it was on matters of peace, and that M. de Rouillé was to follow

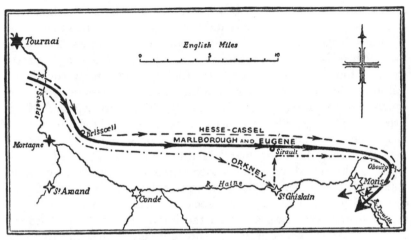

THE MARCH FROM TOURNAI TO MONS

him, but it isn't so, and people of the first importance have told me that M. de Boufflers had left, in consequence of a letter written by M. de Villars to the King a week ago saying he had certain information that the plan of Prince Eugene and Lord Marlborough was to attack the army and offer battle as soon as the citadel surrendered.

M. de Villars hinted to the King that, however fine his army might be, he would prefer that so vital an action was not fought entirely on his responsibility, and asked the King to send him a general trustworthy to share the honour with him. . . .

There is talk of dividing our Army into two bodies. The reason for believing this is that *M. de Boufflers has brought his cuirass and his weapons with him*, and that he must have some plan on hand.[1]

The fact that this probably did not reach headquarters in time in no way detracts from the surpassing quality of the information.

Villars, awaiting at Quiévrain the arrival of part of his infantry

[1] Blenheim MSS.

under D'Artagnan, spent the 7th in a reconnaissance in force towards Hesse-Cassel's position. Boufflers had, indeed, arrived, bearing with him in his person the proof of the King's willingness for battle. During the evening Villars advanced with his army, and lay ten miles from the Allies on the front Montrœul-Athis. The fact that Boufflers had joined the French army reached Marlborough within a few hours. He therefore continued his southward march, and halted for the night on Hesse-Cassel's left on the line Ciply-Quévy. The armies were now eight miles apart in gently undulating

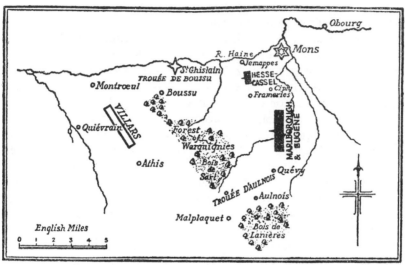

EVENING OF SEPTEMBER 7, 1709

country. Between them lay a broad belt of forest, through which there were but two passages (*trouées*). The first, called the Trouée de Boussu, was between the Haine and the Forest of Warquignies. The second was the Trouée d'Aulnois, in which stood the village of Malplaquet. With the modern rifle and tactics of infiltration, these woodland tracts would be an assistance to the attack. Nothing would be worse for assailants than the open ground of a gap. But in the eighteenth century, with its firearms deadly only at close quarters and with its rigid formations, woods were considered sure barriers of defence. Flanks resting on woodlands were generally considered secure. If Villars wished to attack elsewhere than through one or the other of the gaps, he must make a long march round, and eventually attempt the river lines of the Haine and the Trouille.

On the morning of the 8th a Council of War was held at the allied headquarters at Quévy, in which it was decided that to cover the siege of Mons Eugene should block the exit of the Gap of Boussu, and Marlborough that of the Gap of Aulnois. As Villars on that day faced the former gap Marlborough must keep close to Eugene. Accordingly during the afternoon Eugene occupied the heights of Quaregnon, while Marlborough camped between Genly and Quévy. A French general captured by the patrols stated openly that Villars had the King's leave to fight.

Marlborough seems to have had at this moment no fixed plan of action. His letters show no expectation of battle.[1] He and Eugene were waiting upon events. If they had been content merely to make the siege of Mons they could during the 8th and 9th have constructed a line of circumvallation either in the woods and across the gaps or behind them. But this was not their object. They wanted to bring about a battle in the open, and to hold themselves loose so as to be able to encourage and accommodate Villars, if such was his purpose. No attempt was therefore made to take up a defensive position. Such a step would have prevented a battle. They cherished the hope that Villars would advance through one or other of the gaps, and that then they could fall upon him. They did not want to do anything which would deter him from this. Still, we can hardly think they believed he would do so. The heroic Marshal, while breathing fire and slaughter and inspiring his troops with the spirit of the offensive, never had any such intention. He was only doing what he had done several times before, and was to do afterwards on notable occasions—namely, advancing to close proximity in the hopes of finding a weak body of the enemy in his clutches, or some other exceptional advantage. Marlborough and Eugene during the 8th were evidently tempting him; and for the sake of doing so they allowed him to occupy the forward edges of the woods by the Gap of Boussu—that is to say, they would let him without dispute make of this gap a gateway which he could open when he chose, and through it debouch and deploy for battle. But this was too good to be true.

Villars, who had to halt for supplies, and fed his troops with the greatest difficulty, contented himself again with a cavalry demonstration. His patrols and squadrons came in contact at many points with the cavalry of the Allies, and the numerous sharp minor collisions which took place showed the tension of the great masses

---

[1] Marlborough to Godolphin, September 7; *Sarah Correspondence*, ii, 381.

now brought so close together. He had seen the Gap of Boussu left open to him on the 8th. During the night which followed he sent Luxembourg with a strong force of cavalry to seize the forward edges of both the gaps, thus securing to himself the power to debouch at either. It cannot be supposed that Marlborough and Eugene, watching the scene on horseback from hour to hour during the preceding day, permitted him to do this by negligence. Evidently they meant deliberately to leave both doors open for him to come through either into a battle arena. At dawn on the 9th Villars learned

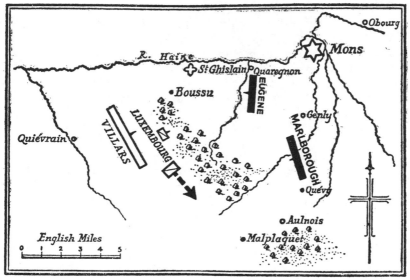

EVENING OF SEPTEMBER 8

that both the gaps were in his possession. He marched forthwith to his right in four columns ready for immediate deployment, and occupied the Aulnois gap with his whole army.

Early on the morning of the 9th both Eugene and Marlborough were writing letters.

Eugene to the Emperor

His Imperial Majesty will have learned from other sources how the armies have remained stationary. But I am this instant about to mount my horse. . . . In fact, the enemy is near, although up to now he has hazarded nothing, and remains behind his fortresses and entrenchments, . . . From our side, since we do not know well the lie of the land, we dare even less take any risks. The terrain is very

uneven, and cut up by many small brooks and ponds swollen by the
bad weather, and is full of water and gullies, paths and defiles, so that
one cannot march directly forward. But I am about to go off with
my lord Duke under heavy escort to review the situation thoroughly,
so that we can come to such a decision as will be to the benefit of the
Common Cause. . . .[1]

Marlborough's letter was to Sarah.[2] She had upbraided him for
not writing to the Queen to complain of the treatment she was
receiving. Apparently she had reproached him with lack of zeal for
her interests.

I am obliged to you for the account you give of the building of
Blenheim in yours of the 21st, and the farther account you intend me
after the Duke and Duchess of Shrewsbury have seen what is done.
You will see by my former letters, as well as by this, that I can take
pleasure in nothing as long as you continue uneasy and think me
unkind. I do assure you, upon my honour and salvation, that the only
reason why I did not write was that I am very sure it would have had
no other effect than that of being shown to Mrs Masham, by which she
would have had an opportunity of turning it as she pleased; so that
when I shall speak to the Queen of her harsh behaviour to you she
would have been prepared. I beg you to be assured that if ever I see
the Queen I shall speak to her just as you would have me; and all the
actions of my life shall make the Queen, as well as all the world,
sensible that you are dearer to me than my own life; for I am fonder
of my happiness than of my life, which I cannot enjoy unless you are
kind.[3]

At this moment the news that Villars was moving came in and
Eugene arrived. Marlborough's horse was brought, and, with an
escort of thirty squadrons and four hundred grenadiers under the
Prince of Auvergne, the two commanders rode out to the Mill of
Sart to reconnoitre. They reached this point about eight o'clock.
As the fringe of their cavalry patrols approached the village of Malplaquet, in the Aulnois gap, they came in contact with Luxembourg's
outposts. Auvergne with a heavier force brushed through the
hostile screen and found himself confronted by strong bodies. To
the westward he or his officers discerned the French army marching
towards the Aulnois gap and the plateau of Malplaquet. As far as
they could tell, the enemy seemed to be about to advance through

[1] *Feldzüge*, ii, Series II, App., 257.
[2] This letter is dated September 10: but its contents show that the first part was
written on the morning of the 9th.
[3] Coxe, v, 68–69.

the forest clearing into the open country towards Mons. Thereupon Marlborough ordered the concentration of the Allies. Only his left, composed mainly of the Dutch under Dopff, could immediately come into line. The right could not come up for several hours, and Eugene's army lay six miles farther to the north. The concentration, according to Orkney, was delayed by "prodigious dusty rain," through which the troops marched incessantly. At 2 P.M. the French batteries, which had now gathered in strength about Malplaquet, began to cannonade Marlborough's left, who, as they were without artillery, could not reply.

This situation has been represented by several writers as critical for the Allies.[1] It is suggested that if Villars had advanced through the gap and deployed his forces he could have beaten the confederate army in detail; but this is nonsense. Marlborough's left, unencumbered by artillery, could have fallen back as fast as the French could advance, and as they receded would have accelerated the concentration of the allied army. Villars himself could not have forced them to battle till they were willing. Nothing could have prevented them from reoccupying, for instance, their former position from Genly to Quévy with their whole united strength. It is certain that this was exactly the kind of situation which Marlborough and Eugene desired. They could then, at dawn on the 10th, have fought that general battle in the open which had never been offered to them since Ramillies. The whole of the allied movements on the 8th and 9th show beyond all question that Marlborough and Eugene had only one object and hope—namely, to entice Villars to go through one or other of the gaps into the plain of Mons, and then fall upon him.

But Villars was far too good a soldier to be caught in that way. He never for a moment contemplated attacking the Allies, or even the risk of an encounter battle, in the open. Under such conditions his ragged, ill-found army, however brave and trained, was no match for the perfectly equipped veteran forces of the Allies. He saw, as well as we see to-day, that the great Captains opposed to him had left these gaps open because it suited them that he should go through them. It is, indeed, surprising that Marlborough and Eugene should have even appeared to take Villars's offensive seriously. Allowance must be made for the atmosphere of excitement which rises to explosion-point when great masses of armed, eager men are manœuvring in close contact with one another, and when the fall of the thunderbolts is expected and even longed for

[1] Even Sautai and the deeply instructed Taylor.

by all. Accordingly Villars sat down in his gap. His troops were marching up all day. His artillery continued to fire on Marlborough's left, which stood in position against his front. During the afternoon the English and Dutch batteries came up, unlimbered, and began to reply in increasing numbers. Thus night fell.

Pelet makes the odd statement that Villars was mistaken about the width of the gap, and thus was "forced" to occupy the woods on either side with infantry. It is surprising that he should have made such an error, or that he should have regarded the occupation of the woods on either flank of the Malplaquet position as anything but a vital duty and an important advantage. During the night he began to fortify his position across the gap. He dug the deepest ditches and built the highest parapets that time allowed. The woods on either side he defended by successive lines of smaller trenches, and with abattis.[1]

Early on the morning of the 10th it was seen that Villars had already begun entrenching himself, and all prospect of his attacking faded. The allied Commanders had now to decide first whether they would themselves assault his position, and whether they should do so at once or wait until the next day. On the one hand, the French defences were growing hourly; on the other, General Withers with nineteen battalions and ten squadrons was marching from Tournai, and could not join the army until very late that night. According to some accounts, Marlborough was for attacking at once, and Eugene for awaiting Withers.[2] The matter rested between the two comrades, and neither of them has left any statement of his individual views. They worked together, and never claimed credit at each other's expense. Whatever passed between them is therefore unknown. In the outcome, "the Princes" resolved to wait until their whole army was assembled, and to hold a council of war that night to decide the question of battle. Such a council was necessary in view of the constitution of the army and the stipulations of the Dutch. The Dutch Deputies had remained behind at Tournai, and Goslinga alone reached the army.

All through the 10th the cannonade continued in the centre of the army, and several hundred casualties were inflicted on either side. Marlborough and Eugene spent the day examining the French

[1] Trees felled and stripped, and with their sharpened branches pointing towards the enemy: the wire entanglements of those days.

[2] The Austrian official account (*Feldzüge*, Sees II, ii, App., 101) says that orders had already been issued for the attack when Marlborough countermanded them. This is clearly an error.

position. Breastworks were constructed for the attacking batteries. Towards evening the guns fell silent, and an incident occurred upon which many accounts dwell. The French general Albergotti, riding round his outposts in the Wood of Taisnières, sent an officer to tell the allied pickets that he would like to talk to one of their generals. The officer was fired upon and withdrew. But a little while later there arrived from the Allies a trumpeter with a flag of truce in due form to say that, if Albergotti desired it, the Prince of Hesse, the Electoral Prince of Brandenburg, and General Cadogan would be delighted to converse with him. The parley which followed spread far along this part of the line. Rumour ran that peace had come, and several thousand men from the two armies, who the next day were to show each other little or no quarter, came eagerly together in a strange paradox of human emotions, embracing and exchanging gifts and salutations with lively curiosity and goodwill.[1] While this fraternization was in progress it was noticed or suspected by the French that several Ally officers were making notes and sketches of the ground, its defences and defenders, and Cadogan was seen to be looking about him in all directions. As soon as Marshal Villars heard of the parley he at once sent orders to break it off, and asserted that Cadogan had only allowed it in order to have the chance of reconnoitring the French left and its incomplete entrenchments. However this may be, the prime responsibility clearly rests with Albergotti.

In the meanwhile the measures which Marlborough took had all been directed to a battle on the 11th. Instructions were sent to Withers to press his march. In order to have an uninterrupted line of retreat upon Tournai in the event of a repulse, Marlborough determined to take Saint-Ghislain by storm. About two thousand men, collected under General Dedem from the battalions blockading Mons, marched accordingly upon this post. Its garrison had been reduced by Villars to two hundred men, and about nine in the evening it was carried "sword in hand,"[2] the garrison being accorded

---

[1] "A cry of 'Peace, peace—it is peace' began on the right wing of the army, and was caught up and repeated along the whole line. Officers and soldiers ran forward from all the regiments to the enemy entrenchments, which lay a short gunshot in front of us, and began to speak to their friends and acquaintances in the French army. The French sprang joyfully upon their entrenchment, and I too rode forward with a close friend. However, when we retired the French fired a full volley, and wounded my horse high up in the buttocks, so this peace was within a hair's breadth of costing me my life." (From an account by Bellingk, quoted in Alexander Schwencke, *Geschichte der Hannoveraschen Truppen im Spanischen Erbfolgekriege* 1701–14 (1862).)

[2] Hare Papers, *H.M.C.*, p. 229.

quarter. Withers actually passed through Saint-Ghislain after its capture, and camped four miles beyond the Haine.

At the Council of War Marlborough and Eugene urged a general attack the next day. Goslinga, who represented the Republic, vigorously supported them. Such a combination of authority was not questioned by the other generals present, and the momentous resolve was taken unanimously. There was no obligation upon them to fight. They had only to sit still and let Villars watch them choke Mons into surrender. There had been half a dozen situations in the war when a great battle could have been fought on no harder terms— nay, on terms less hard—and several others were to occur afterwards. Both sides wanted to fight. Villars made the greatest contribution in his power by coming forward into the gap. Marlborough and Eugene, pressed by their Governments, were in the mood to accept his challenge. How many times of which we know nothing had they perhaps found it impossible to procure an agreement upon decisive action? Now they had the pugnacious Goslinga with them, and alone. Never might such an opportunity return. Now was the time to end the war at a single stroke. Even if conditions were not entirely favourable they believed they were strong enough to beat and ruin the last remaining army of France.

At some moment during this tense day Marlborough resumed his interrupted letter to his wife. "Having writ thus far, I have received intelligence that the French were on their march to attack us; we immediately got ourselves ready. . . . I do not yet know if I shall have an opportunity of sending this letter to-night; if not I shall add to it what may pass to-morrow." He ended with a gesture which may seem extravagant to us, but which might well have served as his farewell to Sarah, and would have been precious to her. "In the meantime I can't hinder saying to you, that tho' the fate of Europe if these armies engage may depend upon the good or bad success, yet your uneasiness gives me much greater trouble."[1]

Eugene's diary records:

> Orders to attack the enemy to-morrow in the name of God. My lord Duke of Marlborough's armies, the Imperial Troops, and the corps from Tournai, which is to make a special attack, are to be let loose upon the enemy. . . . All attacks to begin at daybreak, when everything must be in readiness. The signal will be a salvo from the entire British artillery, which will be taken up by the Dutch cannon.[2]

[1] September 10 (continuation of letter quoted at p. 596); Coxe, iv, 69.
[2] *Feldzüge*, Series II, ii, 101.

Chapter Nine

THE BATTLE OF MALPLAQUET

1709—SEPTEMBER 11

B Y the first light of dawn all the troops were already under arms and in their stations. But with the sun a dense fog rose from the fields and marshy places, shrouding the loaded woods and the two hundred thousand men who awaited the signal to fall upon one another. In the allied army of many nations the ministers and priests of almost every communion known to Christendom—Church of England, Presbyterian, Dutch Calvinist, Huguenot, Lutheran, Roman Catholic—performed their solemn offices at the heads of the regiments. So perfect was the harmony which the ascendancy of Marlborough and Eugene exercised upon all minds that these soldiers of different races, creeds, and Governments—English, Scots, Irish, Danes, Prussians, Hanoverians, Hessians, Saxons, Palatines, and Dutch—acted together as if they were the army of a single nation. Opposed to them was the greatest Power of that age, at length brought low, but finding in desperation new, unmeasured sources of strength from its valiant people. The French stood at the gateway of France—almost along the line where the frontier runs to-day—prepared to dare all to shield their land from invasion. With the French army were a few brigades of Irish exiles, and of troops driven out of the Electorates of Bavaria and Cologne, but all were united in the Catholic faith and in long military comradeship. While they ate their meagre bread, they mocked the plenty of the allied camps and the rum and brandy rations customary there on battle days. The standards of the Maison du Roi bore Louis XIV's challenging motto, "Nec pluribus impar." Never was it more bravely sustained than at Malplaquet.

During September 10 the French line had been minutely studied by "the Princes" and the allied Command. Marlborough's conception was in principle the battle of Blenheim adapted to a new field. The enemy's wings were to be assaulted until Villars was induced by this pressure to weaken his centre. The centre was then to be pierced by the reserve of the infantry (in this case mainly the British),

601

and its earthworks occupied. Out of a hundred guns no fewer than thirty-seven were assigned to move and work with the attacking infantry. The enormous cavalry army, nearly thirty thousand strong, was then to pass through the gaps in the defences, and fight a sabre battle with the French cavalry in the plain beyond. If the French

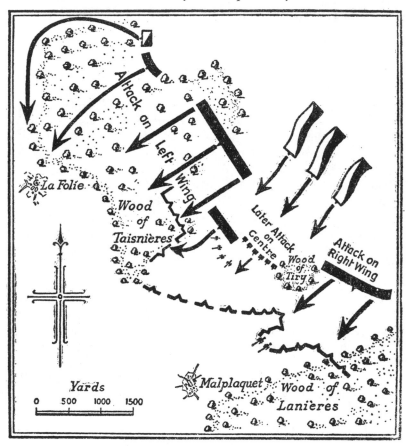

MARLBOROUGH'S PLAN OF ATTACK

cavalry were routed, all their troops drawn into the two flanks would be cut off, as had happened to the French right at Blenheim. We can see the methods and experience of that day alive in the minds of Marlborough and Eugene. The line of redans which Villars had built across the gap were to Marlborough the reproduction of the obstacle of the Nebel. He proposed when the moment came to seize and hold these positions with infantry, and, covered by their fire and by artillery, to form his whole cavalry on the far side for the final stroke. At Blenheim he was suffered to do this without opposition at the passage. Now he might have to fight hard for his debouchment. Apart from this, the gambit of the battle was almost the same. But Marlborough, and still more Eugene, had behind him a vast experience of war. If they had a plan it was to be no rule. The measureless chances of action would certainly create better or worse situations with which they felt competent to deal. Whatever they may have said or written, both looked out upon the day with zest and thrill, and, casting care aside, rejoiced in the intensity of risk, will, art, and action which lay before them. Moreover, here must be the end of the long war, and rest and glory after toil. All should be staked. Nothing should be neglected, and nothing should be withheld.

The curtain of fog by all accounts was regarded as highly convenient for the drawing up of the allied troops. For the main attack of the right wing the lines of battle were three deep: for the secondary but still heavy attack by the left wing, two deep: and in the centre, where it was hoped to give the decisive stroke, only a single line. To this centre, covering a third of the front, Marlborough assigned only nineteen battalions out of a hundred and twenty-eight. But these battalions, which he kept under the strictest personal control, were thirteen English, two foreign, and four Prussian, and constituted his only infantry reserve. He himself would stand near the redcoats and use them for the culminating stroke. Behind this slender infantry line were massed over two hundred squadrons of cavalry and the main artillery of the confederate army.[1]

---

[1] British regiments at Malplaquet (the grouping is that for the campaign of 1709, and was altered for the battle):

{ Scots Greys, 3 squadrons.
{ 5th Royal Irish Dragoons (later Royal Irish Lancers), 2 squadrons.

{ King's Dragoon Guards, 2 squadrons.
{ 5th Dragoon Guards, 2 squadrons.
{ 7th Dragoon Guards, 2 squadrons.
{ 6th Dragoon Guards (later Carabineers), 1 squadron.
{ 3rd Dragoon Guards, 2 squadrons.

    Total: 14 squadrons (about 2000 men).

{ 26th Foot (Cameronians).
{ (Two foreign battalions).
{ Prendergast's Foot.

{ 1st Batt. 1st Guards.
{ 1st Batt. Coldstream Guards.
{ 1st Batt. 1st Foot (Royal Scots).
{ 37th Foot (Hampshire Regiment).
{ 10th Foot (Lincolnshire Regiment).

As the sun gained power the mist dispersed. Broad daylight lapped the field, bright with symmetrical masses of uniformed men and the sparkle of standards and blades. On both sides the famous leaders presented themselves to their soldiers. In the well-known figures of Marlborough and Eugene the confederates saw the assurance of certain victory. In Villars and in Boufflers the French army recognized the two foremost heroes of France. The artillery began to fire about half-past seven, and gradually grew far louder than on the previous days, until at nine o'clock Marlborough ordered the Grand Battery to fire the signal salvo, and the battle began.

The Wood of Taisnières points north-eastward a projecting tongue. This salient, the scene of the fraternization of the day before, held by the five brigades of Albergotti, was Marlborough's first objective. Upon the edge of this his forty-gun battery concentrated its fire. Schulenburg, with forty battalions, three lines deep, marched against its northern face; and Lottum, with twenty-two battalions,[1] after moving as if to attack the French centre, was to change direction to his right, and assault it from the eastward. When Lottum turned to his right Orkney with his fifteen battalions would cover Lottum's left shoulder, which might otherwise have been exposed. At the same time, beyond Schulenburg's right, the detachment of nineteen hundred men from Mons entered an unoccupied part of the wood, and upon the extreme right Withers, with nineteen battalions

---

{ 2nd Batt. 1st Foot (Royal Scots).
{ 23rd Foot (Royal Welch Fusiliers).
{ Orrery's Foot.

{ 3rd Foot (Buffs).
{ Temple's Foot.
{ Evan's Foot.
{ 16th Foot (Bedfordshire and Hertfordshire Regiment).

{ 8th Foot (King's Regiment).
{ 24th Foot (South Wales Borderers).
{ 21st Foot (Royal Scots Fusiliers).
{ 18th Foot (Royal Irish).

{ 15th Foot (East Yorkshire Regiment).
{ 19th Foot (Green Howards).

Total: 20 battalions (about 12,000 men).

The English artillery: 40 guns, about 1000 men.

Total British: 15,000.

[Fortescue, *A History of the British Army*, i, 527.]

The whole army aggregated 253 squadrons, 128 battalions, and 100 cannon, or about 110,000 men on the preparatory line 6000 to 7000 yards in length.

[1] Including Argyll's British brigade (the Buffs, the King's Regiment, and probably Temple's).

and ten squadrons, began to march through the forest in the direction of the La Folie farm, with the object of turning the left of the whole French army. Thus eighty-five allied battalions were simultaneously launched upon or into Taisnières Wood, of which more than sixty attacked the comparatively small tongue-shaped salient.

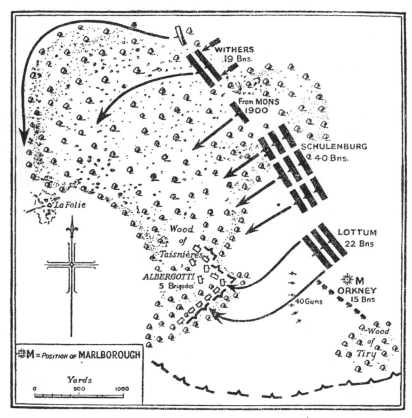

THE ATTACK ON THE WOOD OF TAISNIÈRES

The allied forces outnumbered the French in the Wood of Taisnieres by four to one, and Marlborough might well have expected a speedy result.

Marlborough and Eugene in their battles understood one another so well that each exercised a supervision over the entire field. But although there was no formal division of spheres, Eugene assumed the direction of this great operation upon the right, while Marlborough, with his headquarters staff, conducted the general battle from a slight eminence about half-way between the Grand Battery and the village of Blaregnies. From this dangerous but convenient spot, a little behind Orkney's corps, he was able personally to ensure the safety of Lottum's exposed flank, thus preserving his contact with Eugene, and at the same time to survey, or receive information from, the rest of the front.

Schulenburg's Germans marched firmly to the assault. This oblong mass of over twenty thousand men had eight hundred paces to cross before they came to grips. The five brigades of Albergotti met them according to the tactics of their commanders and the nature of the ground. Here the French charged forward; there they stood behind their entrenchments and reserved their fire till pistol range. But, however it befell, the clash was savage and the slaughter heavy. Two of the three major-generals and all the colonels of Schulenburg's first line were killed or wounded as they led their men inexorably forward till they were stopped by lead or steel. The opposing battalions grappled with each other. The fringe of the wood blazed with fire and smoke. The survivors of Schulenburg's first line recoiled, rent and ragged. But the second, following at two hundred paces under Eugene's personal direction, bore them forward in a double wave. "The Imperial grenadiers, circling the treacherous boggy ground, streamed into the wood upon the outermost flank."[1]

La Colonie, the "Old Campaigner," to whom we have often recurred, was posted with his Bavarian brigade behind the redans, and watched the advance of Lottum's twenty-two battalions.

> As soon as this dense column appeared in the avenue, fourteen guns were promptly brought up in front of our brigade, almost in line with the regiment of Garde Française. The fire of this battery was terrific, and hardly a shot missed its mark. The cannon-shot continued to pour forth without a break, plunged into the enemy's infantry, and carried off whole ranks at a time; but a gap was no sooner created than it was immediately filled again, and they even continued their advance upon us without giving us any idea of the actual point determined on for their attack. At last the column, leaving the great battery on its left, changed its direction a quarter right and threw itself precipitately into the wood on our left, making an assault upon that portion which had been breached.[2]

The French under Albergotti resisted with the utmost tenacity, and the defences proved their value. Sheltered behind the breast-

---

[1] *Feldzüge*, Series II, ii, 103.   [2] *Chronicles of an Old Campaigner* (trans. 1904), p. 338.

works, they fired steadily into the great numbers of assailants, who struggled through the abattis and tried to re-form a fire front at close quarters. To the surprise of the allied generals, the first onsets of both Schulenburg and Lottum were brought to a standstill either on the fringe of the wood or in the open ground before it. Their

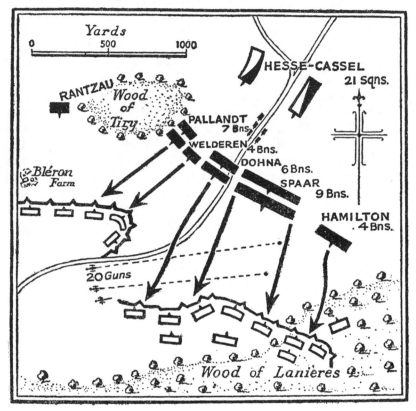

THE DUTCH ATTACK

second and third lines bore them forward again. Generals and colonels sacrificed their lives with the highest devotion. Eugene, riding into the severity of the fire, reorganized and forced on the attack by weight of numbers, regardless of losses. On the other side Albergotti's reserves were thrown into the struggle.

The attack by the allied left was timed to start half an hour later than that of the right. It had originally been intended to reinforce the Dutch in this quarter by Withers' nineteen battalions from

Tournai. The fatigue of these troops after their long, rapid march from the fortress, the late hour on the 10th at which they approached the main army, and the advantage of turning the French left flank by a wide movement had induced a change of plan. Withers was to act upon the right, and the Dutch attack was to become secondary in importance. For this reason it was ordered to halt just outside the range of grapeshot for half an hour after Schulenburg and Lottum had begun. All the officers in the Dutch army looked with pride and loyalty to the gallant figure of their young Prince. Those elements in Holland which wished to keep the house of Orange in the shade were represented by the aged General Tilly. About half-past nine, therefore, the Prince of Orange, without waiting for the consent of General Tilly and accompanied by the fiery Deputy Goslinga, led forward thirty battalions of the Republic with several batteries, the Scots brigade[1] being up on the left. As the left of the attack skirted or penetrated the Wood of Lanières a withering fire burst upon them. Here, in line with the Highlanders, fought the redoubtable Dutch Blue Guards, the flower of their army. The Prince of Orange had most of his staff shot around him. General Oxenstiern fell dead at his side. The Prince's own horse collapsed, and he advanced on foot. The entrenchments before him, three lines deep, were held by some of the finest troops in French service—men of Picardy, of Navarre, of Piedmont, and the French Royal Marines. These considerably outnumbered their assailants. In fact, on this wing the French had sixty battalions against thirty Dutch.

As the Dutch attack advanced in magnificent order it passed on its right hand the salient of the French line on the spur south-west of the Wood of Tiry. Beyond this wood there is a long, shallow trough of ground, about two hundred yards wide, which strikes obliquely across the path the Dutch took. Concealed at the head of this trough was a nest of French batteries mounting twenty cannon. From these there now burst a horrible flanking fire of cannon-balls and grape-shot which tore through the Dutch and Scottish ranks, killing or wounding thousands of men as they moved in faultless discipline towards their goal. The ground was soon heaped with blue uniforms and Highlanders, over whom the rear of the attack moved forward steadfastly, paying their toll. Nevertheless the young Prince, his surviving generals, and Deputy Goslinga arrived, with the mass of the Dutch and the Scots, before the French entrenchments, endured their volleys at close quarters, tore away the

1 These were the Scottish troops in the Dutch service.

608

abattis, stormed the parapets, and captured the works. But they were now too few. The reserves of Navarre and Picardy charged forward in counter-attack, not only upon the front of the Dutch-men, but out of the Wood of Lanières on their left flank; while always around them the scourge of the French batteries smote upon their right and upon the troops advancing in their support.

A retreat in good order began. The generals set the highest example. Spaar was killed; Hamilton wounded. Tullibardine fell amid his clansmen; General Week was killed. The Swiss general Mey was hard hit. The whole allied left wing fell back slowly, receiving terrible punishment, over the ground which they had traversed, now thickly strewn with the corpses or writhing bodies of their comrades. They might have fared even worse, for the French pursued them with vigour, but for the fact that the Prince of Hesse-Cassel, with the twenty-one squadrons of cavalry assigned to this flank, was perceived by the enemy, drawn up and seeking the moment to charge. Thus covered, the Dutch halted their deliberate retreat, and faced about. They had lost in half an hour at least five thousand men. Among the Scots there was an equal carnage. But the Prince of Orange would not be denied. His second horse shot under him, he seized the standard of the wounded Mey, ordered a second attack, and led it forward in person on foot. Once again the faithful battalions ran the gauntlet of the batteries firing along the trough. Once again they reached the French en-trenchments. Foremost of all their heroic prince planted his standard upon the parapet. Once again the counter-attack swept them back-ward, this time in grave disorder. Once again Hesse-Cassel with his cavalry checked the pursuers.

On the right of the Dutch attack Baron Fagel with Pallandt's seven battalions stormed the defences of Bléron Farm; but they in their turn were driven out by the French counter-attack. Rantzau commanded the four Hanoverian battalions on the right of the Dutch. Although he did not belong to the left wing and was in Marlborough's reserve, he had sent two of his battalions to assist them. They had suffered severely in the slaughter. "Monsieur de Goslinga," he wrote when his conduct was afterwards questioned,

> passing at full gallop, came to me and asked me if I did not wish to advance; I answered that he could see quite well that I was advancing, that it might please him to order the Prussians on my right to make the same movement, and to march forward like me, considering I had too little with two battalions to carry through the affair alone.

Monsieur de Goslinga thereupon stopped a moment, and in his confidence of victory, or perhaps seeking to encourage the soldiers, shouted, "La bataille est gagnée, ha! Les braves gens!" After which [says Rantzau somewhat maliciously] he departed, all the more quickly since the enemy had forced our left [*i.e.*, the left of Fagel's assault] to abandon the entrenchment.[1]

Thus upon the left there was a complete and bloody repulse. This is the moment when the French consider that Boufflers, who was on the spot, should have ordered a general advance of their right wing, which he commanded. It was certainly not from want of spirit that he did not do so. He did not feel entitled to make so great a change in the plans of the Commander-in-Chief without consultation, and for this there was no time. The opportunity passed without being tested.

At ten o'clock, while the Dutch were in their agony, Schulenburg and Lottum renewed their onslaughts upon the Taisnières salient. This time Schulenburg broke into the north face of the wood, and his whole command vanished into it. Lottum's corps also fell on, but were again brought to a standstill "torn and exhausted."[2] Their position in the open, almost at right angles to the French centre, harassed by artillery fire from both their front and left flank, became critical. Orkney, who, though not himself actually engaged, was close at hand, sent two more British battalions[3] to support and extend Lottum's left. While these troops were making their way through the marshy ground, Chemerault, the French general commanding the left of the line of redans, saw a chance. He formed a counter-attack of twelve battalions, and was about to launch it upon Lottum's exposed left flank. But meanwhile Marlborough had himself ridden forward with the Prince of Auvergne's thirty squadrons of Dutch cavalry, whom he placed in readiness to charge the French counter-attack. Marshal Villars, who on the other side had also reached this crucial point, seeing the redcoats extending to their right, and this large cavalry force, which Chemerault had not noticed, ready to charge, stopped the counter-stroke and ordered the twelve battalions back—but not to their redans. "I saw," he declares, "that our infantry was losing ground in the wood, and I posted these twelve battalions to receive them when they came out of it."[4] The denudation of the French centre had begun.

---

[1] Rantzau to Bülow; Lamberty, v, 370. [2] *Feldzüge*, Series II, ii, 104.
[3] One battalion of Guards and one of Royal Scots. [4] Villars, *Mémoires*, iii, 70–71.

With conspicuous zeal Argyll's brigade and Orkney's two battalions plunged into the Wood of Taisnières at the root of its tongue.[1]
"The English brigade," says the *Feldzüge* account, "was in support
and gathered Brandenburg's troops to a renewed storming."[2] Thus
they drew forward with them in their movement the whole of Lottum's corps, which, like that of Schulenburg, now disappeared
among the trees and undergrowth. The conditions inside the salient
were indescribable. Within a triangle, no side of which exceeded six
hundred yards, there were at least seven thousand men lying killed
and wounded, more than thirty thousand allied infantry in almost
solid masses, and four or five thousand French survivors. More than
half the superior officers had fallen. The wounded of both sides,
officers and men, were bayoneted and plundered. The screams of
the injured, the roar of the mob of combatants, the crash of musketry,
resounded from this smoking inferno, in which half the allied foot
had become engulfed.

Argyll's brigade sustained heavy losses—in fact, Sir Richard
Temple's regiment lost more men that day than any other single
British battalion. They performed prodigies; but their high spirits
took a savage form. "They hewed in pieces," wrote a German
observer, "all they found before them, . . . even the dead when
their fury found no more living to devour."[3]

Such was the situation which Marlborough from his post a fur-
long behind the Grand Battery surveyed upon his right. Here amid
the cannon-balls he sat his horse, waiting for the moment to strike
at the French centre. He must for some time have felt serious concern at the numbers of his troops which were being absorbed in the
Taisnières Wood, and by the carnage and chaos which reigned there.

---

[1] It is unlikely that Argyll was actually in command of his own brigade. As a
lieutenant-general he would have a wider authority in Lottum's attack.

[2] Corporal Matthew Bishop has left a picturesque account: "The Enemy had the
advantage of the wood, which would have rendered them capable of destroying the
greatest part of us, had they not been intimidated. When we came near the wood, we
threw all our tent poles away, and ran into it as bold as lions. But we were obstructed
from being so expeditious as we should, by reason of their artful inventions, by cutting
down trees and laying them across, and by tying the boughs together in all places. This
they thought would frustrate us, and put us into disorder, and in truth there were but
very few places in that station in which we could draw up our men, in any form at all;
but where we did, it was in this manner. Sometimes ten deep, then we were obstructed
and obliged to halt, then fifteen deep or more, and in this confused manner we went
through the wood, but yet all in high spirits." (*The Life and Adventures of Matthew Bishop*,
p. 208.)

[3] Lichtenstein family's archives; *Feldzüge*, Series II, ii, 104–106.

Towards half-past ten he began to feel uneasy also about his left. He knew that the first attack of the Dutch had been repulsed. He had not intended this attack to be pressed to the same extremity as that of his right. It was, however, an essential part of his plan that the fighting even on the left flank should be serious and heavy. Only by these brutal pressures would the two French Marshals be forced to denude their centre. He had not, however, prepared himself at all for the catastrophe which now broke upon him.

He had already begun to ride towards the left wing when Goslinga, indignant, excited, stained with battle, met him a little short of the Wood of Tiry, before which Rantzau and his battalions were posted. The brave, vehement Deputy told his tale. To anyone who had been through that double repulse it must have seemed that the Dutch corps was virtually destroyed. Goslinga added that the Prince of Orange was organizing a third attack. He demanded immediate reinforcements for the Dutch. Apparently he complained of the change of plan which had deprived them of Withers' corps. It is very likely that he also reported that when he had urged Rantzau to advance with his two remaining Hanoverian battalions Rantzau had not complied. The Captain-General bore the tidings with his usual composure. He calmed the passionate Deputy, and brought him along with him. About this time Eugene, warned of what had happened on the left, overtook Marlborough. Together they reached the point where Rantzau was in action. "Presently," writes Rantzau, "this Prince and the Duke of Marlborough passed on their way to the left wing. Monsieur de Finck, Lieutenant-General, received from them the order [for me] not to quit the post where we now were, unless my lord Duke should make us march himself."[1]

Marlborough, Eugene, and Goslinga then rode on through the streams of Dutch wounded staggering from the battle, or returning bleeding to resume their places in the ranks, to the point where the survivors of the Dutch command gathered around the indomitable Prince. They found consternation both at the appalling losses and at the young Prince's resolve to renew the attack. Together they forbade the further effort, and ordered the left to stand still under the protection of Hesse-Cassel's squadrons.[2]

---

[1] Lamberty, v, 372.

[2] Lediard (ii, 495) asserts that Marlborough promised to send Withers to the left as a reinforcement. If so, it was to soothe the Dutch indignation, for he knew only too well that Withers was launched beyond recall into the woods nearly four miles away.

Then the two Chiefs returned to the centre and the right. Perhaps they galloped, for the crisis of the battle approached. Eugene hastened back to the Wood of Taisnières. Marlborough resumed his former position behind the Grand Battery. It was now half-past eleven of the clock on a fine summer's morning.

Eugene found that progress had been made in Taisnières Wood, Weight of numbers had prevailed over both the obstacles and the French resistance. The French had been driven out of their second position behind the tongue, and the allied line was rolling forward yard by yard, extending as the wood broadened. General Withers with his separate corps, including three British battalions and the Royal Irish, who were some way behind, had entered the wood on the extreme right and encountered little resistance. Eugene had sent him ten additional squadrons, which with his own ten were making their way by a wide circle round the woods and also moving towards La Folie. This movement as it progressed tended to turn the whole hostile position.

A combination of forces was thus developing against the left of the French army which if not broken would be fatal. Marshal Villars watched this with deepening anxiety. He felt the left of his centre was about to be exposed. He responded to this dire pressure exactly as Marlborough had planned and expected. First he sent to Boufflers for reinforcements, but that Marshal, in grapple with the Dutch, could send him none. Villars then resorted to the desperate expedient of taking the remaining troops out of the redans of his centre and throwing them against the Wood of Taisnières to stem the allied advance. He, or others acting on his authority, drew first the Irish brigade, the Champagne brigade, and later La Colonie's Bavarians, and sent them to reinforce Albergotti's remnants. Some of these troops, as will presently be seen, ranged widely in the wood, but their main attack fell upon Lottum. Both Lottum and Schulenburg were heavily checked. The dense but much disordered allied line wavered and recoiled. Eugene was at hand. He rode forward into the front line rallying the German Imperialist troops. It was now that a bullet grazed him behind the ear. He was not disabled. He refused to withdraw. "If we are to die here," he exclaimed, "it is not worth dressing. If we win, there will be time to-night." Step by step, with hideous losses, all the allied nations fighting in the wood resumed their advance, and shortly before noon arrived in a ragged but heavy line at the edge of the plain.

613

"The wood being forced," says Schulenburg, "I found myself on the other side towards the enemy's lines, where I managed to bring up by a kind of miracle seven big cannon which I had with me, by which I did not fail to do great harm to the line of French

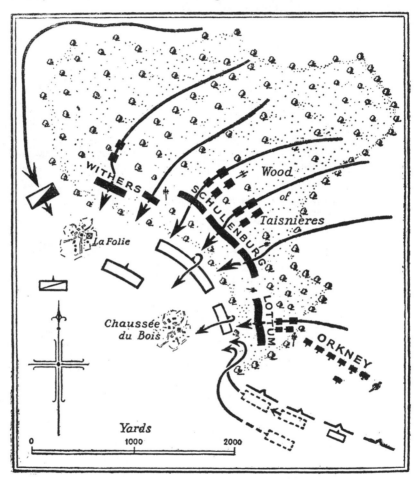

THE ALLIED RIGHT IN THE WOODS

cavalry."[1] This battery began to fire with highly disconcerting effect from the southern flank of the line. At the same time the twenty squadrons of cavalry in Withers' force were making their way round the western edge of the Taisnières Wood towards the French extreme left flank behind it. The remainder of Albergotti's

[1] Schulenburg, Part II, 417.

corps, driven out of the wood, formed on a prepared line and on their reserves three or four hundred paces from its farther edge. For a space of perhaps an hour all the forces on this wing were occupied in rearranging their disordered lines and preparing for a further clash.

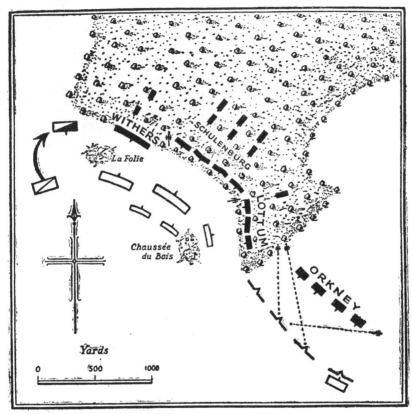

THE ALLIES REACH THE EDGE OF THE WOODS

La Colonie shows us very plainly the working of the remorseless pressures upon the French centre.

By the time the Irish Brigade had got well into the wood it was considered to be hardly sufficient as a reinforcement by itself, and an order came for us to follow it, although there was no one else to fill our place, which would be left open to the enemy. When the first order was brought to the brigade-major, who reported it to me, I refused to obey it, and pointed out the absolute necessity that existed for our maintaining the position we were holding; but a lieutenant-general then arrived on the scene, and ordered us a second time to march off, so sharply that all our remonstrances were useless.[1]

By noon Schulenburg's troops were reassembled and drawn up beyond the wood "where one saw the open country."[2] Their front stretched from the village Chaussée du Bois to La Folie, and the enemy's line stood before them at a distance of two to three hundred yards. Lieutenant-General Wackerbarth, who commanded Schulenburg's first line, is responsible for an erroneous statement which has confused some Continental accounts: "The nineteen battalions from Tournai who ought to have been on my right came out of the wood eventually on my left, so that I became the right of the whole army."[3] In the depths of the wood, by one of the strange coincidences of history, the Royal Irish met and defeated the French Royal Irish Regiment—famous in the war as the "Wild Geese."[4]

[1] La Colonie, p. 339.

[2] Wackerbarth's account in Schulenburg, Part II, 416.

[3] Wackerbarth's statement that Withers' whole force missed their way and came into line on his left, and that he was the right of the army, is adopted by the French official historian, Sautai. It contradicts all extant British accounts. It seems incredible that Withers, with his large force of nineteen battalions, could have come right across behind Schulenburg's line at the edge of the wood or could have found room to come into action between the corps of Schulenburg and that of Lottum. One can only conclude that Wackerbarth arrived at the edge of the wood before Withers had debouched, thought he was himself the right of the army, and that as he was soon wounded he did not witness the later developments in this quarter. It may be also that some of Withers' battalions strayed to their left in the confusion, and that Wackerbarth mistook the part for the whole.

[4] Captain Parker has left a clear account. "We happened to be the last of the Regiments that had been left at Tournay to level our approaches, and therefore could not come up till the Lines were all formed and closed, so that there was no place for us to fall into. We were ordered therefore to draw up by ourselves on the Right of the whole Army; and when the Army advanced to attack the enemy, we also advanced into that part of the wood, which was in our Front. We continued marching slowly on, till we came to an open in the wood. It was a small plain, on the opposite side of which, we perceived a Battalion of the enemy drawn up. Upon this Colonel Kane, who was then at the head of the Regiment, having drawn us up, and formed our Platoons, advanced gently towards them, with six platoons of our first fire made ready. When we had advanced within a hundred paces of them, they gave us a fire of one of their ranks; Whereupon we halted, and returned them the fire of our six Platoons at once; and immediately made ready the six Platoons of our second fire, and advanced upon them again. They then gave us the fire of another rank, and we returned them a second fire, which made them shrink; however, they gave us the fire of a third rank after a scattering manner, and then retired into the wood in great disorder; On which we sent our third fire after them, and saw them no more. We advanced cautiously up to the ground which they had quitted, and found several of them killed and wounded; among the latter was one Lieutenant O'Sullivan, who told us the Battalion we had engaged, was the Royal Regiment of Ireland. Here, therefore, there was a fair trial of skill between the two Royal Regiments of Ireland; one in the British, the other in the French service; for we met each other upon equal terms, and there was none else

Marlborough was still uncertain of the position in the centre. He doubtless knew that the Wood of Taisnières was cleared of the enemy. But more than four-fifths of his infantry were either repulsed with the Dutch or so deeply committed on the right as to be beyond manœuvring control. He now resolved to ride swiftly through Taisnières Wood to where Schulenburg's battery was heard to be firing, in order to see the condition of his right wing, and above all from this new angle the state of the enemy's centre. As he picked his way through the terrible wood, encumbered with slain, filled with the groans and piteous cries of the wounded, he met Eugene. Schulenburg describes how the two Commanders both joined him on the inner edge of the wood at about a quarter to twelve.

A great situation disclosed itself. Beyond the wood to the southward, perhaps three hundred yards away, a strong French line of battle of apparently forty or fifty battalions had been formed to deliver the supreme counter-attack on the remaining forces of Lottum, Schulenburg, and Withers. The forces now facing each other in array at a few hundred paces in this part of the battlefield amounted to perhaps twenty-five thousand men on each side. But the vital fact lay in the centre.

"I can indeed," says Schulenburg in his account,

---

to interpose. We had but four men killed, and six wounded; and found near forty of them on the spot killed and wounded.

"The advantage on our side will be easily accounted for, first from the weight of our ball; for the French Arms carry bullets of 24 to the pound; Whereas our British Firelocks carry ball of 16 only to the pound, which will make a considerable difference in the execution. Again, the manner of our firing was different from theirs; the French at that time fired all by Ranks, which can never do equal execution with our Platoon-firing, especially when six Platoons are fired together. This is undoubtedly the best method that has yet been discovered for fighting a Battalion; especially when two Battalions only engage each other." (*Memoirs*, pp. 138-140.)

It is impossible to tell in what part of the wood this fight took place. We know that the French Irish brigade had moved from the redans into the wood on their left. They could hardly, therefore, have come into action at any time against Withers' command, which was fighting nearly two miles away—about La Folie. In fact, General Saint-Hilaire in his account states plainly that he saw them in action on the *right* of the French left wing at the time when Villars was wounded, and that they were "the only troops who stood firm, and did not break" (Saint-Hilaire to the Duc du Maine (Quesnoy, September 12, 1709), cited by Sautai). It would seem, therefore, that the British Royal Irish, entering the wood separately, lost touch with the rest of Withers' corps and, attracted by the heavy firing, made their way to the left of the wood. Here they would easily meet part of the French Irish brigade. Here also they might have been seen by General Wackerbarth, who on hearing that they were in Withers' corps concluded mistakenly that that corps had come into line upon his left, instead of, according to their orders, upon their right, as no doubt they did.

describe the circumstances of this battle which I watched *de haut en bas et à mon aise*. . . . As soon as my lord Duke heard these cannons roar from this point, he came with Prince Eugene to see me. The Prince, coming up, said, "Truly Lottum has struck a decisive blow" [*a fait un coup de partie*], to which I answered there and then, "If it is a decisive blow, you owe me something for it, because not only have we made the French cavalry on our front retreat by our cannon fire, but I have also taken pains to enfilade a good part of the entrenchments of the enemy which cross the plain. Thus, Monseigneur," said I to my lord Duke, "the French having abandoned these entrenchments, don't delay to have them occupied—of course along the reverse—by several battalions as fast as possible, I beg you."[1]

So once again the moment had come when, the whole of the enemy's infantry being fully engaged and their centre naked, Marlborough still had under his hand a decisive reserve of fresh troops of the highest quality. Much is contradictory and most things uncertain in this vast, dark battle; but we know definitely that Marlborough was with Schulenburg at the edge of the wood somewhat before noon, and that a few minutes after twelve he was back at his former post behind the Grand Battery giving a series of orders which snatched victory from the jaws of defeat. He ordered Orkney to advance with the British corps and several Prussian battalions upon the line of redans. He rearranged the artillery in the centre so as to bring cross-fire to bear upon these works. He ordered Auvergne with his thirty squadrons to follow immediately behind Orkney. He summoned Hesse-Cassel from the left to keep pace with Auvergne. He ordered the whole mass of the cavalry to be ready to advance. He must now have felt, as in the afternoon at Blenheim, that in spite of all mischances and disasters victory was in his hands.

The British and Prussian infantry had hitherto stood in array under severe cannon fire, close to the battle-front. On Marlborough's order Orkney led them forward in a single line of battalions upon the redans of the French centre, from which they had noticed for some time neither smoke nor fire had come. Now their Hussar patrols cantered forward, and here and there got round or into some of the works and signalled that they were empty or weakly held.

"It was about one o'clock," says Orkney, "that my thirteen battalions[2] got up to the retrenchments, which we got very easily; for as we advanced they quitted them and inclined to their right. . . .

[1] Schulenburg, Part II, 417.   [2] Eleven British and two foreign.

618

We found nothing to oppose us, however. Not that I pretend to attribute any glory to myself (for it was the nature of our situation), yet I verily believe that these thirteen battalions gained us the day, and that without firing a shot almost." But this advantage had not come by chance to the gallant Orkney. It was the gift of Marlborough's genius dominating at last the confusion of the battle.[1]

Among the British battalions which now delivered the decisive stroke were the Cameronians, and we discern the sombre, stately figure of Major Blackadder, inspiring his men and communing with

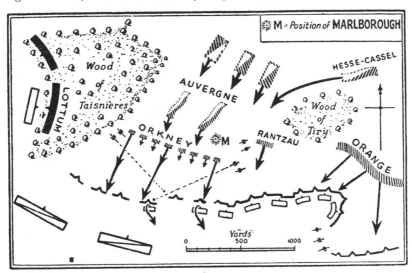

ORKNEY'S ATTACK

his God, his eye fixed upon the Amalekites in another "Ebenezer" of his life.

"It was," he writes,

the most deliberate, solemn, and well-ordered battle that ever I saw— a noble and fine disposition, and as nobly executed. Every man was at his post; and I never saw troops engage with more cheerfulness, boldness, and resolution. In all the soldiers' faces appeared a brisk and lively gaiety which presaged victory. The Lord of Hosts went forth at our head as Captain of our host, and the army followed with a daring cheerful boldness, for we never doubted but we would beat them. Providence ordered it so, that our regiment was no farther engaged than by being cannonaded, which was, indeed, the most severe that ever our regiment suffered, and by which we had considerable loss.

[1] See "Letters of the First Lord Orkney," *English Historical Review*, xix (1904).

But the soldiers endured it without shrinking, very patiently, and with great courage. For my own part I was nobly and richly supplied, as I have always been on such occasions, with liberal supplies of grace and strength, as the exigencies of the day called for. *I never had a more pleasant day in my life.* I was kept in perfect peace; my mind stayed, trusting in God. All went well with me; and not being in hurry and hot action, I had time for plying the throne of grace, sometimes by prayer, sometimes by praise, as the various turns of Providence gave occasion; sometimes for the public, sometimes for myself. I did not seek any assurance of protection for my life; I thought it enough to believe in general, to depend with resignation, and hang about His hand.[1]

But if the major had never passed a more pleasant day, it fared otherwise with his colonel. Cranstoun, whose able letters and criticisms have been several times quoted here, was at the head of his stern regiment. A round shot, about the size of a cricket-ball, such as are still picked up on this old battlefield, struck him in the left breast, coming out at his back. He fell from his horse before Blackadder's eyes without a word. The command devolved upon Blackadder. "A thousand shall fall at thy side," he murmured, "and ten thousand at thy right hand, but it shall not once come near to thee."[2] Thus uplifted, in the temper of the Ironsides, he led forward his men.

The French Guards, resplendent in their new uniforms, who were posted some distance behind the redans, did not attempt any counter-attack, incurring thereby bitter ridicule and reproach from the French army. Only upon the British left was there any resistance; and all the entrenchments in the enemy's centre were captured with small loss. The Dutch infantry on the left, torn by their fearful losses but with undaunted spirit, were led for the third time to the attack on the corpse-strewn triple entrenchments by their Prince and their surviving generals. All accounts speak of the ardour of these troops, who had to be restrained rather than incited. "As at the beginning of the battle, so now, the Dutch bought with their blood every step of the broad earth, and in the end the French right wing had to abandon the field to such death-defying courage."[3] Hesse-Cassel with his twenty-one squadrons was already passing the gaps upon the left of the line of redans, and unless arrested would speedily take the hitherto victorious French right wing and their defences in flank and rear.

[1] A. Crichton, *The Life and Diary of Lieutenant-Colonel J. Blackader* (1824), p. 350.
[2] Blackader, p. 352.   [3] *Feldzüge*, Series II, ii, 107.

By a quarter past one the British battalions held the front face of all the redans. The intervals between them became so many gateways through which the allied cavalry could debouch and endeavour to form line on the plain beyond. The cross-fire of their supporting batteries afforded them some measure of protection during this critical operation. The Prince of Auvergne, with his thirty Dutch squadrons, had followed close behind the British infantry, and began to pour through the gaps and deploy for the

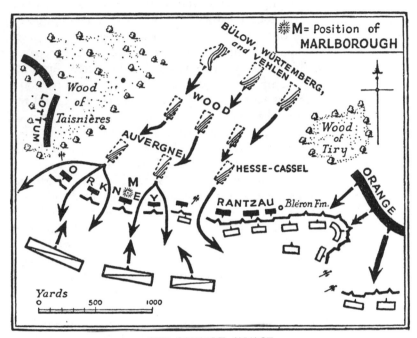

THE CAVALRY ATTACK

charge. Close behind came General Wood with the whole of the British cavalry. Rolling forward behind them again marched the heavy columns of the Prussian and Hanoverian horse under General Bülow, and the whole body of the Imperialist cavalry under the Duke of Würtemberg and Count Vehlen; in all, pressing forward at this point, more than thirty thousand horsemen, the equivalent of seven or eight modern cavalry divisions. This combination of horse, foot, and guns recalls the central attack at Blenheim. The perfect execution of these complicated manœuvres in the roar and crash of the great battle, the discipline and mutual loyalty of all these troops of different nations, justly won the admiration of their enemy, and deserve the proud glance of history.

Marlborough with his staff had ridden forward to a point near one of the redans where he could regulate this new and decisive phase. The struggle of the infantry was mainly over, and a cavalry battle, far larger even than Ramillies, the greatest, in fact, of which there is any example, was about to begin.

While all this was in progress in the centre the much diminished and somewhat disorganized forces of Lottum, Schulenburg, and Withers, in line beyond or along the southern edge of Taisnières Wood, faced the counter-stroke which Marshal Villars had prepared at so heavy a cost to his army. The Marshal had collected upwards of fifty battalions, composed of the remains of Albergotti's five brigades, all the troops he had withdrawn from his centre, and the French reserves which had hitherto been posted in this quarter of the field. The two lines along a mile of front faced each other, often at no more than two hundred yards' distance. Beyond La Folie, and in full view of the greater part of the French left wing, a cavalry episode cheered the arms of France. General Miklau, with the squadrons of Withers, had at length made his way round the forest belt, and his leading squadrons were already deployed to attack the left flank of the hostile infantry. Upon him fell eight squadrons of French carabineers. They caught Miklau in flank in the act of deploying. At least six squadrons of the allied horse were cut to pieces, and the rest driven from the field, the bulk taking shelter in the woods. No mercy was shown by the victors, and the wounded were slaughtered on the spot.

As the whole French line braced themselves to attack there arrived from the centre the veteran artillerist Saint-Hilaire. The tale he told to Villars was terrible. The redans were empty. Masses of the English were already breaking into them. He had only by minutes saved his guns from capture. The Marshal, resolute as ever, saw no remedy but to lead forward twelve battalions which were at the moment in his hands as part of his general counter-stroke. Opposite to him at the edge of the wood was Eugene, who, with all the troops he could control, prepared to meet the French in full career. The whole front came into close, intense fire action, quivering and writhing under the effect of the volleys, while the dead and wounded sank upon the ground.[1] Marshal Villars and his staff, riding forward,

---

[1] Corporal Bishop tells a tale: "They returned our volley with great success. I may

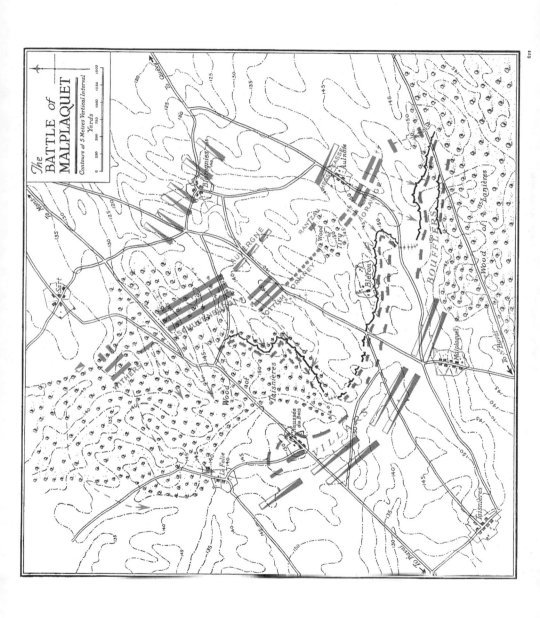

The
BATTLE of
MALPLAQUET

Contours at 5 Metres Vertical Interval
Yards

caught a blast of fire. His horse fell dead, and a bullet smashed his left leg below the knee. At the same moment Albergotti fell from the saddle with a broken thigh, and General Chemerault was killed. Aides-de-camp and a surgeon ran to the prostrate Marshal. He refused to quit the field. A chair was found in a cottage hard by. Seated in this, he endeavoured to conduct the battle, but the agony of his wound was overpowering. He swooned, and remained so long unconscious that they carried him away. He did not recover consciousness until he was in the hospital at Quesnoy. In his own words, "That is all I know about the end of the battle."

There is no doubt that the fall of the illustrious Commander-in-Chief and the simultaneous loss of Albergotti and Chemerault disorganized the French command at the supreme moment of their counter-attack. It is natural that French writers, then and afterwards, should claim that but for this they would have won the battle. But the troops who stood before them were tough and bitter, certainly as numerous, infuriated by their losses, flushed by success, and with Eugene at their head. They would not easily have been driven back into the wood, certainly not through it.

After an interval of paralysis Puységur, the staff officer whose reputation after Oudenarde still stood high, assumed direction of the French left wing. He organized and ordered a methodical retirement. Some regiments marched to within twenty yards of the Allies to fire their final volley before retreating, but within a quarter of an hour of Villars's wound the fifty battalions with their supporting cavalry had retired in good order out of all contact. The Allies, still clogged by the confusion of their passage of the wood, were in

---

say it, for my right and left hand men were shot dead, and in falling had almost thrown me down, for I could scarce prevent my falling among the dead men. Then I said to the second rank: 'Come, my boys, make good the front.' With that they drew up. Then I said: 'Never fear, we shall have better luck the next throw.' But I just saved my word, for my right hand man was shot through the head, and the man that followed me was shot through the groin, and I escaped all, though nothing but the Providence of God could protect me. Then our rear man was called up to be a front; but the poor man was struck with a panic, fearing that he should share the same fate as the others did. He endeavoured to half cover himself behind me, but I put my hand behind me and pulled him up, and told him, that I could no ways screen him, for he was sensible a man behind me was shot. By strong persuasion I prevailed upon him, so that he was not in the least daunted, but stood it out as bold as a lion. We received a great many volleys after that, and one time I remember it wounded my Captain and took my left hand man, and almost swept off those that were on my right, so that it left the man that was intimidated, and myself alone. Then I said: 'Come, Partner, there is nothing like having good courage.' So we filled up our ranks in a regular form, and when we had so done, we fired upon them briskly and with great success." (*The Life and Adventures of Matthew Bishop*, p. 211.)

no condition to pursue. Eugene himself ordered them to remain halted, and to consolidate, and hastened to join Marlborough in the new focus of the battle.

From early morning onward the French cavalry on the plain behind the centre had suffered severely from the allied cannonade. The slopes of the ground were such that many cannon-balls which ricochetted from the crest of the redans flew onward, cutting cruel gaps in the closely formed squadrons. The allied cavalry did not suffer in this way, for the ground on which they had waited was not exposed to this glancing fire. Nevertheless, the French horse was almost as numerous as the Allies'. The French also had the advantage

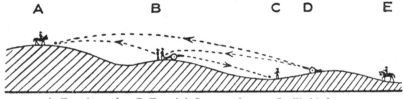

A, French cavalry; B, French infantry and guns; C, allied infantry;
D, allied guns; E, allied cavalry.

*From " Marlborough's Battlefields Illustrated: Malplaquet." by Major A. H. Burne, D.S.O., R.A.,
in " The Journal of the Royal Artillery," vol. lx, p. 48.*

of being able to attack in superior strength an enemy while forming. It was indeed with relief and pent-up wrath that the brilliant squadrons, which had so long borne their punishment from the cannon, found at last a foe to strike. Marshal Boufflers, learning that the supreme command had devolved on him, placed himself at the head of the Maison du Roi, and as soon as Auvergne had formed twenty squadrons beyond the redans, charged him with these splendid troops.

Orkney, whose battalions now manned the whole line of redans, watched the scene at close quarters. "Before we got thirty squadrons out they came down and attacked; and there was such pelting at one another that I really never saw the like." Auvergne's Dutch squadrons were driven back upon the redans, and through the intervals between them. But here the pursuers were stopped by the steady fire of the British infantry and guns. As they recoiled the allied cavalry poured forward again through every gap. General Wood came up with the British cavalry. The fighting was now almost entirely with the sword. Orkney's laconic, veteran style reveals how deeply he was stirred: "We broke through them, particularly four squadrons of English. *Jemmy Campbell, at the head of the Grey Dragoons, behaved like an angell, broke through both lines.* So did Panton, with little Lord Lumley at the head of one of Lumley's and one of Wood's."[1] The struggle ebbed and flowed. The Maison du Roi, with Boufflers fighting sword in hand at their head, again drove back the Dutch, British, and Prussian horse, and repeatedly

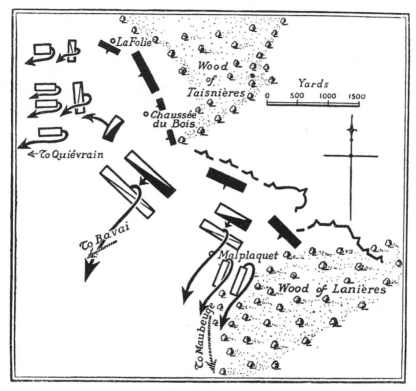

THE FRENCH RETREAT

prevented them from deploying in sufficient numbers. But the triumphant cavaliers were brought each time to a standstill by the disciplined platoon firing of the British infantry. "I really believe," says Orkney, "had not ye foot been there, they would have drove our horse out of the field."[2]

Six separate times did the French charges prevent the main body of the allied cavalry from forming on the plain. Marlborough had

[1] "Letters of the First Lord Orkney," *English Historical Review*, xix (1904).
[2] *Loc. cit.*

led up in person the British and Prussian squadrons. Now Eugene arrived with the whole Imperialist cavalry. Hesse-Cassel had established himself on the left of the line. Boufflers, at last convinced of the impossibility of charging home and producing decisive results against the well-posted and well-trained infantry on the redans, withdrew the mass of the French cavalry to the heath of Malplaquet, a few hundred yards farther to the southward. Here the cavalry conflict renewed itself in continuous charges for over an hour.

But meanwhile the main battle had been decided. The French left was already in full retreat upon Quiévrain. On the other flank Hesse-Cassel's squadrons now threatened the rear of the French right wing. The Prince of Orange in his final attack led his heroic fellow-countrymen over the three lines of trenches. The aged, noble Boufflers, unshaken by his prodigious exertions, did not forget his duty as Commander-in-Chief. Both his wings were in retreat. His centre was pierced, his cavalry outnumbered, pressed backwards, but still in order. He devoted himself with his cavalry to the task of covering the general retirement which was now in progress. By three o'clock the French were marching in three directions upon Quiévrain, Bavai, and Maubeuge.

So severe and sternly contested had been the battle that the Allies could not pursue. The infantry of both wings were fought to a standstill. The intact British battalions in the centre were the sole link between the two disorganized wings. The cavalry pursued as far as the Hognon stream, but the French had organized strong rear-guards of infantry, and their cavalry, though worsted, was still formidable. Marlborough and Eugene were both convinced that they could ask no further sacrifices of their troops. The battle was won, and the victors camped upon the bloody field. Marlborough sat down in his tent near the Mill of Sart and finished the letter he had been writing to Sarah at intervals since the morning of the 9th. The facsimile opposite shows how little his careful handwriting had been affected by the ordeal through which he had just passed. The intense strain of the two days' manœuvre and battle, the long hours at close quarters under the cannonade, the tumult and collision of the cavalry masses, the thirty or forty thousand killed and wounded men who cumbered the ground, the awful stake which had been played, left his sober poise undisturbed, his spirit calm. He re-read what he had written the day before, took up his pen, and added:

not yet know if I shall haue an opportunity
of sending this letter to night if not I shall
add to it what may passe to morrow, in the
meane time I cant hinder saying to you, that
tho the fate of Europe if these armys ingage
may depend upon the good or bad succeß,
yet your vneasineß giues me much greater
trouble. [After the battle.] I am so tired that I haue but
strengh enough to tel you that we haue
had this day a very bloody Battaile, the
first part of the day we beat their
foot, and afterwards their horse
God almighty be prais'd, it is now in
our powers to haue what Peace wee
please, and I maybe pretty well asur'd
of never being in another Battel but
that nor nothing in this world can make
mee happy if you are not kind

Sept. th 11. 1709

JOHN TO SARAH AFTER MALPLAQUET
Blenheim MSS.

Sept. 11, 1709

I am so tired that I have but strength enough to tell you that we have had this day a very bloody battle; the first part of the day we beat their foot, and afterwards their horse. God Almighty be praised, it is now in our powers to have what peace we please, and I may be pretty well assured of never being in another battle; but that nor nothing in this world can make me happy if you are not kind.[1]

[1] Coxe, v, 70.

Chapter Ten

THE EBB-TIDE

1709—AUTUMN AND WINTER

EUROPE was appalled at the slaughter of Malplaquet. The battle of Landen, to which its features have sometimes been compared, had not been nearly so bloody. The losses of the Allies were returned at twenty-four thousand officers and men; those of the French were not fewer than twelve thousand, and probably nearer fifteen thousand. Not until Borodino in 1812 was the carnage of this day surpassed. Our modern mass minds, brutalized by the tenfold figures of the Great War, spread over wider fronts and often weeks of fighting, measure only with some difficulty the shock which the intricate polite society of the old world sustained.[1] Upon no one was the impression of the slaughter more deeply marked than upon Marlborough. It disturbed his mind; it affected his health; it changed his sense of values.

---

[1]   *Marlborough to Townshend*

September 11, 1709

★The bearer [Major-General Gronstein] that is sent by the Deputies has been an eyewitness of the greatest part of the action. It has been more opinionated than I have seen, so that it has been very bloody on both sides. My next must give you the particulars, for I am so tired that I can hardly hold my pen.

P.S. We have so beaten the French that I beg you will tell the Pensioner that it is now in our powers to have what peace we please. [Add. MSS. 41178, f. 65.]

September 13

★. . . I may let you know that the gain of this battle is very glorious for the arms of the allies, but our foot has suffered extremely, especially the Dutch more than any other nation, for though they acted with very great courage they had not the good fortune to force the enemy's retrenchments, so that their horse could not act. As I do not yet know what account the deputies and their generals give I beg you will say nothing of what I write. The French are so beaten and discouraged that I do not doubt of the pensioner hearing very quickly from Mon^sr. de Torcy; I believe on both sides there has been more men killed and wounded in this battle than in all the battles since the war, for there was very little quarter given on either side. The Dutch generals blame some of the Hanover Battalions, otherways all has been very friendly in seconding each other, as if they had been the same nation. Except at Blenheim I never see the French do so well, for after the greatest part of their foot was beaten their horse charged several times and beat a good many of our squadrons. The whole Household charged twice. In the last we beat them so that they have suffered very much. . . .
[*Ibid.*]

628

As he rode through the ghastly woods of Taisnières, or up the trough across which the Dutch had attacked, the heaps of stripped corpses affected him profoundly.

"The day," wrote Goslinga on September 13, "was very bloody, and disputed for more than six hours with more obstinacy and uncertainty of result than I know how to describe. The Princes and generals who saw yesterday the left of the battlefield were horror-struck to see our men stretched before the entrenchment and within it in their ranks as they had fought."[1]

A foreign writer says:

> There where the Dutch Guard battalions had stood lay about twelve hundred terribly mutilated corpses, most robbed of their clothes, in rows before the French entrenchments. The bodies of those who had been foremost seemed to have been mown down, having toppled forward in their ranks against the enemy breastworks. Behind them the ditch was so thick with corpses that no inch of soil could be seen. Add to such a sight the shrieks and groans and sighs of the badly wounded, and one can get some idea of the horror of the night which followed the battle of Malplaquet.[2]

All his long years of war—almost from childhood—had not been able to impart to Marlborough that detachment from human suffering which has often frozen the hearts of great captains. Considering all the rough work he had had to do, he was astonishingly sensitive. He had none of the fanatical ruthlessness of Cromwell at Wexford and Drogheda. He could not, like Napoleon on the field of Eylau, remark unconcernedly upon the physique of the dead, "Ce sont de la petite espèce." "It is melancholy," he wrote, "to see so many brave men killed, with whom I have lived these last eight years, when we thought ourselves sure of a peace."[3] He was unmanned by the plight of the wounded, of whom at least fifteen thousand of all nations and both armies were left upon his hands. "I have hardly had time to sleep, being tormented by the several nations for care to be taken of their wounded."[4] His resources and the science of those days were hopelessly inadequate. For days the woods were crawling with shattered beings. From all sides it is testified that he did his utmost to succour them. He invited Boufflers to send wagons without formality or delay to take back all French wounded, officers or men, upon the simple promise not to serve

[1] Goslinga to Heinsius; Heinsius Archives.   [2] Arneth, ii, 88.
[3] Marlborough to Godolphin, October 3; Coxe, v, 73.
[4] *Ibid.*; *loc. cit*

again. He sent back the wounded Irish himself. He took all the money in his military chest and spent it on relief. His behaviour at this time was greatly respected in all countries. It was known how hard and well he had fought in the battle,[1] and also that his compassion for the wounded was sincere.

Marlborough, like his army, was morally and physically exhausted by the battle. He had fought it with all the skill and vehemence he had shown at Blenheim. His plans had proved successful. He had won at every point. The enemy had been beaten out of all their defences and driven from the field as a result of the heart-shaking struggle. But they had not been routed: they had not been destroyed. They had got off as an army, and, indeed, as a proud army. They retreated, but they cheered. They were beaten, but they boasted.

Villars has been blamed by many French writers for fighting a defensive battle; but what he did was in fact to make the best use of his forces. In particular Feuquières, the most pretentious censorious, and misleading of military critics, has outlined fancy schemes either for a French attack beyond the woods or for a broader line of defence behind them. Modern thought may, on the contrary, regard Villars's decision as both simple and sensible, as all great things in war should be. Unable to face the Allies in the open, he contrived to bring about the main trial of strength under conditions which were most costly to them. Resting his wings upon the woods and covering his centre with intermittent entrenchments, he presented a front which no army but that commanded by Marlborough and Eugene, with superior numbers and eight years of unbroken success behind them, would have dared to attack. He exacted from the Allies a murderous toll of life by his entrenchments and abattis; but all the time he fought a manœuvre battle around and among these created or well-selected obstacles. By a prodigy of valour, tactical skill, and bloodshed they drove him from the field. The victory was theirs; but not one of the allied generals, if he could have gone back upon the past, would have fought the battle, and none of them ever fought such a battle again.

England was inured to victory, and France to defeat. The Allies were discontented at not having gained all. The French were elated at having escaped with so much. Boufflers wrote triumphant letters to Louis XIV. A cruel ordeal beset Villars. His shattered leg and

---

[1] ★ "Les princes se sont bien exposés."—Goslinga to Heinsius, September 13 (Heinsius Archives).

knee-joint involved him in protracted suffering, and for many days his life hung by a thread. He tells us in his memoirs with simplicity and dignity something of what he endured in the two months after he regained consciousness at Quesnoy: how he prepared himself to edi, and thereafter at least to lose his leg. He tells us how one morning the surgeon, pretending he was only about to dress his wounds, suddenly ordered his assistants to seize the Marshal and hold him down upon the table, lest his movements under pain should hamper them, and how then they bared the whole bone and ascertained the exact path of the bullet. At last he turned the corner. In the meanwhile he was brought to Paris by slow stages. As his litter was carried through the war-stricken French towns he was greeted with tributes of reverence and honour, which he enjoyed and had deserved. He too wrote letters exulting in the battle-day.

The Dutch bore their losses with fortitude. The "High and Mighty Lords" wrote their acknowledgments and thanks to Marlborough in the most flattering terms. Their leaders did not play false to their own responsibility in pressing their Deputy-Captain-General for action. It is strange, when the strength of the Peace Party in Holland in earlier and easier years is remembered, that it seemed to lose its influence now. Whereas for some years it had been Marlborough's preoccupation to keep the Dutch from making peace, we see them during the last four years of the war the most steadfast and unrelenting of all the Allies.

Still, the slaughter cast a dark shadow over the Republic. "Ye joy here," wrote Horatio Walpole from The Hague (September 17),

> doe not appear proportional to the success; for ye cries of widows, orphans and tender virgins, deprived of their husbands, fathers and Gallants prevail so much among this phlegmatic nation that I believe the beaten French will carry off their disgrace with better Countenance than ye Dutch triumphant express their Glory; but to say the truth the Dutch troops suffered extreamly: they have not a hundred men in each Battalion, one with another, left out of 30 that engaged fourscore of ye French: wth ye greatest bravery and resolution, but not being supported were cut to pieces; and the clamour here is very great against ye troops of Hanover whose turn it was (as is sayd) to sustain them; but they could not be persuaded to advance though the Prince of Nassau sent to them, upon which that young Hero once more rallyed his broken forces and taking colours in his hand advanced alone a hundred paces before them and so animated the poor soldiers that they entirely routed the ennemys great numbers.[1]

[1] S.P., 84/233.

When Goslinga, visiting his friend Slingelandt, ventured to scold him for cutting down so many fine trees upon his property, Slingelandt answered pointedly that he too might have thought before he consented so lightly to allow the battle of Malplaquet, knowing as he did "the two Princes and the way they looked upon these sort of things."

Goslinga himself was robustly impenitent. He wrote sharply to Heinsius when the latter seemed disappointed with the campaign:

★We shall be very well pleased if we finish by taking Mons. Is it in fact such a small thing to take two of the strongest places in Europe, and win one of the most obstinate and bloody battles ever fought? You appear, however, to suppose that we can march straight to Paris. In truth let me tell you: an army does not march like a traveller, finding bed and board at every stage.[1]

No one disputed that a great victory had been gained, and that nothing that the courage of soldiers and the skill and devotion of Chiefs could give had been withheld. But equally no one doubted that it had cost more than it was worth, and that it cast a lurid reproach upon the failure to make peace in the spring, when all was so near. For a month the impression of triumph was strong in London. There were loud rejoicings, and every one believed that peace was at hand. But the Tories soon recovered from their set-back. They thought to represent the battle as a positive disaster. Although the British casualties were under two thousand, they made far more outcry about it than the Dutch, with four times that number. We can get an idea of their curdled venom from a letter which one of them, Sir Thomas Mansell, wrote to Harley (September 26): "When I first heard that we lay upon the field of battle, I concluded our victory could not be great, when we contented ourselves with that single honour; and could a great man have found in his heart to have parted with intelligence money, they would either have fought two days before or two days after they did."[2] In these circumstances the Queen had little difficulty in concealing her enthusiasm for the victory. ★ "I do agree with You," Marlborough wrote to Sarah (October 3), "that mrs Morley might have taken notice to You of the Victory and have shown some concern for my being safe. If I do not mistake, it was much the same behavior last Year after the Battle of Audenard . . .; I desire You will return my compliments to mr Maynering and lett him know that the Pr. of Savoye and his humble sarvant cals the late battle by the name of

[1] September 17, 1709; Hague Archives.   [2] Portland Papers, *H.M.C.*, iv, 27.

Taisnière."[1] However, this last was not a matter upon which either the "Prince of Savoye" or "his humble sarvant" was found to have the final word.

When Argyll came home at the end of the campaign he attacked Marlborough in bitter terms in the House of Lords for having mismanaged operations and squandered life. But the Whigs used their party and Parliamentary power to the full. They declared Malplaquet his signal and culminating triumph. They voted him the thanks of both Houses of Parliament. They celebrated the battle with all the resources and ability of their party and all the machinery of State. The Tories, outmatched by this exuberance, could but look down their noses and mutter insults and calumnies. The *Tatler* made a witty parody upon the French boastings in Boufflers's and Villars's letters.

> This is to let Your Majesty understand, that to your immortal Honour, and the destruction of the Confederates, your troops have lost another battle. Artagnan did wonders, Rohan perform'd miracles, Guiche did wonders, Gattion perform'd miracles; the whole Army distinguished themselves, and every body did wonders. And to conclude the wonders of the day, I can assure your Majesty, that tho' you have lost the field of battle, you have not lost an inch of ground. The Enemy marched behind us with respect, and we ran away from 'em as bold as Lions.[2]

Colonel Cranstoun's death made a vacancy to which Major Blackadder had claims. The faithful officer waited upon the Duke, comporting himself with pious dignity. He knew that "promotion comes not from the east nor from the west"; nevertheless his diary and his letters to his wife show a natural anxiety. The claimants were busy and pressing, and he feared lest influence and favour should outstrip him. If so he was resigned. "Let others, whose talent it is, get places and posts by assurance and forwardness. I shall have mine by modesty or want them, for I cannot force nature. . . . This winter probably will make you either a Lieutenant-Colonel's Lady or a Farmer's Wife."[3] But valour was rewarded; all was well. Merit prevailed. Providence, acting through Marlborough's hands, guarded his interests. In October he was promoted to the command of the Cameronians, in which famous regiment his name should live.

The battle upheld the credit. ★ "I have agreed with the Bank," wrote Godolphin to Marlborough (September 16), "to circulate

[1] Blenheim MSS.   [2] Lediard, ii, 193.   [3] Blackadder, p. 363.

four hundred thousand pounds more in Exchequer bills pursuant to the latitude given by the Act of Parliament to contract with them to any sum not exceeding one million two hundred thousand pounds. This is one good effect of your battle."[1] And (September 20):

> . . . I shall only add, that upon the strength of your victory, I spoke yesterday to the Bank, that pursuant to the latitude given in the last session of Parliament, they would now contract with me for the circulating of £600,000 more in Exchequer bills to the carrying on the public service. What I said seemed to be pretty well received, and I hope it will succeed; but upon that occasion Sir Gilbert Heathcote, who is Governor, said to me, "Pray, my Lord, don't let us have a rotten peace." "Pray tell me," I answered, "what you call a rotten peace?" "I call any thing a rotten peace," he said, "unless we have Spain, for without it we can have no safety, and now we have them down, let us keep them so, till we get quite out of the war." "But, Sir Gilbert," I said, "I want you a little to consider the circumstances of the Duke of Marlborough and me; we are railed at every day for having a mind, as they call it, to perpetuate the war, and we are told we shall be worried next winter, for refusing a good peace, and insisting upon terms which it was impossible for France to perform." He replied very quick, "They are a company of rotten rogues that tell you so; I'll warrant you, we'll stand by you."[2]

After Malplaquet the French retired behind the line of the Rhonelle, which formed a part of Villars's defensive lines. The Allies were free to open the siege of Mons. Boufflers began to extend his defences from Valenciennes to the Sambre with a view to protecting Maubeuge. Marlborough wished to forestall him in the interests of a future campaign. He therefore, as he tells us, would have preferred to leave Mons and besiege Maubeuge. However, he convinced himself that this was impossible until Mons was taken. French writers assert that the Dutch were inclined to abandon the siege of Mons. Marlborough and Eugene insisted upon its prosecution. The battle had been offered by Villars in order to save Mons, and Mons must fall, if only to prove that Villars was beaten. Besides this, it was of real importance to maintain the pressure upon France to the end of the campaign in the interests of the peace negotiations. Accordingly it was decided to persevere. The siege-train had been ordered before the battle to descend the Scheldt from Tournai to Brussels and thence journey by road to Mons. It could not, however, arrive till September 25. Meanwhile the siege-works were completed and all preparations made for the attack.

[1] Blenheim MSS.   [2] *Sarah Correspondence*, ii, 391.

Marlborough exchanged eighteen battalions which had suffered the most at Malplaquet for twenty-four others drawn from the various garrisons. The numerical strength of his army was thus restored. Boufflers managed to slip two battalions into Mons before the investment finally closed. He also reinforced the garrisons of Condé, Maubeuge, Charleroi, Douai, and Landrecies at the expense of Ypres and Aire, and strengthened his weakened formations with men drawn from all his garrisons. Even so his strongest battalions

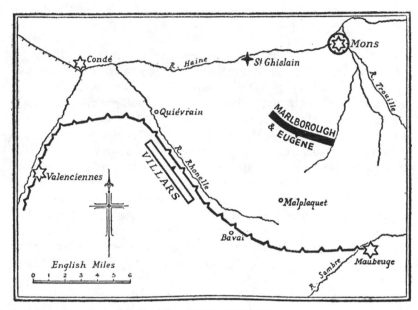

THE SIEGE OF MONS

could muster only four hundred men each. Eventually he collected forces under Luxembourg in the neighbourhood of Charleroi to threaten the communications of the Allies with Brussels and to harry their foragers. Eugene, Orange, and Hesse undertook the siege with 31 battalions and 31 squadrons, another 27 battalions being added later. Marlborough with the covering army lay to the south and south-west. The siege-train arrived safely, and on the 25th the trenches were opened. On this day Cadogan, whose duties took him always into the most dangerous places, was wounded.

John to Sarah

Sept. 26, 1709

★After a great deal of trouble we have at last gott some part of our

635

artillerie from Bruxelles so that we open'd last night the trenches, where poor Cadogan was wound'd in the neck. I hope he will do well, but til he recovers it will oblige me to do many things, by which I shall have but litle rest. I was with him this morning when thay drest his wound. As he is very fatt there greatest aprehension is growing feaverish. We must have patience for two or three dressings before the Surjeans can give their judgement. I hope in God he will do well, for I can intierly depend upon him. We have now very good weather one month [of] which wou'd finish this campagne, and keep the men we have in good health, which is very necessary for by the battel some of our Redgts are very weake.[1]

Marshal Boufflers wished to make an effort to break the siege, but Louis XIV was more concerned for the safety of Maubeuge. He and his military advisers agreed with Marlborough upon the importance of this place. The King told Boufflers that he might risk another battle if necessary to save it. Boufflers thought Maubeuge was strong enough to last out the campaigning season. Meanwhile the siege of Mons progressed steadily, and the breaching batteries performed their remorseless task. At the end of September Berwick, who had been sent to assist Boufflers, personally reconnoitred Marlborough's covering position. He reported that it was too strong to be attacked. On October 20 Mons capitulated. The French army concentrated to protect Maubeuge, but Marlborough had already decided, owing to the bad weather, the hardships of the siege, and the lack of forage, to disperse the army into winter quarters. "I am glad to tel You," careful as ever, he wrote to the Treasurer, "that we have sav'd this Yeare above one-third of the Monys given by Parl: for the additional ten thousand men."

Perverse fortune dogged the Allies in Spain. The news of Galway's defeat at the Caya had cast its malign influence upon the negotiations in the critical days of May 1709. At any time during the rest of the campaign a good success in the Peninsula would have brought peace to Europe. The almost unbearable strain upon France in Flanders and the course of the peace negotiations imposed a strict defensive upon the French troops in the Peninsula. As the summer wore on Louis XIV felt himself compelled, alike by war and policy, to recall all his troops to France. Thus every condition seemed favourable to the gaining of the precious and indispensable victory. Yet it was denied.

Blenheim MSS.

Although war had been resumed upon the greatest scale, negotiations for peace were unceasing. Torcy and Rouillé had returned to France in June, but Petkum maintained an active correspondence with both sides. The immediate object was to bring about a renewal of the conference. It must be remembered that the breaking-point had not been about the evacuation of Spain: both sides were agreed upon that; but upon the method or guarantees for procuring this evacuation. The new discussions played around various alternatives to the obnoxious Article XXXVII. In principle, the French were prepared to give some cautionary towns in France, but were neither ready nor able to give similar cautionary towns in Spain. The Whigs and the Emperor, bringing the Dutch along with them, continued to insist upon Spanish towns being yielded. A further obstacle was the French demand that there should be an immediate armistice, which the Allies would by no means entertain. Thus both before and after Malplaquet the summer and autumn passed in futile interchanges.

It is not true that, as some writers have assumed, the battle made the French more ready to yield. On the contrary, in Torcy's correspondence we read, "The last battle has rather raised the courage of the nation than weakened it" (September 27).[1] The hopes of the French were, however, fortified by the prospect of a new Northern war, consequent upon the defeat and internment of Charles XII, which would lead to the withdrawal from the allied armies of important German contingents. With the close of the campaign and the dispersal into winter quarters the French request for an armistice virtually conceded itself, and the negotiations took a more hopeful turn.

Marlborough's share in these transactions is plain beyond the slightest question. He did not consider himself in a position to press his own views in any formal manner. Throughout he acted in strict submission to the instructions he received from home, and in repeated letters he enjoined this course on Townshend. Secretly, behind the scenes, he did his utmost to procure such mitigations in the allied demands as would enable the Conference to reassemble. In repeated personal letters to Heinsius and to Townshend he declared that the demand for cautionary towns in Spain was beyond the power of the French King to meet, and that to insist upon it was in fact to will the continuance of the war. He was quite ready to fight a separate campaign in Spain, and foresaw no serious

[1] Legrelle, v, 486.

difficulty in driving out Philip V once peace had been made with France.[1]

It seems probable that Eugene was, as usual, in agreement with Marlborough, and if the two Captains and Heinsius could really have handled the negotiations unhampered by London and Vienna the vital result might have been won. In November these three together procured the sending of Petkum to Paris. This was the first peace initiative to come from the Allies. They could give Petkum but little latitude. Article XXXVII and its companions prescribed a time-limit of two months in which Louis XIV must take positive steps for the evacuation of Spain. Petkum was authorized to withdraw this condition. The concession was small, but the spirit in which it was offered, and the sending of Petkum, were tests of the sincerity of the French will to peace. Had Torcy and his master been in the mood to which the famine had reduced them earlier in the year the path to a general treaty would have been opened. Petkum and his proposals were, however, coolly received in Paris. All that the French Court would yield was an admission that the substance of the preliminaries might form the basis of a renewed Conference. At the same time they began to talk as if not merely the outstanding points of difference, but the whole preliminaries would be opened for rediscussion at such a Conference. Heinsius sustained the impression of a rebuff, which he roughly retorted upon the disappointed Petkum on his return.[2]

Marlborough felt convinced of the French insincerity. Both at The Hague and in London tempers rose, and declarations were made of the allied resolve to continue the war with the utmost vigour in 1710. On December 14 the Dutch sent a bellicose message to Queen Anne. In face of this attitude the French became more conciliatory. Their hopes of the Northern distraction proving effective had faded,[3] and in January they made a definite offer to

---

[1] *Marlborough to Godolphin*

October 7, 1709

★. . . It is most Certain that the great and only difficulty of the Peace is the Evacuating of Spain. I beleive it was in the power of ffrance at the beginning of the treaty to have given us permission of severall places in Spain, but how shamfull a part that must have been I leave to others Judgement. It is certain there is no relying on ffrench sincerity, so that I see no so good end as the takeing measures for the forcing them out of Spain. [Blenheim MSS.]

[2] See Legrelle, v, 487.

[3] "God forgive those who will be responsible for breaking negotiations upon the false assumptions about affairs in the North."—Petkum to Rouillé, December 10 (Legrelle, v, 492).

agree to all the preliminaries provided that the difficulties of Article XXXVII were first of all surmounted. The allied chiefs debated this in stormy session at The Hague. The Dutch peace party, headed by Buys and van der Dussen, put extreme pressure upon Heinsius to bring about a conference, and even declared that neither the Province of Utrecht nor the city of Amsterdam would vote the supplies for the new campaign unless this was accomplished.

We have only fleeting glimpses of Marlborough's part in these debates. It is certain, however, that while helping Heinsius to moderate the vehemence of Buys and the Dutch peace party, he also desired to give them satisfaction in the main. He, in fact, sponsored the proposal that should the conference be reached Buys and van der Dussen, the two chief advocates of peace, should themselves conduct the negotiations. This would give the greatest opportunity for obtaining a settlement if one were to be had, and, if not, would satisfy the peace party that all possible had been done to procure it. This course was eventually adopted.

Whatever disputes there might be about the consequences of Malplaquet, one fact was certain: peace was no nearer than in June. A far more potent current than any that set from that battlefield was now flowing. It was becoming evident to the world that Marlborough's authority was being undermined. The effect of this conviction upon the fortunes of the war was instant and constant. The French began to feel that they could afford to wait. Marlborough's need was to create for himself an independent position at the head of the Alliance before his authority vanished at home. It was a grim race.

As early as May 1709 he had sent Craggs to London to make a quiet search in the Privy Seal offices. He hoped to find a precedent for a life-appointment as Captain-General. Craggs' reply of May 20 was markedly discouraging:

*I have been endeavouring to find out General Monck's commission and it was neither in [illegible] or Privy Seal offices, but removed to the Rolls. I find it is only during pleasure. I send your Grace the enclosed Dockett on the contents of the commission and all that I can learn from my Lord Chancellor's opinion is that a commission during life is a new instance and liable to malicious construction, and yet I dare say there is twenty to one would think you ought to have a great deal more. . . .[1]

[1] Blenheim MSS.

And a month later, in answer to the Duke's more formal application to the Lord Chancellor, the latter wrote (June 23):

    *In obedience to your Grace's commands I have made as much
search and inquiry as I could without too much observation concerning the point you last did me the honour to discourse upon, and I
cannot find it was granted at any time otherwise than during pleasure.
Except [unless] the office of Constable should be looked upon as
precedent which since the thirteenth of Henry VIII has never been
granted but on special occasions and then immediately [withdrawn]
[I] do not think your Grace will think the ancient usage nor that obsolete
office to be any guide in the present question.[1]

Nothing could have appeared less auspicious. Both authorities
consulted, one Marlborough's close personal adherent, the other
his most friendly Cabinet colleague, were independently adverse.
For some months the matter slumbered. The urgency of the European situation in the autumn led him to thrust it forward again. In
October he applied directly to the Queen, and when she refused his
request he made a strong protest against the adverse influences
which he declared had been used against him. Continental historians
have complained that Coxe has not published these letters in his
voluminous Marlborough correspondence. But, in fact, no one
has been able to trace them. Considering how regularly all correspondence with the Queen was preserved by the Duke or Sarah, it
is a fair assumption that these records were destroyed. Certainly
the request could not have been made in worse circumstances nor
at a worse time. It was just the kind of demand which Marlborough's
enemies would have wished him to prefer, and which Harley could
safely advise the Queen to refuse.

The Queen to Marlborough

WINDSOR
October 25, 1709

    I saw very plainly your uneasiness at my refusing the mark of
favour you desired, and believed from another letter I had from you
on that subject you fancied that advice came from Masham; but I do
assure you you wrong her most extremely, for upon my word she
knows nothing of it, as I told you in another letter; what I said was
my own thoughts, not thinking it for your service or mine to do a
thing of that nature; however, if when you come home you still continue in the same mind I will comply with your desires. You seem to

[1] Blenheim MSS. Mentioned by Coxe, v, 117, and W. T. Morgan, *English Political
Parties* (1703–10), p. 374.

be dissatisfied with my behaviour to the Duchess of Marlborough. I do not love complaining, but it is impossible to help saying on this occasion I believe nobody was ever so used by a friend as I have been by her ever since my coming to the Crown. I desire nothing but that she would leave off teasing and tormenting me, and behave herself with the decency she ought both to her friend and Queen, and this I hope you will make her do. . . . Whatever her behaviour is to me, mine shall be always as becomes me. Since I began this I have received yours by the Duke of Argyll, and have told him he shall have one of the vacant Garters, and have enjoined him secrecy.[1]

The Queen added:

*I am very sorry for ye resolution you have taken of quitting my service when ye War is ended but I hope when you have talked with your best friends here you will be prevailed with to alter it. It is not to be wondered at you should be incensed against poor Masham since the Duch^{ss} of Marlborough is soe, and has used her soe very hardly as she has don for some yeares past wch I know she does not deserve, but it is vane to go about vindicating one against whom there is so great a prejudice, onely this I must say yt I dare be answerable, she never said to Mr Harley or anybody, what you are informed she did and [I] will ask her about as soon as I see her.[2]

From the terms of this refusal it is clear that Marlborough's request to be accorded the Captain-Generalcy for life was coupled with a declaration of his resolve to retire at the end of the war. There is no reason to doubt the sincerity of this intention, and in any case the Queen could have held him to it. There is not, nor has there ever been, power in a sovereign to make an irrevocable grant. Crown and Parliament together cannot be bound by any law. If, then, a future revocation of the grant were to turn on the question only of fair dealing, Marlborough's expressed resolve to retire would have afforded the fullest justification to the Queen. Therefore, the request which Marlborough was making, however unseasonable, was by no means improper. It might have given him the authority which he needed to bring the war to a satisfactory end. It would have largely re-established his credit among the Allies and his prestige with the enemy. It could only conduce to national and international advantage. Yet, on the other hand, what doors it opened to malice! It not merely exposed the Duke to a direct and painful rebuff, but it afforded Harley fertile occasions of working on

---

[1] Marlborough Papers, *H.M.C.*, 43 (*a*).   [2] Blenheim MSS.

the Queen's fears and of convincing her that she was losing her rights and prerogatives by needless subservience to an insatiable family.

The fact that the request had been made was judiciously imparted to hostile circles, together with its worst construction. Violent party opponents, proud nobles, disaffected officers, found it easy to believe that Marlborough harboured some prodigious design against the State. Was he not already "an overmighty subject"? Had he not power enough? Would nothing satisfy him under the Crown? The case of General Monk, already mentioned by Craggs, occurred to many minds. It was well known how Charles II had feared his power, and how his brother and eventual successor had urged him to curtail it. But other more sombre precedents might be invoked in warning. Many were alive whose youth had been spent under the rule of Oliver Cromwell and his major-generals. Never again must England sink into such military bondage. The Queen, probably by Harley's suggestion, consulted various great men outside the Government, and especially those who would be most inflamed upon the issue. The Duke of Argyll, on leave from the Army, was one of these. This fiery soldier, in no way conciliated by Marlborough's procuring him promotions and the Garter, replied in language whose extravagance was calculated to inspire the Queen not only with lively alarms, but also with combativeness: "Your Majesty need not be in pain, for I would undertake whenever you command to seize the Duke at the head of his troops and bring him away dead or alive."[1]

In the Tory coffee-houses the story was spread that Marlborough sought to subvert the Throne. "General-for-life" was but the stepping-stone. He would be King. "King John II" was the latest term of abuse cast upon him.[2]

While freeing Marlborough from all the graver imputations, it is impossible not to be surprised that he should have exposed himself to such dangers. How could he not have foreseen the fate of his request? His surefooted judgment had gone for once astray. Was this a proof of his inordinate pretensions, or was it a measure of the difficulties by which he was being overcome, and of the forlorn expedients to which he was reduced to carry through his task in the dusk of his power?

---

[1] Swift, *Memoirs relating to the Change in the Queen's Ministry in* 1710 (edited by Temple Scott, 1897–1908), p. 373.

[2] Thomas Hearne, *Collections* (edited by C. E. Doble, 1889), ii, 265.

The impending Barrier Treaty between England and Holland was bound to aggravate the dissensions of the Alliance. Marlborough's opposition to it was inveterate. In all his extant letters he gives as his reason the fear that the Dutch, once satisfied, would make a separate peace. He wrote this regularly to Godolphin, to Sunderland and Townshend. But there can be no doubt that his main reason was, as always, the ill effect which the Dutch Barrier in its extreme form would have not only upon the Imperialists, both at Vienna and in Spain, upon the Emperor and his brother Charles III, but also on the King of Prussia. It was more than ever indispensable to Marlborough, if he was to preserve any further influence with the rest of the Allies, not to be associated with it. He therefore refused his signature and remained at Brussels on October 29, when the document was signed by Townshend alone.

But he went further. The essence of the Barrier Treaty was that it should remain the secret of the Sea Powers. On November 14 Marlborough quitted the army and reached The Hague on a three days' visit. He took the Prussian Commissioner, General Grumbkow, with whom he was on the best of terms, in his coach. At The Hague he met both Eugene and Sinzendorff. It is almost certain that he disclosed to all three the character of the Barrier Treaty which now awaited ratification by the British Cabinet.[1] It was, of course, inevitable that during the impending discussions in London, to which so many persons would be parties, the news would eventually reach the allied Courts. But Marlborough evidently wished to be the purveyor himself, in order first to raise Imperial and Prussian opposition to the treaty at the earliest moment, and, secondly, to make Vienna and Berlin feel that he was true to the Alliance and scrupulously careful of their interests. Thus only could he preserve that confidence in himself on the Continent without which neither the armies nor the signatory states could be held together. Such dissociation from colleagues at home and from his fellow-plenipotentiary Townshend on the spot, unpardonable in persons of secondary status, and in any case open to stricture, is to be justified only by Marlborough's supreme position in the heart of the Alliance and his ceaseless, unswerving zeal and care for its interests.

Meanwhile Harley pursued his designs. Notwithstanding his astute and laborious calculations, success came to him by a path different from that he had prepared. It was no doubt a reasonable

---

[1] See Geikie, p. 169 n.

expectation after so many years of deepening war that the turn of the peace party would come. This accorded tolerably well with the composition and temper of the Tories. The Jacobites, veiled or avowed, were naturally so inclined. The Rochester Tories were against the kind of war which Marlborough had forced them to wage in Flanders. Party men were able to press Spain as an exciting alternative to Marlborough's theme, and all the country gentlemen, however patriotic, felt the hard bite of aggravated taxation. The exploitation of war-weariness in all its forms was a policy which seemed capable of uniting the Tory forces, and was also likely to profit by time and chance. Thus Harley ruminated, resolved, and acted.

Not only were the Tories inclined to peace, but several eminent Whigs, who were watching all the Queen's motions, might be easily gained upon this line. Of these the greatest was Shrewsbury, at this time a sincere advocate of peace. He was in the opinion of all men a prize of the first order. Finally an agitation for peace enabled the whole propaganda against Marlborough to be used to the fullest advantage. The General—thus it ran—was prolonging the war for his own profit. Military men raised by the luck of battle to dizzy heights were naturally prone to preserve the conditions upon which their authority and affluence alike thrived. How many good opportunities of obtaining all the objects of the war by sagacious and even glorious peace had not Marlborough burked! He could have had a good peace after Ramillies; he could have had a better peace before Malplaquet. Even now everything could be obtained by a sincere negotiation. But nothing could be expected except a continuance of the slaughter and taxation, and the ever-mounting indebtedness of the landed gentry to the money-power, while the General ruled all. Here, then, was Harley's political campaign, and to it he devoted himself with slow-burning zeal and shuffling skill.

However, the peace movement encountered obstacles none the less serious if submerged. First, the Tories, for all their party spite, were powerfully affected by the impression of England leading Europe, of redcoats beating the French, and some, politics apart, could scarce repress a cheer for the Duke of Marlborough. Secondly, the Ministry presented an oblique front to the peace talk. They too, so they declared, were striving for peace. Indeed, indefatigable negotiations, fathomless to outsiders, were unceasing. Discussion must therefore turn, not upon a vague desire to escape from war burdens or hardships, but upon particular points of the Treaty. And who had cried loudest for "No Peace without Spain" but Rochester and his Tories? Many Tories prided themselves upon being what Marlborough called "good Englishmen." War under Marlborough, however costly, had spelt glory. No would-be Minister dared openly cast away the fruits of eight dazzling years. Evidently this part of the case had to be stated by the Tory leaders with discretion.

Thirdly, there was the Queen. It was engrained in Anne that her security upon the throne depended upon the stunning defeat of France. All her reign she had pursued this course and had prospered. If she felt her own position greater, more solidly founded, if she found all the princes of Europe attentive to her slightest mood, it was because of her wonderful success in war which Marlborough had unfailingly brought to her. True the Queen was tired of the ordeal. She was galled by the submissions to Marlborough, and still worse to the Whigs, which it required. Had she not exclaimed on the day of the Oudenarde dispatch, "Lord, when will all this dreadful bloodshed cease?" None the less she remained deeply conscious that her sovereignty and British national greatness were founded upon undoubted victory in the war, and that this victory in one form or another, as long as Marlborough was her servant, was almost certainly within her grasp.

Therefore Harley, working steadily through the whispering Abigail, found that his peace talk gained only a lukewarm, doubtful, and hesitating response. The Queen made difficulties about back-stair audiences. Abigail flitted to and fro with explanations that "my poor Aunt" was "short of ready money [courage]," and that she allowed herself to be overborne by the cruel pressures of her Ministers and General.

Abigail Masham to Robert Harley

September 4, 1709

My friend [the Queen] will not consent to my going from hence till I go to lie in, which will not be till the middle of this month, the soonest, for she says I am so near my time the journey may disorder me so much that I may not be able to come hither again, and for that reason she won't let me go. I did not write you this before because I have been in hopes every day of bringing her to give me leave. . . . I can't tell you what use my friend has made of the advice was given her in your letter, but she heard it over and over. She keeps me in ignorance and is very reserved, does not care to tell me any thing. I asked her if she had gratified my Lord R[ochester] in what he desired; she answered, yes, he was very well satisfied, but told me no more. I shall tell her what you said to Mr Masham when I have an opportunity. You may venture to write anything and direct for him, perhaps they will not have the curiosity to open his letters; but make use of the names you sent me. I am very uneasy not to see you before you leave London, but it is impossible for me to do it. Mr M[asham] presents his most humble [service] to you, and we both wish you a good journey, and safe back again.[1]

Even the slaughter of Malplaquet did not affect the Queen, nor, indeed, her people, as deeply as might have been hoped by the Tories. British troops had been few and their losses comparatively small. It was the Dutch, the Prussians, and the mercenaries whom England set in motion and directed who had shed their blood. The British casualties at Malplaquet had been under eighteen hundred. Marlborough's fame, his influence upon the Continent, his comradeship with Eugene, had compelled the tremendous event. The war was not all loss or waste to the British realm, and it was no use for Mr Harley to pretend the contrary.

In the winter of 1709 it was by no means clear that the Tory Opposition could ride back to power upon a hasty peace. At the end of October Harley was discouraged, and Abigail could give him no comfort. But if the peace agitation failed, what other course was open? There was always one sure issue which could be raised —"The Church in danger." On this the strongest elements in the Tory Party and the immense power of the country clergy could be rallied. Harley, however, was the last man to choose such a cry. Had he not at all times striven to modify the rancour of the Church against the Dissenters? Had he not, with St John in his train, joined Marlborough and Godolphin in 1704 on the definite basis that the Occasional Conformity Bill should be shelved or defeated? Was he not himself of Dissenting stock? Those who had opposed him most among the Tories were those very Highfliers with whom the contest between Church and Chapel was a perennial crusade. As Harley viewed the situation in October 1709, nothing could have seemed less propitious than bringing the Church question to the forefront of politics, or using it as the vehicle of success at a General Election. It would certainly unite the super-Ministers, the Whigs, and the moderates. It would divide the Tories. The Catholics would lose interest; the moderates or "whimsicals" would fall away; and Harley would be left alone to share misfortunes with Rochester and the High Church. Yet the caprice of events was to draw him into this very quarrel and to yield results beyond his dreams.

Since June the Whigs had demanded the Admiralty, over which Pembroke had presided after Prince George's death, for Orford.[1] This actor in the Revolution, and hero too of the battle of La Hogue, was the sole member of the Junto who had not regained the Council Chamber. The Queen, remembering his attacks upon her late husband's administration, employed all her means of resistance. Marlborough and Godolphin, deeply concerned by the flaring party complexion of the Government, tried to stave off the appointment. But the Whigs used their power in the Government and in the House of Commons in their usual hard, decisive way. "If the business of the Admiralty," said Halifax, "be not set right, it will be impossible for Lord Somers to continue in his employment."[2] A point was reached when Marlborough and Godolphin had to throw their weight in with them. Marlborough advised the Queen to yield.

At length she gave way. She had a grievance against Sir John Jennings, a competent captain who was also proposed as a member of the Board. He was involved with those who had criticized her husband's administration. She consoled herself by insisting on his exclusion. Orford was nominated head of the Admiralty on November 8. All five members of the Junto—the five tyrant Lords—sat with Queen Anne at the council board. Now at last this long confederacy declared itself satisfied. There was a momentary lull. Political stabilization seemed to be achieved, the tension eased. The Queen even smiled at Sunderland. Sarah reported the prodigy. Marlborough had no illusions. "I believe," he replied to his wife (November 1),

> her easiness to Lord Sunderland proceeds from her being told that she can't do other than go on with the Whigs; but be assured that Mrs Masham and Mr Harley will underhand do everything that can make the business uneasy and particularly to you, the Lord Treasurer, and me.[3]

The end of 1709 marked the zenith of Britain in Europe, of the Whigs under Queen Anne, and of Marlborough's career. Thereafter

---

[1] John to Sarah, June 4; *Sarah Correspondence*, i, 175.
[2] *Ibid.*, i, 241.　　　　　　　　　　[3] Coxe, v, 105.

all fell with odd rapidity. The victorious Alliance moved forward with ever-growing disunity and ever more unreasonable pretensions. The Whigs were driven from office; Marlborough was hounded down; and glorious England turned renegade before all men. But the winter sun shone with fitful brightness.

Chapter Eleven

THE QUEEN'S REVENGE

1709—AUTUMN AND WINTER

QUEEN ANNE brooded and planned revenge upon the Whigs. Her power, founded upon Marlborough's victories, was immense. The Courts of Europe studied her whims; the fierce parties in Britain competed for her smile. But there is a cruel sketch of her about this time, oppressed with sorrow and physical suffering, struggling under her burdens, which commands sympathy and mocks pomp. "She appeared to be the most despicable mortal I had ever seen in any station. The poor lady as I saw her twice before, was again under a severe fit of gout, ill-dressed, blotted in her countenance, and surrounded with plaisters, cataplaisma, and dirty-like rags."[1] From the autumn of 1709 onward the Queen felt herself capable of driving out the Whigs if she could take her time and have good advice. Thereafter she thought about little else. These Whigs had forced themselves upon her. They had intruded into her Council of State. They had used without scruple the power they had from majorities in both Houses of Parliament to override her sovereign pleasure about the personages she thought fit to employ. Not only were her wrath and prejudice directed against the Whigs, but they fell upon Godolphin, her Lord Treasurer, who had been their tool. Marlborough, although not upon this plane, had lent his weight to the Lord Treasurer and shared his disfavour. As for Sarah, the Queen was utterly worn out by her arguments and admonitions. She desired above all things never again to hear her voice or see her handwriting. Nothing remained of that remarkable partnership except the opportunities of quarrel; and these were nearing their end.

When they met at great functions, or when Sarah's offices required her attendance, appearances were preserved. Sarah was a State and political personage. Her dismissal might be followed by Marlborough's resignation and a crisis in Parliament and throughout the Alliance. Even the rumours that she was in disfavour stirred Europe.

[1] *Memoirs of Sir John Clarke*, pp. 71–72.

The Queen did not feel strong enough to face such contingencies in the autumn of 1709. Had Sarah discharged her duties with respectful formality, avoided all intimate or controversial topics, and remained in the country as much as possible, a tolerable relationship between the two women might have been preserved. But Sarah's judgment was warped by her hatred of Abigail, and she was tormented out of all prudence or proper self-respect by jealousy of her triumphant rival. She obtruded herself upon the Queen; she protested her party views; she asked for petty favours, and attributed the refusals to the influence of Abigail. Abigail Masham had become an obsession to her, and she acted as if it were possible to tear the Queen away from her by force. Thus what might have been a dignified if frigid association became a violent and protracted annoyance to the Queen. At every rebuff or repulse Sarah wrote of her grievances to her husband, and urged him, as he loved her, to take up the cudgels on her behalf. All the advice he gave was sound. He begged her to stay away from Court, not to accost or write to the Queen, to remain as quiet as possible and ask no favours. This was advice which Sarah could not bring herself to follow.

"I would go upon all-four to make it easy between you," wrote the Captain-General (August 19), "but for credit, I am satisfied that I have none; so that I would willingly not expose myself, but meddle as little as possible." (August 22) "Be obliging and kind to all your friends, and avoid entering into cabals, and whatever I have in this world, if that can give you any satisfaction, you shall always be mistress of, and have the disposing of that and me."[1]

[*August* 26]

. . It has always been my observation in disputes, especially in those of kindness and friendship, that all reproaches, though ever so reasonable, do serve to no other end but the making the breach wider. I can't hinder being of opinion, how insignificant soever we may be, that there is a power above which puts a period to our happiness or unhappiness; otherwise, should anybody, eight years ago, have told me, after the success I have had, and the twenty-seven years' faithful services of yourself, that we should be obliged, even in the lifetime of the Queen, to seek happiness in a retired life, I should have thought it impossible.[2]

The British envoy to the Court of Hanover, Mr Howe, having died, Sarah, ignoring these sagacious counsels, unfolded to Anne the hard case of his widow, and suggested a pension and apartments

[1] Coxe, v, 168–169.　　　　　[2] *Ibid.*, 108–109.

in Somerset House. The Queen said stiffly it was a matter for the Lord Treasurer. Sarah then asked for some vacant lodgings in St James's Palace for herself in order to make a better entrance to her own apartments. The Queen, as Sarah no doubt knew only too well, had promised these to Mrs Masham's sister. Sarah said they had been reserved for her when they fell vacant. "I do not remember that I was ever spoken to for them," said Anne. "But, supposing that I am mistaken, surely my request cannot be deemed unreasonable," said Sarah. "I have a great many servants of my own," rejoined the Queen, "and some of them I must find room for." "Your Majesty, then, does not reckon Lord Marlborough or me among your servants?" This was picking a quarrel, but Sarah persisted. "It would be thought still more strange were I to repeat this conversation and inform the world that after all Lord Marlborough's services your Majesty refuses to give him a miserable hole to make a clear entry to his lodgings. I beg, therefore, to know whether I am at liberty to repeat this to any of my friends." The Queen, much ruffled, after a long pause said she might repeat it. "I hope your Majesty will reflect upon all that has passed," said Sarah, leaving the room.[1]

The impropriety of Sarah's manner in a subject addressing the Sovereign must be judged in the light of her love and intimacy dating from childhood's days; but the folly of her persistence needs no comment. It did not end here. Sarah resorted to her pen, which was pointed and tireless. She lectured the Queen on the duties of friendship. She dwelt upon the sin committed by those who took the Sacrament while still at enmity with their fellows. She demanded to know by what crime she had forfeited the royal favour. She furnished a lengthy memorial setting forth her services over more than a quarter of a century. But nothing that she could do served any purpose but to confirm the Queen in the position she had adopted. "It is impossible," wrote Anne, "for you to recover my former kindness, but I shall behave myself to you as the Duke of Marlborough's wife, and as my Groom of the Stole."[2]

All this account comes to us from Sarah herself. It proves her as wrong-headed in defending her case to posterity as in pleading it with Queen Anne. The breach was now open and scandalous, and all the ambitions of a rival, of a clique, and the interests of a great political party were concerned to keep it so.

The accomplishment of the Queen's political purpose was by no

[1] Coxe, v, 110–111. [2] *Loc. cit.*

means easy or free from risk. The Government commanded the ability of the great Whig lords, and behind them lay the force of the Whig organization. This included not only the City, with its mysterious power of manufacturing credit, but also the Dissenters, who might upon occasion become the Ironsides. Besides this both Houses of Parliament—the Commons but one year old—were capable at any time of taking sharp and measureless action against the Court, of refusing supplies to carry on the war, of arresting and impeaching friends of the Queen, or having her gentlewoman, the comforting Abigail, dismissed or sent to the Tower. Above all, Marlborough stood at the head of the armies of the Grand Alliance, apparently invincible, indissolubly wedded to Godolphin, to the Whigs, to the Parliamentary system, as well as to Sarah.

This was a great combination for the Queen to confront. Such was her confidence in herself and in her majesty and prerogative that she set herself without hesitation to overthrow it. But she must have good advice. Her intentions could only be carried through by a parliamentarian of profound astuteness and skill. Mr Harley's experience of the House of Commons was unequalled. His management when Speaker or Secretary of State had repeatedly been attended by success. Although he did not control the Tory Party, he had it all behind him now. With the Queen's favour he was, in fact, the head of an alternative Government. He alone would know how to play the Queen's very difficult game. She must act upon his advice. How could she, a woman, cope otherwise with great questions and great figures? But happily at the Queen's ear, always at hand, there was Abigail, Harley's relation and dear friend, whispering slander against the Marlboroughs, waiting hand and foot upon her, always available to carry messages or to arrange interviews. Up and down the backstairs Abigail conducted Harley, or carried his counsels to the Queen.

The successive steps by which the Queen sought and compassed the destruction of her Ministers were calculated and timed with remarkable address. At every stage her action was measured by the growing Tory strength in the country. This process continued remorselessly through the autumn of 1709 to the winter of 1710. This gradual but persistent change from Whig to Tory was only possible because the doctrine of collective Cabinet responsibility was in its infancy. The Lord Treasurer had many of the duties but few of the powers of a modern Prime Minister. His colleagues at the council table felt little loyalty to one another or to him. The Queen had no thought of loyalty to her Ministers, nor to the Parliament which voted her great supplies by their majority. To break and turn them out upon the advice of secret counsellors and by intrigue, veiled under deceitful protestations of confidence and regard, was her unswerving aim. She pursued it with almost total disregard of the consequences to the war, upon which she had spent so much of her subjects' blood and treasure, or to the princes of the Grand Alliance, to whom her royal faith was pledged. Queen Anne conceived herself as entirely within her rights in cleansing herself from the Whigs whom she detested, and also in punishing the two great super-Ministers who had helped to force the Whigs upon her. In behaving thus the Queen violated every modern conception of the duties of a constitutional monarch, and also most of the canons of personal good faith. Nevertheless, neither she nor her subjects felt the same repugnance to these methods as we do to-day. Royal favour was like the weather. It was as useless to reproach Queen Anne with fickleness and inconstancy as it would be to accuse a twentieth-century electorate of these vices.

So complete a transformation in little more than a year of a Government unquestionably sustained by majorities in both Houses could not have been effected if the threatened Ministers had stood together and acted resolutely in their own defence. It would probably have been possible in the early stages to confront the Queen and her secret advisers with an issue. Marlborough, with his sure instinct, was, as we shall see, most anxious for a decisive trial of strength on well-chosen ground. But at every stage the timidity of Godolphin, and the jealousy and selfishness of the Whigs towards one another, prevented any combined front from being formed. Harley, with extraordinary subtlety, managed to present always baffling and oblique issues, never hesitated to recede here and there for the moment, led the Queen to be prodigal in assurances of goodwill and promises to go no further, and thus edged and wedged the doomed administration inch by inch and week by week down the slope towards the disastrous general election which a dissolution against the advice of Ministers could at any moment precipitate.

Party historians, Whig and Tory, have had their say. Modern opinion unitedly condemns the failure to make peace both before and after Malplaquet. But no one can read without disgust and censure the shameful tale of the Harley-Abigail intrigue. Harley, as we have seen, was now master of the Tory Party. All its various circles from Jacobites to moderate Churchmen and patriotic fox-hunters were agreed that the Whigs should be turned out and the war stopped, whatever might happen to Marlborough or to the Allies. Queen Anne had become a traitor to her own Ministers. Harley and the Opposition, agitating from below, received a grand encouragement from above.

Two main methods were pursued by Harley. The first was a villainous propaganda against Marlborough, or what was more easy, 'the Marlboroughs.' Here was this pair and their offspring holding the Queen in bondage, engrossing to themselves all the sunlight of the realm. Here was this General gathering with his covetous hands filthy lucre in fabulous quantities. He was prolonging the war for his own advantage. He had prevented a triumphant peace in order that he might batten on the public fortunes at the head of the army, which, it must be admitted, he sometimes conducted with diabolical skill, but—as Harley did not shrink from hinting—with doubtful courage. Even to this level did he sink. The General had now at Malplaquet contrived a battle, which for its brutal slaughter was without compare, in order that he might line his pockets with the profits of favouritism and corruption, through filling the commissions of those he had led to death. Now this ogre, in base ingratitude to the Queen to whom he owed all, in treason against the kingdom and Parliament, was secretly aiming at the Crown. A new Cromwell dictatorship was his goal. See how the mob cheered him when they had the opportunity. Parliament itself must be on its guard against an ambitious adventurer, who had betrayed in turn every party and every prince he had served. Such, in insidious forms, was the nourishment which Harley fed to Abigail, and which Abigail fed to Anne.

For the rest there were the Whigs, the party foe, a cabal of wealthy nobles, an obsolete expression of the forces which had cut off the head of King Charles the Martyr, now allied with the profiteers and moneylenders of the City and the Bank of England. These were piling up ceaselessly a gigantic debt, of which they were the usurers, which soon would equal in its dead weight and in its interest the whole value of the land and annual food of England. These same Whigs were at heart not only republicans but atheists. It might be going too far to suggest they were the only evil-livers in the land; but still, their standards of morality were drawn at a level which, if accepted for a generation, would destroy the Church of England and debase the British breed.

Ought not the Queen to count for more? Ought she not to be mistress in her own realm? Could she not free herself with loyal aid from the trammels in which Whig majorities in the Commons and the Lords had entangled her? Then England might also be freed from the recreant, self-seeking, and blood-sucking allies who sheltered behind her sword—victorious no doubt—who pursued aims which had no longer any interest for the British Isles. Let the Queen use her undoubted rights and power, let her throw herself with confidence upon the love of her people; and the hateful toil of war would end, peace could be made upon unchallenged victory, and plenty would cheer manor house and vicarage alike. Such was the propaganda, a mixture of fact and malice, pressed upon Queen Anne from many quarters, urged by Harley in his backstair consultations, and counselled by Abigail at the Queen's bedside as she smoothed the pillows and removed the slops.

Side by side with all this lay a plan of action profoundly studied and step by step brought into execution. Fortified by the unfailing favour of the Queen, Harley now began to tamper with the Whig weaklings. The Duke of Somerset was a Cabinet Minister. Although a duke and wealthy, he had never reached beyond a secondary sphere in national politics. A searching process of reciprocal canvassing and criticism proceeded within the ranks of the aristocracy. Society and politics coincided through the entire field. In that keen, well-informed atmosphere personal defects were soon descried. Somerset's intelligence was limited, but he was independent, ambitious, bold, and could upon occasion be both violent and forcible. The insulting manner in which he had driven Harley from the Cabinet in 1708, when Marlborough and Godolphin had stayed away, had played its part in history. His wife was becoming the Queen's close friend. The seduction of the Duke of Somerset from the Whigs and his separation from Marlborough and Godolphin were objects of high political importance.

Harley knew all about the Duke of Somerset. He measured shrewdly both his smaller qualities and his large potential usefulness. For more than a year Somerset was led to believe that he might become the head of some great Ministry, truly national, combining the best in all parties, for causes with which, until they were defined, none would disagree. No records are available of Harley's approaches to Somerset. But we know that the Queen—no doubt by Harley's guidance—began to show him exceptional favour from the end of 1709. She was repeatedly closeted with him. She listened with unwearied patience to all the advice he had to give. He basked resplendent in the royal grace. Godolphin wrote drily to Marlborough that Somerset seemed to be more hours each day with the Queen than away from her. Already because of his airs he was spoken of in the Court as "the Sovereign." We are witnessing an early eighteenth-century example of the process, familiar to twentieth-century democracy in every land, by which a pretentious, imposing mediocrity can be worked up into a national leader. The Duke of Somerset enjoyed the treatment, and while sitting at Council with Marlborough, Godolphin, and the Whigs, upon the assumption of amity and good faith, he actively, crudely, and obviously played Harley's game. Lord Chancellor Cowper has passed a severe judgment on him. "On the whole he appeared a false, mean-spirited knave, at the same time he was a pretender to the greatest courage and steadiness."[1]

Somers may also have been toyed with. "Mr Erasmus Lewis told me," says Carte (April 10, 1749),

> that at the latter end of 1709 or beginning of 1710, Queen Anne sent for lord Somers, and told him, as they were alone, she having an opinion of his judgment and impartiality, desired him to tell her his opinion of the Duke of Marlborough. He said he would; and told her that he was the worst man that God Almighty ever made; that his ambition was boundless and his avarice insatiable; and that he had neither honour nor conscience to restrain him from any wicked attempt, even against her person, as well as against his country, etc. Somers (as the Queen was weary of the duchess) expected to be made first minister, but was baulked. The Queen had expressed herself advantageously of his honour, integrity, and capacity.[2]

But this is doubtful authority.

The next to be detached was Earl Rivers. Godolphin, with his unique experience of the pettiness and baseness of noble persons, and also of others where office is concerned, was early apprised of the alienation of Rivers. In his apprehension he proposed to Marlborough that Rivers, who was a general of some repute, should replace the much aspersed and grievously mutilated Galway as Commander-in-Chief in Spain. Marlborough was by no means incapable of a political job. The old, trained courtier had seen the like without undue aversion for more than forty years. But he had the prejudice which all good soldiers have against putting inferior

[1] William, first Earl Cowper, *Diary*, p. 50.
[2] James Macpherson, *Original Papers* (1775), ii, 283.

men in command of troops. Moreover, he was loyal to Galway. Although he had criticized severely Almanza and some of his other operations, he none the less believed that this Huguenot refugee and hero was one of the finest warriors in that age of ceaseless war. Marlborough did not readily hold with the modern doctrine, popularized by Napoleon, that generals must be judged by results. He therefore upheld Galway, and with many regrets left Lord Rivers on Godolphin's hands. Henceforward Rivers, while preserving his position as a leading Whig, acted in the interests of the Tories.

A far greater figure was the Duke of Shrewsbury. No one could charge him with ignoble ambition. Some twenty years before he had been King William's Secretary of State, and known to all as "the King of Hearts." In unaffected dislike he had cast away office and power. He had repeatedly refused to resume the burden. He had quitted the island. Amid the monuments, pleasures, and cosmopolitan society of Rome he had been for years the prototype of an English grandee. Noble in the technical sense, of vast wealth, bland, affable but remote, detached from his surroundings, disdainful to politics, but with his historic, formidable record, the Duke of Shrewsbury had brooded agreeably upon the Roman scene.

Upon Queen Anne's first coming to the throne Marlborough's resolve had been to bring him into the highest place next to Godolphin. But Shrewsbury preferred his idle life in Rome. He had married an Italian lady whose previous morals had not escaped gossip or even scandal, and whose manners were in all quarters judged lively to the point of being deplorable. In December 1705, when Shrewsbury passed through The Hague, Marlborough had made renewed attempts to rally him to the Administration. Nothing, not even the comical little creature he had espoused, could deprive him of his political status. Shrewsbury had now returned to his great estates in England. Again Marlborough endeavoured to enlist him in the Government. Would he not, perhaps, at least be Master of the Horse? There would be no need for him to do business, or suffer any personal inconvenience. But Shrewsbury amid profuse expressions of friendship had preferred a private life. On another occasion in 1709 Marlborough had spoken to him of the undue claims made by the Whigs, and had dwelt on the importance of having moderate men in the Government. It seemed that this conversation was to be the forerunner of others.

Shrewsbury, whose interest in politics was now being revived by his desire to carry his Italian wife into the forefront of haughty

English society, had perhaps been conscious of waiting for some time. Marlborough for his part had found the Junto, upon whom his policy had come to depend, by no means eager to admit Shrewsbury to their circle. True he was a famous Whig and one of King William's most trusted Ministers. But was it, they asked themselves, for his party colour and services that Marlborough sought to include him in the Government? Was it not rather because he had let that colour fade, and was at heart as ready to work for national as for party purposes? The Lords of the Junto might have accepted Shrewsbury as a mild Tory, but in 1709 they had no relish for him as a Whig. They saw in this idea of Marlborough's only another attempt to build up the strength of the super-Ministers against honest party men. At any rate, Marlborough never resumed his conversation with Shrewsbury, and Shrewsbury was perfectly free to allow his own weight and standing to play their just part in political events.

But Shrewsbury's value to Marlborough's system was also his value to Harley. Shrewsbury was the man of all others to break the Whig phalanx. He was the wedge to drive deep into the official array. Before the end of 1709 Harley had reached a tolerably good understanding with this timid, gifted magnifico. Here was a Whig who cared nothing for the Junto. Here was a Whig whose name was revered throughout that party but who took no further interest in its fortunes. Here was one who could be introduced into the Government as a friend who was in fact their foe. "I am sensible how far I am from being able," wrote Shrewsbury to Harley (November 3), "to act any considerable part in the good you mention, but shall always be ready to concur with you in everything that may be for the interest of the public, being convinced nobody can wish better to it nor judge better of it than yourself. I do not doubt but the generality of the nation long for a peace. . . . Some opportunities have already been lost."[1]

The Houses met on November 15. The Queen for the first time since her husband's death opened Parliament in person in royal and war-time pomp. Her speech from the throne, though read, as some noticed, in faltering tones, was all that a Whig Parliament could wish. French duplicity had used the peace negotiations in an attempt to provoke dissension among the Allies. Their designs had failed. The war had been renewed with greater resolution. A splendid victory had been won, and peace was now only the more needed

[1] Bath Papers, *H.M.C.*, i, 197.

by the enemy. But the war was still going on, and the final effort was required. The Queen appealed for generous supplies.

The Whigs excelled in Parliamentary stage-management. Under their influence the House of Commons resolved, contrary to all custom, to present the Address to the Sovereign on the very same day. Both Houses then proceeded to extol Marlborough. Never in the whole course of the war had the Commons expressed thanks to their General in such glowing terms. They exalted the victory of Malplaquet. They praised his skill and valour. Fifteen of the most distinguished members of the House were deputed to wait upon him with the thanks—against which no single speech had been made —of the most powerful assembly in the world. The Lords vied with the Commons. When Marlborough returned and came to the Upper House on November 17 Lord Chancellor Cowper outstripped all the eulogies he had earned in eight years of invincible war. Klopp rightly says, "This day may be called the supreme and also the last pinnacle of Marlborough's career."[1] Barely two years were to pass, and two more unfailing campaigns to be fought, before he was to be dismissed from all his offices, his faithful generals superseded or cashiered, and he himself charged with peculation and eventually driven from his native land in obloquy.

Hoffmann, the Emperor's Minister, saw beneath the structure of this fine parade. "This extreme politeness," he wrote, "is, to speak exactly, a result of the pleasure which the Whigs have derived from the appointment of one of their friends as Lord High Admiral; and," he added, with less foresight, "this satisfaction promises everything we can desire."[2] More than six million pounds—at which Europe gasped—was voted for the war with the utmost concord and dispatch. "Our Parliamentary business is going wonderfully [*à merveille*]," wrote Marlborough (November 25) to Count Maffei.[3] He told Hoffmann that he believed the session would end six weeks before its usual time. Whig ascendancy was a dangerous medicine; but it certainly seemed at first to work.

---

[1] Klopp, xiii, 370.   [2] Hoffmann, December 20; *loc. cit.*   [3] *Dispatches*, iv, 657.

Chapter Twelve

MORTIFICATIONS

1709–1710—WINTER

TWO unforeseeable but eventually devastating episodes now occurred in which the Whigs showed weakness and unwisdom. For the first they had only themselves to blame. The part played by Dr Sacheverell in the history of the Church of England is out of all proportion to his moral or mental stature. It exercised an influence which lasted for several generations. After the trial of Sacheverell no British Government, even during all the long reign of the Whigs, dared to make an attack upon the Church of England. The Dissenters, though immune from persecution, were for five generations tolerated only upon the characteristic British device of an Act of Indemnity passed from year to year, like the Army (Annual) Bill. It was not until the nineteenth century was well advanced that the religious disabilities of Nonconformists and Catholics were removed; and then only by Tory hands.

Noorden has drawn us a picture of Sacheverell more lively than is found in our own histories.

> His learning was shallow, but his bold forehead, his audacious words and puffed-up pride, the unction which oozed from him as he walked or preached, the Parsee-like play-acting and elaborate gestures, the whole personality set on calculated effect, made him appear to emotional women and simple men as a piece of incarnate saintliness. Others regarded him as a charlatan. His view of God and the world was comprised in the ancient and tenacious papistical Oxford principles: "The priest God's vessel; no salvation without priestly mediation; the death-wounds of Charles Stuart equal to the wounds of Christ; the Nonconformist sects the devil's brood." Nature had endowed him with a craving for sensation which was hereditary in his family. He was a climber thirsting for martyrdom without peril: more noise more honour.[1]

On November 5, 1709, Sacheverell preached a sermon in St Paul's

[1] Noorden, iii, 638.

before the Lord Mayor of London on "the perils of false brethren in Church and State."

"I remember," wrote a Whig observer, "he sate directly against me during Prayers, and I was surpriz'd at the Fiery Red that overspread his Face, (which I have since seen fair and Effeminate enough) and the Gogling Wildness of his Eyes. And I may truly say, He was (if ever Man) transported with an Hellish Fury."[1] There was no remarkable doctrinal departure in the sermon. It represented the views of the main body of the English country parsons. The Doctor had preached it in Oxford four years earlier, in 1705, without its attracting any attention. But now he added certain hostile allusions to Godolphin, who was classed among the "false brethren" as the "wily Volpone." The Treasurer had long been nicknamed "the Fox,"[2] and was thus easily identifiable. It was not only Guy Fawkes Day; it was the anniversary of William III's landing at Torbay. Whig ears were all attention. There was a sounding-board for words which otherwise would have passed unnoticed. The Tory Party was boiling and bubbling under the rule of their party foes, and under the illicit, but all the more thrilling, favour of Queen Anne. The Reverend Doctor was well aware that he was playing high politics. His move, though perhaps spontaneous, was a recognizable feature in the general Tory attack. The Lord Mayor listened without noticeable discomfort. But when the sermon was printed, with a dedication to himself, and when no fewer than forty thousand copies were sold or distributed in a few days, he made haste to dissociate himself from these dangerous manifestations.

Interest spread throughout the country. "We long here," wrote the Jacobite Hearne (November 19), "to see Dr Sacheverell's V[th] of November Sermon preach'd upon these Words, In perils amongst false Brethren. Upon which Words I remember he formerly preach'd at S[t] Marie's and 'tis said 'tis the very same Sermon, only with some Alterations and Additions. It makes a great Noise, and several give out that he will be prosecuted, but that you know best at London."[3]

Sacheverell's discourse threw the Whig Party into a rage. They were in the full pride of place and power. They viewed the sermon as a challenge, not only to their Government, but to the very principles of "the Glorious Revolution of 1688." Party men may

---

[1] Quoted in W. T. Laprade, *Public Opinion in Eighteenth century England* (1936), p. 51.
[2] Volpone is the chief and most odious character in Ben Jonson's satire on avarice *Volpone, or The Fox*.   [3] Hearne, p. 312.

be forgiven for party passions, but cooler heads and broader views are required at the summit of affairs. An Opposition would naturally welcome just this kind of discussion; but it was not for a Government in full career and at the.height of war to indulge them. Obviously the wise course was for Ministers to ignore or belittle the whole affair, and perhaps set one of their minor supporters to deliver a counterblast. There were, however, in the Cabinet Council several elements which did not conform to reason.

Godolphin was deeply sensitive about attacks upon his phantom Tory orthodoxy. He was naturally disquieted by the state of his relations with the Queen. He had the feeling that he was being singled out and marked down as a victim of Tory vengeance. He was therefore in a state of lively indignation. It happened to suit some at least of his Whig colleagues to indulge and even to inflame his wrath. Wharton and others thought that Whig interests would be served by making the Treasurer break his last contacts with the Tories. Marlborough had not returned from the front when the matter was first discussed by the Council. Sunderland was, as usual, a zealot. The Whig Party, Wharton as the leading spirit, clamoured for spirited action. It was decided to pursue Dr Sacheverell. In December articles of impeachment were exhibited against him by the majority of the House of Commons.

The Government's tactical error was understood by the Tories from the first. "So solemn a prosecution for such a scribble," wrote Dr Stratford, tutor to Harley's son (December 21), "will make the Doctor Sacheverell and his performance much more considerable than either of them could have been on any other account."[1] As was well said at the time, "the Whigs took it into their minds to roast a parson, and they did roast him, but their zeal tempted them to make the fire so high that they scorched themselves."[2]

The second episode, though ranking much smaller in history, nevertheless cut deeply into the sequence of events. The mortifications for which Marlborough's secret information had prepared him began almost as soon as he came home. In January Lord Essex died, and the Lieutenancy of the Tower, together with the Oxford Regiment,[3] became vacant. Upon these, as on all other military appointments, it was the unvarying custom for the Captain-General

---

[1] Portland Papers, *H.M.C.*, iv, 530.
[2] Burnet, *History of His Own Time* (1833), v, 443.
[3] Now the 4th Hussars.

to advise the Queen. Marlborough, having in his mind the interest of the Ministry in conciliating Somerset, planned to give the Tower to the Duke of Northumberland, and the regiment to Somerset's son, Lord Hertford. Whether apprised of this or not, the Queen's backstair advisers thought otherwise. Their candidate for the Tower was Lord Rivers. They would find in his appointment a means of displaying their power to reward new adherents. Rivers waited on Marlborough and asked for his recommendation. Marlborough replied affably that the office was not one of sufficient importance for him, and that he hoped to serve him better on a future occasion. Rivers then asked permission to plead his own suit to the Queen. Marlborough, assuming naturally that no appointment would be made without his advice first being sought, and resolved to advise against Rivers, consented. But when almost immediately afterwards he had an audience and submitted Northumberland's name, the Queen answered forthwith, "Your Grace has come too late, for I have already granted the Lieutenancy to Lord Rivers, who has assured me that you had no objection to him."[1] Marlborough saw at once that he had been tricked. He protested, but the Queen declined to recede from her promise to Rivers. That same day the Queen sent him a written message desiring him to appoint to the vacant regiment no other person than Colonel Hill, Mrs Masham's brother.

It was obvious that an insult of the most carefully studied character was intended by the Queen's secret advisers. But the issue ran much deeper than this. In an army in which the leading officers were regarded as the champions of two fiercely struggling parties, whose exploits were cheered or disparaged according to their political colour, it was utterly impossible to maintain discipline or safely to conduct operations except upon the basis of all these men knowing that in their military fortunes the Commander-in-Chief was supreme. It was bad enough that the prowess of the Tory or even Jacobite Webb should be vaunted against the services of the Whig Cadogan in the House of Commons. But these unseemly proceedings could not be extended to the British Army in the field without destroying its efficiency. There was already much talk of Mrs Masham's growing influence, and of Sarah's loss of favour. "The dispute was not between the Queen and my lord Duke, as some will have it, but whether Mrs Masham and her party should have a disposal of all the vacancies in the army, and, by degrees, of everything

---

[1] Coxe, v, 126.

else."[1] The appointment of Mrs Masham's brother to a regiment over the heads of many more competent and experienced colonels was nothing less than a signal to the Army that Marlborough no longer possessed the confidence of the Queen, on which his authority over the British forces stood. The evil of such a demonstration would swiftly extend to the Allies, spreading doubt and discouragement as it travelled. Already the enemy were watching with eager eyes for every sign that the power of their antagonist was waning. The proposed appointment of Abigail's brother to a regiment might well be fatal to the campaign for which the largest armies yet seen were soon to assemble.

Marlborough therefore refused point-blank. He informed his Whig colleagues of his inflexible resolve, and they promised to stand by him. Sunderland, perhaps because he already had a sense of a threat to himself, was especially vigorous. Somers offered either to go with the Captain-General to the Queen or to make a separate intercession. Thus sustained, Marlborough sought a second audience. He pleaded his case with his usual skill and force. He warned the Queen that, apart from the military impropriety of appointing so young an officer on favour over the heads of others with better claims, the event would in the circumstances "set up a standard of disaffection to rally all the malcontent officers in the army." He appealed to the Queen that after all his services he should not be treated thus. Anne remained obdurate. She did not show the slightest sign of sympathy, still less of yielding. Coldly and harshly she ended the discussion with the words, "You will do well to advise with your friends." "He could not draw one kind expression from her."[2] Marlborough left her presence in extreme distress. The peering courtiers in the antechamber noticed that that serenity which neither the heat of battle nor the endless vexations of business had ever disturbed had for the moment deserted him.

He now took a firm decision that the Queen must either dismiss Abigail or himself. On this he invited the Whigs and Godolphin to rally. There is little doubt that he measured the situation rightly. Unless they all stood together and drove Abigail out, their destruction by the intrigues of which the Queen was at once the head and the tool was certain. What better ground could be chosen for Parliament with its Whig majority in both Houses, for the nation at large,

---

[1] *Morrison Papers* (Second Series), ii, 81; quoted in W. T. Morgan, *English Political Parties* (1703–10), p. 380.
[2] *Account of the Conduct of the Duchess of Marlborough*, p. 272.

and for Europe, than this contrast between the illustrious Commander at the head of the Grand Alliance and the spiteful ingrate of the bedchamber? Marlborough's military eye recognized this as an occasion, which might never return, for "venturing all" as on a day of battle. He therefore, without the ceremony of leave-taking, left London and drove down with Sarah to Windsor Lodge on January 14. But the Whigs failed him; and so, from the best of motives, did Godolphin. The Junto, so pertinacious and united in forcing their way into office, were divided and irresolute upon the method of holding their positions. Godolphin laboured for a compromise behind the scenes. Neither he nor Somers attended the meeting of Ministers which Marlborough had arranged. Somers preferred to remonstrate with the Queen himself. Sunderland alone was vehement for action. These divergencies paralysed the Ministers. When the Cabinet met next day Marlborough's place was empty. We have seen what had happened two years before when he and Godolphin had absented themselves in order to force Harley's resignation; but now events ran differently. No Minister interrupted the business to draw attention to the General's absence. They looked at each other and at the Queen, and said no word. The business proceeded mechanically, and the Council separated as if nothing unusual had happened. By this neglect to take united action, as much as by their foolish prosecution of Sacheverell, not only the Whigs but Godolphin settled their own speedy downfall.

Alone at Windsor Lodge with Sarah, Marlborough penned his ultimatum to the Queen. His first resolve and his best was to end the letter with the words, "I hope that your Majesty will either dismiss Mrs Masham or myself." He sent this draft to Godolphin with injunctions to show it to the Whigs, rally them to it, and present it to the Queen. All the Ministers except Sunderland seem to have lost their nerve. Godolphin was obsessed with the feeling that his sole duty to his friend and to the nation was to patch up the quarrel. He therefore damped and divided the meetings of Ministers, which were held at Devonshire House. He absented himself and persuaded others not to attend. Meanwhile, as he did not himself dare broach the matter, he implored Somers to expostulate with the Queen. Somers has left a full account of what he said, or wished to have said, to the Queen. His eloquence loses nothing in the record. "And may I," said he, "take the liberty to observe that the Duke of Marlborough is not to be considered merely as a private subject, because all the eyes of Europe are fixed upon him, and business is transacted with him under the notion of one who is honoured with your Majesty's entire trust and favour; and as men depend on all which he does? The army also unanimously obeys him, because the soldiers look up to him for advancement."[1] Anne listened coldly. She made a few perfunctory remarks about her regard for Marlborough and his great services, but for the rest she maintained an adverse reserve.

An agitated correspondence now ensued. Godolphin's letters betray his distress. "I am in so great a hurry," he wrote to Marlborough (January 16), "and my thoughts so much distracted with the confusion I see coming upon everything, and everybody equally, that I have neither had time to write nor a mind enough composed to write with any sort of coherence."[2] It is only rarely we find Sarah's letters preserved. In this episode her correspondence with Maynwaring, her secretary, shows her clear-cut view.

Sarah to Maynwaring

January 1710

The Queen gives no answer to Godolphin's representations; she says she will send for Somers. . . . I conclude you will wonder with me why these lords . . . should think it reasonable for Lord Marlborough to come. I am sure if he does I shall wish he had never proceeded in this manner, but have gone to council in a cold, formal way, never to the Queen alone, and declared to all the world how he was used, and that he served till the war was ended only because he did not think it reasonable to let a chambermaid disappoint all he had done.[3]

She sought to enlist the Whigs wholeheartedly in her husband's support by holding out the hope that he would range himself definitely with their party.

Thursday morning, January 19

. . . If this business can be well ended, which I much doubt, there must always be an entire union, as I have ever wished, between Lord Marlborough and the Whigs; but he will not say so much as he thinks upon that subject at this time, because I believe he imagines it would have an ill air, and look like making a bargain for help; and I am of that mind too. But if this matter were settled, interest as well as inclination would make them friends as long as they lived.[4]

Meanwhile the news that Marlborough had left town caused a stir in Parliament. Sunderland and some of Marlborough's partisans

[1] Coxe, v. 131. [2] *Ibid.*, 135. [3] *Sarah Correspondence*, i, 289. [4] Coxe, v, 134.

began to talk of an address to the Crown praying for the dismissal of Mrs Masham by name. Marlborough never lent himself to this; he was ready to put the issue to Anne personally and, if possible, in the name of his colleagues, but he certainly never contemplated or countenanced the harsh measure of a Parliamentary demand. Even Sarah, usually so downright, drew the line at this. Nevertheless it was the only movement of any effect which was contemplated. If it had been encouraged by the force of a united Cabinet it might have been successful. The reactions in Parliament were impossible to forecast. The point, though vital to a Commander-in-Chief, was a narrow one, and acquired its sharpness from personal stresses only vaguely known to Parliament. However, the mere rumour that such rough action was being discussed filled the Queen with lively alarm, and we may be sure that Harley liked the prospect as little. If the brunt fell upon Abigail, if Abigail were driven from the Queen's ear, the whole political deployment now prospering so well would be ruptured. Abigail was the vital link. It was not thought wise to expose her to what might at this stage be a shattering blow. From the moment that Queen Anne heard these ugly tales her temper altered. She sent again for Somers. "I do assure you that I feel for his Grace as much kindness as ever; yet I am much surprised at the great offence which is taken at my recommendation, and when Lord Marlborough comes to town, I will endeavour to convince him that my friendship for him is as entire as he can desire."[1]

All his colleagues now begged Marlborough to come back to London. This he steadily refused to do. He was disconcerted by the evident lack of support which the Whigs would give him. At the same time he would not, for the reason Sarah mentioned, join himself definitely to their party. He, however, yielded to the adverse currents and ebbing tide so far as to excise from his letter the decisive sentence which said, in effect, "Either dismiss Masham or me." The letter now went forward to the Queen in a modified form.

Marlborough to the Queen

MADAM,

By what I hear from London I find your Majesty is pleased to think that you are of the opinion that you are in the right in giving Mr Hill the Earl of Essex's regiment. I beg your Majesty will be so just to me as not to think that I can be so unreasonable as to be mortified to the degree that I am, if it did proceed only from this one thing.

[1] Coxe, v, 134.

It must be a prejudice to your service, while I have the honour to command the army, to have men preferred by my professed enemies to the prejudice of general officers of great merit and long service. But this is only one of a great many mortifications that I have met with, and as I may not have many opportunities of writing to you, let me beg your Majesty to reflect what your own people and the rest of the world must think who have been witnesses of the love and zeal and duty with which I have served you when they shall see, after all I have done, it is not able to protect me against the malice of a bed-chamber woman.[1]

On January 20, before this reached her, Anne summoned Godolphin and declared, "After deep consideration of Lord Somers's suggestion I am resolved not to insist on the appointment of Colonel Hill to the regiment. Inform the Duke of Marlborough that I will tell him myself if I see him soon, as I hope I shall." Godolphin replied, "I wish that your Majesty had communicated this to the Duke of Marlborough at an earlier period, as he would then doubtless have been satisfied; but as I am afraid that at present it will not have such good effect, I must request your Majesty to write to him yourself." The Queen only said, "I will tell it to him myself when I see him."[2]

Marlborough's letter now arrived. Its severe and challenging tone, joined to his prolonged absence from the Court, made an impression upon the Queen. She and those behind her saw that, merely by remaining in the Ranger's Lodge for a few days longer, he could create a Parliamentary situation out of which might emerge a direct public attack on Masham. The Queen, therefore, sent again for Godolphin. She showed him the letter. He said, "It is a very good letter." "Do you think," said the Queen, "the conclusion of it is good?" "It shows," said the Treasurer, "that he is very much mortified, and I hope your Majesty intends to answer it." The Queen said, "Yes, but should I not wait for an answer to the message which I sent by you?" "With humble submission," replied Godolphin, "I think not." After a pause the Queen closed the conversation by saying, "I will write to the Duke and send the letter to you to-night." But she did not write. Marlborough, convinced that this was a fatal turning-point, and also that his foes behind the Queen were no longer sure of their ground, was still obdurate. It was no longer a question of a regiment for Hill. Masham must go.

But now, armed with the Queen's surrender upon the immediate

---

[1] *Conduct*, p. 275.   [2] Coxe, v, 143.

issue, Godolphin and almost all his colleagues insisted upon Marlborough's return. Plainly he had gained a victory, and certainly they could argue that his position with the Army was entirely safeguarded. It would be long, they supposed, before such an attempt to undermine his authority as Captain-General would be renewed. Marlborough and Sarah saw clearly that this was no longer the crux. Anne, once again forced to submit to Ministerial control, would be only the more resolved to break it. He might have carried the incidental point, but Harley's opportunities of mischief were endless so long as Abigail had the Queen in her empoisoned hands.

We must not underrate an ordeal in which women are concerned, when one of the women is a Queen whom every one reveres, when one great party stands ready to exploit the situation, when two-fifths of either party would rally to the cry, "No bullying of the Queen. Is she not even able to nominate a colonel to one of her regiments? Is all jobbery to be reserved for the favourites? Besides, has she not already given way?" We can easily see across the centuries the undercurrents which terrified the Whigs and Godolphin, and led them all to caress and coerce Marlborough into acquiescence. Against his truest instincts and the plain facts he yielded to the intercession of his friends, and thus exposed himself and them to the inveteracy of their foes. Never did the chance return of taking Abigail by the scruff and Harley by the throat.

So all was settled to the general acceptance. Marlborough returned to London, and on Tuesday, the 23rd, was received by the Queen with more smiles and favour than he had known since Ramillies. The Whigs purred to one another in short-sighted relief. Godolphin felt that he had averted a catastrophe. Harley comfortably cast up the balance of gains and losses. Marlborough knew that he and his policy were doomed. He and all he stood for were henceforward only prey to time and occasion.

There now arose a general wish that the Duke should cross the seas for The Hague and to the Army. Some said it was a manœuvre of Harley's to get him out of the way before the Sacheverell trial began. But there is solid proof that Parliament was deeply concerned both about the peace negotiations and the approaching campaign. The Dutch were known to be calling for him with insistence. Partly in the desire to enhance his authority, partly to free him from the political brawl which was now imminent, his best friends agreed with his worst foes that he should be gone. An address was carried to the Queen by the Whigs praying that Marlborough should be sent forthwith to supervise the peace negotiations. "We cannot fail," declared the Commons, "to make use of this opportunity to express our sense of the great and unparalleled services of the Duke of Marlborough and to applaud your Majesty's great wisdom in having honoured the same person with the great characters of general and plenipotentiary, who, in our humble opinion, is most capable of discharging two such important trusts."[1]

According to Hoffmann, these terms were used in order to uphold the prestige of Marlborough on the Continent after all the recent bickerings, the rumours of which had been greedily lapped up abroad. The Duke himself must indeed have been glad to quit the darkening scene in London. Instead of having to grind and squeeze his honoured royal mistress amid the deceits, intrigues, and brutalities of party warfare, he could become again Prince, General, Plenipotentiary, with the magnates of Europe waiting upon his action, and brave armies impatient for his presence. When before sailing he was asked who the plenipotentiaries would be, he replied gaily and grimly, "I think there are about a hundred thousand of us." But his real battleground was in England. It was at Westminster and in Whitehall that the fate of the war now lay. The Queen had replied coldly to the Commons' address. She had refused the laudatory draft which Godolphin had laid before her. She preferred terms which followed as closely as possible the rejected Tory amendment. "I am so sensible of the necessity of the Duke of Marlborough's presence in Holland, at this critical juncture, that I have already given the necessary directions for his immediate departure; and I am very glad to find that you concur with me in a just sense of the Duke of Marlborough's eminent services."[2]

The coast was now clear for Harley and Abigail, and the impeachment of Dr Sacheverell was about to begin.

[1] *Parliamentary History of England*, vi, 892.   [2] *Ibid.*, 894.

Chapter Thirteen

SACHEVERELL AND SHREWSBURY

1710—SPRING

SACHEVERELL'S trial began in February. A battle royal on party principles was now joined. At the root lay the question, was the Monarchy founded in divine right or upon a Parliamentary title? Both sides had to face complications. Sacheverell had preached the doctrine of non-resistance to royal authority "in the highest strain."[1] This led him into a tangle; for he and all the Tories who were not Jacobites or Non-jurors had solemnly accepted the Revolution, and without it the Queen, from whom the Tories hoped so much, would not possess the Crown. Therefore he had to argue that 'resistance' had played no part in the driving out of one King and the setting up of another. James II had gone of his free will, and William III had come with no design of conquest. Had it been otherwise, he asserted, the Revolution would have been black and odious. Thus non-resistance, puffed so high in theory, appeared in practice to produce results with which the most ardent revolutionary might be content. But if this absurd hypothesis failed, as fail it must, then nothing stood between the Revolution and all Dr Sacheverell's offensive censures. The preacher had used this subterfuge to indict the Revolution without apparently repudiating it.

The Whig managers of the impeachment for their part were bound to challenge the Tory doctrine of non-resistance in the most strenuous fashion. They declared that resistance ratified by Parliament had brought Henry IV, Henry VII, William III, and Queen Anne herself to the Throne. But then they must remember that their leaders were the Queen's Ministers, and that neither Queen Anne nor any other sovereign could relish open-mouthed championship of the right of subjects to rebel. They were the more anxious to extol the strength of the Queen's Parliamentary title; and as the case proceeded they were drawn into a series of admissions about the birth of the Prince of Wales which struck at the

[1] Burnet, v, 421.

671

whole popular foundation of the Whig case. They boldly declared that but for the Act of Parliament, not the Queen, but her brother would reign. In right of blood his claim, they affirmed, was just. Where, then, was the famous warming-pan, still worn on political fête-days in farthing miniature, and where all the laboured significance of the word *prætensus*? The warming-pan was brazenly discarded as a lie that had served its purpose. Polite society had for some time ceased to believe it; but for the Whigs to proclaim their own work of falsehood to the nation was a grave imprudence. The Tories also were distressed. They had salved their consciences in acting with the Whigs in the Revolution with doubts and aspersions on the legitimacy of the Pretender. These serviceable fictions alone reconciled for both parties the hereditary and Parliamentary rights of Queen Anne. Now they were swept away, and by the very party which had triumphed through exploiting them! The effect in the constituencies was deeply harmful to Whig interests. They could be taunted as self-confessed liars. Moreover, the Succession settlement was weakened by the avowal that the rightful King was for ever to be excluded because of the misdeeds of his father.

Lastly, the effect upon Anne was adverse to the Whigs. Henceforward she accepted the fact that her brother was legitimate. All the more, therefore, did she rest herself upon the Church of England. All the more did she see in protecting that sacred structure alike from Popery and Dissent her sole spiritual claim to wear the Crown. All the more was she tempted to favour her brother's right to succeed her, and thus make final amends to the shade of her father at the expense of her bugbear, the Elector of Hanover. In the autumn of 1710 she would ask that the expression in an address from the City of London "that her right was Divine" might be omitted "as she could by no means like it."[1] But at the same time she clung with even greater devotion to the Church as her comforter under the pricks of conscience, and to the Tories as her shield against republican principles. However, the Queen preserved strict neutrality in public. "I was with my aunt [the Queen]," wrote Abigail to Harley (February), "last night on purpose to speak to her about Dr S[ache-vere]ll and asked her if she did not let people know her mind in the matter. She said no she did not meddle one way or other, and that it was her friends' advice not to meddle."[2]

Behind all the intriguing doctrinal issues, from which our ancestors derived so much refined mental occupation, lay the broad dis-

[1] Bath Papers, *H.M.C.*, i, 199. [2] Portland Papers, *H.M.C.*, iv, 532.

contents of the people. The war pressed heavily upon the masses. The harvest of 1709 had been bad; the price of bread was almost doubled;[1] the taxes on the countryside were heavy. The press-gang was hot for the fleets, and under veiled forms compulsion chiefly recruited the armies. The distresses of the poor had been aggravated by the arrival of twelve thousand refugees from the ravaged Palatinate, to whom much charity already needed at home was directed. Alien immigration, it was said, deprived the poor of their meagre relief. Hatred of the unhappy foreigners rose in the streets. The London populace was against the Government. All grievances were ruthlessly exploited and inflamed by the resources of a great party. The long-drawn-out impeachment of Sacheverell made him the focus of nation-wide opinion, and the symbol of all that was hostile to the Whig Administration. Events and mismanagement tended to prolong the proceedings. Instead of a hearing at the bar of the House of Lords, it was resolved to fit Westminster Hall for a ceremony of the utmost formality. This required weeks of work from carpenters. The planning of the 'scaffolds' was entrusted to Sir Christopher Wren. The Queen had a special box built for herself. She refused vigorously to allow a gallery to be constructed above it. "She would have no one over her head," so the saying ran.[2]

From the earliest stages of the trial Sacheverell's popularity with the crowd became obvious. Admitted to bail, he made a daily progress to Westminster escorted by enthusiastic throngs. The poorer people pressed to touch his hands or garments. When the Queen's sedan chair threaded its way through the multitude her subjects beset her with loyal shouts and cries of "We hope your Majesty is for the Doctor." Inside the Hall Sacheverell's unctuous eloquence drew tears of partisan piety from Tory ladies, while the Whig beauties soon found the legal arguments tedious. Rioting broke out in the streets. The pews of Dissenting chapels were made into bonfires. Bishop Burnet saw one man cleave another's head with a spade upon the learned issue. Threats to sack the palaces of the Whig nobles were freely uttered.

"This uneasy trial of Sacheverell," wrote Godolphin to Marlborough (March 5), "does not only take up all my time, but very

1   PRICE OF WHEAT (PER QUARTER)

| 1706, 23s. 9d. | 1708, 37s. 11d. | 1710, 71s. 6d. | 1712, 42s. 5d. | 1714, 46s. |
| 1707, 26s. | 1709, 71s. 11d. | 1711, 49s. 6d. | 1713, 46s. 9d. | |

[Ernle, *English Farming, Past and Present*, p. 440.]

2 *Wentworth Papers*, p. 111.

much impairs my health, and how it will end I am not at all certain. But I certainly wish it had never begun."[1] And (March 17) "The Duke of Somerset labours hard against us."[2] "I believe," wrote John to Sarah (March 13/24), "the behaviour of the Duke of Somerset, the Duke of Argyll, and Lord Rivers, are true signs of the Queen's being of their mind, which must inevitably bring a great deal of trouble to her. I do, with all my heart, wish I had not recommended the Duke of Argyll, but that can't now be helped; nothing is good but taking measures not to be in the power of ungrateful people." And the next day: "I can't think it possible that the duke of Somerset will give his vote or opinion for the clearing of Sacheverell; if he does, there is nothing he would not sacrifice to have power: his behaviour in this matter will be a true weathercock of the Queen."[3] On March 23 Dr Sacheverell was found guilty by sixty-nine to fifty-two, a majority of seventeen votes. A motion to incapacitate him from preferment in the Church for three years was lost by one. "So all this bustle and fatigue," exclaimed Godolphin, "ends in no more but a suspension of three years from the pulpit, and burning his sermon at the Old Exchange."[4]

The Sacheverell trial was a Whig disaster of the first magnitude. Beyond all doubt it turned the scale. They had hoped by a careful restatement of party fundamentals to rally all moderates and waverers, particularly in the Lords. The division lists on the impeachment showed only too plainly their miscalculation. Sacheverell was now the hero of the day. A lucrative living was bestowed on him by a Tory admirer. His journeys through the country were a triumphal progress. He was welcomed by thousands of ardent Churchmen at every town, and often also greeted by mobs who hailed the mixture of religion and politics for which he stood by riotous demonstrations against the Government.

It was at this inauspicious moment that Sarah came into final collision with the Queen. Feeling that her personal relations had become impossible, she had in February induced her husband to ask the Queen, first, to allow her to remain as much as possible in the country, and, secondly, that at the conclusion of peace she might resign her offices in favour of her two daughters, Lady Rialton and Lady Sunderland. Sarah affirmed that Anne had promised her this reversion upon a former occasion. The Queen, who was bidding farewell to her General starting for the wars, readily agreed to the first, but upon the second contented herself with saying that she hoped

[1] Coxe, v, 154. [2] Ibid., 15 [3] Ibid., 157 et seq. [4] Ibid., 156.

the Duchess would not leave her service. When later on, however, Sarah pressed for more precise assurances and mentioned a promise, the Queen said first, "I do not remember that I was ever spoke to about it." On being further pressed she ended the discussion by saying impatiently, "I desire that I may never be troubled any more on the subject."

Sarah, when she had returned fuming to the country, commented at table freely upon public affairs, and was by no means careful what she said about the Queen. It was a definite part of the Harley-Abigail campaign against her to report to Anne anything likely to make ill-will, and it is certain that their tales lost nothing in the telling. At the Court Sarah was accused of uttering atrocious sentiments and calumnies against her mistress. Indignant, she demanded an audience to clear herself. The Queen did her best to avoid seeing her. She found three separate hours unsuitable, named a fourth, and cancelled the appointment on the grounds that she was going to Kensington. Sarah followed her there, and asked the page of the backstairs to tell the Queen she begged to be received. Then she sat down, according to her account, in the window, "like a ·Scotch lady with a petition, instead of a trusted and lifelong confidant."[1] After a long interval she was admitted.

All accounts of what followed are based upon Sarah's narrative in her *Conduct of the Duchess of Marlborough*, which she published in 1742.[2] The Queen began by saying, "I was just about to write to you." As Sarah tried to unfold her case Anne said, "Whatever you have to say, you may put it in writing." She repeated this interruption four or five times. Sarah protested that she only wished to clear herself from false aspersions. The Queen turned away her face from her. Sarah declared that there were those about the Queen who had made her believe that she had said things of her which she was no more capable of saying than of killing her own children, and "that I seldom named her Majesty in company, and never without respect." To this the Queen observed generally, "Without doubt there are many lies told."

Sarah then pressed to know what exactly it was that she was alleged to have said. The Queen used the second formula which her advisers had no doubt suggested. Sarah in her letter asking for the audience had written, "What I have to say in my own vindication will have no consequence in obliging her Majesty to answer."

[1] Blenheim MSS., quoted in S. J. Reid, *John and Sarah, Duke and Duchess of Marlborough*, p. 322.   [2] *Conduct*, p. 279.

Fastening upon this, the Queen repeated again and again, "You desired no answer and shall have none." To all protestations and entreaties she made this unchanging reply. At length she moved towards the door. On this, in Sarah's words, "when she came to the door I fell down in great disorder. Streams of tears flowed down against my will and prevented me speaking for some time." There may have been a moment when Anne relented, for she certainly stayed and listened further. But presently, recovering herself, she repeated again and again her parrot sentence, "You desired no answer, and you shall have none." At last Sarah could endure it no longer. "I am confident your Majesty will suffer for such an instance of inhumanity." "That will be to myself," said the Queen. These were the last words ever interchanged between the two women. They never saw each other again.

"After I had come out from the Queen," says Sarah, "I sat me down in the long gallery to wipe my eyes, before I came within sight of anybody."[1] She recovered her spirits before her temper: Gaultier reported that she "left the palace like a fury."[2]

Throughout the spring and summer an outpouring of addresses, organized by the Opposition, and expressing Tory sentiments and fervent loyalty, flowed to the Queen from all parts of England. Anne was delighted with these manifestations. She frequently received the deputations in person and made no secret of her sympathies. Even Lockhart, the leader of the Scottish Jacobites in the Commons, was welcomed by her. "Her Majesty," he writes,

> seem'd very well pleased, gave a gracious return to the address, and then told me, tho I had almost allways opposed her measures, she did not doubt of my affection to her person, *and hop'd I wou'd not concurr in the design against Mrs Masham or for bringing over the Prince of Hannover.* At first I was somewhat surprized, but recovering my self, I assur'd her, I shou'd never be accessary to the imposing any hardship or affront upon her.[3]

Shrewsbury had hitherto been a frequent visitor to the buildings at Blenheim. He lived but a few miles away at Heythrop. Lately his visits had ceased; and Sarah could only guess whether this was due to general politics or to her incautious disparagements of the Italian Duchess. While the Sacheverell trial hung in the balance, and

[1] Blenheim MSS., quoted in S. J. Reid, p. 327.
[2] F. Salomon, *Geschichte des letzten Ministerium Königin Annes*, p. 24.
[3] *Lockhart Papers* (1817), i, 317.

when popular opinion ran strongly against the Government, it had
been a matter of widespread curiosity which way the Duke of Shrewsbury would vote. He voted for acquittal. No one could reproach
him for this. He was a free man. His vote on the merits was right
and in harmony with the public mood, but the fact that one of King
William's most renowned Ministers walked through the lobby of
the House of Lords against Sacheverell's impeachment showed
many people that the impeachment was as wrong as every one now
saw it had been impolitic.

What set London agog was not Shrewsbury's vote against the
Government, but its sequel. On the afternoon of April 14 Anne
sent for the Marquis of Kent and deprived him of his office of Lord
Chamberlain. He could be consoled with a dukedom. The next
morning Shrewsbury, within seven weeks of his hostile vote on the
key issue of Sacheverell, was appointed in his stead. In this period
the Lord Chamberlain, with his constant access to the Sovereign
and his immense social and ceremonial power in the Court, was an
officer of State almost as high as the Lord Chancellor. That such an
office should be in hands independent of the Ministry and of the
harassed Treasurer and First Minister was a political change of the
first order. The Queen, sustained by her secret advisers, did not
even mention the matter to Godolphin beforehand. She wrote to
him (April 13) of her desire "to allay the heat and ferment that is
in this poor nation. Since you went to Newmarket," she continued,
"I have received several assurances from the Duke of Shrewsbury
of his readiness to serve me upon all occasions, . . . which offer I
was very willing to accept of, having a very good opinion of him,
and believing he may be of great use in these troublesome times. . . .
I hope that this change will meet with your approbation, which I
wish I may have in all my actions."[1]

The Treasurer on this wrote to the Queen in the most vehement
terms:

> Your Majesty is suffering yourself to be guided to your own Ruin
> and Destruction, as fast as it is possible for them to compass it, to
> whom you seem so much to hearken. . . . There is no Man [he said
> of Shrewsbury] of whose Capacity I have had a better Impression; nor
> with whom I have lived more easily and freely for above twenty Years.
> . . . [And] to bring him into your Service and into your Business at
> this Time, just after his being in a publick open Conjunction in every
> Vote with the whole Body of the Tories, and in a private, constant

[1] Coxe, v, 215–216.

Correspondence and Caballing with Mr Harley in every Thing, what Consequence can this possibly have, but to make every Man that is now in your Cabinet Council, except [the Duke of Somerset] to run from it as they would from the Plague.

He concluded with "two humble requests":

The one, that you will allow me to pass the Remainder of my Life always out of London, where I may find most ease and Quiet. The other, that you would keep this Letter and read it again about next Christmas, and then be pleased to make your own Judgment, who hath given you the best and most faithful advice.[1]

But how could Godolphin resign? Was not Shrewsbury exactly the element with which he and Marlborough had wished to strengthen the Government? Was he not a national statesman who would keep the Queen high above the "merciless men" of both parties? Had not Marlborough himself half a year earlier wished for such a development? The doctrine that the Sovereign acts only on advice of Ministers responsible to Parliament was in its infancy. How could Godolphin boggle at a lapse in procedure, however unpleasant, however menacing? The first conclusion of the Junto, particularly of Sunderland, was that Shrewsbury's appointment was a stroke by Marlborough and Godolphin to reconstruct the Ministry at their expense. This opinion seems to have been widely held outside ministerial circles.[2] The Junto were therefore suspicious and dumb.

When Godolphin reached London on the 16th it was the Queen who was the first with reproaches. "He had shown," she remarked, "more uneasiness in the new appointment than any of his colleagues." When the Queen assured him that she intended no further changes Godolphin's rejoinder was laconic: "The reports of the town run high on that subject." His dismissal from the royal presence was cold and formal. When he met Somers and Sunderland he found them alive with distrust. His agitated manner and downcast mood convinced them that his fortunes were not divorced from theirs. There remained an even greater fear—the dissolution of Parliament. This now became the dominant factor. After Sacheverell the Whigs did not dare to face the country. They had forced themselves upon the Queen in the name of Parliament and the electors. They were now unsure of the electors; and they knew the Queen could soon get rid of the Parliament, already in its second

[1] *Conduct*, p. 291.   [2] Maffei's letter of May 23 to Marlborough; Coxe, v, 221.

year. There was nothing for it but to make the best of Shrewsbury and hope to conciliate him. "I have seen Lord Somers and Lord Sunderland to-day," wrote Godolphin to Sarah.[1] "Both appear to me to be mortified as much as myself, but thinking it reasonable enough to dissemble."

Moreover, Shrewsbury was profuse in his expressions of friendship for the Lord Treasurer and of admiration for the General in the field. He wrote in the most ceremonious style to Marlborough. In a soothing interview he half persuaded Godolphin that he meant to work with him. Godolphin, therefore, submitted to what was none the less a royal affront to his office and status and a searing mark of his loss of credit with the Queen. "I have seen the Duke of Shrewsbury," he wrote (April 17). "I find most people are of opinion that he will like very well to live easily with us, and I am not unapt to think so too. But I think 'tis very plain that he comes in by Mr Harley."[2] And on April 20: "The Lord Chamberlain was extremely full of professions to you, to me, and to Lady Marlborough; and that by whatever door he came in, it was always with an intention and a desire to live well with us three. I answered with compliments from you and me. . . . His Grace protested most solemnly to me that he never had spoken one word to Abigail in his life."[3]

Marlborough, banging away at Douai with the daily chance of a decisive battle upon his hands, had no doubts about what the new appointment meant. Shrewsbury had been brought into the Government not as *his* man, but Harley's. He foresaw from the instant the truth, which was the worst. "I am very much surprised," he wrote to Godolphin (May 5), "at the courage of the Duke of Shrewsbury to come so freely into the storm: I think you and I may see very plainly by neither the Queen's nor his ever taking notice of it to us, that they have another scheme than what would be approved of by us."[4] And to Sarah: "If I know anything of the temper of the Queen, she would not have made this step, but that they are ready to go into all the extravagances imaginable. The chiefest care now should be, that the Parliament be preserved; for if that cannot be obtained, which I very much doubt, nothing will be worth the managing. Of all things, the Whigs must be sure to be of one mind, and then all things, sooner or later, must come right."[5]

Shrewsbury lavished reassurances upon Marlborough. After all,

[1] Coxe, v, 219.   [2] *Ibid.*, 223.   [3] *Ibid.*, 224.   [4] *Ibid.*, 225.   [5] *Ibid.*, 226.

they had much in common in the past. Both at the peril of their lives had been in correspondence with King William. Each had played an historic part in driving out Popery and King James. Both had in remorse or reinsurance kept alive under the shadow of treason their correspondence with the exiles at Saint-Germains. Both had faced a mortal danger at the time of the Fenwick trial. Marlborough had borne the strain imperturbably. Shrewsbury had crumpled beneath it. In his nervous depression he had abandoned public office. Marlborough had marched on through dark years to world glory. The pair had everything in common, except that they were to sit in the same Cabinet in opposite interests. But even this glaring fact, which Marlborough discerned so plainly, was veiled by ceremony and soothing protestation. At no moment was any issue presented upon which Marlborough could make a stand either to the Queen or to the new Lord Chamberlain. All had to be passed off with bows and compliments.

Chapter Fourteen

THE NINTH CAMPAIGN

1710—MARCH—SEPTEMBER

ONCE again the great armies assembled, and now more numerous than ever. Although the plans of the Allies contemplated converging inroads upon France from the Rhine, from Dauphiné, and upon the coast, all gravitated irresistibly to the main theatre. Apart from the separate, self-contained war in Spain, all the subsidiary operations languished. Marlborough's diminished authority was incapable of infusing vigour into them. The Elector of Hanover threw up the command of the Imperial forces on the Rhine on the ground that they were relegated to a minor rôle. Even with a superiority of three to one he had only gaped at his opportunities in 1709. Victor Amadeus of Savoy felt that this was a season for politics rather than for war; and M. de Seissan, a French refugee of some mark, who had undertaken to raise the Cevennes, never found himself provided with the means to undertake this task.

All lay in the north and among the fortresses. Here Marlborough and Eugene would war with Villars supported by four other marshals; and every scrap of force that could be gathered by the war-wearied combatants was hurried to their respective camps. The confederate army marshalled 155 battalions and 262 squadrons, with 102 cannon, 20 howitzers, and 40 pontoons.[1] France, rightly judging the impotency of the minor theatres, claimed to have available for Villars's command no fewer than 204 battalions, 308 squadrons, and a full proportion of artillery and pontoons. Villars's own statements of his strength vary. When making head against Marlborough and Eugene he boasted of a great superiority: in his memoirs he declares himself the weaker by 40,000. There is no doubt that the allied armies were far better equipped and supplied and thus stronger in war-power than their opponents, and all the movements of both sides were based upon this fact.

---

[1] Marlborough, 110 battalions and 161 squadrons; Eugene, 45 battalions and 101 squadrons.

European and English public opinion expected that the two great commanders, superior in skill and in the numbers at their command, would soon bring the war to an end; but the task was not so easy. The dangers and cost of assaulting bravely held entrenchments were rated at a new high level after Malplaquet. The campaign still lay in the second and third lines of the French fortress zone, with all the obstinacies and time-losses that must be encountered there. The problem of feeding and foraging their enormous armies in ruined, famine-stricken regions confronted these lords of thirty or forty thousand cavalry with rigorous limitations. Eighteenth-century warfare had reached its maximum and its culmination as a result of squandered opportunities both of victory and of peace, and of a will-power on both sides which was alike unreasoning and indomitable. Meanwhile at Gertruydenberg the diplomatists and plenipotentiaries, surrounded by a host of agents and busybodies, official and unofficial, manœuvred sedately around the clauses of the peace treaty, incapable as were the armies of reaching a decision.[1]

---

[1]   *Marlborough to Godolphin*   HAGUE
                                                    March 1st, 1710
★You will see by the enclosed intercept'd letter from Monsr Torcy that I shall not be able til the next post of giving the Queen any account of the Negotiations; these people continu resolv'd to have a Peace if it may be had for Sicilly and Sardagn [Sardinia], by which I think it is absolutely necessary for the Queens Service that the Parl: shou'd be setting, for shou'd it be refus'd or grant'd without the knowlidge of Parl: I fear it might cause very great uneasiness, but You on the place can best judge, which will be best to continu the setting or to make a short prorogation.

                                                            March 11
★. . . The Pensioners are expected back this night or to-morrow morning early to make their rapport. We know already that the French sent last night an express to their King. What I can observe of the Pensioner and others is that they seem resolved not to comply with France in such a peace as may leave the war in Spain. Though at the same time they tell me that there is an impossibility of continuing the war. However they are very desirous of doing all in their power for our taking the field early and I expect Cadogan and the undertakers for the forage and wagons to be here on Thursday so that I may give the necessary orders that nothing may be wanting, . . . for I think the only good step we can make towards a peace is to get early into the field. . . . Gromko [Grumbkow] has in great confidence given me a relation of the offers the King of France has made to his master. . . .

                                                            March 12
★I have just now come from the Pensioners when Monsieur Buys and Van Derdussen have made their rapport. . . . I think the French have it still in their power to amuse and cheat us. But if they should be in earnest to have a peace and that they will be contented with Cicilly for the Duke of Anjou you may assure the Queen that in my opinion every man in this State will be for it. And I am very much afraid that if the French will insist upon more they will even in that case find very many friends in this country. . . . I think it absolutely necessary that my Lord Townshend and I should have positive orders how far we may agree to any consideration for the Duke of

Two alternatives offered themselves to the Allies for the final penetration of the French fortress zone (see map, p. 685). The first, which no doubt Marlborough would have favoured because of the use he could make of British amphibious power, was near the coast, down the Lys by Saint-Venant and Aire, aiming at the creation of a new reinforcing base at Abbeville. This movement would turn the left and cut in behind the principal fortresses of the French barrier. It would also avoid the fortified line which Villars was preparing from La Bassée to Douai. A right-handed operation of this kind, however, though very agreeable to English interests and to the true strategy of a combination possessing the command of the sea, exposed the whole of Brabant to a northward thrust by strong French forces. The other choice was to punch at the French centre up the Scarpe to Douai and towards Arras, with further inclination towards Cambrai. Advance by this route was the most direct invasion of France. It covered Brabant and the Spanish Netherlands from French counter-strokes, and it threatened simultaneously five or six fortresses essential to the French defence, any of which might be attacked, all of which must be heavily garrisoned. Both routes led into unravaged regions where the advancing armies could feed

---

Anjou. . . . By what Count Sinzindorff says to me it is very plain that the Court of Vienna had much rather not have a peace with France than to allow any part of the Monarque of Spain to the Duke of Anjou.

March 14

★. . . My Lord Townshend and I had a conversation with the Pensioner last night where he owned to us very freely that he did not believe that France had sincere intentions of evacuating Spain. But if they could or would do it for Sicily, he looked upon it as a great happiness. He assured us that nobody but ourselves knew of his opinion on this particular; for till the French should make a positive declaration he thought it dangerous even for the knowledge of Vanderdussen and Buys.

March 19

★This morning the Pensioner brought me a letter he had received from the French ministers at Gerturenberg. . . . I think everybody is convinced that the chief design of France is to cause a division amongst the Allies; the Imperialists are very desirous of making a peace with France upon the conditions they offer of giving four cautionary towns in their country, and the States General are as positive in putting an end to the war at once by giving the Duke of Anjou a *partage*.

HAGUE
April 5, 1710

★I shall not trouble You with the reflections of these people on the occasion of Sacheverelle. Thay turn every thing to be a reason for Peace, which thay will have, if the ffrench be in earnest. Petkome return'd yesterday from Gertruydenberg. He thinkes ffrance is desirous of a seperatt Peace [*i.e.*, a peace made by all the Allies with France apart from Spain], provid'd we will be content'd with the four Cautionary towns, or that thay will evacuat Spain if the D. of Anjoue may have a reasonable Partage. These people are I believe unanimously resolv'd to give him Sicily and

themselves for many weeks. Both were sustained by good waterways. Marlborough controlled the Lys up to Armentières, and the
Scheldt to beyond Tournai. By either of these rivers he could draw
through Ghent the whole resources of the confederacy, and carry
forward supplies, siege-trains, and munitions with ease and sureness.
Upon the whole, the central punch, if successful, would lead into
better ground for the operation of all arms, and especially the
cavalry, then so dominant a factor. Thus the strategic choice was
evenly balanced; but the political needs of the Dutch to have the
main allied army between their regained territory and the enemy
was decisive. There is no evidence that Marlborough at this time
pressed seriously for the coastal movement. The councils of war
were guided by him and Eugene towards the French centre. This
meant the siege of Douai, followed if successful by that of Arras.
There was complete agreement upon this.

The French placed four armies in the field—in Roussillon under
Noailles, in Dauphiné under Berwick, on the Rhine under Harcourt,
and the great mass under Villars, when he was fit enough, in the
Netherlands. Owing to the stringency of food, forage, money, and
equipment, these armies were to stand everywhere on the defensive.

Sardain, but I believe the Pensioner thinkes the ffrench are not in earnest, which makes
him very uneasy, not knowing how to gett ride of these Plenepotentiarys. Comte
Senzindorf Ld Townshend and my self are to be att the Pensioners at four aclock where
Vanderdussen and Monsr Buys are to be. I believe it will be resolv'd that thay shou'd
this evening or to morrow morning return to Gertruydenberg, in order to endeavour
the knowing if the ffrench have any thing else to offer. I hope thay will speak so
plainly that att their return, we may on tuesday lett you know if these Negotiations
are to Continu; Pr: Eugene is expect'd here next tuesday.

John to Sarah

HAGUE
April 12, 1710

★I am sorry to see in all Yours the Condition things are in, in England, I am afraid
it maybe one of the things which incorages ffrance in the resolution thay seem to be
in of carrying on the Warr. I am to leave this place on Munday, in order to be at
the head of the Army the friday following which is above a month sooner than we
have ever taken the field since this Warr.

Marlborough to Godolphin

HAGUE
April 13, 1710

★You know that these people are so very fond of Peace, that when ever the ffrench
will be reasonable, we shall have it, *which in my opinion is as absolutely necessary for the
Queens service as for these people*. Pr. Eugene has said what he can to persude the impossibility of ending this War, but by a seperat Peace with ffrance [*i.e.*, leaving Spain
to be conquered afterwards]. We shall see in one month after we have been in the
field, not only the humour of the ffrench, but of these people also. The Imperiallist
Continu very obstinat, in never Consenting to any Partage.

[All the above letters are from Blenheim MSS.]

In the main theatre the winter was spent in strengthening the fortresses and collecting supplies. In March Berwick was offered the
command till Villars had recovered sufficiently. Berwick demanded
authority to assemble and forestall the impending attack. As this
was contrary to Louis XIV's general conception of a defensive
campaign, he was not encouraged, and proceeded, as originally

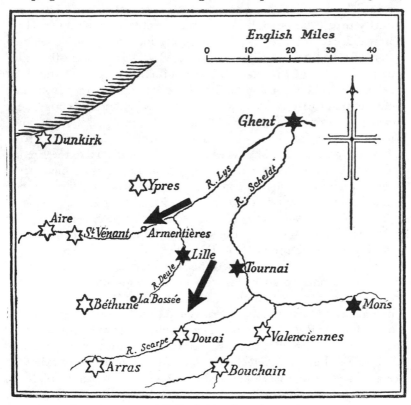

THE CHOICE IN 1710

proposed, to his command in Dauphiné. Marshal d'Artagnan, who
had succeeded to the title of Duc de Montesquiou by which he was
in future to be known, was therefore placed in charge of the preparatory phase. He reinforced La Bassée and Ypres, with some difficulty
persuaded Louis to let him use men and money to strengthen the
lines about La Bassée, and clamoured for everything needed for
war. Montesquiou as yet could only feed 40 battalions and 40
squadrons upon this front, and that for a short time.

Marlborough, arriving at The Hague, decided to take the field at the end of March. He ordered Albemarle, who had been in command of the British troops in Flanders during the winter, to seize Mortagne and Saint-Amand, on the Scheldt, so as to open the water communications for a siege of Douai. Albemarle captured Mortagne on April 14. It was retaken the next day by Luxembourg, and finally mastered by the Allies on April 18. Saint-Amand, surrounded by inundations, was not yet found assailable. This preliminary thrust did not relieve the uncertainties of the French High Command. It might equally well be a feint down the Scheldt to cover an eventual movement by the Lys. However, the confederate army began to assemble around Tournai, and in the third week of April Marlborough and Eugene arrived together from The Hague at that fortress. In spite of the late spring and the consequent shortage of forage, they had decided to begin operations at once without waiting for all their troops to arrive or for the grass to grow.

To besiege Douai it was necessary first of all to pierce the French defensive lines. Only half the allied army had yet assembled; sixty thousand men were still to come, but it was known that the French would be largely immobile for some weeks, and a great operation to pierce their lines was planned, albeit with incomplete forces.

The map opposite shows the situation in the middle of April.

"I hope to date my next on the other side of the lines,"[1] wrote Marlborough on the 20th, when the Allies advanced. The Duke of Würtemberg and Count Feltz, with 15 battalions and 50 squadrons, were sent ahead to the Deule. The army followed in four columns. The next day Würtemberg, accompanied by Cadogan, entered the French lines at Pont-à-Vendin. The defenders retired without fighting. Feltz failed at Pont-Auby, but Eugene, coming up in heavy force, crossed at Courrières and Saut, and the main army followed across these captured bridges and pressed on to the south of Lens, where it halted before the Vimy Ridge after a thirty-mile march, Montesquiou, who was evidently not expecting so early an attack and could not in any case command the means to resist it, was caught foraging, and retreated across the Scarpe at Vitry, breaking his bridges behind him. On the 22nd the advance continued. Montesquiou, now joined by Luxembourg, withdrew precipitately, his front ruptured and his forces overweighted. On this day the Allies followed him across the Scarpe at Vitry, and camped on the south bank. Eugene remained north of the Scarpe to invest Douai from that side. Thus in three days Marlborough had advanced forty

Coxe, v, 181.

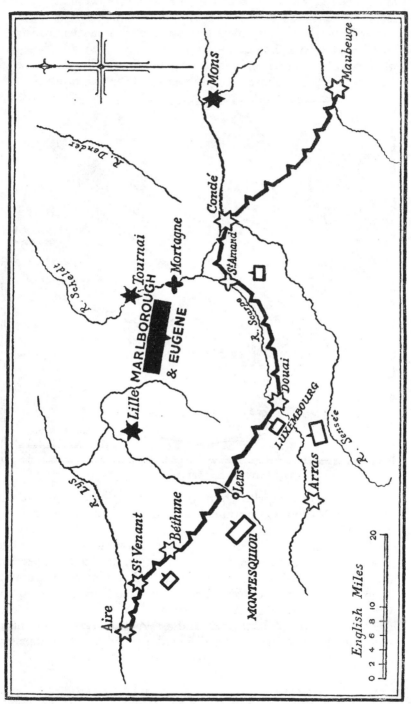

THE SITUATION IN APRIL 1710

miles, and had crossed the Deule and the Scarpe without fighting. Douai was already almost isolated. Montesquiou could not attempt to stand along the Sensée. All the water from this river had been diverted to fill the inundations around Douai, and the river-bed was passable almost everywhere. He therefore fell right back to Cambrai. Here the shortage of supplies and the loss of all his for-

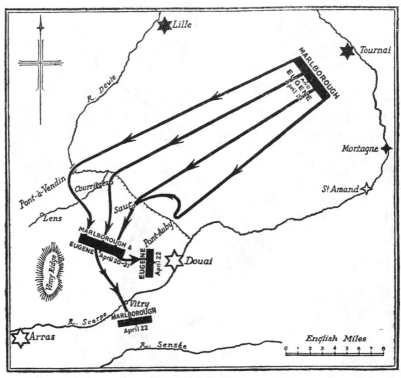

THE ADVANCE: APRIL 19–22, 1710

ward magazines compelled him to disperse the greater part of his army, and Marlborough could begin the siege of Douai in most favourable circumstances.

This masterly movement of extraordinary rapidity was made possible only by dry forage brought by water. It succeeded because it was launched before the enemy could feed on the ground enough troops to man their extensive lines. All these fortifications, upon which so much labour had been spent, proved perfectly useless. They were simply walked over, and a very great tract of country, which might well have been disputed for the whole campaign, passed at a stroke into Marlborough's possession. We are often told of the leisurely and ceremonious methods of eighteenth-century war. Here are movements of large armies as swift and sudden as any in military annals.

John to Sarah

LENS
April 21, 1710

In my last I had but just time to tell you that we had passed the lines. I hope this happy beginning will produce such success this campaign as must put an end to the war. I bless God for putting it into their heads not to defend their lines; for at Pont de Vendin, where I passed the Mareschal d'Artagnan was with 20,000 men, which, if he had stayed, must have made it very doubtful. But, God be praised, we are come here without the loss of any men. The excuse the French make is, that we came four days before they expected us.[1]

Marlborough to Godolphin

LENS
May 1, 1710

*I have receiv'd none of Your letters since my last, nor nothing new has pass'd here. Our Canon both from Gand and Mons, cou'd not be coming forward til to morrow, so that we hope to have part of them here about the eighth, and that we might not Continu intierly Idel. Tho it be against the rule to open the trenches before we have our Canon, we think of doing it tomorrow, or the next day at farthest, for if it were possible we wou'd faine be masters of this town in this month of may.[2]

Douai was a fortress of the first order, well prepared and supplied for a siege. The Deule and the Scarpe were joined by a canal in the town, which was therefore an important key to the waterways. It was protected by a number of strong outlying posts, and by Fort Scarpe, a large detached work which guarded the north-western approaches. Water played a great part in its defences, and the inundations severely limited the sectors open to the attackers. General Albergotti commanded the fortress with a garrison of over eight thousand men, comprising 17 battalions in Douai and 3 in Fort Scarpe.

The lines of circumvallation were completed on April 28. Forty battalions and as many squadrons under the command of the Princes of Anhalt and Orange conducted the siege, which Marlborough and Eugene covered. It was generally hoped that the town would be

---

[1] Coxe, v, 184. [2] Blenheim MSS.

reduced before the grass grew and Villars could assemble an army strong enough to attempt relief; but the siege-train of two hundred guns, including 80 heavy pieces, did not reach the camp till May 9. The fact that the French had control of the sluices made water communications difficult. They were also able, by galleys from Condé operating down the Scheldt, to threaten water convoys moving south from Tournai. Marlborough therefore collected large

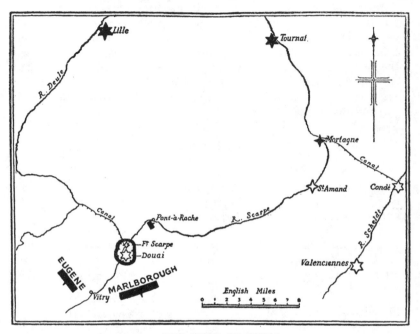

THE SIEGE OF DOUAI

quantities of wagon transport, and also developed the water communications up the Deule from Lille. The heavy batteries began to play on May 11.

Louis XIV hoped that by this time Montesquiou would be strong enough to impede the task of the besiegers. He was answered that the Allies, even after undertaking a siege, were still superior, and that the French army could not yet take the offensive. Villars arrived at Péronne on May 14, and took command. His army could not be fully assembled till the end of the month. Although strategically the great King was upon the defensive, the idea of a battle to relieve Douai, if a good chance offered, was cherished. Berwick, recalled from Dauphiné, joined the army for the same purpose as Boufflers before Malplaquet. Commanders-in-chief fought so hard in the battles of those days that it was indispensable to have a recognized understudy fully versed in the part. The gallant Villars was still suffering from his wound. His knee discharged, and from time to time threatened an abscess. He had had a steel "machine" made which held the joint rigid on horseback. He could not ride for more than two hours without fatigue and pain. But he was none the less overflowing with vitality and what in any man less brave and skilful would be called braggadocio. His army began to draw together around Cambrai. Far from minimizing his forces to safeguard his reputation, he declared that he was at the head of 160,000 men. Actually he had a little over 100,000.

    *"The Marishal de Villars," Marlborough wrote to Slingelandt (May 12), "is expected in a day or two on this frontier. We shall be able to guess by his first motion what his orders and intentions are. We are taking the necessary precautions for the receiving him, but til I see him on the plains of Lenz, I can not bring my self to believe thay will run soe great a hazard as a battel on these plains, *where two lucky houres might deside the fate of ffrance.*"[1]

Innumerable sieges took place in these long wars, and most of them were merely matters of routine. But the siege of a fortress as strongly garrisoned as Douai, with the two main armies in close contact around it, created a situation in which on any day one of the decisive battles of the world might explode. The fact that no great battle was fought does not mean that an intense trial of strength and skill was not proceeding between these armies, upon whose interplay all European eyes were fixed. Marshal Villars rejected the idea of a move against the allied left by crossing the Scheldt about Valenciennes. This would enable practically the whole of the besiegers to join the covering armies, while still leaving Douai isolated. He could not hazard forcing the Scheldt in the face of such opposition. He rejected also a move against the allied centre by crossing the streams of the Sensée and the Moulinet under virtually the same conditions. He resolved, therefore, to move round the allied right between the Scarpe and Lens, while leaving a force at Bouchain which, if Marlborough withdrew his besiegers from that side of Douai, could march into the place with men and supplies, and break the siege. Thus he hoped to pin the besiegers to their task at no great expense in numbers, and to bring a superior field

---

[1] Hague Archives.

army to bear upon Marlborough and Eugene in the region of their communications.

According to Villars, Berwick and Montesquiou deprecated a battle, and Villars admits in his memoirs that he did not mean to fight one. He thought, however, that it would do his army good to march up to close contact with the enemy, and that if they were found well posted he could easily retire. He represented his manœuvre from the outset to his colleagues as a reconnaissance with the whole

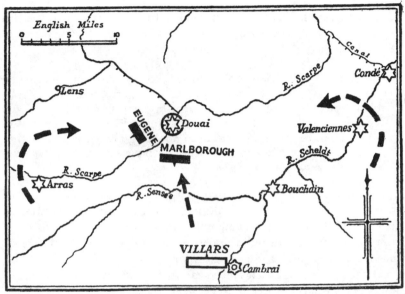

VILLARS'S CHOICE OF ACTION (MAY 1710)

army. Announcing by word and manœuvre that he intended to attack from Bouchain, he concentrated forward in that direction, brought in all the troops from Arras, and advanced north-westward full of menace. The Ally cavalry patrols detected, as Villars desired, the eastward march of the Arras detachment. Marlborough and Eugene personally reconnoitred all the possible battlefields between Douai and the front Valenciennes-Arleux, and the confederate army was deployed in that direction. Only 30 battalions were left at the siege and 12 squadrons at Pont-à-Rache. The whole of the cavalry, which had been feeding its horses from the Deule barges south of Lille, was also brought across the Scarpe by Vitry.

As this confrontation developed day by day both sides received strong reinforcements: Villars from the Rhine and Dauphiné; Marlborough of the Hessians on the spot, of the Palatines coming into Brabant, and of several cavalry regiments which Eugene had summoned from the Rhine. By May 22 the armies faced each other, Marlborough and Eugene being astride of the Scarpe. These two Commanders, acting as ever in the most perfect harmony, of course realized that Villars might only be making a feint, and one fine night would move suddenly back to the west. They therefore built no fewer than twenty bridges across the Scarpe between Vitry and

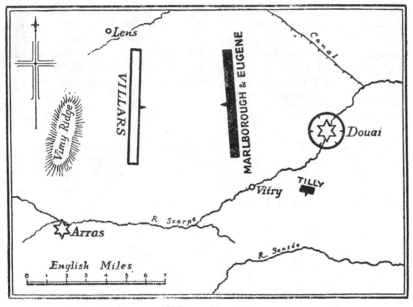

MAY 27–30, 1710

the lines of circumvallation, so that their whole army, moving on interior lines, could swing round to the new quarter of the compass without the slightest impediment.

On May 25 Villars made this move. Under the cloak of darkness he crossed the Scarpe by eight bridges just east of Arras, and debouched into the plain of Lens. On May 27 the three French marshals, Villars, Berwick, and Montesquiou, reconnoitred the allied right wing and, not liking the look of it, continued their left-handed movement towards Lens. Simultaneously Marlborough and Eugene extended their right, drew in the bulk of the siege troops, and formed a front facing west, leaving only the Dutch under Tilly south of the Scarpe. On May 30 Villars advanced directly to within

693

barely two miles of the confederate line, which was now covered by a chain of redoubts. Simultaneously Albergotti began a series of vigorous sorties from Douai. Marlborough none the less brought up Tilly and the Dutch troops, and battle from all appearances seemed imminent. Both the allied Commanders feared this was not true. But Marlborough's letters still convey a sharp impression of this crisis of war.

"This minute they bring me word," he wrote to Godolphin (May 22),

> that the French have passed the Scheldt, and are marching this way; they must make one motion more if they will attack us. Whatever may be the success, pray assure the Queen that, for her sake, as well as my own, I shall do my best; for, if we have a battle, this must decide the fate of almost all Christendom. . . . May the great God of battles give us success![1]

And (May 26):

> Marshal Villars's army increases every day; those that are not yet come have ground marked for them in the line, which is above eight miles long. He gives out that his army will be 160,000 strong. It is certain they have a great number of battalions; but I believe, by the sickness they have at this time in their foot, we have as many men as they. . . .
>
> I am this day threescore; but, I thank God, I find myself in so good health that I hope to end this campaign without being sensible of the inconvenience of old age.[2]

Marlborough to Townshend

June 1, 1710

★Marshal de Villars last Friday left his baggage at Arras with an intention to have attacked us that day, but when he came so near as to see us, he changed his mind, and has since called two councils of war. *The enclosed will let you see their opinions*, which I desire might be shown to nobody but the Pensioner, Count Sinzindorff and Slingelandt; *I have it from a hand that has never failed me, it is the same that gave the first notice of the expedition of Scotland, as also that of Brussels, so that I rely on this paper and hope to be informed of the King of France's answer.* The Prince of Savoy thinks we should resent the insincerity of the King of France, who at the same time he amused us with a sham negotiation gives orders to his general to venture battle.[3]

And (June 2):

[1] Coxe, v, 193.   [2] *Ibid.*, 194.   [3] B.M., Add. MSS. 41178, K.

The enclosed is what was sent to the King of France two days ago.[1] If the Court should insist on attacking, his army is so near that he may be with us in two hours' time; however, we think ourselves so securely posted that we have sent the troops back for the carrying on of the siege. . . . I thank God I have my health; but what I hear from your side of the water gives me so much uneasiness that *I am not so fully pleased with those sanguine thoughts as formerly, that God would protect and bless us;* but with all my soul I pray He may, and shall very freely venture my life that we may have success.[2]

All day the great masses watched each other within cannon, and at some points within musket, shot. The French marshals, including Villars, were agreed that the Allies were too strong to be attacked, and in the evening the French withdrew out of immediate striking distance. This was no doubt a wise decision. The question arises, however, why if the numbers of men were approximately equal, as Marlborough writes, he and Eugene did not themselves advance and attempt to force a battle. The answer must be that they did not intend at this time to run any supreme risks. They thought the war was certainly won, and that they need only continue to conduct it successfully to compel a peace. Time, they believed, was on their side. There was no warrant for staking the overwhelming advantages that had been gained. This reasoning was no doubt sound upon all the military facts. Perhaps Marlborough was not himself satisfied with it. His mind was oppressed by the hostility of the Queen and the growing power of his foes in England. He did not feel that confidence in victory which had inspired him at Blenheim and Ramillies. "I am not so fully pleased with those sanguine thoughts as formerly, that God would protect and bless us," is a sentence which shows that the strains and stresses to which he had been so long subjected had worn him down. Had he felt the same need and urge for battle as in his campaign of 1705 it is by no means certain that Villars could have paraded and promenaded north of the Scarpe with impunity.

As part of the siege works, a dam had been built across the Scarpe at Biache to turn the waters for a time into the neighbouring marshes and thus prevent the flooding of the trenches. This dyke was defended by a fortified post. Villars was attracted by a plan to overpower this post, destroy the dam, and with the pent-up waters

---

[1] This must have been a letter intercepted or betrayed at the front. There were evidently two spies, one in the camp and one at the Court.

[2] Coxe, v, 195.

break an important bridge behind it, as a prelude to an attack on the allied sector between the Scarpe and the Sensée. Oddly enough, at the same time Marlborough began to feel uneasy about Biache and this particular dam. On the morning of June 2 he rode thither himself with Count Tilly. He reinforced the garrison with eighty men, and personally gave orders to the commanding officer to defend himself to the last extremity, assuring him that he would be supported in good time. The very same night about nine o'clock it happened that the enemy attacked. Whether from cowardice or treachery, the officer surrendered the post without any resistance, and with six officers and 150 men was taken prisoner. The dam was partly broken, and some waters released before the counter-attack drove out the intruders. The bridge, however, was not swept away by the scour. The incident is of interest because, unless it was pure coincidence, it not only illustrates Marlborough's attention to detail, but is another example of the uncanny efficiency of his Secret Service.

The siege of Douai was strongly contested. Albergotti is said to have made no fewer than thirty-two sallies during its course. But the Prince of Anhalt's attack in particular progressed steadily. The covered way was mastered by the middle of June, and on the 19th two important ravelins of the inner defences were stormed in a bloody assault. During the night of the 24th the besiegers were so much the masters that they were filling up the 'capital ditch' and building galleries across it. On the morning of the 25th Albergotti beat a parley, offering to surrender Douai but not Fort Scarpe. This was refused, but after some haggling he yielded, and on the 26th articles of capitulation were agreed.

On the morning of the 29th General Albergotti marched out with 4527 effective men. He led his troops past Marlborough and Eugene with mutual salutations. After having ridden some little distance he turned back and joined the two Princes, and all proceeded to dine together, while the survivors of the garrison made their way to Cambrai, escorted to the French lines by some squadrons of allied horse.

The losses of the siege had been severe. Albergotti had lost a third of his men. The Allies had paid eight thousand casualties for the acquisition of the fortress; but, what was even more costly, they had consumed the whole of May and June, and their campaign, which had started so early and so brilliantly, was now a month behind their plans. Marlborough's depression was extreme. "I long," he wrote to Godolphin (June 12), for an end of the war, so God's will be done; whatever the event may be, I shall have nothing to reproach myself, having with all my heart done my duty, and being hitherto blessed with more success than was ever known before. *My wishes and duty are the same; but I can't say that I have the same sanguine prophetic spirit I did use to have*; for in all the former actions I did never doubt of success, we having had constantly the great blessing of being of one mind. I cannot say it is so now; for I fear some are run so far into villainous faction that it would give them more content to see us beaten; but if I live I will be so watchful that it shall not be in their power to do much hurt. The discourse of the Duke of Argyll is that when I please there will then be a peace; I suppose his friends speak the same language in England, so that I must every summer venture my life in a battle, and be found fault with in the winter for not bringing home peace, though I wish for it with all my heart and soul.[1]

Not only the resistance of the fortress but the ravages of typhus had smitten the besiegers. "My last quarters," wrote Marlborough to Godolphin (June 16),

infected a great many of my servants by which I have lost Groffy, my steward, and poor Turliar [his dog]; but the rest are recovering. It is impossible, without seeing it, to be sensible of the misery of this country; at least one-half of the people of the villages, since the beginning of last winter, are dead, and the rest look as if they came out of their graves. It is so mortifying that·no Christian can see it but must with all his heart wish for a speedy peace.[2]

Harley's tentacles now extended in all directions. He had brought into being a group of officers clustered around the Duke of Argyll who were actively disloyal to the Commander-in-Chief, under whom they were serving, and eagerly bidding for promotion in the Army from the régime that was rising into power.

Orrery to Harley

CAMP BEFORE DOUAY
June 21, 1710

Mr Benson will be able to give you a good account of our affairs here, having been in the camp with us about six weeks, where he has been several times entertained by the Vicar-General [a sneering allusion to Marlborough's wish for the Belgian Viceroyalty] and often had discourse with him. I think I already observe an alteration in the behaviour of this great man and his friends upon the prospect of the change in England. They seem to affect a greater air of civility than

[1] Coxe, v, 197.   [2] *Ibid.*, 198.

they once thought they should ever have occasion for, and I am apt to think they will in some little time make overtures of accommodation; for I am persuaded that, though the General should entirely lose his power, he will do all he can to keep his place.

The Duke of Argyll and I have yet had but very little correspondence with him, and we have no inclination to have any with him for the future, further than the duty of our posts obliges us to; *but it is the custom for all officers when they quit the camp to ask his leave, which is a ceremony we would willingly omit if we could. The only way I think for us to be dispensed with in that respect is for the Queen by letter or any other proper method to signify to us her leave to go out of the camp and return to England when we think fit.*

I have lately written to H[enry] S[t John] about my being made a Major-General. . . . I am plainly left out in this last promotion out of pique which has stopped at me though there are not Major-Generals enough upon this establishment. . . . I don't desire it for my own particular advantage. . . .[1]

And again from the camp before Béthune (July 31):

Some time ago I writ to H. St [John] pretty earnestly to let him know how necessary I thought it was that some restraint should be put to that exorbitant power Lord Marlborough has in the army. I am every day more convinced of that necessity, for he plainly disposes of preferments here with no other view but to create a faction sufficient to support him against the Queen and her friends in case every other prop should fail.

I mentioned at the same time my promotion of Major-General which I think I have no ill title to, and which I suppose upon the first application to the Queen will be granted. It will be of use to encourage her friends here and will add a little to the present mortification of his Highness.[2]

It is not often that personal motives are so nakedly exposed.

The flow of Ally reinforcements was continuous. Marlborough replaced the weakened regiments from his numerous garrisons, and in the first week of July he and Eugene stood at the head of 182 battalions and 284 squadrons, all in good strength, a total of 120,000 men. It was still their intention to strike at Arras, the keystone of the last line of the French fortress barrier. In the face of bad weather it took a fortnight from the fall of Douai to recondition the army, to replenish its food and forage, and to place it upon a new front north of the Scarpe between Douai and Lens. On the

---

[1] Portland Papers, *H.M.C.*, iv, 544. [2] *Ibid.*, 553.

12th the Allies moved forward past and over the Vimy Ridge, and lay along the Scarpe with Arras in full view. Villars, denuding the French garrisons not immediately threatened, had concentrated an even larger army in his new lines stretching along the Crinchon stream from Arras to the Somme. These fortifications, held in force by the main army of France, offered bluntly to the Allies another Malplaquet. Upon the acceptance or refusal of this challenge the

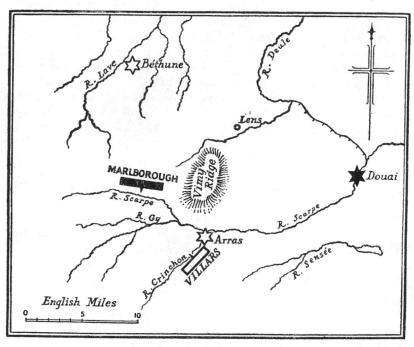

JULY 12, 1710

decisive character of the campaign depended. Afterwards, as will be seen, Argyll attacked Marlborough for timidity in not having besieged Arras, as he had already attacked him for temerity in fighting at Malplaquet; but at the time the allied high command was united in declining to play so high a stake as the great frontal attack upon the whole French army in its entrenchments which was the needful preliminary. All were agreed that the French position was too strong to assault. General Kane, a competent officer not involved in the highest affairs or intrigues, says, "Villars's army much outnumbered ours, and he retired behind the Sensée, so that there was no coming at him nor laying siege to Arras." It was therefore resolved to lay siege to Béthune, a place of minor importance on the southern tributary of the Lys, which opened a waterway for a subsequent attack on Saint-Venant and Aire. This decision was in fact a reversion to the discarded alternative of a coastal advance, at a season too late to reap its rewards. Marlborough revolved deeply an attack upon Calais and Boulogne. Political deterrents were added to the military difficulties. He wrote to Godolphin (August 2):

> You may be assured that the King of France is so encouraged by what passes in England that he has taken a positive resolution for the continuation of the war, and reckons upon my not being employed this next campaign. The little consideration that the Queen has for you and me makes it not safe for me to make any proposal for the employing those regiments now in the Isle of White; though, if things were formerly, I could attempt a project on the sea-coast that might prove advantageous. But as everything is now, I dare attempt nothing, but what I am almost sure must succeed; nor am I sure that those now in power would keep my secret.[1]

Béthune, which was defended by fifteen battalions, was invested on July 15, and capitulated on August 29.[2] The siege was bloody, and cost 3500 men, apart from sickness and desertion. Villars continually threatened a battle for its relief, but he, like the allied commanders, was not prepared to "venture." Once again, after the capture of Béthune, Marlborough and Eugene pondered the question of a general assault upon the French entrenchments, and once again they decided not to try. "Our sickness continues," wrote Marlborough to Sarah (August 28), "but I thank God I have my health, and will take the best care I can to keep it. My poor coachman, that has lived so long with me, died of this fever yesterday; and poor Daniel, my favourite cook, is not yet recovered; but they hope he will."[3] Although there had been no battle, the losses of the campaign had been heavy: eight thousand at Douai, 3500 at Béthune, and fourteen thousand sick or deserted. Nevertheless, while resign-

---

[1] Coxe, vi, 342.

[2]   *Argyll to Harley*

August 29

The town of Béthune has designed to capitulate, so we shall have it in a day or two. What our mighty Prince of Blenheim will think of doing afterwards, I know not; but if we pretend to take any more towns, our infantry will be quite destroyed and our horse so much out of order that we shall be obliged to stay as long in garrison next spring as the enemy, and I don't know but his Grace may think it his interest to have it so. [Portland Papers, *H.M.C.*, iv, 569.]

[3] Coxe, v, 332.

ing the main objective, and in spite of "a very unlucky accident,"[1] they felt strong enough to attack two fortresses at once.

On September 6 Anhalt with forty battalions and as many squadrons besieged Aire, and Nassau-Friesland (the Prince of Orange) with twenty battalions and five squadrons Saint-Venant.

Of the two towns Aire was incomparably the stronger, and held a garrison of fourteen battalions, double that which defended Saint-Venant. Marlborough stood midway between his sieges and Arras. Upon the whole, this phase offered Villars his best opportunity. With sixty battalions and forty-five squadrons withdrawn from the allied army for the sieges, and with all Brabant exposed except for its fortresses, the possibility was open to him of taking the offensive. He suggested this course to Louis

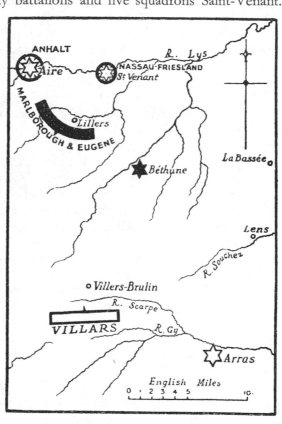

SIEGES OF AIRE AND SAINT-VENANT

XIV, but in a half-hearted manner. The King, who was watching the English Court even more closely than the fighting front, would not

---

[1]   *Marlborough to Godolphin*

Sept. the 22nd, 1710

★Since my last we have had no letters from England. Wee have here had a very unlucky accedent. Great part of our powder and amunition that was for the carrying on of these two sieges, came from Gand on thursday last escort'd by 1200 foot and 450 horse on friday thay were attack'd by the Enemy and beaten, so that the powder was blown upp, and the rest of the store ships sunk; I have sent to Lille Menin Tournay and Doway to see what stores we can have from those places, for Pr Eugene and my self are resolv'd not to raise this siege as long as we have any hopes of getting powder

allow him to run such risks. Villars therefore contented himself with harassing the communications, and one sharp action occurred with Eugene's foraging parties and their escorts, in which the French sustained a rebuff. Saint-Venant fell on September 30. Aire made a more obstinate and formidable resistance. The slaughter was heavy, and the weather terrible. "Our poor men," wrote Marlborough, "are up to their knees in water." It was not until November 9 that the capitulation was signed. The garrison had lost more than a third of its strength, and the Allies nearly seven thousand men, apart from sickness. Villars, whose wound required repeated attention, had handed over the command of his army to Harcourt after the fall of Béthune some six weeks earlier. It was now too late to attempt an advance on Abbeville and the creation of a new base there, and both armies dispersed into winter quarters.

Although this campaign, so costly in casualties and disease, was conducted impeccably by Marlborough, and the results achieved were substantial, it was nevertheless a disappointment. That Marlborough and Eugene with 120,000 men should not have been able to bring the enemy to battle or take Arras seems surprising in view of the achievements of their great years. Reasons other than military must be invoked in explanation. Marlborough, ageing rapidly, undermined at home, uncertain of the loyalty of some of his principal officers, could bring himself to do no more than play military chess with his accustomed skill, and wait for the enemy to make some fatal mistake. If he had run the supreme risk, if he had hurled his army upon the French entrenchments, or if, repeating his manœuvre of 1705 and carrying eight days' supplies in his wagons, he had marched through the intervals between the French fortresses and forced a crisis, he might have ended the war at a stroke, or, on the other hand, have ruined all. No one can pronounce. The authority of the twin Captains cannot lightly be set aside by posterity. What they deemed imprudent must certainly have been perilous. What they declared to be impossible was probably beyond the reach of mortal man.

---

enough to make the trenches, but what gives me the greatest uneasiness is that this misfortune may make our designe on the Cost impracticable, but I am so desirous of executing it, that you maybe sure if it be possible, it shall be attempt'd; but my head at this time is so full how to gett the necessary stores for the carrying on of this siege, that I cant think of any thing else for some few days. [Blenheim MSS.]

Chapter Fifteen

SUNDERLAND'S DISMISSAL

1710—APRIL—JULY

HITHERTO the forces gathering against the domestic system and foreign policy of Marlborough and Godolphin had been numerous and powerful, but disunited. After the trial of Sacheverell they became sentient and focused. There emerged the same group of powerful nobles loosely attached to either party which had played its part in 1708 and was to do so again in 1714. But this time their weight was cast on the Tory side. The encouragement which the Queen gave to almost all elements hostile to her own leading Ministers offered prospects of favour and power to both honest antagonism and selfish aims. To control the government of Britain, which Marlborough's sword had raised so high, was an attraction captivating the great nobles and magnates of the day. At the root lay Harley with the Tory Party, and now, somewhat incongruously, with the Church. The jealous or disaffected officers in the Army found their leader in the Duke of Argyll. In the Cabinet the Duke of Somerset was incited by the craft of Harley and the smiles of Anne to pursue his dream of heading a Government. He found support at this time from the Duke of Newcastle, Lord Privy Seal. He saw himself upon the high road to mastery; he did not hear the slighting comments which those whom he aspired to lead, and whose interests for a time he served, were accustomed to make upon him behind his back. Already, as has been described, Shrewsbury had begun in his cautious manner to work with Harley. All these men in the months following the Sacheverell fiasco 'entered into measures'—to use their dignified expression—with one another. Harley, in close touch with St John, guided from the House of Commons; Argyll glared in the camp; Somerset flaunted himself at the Court; and Shrewsbury lent an aspect of prudence and disinterested moderation to the whole cabal. A novel term now came into British politics. The five Whig lords had been called the Junto. The new group was nicknamed the Juntilla. "There is a Juntilla in imitation of the Junta," Count

Maffei[1] wrote to Victor Amadeus, "and the Duke of Somerset, who is called by the nickname of 'the Sovereign,' plays the figure of a chief, although the others, who are of his society, make him depend on their counsels, and only make use of him to inspire the Queen with what they think proper."[2]

Behind them gathered a train of minor figures, peers and Members, some in the Ministry, some in the Army, all in high expectation of office or promotion. Among these the Earl of Orrery, Earl Rivers, and Earl Poulett were the most prominent and bitter. Orrery and Rivers were general officers of the army. Rivers had made the campaign of 1702 under Marlborough, who promoted him lieutenant-general. Hoping to advance more rapidly, he procured Marlborough's aid in obtaining the command of the 'descent' planned by Guiscard on the French coast in 1706. When this force was diverted to Spain he found himself confronted with the choice of serving under Galway or returning home. He preferred to return home after disparaging Galway to the best of his ability at the Court of Charles III. In April 1708 Marlborough nominated him to the Queen for promotion to general of horse, and also had him sworn a Privy Councillor. This ambitious man foresaw the downfall of the Whigs, and by the winter of 1709 was intimate with Harley and active in his interest. We have seen how serviceable this interest proved to him when the post of Constable of the Tower fell vacant. Thenceforward he became the unscrupulous and virulent enemy of the Commander-in-Chief under whom he served, and to whom his whole rise had been due. Macky says of Rivers:

> He was one of the greatest rakes in England in his younger days, but always a lover of the constitution of his country; is a gentleman of very good sense and very cunning; brave in his person; a lover of play, and understands it well; hath a very good estate and improves it every day; something covetous; a tall, handsome man and of a very fair complexion;[3]

to which Swift adds "an arrant knave in common dealings, and very prostitute."[4]

Earl Poulett, nicknamed "Swallow," had played some part in the Union with Scotland in 1706, and was a Tory politician of minor consequence. Macky describes him as "a mean figure in his person,

---

[1] The Savoyard Minister in London.   [2] Coxe, v, 224.   [3] Macky, pp. 57–58.
[4] When he died prematurely in 1712 his will created a stir. He left nothing to his family, but distributed a fortune among twenty ladies, described by Swift in less flattering terms.

and not handsome." He rarely spoke in Parliament, but was busy behind the scenes. He was one day to make a speech which got him into trouble.

Apart from Argyll and Orrery, who were actually serving in Flanders, these personages were not acting beyond their rights. Harley's combination, however disreputable and clandestine in its methods, is not to be dismissed as mere intrigue. It represented powerful forces in the land, and stood for a definite and arguable policy both at home and abroad. Harley had never diverged from the principle on which he had accepted the Secretaryship of State before Blenheim, of a broad-based centre administration to serve the Queen and make her independent of the extremists of either faction. This had also been the conception of Marlborough and Godolphin, but they had been forced to abandon it, and had become the agents or prisoners of the Whig Junto. They had done this against their will and better judgment; but the fact remained that they had done it. Neither had the Queen altered her general position of wishing to reign above either party with the assistance of leading statesmen from both sides. Harley had received in the Sacheverell turmoil an unexpected and most powerful source of strength from the excited and now arrogant Church party and clergy. This did not harmonize with his general view, but it was none the less welcome and potent. Nor could even the Jacobites be disdained. They proffered their goodwill to a movement which promised to them the disintegration of the European coalition which had so long waged successful war against their true King—as they saw it—and against the chivalrous French monarch who had sheltered him, and who championed the Catholic faith.

But apart from self-interest and the wish to acquire control of the State the main bond between all these diverse elements was a common desire for peace. Harley's policy was to stop the war. Shrewsbury was convinced not only that it should stop now, but that it might have been stopped in the spring of 1709. The Tory Party wanted peace, but peace with British profit. The Queen was the least convinced upon the peace. Her chief desire was to free herself from the Whigs, and now from the Marlboroughs, and to reign—to quote the phrase by which she was allured—"as Queen indeed." But she had been too long in the war to think lightly of the abandonment of its aims. She was convinced that only by unquestionable victory could her throne be safe; and she saw no means of accomplishing this end but through Marlborough.

Therefore, while the successive steps which Anne took to achieve her personal aims, or in response to the pressure of forces round her, wore the aspect of deliberate design, they were in fact only tentative, and were limited at every stage by the fear of a break-up of the Alliance or a financial collapse in the City of London.

In the winter of 1709 the leading members of the so-called Juntilla believed that a good peace was procurable at will. They continued to nurse this conviction in the spring of 1710; but although they remained eager for peace, they became, as the summer wore on and they approached nearer to direct responsibility, increasingly doubtful whether it could now be obtained on any terms which the nation would accept. They were not blind to the fact that as they weakened Marlborough, and as the shadow of his approaching fall spread across Europe, the goal they sought receded. They were in close enough contact with affairs to feel the stiffening of the French attitude. At length they realized that there was no chance of their being able to present a good peace to the nation before the election. To present a bad peace was to ruin their chances. Therefore, like the Queen, they reached the conclusion that the war must be continued for the present, and this in its turn imposed a certain restraint upon their action.

In this, rather than in any lack of power, lies the explanation of the gradualness with which the change of Government was effected. For, after all, it was upon the election that all political fortunes depended. All the news from the country was bad for the Whigs. There was keen political excitement and a great deal of discontent. The Tory Party was active and confident, and the Church vehement. The Whig leaders knew all this as soon as their opponents, and were completely unnerved thereby. With the estranged Queen on one side and a hostile electorate on the other they felt that they were doomed. They and their majorities in both Houses stood upon a trapdoor, and at his selected moment Harley could draw the bolt. This sour fact explains, though it does not excuse, their lack of loyalty to one another. Their only choice appeared to be either to resign together and at once or to be dismissed piecemeal. They drifted into the latter course largely because of their hope that the normal life of the Parliament on which alone they now depended might be preserved, and also that perhaps Marlborough, whom they had ridden so hard in the previous year, might produce some new victory which would once again retrieve all. In this unhappy plight they passed the summer.

With the appointment of Shrewsbury the Queen felt that she had gone far enough for the moment. She would not be pressed into action which would lead to Marlborough's resignation. Neither would she free herself from the "bondage" of Sarah and the Whigs to submit to another thraldom of the Somersets and the Tories. She was well aware that the disgrace of Marlborough and his wife would not bring the country any nearer to the peace she was beginning apprehensively to contemplate. Harley had, therefore, to move with caution. Access to the Queen had been increasingly difficult since the rise of the Somersets at Court. A doleful letter from Abigail reveals this.

Abigail Masham to Robert Harley
April 17, 1710

I am very uneasy to see you, but my poor aunt [the Queen] will not consent to it yet; she puts me off from time to time, which gives me a great deal of trouble. I think it necessary for her service as well as my own for us to meet, for a great many reasons; therefore I have a mind to do it without her knowledge and so secret that it is impossible for anybody but ourselves to know it. I would come to you to-morrow night about eight o'clock to your own house if you approve of it, but if you have made any appointment with company, any other night will serve me. Send this person to me to-morrow about ten in the morning to let me know your resolution what I must do.[1]

If Shrewsbury, Somerset, and Harley could agree upon the next move, and gain the Queen's support for acting, another Ministerial change would follow. Strenuous efforts were made throughout April and May to create this situation. Harley had his internal difficulties. The high Tory feeling aroused by the Sacheverell trial, unless carefully managed, might swamp his moderate schemes. His secret correspondence with Buys and the peace party in Holland had led to hostile comment in the House of Commons. There had been mutterings even of impeachment.[2] Opinion among the Whigs was divided. Godolphin still hoped, though faintly, for an understanding between Shrewsbury and the Whigs. But how was this to be achieved? His own position became daily more embarrassed. He was reading one day to the Queen a reference in one of Townshend's letters which mentioned rumours that the Treasury was to be put in commission. "She gave a sort of scornful smile," wrote the Treasurer,

[1] Portland Papers, *H.M.C.*, iv, 540.
[2] See *The Wentworth Papers*, p. 112.

but did not think fit to say a word to me upon it, and, perhaps, it is not yet in her intentions or thoughts; but what she may be brought to in time by a perpetual course of ill offices and lies from Mr Harley and his friends, and no pains taken by anybody for me, to break the force of those impressions, I am sure I cannot answer. But this I know, that as long as you are abroad in the field, and that your army cannot be regularly paid but by my particular care and endeavour, no slight provocation shall prevail with me to quit my post. . . . But the insolency of Mr Harley and his creature is inexpressible. The Duke of Argyll's brother [Lord Islay] and Lord Rivers, and that sort of cattle, have as little management [*i.e.* decent behaviour] here as you say he has abroad.[1]

Marlborough to Heinsius

May 8, 1710

★. . . Your desiring my thoughts as to what effect the change in England may have as to the common cause God only can tell, but to you as a friend I own very frankly that I do not like it, and do from my soul wish that we had a good peace; I am sure you do me the justice to believe that I shall lose no opportunity this campagne that may bring it to that happy end.[2]

Sarah had retired to Windsor Lodge after her parting from the Queen in April. She was now disillusioned of the Whigs, and impatient at their weakness and vacillation. She despised the individual attempts they made to stand well with Somerset at the expense of Godolphin.[3] She remained convinced that there was no comfort to be drawn from Shrewsbury. With sure instinct, she distrusted his affabilities, she recognized him throughout as an enemy. She was disgusted when the Whigs in their distress suggested even that she should seek a reconciliation with Abigail. Sunderland had toyed desperately with the idea of joining forces with Somerset. He had a three hours' conversation with him, as between colleagues, and reported hopefully that Somerset had spoken with great coldness of Shrewsbury, and had declared that he had only met Harley once at Argyll's house. Sarah was sure that her son-in-law was allowing himself to be deceived.

She now became the object of Whig solicitations to return to Court. We have need of "a good advocate with the Queen," wrote Lady Cowper (May 14).[4] Godolphin frequently advised her to come to town, and Maynwaring constantly warned her of the dangers

---

[1] Godolphin to Marlborough, May 5/16, 1710; Coxe, vii, 227–228.
[2] Heinsius Archives.   [3] Maynwaring to Sarah; *Sarah Correspondence*, i, 316–317.
[4] *Ibid.*, 313.

of leaving the field open.[1] But Sarah at this time followed Marlborough's advice to keep clear of the Court and leave the Queen alone. She shared to the full his prescient pessimism. She took such pains to have her letters destroyed that history is indebted to Maynwaring for preserving the following sprightly epitome.

Sarah to Maynwaring
Saturday Morning, the 20th of May, 1710

. . . What you write to-day of "The Sovereign" [Somerset] and his company at dinner, is not of a piece with the last letters; and 'tis certain if 89 [the Whigs] think of continuing in the Government, that fool must be exposed and run down: there is no other way to deal with him; *but as long as* 89 *fear an ill Parliament*, nothing can be done but by gaining 28 [the Duke of Shrewsbury] which I believe is impossible, tho' I find 6 [Sunderland] is pretty well satisfied with him. I wish I may be mistaken in my opinion. But what a melancholy reflection it is for 89 that now their fate depends upon gaining a man, that t'other day they would have flown over the top of the house if anybody had proposed his coming into employment. *Since* [either] *their bottom is not very strong*, or else we apprehend shadows; if the first, I think they have been very much to blame to 38 [Godolphin] and 39 [Marlborough]; if the last, they must yield to 28 [Shrewsbury], just come into the service.[2]

There was the root of the matter. They "fear an ill Parliament. . . . Their bottom is not very strong." Was it, then, for these men of straw that she had toiled so long, to find that, having grabbed all at her expense, they could not even stand themselves, but must drag down Marlborough and Godolphin with them?

The Duke, from the impressions he could derive at the front, had still not entirely discarded hopes of Shrewsbury. He enjoined his wife not to be offended by the ignominious suggestions of the Whigs in their despair. He saw the whole scene with sombre vision; everything he wrote came true.

Rumour was now busy at Court and in the coffee-houses that Sunderland would be the next victim. Tory addresses were being framed against him in the City, in Surrey, in Shropshire. Tory partisans assailed him throughout the country. The talk was that the fall of Sunderland would be the prelude to the dismissal of the Parliament. Marlborough had heard of this in the camp from the high language of Argyll and his clique of officers.

[1] *Sarah Correspondence*, i, 336.   [2] *Ibid.*, 332–334.

John to Sarah

May 18/29, 1710

... To be emperor of the world I would not give reason for people to believe any consideration would make me truckle to Mrs Masham. I can, for the good of my country and friends, live so as not to seem to know they are in the world. ...

If Shrewsbury intends to keep any measures with you and me he will make it his business not to suffer Sunderland to be removed, but when the time may be proper for the taking off of the mask his being put out will be the first step.

I have so resented the behaviour of 221 [the Duke of Argyll] that nobody converses with him but such as are angry with me.[1]

About a week later the following note reached Harley:

Somerset to Harley

KENSINGTON
May 24, 1710

The Duke of Shrewsbury says you desire to talk with me, so let me know before eight o'clock if you can be at home, or at Northumberland House, this night at nine, accordingly I will come from hence. In case you choose to come to me I will have a servant to conduct you, and if I come to you, then have your back door open for me; but if this notice has not the good fortune to fall into your hands by eight o'clock, then any time you shall appoint to-morrow morning I shall obey.[2]

Unknown as yet to Marlborough, Shrewsbury had taken his first important step. He had brought together Harley and Somerset, and he provided easy access for Harley to the Queen. At the head of the Juntilla a powerful triumvirate had come into being. A further attack could now be launched against the Whig holders of office. Sunderland was to be dismissed, and the hostile forces also felt themselves strong enough for another affront to Marlborough, which should produce a separate trial of strength.

After the campaign Marlborough had submitted a series of promotions to encourage the Army. He had, however, stopped on the roster only one short of the names of Mrs Masham's brother, Colonel Hill, and of her husband, Colonel Masham. Harley and Somerset were not slow to point this out to the Queen. They saw, and so did she, an opportunity of renewing under more favourable conditions the rankling issue that had been fought out earlier in the year. The Queen invited Marlborough to propose both names,

---

[1] *Sarah Correspondence*, i, 326–327.   [2] Portland Papers, *H.M.C.*, iv, 542.

and meanwhile she delayed signing the whole list of promotions. Marlborough immediately complied in the case of Masham, but raised objections to Hill which were certainly justified on military grounds; for even in those days of favour such an appointment would create a scandal in the Army.

While Cardonnel was at the front Walpole acted as Secretary-at-War.[1] The Queen sent for him. She remarked that if the promotion list were stopped only one short of Mrs Masham's brother it would be thought by all the world to be done out of prejudice to him. She then told Walpole "to notify her Secretary of State for three more commissions of Brigadiers."[2] Walpole knew that Sarah had not been satisfied with his attitude about the Hill promotion in January. He was sincerely attached to the Whig interest, to Marlborough, and especially to Sarah, to whom he felt himself indebted for his advancement, and of whose reproaches he stood at this time in awe. He therefore expostulated boldly with the Queen, reminding her that she had already told him that, though she wished Colonel Hill to be Brigadier, she would not insist upon it if the Duke objected. With his quiet force, already noticeable, he used all the arguments about the mortification such a step would be to the Commander-in-Chief, and how it would lessen his credit and authority in the Army. "I shall be in a very unhappy circumstance," he wrote to Marlborough, "if I venture to say that to the Queen which perhaps few servants have done, and at the same time shall be thought to act a trimming game." There is no doubt that he went very far in his remonstrances, and also that the Queen was shaken thereby. She consented at length not to order the three extra commissions until Walpole had been able to write to Marlborough about them. Till then, however, she would sign none of the other commissions. At this point she blurted out that she had stopped them in order to force the Hill promotion. Walpole continued to protest, and the Queen had misgivings about the admission she had made. She no doubt saw how it might be represented that she was holding up the entire promotion of the Army in order to favour Abigail's brother.

"She commanded me strictly," wrote Walpole to Marlborough, "not to tell anybody, in particular not to let you know that she stopped the commissions on this account, but would have it thought, as it hitherto has been, that the delay was accidental." Walpole ends his letter to Marlborough:

[1] Coxe, *Memoirs of Sir Robert Walpole* (1798), i, 23 *n*.　　　　　[2] *Loc. cit.*

As my obligations to the Duchess of Marlborough are so infinite that I would rather dye than deservedly lose her good opinion, soe I beg if my judgment may sometimes lead me to think what is not altogether agreeable to her, you will not expose me to her resentment, if you doe not distrust my sincerity, which, believe me, you never shall have reason to doe.[1]

The busy circles at Court were soon astir with this new mischief. We may admire the cleverness of selecting a point which at the same time enlisted the Queen's affection for Abigail, revived her vexation over the January dispute, and threatened Marlborough with a thrust which must, if it went home, humiliate him before his army. Moreover, this was the very point on which it had already been found impossible to marshal Whig resistance. It seemed to the Whig leaders no more, one way or the other, than a petty piece of patronage—of which there was plenty—and a chance of pleasing the Queen cheaply. They were concerned that Marlborough should take it so seriously. They did not see that it would rot the Army, and treated it entirely as a matter to be smoothed. Marlborough's daughter, Lady Sunderland, was no doubt expressing the prevailing view in Whig circles when she wrote her mother in the last days of May:

When I heard the report mamma speaks of, of Mr Masham's having something given him in the army, I did not think it wrong (as the world is made) for papa to humour the queen in it; but for the other [an accommodation with Abigail] I own I hoped it an impossible thing for you ever to be reconciled to such a creature even if it could do good, but that is impossible; it would, may be, let her do the mischief underhand. I dare say nothing will be ever right, but the removing her; and if that can't be, I hope she will join with the Tories and not with the Whigs, and then it won't be in their power to ruin all the world when there is a peace.[2]

And Godolphin to Marlborough (June 2):

I find by Mr Walpole, that you have not been easy in the matter of Abigail's brother. I am sorry for it, because it puts a difficulty upon your friends here, and nothing would so much gratify your enemies. The question is not so much what is wrong and what is right, but what gives a handle to the Duke of Somerset to tell lies, and make impressions, where nobody has the opportunity of setting it right, or so much as of knowing it till it is too late.[3]

[1] Coxe, *Walpole*, i, 23 *n*.   [2] *Sarah Correspondence*, i, 273–274.
[3] Coxe, v, 237.

Meanwhile Marlborough, in reply to Walpole, gave reasons which might seem unanswerable.

CAMP BEFORE DOUAY
May 29th, 1710

. . . The trew reason for my restraining the promotions of brigadiers to the 25th of March, was not only from the numbers and confusion it must have occasion'd amongest the queen's subjects, but also have given great disatisfaction to all the forainers, this army being compos'd of eight different nations, and next to the blessing of God, we owe all our success to our unanimity, which has been hethertoo, as if in reallity we were but one nation, so that I beg her majesty will be pleas'd to allowe of its stoping at the 25th of March; and as soon as a promotion can be made with any coullor of reason, I shall be sure to take care of those mention'd by the queen.[1]

Anne was conscious of the weight of these reasons which Walpole urged resolutely upon her. "The Queen was," wrote Walpole to Marlborough, using ciphers for names,

not a little at a loss what to do and seemed both unwilling to comply or deny; at last desired it might be done, but in the softest manner that was possible. The commission is therefore to be taken out by me and sent over to you to be delivered at the end of the campaign or when he shall think fit. The Queen promised to write this night to you to assure you that no mortification was meant; and I must say that in this and the last conference there seem'd a great struggle betwixt the desire of doing the thing and not putting a mortification upon you.[2]

Marlborough, painfully aware of his lack of support at home, was so far mollified by these expressions that he published the commission at once. Colonel Hill became a Brigadier. The Army did not, however, receive any immediate benefit from his military skill. He repaired at once to Spa to undergo a thorough cure before subjecting himself to the rigours of active service. As this treatment did not quite carry him on till the end of the campaign, he found it necessary in due course to write to Marlborough:

BRUSSELS
October 29, 1710

★The benefit I hoped to receive by the waters made me stay as long as my pass would permit me. Since I was come to this place every one tells me the Army after the siege will break up. If so, I hope your Grace will excuse my coming back to the camp and give me leave to

---

[1] Coxe, *Walpole,* ii, 19.   [2] *Ibid.,* 22.

713

go for England which I humbly submit to your Grace and shall wait here for your orders.[1]

The Triumvirate at the head of the Juntilla found the Queen very ready to get rid of Sunderland, and relieved that they thought it could now be safely done. The question of his successor was more delicate. Harley, true to his plan of a Government of the Centre, wished to offer Sunderland's Secretaryship of State to the mild Whig Newcastle. The Tories pressed hard for a wholehearted member of their own party. Anglesey and "Swallow" Poulett both heard their claims discussed in their presence at Harley's house. Harley had need of all his tact. Anglesey was too extreme to suit his combination in the vacant office. Such a choice would alienate all middle opinion. He made Poulett, who really had no chance, flatter himself with the idea that he should make a high-minded and voluntary sacrifice of what he was in no case going to receive. It was difficult, he suggested, to bring in a man so close a friend of his as "Swallow."[2] If he must have a Tory Harley preferred a colourless figure.

Godolphin, still wearily confiding, in spite of Sarah's scepticism, in Shrewsbury's benevolence, saw no other way to save Sunderland than that Marlborough should appeal to the Lord Chamberlain. Marlborough's remaining influence was begged in aid all through the summer not only by Godolphin but by the Whigs. He had no illusions: but out of loyalty he complied with his friend's request. He wrote to Shrewsbury. The letter is not extant. It would in any case have been futile. Actually it arrived too late. Sarah's disapproval of such a gesture was anticipated, and the letter was kept secret from her. "Lady Marlborough," wrote Godolphin, "has been, and is still, so much dissatisfied with the Duke of Shrewsbury that I thought it would rather do hurt to acquaint her with your letter to him." Shrewsbury contented himself with disclaiming all responsibility. He threw the blame on Abigail. ★ "She could make the Queen," he remarked to Sarah, "stand on her head if she chose."[3] By June 1 Godolphin was certain of Sunderland's coming dismissal, and that the question of a successor alone caused delay.

"I am told," wrote Sarah to Maynwaring (June 1), "that the persecution against Lord Sunderland is renewed again, with more violence than ever. . . . I conclude the Duke of Shrewsbury, Lord

---

[1] Blenheim MSS.
[2] See Poulett to Harley, Portland Papers, *H.M.C.*, iv, 542–543.
[3] A later narrative of the Duchess of Marlborough (Blenheim M SS.).

Halifax, the Duke of Newcastle and Mr Harley are pretty near of one mind."[1] Sarah was entitled, according to her and also our ideas, to apply the word "violence" to the turning out of Ministers who still possessed effective majorities in both Houses. Her own "violence" was of a simpler character. About this the tale-bearers were again active.

Martha, Lady Mansell,[2] *to Harley*

May 28, 1710

I am almost fright'd to death with the threats of a great Lady who is now retired from Court, which one that lately came from the Lodge tells of. In a little time she says she shall return with as full power as ever, and that both you and every friend you have shall feel the effects of her utmost revenge. Lady Orkney is often with her, and at the table begins a health to her and all that's for the Duke's interest, and total destruction to those that are not for it.[3]

It cost Harley nothing to bring the Whigs into these discussions, and feed them with false hopes. Somers was clearly ready to preserve his own position by agreeing to sacrifice Sunderland. He none the less obtained from Godolphin another payment of a thousand pounds from the Secret Service fund the receipt for which is dated June 14—the day before Sunderland's dismissal.[4] Somers evidently thought himself safe whatever happened, and that a moderate Government would include leading Whigs. He became anxious that Marlborough should not by a resignation create a crisis which would render this impossible. He wrote to him (June 6) urging his concentration upon the campaign, as the sole chance was a victory in the field. "You have done wonders for us, and I hope you are resolved to complete them, and I am sure you will do all that is possible. It is very natural to say then, why is the Duke of Marlborough so imprudently interrupted when he has the cause of all Europe upon him?"[5]

Somers might urge Marlborough to hazard another battle to save the political situation. But this was exactly what Marlborough would not do. He allowed nothing to disturb his duty to the Army. The military facts alone could render a battle possible. He was coming increasingly to regard his military fame as all that might

[1] Blenheim MSS.

[2] Wife of Sir Thomas Mansell, a Welsh Tory neighbour of Harley's, Comptroller of the Household, and a Lord of the Treasury. *The Wentworth Papers*, p. 133.

[3] Portland Papers, *H.M.C.*, iv, 542.   [4] P.R.O., T48, Secret Service.

[5] Coxe, v, 255.

soon be left him. ★"I am with drawing my self," he wrote to Godolphin (June 5), "as fast as the Service will permit, out of all that sort
of intelligence with the foraine Courts, so that it may naturally fall
into the hands of the two Secritarys."[1] Isolated and unsupported,
Marlborough awaited the impending blow. That it might injure
his authority with the Army to the utmost, Argyll spread through
the camp that the Queen was weary of Marlborough's services,
"which would quickly appear by the removal of Lord Sunderland."
Sad, toiling, prescient, the Captain-General watched narrowly the
operations of the great armies, never being drawn by one hair's-
breadth from his professional art.

John to Sarah

June 15

All my friends write me that I must not retire, and I myself think
it would do great mischief if I should quit before the end of this campaign. But after the contemptible usage I meet with, how is it possible
to act as I ought to do? Would not you have some time ago thought
anybody mad that should have believed it would ever have been
in the power of Mr Harley and Mrs Masham to make the Whigs to
remain tamely quiet? They are mistaken if they think this is to go no
farther than the mortifying of you and me; *for their ruin, and a new
Parliament, is most certainly the scheme. For my own part I have nothing
to advise: for if the Whigs suffer Lord Sunderland to be removed, I think
in a very short time everything will be in confusion.*[2]

And (June 19):

★If I were to make the choice, I had much rather be turn'd out,
than that Ld. Sund: shou'd be remov'd, so that I hope all my friends
will struggle with all their might and power, for if this point be carry'd
there nothing disagreable and ruinus but must be expect'd.[3]

To please Godolphin Marlborough wrote him one more letter
(June 9/20) which the Treasurer could read to the Queen.

I am sorry Lord Sunderland is not agreeable to the Queen; but his
being, at this time, singled out, has no other reason but that of being
my son-in-law. When this appears in its true light, I am very confident every man in England will be sensible that my enemies have
prevailed to have this done, in order to make it impossible for me,
with honour, to continue at the head of this glorious army, that has,
through the whole course of this war, been blessed by God with
surprising successes.[4]

[1] Blenheim MSS.   [2] Coxe, v, 258.   [3] Blenheim MSS.   [4] Coxe, v, 259–260.

There was no response. The choice had at last been made. It had fallen upon Lord Dartmouth, son of Marlborough's Jacobite friend of Revolution days. He was a respectable man, a moderate Tory politician, whose significance at this juncture depended upon the fact that his father had died in the Tower for the cause of James II. He himself mentions that the decision had been delayed a month. While Godolphin was ignored, the Whigs had been consulted. They, of course, objected to Anglesey; the Queen was against the famous but somewhat obsolete candidate Nottingham; Newcastle had fallen into the background; the ridiculous Poulett had offered himself in vain by a series of mock renunciations. Finally Somers, on behalf of the Whigs, was authorized to agree to Dartmouth.[1]

On the morning of June 14 Boyle was sent by the Queen to take the seals from Sunderland. At such a moment his strict party principles and stiff personal character stood him in good stead. He quitted office with dignity and, indeed, with scorn. No accusation could be made against him. No pretext but the Queen's dislike could be adduced. Anne therefore offered him a pension of three thousand pounds a year. Sunderland's answer was becoming: "If I cannot have the honour of serving my country, I will not plunder it." Great employments lay before him in another reign. Meanwhile he had his library to amuse him.[2]

The Queen had written to Godolphin (June 13), telling him of her intention, and asseverating there was no idea of removing Marlborough from the command.

> It is true indeed that the turning a son-in-law out of his office may be a mortification to the Duke of Marlborough; but must the fate of Europe depend on that, and must he be gratified in all his desires, and I not in so reasonable a thing as parting with a man whom I took into my service with all the uneasiness imaginable, and whose behaviour to me has been so ever since, and who I must add is obnoxious to all people except a few?[3]

And the next day:

> I have no thoughts of taking the Duke of Marlborough from the head of the army, *nor I dare say nobody else; if he and you should do so wrong a thing at any time, especially at this critical juncture, as to desert my service, what confusion would happen would be at your doors, and you alone*

[1] Burnet, vi, 6 *n.*
[2] Boyer, *History of the Reign of Queen Anne digested into Annals*, ix, 228–230.
[3] Marlborough Papers, *H.M.C.*, p. 43 (*a*).

would be answerable and nobody else; but I hope you will both consider better of it.[1]

The Queen could write this to her faithful, lifelong servant, although she had determined to get rid of him and, in fact, did so in a couple of months.

England was still at war and at the head of the Grand Alliance. All from the Queen downward showed themselves under extreme anxiety. What would Marlborough do? Veritable entreaties from every side were made to him not to give up the command. The Whig leaders feared the danger of his instant resignation. On the day of Sunderland's displacement they and Godolphin held a meeting at Devonshire House and drafted a joint letter beseeching him to stay at his post. This was now their only hope, both for themselves and for their Cause.

June 14/25, 1710

. . . We find ourselves so much afflicted with this misfortune that we cannot but be extremely sensible of the great mortification this must give you at this critical juncture, when you are every moment hazarding your life in the service of your Country, and whilst the fate of Europe depends in so great a degree on your conduct and good success: but we are also as fully convinced that it is impossible for your Grace to quit the service at this time without the utmost hazard to the whole Alliance. And we must therefore conjure you by the glory you have already obtained, by the many services you have done your Queen and country, by the expectation you have justly raised in all Europe, and by all that is dear and tender to you at home, whose chief dependance is upon your success, that you would not leave this great work unfinished, but continue at the head of the Army. This we look upon as the most necessary step that can be taken to prevent the dissolution of this Parliament. Your Grace's compliance with this our earnest request would be the greatest obligation to us, and all that wish well to our country. And you may depend upon it that the contrary will be the greatest satisfaction to your enemies.[2]

This was signed by Cowper, Godolphin, Somers, Newcastle, Devonshire, Orford, Halifax, and Boyle.

Heinsius added his appeal.

June 21/July 2

*I beg you not to give way to vexation, but on the contrary to prove by the continuation of your service that you take the common cause more to heart than the resentment you feel in yourself.[3]

[1] Marlborough Papers, *H.M.C.*, p. 43 (*b*). [2] *Conduct*, p. 301. [3] Heinsius Archives.

The Emperor was the most insistent of all. "Illustrious Cousin and most dear Prince," he wrote (July 16),

> . . . can your affectionate heart, even for a moment, indulge the thought of such terrible calamities, both to the public weal and yourself? by which the whole fruits of the war, acquired with such labour and glory, would be exposed to the utmost peril; and the almost desperate cause of the enemy, to the eternal reproach of your name, would resume new strength, not to be overcome by future exertions. I am willing to believe, on the contrary, that you will continue firm to the public weal; and be convinced, that whatever aid, favour, or authority, I can ever confer, shall be given to you and yours, as the Prince of Savoy will tell you more at large.[1]

Marlborough had never doubted, as we know, that he must hold his post till the end of the campaign. At Godolphin's request he had once again threatened resignation. It had been of no avail. All the time his own mind was clear: Sunderland would be dismissed, and he would have to stay. A collapse in the field and the break-up of the Alliance might have been the consequences of his retirement. No one then or since has ever doubted that it was his duty to stay. But with what melancholy feelings did he face the closing circle of jealousy and malice which after so many glories, with full success in view, and while all the world wondered, was to be his reward. To Sarah, beloved wife and faithful comrade, he wrote his heart. In tragic letters he warned her of the dangers to which she might expose herself and him in their native land, "in a country amongst tigers and wolves." He had evidently through some secret channel received evidence of Somers' double-dealing.

John to Sarah

July 3, 1710

. . . However uneasy or disagreeable it may be to me to continue in the hurry of business, I have not been so blind with passion but that I foresaw the impossibility of my retiring at this time without inevitable ruin to the whole; so that I will comply with the desire of the lords. But I am in no ways convinced that my continuing will save the Parliament; for Mr Harley and his friends know the whole depends on that. . . .

I have had information concerning Lord Somers, which I would trust nobody but yourself with, and that can't be till we meet. Be upon your guard as to what you say to him, and let nobody know that I have given you caution.

[1] Coxe, v, 282–283.

For God's sake let me beg of you to be careful of your behaviour, *for you are in a country amongst tigers and wolves.* You have my wishes, and shall have my company whenever I can be master of myself. . . .[1]

And (July 5): "*Keep your temper, and if Parliament continues, we will make some of their hearts ache.*"[2]

But he could hardly expect that this point had escaped his foes.

John to Sarah

July 7

Yesterday being thanksgiving day, I was in devotion, and earnestly hope God will forgive what is past, and strengthen our hearts; so that for the time to come we may bear with patience the ingratitude we have met with, which He no doubt in due time will punish; for we, I fear, have so justly merited His anger, but no ways have we deserved this usage from the Queen. We must look upon this correction of His as a favour, if it atones for our past actions. As I would not be a favourite, were it in my power, my daily prayers shall be that you and I might be so strengthened by His Grace, that the remainder of our lives might be spent in doing good, by which we might at last be acceptable to Him.

You do not give any account of how you are to pass this summer; I should hope it would be with your children, as much as possible, so that you might not be alone, which might give you so much occasion for the spleen. Whilst the Queen is at Windsor I think you should avoid being at the Lodge; but pray do whatever shall make you most easy.[3]

And to Heinsius (July 5):

★I have taken the resolution of continuing at the head of the army as long as it is possible, & so I have write to my friends in England: but should these new favourites proceede so violently as to break this present Parl. with what heart can I act? For God's sake make M. Vriberg talk boldly on this subject for our all depends on it. . . . If we can preserve the Parl. I should hope everything might be retrieved, but unless that can be done, I fear very great confusion.[4]

And (July 31):

★You will know by what I have desir'd Ld. Townshend to tell you, that our affaires in England are in a very desperat condition. I am impatient of receiving your friendly advice. . . . The measures taken are not to turn the Ministers, as thay Call them, out, thav having no power, but by the authority of the Queen to remove all their

[1] Coxe, v, 268–269.　　　　　　　　[2] *Ibid.*, 272
[3] *Ibid.*, 267–268.　　　　　　　　[4] Heinsius Archives.

friends, by which thay use them more Contemptably then if thay were turn'd out; I cou'd bare my share of it with patience, if I did not see immediate ruin to the Common Cause.[1]

Ailesbury was still living in Brussels when Marlborough returned from the front at the end of this successful but disappointing campaign. The old Lord was offended, because, although he had always written to the Duke and offered his congratulations after every one of his victories, Marlborough had neglected to condole with him on the death of his wife. Ailesbury was in two minds about calling upon him. He wished to show his resentment. On the other hand, he was loath to join in the general desertion of a falling man. He passed two or three days in some distress of mind, but when "by the cannon at three in the afternoon I knew he was arrived" pride and resentment overbalanced, and "go to him I did not." "About eight next morning he sent an old servant of his for to know when he could come to see me, and without any apology I said I would expect him. . . ."

He generally went out in the morning, for he supposed (and I not) that his levée would be crowded as heretofore; so about ten I dressed myself, and just as they were beginning to shave me, my Lord came in, for as to his levée, there was but two or three insignificant persons as I was told—a true emblem of this selfish and flattering world, and 'twas because I would not be like those time-servers that I was so uneasy, as I before mentioned, on his approaching near this town.

After obliging compliments Ailesbury said:

"My Lord, you seem melancholy; that belongs to none but me. I thought you understood an English Court better than to be surprised at changes. As for our laws, they are excellent, but as for the Court, one is as sure of keeping an employment at Constantinople as in London. As you know by experience, when the Whigs were triumphant the Tories fell to the ground, and now can you wonder that the Whigs have found the same fate? . . . You have a fine family and a great and noble seat; go down thither, live quietly and retired, and you may laugh at your enemies. Lay yourself at the Queen's feet, and let her dispose of you as she shall think fit, and know by experience that she is a most gracious Princess." "One might imagine [replied Marlborough] that you had seen the letter I wrote to the Queen on this last subject matter, for 'tis wholly agreeable to the advice you have given me. I am sorry that my papers are gone with my heavy baggage to Holland, by Gant, or I would have shown you

[1] Heinsius Archives.

the copy." I concluded with an old English term, "Say, and keep to what you say." He stayed a day or two, being here with his friend Prince Eugene of Savoy.

Ailesbury writes contemptuously of the magnates and allied functionaries in Brussels:

In his greatness some few kept up to their birth, but all the rest were ready to lick the dust off his shoes, and then abandoned him at his fall. By the continued wars and little intermission, the nobility and gentry were ruined in a manner, and they sought after preferment like a hungry dog after a crust, and made servile court also, with the hopes that their estates might be better preserved from plundering. Besides that they have a natural itch towards preferments, and think it is a disgrace to be without one, set aside the profits that may come in by it. On the whole they were wholly subservient towards this Lord and the States Deputies of Holland, and in a mean manner, and to see how they deserted this Lord was shameful—at least in my eyes that, God be praised, could never do a mean thing, and that is all I can glory in.[1]

These strictures were founded upon fact. Marlborough was so disgusted by the treatment accorded him that he avoided passing through Brussels during the campaign of 1711. And so Ailesbury never saw him again.

[1] Earl of Ailesbury, *Memoirs* (1890), ii, 62–65.

Chapter Sixteen

THE ALARM OF THE ALLIES

1710—JUNE AND JULY

THROUGHOUT this summer the eyes of Europe were fixed upon London in hope or fear. It was realized at Versailles, as well as in every allied capital, that a profound change in the government and policy of England was in progress, and that Marlborough's power was passing. For nine years, in a world war on the largest scale yet known, he had been the central managing force against France. He had struck the main blows himself, and in his hands Britain had become the keystone of the confederate arch. Now, as the result of processes which to friend and foe alike were mysterious and, apparently, irrational, the will-power of the Islanders, for so long the supreme factor in the struggle, seemed about to fail, or even to be exerted in the contrary direction; and this at the moment when all that it had sought was in its grasp. "The fearful carnage of Malplaquet," says Klopp, "was less important to the development of the peoples of Europe than the bloodless change of the Ministry in England which began with the dismissal of Sunderland."[1]

"The driving cog of this great cabal," wrote Hoffmann to Vienna,

is Sir Robert Harley, and beside him the Dukes of Shrewsbury and Somerset, Lord Rivers and Peterborough, together with the favourite Mrs Masham. There would be much to say against the integrity and capacity of most of them. This cabal has gained control of the Queen to such an extent that it has the power both to make a complete change in the Government and to dissolve Parliament. But its members lack the courage to push affairs so far at one stroke. For in that case bad results at home or outside the country would bring such grave responsibility that the Tories would not be sufficiently strong in a new Parliament, and perhaps also not prepared, to rescue the cabal. . . . But if the cabal proceeds further, it is certain that neither Marlborough nor Godolphin will be able to remain in office.[2]

The Juntilla were voluble in reassuring the Allies. They tendered

<hr>

[1] Klopp, xiii, 440.   [2] Hoffmann's dispatch, July 11; Klopp, xiii, 452.

explanations of Sunderland's dismissal to the ambassadors in London. "This morning," wrote Count Gallas (June 13),

the Duke of Shrewsbury came to see me to tell me in absolute confidence in the name of the Queen that she intended to dismiss Lord Sunderland, the Secretary of State. She anticipated that owing to the relationship between Lord Sunderland and Marlborough this change would be widely discussed, and I was to assure the Emperor and the King of Spain that the object was not at all to diminish the prestige of Marlborough, which the Queen wished to preserve. The Queen was, moreover, resolved not to weaken the position of England in the international sphere. The affair was a purely personal one, affecting Lord Sunderland only: the Queen had kept him in her service till now merely out of respect for Marlborough.[1]

"It is not to be imagined," said Shrewsbury, "that the Queen would depart from her settled policy to the detriment of the Common Cause." He reiterated this statement. The Imperial Ambassador replied politely that any anxieties he might have had were removed by the fact that a man of Shrewsbury's moderation held the ear of the Queen. Shrewsbury assured him that his influence would always be used in favour of the Imperial House, and if more war were needed he would certainly vote for it. He added, however, "England is badly in need of peace."

These last words more than undid, in the mind of Gallas, the effect of all that had been said before. Peace no longer depended upon England. The decline of Marlborough's authority had caused an instantaneous revival of the spirit of the French Court. At Gertruydenberg their plenipotentiaries were adopting each day a more haughty tone. Gallas ended his reports to Vienna and Barcelona with the words, "I am very much afraid grave results may follow."

Hoffmann[2] was also present. He formed an even more unfavourable impression.

This visit to Count Gallas is most astonishing. If the Queen really does not intend to proceed further, there is no need for her, merely because she dismisses one single Minister, to give such assurances to the allied Powers. The visit, therefore, suggests that she may have other intentions. . . . Moreover, the movements and intrigues throughout the kingdom render it impossible for stability to be reached without a complete change. The Tories intend to secure the dissolu-

[1] Klopp, xiii, 437.
[2] Hoffmann, it will be remembered, was the Imperial Resident in London. Gallas was an Imperial Envoy on special mission.

tion of the present Parliament and the summons of a new one. If they succeed, this gives them control of the Government; thus the Queen will no longer be able to select moderate men of both parties. . . .

It is difficult to foresee the attitude which Marlborough and Godolphin will take. As long as the war lasts both of them will be needed; for if the Treasurer were dismissed, the credit which is the real basis of the wealth of the country at this moment, would simply collapse, and everything would be plunged into the utmost confusion. Events here have already had the result that France is stiffening.[1]

Sunderland's successor, Lord Dartmouth, was a mild nonentity. "It does not matter," wrote Gallas, "whether one talks to him or not." Hoffmann mentions the rumour that the Tories only thought of keeping him in his position for the time being, in order to prevent "too much uproar at first."[2] "In this affair," reported Gallas, "all hopes and fears are set upon the question of whether the Queen will confine the changes to Sunderland."

Gallas gives an account of a dinner on June 27, to which he, together with the Portuguese and Florentine ambassadors, was invited by the Duke of Shrewsbury. Shrewsbury lived in Kensington Palace, in attendance as Lord Chamberlain upon the Queen. His Duchess received her guests, and conducted them to the Queen's rooms. There they found Shrewsbury and Somerset. Somerset, in the presence of the ambassadors, spoke to Shrewsbury about Godolphin in such bitter terms that Gallas realized that Godolphin's fall was also intended. In the midst of this the Queen entered. Dinner was announced. The Queen motioned Count Gallas to her side as they left the room. She told him she wished to repeat the promise which the Duke of Shrewsbury had made in her name. The Count might assure the Emperor and the King of Spain that she would never change her opinions, and would always be on the side of continuing the war till a good and honourable peace had been secured; nor would she bring anything to pass which would embarrass the Common Cause. Gallas expressed his thanks, and they seated themselves for dinner.[3]

After dinner Gallas found the Duke of Shrewsbury in animated conversation with the Portuguese ambassador. Shrewsbury emphasized the need for England to make peace so much that the Portuguese asked in surprise, "What is this intended to show?

[1] Hoffmann's dispatch, June 24; Klopp, xiii, 437–438.
[2] Hoffmann's dispatch, June 27; *ibid.*, 442.
[3] Gallas, July 1; *loc. cit.*

Do you wish to make peace without driving the Duke of Anjou from Spain?" "Certainly not," replied Shrewsbury, taken aback; "we ask for a good but a rapid peace." "Such language is common here," added Gallas, "and they talk as though they had peace in their hands—as though other persons were diligently prolonging the war. The majority of the English nation is now urgent in its demand for peace. The new party find peace very desirable owing to the turmoil they have caused in the country."[1] Although Shrewsbury was the only newly appointed Minister, the foreign ambassadors in June began to speak of the Juntilla as "the new Government."

The same assurances were given to the other ambassadors. Vryberg, the Dutchman, alone appeared content. He believed no further changes would follow. In conversation with Gallas and Hoffmann he dwelt upon the great influence that the Treasurer still had with the Queen. "This is correct," wrote Hoffmann.

> The Treasurer goes daily to Court, usually twice, and speaks to the Queen in her Cabinet. He would be much too shy to do so, if he felt that the Queen did not trust him. As long as this Minister is heard, we may hope that the Queen will not be led to take any unsound decisions while surrounded by these new persons who have nothing else on their lips than the need for peace.[2]

While the allied diplomatists strove thus to console each other, and their Governments dwelt in suspense, while the great armies lay in close contact and ready for battle upon any day, the conference at Gertruydenberg had been proceeding. On March 9 the French envoys had met Buys and van der Dussen on a yacht at Moerdyk. The ensuing negotiations were vitiated from the outset by an underlying dualism: the French were primarily concerned with compensation for Philip V and attempting to gain this before discussing terms for the evacuation of Spain, while the Dutch were anxious to secure satisfactory guarantees concerning Spain, and accused the French of dishonesty when they tried to shift the emphasis of the negotiations on to the issue of compensation.

It is possible that the Allies would have agreed to provide Philip with an alternative realm after a satisfactory plan of evacuation had been settled. Marlborough, however, was sceptical of this. In close touch with opinion in Vienna through his private correspondence with Brigadier Palmes, our envoy there, he knew that the Austrians

---

[1] Klopp, xiii, 443-444.
[2] Dispatches of Gallas and Hoffmann, July 1-4; *ibid.*, 444.

would never consent to give up Sicily to Philip. This, they declared, would make Naples strategically untenable. His conversation with Sinzendorff strikes an ironic note, in which he very rarely permitted himself to indulge. "If," he remarked to the Austrian envoy, "there were a favourable territory with which to endow Philip, which is not Belgium, Spain, the Indies, nor Naples, nor Sicily— and, of course, the Duchy of Milan cannot be touched—England would agree to the arrangement."[1]

The conference at Gertruydenberg had begun with the Dutch, represented by their peacemakers, more stiff than they had been at any previous time. It continued during the whole of the siege of Douai, but thereafter a potent tide carried the French into marked recalcitrance. Louis XIV became increasingly convinced that Queen Anne's heart was changed, that the Whig power was menaced, and above all that Marlborough was no longer master of events. From this time forth the discussions degenerated into elaborate grimaces, and ended in bitter mutual distrust of each other's good faith by both the French and Dutch negotiators.

Petkum tried in vain to persuade the French to be more accommodating. He saw his long efforts at mediation going for nothing. But after the fall of Sunderland the governing circles in France thought of little more than throwing the odium of the final breach upon the Dutch.[2] It was necessary to make a case for the French people. The larger calculations of Versailles were based upon domestic affairs in England. Time would bring them the ultimate victory. In July, alleging that the Dutch were impossible, Louis XIV brought the conference to an end. In replying to Petkum's shrill remonstrances the French envoys at Gertruydenberg revealed their true motive. "We see things quite differently," they wrote; "we are convinced that in a short time you will see the English commander dismissed in disgrace, or treated in such a way that he will be unable to continue to serve with honour, and that further the present Ministry will fall, and Parliament will be dissolved."[3]

Their calculations were not belied.

On June 15 four Directors of the Bank of England, headed by Sir Gilbert Heathcote, sought an audience with the Queen. Newcastle

[1] Sinzendorff's dispatches, March 27; Austrian State Archives. *Cf.* Noorden, iii, 668.
[2] Lediard, who met Petkum in 1719, quotes (ii, 283) a letter of his saying of the French, "The gaining of time was their chief point, and every pretence of delay contributed, in their opinions, to the interest of their master."
[3] Klopp, xiii, 447.

countenanced and introduced them. The Directors exposed the danger of a financial panic. The rumours, they said, of a change of Ministry were undermining all credit. What would happen if the foreign holders of bank-stock threw it upon the market? This wonderful new credit system, which seemed to conjure wealth and power from the very air, which every country in the world regarded with astonished envy, was at once the object of hatred and worship. Even those who hated it most bowed with awe at the shrine of the then Young Lady of Threadneedle Street, who could cast among her votaries the means of building fleets and marshalling armies, of battering down fortresses, and building fine houses for noblemen, or paying their debts, and, indeed, every other enjoyment and necessity. The fox-hunting squires and the old-world Jacobites might rail at the money power. The Tory Party might feel in its bones that all the land of England was, through the growth of national debt, becoming mortgaged to a kind of London Shylock. Still, no set of men could be found who would dream of taking office without this marvellous credit apparatus at their disposal.

The Queen was sensibly affected by the bankers' protests. In her reply she assured them that she did not intend to make further changes. This was at once interpreted as excluding not only changes of Ministers, but a change in the Parliament. The rumour caused widespread relief. We can see how shrewd and deeply informed was Hoffmann from the fact that he reported that the Queen's assurances did not cover "the life of the Parliament."

> Almost every one considers that the dissolution of Parliament is certain, and already the excitement over the Election is as great throughout the Kingdom as though the dissolution had already taken place. But it is said that this event will not take place till September, so we may still hope that difficulties will arise in the meantime sufficient to restrain the Queen, if she really has this intention.[1]

When Harley heard of this bankers' deputation he was indignant and at the same time, considering his own behaviour, comical. "This is a matter of a very extraordinary nature," he wrote to Arthur Moore, a Commissioner of the Board of Trade, of whom we shall hear later (June 19), "that private gentlemen (for it cannot be conceived for their own sakes that the Bank deputed them) . . . *should have the presumption to take upon them to direct the sovereign.* If

---

[1] Hoffmann's dispatch, June 27; also that of July 4; Klopp, xiii, 442.

this be so let us swear allegiance to those four men and give them a right to our passive obedience without reserve."[1]

During the whole of Anne's reign members of both parties had sat together in the Government. The proportion varied with the complexion of Parliament. Hitherto the assumption had been that they worked together for national purposes. At this juncture we see one set of men holding the great offices, and at their side or close at hand another set, encouraged by the Queen, whose whole purpose was to drive out the Ministers, and become themselves the masters of the Government, and if possible of Marlborough's services.

The position of Godolphin, fatally weakened by the Sacheverell trial, had now become entirely devoid of strength or dignity. The Queen still listened to him on great business, but no longer allowed him the slightest influence on patronage of any account. He had submitted to Shrewsbury's being appointed Lord Chamberlain without his having been consulted. He had protested, and his protest had been ignored. He had striven hard to save Sunderland, but Sunderland had been dismissed. Even in minor offices under the Treasury his nominations were not accepted. Any step which he might wish to take to placate hostile colleagues or opponents was barred by the backstair counsellors, who were resolved not to allow him to strengthen or even mitigate his position. He knew that all about him was intrigue, that the Queen no longer valued his advice, and that his dismissal was so constantly discussed that even British ambassadors abroad reported the tale in their dispatches to London. Yet after nearly a lifetime of high office he still held stubbornly to his post. This was not from any base or small motive. He believed that only by his control of the Treasury could Marlborough receive the regular supplies without which neither his army nor the war could be maintained. For the sake of his friend and of the allied cause he endured every conceivable humiliation, and was resolved to persevere to the end, hoping that it would not be distant. "But," he wrote to Marlborough, "it will be no great surprise to you to hear in some very short time that I am no longer in a capacity for doing you any further service."[2]

Marlborough had been persuaded from all quarters to retain his command, and the Parliament had so far been preserved. The Queen had promised that no further changes should be made. The Whig leaders at home had little hope but to procure delay. If they could

---

[1] Portland Papers, *H.M.C.*, iv, 545.   [2] Coxe, v, 313.

keep Marlborough and prevent a dissolution of Parliament two things were possible. There might be a victory in the field, and an atmosphere for negotiations re-created; or else the Ministerial reconstruction would take the form of a broad-bottomed administration including Harley, the moderates of the Court party, and the more pliant Whigs. But threatening electoral disaster demoralized the individual members of the Whig Party. The first Whig definitely to take a favour from the new power was Halifax. He had shown rancour towards Marlborough since the time of Townshend's appointment to The Hague. At the beginning of July, having, as he protested, convinced himself that the credit of the country was not endangered, and that the present Parliament would continue, he cheerfully accepted the post of Townshend's colleague at The Hague. He too nursed the illusion that a "Whig game was intended at bottom."

Godolphin reported the new appointment to Marlborough.

Godolphin to Marlborough

July 3 [1710]

. . . It is my opinion our governors do believe they have given so just occasion of offence to our present Parliament that there can be no safety for them without having another, so constituted as to sanctify and approve what they have done; and the sooner they go about that the more likely they think themselves to succeed in it, and I think so too. . . . I find by the Queen this morning, and by Lord Halifax himself yesterday, that the Lord Chamberlain has prevailed with her Majesty to add him immediately to Lord Townshend. This is yet a secret here to everybody, . . . but as Lord Halifax has told me the story of that affair, I don't dislike it at all, for he has given me his word and honour he will be entirely firm to the Parliament.[1]

Halifax himself hastened to make out to Marlborough that his appointment was in the nature of a bargain with political opponents, and that the price he had exacted for a seeming departure from Whig interests was the continuance of the Parliament. But Marlborough was not in any way deceived. To Sarah he wrote, "Lord Halifax being employed in the way he is, it seems to me very extraordinary; for I can't comprehend how it sh'd be agreeable either to the Whigs or Tories; or that he himself at this juncture sh'd care to be so employed: but so many extraordinary things happen every day that I wonder at nothing."[2] Godolphin and his principal Whig colleagues resolved to use their remaining strength against the

[1] Coxe, v, 296–297.   [2] July 24; *ibid.*, 298.

approaching Dissolution, and to save their resignations for that. The Treasurer was clear that, whatever happened, Marlborough should remain at the head of the Army. "The madness," he wrote to Marlborough (July 24), "continues as fierce as ever against the Parliament; and most people that I talk with think that extremity is now very near."[1]

And (July 31):

> The Queen seems . . . to look upon it only as a personal contest for power and favour, and whether the Whigs or Tories shall have the greatest sway; and though it may make a little shock at present, yet all that will be set right, and recovered again by the new Parliament, which will be entirely at the Queen's disposal, and have nothing so much at heart as to deliver her from the tyranny of the Whigs and their supporters. This is the language and the scheme. When it comes to be executed, the Lord Chancellor, Lord President, the Duke of Devonshire, and myself, seem resolved to retire, as what may most effectually contribute to a good Parliament.
>
> Now, as to you, I think your conduct must be quite the contrary. You must still represent the mischief of this measure, and the ill consequences of it with the allies, and most particularly with the States and the Emperor, etc.; but, at the same time, continue to give assurances of your best and most faithful services.[2]

During this period the powerful, baffling influence of Shrewsbury made itself felt at almost every stage. His natural timidity and air of disinterested detachment, the ease and grace of his conversation, the part he had played in great events, all made their impression upon every one. He bore himself as if he were every one's friend, a thoroughly good fellow, whose only wish was to make every one live happily together at home and bring about peace with honour abroad. He soon disarmed Godolphin of his suspicions. The Treasurer till the very moment of his fall regarded him as the best hope of maintaining a steady policy and putting the brake on Harley's intrigues. Marlborough could not clear his mind of the belief first that Shrewsbury was his friend, and secondly that his sagacity would prevent him from wrecking the war and the Grand Alliance. He could not rid himself of those memories of William III's time in which he and Shrewsbury had shared deadly secrets and anxieties together. As Marlborough during his years of power had at all times been anxious to have Shrewsbury in the Government and had made several overtures to him, he could not easily feel

[1] Coxe, v, 314. [2] Ibid., 314–315.

uncomfortable about one to whom he had always wished well. Thus when Godolphin emphasized the vital importance of Shrewsbury's aid and urged Marlborough repeatedly to use his influence with him, he complied easily—too easily.

Sarah was the only one who throughout was sure that Shrewsbury was an opponent and 'Harley's man.' She herself had perhaps contributed to bring this about. Until the end of 1709 they were on close neighbourly terms, Shrewsbury calling frequently upon her, and bringing his new wife with him. Caustic comments about people rose readily in Sarah's mind and were with difficulty restrained upon her tongue. Shrewsbury's Italian Duchess was a tempting, provocative topic. When we remember the enormous discontented interests concerned in bringing Shrewsbury and Harley together against Marlborough and Godolphin, it is not strange that telltales were found in this case, as with the Queen, to make the worst of anything she said. At any rate, shortly after Shrewsbury joined the Government, and after Sarah's final quarrel with the Queen, the visits from Heythrop to Blenheim had come to an end in a marked manner. Godolphin thought this was due to the new Lord Chamberlain's not wishing to impede his favour with the Queen by civilities to her bugbear Sarah. Probably, however, Shrewsbury's wife played the greatest part in this coldness. She wished to be a great person at the English Court, to be everywhere received and flattered. This was not to be gained by social arts alone; and such as she possessed repelled. Political power was needed to carry her into the highest circles. Her husband had but to seek such power for it to be his. Thus it may well be that she stirred him to action, and also, having heard some of Sarah's pointed remarks about her, inclined him to the anti-Marlborough camp, where he was always welcome.

Whether or not Sarah had pricks of conscience about her indiscretions, she was from the beginning sure that Shrewsbury was irrevocably engaged in the opposite interest. She continually warned her husband and Godolphin not to be deceived by his bland manners and conciliatory professions. She waxed so hot about this that Marlborough and Godolphin did not vex her with the sight of her husband's letters to Shrewsbury. It is often wise for a man in a great position to invoke by personal appeal, written or spoken, the aid of a powerful colleague, presumably a friend. But to make several such advances without any adequate response is only to reveal weakness and invite hostility.

732

"If," Marlborough wrote to Godolphin, "after the two letters I have written to the Duke of Shrewsbury I must be mortified, I am resolved to give no farther trouble, but conclude him to be as mad as the rest. I must own to you my weakness, that I can so little bear mortifications that it is all I can do to keep myself from being sick."[1] And to Sarah (July 17), "It is impossible to be more sensible than I am of the outrages I meet with; but since everybody thinks I must have patience I must suffer for three or four months. . . . I was in hopes you had taken your resolution of staying in the country till my return, and of never being prevailed upon again to write to the Queen, which I beg you will continue firm to; for as things are now, you must expect neither reason nor justice, but, on the contrary, all the brutality imaginable. I am forced to give over writing, fearing my temper might lead me to say what, in prudence, is better to let alone, in so base an age."[2] And (July 22/August 2), "The king of France is so heartened by our late proceedings in England, that all the letters from Paris mention the great applications for carrying on the war."[3]

[1] Coxe, v, 312. [2] *Ibid.*, 309. [3] *Ibid.*, 311.

Chapter Seventeen

THE FALL OF GODOLPHIN

1710—JULY AND AUGUST

BOTH sides now looked abroad. Harley and what was now being called the Court party had for some time felt the need of giving Hanover favourable impressions of their views and intentions. The opportunity came during the summer. Mr Howe's successor at Hanover must be a fit person to prepare so important a Court for coming changes. Accordingly the Queen wrote (June 25) to Godolphin:

> ★You spoke to me some months ago that Sir Philip Meadows might be sent to Hanover. There being a man who is known to everybody in that court, I think it more proper to send him thither at this juncture than one who is a stranger to them—Cressit. I would not give my orders to Mr Secretary Boyle in this matter until I had first acquainted you with my intentions.[1]

Godolphin, though fully aware of the purpose of the appointment, perforce acquiesced, and a few days later Cresset was made envoy to Hanover. He wrote to the Elector that his mission was one of goodwill.[2] He was, however, going as an envoy not so much of Great Britain as of Harley and the Juntilla. He was to carry with him from the Tory leaders pledges of loyalty to the house of Hanover. But the pith of his task was to propose to the Elector that his Highness should succeed Marlborough as Commander-in-Chief of the main armies. Although these experienced politicians did not share the fears they excited in the Queen and expressed in the Court and the clubs that Marlborough might become "a second Cromwell,"[3] yet the shadow of his renown lay heavy upon them. While he stayed his power was massive; if he went the void would be grievous. In that case what could better convince the nation that no Jacobite restoration was intended than the appointment of the Hanoverian heir to the highest command; and what could better commend the unofficial rulers to him than the offer? It was well

[1] Blenheim MSS.   [2] See Salomon, p. 35.
[3] These rumours extended to Versailles. See Klopp, xiii, 364; Macpherson, ii, 189.

known that the Elector had been offended by Marlborough's secrecy before Oudenarde. It was hoped that he was jealous of his fame. If so this proposal, made with so little concern for the public interest, might be tempting.[1] "I hope you will be very particular," wrote Shrewsbury to Harley on July 22, "in your instructions to Mr Cresset, as well as for Holland as Hanover, where I hope he may be very useful."[2]

But on July 25 Cresset, whose plans for sailing were not noticeably aided by the Whig-controlled Admiralty, suddenly died. Before expiring he was able to seal up all his papers and send them to Harley. Harley showed remarkable concern until they were safely in his hands. Indeed, the Juntilla were strangely excited. "The death of Mr Cresset," wrote Peter Wentworth to his brother, Lord Raby, "was a great disappointment to some people, and reported by way of jest that he was poisoned by the Whigs."[3]

Somerset to Harley

July 26 [1710]

On this most unfortunate occasion of Mr Cressett's death it is absolutely necessary you do come to the Queen and to the Duke of Shrewsbury's at or before nine o'clock this night. We have talked it over and do conclude it to be of so very great consequence that somebody ought to go immediately to Hanover and in his way discourse the Pensioner too on the present change of persons and of the Parliament, . . . and who hath the honour to be in the Queen's confidence. If it be thought a right thing neither the Duke of Shrewsbury nor myself will decline it, but on the contrary either of us will go very cheerfully, as we don't doubt that my Lord Poulett will say and do the same—to go within less than ten days and to return in less than six weeks. I give you this short hint of our thoughts that you may prepare your own against nine o'clock.[4]

On the other side as early as June Walpole had suggested to Marlborough that pressure might be brought to bear by the allied Governments upon the Queen to save the Ministry and the Parliament. Formal occasion was given for such intervention by the Queen's voluble assurances, after Sunderland's dismissal, that no further alterations in the Ministry would be made. Marlborough saw the objections to this course. Knowing the Queen as well as he did, he feared that she might easily be led to resent such interference

---

[1] See Harley's letter to Newcastle, August 10; Portland Papers, *H.M.C.*, ii, 214.
[2] Bath Papers, *H.M.C.*, i, 198.　　　　[3] *The Wentworth Papers*, p. 128.
[4] Portland Papers, *H.M.C.*, v, 552.

in her affairs. Still, all the Allies were extremely alarmed: they wished to take advantage of the opening offered to them, and Marlborough lent himself to the process. If it were to be done at all it must be done thoroughly. He therefore communicated with all the Courts with whom he was in close contact. In particular he addressed himself to Eugene, who wrote at once to the Emperor (July 23):

> The confused state of affairs in England has come to a head. The Queen cannot any longer put up with the Whigs and the Marlborough party, although she still has a certain, though less, consideration for the person of my lord Duke himself—which may perhaps be a reason for hesitating and postponing the issue. Otherwise Parliament will be dissolved, and the said Whigs, together with all those friendly to Marlborough, will be removed from their offices. . . .
>
> We have learned from my lord Duke and elsewhere that the situation in England is of such danger and consequence that a [Ministerial] revolution is without doubt to be feared this coming winter, or else the Queen must undergo a complete change of front. . . . The Tories intend absolutely to bring about peace, to get the upper hand, and completely destroy the Whigs—but the Whigs and our whole work itself can only be preserved through the continuation of the war. It is certain that the majority of the Tories are followers of the Prince of Wales, . . . and that according to all appearances they must act in concert with him and with France.[1]

As a result of these representations Joseph wrote a personal letter to the Queen, and also ordered Gallas to act directly under the control of Eugene and Marlborough.[2]

Though Marlborough showed both reluctance and misgivings, he certainly did his best to marshal the Allies on the front proposed. "Prince Eugene on this occasion," he says, writing on July 10 to Sarah, "has been very kind, and tells me that he is sure his Court will act as I will have them. But I am of opinion, as in most things, the less one meddles the better."[3]

Godolphin had suggested to Marlborough (June 16/27) the lines which the reply of the States-General to the Queen's assurances might follow:

> The best use which we think can be made of this is for the States to return an answer by Vryberg that they are very much concerned for what has happened to Sunderland, who was known to be so great a friend to them and the Common Cause; that they are very glad to

[1] *Feldzüge*, Series II, iii, App., 208–209.   [2] Joseph's letter in Klopp, xiii, 552–554.
[3] Coxe, v, 281–282.

hear the Queen has no intention to make further changes; but if there is to be the least thought of parting with the Parliament, as it is very industriously spread in that country by the friends of France, it will be utterly impossible to hinder these people from running into peace, just as France wishes, leaving England and the Queen to shift for themselves, without any security against the pretensions of Louis XIV.[1]

This appeal against a dissolution was going a long way, and certainly lay open to the Tory retort of foreign interference in British affairs.

Similar replies to the Queen's assurances were drawn up in all the Courts concerned. The Dutch were the first, on July 15, to present their version to the Queen at Kensington. Vryberg had asked Godolphin's advice beforehand. Godolphin unwisely sent him to Somerset, and thus the Juntilla became aware of the contents of the resolution of the States-General before it reached the Queen. They saw their opportunity. Almost as soon as the step had been taken Godolphin realized it was a mistake. Vryberg was made conscious of a rebuff. The Queen took the paper only with the remark, evidently prepared beforehand, "This affair is of such importance and of such a nature that it will require some time to reflect upon it maturely, and give an answer to it." Forthwith the tale was spread throughout the Court that the Dutch Ambassador had presented a note intruding upon the Queen's own business. In vain did the ambassadors endeavour to counteract this injurious tale. This was no advice initiated from abroad. It was simply the grateful reply to the Queen's freely given assurances. Besides, were there not matters of common interest to all members of the Alliance? Would not the people of England feel concerned if the Emperor wished to dismiss Prince Eugene, or the States-General Pensionary Heinsius? The rejoinder which was made to this shows how the threat of a Parliamentary address about Mrs Masham rankled. Conditions in England, said the Juntilla adherents, are different from all other countries. Here an attempt has been made to coerce the Queen in the choice even of her own personal attendants. "Still," answered Count Gallas,

> though this plan may have been made, we have seen that it was not executed, and however unacceptable it may have been to the Queen, it is not to be compared with the feelings which her Majesty would have if, as the result of a step taken by her, the welfare of the whole nation—indeed, of all Europe—were plunged into the gravest peril,

[1] *Sarah Correspondence*, ii, 445.

and the high name and reputation which she had won in conjunction with her previous advisers was sullied and lost before the world.[1]

The Elector of Hanover was the next to reply. His language was extremely blunt. He wrote through Bothmar, his Ambassador at The Hague, that he hoped the Queen did not intend to make any further changes in a Ministry which deserved so well of her, and in a Parliament which was so excellently disposed. It was no part of Harley's politics to become involved in an argument with the heir to the throne; and the Hanoverian reply was left unanswered. The King of Prussia wrote far more ceremoniously. The representations of Lord Raby, now working for the Juntilla interests in Berlin, had been effective. Frederick I confined himself to thanks for the assurances, and disclaimed any idea of judging the Queen's internal policy. He notably avoided all references to a dissolution of Parliament. This impeccable document was shown in mute rebuke by the new favourites to Vryberg, so that he might compare it with his own.

During July the Whigs had been baffled by elusive negotiations, the effect of which was to play upon their individual ambitions and jealousies and to divide them from each other by flattery and false hopes. Harley and Shrewsbury were adepts in this, and the Queen was freely used to play her part. All the talk was for a "broad-bottomed" Ministry of moderate men, including, of course, the best men of both parties. There was truth as well as cajolery in this. It was what Harley at heart preferred. From day to day the rumours of a dissolution faded or advanced, according as the Queen would go to Windsor or stay at Kensington. But at the core all was settled. Harley meant to have a new Parliament. Nothing could be achieved without that. He was acutely aware of the danger of dwelling with the existing hostile body, which, once reassembled, might act with the vigour of self-preservation against the secret advisers of the Queen. It must never meet again. In his letters at this time Godolphin assumed that he would one day be confronted with the Queen's commands for a dissolution of Parliament, and that then would be the moment when he and the Whig leaders would make their united stand. But this was not the way in which Harley meant to approach the crisis.

The practice of 'making' elections did not begin or end with the eighteenth century. The Lord-Lieutenants and sheriffs on such

[1] Gallas, July 15; Klopp, xiii, 453.

occasions played a great part in England. So sure had the Whigs been of themselves in 1709 that they had allowed many Tory sheriffs to be chosen all over the country, reserving their own nominations for 1711, the normal election year. The Lord-Lieutenancies were still, however, mainly Whig. Harley felt the need of changing them, as much as possible, before the appeal to the electors was made. But here Godolphin was an obstacle. He was reserving all his strength to resist the election, and striving, on Marlborough's advice, for the "life of the Parl." He would certainly not alter the Lord-Lieutenancies to suit the Tories. Thus, if the election was to come, if the Queen was to be rid of the Whig Parliament, and the Lord-Lieutenancies were to be largely changed for that purpose, Godolphin must first be driven out; and he must be driven out in ample time for partisanship to be well directed. The old Treasurer, knowing every inch of the ground, blocked the path of dissolution. Therefore he must go. The shock would be taken on the personal issue, and not upon the general question of dissolution.

Harley was "in almost daily attendance upon the Queen."[1] His brother, Edward Harley, has left a monograph from which we learn that the Queen's letter dismissing Godolphin was prepared in the early days of July.[2] But again the difficulty was to find a successor who would satisfy the competing influences at Court. Harley did not feel strong enough as yet to take the chief post. Once he did so the Tory demands upon him would have passed all bounds. Defoe in his reports dwelt on the importance of assuring people "that moderate counsels are at the bottom of all these things; *that the old mad party are not coming in*; . . . that toleration, succession or union are not struck at, and they may be easy as to the nation's liberties."[3]

If Harley stood aside, Shrewsbury was the obvious choice. All his life he had shrunk from the responsibilities and even more from the toil of high office. He hastened to decline, and enlarged on his view in a letter to Harley, written after one of the many secret conclaves held at Kensington Palace. "I have ten reasons, every one strong enough to hinder my doing it. . . . In my mind you should be at the head, because you then come naturally into the Cabinet

[1] Portland Papers, *H.M.C.*, ii, 211.
[2] "An Account of the Earl of Oxford by his Brother," B.M., Lansdowne MSS.; Portland Papers, *H.M.C.*, v, 647 ff.
[3] Defoe to Harley, July 28, 1710; Portland Papers, *H.M.C.*, iv, 552. Defoe was employed by Harley to travel round England and Scotland and send in reports on the state of political opinion.

Council, where you are so much wanted; and every one of the other Commissioners [of the Treasury] should be persons able to serve not only at that Board but in one of the Houses of Parliament."[1] The plan of putting the Treasury in commission had, moreover, the advantages of satisfying several claims so balanced as to be awkward. "Swallow" might here find the solatium for his imaginary sacrifice of the Secretaryship. It was accordingly adopted. Sir Thomas Hanmer, a moderate Tory, was offered by Shrewsbury a junior Lordship on the Treasury Commission on August 2.[2] Hanmer declined, but the fact shows that the whole scheme was now complete. All that remained was to strike the blow. The Whigs, like many others, were still lulled with the notion that any further changes would be moderate in character. Newcastle seemed reassured. Halifax prided himself on being mediator between his colleagues and the moderates at Court. He and the Whigs had been encouraged by the prorogation of Parliament, and the consequent postponement of the dreaded dissolution.

But now an incident occurred which brought the whole matter to a head. Gallas had received from the Emperor the letter which Joseph I had written on the lines suggested by Eugene in replying to the Queen's assurances after Sunderland's dismissal. The Emperor, writing with his own hand, allowed himself great freedom in commenting on the Ministerial changes and deprecating the dissolution. Gallas was so apprehensive of its effect that he did not present it until Eugene and Marlborough, as well as Godolphin, had approved it. Their advice was wrong. This was just the kind of letter which Harley had been waiting for. A foreign potentate, the most backward of all in discharging his obligations to the Alliance, had intruded upon the prerogative of the Queen of Great Britain! It was decided to follow exactly the opposite course from that urged by the Emperor, and to dismiss Godolphin.

Gallas presented his letter on August 1. In the interval, while, unknown to the world, the Treasury Commission was being finally settled, he had a conversation with Shrewsbury. Shrewsbury suggested that the Emperor's letter had not come from Vienna. He hinted that it was not the spontaneous expression of a sovereign's personal feelings, but a document concocted by interested persons. In this he was, as we have seen, not far astray. Gallas, of course, said, "The Emperor did not need to be asked by others to write

[1] Shrewsbury to Harley, July 22, 1710; Bath Papers, *H.M.C.*, i, 198.
[2] Sir Henry Bunbury, *Memoir and Correspondence of Sir Thomas Hanmer*, p. 127.

this letter, for my reports of the real state of affairs give him sufficient cause for anxiety." He pointed to the Emperor's own handwriting. "Surely," he said, with more force, "I am the last person
to whom such reproaches [about interference] should be addressed.
For of all the ambassadors here I can give the most examples of how
the Queen has intervened in matters of slight importance, now with
the Emperor, now with the King of Spain, without either the Emperor or the King having ever taken amiss what was written with
good intention for the Common Cause." He protested that a dissolution at this moment would violate the assurances he had
received in June. "Foreigners," said Shrewsbury, "have strange
ideas of our affairs. Do you imagine that the whole welfare of England depends upon the five hundred persons who are now sitting
in the Commons? I tell you that the whole of England knows its
interests and realizes fully that this war must be pursued with energy
until a good peace can be secured. But peace must be accepted as
soon as possible. Meanwhile it is a difficult request to make to the
Queen that she should retain in her service persons who are opposed
to her." "Will the Queen," asked the Ambassador, "impose upon
the Emperor and the other allies the danger of losing all the advantages they have won?" Gallas reports that Shrewsbury gave him a
reply "from between his teeth, which was not easy to understand,
but his look revealed to me the truth." He wrote at once to Prince
Eugene, "My fears are greater than my hopes."[1]

The fractious and gallant Lord Raby had now completed his
embassage at Berlin. He had for some time past transferred his
loyalties to Harley. It was, however, Godolphin's duty to provide
him with some employment, and a vacancy occurred at the Board
of Trade. "Lord Raby is not very easily satisfied," he wrote to
Marlborough (July 27), "and if he were, it is not in my power to
do him much service. I took occasion to mention his name for the
present vacancy in the Board of Trade, but it would not do. I
suppose that is for some favourite that is to be provided for."
"Is it possible," commented Marlborough (August 2), "that you
can be so sunk in the Queen's opinion, that she will make any commissioners of trade, or any other that belongs to your office, without first consulting you?"[2]

[1] Klopp, xiii, 463.
[2] Coxe, v, 303.

Marlborough to Heinsius

July 26, 1710

★By this post I am not favour'd by any from you, but Ld. Townshend has given

The Treasurer was aware that the Court party were plotting his dismissal and disputing about his successor at the busy, furtive conclaves in the Queen's apartments. There was a slender hope that she would desist for fear of the effect abroad of such a change. Indeed, for some days she seemed to wish to deceive him by a return to her former cordiality. She spoke of the importance of "a moderating system," and even hinted vaguely that he should be reconciled with Harley. That this was designed to draw Godolphin from the Whigs is suggested by the report which Shrewsbury conveyed through Halifax to Godolphin that the Queen was resolved to make him and Harley agree. Amid these lures and traps the Treasurer held his head high and transacted his business as usual. But the end had come. There seems to have been a Cabinet on the 6th at which he had an altercation with Shrewsbury, reproaching him with "French counsels." The Queen intervened on Shrewsbury's side, and Godolphin continued to argue, and this time with her. On the morning of August 7 he called upon the Queen, and afterwards penned a perplexed note to Marlborough: "I think the safety or destruction of the Parliament remains still under a good deal of uncertainty."[1] In the evening he again sought the Queen's presence, and for two hours he harangued his Sovereign upon the evils of government by secret cabals, and closed by asking, "Is it the will of your Majesty that I should go on?" The Queen replied without hesitation, "Yes."[2] She had for nearly a month been lending herself to all the arrangements for putting the Treasury in commission. Men had been sounded: men had been chosen. For some days at least everything had been settled. The next morning one of the Queen's servants brought Godolphin a letter.

The Queen to Godolphin

KENSINGTON
August 7, 1710

The uneasiness which you have showed for some time has given me very much trouble, though I have borne it; and had your behaviour

---

me a very perfect account of all that has pass'd. The ffrench letter is calculat'd a good deal for England. I pray God it be not in concert with some of our new Ministers; if thay continu in the full power thay now have, we must expect every thing that is bad; as I have taken the resolution of being guid'd by my friends, and particularly by you, I shal rest quiet; other ways I like nothing that is doing in England. By the last post I had an account of Ld. Cunningsbey's being turn'd out to provide for Ld. Anglessy who is thought one of the greatest Jacobits in England, and I am prepar'd to hear every thing that is disagreable. [Heinsius Archives.]

[1] Coxe, v, 320–321.   [2] *Loc. cit.*; from a letter of Godolphin's (August 7).

continued the same it was for a few years after my coming to the crown, I could have no dispute with myself what to do. But the many unkind returns I have received since, especially what you said to me personally before the lords, makes it impossible for me to continue you any longer in my service; but I will give you a pension of four thousand a year, and I desire that, instead of bringing the staff to me, you will break it, which, I believe, will be easier to us both.[1]

Thus ended an association which had lasted for more than thirty years of Anne's life, had been a prop to her in times of trouble both under King James and King William, and in her own reign had helped to make her Throne unsurpassed in Europe. Mr Montgomery took a few hours to sign and settle a good many minor things; then he broke his staff and cast the fragments in the grate. He had stood by Marlborough to the end. Harley became Chancelor of the Exchequer and in all that mattered First Minister.

The Queen to Marlborough

KENSINGTON
August 8, 1710

The Lord Treasurer having for some time shown a great deal of uneasiness in my service, and his behaviour not being the same to me as it was formerly, made it impossible for me to let him keep the white staff any longer, and therefore I intend him this evening to break it, which I acquaint you with now, that you may receive this news first from me, *and I do assure you I will take care that the army shall want for nothing.*[2]

Godolphin to Marlborough

Tuesday, August 8, 1710

I believe it will be no great surprise to you, after the steps made here of late, to hear the Queen has this morning, been pleased to dismiss me from her service. . . . What I am chiefly concerned for just now is, that you should take this matter in the manner that is most advisable for yourself and all the world besides.

It is my opinion that you should represent to the Queen that it is impossible for anybody to imagine but you must be affected by this stroke in the most sensible manner, . . . *but by no means to think of leaving your post* till you have had an answer from the Queen to this letter, from which you will be best able to judge what step you are next to take.[3]

And (August 9):

Though my circumstances at present are a little discouraging, yet

_____

[1] Coxe, v, 322.   [2] *Loc. cit.*   [3] *Loc. cit.*

nothing can ever make me neglect doing what is best for the whole, or thinking of everything that may be most for your honour and safety.[1]

It would be idle to portray Godolphin as a powerful and dominating personality, fitted for the contentions of a tumultous period. He was an honest servant of the State, loyal and faithful to his friends and to his duty. He had unrivalled knowledge and experience of affairs. He was a most able and circumspect finance Minister. The means by which he provided the immense sums required for the war, at a time when taxation was narrowly limited in character and degree, and when the credit system was in its mysterious infancy, must be regarded as a splendid public achievement. In that lax age his personal integrity shone as an example. He more nearly corresponds to the great civil servants of the present day than any of his contemporaries. He quitted his nine years' administration of wartime finance, with all the opportunities of self-enrichment by speculation or by taking presents, apart altogether from direct corruption, without reproach and with barely a thousand pounds a year. In days when a Paymaster-General, by merely using according to custom the interest on the moneys which passed through his hands, could amass an enormous fortune Godolphin walked out of the Treasury poorer than he had entered it. Although addicted to cards and betting and a passionate lover of the Turf, he always played for modest stakes and lived at the height of power with admirable frugality. Queen Anne's offer of a pension of four thousand pounds a year was never implemented. It is uncertain whether she did not give it or he would not have it. But by a curious coincidence his immediate family wants were provided for. He was dismissed on August 7, and ten days later the death of his elder brother brought him an inheritance of four thousand pounds a year.

John and Sarah regarded themselves as responsible for his well-being. Their houses were at his disposal. He spent a good deal of the remaining two years of his life at Holywell. His chief concern was to prevent Marlborough from giving up the command of the army, and to try to help him through his influence with Boyle and in other ways. He was not, however, able to play any strong part in Parliament. He left the defence of his finance in the competent hands of Walpole, in whose qualities and future he had unbounded belief. In every respect his conduct after his dismissal was a model of good temper and disinterested care for national interests.

[1] Coxe, v, 323–324.

Chapter Eighteen

MARLBOROUGH AND HANOVER

1710—AUGUST AND SEPTEMBER

W HEN the ability of the Whig Party, their resolute majorities in both Houses of Parliament, their lively association with the prosecution of the war and the Hanoverian Succession, are considered, it is surprising how easily and tamely they allowed themselves in a few months after the trial of Sacheverell to be chased from power. This can only be explained by the astute and perfectly measured tactics of Harley. When the story which the last three chapters have recounted is reviewed, he does not seem to have made a single mistake in choosing his ground, in timing his action, or in dealing with the Queen, the Tories, and the Whigs. He was not the chief of the Tory Party in a formal sense. They regarded him to some extent as a deserter who had fallen out with his new friends, and been returned to them at a discount, though endowed with the priceless favour of the Queen. They never cared much for a leader who had been brought up a Dissenter, was notoriously broadminded about the Church of England, and had thrown his weight against the Occasional Conformity Bill. Moreover, the new ferment which the Sacheverell trial had raised in the country, spreading and strengthening throughout the summer of 1710, sustained those very Tory elements which it was Harley's avowed policy to keep in subjection. As the prospect of power drew nearer, the Tories who had adhered to Rochester and Nottingham since these Ministers had been expelled from the Government in 1703 and 1704 felt that the victory when gained belonged to them. Harley acquired merit with them because through his command of Abigail, and through Abigail of the Queen, he was able to procure the transference of power. They admired his management, and chuckled appreciatively over his devices and deceits. They were glad that he should render them these valuable services. They were not aware that he proposed to make them serve him.

Harley's adroitness was constantly shown in his handling of the clusters of crude, inexperienced, but none the less determined claimants who presented themselves as the various appointments were successively vacated by the Whigs. He succeeded in giving the Tory leaders the impression that the moderate Government of the centre for which he was working was purely transitional; that a frontal attack on Marlborough, Godolphin, and the Whigs would certainly be repulsed; that he must detach important Whig Ministers if he was to carry the Queen; and that, above all things, nothing must be done which would fatally cripple credit or the war. It would be easy thereafter, he let it be thought, to take the further steps, and give 'the gentlemen of England' their full satisfaction. But this was not at all what he meant to do.

This same complicated scheme which held the Tories in leash was also nicely adapted to the confounding of the Whigs. The allied ambassadors, one and all, were astounded that these great statesmen and Parliamentarians allowed themselves to be set at odds with one another, and hoodwinked and tricked until they degenerated into a rabble—no one thinking of anyone but himself. No doubt the Whig fear of the Queen on the one hand, and of a General Election on the other, was harassing in the last degree. Still, at any time in the first six months of 1710 Marlborough, Godolphin, and the Whigs, if they had acted together upon any one of the provocations they received, could have raised a Parliamentary storm before which Queen Anne might well have had to bow. But Harley's skill never presented a direct issue on which they could *all* fight. His attacks were always oblique. First, over the Hill promotion, he isolated Marlborough from his colleagues. How could the whole Government resign upon the petty question (as they conceived it) of the appointment of a brigadier to gratify the Queen? His second attack was upon Godolphin. The appointment of Shrewsbury behind the back of the Lord Treasurer, virtually Prime Minister, was an open, deadly blow at Godolphin's authority. On the other hand, as we have seen, Shrewsbury was exactly the man against whose appointment no united objection could be raised. Marlborough had always wished to have him in the Government. He was a Whig, foremost in the Glorious Revolution. He had been King William's trusted Minister. He was eminent, he was detached. How could the Whigs resign in a body to prevent so famous a figure joining the Queen's Government in an office, that of Lord Chamberlain, which peculiarly concerned her Majesty and her Court, merely because the process of consulting the Lord Treasurer had been omitted? By these two blows, the second of which was accepted with submission, the two super-Ministers were divided from the main body of the Government and the Parliamentary forces at its command.

It was not until the effects were thoroughly understood throughout the political world, and signals of encouragement had been given to all the forces of opposition whether at the front or in Parliament, that Harley assailed the Whig phalanx. Here again the selection of Sunderland for extrusion was judicious. Sunderland, a rasping figure, an uncomfortable colleague, was obnoxious to the Queen, had no popularity with the Whig Party, and, though Marlborough never pressed for him, would not have entered the Government had he not been Marlborough's son-in-law. By this time, too, the whole foundation of the Government had been so much shaken that his dismissal caused far more trouble in the Grand Alliance than it did in British politics. His fall not only broke in upon the Junto, but was everywhere taken as an affront to Marlborough, and a sign that his ascendancy over the Queen had departed. The dismissal of Sunderland by the royal authority, without the advice of any of the responsible Ministers, was a striking event; and when it was endured by all his colleagues without any protest, except from Marlborough and Godolphin, it was obvious that no Whig Minister was safe.

In the two months' interval between the dismissal of Sunderland and that of Godolphin every one of the Whig Ministers, except perhaps Orford and Wharton, was played with by Harley in the most ingenious fashion. After what they had swallowed they were bound to base their hopes upon a moderate central Administration. Each was made to feel that his chances of inclusion depended upon his behaviour. Several were mocked with the hope of becoming the head of the new Government. Somerset above all deluded himself in this way. Somers also had the pleasing vision of bestriding both parties with the favour of the Queen, and having at his disposal the services of Marlborough in the field. In both these cases Anne, under the guidance of the backstairs, played an artful part. In long and frequent audiences she made both the Duke of Somerset and the Lord President Somers feel that they each might be indispensable to fill Godolphin's place. Halifax was early induced to accept small favours from the rising power. The Duke of Newcastle sincerely desired a Government of both parties, and he was the only one of all the Whigs that Harley really meant to keep. His daughter eventually married Harley's son. He succeeded in keeping him till he

747

was not worth keeping any more. Only Cowper, the Lord Chancellor, seems throughout to have acted with simplicity and courage. He held on till the end, but left with dignity.

The prejudices of most of these men were during July skilfully turned against Godolphin. He was evidently marked as the next victim. The Whigs had never cared for him, and they found it easy to ascribe their growing misfortunes to his clumsiness with the Queen. Had not "Volpone" also been foremost in urging the ill-starred prosecution of Sacheverell? Thus the fourth stroke was triumphantly delivered by Harley, and Godolphin had to throw his broken white staff in the grate. Even now the idea of a "broad-bottomed" Administration was used to tantalize the remaining Whigs. Harley did this with perfect ease because it was what he wanted himself. He realized, however, that whether he would succeed in his wish entirely depended upon the character of a new House of Commons.

Meanwhile Harley, Shrewsbury, and Somerset all felt the need of establishing relations with Hanover, and after Cresset's death, which caused a month's delay, their choice fell upon Lord Rivers. But the rumour that Marlborough was to be superseded had already travelled far in Europe. At the end of August the Amsterdam *Gazette* announced that Lord Rivers had been sent to offer the Elector the command of the armies in Flanders. This created consternation throughout the Alliance. Meanwhile the Juntilla became less sure of their ability to do without Marlborough. It was certain that the war was going on, and they could not afford to be without a General. Certainly they did not wish to offer the main command to the Elector and be refused. Without knowing of the Amsterdam disclosure, but upon the same day,[1] they deleted from Rivers' instructions the section containing the invitation. Rivers was authorized to use his discretion on the spot. He left London in the first days of September. He bore with him a ceremonious letter from the Queen, also letters from Shrewsbury and Rochester expressing in fervent language their friendship and devotion to the house of Hanover. Passing through The Hague, he saw Heinsius. The Pensionary at once reported to Marlborough as follows:

Heinsius to Marlborough

Sept. 13, 1710

★I ought to tell you that Lord Rivers, passing through here to

[1] August 24/September 4.

748

Hanover, has assured me that the change [of Government] has not led to any alteration in the public will to procure a good peace, and has also made me aware in his talk that he has no instruction to speak in Hanover about the command of the Army, as the rumour had run; by this I have been much relieved, for it disposes of all the anxieties we have felt on this subject, and the Elector will no longer be embarrassed.[1]

Marlborough had not been in any way disquieted by the Rivers mission to Hanover, or by the rumours which attended it. First, he was sure that he stood on strong ground with the Elector, and, secondly, he did not seem to mind being superseded by him. He may well have contemplated serving under him as his Chief of Staff, as he had been willing to do in 1707, and earlier, in 1702, under Prince George of Denmark.

John to Sarah

August 21, 1710

. . . You mention again in yours the great desire Lord Sunderland has of having me well with the Elector. You may assure him that I have more real power with his Highness than any man in England; and I have been assured that I may depend on his not accepting anything that may be uneasy to me. But this should not be spoken of, for the very foundation of Mr Harley's scheme depends very much on this.[2]

And (September 4):

My last letters from The Hague say that Lord Rivers was expected everyday; the Amsterdam *Gazette* says he is to offer the Elector of Hanover the command of this army. I wish so well to my country, and have so great a respect for the Elector, that if I could any ways contribute to the making him successful, I should cheerfully do all in my power, without any thoughts of reward, but the gaining his esteem, enjoying quiet afterwards, and contemning the ungrateful malice of my enemies.[3]

And again to Godolphin (September 4):

The Amsterdam *Gazette* has acquainted the world with Lord Rivers' errand to Hanover. I own I wish the thing might be made practicable; since it is what might reasonably free me from the incumbrance I now lie under. Besides, I have of late received so many civilities from the Elector of Hanover that I should be glad to use my best endeavours to make it easy to him; but I think the Dutch and Prince Eugene would never be brought to agree to it, though the Queen should declare

---

[1] Heinsius Archives.   [2] *Sarah Correspondence*, i, 364.
[3] *Ibid.*, 372.

never so much in favour of it. My resolution is to be careful of behaving myself so in this matter that the Elector may take it kindly of me.

I am here lodged at the abbey of St Andrew very much to my liking; but it is so near the town that I fear the noise of the cannon and small shot, when the attack begins, will be troublesome. . . . The certainty of a new Parliament makes everybody that has any interest desirous of going for England; if I refuse, they will take it unkindly; and if they go, I shall lose the service of a great many.[1]

These secret letters to his wife and his greatest friend, before whom pretences were alike needless and useless, show that he did not cling to his command if any reasonable arrangement could be made to replace him. Indeed, he probably felt that, serving under the Elector, and in combination with him, he might still find the means of preventing the disaster which now threatened the fruits of all his labours and the allied cause.

The Hanover Court were convinced, and even ardent, supporters of Marlborough. "They are," wrote Horatio Walpole to his brother, the Secretary-at-War, "very much alarmed at the late proceedings in England and think it is time to look about them, being apprehensive of 54 [Harley], and are almost ready to declare for 89 [the Whigs]." And again, on August 18: "I think 39 [Marlborough] should be very diligent in making his court there, which I am afraid was formerly a little neglected, and I am persuaded he will find all imaginable regard and confidence from thence."[2]

Any resentment which the future King George I may have harboured against Marlborough about the Oudenarde campaign played no part in this crisis. The aged Electress and her son decided to send a special envoy to London to watch over their interests and report upon the new Ministers. This envoy was the trusted Bothmar, who used his opportunities to such advantage that for twenty years after the accession of George I he founded or marred the political fortunes of British Ministers. But before Bothmar repaired to England he must first be saturated with Marlborough's views. For this purpose a sojourn of no less than three weeks at his headquarters was deemed necessary. Robethon, for ten years confidential secretary to the Elector and Marlborough's intimate correspondent, was instructed to arrange this.[3]

[1] Coxe, v, 329.   [2] Coxe, *Walpole*, ii, 32–33.
[3]   *Robethon to Marlborough*

HANOVER
August 29, 1710

★M. de Bothmar will start to-morrow from The Hague and will be here on Septem-

The Elector went out of his way to write to Marlborough upon the main issue (September 8), "I hope that nothing will be capable of inducing the Queen to take the command of her armies from a general who has acquitted himself with so much glory and so much success, and in whose hands I shall always see it with pleasure."[1]

Rivers arrived in Hanover on September 18, and was politely received. After presenting his letters and reiterating the assurances they contained, he suggested to the Hanoverian Prime Minister, Count Bernsdorf, that the Elector might reply to Queen Anne in the following terms: "I would esteem myself infinitely happy if I could find the means of showing her, by effects, the zeal which I have for her service; and the greatest favour which her Majesty can do me is to put me in a condition of being able to be useful to her." This was, of course, a device for offering the command without definitely committing the British Government to dismissing Marlborough, or running the risk of receiving a refusal from the heir to the throne. The Hanoverian Court had been well informed about the mission, and the Elector had prepared himself for an invitation to the supreme command. He had already decided upon, and drafted, his answer. It was a reasoned refusal. "His Electoral Highness leaves her Majesty to judge whether the zeal which she has always shown for the Common Cause ought not to decide her to allow the war to be finished by a general who has pressed it thus far with so much success, and who has won the confidence of her Majesty's Allies."[2]

The diplomacy of the Juntilla had saved them from this rebuke.

---

ber 3. He will be able to stay three weeks before returning to The Hague to embark as soon as possible for England. We shall arrange here with him in what way he can converse at length with Your Highness before crossing the sea, and what pretext can be found for him to make a stay with the army. Our Ministers (as well as the Minister himself) understand how useful it will be to His Highness [Prince Eugene] that this envoy before taking up his duties should have the honour of consulting with you and profiting by your lights [*lumières*] upon the disastrous conjunction in which British affairs lie at present, more dangerous than ever since the dismissal of the Treasurer. M. de Bothmar having forwarded the letter which he has received from Your Highness, I have not failed to communicate it to my master, who has been deeply impressed by the strong and agreeable terms of which you make use to mark your devotion to his interests. He has ordered me to thank you in his name. In truth he takes the English affairs far more to heart than he has ever done, and he has ideas which are very just and clear-cut. He counts much upon the goodness which he hopes Your highness will have to guide M. de Bothmar upon this new ground, so slippery and so embarrassed. If during the three weeks that this Minister will pass with you Your Highness has anything on which you wish him to receive instructions [from the Elector] I beg that your letters should be sent to me through General Major St Laurant, feeling sure that they could not be in better hands. [Blenheim MSS.]

[1] Macpherson, ii, 191.   [2] *Loc. cit.*

The Elector rejected the words which Rivers suggested, and wrote only a ceremonial letter of thanks to the Queen. Rivers, who was found to be the bearer to the Elector neither of an offer of the command nor of an invitation to visit England, was treated with some coolness. His deprecations of Bothmar's impending visit to Marlborough's headquarters and to London were ignored. He was allowed to leave amid civilities, but without the customary present.[1] Thus words were paid with words.

Marlborough's judgment was in no way distorted by the Hanoverian favour and confidence shown him in these days. He saw that the true interest of the Elector was not to give himself to either party, but to be courted by both. His letter to Sarah of September 13, although marred by one bitter phrase, is as profound and clairvoyant a document as any he ever penned.

John to Sarah

Sept. 13, 1710

I believe you judge very right that the Queen has deferred her resolution of putting you out till my return. But if there be any pretence [pretext] given, they will do it before; for they are impatient of having that blow given. The Queen is as desirous and as eager in this remove as Mr Harley and Mrs Masham can be. I do by no means approve of the behaviour of the Duke of Shrewsbury in this whole matter; but remember, as Lady Peterborough used to say, that I tell you that *he will be, as well as the Duke of Somerset, duped; for nobody has a real power but Mrs Masham and Mr Harley.* In my opinion, all reasoning serves but to cheat ourselves; for no good judgment can be made, when one has to do with Mrs Masham and Mr Harley; so that the only measure in which you and I may be sure of not being deceived is to know the truth, that whatever can be done to make us uneasy will be attempted.

I am of opinion that the King of France has taken his resolution not to think of peace till he sees, this winter, the behaviour of England. *You must not flatter yourself that the Elector of Hanover is capable of acting a vigorous part. I believe he will show that he esteems me; but at the same time, will be desirous of meddling as little as possible with the affairs of England, for which I cannot much blame him, for not caring to have to do with so villainous a people.*

I am still of the opinion that the only good you can do is to be quiet, by which you will give them no handle to use you ill before my return.[2]

Harley's control of the Exchequer gave him an immediate means

---

[1] Cowper, *Diary*, p. 49 (October 26, 1710).   [2] Coxe, v, 397.

of putting pressure upon Marlborough in a most sensitive spot. Hitherto the building of Blenheim Palace had proceeded steadily in accordance with the Queen's original commands. She herself had chosen the architect, and personally interested herself in the design. Indeed, she had had a model made and set up in Kensington Palace. According to a deep law of nature, the architect's estimate of £100,000 fell far short of the realized expense. By June 1710 £134,000 had already been spent, and the work was but half completed. The continual payments from the Exchequer had become galling to Parliament. The "golden mine of Blenheim" was harped on by Tory members of the House of Commons when in opposition. Now they had the power. The new Treasury Board as one of their first acts suspended the payments. With much cleverness a trap was laid, in which, wary as they were in money matters, John and Sarah were eventually to some extent entangled.[1] Vanbrugh was induced to write to the Duchess dwelling upon the injury and loss which a temporary interruption of the work would cause, and pleaded seductively that she should give him a letter declaring that, whatever might happen, the workmen should not suffer. At the same time the workmen and smaller contractors were prompted to apply to Marlborough for the payment of their wages and bills which had fallen into arrears. Their plight was cruel.[2] If either Marlborough or his wife had committed themselves in the slightest degree to this responsibility they would have found themselves saddled with the whole remaining burden. But both declined to involve themselves. "Instead of complying with him," noted Sarah on Vanbrugh's letter, "I stopped the works in 1710, until the Crown should direct money for it." "Let them keep their heap of stones," said Godolphin.[3]

Marlborough was insistent in advising his wife not to give any

[1] Coxe (vi, 370) shows in detail the alleged interferences, extending from 1705 to 1710, on which Ministers relied in their efforts to transfer the responsibility for the arrears for Blenheim from the Crown to Marlborough.

[2] *William Stratford, of Christ Church, Oxford, to Edward Harley (his former pupil)*
August 21, 1710

The debt to the workmen at Blenheim that is known is above £60,000. They owe to Strong the mason for his share £10,500. It will go hard with many in this town and the country who have contracted with them. Their creditors begin to call on them, and they can get no money at Blenheim. One poor fellow, who has £600 owing to him for lime and brick, came on Saturday to Tom Rowney [Member for Oxford] to ask for a little money he owed him. Tom paid him immediately. It was about £5. The fellow thanked him with tears, and said that money for the present would save him from gaol. [Portland Papers, *H.M.C.*, vii, 14.]

[3] Reid, p. 345.

directions to the builders which might be treated as interference. "My opinion is," he wrote, "that you and I should be careful of leaving the disposition of carrying on the building at Woodstock to the Queen's officers. . . . It is our best way not to give any orders, but to let the Treasury give what orders they please, either for its going on or standing still." Even the action of Sarah in stopping the works and discharging the workmen seemed to him imprudent.

> It no way becomes you or me to be giving orders for the Queen's money. . . . You know my opinion, that neither you, nor I, nor any of our friends ought to meddle in their accounts, but to let it be taken by the Queen's officers, as they always ought to be. She is the mistress of her own money, and consequently of the time of finishing that house. Whilst Lord Godolphin was in, and I had the Queen's favour, I was very earnest to have had it finished; but as it is, I am grown very indifferent. For as things are now, I do not see how I can have any pleasure in living in a country where I have so few friends.[1]

Marlborough had set his heart upon this mighty house in a strange manner. Sarah considered it as his "greatest weakness." It certainly gives us an insight into the recesses of his being. There is no doubt that the desire for posthumous fame, to "leave a good name to history," to be remembered long generations after he had passed away, was in these years his strongest passion. At his age he could not hope to enjoy Blenheim much himself. Several years must pass before it could even offer the comforts of Holywell. It was as a monument, not as a dwelling, that he so earnestly desired it. Hence the enormous thickness of the walls and masses of masonry in Vanbrugh's plan had appealed to him, and had probably been suggested by him. As the Pharaohs built their Pyramids, so he sought a physical monument which would certainly stand, if only as a ruin, for thousands of years. About his achievements he preserved a complete silence, offering neither explanations nor excuses for any of his deeds. His answer was to be this great house.

This mood has characterized dynasts in all ages, and philosophers in none. Remembrance may be preserved to remote posterity by piling great stones on one another, and engraving deep inscriptions upon them. But fame is not to be so easily captured. Blenheim cost him dear. It weakened him in his relations with hostile Ministers. It exposed him to mockery and malice. The liability for its expense was turned as a weapon against him. In after-years he was forced

[1] October 25, 27, and 30; Coxe, v, 350–351.

into unsuccessful litigation with the Crown. In his will he had to leave £50,000 to complete the work otherwise derelict. Indeed, his happiness lost much, and his fame gained nothing, by the building of Blenheim. However, Blenheim stands, and Marlborough would probably regard it as having fulfilled its purpose if he returned to earth at this day.

Chapter Nineteen

DISSOLUTION

1710—AUGUST—OCTOBER

THE last hope of the now ignominious band of Whigs lay in averting the dissolution. To the end they continued to flatter themselves that this would not be forced upon them. Their very apprehension might in itself have confirmed their opponents. Harley knew well from the beginning that without a dissolution he could do nothing, and, indeed, that his path was perilous. The Whig Parliament had no opportunity of coping with the situation created during the summer. They had separated in May. Harley did not dare to let them meet again. Parliaments were dangerous instruments in those times, and rarely had a House of Commons more just grounds for complaint against the Crown. They must therefore be prorogued until they could be dissolved. Harley had no choice in this. It is remarkable that he persuaded so many of the remaining Whig Ministers, now become his colleagues, that the issue still stood in doubt. Then, when the moment was ripe and none could resist, the final blow was struck. Somerset woke up to the fact that he had been fooled, as he deserved. The scales of illusion fell from Somers's eyes. Newcastle had for some time taken refuge in absence. Halifax had become futile and even contemptible. The old Admiral, Orford, and the sharp-tongued libertine Wharton were ripe for the sickle. All this proceeded behind the back of Parliament and through advice tendered to the Queen by a man who, having no constitutional right to advise the Sovereign, tampered with her through her dresser.

The dismissal of Godolphin had been the necessary preliminary to changing the Lord-Lieutenancies in the interests of the new Government at the elections. On September 5/16 Godolphin was supplanted in the Lord-Lieutenancy of Cornwall by Rochester. The Whig Duke of Bolton was deprived of three Lord-Lieutenancies, two of which were given to the Duke of Beaufort, an ardent Tory. General Webb, the gallant Jacobite of Wynendael, became Lord-Lieutenant of the Isle of Wight. These changes were typical and significant. New sheriffs now became the returning officers in a good many counties. Nevertheless, in the advent of the fight there was a resurgence of hope among the Whig leaders.

Sunderland, inveterate optimist, wrote to Marlborough (August 10), "By all accounts from the counties there is like to be a good election."[1] "The stocks fall so much," wrote Godolphin to Seafield, a Scottish peer (August 10), "and our people suffer to that degree that they begin to be enraged at what is doing. . . . I have great hopes we shall have a good Parliament here."[2] Marlborough responded a little to the combative mood. He wrote to Sarah (August 11), *"What has been said by the Duke of Shrewsbury, that he knows the way home, he may by it cheat himself; for a ruined people may be angry."*[3] He gave precise directions about the return of Cadogan for Woodstock,[4] but on the general result he had no illusions. He warned Sarah (August 18), "My intelligence is very positive, that there will be a new Parliament, and that you must not flatter yourself, but expect everything that can be disagreeable personally to yourself; for there is no barbarity but what you and I must expect."[5] And (August 25), "The Queen will risk England rather than not vex you. She has at this time no resentment but to you, me, Lord Treasurer, and our children. God knows how little I have deserved this, and his will be done."[6] And to Heinsius (September 8), ★ "A New Parl. is so sure that all the officers that have interest to be chosen have desired leave of me to goe for England to take care of their Elections. . . . My Lord Godolphin assures me that the chief member of the Bank has promised him that they will lend moneys for the subsistance of this army during this campaigne."[7] He had evidently obtained a new source of secret information.

Marlborough to Godolphin
Aug. 16, 1710

. . . I am informed that Mr Harley, in his conversations, keeps no

---

[1] Coxe, v, 346.   [2] Seafield Papers, *H.M.C.*, p. 209.   [3] Coxe, v, 311.

[4] *John to Sarah*

August 16, 1710

. . . I beg there may be no alteration made at the election of Woodstock; for I intend Cadogan shall come to England with me. 39 [Marlborough] shall expect more assistance in 87 [Parliament] from 197 [Cadogan] and 202 [Macartney] than any other Members, for they have both honesty and courage to speak the truth; so that I do earnestly desire that these two men may be chose preferable to all others, with which I desire you will lose no time in acquainting 38 [Godolphin], and that I beg it of him as a particular favour that he would take care of securing an election for 202, for 39 does think it absolutely necessary to have him early in 108 [England] this winter, of which he will take care. [*Sarah Correspondence*, i, 363.]

[5] Coxe, v, 330.   [6] *Loc. cit.*   [7] Heinsius Archives.

sort of decency for you or me, by which it is plain that the Queen
has no design of reconciling you and Mr Harley, as was mentioned to
me in a former letter. . . . When I see you, you shall have the particulars, how I came to be informed of this business. . . . I beg you
will never mention this to anybody; for though I think I shall have the
glory of saving the Queen, she must know nothing of it; for she
certainly would tell so much of it to Mrs Masham and Mr Harley,
that they would for the future order it so that I should not come to
know, which, *otherwise, I shall know, all that passes.*

Our extravagant behaviour in England has so encouraged the
French that they take measures as if the war were but just beginning;
so that our new Ministers will be extremely deceived, for the greater
desire they shall express for peace, the less they will have it in their
power to obtain it.[1]

And (August 30), "I hope and believe you think so well of me
that after this campaign we may yet for some few years live in more
quietness than these new vipers would have us."[2]

To the influence of the Queen and the Court, to the new Lord-
Lieutenancies and the Tory sheriffs, the Tories now added an effective piece of electioneering. A rowdy triumphant progress was
organized for Dr Sacheverell from London to the lucrative living
in Shropshire with which he had been presented. This went well.
At every town and village through which he passed the whole force
of the Tory Party was used to make a violent demonstration. The
nobility, the gentry, and the clergy found themselves able to draw
the mass of the people in their train. These had no votes, but by
their enthusiasm and turbulence they gave a formidable encouragement. Multitudes greeted the Doctor. The roads and hedges were
lined with cheering peasants; the steeples were illuminated or be-
flagged. Cavalcades of fox-hunters and yeomen escorted his coach.
Mayors received him with ceremony. He passed from feast to feast.
The excitement and passion became intense. The old mood of the
Restoration seemed to have returned.

Towards the end of September the Queen, emboldened, yielded
herself finally to Harley's political management. For some days her
blandishments to Somers had ceased. The Lord President was conscious of a disdain, perhaps not undeserved. On the 19th under
evident pressures he resigned, and with him the Duke of Devonshire, the Lord Steward, and Boyle, Secretary of State. The next
day, when these three hopers against hope had been succeeded in

[1] Coxe, v, 304–305.　　　　[2] *Loc. cit.*

their offices by the Earl of Rochester, the Duke of Buckingham, and Henry St John, who became a Secretary of State, the Council met to swear the new Ministers. No sooner was this ceremony completed than the Queen declared that she had determined upon a dissolution. She caused a draft proclamation to be read. The Lord Chancellor, Cowper, got up to protest. Orford, Lord High Admiral, and Wharton, Lord-Lieutenant of Ireland, veteran chiefs of the Junto, were ready to support him. But before Cowper could even begin the Queen rose to depart, and the sitting came to an end. Wharton and Orford sent in their resignations in the afternoon. These were at once accepted. The Duke of Ormonde was appointed to Ireland instead of Wharton, and the Admiralty was placed under a commission of Tories. On the 22nd, the proclamation having been printed, the Queen commanded the Lord Chancellor to affix the Great Seal to it. Cowper objected. The proclamation declared that the Queen's Council had given its consent. He knew this was not correct: the matter had not even been discussed in the Council. He could not therefore set the Seal to it. He tendered it instead to the Queen, thus resigning his office. No Whig Minister comes out of this story so well as Cowper. Harley was at his wits' end to find a successor. The Queen meanwhile declined to accept the Seal, and a solemn comedy of pushing it to and fro followed. Cowper's diaries tell the story to his credit.

September 22

. . . She strongly oppos'd my doing it, giving it me again at least 5 times after I had laid it down, & at last would not take it, but commanded me to hold it, adding, "I beg it as a Favour of you, if I may use that Expression": on which I took it again. . . . The Reason of all this Importunity, I guess, proceeded from the new Miny. being unprepar'd of a Succr. that wod. be able to execute the Office well . . . : so, much to my Disatisfaction, I return'd home with the Seal. But the next day I gave up the Seal, on my Knee; which the Q. accepted.[1]

For the time being the Lord Chancellorship, like the Treasury and the Admiralty, had to be put in commission. As the Commissioners could not confirm what had taken place before they entered office, a second proclamation was printed containing the first. Well might the Imperial Ambassador remark, "If the great men who are being dismissed are compared with those who replace them, one cannot help wondering that such a change has taken

[1] Cowper, *Diary*, p. 46.

place. Everything here appears so confused and unstable that the situation seems unlikely to last."[1]

But one figure of outstanding abilities, "above the common herd," as he would himself have expressed it, St John, had now reached a commanding station.

"Mr St John's heart will be at ease," wrote Stratford to Edward Harley (August 17); "he will be in the post he has long wished for. I pray God he consider himself under his new character, a Secretary of State must not take all those liberties one of War might think perhaps 'proper to his station.'"[2]

The Tory Don paid frequent visits to St John's "poor disconsolate" wife in Berkshire and found his hopes vain. "I met nothing there," he wrote again in 1711, "but sorrow and disorder. That unfortunate gentleman is more irregular if possible in his private than public capacities."[3]

The appointment of the aged, ailing Rochester, uncle of the Queen, to be Lord President, showed clearly the party tendency which would govern the Administration. Rochester had been out of office since 1703. He had sought to keep England out of large Continental operations. If she must fight, let it be on the oceans; and there let her make conquests in the vast New World. Peace and isolation if possible, but, if not, at worst a half-hearted war— such was the policy and strategy of Rochester. For the rest, he represented the Church of England in its highest expression. No one but Rochester seemed able to answer for a Tory Parliament. But Rochester was a man of the strictest principles. He could have no accommodation with the Whigs, whom he abhorred as republicans, atheists, war-mongers, war-usurers, and friends of the Dissenters. He warned the Queen that she must have an honest party Government, and no nonsense about tame Whigs or non-party moderates, however eminent. All this must, however, await the result of the polls. Parliament was dissolved on September 30.

At this time Marlborough had developed a friendship with the Earl of Stair. Stair was a man of remarkable ability, and afterwards under George I one of the most capable ambassadors Britain ever sent to Paris. He was now serving under Marlborough, and the Duke began to use him as his confidential agent when on leave in London.

---

[1] Dispatches of Gallas and Hoffmann, October 10; Klopp, xiii, 488.
[2] Portland Papers, *H.M.C.*, vii, 12.
[3] *Ibid.*, 39.

DISSOLUTION

Stair to Marlborough

LONDON
September 22, 1710

★Your Grace will know the changes that have preceded and followed the dissolution of Parliament which happened yesterday without one word being spoke at Council, for the Queen rose upon the moment the proclamation was read. The Queen this day refused My Lord Chancellor's demission but it is not believed he can be persuaded to continue. Lord Orford laid down this morning. . . .

I saw Lord Poulett this morning who professed himself your faithful servant with great kindness and affection. Your Grace's presence here will be very necessary to calm things before the sitting down of the Parliament. The delay of dissolving Parliament has been a great disadvantage to the new party. The Whigs have recovered themselves and are united and bold.[1]

Up till the moment of Godolphin's dismissal Somerset had acted confidently with Harley and Shrewsbury. But as Harley's ascendancy with the Queen became obvious Somerset's eyes, though clouded by vanity, were opened. The brilliant prospect he had seen for himself at the head of a Ministry of both parties, the prime favourite of the Queen, and revered as the honest man whom the whole nation trusted, faded with disconcerting swiftness. Somerset now foresaw that in the present weakness and confusion of the Whigs, to which he had himself so largely contributed, an election might yield a Tory Parliament. Such a Parliament would certainly not accept him as leader. He therefore set himself to oppose the dissolution; but he was overborne. He had played his part; his usefulness was exhausted. When the dissolution was announced his fury knew no bounds. Without resigning his office of Master of the Horse he gathered the Whig ex-Ministers at his house and announced his intention of fighting the election hand in glove with them. He would do his best, he said, to keep as many Tories and Jacobites out of Parliament as possible. On such occasions help from almost any quarter is welcomed, and even the most recent quarrels are forgotten. Somerset went off "in a pet to Petworth" and flung himself into the election fight against Harley, while his Duchess wrestled vigorously but vainly with Abigail for the Queen's favour.

But Harley's electioneering was as good as his intrigues. The very counties in which Somerset had considered his influence supreme were those through which Sacheverell had made his progress.

---

[1] Blenheim MSS.

Somerset found himself confronted with an angry opposition who declared he was "against the Doctor," and at the polls his candidates went down like ninepins. His short-lived power was gone. He had been one of the chief factors in the ruin of his own party. It had profited him nothing. All he had done was to set the Tories over them and himself alike. Nevertheless the Duchess of Somerset's relations, and to some extent his own, with the Queen were such that he did not resign; nor did Harley think it wise to proceed to extremities against him. He and his wife actually continued for a year and a half in their offices, backbiting and slandering their new colleagues with the same bitterness as they had their old.

The passion of the election exceeded anything that had been known since the days of Charles II. Indeed, old men thought the savagery of the Civil War had returned. "By the accounts you give," wrote Godolphin to Seafield (October 12), "and by what we find, all the most arbitrary proceedings in the elections are to be expected, but how anybody can think that is long to be maintained in our country and in this constitution is to me, I confess, a very great riddle."[1] "There never was so apparent a fury," Craggs reported to Marlborough (October 13), "as the people of England show against the Whigs and for High Church. Those that voted for Mr Stanhope at Westminster were knocked down; Sir Richard Onslow has lost it in Surrey, and I believe in Parliament they will exceed two to one."[2] "Nor do we fight," wrote Defoe, "with cudgels only as at Marlow Whitechurch etc., . . . but with swords and staves as at Coventry, with stones and brickbats as at other places. Even our civil war . . . was not carried on with such a spirit of fury as is now to be seen."[3] "In a great many of the elections," Peter Wentworth told Lord Raby, "the nonconformists have voted for the Torys, and 'tis thought it proceeds from the assurance Mr Harley has given their preachers that there shall be nothing this Parliament done against them, but their tolleration keep inviolable."[4]

The contest at Woodstock was complicated by the fact that, the Government having cut off supplies and Sarah having stopped the building of Blenheim, the workmen and labourers had been summarily dismissed unpaid. This had upset the neighbourhood. Marlborough's estate agent, one Travers, placated these unfortunate people by distributing three hundred pounds on account of what was

---

[1] Seafield Papers, *H.M.C.*, p. 211.   [2] B.M., Coxe Papers, xxxiii, 102.
[3] Defoe, *A Weekly Review*, vii, 333–337.   [4] *The Wentworth Papers*, p. 151.

owing to them by the Treasury, and Marlborough's candidates were both returned by the handful of freeholders who formed the double constituency.[1]

The Tory Party, united and inflamed, proved itself, as Marlborough had for years believed, definitely the stronger part of the nation. In Westminster the Whig General Stanhope, absent upon the Spanish front, was defeated by the Tory General Webb, amid scenes of ruffianism. Newcastle and all the Whig moderates were rallied. But far and wide throughout England the Whigs were overwhelmed. Bishop Burnet was frightened by a High Church mob. Sir Gilbert Heathcote, director of the Bank, representative of the hated money power, was insulted in the streets. All Wharton's candidates were thrown out in Buckinghamshire.[2] In Scotland, where Hamilton and Mar worked for Harley, "the Whigs, to the fears of Popery and the Pretender, added the danger that Presbytery was in. The Tories spoke little above board, but underhand represented that *now or never was the time to do something effectually for the King, and by restoring him, dissolve the Union.*"[3]

[1] *Travers to Marlborough*

Woodstock
Sunday, Oct. 8, 1710

★Yesterday Lt. Gen. Cadogan and Sir Tho Wheate were elected here without any of the opposition lately threatened by the adverse party, and I sent for the chief of those who had chosen the present Mayor out of course, and were for excluding Sir Tho and choosing me in spite of all my representations to the contrary. With much ado I persuaded them to desist, and not so much as to name me. So all was done quietly and I congratulated the Freemen on their choosing two such worthy members, and thanked them in the name of the High Steward for this mark of their affection and respect for him.

When I came hither on Friday morning I found the scene much changed from what Mr Vanbrugh and Mr Hawkesmoor had told me, and whereof I gave your Grace an account from Henley by last post. The people who had been turned off without their wages were full of complaints and tears and then threats and violence—and Lord A. having very much importuned a neighbouring gentleman to stand, and Sir John Walter having called here last Tuesday with Sir Rob. Jenkinson and others and declared he would set up an honest gentleman there being now a proper occasion for it, Blenheim being indeed under a cloud, and Sir Thomas Wheate being so apprehensive of their surprising us that he had sent expresses to all the gentlemen and other foreign freemen who are our friends to come in to our assistance.

To prevent therefore any tumult that might be set on foot at the Election, and in compassion to so many poor starving people . . . I borrowed £300 here on my own credit and ordered the Comptrollers to pay off the poor labourers and to divide the overplus among the most necessitous of this town. . . .

I am glad that I called here because I am told that the people in my absence would have insisted on a Pole which before I could not have believed, besides the satisfaction of having stopped the clamour and relieved the necessity of a great many poor wretches. [Blenheim MSS.]

[2] Portland Papers, *H.M.C.*, ii, 223.   [3] Lockhart, i, 319.

Two hundred and seventy Members lost their seats. In the new Parliament the Whigs were not a third of the House of Commons. It was proved, indeed, that "the Whigs had no bottom." When this was realized the stocks fell by 30 per cent., and the Bank refused to discount any foreign bills.[1]

Thus was ended, by the power of the Queen and, as it now appeared, by the will of the electorate, the ever-famous Administration of Marlborough and Godolphin, which for eight years had led the league of European nations to victory against the exorbitant power of France, which had made the British Island one United Kingdom, and had raised Great Britain from despondency and weakness to the summit of world affairs. The old Treasurer had retired to Newmarket. Marlborough, entangled in the war, wedded to the Army, claimed by the Allies, remained to struggle on, like a weary, baited bear chained to the post. The Continent, which had long yielded itself to the strong impulse of the island Power, without comprehending the causes of its inspiration and mysterious strength, was now staggered by what seemed to be a meaningless disintegration, the result of a bedchamber intrigue.

Queen Anne, after the intense personal stresses of the conflict which had raged about her, and perhaps also in her own conscience, and in which her will-power had played the decisive part, withdrew to Hampton Court to recover her strength and balance. By all accounts she was enormously relieved and gratified by the results of her exertions. She was not the only Sovereign to rejoice. Louis XIV knew that at the eleventh hour he had been saved from utter ruin. When he heard that the Queen had dissolved the Parliament he sent for Mesnager, his former agent at The Hague, to read him the news. "It is impossible," wrote Mesnager,

> for me to describe the transport of joy the King was in upon reading that part, [viz.] the dissolving of Parliament; "Well," says the King, "if Monsieur Harley does that, I shall say he is un habile homme, and that he knows how to go through what he has undertaken; Mesnager," adds the King, turning to me, "it is time you were in England;" I could not interpose for some time, the King was so full of this news, and talked so fast; sometimes to himself and sometimes to me, and as I was going to speak the King bade me attend in an hour; so I withdrew, and the King went to another apartment. I understood afterwards that his Majesty went to Madame de Maintenon's lodgings to give her part in the news he had received, and perhaps to

[1] Portland Papers, *H.M.C.*, ii, 223.

consult with her what measures should be taken in this important juncture.[1]

Marlborough had measured rightly the whole sequence of events from the beginning. He lent himself to various requests made to him by Godolphin and other Whigs. From time to time he wrote letters to the Queen or to Shrewsbury. But at no moment did he deceive himself. As far back as the summer of 1709, when he saw that Abigail had supplanted Sarah in the Queen's favour, he knew that, unless some extraordinary step was taken, his system was doomed. When the Queen was instigated to make the Hill appointment he chose that moment and that ground, unsatisfactory though they were from some points of view, for the decisive fight. If Godolphin and the Whigs had rallied to him when he quitted the Cabinet and retired to Windsor, the Queen would in all probability have been compelled to amend her courses. Parliament was in session, the campaign was about to begin, the Government was intact. Then was the chance, which never recurred, of bringing everything to a head. It would not have been necessary, in Marlborough's opinion, to proceed against Abigail by a Parliamentary address, and neither he nor Sarah advocated that course. The pressure which the whole Ministry could have brought upon Anne to choose forthwith between her responsible Ministers and her backstairs advisers would almost certainly have been irresistible. Abigail could have been chased from the Court, and Harley exposed before Whig majorities in both Houses.

[1] *Minutes of the Negotiations of Monsieur Mesnager at the Court of England towards the Close of the Last Reign* (1717), p. 61.

The Bavarian Agent in Paris to the Elector of Bavaria

October 18, 1710

The King received, this Day, certain Advice from England, that the Parliament is dissolved, and that the proposed Changes in the Ministry will take Place. . . . It is not at all doubted but that the Duke of Marlborough will give up the Command of the Army, and the more as the now ruling Party will leave no Stone unturn'd to induce him to it. . . . And if the Duke of Marlborough should resign the Command of the Army, in whom else can they have so entire Confidence? I don't know a single Person fit for the Post; for besides being a good Officer, he must likewise be an able Minister, one who has Credit with and Influence over the Confederated Princes, which they will not find united in any one besides the Duke of Marlborough. If the Duke of Hanover should accept of it, he will never agree with Prince Eugene; And thus we shall see Matters absolutely put on a new Face. . . .

The Duke of Berwick, who had early Notice of this Event, has wrote to Monsieur de Torcy, to desire him to represent to the King, that now would be a proper time to attempt a Descent, not in Scotland, but in England; and that he was very willing to put himself at the Head of 20,000 Men, and be secure of Success in carrying over the King of England. [Lediard, ii, 286.]

As things fell out, the Ministry suffered the worst of both courses. The Queen was filled with fear and resentment at the rumour of a Parliamentary address against her cherished Abigail. When this menace proved to be unfounded her fears passed, but her resentment remained. Nothing that had ever happened before had smitten her so deeply as this. All her quarrels and scenes with Sarah, all the interminable correspondence, all the political stresses attending the dismissal of Harley in 1708, and the forcing upon her one after another of the lords of the Junto—all these were upon a lower plane. The alleged attempt to set the House of Commons upon Abigail, and upon her for sheltering Abigail, was, she felt, a mortal affront. Repeatedly in this long-drawn crisis we find the rancour which this episode aroused, hardening her against her Ministers, and severing the last personal ties which united her to Marlborough. It enabled Somerset week after week to pour into her eager ear tales of this outrageous design to rob her of her own personal friend and attendant. How easy for Harley to warn her of Marlborough's alleged desperate ambition! Her grandfather had perished on the scaffold; her father had died in exile. Marlborough, at the head of the armies and of the Grand Alliance, was far greater in power than Cromwell before he became Lord Protector. Deposition in favour of the detested Elector, a republic of the Whigs, a dictatorship of Marlborough, were all bugbears which could be used to aggravate her anger and her alarm. And, on the other hand, what alluring prospects had been unfolded to her, not only by Harley, but also by the unwitting Somerset, and perhaps by Somers! The over-mighty subject should be put down; a Government above party, of her own choosing, should be established; the royal prerogative should be erected again on a new foundation. She would be Queen indeed.

Chapter Twenty

THE NEW RÉGIME

1710—OCTOBER–DECEMBER

YOU may venture to assure everybody," declared St John, the newly chosen Secretary of State, "that credit will be supported, the war prosecuted, the Confederacy improved, and the principle in which we engaged preserved as far as possible. Our friends and enemies both will learn the same lesson, that however we differ about things purely domestic, yet we are unanimous on those points which concern the present and future happiness of Europe."[1]

Behind these words of high resolve and reassurance the new Ministers were intent upon making peace. But even before they had obtained power they had become convinced, though with much reluctance, that the war would go on for some time, and that peace was more distant than before their intervention. In these circumstances they found it convenient to upbraid the Allies upon their many obvious shortcomings. They proclaimed that England would show even greater vigour in the war than under the late Administration. All the more was it necessary that her allies should act up to the highest standard of their obligations, and should be made to, at all costs. "The most popular thing for England," wrote Harley, with much candour, "is to press all the Allies to keep exactly to what they have agreed to do in their Treaties. The partiality to them has been much complained of, and the pressing relentlessly to their exact performing is the likeliest way to obtain peace."[2]

This certainly was a sound policy for men who did not care very much what kind of a peace it was. Nevertheless, the complaint of England against her allies, especially the Empire, was only too well founded, and a certain tonic was administered to them by the attitude of the new Government. England had got into the position

[1] St John to Drummond, October 13, 1710; *Letters and Correspondence of Viscount Bolingbroke* (edited by G. Parke, 1798), i, 5.
[2] "Mr Harley's Plan of Administration" (October 30, 1710); Earl of Hardwicke, *Miscellaneous State Papers* (1778), ii, 485. This programme was read by Harley to the Queen at Windsor.

of begging them to follow her. The change of government, which occasioned so much waste of power, at least reversed this process: the Allies now begged England not to desert them. St John was especially anxious to whip up the Empire. His mood towards Austria was always hostile, and his language harsh. He found it more congenial to harry the Allies than the enemy.

Upon universal appeal and overwhelming reason Marlborough had retained his command under the new Administration. He had every proof that they hated him and the cause which he upheld; but they also at the same time feared and needed him. In his head-quarters, from which he was conducting the sieges of Aire and Saint-Venant, he awaited their orders. At first these were expressed very roughly. St John in particular seemed to find a strong satisfaction in displaying himself as master of the great man who had favoured his early career, admitted him to his comradeship, helped him with his debts, and, indeed, almost adopted him as his son. All his letters about Marlborough at this period are of a scornful and often spiteful character. He wished at once to patronize him and to make him feel the humiliation of his new position. We shall see that some months later, under political strain, he changed his note and flattered, proffering his false friendship, as if he were back in the buoyant days of the Blenheim campaign.

The new Ministry, however, pursued contradictory and ambigu-ous courses towards their General. They would have rejoiced if they could have flung him out, and set the Elector, George Louis, in his place; but that could not be done. They were conscious of serious danger in dismissing Marlborough before finding a substi-tute whom England and the Allies would accept. On the other hand, they wished to bend him, break him, tame him to their yoke. They sought to foster a faction against him among his generals and colonels. They laboured to show the Army that his political power was gone. They took the whole business of promotion out of his hands. They set up a board in London under the Duke of Ormonde, his political opponent and professional competitor, to scrutinize and decide the claims of all officers for promotion. They dismissed or removed from their special appointments his most trusted and competent brigadiers and rising officers. They appointed in their stead those who had been personally disloyal or offensive to him in the campaign, or who had insulted him in Parliament. If there was anyone on whom he specially relied they removed him. If a man could be found who was particularly obnoxious they thrust him forward as near to the Commander-in-Chief as possible. They even made a virtue of this by pretending that Marlborough was making by favouritism an army to subvert the Crown and Constitution. The Queen herself, they hinted, was in danger from his favouritism. Above all, Abigail's brother and husband, Brigadiers Hill and Masham, sailed forward upon this breeze.

If Marlborough endured this treatment his authority with the Army must, they thought, be fatally wounded. If, on the other hand, he found the treatment intolerable, let him resign. They saw that if he resigned he would put himself in the wrong. To dismiss him was dangerous: to provoke his resignation comparatively safe. Then they could have filled England with the cry that he had deserted his post on party grounds, that he had cast away the cause of the Allies, that he had ruined the peace which otherwise was in their hands. Any disaster in the field which followed his withdrawal they could lay on him. In fact, their conduct towards him during their first months exceeded in malice and in meanness anything which is known—and it is a wide field—in the relations of a British general with a British Government. In all this the most poisonous was St John.

Marlborough, though he writhed and groaned under the ordeal, was in no mood to yield his enemies any advantage. He held on to his position with the tenacity with which he had fought the siege of Lille two years earlier. Surrounded upon every side by foes, the worst—his own countrymen—at his back, exposed to all the hazards with which war between equal armies confronts a general, feeling the French spirit rise every day as his political weakness became known, watching the peace which would have released him steadily recede, he repressed all impatience, and disdained or ignored every insult. But can we wonder that in such distress he would have welcomed serving under the Elector of Hanover, or transferring the command in the best conditions to him?

In his steadfast attitude he gained comfort from the great companions with whose aid he had waged the long war. Heinsius usually presents himself to us as a prosaic, austere, and even bleak personality; he had been in conflict with Marlborough over the Barrier since 1709; but we now see him showing every sign of personal sympathy.[1] The Elector of Hanover, recognized future

---

1 ★We have just heard with much surprise that the Lord Treasurer has been deprived of his office, which shows clearly enough what will follow. I am much relieved to know that you are resolved to remain at the head of the Army whatever happens. I have to-day talked with Lord Townshend, who holds the same view. I will not fail to speak to him to see what can be done to make it public. [Heinsius Archives, August 23, 1710.]

master of these arrogant Ministers, and the King of Prussia gave him unswerving support. The Elector declared publicly as a member of the Grand Alliance that unless Marlborough remained in command of the armies he would withdraw his troops. Frederick I spoke in a similar spirit. Eugene, who was not the master of armies, could only publish his resolve not to serve in Flanders except with Marlborough. As for the Dutch, their remonstrances on Marlborough's account had already strained their relations with our queer Queen and her new circle.

Sarah, above all a pugnacious politician, soon in the excitement of the election began to regret that her husband was still the servant of the new Government. But these were unreasonable reflections upon a decision so deliberately adopted. Marlborough's reply was overwhelming.

John to Sarah

Oct. 4, 1710

I find by what Mr Maynwaring has said or writ to you, you are jealous of my acting so with Mr Harley or the Tories, as that the Whigs may have reason to be angry. In the first place, I should not, at this time, have been where I am, if it had not been unanimously desired by all the heads of the Whigs. By the same advice, I have made steps to the Elector of Hanover, who has entered very kindly into my concerns. The States, the Emperor, and the Elector, all three have engaged me to continue with the army, which I suppose is, and will be approved by the Whigs; for I am resolved of doing nothing but in concert with them. I detest Mr Harley; but think I have lived long enough in the world to be able to distinguish between reason and faction.

Nothing is more desired by me than to be quiet; my greatest concern is, if possible, to avoid the harsh usage which is most certainly resolved to be put in practice against you, for whom I must ever be more concerned than for all other things in this world. . . . We are in circumstances that require great temper, by which I hope we may at last overcome our enemies.

Blenheim continued to be a source of vexation and embarrassment.

---

*I am much relieved that you have been told yourself that nothing ill is intended as far as you yourself are concerned, at least until you are back in England, for I believe your presence will dissipate all that, and that you will be in a position to prevent it; which I hope and wish with all my heart.

France shows no sign of wishing to resume peace negotiations. I do not know whether as you think they wish first of all to see the behaviour of the new Parliament, or whether they are waiting on the course of the campaign in Spain. [Heinsius Archives, September 20, 1710.]

I think that those that take care of the building at Blenheim, when the winter season and the want of money makes the work to cease, should take care to cover the works, so as what is already done may receive no prejudice, and then it may remain *as a monument of ingratitude*, as Mr Van. calls it in his letter. I hope the wainscot and every other thing, in your apartment and mine, is finished so that we may live in that part of the house in the spring.[1]

We are masters of St Venant, and I yet hope we shall have Aire by the 20th.[2]

Sarah was pleased to find her husband so apparently indifferent to the fate of Blenheim. "My lord Marlborough," she wrote to Godolphin,

approves very much of all that I said to Mr Travers upon the subject of Woodstock, and I suppose will not be less of that mind when he sees the letters that Mr Joyns writ, to fright me into sending them money. He adds that they may pull down what they have built, if they please, he will never contradict it, which I was glad to see; for I think that building was the greatest weakness my lord Marlborough ever had, and, being his passion, I am pleased he has overcome it; and, I believe, these Ministers thought to ensnare him by it.[3]

We have seen the unsoldierlike letter written by Lord Orrery in June, suggesting that the Queen should give him and Argyll leave to quit the Army without reference to the Commander-in-Chief.[4] This seed bore fruit.

Marlborough to Godolphin

Oct. 4, 1710

Everything is done to lessen my credit here. By the last post Mr Secretary wrote, by the Queen's order, to acquaint Lord Argyll that his friends have desired leave for him to come for England, and she had allowed of it. This is so very extraordinary a step that even the Duke of Argyll came to me yesterday to assure me that he had made no application, and that, when he should desire to go for England, he should apply to me for my leave. The folly and ingratitude of the Queen make me sick and weary of everything.[5]

---

[1] William Stratford in his party outlook interpreted these affairs in his letters to Harley's son, Edward, so as to throw an unwarranted odium upon Marlborough. "In one month more, Blenheim would have been covered so as to be secure against any injury from the weather. Their orders were positive to break off, and if it continue in the condition it is left, the frost and wet will ruin all that has been done this summer." (Portland Papers, *H.M.C.*, vii, 20.)

[2] Coxe, v, 354.
[3] *Ibid.*, 358–359.
[4] See p. 698.
[5] Coxe, v, 360.

The Duke of Argyll, for all his bitterness, had not behaved in the unmilitary fashion the Queen had been induced to authorize. There was a strong opinion in the camps on questions of disciplinary etiquette, and a prominent man, a famous warrior like Argyll, would lower himself in Europe by any gross misbehaviour. But, though he had not been as forward in casting contumely as the Secretary of State wished, he was none the less a few weeks later gazetted General of Infantry in the British Army. Hoffmann, whom nothing escaped, wrote:

> After everything that has taken place between him and Marlborough during the last two campaigns, the appointment will cause Marlborough vexation. That is, however, what it is meant to do. He will be insulted until he resigns voluntarily. Those responsible for the changes here do not intend to let him remain in his high position, because they fear his revenge. The real Tories might tolerate him, although only in such a fashion that he was completely dependent upon them. He cannot, however, be so on account of the Whigs. His position is therefore extremely complicated.[1]

One day this winter in the House of Lords Lord Scarbrough, who had been now Whig, now Tory, but always a malcontent, proposed incontinently that the Lord Chancellor should be directed to send the Duke of Marlborough a letter of thanks for the great successes of the year. Argyll, who had by now returned, objected at once to the motion. "What reason," he asked, "can there be for such a message of thanks, unless custom is to be made the reason? Four strongholds have no doubt been captured; but only one of them, Douai, is of importance. The other three have cost the best blood of the army." Two other Generals, both opponents of Marlborough, Lords North and Grey, supported Argyll, and Scarbrough, who had acted without any authority or preparation, withdrew his motion.[2] On this, as St John acidly observes in his correspondence, "One would imagine Lord Scarbrough was hired by somebody who wished the Duke of Marlborough ill to take so ill-concerted and ridiculous a measure."[3]

A third calculated affront followed a few days later. Informers had reported that three of Marlborough's general officers, Meredith, Macartney, and Honeywood, the first two Members of Parliament, had in the camp drunk to the health of the Duke of Marlborough,

---

[1] Hoffmann's dispatch, November 4; Klopp, xiv, 3.
[2] Hoffmann's dispatch, December 12; Klopp, xiv, 17.
[3] St John to Drummond, Nov. 28; *Bolingbroke Correspondence*, i, 24.

and confusion to the new Government and Mr Harley. Such toasts were common at that time among both parties in the armies, and no notice had ever been taken of them. Without any attempt to establish the facts, or to allow the officers to deny or excuse them, they were immediately cashiered. The orders, in the name of the Queen, were sent through Marlborough under seal, to be delivered by him unopened. He only learned from the officers what their punishment had been. These three young generals were among the very best who had risen in the fierceness of the fighting, and they were also Marlborough's personal friends. There was much astonishment at this measure, both in the army and at home. "All officers," reported Hoffmann,

> speak on behalf of the three. If generals are cashiered on information supplied by an informer, even the most guiltless are no longer secure. Macartney admits freely that he had drunk to the confusion of Marlborough's opponents. But if they mean to punish these said officers they must punish almost the whole army.[1]

It was not, however, the officers at whom Harley and St John were aiming. They were attacking Marlborough. In order not to inflict needless suffering upon subordinates they therefore allowed the three generals to dispose of their commissions under the purchase system, thus saving them from financial ruin. The opportunity was taken of giving Lord Orrery one of the vacancies thus created. Thus he gained the major-generalship for which he had striven so assiduously.

It was a reasonable expectation that Marlborough's treatment at this time by the Queen and Government would have rendered his position impossible by destroying his credit with the Army while heavy operations were proceeding. He himself certainly feared that this would be the result. Curiously enough, the reverse happened. Never in the height of his success was there such a rally to him throughout the allied armies as in these winter months. Apart from the group of intriguing officers round Argyll, all ranks sought occasion by the strict performance of their duty to prove their discipline, and show their respect for their General. In that glorious army of veteran soldiers drawn from eight nations, welded together by so much war for causes which for the most part they comprehended and espoused, the malignant timeservers and backbiters became lepers. Dutch Deputies and foreign generals now supplied

[1] Hoffmann's dispatch, December 30; Klopp, xiv, 23.

Marlborough by their alacrity with the support hitherto forth-coming from home; and, far beyond the Army, there spread through all the signatory states of the Grand Alliance a vehement resolve that he should not be taken from them before the fruits of their efforts were gathered in.

One has a sense at this time of the magnitude of the power which was being wantonly destroyed. The British oak had struck its roots so deep in Europe, its branches spread so far, that even the lopping off of tremendous limbs and the undermining or severing of one root after another still left it erect, the feature of the landscape. Marlborough's faults and limitations have not been, need not be, concealed; his misfortunes now crowded upon him; but he remained the champion of Europe against the military dictatorship of Louis XIV; and, apart from his enemies in England and France, all the nations looked to him.

As the weeks passed those who had risen by the methods we have described found themselves, in their turn, oppressed by the weight of official cares, and disturbed by the temper of their own new-found Parliament. The landslide of the elections had carried affairs far beyond that moderate, middle dispensation which Harley and the Queen, to say nothing of Marlborough and Godolphin, had always desired. The year 1708 had produced a sultry Whig House of Commons: 1710 showed a red-hot Tory domination. From the backwoods of England, from the acres which they cultivated with hard authority and exemplary skill, came in unforeseen numbers and in uncontrollable temper the backbone of England, the Tory squires, blessed by the Church they had sworn to defend. Their hatred for the Whigs was at once instinctive and religious. The process of electioneering had, however, exercised an educative function. They had catered for the Nonconformist vote; they had boasted that the national credit would be safe in their hands; and though they disapproved of Marlborough's tactics and strategy, as well as his character and politics, they were at first genuinely anxious to beat the French, and not to show themselves less compe-tent than their opponents.

We can see how irresistibly the character of the new House of Commons impressed itself upon the Queen and her advisers. All ideas of co-operation with moderate Whigs, upon which Harley had traded so successfully before the election, had been swept to limbo by one stroke of the national wing. All plans for an equi-poise of parties, and their impartial control by the Queen's favourites

at the Court, vanished like the smoke of a quenched fire. This was
not Harley's Parliament. St John felt far more at home with the
new majority. When Sarah saw St John in a large company just
before he became Secretary of State, she said "in her manner which
was often the reverse of polite,"[1] "There goes an ungrateful
rogue." St John seemed resolved to prove that this was true. He
availed himself of Harley's apparatus for collecting dispassionate
information from many quarters through trusted agents. In Holland Harley had an agent, one John Drummond, a Scottish merchant
and resident of high standing, very shrewd at finding out facts, and
blunt in reporting them. Drummond, who was used as a channel
between the Ministry and Marlborough, wrote to both Harley and
St John.

John Drummond to Harley

AMSTERDAM
November 1/12, 1710

What is it are we to imagine that hinders or will hinder their [the
French] new proposals, but what they write us every day, viz. the hopes
they have of the divisions in England and that the Duke of Marlborough
will be made so uneasy as to be obliged to retire and abandon the army,
who they know has been no less instrumental in keeping the Allies
together than in his success in the field? It is not for his person, but
for the public good that I argue or presume to meddle in so important an affair, for well do I know all his vices as well as his virtues,
and I know as well that though his covetousness has gained much
reproach and ill-will on this side of the world, yet his success in the
field, his capacity or rather dexterity in council or in the Cabinet, and
his personal acquaintance with the heads of the Alliance and the faith
they have in him, make him still the great man with them, and on
whom they depend. I can tell you with certainty what I meet in daily
conversation, that you will have little money to expect from this
[Government] if he stay at home, that they wish with all their hearts
almost any sort of peace before he be taken from them, that there is
no Englishman who they have any opinion of for the command of an
army but himself, that his agreeing so well with Prince Eugene is
one of their greatest contentments and to make a new acquaintance
and intimacy of such a nature with any one is what they fear and
abhor the thoughts of.

Pensionary Buys came to me two days after Lord Rivers left this
place almost with tears in his eyes, saying "Lord! what shall become
of us. Lord Rivers would give me no satisfaction that the Duke
shall return. For God's sake write to all your friends, let him but

[1] Klopp, xiv, 31.

return for one campaign till the French but once make new proposals,
let the Queen afterwards do with him what she pleases, but must the
safety of us all be put in the balance with personal pique which perhaps
may be reconciled if rightly gone about?" I hope the Queen will
forbear her farther resentments till a better occasion, though justly
deserved by him and all who belong to him. Baron Gersdorff was last
day here: he is Envoy at The Hague for the Elector of Saxony or King
of Poland; he assured people in a general assembly or society that
his master would recall his troops if the Duke was not to command.[1]

This letter smote Harley. For all his love of dissembling, artifice,
and intrigue, to which was soon added inveterate drunkenness, he
was nevertheless a man built on a large scale and of a nature not
wholly divorced from the life of Britain. He was not at all like
St John, a brilliant, fugitive rascal, prone to bully or grovel with
equal facility according to circumstances or mood. Also Harley
felt himself the man responsible. On him lay the burden. He had
been wronged. He had resented his injuries. He had avenged
them. But he felt himself morally as well as constitutionally accountable to Parliament and in some degree to history. One is at first
astonished at the freedom with which this powerful Minister,
having through Abigail entire control of the Queen, and thus
through his adroitness of the British system, unbosoms himself to
the outspoken John Drummond at Amsterdam. But, of course,
this letter was meant for Marlborough.

Harley to John Drummond

November 7/18, 1710

. . . As to any reconciliation between me and the [Duke of Marl-
borough], give me leave to say that I were unworthy the Queen's
service should I not live with anyone that her service or the public
good requires. I do solemnly assure you I have not the least resentment towards him or anyone else. I thank God my mind puts me above
that. I never did revenge injuries. . . . In one word I do assure you,
I can live and act with the Duke now in the same manner and with
the same easiness as the first day that ever I saw him. . . .

I have upon many occasions since shewn by actions relating to his
particular affairs of Blenheim that I am far from resentment. But this
I find by experience, those who have done injuries are more difficult
to be reconciled than those who have received injuries, and hatred,
the more groundless and unreasonable it is, the more durable and
violent it most times proves. Now I have opened to you my heart

[1] Portland Papers, *H.M.C.*, iv, 620–621.

upon this subject and do again assure you that no resentment of mine shall ever obstruct the public service or hinder the co-operating with any one for the good of the common cause. . . .[1]

Negotiations were therefore set on foot with Marlborough, with the object of reaching a basis upon which he should command the armies in the now inevitable campaign of 1711

John Drummond to Harley

AMSTERDAM
November 29/*December* 10, 1710

. . . Mr Secretary St John will have acquainted you with what I wrote him of my discourse with [Marlborough]. . . . He has faithfully promised both to the Grand Pensionary and to Buys that he is resolved to live with you if you will make it practicable or possible for him; he will not enter into the heats of party debates, but will go heartily and sincerely into all the measures that may be esteemed proper for carrying on the war, but for other votes he will be at his free liberty. . . .

This he consented to, and desired me to write very plainly that he was pretty much desponding, and yet seemed well resolved to carry on the war he had so successfully brought this length, by sticking to her Majesty's service as long as even his greatest enemies should think it possible or practicable for him. . . .[2]

St John, into whose hands the transaction now fell, was far from satisfied with what he heard of Marlborough's attitude. "There is, I dare say," he wrote to Drummond,

no one disaffected man in the Queen's dominions, but who will engage to be of no party, to vote as he finds things first, to be as hearty as any man where the Queen's honour, or the nation's good is concerned. These are vague and uncertain propositions, which tie him down to nothing. . . . If he comes home and disengages himself from the Whigs; if he puts a stop to the rage and fury of his wife, in short, if he abandons all his new and takes up with all his old friends; by the Queen's favour, and by the remains of regard for him which are preserved in the breasts of several people, he may not only stand his ground, but, in my humble opinion, establish himself in as lofty a situation as it becomes a subject to aspire to: but if he imagines that people will any more be caught with general and inconclusive discourse, if he thinks that people will any more engage to him whilst he lies under no engagement, nor gives any security to them; depend upon me, for once he will find himself deceived.[3]

[1] Portland Papers, *H.M.C.*, iv, 623.   [2] *Ibid.*, 634.
[3] November 28/December 8; *Bolingbroke Correspondence*, i, 26.

Marlborough stayed as long as possible at The Hague, and kept the seas between him and his ferocious fellow-countrymen. Here, at least, he found a friendly and grateful Government. Here he remained a European figure, whose gleams were not yet extinguished in the British fog. But the crux was still to come. Harley owed everything, including his daily existence as a Minister, to the Queen, and Anne's fondest wish at this moment was to dismiss Sarah from her appointments, and make sure she never would see that once dearly loved being again. Mrs Masham kept Anne intent upon the point. Therefore Harley, who was by now earnest to obtain Marlborough's services in the new campaign and to use his shield with the army to cover clandestine negotiations for a separate peace, had still one more ugly difficulty to overcome. Sarah must go. She must be stripped of her offices: she must give up the Gold Key. This the Queen demanded at all costs. Could Marlborough ever be brought to consent to this? His love for his wife was well known: his submission to her was a proverb. Would he, could he, force her to resign? If so, the last obstacle was removed. A working arrangement could be made between him and the Ministry. He should lead the army in the final campaign which Britain would fight. At the worst he would uphold the front; at the best some new astonishing event might repair the disaster which the change of Government had palpably caused.

Harley and St John—for these are the two who now counted —therefore pursued their policy of bargaining and affronts, of baits and insults, of compliments and threats, and neither they nor anyone else knew what Marlborough would do.

No view of the problems of the new Ministry is intelligible without the Spanish scene. Stanhope's visit to England at the end of 1709 gave him a gloomy impression. As one of the managers of the Sacheverell impeachment, he felt the hostile surge of popular feeling. Towards the end of March he left for his command in Spain. He stopped at The Hague to discuss the main strategy of the war with Marlborough and Eugene, and particularly to impress upon the latter the need for further Austrian troops in the Peninsula. Accompanied by Craggs,[1] he sailed from Genoa in the middle of May for Catalonia with £80,000 in bullion, a thousand German troops, and considerable corn supplies. At the end of the month he reached the allied headquarters. Starhemberg, on the Aragon

---

[1] The younger.

border, had under his command about eighteen thousand well-equipped troops, while beyond the river Segre, at Lerida, Philip had been able to concentrate twenty-two thousand Spaniards. For two months Stanhope pleaded for a general advance. Fresh from home politics, he knew the urgent need for an offensive, and as a soldier he longed to take advantage of the complete absence of French troops from the country.

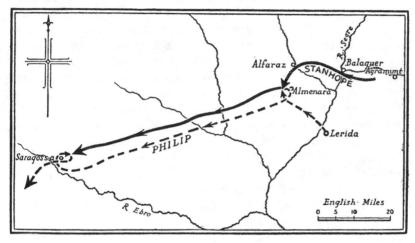

ALMENARA AND SARAGOSSA

At length, in July, Norris's fleet in the Mediterranean brought over reinforcements, and Stanhope was allowed to advance across the Segre at Balaguer, and race with his English dragoons for the bridge of Alfaraz, some twelve miles distant. The capture of this key point would cut off the enemy from North and West Spain. Upon this movement the campaign opened. By the morning of July 27 the whole allied army had crossed the bridge unopposed. Philip from Lerida reached Almenara, two miles short of the bridge, on the same day. Since noon Stanhope had been arguing and shouting and threatening to leave the country if Charles took no action. Just before sundown he wrested from his reluctant colleagues the order for a cavalry charge.

At the head of twenty-six squadrons he gave the signal. Wave upon wave of dragoons swept up the hillsides flanking the Bourbons' positions, and forced their whole army into flight. The opposing cavalry leaders met in personal combat, and Stanhope cut the

779

Spaniard down.[1] "If we had had two hours' daylight more . . . not one foot soldier of their army would have escaped."[2]

Lerida was now untenable, and Philip retired on Saragossa, pursued by the allied army. On the evening of August 19 a second action was fought under the walls of the provincial capital. After three hours the whole Spanish army fled in disorder into Castile. Almanza had been avenged. The way to Madrid lay open. A week after the victory at Saragossa there was a decisive council of war.[3] Stanhope held the view, which the year before had been Marlborough's, that Charles's forces should march at once to Madrid to meet Galway's force from Portugal. The reduction of Spain was the more urgent after the breakdown at Gertruydenberg. But Starhemberg declared for more cautious moves. He proposed to halt at Saragossa. "Conquests should be made step by step, and not by springs and bounds." Valencia should be reoccupied. Philip's communications with France should be cut, and the remaining Bourbon strongholds in Northern Spain systematically reduced. The majority of the council voted with the imperious English leader, flushed by his recent successes, and Charles reluctantly consented to the general advance on Madrid.

Winter was at hand when, at the end of September, Madrid was reached. The communications to the sea-coast were seriously lengthened, and the Spanish population implacable.[4] Above all, a new leader had arrived at the Bourbon headquarters at Valladolid. Vendôme, in disfavour and retirement since his defeats in 1708, was now by Villars's advice sent to Spain with high authority and the hastily collected French garrisons of Navarre. At the final crisis of the war in Spain he was to save the cause of Philip V. His arrival was greeted with enthusiasm by the Spanish at Valladolid. Swiftly concentrating the Bourbon army, he marched southward to prevent a junction between the allied army in Portugal and that in Madrid. Stanhope was moving southward to the point of junction at Almaraz when the French forestalled him. The English army in Portugal, awaiting a successor to the disgusted Galway in the person

---

[1] Probably the Duke of Sarno; but this is disputed. See note in B. Williams, *Stanhope*, p. 96.

[2] Dispatch to Dartmouth; quoted in Williams, p. 95.

[3] On the controversy over the date of the fatal council see Landau, *Geschichte Kaiser Karls VI als König von Spanien* (1889), p. 572; Parnell, *The War of the Succession in Spain* p. 284; and Williams, p. 99 *n.*

[4] For stories of outrages perpetrated by the heretic invaders see Williams, p. 101, and especially Landau, p. 575.

of Lord Portmore, had made no forward movement over the frontier. The Portuguese withdrew into 'summer quarters,' and Stanhope was forced to return to Madrid, leaving Vendôme free to encircle the Spanish capital and the Allies by cutting the communications with Catalonia and the coast. Thus in a few weeks the whole state of the war in Spain was transformed.

Stanhope's proposal to winter in Castile was overruled by the

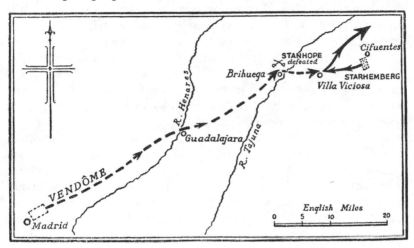

BRIHUEGA AND VILLA VICIOSA

council of war; and at the beginning of December it was decided to retreat into Aragon, a hundred and fifty miles away. Harassed by Spanish irregular bands, short of supplies and money, the allied forces quitted Madrid on December 3. Owing to the scarcity of forage in the devastated countryside they marched in three parallel columns, the Spanish and Portuguese levies on the right, Starhemberg in the centre, and Stanhope on the left. Stanhope, with 4500 men, halted for the night of December 6 at the old Moorish town of Brihuega to rest his troops and bake bread. Starhemberg lay at Cifuentes, five hours' march away over hilly country. The columns had been harried on their march by Spanish bands. The last that had been seen of Vendôme was near Talavera, seventy miles south of Madrid, and when on the morning of the 8th horsemen were seen on the heights around Brihuega, Stanhope assumed that they were the familiar Spanish irregulars. At midday, however, Vendôme's artillery began to fire upon the town. What had happened?

781

On the day that the Allies were leaving the northern suburbs of Madrid Vendôme and Philip had entered the capital from the south. The Marshal hurried the King out of the town in keen pursuit of the allied columns, and at the head of his cavalry plunged across the flooded Henares at Guadalajara. Hearing from his advanced Spanish detachments that they had found Stanhope at Brihuega separated from Starhemberg, he marched incessantly to the scene. A little after midday he arrived with some ten thousand men on the hills above the town. The English general prepared himself for the worst. One of his officers made his way through the enemy lines to warn Starhemberg that Brihuega could not be held for more than twenty-four hours. With no artillery, and a mile and a half of crumbling mud walls and ancient Moorish castle, Stanhope made the best dispositions in his power. Trenches and pits were dug in the streets, houses and church steeples fortified.

By evening over a thousand shot had been fired into the town. An offer of surrender was refused. The next morning the French cannon were brought to close quarters, and a crashing bombardment smashed in the northern gates. The assault began. Not until the evening of the 9th did the Spaniards pass through the breaches and street fighting begin. The Spanish cannon were now mounted inside the walls to rake the streets with grape. Amid the cannonade and blinding smoke from damp wood, lit to baffle the besiegers, the British infantry were driven step by step from their fortified houses and barricades into the citadel. With the town burning, their ammunition nearly exhausted, and over six hundred casualties, Stanhope and his troops surrendered as prisoners of war.

Starhemberg had received the message from Brihuega, but, waiting for his artillery, refused to march until midday on the 9th. He arrived in the neighbourhood at nightfall, a few hours after Stanhope's surrender. After a fierce battle round the village of Villa Viciosa with Vendôme's victorious troops, in which the Bourbon army lost more than four thousand men, Starhemberg was left in possession of the field. An admirably executed retreat into Catalonia followed, and at the beginning of January 1711 he reached Barcelona with a remnant of eight thousand men.

Thus swiftly had the tables been turned. The allied offensive had ended in disaster. Vendôme and the people of Spain had settled the Spanish succession in their own way.

Chapter Twenty-one

THE GOLD KEY

1710–11—DECEMBER AND JANUARY

AFTER a rough three days' passage Marlborough, accompanied by Bothmar, on December 26/January 6 reached Sole Bay. He had memories of these waters, where forty years before he had, as an ensign in the Grenadiers, fought under the Duke of York in the flagship *Prince* in that hard naval battle.

Forty years of service in the British Army, forty years of toil and hazard, facing so often the cannon and the greater risks which beset responsible persons: and now, with a lifetime behind him, back again at Sole Bay, with far more troubles than had burdened him upon the bloody decks of the flagship! What would await him in his native land, the England whose foes he had always confronted, and always beaten? The skies were sullen, and a wintry gale whipped the roadstead. The repository of power, the Queen, his foe; the Parliament, counter-check upon the Crown, ranged in bitter hostility; the Government, a confederacy undecided whether to exploit all the power he had gathered or squander it and him.

One fearless face he saw, one smile of supreme welcome—Sarah. Yet the immediate decision required of him was to procure her expulsion from the high political offices she had won by nearly thirty years of service to Queen Anne. No wonder he bent under this impact. No wonder foreign ambassadors found his countenance changed, and many calculating observers thought that he would soon die. After having lifted Britain to a height hitherto undreamed of, he came home to a society which could have treated him no worse if he had ruined, instead of rebuilt, the State.

Modern opinion is placidly astonished that these eighteenth-century combatants should have cared so much for political sway. Why should not Marlborough dismiss to the devil Abigail, Harley, and St John, and the envenomed hive that buzzed around them, and post home to have a merry Christmas with Sarah and his family? Why struggle further, and by struggling suffer measureless

783

strains and unending insults? Let these hornets sting each other and themselves—as, indeed, they were soon to do. Nowadays every one would say 'Resign!' But this was the eighteenth century, when the birth-thrust of the Island people was in its prime. The will to rule was strong; it coursed in the veins of all the able men who formed the high circle of England. To rule, to conquer, not to lose the game for self or Empire, was their part. In Marlborough's breast also lay the heavy obligations he had contracted in Europe. Twenty-six signatory states of the Grand Alliance, eight nations actually at the moment in his army, absolute victory at last in reach, defeat and confusion advancing in insolent array; impossible to give in, to beat the chamade, to march out even with the honours of war—were they offered. One more effort must be made, one more campaign must be fought; who should say that another Blenheim, another Ramillies, might not lie in the spring? At the worst, the front would be held, and these traitor Ministers—for as such he regarded them, and as such they were to be regarded by two generations of Englishmen—would have the chance to make a reasonable peace.

When we depict Marlborough under the impression of a hostile England, it must be remembered how few were those who had the right in those days to speak for the nation. The peasants and other working-people were not admitted to national affairs. But in many a cottage and in almost every tavern Marlborough's old soldiers had spread his fame, and after nine years of victory he was a hero to the populace. There were the French, so powerful, so dangerous, so arrogant; there was the Pope, and the fires of Smithfield (and who had not read, or been told of, Foxe's *Book of Martyrs*?); there was the Pretender, and his warming-pan! The war was long, the times were hard, but "Corporal John" led the redcoats to some purpose. Even in this dark hour Marlborough could not pass through a village without tumultuous manifestations of regard and admiration from its inhabitants. In those aristocratic days it was considered by Whigs and Tories alike a crime to use what was called the 'mobile,' or mob, in politics. Thus the Duke always after his great successes slipped home by unexpected routes. However, on this occasion as he drew near London crowds gathered about his coach, and the news of his coming spread and ran before him. The people accompanied him in growing numbers. In the City the doors and windows were filled with cheering men. Cries were raised continually, "God bless the Duke of Marlborough!" With these mingled others in the Whig tune—"No wooden shoes!" "No Popery!" Marlborough was well aware of the embarrassments to which such a demonstration would expose him. He would be accused of leading the rabble to coerce the Queen. He therefore, instead of going direct to St James's, turned to Montagu House, and before visiting the Queen waited some hours for the populace to disperse.

Hoffmann's account is authoritative.

LONDON
9 *Jan.*, 1711

★The Duke of Marlborough . . . landed on Epiphany Day. As he drove through this town he was welcomed with great rejoicing by crowds in the streets, who pressed round his carriage in such great numbers that in order not to arrive at St James's Palace, wherein he now resides, accompanied by such a mob, whereat offence might have been taken, he considered it best to drive by side roads to the house of his son-in-law, the Duke of Montagu, and to remain there until the crowd had dispersed again, after which he drove in a hired carriage to his house and went into the Queen's presence, but remained with her Majesty only a quarter of an hour. . . . People think him very much thinner and greatly altered, to which his fatiguing journey, when he had no sleep for five nights, may also have contributed.

Since the bad tidings of affairs in Spain have spread, it is noticed that people speak with more moderation and consideration about the Duke than was the case before this change.[1]

When the next day Marlborough entered upon business with the Queen the conversation was pretty stiff. "I am desirous," said Anne, repeating the formula agreed at the Cabinet, "you should continue to serve me, and will answer for the conduct of all my Ministers towards you. . . . I must request you would not suffer any vote of thanks to you to be moved in Parliament this year, because my Ministers will certainly oppose it." Marlborough replied, "I shall always be ready to serve your Majesty, if what has recently passed should not incapacitate me."[2] It was thus understood that he would accept the task of commanding the armies in the coming campaign, and would sit in the Cabinet with the new Ministers. He remained a few days in London. All the Ministers called upon him except Harley. Harley sent a message to say that he would prefer they should meet as if by accident at the Council or the Court, after which he would pay his visit. This method was observed. "The Duke had a very cold reception last night," wrote Harley to New-castle (December 29). "This day he had by appointment an audience for an hour and a half. He made great professions of compliance.

[1] Blenheim MSS.   [2] Coxe, v, 405.

That was told him which you advised. How long he will keep his temper I cannot tell. Certainly he has advisers who will ruin him, and while we are keeping all things in temper, they will drive it to extremity."[1]

Any inclination on the part of Ministers to treat with fairness the work of their predecessors was resented by the ardent Tory majority. No fewer than two hundred and seventy members of the former House of Commons had lost their seats. There had arrived from the constituencies a strong body of rural Tories, many of them quite young, who firmly believed that the intrigues of the Dissenters were destroying the clergy, that the money power of the City was devouring the landed gentry, and that it was their duty to respond to the Queen's appeal for rescue from these base conspirators. Sentences had been put in the Queen's speeches to give this vehement contingent some verbal satisfaction. Such tactics had only fanned the flame. These raw, untamed, horribly zealous Tories came together in an association. Because of the strong ale brewed in the country houses in October, a small Jacobite coterie had come to be called the October Club. The newcomers joined it, quadrupled its membership, and became group-conscious. They met together in their taverns and private houses, and formed a confederacy in which the minority on any issue bound themselves to act with the majority. They conceived themselves to be at once the purgers and the saviours of the nation. Although the bulk of their talk was current party politics, they comprised within their body or covered externally all the latent Jacobite elements in the realm. It was well said of them they were Jacobites when drunk and Tories when sober. They became immediately formidable in the House of Commons.

The high circle of Ministers and ex-Ministers, most of whom were only slightly attached to party, except at election times, and several of whom were involved in the great transactions by which England had risen to mastery, were alarmed and perplexed by this development. They found themselves confronted by a mass of resolute, thick-headed, earnest gentlemen, who actually believed in the propaganda which had served its purpose at the election. Harley was deeply embarrassed. He, like all other Prime Ministers in such circumstances, having attained power, wanted to be quit of electioneering rant, and do his duty by the national issues. But, as often happens, the rank and file demanded that action should follow the 'will of the nation' and the guidance they had received from their

[1] Portland Papers, *H.M.C.*, ii, 224.

leaders. Harley, St John, and Shrewsbury had found it congenial and also necessary to feed and even fan this temper. They had told the electorate that the financial record of the Marlborough-Godolphin Administration was profligate, incompetent, and corrupt. How, then, asked their followers, could matters stop at this point? How could prominent and aggressive members of the party responsible for these offences actually remain in office?

This mood turned in particular against Walpole, who not only had taken so active a part in War Office and Admiralty business, but had often expounded or defended the whole financial policy of the late guilty Administration. Walpole adhered stubbornly to Marlborough. He was a Whig, but also a rising Minister whose qualities had made a deep impression upon the new Cabinet, and particularly upon Harley. He had fought on the Whig side at the election. Nevertheless, in the unformed practice of those times he still retained his office as Treasurer to the Navy.[1] At this moment almost the sole survivor in office of the Whig Administration, and one of Marlborough's few remaining friends, Walpole worked behind the scenes. But the impression of his personality wrung from Harley the tribute, "worth half his party." He was now the only Whig Commoner that he wished to keep. In January the pressure of the October Club forced Walpole out of the Ministry. This was indirectly another mark of hostility to Marlborough.[2]

The tactics of trying to throw blame upon the late Administration were carried by Harley and St John into another field. The sudden overturn in Spain made it necessary to seek scapegoats. When in the previous September tales of the victories of Almenara and Saragossa had reached London the new Ministers, who obviously had been in no way concerned in them, appropriated the credit as their own. Now black disaster had supervened, and they were

---

[1] He had been appointed in 1709 on the death of Sir Thomas Littleton.
[2]   *Cardonnel to H. Watkins (Secretary to the British Embassy at The Hague)*
                                                                WESTMINSTER
                                                                Jan. 2, 1711

★I have not [been] edified much since our being here. To day Mr Walpole had his Dismission by a letter from Lord Dartmouth, 'tis said Mr Freeman will succeed [*i.e.*, follow] him.

Lord Rochester, Duke of Shrewsbury, Duke of Buckingham, Ld Pawlet and severall others have been with my Lord Duke & given each other mutual assurances of ffriendship, but Mr Harley keeps off, so that I am very doubtfull whether it may be practicable for his Grace to continue at the head of the army. I rather encline to believe it will not, tho' he has given assurances to the Queen and to these Lords that He is very ready & willing to joyne with them in whatever measures may be thought most advisable for the Publick good. [Blenheim MSS.]

conscious that as they had been five months in office some part of
its burden might lie on them, more especially as they had been so
eager to claim the honour of previous successes. They therefore became anxious to carry the discussion of Spanish affairs back to the
year 1707, to the defeat of Almanza and the failure to take Toulon.
They considered that the House of Lords, in which there was a substantial though latent Whig majority, might well be tested upon
these issues. They found in Peterborough an admirable exponent
of reproach about everything that had been done in Spain. Peterborough was high in favour with the new Government. He was
actually under orders to proceed to Vienna as ambassador and plenipotentiary, charged especially to reconcile the Emperor and the Duke
of Savoy. He had nursed for nearly four years his grievances, and
was eager to profit by this favourable atmosphere. Ministers moved
the Queen to send a message to the Lords deploring the defeat at
Brihuega, and calling for measures to repair the misfortune. The
departure of Peterborough was postponed by a resolution; and a
series of debates ensued, of which he was the centre, and from which
he emerged amid stentorian party applause.

We have already[1] described Peterborough's conduct in Spain
and Savoy during 1707. Modern studies have marked it with an
abiding stigma. But Peterborough now had a Government ardent
in his cause, a friendly House of Lords, and a mass of controversial
documents already largely given to the world on his behalf by his
champion, Dr Freind. He forthwith exposed his whole indictment
of the war policy of the Marlborough-Godolphin Administration in
the unsuccessful year 1707, and in particular he attacked Galway and
Stanhope, upon whom he laid the blame of Almanza and indirectly
of the failure at Toulon. Thus, instead of having to defend themselves over their own disasters, the news of which had lately reached
Britain, the Ministers were able to concentrate attention upon events
which, for good or ill, were decided by other Ministers four years
earlier.

The debates in the Lords were long and patient. No doubt the
reports which have come down to us are greatly abridged. Still,
there was an immense series of short debating speeches in which all
the great men on both sides, and, indeed, every peer of prominence,
took part. The issues were confused. Peterborough accused the
late Ministers of having urged an offensive in Spain at a time when
all should have been concentrated upon Toulon. He attacked Gal-

---

[1] Vol. III, p. 230.

way with ferocity. Marlborough, who, as we have seen, had disapproved of Galway's action at the time, could not sit silent under this injustice. He interrupted the proceedings. "It was," he said, "somewhat strange that generals who had acted to the best of their understandings, and had lost their limbs in the service, should be examined like offenders, about insignificant things." And a few days later, when all the enemies who had now come into power had exhausted their venom upon the greatest Government that had ever ruled in England, and upon the unfortunate, mutilated, broken Huguenot refugee, who nevertheless was one of the best-proved fighting generals in Europe, Marlborough said that he could not "perceive the tendency of the inquiry demanded; but if they designed to censure persons who had acted to the best of their understandings, they would have nobody to serve them."

The discussion proceeded for several days, and raised the false point of whether the Ministers of 1707 had or had not ordered an offensive war in Spain, and this without any attempt to define what kind of operations would constitute an offensive or a defensive, or which strategy would have best served the general cause. Peterborough, holding to his main contention that he had opposed the advance which had been followed by Almanza, sought to make this advance appear the same as a general offensive. He likewise suggested that he and the Duke of Savoy had hatched together a grand plan of their own, by which the forces attacking Toulon might have been vastly strengthened and success assured. Marlborough's reply is preserved verbatim:

"My lords, I had the honour of the Queen's command to treat with the Duke of Savoy, about an attempt upon Toulon, which her Majesty, from the beginning of this war, had looked upon as one of the most effectual means to finish it. And I can assure you that in the whole negotiation, with his Royal Highness's Ministers, one of whom, Count Briançon, is dead, the other, Count Maffey, is now here, not one word was spoken of Spain, where the war was to be managed, upon its own bottom, as well as that of Italy; and both independently upon one another. As for the war in Spain, it was the general opinion of England that it should be offensive: And as to my lord Peterborough's projects, I can assure your lordships that one of the greatest instances that Holland and Savoy made was that the Emperor, and we, should not insist upon an expedition to Naples, which might hinder the other design. My lords, my intentions were always honest and sincere, to contribute all that lay in my power, to bring this heavy and expensive war to an end. God Almighty has blessed my endeavours with success: but if men are to be censured when they give their opinions to the best of their understandings, I must expect to be found fault with as well as the rest. My lord Galway, and everybody in Spain, have done their duty: and though I must own, that lord has been unhappy, and that he had no positive orders for a battle; yet I must do him the justice to say that the whole Council of War were of his opinion, to fight the enemy before the coming up of the Duke of Orleans with a reinforcement of 9 or 10,000 men. On the other hand, I must confess I do not understand how the separating of the army would have favoured the siege of Toulon."[1]

Here Peterborough interrupted. "There was a necessity," he said, "of dividing it to go to Madrid." Marlborough rejoined, "I will not contradict that lord as to the situation of the country: *but this separation of the army could not be in order to a defensive but to an offensive war; which, in my opinion, was the best way to make a diversion, and thereby hinder the French from relieving Toulon.* But after all, that unhappy battle had no other effect than to put us upon the defensive; for the French troops that were detached from Spain never came before Toulon."

There is no part of this terse statement that is not valid. Peterborough's pretence that he had enjoyed a superior secrecy with the Duke of Savoy was politely but remorselessly exposed. We have seen[2] the inconvenience which he caused by his advocacy of an expedition to Naples and the withdrawing of troops for this purpose from Spain. Secondly, Marlborough showed that the advice which Peterborough boasted of having given at the council of war— namely, the dividing of the army for a march upon Madrid—was essentially advice for an offensive. Thirdly, he declared that an offensive policy in Spain, whether pursued by the Galway or the Peterborough method, was best calculated to free the siege of Toulon from interference. Finally, he affirmed that even after the defeat of Almanza none of the French troops withdrawn from Spain were able to arrive in time to take part in the defence of Toulon. These arguments did not, however, produce a decisive impression upon the majority of the Lords, and in the upshot, against the protest of thirty-six peers, Peterborough was honoured by a resolution thanking him for his services, and Galway and the generals who had supported him were censured for their action. Harcourt, the Lord Keeper, in congratulating Peterborough on the vote of the House, took occasion to gibe at Marlborough, by eulogizing

---

[1] *Parliamentary History*, vi, 276-277.　　　　　[2] Vol. III, p. 218.

Peterborough's "magnanimity" in accepting the public thanks "unalloyed by any other reward." The process of being wise after the event, and, as was complained of in the debate, judging men by events and not by their conduct, also reflected upon the Marlborough-Godolphin Administration. This was the more wounding because the Whigs had a definite, though at this time disorganized, majority in the House of Lords.

Meanwhile the correspondence of Ministers shows their relations with Marlborough almost from day to day.

"As for the great man [Marlborough]," wrote John Drummond to Harley (January 16), "deal with him as he deserves. I have nothing more to say for him. I believe his wife may advise him sooner to curse God and die than be reconciled to you. If he let such a wife and such a son-in-law manage him, may he fall in the pit they have digged for him."[1]

And St John to Harley (January 17):

> My lord Marlborough desired me to write you word that he would come to my office whenever you pleased to appoint, that he had something of moment to say to you and to me together. I find by the Duke of Shrewsbury that he is desirous to have some of the horse guards over with him the next year, in expectation of a battle, and horse being the only article wherein the enemy can pretend to be equal to us, I hope the Queen will let the Scotch, at least a detachment of them, go. Besides these he may have some squadrons of dragoons; and I think after that he cannot grumble if we take five battalions for our attempt upon Quebec. . . . I am preparing a state of the General Officers, and if she pleases will break Lord Marlborough's faction, by doing what is right in its own nature, and without giving him any just mortification as General.[2]

This unpleasant mood of the Secretary was soon to undergo a change. Meanwhile his thoughts upon Quebec were to open a new and discreditable story. He has given his own account of the interview at which he patronized, lectured, and even threatened the illustrious chief to whom he owed his earlier advancement.

"The great man has been told by the Duke of Shrewsbury," he wrote to Drummond (January 23),

> by Mr Harley, and by your humble servant, that since the Queen agrees to his commanding the army, it is our duty, and in the highest degree our interest, to support him, if possible, better than he ever yet was, and that he may depend upon this. . . . He was told at first

[1] Portland Papers, *H.M.C.*, iv, 655.   [2] *Loc. cit.*

that he had nothing to reproach us with, that his wife, my lord Godolphin, and himself, had thrown the Queen's favour away, and that he ought not to be angry if other people had taken it up. He was told that his true interest consisted in getting rid of his wife [*i.e.*, from her offices], who was grown to be irreconcileable with the Queen, as soon as he could, and with the best grace which he could. He has been told that he must draw a line between all that has passed and all that is to come, and that he must begin entirely upon a new foot; that if he looked back to make complaints, he would have more retorted upon him than it was possible to answer; that, if he would make his former conduct the rule of his future behaviour, he would render his interests incompatible with those of the Queen. What is the effect of all this plain dealing? he submits, he yields, he promises to comply; but he struggles to alleviate Meredith's disgrace,[1] and to make the Queen make a less figure by going back than she could have done by taking no notice at all of the insolence of him and his comrades. He is angry at the Duke of Argyle's being appointed to command in Spain, and would, I suppose, have him punished, for acting on a plan which we have all, even the Queen herself, been concerned in. In short, to finish this description, I doubt [*i.e.*, suspect] he thinks it possible for him to have the same absolute power which he was once vested with, and believes, perhaps, that those who serve the Queen are weak enough not to see the use that he would make of it. Once more, by all the judgment which I can form, the exterior is a little mended; but at heart, the same sentiments remain, and these heightened and inflamed by what he calls provocations. We shall do what we can to support him in the command of the army, without betraying our mistress; and unless he is infatuated, he will help us in this design; for you must know that the moment he leaves the service and loses the protection of the Court, *such scenes will open as no victories can varnish over.*[2]

These last words were the threat, in terms brutal enough, that the new Ministers had beneath their cloaks some exposure which they would make unless Marlborough was submissive. No doubt they had already begun to prepare a case against him for peculation. They may also have heard from their own Jacobite sources that he still retained some contact with Saint-Germain. Once they were in secret relations with France, they might easily hear of his 1708 correspondence with Berwick about peace and about the *douceur* which he had twice rejected, but also in the interval had mentioned.

All these matters will be dealt with in their place. It is only

---

[1] Meredith was one of the Whig officers who had been recently cashiered for attacks on the new Government.

[2] *Bolingbroke Correspondence*, i, 77.

necessary at this point to observe that Marlborough's actions were not in the slightest degree influenced by such menaces. Throughout he behaved exactly as he would have done if there had not been the least substance in them, or even any colourable show. As long as he conceived himself bound to the Grand Alliance, he served the Ministers to the best of his ability in the field. Once he determined to oppose the peace and break with Harley and St John, he faced with his eyes open whatever they thought they could do.

With the change of Government came also a change in the Press. During the Marlborough-Godolphin epoch the newspapers, such as they were, and the general complexion of the news-letters had been coloured to favour the Government. The various hostile pamphlets that had appeared had been in the nature of libels frequently prosecuted by the Executive, or Jacobite publications adroitly skirting the verge of treason. But now authority had changed sides; and in St John the new Administration possessed a patron of literature and a writer of high distinction. St John, young or old, triumphant or downcast, Minister or exile, Jacobite or Hanoverian, applauded or attainted, always lived in a circle of brilliant writers whom he cultivated, whom he often supported, and who followed with genuine admiration the glint of his star. He now, with all the power of Secretary of State, threw himself into the Press affair. The Tories must have a service of newspapers, news-letters, and pamphlets which should turn the tables upon the writers of the outcast régime. Already in August 1710 he had set on foot *The Examiner* in answer to Addison's *Whig Examiner*. This weekly sheet declared its purpose "to examine some of these [Whig] writings with an evil tendency either to religion or to Government." Prior, Freind (Peterborough's eulogist), and Oldisworth, all old Westminster School boys, formed a capable staff. But *The Examiner* made no real play until, first, they were protected by the new men in office, and, above all, until they were taken charge of and inspired by Swift.

In November 1710 Swift began on the tide of the Tory victory to throw himself into *The Examiner*. He meant to make it, if not the brightest, at least the most envenomed sword that struck at Marlborough, Godolphin, and the Whigs. Marlborough, still at the front, was, of course, his largest, most vulnerable, and most sensitive target. The pen of a brilliant writer, loaded with official information and driven by a strange malignancy, stabbed ruthlessly at the great figure who filled the British horizon and played, next to Louis XIV, the greatest part in Europe. In his celebrated No. 17 of *The Examiner* Swift addressed himself in his biting, robust English to the complaints made by the extruded Whigs that Marlborough had been treated with ingratitude.[1] The mordant cleric set himself to prove that Marlborough had not hitherto been the victim of British ingratitude; and he did it in a style which showed his desire to repair this neglect. In pages read by all who took part in English public life he first challenged the claim (which Marlborough had never made) that the Army, military officers, or a commander, however renowned, should presume to meddle in the political government of Britain. That was for the Queen, and for the Queen alone, subject, of course—though this was not mentioned—to such influence as Abigail might exert. Swift suggested to an audience eager to listen that Marlborough was seeking to subvert the State and make himself a second Cromwell. Who was he to match his weight against the authority of the Ministers of the Crown? The greater his power, the more speedily should it be reduced.

Upon the question of ingratitude, which Marlborough had not mentioned, except in his secret letters, but which naturally arose in men's minds from the treatment he was now receiving, Swift descended to the bluntest details. Every one is familiar with the balance-sheet which he drew up of the rewards given in ancient Rome to successful generals and the actual disbursements which England had made to Marlborough. The Roman gratitude, with its frankincense and earthen pots to burn it in, its bull for sacrifice, its embroidered garment, its crown of laurel, its statue, its triumphal arch and triumphal car (valued as a modern coach), was estimated as worth £994 11s. 10d. The Bill of British Ingratitude, comprising Woodstock, Blenheim, the Post Office grant, Mindelheim, pictures, jewels, the site of Marlborough House, and current employments, amounted to £540,000. In all conscience, was this not enough?

The reply made by the scribes of the late Ministry drifted down unfavourable channels. *The Medley*, which attempted to match *The Examiner*, tried to set off against this £540,000 the value of the several battles won by the Duke, and "twenty-seven towns taken" reckoned at £300,000 a town. Thus a total was reached of £8,100,000, which by deduction left the British nation the debtor to Marlborough by £7,560,000. Such computations were unconvincing, and the whole damage of the attack remained. Marlborough, who knew

---

[1] Swift, *Works* (edited by Temple Scott, 1897–1908), ix, 92.

himself powerless, and was only holding his command in the hope of preserving his European system and all that had been gained in the long war, was most painfully affected both by Swift's attack and the defence which was offered. He had certainly built up a great fortune in the process of raising England to her new status and to the primacy of Europe. But he had never represented the military as opposed to the civil power. He had always embodied both. Since the last year of King William he had been the Plenipotentiary appointed by the Crown and Parliament, and since 1702 he had in fact, if not in form, been the chief Minister of the Queen. It was a poignant ordeal to command the army against the might of France, with potential disaster in the field often at no more than a few hours' distance, while being assailed by scurrilous pamphleteering instigated by the Ministers who still sought to profit from his services.

By the winter St John had also started *The Post Boy*, which with equal virulence, but with less style and force, pursued the same quarrel. Harley too had his newspaper, *The Review*; and another writer of the Augustan age of English letters, in his way as great as Swift, and like Swift living with us to-day, Defoe, assailed Marlborough in a different key from this quarter. These famous penmen, aided by clusters of bristling subordinates, vying with one another, laboured week by week to portray him to the excited, prosperous, triumphant public which his victories had called into being as a monster of covetousness and bloodthirsty iniquity.

These were not days when public men could afford to disdain the Press. It was a poisoned dagger at the disposal of gifted and unscrupulous magnates. There were no correctives, apart from State prosecutions and the pillory. There was no broad, tolerant public opinion to rebuke violent excesses, or cast a shield of respect over the great man of the day. He could be hounded down with brutality before a highly cultivated audience of three or four thousand well-to-do persons.

But the depths of insult were plumbed by the notorious Mrs Manley, who had published in May 1709 *The New Atlantis*, a scurrilous and indecent chronicle of society under Charles II with frequent references to Marlborough's early escapades. Mrs Manley was at this time living with the printer of *The Examiner*. She was thus in close touch with Swift, who drew inspiration from her knowledge and from a kindred mind. Swift repaid her with constant aid and guidance, and used her to write obscenities and insults beyond the wide limits which he set himself. That she was also patronized by

Harley is shown by her subsequent appeals to him for money after the death of the Queen.

Marlborough always intended to keep the command for the new campaign provided that due authority was given him, and the Army properly paid and maintained. The Ministers, forced by public opinion, by the Allies, and by the pressure of events, were now ready to give him satisfaction upon these points. Marlborough, however, held the whole issue in suspense in the hope of preventing Sarah from being deprived of her offices. His greatest and chief motive was his affection for her; his second, his instinctive dislike of losing a point in the political struggle. These offices were vantage grounds of power. The mere quitting of them was serious. Their speedy occupation by the enemy was worse. Thirdly, there was the renewed insult and proclaimed loss of favour with its consequent injury to his prestige in all quarters. The Ministers who saw all this naturally feared that he would refuse the command if his wife were dismissed. On the other hand, the Queen cared about nothing in the world so much as getting rid of Sarah at once and for ever. In the plight to which things had come this passion can readily be understood.

Marlborough therefore, keeping his own counsel, resolved to try all in personal ordeal with the Queen. Sarah, for her part, was resolved not to make her loss of office the cause of her husband's resignation, with its measureless reactions at home and abroad. She wrote a most humble letter of contrition and apology, begging in abject terms to be allowed to retain her offices, and promising most solemnly never to vex the Queen upon the old topics of controversy.[1] On January 17, 1711, the way having been to some extent prepared by one of the Queen's doctors, Sir David Hamilton, Marlborough presented this letter to Anne. With delay and obvious reluctance the Queen opened it, read it, and replied, "I cannot change my resolution."

It is painful to record what followed. It can only become comprehensible in the atmosphere of adulation and obsequious servility which surrounded the monarchs of those days. "I would go upon all-four," Marlborough had written in the autumn, "to make it easy between you." He now made this undertaking good. The invincible captain, and statesman who for ten years had led Europe against France, now fell on his knees at the Queen's feet in personal supplication for his wife's employment. He used those arts of persuasion

[1] Coxe, v, 410.

and appeal so long renowned in the greatest matters. He used them in vain. The Queen declared that her honour was involved in Sarah's dismissal. She demanded that the Gold Key of the royal wardrobe should be delivered to her within three days. Marlborough begged at least for ten, and Anne rejoined that it should be two. "I will talk of no other business till I have the Key," she said.

What a contrast does this picture of Marlborough's humiliation, better suited to an Oriental setting than to a Christian land, present to the glittering scenes of war, where the veteran armies marched and manœuvred, steel flashed, drums rolled, and famous generals and princes saluted or stood attentive to the orders of their chief! Yet this obsequious grovelling to royalty was an essential part of the pathway to the bright fields of power and action in an age when royal favour dominated all. Let us make haste to draw the curtain upon an unnatural spectacle which reduces the stature of a soldier without raising the majesty of a queen.

Marlborough went home to tell Sarah that he had failed. "The Duchess," says Archdeacon Coxe, "now felt the necessity of acting with the dignity becoming her spirit and character." It was time. According to some accounts, she flung the key on the floor, and bade her husband take it back at once. The victor of Blenheim and Ramillies picked it up, and made haste to comply. Sarah's offices were divided. Abigail became Keeper of the Privy Purse, and the Duchess of Somerset Groom of the Stole.

The Ministers were greatly reassured to find after some days that Marlborough did not resign; but for several weeks all remained uncertain. "Compliments are paid," explained Marlborough to Gallas, "but no declaration has been given which could convince me that I am being seriously asked to continue to serve. Everything rather appears to be directed to force me to refuse my obedience, so that they may fall upon me and obtain all the advantages which would follow from my refusal. If I am dismissed, the present advisers of the Queen will have to answer for it to the country."[1] The ambassador remarked in his dispatch on this conversation:

> It becomes daily more apparent that the reflex of the Queen's animosity against the Duchess falls back so heavily upon her husband that if he is left in command it will merely be out of fear of public opinion, which demands his retention. . . . So I think that Marlborough will be kept in command, but in such a manner that he has hardly anything more than the mere name. He will be surrounded

[1] Marlborough to Gallas, January 27; Klopp, xiv, 27.

with declared foes, and a beginning has already been made by sending Lord Orrery to replace his friend and supporter Cadogan. He will be pressed in every possible manner and attempts will be made to maltreat him so that at last he may be brought by some means to resign, or else die of anger and disappointment. *Very good progress has been made towards this last object, for Marlborough has suffered so much that he no longer looks like himself.*[1]

Gradually a settlement was reached. In spite of the libels with which they assailed him through their pamphleteers, in spite of the adverse Parliamentary debates and of all the floutings and intrigues of the Court and Society, he was found willing day by day to concert with Harley, St John, and the rest the necessary measures for the campaign. Over £6,000,000 was voted by the House of Commons for the war, and solemn promises were made to Marlborough that full and punctual payments should be made for all the services upon which the Army depended.

It must have been with a long breath of relief that he quitted those scenes of sneers and self-abasement which he had endured in London for the headquarters of the allied army, where upon all sides he was received with the highest ceremony and respect.

[1] Gallas, January 27; Klopp, xiv, 27.

Chapter Twenty-two

THE DEATH OF THE EMPEROR

1711—APRIL AND MAY

Marlborough met Robethon at The Hague. He took him in his coach on the drive to Scheveningen, and talked to him for two hours in all the intimacy of their association and common interests. Robethon's report to the Elector of Hanover of this conversation reveals Marlborough's feelings and intentions at this hour, and, indeed, the English scene, far better than any other record we have. Also, which is very rare, we hear him speak.

"I am ashamed [he said] of my own people and the black calumnies with which each party tears the other. But what grieves me most is the real danger in which my unhappy country lies. I call God to witness that I love the Queen and my country with devotion, and it is from this motive that I have made so much effort to keep my post. Nothing would have been easier for me than to throw England into confusion. For the Whigs believed that I should quit my functions in disgust and make common cause with them against the Court, while the Tories flattered themselves that in order to keep office I would join absolutely with them and declare myself against the Whigs. But I have done neither the one nor the other. A third course which would have been more to my liking than any other was to retire to the country and to withdraw myself absolutely from everything. Things would perhaps have taken such a turn (the command being in other hands) that all would have conduced to my fame, and I should have been missed. That would no doubt have been the surest means of avenging myself upon my enemies. But the public and my country would have suffered, and I thought that I owed them the sacrifice of preferring to serve with discomfort and to expose myself to unfortunate events, although I know how ready the new Ministry will be to blame me for them. Another very strong reason which decided me is my interest in the succession. For I believe that I can be useful in that by remaining in my post, and preventing it falling into evil hands.

"But [he added] do not deceive yourself. This party of the Prince of Wales is very strong. No one dares speak openly for him. That

799

would be treason. But we who know the ground know also the intentions and motives which cause the different manœuvres we see now in England. The party of the October Club is dominant in the Lower House. These are the country gentlemen, so called because of their ardour and because the strongest beer is brewed in the month of October. These fellows have carried several divisions against the Whigs and the Court together. Of these Octobrists the greater part are Jacobites. *The others aim at living like their ancestors when England took no part in external affairs.* All of them are weary of the taxes and seek a speedy peace. The Queen's Ministers are in the same mood, Shrewsbury among them. Rochester's idea is that England ought to remain neutral during this war and watch others fight. You know this President of the Council and how much he liked to lead and govern; but he is greatly changed. He has become old, infirm, and timid. He does not lead at all in the Cabinet Council, and never speaks there in a decisive tone. Neither does Harley. He never speaks except upon Treasury or Parliamentary business and then only with extreme timidity. Each fears to venture too far and thus lay himself open to others. The result is that no one takes the direction and all drifts at hazard. Lord Shrewsbury is even more timid than these two. The Duke of Buckinghamshire is bold enough, but he has neither the capacity to steer the ship nor enough reputation to make others follow him. The Duke of Queensberry is a nonentity. Only the Secretary of State, St John, applies himself to business, and being a man of talent, will soon learn how to deal with it. You in Hanover would do well to look after him. He speaks more boldly to the Queen in Council than anyone else.

"Harley and his relation Mrs Masham are by no means Jacobite. If this man had the choice, he would prefer the Protestant Succession to the Prince of Wales, and if by joining himself with the Whigs he could form a party stronger than that of the Tories, he would do it to-morrow. But the Tory Party (or rather, the Octobrists) is so strong in the Lower House that it is to be feared that Harley, who will always sacrifice everything to his ambition and private interests, will be obliged, if he is to keep his place, to devote himself to them, and to embrace all their schemes; and then the Prince of Wales' business might move so quickly that there would no longer be any remedy.

"This is not to say [added the Duke] that I believe that the Queen is for the Prince. Her interest is to reign quietly, and to consolidate after her the Protestant Succession, and I am sure that this is also her intention. For to make an agreement with the Prince of Wales that he should reign after her would be to risk her own freedom, and even her life, by delivering herself to the impatience of the party which wishes to secure the Throne for the Prince. But the Queen is a woman; she can be deceived; she can be led where she does not think she is going. I cannot describe to you to what degree her favourite and Mr Harley control her. They can raise and lower her mood at their pleasure. The poor Queen has still from time to time this winter had openings of heart to me, which have made me realize to what a point these people have laid hold of her mind. In a word, the time will come, and perhaps sooner than anyone thinks, when it will be necessary that his Electoral Highness should appear and testify publicly that he has the Succession at heart.

"We regard the Elector as an honest Prince, incapable of falsifying the expectations we have of him. He has accepted our Succession, and following the advice of his friends, when the time comes, he will always be the Master of the saving of England, and perhaps of all Europe. Never will his friends abandon him, unless he abandons them first."

He disapproved [says Robethon] and cast far aside the suggestions of Lord Sunderland, whether for the taking into the Hanoverian service the three cashiered generals, or for giving pensions to several impoverished lords. "All these [said he] are miserable palliatives. We must have a cure which goes to the source of the evil, and which must be applied when the real moment comes."

I then pressed him to declare himself more fully upon this point. He said that the time was not yet, that we should make "a watching war" [la guerre à l'œil] and be in a condition to act according to the situations which might present themselves; and that the best policy for the present was for your Highness to humour the Queen as much as possible, and to live with her Majesty and with her Ministers on the best of terms.[1]

In April an event occurred which cut to the tap-root of the European quarrel. The Emperor died of the smallpox.

MENTZ [MAINZ]
April 23, 1711

. . . On the 16th at daybreak [wrote Eugene to Marlborough] . . . he was believed to be out of danger. The same day, towards evening, his malady increased, and he died next morning at eleven. Your Highness knows what a blow this is to the affairs of Europe; but it is still more severe to those who had the honour to serve him, and particularly to me, who have always felt a strong attachment to his person. I received, in consequence, an express from the Empress-Mother, who governs in the name of King Charles, to come and confer with the Elector of Mentz, and to take the command of the Empire, as marshal. I am, therefore, going to-morrow. . . . I send an order to Count Felz to obey your Highness in all things until my arrival.[2]

[1] Robethon to the Elector of Hanover, March 21, 1711; Klopp, xiv, 672–677.
[2] Coxe, vi, 16–17.

All military plans were cast into the melting-pot. ★ "It would be very necessary," Marlborough wrote to Heinsius (April 29), "for me to *know from England* as well as from *Holland* how far this death of the Emperor is to have any influence on our operations. . . . [One should] lose no time *in sending a Deputation to the Queen in order to regulate everything with that end.* . . . No siege can be ventured till this is settled."[1]

By the death of the Emperor Joseph his younger brother, the Archduke, now fighting for the crown of Spain as Charles III, became sovereign of the hereditary dominions of the house of Hapsburg, comprising Austria, Hungary, Bohemia, and Silesia. It was presumable that he would be elected Emperor of the Holy Roman Empire by the German Electoral princes. The Imperial Office had usually gone to the heir of the hereditary Austrian dominions. Although Prussian ambitions might stray in this direction, they were never to be achieved. The other potential rival, the Elector of Bavaria, expelled alike from Bavaria and Belgium, was a fugitive from Marlborough's sword. There does not seem to have been any serious doubt throughout Germany, or, indeed, at The Hague or in London, that Charles III would be elected Emperor in natural succession to his brother. The exertions of Prince Eugene, in fact, procured the support of all the Teutonic Electors.

But how had this affected the Allies and the war into which they had all become welded? Many British historians or writers have suggested that the prime cause of the quarrel had disappeared, and that there was no further reason for pursuing it. The Crowns of Spain and the Empire were now united in a single person, who would from Vienna rule half the world. Where, then, was the balance of power? Was not this aggrandizement of the Hapsburg family an evil of the same order as the union of the Crowns of France and Spain? Was the Grand Alliance—and in particular were Holland and Britain—to continue fighting to bring about this result? It has therefore been generally argued that the death of the Emperor Joseph was an overwhelming justification for a speedy peace.

But these fancies ignore the practical facts as they impinged upon the actors of that day. First, Charles III was King of Spain only in name, and ruler of the Indies and controller of the Mediterranean only by the navy of Britain. Secondly, if he should ever acquire these titles in a treaty of peace, he would be no menace to the Sea Powers. They were not afraid of him. All too plainly they had seen the weak-

[1] Heinsius Archives. Marlborough's underlining.

ness of the Empire. They had carried it on their backs; they had kept it alive with their money. Blenheim had saved Vienna. Marlborough in Flanders had gripped the main military power of France for eight campaigns. Even so the Empire, which was to have been the mainstay of the original Alliance, had barely preserved a coherent existence. Therefore the spectacle of nominal unions of states and dominions under the Vienna Court and the Imperial Crown caused no real alarm to the Allies. They all accepted the prospect with hardly a tremor. The Germanic states naturally did not object to the Holy Roman Emperor of their choice becoming possessed of whatever Spanish dominions he could seize and rule. The Dutch never seem to have feared a union of Spain and Austria or regarded it as comparable to the control and exploitation of Spain by France. Even the Tory Ministry in England, already involved in their secret negotiations with France for a separate peace, never hesitated to accept the amalgamation under one Crown of Vienna and Madrid if it could be obtained. On the first day that the news was received in London the Imperial Envoy, Gallas, received immediate and explicit assurances that the British Cabinet would support the election of Charles III to the Empire and in no way abandon his claims to Spain and the Indies.[1]

Nevertheless the death of the Emperor, so far from bringing peace nearer, drove it farther away. It completely ruptured, as we shall see, all plans for a decisive campaign in Flanders. It stimulated Louis XIV, and furnished him with a verbal argument against the logic of the Allies. It convinced him that he would be able to defend his northern fortress-line through the whole of 1711, and therefore that his remaining strength would outlast Marlborough's dying favour.

The practical point which vexed and baffled the Allies was confined to the Spanish theatre. Stanhope was a prisoner in Bourbon hands, and the Tory Ministers, much to Marlborough's disgust, showed no eagerness to effect his exchange. The English troops were become leaderless. The allied forces were in a luckless state, unpaid and unreinforced, huddled in small Catalonian garrisons behind crumbling walls. Of the £1,500,000 voted by Parliament for the war in the Peninsula, none had been laid out. Only £200,000 had reached the army, and that had been seized by British ships from Genoese galleys and forcibly borrowed from the Italian bankers. The Tory indictment of the Whig generals, Galway and Stanhope,

---

[1] Report of May 8; Klopp, xiv, 92.

in the Lords at the opening of the session of 1711 had been conducted with partisan vigour by Peterborough and Argyll. It seemed only fitting that the bristling Campbell, aflame with martial ambition, should be chosen by the new Government to take over the command of the English troops in Spain. His factious conduct in Flanders prevented him from serving under Marlborough, and his indiscriminate incursions into high politics made his continued presence in England uncomfortable to his associates. On January 11, 1711, he had received from the Queen his appointment as commander-in-chief of the English forces in Spain, with emoluments amounting to £20,000 a year. Peterborough, airily self-confident as he was, had shown little eagerness to offer himself. He knew too well that Spain was the grave of military reputations, and his own, though vindicated by a party majority, was none too robust.

Confident in the support of the new Administration, Argyll left England at the end of March. He did not perceive that the Spanish military deadlock would enable the Tory Ministers to stop insisting on "no peace without Spain." Travelling overland through Holland and Italy, he arrived at Genoa early in May. In conversation with the English agents and Italian bankers he learned the financial, administrative, and above all military chaos that awaited him. On May 9 he wrote to St John that only £40,000 had reached the troops in Spain since Saragossa, adding, "I doe not wish to ruin my reputation." On landing at Barcelona on May 29 Argyll wrote a complaining letter to the Queen. "I found neither money nor credit to subsist your army, which is starving for want of pay, being four months behind of this, not to mention what is due to them on account of former years. . . . I must confess, Madam, this accident was very surprising to me, having received positive assurances from your Majesty's Ministers that measures would be taken to supply this service as well as any other."[1] With five thousand ill-equipped and unpaid troops, Argyll joined Starhemberg in the field. The Austrian general, with about twenty-one thousand men under his command, was engaged in desultory fighting with Vendôme to hold the roads across the Catalonian frontier to Barcelona and Tarragona. All through the summer and autumn the armies marched and countermarched around the mud walls of the frontier village of Pratz del Rey.

Thus precariously Charles III at Barcelona still maintained a foothold in his kingdom. Outside Catalonia all Spain was against him. If

---

[1] Argyll to the Queen, May 14 (N.S.), 1711; Morrison MSS., *H.M.C.*, p. 471.

he left Spanish soil the Duke of Anjou would rule almost without opposition. The military verities were altered by the death of the Emperor only to the detriment of the Allies. Charles's place was now in Vienna. His duty to his home country, and, indeed, to the Alliance, urgently required his presence there. Wratislaw and Eugene wrote in the name of all the authorities who constituted the Imperial State to demand his immediate return. It is to the credit of the Archduke that he set so much store by the Spanish and Catalan loyalties he had won. His blood was up, and urged him not to desert Spain for the Empire; but rather all the more to use the Empire to conquer Spain. He therefore concealed his intentions as long as possible; and when after five months' delay, waiting for English subsidies and in the hope of opening an effective campaign, he was obliged to sail from Barcelona on his journey to the Imperial capital, he left his bride as the symbol of his authority and the pledge of his return. On the day he landed at Genoa (October 12) he was elected Emperor at Frankfort as Charles VI.

One of the by-products of the Emperor's death was to furnish Harley and St John with a specious argument for their secret negotiations with France. If the Allies' candidate for the Spanish throne was simultaneously driven out of Spain and translated to the summit of the Empire, was there not a lively prospect of his making a direct settlement with France on the basis of his keeping the Milanese, Naples, and Sicily—in fact, Italy—together with the Netherlands, and leaving the Duke of Anjou (Philip V) in form, as well as in fact, ruler of Spain and the Indies? The French had offered these terms to Charles in 1706, and again in January 1711. He had remained loyal to the Alliance. This was just the solution which Tories as well as Whigs in Parliament had been brought to regard as most abhorrent to British interests. The strong naval power of France would assert a real authority over the Spanish Indies, and an estranged Hapsburg monarchy at Vienna would from its Italian dominions obstruct British trade in the Mediterranean and all that movement to the East which was to flaunt a vision of fabulous wealth before the eyes of a triumphant generation. Thus it could be urged that England too must be in secret parley with Versailles.

Such arguments enrich debate, but darken counsel. The sole remedy for the embarrassments of the Allies at this juncture was a remorseless punching at the heart of France, the shattering of her remaining armies, and the deep invasion of her territories. A continuance of this pressure, upon the proclaimed decision that

Marlborough would be upheld to the end, would at any time have re-created the opportunities lost at The Hague at the beginning of 1709, and again at Gertruydenberg in 1710. But the Tory Government were now furnished with a supply of convenient words, which they could parade as a substitute for necessary deeds.

Most commentators, including especially Tory apologists and later pacifist writers, treat the question as if England could have had peace for the asking. She could, indeed, secure peace by the sacrifice of most of what she had gained and by the desertion of her Allies. But the Court of France, and even the aged Monarch at its head, were now once again thinking in terms not of peace, but of victory. It was not, indeed, to be such a victory as seemed already gained in 1701; but they saw before them a treaty incomparably superior to anything attainable in 1706 or 1709 or 1710. This realization imposed itself by successive severe gradations upon these new British Ministers who in the previous summer and autumn had thought that all was for them to take or leave. Now Harley, St John, and Shrewsbury understood that they had got to go on fighting. The Queen, if indeed she had ever wavered, had never lost that conviction. They might negotiate underhand with France, but fight all the time they must. Thus we see during the summer of 1711, and when the campaign opened, a remarkable smoothing over of their differences with Marlborough. Only by the power of his sword could they extricate themselves, without arousing British fury, from this wearisome war. We therefore witness a series of overtures of goodwill to Marlborough which were sincere because they corresponded to a real need. Indeed, a competition arose in this sphere also between Harley and St John. They vied with one another, and Shrewsbury joined them, in phrases of conciliation and friendship. Marlborough's advice was asked upon the international scene. It was intimated that the building of Blenheim would be resumed. The indispensable General must be kept in good humour. "Thou shalt not muzzle the ox when he treadeth out the corn." This imposed a similar behaviour upon Marlborough and his wife.

John to Sarah

HAGUE
April 16, 1711

The reason of my desiring you not to name any of the Ministers in any of your letters is from the certain assurances I have of their opening all the letters which come to me. I know you are very indifferent as to their opinion of yourself; but the concern you have for me must in kindness oblige you never to say anything of them which may give offence; since whilst I am in the service I am in their power, especially by the villainous way of printing, which stabs me to the heart; so that I beg of you, as for the quiet of my life, that you will be careful never to write anything that may anger them; and for your own satisfaction, *be assured that I know them so perfectly well that I shall always be upon my guard.* But whilst I serve I must endeavour not to displease; for they have it so much in their power to vex me that I must beg you will, for my sake, be careful in your discourse, as well as in your letters. . . . My thoughts are that you and I should endeavour all we can not to have enemies; for if we flatter ourselves with the having many friends, it is not to be expected when favour is lost, as ours is entirely.[1]

These wise injunctions were only partly followed by Sarah. Having been deprived of her offices, she had to quit her lodgings in St James's Palace where she had lived so long. In her vexation she ordered the brass locks which she had fitted to the doors at her own expense, the mirrors, and the marble chimneypieces to be removed with the rest of her property. When Marlborough heard of her intentions he wrote at once (May 24) in a sterner tone than he used to her on any other occasion.

> Your letter . . . speaks so freely of Mr Harley that I am sorry to see that you have already forgot the earnest request made by me. . . . The prints being governed by Mr St John and Mr Harley, they must be disagreeable as long as these two see and hear what you speak and write.
> I am sent word the Queen is desirous of having the lodgings at St James's, so that I desire you would give directions for the removing of the furniture, as the Queen intends to join some part of them to her own lodgings. I beg you will not remove any of the marble chimney-pieces.[2]

Sarah obeyed, and the marble chimneypieces remained. Otherwise she removed every scrap that belonged to her. She took pains to procure a written statement from the Court official who took over the apartments that "all the chimney-pieces and slabs, wainscot windows and floors, were left in the same condition" as when she had lived there. But the tale of her first intentions and the fact of the brass locks being stripped from the doors were used against her by her enemies with mischievous effect. When Maynwaring remarked to Harley that he hoped the veto on the building of Blenheim was

[1] Coxe, vi, 8–10. [2] Coxe, v, 417.

likely to be lifted, the Chancellor of the Exchequer replied, "So it was, till this late bustle about the lodgings. . . . The Queen is so angry that she says she will build no house for the Duke of Marlborough when the Duchess has pulled hers to pieces, taken away the very slabs out of the chimneys, thrown away the keys, and said they might buy more for ten shillings."[1] But he added that he would do his best to placate the Queen, and told Maynwaring to tell this to Marlborough.

Harley kept his word, and Marlborough expressed his gratitude in graceful terms. "I am extremely obliged to you for the assurances you give me that the building of Blenheim shall not be neglected. I cannot dissemble the desire I have to see that monument of her Majesty's goodness, and the nation's acceptance of my service, brought to some degree of perfection."[2] There were other matters about which he had to appeal to the Minister. "Upon my word and honour I am no ways ambitious of power, but if it be not made visible to the officers that I have the Queen's protection, it will make it very difficult for me to preserve that discipline in this army which is for her service, which I have very much at my heart."[3] And (June 11/22), "I am very sensible how necessary good husbandry is in the vast expense we are at. I have hitherto heartily endeavoured to put an end to it, and assure you that while the nation is obliged to bear that heavy burden, it shall be my constant study to manage that part of the war I am concerned in with the utmost frugality." Harley replied with equal cordiality.[4]

The good relations thus temporarily re-established between Marlborough and the Government formed a basis at home upon which the campaign could be conducted. But the balance now leaned heavily against the victorious Allies, and Marlborough's letters to Godolphin show his gloom and despondency. His health was poor. The news of Rochester's death, which occurred suddenly at this time, aroused sombre thoughts. (May 25) "*I see Ld. Rochister is gone where wee must all follow. I believe my journey will be hastn'd by the many vexations I meat with. I agree intierly with You that men are never want'd. I am sure I wish well to my country, and if I cou'd do good I shou'd think no pains to much, but I find myself dekay so very fast, that from my heart and soull I wish the Queen and my Country, a Peace. . . . I have already told You that wee are very considerably weaker and the Enemy much stronger then the

[1] Coxe, v, 419.   [2] Bath Papers, H.M.C., i, 203.
[3] Ibid., 202.   [4] Ibid., 204.

last campagne, so that God only knows how this may end."[1] And (May 4), "Since constant success has not met with approbation, what may I not expect when nothing is done!" But with that sense of resolve which so often emerged from his depression, and was the prelude to great exploits, he added, "As I rely very much on Providence, so I shall be ready of approving all occasions that may offer."[2]

[1] Blenheim MSS.   [2] Coxe, vi, 23–24.

Chapter Twenty-three

HARLEY AND ST JOHN

1711—FEBRUARY—AUGUST

I N the summer of 1710 a small expedition approved by Marlborough and Godolphin, and consisting only of a regiment
of marines and a few ships under Commodore Martin and
Colonel Nicholson, had with the aid of the New England
colonists very successfully captured Acadie (Nova Scotia) and Port
Royal (Annapolis) from the French. The Commodore returned to
London with the good tidings and four Red Indian chiefs. These
were a great success in London, and the word 'Mohawk' came into
fashionable use. St John's interest in the New World was aroused.
He sought an opportunity for a larger oversea expedition which
should illustrate the Tory conception of how wars should be waged.
He was already busy at these schemes in the winter of 1710.[1]

Harley was from the outset adverse. He knew that Marlborough
would oppose grave reasons to weakening the army by the withdrawal of battalions from Flanders and the diversion of drafts
already prepared in England. As Chancellor of the Exchequer he
had a special right to intervene. His brother Edward Harley,
"Auditor Harley," as he was called, being an official in the Treasury,
he obtained full and early information about St John's requests for
money. The Auditor noticed that St John was working with and
through Arthur Moore, a Commissioner of Trade and Plantations
and Member for Grimsby, a man renowned neither for birth nor
conduct. Thus advised, the Chancellor resisted. "Pray do me the
justice to believe," wrote St John to him, "that I am not light or
whimsical in this project. It will certainly succeed if the secret is
preserved, and if it succeeds you will have done more service to
Britain in half a year than the Ministers who went before you did in
all their administration."[2] The proposed expedition was not brought
before the Cabinet, but in February and March St John repeatedly

---

[1] His order to the Ordnance to prepare stores, the first step, is dated September 10,
1710 (B.M., Add. MSS. 32694).
[2] Portland Papers, *H.M.C.*, iv, 652.

pressed it upon Harley, and Harley raised one objection after another. Marlborough, having made his protest, resigned himself to the loss of the troops and sought Harley's aid in securing some foreign substitute.

Though preparations were moving forward, the project was still in suspense when a sudden event assisted it. Harley became the victim of a murderous attempt. The so-called Marquis de Guiscard had languished in London since the abandonment of his plan for the descent on Charente to raise the Cevennes in 1706. This adventurer, ex-priest, pretended noble, lieutenant-general in the Austrian service, had temporarily held the command of an English regiment, and on the failure of the enterprise had been granted a pension. He had since lived a profligate life about town. St John, before quitting office as Secretary-at-War, had already made him a boon companion. They dined and diced together. They courted the same mistress, but with so negative a rivalry that their first quarrel was about disclaiming the paternity of a bastard child. Guiscard, whose real name was de la Bourlie, brooding morosely over his vanished importance, set his hopes upon St John's arrival in power. Their difference over the penalties of gallantry had not long interrupted convivial relations. Guiscard imagined that the new Ministers would do him justice. His pension of five hundred pounds a year was irregularly paid. He complained that it was too small. Harley, whose weakness inclined to wine rather than to women, disapproved of Guiscard's disorderly life, and sorrowed that his name should be so frequently linked with that of the Secretary of State. As a contribution to public morality he reduced Guiscard's pension from five hundred to four hundred pounds. The new Government must stand on a firm moral foundation.

Guiscard saw it all in a different light. He opened a traitorous correspondence with the enemy. The channel through which his reports were directed is of interest to this account. The reader will remember Catharine Sedley,[1] the heiress upon whom the youthful John Churchill's eyes had been directed by his family; but he had preferred the penniless Sarah. Catharine, in spite of being "tall, plain, thin, angular," had made a career for herself as one of the mistresses of James II. She was created Countess of Dorchester, and in her later prime she married Sir David Colyear, afterwards in 1703 Lord Portmore. Portmore had been appointed in July 1710 Galway's successor in Portugal. Guiscard seems to have known

[1] Vol. I, pp. 115–116.

Catharine well enough to ask of her the favour of transmitting in the diplomatic postbag through her husband at Lisbon a letter addressed to a French banker named Moreau. Lord Portmore had the curiosity to open the letter, and Guiscard's treachery was exposed. He warned his wife, who intercepted other packets entrusted to her by Guiscard. The first letter some weeks later was brought on the waves and winds to Harley. He wrote at once on March 6 to Marlborough.

March 6/17, 1711

★There is fallen into my hand a letter wrote by Msr Guiscard to Msr Croissy at ye Court of France: & with it a letter from an officer in Flanders to Guiscard containing intelligence of the operations impending there, as Guiscard does of what intelligence he can learn on this side. He is very particular about Msr Seissan[1] & his designes; he proposes methods to discover his correspondence in France, he proposes an invasion of the Queens dominions; the particulars are impossible to be set forth till yr Grace sees the Copys wch shal be sent by the next, in the mean time the best care is taken to intercept what goes by this nights Post; your Grace knows best what warning is necessary for Msr Seissan who seems to be in some danger had this villanous mans letter been sent: I am in hopes also to discover what officer of this Army it is who makes Guiscard the channel for his intelligence: I beseech your Grace upon this extraordinary occasion to pardon the length of this letter.[2]

Two days later was Queen Anne's Accession Day. The Chancellor of the Exchequer paid his visit to the Queen at St James's Palace. On the way across the park, where the ornamental lake now lies, he looked out of his sedan-chair and observed the "Marquis de Guiscard" parading with the quality. He was angered. He obtained a warrant from the Queen for his immediate arrest. A Cabinet committee to examine him was convened for two o'clock. Harley had forgotten the anniversary, and had visited the Queen dressed as if the Court were still in mourning. He hastened to repair this oversight by donning a new blue-cloth coat with a fancy waistcoat heavily embroidered with floral decorations in gold and silver. This was a lucky impulse. He wrote to Newcastle, "Mons Guiscard is taken up for High Treason. The Lords are sent for to examine him immediately. Your Grace's presence is desired here."[3]

[1] The French *émigré* whom it was intended to employ in a descent upon the French coast.
[2] Blenheim MSS.
[3] Harley to Newcastle, March 8, 1711; Portland Papers, *H.M.C.*, ii, 225.

In the meantime Guiscard had been arrested. When he saw St John's well-known signature at the foot of the warrant he was transported with fury. "Kill me on the spot," he said to the messengers, who, however, conveyed him in custody to the Secretary's office in the Cockpit. Here, while waiting for the Council to ·assemble, he was given some food, and managed to secrete a penknife. When brought before the Cabinet committee he was placed facing the light, and Harley changed places with St John the better to observe him. Not one only, but a series of treacherous letters was brought in evidence against him, and the case was soon so clear that the bell was rung for the messengers to take him to Newgate. At this moment he appealed to St John. His manner suggested a confession. Might he speak with him in private? St John, with all their joint memories in his mind, indicated that this business was official. "This is hard," exclaimed Guiscard. "Not one word." A desk separated him from the Secretary of State; but as he was being conducted from the room he leaned over Harley's right shoulder and, crying, " J'en veux donc à toi [Then I'll take it out of you]," stabbed him in the breast with his penknife. The heavy gold and silver embroidery, reinforced by some swathings of flannel, and the fortunate interposition of the Chancellor of the Exchequer's breastbone, broke the penknife, and a second more shrewdly directed stroke produced no more than a bruise. Harley collapsed from the force of the blow.

A scene of wild confusion followed. The Ministers drew their swords and fell upon Guiscard. St John thrust him through the arm, but both the Dukes of Ormonde and Newcastle plunged their swords into his body. Some rushed out for assistance. Others stood upon the tables for greater security or a better view. St John made to give a second thrust, and plainly meant to kill him on the spot. "Swallow" Poulett intervened, crying, "Do not kill him; keep him for an example." So hot was the Secretary of State that his sword, according to Swift, was taken from him broken. Burly messengers arrived, one of remarkable physical strength, and felled the miscreant to the ground. "Why didn't you finish me?" he cried to Ormonde. "This is not a gentleman's affair," replied the martial Duke; "you will be dealt with by others."

By all accounts St John's excitement and passion were uncontrollable. Rushing out to call a surgeon, he "ran away in the utmost confusion to St James's, went to Mrs Masham's lodging in much fright, . . . rested a little, and then hasted to assure the Queen that

Harley was not dead."[1] Indeed, Harley's injury was not at all serious. He himself preserved a perfect composure. He asked the surgeon whether his wound was mortal, gave instructions for the Frenchman's wounds to be dressed,[2] and sent word to his sister to go to dinner without him.

Marlborough to Harley

HAGUE
March 24, 1711

★ . . . The discovery you have made of the villany of Mons. Guiscard I hope may bring to light such officers as are ill inclined in ye Army, that they may all have their just reward. You will have seen by whatt I wrote to ye Duke of Shrewsbury the 13th of this month that Monsr Seissan is gone post to Turin, as soon as he returns I shall not fail to warn him to be upon his guard. Mr St John will have told you how uneasy I am to find We shall have upwards of Thirty Battalions in ye Field less than the last year, while the Enemy will certainly be more numerous; therefore I hope I shall be impower'd to replace ye Five Battalions that are going from hence; however you may be assured I shall be careful to lay hold of every opportunity that may offer for the publick good. I must not conclude without returning You my thanks for your kind promises to Vanbrook & Mr Travers.

P.S. Since I clos'd this I have an account from Mr St John of the barbarous Villany of Guiscard. I thank God he could not effect his design & that You escap'd so well, since he writes me he hopes You are in no manner of danger. However I shall be uneasy till I hear You are recover'd.[3]

This episode proved of far-reaching importance. It raised Harley from out of the midst of his embarrassments to the pinnacle of public sympathy. At the moment when all his enemies and many of his supporters were turning upon him he became the object of national solicitude. In those days, antiseptic treatment being unknown, any wound was dangerous. Harley certainly took a long time to recover. Britain waited at his bedside. The Tory Party threw themselves into the public mood with hearty zeal. Previous grievances were brushed aside. The Chancellor of the Exchequer, who had the safety and solvency of the country in his hands, had been the object of an assassin's knife. A foreigner, a Frenchman, a Papist—or so they said—had struck a felon's blow at the hope of Britain. The whole

---

[1] Portland Papers, *H.M.C.*, iv, 670. See also Swift, *Works*, ix, 207–214, for an anonymous essay on the Guiscard affair, written probably by Harley.

[2] Guiscard died of his wounds and their neglect in Newgate. (Coroner's deposition, March 28, 1711; in Portland Papers, *H.M.C.*, iv, 668.)

[3] Blenheim MSS.

Government felt the advantage of this wave of sentiment. It struck St John quite differently, and there followed a ridiculous competition between him and Harley and their respective partisans for the honours of potential martyrdom in retrospect. St John claimed the blow was meant for him. The Harleyites rejoined that it struck Harley. St John and his friends dwelt upon the fact that his signature had been upon the warrant, and that only Harley's changing places with him had saved him from the attack. They pointed out that it was St John whom Guiscard had asked to see alone. They were unfortunately not able to make their full case and emphasize the personal intimacy which had subsisted between the pair. That would have led them on to uncertain ground. But it became an act of faith with St John's adherents that he was the real martyr in the public cause, and that it was to him that sympathy and popularity should rightly be directed.

Harley lay in bed and said nothing. His case was that he had in fact been stabbed; his blood and not St John's had flowed; it was his breast that was bruised; his wind that had been taken by the force of the blow. These were solid titles to public esteem. The Queen, responding to a strong favourable current, and certainly not against his advice, created him Earl of Oxford and Mortimer, and Baron Harley of Wigmore Castle. Aristocratic circles might be mildly scornful of these high-sounding names, and critics conned with unusual attention the genealogies which the College of Heralds prepared. But more important than these honours was the appointment which the Queen hastened to make of her Chancellor of the Exchequer to the office of Lord High Treasurer, vacant since Godolphin's dismissal. Thus Harley became in form, as well as in fact, First Minister of Great Britain.

A kind of equipoise was reached in the Tory Party between the claims of Oxford and St John to be Guiscard's true quarry. So nice was the balance that the pamphleteers were forced to announce that honours were even. Swift, who had thought of publishing his vivid account of the scene in *The Examiner*, felt his allegiance divided and refrained. He confided the task of writing a pamphlet to Mrs Manley, whose scurrility was still the talk of the town. "I had not time to do it myself, so I sent my hints to the author of the *Atlantis*," he wrote to Stella.[1] Later in the year he terms the pamphlet "an account of Guiscard by the same woman, but the facts sent by Presto [himself]."[2] The gentle authoress was in a position to appreciate the

Journal to Stella, April 16, 1711.   [2] *Ibid.*, Novembr 3, 1711.

delicacy of her task. "It would appear reasonable to suppose," she wrote, "that if upon the pretence of confession Guiscard could get Mr St John to withdraw, Mr Harley might possibly be of the Party, and he have the chance to murder both before they could be assisted." She also stated that after Guiscard's second blow on Oxford's chest he had rushed on St John, "thus seeking the destruction of those two dreadful enemies of France." Louis XIV, after all these years of war, still reigned over twenty million Frenchmen, and made head against the bulk of Europe. In all his dominions there were certainly no two lives which he was more concerned to preserve than the rival victims of this outrage. They had been for some time his only hope of victory.

While Oxford was recovering from his wound the direction of affairs fell into St John's hands. He acted with secrecy and decision. He set to work to organize the largest expedition which had yet crossed the Atlantic. He wished to get it off while the Chancellor of the Exchequer was still on the broad of his back. Suddenly he became all smiles to Marlborough. He entertained Mr Craggs, the Duke's confidential agent. He extracted the five battalions. The contrast of what he wrote to Marlborough on March 27 with his letter to Harley of January 17[1] is a characteristic example of his volatile caresses and scowls.

"Your Grace may be assured of my sincere endeavours to serve you *and I hope never to see again the time when I shall be obliged to embark in a separate interest from you.* Craggs dined with me to-day: we were some time alone. . . . Mr Lumley will have been able to tell your grace how sincerely I wish you established on that bottom, which alone suits the merit and the character of a man like you. I do not believe there is any inclination wanting in the persons mentioned by your grace, and confidence will soon be restored."[2]

It would almost seem that St John hoped while his rival was out of action to gain Marlborough to himself. Meanwhile the expedition progressed. Ten ships of the line, with their frigates and smaller vessels, and thirty-one transports bearing more than five thousand troops, were assembled in the Channel. St John managed the affair personally. "As that whole design," he wrote to Drummond later (June 26), "was formed by me and the management of it singly carried on by me, you will easily imagine that I have a sort of paternal concern for the success of it."[3] So great was his desire for secrecy

[1] P. 791.   [2] *Bolingbroke Correspondence,* i, 128–133.
[3] *Ibid.,* 264–265.

816

that the Admiralty Board were in no way consulted, and were therefore able subsequently to disclaim all responsibility.[1] Secrecy achieves its highest effect in amphibious war. There were other advantages. "As these preparations," wrote St John, "both for land and sea were kept private and went almost singly through my hands, so it fell to me therefore to contract on this occasion by the Queen's command."[2] It was certainly also important that prying eyes should not peer into this part of the affair.

The goal of the expedition was to be Quebec. If the conditions of the main war allowed it, if the plan were shrewdly elaborated, the carrying of the war into the heart of the French dominions in North America and the capture of their capital would be a trophy. But St John had in view a more vital objective. To capture Quebec was a deed of fame, but it was far more important to capture Abigail. Although allured by the hope of glory and sustained by the assurances of substantial illicit pecuniary gains, the Secretary of State, to do him full justice, regarded these aims as definitely on a lower plane than his designs for obtaining supreme power. He felt himself master of the House of Commons. He was its favourite speaker, better than anyone else, far better than his chief. He could express the dumb, pent-up fury of the mass of the Tories. But Harley still had the Queen. He had got her through Abigail.

Why should not St John lay his hands upon this magic charm? In this expedition lay the chance. All was secret—plans, numbers, destination, contracts—all was in his private control. It remained to choose a commander for so important an enterprise. But could there be any doubt about that? In Brigadier John Hill—the "four-bottle man," as he was reputed—St John discerned all the qualities requisite for the high task. Hill had no intention of going back to Flanders, and a foreign mission was already at his disposal. He was Abigail's well-loved brother. Like her, he had been educated and fostered by Sarah's incontinent benevolence. His appointment would be an intense gratification to Abigail. It would give Jack a chance of military glory. It would prove to her where her true friend could be found. It was all the more valuable as an act of faith because Brigadier Hill's credentials would not in ordinary circumstances have gained him so brilliant an opening. Moreover, as Harley was against the expedition he would also tend inevitably to be against this grand opportunity for Brigadier John Hill. Some time in April Hill received the command.

[1] J. Burchett, *Naval Transactions*, p. 778.   [2] *Bolingbroke Correspondence*, i, 253.

St John was also careful in choosing his admiral. Rear-Admiral Hovenden Walker, like his military colleague, had not any notable war achievements to his credit, but he was known to be an extremely sound Tory and the kind of officer who would not be offended if in private he were called a Jacobite. He was accordingly knighted in April, and with the Brigadier sailed out to the West at the beginning of May 1711 in a fleet comprising nine battleships and forty trans-ports carrying seven regiments, in all six thousand strong. It is not certain that St John had succeeded in preserving the secrecy to which he rightly attached so much consequence. He had, of course, been obliged to talk it over with his journalist friends. The *Examiner* staff had information of which the Admiralty were not apprised. Swift was none too sure that the leakage might not have extended farther. "Our expedition fleet is but just sailed: [I] believe it will come to nothing. Mr Secretary ... owns four or five princes are in the secret; and for that reason I fear it is no secret to France. There are eight regiments; and the admiral is your Walker's brother, the midwife."[1]

Thereafter the silence of the Atlantic Ocean, which in those days was profound, lapped the expedition for many weeks. St John had sent it off before Harley got well. He was contented. Abigail too awaited results with high hopes. She thought of all Sarah had been able to do for her husband when she had the Queen's ear. Now Abigail would bring her brother, at whom so many had mocked, into the van of great affairs. It would be made clear that victorious commanders were made by royal favour, and that now she had the favour. Her only sense of vexation arose from Mr Harley's want of enthusiasm. Considering all she had done for him—put him where he was, made him master of England, shown him how to turn the tables upon old Marlborough and Godolphin—surely it was shabby of him to object to this small expedition, the chance for her brother, and the compliment to herself. Anything was possible if the leverage she had now was properly used. The triumphant return of Brigadier Hill, with a victory gained in accordance with Tory strategy, would raise him to such a pitch that who should say where he would stop, once the Queen could do without Marlborough.

The political aspects of the Quebec expedition are far more important than its military fate. The arrival of this magnificent armada in Boston Harbour towards the end of June aroused from the New England colonists a wave of Imperialist enthusiasm. For the first time large forces from the Mother Country had been sent

[1] *Journal to Stella*, April 29, 1711.

to attack the French possessions in Canada. The success of 1710 had been gained with modest means. But here at hand was the power of Britain, at that time deemed invincible. The New Englanders made haste to do their part. Men flocked to the militia. A colonial force was set on foot to march overland and make good the conquests to be expected from the fleet and the regular troops. Under the command of Colonel Nicholson a strong column started northward from Boston with great alacrity. Unfortunately, Admiral Walker was not acquainted with the navigation of the St Lawrence, nor was he successful in finding efficient local pilots for those waters. When he reached the mouth of the river he was beset by fog, and also alternately by gales. "For God's sake," wrote Hill (August 12) to St John, "let me come home when I have done my business."[1]

On August 22 in thick weather a land officer on board the flagship, the *Edgar*, saw breakers to the westward, and in great haste went and told the Admiral. "But [he]," writes Walker candidly, "being a land captain, and [I] depending on the judgment of Captain Paddon of the flagship, I had little regard to what he said. . . . However, he came down a second time desiring me for the Lord's sake to come on deck myself, or we should certainly be lost. So I put on gown and slippers and went on deck and made sail, and clawed off the land."[2] Eight transports went on the rocks, and nearly eight hundred of Marlborough's much-needed soldiers were drowned, together with many men of the crews. This loss quenched the spirit not only of the Admiral, but also of Brigadier John Hill. They had recourse to a council of war on the flagship. It was then realized they had only been provided with three months' stores and provisions, of which the greater part was already consumed. Even if Quebec were captured, which was not impossible, a winter there with any serious force required preparations which, unhappily, had not been made.

The council of war came to a unanimous decision. It was to go home. They executed it with promptitude.[3] The land column from New England, which was marching forward and had reached the neighbourhood of the border, heard after a while that the enterprise was abandoned. They were therefore forced to retrace their steps. Opinion in Boston formed itself unfavourably to these methods of oversea warfare. In the few weeks that the Admiral and the Brigadier had been in the harbour quite unpleasant relations had sprung up

---

[1] S.P., 42–68. Details in Walker's *Journal* (1720).
[2] *Loc. cit.*   [3] *Journal to Stella*, October 6, 1711.

between the British and colonial authorities. The British thought the colonists awkward, uncouth, narrow, and hypocritical. The colonists thought the British haughty and incompetent. Both sides expressed their opinions, and nothing occurred in the operations to contradict them. The aftermath of the Quebec fiasco was markedly unhelpful to the British reputation in the New World.

Although some disquieting reports had reached England in September, it was not until the middle of October that the bulk of the expedition regained their native shores. The Admiral lost no time in disembarking from his flagship in order to explain matters at Whitehall. In this he was lucky, for the vessel (through a thief among the crew dropping a light when stealing gunpowder from the magazines) blew up at Spithead with a total loss of five hundred men.[1] There, however, his good fortune stopped. His professional conduct was not admired even by his Tory friends; and when the Whigs returned in 1714 he was not only struck off the list of Admirals, but even deprived of his half-pay.

Thus failed St John's only military design. He had, however, secured a personal advantage which in his eyes far outweighed this mischance. He had got Abigail. The waiting-woman had shared his hopes, his suspense, and his disappointment. When she learned that her brother, in spite of her favour, had not brought home a victory like Blenheim or Ramillies, she wept. She was irritated by what was brought to her of Sarah's caustic comments. In this quarter little was left unsaid. Nothing was forgotten of how Sarah had paid for the first gentleman's shirt Jack Hill ever put on his back, and how he was the fool of his large, indigent family, which she had unwisely saved from the gutter. But what really angered Abigail was the outrageous manner in which Oxford seemed inclined to dissociate himself from the whole adventure. He was reported to have betrayed unseemly mirth upon various occasions—not only in his cups. He had even used serious terms in criticizing the arrangements for the expedition and the personnel to whom it was confided. Abigail felt that here was lack of gratitude indeed.

He had, however, some reason. There was found among Harley's papers, published only in 1899, the following note, which had evidently served as the basis of a statement he sent to the Queen shortly before his dismissal in the summer of 1714. Allowance must be made for his antagonism at that time to St John. The facts, however, speak for themselves.

[1] *Journal to Stella*, October 16, 1711.

June 4, 1711, three days after, Robert Harley being Treasurer, comes a demand for £28,036 5s. (all his and Lord Rochester's endeavours to stop the expedition had been fruitless) for clothes sent to Canada. The Treasurer sampled payment (with very good reason): upon this Mr Secretary St John came with much passion, as also Mr [Arthur] Moore, who said it was hard he should be made the first example. This made me have some suspicion, but Mr Secretary procured the Queen's positive pleasure to have it paid, as appears by his letters: and June 21, the Queen signed a warrant for it. However the Treasurer took all the precaution he could to find out the truth, but the things being conveyed away, and no further light to be found, the 4 of July the [money?] was ordered, pursuant to the Queen's warrant. Upon the return from that expedition, it was discovered that the whole had cost but £7000 and that £21,036 5s. was divided between them. I have borne the larger upon this because it was the only occasion for their anger; though it occasioned much more mischief; for those who had unjustly got this, being masters of the secret of the treaty of peace, laid it out upon stock, where was most lost [i.e., the use of an official secret for a speculation which failed].[1]

Although Harley had been sorry to lose Walpole, an attack upon Godolphin's finance was the necessary foundation for his own schemes as Treasurer. He therefore yielded himself to the spirit of his majority, and plans were prepared for a great exposure of the misdeeds of the former Administration. Guiscard's attack forced Harley to his bed, but the plan came into operation. On April 4 Auditor Harley alleged in the Commons that thirty-five million pounds of public money remained without account. This figure staggered both the House and the political world out of doors. It was as if three or four thousand millions had been declared un-accounted for in the closing phases of the twentieth-century World War. Parliament was given the impression that the whole of Godolphin's stewardship of the Treasury had been one vast muddle, out of which enormous gains had enured to private persons. Passions ran high, and days of violent debate ensued. The villains—so urged the October Club—who had prolonged the war for their own enrich-ment and robbed the public till should at all costs be hunted down. Blood should flow in expiation of their crimes as it had done in public quarrels some sixty years before. Five or six heads, they cried, should fall; and the Ministers who had made the charges were startled to find that this war-cry was meant to be taken literally. These angry country Members clamoured for acts and not mere words of vengeance.

[1] Portland Papers, H.M.C., v, 465.

Four days after Guiscard's outrage it was proposed in the Commons that a Committee should be appointed to examine the public accounts. Seven of the Tory rank and file were selected, the most prominent being Lockhart and Shippen, both Jacobites, who were well pleased to discredit the existing régime.

St John was in general fully prepared to exploit the temper of the new Parliament, and from its beginning had become conscious of rivalry now rising into antagonism with Harley. But this story of the unaccounted thirty-five millions did not command his acceptance. He knew it was rubbish. All the accounts were in existence. The process by which the Treasury examined them was intolerably slow, but also, it is claimed, extremely sure. Malversation was inexorably brought to the notice of Ministerial chiefs some years after the culprits had passed away or were involved in other combinations. Walpole analysed this monstrous figure of thirty-five millions and showed that part of it came from the time of King Charles II, that the bulk was from the reign of William III, and that in no time were the accounts so regularly cast up as under Godolphin. Fourteen or fifteen millions of accounts were with the Paymaster, Brydges. Only four millions altogether had not been finally scrutinized and admitted, and these four millions were at the moment being dealt with by the Lord Privy Seal, the Duke of Newcastle, who had practically arrested the progress of business for fear of being committed to any impropriety. Walpole's answer, although not published at the time, has been regarded by historians as conclusive.

St John was aware of all these facts. He had also his own point of view on the matter. He had been Secretary at War from 1704 to 1708. Brydges had been a principal civil servant at his side. He was also a personal friend who was commonly supposed to lend him money. The whole of this vast accountancy had passed through Brydges' hands. He was the crux on which all had turned. St John recoiled from the thought that the impact of these absurd allegations should fall upon him. Contrary to his political game, and to the disappointment of his enthusiastic backers, he set himself to shield Brydges from this storm. At this time when he was the chief, most capable, most brilliant actor, and in full possession of the stage, he administered to his own close supporters and particular faction in Parliament and out of doors a series of shocks. He was the man they had expected to lead the assault. Instead he was the one who broke it. With a wealth of official and Ministerial knowledge, he defended Brydges, and thereby the whole system and course which had been followed. This is the most becoming incident in his brief, spectacular official career. It was not only in its public aspect disinterested; it ran counter to his interests. Swift, who never indulged such weaknesses in matters of faction, candidly explained the disaster to Stella.

> I am heartily sorry to find my friend the Secretary stand a little ticklish with the rest of the Ministry: . . . Mr Secretary, in his warmth of speech, and zeal for his friend Mr Brydges, on whom part of the blame was falling, said, *he did not know that either Mr Brydges or the late Ministry were at all to blame in this matter; which was very desperately spoken, and giving up the whole cause;* for the chief quarrel against the late Ministry was the ill management of the treasure, and was more than all the rest together.[1]

All this was vexatious to Harley, who from his couch of recuperation brooded upon his great financial schemes, to which he deemed the dark background of Godolphin's misdeeds most important. Whether this idea crossed the mind of the Secretary of State is not known. It is, in any case, fastidiously severe to impute bad motives to good actions.[2]

Harley's recovery opened a new phase in the political history of this memorable year. He returned to the House of Commons on April 26, and received the congratulations of Speaker Bromley amid a general ovation. The outburst of sympathy which Guiscard's outrage had evoked had markedly strengthened his position. In the competition for the martyrdom he emerged justly and decisively the winner. St John, on the other hand, had disappointed the keenest partisans. Harley did not, however, rely upon this fleeting mood. During his convalescence, aided by his brother the Auditor, he had prepared a financial scheme of high political significance. This

---

[1] *Journal to Stella*, April 27, 1711.

[2] Brydges acknowledged to Marlborough the help he had received from the Duke's Parliamentary friends:

★"I am to return Y. G. my most humble thanks for ye support I received not long ago from your friends in Parl. For this kindness of theirs I stand indebted to Y. G. upon whose account I take it for granted they exerted themselves in my behalf. How far I am to be affected by ye Votes wch past, I know not yet, but I am confident, I made it appear to ye world, I could not justly be included in them, since my accounts have been all given in, wch is as much as can be expected, & I may say, more forward by far than ever any of my Predecessors were: but let what will happen to me, if their animosity was level'd only at me, & w. be satisfy'd with ye sacrifice of one so low as I am, I sh. submit, & retire from business with as much pleasure as I came into it. ' (Stowe Collection, 57, v, 89–93; Huntington Library, California.)

scheme owed its inspiration to the genius of the author of *Robinson Crusoe*. Defoe's imagination was captivated by the South Seas. In the West Indies and in the vast lands of Central and South America lay the opportunities of fertile trade and fabulous wealth, both lying within the domain of the Royal Navy. These wonderful regions, hitherto exploited only by the decadent Spaniards, needed an ample supply of slave labour to make them immediately profitable. Hitherto the Queen's ships, in order to weaken Spain, had hampered the importation of negro slaves from West Africa into the West Indies and South America. In the future the Navy would keep the seas clear for this traffic, of which the financial rewards seemed likely to be immediate and enormous.

Harley, thus stimulated, conceived as a supreme new feature in the treaty of peace the assent of Spain to a British slave trade across the South Atlantic on a hitherto undreamed-of scale. Instead of dreary wrangles about the towns of the Dutch Barrier, or the negative satisfaction of dismantling Dunkirk, there would be presented to the Tory eye the glittering prospect of wealth and of oversea acquisition. The Allies might suffer, France might revive, accusations might be made of ill-faith; but here was something for Britain, swiftly realizable, and also distributable among the fighting forces of the Tory Party. Here was something which would salve consciences, perhaps to be distressed by other peace conditions, and reconcile the whole majority behind the Ministers to the treaty which in one form or another Harley was resolved to make.

There was another and more subtle advantage. The apparatus of credit which fascinated London and dazzled Europe had hitherto rested entirely with the merchants and the 'moneyed men' who formed the most powerful wing of the Whig Party. As long as this continued the Tories could never be masters in their own house. The 'gentlemen of England' would always have to go hat in hand to the magnates of the City and of the Bank of England. To escape from this thraldom a substitute must be found. One, the Land Bank, had already been tried under William III. It had failed dismally. Here in the South Seas would be provided an alternative foundation for a Tory money-power which would manufacture credit and sustain a vast public stock, to whose fortunes large numbers of the ruling classes would owe their allegiance and an agreeable addition to their incomes. Moreover, whereas the Whig money interest seemed to thrive on Continental war and the piling up of debt for destructive activities, the new Tory moneyed interest would be inextricably interwoven with peace, with a peace treaty, and with the native Tory policy of isolation from Europe and expansion overseas.

This, then, was Harley's design. The method was simple. Following the precedent of the East India Company, a new South Sea Company was to be created. It would enjoy a monopoly of trade rights, and in this case especially of trading in slaves with Central and Southern America. The Company was also to be assigned in perpetuity the revenues from certain taxes. In exchange for these benefits the directors were to assume the burden of a ten million pounds floating debt, upon which they were to pay to stock-holders agreeable to the transfer interest at 6 per cent. Thus the nation would be relieved of what seemed a gigantic burden; a new stream of wealth would be drawn to London, and a rival financial institution, loyal to the Tories and favourable to peace, would be brought into being against the Bank of England.

The Chancellor of the Exchequer had unfolded this scheme, in his last important speech as a Commoner, to the House of Commons on May 17. It commended itself very seriously to all sections in the Tory Party. Harley's reputation as a financial "sorcerer"—to quote Sarah's searching comment—was established. There was much to be said against the finance of the South Sea scheme, and it played its part in the catastrophic Bubble of 1720. There was everything to be said, according to modern ideas, against its decency and morality. But nothing could be urged against its political astuteness. It lay harmoniously in the Tory interest from every angle.

Harley and his Administration—for such in fact it was—at this time sustained two serious losses. On May 2 its nominal head, Rochester, had died, and in the first week of July Newcastle fell from his horse and followed him to the grave. Rochester in his closing year was the most moderate of the Tories, and the one who of all others could restrain the violence of the Church. Newcastle was the least partisan of the important Whigs. He possessed much influence with the Bank of England. His death left a gap which no Whig of eminence was now willing to close.

These Cabinet vacancies had to be filled, and a keen struggle followed between Oxford and St John upon the character of the new appointments. The Secretary of State, backed by the majority in the House of Commons, pressed for full-blooded characteristic Tory names. Oxford laboured to frustrate them. Strengthened by the halo of his martyrdom, with the repute of his finance and the continuing favour of the Queen, he desired to preserve some central elements in the Cabinet. He proved at the moment strong enough to fill the two great offices as he wished. Rochester was succeeded by the Duke of Buckingham. "John o' Bucks," as he was called, was a typical man of the centre. It was said that his independence was such that he could be turned out of any Government without offence to either party. In the Spanish debates in January he had shown marked friendliness and respect to Marlborough, and had paid him high compliments, followed by an interchange of cere-monial bows. Thus here also the appointment conformed to Harley's desire for an accommodation with Marlborough, at least while the great operations of the campaign were in progress.

Newcastle's place was filled in a manner deemed equally surprising and astute. The reader may remember that when Marlborough in 1707 paid his visits to Charles XII of Sweden he relied for his special information about the Swedish Court upon the Rev. John Robinson, who had for many years been chaplain to the English Embassy at Stockholm, and had awaited Marlborough's arrival at the Swedish encampment outside Leipzig.[1] Robinson left a valuable record of the conversations between the two commanders. Since those days he had become Bishop of Bristol, a preferment due less to his ecclesi-astical than to his diplomatic attainments. He was certainly an extremely able man, well versed in the politics of Europe. Harley's choice had, and was meant to have, a further significance. Since Archbishop Laud, of blessed Tory memory, no bishop had sat in the Royal Council as a Minister. The appointment of the Bishop of Bristol to be Lord Privy Seal made a profound impression upon the Church party. Once again it threw open to the Church of England those doors to secular power which had clanged to so harshly in 1641, and were soon again to be closed for ever. The fact that the Bishop was a sensible, lay-minded man of manageable principles was agreeable to Oxford, and not in the circumstances objectionable to the Church party. They held it as a symbol of a return to the good old times.

In a period when personalities were considered of first conse-quence in public office, when every aspirant was scanned and can-vassed with great knowledge, and from many points of view, the rearrangement of the Cabinet by Oxford in the summer of 1711 must be considered masterly. In the wake of these successes it was easy for the Lord Treasurer to fill his own vacancy at the Exchequer with

---

[1] Vol. III, p. 224.

an obscure but blameless Member, one Robert Benson, brother-in-law of Lord Dartmouth, "a giver of good dinners," and above all a firm adherent of the Lord Treasurer's fortunes and system. As an exiguous sop to the October Club he was content to fling the Mastership of the Buckhounds to St John's associate, Wyndham.

Chapter Twenty-four

GENERAL ONLY

1711—MARCH—JULY

I ONCE heard the Duke of Wellington asked," wrote the historian Stanhope in 1836, "whether he thought Napoleon or Marlborough the greater general. 'It is difficult to answer that,' he replied. 'I used always to say that the presence of Napoleon at a battle was equal to a reinforcement of forty thousand men. But I can conceive nothing greater than Marlborough at the head of an English army. He had greater difficulties than I had with his allies; the Dutch were worse to manage than the Spaniards or the Portuguese. But, on the other hand, I think I had most difficulties at home.'"[1]

Chroniclers must measure justly the immense efforts necessary to mount and sustain the campaign of 1711. It involved the final consumption of Marlborough's power. In spite of the savage party antagonisms in England, in spite of secret negotiations, in spite of exhaustion and war-weariness, the Common Cause and the Captain-General once again had the strength to draw the great armies to the field. A lull imposed itself on faction. The whispers of intrigue were for a space stilled. Indeed, even the doubters felt that France would not be able to withstand the persistent force and culminating momentum of the Grand Alliance.

Before the end of March the movements of the French and the news from the frontier seemed to indicate a design to besiege Douai before the Allies could take the field. Marlborough countered this by sending Cadogan with a covering force of twenty thousand men to the plains of Lille and strengthening all his positions along the Scarpe. This done, he plunged into the business of bringing the army into the field at the highest strength. He wrote repeated personal letters to all the signatory states about their contingents. He made arrangements for the pay of the troops and auxiliaries, for the accumulation of food and transport, for the posting of recruits and

---

[1] Earl Stanhope, *Miscellanies*, pp. 81–87; see also in this work Wellington's considered amplifications of his original remark.

drafts, and for the armament of the fortresses taken in the last campaign. Fifty pages of his letters during the six weeks he remained at The Hague are printed in the *Dispatches*. He also opened the cordial correspondence with the new Ministers which he maintained throughout the campaign. Every few days he wrote at length to St John in terms of deference and goodwill. In fact, he gave the new Secretary of State far fuller accounts of this campaign than he had ever sent to his predecessors. His further correspondence with Oxford will require to be studied later. Like his letters to Shrewsbury and Poulett, it shows the enormous pains he took to conciliate those who had been his opponents but under whom he had agreed to serve, and to create a basis of mutual confidence upon which he could act. The Ministers for their part replied in the most complimentary terms, and anyone reading by itself the correspondence of this summer would have no inkling of what had happened at the beginning of the year, or of what was to happen at its close.

In February the Queen was moved to send a letter to the States-General in which she commended Marlborough to them in high terms, and affirmed her unswerving confidence in his skill and her resolve to support him. Consideration was also shown to Marlborough's position at the head of the Army; and the clique of officers who had gained favour by backbiting him in 1710 were given higher but other employment. Argyll had been sent to Spain. Orrery was withdrawn from the Army and ousted Cadogan in diplomatic functions at The Hague. We find him almost immediately in polite and ceremonious relations with the Duke. A working basis, at any rate, was formed for the purposes of the war between Marlborough and his political opponents. Thus the campaign of 1711 shows Marlborough as General only. Could he under these conditions succeed? The question as the Whigs viewed it at the time is illuminated in Lediard's pages. He quotes a letter written before this campaign.

> Some Persons would still pretend to put a good Face upon the Matter, and do not question, from the Duke of Marlborough's past Successes, but that he will yet frighten our Enemies into an Honourable Peace: But, I am afraid, he is not likely to do so much, at this time, when the Enemy are encouraged to take Heart afresh, the Allies full of Jealousies and Fears, and himself extreamly mortified; Things are not the same, any more than the Usage he meets with: When he is uneasy in his Thoughts, undermin'd in the Favour of his Sovereign, and vilely misrepresented to the People: When his Want of Interest at home

makes it impossible for the Allies to depend upon the Hopes he gives them; When he is without Authority in his Army, where it is made criminal to espouse his Interest, and to fly in his Face is the surest means to Advancement; When it is meritorious in his Officers to cabal against him, and the most factious will be thought the most deserving: With what Heart can a Man, in these Circumstances, serve? Or, what Success can be expected from him, when he is to depend upon professed Enemies for his Support?[1]

The capture by the Allies in 1710 of Douai, Béthune, Aire, and Saint-Venant had marked a further piercing of the French fortress barrier. At the point of maximum penetration only Arras and Cambrai stood in the way of the long-sought allied march into the heart of France. Their command of the sea enabled the Allies, if they should invade upon a narrow front, to replenish their advancing armies by opening new bases on the sea-coast at Abbeville or even at Havre. The conclusion of peace between the Empire and Hungary promised to free Imperial troops for the main theatre. The adjustment of the differences between Victor Amadeus and the Imperial Court made it likely that the crafty and powerful Duke would act with vigour in Dauphiné.

Marlborough longed for the arrival of Eugene. In repeated letters he begged him to hasten his journey. On March 9 there is a postscript in his own handwriting: "Au nom de Dieu, mon prince, hâtez votre voyage autant qu'il sera possible."[2] Amid all the relaxations of success, when none of the Allies was frightened any more, the spectacle of Marlborough and Eugene within the French frontier at the head of a hundred and forty thousand men seemed once again to bring an absolute decision within reach.

But even before the death of the Emperor these prospects became overclouded. First, Augustus II of Poland and Frederick IV of Denmark were eager to profit by the enforced sojourn of Charles XII of Sweden in Turkey. The Empire, by now relieved from the Hungarian drain, found a new cause of disquiet. A "corps of neutrality" of the various states involved was required to ward off these northern perils. This force was formed mostly at the expense of the army in Flanders. Queen Anne's new Ministry withdrew the five British regiments from Marlborough for Abigail's brother's expedition to Quebec. But worst of all was the behaviour of the King of Prussia. In the crumbling of the Alliance he dabbled in that kind of blackmail which has a semblance of right behind it. King

---

[1] Lediard, ii, 290. The writer's name is not mentioned.　　[2] *Dispatches*, v, 266.

William III of England had bequeathed his whole family inheritance to his cousin, the young Prince John William Friso of Nassau, whom we have seen in action at the head of his Dutchmen at Oudenarde and Malplaquet. But the King of Prussia contested this will, and, as the only surviving grandson of Prince Henry of Orange, claimed the whole inheritance. He had already in the course of the war occupied considerable portions of it.[1] He now demanded from the States-General formal recognition of these claims, and some others besides. Failing satisfaction, he would withdraw the twenty thousand troops which, under the bold Anhalt, played so large a part in Marlborough's combinations.

Marlborough, himself hunted at home, had to compel the Dutch to submit to this ill-usage. At this moment he is seen struggling with both sides. Notified from Berlin of Frederick I's veto upon the march of the Prussian troops, he wrote to the King (March 27):

> I must not lose a moment to mark to your Majesty with all respect, that the standstill order to your troops, if not revoked, spells not only the ruin of the coming campaign, but also without doubt that of the Grand Alliance. I am sure that this is not the desire of your Majesty, who up to this moment has contributed with so much zeal and glory to procuring a balance in Europe, upon which our posterity can dwell in peace for many a long year.

He then promised his utmost exertions with the Dutch, and ended:

> Thus I beg most humbly to your Majesty to be so good as to give orders to your troops to begin their march forthwith by the routes prescribed, so that we do not lose by a single stroke the fruit of so much blood and treasure spent, and are not forced to subscribe to a shameful and ruinous peace. This is the mercy which I venture to claim from your Majesty's loyalty and virtue.[2]

At the same time he wrote repeatedly to the young Crown Prince of Prussia, whom he had captivated during the campaign of 1709.

It is not necessary here to probe the merits of the dispute about the Nassau inheritance. Holland itself was divided upon the issue. The provinces which favoured the re-creation of a strong Stadtholder were for the young Prince, but the majority were for giving way to the Prussian demand as an exigency of the war. Passion ran high in Berlin. When Eugene said to General Grumbkow, "Why don't you

---

[1] He had seized Lingen. The dispute at the moment was over the recognition by the Dutch province of Overyssel of his occupation of the border county of Mörs and castles in Guelderland. See Klopp, xiv, 147–149.

[2] *Dispatches*, v, 284–285. See his letter of the same date to Cadogan.

advise your King to show generosity to the Prince and give way?"
that tough but thoroughly well-disposed officer replied, "I shall be
particularly careful not to give such counsel; for it would carry me
to Spandau [the Prussian Bastille]." All hanging in the balance, the
young Prince of Orange was begged to come from the army to
The Hague to make a composition. On Marlborough's appeal[1] he
accepted the invitation, but in crossing the Rhine estuary near
Moerdyk a squall capsized his vessel, and though most of his retinue
saved themselves, the heroic Prince, whose life was so important to
Holland, and his adjutant were drowned. He must have used up all
his luck at Malplaquet. This tragedy at least ended the deadlock.
The claims of his infant daughter and young widow were, after some
pious formalities, sacrificed to the public need; Frederick I was satisfied, and after a vexatious delay the Prussian troops moved to their
place in the allied camps.

There is an incident recorded of Marlborough's relations with the
Prussian commander, afterwards famous as "the old Dessauer,"
which illustrates the Duke's art of managing men and keeping this
army of so many different nations together in perfect accord.

The Prince of Anhalt, of one of the most ancient and noble houses
in all Germany, and an officer of the highest reputation among the
Allies, commanding in chief the Prussian troops, of great fierceness
of courage and a haughty and imperious spirit, took it into his head
upon some occasion or other that the Duke had offended him, and
determined to go and expostulate the matter with him, and express
his resentment according to the conception he had entertained of the
affront. Upon his admittance, his eyes darting fire, the Duke received

[1] *Marlborough to Heinsius*

July 6, 1711

★ *This morning I have spoke with the Prince of Orange & I think that he is now in that
temper that if the States desire his coming to the Hague, he will comply. . . .* As to the Elector
of Bavaria I think it is very plain that every step he made at the Hague was by the
consent & advice of the King of France. As to the detachment sent to the Rhine,
the French have sent more Battalions & we more squadrons, so that upon the whole
I think they are pretty equal; but I must beg you to consider that if we shall resolve
to make detachments equal with the French, we then put it in their power to carry the
war where they please, which I am sure is not the interest of England & Holland.
This is only for Yourself; it not being proper to argue with the Pr. of Savoye. If the
French shall by their detachments give us an advantage, I hope you are so kind as
to believe that I would make the best use of it, both for the public good as well as
for my own honour.

I do assure you I am very desirous of making a diversion which will be the surest
way of helping the army on the Rhine; is it unreasonable to expect that some troops
should be sent from Hungary thither? [Heinsius Archives.]

him with open arms, and, embracing him, said, "My dear Prince, you have prevented me. I was just sending to beg the favour of your company in order to have your opinion upon a design I have formed for attacking the enemy, which I cannot undertake without your approbation, and assistance in the execution, for there are no troops I depend upon like those you command, nor any general in the army but yourself whose head and heart I can trust so in the conduct of an enterprise of such importance. If your Highness will be pleased to sit down, I will inform you of the particulars of my scheme. Tho' the honour of this visit makes it very agreeable to me, yet if possible

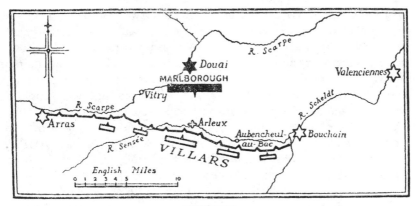

MAY 1711

I am more sensible of the good fortune of it at so critical a time." . . . When the Prince returned, he said to his friends, whom he had informed of his intentions to insult the Duke of Marlborough, "The ascendant of that man is inconceivable. I was unable to utter an angry word; he totally disarmed me in an instant."[1]

Marlborough took the field at the beginning of May with 120,000 men, facing Villars's line from Arleux to Bouchain. This was the most interesting part of the front, for the conquest of Cambrai or Bouchain would effect the deepest inroad into France. Moreover, the inundations of the Sensée were traversed here by two causeways at Arleux and Aubencheul-au-Bac. The strength of the French position was obvious. "The enemy," he wrote to St John on the 7th, "are very busy fortifying and securing all the passages of the rivers, and are being obliged to send a good part of their horse to some distance for the conveniency of forage."[2] "Our chief business at present," said Marlborough, "is to subsist."[3] He fed himself by

[1] Diary; Belvoir Castle MSS. [2] *Dispatches*, v, 330. [3] *Loc. cit.*

the Scarpe through Douai, and was at the same time concerned in passing a heavy convoy of munitions to the newly captured fortresses on the Lys. The French garrison of Valenciennes were but ten miles from the Scarpe, and made several successful raids upon the barges, in one of which they destroyed not only many laden barges but two escorting battalions.

Eugene had joined Marlborough on May 13. The Duke was facing the enemy in the neighbourhood of Douai. The Prussian dispute was at its height, and none of their troops had reached the army. He welcomed Eugene with heartfelt pleasure. But the death of Joseph had disconcerted all plans. The two comrades were to be together only for a few weeks. The Imperial Diet was to meet at Frankfort for the election of the new Emperor. Louis XIV saw that by threatening an invasion he could convulse all German affairs, and with a comparatively small detachment frustrate the impending onslaught from Flanders. He ordered Villars on June 3 to send 15 battalions and 15 squadrons to the Rhine. This shrewd stroke was immediately effective. On June 14 Eugene, with the whole of the Imperialist troops, was forced to march off to the Rhine. At the same time the Dutch, feeling themselves isolated, insisted upon strong garrisons in all the conquered fortresses.

Whereas in March Marlborough had, with his remaining strength and by many personal submissions, begun to concentrate 140,000 men, counting also on the comradeship of Eugene, he now saw himself left alone with but 90,000 men, opposed by a French army certainly 30,000 stronger. His vehement efforts to resist or repair this denudation, both with Vienna and The Hague, exhibited him as a beggar on all sides. His distress could not be concealed. Everything had gone wrong. In the British Government and around the Queen there was an air of singular detachment. Ministers shrugged their shoulders about the war, and threw the burden on Marlborough. He and his Whig friends wanted the war to go on. The Tories had always wished to quit. Out of their patriotism they had deferred to the policies of their opponents for this one more campaign. With what noble superiority to party wishes had they not played their part! Against their better judgment—so they presented it—they had given Marlborough a final chance. If he failed, how right they would be proved. All the time Harley and St John knew that upon his exertions in the field depended their means of making any peace tolerable to the British nation.

Marlborough, in order to divert attention from the departure of

Eugene and his troops, and also to pin Villars to the defence of Arras, marched westward, crossing the Scarpe between Vitry and Douai, and formed his front towards Lens, his right wing resting on the Vimy Ridge. He was now definitely weaker than Villars, and he lay in these broad plains for more than a month reviewing his troops, and drawing them out in line of battle to tempt Villars to an attack, which he had no intention of making. Villars, far from attacking, on June 2 sent 42 battalions and 26 squadrons, including all Max Emmanuel's troops, to meet Eugene on the Rhine, and moved the rest of his army to the neighbourhood of Arras. This still left the French with a small superiority, and ten weeks of the campaign had passed in futility.

Marlborough's conduct of the war at this time is in strong contrast with the aggressive method of his earlier campaigns, and also with the extraordinary exertions he was shortly to display. He was not only depressed by all he heard from England, but he had serious and alarming symptoms of illness. His headaches and earaches were severe. He suffered again from "giddiness and swimmings in my head, which also gave me often sickness in my stomach,"[1] and it may well be that he was not much removed from the stroke which five years later fell upon him. By all accounts he had greatly aged, and was, in fact, worn down by the long, exacting war.

He was also worried lest Sarah should live in Marlborough House before the damp was out of the new walls. "My only design in building that house," he wrote (May 7),

> was to please you; and I am afraid your going into it so soon may prejudice your health, so that you must be careful of having it well examined at the end of September; for should it not be thoroughly dry, you ought to stay one year longer. . . . We have had miserable wet weather ever since we came into the field, and I pity the poor men so much that it makes me uneasy to the last degree, for it can't be otherwise but great numbers must be sick.[2]

All the time he set his mind upon the problem of how to end the war by military means. In his camp at Lens he formed an elaborate strategic and political plan. He sent his friend Lord Stair upon a confidential mission to Oxford. In the first place he was to unfold to the Lord Treasurer, as he now was, a military scheme whereby the bulk of the allied army would, instead of dispersing, spend the winter concentrated upon the frontier. This involved a heavy additional expense in the provision of food, dry forage, and also shelters

---

[1] John to Sarah, May 18; Coxe, v, 27. [2] Coxe, vi, 24.

for the troops and stabling for the horses. It would cost about double as much as the ordinary winter quarters. On the other hand, it would cost the French incomparably more; indeed, they could not match it. It would keep the pressure upon them at its height, and would enable the campaign of 1712 to be begun at the earliest moment and at great advantage. In the second place, Stair was to try to transform the civilities entertained between the Lord Treasurer and the Captain-General into a definite association. Marlborough had, of course, no accurate knowledge of the peace intrigues. The pains which St John had taken to hide these from him had baffled for once his Intelligence service. The handful of men involved guarded their secret with remarkable success. Marlborough could therefore look upon the arrangement with Oxford as the sole means of undoing the harm that had been done by the change of Ministry and of prosecuting the war to a satisfactory conclusion.

The military project was easily settled.[1] But the political overtures which Marlborough made to Oxford encountered an insuperable obstacle. Oxford knew that he could not carry Marlborough with

[1] *Stair to Marlborough*

July 24, 1711—*Tuesday*

★On Saturday I saw my Lord Treasurer at his own house just before he went to Windsor. I delivered your Grace's letter and offered him the memorial with all the other papers, but he refused to take them till they had first been put into the Queen's hands; and I received her Majesty's directions as to the persons to whom I was to talk of the project. On Sunday after dinner I had the honour to wait upon the Queen to deliver your Grace's letter. Her Majesty was very inquisitive as to your Grace's health. I gave her Majesty the memorial and other papers and gave her Majesty an account of the contents. The Queen asked certain questions as to the secrecy and how it be kept, having to be done in conjunction with the States, and if the making of magazines would not declare the design. Her Majesty appointed me to wait upon my Lord Treasurer, Lord Chamberlain, and Mr Secretary St John about these papers, which I did on Monday morning at eleven o'clock at my Lord Chamberlain's. I answered several questions that were asked to make the matter plain; the lords seemed convinced that the things proposed were reasonable and that the design if prosecuted could not fail to act. Afterwards I gave them an account of the situation of the war in Flanders and that your Grace intended thus continuing, and at the same time let them know what difficulties there would be in the execution of anything and the uncertainty of success. I told them at the same time that if their lordships would let your Grace know, that it was the Queen's opinion and their own that something was to be risked to bring the French to a battle, it would very much encourage your Grace and would have great influence on bringing the States to the resolution of endeavouring something. I told them further that if anything was to be attempted your Grace would find yourself very much stinted, for you had no power to call from the country whatever might be necessary for carrying on the public service, such as forage to be supplied to the troops, wagons, etc. They thought it was reasonable that my lord Orrery in the Queen's name should move the States to take the like resolution. I saw my Lord Treasurer this morning to know if he had anything to say by me to your Grace; he told me he intended to write himself. [Blenheim MSS.]

him in his peace plans, and if they succeeded he would not need him. Many years later Stair, in a letter written to Lord Marchmont (December 10, 1734), explained this clearly.

> I went to London, and delivered my lord Marlborough's letter to Lord Oxford. After many delays, I had at last a very free conference with his lordship, in which he spoke with great freedom and plainness to me. I thought, by all my lord said, our conversation was to have ended in establishing a very good understanding between my Lord Treasurer and the Duke of Marlborough; but his lordship in the end thought fit to say that he must defer declaring his final resolution upon the whole matter till our next conversation, which he faithfully promised me should happen in a very few days. . . . From day to day I put my lord Oxford in mind of finishing our conversation, but to no purpose. In the interval Mr Prior was sent [to] them back from France, which they took to be a *carte blanche* for settling all the differences of Europe; and, in the end, I was allowed to go back to the siege of Bouchain with a bamboozling letter from my lord Oxford to the Duke of Marlborough.[1]

There is little doubt that what Marlborough proposed to Oxford through Lord Stair was that they should work together *à deux* to fight the war to a finish. Oxford weighed this matter long and anxiously. If the war must go on in 1712 an arrangement with Marlborough seemed indispensable. But the progress of negotiations made in secret gave Ministers increasing confidence that the armies would not be forced again to take the field. Nevertheless, amicable relations were maintained between the Treasurer and the General. These might ripen into close co-operation or wither into antagonism.

Since the changes in London had first been perceived by the French Court, and still more since the Gaultier mission,[2] the whole policy of Louis XIV had been to gain time for the downfall of Marlborough and an English defection to break up the confederacy. Thus, and thus alone, could France be saved. Hence Marshal Villars was forbidden to risk any battle in the open, and only allowed to fight behind parapets. After the siege of Douai in June 1710 the French had begun to construct an immense new line of fortifications and inundations behind and through which they could stand or manœuvre. This line ran from the sea by the Canche river through the fortresses of Montreuil, Hesdin, and Frévant, and thence to the

---

[1] *Marchmont Papers* (1831), ii, 75–82. The letter is of great interest.
[2] See p. 873.

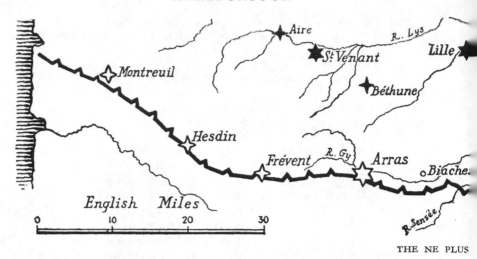

Gy, or Upper Scarpe, west of Arras. It followed the Scarpe to Biaches, turned along the valley of the Sensée to Bouchain on the Scheldt, and thence to Valenciennes. The whole of this ninety-mile front was fortified, not for a siege defence, but for the effective manœuvring of a field army. The many marshes of these days were multiplied and extended by numberless dams, which spread broad sheets of water, or quagmires, more impassable still. The watersheds between the rivers were held by strong ramparts with deep ditches, often doubled, in front of them, and frequent redoubts or strong points. Behind the line, which ran east and west and was almost straight, was a thorough system of lateral roads and bridges, and food and ammunition depots for use in emergency were established.

Beyond Valenciennes the fortifications ran through Quesnoy to Maubeuge, on the Sambre, and thence down that river to Namur, beyond which lay the natural barrier of the Ardennes. But this sector was not likely to be involved in the operations of 1711. The Allies could only approach the lines to attack the strong fortress of Arras in their centre by the riverways of the Lys and the Scheldt, which join at Ghent. They could accumulate supplies in the four fortresses captured in 1710—Arie, Saint-Venant, Béthune, and Douai—and operations on a great scale were almost certainly to be confined to the twenty-five-mile sector Arras-Bouchain. During the whole of the winter great numbers of peasants were employed by the French in perfecting this defensive system, every mile of which was studied with the utmost care. By the spring of 1711

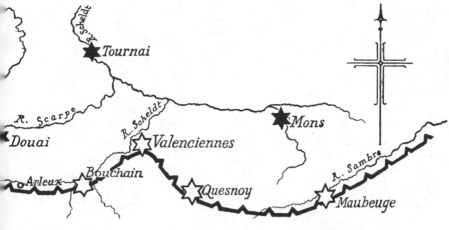

TRA LINES

Villars was so pleased with his lines that he began to boast about them in his usual exuberant style. It was a joke in the armies that Marlborough had bought himself a new scarlet coat of a cut which the tailor described as *ne plus ultra*. Villars, fastening upon this phrase, applied it to his lines, and it was soon on every lip.

Field Deputy Goslinga, who, it will be remembered, believed he had won the battle of Oudenarde and persuaded Marlborough to take Ghent and Bruges in the winter of 1708, had been present at Malplaquet, but had not made the campaign of 1710. In 1711 he reappeared at headquarters and has left a lengthy account of his achievements. He deplored the departure of Prince Eugene, "whose genius for war," he remarks sourly, "is greatly superior to that of the Duke"; and he dwelt upon the discouragement which spread through the army when relegated to Marlborough's sole care. He mentions instances of how as he went about the camps he expressed these helpful opinions to Albemarle, Dopf, and other generals. He induced Albemarle to write a letter to Eugene explaining "in lively colours" the depression of the troops and the other inconveniences and misfortunes which would follow from his departure and begging him to return. Goslinga also wrote in the same terms to his friends at The Hague. These letters, he tells us naively, unhappily fell into the hands of the enemy and were read by Marshal Villars with gusto.[1]

Notwithstanding these unpleasing and injurious activities, Marlborough made a renewed effort to conciliate the hostile Deputy.

[1] Goslinga, p. 116.

Cadogan was instructed to bring him friendly messages, "protestations of friendship and entire confidence," to assure him that "Milord" would treat him in the highest intimacy, and open to him alone all the plans which he might make during the campaign, "that he would consult with me and would be enchanted if I would communicate my thoughts, upon which he would always reflect as they deserved."[1] Goslinga was flattered, and henceforward, as he tells us, he always gave the right advice to Marlborough, and made for him all the plans that succeeded, and many others which would have succeeded if Marlborough had not been too timid or too basely interested in the prolongation of the war to adopt them. In particular, of course, Goslinga thought it would be a good thing to force the enemy's lines. Having reached this profound conclusion, he did not neglect to impart it to the Duke.

> One day finding myself alone with Milord in his room, I referred to the talk I had had with Cadogan and told him that, being at once his servant and friend, *as he knew*, I felt obliged to tell him that now that he was alone and without a companion to share with him the honour of any conquest or successful battle, I should think that it would be in his own interest to try some enterprise and with this object to surprise some part of the enemy's lines; and if ever a sensational stroke [*un coup d'éclat*] had been necessary for his own personal interest as well as for that of the Common Cause, this was the time, . . . when the English Government was using every means to drive out all his relations and friends from the control of affairs, and when he could only by some glorious achievement oblige them to go with him bridle in hand [*bride en main*].

Marlborough, according to the Deputy, concurred in these reasonings. He thanked Goslinga for them and, drawing him towards the map on the wall, examined the military possibilities.

> After some discussion we agreed that an attempt should be made by marches and countermarches to mislead and confuse the enemy, and then by some great and precipitate march cross the Sensée at whatever was the best point.[2]

A few days later Marlborough saw the Deputy again and told him that when the grass was grown so that the army could live beyond the Sensée he would try to cross it either at Arleux or at Aubencheul-au-Bac, or, again, below Marquion stream. Goslinga seems to have been somewhat startled as well as pleased to find

[1] Goslinga, p. 117.   [2] *Ibid.*, pp. 120–121.

these ideas, of which he now conceived himself the fountain, taking shape. To safeguard himself in case things went wrong ("pour me disculper en cas de malheur") "I asked the Duke if he would allow me to confide the design to the Pensionary and M. de Slingelandt and above all to the Prince of Savoy, who was still at The Hague." Marlborough approved this step; the Deputy wrote accordingly, and a few days later received a letter from The Hague expressing general agreement. Milord, says Goslinga, appeared to be very much pleased, and to put matters in train resolved to capture the position of Arleux.

The Duke had, of course, no need to use Goslinga as his channel of communication with Heinsius and Eugene. He had worked with them in the greatest matters for ten years. If he took the pestilent Deputy into his confidence it was because this was a lesser evil than having him spreading doubt and despondency throughout the army, and making all the mischief he could at The Hague.

Chapter Twenty-five

NE PLUS ULTRA

1711—JULY AND AUGUST

THE forcing of long lines was a standard operation until the Great War of 1914. In the old days, when the defence was not greatly superior to the assault, the attacking army feinted one way, and made a forced march by night the other. The interest of Marlborough's campaign of 1711 consists in the artifices and stratagems which he used, and the perfection and true sense of values with which he combined and timed all parts of his schemes. He weighed every factor justly, but most of all he read the character and temperament of Marshal Villars.

The causeway across the Sensée by Arleux has been mentioned. Arleux was a French fort north of the river, and guarded the entrance to the causeway. The lines lay behind the Sensée, itself impassable by its morasses and floods. Marlborough wanted Arleux out of the way. If he took it himself and demolished it, it would be a sure sign that he designed to pass the river there. In that case Villars would man this portion of his lines in sufficient strength, and there could be no surprise. Marlborough therefore sought to induce Villars to demolish Arleux himself. In this seemingly impossible task he succeeded.

On July 6 an allied detachment of seven hundred men captured Arleux and its garrison. The immediate object of this operation was reported by Marlborough to St John to be the breaking of the dam which the enemy had made on the Sensée. No one can say even now that at the time it had a deeper significance. However, having taken Fort Arleux, Marlborough proceeded, not to demolish it, but to fortify it, and on a much larger scale. He placed a strong force under Hompesch ᵥ the glacis of Douai, five miles away, to cover this work. Hompesch was certainly careless, for on July 9 Villars counter-attacked the fort and Hompesch's camp. The fort held out, but Hompesch was seriously cut up and lost nearly a thousand men killed, wounded, and prisoners. Villars exulted publicly, and in his letters to Paris, upon the affront he had inflicted upon his opponent. Marlborough persisted in the fortifying of Arleux; but when these extensive works were completed he assigned only a small garrison of six hundred men to their defence. This clearly wears the aspect of design. Moreover, the Duke now displayed considerable irritation at Hompesch being surprised, and it got about in the allied army, and spread to the French, that he was much upset and very angry. On July 20–21, having recalled Hompesch, he marched his army twenty miles farther to the west, and camped south of Lillers; at the same time he reinforced his garrisons in Douai, Lille, and Tournai, so that he had an exceptional number of troops unnoticed thereabouts. He left his pontoons at Douai. These were certainly definite steps in his plan. They deceived Goslinga, who wrote a letter of protest to Marlborough, complaining of his "remaining so long with folded arms inactive at the head of so fine an army."[1]

More important, they deceived Villars. He too moved his main army a march farther to the west, but at the same time detached a force under Montesquiou to capture Arleux. Villars now viewed Fort Arleux in a new light. He had wished to keep it as a toll-gate to the causeway on Marlborough's side of the river. But now it appeared that Marlborough, far from wishing to demolish it, desired to keep it to prevent an incursion by Villars. If Marlborough had demolished it, Villars would have refortified it. As Marlborough had greatly strengthened its fortifications, Villars thought it would be right to destroy them. This was precisely the reaction which Marlborough had foreseen. With his main army forty miles away, and quite a lot of his troops dispersed within easy reach of Douai, Arleux and its weak garrison was a bait: and the bait was taken. On July 22 Villars attacked Arleux. Instead of using any of the troops which he had within reach of Douai, Marlborough dispatched Cadogan with thirty squadrons and all the Grenadiers from the camp near Lillers to the rescue. Cadogan was too late—Kane even says "he took not such haste as the occasion seemed to require." Arleux was captured by the French, and its garrison were made prisoners of war. Marshal Villars trumpeted to the world this new gross humiliation he had inflicted upon Marlborough, and proceeded to level the peccant Arleux to the ground. At the same time, feeling comfortable about his right, he sent Montesquiou on with his detachment to reinforce Maubeuge and threaten Brabant.

The effect upon Marlborough of this second rebuff was noticed

[1] Goslinga, p. 125.

by all. His customary urbanity and composure deserted him. "He was," says Kane, "very peevish publicly." He was known to be ailing in health, worried out of his wits by politics, and now deeply angered by the severe pinpricks he had received. Spies were everywhere, and his demeanour was reported to the enemy. It was a natural reply to Montesquiou's advance to Maubeuge that Marlborough should send a similar force to the eastward. Accordingly he ordered Albemarle, with twelve battalions and twenty-four squadrons, to Béthune. The French staff saw nothing unusual in this, nor did they notice that, mixed up with Albemarle's movement, much of the baggage of the army and the heavy artillery with a strong escort moved on towards Douai. It now became known that Marlborough had resolved to attack Villars and his lines with the main army in the neighbourhood of Arras. He had for some time past been writing, even to his most intimate friends, that battle would be necessary. On July 26, escorted by two thousand horse, he made a personal reconnaissance of the French lines west of Arras about Avesnes-le-Comte. He took a large staff with him, and rode close enough to have a brush with the French light cavalry. It is noticeable that, though the French force from Maubeuge moved towards Brabant, Albemarle moved no farther east, and Marlborough contented himself with sending a small reinforcement to Brussels. The stage was now set.

Count Tilly, whom Goslinga describes as a brave and loyal man, had his wife with him in the camp. This lady was not only talkative, but suspected, by Goslinga at least, of illicit correspondence with the enemy.[1] Marlborough visited Count Tilly and informed him of his decision to attack Villars in two or three days. Goslinga, who was now in the secret, lunching with an abbé near by, committed the calculated indiscretion of drinking to the great event which would happen two days later, and was pleased to see a young stranger at the table leave very rapidly after the meal. Thus from many sources Villars by the end of July was convinced that Marlborough meant to attack him. It was now too late to recall the French troops sent to Maubeuge, and his Intelligence informed him that Albemarle was still at Béthune, near enough to join the main allied army for the battle. The fact that Albemarle had not moved to protect Brussels seemed to prove that he was needed by Marlborough for a general engagement. Villars thereupon concentrated all his forces upon the sector of the lines west of Arras. His men

[1] Goslinga, p. 125.

worked night and day to strengthen the already formidable defences.
He drew in all cannon and detachments and drained the garrisons
of all the fortresses in reach. The ardent spirit of the Marshal was
highly elated by the prospect of an attack upon his lines. As he
surveyed their immense strength and the superior numbers of the
army he had arrayed behind them he proclaimed on all sides his

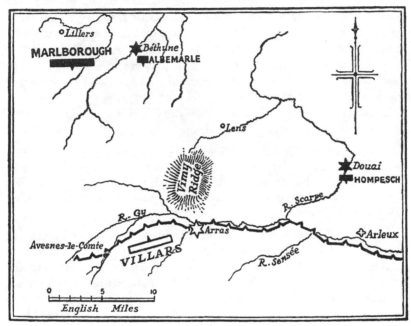

JULY 26, 1711

confidence in the result. He even wrote a letter to the King, for
which he was afterwards ridiculed, declaring that he had brought
Marlborough to the *ne plus ultra*.[1]

On July 30 twelve hundred pioneers were busy preparing the
roads by which the allied army would advance southward; and all
detachments in the neighbourhood were recalled, except those which
lay to the east. Albemarle at Beuvry, near Béthune, received orders
to hold himself in readiness to join Marlborough. Knowing nothing
of Marlborough's plan, he wrote to Drummond (August 1):

> I have just now received orders from Marlborough to rejoin the
> army which marches to-day to attack the enemy within their lines.
> God give us good success in case we undertake this great affair!

[1] Mentioned in Coxe, v, 58.

Marlborough tells me he is resolved to do it, but I declare that I doubt the result, the enterprise appears to me very dangerous, the enemy, in spite of detachments, is yet much superior to us, and it is true that the defection of our army has been terrible this campaign and still continues.[1]

On the 2nd and 3rd the Duke moved forward again and halted abreast of Villers-Brulin within striking distance of the French. He ordered the cavalry to make the thousands of fascines which were needed to fill in the double ditches in front of the French entrenchments. Every preparation was made for battle in both armies. All his commanders, except four or five who were in the secret, were thoroughly misled and deeply alarmed. Defeat was probable; a frightful slaughter certain.

Cardonnel's letter to Robethon on the evening of August 3 may be presented as a masterpiece of discreet ambiguity:

> Monsieur de Villars has assembled all the troops he could, and our advices even say that the garrisons of Ypres and St Omer are in march to join him. Nevertheless, we may probably attempt *to force his lines* before two days are at an end, all possible preparations being made for that end.[2]

On the 4th Marlborough, protected by a large force of cavalry and attended by a numerous staff, reconnoitred the enemy's lines at close quarters. While all eyes were attracted by this spectacle, the field artillery moved off to the eastward in successive detachments. Captain Parker, who was posted with his company, heard of this reconnaissance, and thought there was "something extraordinary in it." He asked his Brigadier for leave to ride out with the Duke.

> This was readily granted, and thereupon I kept as near his Grace as I possibly could. He rode upwards of a league along their lines, as near as their cannon would permit. From thence I could discern plainly by the help of a prospective, that the lines were very strong and high, and crowded with men and cannon, and that the ground before them was levelled and cleared of everything that might be any kind of shelter to those that approached them. Notwithstanding all this, the Duke's countenance was now cleared up, and with an air of assurance, and as if he was confident of success, he pointed out to the General Officers, the manner in which the army was to be drawn up, the places that were to be attacked, and how to be sustained. In short, he talked more than his friends about him thought was discreet, considering that Villars had spies at his very elbow. And indeed some

[1] Portland Papers, *H.M.C.*, v, 62.　　　　　　　　[2] Lediard, iii, 149.

846

began to suspect that the ill-treatment he had met with at home, or the affront he had lately received from Villars, might have turned his brain, and made him desperate. When I found the Duke had almost done, I returned to my post. At this time, I observed General Cadogan steal out of the crowd, attended by one servant only, and he made all the haste he could to camp. I did not think much of this circumstance at that time.[1]

Cadogan, with an escort of forty Hussars, galloped off to Douai. Here he found Hompesch. As darkness fell troops from Lille, Tournai, and Saint-Amand joined the Douai garrison, the whole forming a corps of twenty-three battalions and seventeen squadrons. During the morning, while Marlborough's pioneers were all out preparing the approaches towards the French left, the whole of the field artillery—this certainly seems a great risk—began to move in the opposite direction, and at nightfall Albemarle, instead of being summoned west to join Marlborough, was ordered to march with the utmost speed to Douai. Thither the heavy baggage with its exceptional escort was also proceeding.

That day in the allied camps there was a solemn hush. All were ready to do their duty and pay its forfeits if these were demanded of them. Still, the memories of Malplaquet, and the close survey of the enemy's lines which so many officers had been able to make, led experienced men to wonder whether the Captain-General was in his right mind. There can be no doubt of the readiness of these hard-bitten professional troops to make the frontal assault, and their faith in Marlborough's hitherto infallible skill mastered their misgivings. But when during the afternoon the orders for battle were circulated bewilderment was general. The sun set upon two hundred thousand men who expected to be at each other's throats at daybreak. Villars moved about his army, animating his soldiers for an ordeal which would decide the fate of France. As he considered the position he must have felt, with Cromwell at Dunbar, "The Lord hath delivered them into our hands." All the enemy accounts show that the French soldiers braced themselves in the highest spirit of devotion to conquer or to die, and that their High Command was well content that the supreme stake, decisive for the long war, should on these terms be ventured. As night approached a large body of light cavalry was sent out on the right flank of the allied army, as if to portend some movement towards the west. This was the last thing the French saw before darkness fell.

[1] Parker, *Memoirs*, pp. 153–154. See also Kane, p.85.

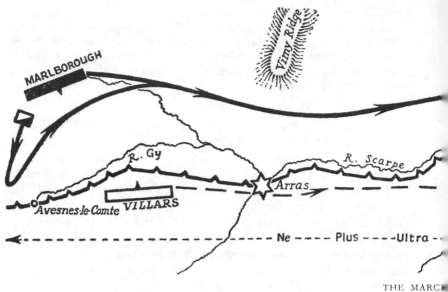

THE MARCH

"At length," says General Kane, "tattoo beats, and before it had done, orders came to strike our tents immediately."[1] The troops stood to arms. Soon staff officers arrived to guide the four columns, and in less than half an hour the whole army was on the march to the left. All through the moonlight night they marched eastward. They traversed those broad undulations between the Vimy Ridge and Arras which two centuries later were to be dyed with British and Canadian blood. The march was pressed with severity: only the briefest halts were allowed; but a sense of excitement filled the troops. It was not to be a bloody battle. The "Old Corporal" was up to something of his own. On they strode. Before five o'clock on the morning of the 5th they reached the Scarpe near Vitry. Here the army found a series of pontoon-bridges already laid, and as the light grew they saw the long columns of their artillery now marching with them.

At daybreak Marlborough, riding in the van at the head of fifty squadrons, met a horseman who galloped up from Cadogan. He bore the news that Cadogan and Hompesch, with twenty-two battalions and twenty squadrons, had crossed the causeway at Arleux at 3 A.M. and were in actual possession of the enemy's lines. Marlborough now sent his aides-de-camp and staff officers down the whole

[1] Kane, p. 85.

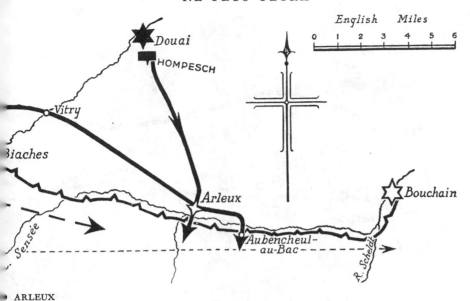

ARLEUX

length of the marching columns with orders to explain to the officers and soldiers of every regiment what he was doing and what had happened, and to tell them that all now depended upon their marching qualities. "My lord Duke wishes the infantry to step out." One must remember that he was dealing with an army composed primarily of men many of whom, though only privates, had for several years, some for ten years, had no other life but the service, and who were keen critics of every move in war. He knew that their comprehension of what he was doing, and what he was saving them from, would gain him their utmost efforts. The whole army marched with every scrap of life and strength they had. As the light broadened and the day advanced, the troops could see upon their right, across the marshes and streams of the Sensée, that the French were moving parallel to them within half cannon shot. But they also saw that the head of the French horse was only abreast of the allied foot. "It was," says Parker, "a perfect race between the two armies, but we, having the start of them by some hours, constantly kept ahead."[1]

Marlborough, putting his fifty squadrons to the trot, hastened on to join Cadogan. His infantry followed with a superb endurance and devotion. Men marched until they dropped, fainting or dying

[1] Parker, p. 155.

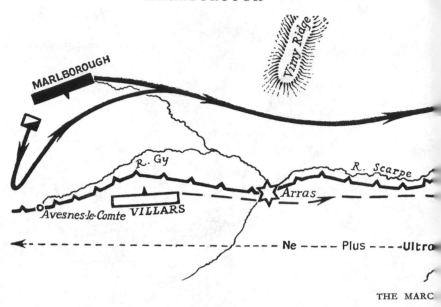

THE MARC

by the road. The track was lined with stupefied soldiers, of whom scores expired from their exertions. Little more than half stayed the course. It was like the rush upon Oudenarde, but far longer. In sixteen hours the infantry of the army marched thirty-six miles, and by four in the afternoon considerable masses had arrived in the new position behind the enemy's lines from Oisy towards the Scheldt.

Villars had not learnt that Marlborough was marching till eleven o'clock that night. All his troops were in the trenches, ready to stand to arms at a moment's notice. He had received a message from Montesquiou, near Maubeuge, that he expected to be attacked at dawn. This was, of course, a delusion. He began to be uncomfortable about the Cambrai-Bouchain area, which, as he says, "was no longer defended." It was 2 A.M. before he was sure where Marlborough was going. He knew at once that he had been forestalled. He ordered the whole of his army to march eastward, and hurried on himself at the head of the Maison du Roi. He was met on the way by the news that the lines had been crossed by an allied advance from Douai, and that large hostile forces of cavalry and infantry were already across the Sensée. On this he pressed forward so rapidly that he arrived on the scene at about eleven o'clock with two or three hundred men. He found Marlborough at the head of a veritable army, long past his lines, and ready to receive him. The

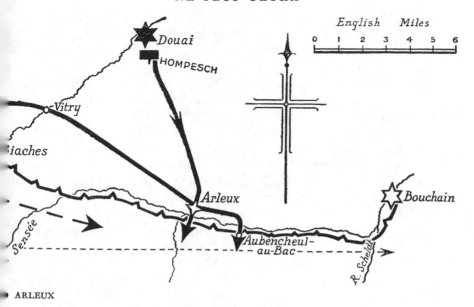

impetuous Marshal lost a hundred of his men, and was within an ace of being captured himself, before he accepted what had happened.

During the 5th of August the bulk of the allied army was crossing the Sensée and drawing up inside the enemy's lines. The whole of the cavalry of the right wing, which acted as rearguard, was employed in bringing in exhausted soldiers, their muskets, and their packs, with which the route was littered, as they had fallen by the way. Villars's main body, after a forced march, was now approaching. The night of the 5th fell on these exertions.

We are indebted to Goslinga for an invaluable sketch of the next morning's proceedings.[1] The Deputy arose at the first glint of dawn (*à la petite pointe du jour*) and proceeded when dressed to Marlborough's quarters; for he felt it his duty to keep him up to the mark. He learned that the Duke had already ridden forth in the dark. The Deputy caught him up after a while and found him accompanied by Hompesch, Bülow, and other principal generals. Marlborough greeted him, and explained that they were going to examine the ground on the front of the army. It looks very much as if the Deputy had overslept himself, but this in no way diminished his self-confidence. "Milord," he records, "said to me out loud, so

---

[1] Goslinga, p. 132.

851

that every one could hear him, 'Now we shall make our siege' (meaning Bouchain): 'our hands are free. I shall use these five or six days which we need for the preparations, in trying to bring the enemy to action.' I loudly applauded this generous resolve," says Goslinga, "and animated the Duke to it. Hompesch did the same." Meanwhile the cavalcade, with its escorting squadrons and patrols, reached the hamlet of Framegies. Here they met two peasants, who declared that the French army was close at hand and advancing. Cadogan and Goslinga climbed the church tower, and even before they reached the top saw a couple of miles away several heavy French columns marching forward and already in the act of deploying. They could even see the colour of their flags. Most of the High Commanders, including Hesse and Würtemberg, had now come up, and all sat their horses awaiting Marlborough's decision. Not so Deputy Goslinga. With all his faults, right or wrong, he was always for fighting; which is something. "Ought you not," he said to Marlborough, "to make all the troops stand to arms, and harness the Dutch artillery, and bring the English artillery as fast as possible across the Sensée?"

Marlborough was a model of politeness and patience in personal relations. Up to now the Deputy had always received bland and even deferential treatment from him. Long night marches, early rising, endless vexations, intense military issues, had not hitherto worn down Marlborough's ceremonious manner. However, on this occasion Goslinga was conscious of a very definite change. "I found him freezing; he answered me dryly [*sèchement*] that there would be time for that, that the first thing was to find out whether the ground made a general attack possible. I answered him," says Goslinga, "that it was always right to be ready," and on this the Deputy turned to Cadogan, looking for his support. "I couldn't get a word out of him [*Je n'en pus tirer une seule parole*]." Hesse offered to reconnoitre with his cavalry. Marlborough contented himself with ordering forty squadrons to stand by. Goslinga, the privileged civilian in the midst of these military men, let himself go.

As for me, seeing this coldness of Milord, and of Cadogan, so ardent by nature but now ice in this rencontre, I said that I should go and warn Count Tilly; and if Milord was agreeable, I would in passing by the left give the order for the army to stand to arms, and to harness and to bring up our artillery: and at the same time recall by a cannon-shot all the foraging parties which were afield.[1]

Goslinga, p. 132.

Goslinga records that Marlborough said to him most coldly,
"All right—you may do it," and that he added as the Deputy rode
off, "I shall expect you for dinner at noon." Was this good manners,
or was it ridicule? Certainly it dismissed very curtly Goslinga's wish
for a battle. Across the centuries one can almost hear the titter
that ran round the circle of high, proud military men, with lifetimes
of war behind them, as the important and self-important Deputy
galloped off to issue his commands. "Don't be late for dinner!"
"What," he said to himself, "dine, when we ought to beat the enemy!"
"I went off quite hotly without listening for anything more."
(Actually he writes *sans attendre réponse*, but the answer had already
been made.) It suited Marlborough well to be alone with his officers.

As it gives so good a picture of the army—all the better because
the impression is unstudied—it is worth while following Goslinga
on his gallop. First he met some subordinate commanders, who
asked, "Is it true the French are forming in battle before us?" "I
told them nothing was more true, and urged them to array their
men." He gave his orders to the Dutch artillery, and then hastened
to the tent of Count Tilly.

> I found him still in bed, but, having made him get up, I explained
> to him the situation. I was not particularly surprised not to find him
> respond to my insistence to come with me at once to Milord. His
> great natural phlegm, augmented by his great age, did not leave him
> any too capable of vigorous action. The defensive was his forte.
> Seeing I should not get much out of him, I told him I should return
> to the front of the army where I had left Milord and most of the
> generals, and that I should await him there. I returned at full gallop,
> and found Milord almost where I had left him. He said to me when
> I accosted him that, according to the reports which the peasants had
> given, the French left was covered by marshes, and their right by a
> deep ravine, and that it would be difficult to attack them.[1]

Goslinga thereupon interrogated the two peasants for himself
and believed that he had extracted a statement from them that
though there was a ravine on the left, there was no marsh on the
right. Marlborough put up with all this, so contrary to the discipline
of an army, and to almost anything that a commander-in-chief is
entitled to expect; but no doubt he saw how surely such behaviour
would put every one on his side. His strategy was just as good on
the smallest scale. All he said was that after the arrival of Count
Tilly they must settle what should be done.

[1] Goslinga, p. 135.

Meanwhile Goslinga hastened from one general to the other "First I tackled Hompesch, and tried to make him stimulate Milord, but he put me off [*mais il battit froid*]." Goslinga turned to Natzmer. All that the Prussian cavalry general, a hard, fierce man of war, hero of the charge at Oudenarde, would say was, according to Goslinga, "We shall have to examine the ground." Natzmer in his own account says, "I supported my lord Duke."[1] Then Tilly arrived with the other Dutch Deputies, and a sort of council of war was held in the open, and it seems on horseback. Goslinga remembered that once, in 1707, Marlborough in a burst of confidence had said to him in effect, "When I don't want to do a particular thing I call a council of war." The Duke now asked for opinions in the reverse order of seniority. All were for battle if the ground permitted it, but the English generals Orkney and Lumley, and Anhalt the Prussian, declared that the ground was too favourable to the enemy, and that the best thing was to cross the Scheldt. Albemarle hedged. Hesse and Würtemberg, according to Goslinga—and the story is taken as he tells it—were for the attack. Thereupon Marlborough spoke for the first time.

He said that there was no possibility of bringing the enemy to decisive battle except by attacking at great disadvantage, and that the only thing to do was to cross the Scheldt and besiege Bouchain. Count Hompesch and the Dutch general Fagel, and even the other two Dutch Deputies, thereupon supported Marlborough. Goslinga protested at length and aloud. "But I spoke in vain," he writes. "Milord held to the resolution which had been taken." It was settled that at sunset the army should cross the Scheldt by four bridges covered by a rearguard of forty squadrons. The generals then dispersed. Marlborough again asked Goslinga to dine with him. "But," says this irate civilian, almost alone among chiefs of war,

> my heart was too full of wrath against his damnable politics, which by avoiding battle only sought to prolong the war, and held out to him the benefits of his continued command of the army, and the ruin of the new English Ministry which could not maintain itself in office if the war went on, because only the Whigs could raise the necessary money from the City. Such were the sad results of having a foreigner in command.[2]

Thus the self-assurance of Goslinga was proof against the almost unanimous opinion of all the captains, and even of his own two colleague Deputies, and, as usual, his chagrin took the form of

[1] Matzmer, p. 168.   [2] Goslinga, p. 141.

imputing dishonourable or corrupt motives to all who differed from him, and particularly to the great man who had—not from inclination, it must be admitted—treated him with so much ceremony and forbearance. The Deputy spread his complaints in all directions and managed to create a good deal of ill-feeling and misconception.

Drummond wrote from Amsterdam to Oxford (August 12):

> I was sitting with the Grand Pensionary when the express came in; he was much concerned at our not fighting, and said, when the States consented to attack the lines, they consented to gain them by force and to fight the enemy. . . . The States Deputies called out to attack, the Duke called a council of war, . . . and his Grace, contrary to his practice throughout all this war, voted not to attack. . . . The Duke may have good reasons for what he has done, besides a great majority on his side of old generals. . . . Count Sinzendorff had some German accounts, which were wrote with malice and passion by what I could hear, and he added as his opinion, that if he were a Prince who had a General who had gained twenty battles, and had been guilty of this one neglect, he would hang him for it.[1]

When the more civil of these criticisms reached his ears Marlborough was deeply offended. He protested to Heinsius (August 13, 1711):

> *I do heartily thank you for your kind congratulations on our passage of the lines. I am persuaded they are very sincere & proceed from a real friendship to me, therefore I cannot help unburdening myself to you that I think I lye under great hardships & discouragement on this occasion, by some letters I have seen from Holland, which seem to reflect on my not making the best use of our advantage by giving the enemy battle as soon as we had passed the lines. I own had it been practicable there is no comparison between the advantages of a Battle, & what we can reap from a siege, but there is not one general or other officer that have the least judgment in these matters but must allow it was altogether impossible to attack the enemy with any probable hopes of success. I cannot but think it very hard, when I do my best, to be liable to such censures.[2]

Let us now judge this episode in the light of modern knowledge. Marlborough had hoped that Villars would be stung into attacking him during the 6th, and, in spite of the severe forced march, he had the army well in hand for this. But it had not been his purpose to fight an offensive battle himself after forcing the lines. His intention was always to move to his left, cross the Scheldt, and besiege

---

[1] Portland Papers, *H.M.C.*, v, 68.   [2] Heinsius Archives.

Bouchain. All his dispositions on crossing the Sensée and the lines—the roads, the bridges, and the bivouacs of his troops—were arranged for such a movement. Of course, if Villars had committed some grave fault, either by attacking or exposing himself to be attacked at a disadvantage, he would have turned aside to deal with him. Nothing of this kind had occurred. Whatever the two peasants may or may not have said, we now know that Villars lay

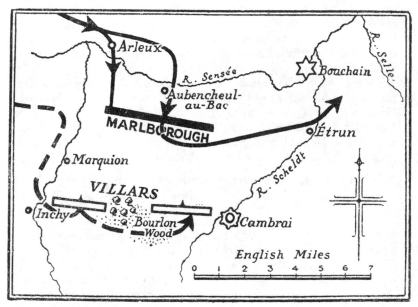

AUGUST 6, 1711

on the 6th with his right on the fortified town of Cambrai, his centre in Bourlon Wood, of which we have heard since, and his left on the marshes and stream behind the village of Marquion, where the Canal du Nord now flows. Villars himself considered that his position was very strong. A modern study of the ground confirms this view. By the afternoon of the 6th he had a substantial superiority in numbers. He had been entrenching his front and preparing abattis in Bourlon Wood since about eight o'clock.

Both armies were tired, but the French had marched along their prepared lateral roads, and the Allies for the most part had tramped across country. Being on outer lines, they had had nearly ten miles farther to go. The allied generals who were consulted had complete confidence in Marlborough, and if he had said "Attack" they would

856

have fallen on in good heart. They would certainly not have wished to venture against his better judgment. The decision was obviously his. It was convenient in the controversy of that time to cite the agreement of all these eminent warriors, but Marlborough alone bears the responsibility. Apart from the natural desire which we all have to witness miracles, there is no doubt he was right. The Allies were under no call to fight a desperate battle. As far as they knew, they had the game in their own hands, if they did not throw it away. Moreover, at this particular juncture Marlborough, although at the head of a smaller army, had gained all his strategic objects. He had ruptured the long-vaunted Ne Plus Ultra line, and was now in a position, albeit inferior in numbers, to undertake a siege. Villars must submit to his will; Bouchain was in his grip. It is, however, remarkable that "Everybody almost except my lord Duke and Cadogan are against this siege."[1]

Villars had now for the moment a choice of evils. He could only protect Bouchain and Valenciennes by moving his army to the right bank of the Scheldt. If he did so Marlborough could besiege Arras. There was no doubt which would be the greater loss. He resigned himself to a siege of Bouchain, and hoped from his safe and near base at Cambrai to interrupt it. In the afternoon of the 6th the allied army marched to its left towards the Scheldt, and by evening eight bridges had been thrown by Étrun. During the night the whole army passed over in heavy rain. Goslinga dilates and gloats upon the confusion of this night march, and tells us that ten thousand men could have routed all. In fact, however, Villars could not pierce the strong cavalry screen, and rested in complete ignorance of what was happening; and the passage of the Scheldt and the investment of Bouchain were accomplished without the slightest loss or even interference. The whole operation was acclaimed at the time, and has since been held to be, an unsurpassed masterpiece of the military art. Indeed, not only in the army but throughout Europe it was regarded as Marlborough's finest stratagem and manœuvre.

[1] Colonel James Pendlebury, Master Gunner, to Earl Rivers, July 27/August 6; Portland Papers, *H.M.C.*, v, 63.

Chapter Twenty-six

BOUCHAIN

Bouchain was an amazing operation. It can only be understood by those who will study the maps and diagrams. Marlborough, having passed the Scheldt during the night of August 6–7, moved round the east side of the fortress and threw a number of bridges across that river by Neuville. He made his main camp between the Scheldt and the Selle, but he immediately pushed his right hand across the Scheldt to the westward, so as to encircle Bouchain. At the same time Villars in superior strength, with at least a hundred thousand men, came to sit down with him at the siege.

On August 8 the Marshal, finding his suddenly captured lines abandoned, and Marlborough committing himself to Bouchain, moved into the angle formed by the Scheldt and the Sensée and established himself there, barely two miles away from the besieged fortress. That same day he sent thirty battalions and proportionate cavalry under Albergotti, whose repute after his defence of Douai stood high, across the Sensée to occupy the high ground at Wavrechin, south-west of Bouchain. This strong force immediately began to construct an entrenched camp. They were separated from Bouchain by the marshes of the Sensée, but through this there ran a winding track called the Cow Path. The French took possession of this, improving it as a route and protecting it, as entrenching was, of course, impossible, by a system of fascinades, never used before or since in war. The parapets on both sides of the Cow Path were made of long faggots bound together for nearly two miles from tree to tree between the willows and rushes which grew in the inundation.[1] Thus constant communication was soon established between the superior relieving army and the strong garrison of the fortress.[2]

Albergotti's position at Wavrechin had an even more important significance. Marlborough's communications ran through Douai,

---

[1] Lediard, ii, 325.

[2] Eight battalions plus 1100 last-minute reinforcements; say five thousand men.

nineteen or twenty miles to the west. They were within easy striking distance of the French in their entrenched camp at Wavrechin. The Scheldt was blocked above him by the fortress of Valenciennes. He had to bring in a siege-train now at Tournai, and also all the supplies and munitions for the siege and for his own army of about ninety

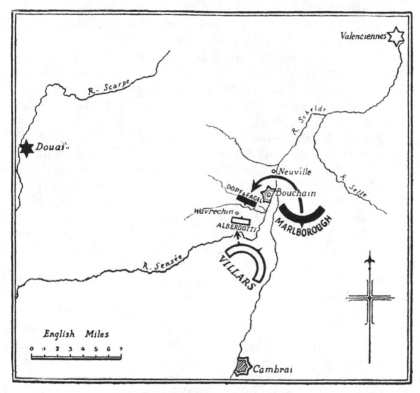

AUGUST 9, 1711

thousand men, from Tournai down the Scarpe to Douai, and thence by wagon convoy from Douai, or, as was arranged later, by a short cut from Marchiennes. Villars could at any time cross the Sensée and march northward, traversing all Marlborough's communications. Marlborough's only remedy in that case would be to come round north of Bouchain and fight a battle. As he must keep at least twenty thousand men in the trenches of the siege, he would have to fight at odds of seventy thousand against a hundred thousand or even more. During the whole of the siege he accepted and often courted this possibility. He must have foreseen all these dangers before deciding on the siege. No wonder even his most faithful followers and admirers in the High Command thought the siege impracticable.

As soon as Marlborough heard on August 8 that the French were crossing the Sensée in force he concluded that Villars meant to cut his communications and bring about a battle. This was, indeed, an obvious move for Villars to make, and it would immediately have forced an encounter in the open field, which Marlborough above all things desired, even at serious numerical odds. He did not mean to fight another Malplaquet, but would have welcomed another Ramillies. He therefore, before finally engaging in the siege, multiplied his bridges below Bouchain, and began moving his main army round to meet Villars somewhere between Bouchain and the Scarpe.

However, Villars had apparently a move either way. If Marlborough came round to the west the Marshal could cross the Scheldt instead of the Sensée by a right-handed instead of a left-handed movement, and once he was ensconced there the siege of Bouchain would become impossible. On the other hand, Arras would be uncovered. Marlborough could then march through Douai direct upon that place. Therefore when Villars began feinting across the Scheldt his gesture did not carry conviction. As long as Marlborough was ready to fight a battle in the open plains west of Douai at heavy odds his plan was sound, and he was master. On any other basis the siege of Bouchain was absurd.

It seemed at first essential to the siege to drive Albergotti out of the Wavrechin position. Dopf had already crossed at Neuville with 30 battalions and 40 squadrons[1] to complete the investment which at Wavrechin was obstructed. Dopf was reinforced during the night of the 8th by sixteen battalions under Fagel; and Cadogan, that trusted Eye, went with him. In this force was the whole of the British infantry. On the morning of the 9th they were ordered to assault Albergotti in such fortifications as he had been able to construct overnight. Here Captain Parker may take up the tale.

> Our British grenadiers were ordered to march up to the top of the hill on the left of their works, in order to begin the attack on that side. Here we were posted in a large high-grown field of wheat, about seventy or eighty paces from their works, expecting every moment, when the signal should be given to fall on.
>
> I must confess I did not like the aspect of the thing. We plainly saw that their entrenchment was a perfect bulwark, strong and lofty,

---

[1] Authorities differ about the actual numbers.

and crowded with men and cannon pointed directly at us: yet did they not fire a shot great or small, reserving all for us, on our advancing up to them. We wished much that the Duke might take a nearer view of the thing: and yet we judged that he chose rather to continue on the other side in order to observe the motions of the enemy on that side, while we were attacking them on this.

But while I was thus musing, the Duke of Marlborough (ever watchful, ever right) rode up quite unattended and alone, and posted himself a little on the right of my company of grenadiers, from whence he had a fair view of the greater part of the enemy's works. It is quite impossible for me to express the joy which the sight of this man gave me at this very critical moment. I was now well satisfied that he would not push the thing, unless he saw a strong probability of success; nor was this my notion alone: it was the sense of the whole army, both officer and soldier, British and foreigner. And indeed we had all the reason in the world for it; for he never led us on to any one action that we did not succeed in. He stayed only three or four minutes, and then rode back; we were in pain for him while he stayed, lest the enemy might have discovered him, and fired at him; in which case they could not well have missed him. He had not been longer from us than he stayed, when orders came to us to retire. It may be presumed we were not long about it, and as the corn we stood in was high, we slipped off undiscovered, and were a good way down the hill, before they perceived that we were retiring; and then they let fly all their great and small shot after us: but as we were by this time under the brow of the hill, all their shot went over our heads, inasmuch that there was not a single man of all the grenadiers hurt.[1]

This episode reveals Marlborough's soldierly qualities as a model for all commanders of British troops. We find him at sixty-one, in poor health, racked with earache and headache, after ten years of war, making these personal reconnaissances within deadly range of the enemy's entrenchments and batteries in order to make sure that his soldiers were not set impossible tasks and their brave lives not cast needlessly away. Although he was the key of the Grand Alliance, he did not consider his life too precious to be risked. It was because his soldiers felt he was watching over them, and would never spare himself where their welfare and honour were concerned, that they were deeply attached to him. His "attention and care," as Corporal Matthew Bishop wrote, "was over us all." Always patiently and thoroughly examining the conditions on the front of the army, unwearied by the ten campaigns, burdened by no sense of his own importance, undiscouraged by the malice of his enemies

[1] Parker, pp. 160–162.

861

at home, he performed to the very end most faithfully and vigilantly the daily duty of a soldier. It was through this rule of conduct that he earned from the rank and file the nickname of "the Old Corporal."

Parker, it must be remembered, was not writing for the Press or the public. His journals lay for forty years in some old trunk and were not printed till long after he was dead. He never spoke to Marlborough during the whole of his service, but watched him only from a distance. He even thought he had been passed over in promotion. His testimony is therefore of peculiar interest.

Perhaps it would have been better if the French had recognized the Captain-General as he rode along the front in the high corn within seventy paces of their entrenchments. One volley, and he would have ranked in our national affections with Wolfe and Nelson. He would have been spared the detestable indignities and maltreatment which his Tory countrymen had in store for him. But there was nothing morbid about Marlborough. He liked living, and was content to take whatever came. It was all in the day's work. Still, if the French had had sharper eyes, the pens of Swift, Macaulay, and Thackeray would have been blunted.

When it was found impossible to dislodge the French from their Wavrechin position, Marlborough consulted the engineers of the army upon whether Bouchain could be taken, and whether it was practicable to persevere in the siege. All answered in the negative except one, Colonel Armstrong, who declared it could be done, and that "he was ready himself to undertake the most difficult part of it." Under the cover of five thousand British troops there was raised in the darkness of the night opposite the French entrenchments a series of "most noble and indeed surprising redoubts with double ditches in which were mounted twenty-four large pieces of cannon, over which at daylight the British standard was flying."[1]

Marlborough now proceeded to wall himself in upon all sides. On August 12 he demanded from the Dutch Council of State six thousand pioneers, or workmen, with their tools, raised by compulsion from the provinces of Flanders, Brabant, and Hainault, and seven hundred additional wagons. "I regret to make these demands upon you," he wrote, "but the service requires it." The Dutch immediately produced all these men for him. Marlborough had prepared an elaborate organization for their control. With their aid and by the labour of the army he constructed lines of circumvallation around the whole of Bouchain, except on the side of the

[1] Parker, p. 163.

southern marsh and along the Selle and the Scheldt, and also double
entrenchments from these lines to the Scarpe, making a protected
area about seven miles long north-west of the siege, through which
he could draw all his supplies, conveyed by water to Marchiennes.
He also entrenched the whole of his camp on the east of Bouchain,
and fortified the Scheldt southward against Villars. The total length
of these lines, which were, of course, additional to all the siege-works,
amounted to over thirty miles. Thus he constructed not only one
fortress around another, but a fortified feeding-area joining him to
his waterways, fortresses, and supplies. These prodigious works,
which came into existence very rapidly during August, could, of
course, only be very lightly held by an army of ninety thousand men.
One may imagine how intense was the effort required to make sure
that whatever section was attacked would be reinforced in time from
the general reserve. At no period in his service was Marlborough
more active than at this siege. At all hours of the night and day
he moved about the astonishing labyrinth which he had constructed
for his protection while he strangled Bouchain.

"The increase of the enemy's army," he wrote to Godolphin
(August 13), "by their draining their garrisons from all places, gives
them so great a superiority that the Deputies thought it proper to
advise with their general how far it might be practicable to persist
in attempting the siege of Bouchain. The greatest number of them
thought the difficulties we should meet with could hardly be overcome. However, we are taking the necessary steps for the siege."
And again (August 17): "We have not yet quite overcome our
difficulties, though we have forced them from several posts; they
have none left but a path called the Cow Path, through a great bog,
at which they can pass only one in front [single file]. . . . If we can
succeed in this siege, we shall have the honour of having done it in
the face of an army many thousands men stronger than we are."[1]

The severing of the Cow Path was a prime essential. Accordingly
the besiegers set out into the morass from both sides, building
fascinades—swiftly copied—step by step till they got near enough
for an attack. Marlborough came himself to direct this curious
operation, and examined its possibilities with scrupulous care. The
water in the marsh was in places up to the necks of the four hundred
grenadiers who assaulted on the 17th. A short officer had himself
carried, a particular target, high on the shoulders of his men. The
fortress cannon fired heavily upon the wading and splashing soldiers

[1] Coxe, vi, 79–80.

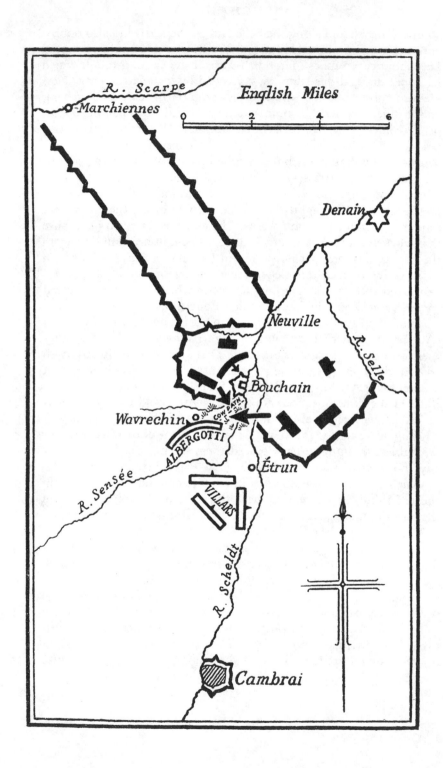

R . Scarpe

Marchiennes

English Miles

0   2   4   6

Denain

Neuville

R. Selle

Bouchain

Wavrechin

COW PATH

ALBERGOTTI

Étrun

R. Sensée

VILLARS

R. Scheldt

Cambrai

as they struggled slowly forward; but the French defenders fled when their advance continued. The Cow Path was taken, and the town completely isolated.[1] "Our greatest difficulties," wrote Marlborough to Godolphin (August 20), "for the siege of Bouchain are over. . . . They are now shut up on all sides."

The siege-train began to arrive from Tournai on August 21. The approach trenches were opened the next day, and the batteries began to fire on the 30th. While Marlborough bombarded Bouchain, Villars bombarded him. "The situation of both armies is so extraordinary," he wrote to Godolphin (September 3),

> that our army which attacks the town is bombarded by the enemy; and we have several posts so near to each other that the sentinels have conversations. The whole French army being so camped that they are seen by the garrison of Bouchain, makes the defence the more obstinate; but, with the blessing of God, I hope we shall get the better of them, and, if they *opinâtre* beyond reason, may be an argument for their being made prisoners of war.[2]

The spectacle of a siege proceeding with two great armies so closely interlocked was unique in the wars of the eighteenth century. It was watched by all Europe with profound interest. The actual reduction of the fortress proceeded with great rapidity. By September 12 the long ordeal reached its end. The governor hung out white flags upon all attacks. He offered to surrender the fortress if he could march out with the honours of war. Marlborough usually accorded such conditions. But on this occasion he determined to inflict upon Villars, under whose eyes the drama proceeded, a rebuke which would be everywhere noticed. He demanded that the garrison should yield themselves prisoners of war. The governor refused, and a terrible bombardment was resumed. The defenders then proposed they should become technically prisoners of war, but should be allowed to reside in France on parole, because the Dutch fed their prisoners so badly. A second time the bombardment was resumed, and after some hours unconditional surrender was made. Two thousand five hundred men marched out of the place into captivity. The Allies had sustained four thousand casualties in the siege. Marlborough was master of Bouchain. It was his last conquest and command.

Meanwhile his relations with Oxford continued apparently to improve. Evidently he tried to indicate that the necessary concessions

---

[1] Coxe, vi, 80.　　　　　　[2] *Ibid.*, 81–82.

might be made to France, leaving Spain to be cleared up later, and that he would undertake this task. "I must confess to you," he wrote to Oxford (September 3), "the last six weeks have given me frequent and sensible remembrances of my growing old; the conscience of my doing my utmost for the Queen's service, the hopes of her Majesty's acceptance and the assurance of your friendship are my chief consolation, and . . . if I can any way contribute towards the putting the war in Spain or any other part of the service on a better foot . . . I pray you will not spare me."[1]

Oxford for his part went very far in his protestations of friendship to Marlborough. He even touched upon the secret negotiations for peace which he was conducting, though his letters attained a very high economy of truth.

August 28/September 8

I have delayed mentioning a particular of great moment because I have no cipher to write to your Grace, but I shall reserve the whole to send by Lord Stair. In general it is this: the French made an offer to the Queen of a general peace, and to do it by the canal of England. The Queen's answer was she would enter into no separate treaty, neither should it be transacted here; she had several things to demand for the good and quiet of her dominions, but she was resolved not to act without her allies, and particularly the States. They [the French] sent a paper in general promising satisfaction to all the allies, in barriers, in trade, and all other articles: this being thought too general, they have sent a man over to explain it: what he says will all be transmitted over by Lord Raby.

And upon the personal issue:

I can say no more than this, that I shall leave it to my actions to speak for me, and so give your Grace demonstration that I am the same man towards you as I was the first day I had the honour of your acquaintance; and I shall as heartily promote everything under your care as I did, or would have done, in any time since I have been known to you.[2]

But all the time poison was working.

St John to Oxford

WINDSOR
September 4, 1711

. . . John Drummond intended to leave Amsterdam this week, so that he will soon be here. Heinsius and Buys both told him their accounts from the army assured them that Torcy was in England. They

[1] Bath Papers, *H.M.C.*, i, 208.   [2] Marlborough Papers, *H.M.C.*, p. 39 (*a*).

both desired the Duke of Marlborough might not be in the secret of the peace, and Buys reflected with warmth on the treatment which he had received from his Grace and from Lord Townshend when the last negotiation was on foot.[1]

One of Oxford's correspondents wrote (September 1711):

At the same time that the outed family are applauded above measure, and bloated on the success at Bouchain, I find they double their malice against your Lordship, and spare no cost to encourage pamphlets against the Ministry. 'Tis a notion in the pamphlet shops that Whiggish libels sell best, so industrious are they to propagate scandal and falsehood. The taking of Bouchain now animates them afresh, 'tis a mighty glorious thing for them to be as long in taking a little town as our ancestors have been in reducing all France; but why is Dunkirk spared all this time? either for treacherous reasons or out of remorse of conscience.[2]

The project of wintering on the frontier had moved forward slowly. The Treasurer showed himself well disposed towards it, and made great play with providing the money and enjoining secrecy. The Dutch, however, were reluctant to promise their contribution. They had become with reason deeply suspicious of the English Government. Marlborough still hoped to persuade them, and might well have succeeded had he been able to return to The Hague immediately after the fall of Bouchain. This was, however, impossible. The English Ministers received the Dutch objections with inward satisfaction. They found themselves in the agreeable position of obliging Marlborough and making a show of favouring his schemes without having to make any substantial exertion. It suited Bolingbroke particularly to throw the blame upon the backward allies. Marlborough in urging his scheme had stated, incautiously perhaps, that it was vital to a successful campaign in 1712. The Secretary of State lost no time in exploiting this admission with the Queen. "If the project has been disappointed," he wrote (September 25), "it has not been so by your Majesty, who gave orders for readily entering into the necessary measures on your part. However, it is of some use to have my lord Marlborough's confession, that we may be disabled from doing anything the next year, and that the enemy may, perhaps, be in a condition to act offensively."[3] This produced the desired effect upon the royal mind. "I think," wrote the Queen to Oxford (September), "the D. of Marlborough shews plainer than ever by this new project his unwillingness for a

[1] Portland Papers, *H.M.C.*, v, 84. [2] *Ibid.*, 94. [3] Coxe, vi, 110.

peace, but I hope our negociations will succeed and then it will not be in his power to prevent it."[1]

Oxford seemed genuinely disappointed. "Ours is a very unlucky situation," he wrote to Marlborough, "that every one is shrinking from the war, and at the same time casting the burthen upon Britain, and yet unwilling to let her have the least advantage. I would to God that our Allies would resolve either to make a good war or a good peace."[2]

Marlborough could do no more than put the facts before Heinsius.[3]

He allowed himself to indulge the illusion that a friendly basis had been established between him and the Cabinet under which he was serving. He seems to have relied too much upon the Treasurer's professions of goodwill. The warfare of pamphlets continued. One praising Marlborough's strategy was thought erroneously by Ministers at home to have emanated from his chaplain, Dr Hare. A virulent counterblast by Mrs Manley was circulated. Marlborough on reading this was thrown into lively and excessive distress.

John to Sarah

Oct. 1711

★I have receiv'd Your letters by Collins, and the print'd paper call'd Bouchain, as also a villinous answer to itt, by which I am of opinion, as I have been for some time, that whilest these barbarous proceedings are in fashon, it were to be wished that we shou'd never apear in print, and endeavour to do all the good we can, without expecting ether favour or justice; it is impossible for me to express the real concern I have had on the account of this barbarous libel, when I am emparing my health, and venturing every thing for the good of my Country.[4]

He appealed, somewhat naively, to Harley to protect him from such attacks while he was serving at the front.

[1] Bath Papers, *H.M.C.*, i, 212. [2] Coxe, vi, 109.

[3] ★It will be in the power of the French [he wrote (September 28)] to have such a superiority as must give the law next campagne, especially if what I hear be trew that you will not agree to the Project sent by Ld. Albemarle, fearing it might be contrary to the Treatys of Contribution made by M. Pesters. It is most certain that the foundation of that Project is to hinder the Enemy from making their magazines, which I think . . . must have given us a good Peace; but if the fact be so by the Treatys of Contribution that they are to make their magazines in quiet, I very much dread the consequences for the next campagne; & am very much afraid that if they make the right use of it, they may retake Bouchain, when our troops are quartered at so great a distance as the Project of the Council of State sends them. I do not flatter myself that any representation of mine shou'd change your resolutions, but I clear my conscience by letting you know what I fear. [Heinsius Archives.]

[4] Blenheim MSS.

Marlborough to Oxford

. . . There are two papers lately published, on your side, and some copies are already got here; the title of one is "Bouchain" and the other an answer to it. I do not know whether your lordship looks into such papers, and I heartily wish they had been kept from me. I am sure you cannot hear of one without the other; and when I protest to you I am no way concerned in the former, I doubt not but you will have some feeling of what I suffer from the latter. . . . The authors of these papers, as well the one as the other, are not only my enemies, they are yours too, my lord; they are enemies to the Queen, and poison to her subjects; and it would be worth the while to make a strict search after them, that the punishment they deserve may be inflicted upon them. But all the remedy, all the ease I can at present expect, under this mortification is that you, my lord, would do me the justice to believe me in no way an abettor or encourager of what has given me a mortal wound; but I will endeavour to bear up under it.[1]

Considering that undoubtedly Sarah through Maynwaring was active in attacking the Government and that the Whig scribes plied their quills with partisan vigour, Oxford was entitled to the full advantage of his reply.

Oxford to Marlborough

. . . I hope my sentiments are so fully known of that villainous way of libelling, I need say little to your Grace upon that subject. When I had the honour to be Secretary of State, I did, by an impartial prosecution, silence most of them, until a party of men [*i.e.* the Whigs], for their own ends, supported them against the laws and my prosecution. I do assure your Grace I abhor the practice as mean and disingenuous. I have made it so familiar to myself, by some years' experience, that as I know I am every week, if not every day, in some libel or other, so I would willingly compound that all the ill-natured scribblers should have licence to write ten times more against me, upon condition they would write against nobody else. I do assure your Grace I neither know nor desire to know any of the authors; and as I heartily wish this barbarous war was at an end, I shall be very ready to take any part in suppressing them.[2]

After Bouchain Marlborough, still hoping to carry out his plan for the advanced winter quarters, had wished to attack Quesnoy. He rode out with the cavalry and reconnoitred the intervening country. He persuaded Oxford to support this further operation.

---

[1] Coxe, vi, 121–122. [2] *Ibid.*, 122–123.

But once again the Dutch in their uncertainty were disinclined to spend more life and treasure. They made no effort to provide the forage and supplies which Marlborough required, and after garrisoning Bouchain and repairing its fortifications he withdrew upon Tournai, and in October sorrowfully dispersed the Grand Army to its normal winter quarters.

He now set out for home. He wrote to Oxford a letter so conciliatory and submissive as to be painful for his admirers to read, but for which there was justification in the tone of Oxford's correspondence.

October 1711

But, my lord, as you have given me encouragement to enter into the strictest friendship with you, and I have done nothing to forfeit it, I beg your friendly advice in what manner I am to govern myself. *You cannot but imagine 'twould be a terrible mortification to pass by The Hague, with our plenipotentiaries there; and myself a stranger to their transactions; and what hopes can I have of any countenance at home, if I am not thought fit to be trusted abroad.* I could have been contented to have passed the winter on the frontier, if the States had done their part; but, under my present circumstances, I am really at a loss what part to take. My lord, I have put myself wholly into your hands, and shall be entirely guided by your advice, if you will be so kind as to favour me with it.[1]

We can see the answer he received from his letter to Sarah of October 22.

★The intelligence You have had as to the particulars of the peace having been sent to me, is without foundation, and I know the intentions of those that now govern is that I am to have nothing to do in the peace. This is what I am extreame glad off, but thay must not know it. . . . As I am now convinced the peace will be conclud'd this Winter, I shall take my measures for living a retier'd life, if it may be in England I shall be glad of it, *if not my business shall be to seek a good climate*, for my Constitution is extreamly spoilt.[2]

He also made a request to Oxford upon a matter petty enough to excite amusement. He had evidently allowed himself to be deceived by the Treasurer's copious affabilities. But this was not the moment to ask for paltry favours.

I entreat your lordship will please to direct Mr Lowndes to send orders to the Custom-house that my baggage, and some small remains of my camp provisions, may pass directly to Whitehall, and be visited

---

[1] Coxe, vi, 111.　　　　　　　　　　　　[2] Blenheim MSS.

there, as has been practised in former years. I flatter myself your lordship will believe me when I promise you I will make no ill use of this indulgence.[1]

"Thus," wrote General Kane, "ended the Duke of Marlborough's last campaign, which may be truly reckoned amongst the greatest he ever made." Natzmer goes even farther. "The year 1711," he wrote, "was certainly the most glorious for my lord Duke. . . . Next to God this success [the passing of the lines] must be attributed solely to his wisdom, and he can be justly given credit for it as a *coup-de-tête*."[2]

Some records of a regimental officer are also available, and are of value.[3]

In after-years Marlborough always looked back to the campaign

---

[1] October 26; Coxe, vi, 114.   [2] Natzmer, p. 328.
[3] From the family records of Lieutenant-Colonel Gordon Halswell.

Captain James Gordon to Lieutenant Swan, Royal Scots Fusiliers
September 12, 1711

★This year the D. of Marlb. has certainly made it appear that as much of the glory of this war is due to him as aniebody else; for you know Prince Eugene had always the vogue before; not that I should pretend to detract from the Sterling merit of that great man, but only I would that every one have his due. Pray give my respects to all my good friends in your Regiment, and oblige your most obedient humble servant.

And to James Murdock, minister of Kirkcordan:

★We have been very busie this Summer; whereas when we took the field we were all persuaded we should be idle; but the D. of Marlborough, who is as famous for Stratagems as ever Ulysses was and more happy in his victories than Hannibal himself, under Providence and good Fortune, would not suffer us to be passive; but on the contrary we have been very active and successful in pushing the enemy, not only within the walls but in the field, having got over their prodigious lines, which nobody thought we should have done without a battel; but having never lost a man in the cause, it is of more consequence to us than any battel we have fought this war, besides the considerable little Town of Bouchain; so the campaign being near an end, we reckon we have no more but to go to garrison very soon; for this end our army is divided up and down the fields.

And the next year:

★How much the D. of Marlborough was traduced and detracted from, amongst 'em, how much his ingenious strategems and notable feats of war were contemned and set at nought witness the Siege of Bouchain. What a simple insignificant [thing] it was reckoned and how contemptibly it was spoken of among 'em; tho' the D. of Ormonde, when he saw and considered it, thought it as signal and remarkable action as he ever either heard or read of, finding that we are thereby near master of the Scheldt, that there are above 76 villages in its Chatelleny, how inconsiderable so ever it be in itself, and what prodigious difficulties there were in the Siege, which sometimes seem'd to be insuperable. I hope Sir Thomas Hammond [Hanmer] is gone home, sensible of a great many mistakes and false opinions abundance of his compatriots labour under, and will endeavour to undeceive 'em, for sure the most part of 'em that has served under the D. of Marlborough must love him for his shining merit and capacity.

of 1711 with pride. The Blenheim tapestries made under his directions assign to the capture of Bouchain a prominence over any of
the great battles he had won. To understand this one must weigh
the facts and figures. An army of perhaps 130,000 opposed by
90,000 could normally undertake a first-class siege, and provide a
covering force which at any time could fight a battle behind entrenchments, or even at a hazard in the open. But for an army of 90,000
to effect the conquest of a fully garrisoned fortress in the face of at
least 96,000 was an overturning of all the rules and experience resulting from twenty-five years of continuous war.

Thus ended the ten campaigns of the Duke of Marlborough,
during which he had won four great battles and many secondary
actions and combats, and had taken by siege thirty fortresses. In
this process he had broken the military power of France, and
reduced the first of military nations to a condition in which they
were no longer feared by any country. He had practically destroyed
the French barrier with the exception of some fortresses of the third
line, and at any time a road into France could be opened. During
the whole of these ceaseless operations of war on the largest scale
the world had seen, or was to see for several generations, confronted
by the main armies of France and their best generals, he had never
sustained a defeat or even a serious check. Hardly a convoy had
been cut up or a camp surprised. The aspect which these affairs
wore to friend and foe alike was that of certain victory in any battle,
siege, or foray he might undertake. The annals of war contain no
similar record.

Here is a tribute which was surely not unwelcome:

Thursday, August 9, 1711

★Dear Grandpapa

I did not write to you before because I could not congratulate you for any victory
but now I heartily do upon that glorious success of passing the Lines performed by
her Majestys Arms under your Command july 25 in the low countries. I hope you
will go on in winning of Battles, taking of towns & beating & routing the French in
all manner of ways, and then come home with a good peace & look back upon those
glorious toils of the battles of Ramellies Bleinheim Schelenberg &c & the sieges of
oudenard Ghent &c. I am now at the Lodge in the little Park & like it verry well
the Birds are verry pretty. I wish you all happiness & good success in all your undertakings. I hope you will think nothing of all this flattery, for it is my thoughts, & I
cant help saying

Happy the Isle with such a Heroe blest
What Vertue dwells not in his loyal breast?

On thursday 2 of August I presented the Banner to the Queen & was received but
coldly. You see I write on tho I have no awnser. Your dutifull Grandson,

[Blenheim MSS.]   W. Godolphin

872

Chapter Twenty-seven

THE SECRET NEGOTIATIONS

1711—JANUARY—OCTOBER

THE negotiations which eventually led to the Treaty of
Utrecht must now be related. In 1715, when under
George I the triumphant, and justly indignant, Whigs
were busily seeking evidence for the impeachment of
Oxford, a "Committee of Secrecy" was appointed to find out how
the negotiations had first been set on foot; and also whether any
overtures had been made by ex-Ministers for a Jacobite restoration
in the event of Queen Anne's death. The object so ardently pursued
was to fix a criminal responsibility upon Oxford which would
deprive him of liberty, if not of life. Hopes centred upon Prior's
papers, which had been impounded by the new Whig Ambassador,
Marlborough's friend, Lord Stair. Prior had been Secretary at the
English Embassy in Paris, and all transactions were believed to have
passed through his hands. Nothing, however, rewarded this
diligent search; all that was found was already public. In 1711 a
letter from Versailles dated April 11/22 had reached London, had
forthwith been brought before the Cabinet, and immediately communicated through Lord Raby to the Dutch. No fault could be
found with this, and efforts to go behind or beyond it proved fruitless. It was not until Torcy's memoirs were published towards the
end of the eighteenth century, when all the actors had been in their
graves for two generations, that the truth, supplemented still later
by research in the French archives, became known.

When Marshal Tallard was Ambassador in London before the
war he had as chaplain a French priest named Gaultier. Tallard,
departing in 1702 upon the rupture between England and France,
left Gaultier, instructing him, in Torcy's words,

to prolong his stay in London as long as he was allowed to dwell
there, to watch events discreetly, and to report to the French Minister
for Foreign Affairs, but to do this with the discretion necessary to
avoid being looked upon and accused in England as a spy; therefore
to write rarely, and in a manner which would not draw upon him

an order of expulsion from England, or other usage even more unpleasant.[1]

Eight years had passed during which the Abbé had faithfully fulfilled his part. After a while he became chaplain to Count Gallas, and was accustomed to celebrate Mass in his Embassy chapel. In this secure position he heard and saw all he could, but wrote seldom to France, and never upon military matters. No one had the slightest idea that he was a French agent. Lord Jersey, a Tory-Jacobite noble of strong French sympathies, had been English Ambassador in Paris after the Peace of Ryswick. He had married a French Catholic, and this lady was accustomed to attend Mass at Gallas's chapel. There Gaultier became acquainted with her. He gained the confidence of the Jersey household, and thus extended his political and social contacts in London. Jersey, though not holding or seeking office, stood well with the new Ministers.[2] In particular he was intimate with Harley, as he then was, and Shrewsbury. When, therefore, he found them eager for peace and looking around for some secret channel to France, he suggested the Abbé Gaultier as a trustworthy emissary. The two English Ministers readily fell in with the idea. They confabulated with Gaultier, and, unknown to any other person, unknown to the Cabinet, unknown even to St John, Secretary of State, they sent him through the lines near Nieuport to Paris, where he arrived on January 7/18, 1711. He was charged to tell Torcy that the new Ministers sought peace and believed it necessary to the welfare of England, and that they would be glad if Louis XIV would propose to the Dutch a renewal of the conferences which had ended at Gertruydenberg in the summer. This time the English plenipotentiaries would make sure the negotiations should not be broken down by the Dutch.

"Who would have said at this time," wrote Torcy in his memoirs,

that the property of that formidable Alliance of the enemies of France and Spain had reached its final limit; . . . that the Supreme Being Who fixes the bounds of the sea and calms when it pleases Him the force of its tides would stop so swiftly the torrent of so many victories; that before two years had flowed away these proud warriors, so drunk with their successes, would, confounded in their designs, restore to the King the most important fortresses they had captured; that there would no longer be any question of their demanding hostages to

[1] Torcy, *Mémoires*, p. 666.
[2] He was to get a pension of £3000 from France for his services (see *Edinburgh Review*, October 1835, p. 15).

guarantee the inviolable word of a great King, nor of proposing as the foundation of a Treaty odious preliminaries; . . . that in spite of the efforts of the Alliance [*Ligue*] and the advantages it had gathered, the grandson of St Louis chosen by Providence to reign in Spain would dwell secure upon his throne, recognized as monarch and lawful possessor of Spain and the Indies by a host of foes, who brought home after so many years of bloody war nothing but the crushing burden of the debts contracted to sustain their vast designs? [1]

Torcy only knew Gaultier from his Secret Service reports.[2] He was greatly surprised to find his own skilful spy in London returning to him in the capacity of envoy from the British Government. Gaultier, departing brusquely from the actual terms of his mission, spoke at once as a zealous Frenchman. "Do you want peace? I come to bring you the means of negotiating and concluding peace independently of the Dutch, who are unworthy of the consideration of the King and of the honour which he has so often extended them by addressing himself to them, and by seeking to pacify Europe through them." "To ask," comments Torcy, "a Minister of Louis XIV if he wished for peace was like asking a sick man attacked by a long and dangerous malady if he wished to get well." He showed, however, far more suspicion of his own employee, Gaultier, than had the two English Ministers. It seemed to him incredible that such proposals could reach him through such a channel. However, the British emissary asked very little. "Give me," he said, "a letter to Lord Jersey. Write to him simply that you have been very glad to learn from me that he was in good health; that you have charged me to thank him for his regards, and to give him your compliments. This letter will suffice by itself for my passport, and for my credentials to listen to any proposals which may be made to you. I will return to London, and bring them back in no time."

Torcy consulted the King, and all was discussed in council at Versailles. There was a natural doubt whether the English advances were genuine, but the opinion prevailed that "the overtures of the new Ministers were less deserving of suspicion, because it was their personal interest that the war which redounded to the prestige of their opponents should end at once." It was decided to give Gaultier his letter. "There do not seem," remarks Torcy, "any objections to writing it, but many in refusing to do so."[3]

[1] Torcy, p. 661.
[2] The Abbé had been reporting regularly to Torcy since about January 1710. See Salomon, p. 50.
[3] Torcy, p. 666.

The Abbé Gaultier did not transact business only with Torcy. With that Minister's assent he also visited Marshal Berwick on Harley's behalf.

"He told me," says Berwick,

> that he had orders to speak to me about the Pretender's affairs, and to concert with me the means of restoring him; but before he entered upon the point, he was to exact a promise, first that no person at Saint-Germain, not even the Queen, should be privy to the matter; secondly, that Queen Anne should enjoy the Crown in tranquillity during her life, provided that she confirmed the possession of it to her brother after her death; thirdly, that sufficient securities should be given for the preservation of the Church of England, and of the liberties of the kingdom. To all this, it may easily be imagined, that I readily consented, and I had the same confirmed to him by the Pretender, to whom I introduced him for that purpose. . . . In order to shew that we would omit nothing, and to give proofs of our sincerity, we wrote to all the Jacobites to join in with the Court. This contributed greatly to make the Queen's party so superior in the House of Commons that everything was carried there according to her wishes.[1]

Gaultier reached London on January 28/February 8. He displayed Torcy's letter to Harley, Shrewsbury, and (it is to be presumed) Jersey, whom alone it apparently concerned. By word of mouth he stated that the French were ready to treat and to come into conference. The two Ministers were disappointed that France was not more forthcoming. Perhaps they realized how very cheapening to their position Gaultier's first mission had been. They felt conscious of a rebuff. Evidently Gaultier was made sensible of their mood, because in a letter dated February 13 he put something not far removed from an ultimatum before his French masters. He wrote that the friendly British Government earnestly hoped that a definite offer of peace would come to them from Paris, and in such a form that it would appear to have arisen spontaneously from France. This alone would enable these Ministers who were running risks by their peace policy to preserve their reputation, both with Parliament and their allies. He had, or affected to have, a hammer with which to drive this nail. The armies were assembling. Marlborough would soon take the field with Eugene at his side. "Be assured," wrote Gaultier (February 27, 1711),

> that you will never have so fine an occasion of ending this quarrel than that which is open to-day; for if the Duke of Marlborough

Berwick, ii, 182–183.

should happen to gain another battle during the impending campaign in Flanders, the Queen with her new Ministers will be obliged to fall back once more into the hands of the Presbyterians, and God knows when we shall have an end to this war.

And, a few days later (March 10), "They [our friends] are always of the same feelings here. . . . What then do you fear?"[1]

Torcy and the French Government, from the King downward, had their fears, but their hesitation was due rather to their growing hopes. Some profound and to them blessed change had occurred in England, and the whole Alliance might collapse. The Great Council which sat around the King, with Madame de Maintenon close at hand, became conscious not merely of relief, but of a wonderful opportunity. In this atmosphere the discussion was hard, and Torcy, who was determined not to lose the thread, or cord even, that had been thrust into his hands, had serious anxieties. A further interchange between the Governments took place without modifying the issue. In the end the shadow of Marlborough taking the field, and the chance which none could ignore of another shattering battle, decided the French to comply with the wishes of the English Ministers. Torcy dwelt upon the Dutch reports—coloured no doubt —of the steadfastness of the new English Government. To break at this point, he wrote, would have been in effect

to preserve to this General the dangerous authority which he had over the troops, and to leave him still in the command of the Armies: it would in any case be difficult to deprive him of it; his reputation was too firmly established, and no capital fault could yet be imputed to him. No general officer in England possessed the same talents, and none could fill his place in the confidence of the Allies. The new Ministers had curtailed his authority; but this rather futile mark of their ill-will in itself showed him that he was feared and that his services were indispensable. He was irritated by the affronts made to his wife, to his allies, to his friends, and by seeing their enemies promoted in their places. They had vexed him still more in cutting off part of the power he had wielded in preceding years, but none the less they had left him enough to revenge himself. The sole way of reducing him to the rank of an ordinary subject, was to make peace.[2]

Thus Torcy records the arguments he had used. They prevailed, and when Gaultier arrived on April 6/17 to procure the reply the

[1] French Foreign Office Archives, "Angleterre," tome 232; quoted in O. Weber, *Der Friede von Utrecht*, p. 27.
[2] Torcy, p. 665.

Council met to consider a formal French proposal for a treaty, first with England, but carrying with it the consequence of a general peace. "As no one could doubt that the King was in a condition to continue the war with honour, it should not be taken as a sign of weakness that his Majesty was prepared to break the silence which he had kept since the separation at Gertruydenberg." Accordingly the King offered to negotiate peace on the following basis: The English should have effective guarantees for the future of their commerce in Spain, in the Indies, and in the ports of the Mediterranean. The Dutch should have an adequate Barrier for the safety of their Republic; and this Barrier should be "agreeable to the English nation"; the Dutch should further have entire freedom and security for their trade. Arrangements would be made in good faith and in the most reasonable spirit to satisfy all the allies of England and Holland. "As the success of the King of Spain's affairs opens new expedients for settling the disputes about the Spanish Monarchy, an effort will be made to surmount the difficulties in this quarter, and to safeguard the commerce and generally the interests of all Powers engaged in the present war." Conferences should be opened at once upon this basis, and the King would treat either with England and Holland alone or jointly with them and their allies, according as England might wish. Aix-la-Chapelle or Liége might be the scene of the conferences for a general peace, at the choice of England.[1]

Gaultier delivered this very important document, dated April 11/22, in London ten days later. Harley was still indoors, absorbed in the financial schemes he was preparing for Parliament. Up to this point his only Ministerial confidant had been Shrewsbury. It was now necessary to inform the Dutch. Shrewsbury had ventured thus far in this delicate and, in those days, dangerous transaction. But now he was determined that the responsibility should be shared with the Cabinet. His wishes prevailed. The French note was brought before the Cabinet and sent to the Dutch "as a paper come to the Queen's hands, without saying how."

It was not until this Cabinet (April 26) that St John, the Secretary of State who has been so often credited with the whole of the peace negotiations, was allowed to enter into them. Hitherto he had been writing to Drummond, now the important link with the Dutch party, assurances for the benefit of the Dutch of the British resolve to prosecute the war to the end, and to make peace only in common. Repressing whatever surprise or resentment he may have felt at

[1] Lamberty, vi, 669.

having been kept in the dark, or possibly not knowing even now of Gaultier's to-ings and fro-ings, he accepted the new position. Harley, while moving towards a very large objective in the mole-like fashion which he enjoyed, had taken little care of detail. Lord Jersey had fed Gaultier with all sorts of suggestions, and made through him offers which went far beyond anything that the two Ministers had contemplated. He had let it be supposed that England would give up Gibraltar and Minorca,[1] and, above all, he had fostered the idea that all these peace parleys, so precious in themselves, were but the preliminary to the succession of the Prince of Wales upon the death of the Queen. In fact, the French Government had been amazed at the language which Gaultier seemed to be authorized to use on behalf of Britain. Now and henceforward the business passed out of these irresponsible hands into the masterly, if unscrupulous, grip of St John. Within a few weeks of the receipt of the French proposal he had taken that complete control of the whole negotiation which he never relinquished until the Treaty of Utrecht was signed.

The Cabinet in general were also at this time apprised of Harley's South Sea project. Buckingham urged that a demand should be made upon the French for "cautionary towns," or more properly 'treaty ports,' in the West Indies and South America, in order that the hopes which were to be aroused might be capable of fulfilment. It was therefore decided to send not only Gaultier but Matthew Prior, who was in St John's particular circle, and had diplomatic experience in France, to Paris, to ask for additional easements and to procure from the French more explicit undertakings upon the commercial aspect. "I always thought it very wrong," said the Queen, "to send people abroad of meane extraction; but since you think Mr Prior will be very usefull at this time, I will comply with your desire."[2] Prior's commission was extensive. Now for the first time, at the beginning of July, there appears a written document on the British side of the negotiations. It was remarkable:

> Le sieur Prior est pleinement instruit et autorisé de communiquer à la France nos demandes Préliminaires, et de nous en rapporter la réponse.
>
> A. R.[3]

This document was, of course, disclosed to the Committee of Secrecy in 1715; and it was immediately noticed that the Queen

---

[1] See French Foreign Office Archives, "Angleterre," tome 233, f. 43.
[2] Bath Papers, *H.M.C.*, i, 217.   [3] P.R.O., Treaty Papers, f. 15.

had given this general and far-reaching authority to a comparatively small personage upon her own sign manual. No Minister cared, or dared, to take formal responsibility for this extraordinary 'power.' Anne was willing as sovereign alone to bear the brunt before Parliament. When in due course Prior in his examination was asked, "Did the Lord Treasurer send you to France?" he was able to reply, "No, I was sent by the Queen." This evidence, coupled with the document, was insurmountable, and after four years Harley's subtlety and foresight stood him in good stead.

Thus empowered, Prior proceeded in the deepest secrecy, which nevertheless was to some extent already penetrated,[1] to Versailles, where he arrived on the evening of July 21. He had three interviews with Torcy. In the first he unfolded the English demands. It was the purpose of the new Government to secure substantial commercial advantages for England by agreement with the French before hampering themselves with claims on behalf of the Allies. England required, first, the right to import African negro slaves into the West Indies and South America, termed in the discussions the Assiento; secondly, the naval bases of Gibraltar and Minorca; thirdly, the cession of Nova Scotia and Newfoundland, and various fishing and trading rights in those quarters; fourthly, the demolition of the fortifications at Dunkirk; and, fifthly, the recognition by France of the sovereignty of Queen Anne. After these requirements had been set forth Prior was instructed to ask for the everlasting division of the crowns of France and Spain, an adequate Barrier for Holland, an especial barrier for the Duke of Savoy, and a barrier for the Empire. Nothing was said about the succession in England; nothing about the Germanic frontiers on the Rhine; nothing about the Emperor's claims in Italy, Spain, Bavaria, or the Netherlands. All this was left for future discussion.

At Prior's last interview Torcy, feeling himself in the presence of a Government which wished to make a separate peace for its own special advantage behind the backs and at the expense of its allies, felt sufficiently emboldened to ask abruptly, "What is France to have from England in return for all this?" In all previous negotia-

---

[1] *Brydges to Marlborough*

June 9/20, 1711

★It is lookt upon here as certain, that there are Propositions in agitation for a General Peace. Y. G. must undoubtedly be apprised of them, if there are, tho yᵉ treaty is carried on with yᵉ utmost secrecy, if there is one, I am inclined to believe, that yᵉ Message which was sent with so much privacy about three weeks ago to Holland was upon that account. [Stowe Collection, 57, v, 89–93; Huntington Library, California.]

tions England had prescribed terms in conjunction with her allies. The atmosphere was different now. A transaction which would be regarded as odious by all except its peculiar beneficiaries, and not a general peace, was on the board, or, rather, under it. Prior, who, though a good poet, was not lacking in diplomatic experience or skill, and who knew France and the French well, was taken aback. Like other Englishmen, he had nursed for some years the feeling, born of unbroken success, that we had only to ask what we thought reasonable to receive it. He replied, "Spain and the Indies for Philip V." "Have you, then," inquired Torcy, "Spain at your disposal?" Prior was astonished at this rejoinder. Torcy pursued his advantage. He read to Harley's envoy the latest batch of Petkum's letters from Holland, from which it appeared, or was made to appear, that the Dutch, fearing an English desertion, were themselves ready to enter into private preliminaries.

No progress was made in these conversations, except that it became clear that Great Britain was entirely resolved on peace and persuaded it could be obtained on the terms she wished; and that France saw enormous opportunities, first from British over-eagerness, and secondly from disagreements among the Allies the moment they became aware of the secret negotiations. Upon the commercial aspect there was a complete deadlock. So it was decided that Prior and Gaultier should return to London, and that the discussions should be resumed there. Mesnager, the French commercial expert, was also to go, but to travel separately. Mesnager entered England without detection, but Prior, by the untutored zeal of a Customs official, was arrested at Dover. He was, of course, released as soon as he produced the warrant of the Secretary of State. But the fact became known outside the close Court and Cabinet circle, and rumour immediately ran rife.[1]

The lengthy document containing Mesnager's instructions was

[1]   *Brydges to Marlborough*

                                                 August 23, 1711

★We have a strong report in town of a secret negotiation of peace being carried on, and that which confirms people in this opinion is the search that was lately made of some persons as they landed upon coming over from France, but were released again upon their producing passes from the Secretary of State and all their papers delivered to him. . . . Mr Prior was declared to be one of the number. I would not trouble your Grace with a matter of town talk if I had not a reason to look upon it as being true and that he went over about three weeks ago with Monsieur de Torcy's secretary, and whether the treaty has been desired by the French and what promises have been offered or asked I am wholly a stranger to.

P.S. There was a Council last Sunday at Windsor and his Grace the Duke of Somerset did not endeavour to come into it. [Blenheim MSS.]

remarkable because it showed that the French only half believed that the English Ministers were bent upon a separate peace. The French still expected that they would be confronted with a demand for general preliminaries affecting all the Allies. If, however, the British policy was really as base and unscrupulous as it had been presented, then very considerable sacrifices would be made by France to secure the effective detachment of Britain from the Grand Alliance. Mesnager therefore had authority on this assumption to concede Gibraltar anyhow, and Minorca or even Corunna in the last resort; to meet the English claims in North America; and to agree, if nothing else would suffice, to the razing of Dunkirk. Furthermore, as something had to be said about the Rhine, although the English had not mentioned it, he was allowed to indicate the cession of Kehl and Breisach as a sop to the Empire and the Germanic states.

Prior met the inner Cabinet on August 18. The discussion was resumed at Windsor the next day, and here, for the first time, St John's co-Secretary of State, Dartmouth, was made party to the negotiations. He was informed, but he was also excluded. St John, who was the most capable Minister, and the only one who spoke good French, wrestled with Mesnager. From August until October these hagglings continued. Mesnager found that the English Minister was undoubtedly resolved upon a private peace for Britain, without worrying too much about the allies. He therefore gradually conceded all that his instructions allowed him. In return he asked that the British Government should commit itself positively, and not merely by indifference, to the compensatory demands which France would make upon the allies of Britain. If England was to have special consideration she must not wrangle with France at any later stage because of the disappointments of her comrades in the war. Mesnager sought to shape the dual preliminaries in this sense, and St John, intent upon the special gains of England, allowed the document to take this form. Shrewsbury, who followed the negotiations with closer attention that the other Ministers, evidently felt increasing uneasiness, particularly about Dunkirk, the Protestant Succession,. and the removal of the Pretender from France.[1] Anne herself was less troubled. "Since I saw you," wrote the Queen to Oxford (September 19), "Lord Chamberlain has talked a good deale to me about the Peace, and I hope he will act very heartily in it, tho' he seems a little fearfull."[2]

[1] Shrewsbury to Oxford; Bath Papers, *H.M.C.*, i, 221. [2] *Ibid.*, 210.

By the beginning of October the results of this process were ready for the Cabinet. A conference to discuss the French offers was held between the Ministers involved. At this meeting Mesnager was led inadvertently into an indiscretion. With some simplicity, he asked what the British Government proposed about the Succession in England, and generally about the Jacobite question. It almost seems that he had not heard of Gaultier's conversation with Berwick. The effect of his question froze the Ministers into silence. For a time not one could think of anything to say. Then St John intervened roughly, and possibly on the spur of the emergency. "It would be impossible," he said, "for England to make peace with a country in which the Pretender was living." That this represented the public position of Shrewsbury and most of the Ministers is undoubted. It was not, however, a decision to which they had deliberately come; nor was it in accordance with the conversation which Gaultier had held in January with Berwick, in consideration of which the English Jacobites in Parliament had given their support to the Ministry during the whole session.

The comment which forces itself upon the student of these times is that this vigorous declaration of inveterate war against any Power which gave asylum to the Prince of Wales was made by the statesman who only three years later was Jacobite Secretary of State at Saint-Germains. St John had the character which enabled him to say anything which the moment required in the most brilliant and decisive manner. He could hit any nail directly on the head with his hammer; which nail did not seem, in his brief heyday, to be particularly important.

The Queen to Oxford

September 24, 1711

I have this business of the Peace soe much at hart, that I cannot help giveing you this trouble to ask if it may not be proper to order Mr Secretary, in case he finds M. Mesnager very averse to the new propossition, not to insist upon it, and if you think it right I hope you will take care Mr Secretary has such an order in my name, for I think there is nothing soe much to be feared as the letting the Treaty goe out of our hands.[1]

It now became indispensable once again to widen the circle of those responsible. Poulett, Bishop Robinson, and Buckingham were for the first time apprised of the work of the year. The upshot of this serious conclave was the general feeling, voiced by Shrewsbury,

---

[1] Bath Papers, *H.M.C.*, i, 218.

that the draft preliminaries, however advantageous, were too shameless for publication. Even St John, while parading his work, admitted that "it required dressing up." Accordingly Prior was sent to Mesnager to rewrite the section which concerned the allies in terms which would throw some cloak, or at least some veil, over their naked, cynical realism. The French emissary was deeply embarrassed. All that he had given to England had been upon the basis of her flagrant public desertion of her allies. Now, having pocketed their special advantages, the English Cabinet wished apparently to be protected from some at least of the strictures which would be passed upon them by their comrades. Mesnager therefore asked for time to communicate with Versailles. However, St John rose to the occasion, and with the compulsive violence of a vital mind induced him to take the responsibility. On October 8 the three documents relating to the English claims, to the interests of the allies, and to the special interest of Savoy were signed between England and France, and approved by the Queen.

Chapter Twenty-eight

HANOVER INTERVENES

THE tale of these times should not be told as if it were wrong for an Opposition to seek to become a Government, or for Ministers at the head of the State to labour diligently for peace. The stigma upon them lies somewhat differently. Just as they had obtained power, not by free debate in Parliament, but by a backstairs intrigue with the Queen, so they sought a peace by a greedy and treacherous desertion of their allies. In the first case, they infringed every principle of Parliamentary government as accepted in Great Britain to-day. In the second, they violated the whole structure of personal and international good faith, of which British Governments have so often prided themselves on being the architects and defenders. All this, however, was but the starting-point. The career of deliberate bad faith for special national advantage, pursued by Ministers whose personal interests were also engaged, had but begun. It was now confined to the words of documents and the mutterings of Cabinet conclaves. Presently we shall see it translated into action in the field and in the face of the common enemy; and few who study it with attention will be surprised at the old French taunt, "Perfidious Albion."

England and France were now agreed upon the preliminaries, and the special interests of England were only too well protected. St John next addressed himself to the task of reconciling the allies to the Anglo-French basis. He thought at first this would be easy. The Dutch, who had hitherto only been shown Torcy's letter of April 11, had passed the summer in uncertainty and suspicion. They had perhaps been inclined to follow the British example of direct and separate contact with France. They had not made any formal complaint upon the terms of the Torcy letter; and St John might reasonably claim that they were not disturbed by it. None of the other allies had been informed at all. Now in October the preliminaries, *apart from the secret Anglo-French agreement*, were circulated to the allied Courts. Vehement opposition developed at once from two quarters. The first was, of course, Vienna. The Emperor protested by every means in his power—and there were many— against the proposal to deprive the house of Hapsburg of Spain and the Indies. On this, as Charles VI or as Charles III, he had a strong case against England. Was it not at the English request that he had gone to Spain to fight so long and hard for the Peninsular monarchy? Had he not twice been proclaimed King of Spain at Madrid? Had not the English Parliament above all other bodies or powers in Europe proclaimed and ceaselessly ingeminated "no peace without Spain"? Yet now England appeared ready to turn her back on all this. Why? Was this the whole of the transaction? Were the so-called French proposals for discussion in fact a bargain already struck between England and France? What lay behind?

Continental historians like Klopp naturally dwell upon the ill-usage of the Emperor Charles; but there is another side. No allied Power had more at stake in the war than the Empire. None had made greater promise to contribute to it. But what had been the performance? Where had been those ninety thousand men whom in the original treaty the Empire had bound itself to maintain upon the Rhine and in the Northern theatre? Where had been that support which the Hapsburg Emperor professed to enjoy from the Germanic states? The feeble, ill-paid armies, never rising above forty thousand, which under unhelpful or incapable commanders had appeared upon the Rhine had been the laughing-stock of friend and foe. The contingents which the Germanic princes should have sent to their supreme liege lord had only appeared in the guise of mercenary troops paid and maintained by the Sea Powers. Nothing had been given freely to the Empire. That decrepit body, paralysed from the outset by the Bavarian desertion and the Magyar revolt, had utterly failed in all its engagements. Vienna itself had been saved by the battle of Blenheim, gained in Central Europe by British soldiers and by contingents maintained by England and Holland. Even the troops which Eugene had led with quenchless valour and unsurpassed skill had been largely provided by the Sea Powers. His Turin campaign was sustained almost entirely by British money and allied contingents. His attempt on Toulon was similarly founded, and there remained much reproach about the ineffectual use of these resources. The Empire had shown itself quite unmindful of the Common Cause, which now played so large a part in their protestations, when they weakened the Toulon expedition for the sake of acquiring territorial gains at Naples. The military convention which they had made with France at the end of 1706 had shown no consideration for allied interests, and had liberated large numbers of French troops, cut off and invested in the fortresses of the Milanese, to face Marlborough in Flanders in 1707.

Klopp, while admitting the woeful facts of physical failure, still claims that the Empire had acted loyally and correctly. This loyal and correct attitude had, however, been maintained while they were carried shoulder-high by the Sea Powers. Perfidy among allies is justly odious, but failure to fulfil solemn undertakings and make adequate contribution to the common cause is not distinguishable, in its consequences at least, from perfidy. No British Government was therefore unprovided with an answer to the Austrian reproach. To bring all this to a point St John had at the end of June asked that eight thousand of the Imperialist troops released from Hungary should be sent to reinforce the Duke of Savoy and encourage his offensive. It was a request which courted a refusal, which the Secretary could turn to good account. "We must look upon a refusal," he wrote with characteristic cant (June 12), "*as an absolute desertion of the Common Cause.*"[1] He could write this while he was corresponding with Torcy upon the basis that the allies were the "common enemy."

It was not from the Empire but from another quarter that the real thrust against the new British policy was delivered. The Elector of Hanover held a far stronger position in everything that concerned England than the Emperor. His troops had fought well throughout the war in the main theatre and in Marlborough's battles. His son had risked his life in the charge at Oudenarde. But far more important than such actions or gestures was the fact that he was the proclaimed constitutional heir to the British throne. All party politics in England revolved around him. We have seen the perfervid attempts of Oxford, Shrewsbury, and St John to gain his good graces. Well might they try; for the Queen's health, for many years precarious, gave no assurance of a lengthy reign. At any time a recurrence of her gout or some other of the maladies by which she was afflicted might remove her from the scene. Where then would be those proud Ministers who had obtained power by her favour and Abigail's intrigues if they now set themselves in direct hostility to the sincere desires and the treaty rights of their future sovereign? Although two generations had passed since the

---

[1] *Bolingbroke Correspondence*, i, 241.

axe had fallen upon an English Minister as the result of impeach
ment for policy apart from rebellion, no one could say that the
practice might not be revived. The fate of the great Lord Strafford
was still vivid in men's minds. The weapons of impeachment and
attainder remained in full existence. They were perhaps blunted
by the insensible but ceaseless march of culture and civilization
which distinguished this great period in our history. But it would
not take long to sharpen the axe on the Tower grindstone. That
these possibilities were never forgotten by the public figures of the
age of Anne is revealed by innumerable references in their letters.
Marlborough certainly never had the assurance that even his victories
could protect him from impeachment. The dispossessed Whigs
from now onward never ceased to declare of Harley that they "would
have his head" should they regain power. The Hanoverian accession would give them power. A quarrel with the sovereign desig-
nate upon the high issue of the abandonment of the war might easily
inspire power with vengeance.

The attitude of the Court of Hanover became at once vehemently
hostile to the peace and to the new advisers of Queen Anne. This
was even so marked as to show a very considerable detachment on
the part of the Elector from his prospects of gaining the British
throne. Evidently by his antagonism to the Tory Ministers, who
would presumably be in office on a demise of the Crown, he tempted
them for their own sakes to look elsewhere for a successor, if that
were possible. They might well face the perils of such a course if
it became the only escape from other equal dangers. Hitherto they
had hoped that the lure of the crown of Great Britain would far
outweigh any pride in the Electoral Hat. It now appeared that the
Elector was at heart a Hanoverian prince rather than a candidate
for the British throne, and that he did not hesitate to base his chances
of succession upon the Whigs and upon Whig policy at home and
abroad. These developments intensified severely the passions of the
British parties during the last years of Anne, until at times they
seemed almost to revive in a gentler period the merciless hatreds
of Charles II's reign and of the Popish Plot.

During these months the whispers had grown in Whitehall.
The allied ambassadors in their anxiety obtruded themselves on
Ministers and asked awkward questions. Oxford was not handy
at replying. He lied obdurately without convincing. Sometimes he
talked confusedly for an hour without creating any impression but
that of mistrust. On October 5, meeting Hoffmann at Court, he

said, "I beg you to see that no time is lost in submitting the plan of campaign for Spain, which has already been asked for a number of times. I am afraid it may arrive too late." Hoffmann smiled sardonically at him. "Have we really got to make a plan of campaign for Spain, when every one here knows that a peace is concluded, or at least certain? Indeed, if rumour is to be trusted, I should not like to carry the news to King Charles." "I should, though," replied the Treasurer genially. "How is that, when Spain and the Indies are to be given to the Duke of Anjou?" "There is no question of that," asserted Oxford, turning sharply away to end the conversation.[1]

St John throughout this interval had been more artistic. He diffused ceaselessly an atmosphere of defeatism and uncertainty. He threw out a continuous stream of hints that the Alliance was breaking up. Every one was playing for his own hand. Only the Queen, of course, as he made out, was faithfully, laboriously, quixotically, adhering to the Common Cause. When Brigadier Palmes, of Blenheim day, returning from Vienna, suggested that opportunity was favourable for capturing Sicily, St John replied, "How do you know that the Court of Vienna is not at this very moment secretly negotiating with France?" To the Savoyard envoy he said, "Are you sure that negotiations are not proceeding in Holland?" And to the Hanoverian he remarked, "I don't say that we have anything in hand, but if we had we should be doing nothing more than what others have long been doing."[2] In this way he rocked and shook all the foundations of the Alliance, and sought to encourage the signatories to break their bond and shift for themselves, well knowing he and his colleagues had stolen the decisive march upon them all. It is an astonishing proof of the basic strength of the structure that it did not collapse entirely during the summer.

His relations with Gallas soon became unpleasant. Gallas was a deeply informed, farseeing, zealous servant of Charles III and of the Empire. His ability and his knowledge made him feared and hated by the Secretary of State, laden with his covert designs. Gallas became conscious that the Government had surrounded him with a network of spies. He mentions some names in his dispatches. He was, however, more successful in finding out the secrets of others than in guarding his own. He was not aware that a trusted servant of his household, the priest Gaultier, who officiated in his chapel, had long been the agent of France, and had now also become the

---

[1] Klopp, xiv, 175.   [2] *Ibid.*, 115.

agent of England. A more deadly seduction followed. Whether or not Gaultier guided St John into the secret circle of Gallas's embassy is not known, though it is a reasonable assumption. At any rate, in the summer of 1711 St John had bribed the first Secretary of the embassy, one Clemente, to betray his ambassador. Clemente delivered to the Secretary of State Gallas's reports to Barcelona and Vienna, together with the cipher which translated them. St John had the advantage of reading in the dispatch of July 31 a very candid account of himself and his principal colleagues, which rings true to-day. Gallas wrote:

> He [Oxford] is so well informed in internal affairs that he may almost be regarded as perfect in that respect, but he knows very little of foreign affairs; yet he is always with the Queen. . . . To talk to Dartmouth is like talking to a brick wall. St John is just the opposite. He investigates everything, takes everything in, and can always be relied upon to make a formal statement. Neither his rank, his credit, capacity, or steadiness make one believe him. Moreover, his arrogance and excessive fiery temper are increasing from day to day to such an extent that one cannot penetrate his real ideas. Besides this, he is given to the bottle and debauchery to the point of almost making a virtue out of his open affectation that public affairs are a bagatelle to him, and that his capacity is on so high a level that he has no need to give up his pleasures in the slightest degree for any cause.[1]

And again (July 31), "The Ministers and the dominant party are enemies rather than friends of the Alliance."[2]

Moreover, Gallas had a plan. He urged that some personality of the highest repute should be sent to London to question Ministers and grip the situation. Obviously Prince Eugene was the man. All through the summer Gallas was suggesting this to his masters. They dallied. Eugene was indeed to come; but too late.

Naturally St John and Oxford were entitled to regard Gallas as a dangerous, inveterate opponent. We need not waste indignation upon the trick of opening, decoding, or suppressing the correspondence of ambassadors, privileged under the law of nations; for this practice did not end with the eighteenth century. St John by October felt free to indulge his resentment against Gallas. The Ambassador had ceased to attend his receptions. Although Gallas was blissfully unaware of St John's information, the two men were no longer on speaking terms. The note setting forth the French proposals was now presented by St John to the allies. Gallas received

---

[1] Gallas, July 17; Klopp, xiv, 116.   [2] *Loc. cit.*

his copy. He treated it with slight consideration. St John expressed his disgust to Raby, created Earl of Strafford in September:

"He calls the proceeding an enigma, and in short, speaks the language which the impertinence of an Austrian Minister, improved by the encouragement and conversation of a saucy faction, might make one expect. It shall be no fault of mine if he does not receive such a reply as, by the decency of it, will give him reason to be ashamed, and as, by the resolution of it, will confound him."[1]

It was the peculiar quality of St John to be able to brand in the most caustic terms in others the exact conduct which he was himself pursuing. To criticize a Government of which he was a member was "to attack the Queen." His opponents were always "a shameless faction." The allies were always guilty of the basest duplicity. He was unfeignedly indignant at the espionage and corruption by which he felt himself surrounded, and to which he made a notable contribution. He could use all arguments and all rhetoric on all sides of all questions, and he did it with a zest and pith which almost enlists us in the cause he championed at the moment. He had good reason to be annoyed when, the day after the French note had been sent in secrecy to the allies, its text appeared in the Whig news-sheet. There was a great sensation. "Both Whigs and Tories in the coffee houses were so astonished at the terms that they looked at each other without speaking. The stocks on the exchange fell several points."[2] Gallas reported that "the publication of the new scandalous preliminaries last Sunday by the *Daily Courant* has made Tories and Whigs terrified and dumb."

The Ministry asserted that Gallas had disclosed the secret. They may well have had conclusive but unpublishable proof at their disposal. Anyhow they had an ample case against Gallas if they wished to get rid of him. They knew from his intercepted letters that he had arranged to have Peterborough shadowed on his mission as ambassador to Vienna. They had had his own opinion of them set before them in terms which to men of intelligence must have appeared particularly insulting because so shrewd. They found, however, a difficulty in dismissing Count Gallas: he had already been recalled. The Emperor Charles VI had summoned him to Vienna. It was possible none the less to inflict on him an affront which travelled round Europe. On October 26 the Master of the Ceremonies announced to him that, "owing to the displeasure his conduct had caused her, the Queen had forbidden him the Court,

---

[1] *Bolingbroke Correspondence*, i, 404.   [2] Hoffmann, October 27; Klopp, xiv, 178.

and would explain her reasons to the Emperor. Announcements from the Emperor through another servant would be acceptable to the Queen."

St John used his *Post Boy* to vilipend the Ambassador, and hold him up to the anger of the Tory Party. Nevertheless, in the solid tolerances of those days Gallas, though excluded from his functions, remained for many weeks in England as a private person. The manners of the eighteenth century permitted the most scathing official discourtesies to subsist by the side of very considerable minor politeness.

Marlborough's overtures, through Stair and in his correspondence with Oxford, had lasted during the campaign. Many persons not privy to these communications believed that an effective combination between the General and the Lord Treasurer would be a supreme advantage to the public. It would afford the best chance either of "a good peace or a good war." It would secure the Hanoverian Succession beyond all question. It would furnish the Queen with a Government of a moderate character, representative of both parties and at the mercy of neither. It certainly fulfilled in home affairs what had been the consistent conviction and desire both of the General and the Treasurer. It was in principle a return to the basis of 1704, without Sarah or Godolphin. But the obstacles were now insuperable.

Marlborough, absorbed in the arduous campaign and unaware of the secret negotiations, had only responded to Oxford's peace feelers by general assurances. He was more than willing to see the obstacles which had wrecked the Gertruydenberg conference swept away, and a broad settlement made in Europe. But that he should be a party to a separate peace behind the backs of the other signatory states never entered his mind. He was the soul of the Grand Alliance. He was enjoying far better treatment at the hands of its members than from his own countrymen. While in England savage party enmities beset him, in Europe he was trusted, admired, and venerated. Oxford, who understood this, did not venture to declare his own true position. He was sure that no common policy on these lines could be agreed between them. He meant to have peace almost at any price, and he now felt certain he had it in his grasp. As the campaign drew to a conclusion the correspondence between the two men had evaporated in civilities.

Each relied on certain forces or processes. Hanover was now

Marlborough's most important stronghold. He still hoped for a friendly arrangement with the Treasurer, but he was determined to preserve his influence there. When at the beginning of October he returned to The Hague and entered its atmosphere of anxiety and suspicion he put himself in the closest contact with the Elector George Lewis. Neither knew what the British Government had done or intended. Both were sure that private negotiations were going on between England and France. How far these were operative, or whether there was a definite agreement on any particular point, was still unknown. It cannot, however, be doubted that Marlborough and the Hanoverian Court were in entire agreement, each spurring on the other, that a separate peace by England at the expense of the allies should be resisted by every means in their power.

On the other side Oxford and St John had their plan. If, as Oxford apprehended, they could not gain Marlborough to their schemes they meant to dismiss and dishonour him; and they believed they had the means to do both. If he would go forward with Ministers upon the path of a separate peace his interests would be protected in every way. If not, then, in the words which St John had used to Drummond earlier in the year, "such scenes will open as no victories can varnish over." Thus Marlborough's choice was either to become the military tool of a disloyal peace or to face the full malice of the Government supported by the Queen and commanding majorities in both Houses. He was somewhat slow in becoming aware of this issue.

His eyes were to some extent opened upon his arrival at The Hague. The partisan attack launched by the new Ministry upon the financial conduct of Godolphin, the fantastic tale of "thirty-five millions unaccounted for," had led to the appointment in the spring of a House of Commons "Commission of Accounts," composed of ardent Tories, headed by Lockhart and Shippen, another red-hot Jacobite. The Lockhart papers and the report which he presented to the House of Commons give a full account of the work of the Commission. Their hope and object was to unearth financial scandals and cases of peculation among their predecessors and opponents. Godolphin was protected from any personal charge by his evident poverty; but Walpole, the truculent and most competent Whig statesman in the Commons, was marked as a target. Above all, Marlborough attracted the thirsty scrutiny of the Tory-Jacobite committee. These volumes have not concealed the many good and valid reasons which the Jacobites had to seek revenge upon him. From the night in 1688 when he rode away from James's camp at Salisbury he had been their most relentless and deceitful foe. His own notorious love of wealth, the fortune he had made, the perpetual annuity voted to him for his victories, the salaries and allowances he drew from so many English military offices and as Deputy Captain-General of Holland, the ten years in which he had managed things in his own way—all proclaimed a broad and fertile field to the inquisitors. It had been known in Government circles for years past that he deducted annually a percentage from the pay of the foreign contingents serving under him and took other perquisites to form an Army fund which he said was devoted to Secret Service of all kinds. Over this, of course, he had complete control. It is the essence of Secret Service funds that no account of them can ever be presented. Thus he could be charged by his political foes with having pocketed as much as he chose of this percentage.

Marlborough does not seem to have been the least disturbed by the holding of the inquiry. He wrote to Sir Solomon Medina, the principal Government contractor, who had been summoned to England, that he was glad he was to be a witness, and would afford any documentary assistance in his power. But either Medina had some grievance about the payments made to him or he was gained to the Government interest. Whatever the cause, he certainly framed his deposition in an injurious and misleading form. He said that from 1707 to 1711 he had paid the Duke of Marlborough on bread and various contracts for the army the sum of 332,425 guilders *for his own use*, and yearly twelve or fourteen wagons gratis "for the use of the Duke himself." He mentioned also quite properly that on each contract he had presented Cardonnel with a gratuity of five hundred ducats, and paid Mr Sweet, the Deputy-Paymaster at Amsterdam, 1 per cent. on all the moneys he received.

As soon as he heard of this Marlborough wrote a full explanation to the Commissioners.

> Having been informed on my arrival here that Sir Solomon de Medina has acquainted you with my having received several sums of money from him, that it might make the less impression on you I would lose no time in letting you know that this is no more than what has been allowed as a perquisite to the general, or commander-in-chief of the army in the Low Countries, even before the Revolution, and since; and I do assure you, at the same time, that whatever sums I have received on that account have been constantly employed for the

service of the public, in keeping secret correspondence, and getting intelligence of the enemy's motions and designs.

He then declared that he had also received 2½ per cent. upon the pay of the foreign auxiliaries during all these years for Secret Service, that he had himself negotiated this agreement in the capacity of plenipotentiary under King William III, and that he held Queen Anne's warrant dated July 6, 1702, for the transaction.

And now, gentlemen [he continued], as I have laid the whole matter fairly before you, and I hope you will allow I have served my Queen and country with that faithfulness and zeal which becomes an honest man, the favour that I intreat of you is that when you make your report to the Parliament you will lay this part before them in its true light, so that they may see this necessary and important part of the war has been provided for and carried on without any other expense to the public than ten thousand pounds a year. And I flatter myself that when the accounts of the army in Flanders come under your consideration, you will be sensible the service on this side has been carried on with all the economy and good husbandry to the public that was possible.[1]

Evidently he supposed his explanation was complete and would be accepted. Anyone considering his behaviour at this time will feel, "Here is a man with a clear conscience who cares nothing for the worst that his foes may do." And this conclusion has its force for us to-day.

His attitude might well have arisen from the hardihood of his nature and those powers of endurance under the most severe pressures which he had shown during the Fenwick trial and on many other occasions in his long, anxious career. Yet this was a matter which was now bound to come to a head, and was sure—unless Ministers turned it aside, as they could so easily do—to involve a cruel ordeal. These Ministers would have blithely purchased Marlborough's support for their policy or his compliance in it, or even his silent neutrality, by relieving him of all vexation. It should not be supposed that St John, for instance, was at all scandalized by what he had learned. He had just netted a large sum of money from the special clothing contract for his Canadian fiasco. Even if he put the ugliest construction on Marlborough's conduct, St John did not think any the worse of him for it. He had long regarded it as a fine blackmailing counter to compel Marlborough to serve and aid the Tory Ministry. It was for this reason he had written his

[1] Coxe, vi, 124–125.

letter in 1711 to the go-between, Drummond, to make Marlborough aware that the new Ministers felt they had him in their hands. If he stood aside from the impending clash, if he retired to Woodstock to superintend the building of his palace, they would no doubt be very ready to give him guarantees against annoyance or molestation.

Both Marlborough's political action at this juncture and his personal integrity must be judged in relation to his knowledge of these facts. He never hesitated at all in the course which he took. He rallied the whole political power of the Allies against a separate British peace. He used all his paramount influence in Hanover, both through Robethon and also directly upon the Electress Sophia and the Elector, to make them dare all against it. He was working in the most complete intimacy and accord with Bothmar. Whatever he afterwards encountered, it was with his eyes open. He did not turn aside by a single step from the policy on which he was resolved. He faced the accusations with which he knew he would be assailed with no more unmanly shrinking than he would a cannon-ball in the field. He meant to throw his whole weight—and it might well be decisive —on the side of the immense forces gathering against the Ministry and their dishonourable negotiations. He seems nevertheless to have imagined that Oxford, whom he had driven from office in 1708 in circumstances of affront and danger, and who now stood in a situation commanding enough, but also precarious, would, merely as a matter of truth and fair play, not misrepresent the facts against him or treat them with prejudice and malice.

Marlborough to Oxford

HAGUE
November 10, 1711

. . . Upon my arrival here, I had notice that my name was brought before the Commissioners of Accounts, possibly without any design to do me a prejudice. However, to prevent any ill impression it might take, I have writ a letter to those gentlemen, setting the matter in its true light, which Mr Craggs will deliver; and when you have taken the pains to read the enclosed copy, pray be so kind as to employ your good offices, so as that it may be known I have the advantage of your friendship. No one knows better than your lordship the great use and expense of intelligence, and no one can better explain it. . . .

My lord, you see I make no scruple to give you a little trouble, which to a temper like yours rather increases than diminishes the pleasure of doing a good office. I do, therefore, boldly claim the benefit of your friendship, and am so sanguine as to expect the good effects of it, which I shall make it my constant business to deserve. The endeavours of our enemies to destroy the friendship between us will double mine to continue and improve it.[1]

With this he enclosed a copy of the formal letter he had written to the Commissioners.

But when truth is stifled under veils of tactics and deceit, and when fair play between man and man has long been devoured by antagonism, such an appeal was not worth making. By this time the Treasurer knew that Marlborough would act against him on the treaty issue. Why, then, should he give up his weapon and the chance of setting a hostile House of Commons loose upon him? "That were some love, but little policy."

The strongest efforts had been made by the Queen's Ministers to reconcile the Elector of Hanover to their courses. Lord Rivers was sent over with the so-called French offer of peace preliminaries. Oxford, Shrewsbury, and even Buckingham, a non-violent but undoubted Jacobite, vied with one another in their professions of devotion to the Hanoverian Succession. Abigail later on, with more comprehension than she ever showed at any other time, explained to Mesnager the root fact that the peace could only be carried under extreme asseverations of the loyalty of the Queen and of the whole Government to the Act of Settlement. This aspect was well understood at Hanover. By no one was it realized more intensely than by the aged Electress Sophia. She must be regarded as the mainspring of Hanoverian policy. That her son also held her views does not detract from this. This resolute, clear-sighted old woman revolted at the fabric of falsehood and hypocrisy which now enwrapped the policy of Britain. She never made a secret of her admiration for Marlborough. When Strafford had on one occasion twitted her "that he saw she belonged to Marlborough's party" she answered with vigour, "If the Queen had made an ape her general, and this ape had won so many victories, I should be on the side of the ape."[2]

In answer to the laboured explanations of the peace policy of the English Government the Electress Sophia remarked to Strafford, "If you had been willing to accept peace on such terms as are printed in the English gazettes a great deal of blood and a great deal of the money of England and Holland might have been saved."[3] The Elector too gave his opinion upon the peace proposals to the Queen, and mentioned that he would send to London a man who

[1] Coxe, v, 126   [2] Macpherson, ii, 347.   [3] Ibid., 267.

was in his confidence. This envoy was, of course, the Baron von Bothmar. To Oxford he wrote in sharply edged terms; he expressed his joy at the Queen's declared resolve to make peace only in common with her allies.

> This is worthy of the behaviour of so great a Queen, and, besides that, is in keeping with your achievements for the general interests of your allies during the course of such a famous war. . . . And you, my lord, are too penetrating to have failed to realize that the fruits of this war will be lost if Spain and the Indies remain in the hands of the Duke of Anjou, for this will soon render France once more in a a state *to give the law to Europe*, and bring to nought all those wise measures which the Queen began in order to secure lasting prosperity for her people.[1]

This language, especially the phrase about France "giving the law to Europe," is familiar to us. It has been already repeated a dozen times in Marlborough's secret letters to Godolphin and Sarah in the last five years. One can hardly doubt its parentage.

Following upon all this, the Hanoverian Court framed a long formal protest to the British Government against according Louis XIV

> a peace glorious to himself, ruinous to the victorious Allies, and destructive to the liberties of all Europe, in acquiring the power of giving a monarch to Spain, of imposing another on Great Britain, and of making the validity of the Crown of the Empire depend on his approbation.[2]

Bothmar, armed with this manifesto, set out for London. He did not travel alone. At The Hague he was joined by Marlborough, and the two arrived together in the closest relations in good time for the meeting of Parliament. Bothmar presented his memorandum to the Secretary of State on November 28. The Ministers were surprised and shocked by this implacable resistance from the one quarter they were bound to respect. They were still more surprised and angered when the very next day they found this document also published and reprinted in successive editions of the *Daily Courant*. The Duchess of Somerset read the document to the Queen. Thus all along the line the struggle was openly joined. The heir to the Throne, the reunited Whig Party, the weight of the Grand Alliance, and behind them all Marlborough, ranged themselves against the separate peace already agreed between England and France.

The political crisis which followed is notable in English history.

[1] Macpherson, ii, 263.
[2] Coxe, vi, 135–136; quoted from an anonymous *History of Europe* (1711), p. 398.

Chapter Twenty-nine

THE POLITICAL CLIMAX

1711—WINTER

THE disclosures by the *Daily Courant* on October 13 of the peace preliminaries said to be 'offered' by France brought the whole question before the nation. The Whig Party was instantly united against the settlement. They had recovered their poise in opposition. They began to feel again that "they had a bottom." If any issue could revive them it was surely the abandonment of the principle "No peace without Spain," which they themselves had accepted from the Tories, and to which many Tories still adhered. The Junto Lords began again to meet in their country houses and to marshal their forces for the session of Parliament. They contemplated a public memorial to the Queen protesting against the negotiations. They were stimulated by the eagerness of all the elements on which they depended, and felt themselves moving upon their main highway in conjunction with all the states of the Grand Alliance.

At this time they gained a welcome, though hardly an exhilarating, adherent of high consequence. The Earl of Nottingham, who had been forced to cede the Secretaryship of State to Oxford in 1704, was, even more than Rochester, a high Tory, and without doubt the leader of the Church of England. He had shared in Rochester's fall, but he had not been restored when the Tories returned to power. He had always disliked a Continental war. In opposition to Marlborough's demands for the Low Countries he had expounded the Tory strategy of leaving foreigners to cut each other's throats on the main land, while England picked up valuable possessions in the outer seas. In 1704 this policy had expressed itself in terms of contact with Portugal and of a major English effort in Spain rather than in Flanders. In fact, though in an entirely different connotation, Nottingham was the parent of the phrase "No peace without Spain," now on all Whig lips. He could therefore, with a a fine show of verbal consistency, place himself upon the Whig side on the dominating question of the hour. But a barrier intervened

899

between him and the Whigs. As lay leader of the Church he was the champion of the Occasional Conformity Bill. If he was to preserve his hold over the clergy, and, indeed, live up to his life-constructed reputation as a man of the highest piety and virtue, he must be true to the Occasional Conformity Bill.

This measure now stood in a totally different light from when it was last successfully burked in 1704. Then it had been—apart, that is to say, from the spiritual and mystic issues involved—a party move of the Tories to hamper the Whigs at the elections and keep them out of public life. Now the settlement of this once bitter controversy might be the means of putting the Whigs in office. Nottingham felt differently about it, and so did the Whigs. The combination between the Anglican Church, headed by a statesman so long ill-treated by the Crown, and all the Whig forces, against the disreputable negotiation casting away the principle of "No peace without Spain," seemed to offer almost the certainty of victory. If the Church could be joined to the Whigs the effects of Sacheverell would be largely effaced. The anxieties of the Queen about her beloved Church would be removed, and an Administration might be formed which would revive the honour of England, and in which Nottingham felt he might with exemplary decorum and consistency play a leading part.

It is a measure of the commotion in the public mind, of the intensity of Whig feeling against the peace, and of their resentment at the manner in which they had been driven from office, that the Junto not only agreed with Nottingham not to oppose the Occasional Conformity Bill, but also carried with them the whole of the Whig Parliamentary party. They were even able in some degree to quiet the Dissenters, against whom it was aimed and supposed to be a deadly blow. All this was another sign of how the stakes were raised by both sides as their passions, intellectual, moral, and unmoral, became ever more vehemently engaged. The Whigs accordingly came to terms with Nottingham. They guaranteed an unopposed passage for the Occasional Conformity Bill in return for his wholehearted opposition to the proposed peace. Rumours that Nottingham was being got at soon reached the Tory chiefs. Poulett was deputed to get into touch with him. His report was not reassuring. "I find Nottingham," he wrote to Oxford in November,

> as sour and fiercely wild as you can imagine anything to be that has lived so long in the desert; I had two hours and a half discourse this forenoon with him and shall acquaint you with it when you please. . . .

I am a great deal concerned how your numbers may answer in our House, for I think the Queen's enemies at present generally understand one another much better than her friends and servants. The adversaries have been a long time prepared for a meeting [of Parliament] which will decide the fate of Europe as well as Britain.[1]

In Whig circles there was wicked glee. Nottingham's health was drunk in bumpers at their banquets and in the Kit-cat Club. His lugubrious countenance and preternaturally solemn demeanour had long gained him a nickname. Wharton, with deplorable levity, remarked, "It is Dismal will save England at last."[2]

Oxford and his friends, aware of the gathering storm, were full of fears for the meeting of Parliament. They could count on the Commons, where the bulk of the Tory Members would stand by them through thick and thin. Even if the parsons were placated by Nottingham the squires would not be daunted. After all, it was the squires who would have to give the votes. But in the House of Lords the forces were nicely balanced. Nottingham would certainly influence a number of peers, and even some bishops might be affected. The Scottish peers therefore acquired particular importance. It was urgent to bring them to London, and it cannot be doubted that appeals for their attendance were sustained by various inducements. Still, it took eight or nine days of hard travel for the chivalry of North Britain to reach the Metropolis. All the Whig forces, on the other hand, would be ready from the first day. Parliament was prorogued from week to week. It should normally have met early in November. People began to say that the Government did not dare to call Parliament together upon their peace terms. This talk travelled to The Hague. It was indispensable that Ministers should announce in the Queen's Speech that the States-General had agreed to a conference after the preliminaries. Strafford declared that the Dutch and other allies were becoming unmanageable. They were ceasing to pay attention to anything he said. Finally Parliament was summoned for December 7, and on this the Dutch, hoping that the Ministry would not survive the ordeal, consented to meet the French at Utrecht in February.

But an even graver anxiety oppressed Oxford and St John. They began to feel uncertain about the Queen. Deeply as she desired peace, she was aware that its dangers might affect not only her Ministers but herself. Had she not been warned repeatedly only a little more than a year ago by Oxford, Somerset, and others that

---

[1] Portland Papers, *H.M.C.*, v, 119. [2] Swift, *Journal to Stella*, December 5, 1711.

Marlborough was aiming at the crown? And had they not assured her that the Whigs whom she had driven from her presence had always been Republicans at heart? Her new Ministers were challenging all those strong forces in the nation which had brought her to the throne, and the great European combination whereby Marlborough had raised her to the head of Europe. From all quarters forces seemed to close in upon her. Every foreign ambassador told the same tale. She knew that she was deceiving and deserting her allies, that her royal word would be a mockery throughout the world.

Abigail's soothings were a comfort to the Queen; but she had another woman friend. The Duchess of Somerset was not in contact with the Queen's person in the intimate fashion of her bedchamber woman; she was rather a trusted social companion. In the year that had passed Somerset's breach with the Ministry had become complete. When, after having worked against them at the election, he had presented himself with effrontery at the Council, St John had got up from the table, saying he would not sit in the room with such a man. He was no more at Cabinet or even at Court. He glowered from Petworth upon the scene of his miscalculations; but his Duchess was daily at the Queen's side, matching Abigail's assurances with Whig admonitions, not easily at times to be distinguished from threats.

On top of this came Nottingham's change of sides, and the prospect that the dear Church entrusted to Anne's keeping would soon gain that safeguard against hypocrisy and blasphemy for the sake of office for which it had so long and so earnestly striven—which the Queen had always wished it should have. The combination of the Whigs with even part of the Church party seemed a strange, unnatural thing. Nevertheless, the Queen felt that for the Whigs to carry the Occasional Conformity Bill meant a sensible mitigation of those sectarian broils which had always vexed her so sorely, and a real victory for the Church. Thus we have in these weeks a host of impressions of keen alarm in Tory circles about the attitude of the Queen. Swift's letters to Stella during December are a mirror of these. "Mrs Masham . . . gave me some lights to suspect the Queen is changed." "The Queen is false, or at least very much wavering." "I have now some farther conviction that the Queen is false, and it begins to be known." "Arbuthnot is in good hopes that the Queen has not betrayed us. . . . But I cannot yet be of his opinion." "The Queen certainly designs to change the Ministry." "We must certainly fall if the Duchess of Somerset be not turned out, and nobody believes the Queen will ever part with her."[1]

A final effort was made to gain Marlborough and some of the Whig leaders. The peace policy must go through, but all personal issues could be smoothed over. The Queen sent for Somers, Halifax, and Cowper. Not one of the Whigs would yield; and Marlborough was bound to the Grand Alliance. When it was found that the Opposition meant to play their hand for what it was worth, Oxford resolved to match their stake—to match it and to overbid it.

Meanwhile the Whigs were preparing night and day for the meeting of Parliament. They now felt themselves strong enough to bid for the crowd. Gone were the days when Sacheverell had been the popular idol. His progress to Shropshire had played a great part in the election of 1710. Now the Whigs would have a procession of their own. November 17 was the anniversary of the accession of Queen Elizabeth, when good Protestants and good Englishmen were accustomed to demonstrate their abhorrence of Popery, persecution, and generally of tyrants and foreigners. A great midnight procession was arranged through London. A thousand pounds was readily forthcoming for the expense. The Duke of Kent, still remembering how he had been thrust from the office of Lord Chamberlain for the sake of Shrewsbury, was a stalwart contributor. Effigies were prepared of the Pope, the Devil, the Pretender, Sacheverell, and Oxford. These were to be escorted through the streets of the City and Westminster by a mighty concourse of Whigs, and burned in proper style.

There was no harm in this. It was but a part of the usual horse-play of English politics. But the Tory Ministers found it a serious addition to their anxieties. They too resolved to turn it to account. They filled the town with rumours that a terrible conspiracy of the Whigs was afoot to depose the Queen and set up an atheist republic. They declared that the rabble would be hounded on to attack the Lord Treasurer's house. They banned the procession, and seized the obnoxious effigies. For this purpose they called out a great body of troops—not only the Guards, but the militia. With many people they made themselves a laughing-stock, but good Tories lashed themselves into fury by contemplating the perils by which they were menaced. The important thing was the effect which fear would have upon the Queen. Up to a certain point it had acted unfavourably to Ministers. Whether beyond that point better results

[1] Swift, *Journal to Stella*, December 21, 1711.

could be secured was a matter on which Oxford thought himself the best judge.

Marlborough landed at Greenwich on the very day that the procession was forbidden. As soon as he heard about it he decided not to come into London. He therefore remained during November 18 at Greenwich Hospital, and waited on the Queen only the next day. Anne gave Oxford her own account of the interview. "The Duke of Marlborough came to me yesterday as soon as I had dined, made a great many of his usiall proffessions of duty and affection to me. He seemed dejected and very uneasy about this matter of the publick accounts, stayed neare an hour and saw nobody heare but my self."[1]

The account which St John received of this audience drew from him the following comment:

> The Duke of Marlborough I have seen once, but it has been in public, so that I am very much a stranger to his Grace's sentiments. I hear however that . . . in his conversation with the Queen he has spoken against what we are doing; in short *his fate hangs heavy upon him;* and he has of late pursued every council [*sic*] which was worst for him.[2]

But it was not only Marlborough upon whom Fate hung heavy. Three years would see a fuller unfolding. Marlborough was to pass the last decade of his life in his Oxfordshire home in honour and splendour. St John was to dwell attainted, in exile, cast off even by the Pretender to whom he had fled, and, with all his matchless abilities, never again in thirty years to speak in Parliament or hold office under the Crown.

At length the day of great debate arrived. Whatever the misgivings of Ministers, these bold and hardy men played their hand magnificently. In the Queen's Speech we discern the literary parade and polish of Bolingbroke, and also that comprehension of all the political values which he shared with Oxford. The Queen read her speech herself. Every statement, every guarding phrase, every word, should be studied by those who wish to bring back again to themselves the passions and artifices of those days in their pristine force. The whole story is there in all its truth, and with all its lies. Every appeal that the Government could make to its supporters, every affront profitable to offer to the other side, found a place in this adroit and provocative declaration. The first sentence contained what was meant to be a cut at Marlborough, and drew out the main lines of party conflict. "I am glad that I can now tell you that

[1] Bath Papers, *H.M.C.*, i, 217.　　　　[2] *Bolingbroke Correspondence*, i, 480.

notwithstanding the arts of those who delight in war, both place and time
are appointed for opening the Treaty of a general Peace." The second
affirmed what was not only false, but known to be false. "Our
allies, especially the States-General, whose interest I look upon as
inseparable from my own, have, by *their ready concurrence, expressed
their entire confidence in me*."[1] This was followed by assurances about
the Protestant religion, the Succession, and by a eulogy on the
blessings of Peace and Plenty in which all might concur.

After the Queen had read her Ministers' speech, which was also
what she meant and wished to say herself, she took an unusual
course. Laying aside her robes, she returned to the House *incognita*,
as the phrase went, and sat in a special box prepared for her. Thus
the Lords would debate her words in her presence, as though in
Cabinet. After the Ministerial proposal of the customary address of
thanks uprose—lank, sombre, cadaverous—Nottingham. High
Tory, High Churchman, trusted leader of the country clergy,
statesman who had now extorted the Occasional Conformity Bill
from the Whigs, carrying with him in that small, narrowly balanced
assembly eight or ten peers in his following, shaking the bishops
where they sat, Nottingham moved his amendment to add to the
Lords' reply the crucial words "that no peace could be safe or
honourable to Great Britain, or Europe, if Spain and the West
Indies were allotted to any branch of the house of Bourbon."

The Government speakers took the line that this was not the
moment to debate the issue of Spain, for which another day would
be found, but rather to thank the Queen for her Speech. Accordingly
they met Nottingham's amendment by moving what is called the
'previous question'—*i.e.* that "the question be not now put." On
this the Government was defeated by a single vote. The debate
which followed is fully recorded.[2] Marlborough sat an impressive
figure through its course. "He was at the head of the Whigs,"
wrote Oxford to Strafford a few days later. He was bound to speak
in any case, but chance gave him an advantage. Lord Anglesey, who
had hastened back with Ormonde from Ireland, spoke late, and said,
"We might have enjoyed that blessing [of peace] soon after the
battle of Ramillies, if the same had not been put off by some persons,
whose interest it was to prolong the war." This repeated the
malignant sentence of the Royal Speech, and fixed the charge directly
upon Marlborough by reference to Ramillies, of which certainly he
had no need to feel ashamed. He had never had much practice in

[1] *Parliamentary History*, vi, 1035.   [2] *Ibid.*, 1035–1046.

speaking, but he was always able to express himself with force and dignity. In those days the weightiest speeches were often the shortest. He rose and said:

"I think myself happy, in having an opportunity given me, of vindicating myself on so material a point, which my enemies have so loudly, and so unjustly laid to my charge before a person [here he bowed to the Queen where she sat] who, knowing the integrity of my heart, and the uprightness of my conduct, will not fail to do me justice. I refer myself to the Queen whether, while I have had the honour to serve her Majesty as general and plenipotentiary, I have not constantly informed her, and her council, of all the proposals of peace that have been made: and have not desired instructions for my conduct on that subject. I can declare with a safe conscience, in the presence of her Majesty, of the illustrious assembly, and of that Supreme Being, Who is infinitely above all the powers upon earth, and before Whom, according to the ordinary course of nature, I must soon appear, to give an account of my actions, that I was ever desirous of a safe, honourable and lasting peace; and that I always have been very far from any design of prolonging the war for my own private advantage, as my enemies have most falsely insinuated. My advanced age, and the many fatigues I have undergone, make me earnestly wish for retirement and repose, to think of eternity during the remainder of my days; the rather, because I have not the least motive to desire the continuance of the war, having been so generously rewarded, and had honours and riches heaped upon me, far beyond my desert and expectation, both by her Majesty and her Parliaments. I think myself bound to this public acknowledgment to her Majesty and my country, that I shall always be ready to serve them, if I can but crawl along, to obtain an honourable and lasting peace; but at the same time, I must take the liberty to declare, that I can, by no means [join in] the measures that have lately been taken to enter into a negotiation of peace with France, upon the foot of the seven preliminary articles; for I am of the same opinion with the rest of the Allies, that the safety and liberties of Europe would be in imminent danger, if Spain and the West Indies were left to the house of Bourbon; which, with all humility, and as I think myself in duty bound, I have declared to her Majesty, whom I had the honour to wait on, after my return from Holland: and therefore, I am for inserting in the address the clause offered by the Earl of Nottingham."[1]

It had been expected that this speech with its profound effect would finish the debate, but the division was not until the next day, and Cowper, Bishop Burnet, and Halifax flung in their discharges

[1] *Parliamentary History*, vi, 1037–8.

in Marlborough's support. Again the couriers for all Europe were waiting upon the result. They left with joyful reports from the ambassadors that the Government had been beaten. Upon the voting the next day Oxford and the Ministers, who had counted upon a majority of ten, found themselves defeated by twelve. In the sensation and stir which followed the voting of all these solid, tough, amazingly capable oligarchs, the Queen rose from her seat in her private box, and the high functionaries pressed forward to attend her. Would she, asked Shrewsbury, give her hand to him to be led from the House, or would she prefer the hereditary Lord Great Chamberlain, Lord Lindsey, to conduct her? "Neither of you," said Anne, and with a wave of her hand she beckoned the Duke of Somerset, still in a sense a Cabinet Minister, but who voted against the Government and the address to the Crown, and who, to quote Swift, "was louder than any in the House for the clause against peace," to lead her forth.

This proceeding staggered every one. According to the rules of this intense game, upon which, be it remembered, the fortunes not only of Britain but of Europe depended, such an event betokened the fall of the Ministry. Wharton, whose rake's character was often redeemed by his mordant wit, had been grimly placing both hands to his neck whenever Ministers rose to speak. Indeed, this was the level upon which politics seemed to stand. Swift remarked in these days genially to Oxford, "I shall have the advantage of you, for you will lose your head and I shall only be hanged, and so carry my body entire to the grave."

Oxford's account to Strafford shows his resentment.

No one of the Court or of the Church party, would enter into the debate about Spain and the Indies, except some few scattering words, desiring that a day on purpose might be appointed for that debate, but the General [Marlborough], putting himself at the head of the Whigs, and his other creatures who have promised to screen him from the discoveries the Commissioners of Accounts have made, would not consent to that; depending upon the money which is given for votes (which is wonderful) and the absence of the Scots Peers, whom the floods have hindered, they pressed the question, and upon the division, carried it, by one vote only; when fourteen of the Queen's servants, who have been kept in by the indulgence showed them [*i.e.*, moderate Whigs], voted that way, and others broke their words, not without sensible reasons; but this goes for nothing; the General and the foreign Ministers have united to blow up this; which will return upon themselves. . . . This proceeding will oblige the

Queen, without reserve, *to use the gentlemen of England*, and those who
are for her prerogative; it will draw marks of displeasure upon those
who have barefaced set up a standard against her.[1]

St John in his letter endorses the charge of bribery, in speaking
of the "cabals of the foreign ministers against the Queen, particularly
of Buys and Bothmar, and of the distribution of money, in which the
last of these was actually concerned." If there was not any truth in
the charge of corruption, it was no thanks to moral scruples on the
part of Bothmar. Though bribing Members of Parliament was carefully considered, the decision was adverse, principally because funds
were lacking.[2]

The sequel to the vote in the Lords marks again the power of the
House of Commons. Against them were the Lords, the allied princes
and sovereigns of Europe, the victorious Commander, all the interest
of the Whig Party, and, it must also be urged, the honour and faith
of Britain to a European League which she had long led. Up to this
point it had been believed that an adverse vote in the House of
Lords on a major issue of confidence would overthrow the Ministry.
But the Tory majority in the Commons cared nothing for all this.
They meant to beat the Whigs and stop the war, and their will
prevailed. Walpole, by ever-growing quality and performance now
become in fact leader of the Opposition in the Commons, had moved
the same amendment to the address on the same day. It was rejected
by 232 to 106. Thus those Ministers who had by backstairs intrigue
and royal favour insinuated themselves into office without due
Parliamentary support had now exchanged this questionable, precarious foundation for a Parliamentary majority, which proved to
them a rock around which all the tides, currents, and waves of
political life swirled in vain. The Queen's undermining gesture after
the division in the Lords revealed her to be wavering on the verge

---

[1] *Bolingbroke Correspondence*, ii, 49.

[2] "Baron Bothmar," wrote Eugene (January 24), "raised the question whether
I could not employ a sum of money for the winning over of certain Members of Parliament, to which end he handed to me a detailed list of fifteen of the same who were to
be brought over by these means. The cost of this amounted to £10,400, with the
condition, however, that payments should be continued every year so long as the war
lasted and this sum of money should be paid to them not otherwise than in the name
of the Elector; for these people reckoned that since he was in the future coming to
the Throne, they could accept and act with the money in this fashion with good conscience. I did not fail to point out to Baron Bothmar that such acceptance came easy
to his master as one who would alone benefit by it; that although I had certain funds
at my disposal, the proposed amount was so large and particularly the commitment
of the future that I for my part was not prepared to offer to do anything whatsoever."
(*Feldzüge*, Series II, v, App. 12.)

of reluctantly deserting Oxford, as she had blithely deserted Marl-borough and Godolphin. But the vote of the Commons restored her nerve. The Crown and Commons together could override all other forces in the realm. This was the fact which after some delay proved decisive.

The division in the Lords took place on December 11. Swift thought that all was over. There was talk of a Somerset-Notting-ham-Walpole Ministry. St John was for some days in the depths. Abigail lifted her hands in helpless consternation. But Oxford, more secretive and baffling than ever, never doubted that with the support of the House of Commons he could command the Queen, and that with the Queen he could beat all opponents. When Swift and others accosted him in these critical days he did not altogether conceal his nervousness, but he always said, "Poh! poh! it will be all right." And thus in his interest it fell out.

Upon Marlborough's speech and vote in the debate on Decem-ber 7, Oxford resolved to proceed to all possible extremities against him. The Lord Treasurer's confidant, Drummond, now in England advising Ministers, wrote that very night to tell Heinsius that Marlborough was to be dismissed from the command of the Army, and that the Duke of Ormonde would take his place.[1] Actually this was not effected for another three weeks. There were two reasons for the delay. The first was to gain time to blacken his character by bringing the report of the Commission of Accounts before the House of Commons. The second was the difficulty of convincing the Queen that she could break him publicly without danger to herself.

On December 15 the Commons called for the report of the Com-missioners of Public Accounts, and on the 17th for the documents on which it was based. This damaging indictment, the most hostile that lifelong foes and faction could devise, was circulated under obligations of secrecy to all the Members on the 21st. The Com-mons were then adjourned for Christmas until January 14. Thus Oxford and St John planned to have one side of the case only under the eyes of those who would judge it for three weeks before any answer could be made. At the same time they hoped that rumours of the gravity of the charges against Marlborough and of scandalous revelations would spread far and wide in an atmosphere of mystery and suspicion.

When these tactics were discerned Marlborough himself published in the *Daily Courant* the letter of justification which he had sent from

---

[1] Drummond to Heinsius, December 7/18, 1711; Weber, p. 140.

The Hague to the Commissioners. The letter made so considerable an impression in that buzzing, excited Court and in the London world that the Government thought it best to publish the report, which was accordingly done on December 29. By this the impression was created that there was a case of peculation disclosed against Marlborough, to which he had an answer, but that the matter must now go forward to a Parliamentary decision. As the Ministers were sure of their majority in the House of Commons, it was obvious that some formal censure upon the Duke was intended, and would be inflicted.

Thus armed, Oxford used all his influence with the Queen. He did not confine himself to the dismissal of Marlborough. He demanded from Anne a simultaneous extraordinary creation of peers, to be sure of a majority in both Houses. The two proposals went forward together. Anne was already inclined to the second. She had been induced to confer an English peerage—the Dukedom of Brandon—upon the Duke of Hamilton. The recipient of this honour claimed the right to sit and vote in the House of Lords as an English peer. No such case had previously arisen. The matter had been sharply debated on December 10. Where majorities were so narrow every vote counted, and the bringing in of Scottish nobles under English peerages was a serious party issue. The Whigs, using their majority, succeeded in defeating this proposal by a majority of five. The Queen, who listened to this debate as to others, took it as an attack upon her prerogative. No one had ever questioned before the power of the Crown to create peers, and the fact that a man was a Scottish peer already could be no disability to him. She therefore agreed to Oxford's plan to overcome the Whigs in the Lords by making twelve additional Tory peers at one stroke. This memorable decision was taken, and its consequences rolled in our history.

The Queen still shrank, though not on any grounds of compunction, from the step upon which the world waited of dismissing Marlborough while all preparations were still going forward for another campaign. Oxford and St John worked upon her fears. In this they went to all lengths in malice and mendacity. They warned the Queen that she had now reached the same parting of the ways which had confronted her grandfather over the execution of the great Lord Strafford. To Charles I's faithless surrender at that crisis they ascribed his ruin and slaughter. To desert chosen and trusted Ministers in the hour of stress was only to redouble all existing difficulties and dangers. The Ministers declared that for their protection not only must the extraordinary creation of peers be made, but that Marlborough should be publicly broken, and that the Duke and Duchess of Somerset should be dismissed from the Queen's presence. Unless this were done, and done at once, they could not guarantee that the Whigs, who were in fact, they suggested, the Cromwellians of sixty years before, with Marlborough at their head, would not thrust her from her throne, and deprive her of her liberty and perhaps of her life. Marlborough, they hinted, would reign in her stead.

These conversations, of which there is no direct record, are reflected in the account which St John wrote to Strafford, the great-nephew and now the namesake of the famous Ministerial victim of Parliamentary wrath.

> Now my pen is in my hand, I cannot forbear saying that I sincerely think this is the most important conjuncture that any Prince has been in since the time that your Excellency's ancestor was attacked by the faction which began with him, and did not conclude their tragedy even with his master. That King sealed the warrant of his own execution, when he gave up his servant, and our mistress has no way of securing herself, but exerting her power to protect her Ministers, who have rescued her from domestic bondage, and are going on to relieve her from foreign oppression. 1 will never deceive you, my lord—I would not do it even in the most pardonable, the most agreeable manner—by concealing real dangers, and giving false hopes; you may therefore depend upon me when I tell you that I think all safe, and the Queen determined.[1]

Such arguments prevailed upon the Queen. Actually Oxford and St John were both sure of her from the 12th of December onward. On their side they agreed to put up with the Somersets retaining office, and threw them in as a makeweight to impress upon Anne that she was "Queen indeed." Marlborough appeared at Court for the last time in Queen Anne's reign on December 30. He was still Captain-General and a member of the Cabinet. No Whigs attended, and he stood alone among his enemies. He was shunned by all. "Nobody hardly took notice of him," wrote Swift, who received an exulting account from his Ministerial friends.[2] Such a spectacle, though entirely in accordance with the character of such tribes, is none the less unpleasant. There he stood, stared at and scorned,

---

[1] December 15, 1711; *Bolingbroke Correspondence*, ii, 74.
[2] *Journal to Stella*, December 30, 1711.

with no protection but his composure and his fame. The Cabinet Council on the following day, with the Queen presiding, recorded the following decision:

> Being informed that an information against the Duke of Marlborough was laid before the House of Commons, by the commissioners of the public accounts, her Majesty thought fit to dismiss him from all his employments, that the matter might undergo an impartial investigation.[1]

That night Queen Anne wrote the letter to her servant and counsellor of thirty years, and the builder of her fame and power, which ended for ever all relations between them. We do not know the terms in which Oxford and Abigail prompted her to write, because Marlborough was so moved by reading them that he flung the letter in the fire.[2] His answer tells the tale.

Marlborough to the Queen

Jan. 1, 1712

I am very sensible of the honour your Majesty does me in dismissing me from your service by a letter of your own hand, though I find by it that my enemies have been able to prevail with your Majesty to do it in the manner that is most injurious to me. And if their malice and inveteracy against me had not been more powerful with them than the consideration of your Majesty's honour and justice, they would not have influenced you to impute the occasion of my dismission to a false and malicious insinuation, contrived by themselves, and made public when there was no opportunity for me to give in my answer, which they must needs be conscious would fully detect the falsehood and malice of their aspersions, and not leave them that handle for bringing your Majesty to such extremities against me.

But I am much more concerned at an expression in your Majesty's letter which seems to complain of the treatment you had met with. I know not how to understand that word, nor what construction to make of it. I know I have always endeavoured to serve your Majesty faithfully and zealously through a great many undeserved mortifications. But if your Majesty does intend, by that expression, to find fault with my not coming to the Cabinet Council, I am very free to acknowledge that my duty to your Majesty and country would not give me leave to join in the counsel of a man who, in my opinion, puts your Majesty upon all manner of extremities. And it is not my opinion only, but the opinion of all mankind, that the friendship of France must needs be destructive to your Majesty, there being in that Court a root of enmity irreconcilable to your Majesty's Government and the

[1] Coxe, vi, 152. [2] Marlborough Papers, *H.M.C.*, p. 16 (*b*).

religion of these kingdoms. I wish your Majesty may never find the want of so faithful a servant as I have always endeavoured to approve myself to you.[1]

The New Year's Day *Gazette* announced the creation of the twelve peers (among whom was Abigail's husband), and the dismissal of Marlborough from all his offices. The Captain-Generalcy, the command of the armies, and his command of the 1st Guards were given to Ormonde. Rivers, who had made a career for himself by his hostility to the chief to whom he owed his rise, became Master-General of the Ordnance. One can imagine the clatter of the factions, the flouts and snorts of the bewigged magnates, of their proud womenfolk, and their literary fighting cocks. They had no lack of fuel for quarrel or gossip, for taunt and rejoinder. But the most pregnant comment was made by Louis XIV: "The affair of displacing the Duke of Marlborough will do all for us we desire."

[1] Coxe, vi, 152–153.

Chapter Thirty

THE VISIT OF PRINCE EUGENE

1712—JANUARY–MARCH

THE impact of the Hanoverian manifesto on the London world was serious. Many Tories were shaken by it. Few there were who did not ask themselves how they would stand when this reproachful Prince was their King and master. If they held together it was for mutual protection. Thus the crisis lasted. The Hanover complaint met its counterblast in Swift's *Conduct of the Allies*. This cool and massive catalogue of all the shortcomings of the Dutch, of the Empire, of the German states, constitutes an indictment filled with just counts. Being primed with the secret information of Ministers, Swift was able to expose the recent neglect of the Dutch to accept their part in Marlborough's scheme of wintering on the frontiers. He represented the allies as a tribe of recreants and spongers who had failed in their engagements and thriven on the victories and subsidies of England. In many ways the booklet was inevitably a tribute to Marlborough. But nothing could have been better devised to create schism in the Grand Alliance at a time when the French were still in arms and the war in progress. No one can dispute many of Swift's reproaches against the allies. But the Dutch at least had an overwhelming rejoinder. Although a far smaller community, they had maintained continuously in Flanders double the army of England.[1] They had

---

[1] A comparative table showing the numbers of the English and Dutch forces in Flanders during the war is to be found among the Strafford Papers in the British Museum (Add. MSS. 22264, f. 67). It is as follows:

	ENGLISH	DUTCH
	(and troops in their pay)	
1702	40,671	110,242
1703 ⎫		
1704 ⎬	50,671	120,242
1705 ⎭		
1706	52,671	121,242
1707	52,790	112,271
	(not including 2600	(not including 12,850
	sent to Italy)	sent to Italy)
1708	58,228	112,271

repeatedly desired to make peace. They had been forced to continue the war by Queen Anne—for that was how they could state it—upon the strange cry, "No peace without Spain," which had arisen from English party politics. They had shed their blood for this to please England. Now they were insulted and about to be deserted. But to the Tories all this was the best October ale. They salved their conscience by abusing their allies.

For all his partisanship Swift was shocked at Marlborough's dismissal. "These are strong remedies," he wrote (December 31); "pray God the patient is able to bear them. The last Ministry people are utterly desperate."[1] And the next day:

> The Queen and Lord Treasurer mortally hate the Duke of Marlborough, and to that he owes his fall, more than to his other faults; . . . however it be, the world abroad will blame us. I confess my belief that he has not one good quality in the world beside that of a general, and even that I have heard denied by several great soldiers. But we have had constant success in arms while he commanded. Opinion is a mighty matter in war, and I doubt the French think it impossible to conquer an army that he leads, and our soldiers think the same; and how far even this step may encourage the French to play tricks with us, no man knows. I do not love to see personal resentment mix with public affairs.[2]

Marlborough bore his graceless treatment with dignity. Apart from the flash of anger which Anne's letter had extorted from him, his bearing was serene and even cheerful. He spoke and wrote as if his affairs belonged to less dismal chapters of history. He felt himself supported by the interest of one of the great parties in the island. He knew that he had the goodwill and confidence of the whole of the Grand Alliance. He was sure the armies he had led, and particularly the British troops, thought well of him. Although no man of spirit cares to have a task of which he is master taken from his hands while still unfinished, he was unfeignedly relieved not to have to risk his military fame and long-strained luck at the beck and direction of Oxford and St John and the rest of his Tory foes. The balm of ease, after ceaseless toil and thought, flowed out upon his soul. Everything in his behaviour shows that the

1709	67,699	122,458
1710	69,247	122,458
1711	65,197	122,458
	(not including 4500 sent to Canada)	

[1] Swift, *Journal to Stella*, December 31, 1711.   [2] *Ibid.*, January 1, 1712.

oft-repeated wishes of his home letters for peace and quiet were sincere. This certainly was his first reaction.

Hompesch, Albemarle, Grumbkow, Schulenburg, Wratislaw, Robethon, all sent expressions of their sorrow or their wrath at his treatment. To them he wrote variants of the same reply. To Hompesch: "You will have already learned my fate, that the Queen has thought well to relieve me of all my employments. I have just been sharply attacked again, but provided that this lets me get home to the country, as I have so long desired, I shall be content with my lot, and indeed shall owe a debt to my enemies."[1] To Albemarle (January 28, 1712): "I . . . am very sensible of the friendly part you take in what has happened to me. The Friday's mail will have brought you an account of what passed on Thursday in the House of Commons. If it procure me a quiet retirement—as you know it is what I have long wished for—I shall be easy in relation to my own fortunes."[2] To Schulenburg (February 22): "So long as my destiny brings no detriment to the public, I shall always be content with it, and I shall count myself more than happy in a retirement where I can reflect ripely on the vicissitudes of this world."[3] And to Robethon (February 22): "Nothing could console or encourage me more than the feelings which you convince me their Electoral Highnesses have towards me."[4] This last was certainly a solid assurance.

It is remarkable that, although while in power Marlborough complained often of his treatment in his secret letters to Godolphin and Sarah, and showed himself so sensitive to the attacks of the Press and the pamphleteers, once he became a private person without responsibility for national interests, no word is ever known to have escaped him of reproach or self-pity. Up till the moment when he was dismissed from his offices we have an enormous mass of correspondence both public and private relating to the war and politics. But henceforth, except for the few farewell letters which have been mentioned, he wrapped himself in almost complete silence. A handful of letters to Sarah in rare intervals of separation, a few on business, a few on politics (mostly to Hanover), one about the Woodstock election, and a few asking for some assistance or protection for faithful servants, or wounded or unemployed officers, are all that have been found during these years of exile and obloquy.

---

[1] *Dispatches*, v, 573. December 28 is the date given by Murray. Marlborough was not dismissed until December 31. It seems that the date has been wrongly transcribed.
[2] *Ibid.*, 574. [3] *Ibid.*, 577. [4] *Ibid.*, 578.

Cadogan's letter to an intimate friend throws an agreeable light on that fine soldier.

HAGUE
24 *Jan.*, 1712

*. . . Wee have Dear Judge in the course of our long acquaintance generally agreed in our opinions of men and things, this makes it easy for me to guess att the indisposition of mind you complain of, and the cause of it. I am deeply affected in the same Part, and by the same Distemper, and am so far gone in it, as not only to be tired of business and Employments, but even weary of Life itself. You know the bottome of my Heart, therefore can better imagine then I describe the afliction and weight of Grief I am under. I am uncertain and I assure you unconcerned as to what becomes of my self. I shall act according to the strictest rules of Gratitude Duty and Honour, in Relation to our Great unfortunate Benefactor, and my Zeal Inclination and desire to serve and suffer for him are equal to the vast obligations and Favours I have received from him. As to the rest, I shall doe as People att Sea when the violence of the storm obliges them to abandon the Helm and cut down the masts, I commit my self to the mercy of the winds and waves. Whether they force me to split on Rocks or whether my good Fortune may throw a Plank in my way to carry me ashore, I am grown so insensible or so resigned as to be no longer in Pain about.[1]

At home the Whigs raised the loudest outcry in their power, and their newspapers strove to contend with the cataract of libels and abuse which the Ministers unloosed. History was searched for a parallel to Marlborough's fall, and the name of Belisarius was now on many lips. Sarah asked Bishop Burnet to explain the allusion to her, and when he told her of the Emperor Justinian's ill-usage of his great general she inquired the cause. The Bishop is said to have replied, "It was because he had the broth of a wife." But perhaps this was only what he thought of afterwards.

The tale of Marlborough's disgrace astounded Europe. It was everywhere, even in France, regarded as a prodigy of ingratitude by a sovereign towards a servant and subject. It had been a strange experience for friend and foe to watch the Queen seemingly tearing down with both hands the whole structure of European policy, the building of which had been the task and glory of her reign. When she proceeded to strike at the architect of her own and her country's fame and power, amazement and scorn were universal.

In the armies which he had led the shock and grief at his

---

[1] Cadogan papers in private possession. "Dear Judge" is most probably the Deputy Judge Advocate, Henry Watkins.

dismissal were painful. General Kane in his *Memoirs* expressed the overwhelming opinion of British officers.

And now, after this great Man had reduced the Common Enemy of Europe to the last Extremity, had taken the last Barrier of his Kingdom, which lay now open to the Allies, his Army dispirited, and their Courage, and his whole Nation in a most miserable Condition; I say, after he had done all these great Things so much to the Honour of the British Nation, was he ignominiously traduc'd, and turn'd out of all Employ, and even forc'd to fly his Country, of which he had been so great an Ornament; and this done by a Set of vile profligate Men, who had insinuated themselves into the Favour of the weak Queen, and were at this Time carrying on a scandalous underhand Treaty with the Grand Enemy of Europe.[1]

This feeling was shared by every rank. All our fighting diarists and correspondents write in the same sense.

Lieutenant Gordon Halswell to Lieutenant Sinclair, Royal Scots Fusiliers

*They are doing strange things in Great Britain. They have over-turned our Captain-General, and meantime we are without a head. They have taken from him all his public Offices, but for what, we don't yet know. They have impeached him in Parliament for several things and yet we don't hear he can be found guilty. It may give a moral reflection upon the unsteddiness of human affairs—a great man and one of the greatest Generals and subjects in the world, stript of his glory in a moment when neither his friends nor foes expected it.[2]

Corporal Matthew Bishop was consternated.

In 1711/12, hearing that our brave Duke of Marlborough was gone to England, I began to be under some Apprehension that he would not return; therefore I concluded the Neck of the War was broke, and that I should be disappointed of the Pleasure of seeing Paris that Year; though we were once in Hopes of arriving to that Honour, had not our Conductor been detained in England. . . . Even none could avoid giving him their Praise; and he was worthy of all, for his good Discipline and good Order; and the greatest Blessing of all, his Success in all his Attempts, which was owing to his profound Knowledge in sending proper Emissaries to observe the Enemy's Motions. *Oh!* said I, *must we part from such a Man, whose Fame has spread throughout all the World?*

On hearing that it was confirmed that he was no longer to command, it terrified my Soul to such a Degree, that I could not rest Night or Day.[3]

[1] Kane, pp. 101–102.   [2] Halswell letters in private possession.
[3] Bishop, pp. 235–236.

The corporal's emotions led him into poetry, and he gave vent to the following lines—often quoted, though their author is usually forgotten.

> God and a Soldier Men alike adore,
> When at the Brink of Danger, not before;
> The Danger past, alike are both requited,
> God is forgot, and the brave Soldier slighted.[1]

But a friend was approaching. Charles III had quitted Spain in October, and assumed his duties as the Emperor Charles VI. At Milan he heard of the French peace preliminaries, and wrote his protest at once to Queen Anne. It was not until he reached Innsbruck a week later, and met his Council of Regency, including Prince Eugene and Wratislaw, that he learned of the dismissal of Gallas. This was regarded by all as a great affront, but opinions were divided as to how it should be met. Eugene urged that no other Ambassador should be sent to London until full amends had been made. But the opposite counsels prevailed, and after two days' discussion the Emperor commanded Eugene himself to go to England and try to restore his relations with Queen Anne. This was, in fact, the plan which the luckless Gallas had urged during the whole summer. Like most of the decisions of the Holy Roman Empire, it was adopted too late. Hoffmann was instructed by courier to prepare the English Court for the impending visit of Prince Eugene.

No guest could have been more unwelcome to Harley and St John than the famous warrior. They knew that his comradeship with Marlborough was proof against all shocks. They were sure that he would cross-question them about their peace negotiations. It was obvious, moreover, that his arrival would comfort and fortify the Whigs. They therefore without delay and by every channel repeatedly tried to prevent his coming. St John sent a stream of letters to Strafford at The Hague to turn him back, and to enlist the Dutch in this task. "Your Excellency is to discourage as much as possible this Prince from coming over. . . . It is high time to put a stop to this foreign influence on British councils; and we must either emancipate ourselves now, or be for ever slaves."[2]

Eugene floated down the Rhine and reached The Hague in the middle of December. Here Strafford delivered his discouragements. Heinsius, completely cowed by the new English attitude, advised the Prince against the visit. A message was given him from St John that, owing to the ferment in men's minds in England, the

---

[1] Bishop, p. 266.   [2] *Bolingbroke Correspondence*, ii, 52.

Government could not be answerable for his safety. Eugene, impelled by further orders from the Emperor, replied by asking for a yacht and a frigate for a convoy. The request was presented to the Cabinet by Hoffmann. At first this was considered as a courtesy which could not be refused. But as the anxieties of Ministers grew their manners declined. Eventually they decided to refuse all assistance. Fresh instructions were sent to Strafford, who was also a member of the Admiralty Board, to deny Eugene all transport or protection on the seas. But this order took some time to reach The Hague.

Eugene's contacts with Strafford were not agreeable. The Prince regarded him with unconcealed suspicion. The preparations and plans for the campaign were at that time under discussion at The Hague. In a conference at which Strafford was present Eugene remarked blandly that he had indeed much to say about military matters, but he could not speak of them in the presence of the English Ambassador, because he did not know whether he was an Englishman or a Frenchman. No more scathing taunt could be conceived. Yet if the conference could have seen the terms upon which Torcy and St John had been corresponding they could not have impugned its justice. For instance, Torcy wrote to Gaultier that Oxford and St John were to be assured in the name of the King that all the manœuvres employed by *the common enemies* were incapable of upsetting his resolves. St John accepted this expression of "the common enemies" as applied to all the allies of England who were unwilling to follow his lead. "It is the desire of the ill-mentioned," he wrote to Torcy, "to arouse this mistrust both among us and everywhere else, but I am not worrying on that account, because it merely depends upon the All-Christian King to render all their efforts vain."[1] In fact, Oxford and St John, dominated by their party struggle, now looked upon the French as friends, and upon their allies, by whose side they were standing in the field, as foes.

Strafford had sustained another rebuff at this time. When he made his statement upon the French preliminaries to the allied ambassadors and secret Deputies of the States-General gathered at The Hague, the Imperial Minister, Baron Heems, audaciously transformed guesses into assertion: "I put it to Lord Strafford that a treaty has already been signed between Great Britain and France. I can tell him the day and the hour on which it was signed. I can tell him the room, how many candles there were burning, how many

---

[1] October 22; *Bolingbroke Correspondence*, i, 454.

seals there were on the document, what was the colour of the wax and of the threads whereby the sheets were bound together."[1] Strafford was completely disconcerted. He remained silent before the company under these tremendous assertions.

Eugene pressed for transport and convoy to England. Strafford, not having received the latest Cabinet decision, left it to the captain of the frigate, to whom he sent an ambiguous note. The captain complied with alacrity; but the voyage was severe. For more than a week Eugene tossed about between Flushing and Harwich, buffeted by the waves and baffled by the winds. This was certainly the longest sea journey which this great man ever endured. The tale of his coming had outstripped him. When he reached Harwich he was told that all the towns between that port and London were crowded with people who had gathered from the countryside to welcome him and to look at him. Here we see with what attention and passion our ancestors followed the great events and heroic figures of their age. They were tough, but they nursed a strong sentiment. News travelled fast and far, and people formed their own opinions.

Eugene also learned of Marlborough's dismissal from all his offices. He was resolved to be a model of discretion; so, instead of landing at Harwich, he coasted round to the Thames. Up the Thames he sailed in the yacht (which the scholarly St John spelt as badly as Marlborough—"yatch" against "yahct"). He was boarded by one of Marlborough's officers, and later by Drummond from the Court. "I had to tell him," reported Eugene to the Emperor,

> that since it was known all over the world what a firm and intimate friendship I had fostered with the Duke of Marlborough, now finding him in misfortune, I could not do otherwise than uphold my friendship with him, lest the world should say, and I leave it as an evil echo after me, that I deserted and abandoned a friend in his hour of sorrow and stress when fortune had forsaken him.[2]

He had thought of landing at Greenwich, but there was a large gathering awaiting him there. He hoped to land at the Tower, but the wharf was black with people; so he came on with the tide as far as the Whitehall Stairs, where no one expected him. He took "the first cab he saw," and drove to Leicester House, the residence of the departed Gallas, which was still maintained to receive him. At Leicester House Marlborough was the first to visit him. They

---

[1] Lamberty, vi, 731.   [2] *Feldzüge*, Series II, v, App., 14.

were long together. The next morning he was to see the Queen. St John had been very ready to "treat him *chère entière*."[1] No doubt he would gladly have taken him round those houses of revelry which he used to frequent in company with the late lamented Guiscard. Such entertainment would certainly not have appealed to Eugene. But at least the Secretary of State conducted him in his own carriage to the Queen.

> She gave me audience in her Cabinet, and I found her somewhat embarrassed and aloof. I explained to her briefly my mission, and finally asked her with which Minister I should converse. I noticed, however, that she must have been primed beforehand, for she gave me as answer that she had resolved that the business already known to me by secret information should be dealt with only in Holland, and she could not depart from this.[2]

The Prince observed that there were other matters besides, and especially the restoring of a perfect harmony between her Majesty and the Emperor. Anne was now being drawn beyond the limits of her Ministerial advice; so she said that her health would not enable her to see much of him, but her Ministers, meaning Oxford and St John, would hear all he had to say.

Eugene was two months in England. He paid several friendly visits to Ormonde at Richmond in the interests of the impending campaign, but his interviews with Ministers were rare. None visited him formally. They contrived to prevent the banquet which the City of London had wished to hold in his honour.[3] But nothing could deprive him of the admiration of all classes and both parties. His anterooms in Leicester House were so crowded with notables, some of whom came a hundred miles to see him, that the floors cracked under their weight. Crowds surrounded the house continuously, and followed him cheering when he walked abroad "in modest dress, very thoughtful or *rêveur*," with "a way to toss his head on the right and the left to be seen of everybody." When he went to the Opera with Marlborough the spectacle of "those venerable and respectfull men sitting in a box together" attracted the eyes of the audience much more than the actors. Even the "rabble which fills the upper gallery, and has always been very rude, stamping, bawling, singing, hissing and the like . . . when he came into his box gave three huzzas, were very silent during the action, and when the Prince went, they gave him three huzzas again." On this

---

[1] *Bolingbroke Correspondence*, ii, 56.   [2] *Feldzüge*, Series II, v, App., 14.
[3] Abel Boyer, *Annals* (1712), pp. 338–339.

Marlborough assured him that it was an honour as good "as a voley of canon or of small shot in others."[1]

Portland, the son of King William's confidant, gave a dinner in his new dining-hall "finished and furnished a purpose," at which Marlborough, Devonshire, Godolphin, Sunderland, Townshend, and several ambassadors were present, and at which "no servant in livery was suffer'd to come and wayt, all that wayted were gentlemen that offer'd themselves, to have an occasion to see the feast." The repast, which began at six, and was held to beat all records both for quality and quantity, was consumed to the ceaseless sound of trumpets and kettledrums, and the entertainment, followed by a ball, continued till five o'clock the next morning. Apparently neither Eugene nor Marlborough would dance. "I don't thinck," writes Portland's anonymous correspondent, "they could kick their heels like Nero or Louis XIV, . . . tho both have very handsomly kicked the Grand Monarch at the great balls of Blenheim, Ramelies, Turin and Blaregnies."[2]

The only important official conference was at Dartmouth's office on January 31. Eugene raised three points: the plan for the war in Spain, whether the Empire should attend the conference, and, thirdly, Gallas. On this last his instructions were humble. The Emperor could not withdraw an ambassador without either a breach or a formal leave-taking. At least this should be regularized by letter. In due course the Ministers replied that the Spanish campaign could only be settled at The Hague; that, of course, all the Allies should come to Utrecht; and as for Gallas, the Queen would not receive his letter. This, then, was all that resulted from the visit of Prince Eugene, which in the previous autumn might have changed the march of events.

Shortly after his arrival tidings had come from Spain. Starhemberg, who had been reputed to be finished, had won a considerable action under the walls of Cardona. The enemy had been repulsed with the loss of his whole artillery. This news made a stir. To Oxford and St John it was most unwelcome. These Ministers, in whose eyes the Allies were "the common enemy," necessarily regarded a British and allied victory as a disaster. The Tory Party, while loyal to their leaders, had never reconciled themselves to the abandonment of the Spanish aim and catchword. Now it appeared the cause was not lost; perhaps we were winning after all. It was in

---

[1] *Willem III en Portland* (edited by Japikse, 1928), ii, 713.
[2] *Ibid.*, 716.

this unfavourable atmosphere that the two ruling Ministers approached the formidable trial of strength involved in charging first Walpole and then Marlborough with peculation. This episode of domestic politics will be reserved for the next chapter. Both before and after it they laboured to raise the "ferment" they affected to deplore to the highest pitch.

During the month of February rumours ran rife in London that Prince Eugene and Marlborough were engaged in a plot to depose the Queen. Torcy gravely records in his memoirs how Eugene was to set London on fire, while Marlborough seized the person of the Queen. He safeguarded himself by the words, "It may be that those who tell these tales were ill-informed." This monstrous story was spread about the capital, and every effort was made by the Government to create a mood of panic which should react in their favour, both upon their majority in the Commons and still more upon the nerves of Anne. At that time there was a set of rowdy, well-born young men who, reviving the memories of the Mohawks whose visit in a previous year has been mentioned, called themselves the Mohocks. These pampered ruffians indulged in various nocturnal escapades; some harmless pranks, others veritable outrages on public decency and order. This was all brought in to create the impression that anarchy and revolution were near. The guards about Kensington Palace were doubled, and cavalry posts were mounted at various points. Harley inflamed his colleagues by reading to them two alleged dispatches of Eugene's, which he said he had intercepted in the post. In these were reported conversations which the Prince was said to have had with Marlborough and Bothmar, replete with references to deeds of violence. The guilty Ministers should, it was said, be 'de-Witted'—a well-understood reference to the lynching of the de Witts at The Hague in 1672. "The destruction of a few worthless fellows now at the helm ought not to stand in competition with the Common Cause. . . . Yea, Bothmar said smiling that it were better that all at the helm were blown up in the air than that should suffer." However, it was added, Count Sinzendorff had written to Prince Eugene "that in his opinion it would not be proper for him to stay here to see the execution of it."[1] Such were the cruder versions spread about the town of what the Lord Treasurer unfolded to the Cabinet.

There was, of course, no shred of truth in all this rubbish. Eugene's reports to the Emperor are preserved in the archives at

---

[1] *Bolingbroke Correspondence*, ii, 147–148.

Vienna, and are printed in the *Feldzüge*. They comprise dispatches written on the dates mentioned to the Cabinet by Oxford. They deal very candidly with English affairs and statesmen, but there is nothing to lend the slightest colour to the rumours of a revolutionary design. At this time the Government had made a speciality of opening the diplomatic correspondence leaving England, and the Lord Treasurer may well have had one of Eugene's dispatches before him and doctored it to the form he required for his purposes. Eugene found much difficulty in communicating with Vienna through The Hague. Queen Anne's Ministers had a much shorter route through the enemy's lines. "The worst and greatest contretemps," wrote Eugene (January, 29) "is that the Ministry receive almost daily letters *via* Calais; thus they can know exactly what is happening at the Congress, while I, all the ambassadors, and the good party must remain robbed of news by contrary winds."[1]

The lie was given to all this chatter and buzz of horrible plots to stimulate the faithful and delude the vulgar when the Queen summoned Eugene to her presence on her birthday, and presented him with a diamond-hilted sword valued at £4000. If Ministerial beliefs had been on a par with their whisperings they must have expected that he would draw it and plunge it into her breast. Nothing of the kind occurred. On the contrary, during his last days in England Oxford made remarkable overtures to Eugene. His methods were characteristic. He got into touch with him through a friend who knew a friend of the Prince's, and by this devious channel arranged that he should visit Eugene up his backstairs in the dark of the night. His demeanour was most cordial, his two-hour talk discursive. But Harley had, as usual, a clear purpose behind his copious verbiage. He did not mean to make a personal enemy of Eugene, or let him leave the country with every contact broken. He exacted from the Prince a return visit. It was arranged with similar precautions, and proved equally sterile. "I entered his own house in the deepest secrecy," wrote Eugene, "through a particular door which is usually kept locked. We talked together confidentially but as there is nothing material to report, I need not go into details."[2]

Two of Eugene's rejoinders during his visit to London which went the rounds and have become well known are typical of the attitude which he consistently adopted. Burnet records that, he having mentioned to the Prince the remark of a Minister that

---

[1] *Feldzüge*, Series II, v, App., 46.   [2] *Ibid.*, 87.

Marlborough had "perhaps been once fortunate," Eugene replied, "No greater tribute could be given him, since he was always successful."[1] When at a dinner Oxford toasted him as "the greatest general of the age," "If that be true," said Eugene, "I owe it to your lordship." Thus always did the famous Prince and warrior proclaim his friendship and admiration for his comrade of so many glorious days.

[1] Burnet, vi, 103.

Chapter Thirty-one

THE PECULATION CHARGE

1712—JANUARY

D URING Prince Eugene's visit the Government continued their campaign of detraction against the late
Ministry, and above all against Marlborough. Next in
their animosity and fear stood Walpole. They knew they
had struck down the great man of their day. It was only after some
years that Harley and St John realized that they had incurred the
implacable vengeance of the great man of the future.

The first report of the Commission of Accounts had been presented to Parliament before the Christmas adjournment. The Commissioners were still at their task. Evidence was tendered to them
which revealed an impropriety committed by Walpole a year
earlier, when he was Secretary-at-War. In a contract for forage
not made by him but for which he was responsible two sums of
£500 had been paid to one of his personal friends, a certain Robert
Mann. There was no suggestion that Walpole himself had benefited
by the money. He had merely endorsed the bills and sent them to
Mann. The explanation was sufficient to clear Walpole of personal
corruption; but it showed a want of delicacy and propriety against
which public servants would nowadays be required to keep especially
on their guard.

On the other hand, the facts were also capable of being presented
in a manner most injurious to the competent, vigorous Leader of
the Opposition, who was every day hitting the Government hard
in the House of Commons, and whose able pamphlet *The £35,000,000
Accounted For* had demolished their case against their predecessors.[1]
The Commissioners hastened to lay the facts before their party
friends. Ministers did not decide their course without testing
the opinion of their supporters. In this Bromley, the Speaker, who
was, of course, elected as a partisan, was adviser. He convened a
party meeting, and laid the facts before it. Many of the members

---

[1] Walpole's two pamphlets in defence of Whig financial administration are published
in Boyer's *Annals*, p. 25.

did not think the case very good, and deemed it unfair to use it against the Leader of the Opposition. This opinion manifested itself strongly as the party discussion proceeded. But Bromley clinched matters by saying bluntly that unless Walpole were got out of the way it would not be possible for the Government to carry through their business. His knowledge was too great, his attacks too damaging. His exclusion was, he said, the *unum necessarium*. On this appeal it was decided to go to all lengths against Walpole.

Accordingly, on January 17 Walpole was heard in his defence, and thereafter it was moved that he was "guilty of a high breach of trust and notorious corruption." An amendment was proposed to leave out the words "notorious corruption." The House rejected this by 207 votes to 155. It was then moved to commit him to the Tower during the pleasure of the House. On this the Opposition moved that the House should adjourn. The Government majority fell to only twelve. A further motion "that the said Robert Walpole be for the said offence expelled from this House" was carried by twenty-two. These figures tell their own tale. A majority of twelve on the crucial division was a poor showing for a Government which had a normal majority of between 100 and 150. Walpole was accordingly arrested and sent to the Tower. His seat was declared vacant, and his mouth was stopped. To keep it stopped as long as possible in Parliament, the House was led to proceed by successive adjournments and did not technically rise until July. Walpole was thus imprisoned for nearly five months in the Tower.

His constituents stood by their member, and he was returned again while still in custody. Defoe, who had a year earlier visited Norfolk, mentions the strength of his influence in the Eastern counties: "Here I am in a land," he had reported, "where the Queen's writ does not run, but only that of King Walpole." The House refused to admit Walpole on his re-election, and declared it void. They maintained their expulsion order during the whole Parliament. This was a great convenience to the Government. It also provided the precedents which were used in the Wilkes case fifty years later. Few even in the Tory Party considered Walpole at all affected in his honour. He was visited not only by the leading Whigs, and of course by Marlborough, but also by many other persons of consequence. His room in the Tower was more like the scene of a levée than a prison. The Ministers had gained their advantage in excluding their most dangerous antagonist from the House of Commons, but they were deeply concerned by the lack of support they had received from their own followers upon the critical division. It was resolved to take much greater care on the next occasion.

This was, of course, their attack upon Marlborough. Oxford and St John were by now alive to the difficulties of branding the champion of Britain in her age of glorious advance. For eight years in succession the House had passed its resolutions of thanks by overwhelming majorities and often unanimously. Every session delegations of its members had waited upon him to express their admiration and gratitude for his services. It was a sharp turn now, after he had been stripped of all office and was a private person, to inflict upon him by a purely party vote an insulting censure which sought to rank him with criminals.

There was another difficulty which affected the Cabinet internally. Brydges, Paymaster and Accountant-General, was, like most of the governing functionaries of that day, a Member of Parliament. No one could speak with greater authority on the issue. He had, indeed, a considerable personal responsibility. He had been attacked the year before in the first flush of the Tory election success. He had been defended by St John, now Leader of the Commons. St John, against the immediate interests of his party and for the sake of doing him justice or other motives, had vindicated Brydges, and pricked the bubble of "the £35,000,000 unaccounted for." Brydges was therefore in an unassailable position. He was still Paymaster. He was working daily with Ministers. He let them know that he would justify Marlborough. It was not easy to foresee what the effect of his intervention would be.

There was nothing for it but, in Oxford's phrase, "to use the gentlemen of England." The question was how far these gentlemen would go. On the one hand, it was believed that by better whipping a good majority could be obtained. On the other, there was a desire to reach some compromise. Mr Speaker Bromley, atcing now very much as his predecessor Oxford had done in previous Parliaments, measured up the forces. Proposals were made to Marlborough's friends in the House that he should acquiesce in the report of the Commission, in which case the censures would be the mildest possible. On the other hand, if he resolved to defend himself and to oppose the Government it was hinted that severe measures would be taken. The 'gentlemen' would be used with vigour. Impeachment was their only weapon, for the Commons could not commit a peer to prison. That there was talk of impeachment is evident. Bromley's letter to Oxford reveals these preliminary discussions.

January 21, 1711

I find nothing will satisfy, nor be taken to be falling gently, that shall go farther than to declare that in consideration of the General's great services the House does not think fit to proceed upon the report. Voting the money on the contract for bread no perquisites, and that the 2½ per cent. is public money and ought to be accounted for, is what he will not hear of; for that is putting him into the power of his enemies, *and he had rather lose his head.* This shews he has great confidence in the solicitations that have been made, and I presume to acquaint your Lordship with it that due care (*better care than last Thursday*) may be taken to oblige the attendance of some, and to engage others on this occasion.[1]

There were personal negotiations.

Brydges to Marlborough

January 10, 1712

★I was this morning with Mr St Iohn whom I found concern'd upon his having heard Yr Grace intended to push for a Vote of Iustification in Parl. He thought it wd be looked upon as an attacking ye Ministry, wch wd engage many, who wd otherwise not appear against you to espouse their interest, & I find by him it will be very difficult to prevent a vote's being carried that ye 2½ pr ct be deem'd publick money, Yr Grace having in effect, he sayd, own'd it in your letter to ye Commissrs to be such. He will have ye honour to discourse you upon it himself, & says if he does not see Yr Grace at his house to morrow before six in ye evening he'l wait upon you at yours.

Mr Sweet has sent me a letter to deliver the Commissioners of Accots wch I'l beg leave to show Y. G. first. The substance of it is that ye 2½ was left in his hands for Y. G. & that he knows nothing of any warrant or authority for deducting it, but took it always to be a free gift of yr troops.[2]

Evidently Marlborough was offered the resolutions which were afterwards passed by the House, with the threat of far worse if he resisted them. He refused point-blank. He was perhaps willing that the House should take note of the report and decline to act upon it because of his previous services. Nothing less than this would satisfy him. He would "rather lose his head." Swift, who was in the swim with St John, wrote to Stella:

[1] Portland Papers, *H.M.C.*, v, 139.
[2] Stowe, 57, vol. vi, pp. 152–153; Huntington Library, California.

The Minister's design is, that the Duke of Marlborough shall be censured as gently as possible, provided his friends will not make nead to defend him, but if they do, it may end in some severer votes. A gentleman, who was just now with him, tells me he is much cast down, and fallen away; but he is positive, if he has but ten friends in the House, that they shall defend him to the utmost, and endeavour to prevent the least censure upon him, which I think cannot be, since the bribery is manifest. Sir Solomon Medina paid him six thousand pounds a year to have the employment of providing bread for the army, and the Duke owns it in his letter to the Commissioners of Accounts.[1]

Somers, under King William, when impeached for his share in the Partition Treaties of 1700, had appeared at the bar of the Commons, and by his eloquence and his facts had converted the assembly. Marlborough had been inclined to follow this precedent, but his friends, including certainly Godolphin, dissuaded him. Passions ran too high. The life of the Government was at stake. Every effort had been made to bring up their reserves. He would only court a greater humiliation by pleading in person before a tribunal bound in self-preservation to proclaim the kind of view which Swift had expressed. He therefore, with Godolphin's assistance, prepared a statement covering every point in the charges in the Commissioners' report. This was no doubt in the hands of his friends, but was not published till some time after.

As this matter affects Marlborough so deeply it is better to record its principal features in his own words:

The first Article in the Report is founded upon the deposition of Sir Solomon de Medina, by which you are informed of a yearly sum paid by him and his predecessor, contractors for Bread and Bread-waggons, to myself. This payment in my letter I have called a perquisite of the general or commander-in-chief in the Low Countries; and it has been constantly applied to one of the most important parts of the service there, I mean the procuring intelligence, and other secret service. . . .

The commissioners are pleased to observe that these sums cannot be esteemed legal perquisites because they do not find them claimed or received by any other English general in the Low Countries. But I must take leave to affirm to this house, that this perquisite or payment has been allowed to the general or commander in chief in the Low Countries both before and ever since the Revolution, to enable him to carry on such secret services. The like allowance was made to

[1] *Journal to Stella*, January 23.

prince Waldeck, whilst he was general of the Dutch army in Flanders; it was made during the last war as well as this. . . .

The Report may have observed very rightly, that, by the strictest inquiry the commissioners could make, they cannot find that any English general ever received this perquisite. But I presume to say, the reason is that there was never any other English general besides mysel who was commander-in-chief in the Low Countries. I crave leave then to say, that this observation in the Report, was occasioned through want of due information in the usage of the army. In receiving this as an established and known perquisite, I have followed and kept up that usage, which I found in the army, when I first entered upon that service; and upon this ground alone I hope that this House will not think that I was unwarranted in taking it.

. . . This allowance to the general can have no influence upon the contract itself, which is actually made and signed at the Treasury, and the price regulated by what the States have agreed to pay for the bread for their forces. I appeal to all the officers who have served with me in Flanders, whether the forces in her majesty's pay have not all along had as much, and as good bread as those of the States, and at the same prices; which everybody will believe to be the lowest that considers the frugal economy of the States, and the small pay of their troops. And therefore I may safely conclude, that if the English have had their bread as cheap as the Dutch, they have had it as cheap as was possible. Nor indeed can it be imagined to be otherwise; for the very supposition of two different prices, paid by different troops in the same army, for the same quantity of bread, would occasion a mutiny. But this whole affair has been so regulated, and there has been so little occasion for complaint, that it is well known our army in Flanders has been duly supplied with bread during the whole war, and has received it with an exactness that will be hardly thought consistent with the secrecy, and suddenness of some of the motions [movements] that have been made.

Now as to the second Article in the Report allow me to observe to you, that it has arisen only from the information I myself gave the commissioners by my letter to them; this matter having relation to that part of the service to which the sums in the former article have been applied; that the Commissioners might have a true state of it, I chose to insert a short Account of it in my letter to them. If I did this voluntarily out of duty to the public, I hope I shall be thought to have given you information upon a certain belief, and I was altogether blameless in the part I have had in it. It will be necessary that I trouble the House with an Account of the time and occasion whence this payment of $2\frac{1}{2}$ per cent. by the foreign troops, commenced. During the last war, the allowances by parliament for the contingencies of the army, of which that of secret service is the principal, was

£50,000 per ann. But this allowance fell so far short of the expense on that head, that upon the prospect of this war's breaking out, the late king assured him [calculated], that this last part of the service never cost him less than £70,000 per ann. However, the allowance of parliament for the whole contingent service during this war has been but £10,000 per annum, £3000 of which or thereabouts has generally gone for other contingencies than that of intelligence. The late king, being unwilling to come to parliament for more money, on that head of the service, proposed this allowance from the foreign troops, as an expedient to assist that part of the service, and commanded me to make the proposition to them; which I did accordingly, and it was readily consented to. By this means a new fund of about £15,000 per annum was provided for carrying on the secret service, without any expense to the public, or grievance to the troops from whom the allowance was made. . . .

This expedient being formed in the manner I have shewn her majesty was pleased to approve it by her warrant, . . . [which] was counter-signed by the secretary of state whose province it belonged to, as the only proper officer. . . .

The true design of this deduction being to supply the secret service, gentlemen, I hope you will observe, that this, together with the sum on the former article of the allowance by parliament, when put together, doth fall short of the allowance given by parliament in the last war upon this head. . . .

I cannot suppose that I need to say how essential a part of the service this is, that no war can be conducted successfully, without early and good intelligence, and that such advices cannot be had but at a very great expense. Nobody can be ignorant of this, that knows anything of secret correspondence or considers the numbers of persons that must be employed in it, the great hazard they undergo, the variety of places in which the correspondence must be kept, and the constant necessity there is of supporting and feeding this service; not to mention some extraordinary expenses of a higher nature, which ought only to be hinted at. And I affirm, that whatever sums have been received on this account, have been constantly employed in procuring intelligence, in keeping correspondence, and other secret service. . . . And though the merit of our successes should be least of all attributed to the general, the many successful actions, such as have surpassed our own hopes, or the apprehensions of the enemy, in this present war in Flanders, to which our constant good intelligence has greatly contributed, must convince every gentleman, that such advices have been obtained and consequently that this money has been rightly applied. . . .

Having given this full and faithful account of the rise and use of this deduction, it must, I flatter myself, appear to everybody that hears me, to have been a real service, as well as saving of money to the public. And though honour is due to the memory of the late king, who formed this expedient, and to her majesty, who approved of it, by her warrant, I cannot, upon this ground, apprehend any imputation to myself, who have pursued this, so much to the advantage of my country. . . .

Upon the whole matter, I cannot but hope this House will find reason to be satisfied with this part of my conduct; and I think it no ill service, that so necessary and important a part of the war, and which has turned to so good an account, has been managed with so little expense to the public; and I may, with the greatest certainty, assure them that all other parts of the service have been carried on with all the good husbandry that was possible. And I believe I may venture to affirm that I have in the article for Secret Services saved the government near four times the sum this deduction amounts to. Which I must reckon so much money saved to the public.[1]

The debate was fierce and solemn. The Members felt that in striking at Marlborough they were striking at the new greatness of their country. On the other hand, what would happen to their party if they did not strike home? But the defence was solid. Sir John Germaine, speaking from the bar, declared that he had served in the Low Countries under Prince Waldeck, and that that General had, as Marlborough declared, received the same perquisites and allowances for the purpose of military intelligence and Secret Service. Sir Charles Hedges, the Tory Secretary of State, who ten years before had countersigned the Queen's warrant under which Marlborough received the $2\frac{1}{2}$ per cent., stood by his action and absolved the former Commander-in-Chief of all impropriety. There was no dispute about the warrant. Then up rose Brydges. No report of his speech is contained in the *Parliamentary History*, but Hoffmann's dispatch, unearthed by Klopp, shows that Brydges was particularly vigorous in emphasizing that the British people owed the information services to the careful expenditure of this money, and in consequence the Army had never been surprised. Brydges dared to say "that the proceedings were a scandal to the British people."[2]

On the other side St John, Wyndham, Hanmer, and Edward Harley urged the infliction of the censure. Not only Whigs, but

[1] *Parliamentary History*, vi, 1088.
[2] Hoffmann, February 5; Klopp, xiv, 254. "Marlborough's friends," reported Hoffmann, "are of the opinion that he cannot be got at by lawful means, and that the whole charge against him is only intended to blacken him in the eyes of the nation and justify his removal."

moderate Tories spoke on Marlborough's side. The House was full to overflowing. No fewer than 435 Members took part in the division, and it was carried by a majority of 276 against 165 that "the taking of several sums of money annually by the Duke of Marlborough from the contractor for foraging the bread and bread wagons in the Low Countries was unwarrantable and illegal." The Government, refusing a motion for adjournment which was moved by the Opposition, also carried "that the deduction of 2½ per cent. from the pay of the foreign troops in her Majesty's service is public money, and ought to be accounted for." On the two heads the sums involved were computed to amount to between £170,000 and £250,000. It remains only to be mentioned that Cardonnel's petty perquisite of 500 ducats, for which there was no excuse but custom, was made the ground for expelling him from the House, and that Mr Sweet, although it was proved that his deduction of 1 per cent. was likewise a customary fee to the Paymaster of the Forces, was ordered to be prosecuted.

Thus the Ministry triumphed, and Marlborough's name was tarnished in history by this cruel, false, and ungrateful censure. The Queen said in her reply to the address communicating the resolution, "I have a great regard for whatever is presented to me by my Commons, and will do my part to redress whatever you complain of." Brydges was so disgusted that he offered his resignation to Oxford, and was only with difficulty persuaded to continue in his key-office.[1]

It would have been natural after such resolutions for the Commons to impeach Marlborough at the bar of the Lords. However, no further steps were taken. One reason at least is obvious. The Duke of Ormonde was now Commander-in-Chief. The Ministers who had just obtained a party verdict against Marlborough authorized Ormonde to draw the same deduction upon the bread contract and bread wagons, and to receive the same 2½ per cent. on the pay of the foreign troops, and to use it for the same purposes as Marlborough had done. Thus, while inducing the House of Commons to condemn his practice, they themselves vindicated him by adopting it.[2]

There is one final refutation of these charges, which has never yet been published. A year later at Utrecht in long procession the Princes and Courts of the Grand Alliance recorded their full approval of the deduction of the 2½ per cent., declared that it was their own money, and that it had been spent to their entire satisfaction.

[1] *Huntington Library Bulletin*, November 11, 1931, p. 124.   [2] Burnet, vi, 104.

The Electors of Cassel and Düsseldorf sent identical letters:

★Although we agreed entirely that this deduction of $2\frac{1}{2}$ per cent. for the Secret Services had been granted without expecting any rendering of account, the nature of the business demanding it, nevertheless we admit that we are fully satisfied and convinced that the said money has been disposed of for the above purposes, and we should think it an injury to the reputation of this great General if we did not declare that his prudent and wise handling of these sums has principally contributed, after the Grace of God, to the gain of so many glorious victories, and to the surprising successes which have accompanied the armies of the Allies during the whole course of this long war.

And in order that a complete and full justice may be done from our side, we have to bear witness that we granted and accorded voluntarily the said $2\frac{1}{2}$ per cent. to the said Duke of Marlborough for the above purposes and without the rendering of account.[1]

Dalwigh, Counsellor of State and plenipotentiary of the Landgrave of Hesse, stated to the Peace Congress:

★I have paid from the amount received for the troops of his Most Serene Highness in the service of her Majesty the Queen of Great Britain $2\frac{1}{2}$ per cent. to the Prince and Duke of Marlborough. But I declare at the same time that this has been paid upon the initiative of his Serene Highness my master himself in consideration of the great services which his Highness my lord Prince and Duke has rendered to the Common Cause in general, and to his Highness and his troops in particular. And thus Mr Sweet has never demanded it by order of the Queen, or of anyone else, not having even the right to do so, this being contrary to the treaties made concerning the said troops.[2]

The Elector of Hanover was even more emphatic:

★Since we feel obliged to bear witness to the truth on the subject of the $2\frac{1}{2}$ per cent. which has been deducted during the war from the pay of the troops which we have had in the service of her Majesty the Queen of Great Britain in the Low Countries: We declare and affirm by this present document that we have voluntarily accorded this sum as a free gift to the Prince and Duke of Marlborough in the quality of General Commander-in-Chief of the Allies. The fact that the other generals in command of allied armies have enjoyed similar gratuities has led to the practice of employing the said $2\frac{1}{2}$ per cent. for the most part in Secret Service work for which one is informed no other provision has been made.

Moreover, we declare that we are fully convinced and satisfied that

---

[1] March 13, 1713; Blenheim MSS.   [2] January 18, 1713; Blenheim MSS.

the Prince Duke of Marlborough has annually applied these sums to the Secret Services according to their destination, and we are persuaded that his wise application of these amounts has forcibly contributed to the gaining of so many battles, to the passing of so many entrenchments and so many lines, successes which, after the blessing of God, are due in great part to the good intelligence and information which the said Prince has had of the movements and condition of the enemy. . . .

GEORGE LEWIS
Electeur[1]

It is to be noticed that these testimonies were recorded when Marlborough had fallen from power and was only a wanderer on the Continent. They were solemnly presented by the allied princes and states to the Peace Congress as an act of justice and as a salute to the General who had served them well.

Professor G. M. Trevelyan has declared that no one ever gave better value to England than Marlborough for every guinea he received. But this is not the point at issue. No single charge of corruption or malversation was ever proved against Marlborough, and the charges on which he was condemned were manifestly disproved. For two years all the malice of a triumphant faction and all the power of the Crown were remorselessly used to make a case against him. The Commission of Accounts ransacked the records of the Army in the confident expectation of finding that he had been accustomed to take a profit upon sales of commissions by officers to their successors, or on promotions to replace officers killed in action. This was one of the libels blatantly proclaimed against him by the Tory pamphleteers. It touched his conduct not only as Captain-General but as Colonel of the Guards. It is incredible that if such abuses had occurred they would not have been brought to light. Any officer who would come forward with a complaint would have been sure of favour from the ruling powers. Marlborough's Whig friends were anxious about this, but no single jot of evidence was found against him in all those long ten years of command. "Few," wrote Burnet, "thought that he had been so clear in that matter; for it was the only thing in which now his enemies were confident that some discoveries would have been made to his prejudice; so

1 Hanover, January 13, 1713. See also Marlborough Papers, *H.M.C.*, p. 16(*a*), for letter of March 23. Similar unpublished letters from the Bishop of Paderborn and Münster (January 7, 1713), from the dragoon regiment commanded by Baron deWaleff (March 9, 1713), and from the envoy of the Elector of Trèves at Utrecht (January 18, 1713) are also preserved in the Blenheim archives.

that the endeavours used to search into these matters proved nothing, but raised the repute of his incorrupt administration more than all his well-wishers could have expected. Thus happy does sometimes the malice of an enemy prove."[1]

But the Tory lie stands upon the journals of the House of Commons. Marlborough's answers and the failure of his accusers did not bar a scandalous prosecution being set on foot against him for the recovery of all these sums expended so well in the British interests. Nor could they prevent a sneer or a smear remaining on the pages of history, and successive generations being content with the loose impression that there was something dishonest in Marlborough's conduct.

Marlborough was careful and thrifty in all he did. He saved money for himself and the public every week. His strictness about the funds, public and private, under his control descended to the smallest details. In a lavish and corrupt age he practised a severe, businesslike economy. He would take presents from the princes of the Alliance, and might even in the event of a peace and in certain circumstances have accepted the rewards of Louis XIV himself for services which were not incompatible with the interests of England. No doubt when, in the occupation of conquered territory, 'safeguards' were granted to individual owners, he took these payments as a kind of prize money. But where public money was concerned his record is impeccable. He is entitled to claim from his countrymen the declaration that he acted with strict integrity and according to his warrant in the administration of all Army funds entrusted to him. If this be challenged, let the contrary case be made.

[1] Burnet, vi, 104–105.

Chapter Thirty-two

THE RESTRAINING ORDERS

THE Tories were now triumphant at home, and on January 29, 1712, their plenipotentiaries, the Bishop of Bristol and Lord Strafford, together with representatives of Holland and the Empire, met the French in conference at Utrecht. None of the Allies knew what secret understandings subsisted between England and France, but when the Marquis d'Huxelles announced the French proposals these were denounced at once as treating the allies of England as if they were vanquished states. The unconditional retention of Spain and the Indies by Philip V was claimed by the French to be finally settled. The rest of the French demands affronted the Dutch, the Germanic Princes, and the Empire. English interests alone were privileged. The anger of the Allies knew no bounds, and in England outside the Court circle widespread wrath was mingled with wider shame. In the Commons the 'gentlemen' "stood by the Queen"; but in the Lords Halifax, in spite of the recent wholesale creation of peers, carried an address to continue the war rather than submit to such terms. This "ill-usage of the Queen" by war-loving factions in factious defiance of her Ministers, as St John viewed it, absolved him in his own opinion from all inconvenient obligations. He and Oxford began forthwith to negotiate a peace treaty with the French, the signature of which would bind the allies or leave them to their fate.

At this moment there occurred in the French royal family a remarkable, and many believed a sinister, series of deaths. The Dauphin, son of Louis XIV, who had played so vigorous a part in breaking the negotiations of 1709, had expired in April 1711, leaving behind him, besides his younger sons (the Dukes of Anjou and Berri), a son and two grandsons, all of whom stood in the direct line of succession to the throne of France, and constituted an immense barrier of probability against the succession of Philip V and the union of the two crowns in a single person. Now, in February 1712, this barrier was almost shorn away. The sequence was amazing.

On February 12 the Duchess of Burgundy, daughter of Victor Amadeus and wife of the new Dauphin, died of smallpox. Four days later her husband, the Dauphin, fell ill. He immediately predisposed himself to death. The next evening he had an altar erected in his sick chamber and received the last succours of the Church. On the 18th he died. Thus there passed from France the amiable Prince who had been the pupil of Fénelon, had muddled with Vendôme the battle of Oudenarde, and was wistfully regarded as the virtuous hope of the French monarchy. The couple who had been so swiftly swept away left behind them two little boys, the elder of whom, five years old, became the third Dauphin in twelve months. The younger was only two years old and very sickly. Both these children were immediately stricken with the malady which had destroyed their parents. It would be natural to suppose that the wife had given the dreaded infection to her husband, and that the children had caught it from them. But when the third Dauphin died in a few days of this scourge the rumour of poison grew, and suspicion against their cousin, the Duke of Orleans, nephew of Louis XIV, was so strong that the King imprisoned Orleans' chemist in the Bastille. It is even said that the Duke of Orleans himself suggested this. Modern opinion may feel that the chemist was ill-used.

Only the sickly and infected infant, aged two, now lay between the personal union of the crowns of France and Spain. His own escape is worth recording. In the words of the Duchess of Orleans,[1] the mother of the suspected Duke,

> When the little Dauphin became quite red with the smallpox and sweated, the doctors opened a vein, and in consequence of this operation the poor child died. . . . His little brother had exactly the same illness. While the nine doctors were busy with the elder child, the nurses locked themselves in with the younger prince. Yesterday, the 9th, the doctors wanted to open a vein because the child had severe fever; but the governess, Madame de Ventadour, and her deputy, strongly opposed this, and steadfastly refused to permit it, and only kept him nice and warm. So this child was saved[2]

—to become eventually Louis XV.

In a period when the affairs of the world were largely swayed by dynastic events this strange succession of deaths upon the main highroad of European history paralysed France and staggered all

---

[1] Elizabeth Charlotte de Bavière.
[2] Klopp, xiv, 304; quoted from a letter of the Duchess of Orleans (March 10).

other countries. One could hardly follow the succession of blows, and as the couriers arrived with their tidings at every capital the general conclusion, for which no proof has ever been advanced, was that Orleans had poisoned the whole lot. It was even reported that the aged monarch was himself a victim.

Nothing could be more embarrassing to Oxford and St John than these deaths in France. The French royal family, with whom they were in deep confederacy, had virtually disintegrated before their eyes. The security against the union of the two crowns, which they had so confidently paraded in the persons of the Duke of Burgundy and his two sons, had almost vanished. Whatever virtue there had been in a French declaration that the Crowns should never be combined seemed to have been destroyed beforehand by the most inexorable of facts.[1]

As no one expected the infant Prince to live, and as even the Tories could not stomach the union, imminent as it appeared, of the Crowns of France and Spain in the person of Philip V, the English Ministers proposed that Philip should renounce the throne of France for himself and his heirs. But now the French lawyers affirmed that such a declaration was contrary to the principle of the French monarchy and was necessarily invalid. St John and Oxford then proposed that Philip V should renounce the throne of Spain on accession to that of France, in which case France would receive compensation in Italy, and Spain would fall to the Duke of Savoy. The advantages offered to France in Italy were so substantial that Louis XIV agreed that the proposal should be made to Philip. The concession cost him little. It captivated the English Ministers, who saw themselves suddenly within reach of diverting Spain and the Indies from the house of Bourbon and vindicating after all the "No peace without Spain" cry, thus completely cutting the ground from under the Whigs. On May 28, while the messengers were riding to Madrid, Oxford told the Lords that peace upon these lines was near. But a new surprise was in store. Philip V chose at all costs to retain the crown of Spain, which he had gained with his sword and with the love of the Spanish people through so many cruel years of war. All solutions were therefore destroyed, and Europe was confronted with the double deadlock which perhaps Louis XIV had foreseen—that Philip could not renounce the crown of France and would not renounce the crown of Spain. Upon this all the Allies called for the renewal of the war. No basis of peace,

---

[1] See Portland Papers, *H.M.C.*, iv, 672–677.

no treaty of any kind, was in sight. The armies were, in fact, already assembling, and such was the feeling in England that the Ministry ordered the Duke of Ormonde and the British forces to join them. Thus the only result of the Tory peace effort and intrigue with France, for the sake of which they had supplanted Marlborough and Godolphin and rendered their country odious to all its allies, had been to condemn all Europe to two more campaigns.

Ormonde reached The Hague on April 9, and assumed command of the British-paid forces, all of which, with the rest of the allies, were now marching to the points of assembly. Ormonde's orders were to see the Pensionary and

> express to him the Queen's resolution of pushing the war with all possible vigour, until the enemy should agree to such terms of peace as might be safe and honourable for herself and her allies; to assure him that he was prepared to live in a perfect and good correspondence with all the generals of the Allies, and particularly with those of the States; to desire the Pensionary to inform him what plan had been agreed upon for the operations of the campaign; and as soon as he arrived at the frontier, to meet with Prince Eugene, and such others of the generals as should be in the secret, and with them to concert the proper measures for entering upon action.[1]

To these forthcoming declarations the Dutch Council of State replied with some stiffness:

> That there was no particular resolution taken as to the operations of the campaign, but they left it to their generals, who with their deputies were to act in concert with the generals of the Allies: and that they had given orders to their generals to live in a good correspondence with his Grace.[2]

The Dutch and other allies excused themselves to Ormonde for having made Prince Eugene Generalissimo. They explained that in practice Ormonde and the Prince were now "upon an equal foot." Cadogan, though excluded from the list of lieutenant-generals, offered—no doubt at Marlborough's desire—his services to the new Commander-in-Chief, who was allowed by the Government to accept them. The allied army, concentrating beyond Tournai, amounted to 122,000 men, with 120 field cannon, apart from the siege-train. Against them stood Villars with 100,000 men, ill-equipped and with a weak artillery.[3] When on May 17 Ormonde met Eugene at Tournai the physical ascendancy of the Allies was evident, and the

---

[1] Tindal, *Continuation of Rapin's History*, xvii, 495.
[2] *Loc. cit.*   [3] See map on opposite page.

purely military prospects bright. It was agreed to pass the Scheldt behind Bouchain, and to advance towards the enemy, either to attack him if he were ill posted or to lay siege to Quesnoy, a small but effective fortress ten miles south of Valenciennes.

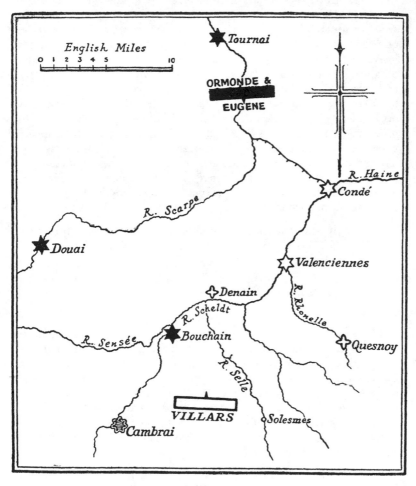

MAY 1712

Ormonde had thus been enabled to take the field in favourable conditions and upon honourable terms. Only a few days before Eugene had recorded his opinion that he was "the finest cavalier and most complete gentleman that England bred, being the glory of his nation."[1] But already St John had begun to make him aware

[1] Portland Papers, *H.M.C.*, v, 157.

of the purposes for which he was to be used. On April 16/27 he wrote:

> I find by very certain intelligences from Holland that the Dutch Ministers are not without their fears of their new General [Prince Eugene]. They begin to consider that he is a Papist, and a German, at least in interest. That the Emperor, his master, has nothing to lose on the side of the Netherlands; that a battle won may give ground for insisting on higher terms than the House of Austria is now likely to obtain; that a battle lost may still contribute to prolong the war, and that in either case, the expense of blood will fall to the share of the Queen and States. I am of opinion that these reflections have occasioned private directions to their [the Dutch] General, to use more caution than the Prince will perhaps approve. This measure, your Grace sees, is not very consistent with the compliment made him, . . . in the name of the States, of an unlimited command. We hardly think the enemy would have taken the posts in which they now are, if they had not had a prospect of subsisting in them, till there is forage on the ground.[1]

Thus nicely did the Secretary labour to sow distrust between Ormonde and Eugene and prevent active operations.

On April 25/May 6 St John wrote again desiring Ormonde to make sure that all the foreign troops paid by Britain should be kept under Ormonde's direct command—*i.e.* not merged with the similar mercenary forces in the Dutch pay:

> There can be no need for me to enter into the grounds which we have in this conjuncture to be jealous of Prince Eugene's conduct; your Grace sees and knows them all better than I can repeat them. But on this occasion the Queen directs me to inform your Grace that she thinks you are to be more cautious for some time of engaging in an action, unless in the case of a very apparent and considerable advantage, because you will be daily strengthened by the arrival of the Imperial troops. It is but just that these should have their part, if anything of that kind is to happen.[2]

In reply to this Ormonde reminded the Minister that in his instructions he "was ordered to act in conjunction with the Allies, in prosecuting the war with vigour; so that, should there happen a fair opportunity to attack the enemy, he could not decline it, if proposed by the Prince and States." And a few days later: "If there be a good opportunity to attack the enemy, and get into France, by the way of Champagne, I am sure the Prince and the States will

---

[1] *Bolingbroke Correspondence*, ii, 267–268.   [2] *Ibid.*, 274.

press it, unless they hear from England that the peace is near being concluded."

The armies were now in presence of one another, and on May 10/21 St John wrote the following letter to Ormonde:

> Her Majesty, my Lord, has reason to believe that we shall come to an agreement upon the great article of the union of the two monarchies, as soon as a courier, sent from Versailles to Madrid, can return; it is therefore the Queen's positive command to your Grace that you avoid engaging in any siege, or hazarding a battle, till you have farther orders from her Majesty. I am, at the same time, directed to let your Grace know that the Queen would have you disguise the receipt of this order, and her Majesty thinks that you cannot want pretences for conducting yourself so as to answer her ends, without owning that which might, at present, have an ill effect if it was publicly known.

This was the notorious restraining order which later formed the principal article in St John's impeachment. But the postscript is not less remarkable:

> P.S. I had almost forgot to tell your Grace that communication is given of this order to the Court of France; so that if the Mareschal de Villars takes, in any private way, notice of it to you, your Grace will answer accordingly. If this order is changed on either side, we shall, in honour, be obliged to give notice of it to the other.[1]

To Gaultier St John was even more explicit. "I asked Mr St John," wrote Gaultier to Torcy (May 21), "what Marshal Villars should do if by chance Prince Eugene and the Dutch attempted some offensive. He answered that there would be nothing to be done but to fall upon him *and cut him to pieces, him and his army*."[2]

It would have been a grievous, though a permissible, measure to tell Eugene, the States-General, and other members of the Alliance that the British forces would not fight until the peace treaty was settled one way or the other. But for an English Minister, acting in the name of the Queen, to conceal from the Allies his intention, while disclosing it secretly to the enemy, was in fact to encompass the defeat of Eugene and the slaughter of the allies and comrades with whom the British troops had so long stood shoulder to shoulder. Nothing in the history of civilized peoples has surpassed this black treachery. The punishment meted out in after-years by their countrymen to the criminals concerned may lighten, but cannot efface, its indelible stain.

---

[1] *Bolingbroke Correspondence*, ii, 319–320.   [2] *Edinburgh Review*, October 1835, p. 9.

Ormonde, so popular and magnificent, so gallant in his youth, now showed himself the weak, base creature he was at heart. With his eyes open he lent himself to this shame; and it was no thanks to him that Eugene and the allied generals to whom Ormonde was bound in soldierly faith did not in fact suffer the fate wickedly contemplated by St John. But the Prince, who had so much experience of war and treachery, was vigilant; and the Dutch, fortunately for themselves, were wary. It was noticed that Villars, although but a league away from the superior confederate army, took no trouble to entrench his camp, and sent out no reconnaissances to test the strength of the allied forces. He lay as if to invite attack. He might well do this, for, according to St John's assurances through Gaultier and Torcy, as well as from the communications he had directly with Ormonde, he had a right to suppose that not only the redcoats but all the British-paid forces, numbering between forty and fifty thousand men, or nearly half Eugene's army, would desert at the moment of battle, and leave the rest an easy prey—in St John's words, to be "cut to pieces."

The apparent imprudence of so capable a general redoubled the suspicions of the allies. Eugene resolved to put Ormonde to the test. The Duke, though consenting to dishonour, was no adept in deceit. He failed at once as hero and as cheat. He could not meet Eugene and the allied generals as guests at his table without revealing his embarrassment. He could not withstand the hard questions which the Dutch Deputies asked in formal interviews. When a reconnaissance in force showed that the French army, only four miles away across a plain, lay without entrenchments of any kind, and Eugene, supported by all technical opinion, had proposed an advance and a battle, he wrote pitifully to the Secretary of State (May 29):

> You may easily imagine the difficulty that I was under to excuse the delaying a matter, which, according to the informations I had from the quarter-masters-general, and several other general-officers, that went out with the detachment, seemed to be so practicable. The best excuse I could make was Lord Strafford's sudden voyage to England, which gave me reason to believe there must be something of consequence transacting, which a delay of four or five days would bring to light: and therefore I desired they would defer this undertaking, or any other, till I should receive fresh letters from England.[1]

But when he made this answer in the camp Prince Eugene and

[1] *Mémoires du duc d'Ormond*, i, 203.

the Dutch Deputies told him plainly "that his answer was agreeable to the suspicions they had for some time entertained, particularly since the express of the 24th, which they knew had brought him letters from England." Ormonde could only keep on saying "that before he entered upon action, he should be glad to receive letters from England, which he expected every moment." In this plight the affairs of the confederate army remained for several days. When on June 7 the expected letter from St John came it only expressed "the impatience her Majesty was in to hear whether the orders, sent on May 10, came safely and early to his hands, and the assurance she had of his punctual obedience to her commands in so nice and important a conjuncture." Ormonde had already described to St John the distrust among the allies by which he was encompassed. Now he struck a note new to the Secretary:

There are several among them who do not hesitate to say aloud that they have been betrayed. I am afraid that if the conclusion of peace is postponed, *I shall find myself Commander only of the British national troops*. I am strengthened in this fear by the fact that the Elector of Hanover is strongly opposed to the peace, and will let his troops serve with the Dutch. I am also doubtful whether we can win over the Danes.[1]

He ended with a belated and irresolute suggestion:

You may guess how uneasy a situation I am in; and, if there be no prospect of action, I do not see of what use I am here; and, if it suit with her Majesty's service, I should be glad I might have leave to return to England.

He did not know how far men's minds had travelled upon the frenzy of despair which convulsed the councils at The Hague—councils secret now from those deemed "the English traitors." It was, in fact, seriously planned to disarm and arrest the twelve thousand British troops in Flanders. The famous redcoats whose martial honour stood so high in those professional camps were to be seized as hostages against the faithlessness of their Government. Primoli[2] reported to Gallas from The Hague on June 7:

Welderen and Hop have set out for the army. It appears they have the intention of disarming the English. If one can win over the rulers of Hanover and Denmark, it is certain one would carry this out. Only Prussia is frightened of this. My view is that such a blow would have a very good effect in London. They are so blinded at the moment

[1] *Mémoires du duc d'Ormond*, i, 207.   [2] Gallas's secretary.

there by the duplicities of the Ministry that they do not see through their intrigues. The enclosed letters directed to me from London full of questions prove this. If this were done they would then become aware of the treachery which these Ministers are plotting equally against the common welfare of the Alliance as against the real interest of England.[1]

This desperate project, hitherto recorded only in Continental histories, fortunately came to naught. That it was known to St John is shown by a sentence in his letter to Harley of this same date: "Some are even saucy enough to insinuate so far as to attempt seizing the British troops in Flanders."[2] To such a point had the Queen and her new friends brought the Common Cause.

Rumours of the deadlock at headquarters travelled far and fast. Even "the gentlemen of England" were upset at the idea of a British Commander-in-Chief standing in the line with his allies but forbidden to give them true aid and succour. On May 28/June 8 Halifax brought the whole business before the Lords. He recounted the memorable victories of the Allies which had brought the "common enemy" of Christendom to extremities. He declared these prospects totally defaced by the orders given to the Queen's General not to act offensively against the enemy. On this there was much questioning of the Government whether in fact any restraining orders had been given to Ormonde. The Lord Treasurer said

> that they who had the honour to serve the Queen could not reveal the orders she gave to her General without a particular direction from her Majesty; and that in his opinion those orders were not fit to be divulged. However, he would adventure to say that, if the Duke of Ormonde had refused to act offensively, he did not doubt, but he had followed his instructions: and it was prudence not to hazard a battle upon the point of concluding a good peace, especially considering they had to deal with an enemy so apt to break his word.

This was pretty blunt. St John in the Commons had no mind to go so far. He covered himself with denials, which were accepted by his supporters, and, as Swift said, "these all went swimmingly." In the Lords the matter was more sharply probed. Wharton, fastening upon Oxford's allusion to the treacherous character of the French, interrupted with the pertinent question, "Whether it was not better to push such an enemy with the utmost vigour till he was reduced to the method of dealing honestly?" Oxford became even more candid. "Though the Duke of Ormonde may have refused to

---

[1] Klopp, xiv, 332.　　　　[2] *Correspondence*, ii, 374.

hazard a general action, yet I can be positive he would not decline joining with the allies in a siege, orders having been sent him for that purpose." This eminently civilian idea that a siege is a compromise midway between a battle and a treaty gave Marlborough his opening. He had come to the House resolved to support or second Halifax. He now rose and said, "I do not know how to reconcile the orders not to hazard a battle and to join in a siege to the rules of war, since it is impossible to make a siege without either hazarding a battle in case the enemy attempt to relieve the place, or shamefully raising the siege."[1] He continued:

"Altho' the negotiations for peace may be far advanced, yet I can see no reason which should induce the Allies or ourselves to remain inactive, and not push on the war with the utmost vigour as we have incurred the expense of recruiting the army for the service of another year. That army is now in the field, and it has often occurred that a victory or a siege has produced good effects and manifold advantages, when treaties were still farther advanced than is the present negotiation. And as I am of opinion that we should make the most we can for ourselves, the only infallible way to force France to an entire submission is to besiege and occupy Cambrai or Arras, and to carry the war into the heart of that kingdom. But as the troops of the enemy are now encamped, it is impossible to execute this design, unless they are withdrawn from their position; and as they cannot be reduced to retire for want of provision, they must be attacked and forced. For the truth of what I say I appeal to a noble Duke [looking at Argyll], whom I rejoice to see in the House, because he knows the country, and is as good a judge of these matters as any person now alive."[2]

Argyll, newly returned from Spain, responded to this appeal, though in a manner different from what Marlborough may have hoped.

"I agree with the noble Duke [he said] that it is impossible to remove them, except by attacking and driving them away, and until that is effected, neither of the two sieges alluded to can be undertaken. I likewise agree that the capture of these towns is the most effectual way to carry on the war with advantage, and would be a fatal blow to France."[3]

He then reproached Marlborough for not having taken these towns in the campaign of 1710, instead of wasting much blood and

[1] *Parliamentary History*, vi, 1132. See also Coxe, vi, 197, and Lockhart, i, 392, for a better reporting of the debate.

[2] Coxe, vi, 191.

[3] *Parliamentary History*, vi, 1132.

treasure for the sake of Béthune, Aire, and Saint-Venant—"dove-cotes," as the critics were wont to class them. Argyll's rejoinder, delivered with force and fire, made a marked impression upon the House. Here was a General of proved courage and long experience, who had fallen out with the Ministry, who was no longer in command, and who nevertheless stood up to the great Commander and supported the Government policy. The Lords had no knowledge of what St John had written to Ormonde, still less of what he had written to Torcy. The balance of opinion was that it was not unreasonable for the British to hold the allies back at such a moment. Another Malplaquet, with peace on the threshold, would be unendurable. Granted the long way we had journeyed in negotiation and the limited knowledge of the House, this was a not unnatural conclusion. Nottingham said "that he could not comprehend why orders had been given to our General not to fight, unless certain persons were apprehensive of weakening the French, so far as to hamper themselves in bringing about designs which they durst not yet own." The Duke of Devonshire remarked "that, by the proximity of blood, he was more concerned for the Duke of Ormonde's reputation than any other; and therefore he could not forbear declaring he was surprised to see any one dare to make a nobleman of the first rank, and of so distinguished a character, the instrument of such a proceeding." But Halifax, not relishing the prospects of a division, was now willing to withdraw his motion. This was not allowed. In the closing moments "Swallow" Poulett flung the grossest insult at Marlborough which his busy brain could frame.

"Nobody [he said] could doubt of the Duke of Ormonde's courage and bravery; but that he was not like a certain General, who led troops to the slaughter to cause a great number of officers to be knocked on the head in a battle, or against stone walls, in order to fill his pockets by disposing of their commissions."[1]

Finally Oxford, speaking again, gave the most positive assurances that neither he nor the Government would ever engage in a separate peace. His words were remarkable: "Nothing of that nature was ever intended; for such a peace would be so foolish, villainous, and knavish that every servant of the Queen must answer for it with his head to the nation." "The Allies," he assured the Lords, "are acquainted with our proceedings, and satisfied with our terms." Wharton, whose interventions were always pointed, besought the Lords to bear in mind these words "foolish, villainous, and knavish,"

[1] *Parliamentary History*, vi, 1132.

and also the words "answer for it with his head." Ministers obtained a majority of sixty-eight to forty. But Parliament and the nation did not know what the Government had done, and what the Allies, now paraded as in contented accord, were really thinking.

Marlborough had sat silent under Poulett's taunt. It was evident that it was not one to be answered with words. As soon as the House was up he sent Lord Mohun to Poulett with an invitation, in the style of those days, "to take the air in the country." Poulett had not been expecting such a retort. "Is this a challenge?" he asked. Mohun replied that the message explained itself. He added, "I shall accompany the Duke of Marlborough, and your lordship will do well to provide a second." A tragic episode was soon to prove that when Mohun spoke in this way he was in earnest. Affairs of this kind were usually kept by gentlemen secret from their wives. Poulett was, however, unable to conceal his agitation. Lady Poulett acted promptly and with the zeal of an affectionate spouse. She wrote no fewer than five letters to the Secretary of State, imparting the unhappy position in which her lord now found himself. Although he was twelve years younger than Marlborough, he felt politics ought not to take this unpleasant turn. In her first letter his wife begs Lord Dartmouth "to order the guards to be ready upon two noblemen's falling out; she will listen when Lord Mohun comes, and will send a more speedy and exact account." Her next note runs, "I listend and itt is my Lord Mallbouro that has challings my Lord by Lord Mohun. Pray lett him be secured immedatly." In a third note, headed "Saturday morning," Lady Poulett again urges Lord Dartmouth to send guards, and adds, "the Treasurer must make itt up with Halifax . . . that noe more quarills happens one this occasion which I hope you and the Queen will prevent for the present. Pray burn my letters and send the very next gard att hand to secure my Lord and Lord Mohun."[1]

Thus energetically did Lady Poulett arouse Dartmouth to a just sense of the impending danger. The Secretary of State went at once to Marlborough, and personally requested him "not to stir abroad." To reassure the Pouletts two sentries were forthwith placed outside their house. These measures taken, the Queen was informed.[2] She sent Marlborough a royal command that "this might

[1] Dartmouth Papers, *H.M.C.*, 309.
[2] *Cardinal to Watkins*

WESTMINSTER
June 3, 1712

★It seems the Earle Pawlet was pleas'd to take this occasion to reflect very grosly

go no further," and to require his word to that effect. Here were other "restraining orders." Eventually some sort of apology was made by Poulett. In this age of duelling, and while charges of selling commissions were actually the subject of official investigation against Marlborough, it was hardly possible to imagine a more just provocation than Poulett's words. This did not prevent Swift and his *Examiner* pack from crying out in scandalized virtue against party duels.

---

upon my Lord Duke as if his Grace had fought so many battles and expos'd so many men's lives against Stonewalls with no other view than the disposal of Commissions. This is the Substance of wt I have heard, but 'tis reported to have been much worse & utter'd in the most brutal manner. What grounds there could be for anything of this kind you are as good a judge of as anybody. His Grace thought his honr so farr concernd that the next morning he sent Lord Mohun to tell Lord Pawlet his Grace expected satisfaction, but the two Lords could not see each other till Saturday morning, when 'tis said Lord Mohun us'd pretty plain language. By this time it had gott Wind. Centries were posted att Ld Pawlet & Ld Mohun's, tho' the latter was not at home. Ld Dartmouth was sent att the same time to his Grace. Thus by Her Majestys interposing Her authority I think all is put up again, but it is reported Lord Pawlet is order'd to make some appology the first time they meet in the House. [Blenheim MSS.]

Chapter Thirty-three

THE BRITISH DESERTION

1712—MAY–JULY

WHILE the Lords' debate was in progress Eugene and the Deputies, having put Ormonde to the test of a proposed battle and found him wanting, decided to besiege Quesnoy. They acted independently of the Captain-General. On June 8 they crossed the Selle, and began the investment. Ormonde compromised. He allowed seven battalions and nine squadrons in the joint pay of England and the States to take part in the siege, and lay with the rest of his forces between the French position and that of the besiegers, as if he were in fact a covering army. The enemy commander took this much amiss. He regarded it as a breach of the dishonourable understanding into which the British general had entered.

> I have received several advices that Quesnoy is invested, and that part of the troops in your Grace's army are employed in that service. By the order of the King, I desire to know of you if any of the troops under your command have a share in undertaking or forming that siege; for I cannot believe Prince Eugene would venture to attempt it only with the forces he commands. Pray explain your position to me, so that I may know how to act if Prince Eugene perseveres in the siege.

This request of Marshal Villars was reasonable. He had a right to know whether the English were friends or foes. He had been formally apprised by her Majesty's Government that treachery was afoot. He may be pardoned for wishing to make sure against whom it was designed. To these expostulations Ormonde returned an answer worthy of himself and of the policy he served. He wrote:

> That as the Marshal observed himself of what consequence it was to keep this affair secret, he would leave him to judge whether he could have done it better than by the conduct he observed. It was true that for the siege of Quesnoy, which it was not in his power to prevent, he had furnished some troops, which were paid in part by the States, but not one single man solely in the Queen's pay.[1]

[1] Pelet, xi, 462–463.

Villars on this put to the British Commander-in-Chief from the opposite standpoint the same blunt question with which Eugene and the Dutch Deputies had plagued him for a fortnight. He intimated that it was his military duty to interrupt the siege, and that as the English General ought not, according to the understanding, to hamper him, the King of France would expect him to strike. But to this Ormonde made no response. There is no need to waste sympathy upon him. No decent, honest man would have done this work. When he had received the command the Tories boasted that he would soon show himself a finer soldier than the Duke of Marlborough. These pages have fully described his military performances. There remained only to pay the forfeit.

The siege of Quesnoy proceeded apace, and so did the English negotiations, which, now abandoning all pretence, were on the verge of a separate peace. Ormonde, seeing that Quesnoy was approaching its last straits, wrote to Eugene "that the British forces would continue with the army provided that he abandoned the siege." Eugene answered "that instead of relinquishing the siege, he would cause it to be prosecuted with all imaginable vigour." This ended correspondence between the two Commanders. Eugene, seeing the close and constant communication which took place between his ally and the enemy, gradually disentangled his forces from Ormonde's, and took all proper measures for his own security. At this time he let it be known "that he would be glad if the English would march off, they being now only a burden to the Netherlands."

A struggle began in the heart of this valiant, renowned confederate army for the foreign troops in British and in British-Dutch pay. But there was never much doubt of the issue. The private soldiers felt the same scorn and hatred for the behaviour of their caitiff allies as the generals and princes who led them. Ormonde knew that if the armies separated he would be followed only by the British nationals. He also knew what their feelings were. He had, however, another anxiety upon a nice point of perverted honour. In all the agreements made between St John and Torcy, as well as in the contacts he himself had had with Marshal Villars, the assumption had always been that when Great Britain quitted the front at least forty thousand men would be withdrawn from the allied army, and that Prince Eugene and the Dutch would thus lie at the mercy of greatly superior French forces. On this basis the separate peace treaty was to be concluded. On this basis King Louis XIV consented to surrender Dunkirk to a British garrison. But now Ormonde felt he could only desert in pursuance of his orders with the twelve thousand English. This defection, falling so far short of the expected quota, would leave Prince Eugene with a still respectable army. How then would France behave? Would Dunkirk be delivered? If not, on which port should the British retire? Oppressed by these problems, Ormonde did his best. On June 28 he sent written orders to the generals of the foreign troops in British pay to hold themselves and their men in readiness to march. With the exception of four squadrons, one regiment of dragoons, and one battalion, all answered unanimously "that they could not follow him nor separate from Prince Eugene without express orders from their respective princes." Some of the generals who were princes sent insulting replies. On July 1 the Allies stormed the counterscarp of Quesnoy, and the place surrendered, its garrison of nearly three thousand officers and men becoming prisoners of war.

At length the day of the parting came. In the middle of July Prince Eugene issued orders for a march, and Ormonde prepared to announce on behalf of England that an armistice had been arranged between the French and British Governments. He set his columns in retreat upon the north. He was followed only by a handful of the foreign troops. These mercenaries, from the poorest private upward, although warned that a half of their pay would be cut, resolved in a spasm of pride to stand by Prince Eugene and the Common Cause.

The misery of the redcoats has often been described. Under an iron discipline the veteran regiments and battalions, whose names had hitherto been held in so much honour in the camps of Europe, marched off with downcast eyes, while their comrades of the long war gazed upon them in mute reproach. The strictest orders had been given against recrimination, yet the silence struck a chill in the hearts of British soldiers whom no perils had daunted. But when they reached the end of the march and the ranks were broken terrible scenes were witnessed of humble men breaking their muskets, tearing their hair, and pouring out blasphemies and curses against the Queen and the Ministry who could subject them to that ordeal. Others of these rough fellows—the scum, we are assured, of our country—sat on the ground weeping with rage and grief when they thought of all they had dared and suffered, and of "the Old Corporal" who had led them on.

St John saw the episode from a different angle. To Harley's relation Thomas at The Hague he wrote (July 11/22), in a letter which gives us as accurate and revealing a measure of his nature as any upon record, the following sentence: "For the foreigners to desert her Majesty whilst her bread was in their mouths and her money in their pockets, to leave her subjects exposed for ought they knew to the attempt of the enemy, this the Queen looks upon to be such an indignity, such a violation of all faith, that she is resolved to resent it in the manner becoming so great a Princess."[1]

No humiliation was spared the retreating British troops. Tournai, Mons, and other conquered fortresses shut the gates in their faces, though, as Millner relates, "they handed over their walls . . . some things which our men most wanted." In retaliation Ormonde seized Ghent and Bruges. Meanwhile the egregious Jack Hill, with a squadron of the fleet and a few battalions, had occupied Dunkirk; and Swift could write obsequious letters to Abigail complimenting her as "the governess of Dunkirk."

Thus did St John carry through the policy to which he had bent himself. There was only one Englishman in that age, or perhaps in any period of our history, who had all the qualities necessary to carry such a policy to completion. It was a momentous contribution to the history of England and of Europe. It belongs by right to him. He bore its weight during the many years he was yet to live, and he bears it in history. When later in the year he was attacked in the House of Commons for carrying on the negotiations "in a fantastic and treacherous manner" St John said

> he hoped it would not be counted treachery to act for the good and advantage of Great Britain; that he gloried in the small share he had in these negotiations; and whatever censure he might undergo for it, the bare satisfaction of acting with that view would be a sufficient recompense and comfort to him all his lifetime.

It is not often that statesmen are taken by Fortune so strictly at their word.

The fact that twelve thousand British had been withdrawn from the army did not deprive the Allies of their numerical preponderance or of their superior equipment and immense supplies. The preparations to carry the war into the heart of France which Marlborough had urged, and to some extent procured, had resulted in the creation of immense magazines on the Scarpe and the Scheldt in the region south of Tournai. Being in control of the whole

---

[1] Portland Papers, *H.M.C.*, v, 201.

navigation of the Scarpe to Bouchain, Marlborough's administration in 1711 had constructed a veritable fleet of enormous barges called 'bilanders,' capable of moving a siege-train and supplies with an ease and upon a scale hitherto unequalled. The principal magazine was established at Marchiennes, north of Douai on the Scarpe. Here were collected

> above a hundred bilanders, a hundred pieces of cannon, three hundred waggons with their harnesses, the hospital of the army, and in the storehouses or in the bilanders a prodigious number and quantity of bombs, grenades, bullets, musket-balls, powder, corn, meal, hams, bacon, cheese, butter, beer, wine, brandy, merchandise, ladders, hatchets, bills, planks, match, flint, and, in a word, all sorts of provisions necessary to make two sieges, and there were likewise a good number of horses.[1]

All the fortified places in the forward areas had been loaded with munitions, food, and forage for Marlborough's further advance.

However, Villars, lying on the Arras-Cambrai front, was well posted to oppose the operations of Eugene's weakened army. After Ormonde's departure Eugene marched south-east and invested Landrecies. His line of communications ran by water from Tournai through Saint-Amand and Marchiennes, on the Scarpe, and by road through Denain, behind Bouchain on the Scheldt, to his new conquest of Quesnoy. Anyone can see from the map that a siege of Landrecies was a venturesome effort. Although the Prince held the fortresses of Douai and Bouchain as a shield towards the enemy, and further had constructed a line of defences from Douai to Neuville, he was presenting nearly sixty miles of communications to a flank attack by Villars; and once he was engaged in a new siege this attack could be delivered in superior force. In consequence Eugene had to denude the garrisons of his fortresses and fortified positions to a dangerously low level. He had also to weaken the field army in order to make good this long, vulnerable line of communications. Lastly, he had in his rear the still untaken fortresses of Valenciennes and Maubeuge, which, without Ormonde's aid, he had not been able to besiege.

The disasters which now overwhelmed the campaign have cast a cloud upon Eugene's military record, and led at the time, and since, to unfavourable comparisons between him and Marlborough. The explanation is no doubt the passion to achieve success, in spite of the manner in which he had been treated, which laid hold of

[1] Lediard, iii, 319

Eugene and led him into risks which ought not to have been run. His was the strategy of exasperation.

A brief account will suffice of the melancholy three months (mid-July to mid-October) in which the allied army under Eugene lost more than had been gained in the three preceding years. As soon as Landrecies was invested on July 16 Villars crossed the Scheldt and encamped on the Selle near Cateau-Cambrésis. From here he began preparing the roads from the Selle to the Sambre and bridging the Sambre in many places above Landrecies. This portended an attempt in force to relieve that place. Eugene was not disquieted by this, for Villars's movement brought the two main armies into close contact, so that a battle could be fought in which Eugene's far more exposed communications would not tell against him. He was glad to see the French working parties across the Sambre. It was evident that if Villars moved into that region the French communications would be exposed almost as much as those of Eugene. He therefore withdrew his covering troops a little nearer to the siege and prepared himself for battle in and about his lines of circumvallation.

On July 22 the French army crossed the Selle about sixty thousand strong, and marched eight columns along their prepared routes to the Sambre a few miles south of Landrecies. Night fell on the appearance that this movement would continue the next day, but under the cover of darkness Villars marched in the opposite direction. He retraced his steps to Cateau-Cambrésis; he descended the Selle, all the crossings of which had been occupied by his cavalry, and during the night of the 23rd his vanguards crossed the Scheldt north of Bouchain by Neuville. At seven o'clock on the morning of the 24th he approached in superior force, increasing every hour, the allied fortified camp at Denain. Denain was a vital point in Eugene's communications. It was behind the left of the entrenched line he had thrown from the Scheldt to the Scarpe at Douai. Seventeen battalions and twelve cannon, eight thousand men in all, under Albemarle were assigned to its defence. The position was strong and carefully prepared, and had been reinforced by Eugene only a few days before. It was, however, too large to be defended by a detachment against an army, and an army was now rapidly deploying before it.

Eugene did not receive the news of Villars's doubling back till the early morning of the 24th. He immediately ordered his whole movable force to march from Landrecies to the succour of Denain, and rode over himself to the threatened position. He found Albemarle now gravely concerned. The French advance guard was already close to Neuville, and heavy columns of foot were rapidly crossing the Scheldt. Eugene saw that Albemarle if seriously attacked must retreat to the east bank. He therefore posted the seventeen squadrons of cavalry he had brought up from the Abbey of Denain on the heights on that side to cover Albemarle's infantry when they had crossed. In order to clear the way for such a withdrawal he ordered all the baggage to cross at once by the single existing pontoon bridge. These orders given, Eugene galloped back to press the march of his own army, which was by now striding along the fifteen miles which had separated them from Denain. He had hardly left the scene when the French attack on Neuville began. Four ally battalions guarding the lines were routed, and an important convoy sheltering behind them was captured with five hundred prisoners. Albemarle, after an attempt to succour the convoy, regained the Denain defences and manned the ramparts. Before these the French army was now drawing up in line of battle.

It was often asked that year in the camps why there was only one pontoon bridge behind so considerable a force as seventeen battalions. The explanation which was commonly given did not redound to Ormonde's credit. It was known that on the evening of the day on which he had declared the cessation of arms he sent to Denain for all the pontoons he had lent Albemarle. The most earnest appeals of Eugene and the Dutch Deputies could only procure a respite of eight days before these invaluable copper boats were removed. It was alleged that, on the day they left, two French engineers in disguise went with the party which fetched the pontoons away, that they spied out the whole position, and discovered especially that there was only a solitary bridge behind it. Though Ormonde always declared he knew nothing of this, it was the talk in the army and in the allied Courts that the plan had been concerted between the British and French commanders. This was not true; but if it had been true the event would not have been more disastrous.

By noon, the French deployment being complete, Villars attacked with thirty-six battalions in three columns supported by six more. When told that fascines were lacking to fill the ditch he cried out vehemently, "We will fill them with our bodies." The whole line, drums beating, advanced six or seven hundred paces without firing until within half musket shot of the ramparts. The defenders discharged their cannon loaded with canister and three volleys of musketry. The French faced this fire unflinchingly and in perfect order. Undeterred by several hundred casualties, their muskets slung, and sword in hand as at Steinkirk, they scrambled across the ditch and stormed the parapets. The allied troops, mostly Germans, with some Dutch, had all fought well in previous campaigns; but now after a weak resistance they fell back in serious disorder to their second line of defence, and an immediate retreat was ordered upon the bridge. The French, intoxicated by the first draught of victory they had tasted in Flanders for ten years, re-formed, and renewed their attack with fury. Even now the bulk of Albemarle's men might have escaped. But the bridge had broken under the hurried motions of the transport, and the whole of his force was pinned between the now overpowering masses of the French and the river. The Scheldt here flows sluggishly but very deep, and between banks six or seven feet high with no sloping shores. Whole battalions were driven into the water and perished. Four generals, including the brave Count Dohna and Count Nassau-Woudenberg, who might have swum the river on their horses, were dragged down by swarms of drowning men. Albemarle and a score of distinguished officers were made prisoners. Of the rank and file 1000 were killed, 1500 drowned, and 2500 surrendered. Out of Albemarle's whole force scarcely three thousand escaped. The French losses did not exceed four hundred. Eugene, his army still three hours away, was unable to intervene, and the Prince remained a sombre spectator on the farther bank.

Such was the victory of Denain, the only one gained by the French in the Low Countries since the wars of King William III. Voltaire declared that it was more essential to the safety of France even than the Treaty of Utrecht, and that if Villars had his due he would be called the saviour of his country. "Denain," said Napoleon a hundred years later, "saved France." Eugene's communications were severed. He was soon forced to raise the siege of Landrecies. Marchiennes, with its enormous magazines and transport, lay in Villars's grip. In the next few days all the strong posts of the Allies on the Scarpe were taken by the Marshal. Anchin, Pont-à-Rache, Hasnon, Mortagne, and Saint-Amand were all captured full of stores and with their garrisons. Marchiennes resisted till July 31, when five thousand men surrendered as prisoners of war, and the whole supplies for the campaign, "enough for two sieges," fell into the hands of a gallant enemy, long unused to such plenty.

On August 12 Villars laid siege to Douai. This superb fortress, which had afforded the main trial of strength for the great armies in

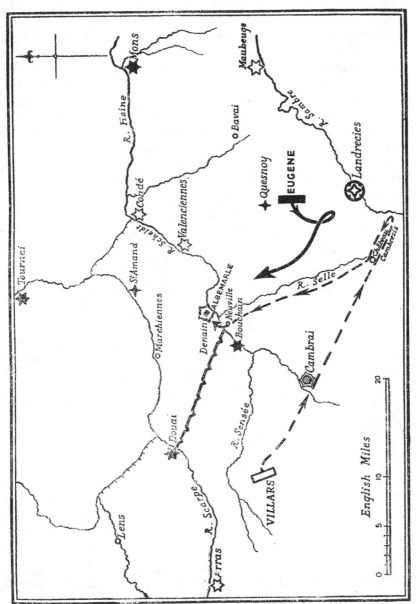

THE SURPRISE OF DENAIN

the year 1710, and had cost fifteen thousand men to take, was found garrisoned by only six battalions, and in spite of Eugene's efforts for its relief fell on September 8. Quesnoy, sole success of the campaign of 1712, surrendered on October 4. Bouchain, Marlborough's masterpiece of 1711, resisted for only eight days. In fact, the entire structure of the allied military power beyond the French frontier was torn to pieces, and the whole ascendancy and initiative passed to the amazed, resuscitated enemy. Besides seventeen battalions destroyed at Denain, upward of forty were surrendered with these fortresses, making a loss of fifty-seven battalions, or one-third of the units of the army, in these few months. Well might Louis XIV write to the Archbishop of Paris calling for solemn services of thanksgiving. Amid their loud *Te Deums* the old monarch, delivered from ruin, might have found a place for the trinity of serviceable agents through whom the wonders of the Almighty had been performed—Abigail, Harley, and St John.

The Old Campaigner, La Colonie, fought in the action of Denain and has left a vigorous and picturesque account of the assault. His regiment encamped on the field of battle for ten days. There was anxiety lest the great numbers of corpses rotting in the Scheldt should block up the locks at Valenciennes and elsewhere and bring about an epidemic. An order was therefore issued that all soldiers who knew how to swim, and cared to dive for the bodies of their drowned adversaries, would receive thirty sols for each corpse, "besides what spoil they might find on the same." This sport proving popular, an immense trench of great depth and width was dug into which the bodies withdrawn from the water, excepting those of the four generals, were thrown. This gruesome sketch seems suited to the general theme.

Not only victory but discipline had quitted the Allies and the British army with Marlborough. No sooner had his régime of alleged stinginess and peculation come to an end than for the first time the quality of the bread supplied to the troops gave rise to bitter and widespread complaint. The sudden deterioration in the husbandry of the army makes a mark which runs through the diaries and letters of officers and soldiers alike. During the month that Ormonde was immobile at Cateau-Cambrésis, negotiating with Villars, his troops fared ill, and their temper became morose.

The soldiers had nothing now to do but their Quarter-guard duty, and from a rising ground in front of our Camp, had a fair view of that rich part of France, which they reckoned they had dearly earned the plunder of. They were greatly exasperated at the disappointment, and were continually murmuring at those who brought them within sight of the "promised land," as they called it, and yet would not suffer them to taste the "milk and honey" it abounded with. Here they often lamented the loss of the "Old Corporal," which was a favourite name they had given the Duke of Marlborough; and to make the matter worse, through the carelessness of the contractors, their bread was so intolerably bad, that it was with great difficulty the officers could restrain them from mutinying. This prepared them for mischief, and they were resolved to pay a visit to France, before they left the quarters they were then in. As forage grew scarce in our Camp, and none was to be had near us but in Picardy, we had liberty by the favour of Villars to forage in that country. It nettled our soldiers that their General should condescend to ask leave: however they were determined to lay hold of this opportunity of tasting some of the sweets of France.[1]

This mood led to a horrible outrage.

Upon all foragings a strong detachment was sent out the night before, under the command of a general officer, to keep the foragers within bounds, to cover them from the enemy, and to prevent irregularities and abuses. When the detachment marched off, a number of soldiers of all nations stole out of Camp with their arms, they chose officers and swore obedience to them, their principal care being to keep at a distance from the covering detachment. Among these one party of of British soldiers, to the number of six hundred, came to a village called Molain, where the inhabitants were in arms, and had barricaded all the avenues to the town. Upon this an engagement ensued, in which some of the soldiers fell; this enraged the rest to that degree, that they rushed up to the barrier and drove the inhabitants into the church; but as they again fired from thence, in their fury they set fire to the church, burnt it to the ground, and upwards of four hundred persons perished in the flames; then plundering the town, they set it on fire; and as it grew dark, stole privately into Camp. Two days after, a complaint was made to the General, and the affair was inquired into, but no discovery could be made. This was a taste of what France might have expected, and I mention it for that purpose only; for the action in itself is utterly inexcusable.[2]

Later in the year a grievous mutiny actually broke out among the British troops in Ghent, provoked in the first instance by "the extreme badness of their bread."

[1] Parker, pp. 175-176.   [2] *Ibid.*, pp. 176-177.

This prepared them [says Parker] to mutiny; and some sly villains, finding the generality of them in this disposition, artfully insinuated that they had a considerable arrear of pay due to them; that the War being over, the greater part of them would soon be disbanded, and that consequently they must expect to lose all that arrear unless they did themselves justice while they had their arms in their hands. This took with the giddy unthinking part of the soldiery, and a villainous and bloody design was formed.[1]

Fortunately the authorities were warned in time, and after some days of crisis three thousand men, armed and in mutiny, were surrounded by cavalry and cannon, and forced to surrender at discretion: whereupon ten of the ringleaders were executed on the spot.

Corporal Matthew Bishop, who was serving in Ghent at the time, gives an independent account and takes occasion to point his moral:

At that Juncture of Time there was a great Disturbance at Ghent amongst the Soldiers, which occasioned some to suffer Death. On hearing that News, I could not contain myself any longer without observing to the first Officer I met with, *Sir, with submission, what can be the Meaning that all our Garisons are disturbed in this Manner? It is an Instance that never happened during the Time of the Duke of Marlborough.* The Officer replied, *There is no accounting for it*; . . . O the Duke of Marlborough that gained the Love of all Men, knew better, than to put it in any one's Power to upbraid him; for all his Men in general were obsequious. Now they are become refractory, and neglect their Duty.[2]

For his services in the campaign the thanks of both Houses of Parliament were solemnly voted to the Duke of Ormonde.

The separate preliminaries of peace between England and France being now agreed, and England having arranged an armistice for herself in the field and quitted the allied front, it seemed that St John's labours had achieved their first stage. He looked about him for reward and advancement. He intimated to Oxford and the Queen that he would find it agreeable to be raised to the peerage by the revival of the family earldom of Bolingbroke which had just lapsed in the older branch. Oxford would have been wise to comply fully with these desires. He was, however, already conscious of St John's jealousy and latent antagonism. It is one of the self-indulgences of unworthy men in power to pay off such minor scores when opportunity seems to offer. Therefore Oxford, with his remaining influence, moved the Queen to demur to the grant of an

[1] Parker, p. 187.   [2] Bishop, pp. 264–265.

earldom, and accord instead a viscounty. St John was deeply angered by this slight. He saw at length how foolish he would be in quitting the House of Commons, the seat of his direct power upon the Tory Party. It is astonishing to modern eyes that this realization should have come to him so late in the day. The honour and status of a peerage were in this period invested with a glamour and splendour which has since become markedly diminished. The House of Lords, though already decisively overmatched by the Commons, was still the scene of an immense, sedate, and elegant power. St John had yielded to this mood. He had been rebuffed in the manner which he could least easily resent. By all the standards to which he subjected himself in asking for a peerage, the double elevation to a viscounty was enormous. Yet he was dissatisfied— and with good reason. Even a dukedom would not have compensated him for leaving the House of Commons, where his eloquence and partisanship made him in the absence of Oxford supreme.

He now wished to withdraw his request. He was informed by an elaborate grimace of State that the Queen's pleasure had already been exercised for his ennoblement. To decline a viscounty would be to affront the majesty of the realm and the whole nobility. To take such a step upon the difference between a viscounty and an earldom, which was the only reason he could now advance, would be to give offence to the social world in which he moved. Besides, becoming first a viscount was no reason why he should not later on become an earl or better. Thus in July 1712 St John quitted the House of Commons for a more exalted sphere. He did so with the chagrin and latent malice of one who instead of thirty pieces had received only twenty-five.

A week later the battle of Denain let loose its tide of disaster upon the Allies. While Eugene recoiled and Villars advanced from one success to another, it was thought suitable that the new Viscount Bolingbroke should proceed to Paris with an imposing retinue as Ambassador Extraordinary. This step was calculated to give the most marked encouragement to the French and to strike a further wounding blow at the deserted and collapsing allies of twenty years of war. It commended itself to the new Viscount as an opportunity of posing upon what was still the most splendid scene in the world, and also of revelling in those pleasures which French society carried to their highest pitch.

Apart from these advantages his mission was sterile. He was welcomed at the French Court with all the gratitude he deserved. The

King and the highest nobility lavished their favours upon him. His gallantries were viewed with an indulgent eye, though his habit of boasting about them excited comment. Torcy, however, extended him a spacious hospitality. He was the guest of the Foreign Minister's aunt, Madame de Croissy, and here he was entertained by the famous beauty Madame de Tencin, who became his mistress. Madame de Tencin was also a good servant of France, and her liaison with Bolingbroke opened to Torcy then and thenceforward another intimate view into the governing system of Britain. The granting of passports to visit France after the long war, and with so many business prospects opening, was in the gift of the Secretary of State. Bolingbroke was able during his visit to Paris to put the system on so satisfactory a footing that, as we learn from Prior, he netted for himself as much as three thousand pounds in a single year. In public affairs all he gained was an extension of the armistice for an additional two months. This enabled the disasters which befell the allies to come to their full fruition during the campaign.

Chapter Thirty-four

MARLBOROUGH LEAVES ENGLAND

1712—JUNE–DECEMBER

THE presentation of the proposed terms of a separate peace to Parliament on June 6 forced from Marlborough his last public action during the remaining life of the Queen. These terms were a shock to many supporters of the Government, but the Ministerial defence, the realization that the main issue was decided and that the Tory policy had prevailed, commanded great majorities in both Houses. Marlborough made his protest and declared, "That the measures pursued in England for a year past were directly contrary to her Majesty's engagements with the Allies, sullied the triumphs and glories of her reign, and would render the English name odious to all other nations."[1] This is the only record that exists of his speech. Strafford replied with asperity, saying "That some of the Allies [meaning the Dutch] would not show such backwardness to a peace as they had hitherto done but for a member of that illustrious assembly [meaning the Duke of Marlborough] who maintained a secret correspondence with, and endeavoured to persuade them to carry on the war; feeding them with hopes that they should be supported by a strong party here."[2] Cowper, alluding to Strafford's foreign mode of speech, rejoined "That the ex-Ambassador had been so long abroad that he had almost forgotten, not only the language, but the Constitution of his own country. That, according to our laws, it could never be suggested as a crime . . . to hold correspondence with our allies; . . . whereas it would be a hard matter to justify the conduct of some persons in treating clandestinely with the common enemy."[3]

Nothing could, however, stem the tide, and the treaty terms were approved in the Lords by no fewer than eighty-one to thirty-six. Twenty-four lords recorded their formal protest. Among them are the names of Somerset, Godolphin, Devonshire, Haversham, Wharton, Marlborough, Nottingham, Mohun, Townshend, and Cowper. The majority ordered this to be expunged from the

---

[1] *Parliamentary History*, vi, 1146. [2] *Loc. cit.* [3] *Loc. cit.*

journals of the House, but the powerful nobles and politicians concerned, defying Parliamentary laws, had the terms of their protest circulated throughout the country, and only printers and publishers were punished for the offence.

Having thus placed himself on record, Marlborough withdrew finally to the country. Blenheim was, of course, only a skeleton, and all work upon it stopped. But he still had his house at St Albans, and Marlborough House, in London, had been open for nearly a year. He lived during the summer months in rustic pomp at Holywell, observing with impassive eye the procession of military disasters which fell upon the Allies, and the destruction of his achievements in the campaigns of 1710 and 1711. On Blenheim Day he gave a feast, which Godolphin, Cowper, Walpole, and a large company attended. He had pitched his campaigning tent upon the bowling-green. In this historic tabernacle most of the great decisions of his ten campaigns had been taken. The tent, we are told, "was magnificent, being of Arras-work, and very curious in its kind."[1] It stood there the rest of the summer, and sightseers resorted to it in crowds from the countryside at a fee of sixpence. The hostile Press declared he was using army tents to shelter his faction and to amass greater opulence. The venom and scurrility of the attacks made upon him by the Government-paid or otherwise procured writers from Swift downward exceeded anything known before or since. If he had been the vilest criminal, if he had been guilty of cowardice or treachery in the field, if he had led the English armies to a series of shameful defeats, nothing more could have been said against him. *The Examiner* wrote of Malplaquet (April 13):

> What a deplorable Sight it was to see Men with their Limbs shot off lying upon the Field in such an abandoned, wretched Condition that Ravens and Crows have fallen upon them for Carrion. Wanting proper Persons to dress their Limbs, their Wounds putrefied to such a degree that Dogs gnawed their Flesh while they were yet alive. Amidst this Torture, thousands expired that might have been preserved if the General had not sunk the Money designed for Medicines and Surgeons. No Age, no Country, how barbarous so ever, hath ever given us such an Instance of Cruelty and Avarice.[2]

Another passage in this organ of St John's roused the indignation of Captain Parker:

> That the Duke of Marlborough was naturally a very great coward: That all the victories and successes that attended him, were owing

---

[1] Lediard, iii, 291–292.   [2] Quoted in Laprade, p. 120.

to mere chance, and to those about him; for whenever he came to be engaged in action, he was always in a great hurry, and very much confounded upon every little emergency that happened; and would cry in great confusion to those about him, "What shall we do now?"

"Had I not read these very words," wrote the Captain, "I should never have believed that any man could have the face to publish so notorious a falsehood."[1]

During the autumn Marlborough resolved to leave England. There was then, and has been since, much controversy about his reasons, and so many can be given that a certain air of mystery still shrouds the event. There are, as usual, two contradictory explanations for his action. The first is that he wished to go, that the Cabinet would have prevented him, but that Harley secured him his passport from the Queen. Alternatively, it is said that he did not wish to go, but that Harley, fearing to have him in the country, forced him into exile by the threat of using letters or information supplied by the French Government either of Marlborough's correspondence with Saint-Germains or of his offers to make peace in 1708.

Both these theories are plausible. Marlborough would certainly have liked to live in England; but this ceaseless girding and insult directed upon him by the Court and the Ministry, with all their resources, was not calculated to make life pleasant even in the country in summertime. Winter was now drawing near, and with it the reassembly of a Parliament eager to hound him down, and ready to approve every new affront or injury which Ministers might suggest. Although the Whig nobility, the bulk of the officers who had served under him, and the mass of ordinary folk were still friendly, and as the social scale was descended enthusiastic, a definite change had been produced during this year by the torrent of calumny unloosed and impelled against him.

In those days of brief triennial Parliaments a new election was distant but a year. If Marlborough remained in England nothing could prevent his greatness from becoming the most obvious target. Instead of the bolts and balls he was accustomed to face in the field, he would find himself in the midst of a filthy warfare of slander and abuse. The election of 1713 might well be fought on fouling his name and reputation. The worst motives would be imputed to whatever he did. If he exerted himself it would be his disappointed malice; if he remained silent it was no doubt his guilty conscience. All these long years of camp and march we have seen

[1] Parker, p. 168.

in his letters the longing for home and peace—the peaches ripening on the wall, the great building at Woodstock growing from day to day, rest with children and Sarah at his side. But this prospect now seemed to be defiled. He could not at this time find happiness or even peace in England.

A second set of arguments arose from the political outlook. The Queen was ageing fast. Her health was such that almost any month might see a dangerous crisis. The whole issue of the Succession had now again been called in question by the Parliament of Tory squires, and by the profound quarrel which the two ruling Ministers were developing against their allies, and their deep understandings with the enemy. The Tory policy which Harley and St John, however ill-wed, were unfolding step by step must reach its crisis before long. The two Englands stood against one another, and were being inflamed to hatred and violence by every art which Government authority or high party influence could command. Marlborough could not live at home without the active protection of one or the other of the violent factions. Naturally he must incline to the Whigs; and if so he must endure ceaseless persecution from the Ministers, and from the Queen into whose ears their lies and hatred were daily poured. Already he was beset by observers and spies. Every person who visited his house, every call he paid, even the days when he kept indoors—all were eagerly reported to Whitehall.

There was a fierce spirit among the veteran officers of the Army now at home in England. Some had been forced to resign their commissions; others had seen promotion go on party grounds to their rivals, their juniors, and, as they judged, their inferiors. They felt that the fruits of the long struggle which had been won, and in which they had risked their lives, were being wantonly cast away, and that the military fame of England, till now glorious, was being dishonoured. The idea that the British Army, which had borne itself so proudly on the Continent, had become odious in all the camps for deeds of baseness and deceit obsessed their minds. These were hard men, wrought by a lifetime of war, to whom bloodshed was a profession. Their swords were at their sides as they paced the streets of London. At any moment—in the park, in the coffee-houses, in the taverns—taunts might be thrown and passions break loose, and a bloody deed be done. Whatever happened would be laid to Marlborough's account. To leave the country was to be free from all this. The whole Continent regarded Marlborough as a prodigy. The lustre of his victories, the sagacious consistency of his policy, the enormous changes in the relative power of nations which had followed from his conduct, assured him a reverential welcome everywhere outside France. He was rich; money could be transferred abroad; there was Mindelheim, which he had never seen. In England he was a prey. In Europe he was a Prince. Here, then, was peace and a broad sanctuary. Why tarry among foes and fogs?

A third, more directly practical reason for his going abroad is apparent in the State suits set on foot against him. The Attorney-General was slowly moving forward the prosecution which, pursuant to the resolution of the Commons, required that Marlborough should repay to the Exchequer all the moneys he had expended upon the Army intelligence service in a ten years' successful war. This might well confront him with a judgment to find more than a quarter of a million sterling. Another suit, equally vexatious, had been started against him by the Crown about the expenses of the "monument of national gratitude," Blenheim. Careful as he had been, it was alleged that when the Government payments were in arrear he had written from the front to keep the workmen in employment for a few weeks upon his orders or Sarah's, or otherwise had interfered. The Queen was now moved to use this against him. A process to require him to repay at least £30,000 was on foot. If he left England these processes might be suspended. If he remained at home and at variance with the Ministry he might be sensibly impoverished. One could not tell the lengths which malice would go as it fed upon triumph.

These causes seem a sufficient reason for any man's departure from his native land. But Marlborough's traducers have found others in addition.

During the debates about the peace, in opposition to it, M. de Torcy acquainted Lord Oxford, that after the Duke of Marlborough had hindered the peace of 1706, when it should have been made, he had treated with the French court to make them one, and was to have two million of crowns for it. . . .

When M. de Torcy discovered this, the King of France allowed Lord Oxford to make use of it, to send the duke of Marlborough abroad; but insisted that his life should not be touched; and so it was. They had a meeting at Thomas Harley's house, in James street, Westminster, Oxford coming to the street door, in his coach, the Duke of Marlborough in a chair to the garden door opening into the park; it was then resolved, that the duke of Marlborough should go abroad. Prince Eugene and Lord Wharton both said, on the occasion, that the Duke of Marlborough had not a clear conscience, or he would not have submitted to that step.[1]

The authority for this is Oxford's secretary, Erasmus Lewis, a serious witness. The arrangements for the meeting are certainly characteristic of Oxford. Moreover, there is no doubt that a meeting took place, for Marlborough, writing to Oxford from Antwerp on December 4/15, 1712, says, "*When I had the honour of seeing you last*, I told you that the disappointment of Mr Cadogan's company would hinder my going to Italy this season."[2] At this meeting, it is alleged, Oxford blackmailed Marlborough into leaving the country.

If this story be true Oxford must have had an easy task. He was forcing an open door with a battering-ram. It cannot be thought at all surprising that the French should at this time, as at others, wish to strike down Marlborough, nor that they should place incriminating letters, if they had them, at the disposal of their English confederates. "This man," they might have said, "who is heading the resistance to peace, was ready enough to make one, less than four years ago, if he had got two millions out of it." It would be beyond human nature that a monarch and Government in dire straits, with an exhausted nation behind them, should respect such a pledge of secrecy to their arch-foe now driven from power.

Against this view, however, there are a number of facts. Marlborough had exacted the return of his original letters from Berwick, and there is no reason to suppose that Berwick, punctilious in a matter of honour, especially towards a kinsman and a soldier for whom he had profound admiration, did not comply with this condition. There would, of course, remain any disclosure the French Court might make about the negotiation; but all this could be denied, and the assertions of a war enemy have never been taken as good evidence. Secondly, Marlborough himself wished, on the grounds which have been set forth, to leave the country, so that there was no necessity for Oxford to put pressure upon him. Thirdly, apart from Oxford himself, the "major part of the Ministers, particularly Mr St John, was against it, being afraid of his Grace as well abroad as at home and thought their power would secure them better against him here."[3] It was Oxford who, behind their backs, procured Marlborough's passport from the Queen, and took pains to obtain Marlborough's personal acknowledgment to him for it.[4] Anne

[1] Carte's Memorandum Book; Macpherson, ii, 85.   [2] Bath Papers, *H.M.C.*, i, 225.
[3] Boyer, quoted by Lediard, ii, 294–295.   [4] *Loc. cit.*

was favourable to Marlborough's wish and remarked, "He did wisely."[1]

The pass permitted Marlborough to go into foreign parts,

> whithersoever he may think fit, together with his suite, and committed him to the good offices of kings, princes, republics and Her Majesty's Allies as well as to commanders etc. her own subjects. Allowance to go freely and commodiously wherever his need requires, and states that such good offices shall be acknowledged and returned when opportunity serves.

It is dated from Windsor Castle on October 30, 1712, and countersigned "Bolingbroke." This did not prevent the Secretary of State sending the following message of November 11 through Gaultier to Torcy:

> The Duke of Marlborough has asked permission from the Queen to quit the kingdom, and that, after a good deal of contest and consideration, her Majesty has given him leave. He is to pass by Ostend, Bruges, Ghent, Brussels, and Liége to his principality [of Mindelheim], thence through the Tyrol to Venice, and finally to Naples, where he is to sojourn as long as he pleases. Such is the route which has been traced out for him without permission to pass anywhere else.[2]

To describe Bolingbroke as a good liar would be a mis-statement. He scattered his lies with such profusion that he wasted them.

Another link with England had been snapped by the death of Godolphin on September 15, 1712. Boyer says that

> he died at St Albans, having been long afflicted with the stone in the kidneys. . . . Notwithstanding the clamours which were raised against him, his administration was found thoroughly clear, sound and unattackable; so that as he lived, he died with an unblemished character, to which the most candid of his enemies paid a due respect.[3]

Walpole visited Godolphin during his last illness at St Albans. As Godolphin lay dying he turned to Sarah and said to her, "If you ever forsake that young man, and if souls are permitted to return from the grave to the earth, I will appear to you, and reproach

[1] Cowper, *Diary*, p. 54.
[2] Letter dated November 11, 1712, French Foreign Office Archives; quoted by Stanhope, *Reign of Queen Anne*, p. 539.
[3] Boyer, p. 392.

you for your conduct."[1] But Sarah quarrelled with every one before her life was over. Godolphin was not buried for three weeks. His embalmed body lay in the Jerusalem Chamber until a sufficient number of Whig Knights of the Garter could come to Westminster to bear the pall, "for they don't find the Tory Knights so ready to come to town a purpose."[2] He was interred in the Abbey on October 7, the Dukes of Marlborough, Devonshire, Richmond, and Schomberg bearing up the pall.

Sarah's tribute deserves record.

> He had conducted the Queen with the care and tenderness of a father or a guardian through a state of helpless ignorance and had faithfully served her in all her difficulties before she was Queen, as well as greatly contributed to the glories she had to boast of after she was so. . . . He was a man of wonderful frugality in the public concerns but of no great money above his paternal estate. What he left at his death showed that he had been indeed the nation's treasurer and not his own.[3]

On November 15 a shocking event occurred which must have reconciled Marlborough to leaving England. The Duke of Hamilton, newly created Duke of Brandon, a man of great charm and quality, a strong Jacobite, had been nominated Ambassador to France, and, having asked the Pretender's leave before accepting the post,[4] was soon to start for Paris. He thus became the central figure in the plans of the Ministry. A quarrel about a disputed estate arose between him and Lord Mohun, who had so lately visited Poulett with Marlborough's challenge. The result was a duel justly described in the annals of the age as "terrible." They met at daybreak in Hyde Park. Colonel Hamilton attended the Duke, and Mohun's second was General Macartney, Marlborough's faithful officer, who had been broken for drinking "confusion to the Whigs." The Duke of Hamilton proposed that the seconds should not fight; as, however, they both desired to do so, he consented, and the two pairs attacked each other with their rapiers. Almost immediately Hamilton killed Mohun, but at the same time he received himself a wound of which he died in a few minutes. Swift says:

> The dog Mohun was killed on the spot; and [while] the Duke

---

[1] Coxe, *Walpole*, i, 42.　　　　[2] *The Wentworth Papers*, p. 302.
[3] Essays by Sarah included in *Sarah Correspondence* (ii, 125–126).
[4] *English Historical Review*, i, 768.

was over him, Mohun shortening his sword, stabbed him in at the shoulder to the heart. The Duke was helped toward the cake-house by the ring in Hyde Park, . . . and died on the grass, before he could reach the house; and was brought home in his coach by eight, while the poor Duchess was asleep.[1]

This tragedy produced a furious commotion. The Tories declared that Macartney had stabbed Hamilton as he lay on the ground. Both seconds fled the country. The hue and cry was raised after Macartney, and Bolingbroke paid a bill for the efforts made to apprehend him. He escaped to the Continent, knowing that he would certainly not receive fair treatment from the dominant faction. After the accession of George I he returned and submitted himself to justice. He was tried and acquitted, and his name cleared.[2] But now, in 1712, every effort was made to cast further aspersions upon Marlborough. He was the centre, said the Tories, from which the bullies of the Flanders army derived their inspiration in murdering the Queen's Ambassadors. At the coroner's inquest it was insinuated that he had been privy to the challenge sent by Mohun to Hamilton. The fact that both Mohun and Macartney were near to him in sentiment and association lent colour to these utterly unfounded suggestions. To free himself from such an atmosphere, where furious men of the sword were eager to engage the political opponents who they conceived had ruined them and their country, was surely one of the motives which had made him resolve to leave a land so torn at the height of its success with feud and hatred.

Marlborough conveyed most of his settled estate to his sons-in-law. He transferred £50,000 to Cadogan at The Hague, so that, as Sarah wrote, he should not be without the means of sustenance "if the Stuart line were restored." On November 24 he set out with only a few servants for Dover. Sarah was to follow later. Contrary winds detained him for a week, but on December 1 he embarked upon the ordinary packet-boat without any attention except the salute of its captain. No record exists of his reflections upon this melancholy voyage.

Sarah in her will prescribed as the condition of any biography of her husband that no single line of poetry should be quoted in it. Nevertheless, the valedictory verses which Addison wrote deserve inclusion on every ground.

[1] Swift, *Journal to Stella*, November 15, 1712.
[2] The Privy Council minutes on the duel in Dartmouth Papers, *H.M.C.*, p. 311.

Go, Mighty Prince, and those great Nations see,
Which thy Victorious Arms before made free;
View that fam'd Column, where thy Name engrav'd,
Shall tell their Children, who their Empire sav'd.
Point out that *Marble*, where thy Worth is shown
To every grateful Country, but thy own.

O Censure undeserv'd! Unequal Fate!
Which strove to lessen *Him* who made *Her* Great;
Which pamper'd with Success, and Rich in Fame,
Extoll'd his Conquest, but condemn'd His Name,
But Virtue is a Crime, when plac'd on high;
Tho' all the Fault's in the Beholder's Eye.[1]

[1] Lediard, iii, 297.

Chapter Thirty-five

EXILE

1713

THE captain of the packet-boat on arriving at Ostend the
next morning hoisted her ensign on the topmast-head.
This was taken as a signal that Marlborough was on board.
Forthwith all the cannon on the sea-front fired a salute,
and on the ship entering the harbour the artillery of the ramparts
fired three salvos. Cadogan and the Governor with a great crowd
received Marlborough as he landed. When the next day, December 13, he set out for Antwerp not only did all the Dutch cannon
fire again, but even the English ships in the harbour as well.[1] At
Antwerp he was met by the governor, the Marquis of Terracena,
who had come over to the allied cause with the rest of Belgium on
the morrow of Ramillies. The Marquis offered in the name of the
Emperor all the honours due to sovereigns. Marlborough declined
these dangerous compliments; but the mass of the people thronged
about him, acclaiming him as their deliverer and champion. This,
indeed, he had been, against not only the French but also the Dutch.

From Antwerp he wrote to Oxford asking again that Cadogan
might be released from his duties to travel with him as his companion.[2] The brave, generous Irish soldier, who was never found
wanting in fidelity or chivalry, gladly cast away any prospects he
might have under the Tories in order to accompany his old chief.
"The Duke of Marlborough's ill-health," he wrote to Oxford, "the
inconvenience a winter's journey exposes him to, and his being
without any one friend to accompany him, make the requesting
leave to wait on him an indispensable duty on me, who for so many
years have been honoured with his confidence and friendship, and
[owe] all I have in the world to his favour."[3] The Ministers were
not unwilling to oblige him. The Queen's permission was granted;
but Cadogan was shortly afterwards dismissed from all his appointments.

[1] Lediard, iii, 297. [2] Bath Papers, *H.M.C.*, i, 225.
[3] Portland Papers, *H.M.C.*, v, 257.

977

So enthusiastic were the demonstrations of the Belgians that the Duke, mindful of the long arm of Queen Anne's Government, took by-roads on his journey to Maestricht. Here in Dutch territory he found the whole garrison drawn up to receive him. General Dopf attached himself to him in the name of the States-General, and with Cadogan conducted him upon what became perforce a triumphal progress. On the journey to Aix-la-Chapelle all the cavalry forces within long marches came out to ride with him; and in the town of Aix, then so small as to be described by Lediard as "a poor, obscure village," the peasants from the surrounding country crowded in, curious and wondering. A saying ran about Holland and Belgium at this time, "Better be born in Lapland than in England."[1]

From Aix-la-Chapelle Marlborough wrote to Sarah. She had much to arrange before leaving England, and he missed her greatly. "The port of Ostend," he wrote, "is never shut by the frost and that of the Brill very rarely. . . . This frosty weather makes the sea calm, and the roads as good as in summer; so that I could have wished we might have got to Frankfort before the thaw, of which I now despair."[2]

John to Sarah

AIX-LA-CHAPELLE
Jan. 21, 1713

*Since the 20th of the last month I have receiv'd no letters from England, so that I am altogether ignorant where You maybe that I am resolv'd to write no more til I hear from You. Wee have now a thorough thaw. You will find the ways extreamly bad, and as this place is extreamly durty I have resolv'd to go to Mastrick the begining of the weak, and there to expect You. I send this letter to Ostend in hopes it may meet You there, for affter all the advises Your friends may give You, I cant but think that You will find that the most Convenient place for Your landing will be Ostend, where I wish You in safety with all my heart, so that I may have the happyness of having Your Company.[3]

John to Sarah

MAESTRICHT
Feb. 5, 1713

If you have observed by my letters that I thought you would have left England sooner than you have been able to do, I hope you will be so kind and just to me, to impute it to the great desire I had of having the satisfaction of your company. For I am extremely sensible of the obligation I have to you, for the resolution you have taken of

---

[1] Blenheim MSS.   [2] Coxe, vi, 227.   [3] Blenheim MSS.

leaving your friends and country for my sake. I am very sure, if there be anything in my power that may make it easy to you, I should do it with all imaginable pleasure. In this place you will have little conveniences; so that we must get to Frankfort as soon as we can. I wish we may be better there; but I fear you will not be easy till we get to some place where we may settle for some time; so that we may be in a method and orderly way of living; and if you are then contented, I shall have nothing to trouble me.[1]

Sarah joined her husband in the New Year.[2] He had impatiently and eagerly awaited her arrival in Maestricht. Together they wended through Germany, always being received with respect and pleasure by the inhabitants and with salutes and ceremonies by the rulers.

Sarah's letters from exile are a refreshing counterpart after forty years to the love-letters which she wrote to the young officer of the Guards. The rabid politician, bitter controversialist, fierce mentor and rebuker of the Queen, the tyrant of the Court and of society, recede. We find a mellow and philosophical personage, sometimes scornful but entirely self-possessed, content for the most part with life as it offers itself each day. Her two principal correspondents in England were Mrs Clayton, wife of one of the Duke's estate agents at Woodstock, and one of her cousins, Mr Jennings, who had driven down with her to Dover and had seen her on board the packet for Ostend.

She reacted in a lively fashion to her Continental impressions. "All the Places one pass's thro in these Parts," she wrote to Jennings (February 12),

have an Air very different from London. The most considerable People I have seen have but just enough to live, and the ordinary People, I believe, are half-starved; but they are all so good and so civill that I could not help wishing . . . that they had the Riches and the Libertys that our wise Cittyzens and Countrymen have thrown away, or at best put in great Danger, . . . and tho the Generality of them I have seen are Roman Catholicks, they fear the Power of France so much that they drink to the Protestant Succession, and the Honours they have don me in all Places upon the Duke of Marlborough's Account is not to bee imagined, which is not disagreeable now, because as it cannot proceed from Power, it shews that he made a right Use of it when hee was General.[3]

[1] Coxe, vi, 229.
[2] She applied to Dartmouth for a passport on January 29. (Dartmouth Papers, *H.M.C.*, p. 315.)
[3] *Letters of Sarah, Duchess of Marlborough, at Madresfield Court* (1875), p. 25.

Husband and wife both stayed some time at Aix-la-Chapelle, where John had "the advantage of one month of the hot baths."[1] "I cannot end my letter," says Sarah (March 31),

without giving you some Account how I pass my Time in this Place, which is in visiting Nunnerys and Churches, where I have heard of such Marvells and seen such ridiculous Things as would appear to you incredible. . . . Tis so much beyond all that I ever saw or heard of in England of that Religion which I am apt to think has made those Atheists that are in the World; for tis impossible to see the Abuses of the Priests without raising strange Thoughts in one's Mind, which one checks as soon as one can; and I think tis unnaturall for any Body to have so monstrous a Notion as that there is no God, if the Priests (to get all the Power and Mony themselves) did not act in the Manner that they doe in these Parts, where they have three Parts of all the Land in the Country, and yet they are not contented, but squeeze the poor deluded People to get more, who are really half-starved by the vast number of Holydays in which they can't work, and the Mony they must pay when they have it, for the Forgivenesse of their Sins. . . . In one Church where I was lately, there were 27 jolly-face Priests that had Nothing in the World to doe but to say Mass for the living, and to take the dead Souls the sooner out of Purgatory by their Prayers.[2]

At Frankfort, which they reached in May, they were not far from the war. "I am come just now," wrote Sarah (May 14, 1713),

from a Window from which I saw a great many Troops pass that were under the Command of P. Eugene. They paid all the Respects as they went by to the D. of Marl. as if hee had been in his old Post. The Men lookd very well. . . . To see so many brave Men marching was a very fine Sight, it gave me melancholly Reflections, and made me weep; but at the same Time I was so much animated that I wishd I had been a Man that I might have ventured my Life a thousand Times in the glorious Cause of Liberty, the Loss of which will be seen and lamented too late for any Remedy; and upon this Occasion I must borrow a Speech out of Cato: "May some chosen Curse, some hidden Thunder from the Shores of Heaven, red with uncommon Wrath, blast the Men that use their Greatness to their Country's Ruin." . . .

When I had written so far I was calld to receive the Honour of a Visit from the Elector of Miance. I fancy hee came to this Place chiefly to see the D. of Marl. His shape is, like my own, a little of the fatest, but in my Life I never saw a Face that expressed so much Opennesse, Honesty, Sense, and good Nature. . . . I can't help repeat-

<hr>

[1] Bath Papers, *H.M.C.*, i, 225.　　　　　　　　[2] *Ibid.*, 28.

ing Part of his Compliment to the Duke of Marl., that he wished any Prince of the Empire might bee severely punished if ever they forgot his Merit. The Civillitys are so great that are paid him by all sorts of People, that one can't but reflect how much a greater Claim he had to all manner of good Usage from his own ungrateful Country. It would fill a Book to give you an Account of all the Honours don him as we came to this Place by the Ellector of Solms, and in all the Towns, as if the D. of Marl. had been King of them, which in his Case is very valuable, because it shews tis from their Hearts; and if hee had been their King hee might have been like others, a Tyrant.[1]

May 16, 1713

I am not uneasy as you think upon Account of the Time that is so heavy. . . . Mr Cowley . . . says 'tis very fantastical and contradictory in human Nature that People are generally thought to love themselves better than all the Rest of the World, and yet never can indure to bee with themselves; . . . but tho' I love Solitude more than ever, I would not have you think that I don't wish earnestly to see my Friends, and to be in a clean sweet House and Garden, tho' ever so small, for here there is Nothing of that kind; and in the Gardens, tho' the Hedges are green and pretty, the Sand that goes over one's Shoes is so disagreeable that I love to walk in the Roads and Fields better, where the D. of Marl. and I go constantly every Day in the Afternoon, and stop the Coach and go out wherever wee see a Place that looks hard and clean. 'Tother Day we were walking upon the Road, and a Gentleman and his Lady went by us in their Chariot who wee had never seen before, and after passing us with the usual Civilitys, in half a quarter of an Hour or less they bethought themselves and turnd back, came out of their Coach to us, and desired that wee would go into their Garden, which was very near that Place, and which they think, I believe, a fine Thing, desiring us to accept of a Key. This is only a little Tast of the Civillity of People abroad, and I could not help thinking that wee might have walk'd in England as far as our Feet would have carryd us before Anybody that we had never seen before would have lighted out of their Coach to have entertained us. . . .

I am confydent I should have been the greatest Hero that ever was known in the Parliament House if I had been so happy as to have been a Man; as to the Field, I can't brag much of that sort of Courage, but I am sure no Mony, Tittles, nor Ribons should have prevaild with me to have betrayd my Country, or to have flatterd the Villains that hav don it. . . . This long Letter upon Nothing will make you think that tis no Wonder my Time does not lye upon my Hands, since I can employ it so idly, but that is no Argument for my troubling you so much.[2]

[1] Bath Papers, *H.M.C.*, i, 31.   [2] *Ibid.*, 37–38.

Cardonnel's wife had died, and Marlborough wrote (July 24):

> I would have written to you sooner, dear Cardonel, if I had believed it possible to say anything to lessen your grief; but, I think, of all worldly misfortunes, the losing what one loves is the greatest, and nothing but time can ease you. However, I could not deny myself any longer the satisfaction of writing to assure you that I shall always be very sorry for anything that is a trouble to you, and that I long for the opportunity of assuring you myself that I am your humble servant and faithful friend.
>
> P.S. The Duchess of Marlborough desires me to assure you of her true friendship and concern for you upon all occasions, and she would have wrote herself, but she thinks this will be the least troublesome to you.[1]

From May till the end of the year Marlborough and his wife lived quietly in Frankfort. The Duke paid a visit to his principality of Mindelheim, and was received there with royal honours. All this time the decoration of Marlborough House was proceeding, and the celebrated Laguerre was painting the battle-scenes upon the staircase and the hall. "I am very desirous of having it finished," wrote Sarah from Frankfort (June 17, 1713),

> tho the giving all the Trade and Power to France does not look as though I should ever enjoy it. However, I have this Satisfaction Mischiefs that are coming upon my Country, and having nothing to reproach myself with, nor nothing in my Power that can doe any good, I am as quiet and contented as any Philosopher ever was. But, at the same time, if I were a Man I should struggle to the last Moment in the glorious Cause of Liberty; for if one succeeds tis a great deal of Pleasure, and if one fails tho one loses one's Life, in that Case one is a Gainer, and when one considers seriously tis no matter how or when one dyes, provided one lives as one ought to doe.[2]

> *October* 27, 1713
>
> . . . I should be very well contented to live out my short Span of Life in any of my country Hous's. This is a World that is subject to frequent Revolutions, and tho one wish's to leave one's Posterity secure, there is so few that makes a suitable Return that even upon that Account . . . one need not be unhappy for Anything that is not in one's Power to help.

Gradually, however, homesickness got the better of her "phylosophy," and she uttered a cry of pain more audible because of its restraint.

[1] Coxe, vi, 244.　　　[2] *Ibid.*, 41.

The best Thing I have heard is that those Men who have been so bold in betraying this Country have been much frightnd of late, but I have heard that some of them were never counted very valiant, and tis the Nature of Cowards, I believe, never to think they have Security enough when the least Danger appeares. . . . But I am intirely of your Mind that wee shall soon bee out of the Pain of Uncertainty. I wish I could as easyly believe that I shall bee contented when I have lost all, and am forced to live the rest of my Life in these durty Countrys. I am now in some Doubt whether my Phylosophy will goe so far as that, tho it has been sufficient to support me against all that the worst of Men or Women have don, and tho I know one shall bear whatever one can't help, I pray most heartily that I may not be tryd any further, for tis quite another Thing to hear that one is never to see England nor one's Children again . . . than it is to leave a disagreeable Court, when one knows one has not deserved ill Treatment, and only to make a Sort of a Pilgrimage for a little while, hoping to see Justice don upon some of one's Enemys.[1]

The hardest forfeit was not, however, to be exacted.

There are three aspects of Marlborough's life at this time which require scrutiny. First, his contacts with England; secondly, his relations with Saint-Germains; and, thirdly, his association with Hanover. Upon all these there has been much discussion.

Cadogan was his chief agent and most faithful friend. The rugged Irish soldier who had borne the brunt of so many serious days had been for twenty years in Marlborough's circle and for ten his right-hand man. He lost his employments; yet he still preserved connexions with Ministers to which they attached importance, and which were serviceable to Marlborough. Cadogan shared in the main Marlborough's exile, but was able to pass to and fro from Germany to England through Holland, or even through Dunkirk, being everywhere received as the honoured Quartermaster of the army in famous days.

Stanhope ranks next in Marlborough's system. The immense personal force and versatility of this man grows on all those who study his vivid career. He was as straight as a die. Sincere, ardent Whig and Protestant, warrior, diplomatist, and statesman, he was certainly one of the greatest personalities of the Age of Anne. Marlborough placed full confidence in him, and he was upon the whole his foremost champion in London. Yet this attachment was not due so much to personal regard or admiration as to a conviction

[1] Coxe, vi, 43.

that Marlborough's sword and the Protestant Succession were one. All the Whigs valued Stanhope, from the ageing Lords of the Junto to the new generation of brilliant men who were now approaching their prime. They knew that in the Cause he would stop at nothing that honour allowed.

The third was Sunderland. His disloyalties to Marlborough in the days of prosperity had arisen mostly out of his superabundant Whiggery. This characteristic, which Queen Anne found so obnoxious, and which in former years had been a marked inconvenience to Cabinet business, now in Opposition left the former Secretary of State with a secondary but none the less unshakable position in the heart of the Whig Party. Well may they have said to him as misfortunes fell in successive sheets upon them, and as their resentments smouldered with a fierceness we can hardly understand, "You were indeed right when you wished to use our Parliament against the accursed Abigail." Sunderland's ties with Marlborough were those of husband of his daughter and father of his heir. Walpole was another Whig in a close intimacy with the great absentee. The able Stair, leading the Whigs in Scotland—the danger-point of Jacobite intrigue—and the younger Craggs, the faithful envoy of many missions, were also in frequent movement between Frankfort or Antwerp and London.

Nearly all these men, now in this chilly period, had sunshine days before them. Cadogan would be Captain-General, Stanhope Secretary of State and head of a Government. A similar experience awaited Sunderland. Before Walpole there spread that long reign of power which consolidated the achievements of Marlborough's wars, and laid the foundations on which the great Chatham was afterwards to build the further expansion of England. Stair was to become one of the most capable ambassadors our Island has ever sent to Paris. Craggs attained a Secretaryship of State. To all these men during the years of evil Marlborough was a figure of unfading fame, and if occasion should serve of immense importance.

It seems unnatural that, with these masterful, virile Whig associates and all that the near future seemed to hold in store, Marlborough should still have cultivated those undefined, mysterious, and to a large extent meaningless relations with Saint-Germains which never ceased from 1689, when William was enthroned, to 1716, when Marlborough sank into bowed old age. His communications with the cast-out Court, his asseverations of sympathy, his cruelty of mocking hopes, his blandishments and moon-shine promises, continued in an airy way. During his stay at Frank-fort he was in touch with Mary of Modena, with his nephew Berwick, and with the pretended Prince of Wales. In this phase there are no letters of Marlborough's, authentic or forged; but the Stuart archives, the Macpherson documents, and Berwick's memoirs all show us the repercussion upon the shadow Court of occasional communications received from Marlborough—always referred to in their code as "Monsieur Malbranche." He is from time to time visited by an agent, who converses with him, reports the gist, and returns with conciliatory replies. These interchanges were initiated by the Jacobite circles themselves. Soon after the Duke was dis-missed from his posts at the beginning of 1712 Middleton, the Pretender's Secretary of State, had written to him that the King and the Queen-Mother were convinced that it must be a source of grief to him that he had not followed their advice in paying his debt to them while he had the means at his disposal. They regretted his misfortune, but the King had great confidence in him and awaited his assistance; for even if his power had vanished, his ability and experience would be of great value.[1]

From Berwick's letters we see that Marlborough asked the banished Prince and circle to trust him as a friend who always cherished the hope of being of service. He suggested to them that they should use their influence, and that of the French Government, to assuage the hostility of Oxford towards him. He pointed out that the Tory Government had all his estates and property in their power, that he was pursued by a Crown lawsuit which might beggar him, and that unless they could help him he would be forced to make some bargain with Harley which would prevent him from achieving his lifelong aspirations for their good. Finally he sought a pardon from James III which would protect him in the event of a restora-tion.[2] These protestations did not deceive Saint-Germains. They had endured twenty years of them. On the other hand, they were in no condition to reject any assurances of goodwill. In their for-lorn plight, with the desperate project of an invasion of Britain always in their minds, it was better to be cheated again by Marl-borough than to feel once and for all certain he was their foe. They nursed the illusion that a day would come when by a sweep of his arm he would undo the past. But this was but a daydream. They had little to give but words, which seemed an equitable return.

[1] Macpherson, ii, 297.   [2] Stuart Papers, *H.M.C.*, i, 278–279.

Berwick's letters speak always slightingly and sceptically of Marlborough's assurances, and yet they give the impression that Berwick is always pleading his uncle's cause at Saint-Germains. He thought it best to do so in an offhand manner. We know this gentleman is only playing with us. Still, it may suit our interests to work upon his fears. Let us pay him words for words. Above all, we must never regard him as a man either to be totally trusted or to be considered of no power or value. Had Berwick been a perfervid advocate of Marlborough, his ardour would at once have been discounted because of their kinship, and by the soldierly esteem which was known to subsist between them as military men. Thus what Berwick advised was done, and back went the messenger with polite comfortings, the counterpart of what Marlborough had proffered.

Historians have made great play with this shadow traffic. They have sought to represent it as a prodigy of infamy and deceit, and have even alleged that Marlborough was at all times ready to serve the side that won. But there is no truth in this. That Marlborough would have been glad to end his days at Blenheim Palace even if Parliament had brought back the Stuart line may be true. He did not wish to die abroad in poverty, or to be victimized and stripped at home; but he never meant to allow a Jacobite restoration if by his utmost exertions he could prevent it. This is what invests his whole relationship to Saint-Germains with an air of heartlessness and hypocrisy, which was habitual and persisted in long after his gestures had ceased to count in any effective degree.

Why did he do it? At this stage he must have realized that the risk of such correspondence far outweighed the reality of any benefits he could personally receive. It might estrange him from all his Whig colleagues. It might ruin his interests with the future Hanoverian King. It is possible only to surmise the answer. There is, however, a theory which fits all the facts of twenty years. These contacts with the Jacobite Court were to him a window of indispensable intelligence. We have seen how on the eve of the Blenheim march he was closeted with the Jacobite agents, and how he learned from them in return that Berwick was to serve in Spain and would not be sent against him in Germany. Is it certain that the Paris spy whose deadly information has been mentioned so frequently, and who clearly moved in the innermost circles of Court politics and fashion at Versailles, was a Frenchman, and not an English Jacobite of rank, busying himself in this ceaseless reporting of military and political facts? Might not such an agent have felt

that he was helping his own country at the same time that he
pocketed the Secret Service payments, and might he not have salved
his conscience by the belief that in helping Marlborough he was
helping some one who was perhaps the sole hope at once of a victorious England and a Stuart restoration?

This is, of course, pure speculation, but at this period we find
Marlborough's relations with the Court of Hanover as good as those
with Saint-Germains. We have seen how some of William III's
Ministers maintained correspondence with James II, and showed
King William the letters they sent and the answers they received.
Something very similar occurred at the present juncture. Marl-
borough is hand-in-glove with the Hanoverian Court. All their
principal personages are working in the closest confidence with him.
Bernstorf, Robethon, Bothmar, ask his opinion and act on his
advice. They were as sure that he was in their interests as the
Jacobites were sure they were being fooled.

In these spider's webs of diplomacy and intrigue all the actors
were enveloped. Oxford's and Bolingbroke's relations with Torcy,
begun while they were at war and continued now, were more confidential than any which they had with the Queen, with their allies,
with their colleagues, or with their own supporters in Parliament.
In October 1712 Bolingbroke had asked Torcy to let him have the
names of Whig leaders who were in correspondence with Saint-
Germain.[1] Torcy accordingly approached the Pretender and his
Secretaries. It was vital to the banished Court that the inviolability
of British confidences made to them should be preserved. Honour
apart, one single breach of confidence would have fatally and for
ever debased the currency of treason. The Pretender replied to the
effect that he was a gentleman as well as a king. Nevertheless Torcy
and the French Foreign Office, to whom the poor Jacobites were
daily beholden, managed to obtain either some old letters of Marlborough's or tolerable proofs that communications had passed
between him and Saint-Germains.

Some time in 1713 Harley, himself wooing both the Pretender
and the Elector alternately, sent documentary evidence to Hanover
which he confidently expected would blast Marlborough's dangerous credit in that quarter.[2] When the whole tale of Marlborough's
craft and stratagems is remembered, and how he was renowned for dissimulation, it is indeed astonishing that these revelations should not
have achieved their aim. But they made not the slightest impression.

---

[1] Stuart Papers, *H.M.C.*, i, 248. [2] See Macpherson, ii, 638.

Klopp says, "Marlborough succeeded in an astonishing way in not losing the confidence of Saint-Germains, while at the same time preserving that of Hanover."[1]

But this dictum would be erroneously construed if it were thought that Marlborough was in fact playing a double game. On the one side all was civil sham, and known to be so; on the other, deadly earnest and rightly judged as such. The Electress Sophia reposed absolute faith in him. She regarded him with the highest admiration and regard. Her son, more sceptical, and soured by Marlborough's reticence in the Oudenarde campaign, none the less had no doubt which side he was on. Robethon trusted him implicitly.

Marlborough had hardly reached Frankfort in 1713 when he became deeply leagued with the Hanover Court. "What are the steps in general which we should take here," they asked in a memorial dated March 10, for the Elector's friends in England, communicated to Marlborough through Cadogan, "after we have received the news of the Queen's death? What procurations, patents, or orders should we have ready to be sent then, wherever it will be necessary?" On the assumption that it was necessary that the Electoral Prince (the Elector's eldest son, who had fought so well at Oudenarde, and was afterwards George II) was to set forth immediately on the Queen's death for London, a whole series of searching questions were asked both of the Whigs at home and of Marlborough abroad. "What part would Marlborough choose to act? Would he go directly to London, being one of the Regents, or go along with the Elector?" Meanwhile Robethon asked that he should stay within reach, and that, instead of going to live at Frankfort, he should settle at Wesel.[2]

Cadogan gave answers in Marlborough's name to many of the questions.

> It was the Duke's opinion that the Elector [not the Electoral Prince] should go to England immediately upon the Queen's death, with full powers from the Electress as her lieutenant-general. The kings of England frequently invested lieutenants to govern the kingdom in their absence, with all the authority and power they possessed themselves.[3]

Marlborough intimated that when he was sure of the fidelity of the troops abroad he himself might follow the Elector into England, and leave the Electoral Prince with Cadogan to command them. The following letter shows that these plans were carried far.

[1] Klopp, xiv, 408–410.   [2] Macpherson, ii, 475–477.   [3] *Ibid.*, 478.

Bothmar to Robethon

March 25, 1713

Cadogan thought that the Electoral Prince should not go to take the command of the English troops on the Continent; but that Bothmar should provisionally have powers in his hands to authorize the Duke of Marlborough and himself [Cadogan] to secure these troops and the fortresses they garrison. If the Electress did not choose to sign a commission of that kind it would be sufficient to have one signed by the Elector in her name. The troops upon seeing a parchment with the great seal of his Electoral Highness would readily obey a man so agreeable to them as the Duke of Marlborough. It was not necessary to follow the form used in commissions of that kind in England, nor to write one in English. The Duke of Marlborough's commission and his own were in England, and he could not send copies of them; but it would be sufficient to say in the new patent that he was now invested with the same powers he had formerly from the Queen.[1]

Eventually Sunderland supplied the forms of the patents. Cadogan gave Bothmar the character of some officers. The commandant at Dunkirk, a Scotsman, and two battalions of that nation were thorough Jacobites; but the eight English battalions were well affected, and "would give a very good account of the other two, and of their commandant." Cadogan added that Marlborough recommended the Elector to have some one with the Pretender to send exact and speedy intelligence of everything that happened. Marlborough himself offered to find the man, if the Elector would lay out fifty louis d'or a month, and in the meantime he would try to find out what he could himself. Marlborough named three agents who might be used as spies.[2] His advice was taken with valuable results.[3]

Side by side with Marlborough, the Hanoverians gazed through the window which he had opened and kept open for their benefit and his own. Can we not see how very flat the exposures of the distrusted and detested Harley fell when flaunted before such close confederates? Marlborough could have revealed to the Court of Hanover every word he had spoken to the Jacobite agents without in the least affecting their relations. Indeed, it may well be that he did so.

---

[1] Macpherson, ii, 477.

[2] Their identity is preserved: (1) one of the magistrates of Huy; (2) an Irish officer of the name of Carol, who affects the Popish religion, but is a Protestant in his heart; (3) a Lorraine gentleman, who served in the army under the name of Remiremont.

[3] See the letter of an agent to the Electress dated April 5, 1714; Sir Thomas Hanmer, *Correspondence* (edited by Sir H. Bunbury, 1838), pp. 165–168.

No one can read without regret and repugnance the long, wearisome tale of the frauds and injuries which Marlborough perpetrated upon the house of Stuart. No attempt has been made in these pages to conceal or palliate them. It is enough for his fundamental integrity to prove that from the moment when he warned James II at Winchester in 1687[1] to the day when he welcomed King George I upon his succession in 1714, a period of nearly thirty years, he never swerved from his fidelity to the Protestant Succession. To this he devoted all the power of his sword and his statecraft, and all the network of his subterfuges and deceits. The reader is not invited to admire the seamy side of that intense period, but only to admit that Marlborough's purpose throughout was unchanged.

[1] See Vol. I, pp. 214–215.

Chapter Thirty-six

UTRECHT AND THE SUCCESSION

1713–1714

THE Duke of Hamilton having been killed in his duel with Lord Mohun, a new envoy of high consequence must be found to reside in Paris while armistice ripened into peace. Shrewsbury, whose tastes in these years were noticeably deflected by his wife to scenes of social pomp and glitter, was found willing to accept the task. Bolingbroke's correspondence with him from the beginning of 1713 shows that the extrusion of Dartmouth from the peace negotiations had already become evident. These early months of 1713 were the brightest in Bolingbroke's career. Between the vivid years of audacity, excitement, debauchery, and intrigue and the long grey aftermath of disappointment, exclusion, and futility, they form a gleaming passage. In the state into which he had brought our affairs abroad he was the only man capable of securing any settlement with France. He and his associates had broken up the Grand Alliance, had involved its armies in defeat, and had revived not only French hopes but French ambitions. But for Bolingbroke's statecraft, gambler's-craft, and personality, we might have thrown away the victory without gaining peace. For good or ill the Treaty of Utrecht was better than an indefinite continuance of a broken-backed war. Therefore there were occasions in the spring of 1713 when Bolingbroke's gifts were serviceable to his country. At times, indeed, he seems to speak in ringing tones for that great England whose sacrifices he had mocked, whose interests he had squandered, and whose honour he had lastingly defaced.

Torcy and the French Court, with the old King chastened and tottering in its midst, saw in the bitter quarrels of the Allies the chance of regaining in a few months of successful war and chicane all that had been cut from them by the swords of Marlborough and Eugene. In this mood they dallied in coming to terms. The weeks slipped by. Eugene in the name of the Emperor clamoured for the preparation of the armies for a new campaign. In England Ministers did not dare meet Parliament except upon the basis of a compacted peace. There were no fewer than eleven prorogations. At last Bolingbroke realized that all his blandishments of the French and his camaraderie with Torcy were exhausted. The desperate nature of his own plight if Parliament met while war and peace were alike in chaos startled him to robust action. All his sense of values underwent a swift change. The French, so eagerly courted and praised, fell under his ban. The Dutch, so sourly viewed, so roughly treated, began to acquire a new merit. The fact that each of these Governments looked upon his transition with contempt did not strip it of its efficacy. At the end of February the Secretary of State drew up an ultimatum to the French Court prescribing the final outstanding demands of England. There were the fishing rights off Nova Scotia; there were the monopoly upon the Amazon for Portugal and the addition of Tournai to the Dutch Barrier. These must be met fully and forthwith, or England would rouse all the allies to a renewal of the war. France was neither in the condition nor temper to stand a united onslaught. The resumption by England of her place in their ranks would largely reverse the advantages they had gained by her desertion. Considering how wonderful had been their deliverance, how cruel the strain upon the French people, how worn out their martial strength, to haggle too long over details in the hopes of exploiting the confusion of the Allies would be a folly and a crime from which they shrank. Accordingly, on March 31/April 11, 1713, the peace was signed at Utrecht between France and England, Holland, Portugal, Prussia, and Savoy. England and France signed first at two o'clock in the afternoon, Savoy and Prussia, with Portugal, in the evening, and the Dutch Republic at midnight.

Upon Bolingbroke's younger brother, George St John, was conferred the honour, as Tories saw it, of bringing over the Treaty. On the afternoon of Good Friday, April 3/14, his post-chaise drew up at Whitehall. Covered with dust, he ascended the steps, and Bolingbroke met him in a brief, dear-bought hour of triumph.

What is called the Treaty of Utrecht was in fact a series of separate agreements between individual allied states with France and with Spain. The Empire continued the war alone. In the forefront stood the fact that the Duke of Anjou, recognized as Philip V, held Spain and the Indies, thus flouting the unreasonable declaration to which the English Parliament had so long adhered. With this out of the way, the British Government gained their special terms, most of which would long ago have been conceded, and many of which ceased to have importance after a few years. The French Court recognized the Protestant Succession in Britain; agreed to expel the Pretender from France, to demolish the fortifications of Dunkirk, and to cede various territories in North America and the West Indies—to wit, Hudson Bay, Newfoundland, Nova Scotia, and St Christopher. Perpetual amity and goodwill was declared, and both sides swore not to make war without giving six months' notice. With Spain the terms were that England should hold Minorca and Gibraltar, thus securing to her while she remained the chief sea Power the entry and control of the Mediterranean. Commercial advantages in Spanish South America were obtained, and in particular the Assiento, or the right for thirty years to import African negroes as slaves into the New World. By this it was hoped to build the South Sea Company as a Tory rival to the Bank of England. Spain covenanted not to cede any portion of her dominions to France, and as a corollary England guaranteed the integrity of the remaining Spanish Empire against all comers. A renunciation was made both by France and Spain against the union of the two Crowns. This, as has been seen, now hung for its validity upon the frail child since known to history as Louis XV. Madame des Ursins, unkindly called "the Lady Masham of the Court of Spain," who dominated Philip's wife, and was thus in many ways the core of his indomitable resistance, was rewarded with the Duchy of Limburg. On the other hand, the Catalans, who had been called into the field by the Allies, and particularly by England, and who had adhered with admirable tenacity to Charles III, were delivered over under polite diplomatic phrases to the vengeance of the victorious party in Spain.

The Dutch secured a restricted Barrier, which nevertheless included, on the outer line, Furnes, Fort Knocke, Ypres, Menin, Tournai, Mons, Charleroi, and Namur; Ghent, for communication with Holland; and certain important forts guarding the entrance to the Scheldt. The commercial advantages of trade with Belgium were to be shared between England and Holland. Prussia obtained Guelderland at the expense of Dutch claims. All other fortresses in the Low Countries beyond the Barrier were restored to France, including particularly Lille. Victor Amadeus of Savoy gained Sicily and a strong frontier on the Alps. Portugal was rewarded for feeble services with trading rights upon the Amazon. The frontiers on the Rhine and the fate of Bavaria and the Milanese were left to the decision of further war. Such were the settlements reached at Utrecht in the spring of 1713.

21

The Emperor Charles, indignant at the Spanish surrender, continued the war during the whole of 1713; but the French armies, though themselves exhausted, took the key fortress of Landau, and penetrated into Germany. In March 1714 the Emperor was forced to conclude the Peace of Rastadt, where he entrusted to Prince Eugene the duty of making such terms with Marshal Villars as the situation permitted. By this treaty the Rhine frontier was settled as follows: France regained Strasburg and Landau, and ceded all conquests on the right bank of the Rhine. The Elector, Max Emmanuel, was reinstated in Bavaria, incidentally extruding Marlborough from his principality of Mindelheim. "He laughs best who laughs last." The Milanese, Naples, and Sardinia rested with the Empire. On this basis Europe subsided into a long, if uneasy, peace, and although these terms were not comparable with what the Allies could have gained in 1706, in 1709, or at Gertruydenberg in 1710, they none the less ended for a while the long torment to which Christendom had been subjected.

Bolingbroke's masterly defence of the Treaty of Utrecht and its forerunner, Swift's *Conduct of the Allies*, together with the squandered opportunity of making peace in 1709, constitute a case for the policy of the Tories which, though rejected during the long period of Whig rule, has commanded the respect of later times. Bolingbroke was no doubt right in saying that if the Allies in 1712 had conformed to the new policy of Queen Anne's Government, and had cordially joined with them in making a general peace, the odious events which followed in the field would have been avoided. If they had agreed with him, there would have been no need for him to go behind their backs. If they had desisted from the campaign, England would not have been forced to desert their camps. If they had not incurred the military disasters in the autumn of 1712, the united Allies could have forced France into far more satisfactory arrangements for the Dutch, the Germanic states, and the Empire than were in fact achieved. But all this reasoning stands on a false foundation. They did not conform, they did not agree, they did not desist, and the disasters followed. Was, then, England relieved from all obligations towards them? The solemn condition of the Grand Alliance was that they should make peace in common, and England was by no means absolved by the fact that she suddenly became more anxious for peace than the other signatory states. If the shortcomings of our allies in waging war were as gross as Swift pretends, that was a ground for reproach, but not for betrayal or desertion. It certainly did not lie with England, which for so long had urged the unrelenting prosecution of the war, which had imposed its formula, "No peace without Spain," upon reluctant Dutch and indifferent Germanic states, to blame them for not obediently abandoning their policy because England had a new Minister and Queen Anne a new favourite. The secret and separate negotiations of the Tory Ministers inspired our allies with distrust and anger. It was neither right nor reasonable, therefore, to expect from states smarting under the sense of having been tricked patient, loyal co-operation. If the Tory Ministers had wished to carry their policy, they should have done so straightforwardly, openly, and in concert with their allies. They did not do this, because they had to deceive their own Parliament as well as their allies, and confront them both stage by stage with new situations.

It is not, therefore, upon the terms of settlement in general that censure can found itself. The mean and treacherous manner in which the Grand Alliance had been broken up, with the shameful episodes of violated faith and desertion in the field, inflicted the stigma which was for so long visible on the face of this transaction. Forty years later William Pitt, writing to Sir Benjamin Keene, feeling the odium which still clung to England and infected her every public pledge, pronounced the stern judgment that "Utrecht was an indelible reproach of the last generation."[1]

Marlborough had always believed that unless France was reduced, not merely to temporary exhaustion, but to a definitely restricted power, the wars of his generation would be renewed in the future. This was looking far ahead, but the fact remains that in the century that followed Europe was racked with repeated conflicts and Great Britain fought four separate wars with France, aggregating in all forty-three years of deadly strife. During these wars the first British Empire was largely ruined. Great coalitions were formed against Britain. She was stripped by war and other causes of her vast American possessions. Her existence as a world state was repeatedly in jeopardy, and finally, against Napoleon, she was at one time left alone to face the world. That these indescribable perils were surmounted by the valour and vigour of the descendants of those who fought in the age of Anne unfolds a series of new marvels and prodigies in our island story.

Archdeacon Coxe, writing in 1819, was able to condemn the Treaty of Utrecht and its disreputable concomitants by convincing

[1] Coxe, *Memoirs of the Kings of Spain* (1815), iv, 190.

reference to the events of the previous hundred years. If, he was able to argue, Marlborough had been sustained by his countrymen to the end the "overweening power" of France, the greatest military nation and the greatest block of nationhood which existed, would have been finally reduced to harmless limits. But as the human tale unfolds its chapters of confusion and misfortune, so all proportions and relations fade and change. Writing now, more than a hundred years later, we may perhaps be content that an overweening Germany did not sooner present to us the menace which our ancestors recognized in France. And to-day this same France, so long the terror of Europe, is a precious, indispensable guardian of those very causes of national freedom, religious toleration, and Parliamentary government which in a different combination were all at stake in Marlborough's time. Thus do the very foundations of historical judgments change with the centuries. It is not given to princes, statesmen, and captains to pierce the mysteries of the future, and even the most penetrating gaze reaches only conclusions which, however seemingly vindicated at a given moment, are inexorably effaced by time. One rule of conduct alone survives as a guide to men in their wanderings: fidelity to covenants, the honour of soldiers, and the hatred of causing human woe.

At the time the sense of frustration and of the casting away of the fruits of so much perseverance and good fortune rankled deeply in many bosoms. The fate of the Catalans, abandoned, slaughtered, and oppressed, made a dark page in our records, and even to-day plays its part in the internal affairs of Spain. The fierce debates in Parliament cannot be read without a blush. All might so easily have been made smooth and clean; but the unending cadence of history shows that moderation and mercy in victory are no less vital than courage and skill in war. England in 1713 rejoiced that peace, no matter how, had come at last. The nation as a whole endorsed and acclaimed what Queen Anne and her Ministers had done, and even when under George I the Whigs regained the full and prolonged control of affairs they did not venture, as will be seen, to challenge the settlements which were made.

Early in December 1713 the Queen fell ill. The gout by which she had long been plagued took a new form, and she suffered severe attacks of fever before the abscess formed in her leg. Her condition caused lively alarm in all quarters, but for different reasons. On December 3 Abigail warned Oxford that there was danger. The fortunes of the Ministry hung upon Anne's life; but far greater issues were involved. At this time the quarrel between Oxford and Bolingbroke had not reached the point where the unity of the Tory Party was seriously affected. The Pretender had as yet made no public declaration that he would always remain a Catholic. Hopes of his conversion might well be entertained not only among interested politicians or Tory partisans, but throughout the nation. Most serious of all, neither the Court of Hanover nor the Whigs in Great Britain had made any effective preparations for the tremendous and deadly crisis which must instantly attend a demise of the Crown. No man, not the shrewdest or best-informed, could predict what would happen. The Tories had majorities in both houses; they had a newly elected Tory House of Commons. All the commands in the fleet, Army, and fortresses were in the hands of trusted Tory or Jacobite adherents. Ormonde was Warden of the Cinque Ports, and in close touch with Berwick. A Jacobite governed Edinburgh. The Whig Earl of Dorset had been ejected from Dover Castle. No attempt had been made by the Whigs to organize the nuclei of resistance. They had their Act of Settlement—the law on their side—but that was all.

A wave of fear swept through one half of political England lest they should lose the Queen, through the other lest the Protestant Succession should be subverted, and through both lest civil war, with all its uncountable horrors, should come. It was a quarrel which nobody wanted, but into which all would inexorably be drawn. The French were also on the move. Under pretext of changing garrisons several battalions and all the Irish regiments in the French service moved towards the coastal towns.[1] Abigail's brother, Jack Hill, who was governor of Dunkirk, expatiated on its advantages to French troops as a port of embarkation for England. Faced with this peril, the Whigs looked about them for means of defence. A hurried meeting was held at Wharton's house. Strenuous appeals were made to Hanover by the Whigs in England and by Marlborough from Frankfort. The Electress and her son acted with what vigour was possible. Marlborough and Cadogan both held their provisional commissions to take command of the British forces which remained in the Low Countries. There were troops at Ghent and Bruges, there were troops at Ostend; above all, there was the garrison at Dunkirk. Two of Marlborough's trusted Lieutenants held command under Hill. Colonel Armstrong, the engineer who had distinguished himself in the capture of Bouchain, was Quartermaster-General.

[1] Macpherson, ii, 548.

Colonel Kane, the diarist whose opinions have several times been cited in these pages, commanded the citadel.

Bothmar to Bernstorf

December 16, 1713

Both the Duke of Marlborough and Cadogan have provisional orders from the Electress to take command of the troops and garrison in case of the Queen's death. Cadogan told me it would be proper to have a particular one for Mr Armstrong, Quartermaster-General at Dunkirk, to seize upon that place, and execute the orders of Mr Cadogan.[1]

Marlborough himself travelled from Frankfort to Antwerp, where he established himself at the beginning of December. Here he was in much closer contact with events. He had sent Cadogan to The Hague to learn the "sentiments and thoughts of our friends in England, and to inform himself of the situation of things in Holland." Upon Cadogan's return from The Hague he sent a full account, and formally accepted the Elector's commission as Commander-in-Chief.

Marlborough to Robethon

Feb. 26, 1714

I am very glad to find by him [Cadogan] the Republic takes the alarm, and begins to wake out of the lethargy it has fallen into since the peace at Utrecht. . . . The first and great mark of their present good disposition is their secret resolution to set out, as soon as possible, a strong squadron of men-of-war, for which they have found a very plausible pretext, when their preparations are so far advanced, as to oblige them to own it. They have likewise, in case of her Majesty's death, agreed on the most proper means for assisting his Electoral Highness with their troops.

. . . I have received the commission his Electoral Highness has been pleased to honour me with. I must beg of you to make him my most humble and sincere acknowledgments for this new mark of favour and confidence. I shall make the best use I can of it for his service, in the advancing of which I am always ready to hazard both life and fortune.[2]

Thus we see Marlborough still in the centre of all those forces which he had previously directed, and assisting to weld together the Whigs in Britain, the army in Flanders, the Dutch and the Empire behind the house of Hanover. There can be no doubt of either his acts or his intentions.

It would, however, be a mistake to imagine him at this time as

[1] Macpherson, ii, 519.   [2] *Ibid.*, 569-571.

a fretful, energetic schemer impatiently awaiting a new turn of fortune's wheel. From the moment he had been relieved of his military and European responsibilities he had sensibly aged. He laid down at the same time his burdens and his strength. However painful it might be to watch the squandering of so much that he had gained, he did not despair about what could not be prevented. He yielded himself easily to his new-found leisure. The will-power which for ten years had held the whole movement of Europe upon its course first relaxed and then declined. He enjoyed the placid days as they succeeded one another. Sarah rallied him severely. He had grown, she complained, "intolerably lazy." He would hardly write a letter—not even to his well-loved daughters. But his noble air and the sense of authority and kindliness which his presence conveyed made their impression upon all who met him. Alison records a notable saying about him at this time. "The only things the Duke has forgotten are his deeds. The only things he remembers are the misfortunes of others."[1]

Sorrow too fell upon him in these wanderings. Early in 1714 his third daughter, Elizabeth, Countess of Bridgewater, died of the smallpox scourge. She was his favourite child, and deeply attached to him. All accounts describe her sunshine nature and graceful virtues. When at Antwerp Marlborough received the news of her death his head dropped on the marble mantelpiece against which he leaned, and he is said to have become unconscious.

By the end of January the Queen was clearly better. She had recovered sufficiently to open Parliament in person on February 15. Oxford laboured to reassure the nation that there was no question of altering the Succession, and that the best relations prevailed with the Court of Hanover. No one believed him; and with reason, for at this very time he was through Gaultier offering the Pretender the Throne if he would change his religion. All this, of course, lay in secret; but once Parliament met, the Whigs were able to force the issue of the Succession into the full glare of debate.

In March the Queen fell ill again, and anxiety became intensified. In April the Whigs and the adherents of the house of Hanover persuaded the Hanoverian envoy Schütz to request a writ of summons for the Electoral Prince to take his seat in the House of Lords as Duke of Cambridge. This measure was well conceived. It exposed the Ministers to the utmost embarrassment, and it split the Tory

[1] Alison, *Life of John, Duke of Marlborough* (1852), ii, 247.

Party. Hanmer had been chosen Speaker, and became at once the leader of a strong body of Hanoverian Tories. In the Lords the attack was pressed on the general issue that the Succession was in danger. Argyll, who since his experiences in Spain and Minorca bore resentments against the Ministry as bitter as those he had lately nourished against Marlborough, assailed the Government. He alleged that subsidies were being paid by the Treasury to the Jacobite clans in the Highlands, and that Whig officers were being purged from the Army. So serious was his alarm, so intense his new rage, that he became reconciled with Marlborough. The whole bench of bishops, with two exceptions, voted with the Opposition. The Ministers escaped censure, which in this case was tantamount to an accusation of high treason, only by the twelve votes of the batch of peers created two years before.

The writ for the Electoral Prince, of course, struck the Queen in her most sensitive spot. She was convulsed with distress and wrath. A series of vehement letters in Bolingbroke's haughty style were sent to Hanover. The aged Electress, whose illuminating intelligence had long cast its light upon the European scene, was so painfully affected by their tone that she expired a few days later. The Elector George Lewis was now the direct constitutional heir. By this time Oxford and Bolingbroke had received the Pretender's answer to their invitation to change his religion.[1] His answer was fatal to his prospects, but for ever honourable to his name. It has been well said that his sincerity and honesty should win for his memory the gratitude of the British nation. He repulsed with indignation the suggestion that he should forsake his faith for his crown. When Oxford and Bolingbroke received his reply both realized that there was no hope of a Restoration. Oxford, with hardly a day's delay, renewed perfervid blandishments to the Court of Hanover, Bolingbroke told the French envoy, Iberville, that "people would rather have a Turk than a Catholic." From this moment Oxford seems definitely to have rallied to the Hanoverian Succession and to have endeavoured to bring the Queen to the conviction that it was inevitable. But now he found his influence gone. He had quarrelled with Abigail. He had refused her a share in the profits of the Assiento contract, for which Bolingbroke had led her to hope. She therefore threw all her weight against him, and, dreading the prospects of a Hanoverian monarchy, strove to lead the

---

[1] Pretender's letter dated February 26, 1714; French Foreign Office Archives, "Angleterre," tome 255. Another letter dated March 13; Macpherson, ii, 525.

Queen into Jacobite paths. Here, however, Anne became intractable. She, like every one else, had been staggered by the Pretender's uncompromising refusal to abandon the Roman Catholic faith. She feared that his accession would fatally injure the Church of England, her rock in tribulation. She therefore allowed events to drift on their course, and implored Oxford and Bolingbroke to be reconciled to each other. This, indeed, was but one of the measures their safety required. But their mutual hatreds and charges against each other were too serious to be overridden even by the instinct of self-preservation.

By a strange perversity the Secretary of State continued to the full limit of his great office to take a whole series of measures which, while they gratified Tory partisanship, were consistent only with a Jacobite Restoration. The chief of these was the renewed purge of the Army. Argyll was removed from all his places, and Stair was ordered to dispose of the command of the Scots Greys. A long list of generals, colonels, and captains were ordered to sell their regiments and companies unless they were willing to promise that they would "serve the Queen without asking questions." A scheme, involving the dismissal of seventy-two officers, was set on foot to break up nine Protestant regiments quartered in Ireland, and to create in their place fifteen new regiments of suitable complexion.

On the other side nothing was now neglected. The group of war leaders, Marlborough, Cadogan, Stanhope, and Argyll, were now all acting in unity, and resolved if need be to proceed to extremities. A convention was drawn up between the States-General and Hanover for ships and troops. Stanhope privily organized the French Huguenot officers and men in London. Many veterans discharged from Marlborough's armies were enrolled in secret bands. Argyll and Stair took similar steps in Scotland. It was widely believed that the Regular Army itself, in spite of the purge of officers, would not act against the renowned Chiefs of the great war. A Whig Association was formed comprising a large number of officers who undertook to remain armed and ready at call, and a fund was created to which the merchants of the City largely contributed.

When Marlborough at Antwerp was invited to join this body he declined.[1] His refusal excited surprise at the time, and has been criticized since. It can hardly be doubted that he was wise not to join a purely Whig conspiracy. He was more than ever determined in his freedom not to be enrolled in the ranks of either party. By

[1] See N. Tindal, *Continuation of Rapin's History*, xviii, 167.

any overt action he would have presented the Government with the advantage of reviving the cry that he sought to become a second Cromwell. There is, however, no question where he stood. A more decisive step was in his mind. He had resolved to return to England. "Pray be pleased to take an opportunity," he wrote to Robethon (June 18), "of acquainting his Electoral Highness that my best friends think my being in England may be of much more use to the service than my continuing abroad, upon which I design to return as soon as the Parliament is up."[1]

And (July 9):

> My last letters were very full of hopes that something considerable for the Protestant Succession may yet be done before the Parliament parts; so that I flatter myself that the arrival of Mons. Bothmar may be of great use, the Parliament being likely to set sometime longer than was expect'd. I shall not leave this place till about the end of this month. I followed your directions in acquainting Mr M[olyneux][2] as to the number of the troops [*i.e.* the troops in Dunkirk]. They are all well inclin'd except the two battalions of Orkney.[3]

The air of meaningless mystery which surrounds Marlborough's leaving England also covers his return. It is certain that he took this decision without reference to whether the Queen was dead, dying, or about to recover, and without regard to whether Oxford or Bolingbroke emerged the winner from their struggle. The only consideration which he mentioned was that Parliament should have risen. This would free him from some minor annoyances. Parliament was prorogued on July 9/20, and Marlborough set out accordingly for Ostend.

Sarah was with him. There was no doubt about her sentiments. She was, as ever, the full-blooded Whig, hating the Pope and Pretender with equal zeal. Her motive also was simple. She was burning to get home. The longing to be back in England seemed to have taken possession of her soul. There is no doubt that the moment of Marlborough's return was influenced by this rather than by any deeply calculated plan of action. At first the Continent had seemed to him an attractive change from the English political scene. But after a year this mood had passed. He was not comfortable at Antwerp. ✶ "We had a very inconvenient house," says Sarah, "and before we could remove from thence the Duke of Marlborough was so weary that he took a resolution to go for England."[4] We see

---

[1] Macpherson, ii, 627.   [2] Marlborough's private agent in Hanover.
[3] Macpherson, ii, 632.   [4] Blenheim MSS.

also that he had not the slightest fear of returning home. He asked no one's permission. He made no concealment of his intentions. "The Whigs," wrote one of Swift's correspondents, "give out the Duke of Marlborough is coming over, and his house is now actually fitting up at St James's."[1] He appeared perfectly sure of himself, and that he would be able to deal with the facts of his native land as he found them. He was as cool and matter-of-fact as on the morning of one of his battles. On the other hand, he was in no particular hurry. He was prepared to wait a week or two for a fair wind that would carry him across in a single day. Here too we see Sarah's influence. She hated the sea, and hoped to avoid sleeping on board. It must be remembered, however, that in those times, when a passage might take twelve hours or twelve days, there was a tactical advantage in being able to move fast, once one had moved at all.

Throughout his voluntary exile Marlborough had maintained civil relations with Oxford, and in January 1714 the Treasurer had granted a warrant of £10,000, for which the Duke thanked him, for some resumption of the building of Blenheim.[2] It is possible, though no correspondence exists, that Bolingbroke had also kept contact with him. But there is no truth in the widely made suggestion that his return to England was the result of any understanding or agreement with either of the quarrelling Ministers. In fact, the contrary is easily proved. "Lord Marlborough's people," wrote Bolingbroke to Strafford (July 14), "give out that he is coming over, and I take it for granted that he is so; whether on account of the ill figure he makes upon the Continent, or the good one he hopes to make at home, I shall not determine."[3] The Secretary of State then hinted that Marlborough was in cabal with Oxford, and he used this as an additional means of arousing the prejudices of the Queen against his rival. There is no doubt that the prospect of Marlborough's return was extremely unwelcome to him. To Prior in Paris it was a source of dread. "We are all frightened out of our wits," he wrote, when he at length heard of it, to Bolingbroke, "upon the Duke of Marlborough's going to England."[4]

"It is surprising," wrote Bothmar, already in London (July 16/27),

that the Duke of Marlborough comes over at such a crisis, and does not rather wait until it is seen which of the two competitors will carry it with the Queen; Lord Sunderland himself does not comprehend this. I am told he will be the day after to-morrow at Ostend, in order to

---

[1] Swift, *Works*, xvi, 141.   [2] Bath Papers, *H.M.C.*, i, 244.
[3] Coxe, vi, 112.   [4] August 7; *Bolingbroke Correspondence*, iv, 579.

embark there for this country. Cadogan has been for eight or ten days in the country [*i.e.* out of London]. He is expected back this evening. He said when he went away that the Duke of Marlborough would wait for him at Antwerp. The impetuosity of the Duchess has probably precipitated this journey.[1]

Sarah to Mrs Clayton

July 14, 1714

★This is only to tell my dear Mrs Clayton that we hold our resolution of leaving this place upon Friday next. We shall bee three days going to Ostend and there wait on a fair wind, and wee shall rather stay there than come without a very good one because it is intolerable to goe to bed in those boats; but if we can have such weather, and in the daytime, wee may hope to get to Dover without going to bed, and it will be easy enough to sit upon the deck.[2]

On the road to Ostend an incident occurred. The Royal Irish Regiment, ultra-Protestants from Northern Ireland, and Webb's were both quartered in the castle of Ghent. Captain Parker tells us that "on hearing that the Duke was to pass that way, all the officers of both Regiments went without Antwerp port, and drew up in two lines to pay him our compliments, and shew the respect we still retained for his Grace." The Duke and Sarah rode up on horseback, and spent half an hour talking to the officers "on indifferent matters before resuming their journey."[3]

Sarah to Mrs Clayton

OSTEND
July 30

I am sure my dear friend will be glad to hear that we are come well to this place, where we wait for a fair wind, and in the meantime are in a very clean house and have everything good but weather. . . .

The respect and affection shewn to D. of Marl. in every place where he goes allways makes me remember our governors in the manner that is naturel to do, and upon this journey one thing has happened that was surprising and very pretty. The D. of Marl. contrived it so as to avoid going into the great towns as much as he could, and for that reason were a little out of the way not to go to Ghent. But the chief magistrates, learning where we were to pass, met him upon the road, and had prepared a very handsome breakfast, for all that was with us in a little village where one of their ladys stayed to do the honours, and there was in the company a considerable churchman.

Among the governors of the town there were a great many officers that came out with them afoot, and I was so much surprised and

---

[1] Macpherson, ii, 636. [2] Blenheim MSS. [3] Parker, p. 197.

touched that I could not speak to the officers without a good deal of concern, saying that I was sorry for what they did fearing it might hurt them, to which they replyed very pollitickly or ignorantly, I dont know which, "that it was not possible for them to suffer for having done their duty."

The D. of Marl. is determined to stay here for a fair wind. . . .

I long to embrace dear Mrs C. . . . I have as ill an opinion of public affairs as ever, but I would fain end my life in England with my friends, if I can, and even submit to Popery or anything that cannot be helped.[1]

But while Marlborough and his eager wife waited at Ostend for the fair wind events moved to their decision in England.

[1] Coxe, vi, 295.

Chapter Thirty-seven

THE DEATH OF THE QUEEN
1714—JULY

BOLINGBROKE'S improvidence was unsurpassable. He had used partisan power with the utmost brutality against the Whigs. He had injured and outraged all the allies. He had earned the cold, enduring antagonism of the Hanoverian Court and of the lawful heir to the throne. He had gloried in trampling down every principle and interest which was dear to the new England sprung from the Revolution. Yet he had by no means resolved to bring in a Popish prince. He continued to walk with the Protestant Succession, wondering hopefully if a moment would come to stab it in the back, but not having by any means made up his mind to do so. He had removed from the Army all officers who were anchored to the Act of Settlement, and were the products of the period of glory. From every side he had gathered and promoted avowed Jacobites to the higher positions in the armed forces. Yet he joined himself with the proclamation extorted by public opinion from Queen Anne setting a five thousand pound price on the head of the Pretender if found on British soil. He had declared that the exiled King had no more chance of coming to the crown as a Papist than the Sultan of Turkey, yet all his future and the future of his party could be saved only by the accession of this unyielding Prince. The Queen's life hung on a thread, and he and all the interests he directed hung on that same thread. At any moment all might fall together. He could not see beyond a demise of the Crown, yet at Christmas this had seemed very near. The crisis might at any moment recur.

In these precarious months of 1714 his main activities were to rend the Tory Party by a mortal quarrel with Oxford, and to fan the flames of faction with the Schism Bill. By this measure no Dissenter would be permitted to teach in either public or private schools, or even in private houses. The entire religious education of Nonconformist children would be taken from their parents and handed over to schoolmasters licensed by the bishops. In the House of Commons this attack by the Church upon the Chapel had a great success. The Tory majority and the 'gentlemen of England,' who after winning their second general election thought the world was theirs for ever, affirmed by 237 votes to 126 these principles of religious intolerance oppressing a large and powerful body of their fellow-countrymen. In the Lords the margin was narrow. Bolingbroke exerted his gifts of oratory, but the Bill passed only by 77 to 72. Five of the most eminent bishops of the Church of England voted against it as an act of persecution. This law, so cruel in itself, was to Bolingbroke a move in his strife with Oxford. In Defoe's words, "The Schism Bill was a mine dug to blow up the White Staff." Oxford did not resist its passage. He could not afford to run counter to the excited feelings of the Tory Party. He sat dumb and glowering through the debates. He did not vote. He was preparing his counter-mine. It was of a different character, but might well in the end have proved more deadly.

In the Spanish Trade Treaty were found certain explanatory articles held to be injurious to British commerce. An inquiry was demanded by the Whigs and the merchants into the circumstances which had led to their insertion. The inquiry was resisted with warmth by Bolingbroke. He sought to repulse it in his most arrogant manner; but Oxford supported the demand, and hinted darkly at hidden motives and grave malfeasance. The House of Lords called for the papers relating to the treaty, and for the names of those who settled its details. It was common talk that these were Bolingbroke and his confederate, the Commissioner of Trade, the Irish adventurer Arthur Moore. The Commissioners of the Board of Trade and Plantations and the directors of the South Sea Company were examined. It was discovered that in the original Assiento contract a share of profits was reserved by the Spanish Court; and that this share had not been made over with the rest to the South Sea Company, but retained nominally in the hands of the Treasury.[1]

The Lord Treasurer repudiated all responsibility on their behalf. It was openly alleged that a large sum had been divided between Bolingbroke, Abigail, and Arthur Moore. We now know that the Secret Service funds were systematically raided to meet the needs of the new favourite and Ministers. The Queen's drafts upon these funds for her private purposes during the last two years of Godolphin had been at the rate of £282 a month. During the Tory rule they rose to £976, or more than three times as much.[2] But even this

---

[1] I. S. Leadam, *Political History of England* (1702–60), ix, 219. [2] P.R.O., Treasury, 48.

did not satisfy Abigail. Her transference of allegiance from Oxford to Bolingbroke had been finally determined by the fact that the Treasurer had "refused her a job of some money out of the Assiento contract."[1] In her anger she told him bluntly she would carry no more messages to the Queen for him, and later added, "You never did the Queen any service, nor are you capable of doing her any."[2]

The warfare between the two chief Ministers had thus reached its climax. It was clear that Oxford was determined to expose the Secretary of State, whatever it might cost himself, the Tory Party, or the Queen. In these straits Abigail, urged on by Bolingbroke, acted with vigour. On July 9, the day after the Secretary of the Treasury, Lowndes, had formally disowned all knowledge of where the missing Assiento money had gone, Abigail induced the unhappy, entangled, stricken Queen to come down in person and prorogue Parliament. For the moment a breathing-space was gained, but the autumn session was not far off. Public indignation ran high. The South Sea Company, without even according him a hearing, expelled Arthur Moore from among its directors. Everywhere it was said that when Parliament assembled in the autumn "the Dragon," as Oxford was nicknamed, "would have it all out." One thing was certain—the Ministry as constituted could never face even their own Tory Parliament again. The desertion of the allied armies in the face of the enemy abroad in 1712 could now be matched by an episode equally disgraceful at home. To this shameful conclusion had two evil counsellors led the tottering Anne. And now they were at each other's throats, and the hour of reckoning had come.

"Good God," exclaimed the Duke of Buckingham (after he had been put out of office),

> how has this poor Nation been governed in my time! During the reign of King Charles the Second we were governed by a parcel of French whores; in King James the Second's time by a parcel of Popish Priests; in King William's time by a parcel of Dutch Footmen; and now we are governed by a dirty chambermaid, a Welsh attorney, and a profligate wretch that has neither honour nor honesty.[3]

Many accounts converge upon the conclusion that the final scene in the long debate between Oxford and Bolingbroke at the Cabinet Council of July 27 brought about the death of Queen Anne. Already scarcely capable of standing or walking, she nevertheless followed the intense political struggles proceeding around her with absorbed

---

[1] Lord Mahon, *Reign of Queen Anne*, i, 86, 87.   [2] Swift, *Works*, xvi, 144–173.
[3] Parker, pp. 184–185.

attention. She notified the Lord Treasurer by gesture and utterance that he must surrender the White Staff. The sodden, indolent, but none the less tough and crafty politician, who had overthrown Marlborough and changed the history of Europe, had his final fling at his triumphant rival. For months past he had lapped up the Treasury tales of the corruption whereby the Secretary of State and Abigail were enriching themselves. Some weeks before he had submitted to the Queen a "brief account" of his own conduct, in which detailed charges of peculation were made against Bolingbroke. The swindles of the Quebec expedition in 1711, the naked abstraction at the beginning of 1714 of Secret Service money by Bolingbroke to pay off a mortgage on his estate, the passport scandal, and the gross malversations of Arthur Moore, in which Bolingbroke was deeply involved—all these were at his fingers' ends. And this was the man who should supplant him! In savage tones across the table, both men being within six feet of the Queen, he denounced him to her as a rogue and thief, and in terms of vague but none the less impressive menace made it plain that he would denounce him to Parliament.

Anne was deeply smitten. She had made up her mind, by the processes which have been described, to get rid of this lax but formidable Minister by whose advice and aid she had violated the friendships of her lifetime and stultified the purpose of her reign. But she knew too much about Bolingbroke, his morals, his finances, his malpractices, public and private, to feel that in quitting Harley she had another stepping-stone on which to stand. Certainly she could not appoint to the Lord Treasurership a man whose financial probity was under investigation and in general disrepute. There is little doubt that she was harassed beyond human endurance. She had taken all upon herself, and now she did not know which way to turn. She was assisted and carried from this violent confrontation, and two days later the gout which had hitherto tormented her body moved with decision towards her brain. Oxford went home to scribble doggerel to Swift about the vicissitudes of statesmen. Bolingbroke remained master of the field and of the day—but only for a day.

During forty-eight hours Bolingbroke possessed plenary power at a cardinal point in English history. What did he mean to do? Had he a clear resolve, equal to the emergency, for which he was prepared to die or kill? "Harry" was never of that stuff. There was no Cromwell in him; there was no Marlborough; there was no

Stanhope. He dawdled, he wavered, he crumpled. More than that, his luck ran out.

There is a striking incident recorded of the night of July 28. Bolingbroke, who was in the position of a man charged with the royal commission to reconstitute a Government, had bidden all the rising generation of Whig leaders to dinner at his house in Golden Square. The names of those he had invited are surprising—Stanhope, Craggs, Pulteney, Walpole, Cadogan—in fact, a cluster of Marlborough's friends and adherents and of Bolingbroke's most bitter foes. All these men had been outraged by his conduct. The generals had seen the cause they had fought for cast away. Cadogan had seen his revered chief wronged, insulted, and driven into exile. Stanhope had been superseded. Craggs on Marlborough's missions had been treated with barely disguised contempt. Walpole had been sent to the Tower for five months on a charge of corruption, which at its worst was venial compared to the misdeeds of Bolingbroke. Yet they were all invited, and all except Walpole met round Bolingbroke's table on the night of July 28.

The Secretary expatiated upon his fidelity to the house of Hanover and to the Act of Settlement, and made it clear that places in his new Government would be offered to the company. But surely this was not the end to which his actions for months had seemed to point. He had purged the Army: he had begun to tamper with the Navy. Every one of these Whigs believed that he was plotting to bring in the Pretender, and place him as an avowed Papist upon the throne, in defiance of all the laws and oaths that had followed the Revolution of 1688. If he did not mean this what did he mean? It is pretty plain nowadays that he meant nothing definite—certainly nothing that could become effective at that time. He wanted to build up a situation step by step, so that if his affairs prospered he could move with safety in the direction he desired. But if it became too dangerous he thought he could withdraw with equal facility, and court the Elector of Hanover as easily as the "Prince of Wales." For this he needed power and time. He gained the power, but the time was denied him.

The resolute, able men who sat at his table were not hampered by any of the balancings which obsessed their host. They meant, if it were necessary, to fight a civil war for the Protestant Succession. Their situation was incomparably stronger than when the Queen had first fallen ill at the end of 1713. They had a sworn association; they had arms; they had large funds; they had the whole force of a great party and of strong elements in the national life. For months they had been secretly recruiting Marlborough's veterans—sergeants, corporals, private men. They had several thousands of them on their lists in London, and many others in the Provinces. They had with them nearly all the officers who had led the British troops under Marlborough in ten years of victory. They were in the closest touch with Marlborough, and knew he was on his way to England— would, if need be, take the field at their head. If he could not arrive in time, Stanhope would act. Little recked they of lands or life. Finally, they had the law and the Constitution on their side.

It must have been one of the strangest dinner-parties upon record, and there are many. No one knew the Queen was going to die. No one knew how long she would live. She might live for years. She had been as ill as this at Christmas, and had recovered. At the end Stanhope spoke words of grave and fair import. He offered a soldier's terms to Bolingbroke. Let him put the fleet into the hands of admirals loyal to the Hanoverian Succession. Let him restore Marlborough to the command of the Army and of the fortified seaports. This done, let him enjoy the Queen's favour while she lived, and all would take their chance of office under the future George I without bearing him malice. If not, let him play the other hand, and put it to the test. But Bolingbroke, who had got round so many deadly difficulties in breaking Marlborough, deserting the allies, and carrying the Treaty of Utrecht, and now at last had got rid of Oxford, was by no means ready for such sharp choices. He was obviously incapable of responding with force and sincerity. He fell back on general phrases. As the party broke up Stanhope in all bluntness of after-dinner camaraderie said, "Harry, you have only two ways of escaping the gallows. The first is to join the honest party of the Whigs; the other to give yourself up entirely to the French King and seek his help for the Pretender. If you do not choose the first, we can only imagine that you have decided for the second."[1]

If Bolingbroke had had more time, if the Queen had lived for another six weeks, it seems very likely that he would have brought about—not for any steady purpose or conviction, for at his heart there was nothing but brilliant opportunism, but for his caprice and ambition—what might have been a civil war as cruel and bloody as has ever rent our nation. While he had made every preparation in his power, had even bargained with Torcy for French troops, yet

[1] Salmon, p. 312; W. Michael, *England under George I* (1936), p. 50.

when it came to the point he had neither the soul to decide nor the manhood to dare. We must indeed thank God that our Island story was not seared by a hideous tragedy; that Marlborough's sword and the bayonets of his veterans, that Colonel Blackadder, Captain Parker, Sergeant Milner, Corporal Bishop, and their comrades, were not engaged on English soil against a goodly company of sentimental Jacobites and stout-hearted country squires and their dependants; and that the old quarrel of Cavalier and Roundhead, in different forms but perhaps on a far larger scale, was not renewed again in England. To the brink of this catastrophe our national life was brought by the wickedness and inherent degeneracy of this richly gifted man.

One is surprised to find serious writers describing his actions as if they were deserving of impartial presentment. Whigs and Tories, Hanoverians and Jacobites—it was, they suggest, six of one and half a dozen of the other. Marlborough had won the war; Bolingbroke had made the peace. Great and respectable currents of opinion flowed in either cause, and history, we are enjoined, must with a cool detachment tolerate both points of view. But this weak mood cannot be indulged in a world where the consequences of men's actions produce such frightful calamities for millions of humble folk, and may rob great nations of their destiny. By personal vices of heart and mind, by deeds of basest treachery, by violation of law and public faith, this man St John—unpurposed, unprincipled, miscreant adventurer—had brought his native land to the edge of the abyss, and in this horrid juncture he could not even clothe crime with coherency. Let the lifelong failure and suppression of his bright gifts procure no mitigation of modern censure. Let us also rejoice that poor Queen Anne was now at her last gasp. Just in the nick of time she died. She had lived long enough to strip the name of Britain of most of the glories with which it had shone. She had seen it become odious or contemptible throughout the world. She sank into her mortal collapse with her country in the jaws of measureless tribulation. But luckily she expired while there was still time to save it.

Anne allowed Oxford to take leave of her with some ceremony; but her gout increased, and she suffered from pains in the head. Her six doctors who divided the responsibility were all anxious. "On Friday morning [the 30th]," wrote one of them, Daniel Malthus, "her Majesty rose and in her dressing room between 9 and 10, had two very violent convulsions, one immediately after the other which lasted till 11."[1] Meanwhile the Council met in the palace. They were about to transact business when the door opened, and in marched the Duke of Somerset and the Duke of Argyll. Both were Privy Councillors, but neither of them had received a summons. They declared that the dangerous illness of the Queen made it their duty to proffer their services. The Tory Ministers were taken aback at this apparition. These were not men who could easily be ejected. Somerset was the embodiment of political effrontery and violence. Argyll had been the first man in the storm of Oudenarde. If the Tory Ministers had risen from the table, drawn their swords, and ordered the intruders to depart, they would have been at the level of the crisis. As it was, they were only flustered. Before they could recover, Shrewsbury, who had certainly planned this stroke, was uttering suave phrases of welcome and thanks to the two Dukes for the patriotic impulse which had moved them. With an adroitness which can be discerned across the interval of time, he began to speak of the Queen's health. The doctors must at once be summoned to the Council. The two stranger Dukes should hear for themselves what they had to say. The doctors came, and related at length the various professional tortures they were inflicting upon the patient. By the time they had finished Somerset and Argyll were for all intents and purposes members of the Cabinet. It is noteworthy that these were the same three Dukes, and men of middle views, who had turned the scale in 1710 against Godolphin and Marlborough. Now they acted in an even greater crisis. In each case Shrewsbury was the prime mover, and revealed in different forms the latent power and guile of his nature.

It was obvious that the great business of the day was to advise how the Queen should fill the vacant office of Lord Treasurer. Oxford had delivered up his staff. It had not yet been bestowed upon another. To whom could it go but Shrewsbury? This was no matter of finance. The Succession was at stake, and the prevention of civil war. Shrewsbury was willing to become First Minister during the emergency. What had the Tories, and, above all, what had Bolingbroke, to say? None of them had any conviction. They had no plan. They had taken no resolves. Against them were determined men. Before he knew where he was Bolingbroke was proposing that the Queen should be advised to appoint Shrewsbury Lord Treasurer.

[1] Dr Daniel Malthus to Sir W. Trumbull, August 6, 1714; Downshire Papers, *H.M.C.*, p. 902.

"From near noon," says Dr Malthus, "Her Majesty had her understanding perfect, but from that time answered nothing but aye or no." The doctors were asked "whether she could be spoke to." To quote Malthus, "At the coming out of the fit the Duchess of Somerset desired from the Lords of the Council that they might propose something to her of great moment to her, which granted, some went in, of which the Dukes of Shrewsbury, Somerset, and Argyll were part."[1] Lord Chancellor Harcourt guided her hand as she passed the White Staff to Shrewsbury, uttering, it was untruthfully asserted, the words, "Use it for the good of my people." The Queen then sank into a coma, and the Ministers returned to the council chamber with Shrewsbury at their head. By this transaction, which seemed to move so naturally and perhaps inevitably, Bolingbroke was destroyed. In the morning all power was in his hands; in the evening he was almost an outcast.

The Council sat far into the night. Vigorous measures were taken to ensure the Hanoverian Succession. Messengers were dispatched in all directions to rally to their duty every functionary and officer throughout the land. The fleet was mobilized under the Whig Earl of Berkeley, and ordered to patrol the Channel and watch the French ports. Ten battalions were recalled from Flanders. The garrisons were put under arms, and the train-bands warned. The Dutch were reminded of their treaty obligations. Everything was prepared to proclaim the accession of the Elector of Hanover as George I. These orders bore the signatures not only of Shrewsbury, Somerset, and Argyll, but of Bolingbroke and his Tory colleagues. In the circumstances they could do no less. Indeed, as the ponderous balance had now tilted, their safety lay in showing themselves especially ardent. Throughout the 31st the Council toiled and acted. On this day the Cabinet became merged in the Privy Council. Somers, Halifax, and other leading Whigs took their places at the table. It was now a national body of overwhelming power, none dissenting or daring to dissent. As the day wore on the physicians reported that the Queen could certainly not recover, and that the end was near. All preparations were made with heralds and Household troops to proclaim King George.

Queen Anne breathed her last at half-past seven on August 1. It is sad to relate that her death brought an immense relief to great masses of her subjects. By a harsh coincidence the Schism Act,

---

[1] Dr Daniel Malthus to Sir W. Trumbull, August 6, 1714; Downshire Papers, *H.M.C.*, p. 902.

by which Bolingbroke was to persecute the Dissenters, came into force on that same day. The death of the Queen was an assurance to Nonconformist England that it would be a dead letter. But above all there was the blessed certainty that there would be no Popery, no disputed succession, no French bayonets, no civil war. Without the slightest protest or resistance, the Elector of Hanover was proclaimed Sovereign of the United Kingdom of Great Britain and Ireland.

Chapter Thirty-eight

MARLBOROUGH IN THE NEW REIGN
1714–1716

ALL England awaited the arrival of King George I. An epoch glorious in its prime, shameful in its close, had passed away. The famous Age of Anne, the supreme manifestation of British genius, its virtues and vices, in peace and war, by land and sea, in politics, letters, and architecture, was over. A new scene opens with different patterns, lights, and values. All the old actors quit the stage—some in ignominy, some in splendour. Younger men of high gifts and proved capacity present the drama of national life after the triumphs and intense passions of the war. Milder, easier, more comfortable, less romantic themes rule in British society for many years. England had gained heights in the world that she had never reached before. She sat exhausted after prodigious exertions upon these commanding uplands, and regathered her strength and poise.

The contrary wind which had detained Marlborough for a momentous fortnight was at last changed to 'fair.' He landed at Dover on August 2, and there learned the news of the Queen's death. On this homecoming he did not attempt concealment.[1]

He was everywhere received with demonstrations of welcome and regard. Notables and populace thronged the streets of every town and village through which he and Sarah passed, and when they entered the City they were escorted by hundreds of gentlemen on horseback, a body of grenadiers, the civic authorities, a long train

---

[1] *The Flying Post* (August 5, 1714) reported:

ROCHESTER
August 3, 1714

To-day, about 12 o'clock, the Duke and Duchess of Marlborough passed through this city; they were received with great expressions of joy from the people, especially those at Chatham, who strewed their way with flowers, as they adorned their houses with green boughs, and welcomed them with repeated shouts and acclamations. They were met about three miles from hence by Dr Harris [author of *History of Kent* (1719)] one of our prebendary's, the minister of Chatham, and many other gentlemen of that place and Rochester, on horseback. Dr Harris made a short and congratulatory speech which the Duke returned with all possible condescension and humanity.

of attendant coaches, and an immense concourse of all classes, who accompanied him with loud, unceasing cheers, drowned amid which, we are assured, there were also boos.

The gradations by which Bolingbroke passed from the position of the most powerful and most brilliant Minister to a culprit awaiting his trial succeeded each other with swiftness. His authority had gone. His policy, if he had one, was gone. Indeed, his only hope was to disavow the designs in which he had dabbled. He was still Secretary of State. But soon a black box in Bothmar's keeping was opened with the names of the Regents appointed by King George I to rule the realm till he could reach London. There were twenty-five Regents. Among them was not found the name of Bolingbroke. The list had been drawn up from the Hanover angle. Extreme Whigs like Somers, Sunderland, and Wharton were not included; neither were any of the Tory Ministers. Marlborough was surprised and offended not to be declared a Regent; but, considering that this Council of Regency was to come into being in England only until the King could come himself, and that Marlborough was also beyond the seas at the time the list was drawn, his complaint was ill-founded. The omission of his name, as was soon proved, was neither a slight nor intended to be one.

St John, though he put upon it the best face he could, was not slow in realizing his position. To him, it has been said, the twenty-five Regents were twenty-five Sovereigns. He was directed to send his dispatches to them. Day after day for nearly three weeks he paced the anteroom awaiting their pleasure. Swift, whose world had also clattered about his ears, and who saw the loss of all he had gained by the malice of his pen, warned the stranded Secretary to expect the worst. On August 16 there arrived from Hanover a curt dismissal and an order to deliver up his seals to Townshend. Thereupon, as an indication of what was in store, he was visited by two lords who collected and sealed up such papers as he had not already destroyed and was willing to surrender. He retired to the country, a prey to equally well-founded regrets and fears.

No ceremony was used with the Tory underlings and creatures. Abigail had played little part in the closing scenes of her mistress's life. It was the Duchess of Somerset who took charge of the death-bed and the corpse. Abigail and her husband hastened to the country, carrying with them, it is alleged, a substantial sum of money. She lived in complete obscurity till 1732; but no one can say she had not had her hour. The fate of Mrs Manley was more harsh. "The bill your Lordship was so good to send me," she wrote (August 30, 1714) to her patron, Oxford,

> went immediately to quiet uneasy creditors, and now I have nothing but a starving scene before me, new interests to make without any old merit; Lord Mal—— and all his accomplices justly enraged against me; nothing saved out of the general wreck, for what indeed could I save? your Lordship's bounty being all I ever received from the public for what some esteem good service to the cause; many persons prejudiced, but none in particular thinking themselves obliged.[1]

Oxford in misfortune was sustained by his admirable phlegm, by liquor, and by the intense inward joy with which he watched the ruin of his faithless and lately triumphant confederate. He was more concerned in bringing to light Bolingbroke's peculation in the Quebec expedition than about his own defence. He even seems to have persuaded himself at first that he would find favour in the new reign. In this he was speedily undeceived.

George I landed at Greenwich on September 18, and in the palace by the waterside received the nobility of his realm. At heart this lucky German Prince regarded them all with a comprehensive, impartial distrust and disdain. He had received the news of his accession without excitement and certainly without enthusiasm. He had accepted the British crown as a duty entailing exile from home. He had gazed long and attentively upon the darker side of British politics without understanding the stresses which were its explanation. He had seen both parties competing year after year for his favour in order to advance their own ends. He despised them, alike for their servility and their factiousness. He knew how little they cared for him, except as an instrument, even a tool, in their Island quarrels. They were using him as a convenience, and he would use them as their mood and plight deserved. Between them, as he saw it, they had made England play a part of faithlessness and military desertion which all Europe, friends and foes alike, viewed with sincere and open scorn. They had begged him to leave his Hanoverian home to rule over them. He would be graciously pleased to do so, according to the rules arising from their civil and religious fights. Besides, they were rich, and the great force they embodied might well be made serviceable to Hanover and in the larger European problems. Around him were well-tried counsellors

[1] Portland Papers, *H.M.C.*, v, 491.

like Bernstorf, Bothmar, and Robethon, deeply versed in English political intrigue. He brought with him a pair of ugly and rapacious German mistresses and a son whom he hated like the plague.

He trusted no English statesman. Bolingbroke and Oxford were the men who had betrayed the allied cause—the men of Utrecht. Ormonde was the general who had deserted Prince Eugene. Shrewsbury had played a part of duplicity in breaking up the Grand Alliance. Somers, Halifax, Sunderland, and the rest of the Whigs had all been ready to sell one another for the sake of office. Even the mighty Marlborough, master of war and guide of Europe, had concealed from him the plans of the Oudenarde campaign, and had sought to reinsure himself with Saint-Germains. Thus our new Sovereign took the poorest view of his principal subjects, and set himself to manage them with much perplexity but genuine contempt. And who was he himself, it may be asked, to be their judge? A narrow, vindictive, humdrum German martinet, with dull brains, coarse tastes, crude appetites; a commonplace and ungenerous ruler, and a sluggish and incompetent commander in the field—that was all. Surely his accession, however indispensable, was a humbling experience to the tremendous society and nation whose arm had broken the might of the France of Louis XIV. But these are the penalties of a divided national life.

The political arrangements were made with that expert skill which is best exercised under conditions of unsympathetic detachment. The King of England could not speak a word of English; but he had his own advisers, who now became the repositories of power. They decided in principle to ban the Tories from office, to put the old Whig Junto in the shade, and to bring forward a new generation. Bolingbroke had already been dismissed. When Oxford at length came forward Dorset presented him thus: "Here is the Earl of Oxford, of whom your Majesty must have heard."[1] The King, disconcerted, allowed him to kiss his hand, gave him a frozen stare, and turned away. Ormonde, having already learned that he was stripped of his command, departed from the Court without a word.

Marlborough, on the other hand, had been received with the greatest honour and cordiality. "My lord Duke," exclaimed the King, as soon as he landed, "I hope your troubles are now all over." He was immediately granted an hour's audience, and the first warrant signed by the King reinstated him as Captain-General, Master-

[1] Michael, p. 76.

General of the Ordnance, and Colonel of the 1st Guards. A small incident in these crowded hours shows the agreeable terms upon which he found himself with his Sovereign. Dr Garth, Marlborough's devoted admirer, had for some time been also physician to the King. He was the recipient of the first knighthood conferred in the new reign. He asked as a special favour that the accolade might be given him with Marlborough's sword, and the King complied with this in much good humour. A week later the King was entertained at a banquet at Marlborough House, and in every way showed the Captain-General countenance and favour. There was no doubt more policy than personal friendship in these demonstrations. Nothing could strengthen the new reigning house more at this moment than these proofs that Marlborough was with it. In the British Army, where the veterans had not forgotten Ormonde's desertion of Prince Eugene in 1712, the "Old Corporal" was welcomed back with warm satisfaction; and throughout Europe the States and Princes of the former Allies were impressed with the power and stability of the new Government.

At first the Whigs and Hanoverians were in a mood to revive the foreign policy and European grouping so grievously broken since 1710, but these ideas faded before the realities of a new day. Utrecht was irrevocable. A Ministry was swiftly formed. All the Lords of the Junto were installed in Cabinet posts. Shrewsbury gladly yielded the Treasurer's staff, and resumed the wand of Lord Chamberlain. The Treasury was placed in commission under the Presidency of the none the less unsatisfied Halifax. But the real business of the State, subject to the supervision of the Hanoverian circle, fell increasingly to Townshend, Stanhope, and Walpole. There could be found no three abler men in the full vigour of manhood and prime. Townshend and Stanhope were the Secretaries of State. Walpole, owing to the disapprobation of Bothmar, had to console himself with the lucrative office of Paymaster of the Forces and the patronage that flowed therefrom. Nottingham, "Dismal," was the only important Tory figure in the Administration, and he in Tory eyes was a renegade.

Now was the hour of Whig retaliation. The Tory Parliament, lately dominated by the October Club and swelling with incipient Jacobitism, had been profuse in its asseverations of loyalty to King George and had voted him munificent supplies. They were remorselessly dissolved; and from the new election an overwhelming Whig majority was returned, which, as it fell out, inaugurated nearly forty years of Whig ascendancy. As if the spell which had bound them to life had been snapped with the end of their period, Somers, Shrewsbury, Halifax, and Wharton all died within a few years. Bolingbroke alone survived for more than a generation to gaze forlornly upon the past and mock himself with vain hopes.

His immediate conduct and fortunes deserve a passing glance. The Whig Parliament proceeded to repeat the odious process of recrimination and censure in which four years earlier the Tories under Harley and St John had so wantonly indulged at the expense of Marlborough and Godolphin. A sincere loathing was felt by the political victors for the men who had made the Treaty of Utrecht. Not one of them was ever allowed to hold Ministerial office again. But against the principal authors of the desertion and separate peace the ancient processes of the Constitution were set in motion. Parliament, with the full assent of the Crown, demanded the punishment of the ex-Treasurer, who had negotiated with France behind their backs; of the ex-Secretary, who had, it was alleged, conspired to subvert the Act of Settlement and bring in a Popish prince to the prejudice of the lawful Sovereign; and of the General who had marched away from the allied camps, taking with him the pontoons which might have averted the massacre of Denain. The procedure of impeachment was invoked. The brilliant Bolingbroke's nerves collapsed hopelessly under the strain. At first jaunty and audacious, he tried to carry off all with a gay confidence. He spoke in the Lords with fire and skill. He built the largest bonfire before his house to celebrate the Coronation. He presented himself at the theatre as a patron of the arts, and kept high state in his London house. But a slow, cold fear began to gnaw his heart. He knew how much he owed. He dreaded what he would have to pay. His trepidations led him to an astonishing course. He threw himself upon the magnanimity of Marlborough.

Marlborough was no doubt surprised when the ex-Secretary of State called at his door. A long account stood between them. Marlborough had befriended him in his early career. He had made him Secretary-at-War in the great days. He had helped him pay his debts. He had almost called him his son. He had never done him any injury, and there is no record of any harsh word which he ever spoke about him. On the other hand, no one had pursued Marlborough with more malignity than Bolingbroke. He had helped in his overthrow. He had turned Swift loose upon him to traduce his character and libel his wife. In his hour of authority he had lectured and patronized him. He had written scores of letters about him in terms of hostility and contempt. He had largely destroyed his European work. He had removed him from the command of the allied armies, broken his faithful officers, and involved the British troops in the foulest dishonour. He had led and persuaded the House of Commons, in spite of truth or justice, to brand him for all time as guilty of peculation and corruption. His had been the hand that would have denied him even an asylum abroad. He had even written to Torcy that he would cut off his head, and only a few months before had threatened to send him to the Tower if he set foot in his native land. Now, in all the disreputable inconsequence of his nature, he came to beg his help and advice.

Marlborough was not a vindictive man, but, as Bolingbroke's biographer justly observes, "He would have been either much more or much less than human—he would perhaps have acted with ridiculous weakness—could he in his heart have forgiven Bolingbroke, or have performed towards him a friendly part."[1] The Captain-General received his visitor with his usual good manners. Bolingbroke sought to know how he stood with the new régime, and what his fate was to be. He appealed for aid and pity, under the cloak of seeking advice. Marlborough read him through and through. He had had many opportunities of seeing whether a man was frightened or not; but he was all bows, consideration, and urbanity. Bolingbroke soon felt that at least he had one friend. When this impression was established, Marlborough confided to him the fact that his life was in danger. It was not the purpose of the new King and Government to persecute the Tory Party or punish the Tory leaders as a whole. In the new reign there must be a fair start. But it was felt that an example should be made. Speaking as one known to be deep in the secrets alike of Heinsius and of the Hanoverian circle, he hinted that Oxford and the Whigs had reached an agreement on which Bolingbroke's blood should set the seal. The sole hope for him was to fly the country. There might just be time.

Bolingbroke, already in the grip of fear, was panic-stricken not only by Marlborough's words but by his manner. That very night, after showing himself ostentatiously at the theatre, he set out for Paris disguised as the valet of the French messenger La Vigne. From the packet at Dover he wrote a letter to his friend Lord Lans-

[1] Thomas MacKnight, *Life of Bolingbroke* (1863), p. 439.

downe which as it passed from hand to hand created amazement. "I left town so abruptly," he wrote,

> that I had not time to take leave of you or any of my friends. You will excuse me when you know that I had certain and repeated information, from some who are in the secret of affairs, that a resolution was taken by those who have power to execute it to pursue me to the scaffold. My blood was to have been the cement of a new alliance; nor could my innocence be any security after it had been once demanded from abroad, and resolved on at home, that it was necessary to cut me off.[1]

His life was, of course, in no serious danger, but Marlborough had frightened him out of his wits, and by running away from England he admitted the worst that his opponents could have charged against him. Marlborough had no strong sense of humour, but he must have chuckled over this.

In after-years Bolingbroke publicly denied that Marlborough's warnings had been the cause of his flight. The French Ambassador, Iberville, who arranged it, wrote to Torcy (April 5), "Milord Bolingbroke has just been warned that his destruction is resolved."[2] And (April 12), "He was warned on sure authority that the decision was taken on Tuesday the 2nd to accuse him of high treason, and that they boasted they had enough against him to cut off his head. His head was demanded by the Emperor and the Dutch."[3] And a year later (May 6, 1715), "It is taken as certain that it was Milord Marlborough who warned Lord Bolingbroke of the Cabinet's decision not to spare him."[4]

By his flight Bolingbroke was held to have admitted the worst his enemies could allege. An Act of Attainder was passed upon him. In a few months he became Secretary of State to the Pretender, and held this office during the rebellion of 1715, thus making war upon the country of which he had so recently been a principal Minister. His habit of revealing secret business to his mistresses and his outspoken criticisms of the Shadow Court at Saint-Germains led to his dismissal in 1716 by the Pretender. It was eight years before he was,

---

[1] MacKnight, p. 437.

[2] French Foreign Office Archives, "Angleterre," tome 265, f. 105.

[3] *Ibid.*, tome 268, f. 25.

[4] *Ibid.*, f. 28. Confirmation is available from a totally different quarter. Edward Harley, the Auditor, in his "Memoirs of the Harley Family" says, "The Lord Bolingbroke, by the private negotiations of the Duke of Marlborough and those employed by him, was not only prevailed upon to quit the Kingdom in disguise, but also to deliver up his book of private letters relating to the peace." (Portland Papers, *H.M.C.*, v. 663.)

with some tolerance, allowed to return to England, but the Attainder, though mitigated in respect of his property, debarred him for ever from Parliamentary life.

Oxford's behaviour in adversity extorted respect from all. When it became clear that the new House of Commons would demand his impeachment, and a formidable catalogue of high crimes and misdemeanours was drawn against him with all the skill of the Whigs, guided by the deadly common sense of Walpole, he announced through his brother, Edward Harley, "that he would neither fly his country nor conceal himself, but be forthcoming whenever he should be called upon to justify his conduct."[1] While the process developed against him he regularly attended the House of Lords. Here he was shunned by most of those who had shared the responsibility for his actions and competed for the favours he could formerly bestow. Among these timeservers Lord Poulett, "Swallow," was conspicuous. When eventually the articles of impeachment were exhibited against the ex-Treasurer in the Lords, and a resolution was carried to commit him to safe custody in the Tower, he spoke with a dignity "unconcerned with the life of an insignificant old man,"[2] and declared that with his dying breath he would vindicate the memory of Queen Anne and the measures she had pursued. Edward Harley says that "he fetched tears either of rage or compassion from the greatest of his enemies; the Duke of Marlborough himself saying that he could not but envy him that under such circumstances he could talk with so much resolution." He had much to answer for; but behind him stood the fact that his policy had received the sincere assent of the Queen, and had been affirmed by two successive elections and Parliaments. His coach was accompanied through Piccadilly and Holborn to the Tower by a great throng of the common people, and when the Whigs shouted, "Down with the Pretender!" and "Down with the traitors!" the Tory chorus overpowered them with "High Church!" "Ormonde and Oxford for ever!" The gates of the Tower closed against this excited concourse, and Oxford remained there for a long time.

Marlborough's restoration to the highest military and political functions had been complete. He was the most august member of the Cabinet. He held once more his great military offices. His political friends occupied all the important positions, military, civil,

[1] E. Harley's memoir of Robert Harley, quoted in Michael, p. 23.
[2] Quoted in Michael, p. 128.

and diplomatic. Townshend, Stanhope, and Walpole were the life and soul of the Government. Cadogan held high command under him in the Army. Craggs seemed likely soon to be a Minister. Stair, the capable Ambassador in Paris, was the most prominent of British envoys. Although Sunderland thought himself slighted by receiving no more than the Lord-Lieutenancy of Ireland, Marlborough's numerous relations were so well represented in Ministerial and Court positions as to cause jealousy. His three sons-in-law, Lord Godolphin, the Earl of Bridgewater, and the Duke of Montagu, received respectively the posts of Cofferer of the Household, Lord Chamberlain to the Prince of Wales's Household, and the command of a regiment; and his daughter, the Duchess of Montagu, was Lady-in-Waiting to the Princess of Wales. His levée was as crowded as in the famous years. Once again, affable and bland, smiling and bowing, courteous to all, he was the centre of the Antechamber, "making the same figure at Court that he did when he first came into it."[1] Sarah seldom accompanied him to these circles where she had so long been powerful. She was disillusioned. She had urged her husband not to take any office. "I think," she wrote to Lady Cowper, "anyone that has common sense or honesty must needs be very weary of everything that one meets with in Courts."[2]

The Duke, however, wielded an immense influence whenever he cared to use it. He had the satisfaction—and it must have been a great one—of reinstating in the Army the faithful, war-proved officers who had been the victims of Bolingbroke's purges. With Argyll and Cadogan as his two subordinates, he rearranged and redistributed the commands of the Army, the fortresses and regiments. That this process should be severe and resented by the Tories was inevitable. It was certainly not needlessly vindictive. Marlborough, now as ever, was averse to the partisan treatment of national affairs. If he had been inclined to pursue officers of merit who had been disloyal to him he had the fullest opportunity. But there is no record of such a reproach having been made against him. None the less the control of the Army was brought into harmony with the interests of the house of Hanover and the Protestant Succession. This work, which occupied the winter of 1714 and the greater part of the next year, was soon to be put to a serious test.

In the acrid debates about the size of the standing army he effectively championed against a harsh prejudice the interests of the

[1] Lady Mary Wortley Montagu; quoted in Michael, p. 95.
[2] *Diary of Lady Cowper*, p. 196.

foreign officers who had bravely served him in the wars. "Thus to cashier," he told the Lords, "officers, particularly French refugees, whose intrepidity and skill I have often experienced, many of whom have served during twenty-five years with disinterested zeal and unblemished fidelity, would be the height of ingratitude, and an act of injustice unparalleled even among the most barbarous nations."[1] He also successfully resisted on behalf of the Government the Tory proposal to confine by law all British regiments to their respective stations, saying, "His Majesty having trusted his royal person and family entirely into the hands of the nation, and at the opening of the Session told the Parliament that what they should judge necessary for their safety he should think sufficient for his own, we cannot do less for his Majesty than to leave to his great wisdom and direction the disposal of the few troops that are kept on foot."[2] In this case his appeal was accepted without even a division.

In fact, during 1715 the actual government of the country seemed to be carried on by an inner Cabinet of German and British Ministers, of whom Marlborough, though not the most active, was the foremost. "Under the cover of darkness," wrote Hoffmann, "Marlborough, Townshend, and Bernstorf meet every night at Bothmar's house."[3] Bonet, the Prussian envoy, wrote at the same time, "This quadrumvirate settles everything."[4] Very soon they were joined by Stanhope. This system prevailed during the whole of 1715, and Marlborough dropped out of it through the decline of his energy and the eventual breakdown of his health. He no longer made the same commanding impression upon people. Although he was the King's greatest subject, and in the greatest situations, the actual leadership and conduct of business did not lie in his hands. Nor did he seek to assert it. His life's work was done, and his genius for command and control had gradually departed.

There is ample explanation and excuse in human nature for the wrath with which the Whigs pursued the ousted Tories. But the reaction which followed was formidable. The Tory Party, undoubtedly the stronger, now saw themselves not only stripped of power and office, but censured in scathing terms by those over whom they had lately ruled. They claimed that the country had been with them in the Peace. They were sure it was with them against the renewal of the war. The Whigs, they declared, in their hearts sought to resume the foreign policy of 1710, for which a great standing army

[1] Coxe, vi, 317.   [2] Ibid., 316.   [3] Quoted in Michael, p. 106.   [4] Loc. cit.

and heavy expenditure would be required. Inflamed by the impeachment of their leaders, offended by the foreign aspect of the Court
and the King's hostility to them, the Tories gave way to angers
which stirred in every class and every parish throughout the land.
This violent mood prepared their further undoing, for the Pretender,
misled by their discontents, encouraged by Bolingbroke, proceeded
to claim his rights with the sword. Here is no place to describe the
rebellion of 1715 in Scotland and its suppression. Marlborough as
Captain-General used the whole power of the Army against the
Jacobites. He was no longer fit to take the field himself, nor, indeed,
were the forces and operations upon a scale requiring his presence.
It seemed natural that Argyll should command King George's
forces in Scotland, and thither also Marlborough sent Cadogan
with the six thousand Dutch troops readily furnished by the States-
General under the Succession Treaty.

Marlborough presided over, rather than conducted, the brief
and petty campaign. He rightly predicted Preston as the point at
which the Jacobite inroad from Scotland would be arrested. He sat
daily in the Cabinet and strongly supported the exclusion of the
Duke of Somerset, whose high words about the detention of a
nephew in the Tower had provoked his colleagues. When Argyll's
chivalrous sympathy for his fellow-countrymen in arms against the
Crown made him lax and lukewarm at the head of the Royal forces
in Scotland, Marlborough intervened effectively to have him superseded by Cadogan. The crazy allegation that he trafficked with the
Pretender at this period, though in accord with everything that
Jacobite traducers have said about him, is belied by all his actions
and all his interests. Yet it is an old man whom we now see once
again installed in the highest authority; and the vigour of the Government measures must be ascribed to Ministers in their prime like
Townshend and Walpole, and above all Stanhope.

Political England, which in the spring and summer of 1715 had
been so fiercely discontented with the Hanoverian-Whig régime,
rallied to it in overwhelming decision against rebellion and invasion.
Both parties—one sadly, but none the less decidedly—joined in
protestations of loyalty to King George. A price of £100,000 was
set upon the Pretender, dead or alive. Hundreds of suspected notables
were placed under preventive arrest. The Swedish fleet, in which
Charles XII had planned to come to Scotland with twelve thousand
of his veterans, was attacked and destroyed in Danish waters by
British battleships, allied with the Danish squadron and under the

Danish flag. Ormonde, whose popularity had been counted on to carry all before it in the south and west of Scotland, arrived in France a fugitive, and did not dare even to land again in counties, like Devonshire and Cornwall, in which he had formerly been all-powerful. The ill-starred Pretender, escaping from his flicker of sovereignty in Scotland, dismissed Bolingbroke from a phantom Secretaryship of State. The death of Louis XIV in September 1715 and the accession to power of the Duke of Orleans as Regent fundamentally altered the policy of France towards the house of Stuart, and new combinations opened in Europe which are beyond the scope of this account.

Very little blood was shed in the fighting of 1715, and—according to modern standards—restraint was shown by the Government towards the prisoners they had taken. Two lords only suffered on the scaffold, and a few score of shootings and hangings measured the penalties among officers and the rank and file. Tory England, which had rejected the cause of a Popish prince and had adhered steadfastly to the Act of Settlement, now looked forward to a general election as the constitutional means of voicing just grievances. But in this they were forestalled by the passing of an Act which, with doubtful moral warrant, extended the life of the House of Commons to seven years. In this period the Hanoverian dynasty became consolidated upon the throne, and the Whig Party grew to such ascendancy that they could afford to fight among themselves for the control of the Government. After their able men had jostled each other for some years the scandals which followed the bursting of the South Sea Bubble opened to Walpole a long reign of peace and plenty, sustained by bribery and party management. This period of repose and growth, albeit an unheroic pendant to the glories of the Age of Anne, was the necessary prelude for the renewed advance of Britain to Imperial State under the command of the great Pitt. Thus the scroll unfolds.

Chapter Thirty-nine

AT BLENHEIM PALACE

M ARLBOROUGH'S daughter Anne, Sunderland's wife, who by all the records preserved of her appears in a light of kindness and charm, died of what was called a "pleuritic fever" in April 1716. Her father was broken by the blow. His love for his wife and children stood always first in his life. Sarah also gave way to deep depression. They retired to Holywell alone together. Here on May 28 the headaches and giddiness which had always dogged him culminated in a paralytic stroke. He was at first robbed of both sense and speech. Dr Garth, summoned from London, administered the bleedings and cuppings which were the remedies of those days. Gradually his mind cleared, and bit by bit his speech returned. In the summer he was well enough to be moved to Bath, where the waters did him good, and the natural strength of his constitution largely repaired the lesion in his brain. In November he had a second, even more severe stroke, and it was thought by all that his end had come. But again he made a surprising recovery. He was able after a while to resume the riding which had become second nature to him and was his daily exercise almost to the end of his life. His mind, though its energies were weakened, had rapidly regained its full poise and clearness, but he never recovered the complete power of speech. He could converse agreeably on every subject, and his judgment and sagacity were unimpaired; but, as often happens in such cases, certain words were stumbling-blocks, and as he was not willing to expose this weakness to strangers, he became increasingly silent except in the family circle. He still took a keen interest in public affairs. He voted for Oxford's impeachment in 1717. ★ "He was at this time," says Sarah, "so ill that he could not go fifteen miles without being tired."[1] He had in his old age developed an inveterate dislike of the opponent who had brought him down, and though stricken himself, he used all the influence he could still command to prevent the

[1] Blenheim MSS.

impeachment from being allowed to lapse.[1] Perhaps his own sense of being mentally crippled embittered him. All his life he had been a humane man, whose path was free from the tiresome, baulking shadows of revenge.

On account of his infirmities he sought, as was indeed no more than proper, to give up the Captain-Generalcy. But this did not commend itself to George I. The quarrel between the King and the Prince of Wales was at its height, and the Sovereign could not run the risk of the vacant office being demanded for his son. He therefore begged Marlborough to continue Captain-General, and the Duke in fact held this post, though quite unable to discharge it, until a few months before his death.

Marlborough had nearly five more years of life. He always maintained a considerable state. He attended the House of Lords regularly till November 1721, and lived at Holywell, which was well established and comfortable, or at the Lodge in Windsor Park, which Sarah had considerably enlarged, or at Marlborough House; but all his active interest was in Blenheim. One wing was finished, and the rest was rising slowly year by year. His surviving daughters and their husbands, and now grandchildren growing up, all wished to pay their court to him; but Sarah for one reason and another surrounded him instead with all kinds of quarrels, for which she has left abundant self-justifications. These are recorded with care in the pages of Archdeacon Coxe, and have been even further exposed in the present century by Reid's agreeable narrative. It is not necessary to do more than mention them here.

She fell foul of Sunderland both on family and political grounds. A year and a half after his wife Anne's death he married again—as Sarah thought, beneath him. He made financial settlements which she considered prejudicial to her daughter's children. She reproached him in harsh terms. Sunderland, who had filled so many high offices and lived all his life in an atmosphere of controversy, retorted with an equal command of combative and insulting phrase. When in 1718 he became head of the Government their breach was already final. This did not, however, prevent Sarah from quarrelling simultaneously with Sunderland's principal opponents, Townshend and Walpole, and her animosities pursued these statesmen during the whole of their lives. She accused Craggs, when Secretary of State, of having offered her a gross discourtesy before a masquerade in

---

[1] Edward Harley, "Memoirs of the Harley Family," Portland Papers, *H.M.C.*, v, p. 665.

1712.[1] Craggs denied the story, and the charge was perhaps unfounded, but she hated him well and long. Soon she believed Stanhope, before whom the highest political prospects were open, was intriguing to obtain Marlborough's office of Captain-General, and she abused him heartily on all occasions.

Her dispute with Cadogan was still more painful. He had, she alleged, misapplied, and even partly misappropriated, the fifty thousand pounds which Marlborough had entrusted to him when he quitted England at the end of 1712. He had transferred it from Dutch funds, which later had paid interest at only $2\frac{1}{2}$ per cent., to the loans of the Empire, which yielded 8 per cent. with a proportionate increase of risk. She declared that he had profited substantially by the difference in interest. Dominating her husband in his decline, she demanded a repayment of the capital, by this time greatly depreciated, and asserted her rights at law. Into this sorry story there is no need to pry, though voluminous material and documents exist at Blenheim. It is impossible to deny that Sarah's claims were seriously founded. She gained her action, and Marlborough's brave and faithful comrade, always lax in money matters, had great difficulty in making the necessary restitution.

It can hardly be thought strange that she fell out with her architect, Vanbrugh, as well as with several of the contractors who built Blenheim. She had always, as has been seen, disapproved of a palace on so magnificent a scale. She visited this upon Vanbrugh, whose ambitious design had been the cause of so much friction and embarrassment to Marlborough. When she saw the chaos in which the works stood in 1716 her wrath overflowed. She fought Vanbrugh with zest and zeal. He was a person of some consequence in society with a tongue and pen of venom. Here, then, was another fertile and enduring theme of strife. The building of Blenheim under all the varying relationships of Marlborough with successive Governments

1 "The Impertinence I mention'd (at the time of the Masquerades) [1711 or 1712] was as follows. Lady Anne Spencer and Lady Charlotte McCarty being generally at my Lodgings to amuse the Duke of Marlborough, one of them told me that there were a great many people that went to the Masquerade would come first & shew themselves to me if I lik'd it: Upon which I said, If They pleased; thinking that their Comical dresses might divert the Duke of Marlborough, as well as the Young people; And upon that Several did come, Among which Mr Secretary Craggs came dress'd like a Friar: He sat down by me and ask'd me if He should give me some advice. And then added that He wonder'd (or to that purpose) That I should see the Masquerades, for my enemies might come as well as my Friends. To which I said, Who are my Enemies? Then he answer'd, The Duchess of Montagu or my Lady Godolphin may come, and not knowing them you may give them a cup of Tea or a Dish of Coffee." Sarah's "Green Book," f. 21; (Blenheim MSS.).

no doubt gave opportunity to extravagance, inefficiency, and actual fraud. On the whole, the merits lay on Sarah's side, and she certainly gained several actions against the contractors.

But the saddest quarrels, and those that rent Marlborough's heart, were with her two surviving daughters, Henrietta, Lady Godolphin, and Mary, Duchess of Montagu. Both daughters, while declaring and evincing devotion to their father, treated their mother undutifully and even cruelly. These distresses darkened Marlborough's closing years, but while he tried to soften his wife's severity he always stood by her on every occasion. And she stood by him. All the love and tenderness of her vehement, tireless nature centred upon her failing husband. She waited on him hand and foot. She watched over him night and day. She studied his every wish, except in the one matter which would have rejoiced him most. At one time a sham reconciliation with her daughters was performed in his presence; but love was dead on both sides between mother and children. Sarah prowled around his couch like a she-bear guarding its slowly dying mate, and tearing all, friend or foe, who approached.

These shadows did not, however, fill the picture of Marlborough's decline. There were happiness and pleasure as well. The new generation and their friends were welcome in the half-finished palace. Young soldiers came on visits of courtship or pleasure, or in the hope of seeing the warrior whose deeds resounded through the world. Coxe gives an agreeable account of theatricals where, after its lines had been carefully pruned by Sarah of all immodest suggestion, *All for Love* was acted with much skill. It was in this bright and innocent circle that Marlborough realized some of those pleasures of home of which he had dreamed throughout his campaigns. He himself played cards for amusement, particularly piquet and ombre; while Sarah indulged her taste for more serious stakes. He rode about his wide park and properties often twice a day, or drove behind postilions with his wife. Always he remained a centre of harmony, patience, and gentleness; and always the object of veneration and love, with which pity increasingly mingled.

In 1720 the amazing episode of the South Sea Bubble inflamed, scorched, and seared London society. Sarah, with her almost repellent common sense, forced the Duke out of the market before the collapse, and added £100,000 to the fortune which he and she had gathered. Nor was this feminine intuition. In a blistering letter she wrote, while all English society was bewitched by speculation, "Every mortal that has common sense or that knows anything of figures sees that 'tis not possible by all the arts and tricks upon earth long to carry £400,000,000 of paper credit with £15,000,000 of specie. This makes me think that this project must burst in a little while and fall to nothing."[1] All the Ministers, her enemies, were involved in the scandals and widespread ruin which followed. Sunderland and Craggs were grievously stricken in fame and fortune. Unscathed herself, Sarah gave full rein to her honest indignation. She urged the hounds of public wrath upon the trail of the wrongdoers. But these held high places, and, although hard pressed, were able to retaliate in their own fashion. All her enemies in the Government and at Court laid their heads together. They worked upon the King. To keep her quiet or busy with her own affairs, they set on foot against her, with his connivance, the most fantastic slander that could be imagined. She was in a plot, they said, to bring back the Pretender. She had even sent him a large sum of money. Marlborough, in spite of his health, was summoned by his estranged son-in-law Sunderland, then Prime Minister, to receive this monstrous accusation against his wife.

★ "That winter [1720]," Sarah writes in her "Green Book,"

when the struggle was in Parliament about the Directors and the South Sea (being always mighty averse to that scheme and wishing to have the Directors punished), I talked to all the Parliament men that I knew, wishing that the Parliament would be as honest as they could, thinking that that would help the publick credit, and upon this heed one day I asked a friend of my lord Cadogan how he would be, endeavouring to persuade him that it was his interest to join with the Duke of Marlborough, who was of my mind in all the Proceeding: I did not say one word of any of the ministers that was the least offensive . . ., but my lord Cadogan (who can never forgive me for defeating his design of cheating the Duke of Marlborough of £50,000 which he had in Holland to secure bread in case of forfeiture in England) took this handle with a fruitful invention to go to my lord Sunderland and my lord Stanhope and told them millions of falsities that I had said of them on that subject, which put my lord Sunderland into such a violent passion that he sent immediately to speak with the Duke of Marlborough and said all that can be imagined ill of me to him, and amongst the rest he assured him that I was in a plot to bring in the Pretender and that in the Spanish-Scotch invasion I had remitted a great sum of money for that service, and that the King could prove it. This conversation harassed the poor Duke of Marlborough so much that he came home half dead.

[1] Blenheim MSS.

Nothing could have been better calculated to drive Sarah into fury—she, the lifelong Whig, the foe of Popery! But when she resorted to Court aflame with injured innocence she found herself sullenly received, and her impassioned letter of protest drew from the King only the following curt reply:

St James's
December 17, 1720

Whatever I may have been told upon your account, I think I have shown, on all occasions, the value I have for the services of the Duke your husband; and I am always disposed to judge of him and you by the behaviour of each of you in regard to my service. Upon which I pray God, my lady Marlborough, to preserve you in all happiness.

George R.[1]

"They who play at bowls must look for rubbers." But the behaviour of his nearest and dearest was Marlborough's unceasing distress. No excuse can be offered for the Duchess of Montagu's conduct to her mother. She made a practice of ignoring her even in the presence of strangers.

★After the great illness that the Duke of Marlborough had in 1716 . . . I was determined to bear whatever she would do rather than hinder any of the Duke of Marlborough's Children from comeing to my house when he was sick. And this was so great an encouragement to all manner of ill behaviour, that what I had hid so long They made publick, for They never came to see their Father in a morning, but att the hours when Company was there, going up towards him without taking any notice of me, as if they had a pleasure in shewing everybody that they insulted me.[2]

These disagreeable conditions continued through the years.

The Duchess of Montagu to her Father

Jan. 1, 1721

★I was to wait upon my Dear Father last night, to tell You What I hope You know without my saying it, that I was very sorry not to be at home when You came. If You could have the least pleasure in the Variety of coming here, any afternoon, it would be a great one to Me, and to anybody, I am sure, that You would let meet You. My Lord Sunderland is a very good Whisk player, and my Sister Godolphin can play and would be pleas'd with it, (I know), in Your Company. I hope You will come again, and be so good to let me know when, that I may send to them, or anybody You like. I know my

1 Coxe, vi, 3–8.   2 Sarah's "Green Book," ff. 8–9; Blenheim MSS.

Dear Father can never be with anybody that don't love him, but I am sure there is no body that does it more than

Your most Dutifull

M. MONTAGU

Marlborough to Mary

★I thank You for your Letter my Dear Child, but I observe that You take no manner of notice of your Mother: and certainly when You consider of that, You can't imagine that any Company can be agreeable to me, who have not a right behaviour to Her. This is doing what is right to Yourself as well as to your affectionate Father

MARLBOROUGH

★MY DEAR CHILD,   *January* 2, 1721

Your expressions of duty and tenderness to me would give me the greatest satisfaction if they were joined to that duty and kindness which you really owe to so good a mother: and I am not only concerned but surprised at your manner of expressing yourself about her, when you tell me, she will own to me, she has done things that were never done by any mother, kind or unkind. I know very well how tenderly she loved you and thought it one of the greatest misfortunes of her life that she could not live in such a manner with you as to have those comforts which tis natural and reasonable for every parent to hope and expect from the duty and kindness of their children. . . . Though upon shewing your letter to your mother and enquiring of her what you mean with regard to that very harsh expression "*that she had done what no Mother did*" I can't find that you had any reason for your complaint, but she had a great deal.

Praying God Almighty to turn your heart to what is certainly most just and what has always been my earnest desire.

And later still, in faltering hand:

★I am not well enough to write so long a letter with my own hand; and I believe I am the worse to see my children live so ill with a Mother for whom I must have the greatest tenderness and regard.[1]

None the less the old warrior lived his last spell in sedate splendour, and was not deserted by that Olympian calm which had been his shield in the great days. After all his toil he reposed in much tranquillity and contentment. He devoted to the conciliation of domestic broils those resources of tact and patience which had so long held the Confederacy of Europe united. From the habitable wing at Blenheim he watched the masonry rising up with that daily interest which had in bygone years measured so many processes of battering down; and the distant chink and clang of the hammers

[1] Sarah's "Green Book"; Blenheim MSS.

took the place of the cannonades by which more than thirty of the strongest fortresses in Europe had been infallibly reduced to surrender. But always he was true to the Grand Alliance on which his life had been founded. Never in all the family conflicts did he allow his loyalty to stray from Sarah. There he remained at the end of the long road, on the crest of the hill, trying to bring order out of confusion and reach his just and final peace. Although the evening sky was slashed with storm-clouds, the horizon upon which the light faded was suffused with a gentle and steady glow. Those who loved him and those whom he loved bickered and snapped at one another, while he did his best for them all.

It is indeed astonishing that during all these years when he had so much leisure he should never have left any record, even in conversation, of the critical and disputed passages in his life, nor told his tales of camp and court. Had he done so, it is impossible that some account should not have been preserved. For him the past was the past, and, so far as he was concerned, it might rest in silence. He was by no means indifferent to his fame. His desire "to leave a good name to history" had always been strong within him; but as he looked back over his life he seems to have felt sure that the facts would tell their tale, and that he need not stir himself to do so. He looked to the great stones rising round him into a noble pile as one answer which would repeat itself with the generations. It is the truth that only a single remark of his about himself has survived. One day he paced with failing steps the state rooms of his palace, and stood long and intently contemplating his portrait by Kneller. Then he turned away with the words, "That was once a man."[1]

The span of mortals is short, the end universal; and the tinge of melancholy which accompanies decline and retirement is in itself an anodyne. It is foolish to waste lamentations upon the closing phase of human life. Noble spirits yield themselves willingly to the successively falling shades which carry them to a better world or to oblivion.

The Archdeacon has recounted Marlborough's death in 1722 in the magniloquent terms appropriate to a ducal demise in an age when hereditary aristocracy still ruled the land. Of course, it is more becoming for a warrior to die in battle on the field, in command, with great causes in dispute and strong action surging round; like Charles XII at Frederikshald, like Berwick at Philippsburg, or Wolfe on the Heights of Abraham, or Nelson at Trafalgar.

---

[1] Blenheim MSS., quoted in Reid, p. 413.

But these swift exits are not in human choice. Great captains must take their chance with the rest. Cæsar was assassinated by his dearest friend. Hannibal was cut off by poison. Frederick the Great lingered out years of loneliness in body and soul. Napoleon rotted at St Helena. Compared with these, Marlborough had a good and fair end to his life.

Early in June 1722, at Windsor Lodge, he was attacked with further paroxysms, and though his reason was unclouded, his strength began to fail rapidly. He was aware that his end was near. Around him fierce animosities divided his wife from his daughters. Sarah unfolds a sad account of the final scene.

★The afternoon before her father died, when I had no hopes of his recovery, I was mightily surprised and troubled at what I did not expect, that the Duchess of Montagu and my lady Godolphin were without. . . . I am sure it is impossible for any tongue to express what I felt at that time; but I believe anybody that ever loved another so tenderly as I did the Duke of Marlborough may have some feeling of what it was to have one's children come in, in those last hours who I knew did not come to comfort me but like enemies that would report to others whatever I did in a wrong way. However at the time I thought my soul was tearing from my body and that I could not say many things before them, yet I would not refuse them to come in, for fear I should repent of it. Upon which I desired Mrs Kingdom to go to them and tell them that I did not know what disorder it might give their father to go to him now, but I desired they would judge themselves and do as they liked, but I begged of them that they would not stay long in the room because I could not come in while they were there, being in so much affliction. Mrs Kingdom delivered this message and she told me that the Duchess of Montagu answered that she did not understand her but that if she meant that they were not to see their mother they were very well used to that.

They staid a great while and not being able to be out of the room longer from him I went in though they were there, and kneel'd down by him. They rose up when I came in and made curtsys but did not speak to me and after some time I called for prayers. When they were over I asked the Duke of Marlborough if he heard them well and he answered *yes and he had joined in them.*

After that he took several things and when it was almost dark, these ladies being all the time present, I said I believed he would be easier in his bed, the couch being too narrow, and ask'd him if he liked to go to bed. He said Yes, so we carried him upon the couch into his own room.[1]

[1] Sarah's "Green Book"; Blenheim MSS.

He lay quietly or in a coma for some hours, and died with the dawn of June 16 in the seventy-third year of his age.

His funeral was a scene of solemn splendour and martial pomp. Sarah would not accept the offers of the State, wishing to bear the expense herself; but the nobility, the Army, and the College of Heralds surrounded and followed the funeral car as it made its way through immense crowds to Westminster Abbey. Eight Dukes, Knights of the Garter, followed the Duke of Montagu, chief mourner, and in the procession walked Cadogan, now Commander-in-Chief, and a group of generals who had shared equally in Marl-borough's glories and misfortunes. The coffin was lowered into the vault at the east end of Henry VII's Chapel, and rested there for some years.

Marlborough's death stirred his old soldiers wherever they might be. There was long sung in the taverns a folk-song of his martial deeds. One verse of this shows the feelings of those humble poeple towards their hero.

> Now on a bed of sickness prone
>   I am resigned for to die;
> You generals and champions bold,
>   Stand true, as well as I.
> Unto your colours stand you true
>   And fight with courage bold.
> I've led my men through fire and smoke,
>   But ne'er was bribed with gold.[1]

Sarah survived John by twenty-two years. The story of her life would require a separate study far beyond the limits of this work. She lived entirely for her husband's memory. At sixty-two she was still remarkably handsome, and her high, keen intelligence also exercised a powerful attraction. Lord Coningsby begged her to marry him, and wrote her letters of ardent affection. But she put him aside gently, and their considerable correspondence, which had lasted over many years, comes abruptly to an end in 1723. Another suitor was found in the Duke of Somerset. To this lord of vast possessions, who had played his part in history, she returned her famous answer, "If I were young and handsome as I was, instead of old and faded as I am, and you could lay the empire of the world at my feet, you should never share the heart and hand that once belonged to John, Duke of Marlborough." Somerset

---

[1] I am indebted to Mr H. M. Collier for this version. Others are found in the *Journal of the Folk Song Society*, i, 156; iii, 200; v, 265.

respected her all the more, and she was a help to him in his later marriage.

Although hitherto she had never cared for Blenheim, she made it her duty to fulfil in letter and in spirit Marlborough's wishes for its completion. She threw herself into this task with characteristic efficiency, and the fifty thousand pounds he had left to finish it went double as far as equal sums spent by the Government in previous years. Besides this she herself built a triumphal arch at the entrance to the park from Woodstock. On the rise opposite the palace she set up a pillar of a hundred and thirty feet, surmounted by a leaden statue of the Duke, which looks from the ground no larger than human, but is actually twenty-five feet high. On three sides of the plinth of this fine monument she had inscribed the Acts of Parliament setting forth the gift of Blenheim by the nation and Queen Anne, and on the fourth an inscription recounting the ten campaigns. This inscription is said to be by the hand of Bolingbroke, and is a masterpiece of compact and majestic statement. In fact, it would serve as a history in itself, were all other records lost.

Finally she charged Rysbrack to make for the Long Gallery the celebrated bust of Marlborough, and a statue of Queen Anne upon which, after all that had passed, there were inscribed the words, "To the memory of Queen Anne, under whose auspices John, Duke of Marlborough, conquered, and to whose munificence he and his posterity with gratitude owe the possession of Blenheim."

She was no doubt the richest woman alive in any country, having at least £40,000 a year in the commanding currency of those days. She used her fortune to sustain her ideas and assert her power. She lived in some state in her various homes, and even built, and rebuilt to her liking, a fifth house for herself at Wimbledon. She also gave largely to charity. She built almshouses in Woodstock and in St Albans, and helped a surprising number of people whose misfortunes or qualities appealed to her, some of whose cases have become known. She administered her estates with broad-minded capacity, and distributed her favours among her descendants according to her likes and dislikes, both of which continued to be vehement. Her most remarkable gift was the ten thousand pounds and landed property with which she presented William Pitt, then comparatively a small figure in national affairs, in order to make him independent of Court or Cabinet favour. Although her relish for his attacks upon Walpole affords one explanation of her motive, it is nevertheless an extraordinary fact that in the bloom of youth and in extreme old age her instinct discerned undiscovered genius in the two greatest builders of British imperial power.

After her death, in accordance with her wish, Marlborough's body was removed from King Henry VII's Chapel in Westminster Abbey to the tomb she had built at Blenheim. There they lie side by side in victorious peace.

There is a picture in existence which reminds us of the length of Marlborough's journey. The young officer, there shown bearing the lilies of France in the service of Louis XIV, had done his work. He marched by unexpected paths. He had consolidated all that England gained by the Revolution of 1688 and the achievements of William III. By his invincible genius in war and his scarcely less admirable qualities of wisdom and management he had completed that glorious process that carried England from her dependency upon France under Charles II to ten years' leadership of Europe. Although this proud task was for a space cast aside by faction, the union and the greatness of Britain and her claims to empire were established upon foundations that have lasted to this day. He had proved himself the "good Englishman" he aspired to be, and History may declare that if he had had more power his country would have had more strength and happiness, and Europe a surer progress.

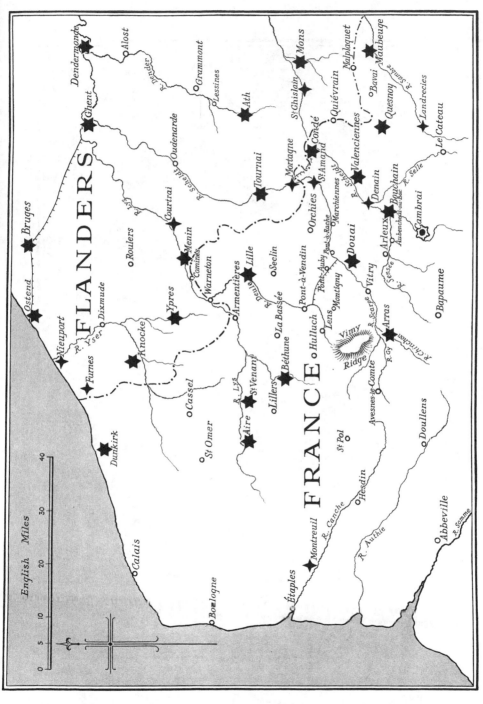

THE WESTERN NETHERLANDS

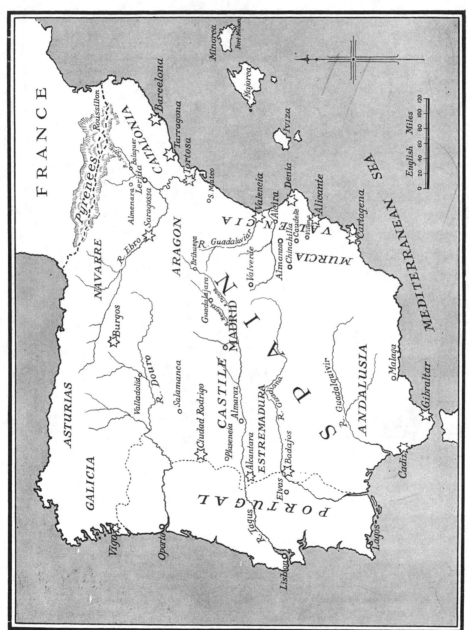

GENERAL MAP OF SPAIN

BIBLIOGRAPHY[1]

I. MANUSCRIPT SOURCES

The Public Record Office
   Secret Service Accounts (Treasury, 48).
The British Museum
   Unedited Coxe MSS.
   Additional Manuscripts [Add. MSS.], 28070 (Godolphin Papers) 28057 (Peterborough), Newcastle's Papers, 41178 (Townshend Papers).
Blenheim Palace, Woodstock
   Marlborough Papers.
   Sarah, Duchess of Marlborough, Papers.
   Sunderland Papers.
Le Ministère des Affaires Étrangères, Quai d'Orsay, Paris
   Correspondance politique, "Angleterre," tome 265; "Bavière," vol. 56.
The Hague Archives
   Heinsius Archives.
   Archives of the States-General (Goslinga and Slingelandt letters).
The Huntington Library, San Marino, California
   Stowe Collection (Brydges Papers).
   Family papers of the Hon. Edward Cadogan.
   Family papers of Lieutenant-Colonel Gordon Halswell.
Staatsarchiv, Vienna
   Grosse Politik (Imperial correspondence relating to Spain; Charles III's letters; Lichtenstein's reports).
Archivio di Stato, Turin
   Gran Bretagna: Envoy's reports.

II. PRINTED SOURCES

AILESBURY, THOMAS BRUCE, EARL OF: *Memoirs*, vol. ii (Roxburgh Club, 1890).

BERWICK, JAMES FITZJAMES, DUKE OF: *Memoirs*, vol. ii (English translation, 1779).

BISHOP, MATTHEW: *Life and Adventures* (1744).

BLACKADER, LIEUTENANT-COLONEL JOHN: *Diary* (1700–28) (ed. A. Crichton, 1824).

BOLINGBROKE, HENRY ST JOHN, VISCOUNT: *Letters and Correspondence* (ed. G. Parke, four vols., 1798).

[1] The dates indicate neither the first nor the current editions of works, but the editions consulted in writing this book. Dates in the footnotes are inserted on the same principle.

BOYER, ABEL: *History of the Reign of Queen Anne digested into Annals* (1709–14).

BURNET, GILBERT: *History of His Own Time*, vols. v, vi (1823).

COWPER, WILLIAM, FIRST EARL: *Private Diary of William, First Earl Cowper* (Roxburgh Club, 1846).

DEANE, J. M.: *Journal of a Campaign in Flanders*, 1708 (privately printed, 1846).

EUGENE, PRINCE OF SAVOY: *Feldzüge*, Series I, vols. vii–ix; Series II, vols. i–vi (Imperial General Staff, Vienna, 1876–81).

FEUQUIÈRE, ANTOINE MANASSÈS DE PAS, MARQUIS DE: *Mémoires* (Paris, 1775).

GOSLINGA, SICCO VAN: *Mémoires* (1706–9 *and* 1711) (1857).

HARDWICKE, PHILIP YORKE, EARL OF: *State Papers* (two vols., 1778).

HANMER, SIR THOMAS: *Correspondence* (ed. Sir H. Bunbury, 1838).

HEARNE, THOMAS: *Collections* (ed. C. E. Doble, 1889).

House of Commons Journals.

House of Lords Journals, vol. xviii (1707–8).

KANE, COLONEL RICHARD: *Campaigns of King William and the Duke of Marlborough* (1735).

LA COLONIE, JEAN-MARTIN DE: *The Chronicles of an Old Campaigner* (translated Walter C. Horsley, 1904).

LAMBERTY, G. DE: *Mémoires pour servir à l'histoire du XVIII siècle*, vols. iii–vi (1735, etc.).

LUDWIG WILHELM, MARKGRAF VON BADEN: *Kriegs- und Staatschriften über den spanischen Erbfolgekrieg* (ed. P. Röder, two vols., 1850).

LUTTRELL, NARCISSUS: *Brief Historical Relation of State Affairs*, vols. v, vi (1857).

MACPHERSON, JAMES: *Original Papers containing the Secret History of Great Britain* (two vols., 1775).

MAFFEI, ANNIBALE, MARQUIS: *Mémoires du Marquis Maffei* (French translation, 1740).

MANLEY, MRS: *The New Atlantis* (1720).

MARLBOROUGH, JOHN CHURCHILL, DUKE OF: *Letters and Dispatches*, vols. ii–v (ed. Sir G. Murray, 1845).

MARLBOROUGH, SARAH, DUCHESS OF: *Account of the Conduct of the Dowager Duchess of Marlborough from her First Coming to Court to the Year 1710* (1742).

—— *Private Correspondence* (two vols., 1838).

—— *Letters from Madresfield Court* (1875).

MORANDI, CARLO: *Relazioni di Ambasciatori Sabaudi, Genovesi, e Veneti* (1693–1713), vol. i (1935).

NATZMER, GENERAL: *Des General Feldmarschalls Dubislav G. von Natzmer Leben und Kriegsthaten* (1838).

PARKER, CAPTAIN ROBERT: *Memoirs* (1683–1718) (1746).

Parliamentary History of England, vol. vi (ed. William Cobbett and J. Wright, 1810) (Hansard).

PELET, J. J. G., and F. E. DE VAULT: *Mémoires militaires relatifs à la succession d'Espagne sous Louis XIV* (1850).

RALPH: *The Other Side of the Question* (1742) (answer to the *Conduct*).

Recueil des instructions données aux Ambassadeurs de France: Hollande, (ed. Louis André and Émile Bourgeois, Paris, 1923).

RÖDER—*see* Ludwig Wilhelm von Baden.

SAINT-SIMON, LOUIS DE ROUVROY, DUC DE: *Mémoires,* vols. iii–iv (ed. Chéruel and Regnier, 1881–1907).

SCHULENBURG, J. M., REICHSGRAF VON DER : *Leben und Denkwürdigkeiten* (two vols., 1834).

SWIFT, DEAN: *Works* (ed. Sir W. Scott, nineteen vols., 1883).

TINDAL, N.: *Continuation of Rapin's History,* vols. iv–vi (1763).

TORCY, JEAN-BAPTISTE COLBERT, MARQUIS DE: *Mémoires* (ed. Michaud and Pouljoulat, 1850).

TREVELYAN, G. M.: *Select Documents for Queen Anne's Reign* (1702–7) (1929).

VILLARS, CLAUDE-LOUIS-HECTOR, DUC DE: *Mémoires* (ed. de Vogüé, 1887).

VREEDE, C. G. (editor): *Correspondance diplomatique et militaire entre Marlborough et Heinsius . . .* (1850).

WENTWORTH, THOMAS (EARL OF STRAFFORD): *The Wentworth Papers* (ed. J. J. Cartwright, 1883).

III. REPORTS OF THE HISTORICAL MANUSCRIPTS COMMISSION

Bath Papers, vols. i, iii (1904). (Harley, Shrewsbury, St John, Marlborough, and Godolphin correspondence.)

Dartmouth Papers (1889).

Downshire Papers (1924). (Queen's death.)

Hare Papers (1895). (Francis Hare, Chaplain-General.)

House of Lords MSS. (Admiralty Papers), vols., vii, viii.

Mar Papers (1904). (Jacobite correspondence.)

Marlborough Papers (1881).

Portland Papers (1897). (Harley correspondence, Abigail letters, newsletters.)

Round Papers (1895). (Petkum correspondence.)

Russell-Frankland-Astley Papers (1900). (Tory correspondence.)

Seafield Papers (1894). (Godolphin letters.)

Stuart Papers, vol. i (1902). (Jacobite correspondence.)

Townshend Papers (1887).

IV. PRINCIPAL WORKS ON JOHN, DUKE OF MARLBOROUGH, AND SARAH, DUCHESS OF MARLBOROUGH

ALISON, SIR ARCHIBALD: *Life of John, Duke of Marlborough* (1852).

ATKINSON, C. T.: *Marlborough and the Rise of the British Army* (1921).

CAMPBELL, K.: *Sarah, Duchess of Marlborough* (1932).

COXE, W. C.: *Memoirs of John, Duke of Marlborough* (1820).

DOBRÉE, B.: *Sarah Churchill* (1927).

DUTEMS, J. F. H., and MADGETT: *Histoire de Jean, Duc de Marlborough* (revised by Duclos) (1806).

LEDIARD, THOMAS: *Life of John, Duke of Marlborough* (1736).
REID, S. J.: *John and Sarah, Duke and Duchess of Marlborough* (1914).
TAYLOR, F.: *The Wars of Marlborough* (1921).
[For a comprehensive list, see Book I, pp. 1008–9.]

V. SECONDARY AUTHORITIES

ARNETH, RITTER VON: *Prinz Eugen von Savoyen* (1864).
BALLARD, GENERAL COLIN: *The Great Earl of Peterborough* (1929).
CARUTTI, D.: *Vittorio Armadeo II* (Turin, 1856).
CORBETT, J. S.: *England in the Mediterranean*, vol. ii (1904).
COXE, W. C.: *Memoirs of Sir Robert Walpole* (three vols., 1798).
ELIOT, H.: *Life of Godolphin* (1888).
FEILING, K. G.: *A History of the Tory Party* (1640–1714) (1924).
FORTESCUE, SIR JOHN: *A History of the British Army*, vol. i (1889).
GACHARD, L. P.: *Histoire de la Belgique au commencement du 18e siècle* (1880).
GEIKIE, R., and I. MONTGOMERY: *The Dutch Barrier* (1705–19) (1930).
HOPKINSON, M. R.: *Anne of England* (1934).
KLOPP, O.: *Der Fall des Hauses Stuart*, vols. xi–xiv (1881–85).
LANDAU, KARL: *Geschichte Kaiser Karls vi als König von Spanien* (1889).
LAPRADE, W. T.: *Public Opinion and Politics in Eighteenth-century England* (1936).
LA RONCIÈRE, C.: *Histoire de la marine française*, vol. vi (1932).
LEADHAM, I. S.: *Political History of England* (1702–60) (1921).
LEGG, WICKHAM: *Matthew Prior* (1921).
LEGRELLE, A.: *La Diplomatie française et la succession d'Espagne*, vols. iv–vi (1892).
—— *Berwick et Marlborough: Une Négociation inconnue* (1893).
MACKNIGHT, THOMAS: *Life of Viscount Bolingbroke* (1863).
MICHAEL, WOLFGANG: *England under George I* (translated 1936).
MILLER, O. B.: *Robert Harley* (Stanhope Prize Essay, 1925).
MORGAN, W. T.: *English Political Parties and Leaders in the Reign of Queen Anne* (1920).
NICHOLSON, T. C., and A. S. TURBERVILLE: *Charles Talbot, Duke of Shrewsbury* (1930).
NOORDEN, CARL VON: *Europäische Geschichte im achtzehnten Jahrhundert*, vols. ii, iii (1870–71).
—— *Historische Vorträge* (1884).
PARNELL, HON. ARTHUR: *The War of the Succession in Spain* (1888).
PETRIE, SIR CHARLES: *Bolingbroke* (1937).
REESE, WERNER: *Das Ringen um Frieden und Sicherheit* (1708–9) (1933).
SAUTAI, M. T.: *La bataille de Malplaquet* (1904).
—— *Le Forcement du passage de l'Escaut en 1708* (1905).
SICHEL, WALTER: *Bolingbroke and his Times* (1901).
STANHOPE, PHILIP HENRY, EARL: *History of the Reign of Queen Anne* (1872).
STEBBING, W.: *Peterborough* (1890).
STRICKLAND, AGNES: *Lives of the Queens of England*, vol. viii (1852).
TREVELYAN, G. M.: *England under Queen Anne: The Peace and the Protestant Succession* (1934).
—— *England under Queen Anne: Ramillies and the Union with Scotland* (1932).

VOLTAIRE: *Histoire de Charles XII* (*Œuvres complètes*, vol. xvi) (1878).
WEBER, OTTOKAR: *Der Friede von Utrecht* (1891).
WILLIAMS, BASIL: *Stanhope* (1932).

VI. ARTICLES

ATKINSON, C. T.: "Marlborough's Sieges," *Journal of the Society for Army Historical Research*, Winter 1934.

BRAUBACH, M.: "Eugen von Savoyen," *Historische Zeitschrift*, Band 154, April 1936.

BURNE, A. H.: "Marlborough's Battlefields Illustrated: Malplaquet," *Journal of the Royal Artillery*, vol. lx (1933–4).

—— "Ramillies and Oudenarde," *The Fighting Forces*, August 1933.

CRA'STER, H. H. E.: "Orkney's Letters," *English Historical Review*, vol. xix, April 1904.

FIELDHOUSE, H. N.: "Bolingbroke and the D'Iberville Correspondence," *English Historical Review*, vol. lii, October 1937.

HARVEY, E. L.: "Letters and Accounts of James Brydges (1705–13)," *Huntington Library Bulletin*, No. 2 (1931).

LORD, W. F.: "Political Parties in the Reign of Queen Anne," *Transactions of the Royal Historical Society*, vol. xiv (N.S.) (1900).

MORGAN, W. T.: "The General Election of 1710," *Political Science Quarterly*, vol. xxxvii (1922).

REYNALD, H.: "Gispert Cuypert," *Revue historique*, vol. ii (1876).

STAMP, A. E.: "Marlborough and Charles XII," *Transactions of the Royal Historical Society*, vol. xii (N.S.).

SYKES, REV. NORMAN: "Queen Anne and the Episcopate," *English Historical Review*, July 1935.

THORNTON, P. M.: "The Hanover Papers (1695–1719)," *English Historical Review*, vol. i (1886).

TREVELYAN, G. M.: "The Jersey Period of the Utrecht Negotiations," *English Historical Review*, vol. xlix (1934).

Review of G. W. Cooke's *Memoirs of Lord Bolingbroke* in *Edinburgh Review*, vol. lxii, October 1835.

INDEX